Personal Insolvency
Law and Practice

Personal Insolvency Law and Practice

Fourth Edition

Stephen Schaw Miller MA (Oxon)
Barrister

Edward Bailey MA, LLB (Cantab)
One of Her Majesty's Circuit Judges

With assistance from:

Tim Akkouh LLB (Lond) LLM (Lond)
Barrister

Emily Gillett LLB (Lond)
Barrister

LexisNexis®

Members of the LexisNexis Group worldwide

United Kingdom	LexisNexis, a Division of Reed Elsevier (UK) Ltd, Halsbury House, 35 Chancery Lane, London, WC2A 1EL, and London House, 20–22 East London Street, Edinburgh EH7 4BQ
Argentina	LexisNexis Argentina, Buenos Aires
Australia	LexisNexis Butterworths, Chatswood, New South Wales
Austria	LexisNexis Verlag ARD Orac GmbH & Co KG, Vienna
Benelux	LexisNexis Benelux, Amsterdam
Canada	LexisNexis Canada, Markham, Ontario
Chile	LexisNexis Chile Ltda, Santiago
China	LexisNexis China, Beijing and Shanghai
France	LexisNexis SA, Paris
Germany	LexisNexis Deutschland GmbH, Munster
Hong Kong	LexisNexis Butterworths, Hong Kong
India	LexisNexis India, New Delhi
Italy	Giuffrè Editore, Milan
Japan	LexisNexis Japan, Tokyo
Malaysia	Malayan Law Journal Sdn Bhd, Kuala Lumpur
Mexico	LexisNexis Mexico, Mexico
New Zealand	LexisNexis Butterworths, Wellington
Poland	Wydawnictwo Prawnicze LexisNexis Sp, Warsaw
Singapore	LexisNexis Butterworths, Singapore
South Africa	LexisNexis Butterworths, Durban
USA	LexisNexis, Dayton, Ohio

© Reed Elsevier (UK) Ltd 2008

Published by LexisNexis

A CIP Catalogue record for this book is available from the British Library.

ISBN 978-1-4057-0152-5

9 781405 701525

Typeset by Letterpart Ltd, Reigate, Surrey

Printed and bound in Great Britain by Antony Rowe Ltd, Chippenham, Wilts

Visit LexisNexis at www.lexisnexis.co.uk

Preface

Many boundary stones in bankruptcy have moved since the last edition. Not the least of these is the attenuated social consequence of bankruptcy itself: since the Enterprise Act 2002, discharge occurs after one year and bankruptcy no longer automatically entails all the disqualifications that it did. Only the bankrupt whose conduct justifies a bankruptcy restrictions order will suffer in full those disadvantages that previously were the lot of the undischarged bankrupt. The EC Insolvency Regulation and the Cross-Border Insolvency Regulations 2006 have founded a different order to the foreign aspect of the subject. We have paid more attention to this topic than in previous editions. The government hopes that the growing problem of the consumer bankrupt will be addressed by four new regimes introduced by the Tribunals, Courts and Enforcement Act 2007 but not yet in force: these schemes are described in the final chapter, though much detail is still to be filled into the framework by subordinate legislation.

By way of change to the form of this book, we have re-ordered the chapters with the aim of treating the topics broadly in the sequence that they arise as the process of bankruptcy unfolds in a typical case. The structure, we hope, will be clearer in consequence.

Although some of the reforms just mentioned have enabled debtors more swiftly to disburden themselves of their debts, no commensurate acceleration has been achieved by us, as authors, in the discharge of our obligations. We express our gratitude to the tolerance, not untested, of the publishers. Thanks are due also to Tim Akkouh and Emily Gillett for their assistance.

We have endeavoured to state the law as at 31 December 2007.

Stephen Schaw Miller

Edward Bailey

19 February 2008

Preface

Summary of Contents

Summary of Contents

Offences

Special regimes

Miscellaneous

PART IV ADMINISTRATION ORDERS AND OTHER DEBT MANAGEMENT ARRANGEMENTS

PART V APPENDICES

Contents

PART I INSTITUTIONS

Contents

x

Contents

Contents

Contents

Contents

Contents

Contents

The bankrupt

Contents

The trustee

Contents

The estate

Contents

Contents

Contents

Contents

Contents

Contents

Contents

Offences

Contents

Special regimes

Contents

PART IV ADMINISTRATION ORDERS AND OTHER DEBT MANAGEMENT ARRANGEMENTS

Contents

PART V APPENDICES

Table of Statutes

References in the right hand column are to paragraph numbers.

Table of Statutes

Table of Statutory Instruments

References in the right hand column are to paragraph numbers.

Table of Statutory Instruments

Table of European and International Legislation

References in the right hand column are to paragraph numbers.

Table of Cases

Table of Cases

Table of Cases

PARA

Table of Cases

Table of Cases

PARA

J

L

Table of Cases

N

P

PARA

S

Table of Cases

Table of Cases

Table of Cases

X

Decisions of the European Court of Justice are listed below numerically. These decisions are
also included in the preceding alphabetical list.

Part I

INSTITUTIONS

Chapter 1

INDIVIDUAL INSOLVENCY REGIMES, BANKRUPTCY COURTS AND OFFICIALS

A   Introduction
B   Current individual insolvency regimes
C   Sources of law
D   Bankruptcy courts
E   Official receivers
F   Secretary of State

A INTRODUCTION

Historical sketch

1.1 The law of bankruptcy has a long history, applying originally only to merchants subject to the Law Merchant which had its roots in Roman law. The first statute was the Bankruptcy Act 1542, and between then and 1861 there were a number of statutes amending the law governing insolvent traders namely persons engaged in the manufacture, distribution and sale of goods. Other debtors were subject to the general law which permitted seizure and sale of property and imprisonment. Minor reforms to this rigorous approach to individual insolvency in the early part of the nineteenth century were followed by the Bankruptcy Act 1861 which applied to all debtors whether traders or not. The foundation of the modern law of bankruptcy is the Bankruptcy Act 1869, enacted in the same year as the Debtors Act 1869 which abolished general imprisonment for debt. The 1869 Act was repealed and replaced by the Bankruptcy Act 1883, the culmination of nineteenth century reforms of bankruptcy law. These reforms, as enacted in the Bankruptcy Act 1914, applied to all cases where a bankruptcy petition had been presented or a receiving order was made before 29 December 1986. The essential aims of the law were on the one hand to protect the debtor's person and his goods from seizure and on the other to ensure that all creditors within the same category of debts received an equal share of the debtor's available estate proportionate to the size of their debts. Provided the debt was due to the creditor at the date on which the bankruptcy is deemed to have commenced the law has never been concerned on the distribution of the bankrupt's estate as to the comparative dates on which the debts were incurred by the debtor.

The Insolvency Act 1986

1.2 Widespread disquiet with the law governing both individual and corporate insolvency and the conduct of professionals as office-holders in insolvency matters led to the appointment in January 1977 of a Review Committee on Insolvency Law and Practice. This committee, the 'Cork Committee', had wide terms of reference to review the law and practice relating to bankruptcy, liquidation and receiverships with a view to introducing a comprehensive insolvency system including less formal procedures both in individual and corporate insolvency. The final report of the Cork Committee[1] made a great many recommendations and detailed proposals for the reform of the law of insolvency some but not all of which are to be found in the Insolvency Act 1986 ('IA 1986'). The enactment of these reforms was not well managed. For present purposes it is important only to note that Parliament first enacted the Insolvency Act 1985. Although one of the main aims of the reforms proposed by the Cork Committee was to harmonise as far as possible the law relating to individual and corporate insolvency, the 1985 Act provided a complete code for the law of bankruptcy, but did not do the same for corporate insolvency. No attempt had been made earlier that year to co-ordinate the codification of the Companies Acts with the enactment of the reforms of corporate insolvency, and while the Insolvency Act 1985 made a number of amendments to the law of corporate insolvency it left the Companies Act 1985 as the governing statute on company winding up. This unsatisfactory and unnecessary state of affairs was resolved by the passing of the Insolvency Act 1986 before the implementation, except in small part, of the Insolvency Act 1985. The respective commencement orders[2] provided that the Insolvency Act 1985 and the Insolvency Act 1986 should come into force on the same day, 29 December 1986, the 1985 Act immediately before the Insolvency Act 1986 which then substantially repealed the 1985 Act[3].

[1]   Cmnd 8558, published June 1982.
[2]   SIs 1986/6, 1986/185, 1986/463, 1986/840 and 1986/1924.
[3]   A reader wishing to check the extent of the previous legislation repealed by the new insolvency law must therefore refer to the Insolvency Act 1985 as well as to the Insolvency Act 1986.

Pre-1986 bankruptcies

1.3 The transitional provisions in the IA 1986[1] provide that the provisions of the IA 1986 do not apply to any case in which a petition for bankruptcy was presented, or a receiving order or adjudication in bankruptcy was made, before 29 December 1986. Such cases continue to be dealt with under the Bankruptcy Act 1914.

[1]   IA 1986, Sch 11, para 13.

The Enterprise Act 2002

1.4 Although there have been a number of adjustments to the law of bankruptcy by amendments made to the Insolvency Act 1986, the changes made by the Enterprise Act 2002 represent a major structural change. The provisions of Part 10 of that Act introduce measures which were canvassed in a discussion paper published by the government in 2000, *Bankruptcy: A Fresh Start*[1]. The changes aimed to contribute to the development of a culture of entrepreneurship and responsible risk-taking. To this end the period from the commencement of bankruptcy to discharge was reduced to one year in all cases. But, in recognition that some bankrupts achieve their insolvency through dishonesty or irresponsibility, a regime for imposing bankruptcy restrictions orders was introduced, analogous to the regime providing for the disqualification of company directors, whereby bankrupts guilty of reprehensible conduct may be subjected to restrictions similar to those applicable to undischarged bankrupts for periods of two to fifteen years. Individual voluntary arrangements were made more readily available by widening the number of persons who might act as nominees and supervisors and a method to enable undischarged bankrupts more easily to establish an individual voluntary arrangement where the official receiver acted as nominee and then a supervisor was introduced. These changes have prompted a wider willingness by individuals to become bankrupt or propose voluntary arrangements, although whether they have generated wider entrepreneurship or other benefits has been questioned.

[1]   March 2000.

The Tribunals, Courts and Enforcement Act 2007

1.4A Recent years have seen an increase in the number of consumer debtors. Existing insolvency regimes are not always best suited to such debtors because of the expense of initiating bankruptcy or an IVA and of afterwards administering it. The problem was addressed in a consultation paper issued by the Insolvency Service 'Relief for the Indebted – An Alternative to Bankruptcy'[1]. The Tribunals, Court and Enforcement Act 2007, not yet in force, introduces three new regimes aimed at debtors whose debts are limited in extent, and substantially amends the county court administration order. These regimes are listed in the next paragraph and are, though not yet in force, explained in Part IV of this book.

[1]   1 March 2005.

B CURRENT INDIVIDUAL INSOLVENCY REGIMES

Outline of regimes

1.5 There are four statutory procedures which may be applied to an individual debtor who is unable to pay his current debts, or is unlikely to be able to pay his future debts when they become due. These are:

(1)   bankruptcy under Part IX of the Insolvency Act 1986, by which the debtor obtains a release for all his bankruptcy debts, he and his estate are protected against legal proceedings and execution at the suit of individual creditors, his estate is realised by the trustee in bankruptcy

and distributed rateably among the debtor's creditors in accordance with the priority of their various debts;

(2) an individual voluntary arrangement under Part VIII of the Insolvency Act 1986 which enables a debtor to enter into a binding arrangement with all his creditors for the implementation of a composition in satisfaction of his debts or a scheme or arrangement for his affairs;

(3) a deed of arrangement subject to the provisions of the Deeds of Arrangement Act 1914, generally in the form of a composition by the debtor with his creditors or the assignment of the debtor's property to a trustee for the benefit of the creditors;

(4) a county court administration order, available as an alternative to bankruptcy since 1883 for debtors whose total debts are very low, the current level being £5,000, and who have a source of income sufficient to enable them to repay these debts over a period of time.

Criminal bankruptcy was abolished as from 14 October 1991 by the Criminal Justice Act 1988, s 101.

1.5A The Tribunals, Courts and Enforcement Act 2007 will introduce four regimes applicable to debtors whose liabilities are low but cannot be met. These are:

(1) an amended version of the county court administration order[1];
(2) an enforcement restrictions order[2];
(3) a debt relief order[3];
(4) a debt repayment plan arranged under a debt management scheme[4].

These regimes are discussed in Part IV below.

[1] TCEA 2007, s 106 substituting a new Part 6 into the County Courts Act 1984 containing ss 112A–112AI.
[2] TCEA 2007, s 107 inserting a new Part 6A into the County Courts Act 1984 containing ss 117A–117X.
[3] TCEA 2007, s 108 inserting a new Part 7A into the Insolvency Act 1986 containing ss 251A–251X and two new Schedules to that Act, Sch 4ZA and 4ZB.
[4] TCEA 2007, ss 109–133.

Insolvent partnerships

1.6 Insolvent partnerships may be administered under a variety of regimes. These are mainly governed by the Insolvent Partnerships Order 1994[1]. They include voluntary arrangements, administration, and winding up as an unregistered company. Where the members are or include individuals, the winding up of the partnership as an unregistered company may proceed concurrently with bankruptcy proceedings against one or more of the individual members. It is also possible for the individual members themselves to present a joint bankruptcy petition. Finally, quite apart from the various processes or combinations of processes governed by the Insolvent Partnerships Order 1994, the individual partners may be rendered bankrupt by separate bankruptcy proceedings against each of them.

[1] SI 1994/2421.

Insolvent estates of deceased persons

1.7 Death does not bring a reprieve from debts. The Administration of Insolvent Estates of Deceased Persons Order 1986[1] governs how such estates may be administered. The administration may proceed under formally constituted bankruptcy proceedings where a petition has been presented against the deceased before his death and an order is made on it or where a petition for an insolvency administration order is presented after his death and such an order is made upon it. But the estate may also be administered otherwise than in bankruptcy, but if so much of the law of bankruptcy will still apply to the administration of the estate.

[1]   SI 1986/1999.

Application to the Crown

1.8 The provisions of the Insolvency Act 1986 bind the Crown in relation to the following matters:

(a)   remedies against, or against the property of, individuals and companies;
(b)   priorities of debts;
(c)   transactions at an undervalue or preferences;
(d)   voluntary arrangements approved under Part VIII of the Insolvency Act 1986; and
(e)   discharge from bankruptcy[1].

[1]   IA 1986, s 434.

C SOURCES OF LAW

Statute and statutory instruments

1.9 Bankruptcy is not known to common law but is a creature of statute. As already mentioned the principal statute is the Insolvency Act 1986 as amended by the Enterprise Act 2002 and other Acts. That statute and the secondary legislation made pursuant to it form the primary source of the law of bankruptcy. Case law determining the proper interpretation of the statute and the instruments made under it supplement this source.

Case law relating to previous statutes

1.10 Parts of IA 1986 introduced provisions entirely different from those in force under the Bankruptcy Act 1914. In particular the method of initiating bankruptcy proceedings by the taking of the preliminary step of serving a statutory demand represented an entirely new point of departure. Thus, the Court of Appeal held that the old law relating to bankruptcy notices had no part to play in the construction of the new scheme:

1.10 *Individual insolvency regimes, bankruptcy courts and officials*

'The new code has made many changes in the law of bankruptcy, and the court's task, with regard to the new code, must be to construe the new statutory provisions in accordance with the ordinary canons of construction, unfettered by previous authorities.'[1]

1   *Re a Debtor (No 1 of 1987, Lancaster)* [1989] 2 All ER 46, [1989] 1 WLR 271.

1.11 In *Smith (a bankrupt) v Braintree District Council*[1], the House of Lords had to determine whether 'other legal process' within IA 1986, s 285(1) included a warrant of commitment issued by a magistrates' court because of the debtor's failure to pay rates. Case law relating to similar language in the Bankruptcy Acts held that there was an implied exception for warrants said to have been issued for the purpose of punishing the debtor rather than enforcing a remedy against him. On the basis of that authority the warrant could not be stayed despite the debtors having been adjudged bankrupt. The House of Lords held that s 285(1) had to be construed afresh. Lord Jauncey of Tullichettle said:

'the legislation now emphasises the importance of the rehabilitation of the individual insolvent, it provides for automatic discharge from bankruptcy in many cases, and it abolishes mandatory public examinations as well as enabling a bankrupt to be discharged without public examination. Thus not only has the legislative approach to individual bankruptcy altered since the mid-19th century, but social views as to what conduct involves delinquency, as to punishment and as to the desirability of imprisonment have drastically changed ... In these circumstances, I feel justified in construing section 285 of the Act of 1986 as a piece of new legislation without regard to 19th century authorities or similar provisions of repealed Bankruptcy Acts.'

Accordingly the previous authority was not followed and a stay was available.

1   [1990] 2 AC 215, [1989] 3 All ER 897.

1.12 However, although case law under the Bankruptcy Acts may be reappraised when construing the Insolvency Act 1986, it is not entirely jettisoned. In a well-known passage Hoffmann J expressed the position as follows:

'one must pay particular attention to the purposes and policies of its own provisions and be wary of simply carrying over uncritically meanings which had been given to similar words in the earlier Act. It does not, however, mean that the language of the new Act comes to one entirely free of any of the intellectual freight which was carried by words and phrases in earlier bankruptcy or other legislation. Decisions of the court upon the meanings of phrases used in Acts of Parliament may come, in the course of time, to give them the quality of terms of art which Parliament may well be assumed to have intended them to bring with them when used in subsequent legislation. In section 265, for example, terms such as "domiciled", "personally present", "ordinarily resident", have had attributed to them, both in the context of bankruptcy and in that of civil procedure generally, a wealth of refined construction which it is difficult to suppose Parliament did not intend equally to apply when those words were used in the Act of 1986. Is there any reason why that should not apply equally to the words "has carried on business?" There does not seem to me to be anything in the policy of the new Act which suggests that in this provision Parliament was intending to give those words a different meaning from those which they had been held to bear under the Act of 1914.'[1]

8

This approach has been cited many times since[2] and underpins the use of pre-1986 authority in this book.

1   *Re a Debtor (784 of 1991)* [1992] Ch 554, [1992] 3 All ER 376.
2   For examples, see *Woodland-Ferrari v UCL Group Retirement Benefits Scheme* [2002] EWHC 1354 (Ch), [2003] Ch 115, [2002] 3 All ER 670 and *Re Modern Jet Support Centre Ltd* [2005] EWHC 1611 (Ch), [2005] 1 WLR 3380.

The 'common law of bankruptcy'

1.13 Despite what has been said above about bankruptcy being entirely the creature of statute, reference is sometimes made to the common law of bankruptcy. The phenomenon in view here is the emergence of rules or principles by way of deduction from the scheme and purpose of enacted bankruptcy law. A clear example is the rule that causes of action do not vest in the trustee as part of the bankrupt's estate where the damages are to be estimated by immediate reference to pain felt by the bankrupt in respect of his body, mind or character, and without immediate reference to his rights of property[1]. In that example, the principle may be seen to be shaped by some principle of common humanity. In other cases, for example the principle that no-one may contract out of pari passu distribution or the rule against double proof, the principle is more clearly derived from and to protect the statutory scheme itself. In any event, principles of this kind either underpin the statutory scheme or operate interstitially within it; they are not wholly free-standing sources of substantive bankruptcy law.

1   *Beckham v Drake* (1849) 2 HL Cas 579.

EC law

1.14 On 31 May 2002 the Council Regulation of 29 May 2000 on insolvency proceedings[1] came into force. Numerous amendments have been made to the Insolvency Act 1986 and to the Insolvency Rules 1986 to reflect the impact of this regulation, referred to in this book as the EC Insolvency Regulation. But as a Council regulation the regulation has direct effect and is therefore an independent source of insolvency making a considerable impact on the extent of the jurisdiction of the court in England and Wales to open insolvency proceedings and as to the effect in England and Wales of insolvency proceedings opened in other Member States where the regulation applies[2]. An important consequence is that, where necessary, reference may be made to the European Court of Justice for the interpretation of the EC Insolvency Regulation.

1   1346/2000/EC.
2   It does not apply to Denmark which did not participate in its adoption and is not subject to it.

UNCITRAL Model Law

1.15 A second significant source of law of international origin is the UNCITRAL Model Law on Cross-Border Insolvency. A modified version of the UNCITRAL Model Law has been given the force of law in Great Britain, that is to say in the legal systems of England and Wales and of Scotland, by the Cross-Border Insolvency Regulations 2006[1] which came into force on 4 April 2006. These regulations too make a significant contribution to simplifying and clarifying the impact of foreign insolvency proceedings on persons and property in Great Britain. Although they derive from a model law, in the sense of a precedent set of rules made available for adoption by any state, the regulations form part of English and Scottish law respectively, having been given force in the conventional manner of enactment pursuant to statute[2] by way of secondary legislation. So the English and Scottish courts, including of course the House of Lords, remain the ultimate arbiter of the true meaning of the regulations but in construing them, regard must be had to their international origin and the promotion of uniformity in their application[3] and the travaux préparatoires and Guide to Enactment prepared by UNCITRAL are admissible for consideration[4].

[1]   SI 2006/1030.
[2]   The enabling power is contained in the Insolvency Act 2000, s 14.
[3]   Model Law, art 8.
[4]   Cross-Border Insolvency Regulations 2006, SI 2006/1030, reg 2(2).

European Convention on Human Rights and the Human Rights Act 1998

1.16 Like other legislation the Insolvency Act 1986 and the Insolvency Rules 1986 must be read and given effect in a way which is compatible with the Convention rights contained in Schedule 1 to the Human Rights Act 1998[1]. Although many cases include argument as to the effect of Convention rights, there are few instances where the outcome has differed in consequence. However, the requirement to consider Convention rights has motivated a more critical approach to the fairness of procedures under the Insolvency Act 1986. A good example is *Hickling v Baker*[2] where the bankrupt was arrested under a warrant issued at a hearing held without notice to him and on the basis of evidence which his trustee in bankruptcy wished to withhold from him. The Court of Appeal reviewed the procedure whereby the court issues such warrants and, although finding the deprivation of liberty ensuing from the arrest justifiable under art 5(1)(b), laid down principles governing the procedure to be followed so as to charge the court with the initiative of bringing the arrested bankrupt for a full hearing, rather than leaving it to him to make an application. The object of ensuring fairness might well have been equally served by consideration of the issues under principles derived from common law but the need to consider Convention rights provided a framework and an impetus to pursue that object which might otherwise not have been present. The Court of Appeal did not determine whether it was justifiable to proceed on the basis of evidence which was withheld from the bankrupt but expressed doubts as to the availability of this practice.

[1]   Human Rights Act 1998, s 3(1) and (2)(a).
[2]   [2007] EWCA Civ 287, [2007] 4 All ER 390, [2007] 1 WLR 2386.

1.17 A signal case where the Convention has had an impact is the change made to IA 1986, s 433 by the Youth Justice and Criminal Evidence Act 1999 whereby a statement given under compulsion pursuant to a requirement contained in the Insolvency Act 1986 or rules made under may not be adduced in evidence by the prosecution unless evidence relating to the statement is adduced by the person who made it. This change was made in light of the decision of the European Court of Human Rights in *Saunders v United Kingdom*[1] that use of such statements as evidence in chief by the prosecution breached a defendant's right to a fair trial. This change was implemented before the Human Rights Act 1998 came into force and was made following the proceedings brought before the European Court of Human Rights pursuant to the Convention.

[1]   (1997) 23 EHRR 313.

D BANKRUPTCY COURTS

Bankruptcy courts

1.18 In England and Wales the courts possessing bankruptcy jurisdiction are the High Court and certain county courts. Each bankruptcy court has jurisdiction throughout England and Wales[1], but primarily it exercises jurisdiction in relation to those proceedings which are allocated to its own insolvency district[2]. The insolvency districts are designated by order by the Lord Chancellor[3], the High Court having jurisdiction over the London Insolvency District and certain county courts[4] having jurisdiction over the various insolvency districts in the rest of England and Wales, these districts for the main being made up of a number of individual county court areas. Wherever it may be, a British warship is deemed part of the parish of Stepney and persons on it are accordingly within the London Insolvency District[5]. Bankruptcy proceedings are not invalidated by reason of the fact that they are commenced in the wrong court, and may be freely transferred between courts having insolvency jurisdiction[6]. Appeals from a High Court Registrar, a district judge of a district registry or from a decision of the county court lie to a single judge of the High Court without the need to obtain permission[7]. Appeals from a High Court judge lie, with the permission of the Judge or the Court of Appeal, to the Court of Appeal[8]. The Court of Appeal has jurisdiction to hear an appeal from the refusal of a High Court judge to extend time for an appeal against the making of a bankruptcy order[9].

[1]   IA 1986, s 373(1).
[2]   IA 1986, s 373(3).
[3]   IA 1986, s 374(1).
[4]   See the County Court Practice.
[5]   *Fraser v Akers* (1891) 35 Sol Jo 477; *Seagrave v Parks* [1891] 1 QB 551.
[6]   IA 1986, s 373(4).
[7]   IR 1986, r 7.47(2). See generally *Practice Direction: Insolvency Proceedings* (amended as from 2 May 2000), para 17 and **Appendix 1**. Appeals from a decision made in a county court exercising jurisdiction over an area within Birmingham, Bristol, Cardiff, Leeds, Liverpool, Manchester, Newcastle upon Tyne, or Preston Chancery District Registries may be filed in the Chancery District Registry of the High Court appropriate to the area in which the decision was made: *Practice Direction: Insolvency Proceedings*, para 17.10(2).

8   IR 1986, r 7.47(2).
9   *Lawrence v European Credit Co Ltd* [1992] BCC 792, CA.

High Court

1.19 The High Court has jurisdiction over the following cases:

(a)   where the petition is presented by a Minister of the Crown or a Government Department and either in any statutory demand on which the petition is based the creditor has indicated an intention to present a bankruptcy petition to that court or the petition is presented in respect of a judgment debt where execution has been returned unsatisfied in whole or in part[1];

(b)   where the debtor has resided or carried on business within the London Insolvency District for the greater part of the six months immediately preceding the presentation of the petition or for a longer period in those six months than in any other insolvency district[2];

(c)   where the debtor is not resident in England and Wales[3];

(d)   where the petitioner is unable to ascertain the residence of the debtor or his place of business[4].

1   IR 1986, r 6.9(1)(a).
2   IR 1986, r 6.9(1)(b) (creditor's petition), r 6.40(1)(a) (debtor's petition).
3   IR 1986, r 6.9(1)(c) (creditor's petition), r 6.40(1)(b) (debtor's petition).
4   IR 1986, r 6.9(1)(d).

1.20 The jurisdiction of the High Court is exercised by the judges of the Chancery Division. The following applications are to be made direct to the judge and unless otherwise ordered are heard in public:

(i)   applications for the committal of any person to prison for contempt;

(ii)   applications for injunctions or for the modification or discharge of injunctions;

(iii)   applications for interlocutory relief or directions after the matter had been referred to the judge[1].

1   *Practice Direction: Insolvency Proceedings*, para 9.1.

1.21 All other applications are to be made to the registrar or the district judge in the first instance who will give any necessary directions and either hear and determine the application or refer it to the judge[1]. All matters and applications heard by the judge are heard in public, except those referred by the registrar to be heard in private or directed so to be heard by the judge[2]. In addition, the following matters must be heard in public:

(a)   the public examination of debtors;

(b)   opposed applications for discharge or for the suspension of the lifting of the suspension or discharge; and

(c)   opposed applications for permission to act as a director[3].

1   *Practice Direction: Insolvency Proceedings*, para 9.2.
2   *Practice Direction: Insolvency Proceedings*, para 9.3(5).
3   *Practice Direction: Insolvency Proceedings*, para 9.3(1)–(3).

County courts

1.22 Jurisdiction over insolvency districts outside the London Insolvency District is vested in designated county courts[1]. For the purposes of the Insolvency Act 1986, the county court has all the powers and jurisdiction of the High Court in addition to its ordinary jurisdiction and its order may be enforced accordingly[2]. Orders of a bankruptcy county court may be enforced in the same manner as a judgment to the same effect[3], and if appropriate in a county court other than the court making the order. Thus where an order is made or process issued by a bankruptcy county court ('the primary court') that order or process may be enforced, executed or dealt with by any other county court ('the secondary court') as if it had been made or issued for the enforcement of a judgment or order made by the secondary court whether or not the secondary court has a bankruptcy jurisdiction[4].

1   IA 1986, s 373(1), (3), see County Courts Directory (HMSO).
2   IA 1986, s 373(2).
3   IR 1986, r 7.19(1).
4   IR 1986, r 7.19(2).

Allocation of work

1.23 The Insolvency Rules 1986 provide[1] that anything to be done under or by virtue of the Insolvency Act 1986 or the Insolvency Rules 1986 by, to or before the court may be done by, to or before a judge or registrar[2]. Formal or administrative acts which are not the statutory responsibility of the registrar may be delegated to the court manager of the bankruptcy court[3]. Within the High Court the allocation of business between the judge and registrar is the subject of a practice direction[4]. No proceedings are invalidated because they have been commenced in the wrong bankruptcy court[5], that is an inappropriate court given the designation of county court bankruptcy districts, not a court having no bankruptcy jurisdiction at all[6]. Once proceedings have been commenced in an inappropriate court, that court may retain the bankruptcy proceedings, or it may transfer the proceedings to the appropriate court, or order that they be struck out[7].

1   IR 1986, r 13.2(1).
2   Note that in the High Court in London the title remains registrar, though in the district registry and county court it is the district judge.
3   In accordance with regulations given by the Lord Chancellor, IR 1986, r 13.2(2); see *Practice Direction: Insolvency Proceedings*, para 9.5. The applications so authorised are: (1) by petitioning creditors to extend time for hearing petitions under IA 1986, s 376; (2) by the official receiver (a) to transfer proceedings from the High Court to a county court under IR 1986, r 7.13; (b) to amend the full title of proceedings under IR 1986, r 6.35 or r 6.47. *Note:* in district registries all such applications must be made to the district judge.
4   See *Practice Direction: Insolvency Proceedings*, paras 9.1, 9.2.
5   IA 1986, s 373(4).
6   *Re Southsea Garage Ltd* (1911) 27 TLR 295. It would seem likely that the whole of the proceedings have to be transferred; it is not possible to transfer any one application, cf *Re a Debtor (26A of 1975)* [1984] 3 All ER 995, [1985] 1 WLR 6.
7   IR 1986, r 7.12.

E OFFICIAL RECEIVERS

Department of Trade

1.24 The Department of Trade and Industry has overall responsibility for the administration of insolvency in England and Wales. Within the Department the relevant work is undertaken by the Insolvency Service. This Service is presided over by the Inspector General who has a supervisory responsibility over all official receivers and qualified insolvency practitioners[1].

[1] The address of the headquarters of the Insolvency Service is 21 Bloomsbury Street, London WC1B 3QW. The addresses of the various offices of the official receivers are given in the Guide to the Insolvency Service obtainable on the Insolvency Service website, the address of which is www.insolvency.gov.uk.

Appointment of official receivers

1.25 Official receivers are appointed by the Secretary of State, subject to the approval of the Treasury as to numbers[1]. The office of official receiver is not a prerogative office under the crown, nor a crown office; it is a statutory office[2]. The salary and terms and conditions of office are under the control of the Secretary of State, again subject to the concurrence of the Treasury[3]. Each person holding the office of official receiver is attached by the Secretary of State from time to time either to the High Court or to a county court having a bankruptcy jurisdiction[4]. Subject to any directions[5] by the Secretary of State, an official receiver attached to a particular court is the person authorised to act as the official receiver in relation to every bankruptcy or winding up falling within the jurisdiction of that court[6]. The Secretary of State is required to ensure that there is, at all times, at least one official receiver attached to the High Court and each county court having a bankruptcy jurisdiction, but he may attach the same official receiver to two or more different courts[7]. This power would, for example, enable an official receiver to deal with all the cases of any particular description falling within the jurisdiction of several courts throughout the country. The Secretary of State is empowered to give directions as to the allocation of business between official receivers and their deputies[8] at the same or different courts so as to enable official receivers to specialise in certain classes of case[9]. An official receiver is almost certainly a public authority for the purposes of the Human Rights Act 1998, s 6. Accordingly, if an official receiver acts in a manner incompatible with an individual's convention right he may be subject to a private right of action[10].

Judicial notice must be taken of the appointment of official receivers or deputy official receivers[11].

[1] IA 1986, s 399(2).
[2] *Re Minotaur Data Systems Ltd* [1999] 2 BCLC 766, 772.
[3] IA 1986, s 399(2).
[4] IA 1986, s 399(3).
[5] Ie under IA 1986, s 399(6).
[6] IA 1986, s 399(4).
[7] IA 1986, s 399(5).
[8] See IA 1986, s 401 and para **1.26** below.
[9] IA 1986, s 399(6).

10 Human Rights Act 1998, s 7(1).
11 IR 1986, r 10.1.

Deputy official receivers

1.26 The Secretary of State may, if he thinks it expedient to do so in order to facilitate the disposal of the business of the official receiver attached to any court, appoint an officer in his department to act as deputy to that official receiver[1]. The conditions and period of the appointment are within the discretion of the Secretary of State, and for the length of the appointment a deputy to an official receiver will usually have the same status and functions as the official receiver to whom he is appointed deputy[2]. An appointment of a person to act as deputy official receiver may be terminated at any time by the Secretary of State[3]. To assist official receivers and their deputies the Secretary of State, subject to treasury approval as to numbers and terms of engagement, may appoint officers of his department to carry out their functions[4]. In the absence of the official receiver authorised to act in a particular case, an officer authorised in writing for the purpose by the Secretary of State, or by the official receiver himself, may, with the leave of the court, act on the official receiver's behalf and in his place in any public or private examination[5], and in respect of any application to the court[6]. In case of emergency, where there is no official receiver capable of acting the registrar of the court may undertake any of the official receiver's functions[7].

1   IA 1986, s 401(1).
2   IA 1986, s 401(2).
3   IA 1986, s 401(3).
4   IA 1986, s 401(4).
5   See IA 1986, ss 290 and 366 and paras **17.28** and **17.48** below.
6   IR 1986, r 10.2(1).
7   IR 1986, r 10.2(2).

Functions and duties of official receivers

1.27 The primary function of the official receiver is to carry out the various obligations imposed on him by the Insolvency Act 1986[1]. Predominant amongst these is the duty to investigate every bankruptcy and to act as receiver and manager of every bankrupt's estate until a trustee in bankruptcy is appointed. In many cases where there are few assets in the estate the official receiver will continue to act as trustee throughout the bankruptcy. Nevertheless, the foremost task of the official receiver is that of investigation of the conduct and affairs of the bankrupt[2], which is carried out primarily through the examination of the bankrupt by public[3] or private examination[4], or the private examination of the bankrupt's spouse or former spouse or of any other person capable of giving information about the bankrupt's business or affairs[5]. The official receiver may act as the nominee in respect of an individual voluntary arrangement proposed by an undischarged bankrupt and as the supervisor of the arrangement if it is approved[6].

1   For the various functions imposed by the IA 1986 see the following sections: 253(3), 262(2), 279(3), 286(1), 287, 288(3), 289(1), (2), (3), (4), 289(5), 290, 293(1), (2), (3), 294(2), 295(1), (4), 296(1), 297(1), (2), 300, 305–349, 365–367, 369–372, 424.

2   IA 1986, s 289(1); if he thinks fit the official receiver should make a report to the court on
     his investigation.
3   IA 1986, s 290.
4   IA 1986, s 366(1); the official receiver may examine the bankrupt privately whether or not
     he is the trustee.
5   IA 1986, s 366(1)(a), (c).
6   IA 1986, s 389B.

1.28 In addition to the functions conferred on him by the Insolvency Act
1986, the official receiver must carry out such other functions as may from
time to time be conferred on him by the Secretary of State[1]. In carrying out his
duties the official receiver must act under the general directions of the
Secretary of State and is an officer of the court in relation to which he
exercises his functions[2]. As an officer of the court the official receiver is
required to act fairly and honourably, and give due allowance to persons
whose claims are contrary to his own interests, even should this mean not
standing on his exact rights in law or equity[3].

1   IA 1986, s 400(1).
2   IA 1986, s 400(2).
3   The principle in *Re Condon, ex p James* (1874) 9 Ch App 609, which applies to an official
     receiver; see *Re Opera Ltd* [1891] 2 Ch 154, CA and *Re Wyvern Developments Ltd* [1974]
     2 All ER 535, [1974] 1 WLR 1097.

Directions and proceedings

1.29 The official receiver may apply to the court for directions in relation to
any matter arising in insolvency proceedings[1]. In carrying out his duties the
official receiver is performing a public law function, and is not susceptible to
control by the court[2]. As holder of a statutory office the official receiver is
empowered to bring proceedings in his own name, and is accorded by law a
right of audience before the court to which he or she is attached. When
bringing proceedings the official receiver is entitled to have his costs taxed as a
litigant in person, and the fact that he is salaried does not result in his costs
being limited to disbursements[3]. Provided that the official receiver is acting in
the course of the bankruptcy proceedings and within the scope of his powers
and duties, he has immunity from suit in respect of his actions and any
statements he may make which are relied on by others[4]. This immunity covers
the official receiver's investigatory work and any reports he may prepare for
the court as well as his getting in the bankrupt's assets[5]. The reasons for the
immunity are twofold; first that it is his duty to state with the greatest
frankness all the matters that he has ascertained in his investigation, and
secondly that the official receiver is performing a duty as an officer of the
court in connection with an inquiry which might rightly be termed a judicial
enquiry[6]. There is no liability on the part of the Department of Trade where
an official receiver in a liquidation, acting on the Department's behalf in the
absence of a liquidation committee, sanctions the defending of proceedings
which in the event cause loss to the liquidator through the incurring of costs,
and the same principle will apply in bankruptcy[7].

1   IR 1986, r 10.3; 'insolvency proceedings' means any proceedings under the Insolvency
     Act 1986 or the Insolvency Rules 1986, r 13.7.
2   *Hardy v Focus Insurance Co Ltd* [1997] BPIR 77.

3   *Re Minotaur Data Systems Ltd* [1999] 3 All ER 122, [1999] 1 WLR 1129, CA.
4   *Mond v Hyde* [1999] 2 WLR 499, CA.
5   *Mond v Hyde* [1999] 2 WLR 499, at p 515G.
6   *Burr v Smith* [1909] 2 KB 306, CA; in *Mond v Hyde* at p 513, the court stated that the first of these two reasons would of itself be a sufficient justification for holding that statements made in the course of a report to the court should be entitled to absolute privilege and carry immunity from suit.
7   *Mond v Hyde* [1999] 2 WLR 499, at p 516.

Statutory succession

1.30 Any property vested in an official receiver in his official capacity vests, on his dying, ceasing to hold office or being otherwise succeeded in relation to the relevant bankruptcy by another official receiver, in his successor without any conveyance, assignment or transfer[1].

1   IA 1986, s 400(3).

The investigatory duties of the official receiver

1.31 On the making of every bankruptcy order, except where there is a certificate of summary administration in force, it is the duty of the official receiver to investigate the conduct and affairs of the bankrupt both before and after the making of the bankruptcy order and to make any report he may think fit to the court[1]. The official receiver also has a duty to make a report to the court where a bankrupt makes an application for his discharge from bankruptcy[2]. In any subsequent proceedings the official receiver's report is prima facie evidence of the facts stated in it[3]. The report is subject to absolute privilege for the purpose of libel proceedings by any person named in it[4]. To assist the official receiver in his investigation, the bankrupt is under a duty to:

(a)   deliver possession of his estate to the official receiver;

(b)   deliver up all books, papers and other records relating to his estate of which he has possession or control, including documents which would be privileged from disclosure in proceedings[5];

(c)   do all such things as may reasonably be required by the official receiver to protect property which cannot be delivered to the official receiver[6];

(d)   give the official receiver an inventory of his estate and such other information as the official receiver may at any time reasonably require and to attend on the official receiver at such times as the latter may reasonably require, including any time after his discharge from bankruptcy[7].

1   IA 1986, s 289(1), (4).
2   IA 1986, s 289(2).
3   IA 1986, s 289(3).
4   *Bottomley v Brougham* [1908] 1 KB 584; *Burr v Smith* [1909] 2 KB 306, CA; *Re John Tweddle & Co Ltd* [1910] 2 KB 697, CA.
5   IA 1986, s 291(1).
6   IA 1986, s 291(2).
7   IA 1986, s 291(4), (5).

The statement of affairs

1.32 The official receiver has extensive duties with regard to the statement of affairs following any bankruptcy order made otherwise than on a debtor's petition. The bankrupt must make out and submit to the official receiver a statement in the prescribed form[1] as to his affairs[2]. The Insolvency Act 1986 provides for the statement of affairs to be submitted within 21 days of the commencement of the bankruptcy but the official receiver is empowered at any time of his own volition or at the bankrupt's request[3] to extend this period, or release the bankrupt from the obligation to provide the statement or any part of it. Where the official receiver has refused to exercise these powers the court may do so on the application of the bankrupt[4].

[1]   See IR 1986, rr 6.59, 12.7, Sch 4, Form 6.33.
[2]   IA 1986, s 288(1).
[3]   IR 1986, r 6.62(1).
[4]   IA 1986, s 288(3); as for the procedure on the application see IR 1986, r 6.62(2)–(7).

1.33 In cases where the bankrupt is unable to prepare a proper statement of affairs by himself, the official receiver may employ someone to assist in the preparation of the statement, or make an allowance towards the expense of the bankrupt doing so, in either case at the expense of the estate[1]. The official receiver may at any time require further information from the bankrupt in writing amplifying, modifying or explaining any matter contained in the statement of affairs[2], verified by affidavit if the official receiver so directs[3].

[1]   IR 1986, r 6.63(1), (2).
[2]   IR 1986, r 6.66(1).
[3]   IR 1986, r 6.66(2).

1.34 If a person without reasonable excuse fails to comply with any obligation imposed in relation to the statement of affairs, he is liable on conviction on indictment to a fine, or on summary conviction to a fine not exceeding the statutory maximum and, on conviction after continued contravention, to a daily default fine not exceeding one-tenth of the statutory maximum[1].

[1]   IA 1986, ss 288(4), 430, Sch 10.

Report to creditors

1.35 The official receiver is required to send a report to creditors with respect to the bankruptcy proceedings and the state of the bankrupt's affairs at least once after the making of the bankruptcy order[1]. A copy of any report is to be filed in court[2]. This report must inform creditors whether a statement of affairs has been submitted and filed in court, or has been dispensed with. In the former case the official receiver must provide creditors with a summary of the statement and any observations he thinks fit to make with respect to it, or to the affairs of the bankrupt in general[3], and in the latter case the official receiver must send to creditors a report containing a summary of the bankrupt's affairs, so far as within his knowledge, and his observations, if any, with respect to it, or to the affairs of the bankrupt in general[4]. The official receiver need not comply with either of these requirements if he has previously reported to creditors and contributories with respect to the company's affairs, so far as known to him, and he is of the opinion that there are no additional matters which ought to be brought to their attention[5].

1 IR 1986, r 6.73(1).
2 IR 1986, r 6.73(2).
3 IR 1986, r 6.75(1).
4 IR 1986, r 6.76(1), (2).
5 IR 1986, rr 6.75(2), 6.76(3).

1.36 The court may, on the official receiver's application, relieve him of any duty imposed on him to report to creditors, or authorise him to carry out the duty in another way[1]. On such an application, the court must have regard to the cost of carrying out the duty, to the amount of the funds available to the estate, and to the extent of the interest of creditors, or any particular class of them[2].

If the bankruptcy order is annulled any duty of the official receiver to send reports ceases[3].

1 IR 1986, r 6.77(1).
2 IR 1986, r 6.77(2).
3 IR 1986, r 6.78.

Official receiver's fees, remuneration and expenses

1.37 A fee is payable to the Secretary of State in respect of the official receiver's performance of his general duties[1]. Fees are also payable to the Secretary of State where the official receiver acts as nominee or supervisor with respect to an individual voluntary arrangement[2].

1 Insolvency Proceedings (Fees) Order 2004, SI 2004/593, art 4, Sch 2, B1 in the Table of Fees.
2 Insolvency Proceedings (Fees) Order 2004, SI 2004/593, art 4, Sch 2, IVA1, IVA2 and IVA3 in the Table of Fees.

1.38 Where the official receiver acts as trustee of the bankrupt's estate or as interim receiver he is entitled to remuneration at hourly rates in relation to a distribution made by him when acting as trustee, the supervision of a special manager and the performance by him of any functions where he acts as interim receiver[1]. The hourly rates vary depending on whether the official receiver is of the London insolvency district or not and are set out in Tables 2 and 3 to the Insolvency Regulations 1994.

1 Insolvency Regulations 1994, SI 1994/2507, reg 35, in force on 1 April 2005 with effect to cases where the bankruptcy order was made on or after 1 April 2005 or the official receiver was appointed as interim receiver on or after 1 April 2005. The regulations in their previous form continue to apply to cases where the relevant event occurred before 1 April 2005.

1.39 The court has inherent jurisdiction to order payment to the official receiver of his costs and charges out of assets held by an insolvent on trust[1].

Any expenses[2] incurred by the official receiver, in whatever capacity he may be acting, in connection with proceedings taken against him in insolvency proceedings are to be treated as expenses of the insolvency proceedings[3]. In respect of any sums due to the official receiver in relation to such expenses, he has a charge on the bankrupt's estate[4].

1   *Re Exchange Securities and Commodities Ltd (No 2)* [1985] BCLC 392.
2   'Expenses' includes damages, IR 1986, r 10.4(1).
3   IR 1986, r 10.4(1).
4   IR 1986, r 10.4(2).

Official receiver's liability for costs

1.40 The official receiver may not be personally liable for any costs incurred by any person in respect of an appeal against his decision with respect to the admission of or rejection of a creditor's proof for dividend[1], nor for the costs and expenses of a public examination[2]. However, where the official receiver is acting as trustee he is subject to the rules as to costs as they affect other trustees[3]. Where the official receiver is made a party to any proceedings he will not be personally liable for costs unless the court otherwise directs[4].

1   IR 1986, r 6.105(6).
2   IR 1986, r 6.177(2).
3   *Re John Tweddle & Co Ltd* [1910] 2 KB 697, CA.
4   IR 1986, r 7.39; this provision is without prejudice to any statutory provision which protects the official receiver against an order for costs.

Contracting out

1.41 The official receiver is enabled to contract out many of his functions to a person authorised by the official receiver in that behalf[1]. The Schedule to the Contracting out (Functions of the Official Receiver) Order 1995, SI 1995/1386, contains a long list of functions which may not be contracted out.

1   Contracting out (Functions of the Official Receiver) Order 1995, SI 1995/1386, art 3(1).

F SECRETARY OF STATE

General functions

1.42 The Secretary of State for Trade and Industry has various functions in relation to individual insolvency which are administered by the Insolvency Service. The Secretary of State is responsible for the appointment, removal, and terms of employment of official receivers[1], and for the qualification of insolvency practitioners[2].

1   IA 1986, s 399(2).
2   See **Chapter 2** below.

Powers to make rules and regulations

1.43 The Secretary of State has wide statutory powers and duties with respect to insolvency rules and regulations. His concurrence is required to the making of general insolvency rules by the Lord Chancellor[1]. More specifically the Secretary of State may make regulations with respect to any matter provided for in the Insolvency Rules 1986 as relates to the carrying out of the functions of a trustee in bankruptcy or interim receiver including, without prejudice to the generality of the above, provision with respect to the following matters arising in bankruptcy:

(1)   the preparation and keeping by trustees and interim receivers of books, accounts and other records, and their production to such persons as may be authorised or required to inspect them;
(2)   the auditing of trustees' accounts;
(3)   the manner in which trustees are to act in relation to the bankrupt's books, papers and other records, and the manner of their disposal by the responsible insolvency practitioner or others;
(4)   the supply by the trustee to creditors and members of the creditors' committee of copies of documents relating to the insolvency and the affairs of the bankrupt, on payment, in such cases as may be specified by the regulations, of the specified fee;
(5)   the manner in which insolvent estates are to be distributed by trustees, including provision with respect to unclaimed funds and dividends;
(6)   the manner in which moneys coming into the hands of a trustee in the course of his administration are to be handled, and the payment of interest on sums which, in pursuance of regulations, have been paid into the Insolvency Services Account;
(7)   the amount (or the manner of determining the amount) to be paid to the official receiver by way of remuneration when acting as interim receiver or trustee[2].

[1]   IA 1986, s 411(1).
[2]   IR 1986, r 12.1(1).

1.44 Such regulations may confer a discretion on the court, make non-compliance with any of the regulations a criminal offence, and make different provision for different cases, including different provision for different areas, and may contain such incidental, supplemental and transitional provisions as may appear to the Secretary of State necessary or expedient[1]. The Secretary of State is also empowered to increase or decrease any of the money sums specified in any provisions of the Insolvency Act 1986[2].

[1]   IR 1986, r 12.1(3).
[2]   IA 1986, s 418(1); the section sets out the seven amounts which may be prescribed for the purposes of bankruptcy.

Role in bankruptcies

1.45 The Secretary of State has a number of specific functions to perform when necessary in the course of a bankruptcy namely:

(a) to make an appointment as trustee, or to decline to do so when requested by the official receiver either following the failure of the meeting of creditors summoned to appoint a first trustee to make such an appointment[1], or when a vacancy in the office of trustee arises[2];

(b) where he has made an appointment as trustee the Secretary of State may remove his appointee by direction[3];

(c) to exercise the functions of the creditors' committee where there is no such committee or when the official receiver is the trustee[4];

(d) maintaining surveillance over insolvency practitioners and their records and accounts[5];

(e) determining the time of release of the trustee where he is the official receiver or where the general body of creditors has resolved against his release[6]; and

(f) issuing a certificate to a trustee stating that it would be inappropriate or inexpedient for the trustee to apply for a charging order over a matrimonial home which the trustee has not been able to realise in order that the trustee may summon a final meeting of creditors despite the fact that this property forming part of the bankrupt's estate has not been realised[7].

[1] IA 1986, s 295(2).
[2] IA 1986, s 300(6).
[3] IA 1986, s 298(5).
[4] IA 1986, s 302(1), (2).
[5] Insolvency Practitioners Regulations 1986, reg 16.
[6] IA 1986, s 299.
[7] IA 1986, s 332.

1.46 An appeal lies at the instance of the Secretary of State from any order of the court made on an application for the rescission or annulment of a bankruptcy order, or for a bankrupt's discharge[1]. There is no general right of appeal to the court from the decisions of the Secretary of State, but any person dissatisfied with a decision in respect of a claim to undistributed assets forming part of the bankrupt's estate which have been paid into the Insolvency Services Account[2] may apply to the court by way of appeal against the decision within 28 days of the notification of the decision[3].

[1] IR 1986, r 7.48(1).
[2] See para **1.47**.
[3] IR 1986, r 7.50.

Insolvency Services Account

1.47 All money received by the Secretary of State in respect of insolvency proceedings is to be paid into the Insolvency Services Account kept by the Secretary of State with the Bank of England, and the Secretary of State controls all payments out of this account[1]. Trustees in bankruptcy are required to remit any money received by them in the course of their administration once every 14 days, or forthwith if the sum received is more than £5,000[2]. The Secretary of State must notify the National Debt Commissioners whenever he considers that there is more money in the account than is needed to meet the needs of the estates of companies and bankrupts and the excess is then paid into the Insolvency Services Investment Account[3]. The Treasury has power to direct the payment out of the Consolidated Fund of sums into the Insolvency Services Account[4]. Any unclaimed dividends or balances too small to be distributed among the persons entitled to receive them are to be paid by the Secretary of State out of the Insolvency Services Account and into the Consolidated Fund[5].

[1]   IA 1986, s 403(1).
[2]   Insolvency Regulations 1994, 1994/2507, reg 20(1).
[3]   IA 1986, s 403(2).
[4]   IA 1986, s 408.
[5]   IA 1986, s 407.

1.48 It has been possible for some time for funds held in the Insolvency Services Account on behalf of a company in liquidation to be placed on an interest bearing account or to be invested in treasury bills or other government securities for the benefit of the estate. This facility has not been available for the benefit of funds held by trustees in bankruptcy. The Insolvency Act 2000[1] has amended the IA 1986[2] to enable the Secretary of State to make rules which will provide for interest to be earned on bankruptcy estate funds or enable such funds to be invested.

[1]   IA 2000, s 13.
[2]   IA 1986, s 406 and Sch 9, para 21.

1.49 The Secretary of State is required to prepare a statement of the sums received or paid by him from and into the account for each year ending 31 March for transmission to the Comptroller and Auditor General before the end of November next following the year in question[1].

[1]   IA 1986, s 409.

Chapter 2

INSOLVENCY PRACTITIONERS

A PROHIBITION AGAINST ACTING AS AN INSOLVENCY PRACTITIONER WITHOUT QUALIFICATION

General

2.1 Before the enactment of the Insolvency Act 1986 ('IA 1986') there were no formal qualifications required of a trustee in bankruptcy or a liquidator of a company. In a significant number of cases company insolvency procedures were abused, either by directors who had grown familiar with the winding-up provisions of the Companies Act or by individuals who advertised themselves as insolvency practitioners and used their appointments to benefit themselves and their accomplices. Complaints were not uncommon as to the disposal of a company's assets to associates at favourable prices perhaps supported by a valuation from supposed independent experts themselves involved with the liquidator. Similar complaints were voiced against trustees in bankruptcy, though the scope for malpractice in bankruptcy was perhaps more limited than in company winding up. There were also complaints of inexperience against trustees and liquidators, particularly from the Department of Trade from whom frequent guidance would be sought from some professional accountants as to the proper administration of the estate. This resulted in delay and imposed additional burdens on an already stretched insolvency service.

2.2 In order to meet this concern the Insolvency Act 1986 introduced a system of licensing aimed at ensuring the professional competence and skill of insolvency practitioners both in individual and corporate insolvency. Only an individual may be qualified to act as an insolvency practitioner[1], though in recognition of the fact that most insolvency practitioners are members of a firm and that they themselves or their firm have employees who will carry out many of the tasks involved in a liquidation or administration the Insolvency Rules 1986 do in a number of cases give specific authorisation for acts to be carried out by employees of an insolvency practitioner or his firm[2]. The individual must either be authorised by virtue of membership of a recognised professional body, and meeting any requirements of that body, or he must hold an authorisation granted by a competent authority. He must fulfil the prescribed requirements as to education and practical training and experience, and he must have in force the required security for the proper performance of his functions. This latter requirement ensures that there is security to meet any claims which may be made by creditors in the event of misfeasance by the insolvency practitioner. An insolvency practitioner will not be qualified if he is subject to one of the statutory prohibitions.

[1]   IA 1986, s 390(1); for the meaning of 'act as an insolvency practitioner' see para **2.5** below.
[2]   See eg IR 1986, r 4.55(3) which permits such an employee to act as chairman of a meeting of creditors or contributories.

2.3 Where the intending insolvency practitioner is a member of one of the recognised professional bodies his application to become an insolvency practitioner will be dealt with by the body concerned. In other cases application may be made to a 'competent authority' for authorisation to act as an insolvency practitioner. At present there is no competent authority for these purposes other than the Secretary of State. He is empowered to grant or refuse applications, or withdraw existing authorisations, but where he proposes to refuse such an application or withdraw an authorisation, he must give the applicant or holder written notice of his intention to do so. The applicant may then refer the matter in effect by way of appeal to the Insolvency Practitioners Tribunal. The tribunal investigates the case and makes a report to the Secretary of State stating what would in its opinion be the appropriate decision in the matter and the reason for that opinion, and the Secretary of State is duty bound to decide the matter accordingly[1].

[1]   IA 1986, s 397(1).

2.4 In order that the work of insolvency practitioners may be monitored by their professional body or the Secretary of State an insolvency practitioner is obliged when acting in relation to any company, to maintain, allow the inspection of and preserve prescribed records[1].

[1]   See the Insolvency Practitioners Regulations 2005, SI 2005/524, regs 13–17.

Acting as an insolvency practitioner

2.5 Only an individual can act as an insolvency practitioner[1]. A person acts as an insolvency practitioner in relation to an individual by acting:

(1)   as his trustee in bankruptcy or interim receiver;
(2)   as trustee under a deed of arrangement made for the benefit of his creditors;
(3)   where a voluntary arrangement in relation to him is proposed or approved under the IA 1986, Pt VIII as nominee or supervisor;
(4)   as administrator of the estate of a deceased individual which is being administered in insolvency[2].

1   IA 1986, s 390(1).
2   IA 1986, s 388(2).

2.6 With respect to partnerships, a person acts as an insolvency practitioner in relation to an insolvent partnership by acting as:

(a)   its liquidator, provisional liquidator or administrator;
(b)   the trustee of the partners;
(c)   where a partnership voluntary arrangement is proposed, as its nominee or supervisor[1].

1   IA 1986, s 388(2A).

Prohibition on acting when not qualified

2.7 A person who acts as an insolvency practitioner in relation to an individual at a time when he is not qualified to do so commits a criminal offence[1]. Where an insolvency practitioner's authority to act is suspended he must immediately vacate any office he may hold as trustee[2]. There are a number of exemptions from the requirement to be qualified as an insolvency practitioner.

1   IA 1986, s 389(1): and is liable on conviction on indictment to imprisonment for a term not exceeding two years or a fine, or to both, or on summary conviction to imprisonment for a term not exceeding six months or a fine not exceeding the statutory maximum, or to both.
2   IA 1986, s 298(6).

Exemption for official receiver

2.8 First, there is an exemption for the official receiver who need not comply with the requirements either for qualification or for the provision of security which must be met by insolvency practitioners[1]. The official receiver is specifically authorised to act as nominee and supervisor of a voluntary arrangement relating to an individual who is an undischarged bankrupt when it is proposed[2].

1   IA 1986, ss 388(5), 389(2).
2   IA 1986, s 389B.

Exemption for certain persons to act as nominees and supervisors in relation to voluntary arrangements

2.9 Secondly, under IA 1986, s 389A, introduced by IA 2000, an individual, who is not qualified as an insolvency practitioner but is a member of a body recognised for the purpose and in relation to whom prescribed security is in force for the proper performance of his functions, may act as nominee or supervisor in relation to a voluntary arrangement. This provision forms part of the amendments introduced to permit persons other than insolvency practitioners to act as business rescue consultants to save small businesses which get into financial difficulties. An individual may not act as a nominee or a supervisor if he is an undischarged bankrupt, subject to disqualification as a director, a patient under an applicable Mental Health Act or lacks capacity to act within the meaning of the Mental Capacity Act 2005.

Exemption for EC Insolvency Regulation liquidator

2.10 Where insolvency proceedings, within the meaning of the EC Insolvency Regulation, have been opened in another Member State, nothing done either in the United Kingdom or elsewhere in relation to those insolvency proceedings involves acting as an insolvency practitioner[1]. So if the liquidator, within the meaning of EC Insolvency Regulation, acts directly in the United Kingdom, he does not act as an insolvency practitioner. If, however, he were to request that bankruptcy proceedings be opened against the debtor in England, the trustee appointed in those proceedings would act as an insolvency practitioner and would therefore have to be qualified.

[1]   IA 1986, s 388(6).

Exemption for foreign representative under the Cross-Border Insolvency Regulations 2006

2.11 Similarly, where anything is done by a foreign representative, within the meaning of the Cross-Border Insolvency Regulations 2006, under or by virtue of those regulations or in relation to relief granted or co-operation or co-ordination provided under them, IA 1986, s 388 does not apply and so the foreign representative does not act as an insolvency practitioner in carrying them out[1]. A supervisory jurisdiction over foreign representatives is conferred by the Cross-Border Insolvency Regulations 2006, Sch 2, Pt 8.

[1]   Cross-Border Insolvency Regulations 2006, SI 2006/1030, reg 8.

B QUALIFICATION AS INSOLVENCY PRACTITIONER

Requirements and disqualifications

Only individuals may act as an insolvency practitioner

2.12 A person who is not an individual is not qualified to act as an insolvency practitioner[1]. A consequence of this is that, although insolvency practitioners may, and often do, carry on practice in partnership, his qualification is personal and any offices to which he is appointed are personal to him.

¹   IA 1986, s 390(1).

Disqualifications

2.13 As a matter of drafting technique IA 1986, s 390 explains who is qualified to act as an insolvency practitioner negatively by stating what persons are not qualified so to act. But in subsections (4) and (5) it sets out matters which may properly be classified as disqualifications. These are as follows. A person is not qualified to act as an insolvency practitioner at any time if at that time:

(1)   he has been adjudged bankrupt or, in Scotland sequestration of his estate has been awarded and, in either case, he has not been discharged;
(2)   he is subject to a disqualification order made under the Company Directors Disqualification Act 1986;
(3)   a bankruptcy restrictions order or undertaking is in force in respect of him[1];
(4)   he is a patient within the meaning of the Mental Health Act 1983 or the analogous legislation in Scotland; or
(5)   he lacks capacity within the meaning of the Mental Capacity Act 2005 to act as an insolvency practitioner.

¹   IA 1986, ss 390(5) and 281A, Sch 4A, para 8.

Authorisation

2.14 No individual may act as an insolvency practitioner unless he is authorised to do so by virtue of membership of a recognised professional body, or by holding an authorisation granted by a competent authority[1]. Further detail about obtaining authorisation is set out below.

¹   IA 1986, s 390(2); the competent authority is in effect at present the Secretary of State; see para **2.22** below.

Security

2.15 Finally, even if authorised to act and not otherwise disqualified, an individual is not qualified to act as an insolvency practitioner unless there is in force security for the proper performance of his functions which meets prescribed requirements[1]. This requirement is discussed further below.

¹   IA 1986, s 390(3).

Authorisation

Two routes

2.16 There are two routes to obtaining authorisation to act as an insolvency practitioner. Either an individual may join and qualify himself to act pursuant to the rules of a recognised professional body or he may apply to the Secretary of State for authorisation.

First route: membership of a recognised professional body

2.17 The original proposals for the compulsory qualification of all insolvency practitioners were that any person who wished to act as an insolvency practitioner, whatever professional qualification he held, was to apply to the Secretary of State for a certificate of authorisation permitting him to act as an insolvency practitioner. Although the intention was that the Secretary of State would delegate his powers of authorisation to appropriate professional associations within uniform guidelines, in consequence of forceful representations made to the government, a self-regulatory basis of obtaining authorisation through recognised professional bodies was established.

RECOGNISED PROFESSIONAL BODIES

2.18 For this purpose, the Secretary of State is empowered[1] by order to declare a body which appears to him to fulfil the statutory requirements[2] to be a recognised professional body for the purposes of authorising individuals to be qualified to act as insolvency practitioners. To be so recognised the body must regulate the practice of a profession and maintain and enforce rules for securing that such of its members as are permitted by or under the rules to act as insolvency practitioners are fit and proper persons so to act and meet acceptable requirements as to education and practical training and experience[3].

[1]   IA 1986, s 391(1).
[2]   Specified in IA 1986, s 391(2).
[3]   IA 1986, s 391(2).

2.19 The bodies declared to be recognised professional bodies for the purposes of the Insolvency Act 1986 are:

(a)   The Chartered Association of Certified Accountants;
(b)   The Insolvency Practitioners Association;
(c)   The Institute of Chartered Accountants in England and Wales;
(d)   The Institute of Chartered Accountants in Ireland;
(e)   The Institute of Chartered Accountants of Scotland;
(f)   The Law Society; and
(g)   The Law Society of Scotland[1].

2.19 *Insolvency practitioners*

1   Insolvency Practitioners (Recognised Professional Bodies) Order 1986, SI 1986/1764, art 2,
Schedule (made under the Insolvency Act 1985, ss 3(2), 10 (repealed) and having effect as
if made under the Insolvency Act 1986, s 392 by virtue of s 437, Sch 11, para 23; the
Interpretation Act 1978, s 17(2)(b)).

2.20 The Secretary of State may withdraw recognition and revoke an order in
relation to a professional body if it appears to him that the body no longer
meets the above requirements[1]. When the Secretary of State makes an order
recognising a professional body under these provisions he must specify the
date from which the order is effective[2]; and in the event that he makes an
order revoking a previous order he may make provision whereby members of
the body in question continue to be treated as authorised to act as insolvency
practitioners for a specified period after the revocation takes effect[3].

1   IA 1986, s 391(4).
2   The order in respect of the professional bodies listed in the text took effect from
10 November 1986.
3   IA 1986, s 391(5).

MEMBER OF A RECOGNISED PROFESSIONAL BODY

2.21 A 'member' of a professional body need not for these purposes be a fully
admitted member of the body. Any person who is subject to the rules of the
body in the practice of his profession is a member of the body for the purposes
of becoming an insolvency practitioner[1].

1   IA 1986, s 391(3).

Second route: authorisation by competent authority

2.22 The Insolvency Act 1986[1] provides that an individual wishing to become
an insolvency practitioner may apply to a 'competent authority' for authorisation to act as an insolvency practitioner. The competent authorities specified
in the legislation for this purpose are (1) in relation to a case of any
description specified in directions given by the Secretary of State, the body or
person so specified in relation to cases of that description[2]; and (2) in relation
to any other case, the Secretary of State[3]. At present no directions have been
given by the Secretary of State in respect of any body or person and
accordingly the only competent authority is the Secretary of State.

1   IA 1986, s 392(1).
2   IA 1986, s 392(2)(a).
3   IA 1986, s 392(2)(b).

APPLICATION

2.23 An application by an individual to become an insolvency practitioner
must (a) be made in such manner as the competent authority may direct; (b)
contain or be accompanied by such information as that authority may
reasonably require for the purpose of determining the application[1]; and (c) be
accompanied by the prescribed fee[2]; and the authority may direct that notice

of the making of the application must be published in such manner as may be specified in the direction[3]. At any time after receiving the application and before determining it the authority may require the applicant to furnish additional information[4]. The authority may approach individual applications on their own merits and need not follow the same procedure in each case[5]. The competent authority has power to specify the form in which information is to be forwarded by the applicant in support of his application and where appropriate may require verification of that information[6]. An applicant may withdraw his application before it is granted or refused[7].

1   The information should take into account the grounds for granting or refusing applications: see para **2.24** below.
2   The prescribed fee is £200 unless the applicant already holds an authorisation, when it is £100: Insolvency Practitioners Regulations 1990, SI 1990/439, reg 9. Any sum received by the Secretary of State must be paid into the Consolidated Fund: IA 1986, s 392(8).
3   IA 1986, s 392(3).
4   IA 1986, s 392(4).
5   IA 1986, s 392(5).
6   IA 1986, s 392(6).
7   IA 1986, s 392(7).

Grant and refusal of authorisation

2.24 The competent authority may grant or refuse an application duly made and supported with all such information as has been required[1]. The authority must, however, grant the application if it appears to it from the information furnished by the applicant and having regard to such other information, if any, as it may have that:

(1)   the applicant is a fit and proper person to act as an insolvency practitioner; and
(2)   the applicant meets the prescribed requirements with respect to education and practical training and experience[2].

1   IA 1986, s 393(1).
2   IA 1986, s 393(2).

2.25 An authorisation granted under the above provisions, if not previously withdrawn, continues in force for such period not exceeding the prescribed maximum of three years[1] from the date of grant as may be specified in the authorisation[2].

1   Insolvency Practitioners Regulations 2005, SI 2005/524, reg 10.
2   IA 1986, s 393(3).

2.26 On the grant of an authorisation to a practitioner the competent authority must give written notice of that fact to the applicant, specifying the date on which the authorisation takes effect[1]. Where the authority proposes to refuse an application, or to withdraw an authorisation[2], it must give the applicant or holder of the authorisation written notice of its intention to do so, setting out particulars of the grounds on which it proposes to act[3]. In the case of a proposed withdrawal, the notice must state the date on which it is proposed that the withdrawal should take effect[4]. A person on whom a notice is served by the competent authority that it proposes to refuse or withdraw an authorisation may, within 14 days after the date of service, make written representations to the competent authority[5]. The competent authority must have regard to any representations so made in determining whether to refuse the application or withdraw the authorisation[6].

[1]   IA 1986, s 394(1).
[2]   Under IA 1986, s 393(4).
[3]   IA 1986, s 394(2); the notice must inform the person concerned of his right to make written representations by virtue of the provisions of IA 1986, s 395(1).
[4]   IA 1986, s 394(3).
[5]   IA 1986, s 395(1).
[6]   IA 1986, s 395(2).

Fit and proper applicant

2.27 In determining whether an applicant[1] is a fit and proper person to act as an insolvency practitioner, the matters to be taken into account include:

(1)   whether the applicant has been convicted of any offence involving fraud or other dishonesty or violence;

(2)   whether the applicant has contravened any provision in any enactment contained in insolvency legislation[2]; for this purpose insolvency legislation means the primary and secondary legislation currently or previously in force in any part of Great Britain which relates to the insolvency of any person;

(3)   whether the applicant has engaged in any practices in the course of carrying on any trade, profession or vocation or in the course of discharging any functions relating to any office or employment appearing to be deceitful or oppressive or otherwise unfair or improper, whether unlawful or not, or which otherwise cast doubt upon his probity or competence for discharging the duties of an insolvency practitioner;

(4)   whether, in respect of any insolvency practice carried on by the applicant at the date or at any time before his application, there were established adequate systems of control of the practice and adequate records relating to the practice, including accounting records, and whether such systems of control and records have been or were maintained on an adequate basis;

(5)   whether the insolvency practice of the applicant is, has been or, where the applicant is not yet carrying on such a practice, will be, carried on with the independence, integrity and the professional skills appropriate to the range and scale of the practice and the proper performance of the duties of an insolvency practitioner and in accordance with generally accepted professional standards, practices and principles;

(6)   whether the applicant, in any case where he has acted as an insolvency practitioner, has failed to disclose fully to such persons as might reasonably be expected to be affected thereby circumstances where there is or appears to be a conflict of interest between his so acting and any interest of his own, whether personal, financial or otherwise, without having received such consent as might be appropriate to his acting or continuing to act despite the existence of such circumstances[3].

1   Or holder if the proposal is to withdraw an existing authorisation, Insolvency Practitioners Regulations 1990, SI 1990/439, reg 4(2).
2   Insolvency Practitioners Regulations 2005, SI 2005/524, reg 5.
3   Insolvency Practitioners Regulations 2005, SI 2005/524, reg 6.

Education and training

2.28 The prescribed requirements which an applicant must meet to qualify for the grant of an authorisation to act as an insolvency practitioner as regards education, practical training and experience[1] are laid down in the Insolvency Practitioners Regulations 2005[2]. They differ depending on whether the applicant has previously been authorised to act as an insolvency practitioner or not. Where the applicant has not been previously authorised he must have passed the Joint Insolvency Examination or acquired a comparable professional or vocational qualification outside Great Britain and have acquired sufficient experience of insolvency work; he must also have a good command of the English language[3]. Where the applicant has been previously authorised, he must have acquired sufficient experience and have completed sufficient continuing professional development[4]. Every holder of an authorisation by the Secretary of State must maintain a record of continuing professional development activity[5].

1   For the purposes of IA 1986, s 393(2)(b).
2   Insolvency Practitioners Regulations 2005, SI 2005/524, Pt 2.
3   Insolvency Practitioners Regulations 2005, SI 2005/524, reg 7.
4   Insolvency Practitioners Regulations 2005, SI 2005/524, reg 8.
5   Insolvency Practitioners Regulations 2005, SI 2005/524, reg 9.

Withdrawal of authorisation

2.29 An authorisation to act as an insolvency practitioner granted by a competent authority may be withdrawn by that authority should it appear that the holder of the authorisation is no longer a fit and proper person to act as an insolvency practitioner[1]. Further, the authorisation may be withdrawn where the holder (1) has failed to comply with any provision in relation to insolvency practitioners and their qualifications made under the Insolvency Act 1986[2]; or (2) in purported compliance with any such provision, has furnished the competent authority with false, inaccurate or misleading information[3]. Any such authorisation may also be withdrawn by the Secretary of State at the request or with the consent of the holder of the authorisation[4].

1   See para **2.27** above for the matters which determine whether a person is fit and proper to act as an insolvency practitioner.
2   Ie IA 1986, ss 388–398.
3   IA 1986, s 393(4).
4   IA 1986, s 393(5).

Transitional cases

2.30 Although there may not be many, if any, such cases today, where an individual began to act as an insolvency practitioner under the law as it stood before 29 December 1986, ie under the Companies Act 1985, he is entitled to continue acting without qualification under the 1986 Act[1].

[1]   IA 1986, s 437, Sch 11, Pt IV, para 21.

Security

Requirements for security

2.31 In order to act as an insolvency practitioner a person must satisfy the requirements for the provision of security for the proper performance of his functions[1]. These requirements are specified in Schedule 2 to the Insolvency Practitioners Regulations 2005[2].

[1]   IA 1986, s 390(3).
[2]   Insolvency Practitioners Regulations 2005, SI 2005/524, reg 12(1).

THE TERMS OF THE BOND

2.32 The bond must be in a form approved by the Secretary of State. It must contain provision whereby a surety undertakes to be jointly and severally liable for losses in relation to the insolvent caused by the fraud or dishonesty of the insolvency practitioner whether acting alone or in collusion with one or more persons or the fraud or dishonesty of any person committed with the connivance of the insolvency practitioner[1]. In outline, the bond must provide for the payment of losses so caused in each case up to the estimated value of the insolvent's assets, subject to a minimum of £5,000 and a maximum of £5,000,000 ('the specific penalty sum') and, in the event that the specific penalty sum is insufficient to meet the claims arising, for a further sum of £250,000 ('the general penalty sum') to be available to meet such claims[2].

[1]   Insolvency Practitioners Regulations 2005, SI 2005/524, reg 12(1), Sch 2, para 3.
[2]   Insolvency Practitioners Regulations 2005, SI 2005/524, reg 12(1), Sch 2, paras 4–8.

RECORDS RELATING TO THE BOND

2.33 An insolvency practitioner must maintain a record of all specific penalty sums that are applicable in relation to any case in which he is acting. The record must contain the name of each person to whom the specific penalty sum relates and the amount of each penalty sum that is in force. The record must be made available for inspection on the giving of notice by any professional body recognised under IA 1986, s 391 of which he is a member and whose rules of membership entitle him to act as an insolvency practitioner, any competent authority by whom he is authorised to act pursuant to IA 1986, s 393 or the Secretary of State[1].

[1]   Insolvency Practitioners Regulations 2005, SI 2005/524, reg 12(1), Sch 2, para 9.

RETENTION OF THE BOND

2.34 The insolvency practitioner must send the bond to the professional body recognised under IA 1986, s 391 of which he is a member and whose rules of membership entitle him to act as an insolvency practitioner or to the competent authority by whom he is authorised to act pursuant to IA 1986, s 393[1].

[1] Insolvency Practitioners Regulations 2005, SI 2005/524, reg 12(1), Sch 2, para 10.

OBLIGATIONS RELATING TO THE COVER SCHEDULE

2.35 The insolvency practitioner must submit to his authorising body[1], not later than 20 days after the end of each month during which he holds office in a case: the information submitted to a surety in any cover schedule related to that month; where no cover schedule is submitted in relation to the month, a statement either that there are no relevant particulars to be supplied or, as the case may be, that it is not practicable to supply particulars in relation to any appointments taken during that month; and a statement identifying any case in which he has been granted his release or discharge[2]. He must retain a copy of the cover schedule so submitted by him in respect of his acting in respect of any company or individual until the second anniversary of his release or discharge in relation to that company or individual[3]. The copy must be produced for inspection on request by: any creditor: if it relates to an individual, that individual; if it relates to a company, any contributory, director or other officer of that company; and the Secretary of State[4].

[1] This means the professional body recognised under IA 1986, s 391 of which he is a member and whose rules of membership entitle him to act as an insolvency practitioner or the competent authority by whom he is authorised to act pursuant to IA 1986, s 393: Insolvency Practitioners Regulations 2005, SI 2005/524, reg 12(1), Sch 2, para 13(2).
[2] Insolvency Practitioners Regulations 2005, SI 2005/524, reg 12(1), Sch 2, para 13(1).
[3] Insolvency Practitioners Regulations 2005, SI 2005/524, reg 12(1), Sch 2, para 11(1) and (2).
[4] Insolvency Practitioners Regulations 2005, SI 2005/524, reg 12(1), Sch 2, para 11(1) and (3).

C EXEMPTIONS FROM THE RESTRICTIVE TRADE PRACTICES ACT 1976

2.36 The provision of insolvency services by insolvency practitioners are given a complete exemption from the provisions of the Restrictive Trade Practices Act 1976. For these purposes 'insolvency services' means the services of persons acting as insolvency practitioners or carrying out the corresponding functions under the law of Northern Ireland[1]. From the date of the coming into force of the Insolvency Act 1986[2], no restriction in respect of any of the following matters is to be regarded as a restriction by virtue of which the 1976 Act applies to any agreement, whenever made:

(1)   the charges to be made, quoted or paid for insolvency services supplied, offered or obtained;

(2)   the terms or conditions on or subject to which insolvency services are to be supplied or obtained;

(3)   the extent, if any, to which, or the scale, if any, on which, insolvency services are to be made available, supplied or obtained;

(4)   the form or manner in which insolvency services are to be made available, supplied or obtained;

(5)   the persons or classes of persons for whom or from whom, or the areas or places in or from which, insolvency services are to be made available or supplied or are to be obtained[3].

¹   IA 1986, s 428(3).
²   Ie 29 December 1986: IA 1986, s 443; Insolvency Act 1985 (Commencement No 5) Order 1986, SI 1986/1924.
³   IA 1986, s 428(1), (2). For the purposes of IA 1986, s 428 expressions which are also used in the Restrictive Trade Practices Act 1976 have the same meaning in the IA 1986, s 428 as in the 1976 Act: IA 1986, s 428(3).

D INSOLVENCY PRACTITIONERS TRIBUNAL

Constitution and purpose

2.37 The Secretary of State is required[1] to draw up and from time to time revise:

(1)   a panel of persons who have a seven-year general legal qualification, within the meaning of the Courts and Legal Services Act 1990, s 71, and are nominated for the purpose by the Lord Chancellor; and

(2)   a panel of persons who are experienced in insolvency matters from which panels the members of the Insolvency Practitioners Tribunal will be selected[2].

¹   IA 1986, s 396(1), Sch 7, para 1.
²   The members may be remunerated for sitting on the tribunal, IA 1986, Sch 7, para 2.

2.38 The power of the Secretary of State to revise the membership of the panels includes a power to terminate a person's membership of either of them[1]. To that extent the power is subject to the provisions of the Tribunal and Inquiries Act 1992, s 7 and requires the consent of the Lord Chancellor. For the purposes of carrying out its functions in relation to any cases referred to it, the Insolvency Practitioners Tribunal may sit either as a single tribunal or in two or more divisions[2]; and the functions of the tribunal in relation to any case referred to it must be exercised by three members consisting of a chairman, who is drawn from the panel of lawyers, and two other members who are to be drawn from the panel of experienced practitioners[3].

¹   IA 1986, Sch 7, para 1(2).
²   IA 1986, Sch 7, para 3(1).
³   IA 1986, Sch 7, para 3(2).

2.38A The Tribunals, Courts and Enforcement Act 2007 seeks to introduce a unified system of administrative tribunals. Under this system there will be a First-tier Tribunal and an Upper Tribunal[1]. The Lord Chancellor is enabled to transfer the functions of some existing tribunals to these new, unified tribunals[2]. He may do so, in particular, with respect to the Insolvency Practitioners' Tribunal[3].

1   TCEA 2007, s 3.
2   TCEA 2007, s 30.
3   TCEA 2007, s 30(2) and Sch 6.

2.39 The Insolvency Practitioners Tribunal (Conduct of Investigations) Rules 1986[1] enable the chairman to carry out anything required or authorised to be done by the Insolvency Practitioners Tribunal in the course of an investigation except:

(1)   the settling of the manner in which the tribunal is to conduct its investigation;

(2)   the hearing or consideration of any representations made by the competent authority or the applicant; and

(3)   the taking of evidence, whether orally or in the form of documents or non-documentary records.

1   Insolvency Practitioners Tribunal (Conduct of Investigations) Rules 1986, SI 1986/952, r 14.

Reference to tribunal

2.40 A person who is served with a notice by the competent authority that it proposes to refuse or withdraw an authorisation, may (1) at any time within 28 days after the date of service of the notice, or (2) at any time after the making by him of written representations[1] and before the end of the period of 28 days after the date of the service on him of a notice by the competent authority that the authority does not propose to alter its decision in consequence of the representations, give written notice to the authority requiring the case to be referred to the Insolvency Practitioners Tribunal[2]. Where such a requirement is made the competent authority must refer the case to the Insolvency Practitioners Tribunal, unless it has decided or decides to grant the application or, as appropriate, not to withdraw the authorisation, and gives written notice of that decision to the person by whom the requirement was made within seven days after the date of the making of the requirement[3].

1   Under IA 1986, s 395(1).
2   IA 1986, s 396(2).
3   IA 1986, s 396(3).

2.41 On referring a case to the tribunal, the competent authority must send to the tribunal a copy of the written notice served by it on the applicant, together with a copy of the notification by the applicant that he wishes the case to be referred to the tribunal, and give notice to the applicant of the date on which the case has been referred by it to the tribunal and of the address to which any statement, notice or other document required to be given or sent to the tribunal is to be given or sent[1]. Within 21 days of referring the case to the tribunal, the competent authority must send to the tribunal such further information and copies of such other documents and records as it considers would be of assistance to the tribunal, and at the same time send to the applicant such further information and copies of such other documents and records; or, if there is no such information or copies, the competent authority must within such period notify the tribunal and the applicant to that effect[2].

[1]   Insolvency Practitioners Tribunal (Conduct of Investigations) Rules 1986, SI 1986/952, r 2.
[2]   Insolvency Practitioners Tribunal (Conduct of Investigations) Rules, 1986, SI 1986/952, r 2(2).

2.42 The applicant must serve a statement of his grounds for requiring the case to be investigated by the tribunal within 21 days after the competent authority has sent to the applicant the above material or, as the case may be, after it has sent to him the notification that there is no such material[1]. The statement of grounds must state:

(1)   which matters of fact, if any, contained in the written notice served on him he disputes;
(2)   any other matters which he considers should be drawn to the attention of the tribunal; and
(3)   the names and addresses of any witnesses whose evidence he wishes the tribunal to hear. The statement must be served both on the tribunal and on the competent authority[2].

[1]   Insolvency Practitioners Tribunal (Conduct of Investigations) Rules, 1986, SI 1986/952, r 3.
[2]   Insolvency Practitioners Tribunal (Conduct of Investigations) Rules, 1986, SI 1986/952, r 3(2).

Investigation by tribunal

2.43 The investigation of the Insolvency Practitioners Tribunal into any case referred to it is governed by the Insolvency Practitioners Tribunal (Conduct of Investigation) Rules 1986[1]. At any time after the reference has been made, the Insolvency Practitioners Tribunal may appoint the Treasury Solicitor and Counsel to assist the tribunal in seeking and presenting evidence in accordance with its requirements, and representing the public interest in relation to the matters before the tribunal[2]. The tribunal investigates the case and makes a report to the competent authority stating what would in its opinion be the appropriate decision in the matter and the reasons for that opinion. The competent authority is required to decide the matter in accordance with this opinion[3].

[1]   Insolvency Practitioners Tribunal (Conduct of Investigations) Rules, 1986, SI 1986/952.
[2]   Insolvency Practitioners Tribunal (Conduct of Investigations) Rules, 1986, SI 1986/952, r 4.
[3]   IA 1986, s 397(1).

2.44 After the receipt of the statement of the applicant or, if no such statement is received, after the expiry of the 21 days in which the applicant must send his statement, the tribunal must investigate the case and make a report by carrying out such inquiries as it thinks appropriate for that purpose into and concerning the information, documents, records and matters placed before it[1].

Any notice or other document required by the Insolvency Practitioners Tribunal (Conduct of Investigations) Rules 1986 to be given or sent may be given or sent by first-class post[2].

1   Insolvency Practitioners Tribunal (Conduct of Investigations) Rules, 1986, SI 1986/952, r 5.
2   Insolvency Practitioners Tribunal (Conduct of Investigations) Rules, 1986, SI 1986/952, r 12.

2.45 The Insolvency Practitioners Tribunal has power to extend the time within which the competent authority or the applicant is required to send any document or perform any act under the Tribunal Rules and such extension of time may be granted after any such time has expired[1].

1   Insolvency Practitioners Tribunal (Conduct of Investigations) Rules, 1986, SI 1986/952, r 13.

Procedure of and methods of inquiry by the tribunal

2.46 Any investigation by the Insolvency Practitioners Tribunal must be so conducted as to afford a reasonable opportunity for representations to be made to the tribunal by or on behalf of the person whose case is the subject of the investigation[1], and in accordance with the rules made by the Secretary of State for regulating the procedure on any investigation by the tribunal[2].

1   IA 1986, Sch 7, para 4(1).
2   See the Insolvency Practitioners Tribunal (Conduct of Investigations) Rules 1986, SI 1986/952, which were made pursuant to the Insolvency Act 1985, Sch 1, para 4 (repealed).

2.47 As soon as practicable after the tribunal has considered the subject matter of the investigation, it must notify the competent authority and the applicant of the manner in which it proposes to conduct its inquiries and in particular whether oral evidence is to be taken[1]. The tribunal must give the competent authority and the applicant a reasonable opportunity of making representations on the manner in which it proposes to conduct its inquiries and such representations may be made orally or in writing at the option of the competent authority or the applicant, as the case may be[2]. After considering any such representations that may be made, the tribunal must notify the competent authority and the applicant whether and, if so, in what respects, it has decided to alter the manner in which it proposes to carry out its inquiries[3]. If, at any subsequent stage in the investigation, the tribunal proposes to make any material change in the manner in which its inquiries are to be carried out, it must notify the competent authority and the applicant[4].

1   Insolvency Practitioners Tribunal (Conduct of Investigations) Rules 1986, SI 1986/952, r 6(1).
2   Insolvency Practitioners Tribunal (Conduct of Investigations) Rules 1986, SI 1986/952, r 6(2).

[3] Insolvency Practitioners Tribunal (Conduct of Investigations) Rules 1986, SI 1986/952, r 6(3).
[4] Insolvency Practitioners Tribunal (Conduct of Investigations) Rules 1986, SI 1986/952, r 6(4).

2.48 For the purposes of its investigation, the Insolvency Practitioners Tribunal (1) may by summons require any person to attend, at such time and place as is specified in the summons, to give evidence or to produce any books, papers and other records in his possession or under his control which the tribunal considers it necessary for the purposes of the investigation to examine; and (2) may take evidence on oath, and for the purpose administer oaths, or may, instead of administering an oath, require the person examined to make and subscribe a declaration of the truth of the matter respecting which he is examined; but no person is to be required, in obedience to such a summons, to go more than ten miles from his place of residence, unless the necessary expenses of his attendance are paid or tendered to him[1].

[1] IA 1986, Sch 7, para 4(2). By para 4(3) every person who (a) without reasonable excuse fails to attend in obedience to a summons issued under the above provisions, or refuses to give evidence, or (b) intentionally alters, suppresses, conceals or destroys or refuses to produce any document which he may be required to produce for the purpose of an investigation by the tribunal, is liable on summary conviction to a fine on level 3 on the standard scale within the meaning of the Criminal Justice Act 1982, s 37 and IA 1986, Sch 10.

2.49 When in the carrying out of its inquiries the tribunal wishes to examine a witness orally, it must give notice to the applicant and the competent authority of the time and place at which the examination will be held, and the applicant and the competent authority are entitled to be present at the examination by the tribunal of any witness and to put such additional questions to him as may appear to the tribunal to be relevant to the subject matter of the investigation[1]. Where the tribunal takes into consideration documentary evidence or evidence in the form of computer or other non-documentary records not placed before the tribunal, the tribunal must give the applicant and the competent authority an opportunity of inspecting that evidence and taking copies or an appropriate record thereof[2].

[1] Insolvency Practitioners Tribunal (Conduct of Investigations) Rules 1986, SI 1986/952, r 7(a).
[2] Insolvency Practitioners Tribunal (Conduct of Investigations) Rules 1986, SI 1986/952, r 7(b).

2.50 After the Insolvency Practitioners Tribunal has completed the taking of such evidence as it considers necessary for the purpose of the investigation, it must give the applicant and the competent authority a reasonable opportunity of making final representations on the evidence and on the subject matter of the investigation generally. Such final representations may be made orally or in writing at the option of the applicant or, as the case may be, of the competent authority[1].

[1] Insolvency Practitioners Tribunal (Conduct of Investigations) Rules 1986, SI 1986/952, r 8.

Conduct of hearings

2.51 At the hearing of oral representations or the taking of oral evidence before the Insolvency Practitioners Tribunal, the applicant may be represented by counsel or solicitor, or by any other person allowed by the tribunal to appear on his behalf[1]. The competent authority may be represented by counsel or solicitor or by any officer of the competent authority[2].

Copies of any written representations made by either side to the Insolvency Practitioners Tribunal in the course of its investigation must be served on the other side[3].

[1]   Insolvency Practitioners Tribunal (Conduct of Investigations) Rules 1986, SI 1986/952, r 9(a).
[2]   Insolvency Practitioners Tribunal (Conduct of Investigations) Rules 1986, SI 1986/952, r 9(b).
[3]   Insolvency Practitioners Tribunal (Conduct of Investigations) Rules 1986, SI 1986/952, r 10.

2.52 The Insolvency Practitioners Tribunal must conduct its investigation in private and, save to the extent that the Insolvency Practitioners Tribunal (Conduct of Investigations) Rules 1986 provide for the hearing of oral representations or for the taking of oral evidence and the applicant requests that any such hearing be in public, no person other than those entitled to represent the applicant or the competent authority or having the leave of the tribunal are entitled to be present at any such hearing[1].

[1]   Insolvency Practitioners Tribunal (Conduct of Investigations) Rules 1986, SI 1986/952, r 11(1).

Reports by tribunal following investigation

2.53 Following a reference to it, the Insolvency Practitioners Tribunal must make a report to the competent authority stating what would in its opinion be the appropriate decision in the matter and the reasons for that opinion[1]. The tribunal must make its report on the case to the competent authority no later than four months after the date on which the case is referred to it unless the competent authority, on the application of the tribunal, permits the report to be made within such further period as the competent authority may notify in writing to the tribunal[2].

[1]   IA 1986, s 397(1)(b).
[2]   Insolvency Practitioners Tribunal (Conduct of Investigations) Rules 1986, SI 1986/952, r 15(1).

2.54 The competent authority may only permit the report to be made within such further period where it appears to that authority that, through exceptional circumstances, the tribunal will be unable to make its report within the period of four months referred to above[1]. The tribunal must send a copy of the report to the applicant or, as the case may be, the holder of the authorisation; and the competent authority must serve him with a written notice of the decision made by it in accordance with the report[2].

The competent authority may, if it thinks fit, publish the report of the tribunal[3].

1 Insolvency Practitioners Tribunal (Conduct of Investigations) Rules 1986, SI 1986/952, r 15(2).
2 IA 1986, s 397(2).
3 IA 1986, s 397(3).

Refusal or withdrawal of authorisation without reference to tribunal

2.55 Where in the case of any proposed refusal or withdrawal of an authorisation the periods within which a person may give written notice to the competent authority requiring the case to be referred to the Insolvency Practitioners Tribunal have expired, the competent authority may give written notice of the refusal or withdrawal to the person concerned[1]. The expiry of the periods referred to is either (1) the expiry of the period for giving notice to the competent authority requiring the case to be referred to the tribunal[2], or (2) where the competent authority has given a notice to the practitioner that it does not propose to alter its decision to withdraw his authorisation despite consideration of his written representations[3], the expiry of the period of 28 days from the date of the service of such notice.

The written notice of the refusal or withdrawal of the authorisation to the person concerned must be in accordance with the proposal in the original notice given to the practitioner[4].

1 IA 1986, s 398.
2 See IA 1986, s 396(2)(a) (see para 2.40 above) ie 28 days after the service of a notice by the competent authority informing the applicant of its intention to withdraw his authorisation.
3 Ie under IA 1986, s 395.
4 Ie under IA 1986, ss 394(2), 398.

E RECORDS TO BE KEPT BY INSOLVENCY PRACTITIONER

Cases where the insolvency practitioner was appointed before 1 April 2005

2.56 In respect of any case where the insolvency practitioner was appointed before 1 April 2005, the provisions of the Insolvency Practitioners Regulations 1990, Pt IV[1] continue to apply to the records which he must keep.

1 SI 1990/439.

Cases where the insolvency practitioner was appointed on or after 1 April 2005

2.57 Where the insolvency practitioner's appointment was made on or after 1 April 2005, he must maintain records in accordance with the Insolvency Practitioners Regulations 2005, Pt 4[1]. It is these rules which are set out below.

1 SI 2005/524.

Records to be kept

2.58 In respect of each case in which he acts, an insolvency practitioner must maintain records containing at least the information specified in Schedule 3 to the Insolvency Practitioners Regulations 2005[1]. He is under a duty to keep the records up to date at all times[2]. So, on taking up office as trustee where another practitioner has previously acted as trustee, an insolvency practitioner must check the state of the records and bring them up to date if necessary. Each record must be capable of being produced by the insolvency practitioner separately from any other record.

[1]   Insolvency Practitioners Regulations 2005, SI 2005/524, reg 13.
[2]   Insolvency Practitioners Regulations 2005, SI 2005/524, reg 13(2).

2.59 The information is specified in Schedule 3 to the regulations under the following heads:

(1)   details of the insolvency practitioner acting in the case;
(2)   details of the insolvent;
(3)   progress of the administration;
(4)   bonding arrangements in the case;
(5)   matters relating to remuneration;
(6)   meetings apart from any final meeting of creditors;
(7)   (in cases of company insolvency) certain matters where a return or report must be made under the Company Directors Disqualification Act 1986;
(8)   vacation of office;
(9)   distribution to creditors;
(10)   statutory returns;
(11)   time recording.

2.60 Extensive records will also be required in order to comply with the requirements contained in the Practice Statement: The Fixing and Approval of the Remuneration of Appointees (2004), para 5.

Period for which the records must be preserved

2.61 The record must be preserved by the insolvency practitioner until whichever is the later of the sixth anniversary of the date of the grant to the insolvency practitioner of his release or discharge in the relevant case or the sixth anniversary of the date on which any security maintained in that case expires or otherwise ceases to have effect[1].

[1]   Insolvency Practitioners Regulations 2005, SI 2005/524, reg 13(5).

Notification of the whereabouts of the records

2.62 The whereabouts of the records and the place, if different, where they may be inspected must be notified by an insolvency practitioner to any professional body recognised under IA 1986, s 391 of which he is a member and whose rules of membership entitle him to act as an insolvency practitioner or any competent authority by whom he is authorised to act pursuant to IA 1986, s 393[1].

[1] Insolvency Practitioners Regulations 2005, SI 2005/524, regs 14 and 15(1)(a) and (b).

Inspection of records

2.63 The records must be produced for inspection on the giving of notice by any professional body recognised under IA 1986, s 391 of which he is a member and whose rules of membership entitle him to act as an insolvency practitioner, any competent authority by whom he is authorised to act pursuant to IA 1986, s 393 or the Secretary of State. Anyone entitled to inspect may take a copy of the record[1].

[1] Insolvency Practitioners Regulations 2005, SI 2005/524, reg 15.

Inspection of practice records

2.64 The Secretary of State has the right to inspect and to take copies of the practice records of any insolvency practitioner who was authorised to act pursuant to IA 1986, s 393. These records are the records which record receipts and payments made by the insolvency practitioner in relation to which he acted as insolvency practitioner pursuant to the authorisation, which record time spent by the insolvency practitioner or anyone assigned to assist him, which relate to any business carried on in the case by or at the direction of the insolvency practitioner, or which otherwise relate to the management of the case. The right extends to records of this kind whether held by the insolvency practitioner himself, his employer or former employer or any firm or other body of which he is or was a member or partner[1].

[1] Insolvency Practitioners Regulations 2005, SI 2005/524, reg 16.

F REMOVAL AND REPLACEMENT OF INSOLVENCY PRACTITIONERS AS OFFICE-HOLDERS

General

2.65 An appointment as an office-holder is a personal appointment. This is the case even where the authorised insolvency practitioner concerned is a member of a firm and has been appointed to office by reason of that membership. An office-holder may leave office by retirement or removal and for a variety of reasons either voluntary or involuntary. For the circumstances in which a trustee may resign his office, see **Chapter 13**, section E below. This section is concerned with the manner in which an office-holder may be removed from office prior to the completion of the insolvency procedure to which he has been appointed, and replaced by an alternative insolvency practitioner.

Supervisor of voluntary arrangement

2.66 The court has power to appoint a qualified insolvency practitioner to carry out the functions of supervisor when it is 'inexpedient, difficult or impracticable for an appointment to be made without the assistance of the court'[1]. This power may be exercised so as to replace one or more existing supervisors or to increase the number of insolvency practitioners acting as supervisor to the voluntary arrangement[2]. The IA 1986 provides that it must be expedient for the court to appoint a person to carry out the functions of the supervisor before an appointment can be made[3]; plainly it will be expedient for an appointment to be made when a supervisor retires, whether voluntarily or involuntarily, for every voluntary arrangement must have a supervisor[4]. The wording of the statute makes it plain that the appointment of a replacement or additional supervisor should primarily be a matter for the creditors. If the voluntary arrangement contains provision for the appointment of an alternative supervisor, the existing supervisor and the creditors will have to follow the relevant terms of the arrangement. If the arrangement has no relevant terms an application will have to be made to the court by the existing supervisor, the debtor or any creditor[5].

1   IA 1986, s 263(5)(b).
2   IA 1986, s 263(6); see *Re A & C Supplies Ltd* [1998] 1 BCLC 603.
3   IA 1986, s 263(5)(a).
4   IA 1986, s 263(2).
5   By originating application under the IA 1986, s 263(5) and/or s 263(3), which enables any of the debtor's creditors or any other person who is dissatisfied by an act, omission or decision of the supervisor to apply to the court.

Trustee in bankruptcy

2.67 In the relatively rare case of a trustee appointed by the Secretary of State, he may be removed from office by a direction of the Secretary of State[1]. In all other cases a trustee may be removed from office only by order of the court, or by a general meeting of the bankrupt's creditors summoned specially for that purpose[2]. Where an application is made for the removal of the trustee by the court there is no statutory requirement that a cause for removal adverse to the trustee be shown[3], neither is there express power in the court to appoint a replacement trustee. However, it was held in *Re A & C Supplies Ltd*[4] both that a cause must be shown, and that the court could appoint a replacement where it removed an existing trustee[5].

1   IA 1986, s 298(5).
2   IA 1986, s 298(1).
3   As is the case under the IA 1986, s 172(2) which does not expressly require cause to be shown for the removal of a liquidator in compulsory winding up, in contrast to the provisions of the IA 1986, s 108(2) governing the removal by the court of a liquidator in a voluntary winding up.
4   [1998] 1 BCLC 603.
5   The case concerned the removal of an insolvency practitioner from appointments both as liquidator and trustee. The court's power to appoint a replacement trustee is to be implied under the IA 1986, s 303(2).

Removal by meeting of creditors

2.68 The statute expressly requires that a meeting of creditors summoned to remove a trustee must be summoned in accordance with the rules[1]. The rules specify that the notice[2] summoning the meeting must (a) indicate that the removal of the trustee is the purpose, or one of the purposes, of the meeting; and (b) draw the attention of creditors to the statutory provisions regarding the trustee's release[3]. The meeting may resolve against the trustee having his release, in which event the trustee will have to apply to the Secretary of State for his release[4]. If the meeting does not resolve against his release, whether or not it agrees to it, the trustee will have his release at the time that notice is given to the court that the trustee no longer holds office[5]. The notice summoning the meeting of creditors must be sent to the official receiver at the same time as it is sent to the creditors[6]. At the meeting a person other than the trustee or his nominee may be elected to act as chairman[7]. It will normally be sensible for there to be an independent chairman, but where the creditors are divided on the issue it may be difficult for a chairman to be found who is satisfactory to both sides. One answer is to invite the official receiver to chair the meeting. Should the trustee or his nominee act as chairman he may not delay the evil day by adjourning the meeting against the wishes of creditors. Once a resolution has been proposed for the removal of the trustee, the chairman of the meeting may not adjourn it without the consent of at least one-half in value of the creditors present (in person or by proxy) and entitled to vote[8]. On the application of any creditor, the court may give directions as to the mode of summoning the meeting, the sending out and return of forms of proxy, the conduct of the meeting and any other matter which appears to the court to require regulation or control[9].

[1]   IA 1986, s 298(1).
[2]   The form of notice to creditors for a meeting of creditors is Form 6.35 in the IR 1986, Sch 4.
[3]   IR 1986, r 6.129(1); the trustee's release is governed by the IA 1986, s 299(3).
[4]   IA 1986, s 299(3)(b).
[5]   IA 1986, s 299(3)(a); notice is given to the court by the official receiver, IR 1986, r 6.131.
[6]   IR 1986, r 6.129(2).
[7]   IR 1986, r 6.129(3).
[8]   IR 1986, r 6.129(3).
[9]   IR 1986, r 6.130.

2.69 The official receiver is to be kept informed, and where he is not the chairman of the meeting, the chairman is required to send him, within three days, a copy of any resolution (a) to remove the trustee, (b) to appoint a new trustee and (c) that the removed trustee is not to have his release[1]. In addition, and also within three days, the chairman of the meeting must send a certificate of removal of the former trustee and a certificate of appointment of any new trustee to the official receiver[2]. The official receiver files the certificate of removal in court[3], and the resolution to remove the trustee is effective as from the day on which the certificate is so filed, this date being endorsed on the certificate[4]. The official receiver may not file the certificate in court unless and until the Secretary of State has certified to him that the removed trustee has reconciled his account in respect of the winding up with that held by the Secretary of State[5]. When the certificate has been filed and endorsed a copy of it is sent by the official receiver to both the removed trustee and any new trustee[6]. Where a replacement trustee is appointed he must give notice of his appointment by advertisement[7] and state that his predecessor has been removed and, if it be the case, that he has been given his release[8].

1   IR 1986, r 6.129(4).
2   IR 1986, r 6.129(4), (5).
3   IR 1986, r 6.131(1).
4   IR 1986, r 6.131(2).
5   IR 1986, r 6.131(4).
6   IR 1986, r 6.131(3).
7   IR 1986, r 6.124(1).
8   IR 1986, r 6.134.

Multiple applications

2.70 Most insolvency practitioners will be appointed to hold office in many insolvencies, both corporate and personal, and in different courts throughout the country. Should an individual practitioner have to cease practising through ill-health, disqualification or retirement, one or more replacements will have to be appointed to each of the outgoing practitioner's appointments. Separate applications to replace the practitioner in each case would be an expensive and time-consuming exercise. Although initially the courts held that a practitioner would have to be replaced on a case-by-case basis where his appointments were spread between different courts[1], the resulting inconvenience has now been avoided by the expedient of transferring all county court proceedings in which the insolvency practitioner has an appointment to the High Court, and replacing the practitioner in all his High Court and county court appointments in one application. The transfer from the county court takes place under the provisions of the County Courts Act 1984, s 41(1). Once all the cases are in the High Court one single order may be made removing the office-holder from his various appointments and replacing him in each case with one or more qualified insolvency practitioners[2]. The court must have regard to the interests of the creditors of the various estates, and where appropriate to do so should impose conditions for the protection of creditors[3]. It was held in *Supperstone v Auger*[4] that an order made by the High Court replacing an insolvency practitioner in multiple appointments may include offices held by him in pre-1986 insolvencies. In that case Mr Justice Park prepared a table showing the statutory sources of jurisdiction for a block order by the High Court transferring offices held by an insolvency practitioner together with a number of explanatory notes. This table and the explanatory notes are reproduced at para **2.80** below.

1   See *Re Bridgend Goldsmiths Ltd* [1995] 2 BCLC 208; *Re Sankey Furniture Ltd, ex p Harding* [1995] 2 BCLC 594.
2   See *Re Bullard and Taplin Ltd* [1996] BCC 973; *Re a Licence-holder, Abbot* [1997] BCC 666; *Re A & C Supplies Ltd* [1998] 1 BCLC 603.
3   *Re Equity Nominees Ltd* [1999] 2 BCLC 19, where the court ordered the new office-holder to write within 28 days to all creditors explaining the effect of the order and the right of creditors to call for a statement of receipts and payments in the trusteeship (Insolvency Regulations 1994, SI 1994/2507, reg 25) and gave the creditors liberty to apply within 28 days thereafter for a reconsideration of the order if there was a 'good ground' on which to do so.
4   [1999] BPIR 152.

Applicant for order

2.71 Neither the Insolvency Act 1986 nor the Insolvency Rules 1986 make provision governing who may apply for an order to remove and or replace an insolvency practitioner. The courts have approached the matter pragmatically, and it appears that anyone with a legitimate interest to do so may make the application. Thus in *Re A J Adams Builders Ltd*[1] the court allowed an application by a liquidator who had been suspended from acting as an authorised insolvency practitioner, the suspended practitioner applying for an order that a colleague be appointed in his place. In *Re a Licence-holder, Abbot*[2] the application was made by the corporate insolvency partner of a firm of accountants, an employee of which had been appointed to act in some 400 matters but whose application to act as an insolvency practitioner had been refused by the Secretary of State[3]. The application was made with the support of the Secretary of State. In *Re Bullard and Taplin Ltd*[4] the application was made by an insolvency practitioner whose partnership had dissolved and whose assets were taken over by another firm. He applied for his replacement in 168 offices by partners in the takeover firm. In *Re Stella Metals Ltd (in liquidation)*[5] the court permitted an application by the Insolvency Practitioners Association to replace from his appointments a former member of the Association who had been suspended from acting as an authorised insolvency practitioner. In doing so the court stated that it would not be desirable to lay down hard and fast rules of general application as to who may apply for the removal and replacement of an insolvency practitioner. In the cases then before the court it was convenient for the Insolvency Practitioners Association to make one application rather than require creditors in each insolvency to make separate applications. However, that did not mean that a recognised professional body would be an appropriate applicant in every case[6].

1   [1991] BCLC 359.
2   [1997] BCC 666.
3   See also *Re A & C Supplies Ltd* [1998] 1 BCLC 603 where the office-holder was expelled from his partnership, and the remaining partners applied for his replacement by continuing partners.
4   [1996] BCC 973.
5   [1997] BCC 626.
6   [1997] BCC 626 at 628H.

Procedure

2.72 The procedure to be followed is set out in the *Practice Direction: Insolvency Proceedings*, para 1.6 which applies where an insolvency practitioner ('the outgoing office-holder') holds office as a liquidator, administrator, trustee or supervisor in more than one case and dies, retires from practice as an insolvency practitioner or is otherwise unable or unwilling to continue in office.

2.73 A single application may be made to a judge of the Chancery Division of the High Court by way of ordinary application in Form 7.2 for the appointment of a substitute office-holder or office-holders in all cases in which the outgoing office-holder holds office, and for the transfer of each such case to the High Court for the purpose only of making such an order. The application may be made by the outgoing office-holder (if he is able and willing to do so), any person who holds office jointly with the outgoing office-holder, any person who is proposed to be appointed as a substitute for the outgoing office-holder or any creditor in the cases where the substitution is proposed to be made.

2.74 The outgoing office-holder (if he is not the applicant) and every person who holds office jointly with the office-holder must be made a respondent to the application, but it is not necessary to join any other person as a respondent or to serve the application upon any other person unless the judge or registrar in the High Court so directs. The application should not be made without notice to the existing trustee, though in an urgent case an additional trustee may be appointed where appropriate[1].

[1]   *Clements v Udal* [2002] 2 BCLC 606.

2.75 The application should contain schedules setting out the nature of the office held, the identity of the Court currently having jurisdiction over each case and its name and number. It must be supported by evidence setting out the circumstances which have given rise to the need to make a substitution and exhibiting the written consent to act of each person who is proposed to be appointed in place of the outgoing office-holder.

2.76 The Judge will in the first instance consider the application on paper and make such order as he thinks fit. In particular he may do any of the following:

(i)   make an order directing the transfer to the High Court of those cases not already within its jurisdiction for the purpose only of the substantive application;

(ii)   if he considers that the papers are in order and that the matter is straightforward, make an order on the substantive application;

(iii) give any directions which he considers to be necessary including (if appropriate) directions for the joinder of any additional respondents or requiring the service of the application on any person or requiring additional evidence to be provided;

(iv)   if he does not himself make an order on the substantive application when the matter is first before him, give directions for the further consideration of the substantive application by himself or another judge of the Chancery Division or adjourn the substantive application to the registrar for him to make such order upon it as is appropriate.

2.77 An order of the kind referred to in sub-paragraph (i) above must follow the draft order in Form PDIP 3 set out in the Schedule to the Practice Direction and an order granting the substantive application shall follow the draft order in Form PDIP 4 set out in that schedule, subject in each case to such modifications as may be necessary or appropriate.

2.78 The applicant is under an obligation to ensure that a sealed copy of every order transferring any case to the High Court and of every order which is made on a substantive application is lodged with the court having jurisdiction over each case affected by such order for filing on the court file relating to that case.

Interested parties may apply to review a block transfer order[1].

It is not necessary for the file relating to any case which is transferred to the High Court in accordance with this paragraph to be sent to the High Court unless a Judge or Registrar so directs.

[1]   *HM Customs & Excise v Allen* [2003] BPIR 830.

2.79 The costs of the application should not fall on the bankrupt's estate or on the assets of any insolvent company, unless the court expressly so orders[1]. In multiple removal and replacement applications, orders for costs have been made against the various estates divided in equal proportions between the various cases involved[2]. Where there are many cases the burden of costs falling on the individual estates will be small. It will, however, be no fault of the creditors that an individual office-holder has to be removed, and in the ordinary course of events the court should look first to visiting any order for costs on the office-holder who has made an application necessary. In *Re Equity Nominees Ltd* the court considered the incidence of costs and was inclined to the view that in the ordinary course of events the cost of replacing an office-holder who had not himself behaved improperly reasonably fell on the various estates as a normal incidence of insolvency. Costs which could not be attributed to any particular estate could properly be divided equally among all the various estates regardless of size[3].

[1]   IR 1986, r 6.132(4) (bankruptcy); IR 1986, r 4.119(5) (compulsory liquidation); IR 1986, r 4.120(5) (voluntary liquidation).
[2]   See, for example, *Re a Licence-holder, Abbot* [1997] BCC 666, where the court imposed a limit of 10% of the realisable assets in any one case.
[3]   [1999] 2 BCLC 19.

Mr Justice Park's statutory sources table

2.80

INDIVIDUALS	Transfer to High Court	Removal of present office-holder	Appoint-ment of new office-holder	See note:
Bankruptcies				
Post-1986 in county court	IR 1986, r 7.11(4) CCA 1984, s 41(1)			1

Post-1986 in High Court	Unnecessary but see note 2	IA 1986, s 298(1)	IA 1986, s 303(2)	2, 3, 4
Pre-1986 in county court	BR 1952, r 21 CCA 1984, s 41(1)			1
Pre-1986 in High Court	Unnecessary but see note 2	BA 1914, s 79(3)	BA 1914, s 79(3)	2, 3, 4
Voluntary arrangements – IVAs				
Post-1986 only in county court	CCA 1984, s 41(1)			1
in High Court	Unnecessary but see note 2	IA 1986, s 263(5)	IA 1986, s 263(5)	2
COMPANIES				
Voluntary liquidations				
Post-1986	Unnecessary	IA 1986, s 108	IA 1986, s 108	
Pre-1986	Unnecessary	CA 1985, s 599	CA 1985, s 599	
Compulsory liquidations				
Post-1986 in county court	IR 1986, r 7.11(4) CAA 1984, s 41(1)			1
Post-1986 in High Court	Unnecessary but see note 2	IA 1986, s 172(2)	IA 1986, s 168(3)	2, 3, 4
Pre-1986 in county court	C(W-U)R 1949, r 45 CCA 1984, s 41(1)			1
Pre-1986 in High Court	Unnecessary but see note 2	CA 1985, s 536(1)	CA 1985, s 536(3)	2

2.81 *Insolvency practitioners*

Voluntary arrangements – CVAs				
(Post-1986 only) in county court	CCA 1984, s 41(1)			1, 5
in High Court	Unnecessary but see note 2	IA 1986, s 7(5)	IA 1986, s 7(5)	2

Abbreviations:

2.81 IA 1986: Insolvency Act 1986

IR 1986: Insolvency Rules 1986

BA 1914: Bankruptcy Act 1914

BR 1952: Bankruptcy Rules 1952

CCA 1984: County Courts Act 1984

CA 1985: Companies Act 1985 (to include earlier Acts consolidated therein)

C(W-U)R 1949: Companies (Winding-Up) Rules 1949

General:

2.82 'Post-1986' and 'pre-1986' refer to after and before the commencement of the Insolvency Act and Insolvency Rules, which was on 29 December 1986.

Notes referred to in the table

2.83

(1)   The court orders a county court matter to be transferred to the High Court for the purpose only of making the order for the removal of the present office-holder and the appointment of the new one. Therefore once the order has been made the matter reverts to the county court.

(2)   If a High Court matter is proceeding in a district registry but is to be included in a block order made by a judge at the Royal Courts of Justice, it would be prudent (though it may not be essential) for the court to direct under RSC Ord 5 r 5(4) that the matter be transferred to the RCJ for the purpose only of making the order for the removal of the present office-holder and the appointment of the new one. Once the order has been made the matter reverts to the district registry.

(3)   The general wording of IA 1986, s 303(2), BA 1914, s 79(3) and IA 1986, s 168(3) is sufficient to empower the court to appoint a new office-holder: see *Re Parkdawn Ltd* (15 June 1993, unreported); *Re Bullard and Taplin Ltd* [1996] BPIR 526 at 528G, and *Re A & C Supplies Ltd* [1998] 1 BCLC 603 at 608e. In *Re APP Services Ltd* (1998, unreported) it was held that it is also sufficient to empower the court to remove an existing office-holder; this is only important in the case of pre-1986 bankruptcies, since in all other cases there are other provisions which confer specific powers of removal.

(4)   The court may exercise the powers conferred by IA 1986, s 303(2), BA 1914, s 79(3) and IA 1986, s 168(3) if the application, though not made by the present office-holder (who is the person specified in the section), is made by another person with a sufficient interest to make it. This includes the proposed new office-holder or a partnership of which he is a member: *Re A & C Supplies Ltd* [1998] 1 BCLC 603 at 608g, 610f–h.

(5)   It is possible that a transfer of a CVA from a county court is never required: see Knox J in *Re Bullard and Taplin Ltd* (above) at 529A–B. However, CVA meetings are reported to a court and recorded on a file at the court: IA 1986, s 4(6), IR 1986, r 1.24(3). The court may be a county court: see IA 1986, s 251 (the concluding part), CA 1985, s 744 ('court'), and IA 1986, s 117(2). Where it might be safest in the case of a proposed block order to direct a transfer to the High Court under CCA 1984, s 41(1).

G PROFESSIONAL NEGLIGENCE

Engagement to advise

2.84 An insolvency practitioner may be retained in order to advise a person concerned as to his solvency. Where retained in this way the practitioner will owe his client a duty of care in contract and at common law to advise with due professional skill and care. Problems can arise where the practitioner goes on to act as office-holder in relation to his former client. First, it is possible that the practitioner will be disqualified from so acting because of duties of confidence which he owes his client. Secondly, even if not precluded in that way from taking on the relevant office, misunderstanding may arise if the possibility that the practitioner may proceed to take on the office has not been addressed in the terms of the retainer[1].

[1]   *Wade v Poppleton & Appleby (a firm)* [2003] EWHC 3159, [2004] 1 BCLC 674.

Acts or omissions while holding office

2.85 The Court of Appeal has held that, in the absence of some special circumstance, an administrator appointed with respect to a company does not owe a duty of care at common law to the creditors of the company[1]. In part the decision depended on the analogy drawn between the position of the administrator and the position of directors who, in general, owe duties to the company but not directly to the members or the creditors. That analogy is not available in bankruptcy. But the consideration that express provision is made in the legislation to compel the administrator to repay money to or compensate the company[2] has equal force in bankruptcy where the trustee may be similarly compelled with respect to the bankrupt's estate pursuant to IA 1986, s 304. In view of this it seems likely that a trustee will not be liable directly to creditors pursuant to a duty owed at common law.

[1]   *Kyrris v Oldham* [2003] EWCA Civ 1506, [2004] 1 BCLC 305.
[2]   IA 1986, s 212.

Chapter 3

PRACTICE AND PROCEDURE IN INSOLVENCY PROCEEDINGS

A GENERAL POINTS

Insolvency proceedings

3.1 By 'insolvency proceedings' is meant any proceedings under the Insolvency Act 1986 ('IA 1986') or the Insolvency Rules 1986 ('IR 1986)[1]. In general, insolvency proceedings differ from litigation at common law in that they relate to the administration of an insolvent's estate for the collective benefit of his creditors. Proceedings in bankruptcy may therefore raise questions affecting the interests of persons who are not parties to them[2]. In the High Court, the Bankruptcy Court is part of the Chancery Division[3].

[1]   IR 1986, r 13.7.
[2]   *Re Busytoday Ltd* [1992] 4 All ER 61, [1992] 1 WLR 683.
[3]   See the Chancery Guide, chapter 19.

3.2 Proceedings brought under the IA 1986, s 423 to set aside a transaction intended to defraud creditors, although arising under the IA 1986, need not be

55

brought in a court having insolvency jurisdiction and may have no connection with any pending insolvency proceedings[1].

[1]   *TSB Bank plc v Katz* [1997] BPIR 147.

Applicable rules of procedure

3.3 The primary set of rules which apply to insolvency proceedings are the IR 1986. These rules are made by the Lord Chancellor with the concurrence of the Secretary of State by statutory instrument and include, amongst other things, provision for regulating the practice and procedure of any court exercising jurisdiction for the purpose of the parts of the IA 1986 which govern individual insolvency[1]. The Civil Procedure Rules ('CPR') do not apply to insolvency proceedings except to the extent provided for by some enactment other than the CPR. In the case of insolvency proceedings the principal relevant enactment is the IR 1986, r 7.51 of which provides that the CPR, the practice and procedure of the High Court and of the county court (including any practice direction) apply to insolvency proceedings in the High Court or the county court as the case may be, in either case with any necessary modifications, except so far as inconsistent with the IR 1986[2]. Other provisions of the CPR which are specifically incorporated, with modifications, are (subject to the IR 1986, r 12.12(1) discussed below) the CPR Pt 6 concerning service[3], CPR rr 2.8 and 3.1(2)(a) concerning time limits and their variation[4], the CPR Pts 43 to 48 concerning costs[5], and (subject to the provisions of the *Practice Direction: Insolvency Proceedings*) the procedure and practice of the Supreme Court relating to appeals to the Court of Appeal concerning appeals[6]. All insolvency proceedings are allocated to the multi-track[7].

[1]   IA 1986, s 412(1), (2) and (3) and Sch 9, para 3.
[2]   IR 1986, r 7.51(1).
[3]   IR 1986, r 12.11.
[4]   IR 1986, r 12.9.
[5]   IR 1986, r 7.33.
[6]   IR 1986, r 7.49(1).
[7]   IR 1986, r 7.51(2).

Bankruptcy petitions

3.4 Special procedure rules apply to bankruptcy petitions. These are set out in the Insolvency Rules 1986 but since they relate only to bankruptcy petitions they are addressed in the **Chapter 8.**

Cross-Border Insolvency Regulations 2006

3.5 Detailed rules of procedure applicable to applications made under the Cross-Border Insolvency Regulations 2006 are contained in Schedule 2 to those regulations. They are discussed in **Chapter 5.**

Practice Direction on Insolvency Proceedings

3.6 A practice direction relating to insolvency proceedings has been issued entitled *Practice Direction: Insolvency Proceedings*, referred to in this book as PDIP. It came into effect on 26 April 1999 and replaces all previous practice notes and practice directions relating to insolvency proceedings[1]. It is updated from time to time.

[1] PDIP, para 1.2.

Forms

3.7 The IR 1986, Sch 4 contains forms which are to be used in and in connection with insolvency proceedings in the High Court and the county courts. Use of the forms is mandatory but may be varied if circumstances require[1]. For example there is no form specific to an expedited bankruptcy petition presented under the IA 1986, s 270 but the prescribed form of petition must be used and varied to include a statement concerning the risk of dissipation of the debtor's assets and to delete, if appropriate, any assertion that there is no outstanding application to set aside the statutory demand on which the petition is based[2].

[1] IR 1986, r 12.7.
[2] *Re a Debtor (No 22 of 1993)* [1994] 2 All ER 105, [1994] 1 WLR 46.

Title of proceedings

3.8 Every proceeding under the IA 1986, Pts IX to XI[1] shall be entitled 'in bankruptcy[2]'. Proceedings relating to individual voluntary arrangements are governed by IA 1986, Pt VIII and therefore should not be entitled with these words.

[1] Ie IA 1986, ss 264–385.
[2] IR 1986, r 7.26(2).

Formal defects

3.9 No insolvency proceedings shall be invalidated by any formal defect or by any irregularity, unless the court considers that substantial injustice has been caused by the defect or irregularity, and that the injustice cannot be remedied by any order of the court[1].

[1] IR 1986, r 7.55.

Computing time

3.10 The provisions of the CPR r 2.8 apply, as regards computation of time, to anything required or authorised to be done by the IR 1986[1]. The CPR r 2.8(2) requires that where a period of time is expressed as a number of days, it should be expressed as clear days. That means that in computing the number of days, the day on which the period begins and, if the end of the period is defined by reference to an event, the day on which that event occurs, are not included[2]. Where the specified period is five days or less and includes a Saturday, a Sunday, a Bank Holiday, Christmas Day or Good Friday, that day does not count[3]. When the period specified by the IR 1986 or PDIP or the CPR where applicable or by any court order for doing any act at the court office ends on a day on which the court office is closed, that act shall be done in time if done on the next day on which the court office is open[4].

[1] IR 1986, r 12.9(1).
[2] CPR r 2.8(3).
[3] CPR r 2.8(4).
[4] CPR r 2.8(5) with modification.

Extending time limits imposed by IA 1986 and IR 1986

3.11 Where by any provision in the Group of Parts of the IA 1986 relating to individual insolvency or by the IR 1986 the time for doing anything is limited, the court may extend the time, either before or after it has expired on such terms, if any, as the court thinks fit[1]. For instance, the period within which a challenge to the approval of an IVA under the IA 1986, s 262(3) has been extended for the purpose of permitting a challenge to be made out of time[2].

[1] IA 1986, s 376.
[2] *Tager v Westpac Banking Corpn* [1997] 1 BCLC 313.

Rights of audience

3.12 Barristers and solicitors holding a higher courts advocacy qualification[1] have unrestricted rights of audience in insolvency proceedings. But solicitors who do not hold a higher courts advocacy qualification are also entitled to appear in bankruptcy proceedings, not only in the county court and in High Court hearings held in private, as is so in any case, but also before any judge of the High Court sitting in bankruptcy. The origin of this right is the Bankruptcy Act 1869, s 70 which enabled every attorney and solicitor of the Supreme Court to appear and be heard without employing counsel in matters before the chief judge or the registrars in the London Court of Bankruptcy. By the Bankruptcy Act 1883, s 93, the London Court of Bankruptcy was consolidated with the Supreme Court of Judicature and its jurisdiction transferred to the High Court. By the Bankruptcy Act 1883, s 181 existing rights of audience were preserved and it was expressly provided that all solicitors or other persons who had the right of audience before the chief judge in bankruptcy should have the like right of audience in bankruptcy matters in the High Court. Hence in *Re Barnett, ex p Reynolds* the divisional court in bankruptcy, which at that time heard appeals from orders of county courts in bankruptcy matters[2] held that a solicitor had rights of audience before it[3]. However, the right did not extend to the Court of Appeal[4]. When the Bankruptcy Act 1914 was enacted, the right was expressly saved[5]. The right was again preserved by the IR 1986, which provided that, subject to provision for official receivers, rights of audience in insolvency proceedings are the same as obtained before the coming into force of the IR 1986[6].

1   See the Higher Courts Qualification Regulations 1998 made on 23 April 1998 by the Council of the Law Society pursuant to the Courts and Legal Services Act 1990, s 27 and the Solicitors Act 1974, s 2. By virtue of the Courts and Legal Services Act 1990, s 31(2)(a), as amended by the Access to Justice Act 1999, s 36, every solicitor is deemed to have a right of audience before every court in relation to all proceedings, but that right is only exercisable in accordance with the qualification regulations and rules of conduct of the Law Society.
2   Bankruptcy Act 1883, s 104(2)(a) as amended by the Bankruptcy Appeals (County Courts) Act 1884, s 4.
3   (1885) 15 QBD 169, 171. The point was not pursued on further appeal to the Court of Appeal.
4   *Re Ellerton, ex p Russell* (1887) 4 Morr 36, CA.
5   Bankruptcy Act 1914, s 152.
6   IR 1986, r 7.52(2).

3.13 Official receivers and deputy official receivers have rights of audience in insolvency proceedings in the High Court and in the county courts[1].

1   IR 1986, r 7.52(1).

3.14 Litigants may appear in person. In relation to proceedings in public, a litigant in person will ordinarily be allowed to have the assistance of an unqualified person, referred to as a McKenzie friend, unless the judge is satisfied that fairness and the interests of justice do not require a litigant to have such assistance[1]. The position is the same whether the proceedings are in court or not unless the proceedings are being held in private, that is what used to be called *in camera*. Where proceedings are in private in that sense, then their nature may make it undesirable in the interests of justice for a McKenzie friend to assist.

1   *R v Bow County Court, ex p Pelling* [1999] 4 All ER 751, [1999] 1 WLR 1807, CA.

B SERVICE

Service

3.15 Special rules govern the service of statutory demands and bankruptcy petitions and these have been discussed in **Chapter 8.**

3.16 In relation to other documents and subject to the rules concerning service by post mentioned below and the exclusion of those parts of the CPR Pt 6 which concern service out of the jurisdiction, the CPR Pt 6 applies as regards any matter relating to the service of documents and the giving of notices in insolvency proceedings[1]. Thus service may be effected by any of the methods recognised in the CPR r 6.2, which are: personal service; first-class post; leaving the document at a place specified in CPR r 6.5; delivery through a document exchange in accordance with the relevant practice direction; and sending by fax or other means of electronic communication in accordance with the relevant practice direction.

1   IR 1986, r 12.11.

3.17 The rules permitting service by post are extended by the IR 1986. For, a reference in the IR 1986 to giving notice, or to delivering, sending or serving any documents means that the document may be served by post, unless under a particular rule personal service is expressly required[1]. By IR 1986, r 13.3(2) it is provided that any form of post may be used unless a specified form is expressly required, but by IR 1986, r 12.10(1) it is provided that for a document to be properly served by post, it must be contained in an envelope addressed to the person on whom service is to be effected and prepaid for either first or second-class post. Thus registered post appears to be ineffective as a method of service. When first-class post is used, the document is treated as served on the second day after the date of posting, unless the contrary is shown; where second-class post is used, the document is treated as served on the fourth day after the date of posting, unless the contrary is shown[2].

[1]   IR 1986, r 13.3(1).
[2]   IR 1986, r 12.10(2), (3).

3.18 The address for service will be the address ascertained under the CPR r 6.5. The IR 1986 provide that a document to be served by post may be sent to the last known address of the person to be served[1]. In the case of an individual, that means his last known place of residence, unless he was the proprietor of a business, in which case, his last known place of business is available as an alternative[2].

[1]   IR 1986, r 12.10(1A).
[2]   See the table to CPR r 6.5.

3.19 Except where the IR 1986 provide otherwise, service of documents in insolvency proceedings in the High Court is the responsibility of the parties and is not undertaken by the court[1].

[1]   PDIP, para 1.3.

Service out of the jurisdiction

3.20 The court has a special power to permit service of insolvency proceedings outside the jurisdiction[1].

[1]   IR 1986, r 12.12(2) and (3).

3.21 This power to permit service outside the jurisdiction is independent of the rules governing whether service may be effected outside the jurisdiction in other civil proceedings. CPR rr 6.17 to 6.35 concerning service out of the jurisdiction (and service of foreign process in England and Wales) are expressly excluded from applying to insolvency proceedings[1]. The EC Judgments Regulation[2] does not apply to bankruptcy.

[1]   IR 1986, r 12.12(1).
[2]   Council Regulation (EC) No 44/2001, art 1(2).

3.22 But a bankruptcy petition may be served with the leave of the court outside England and Wales in such manner as the court may direct.

¹   IR 1986, r 12.12(2).

3.23 Where for the purpose of insolvency proceedings any process or order of the court is required to be served on a person who is not in England and Wales, the court may order service to be effected within such time, on such person, at such place and in such manner as it thinks fit, and may also require such proof of service as it thinks fit¹.

¹   IR 1986, r 12.12(3).

Circumstances in which permission may be granted

3.24 The discretion under IR 1986, r 12.12 to permit service abroad is wider than the powers now contained in CPR Pt 6 concerning the granting of leave in cases falling outside the Brussels Convention to serve out of the jurisdiction and the power under IR 1986, r 12.12 should not be exercised by analogy to those provisions¹. In *Re Howard Holdings Inc*² Chadwick J broke the issue down into two questions: first, is there a real issue between the applicant and the prospective respondent which the court may reasonably be asked to try? Secondly, is there a good reason why England is the proper place for the claim to be litigated? But, while providing a clear and useful approach, the discretion should not be exercised by rigid adherence to these or any other tests. For example, in taking into account the strength of the applicant's case against the respondent, the court may require a stronger case in some circumstances than in others. Thus, in some cases the events which give rise to the claim will have taken place entirely within the jurisdiction and the fact that the respondent is now abroad has no bearing on the substantive matter in dispute. But in cases where the claim itself involves a foreign element, the applicant may be required to show a particularly strong case to justify bringing a respondent into the jurisdiction to answer it³.

¹   *Re Paramount Airways Ltd* [1993] Ch 223, [1992] 3 All ER 1, CA.
²   [1998] BCC 549.
³   *Re Tucker (a bankrupt) (No 2)* [1988] 2 All ER 339; *Re Paramount Airways Ltd* [1993] Ch 223, [1992] 3 All ER 1.

Procedure

3.25 An application under the IR 1986, r 12.12 must be supported by a witness statement (or affidavit) stating the grounds on which the application is made and in what place or country the person to be served is or may probably be found.

3.26 The court need not require that the method of service to be used should comply with the law of the country in whose territory service is to take place:

the paramount purpose is to employ a method which is likely to make the person to be served aware of the proceedings and to enable him to resist them if he wishes[1].

[1]   *Re Busytoday Ltd* [1992] 1 WLR 683.

Appearance to contest jurisdiction

3.27 No provision is made in the IR 1986 for a respondent to appear solely for the purpose of contesting the jurisdiction. But although those parts of the CPR concerned with the granting of leave to serve a defendant outside the jurisdiction are excluded from having effect in relation to insolvency proceedings, there does not appear to be any reason why the CPR Pt 11, concerned with applications to dispute jurisdiction, should also be excluded from applying[1]. As well as considering whether leave to serve abroad was justified, a further question, which a foreign respondent should consider before submitting to the jurisdiction, is whether the statutory provision under which the process or order to be served is brought or made extends to foreign persons located outside the jurisdiction[2].

[1]   IR 1986, r 12.12(1) excludes RSC Ord 11 from applying in insolvency proceedings, but under the RSC, applications to dispute jurisdiction were made under RSC Ord 12 r 8.
[2]   See eg *Re Paramount Airways Ltd* [1993] Ch 223 and *Re Seagull Manufacturing Co Ltd* [1993] BCLC 1139, CA, although in neither of these cases did the argument that the provisions in question did not have extra-territorial effect over foreign persons succeed.

Service abroad on a Member State liquidator

3.28 Permission is not required to serve any process, court order or other document on a Member State liquidator[1].

[1]   IR 1986, r 12.12(5).

Claims made pursuant to IA 1986, s 423

3.29 It may be convenient to mention here that, although not insolvency proceedings, claims made pursuant to IA 1986, s 423 to avoid transactions made with intent to put assets beyond the reach of creditors may be served on defendants outside the jurisdiction without obtaining permission from the court because they fall within CPR r 6.19(2) which governs claims which the court has power to determine under an enactment[1]. Jurisdiction may be founded on this rule even where the impugned transaction took place overseas.

[1]   *Jyske Bank Ltd v Spjeldnaes* [1999] 2 BCLC 101.

Notices

3.30 All notices required or authorised by or under the IA 1986 or the IR 1986 to be given must be given in writing, unless it is otherwise provided or the court allows the notice to be given in some other way[1]. A reference in the IR 1986 to giving notice, or to delivering, sending or serving any document, means that the notice or document may be served by any form of post, unless under a particular rule personal service or a specified form of post is expressly required[2]. However, personal service is permissible in all cases[3]. Notice may be given to a person's solicitor if he has indicated that his solicitor is authorised to accept service on his behalf[4], and service on one of any number of persons acting jointly as the responsible insolvency practitioner is to be treated as delivery to them all[5].

[1]   IR 1986, r 12.4(1).
[2]   IR 1986, r 13.3.
[3]   IR 1986, r 13.3(3).
[4]   IR 1986, r 13.4.
[5]   IR 1986, r 13.5.

3.31 Where in any proceedings a notice is required to be sent or given by the official receiver or by the responsible insolvency practitioner, the sending or giving of it may be proved by means of a certificate, in the case of the official receiver, by him or a member of his staff and, in the case of the responsible insolvency practitioner, by him or his solicitor or a partner or employee of either of them. In the case of a notice to be sent or given by some person other than the official receiver or the responsible insolvency practitioner, the sending or giving of it may be proved by means of a certificate by that person that he posted the notice, or instructed another person, who must be named in the certificate, to do so. A certificate may be endorsed on a copy or specimen of the notice to which it relates[1].

[1]   IR 1986, r 12.4(2), (3) and (4).

3.32 Where under the IA 1986 or the IR 1986 a document of any description is to be sent to a person (whether or not as a member of a class of persons to whom that same document is to be sent), it may be sent as an accompaniment to any other document or information which the person is to receive, with or without modification or adaptation of the form applicable to that document[1].

[1]   IR 1986, r 12.14.

3.33 Where, in accordance with the IA 1986 or the IR 1986, a meeting of creditors or other persons is summoned by notice, the meeting is presumed to have been duly summoned and held, notwithstanding that not all those to whom the notice is to be given have received it[1].

[1]   IR 1986, r 12.16.

C APPLICATIONS

3.34 The provisions described in this section apply to any application made to the court in individual insolvency proceedings under the IA 1986 or the IR

1986 except for a petition for a bankruptcy order[1]. The procedure in relation to bankruptcy petitions is dealt with in **Chapter 8.**

[1]   IR 1986, r 7.1(c).

3.35 There are two forms of application:

(1)   an originating application which is an application to the court which is not an application in pending proceedings before the court, and

(2)   an ordinary application which means any other application to the court[1].

[1]   IR 1986, r 7.2(1).

3.36 An originating application should be used where proceedings are being commenced in which some new substantive relief is sought or new substantive issue raised for determination. An ordinary application is akin to an application made by application under CPR Pt 23 or, in the old terminology, an interlocutory summons or motion[1].

[1]   See *Port v Auger* [1994] 3 All ER 200, [1994] 1 WLR 862.

3.37 Applications should be made in the appropriate form[1].

An application must be in writing. It must state:

(a)   the names of the parties;

(b)   the nature of the relief or order applied for or the directions sought from the court;

(c)   the names and addresses of the persons (if any) on whom it is intended to serve the application or that no person is intended to be served;

(d)   where the IA 1986 or the IR 1986 require that notice of the application is to be given to specified persons, the names and addresses of all those persons (so far as known to the applicant); and

(e)   the applicant's address for service[2].

[1]   IR 1986, r 7.2(2).
[2]   IR 1986, r 7.3(1).

3.38 The application must be signed by the applicant if he is acting in person, or by or on behalf of his solicitor if he is not[1]. If it is an originating application the grounds on which the applicant claims to be entitled to the relief or order sought must be set out[2].

[1]   IR 1986, r 7.3(3).
[2]   IR 1986, r 7.3(2).

3.39 An application must be filed in court[1], accompanied by one copy and a number of additional copies equal to the number of persons who are to be served with it[2]. On the presentation of the application together with the appropriate number of copies the court will fix a venue[3] for the hearing of the application. The application must then be served at least 14 days before the date fixed for the hearing[4]. However, the court may hear an application immediately either if the case is one of urgency[5] or if the relevant provisions of the IA 1986 or the IR 1986 do not require service of the application or notice of it to be given to any person[6]. In the latter case the court may take the alternative course of fixing a venue if it wishes. The court has a general discretion to make an order dispensing with the need to fix a venue[7]. It also has power to authorise a shorter period of service[8]. The court need not fix a venue if the rule under which the application is brought provides otherwise[9].

[1] By virtue of IR 1986, r 13.13(3) 'file in court' means deliver to the court for filing.
[2] IR 1986, r 7.4(1).
[3] IR 1986, r 13.6 defines 'venue' as the time, date and place for the proceeding, attendance or meeting.
[4] IR 1986, r 7.4(2).
[5] IR 1986, r 7.4(6)(a).
[6] IR 1986, r 7.5(1), (2).
[7] IR 1986, r 7.4(2).
[8] IR 1986, r 7.4(6)(b).
[9] IR 1986, r 7.4(2).

3.40 If a venue is fixed, then, unless the court otherwise directs, the applicant must serve on every respondent named in the application a sealed copy of the application, endorsed with the venue for the hearing[1]. The court may give any of the following directions: that the application be served upon persons other than those specified by the relevant provision of the IA 1986 or the IR 1986; that the giving of notice to any person be dispensed with; or that notice be given in some way other than that specified above[2]. These provisions apply with appropriate modifications to an application properly made without notice but where the court nevertheless fixes a venue[3].

[1] IR 1986, r 7.4(3).
[2] IR 1986, r 7.4(4).
[3] IR 1986, r 7.5(3).

Distribution of business

3.41 Anything to be done under or by virtue of the Act or the Rules by, to or before the court may be done by, to or before a judge or the registrar. In individual insolvency proceedings 'registrar' means a Registrar in Bankruptcy of the High Court, or the district judge or deputy district judge in a county court[1]. Except for applications to commit a person to prison for contempt and applications for injunctions or for the modification or discharge of injunctions, all applications should be made in the first instance to the registrar[2]. Applications for committal or for or relating to injunctions must be heard by a judge and should be listed accordingly.

[1] IR 1986, r 13.2(1) and (3).
[2] PDIP, para 9.1(1) and (2) and para 9.2.

3.42 The registrar or district judge will give any necessary directions and may at his discretion, if the application is within his jurisdiction to determine, either hear and determine it himself or transfer it to the judge[1]. When deciding whether to transfer a matter to a judge or hear it himself, a registrar should have regard to the complexity of the proceedings, whether the proceedings raise new or controversial points of law, the likely date and length of the proceedings, the public interest in the proceedings and the availability of the court which is likely to hear the proceedings of relevant specialist expertise[2]. Once a matter has been transferred to the judge, all applications for interlocutory relief and directions should be made to the judge, unless liberty to apply to the registrar has been given[3].

[1]   PDIP, para 9.2.
[2]   Practice Note: The Hearing of Insolvency Proceedings.
[3]   PDIP, para 9.1(3) and Practice Note: The Hearing of Insolvency Proceedings.

3.43 The following matters must be heard in public:

(1)   the public examination of debtors;
(2)   opposed applications for discharge from bankruptcy or for the suspension or lifting of the suspension of discharge;
(3)   opposed applications for permission to be a director;
(4)   all matters and applications heard by the judge, except matters and applications referred by the registrar or the district judge to be heard by the judge in private or directed to be so heard[1].

[1]   PDIP, para 9.3.

3.44 In a case where the petition was presented or the receiving order or order for adjudication was made before the appointed day, the matters and applications specified in the Bankruptcy Rules 1952, r 8 must be heard in public[1].

[1]   PDIP, para 9.3(4).

Court manager's powers

3.45 In the High Court certain matters may be dealt with by the court manager of the bankruptcy court, namely applications by petitioning creditors to extend time for hearing petitions and applications by the official receiver to transfer proceedings from the High Court to a county court or to amend the full title of the proceedings[1]. But in District Registries, all such applications must be made to the district judge.

[1]   PDIP, para 9.5.

Adjournments

3.46 The court may adjourn the hearing of an application on such terms, if any, as it thinks fit[1].

[1]   IR 1986, r 7.10(1).

Directions

3.47 All insolvency proceedings are allocated to the multi-track[1]. Since allocation to that track is automatic, the provisions of the CPR which provide for allocation questionnaires[2] and track allocation do not apply[3]. At any time the court may give such directions as it thinks fit as to:

(a) service or notice of an application on or to any person, whether in connection with the venue of a resumed hearing or for any other purpose;
(b) whether particulars of claim and defence are to be delivered and generally as to the procedure on the application;
(c) the manner in which any evidence is to be adduced at a resumed hearing; and
(d) the matters to be dealt with in evidence[4].

[1] IR 1986, r 7.51(2).
[2] CPR r 26.3.
[3] CPR r 26.5.
[4] IR 1986, r 7.10(2).

3.48 In giving directions as to the manner in which evidence is to be adduced the court may, for example, give directions as to the taking of evidence wholly or in part by affidavit or orally, the cross-examination either before the judge or registrar on the hearing in court or in chambers of any deponents to affidavits, any report to be given by the official receiver or other person[1] authorised to give evidence by report under the IR 1986.

[1] IR 1986, r 7.9.

Further information and disclosure

3.49 Any party to insolvency proceedings may apply to the court for an order that any other party clarify any matter which is in dispute in the proceedings or give additional information in relation to such matter in accordance with the CPR Pt 18. Any party may apply for disclosure from any other party in accordance with the CPR Pt 31. In either case the application may be made without notice being served on the other party[1].

[1] IR 1986, r 7.60.

Payments into court

3.50 The CPR relating to payment into and out of court of money lodged in court as security for costs apply to money lodged in court under the IR 1986[1].

[1] IR 1986, r 7.59.

Consent orders

3.51 In suitable cases the court may make consent orders without the attendance of the parties. The written consent of the parties will be required. If an adjournment is required, either generally with liberty to restore or to a fixed date, the order by consent may include an order for the adjournment. If an adjournment to a date is requested, a time estimate should be given and the court will fix the first available date on or after the date requested. Parties should not assume that the order will be made as requested[1].

[1]   PDIP, paras 16.3–16.4.

3.52 Applications for consent orders to be made without attendance should be lodged at least two clear working days (and preferably longer) before any fixed hearing date. Whenever a document is lodged or letter sent, the correct case number, code (if any) and year should be quoted[1]. A note should also be given of the date and time of the next hearing (if any)[2].

Attention is drawn to para 4.4(4) of the Practice Direction relating to CPR Pt 44[3].

[1]   For example, 123/SD/99 or 234/99.
[2]   PDIP, paras 16.6–16.7.
[3]   PDIP, para 16.8.

D EVIDENCE

Evidence

3.53 In the IR 1986 the form in which evidence is usually expressed to be required is an affidavit, but IR 1986, r 7.57(5) now provides that, subject to certain exceptions, where the IR 1986 provide for the use of an affidavit, a witness statement verified by a statement of truth may be used as an alternative. In relation to individual insolvency the exceptions are: the bankrupt's statement of affairs under IR 1986, r 6.60; disclosure of further information by the bankrupt under r 6.66 and r 6.72; accounts under r 6.65 and r 6.70; proofs of debt under r 6.96 and r 6.99 and examinations under r 9.3 and r 9.4[1].

[1]   IR 1986, r 7.57(6).

3.54 In insolvency proceedings evidence may be given by witness statement or affidavit unless it is otherwise provided by the IR 1986 or directed by the court. However, the court may, on the application of any party, order the attendance for cross-examination of the person making the witness statement or affidavit. If the person in question does not attend after an order for his attendance has been made, his witness statement or affidavit may not be used in evidence without the leave of the court[1]. The court will ordinarily be precluded from disbelieving evidence without cross-examination of the witness giving it. So, where a party proposes to ask the court not to accept evidence given in a witness statement or affidavit, he should seek a direction for cross-examination[2].

[1]   IR 1986, r 7.7.
[2]   See *Long v Farrer & Co* [2004] EWHC 1774 (Ch), [2004] BPIR 1218 as an example of the difficulty which can arise.

Use of reports

3.55 In any case, the official receiver or a deputy official receiver may file a report instead of an affidavit or witness statement[1]. Any report filed by the official receiver in accordance with the IA 1986 or the IR 1986 is *prima facie* evidence of any matter contained in it[2]. Since any statement admissible in proceedings under the law of evidence comprises evidence of its contents, the point of this provision seems to be to give some further force to reports made by the official receiver. What that further force might be is not clear but it would seem that if the official receiver reports that some event has occurred, then, absent any contradictory evidence, the court would not require further proof of the event referred to. Such further proof which would otherwise be required might comprise production of documents or of first-hand testimony showing that the event had occurred. However, the official receiver's report is not conclusive evidence of its contents and may therefore be contradicted by credible evidence to the contrary.

[1]   IR 1986, r 7.9(1)(a).
[2]   IR 1986, r 7.9(3).

3.56 Unless the application involves other parties or the court otherwise orders, certain other office-holders may also give evidence by way of report[1]. In the context of individual insolvency, they are trustees in bankruptcy, interim receivers appointed under the IA 1986, s 286, special managers appointed under the IA 1986, s 370 and insolvency practitioners appointed under the IA 1986, s 273(2). But the IR 1986 do not provide that reports by such persons are *prima facie* evidence of their contents. Presumably, therefore, such reports must conform to the general law of evidence. Given that evidence may now generally be given by witness statement instead of affidavit, the advantage of making a report is somewhat reduced.

[1]   IR 1986, r 7.9(1)(b).

3.57 Reports must be filed in court and served on respondents in the same way as affidavits or witness statements[1]. That is to say, subject to any provision or order otherwise, in the case of an applicant the report must be filed and served not less than 14 days before the date fixed for the hearing, and in the case of a respondent not less than seven days before that date[2].

[1]   IR 1986, r 7.9(2).
[2]   IR 1986, r 7.8(1).

Documents with special evidential status

3.58 A copy of the London Gazette containing any notice required by the IA 1986 or the IR 1986 to be gazetted is evidence of any facts stated in the notice[1]. In the case of an order of the court notice of which is required to be gazetted, a copy of the London Gazette containing the notice may in any proceedings be produced as conclusive evidence that the order was made on the date specified in the notice[2]. Orders of the court may be varied and errors may be made gazetting a matter; in either case the person whose responsibility it was to gazette the order or other matter must forthwith cause the variation of the order to be gazetted or a further entry to be made correcting the error[3].

1   IR 1986, r 12.20(1).
2   IR 1986, r 12.20(2).
3   IR 1986, r 12.20(3).

3.59   A minute of proceedings at a creditors' meeting held under the IA 1986 or the IR 1986 signed by a person describing himself as, or appearing to be, the chairman of that meeting is admissible in insolvency proceedings without further proof. The minute is *prima facie* proof that the meeting was duly convened and held, that all resolutions at the meeting were duly passed, and that all proceedings at the meeting duly took place[1].

1   IR 1986, r 12.5.

3.60   Any document, whether signed by the Secretary of State himself or an officer on his behalf, purporting to be, or to contain, any order, directions or certificate issued by the Secretary of State shall be received in evidence and deemed to be or (as the case may) contain that order or certificate, or those directions, without further proof, unless the contrary is shown[1]. Further, a certificate signed by the Secretary of State or an officer on his behalf and confirming the making of any order, the issuing of any document or the exercise of any discretion, power or obligation arising under or imposed by the IA 1986 or the IR 1986 is conclusive evidence of the matters dealt with in the certificate[2].

1   IR 1986, r 12.6(1) and (2).
2   IR 1986, r 12.6(3).

3.61   Statements of affairs and other statements made pursuant to any requirement imposed by the IA 1985 or the IR 1986 are rendered admissible, in any proceedings, whether or not under the IA 1986, as evidence which may be used against any person making or concurring in making the statement save as evidence in chief in criminal proceedings[1]. For this purpose, statements of affairs are defined as statements of affairs prepared for the purposes of any provision of the IA 1986 which is derived from the IA 1985. The primary provisions in the context of bankruptcy are the IA 1986, s 288, derived from the IA 1985, s 135, which imposes a requirement on a bankrupt where a bankruptcy order has been made on a petition other than a debtor's petition to submit a statement of affairs to the official receiver and the IA 1986, s 272, derived from the IA 1985, s 122, which imposes a requirement that a debtor's petition be accompanied by a statement of the debtor's affairs.

1   IA 1986, s 433.

Filing of Gazette notices and advertisements

3.62   Where an advertisement relating to insolvency proceedings appears in an issue of the Gazette a copy of the issue must be filed in the court where the proceedings are pending by an officer of the court[1]. If a person inserts in a newspaper an advertisement relating to insolvency proceedings, he must file a copy together with particulars to identify the proceedings with the court in which the proceedings are pending[2]. An officer of the court must from time to time file a memorandum setting out the dates and particulars of notices and advertisements, which will constitute *prima facie* evidence that the notice or advertisement was duly inserted in the specified issue of the Gazette or newspaper[3].

[1]   IR 1986, r 7.32(1).
[2]   IR 1986, r 7.32(2).
[3]   IR 1986, r 7.32(3).

E TRANSFER OF PROCEEDINGS

3.63 Where bankruptcy proceedings are pending in the High Court, the court may order them to be transferred to a specified county court[1]. If the proceedings are pending in a county court, they may be transferred by order of that court either to the High Court or to another county court[2]. A transfer to a county court must be to a county court with jurisdiction in bankruptcy[3]. A judge of the High Court may order bankruptcy proceedings pending in a county court to be transferred to the High Court.

[1]   IR 1986, r 7.11(1).
[2]   IR 1986, r 7.11(2).
[3]   IR 1986, r 7.11(3).

3.64 A transfer of proceedings[1] may be ordered by the court of its own motion, on the application of the official receiver, or on the application of a person appearing to the court to have an interest in the proceedings[2].

[1]   Under IR 1986, r 7.11.
[2]   IR 1986, r 7.11(5).

3.65 Where the application is made by the official receiver, he must accompany it with a report made by him setting out the reasons for the application to transfer and including a statement that either the petitioner consents to the transfer or that he has been given at least 14 days' notice of the application[1]. If the official receiver's report satisfies the court that the proceedings can be conducted more conveniently in another court, the court has no discretion but must transfer the proceedings[2].

[1]   IR 1986, r 7.13(1).
[2]   IR 1986, r 7.13(2).

3.66 Where the application is made by some person other than the official receiver, that applicant must give at least 14 days' notice to the official receiver attached to the court in which the proceedings are pending and to the official receiver attached to the court to which it is proposed that they be transferred[1]. The application must be supported by affidavit. The court has a discretion whether to allow the application.

[1]   IR 1986, r 7.13(3).

3.67 The court making an order for transfer under the IR 1986, r 7.11 must, subject to one exception[1], send forthwith to the court to which the proceedings are being transferred a sealed copy of the order and the file of the proceedings[2]. When that court receives the order and the file it must send notice of the transfer to the official receiver attached to it and to the court from which the proceedings have been transferred[3].

1 See below on IR 1986, r 7.14(3).
2 IR 1986, r 7.14(1).
3 IR 1986, r 7.14(3).

3.68 The exception to the procedure set out above is where the High Court makes an order transferring proceedings to it from a county court[1]. In that instance the High Court must send copies of the order to the county court from which the proceedings are to be transferred and to the official receiver attached to that court and to the official receiver attached to the High Court[2].

1 Under IR 1986, r 7.11(4).
2 IR 1986, r 7.14(3).

3.69 When the procedure under IR 1986, r 7.14 has been complied with, the official receiver attached to the court to which the proceedings have been transferred becomes the official receiver in relation to those proceedings in place of the official receiver attached to the court from which the proceedings have been transferred[1].

1 IR 1986, r 7.14(4).

Proceedings commenced in the wrong court

3.70 The IR 1986 make provision for the correct court in which to commence bankruptcy proceedings[1]. Where bankruptcy proceedings are commenced in a court which is, in relation to those proceedings, the wrong court, that court may:

(a) order the transfer of the proceedings to the court in which they ought to have been commenced;
(b) order that the proceedings be continued in the court in which they have been commenced; or
(c) order that the proceedings be struck out[2].

1 IR 1986, rr 6.9 and 6.40.
2 IR 1986, r 7.12.

3.71 Presumably the court would only allow proceedings to continue in the wrong court if the debtor consented or if there was a reason which would be sufficient to justify a transfer to that court.

Transfer of other proceedings

3.72 Where, in relation to an individual, a bankruptcy order has been made by the High Court or an interim receiver has been appointed[1] or bankruptcy proceedings have been transferred to the High Court from a county court, a judge of any division of the High Court may, of his own motion, order the transfer to that division of certain proceedings pending against that individual which are pending in another division of the High Court or in a court in England and Wales other than the High Court[2]. The relevant proceedings are those brought by or against the individual concerned for the purpose of enforcing a claim against his insolvent estate or brought by some other person for the purpose of enforcing any such claim (including any proceedings brought by a mortgagee)[3].

1 Under the IA 1986, s 286.
2 IR 1986, r 7.15(1), (2).
3 IR 1986, r 7.15(3).

3.73 Where proceedings are transferred under this rule the bankruptcy registrar may dispose of any matter arising in the proceedings which would otherwise have been disposed of in chambers or, if in the county court, by the district judge[1].

1 IR 1986, r 7.15(4).

F REVIEWS

Reviews by the same court

3.74 Every court having jurisdiction in bankruptcy may review, rescind or vary any order made by it in the exercise of that jurisdiction[1]. The power thus granted to a court exercising bankruptcy jurisdiction is unique and, in theory, unlimited. Although it is in almost identical terms to the provisions of previous Bankruptcy Acts[2], it forms part of an insolvency regime with a very different philosophy from that which informed those Acts. Hence rules established in case law under those Acts limiting the exercise of the power will not be followed (unless justified under the present regime) but the power is still to be exercised with caution and only in exceptional circumstances[3]. In general, the circumstances must involve some material difference in the facts or evidence which is put before the reviewing court: for instance events which have occurred since the making of the original order or significant facts which, although in existence at the time of the original order, were not brought to the attention of the court at that time[4].

1 IA 1986, s 375(1).
2 Bankruptcy Act 1869, s 71; Bankruptcy Act 1883, s 104(1); Bankruptcy Act 1914, s 108(1).
3 *Fitch v Official Receiver* [1996] 1 WLR 242 esp at 246 and 248–249 from which this and the second and third sentences of this para are drawn. The same test applies in the corporate context under IR 1986, r 7.47(1); see *Re Thirty-Eight Building Ltd (in liquidation) (No 2)* [2000] 1 BCLC 201.
4 *Papanicola v Humphreys* [2005] EWHC 335 (Ch), [2005] 2 All ER 418.

3.75 Ordinarily the review should be conducted by the same judge who made the order under review; but, where appropriate, another judge of co-ordinate jurisdiction has power to conduct the review[1]. In *Re SN Group plc*[2] the vacation judge refused to review a winding-up order made by the registrar on the ground, amongst others, that the role of a High Court judge in such cases was restricted to an appellate function. However, in *Re Dollar Land (Feltham) Ltd*³ a winding-up order made by the registrar was rescinded by a High Court judge without explicitly addressing the question of jurisdiction, and the deputy judge in *Re Piccadilly Property Management Ltd*⁴, having addressed the point, concluded that he did have jurisdiction to review a decision of an inferior court. He emphasised that very few cases would be proper cases for a party to seek a review in a court superior to that in which the order was made; in the ordinary course an aggrieved party should seek his review from the same judge in the same court as made the order otherwise he should appeal to the superior court.

¹   *Mond v Hammond Suddards* [2000] Ch 40, CA.
²   [1994] 1 BCLC 319.
³   [1995] 2 BCLC 370.
⁴   [1999] 2 BCLC 145.

Reviews of bankruptcy orders

3.76 A bankruptcy order may be reviewed and rescinded under the IA 1986, s 375(1). In *Fitch v Official Receiver*¹ the debtors against whom bankruptcy orders had been made sought to rescind on the ground that, after the bankruptcy order had been made, a large body of creditors, including the petitioning creditors, had decided that it would be better if no bankruptcy order had been made (because funds enabling payment of the debts to be made were more likely to be earned by the debtors) and therefore supported the rescission of the order. No known creditors opposed the rescission. The Court of Appeal rescinded the bankruptcy order. However, in a case where the creditor opposed the rescission, it was said at first instance that where the application to review a bankruptcy order effectively amounted to an attempt to circumvent the provisions regulating the circumstances in which a bankruptcy order will be annulled, rescission should be refused². It is submitted that in so far as this point might be taken to introduce into the question whether to rescind under the IA 1986, s 375 consideration whether the requirements of the IA 1986, s 282 have been met, this aspect of the decision should not be followed³. The jurisdictions are distinct and the specific requirements applicable to an application to annul under the IA 1986, s 282 ought not to be applied under s 375. It was sufficient for the decision not to rescind to find, as was the case, that the circumstances were not exceptional. Examples of exceptional circumstances include material change of circumstances and new evidence coming to light⁴ but the category is an open one.

¹   [1996] 1 WLR 242, CA.
²   *IRC v Robinson* [1999] BPIR 329.
³   It is akin to the former approach under the Bankruptcy Act 1914 that there must be circumstances analogous to a scheme of arrangement before a receiving order could be rescinded; see *Re a Debtor (No 12 of 1970)* [1971] 2 All ER 1494, [1971] 1 WLR 1212. In *Re a Debtor (No 32-SD-1991)* [1993] 2 All ER 991, [1993] 1 WLR 314 Millett J declined to continue this approach under the IA 1986.
⁴   *Re Thirty-Eight Building Ltd (in liquidation) (No 2)* [2000] 1 BCLC 201.

3.77 If, on an application to rescind a bankruptcy order, the court rescinds the bankruptcy order, the Secretary of State, although not a party, has standing to appeal[1]. An application to rescind would usually be made to a bankruptcy registrar or district judge, since bankruptcy orders are ordinarily made by them. An appeal from either a bankruptcy registrar or a district judge does not require permission, but if the bankruptcy order had been made by a judge of the High Court, permission to appeal to the Court of Appeal would be required[2]. It is not clear whether the rule relating to an appeal by the Secretary of State enables him to appeal without permission but presumably permission would be required.

[1]   IR 1986, r 7.48(1).
[2]   See para **3.120** below.

Evidence admissible on review

3.78 Before 26 April 1999 an advantage of a review over an appeal was that, in contrast with an appeal[1], fresh evidence might be put before the court because the special conditions[2] which had to be fulfilled in order to admit new evidence on appeal did not apply to a review. Since 26 April 1999 the rules relating to the admission of fresh evidence on appeal have been relaxed to some extent in that those special conditions now represent 'principles rather than rules'[3]. But, given that there is no restriction on the admission of fresh evidence on a review[4], there probably remains some advantage.

[1]   An appeal to a single judge under the IA 1986, s 375(2) was a true appeal: *Re Gilmartin, ex p bankrupt v International Agency and Supply Ltd* [1989] 2 All ER 835, [1989] 1 WLR 513.
[2]   See *Ladd v Marshall* [1954] 3 All ER 745, [1954] 1 WLR 1489, CA.
[3]   *Hertfordshire Investments v Bubb* [2000] 1 WLR 2318, 2325, CA; and see also paras **3.113–3.116** below.
[4]   *Re a Debtor (No 32-SD-1991)* [1993] 2 All ER 991, [1993] 1 WLR 314.

G APPEALS

Appeals[1]

3.79 In bankruptcy, decisions on procedural and substantial questions may be made in a county court by district judges or circuit judges or in the High Court by bankruptcy registrars or judges of the High Court. From a decision of a county court, whether made by a district judge or by a circuit judge, and from a decision of a bankruptcy registrar an appeal lies to a single judge of the High Court[2]. Such an appeal is referred to in the PDIP as 'a first appeal'[3]. No permission is required to make such an appeal[4].

[1]   The procedure governing appeals was changed with effect from 2 May 2000. For transitional provisions in respect of appeals set down in the High Court before 2 May 2000 or where permission was granted to appeal to the Court of Appeal before 2 May 2000, see PDIP, para 17.24.
[2]   IA 1986, s 375(2); IR 1986, r 7.48(2).
[3]   PDIP, para 17.2(1).
[4]   PDIP, para 17.6.

3.80 Decisions by judges of the High Court in the exercise of their juris-diction in bankruptcy fall into two categories: (1) decisions made on appeals from a decision of a county court or a bankruptcy registrar, ie decisions made on a first appeal; and (2) original decisions made at first instance. From a decision made by a judge of the High Court on a first appeal, a further appeal to the Court of Appeal may only be made with the permission of the Court of Appeal[1]. From a decision made by a High Court judge at first instance, an appeal may be made to the Court of Appeal[2] with the permission of either the judge or the Court of Appeal[3]. Although such an appeal will be the first to be made in such a case, it is not 'a first appeal' within the meaning ascribed to that term in the PDIP[4].

1   IA 1986, s 375(2) as amended by the Access to Justice Act 1999, s 55; PDIP, para 17.3(1).
2   The Supreme Court Act 1981, s 16(1).
3   CPR r 52.3(1).
4   PDIP, para 17.3(3).

Appeal by the Secretary of State

3.81 Reflecting the public interest which may exist in an individual's status as a bankrupt, the Secretary of State is given standing to appeal from any order made on an application for the rescission or annulment of a bankruptcy order or for a bankrupt's discharge[1]. Where the Secretary of State makes such an appeal, save that the appellant is a person who was not present at the hearing below, the same procedure applies as in other appeals.

1   IR 1986, r 7.48(1).

Applicable procedure

3.82 Subject to certain modifications, the procedure and practice of the Supreme Court relating to appeals to the Court of Appeal apply to appeals in bankruptcy proceedings[1]. That procedure and practice is now contained in CPR Pt 52 and its Practice Direction. But the CPR Pt 52 and its Practice Direction need to be read in conjunction with the PDIP, para 17[2]. In the case of first appeals, the application of the CPR Pt 52 and its Practice Direction is much restricted[3]. The IR 1986, r 7.49 seems to require further amendment to reflect the procedure set out in PDIP, para 17.

1   IR 1986, r 7.49(1).
2   CPR r 52.1(4).
3   PDIP, para 17.7.

First appeals

3.83 As discussed above PDIP defines 'a first appeal' as an appeal from a decision of a county court (whether made by a district judge or a circuit judge) or from a decision of a bankruptcy registrar[1].

1   PDIP, para 17.2(1).

Procedure governing first appeals

3.84 The procedure governing first appeals is governed by PDIP, paras 17.8–17.23 which apply only to first appeals[1]. The following paras are concerned with that procedure. CPR Pt 52 has only limited application to first appeals in insolvency cases: only paras 5.12 and 5.14–5.20 of the Practice Direction to CPR, Pt 52 apply to first appeals.

1   PDIP, para 17.7.

3.85 But, PDIP incorporates some of the definitions used in the CPR Pt 52, namely 'appeal court' meaning the court to which an appeal is made; 'lower court' meaning the court, tribunal or other person or body from whose decision an appeal is brought; 'appellant' meaning a person who brings or seeks to bring an appeal; 'respondent' meaning (i) a person other than the appellant who was a party to the proceedings in the lower court and who is affected by the appeal and (ii) a person who is permitted by the appeal court to be a party to the appeal; and 'appeal notice' meaning an appellant's or a respondent's notice[1]. PDIP defines 'Registrar of Appeals' as meaning, in relation to an appeal filed at the Royal Courts of Justice in London, a bankruptcy registrar and, in relation to an appeal filed in a district registry, a district judge of the relevant district registry[2]. 'Appeal date' means the date fixed by the appeal court for the hearing of the appeal or the date fixed by the appeal court upon which the period within which the appeal will be heard commences[3].

1   PDIP, para 17.8(a).
2   PDIP, para 17.8(b).
3   PDIP, para 17.8(c).

No permission required for a first appeal

3.86 A first appeal does not require the permission of any court[1].

1   PDIP, para 17.6 and see *Secretary of State for Trade and Industry v Paulin* [2005] EWHC 888 (Ch), [2005] 2 BCLC 667.

Stay pending outcome of appeal

3.87 An appeal does not operate as a stay of any order or decision of the lower court unless the appeal court or the lower court orders otherwise[1]. As mentioned above, permission to appeal is not required for a first appeal[2], but a representative should, if appropriate, seek a stay from the lower court when the order is made. Where it is necessary to seek a stay from the appeal court, it is necessary to make a separate application for the stay by way of ordinary application[3] because para 5.5 of the Practice Direction to CPR, Pt 52 (which permits applications for incidental remedies to be included in the appeal notice) does not apply[4]. If, as may often be so, what is required is not a stay but an injunction pending the outcome of the appeal, the application must be made to a judge of the appeal court, ie to a judge of the High Court[5].

¹ PDIP, para 17.14.
² PDIP, para 17.6.
³ PDIP, para 17.21.
⁴ PDIP, para 17.7.
⁵ PDIP, para 17.19.

Appellant's notice

3.88 An appellant's notice must be in Form PDIP 1[1]. An appellant should take care to include in his notice all the points which he may wish to raise. For at the hearing of the appeal he may not rely on any matter not contained in his notice unless the appeal court gives permission[2] and he may only amend the notice with the permission of the appeal court[3].

¹ PDIP, para 17.9.
² PDIP, para 17.18(5).
³ PDIP, para 17.15.

Appellant's duty to file appellant's notice

3.89 The appellant must file the appellant's notice at the appeal court within (a) such period as may be directed by the lower court or (b) where the lower court makes no such direction, 14 days after the decision of the lower court which the appellant wishes to appeal[1]. The lower court should not normally direct a period longer than 28 days[2]. Where the lower court judge announces his decision and reserves the reasons for his judgment or order until a later date, he should fix a period for filing the appellant's notice at the appeal court which takes this into account[3]. An appeal from a decision of a bankruptcy registrar must be filed at the Royal Courts of Justice in London[4]. An appeal from a decision made by a county court may be filed at the Royal Courts of Justice in London or, if made in a county court exercising jurisdiction over an area within the Birmingham, Bristol, Cardiff, Leeds, Liverpool, Manchester, Newcastle-upon-Tyne or Preston Chancery District Registries, may be filed in the Chancery District Registry appropriate to the area in which the decision was made[5].

¹ PDIP, para 17.11(2).
² Practice Direction to CPR, Pt 52, para 5.19 which is applicable by virtue of PDIP, para 17.23.
³ Practice Direction to CPR, Pt 52, para 5.20 which is applicable by virtue of PDIP, para 17.23.
⁴ PDIP, para 17.10(1).
⁵ PDIP, para 17.10(1) and (2).

3.90 When the appellant files the appellant's notice, he must also file:

(a) two copies of the appellant's notice for the use of the court, one of which must be stamped with the appropriate fee, and a number of additional copies equal to the number of persons who are to be served with it;

(b) a copy of the order under appeal; and

(c)   an estimate of the time for the hearing[1].

[1]   PDIP, para 17.22(1).

3.91 These documents may be lodged personally or by post and shall be lodged at the address of the appropriate venue which are as follows:

(a)   if the appeal is to be heard at the Royal Courts of Justice in London, Room 110, Thomas More Building, The Royal Courts of Justice, Strand, London WC2A 2LL;

(b)   if the appeal is to be heard in Birmingham, the District Registry of the Chancery Division of the High Court, 33 Bull Street, Birmingham, B4 6DS;

(c)   if the appeal is to be heard in Bristol, the District Registry of the Chancery Division of the High Court, Third Floor, Greyfriars, Lewins Mead, Bristol, BS1 2NR;

(d)   if the appeal is to be heard in Cardiff, the District Registry of the Chancery Division of the High Court, First Floor, 2 Park Street, Cardiff, CF10 1ET;

(e)   if the appeal is to be heard in Leeds, the District Registry of the Chancery Division of the High Court, The Court House, 1 Oxford Row, Leeds, LS1 3BG;

(f)   if the appeal is to be heard in Liverpool, the District Registry of the Chancery Division of the High Court, Liverpool Combined Court Centre, Derby Square, Liverpool, L2 1XA;

(g)   if the appeal is to be heard in Manchester, the District Registry of the Chancery Division of the High Court, Courts of Justice, Crown Square, Manchester, M60 9DJ;

(h)   if the appeal is to be heard at Newcastle-upon-Tyne, the District Registry of the Chancery Division of the High Court, The Law Courts, Quayside, Newcastle-upon-Tyne, NE1 3LA;

(i)   if the appeal is to be heard in Preston, the District Registry of the Chancery Division of the High Court, The Combined Court Centre, Ringway, Preston, PR1 2LL[1].

[1]   PDIP, para 17.22(2).

The court's response

3.92 If an appellant files the correct documents and they are in order, the court at which the documents are filed will fix the appeal date and will also fix the place of hearing. It is not clear what the court will do if the correct documents are not filed or they are not in order. Presumably the court will inform the party seeking to appeal who will have to remedy the defect and make any necessary application to extend time for filing the required documents. The court will send letters to all the parties to the appeal informing them of the appeal date, the place of hearing and the appellant's time estimate. The court's letter will invite the parties to notify the court of any alternative or revised time estimate. In the absence of any such notification, the time estimate will be taken as agreed. The court will also send to the appellant a document setting out the court's requirement concerning the form and content of the bundle of documents for the use of the judge[1].

¹   PDIP, para 17.22(3).

Appellant's duty to serve appellant's notice

3.93 Unless the appeal court orders otherwise, the appellant must serve his appellant's notice on each respondent as soon as practicable and, in any event, not later than seven days after it is filed[1]. The appellant must serve his appellant's notice on all parties to the proceedings in the lower court who are directly affected by the appeal[2]. This may include the official receiver or the trustee in bankruptcy.

¹   PDIP, para 17.11(3).
²   PDIP, para 17.22(4).

3.94 The appellant's notice must be served by the appellant or his legal representative. It may be served by any of the methods referred to in the CPR r 6.2, that is to say (a) by personal service in accordance with the CPR r 6.4, (b) by first-class post, (c) by leaving the document in a place specified in the CPR r 6.5, (d) through a document exchange in accordance with the relevant practice direction or (e) by fax or other means of electronic communication in accordance with the relevant practice direction[1]. With the permission of the court, service may be effected by an alternative method pursuant to CPR r 6.8[2]. A certificate of service complying with the CPR r 6.10 (CPR Form N215) must be filed at court immediately after service[3].

¹   PDIP, para 17.22(5)(a).
²   PDIP, para 17.22(5)(b).
³   PDIP, para 17.22(6).

Respondent's notice

3.95 A respondent may file a respondent's notice[1]. He must file a respondent's notice if he wishes to ask the appeal court to uphold the order of the lower court for reasons which are different from or additional to those given by the lower court[2]. A respondent's notice must be in Form PDIP 2[3]. Like an appellant, a respondent must take care to include all the points which he may wish to rely on at the hearing of the appeal in his notice, if he serves one[4].

¹   PDIP, para 17.12(1).
²   PDIP, para 17.12(2).
³   PDIP, para 17.9.
⁴   PDIP, para 17.18(5).

Service of respondent's notice

3.96 Unless the appeal court orders otherwise, a respondent's notice must be served by the respondent on the appellant and any other respondent as soon as practicable and in any event not later than seven days after it is filed[1].

Presumably a respondent's notice may be served by any of the methods available for the service of an appellant's notice. A certificate of service complying with the CPR r 6.10 (CPR Form N215) must be filed at court immediately after service[2].

1   PDIP, para 17.12(4).
2   PDIP, para 17.22(6).

Extensions of time to file an appeal notice

3.97 Where a party seeks an extension of time within which to file an appeal notice[1], the request must be included in the appeal notice. The appeal notice must state the reason for the delay and the steps taken before the application was made. The court will fix a date for the hearing of the application and notify the parties of the date and place of the hearing[2]. The PDIP provides that an application to vary the time limit for filing an appeal notice must be made to the appeal court[3].

1   An appeal notice includes a respondent's notice as well as an appellant's notice by the definition imported from CPR r 52.1(3).
2   PDIP, para 17.11(1).
3   PDIP, para 17.13(1).

3.98 The parties may not agree to extend any date or time limit set by PDIP or an order of the appeal court or the lower court[1].

1   PDIP, para 17.13(2).

Amendment of appeal notice

3.99 Neither an appellant's nor a respondent's notice may be amended without the permission of the appeal court[1].

1   PDIP, para 17.15.

Striking out an appeal notice

3.100 A judge of the appeal court may strike out the whole or part of an appeal notice where there is compelling reason to do so[1]. The appeal court in a first appeal in bankruptcy will be the High Court. By 'judge of the appeal court' is meant a judge of the High Court.

1   PDIP, para 17.16.

3.101 This is the same test as applies under the CPR r 52.9 where it is made explicit that the appeal court will only strike out an appeal notice where there is compelling reason to do so. The CPR permits a judge to act on his own initiative and the procedure applicable to such activity is set out in the CPR r 3.3. Where a party wishes to strike out an appeal notice, he must apply directly to the judge[1].

[1]   PDIP, para 17.19(3).

Security for costs

3.102 Security for costs may be ordered against an appellant or a respondent who appeals but only on the same grounds as security for costs would be ordered against a claimant at first instance[1]. Security for costs will only be ordered against a party if the court is satisfied, having regard to all the circumstances of the case that it is just to make such an order and either that one of the conditions set out in the CPR r 25.13(2) applies or that an enactment permits the court to require security for costs[2]. This changes the law in that before the CPR came into force security might be ordered against an appellant on wider grounds than were applicable at first instance. The CPR r 25.15 eliminates that difference.

[1]   CPR r 25.15(1).
[2]   CPR r 25.13.

3.103 The general conditions giving the court jurisdiction to order security are not discussed here but one may be noted. That is the condition enabling security for costs to be ordered where the claimant is acting as a nominal claimant, other than as a representative claimant under the CPR Pt 9, and there is reason to believe that he will be unable to pay the defendant's costs if ordered to do so. Decisions made under previous rules of court in respect of actions brought by trustees in bankruptcy established that a trustee in bankruptcy was not a nominal plaintiff[1].

[1]   *Pooley's Trustee v Whetham* (1884) 28 Ch D 38, CA; *Cowell v Taylor* (1885) 31 Ch D 34, CA.

Other interim remedies or orders

3.104 The appeal court has in relation to an appeal all the powers of the lower court[1].

[1]   PDIP, para 17.17(1).

Interim applications

3.105 Save for the applications mentioned below, interim applications should be made to the registrar of appeals in the first instance who may in his discretion either hear and determine the application himself or refer it to a judge[1]. Applications for injunctions pending the substantive hearing of the appeal, for expedition or vacation of a hearing date of an appeal, for an order striking out the whole or part of an appeal notice[2] or for a final order on paper following settlement or withdrawal of the appeal[3] should be made directly to a judge[4].

1   PDIP, para 17.20(1).
2   Pursuant to PDIP, para 17.16.
3   Pursuant to PDIP, para 17.22(8).
4   PDIP, para 17.19.

3.106 Interim applications should be made by way of ordinary application[1]. The procedure governing ordinary applications is primarily governed by the IR 1986, rr 7.1–7.10. The prescribed form is Form 7.2 in the IR 1986, Sch 4.

1   PDIP, para 17.21.

3.107 An appeal from a decision of a registrar of appeals lies to a judge of the appeal court, ie a judge of the High Court, and does not require the permission of either the registrar of appeals or the judge[1].

1   PDIP, para 17.20(2).

3.108 A further appeal from the judge would lie to the Court of Appeal[1] but such an appeal would require the permission of the Court of Appeal and would only be permitted if the Court of Appeal considered that the appeal would raise an important point of principle or practice or there was some other compelling reason for the Court of Appeal to hear it[2].

1   The Access to Justice Act 1999 (Destination of Appeals) Order 2000, SI 2000/1071, art 5.
2   The Access to Justice Act 1999, s 55(1). See *Tanfern Ltd v Cameron-MacDonald* [2000] 1 WLR 1311 paras 41–46 for a description of the reasons for the reform made by s 55(1).

Settlement or withdrawal of appeal

3.109 Where an appeal has been settled or the appellant does not wish to continue with the appeal, the appeal may be disposed of on paper without a hearing[1]. The appeal may be dismissed by consent but the appeal court will not make an order allowing an appeal unless it is satisfied that the decision of the lower court was wrong. Any consent order signed by each party or letters of consent from each party must be lodged not later than 24 hours before the date fixed for the hearing of the appeal at the address of the appropriate court. The consent order will be dealt with by a judge of the appeal court[2]. The draft consent order should make provision for costs either in the form of an agreed figure payable in respect of costs or that there be no order for costs. If the parties cannot agree with respect to costs, they will have to attend but, unless good reason can be shown for the failure to deal with costs, no costs will be allowed for the attendance[3].

1   PDIP, para 17.22(8).
2   PDIP, para 17.19(4).
3   Practice Direction about Costs, para 13.4 (replacing the Practice Direction to CPR, Pt 44, para 4.4(4) to which PDIP, para 17.22(8) cross-refers). See also the Practice Direction about Costs, para 13.13(a).

Preparation for the hearing of the appeal

3.110 The appellant is responsible for preparing a bundle for the use of the judge. The form and content of the bundle should follow the requirements of which the court informed the appellant by letter in response to the filing of the appellant's notice. The bundle must include an approved transcript of the judgment of the lower court, or where there is no officially recorded judgment, the document or documents referred to in para 5.12 of the Practice Direction to CPR, Pt 52[1].

¹   PDIP, para 17.22(3).

3.111 If there are documents which the appellant considers must be before the court but which have not been included in the content required by the court, it may be prudent to correspond with the court at an early stage explaining why the documents should be included. Not later than seven days before the appeal date[1] the bundle of documents must be filed by the appellant at the address of the relevant venue and a copy of it must be served on each respondent[2].

¹   As defined in PDIP, para 17.8(c).
²   PDIP, para 17.22(3).

3.112 Skeleton arguments accompanied by a written chronology of events relevant to the appeal should be filed at the relevant venue at least two clear days before the date fixed for the hearing[1]. Presumably 'the date fixed for the hearing' means the same as 'the appeal date', although the appeal date may refer to the commencement of a period during which the appeal will be heard. The skeleton arguments should be prepared in time for the commencement of that period since the appeal may be called on for hearing at short notice[2].

¹   PDIP, para 17.22(7).
²   Cf the Chancery Guide, para 7.24.

Evidence on appeal

3.113 All the evidence which was given at the hearing before the lower court is admissible at the hearing of the appeal. Much of that evidence will be on paper either in the form of a witness statement or as documentary evidence. Where evidence which was given orally is relevant to the appeal, the official transcript of the relevant evidence must be obtained[1]. If evidence relevant to the appeal was not officially recorded, a typed version of the judge's notes must be obtained[2]. Where the lower court or the appeal court is satisfied that an unrepresented appellant is in such poor financial circumstances that the costs of a transcript would be an excessive burden, the court may certify that the cost of obtaining one official transcript should be borne at public expense. The relevant court must also be satisfied that there are reasonable grounds for appeal. A request for a transcript at public expense should be made to the lower court when the order which is the subject of the appeal is given[3].

¹   Practice Direction to CPR, Pt 52, para 5.15 which is applicable by virtue of PDIP, para 17.23.

2 Practice Direction to CPR, Pt 52, para 5.16 which is applicable by virtue of PDIP, para 17.23.
3 Practice Direction to CPR, Pt 52, paras 5.17–5.18 which is applicable by virtue of PDIP, para 17.23. Para 5.18 requires modification since permission to appeal is not required for a first appeal in bankruptcy.

3.114 The appeal court may draw any inference of fact which it considers justified on the evidence[1].

1 PDIP, para 17.18(4).

Oral evidence

3.115 The appeal court will not receive oral evidence unless it orders otherwise[1].

1 PDIP, para 17.18(2)(a). Under the RSC the Court of Appeal had power to receive further evidence by, amongst other methods, oral examination in court: RSC Ord 59 r 10(2). The new provision is not restricted to further evidence.

Fresh evidence on appeal

3.116 Unless it orders otherwise, the appeal court will not receive evidence which was not before the lower court[1]. It is no longer necessary for a party seeking to adduce fresh evidence on an appeal to show that there are special grounds, meaning that the fresh evidence satisfied the conditions laid down in *Ladd v Marshall*[2] but the appeal court will still, in the interests of finality in litigation, have regard to those conditions, treating them as 'principles rather than rules'[3]. The distinction between interlocutory and final decisions which, before 2 May 2000, determined whether the *Ladd v Marshall* conditions had to be fulfilled, is no longer material.

1 PDIP, para 17.18(2)(b).
2 [1954] 3 All ER 745, [1954] 1 WLR 1489, CA.
3 *Hertfordshire Investments v Bubb* [2000] 1 WLR 2318, 2325; and see *Hamilton v Al-Fayed* (21 December 2000, unreported), CA.

Nature and determination of the appeal

3.117 The appeal will be limited to a review of the decision of the lower court[1]. There are two grounds on which the appeal court will allow an appeal: first, where the decision of the lower court was wrong and secondly, where the decision of the lower court was unjust because of a serious procedural or other irregularity in the proceedings in the lower court[2]. The effect of the appeal's being a review of the decision of the lower court is most marked in respect of decisions which turn on findings of fact or the exercise of discretion. The appeal court will not interfere with the decision of the lower court which rests on either of these bases unless it is persuaded that the finding of fact or exercise of discretion by the lower court is perverse. If the lower court has either failed to exercise a discretion or has exercised it erroneously, the appeal court may exercise the discretion afresh if the necessary evidence to do so is before it and the parties have had a proper opportunity to present their cases. Alternatively, it may remit the matter to the lower court for the matter to be considered again and by a different tribunal, if appropriate[3].

1   PDIP, para 17.18(1).
2   PDIP, para 17.18(3).
3   *Re a Debtor (No 32-SD-1991)* [1993] 2 All ER 991, [1993] 1 WLR 314 following *Blunt v Blunt* [1943] AC 517, [1943] 2 All ER 76, HL.

Orders on the appeal

3.118 The appeal court has power to affirm, set aside or vary any order or judgment made or given by the lower court, to refer any claim or issue for determination by the lower court, to order a new trial or hearing and to make a costs order[1]. It may exercise its powers in relation to the whole or part of the order of the lower court[2]. Further, in relation to the appeal, the appeal court has all the powers of the lower court[3].

1   PDIP, para 17.17(2).
2   PDIP, para 17.17(3).
3   PDIP, para 17.17(1).

Appeals from decisions of High Court judges

3.119 An appeal from a decision made by a judge of the High Court, whether the decision was made as an original decision at first instance or on a first appeal, lies to the Court of Appeal[1].

1   The Supreme Court Act 1981, s 16(1).

Requirement of permission

3.120 In either case permission to appeal is required, but as regards an appeal from a decision made by a High Court judge sitting at first instance, permission to appeal may be given either by the judge or by the Court of Appeal[1]. Where it is sought to appeal from a decision made by a judge of the High Court on a first appeal, a further appeal to the Court of Appeal may only be made with the permission of the Court of Appeal[2]. And, although such an appeal will be the first to be made in such a case, it is not 'a first appeal' within the meaning ascribed to that term in the PDIP[3].

1   PDIP, para 17.3(2) and the CPR r 52.3(1).
2   IA 1986, s 375(2) as amended by the Access to Justice Act 1999, s 55; PDIP, para 17.3(1).
3   PDIP, para 17.3(3).

Procedure governing appeals to the Court of Appeal

3.121 The procedure and practice of the Supreme Court relating to appeals to the Court of Appeal apply to appeals to that court in bankruptcy matters[1]. Thus the CPR Pt 52 and its Practice Directions and Forms apply to appeals from a decision of a judge of the High Court in bankruptcy proceedings[2]. Since PDIP, para 17.4 specifically refers to the prescribed forms to be used under the CPR Pt 52, an appellant should use an appellant's notice[3]. Since the procedure governing an appeal in insolvency proceedings to the Court of Appeal is the same as that governing appeals in other civil proceedings, the procedure is not discussed here.

[1]   IR 1986, r 7.49(1) and PDIP, para 17.3(3).
[2]   PDIP, para 17.4.
[3]   Form N161. IR 1986, r 7.49(3) appears to have been overtaken by the changes in the procedure relating to appeals.

H APPLICATIONS AKIN TO APPEALS

Appeal from Secretary of State or official receiver

3.122 An appeal under the IA 1986 or the IR 1986 against a decision of the Secretary of State or the official receiver shall be brought within 28 days of the notification of the decision[1]. Although r 7.50 uses the word 'appeal', the procedure is by way of originating application to the court and the application will be heard by the registrar or district judge unless he directs that it be heard by a judge.

[1]   IR 1986, r 7.50.

Challenging the trustee's acts, omissions and decisions

3.123 The bankrupt, any of his creditors or any other person dissatisfied by any act, omission or decision of a trustee of the bankrupt's estate may apply to the court[1]. The application should be made by originating application. On hearing it, the court may confirm, reverse or modify any act or decision of the trustee, may give him directions or may make such other order as it thinks fit. There is provision in the same terms for challenging the acts, omissions and decisions of the supervisor of an IVA[2].

[1]   IA 1986, s 303(1). See para **18.284**.
[2]   IA 1986, s 263(3).

I COSTS

Application of the CPR

3.124 In general, the provisions of the CPR Pts 43, 44, 45, 47 and 48 apply to insolvency proceedings with any necessary modifications[1]. The CPR Pt 46 concerns costs in cases allocated to the fast-track and, since all insolvency proceedings are allocated to the multi-track[2], is not relevant.

[1]   IR 1986, r 7.33.
[2]   IR 1986, r 7.51(2).

Requirement for detailed assessment

3.125 Where any person's costs, charges or expenses are payable out of the insolvent estate, the amount of those costs must be decided by detailed assessment unless agreed between the responsible insolvency practitioner and the person entitled to payment[1]. In the absence of agreement, the responsible insolvency practitioner may serve notice in writing requiring the person entitled to payment to commence detailed assessment proceedings in accordance with the CPR Pt 47 in the court to which the insolvency proceedings are allocated[2]. The creditors' committee established in insolvency proceedings may resolve that the amount of any costs, charges or expenses payable to any person shall be decided by detailed assessment. If it does so, the insolvency practitioner must require a detailed assessment[3].

1   IR 1986, r 7.34(1).
2   IR 1986, r 7.34(1).
3   IR 1986, r 7.34(2).

3.126 Before making a detailed assessment of the costs of any person employed in insolvency proceedings by a responsible insolvency practitioner, the costs officer shall require a certificate of employment, endorsed on the bill and signed by the responsible insolvency practitioner including the name and address of the person employed, details of the function to be carried out under the employment and a note of any special terms or remuneration which may have been agreed[1].

1   IR 1986, r 7.35(1) and (2).

Payments on account

3.127 An insolvency practitioner may make payments on account to a person employed by him in insolvency proceedings even though that person's costs, charges or expenses must be decided by a detailed assessment or fixed by the court. But, before an insolvency practitioner makes any such payment on account, he must obtain from the person to be paid on account an undertaking to repay immediately any money which the detailed assessment, when it is made, shows to have been overpaid, with interest at the rate specified in the Judgments Act 1838, s 17 on the date payment was made and for the period from the date of that payment to that of repayment[1].

1   IR 1986, r 7.34(3).

Forfeiture of costs

3.128 Every person whose costs are required to be decided by detailed assessment, shall, on being required in writing by the responsible insolvency practitioner to do so, commence detailed assessment proceedings in accordance with the CPR Pt 47[1]. If that person does not commence the detailed assessment proceedings within three months of the insolvency practitioner's requirement, or within such further time as the court on application may permit, the insolvency practitioner may deal with the insolvent estate without regard to any claim by that person, whose claim is forfeited by his failure to commence detailed assessment proceedings[2]. Where in any such case a claim also lies against an insolvency practitioner in his personal capacity, that claim is also forfeited by the failure to commence detailed assessment proceedings in time[3]. Presumably the period of time will run from the date on which the document containing the insolvency practitioner's requirement that the detailed assessment proceedings be commenced is served, or is treated as served[4], on the person to whom it is addressed.

[1] IR 1986, r 7.35(3).
[2] IR 1986, r 7.35(4).
[3] IR 1986, r 7.35(5).
[4] See IR 1986, rr 13.3 and 12.10.

Enforcement officer's costs

3.129 Where an enforcement officer or other officer charged with the execution, has taken a person's goods in execution of a judgment against him but has been given notice of that judgment debtor's bankruptcy before the completion of the execution, the official receiver or the trustee may require the enforcement officer or other officer to deliver up the goods and any money seized or recovered in part satisfaction of the judgment[1]. The costs of execution are a first charge on the goods or money in question[2]. Similarly, if the enforcement officer or other officer charged with the execution has sold the goods or been paid money to avoid a sale and a bankruptcy order is made on a petition presented within 14 days of the sale or payment, the balance of the proceeds of sale or money paid does not inure to the benefit of the judgment creditor but is comprised in the bankrupt's estate after deducting the costs of execution[3]. In either case, the responsible insolvency practitioner may in writing require the amount of the enforcement officer's or other officer's bill of costs to be decided by detailed assessment[4]. Where on the detailed assessment any part of the sum deducted from the proceeds of sale or money paid is disallowed, the enforcement officer or other officer charged with the execution must forthwith pay a sum equal to that which has been disallowed to the insolvency practitioner for the benefit of the bankrupt's estate[5]. The enforcement officer or other officer must commence the detailed assessment proceedings within three months of being required in writing to do so or within such further time as the court may allow. If he does not, his claim for costs is forfeit[6]. Presumably, therefore, if the enforcement officer or other officer charged with the execution has deducted any costs from the proceeds of sale or money paid but by his failure to bring detailed assessment proceedings within the appropriate time, he will become liable to pay the whole amount which he has deducted to the responsible insolvency practitioner for the benefit of the bankrupt's estate.

[1] IA 1986, s 346(2)(a).
[2] IA 1986, s 346(2)(b).
[3] IA 1986, s 346(3).
[4] IR 1986, r 7.36(1)(a).
[5] IR 1986, r 7.36(3).
[6] IR 1986, r 7.36(2).

Protection against personal liability for costs

3.130 In any proceedings it may be necessary for the official receiver or, as is more likely, the trustee in bankruptcy to be a party in order that all persons interested in a matter be bound by such judgment as may be given in those proceedings. Where the official receiver or trustee is joined in proceedings on the application of another party to the proceedings, then, without prejudice to any wider immunity from liability for costs conferred by the IA 1986 or the IR 1986, he shall not be personally liable for costs unless the court otherwise directs[1]. Although the rule appears expressly to address only the case where proceedings are pending between other parties and one of those parties applies to make the official receiver or trustee a party to those proceedings, the court should take the same approach where the official receiver or trustee has been a party, other than as claimant, from the commencement of the proceedings[2].

[1] IR 1986, r 7.39.
[2] It may be argued to the contrary that since the provision in the Bankruptcy Rules 1952, r 92(3) governing this matter did make express reference to actions being brought against the official receiver or trustee, the omission must be deliberate, but it is difficult to see why the situations are different in principle.

Indemnity from the estate

3.131 Expenses properly incurred by the official receiver or the trustee in preserving, realising or getting in any assets of the bankrupt, including those incurred in acquiring title to after-acquired property are payable out of the bankrupt's estate[1]. Such expenses are not properly incurred if sanction was not obtained when required from the creditors' committee and in such case the trustee will not be entitled to be indemnified by the estate in respect of such costs[2]. However, the prudent trustee should obtain an indemnity in respect of costs from a third party because costs of an unsuccessful action to recover assets are not payable out of the estate[3]. Nor are the costs of an action brought in respect of a right conferred on the trustee by the IA 1986 to make a claim which would not have been available to the bankrupt, such as to set aside a prior transaction as being at an undervalue or a preference[4], because such a claim is not made in respect of an existing asset of the bankrupt.

[1] IR 1986, r 6.224(1)(a).
[2] *Re Branson, ex p the Trustee* [1914] 2 KB 701; *Re a Debtor (No 26A of 1975)* [1984] 3 All ER 995, [1985] 1 WLR 6; *Weddell v Pearce* [1988] Ch 26, [1987] 3 All ER 624.
[3] *Re MC Bacon Ltd* [1991] Ch 127, [1990] 3 WLR 646.
[4] *Re MC Bacon Ltd* [1991] Ch 127, [1990] 3 WLR 646.

Security for costs

3.132 The circumstances in which security for costs may be ordered are set out in the CPR r 25.13. Security for costs will not be ordered against individuals solely because they are impecunious. Where a trustee in bankruptcy brings proceedings in his own name he is not a nominal claimant[1] but a debtor under an IVA who brings a claim for the benefit of his creditors may be a nominal claimant and may, therefore, be ordered to give security for costs if there is reason to believe that he will be unable to pay the defendant's costs if ordered to do so.

¹   *Cowell v Taylor* (1885) 31 Ch D 34, CA. See further para **19.18ff**.

Application for costs

3.133 Where a party to or a person affected by any proceedings in an insolvency applies to the court for an order allowing his costs or part of them incidental to the proceedings and the application is not made at the time of the proceedings, the applicant must serve a sealed copy of his application on the responsible insolvency practitioner and, where appropriate, the official receiver may appear on the application[1]. No costs of or incidental to the application shall be allowed to the applicant unless the court is satisfied that the application could not have been made at the time of the proceedings[2].

¹   IR 1986, r 7.40(1), (2).
²   IR 1986, r 7.40(4).

Costs and expenses of witnesses

3.134 No allowance as a witness in any examination or other proceedings before the court shall be made to the bankrupt to whom the proceedings relate. A person presenting a bankruptcy petition shall not be regarded as a witness on the hearing of the petition, but the costs officer may allow his expenses of travelling and subsistence[1].

¹   IR 1986, r 7.41.

Petitions presented by insolvents

3.135 Where a petition is presented by an individual against himself, any solicitor acting for him shall in his bill of costs give credit for any sum or security received from the individual as a deposit on account of the costs and expenses to be incurred in respect of the filing and prosecution of the petition. The costs officer must note the deposit on the final costs certificate[1]. It may be that the individual's own petition is presented between the presentation and hearing of another person's petition. If so and a bankruptcy order is made, no costs will be allowed to the bankrupt or his solicitor out of the estate unless the court considers that the insolvent estate has benefited by the bankrupt's conduct or that there are otherwise special circumstances justifying the allowance of costs[2].

¹   IR 1986, r 7.37(1).
²   IR 1986, r 7.37(2), (3).

Costs of proving debts

3.136 A creditor will bear the cost of proving his own debt, including the cost incurred in providing documents or evidence required by the trustee[1]. However, costs incurred by the trustee in estimating the value of a bankruptcy debt of uncertain value[2] falls on the estate as an expense of the bankruptcy[3]. The court has a discretion to order otherwise[4].

[1]   IR 1986, r 6.100(1).
[2]   See IA 1986, s 322(3).
[3]   IR 1986, r 6.100(2).
[4]   IR 1986, r 6.100(3).

Final costs certificate

3.137 A final costs certificate of the costs officer is final and conclusive as to all matters which have been objected to in the manner provided for under the rules of the court[1]. Where it is proved to the satisfaction of a costs officer that a final costs certificate has been lost or destroyed, he may issue a duplicate[2].

[1]   IR 1986, r 7.42(1).
[2]   IR 1986, r 7.42(2).

J FEES

Fees

3.138 The fees payable in respect of proceedings which relate to individual insolvency under the IA 1986 and the IR 1986 are set out in Schedule 2 to the Insolvency Proceedings (Fees) Order 2004[1]. These apply to cases where the bankruptcy order was made on or after 1 April 2004.

[1]   SI 2004/593.

Individual voluntary arrangements

3.139 A fee of £15 is payable on registration of an IVA. If the official receiver acts as the nominee for the purpose of a proposal for an IVA, a fee of £300 is payable. If the official receiver acts as the supervisor of an IVA, a fee is payable calculated as a percentage of the monies realised whilst he so acts. The current percentage is 15%.

Bankruptcy

3.140 The official receiver's fee is £1,625[1]. The Secretary of State's administration fee is a fee, up to a maximum of £100,000, calculated as a percentage, currently 17%, of total chargeable receipts relating to the bankruptcy, but ignoring the first £2,000 and that part of the total receipts which exceeds the bankruptcy ceiling[2]. The chargeable receipts means the sums paid into the

Insolvency Services Account after first deducting any amounts paid into that account which are paid out to secured creditors in respect of their securities or in carrying on the business of the bankrupt[3]. The bankruptcy ceiling means, in relation to a bankruptcy, the sum which is arrived at by adding the bankruptcy debts, interest payable on them pursuant to IA 1986, s 328(4) and the expenses of the bankruptcy except for any sums spent out of money received on carrying on the business of the bankrupt and the fee payable to the Secretary of State in relation to her administration of the estate[4]. The effect of the ceiling is that the fee levied in relation to an estate which is sufficient to pay all the bankruptcy debts, interest on them and the expenses, is only levied on the part of the estate which needs to be applied in payment of these amounts; it is not levied on the surplus. This will also be relevant in cases where annulment is obtained on the basis that all the debts, interest and expenses are paid.

[1]   This fee is reduced to £812.50 where proposals made by the bankrupt for an IVA with the official receiver acting as supervisor is approved by the creditors; Insolvency Proceedings (Fees) Order 2004, SI 2004/593, art 8.
[2]   Insolvency Proceedings (Fees) Order 2004, SI 2004/593, art 4(1) and Sch 2, Fee B2.
[3]   Insolvency Proceedings (Fees) Order 2004, SI 2004/593, art 1(1).
[4]   Insolvency Proceedings (Fees) Order 2004, SI 2004/593, art 1(1).

3.141 Each request for the purchase of government securities by a trustee in bankruptcy incurs a fee of £50[1].

[1]   Insolvency Proceedings (Fees) Order 2004, SI 2004/593, art 4(1) and Sch 2, Fee INV1 and art 4(4).

VAT

3.142 Where VAT is chargeable in respect of the provision of a service for which a fee is payable, the amount of the VAT has to be paid in addition to the fee[1].

[1]   Insolvency Proceedings (Fees) Order 2004, SI 2004/593, art 9.

Where the bankruptcy order was made before 1 April 2004

3.143 Where the bankruptcy order was made before 1 April 2004, the Insolvency Fees Order 1986[1] continues to apply with modification under transitional provisions[2]. In relation to such cases, the 1986 Order continues to apply with the deletion of all the entries in the Schedule to the 1986 Order except, in relation bankruptcy, that relating to Fee 13 in Part 2 of the Schedule[3]. The 2004 Order does not apply to such cases except in so far as is necessary to enable the charging of fee INV1 and, as regards an IVA proposed by or entered into by the bankrupt, fees IVA1, IVA2 and IVA3[4]. These fees are set out in the Table of Fees in Schedule 2 to the 2004 Order.

[1]   SI 1986/2030.
[2]   Insolvency Proceedings (Fees) Order 2004, SI 2004/593, arts 3 and 4(2).
[3]   Insolvency Proceedings (Fees) Order 2004, SI 2004/593, art 3 and Sch 1.
[4]   Insolvency Proceedings (Fees) Order 2004, SI 2004/593, art 4(2).

Deposit payable on presentation of a bankruptcy petition

3.144 On the presentation of a bankruptcy petition a deposit must be paid by the petitioner to the court in which the petition is to be presented as security for the payment of the relevant fees which may be incurred[1]. In relation to a bankruptcy petition presented by a debtor the deposit is £325; in relation to other petitions it is £390[2]. Unless an insolvency practitioner is appointed under IA 1986, s 273(2) to prepare a report, the court, on receiving the deposit, should pay it to the official receiver attached to that court. Where an insolvency is appointed in that way, the court should retain the deposit and pay the practitioner a fee of £310 including VAT on receipt of the report.

1   Insolvency Proceedings (Fees) Order 2004, SI 2004/593, art 6(2).
2   Insolvency Proceedings (Fees) Order 2004, SI 2004/593, art 6(1).

3.145 The deposit will be repaid to the person who paid if the petition is dismissed or withdrawn unless it is required to pay any fees arising in relation to the appointment of an insolvency practitioner to prepare a report under IA 1986, s 273(2)[1].

1   Insolvency Proceedings (Fees) Order 2004, SI 2004/593, art 6(4).

3.146 If a bankruptcy order is made, the deposit will be returned to the person who made it save to the extent that the assets comprised in the bankrupt's estate are insufficient to discharge the fees for which the deposit is made[1].

1   Insolvency Proceedings (Fees) Order 2004, SI 2004/593, art 6(5).

Validity of requirement to pay deposit

3.147 Debtors presenting their own petition are required to pay a deposit to the court. In *R v Lord Chancellor, ex p Lightfoot*[1] a challenge was made to the validity of this requirement on the footing that it infringed an individual's constitutional right at common law of access to justice recognised in *R v Lord Chancellor, ex p Witham*[2]. In *Ex p Witham* access to the court was sought for the purpose of adjudicating a dispute and establishing the applicant's legal right. It was held that an individual's right of access to justice in that sense could only be abrogated at common law by specific provision in primary legislation or by subordinate legislation pursuant to primary legislation which gave the body making the subordinate legislation specific power to abrogate the right. However, in *Ex p Lightfoot* the challenge failed. The primary reason was that the interest which a debtor has in obtaining the relief afforded by the 'administrative scheme' comprised in the bankruptcy process is not a constitutional right of the sort recognised in *Ex p Witham*. Hence it does not have the same protection at common law from abrogation by ordinary legislation whether primary or subordinate, that is to say legislation which is not expressly stated to have as its purpose the abrogation of the constitutional right in question. As well as addressing the matter on the basis of the common law, the question was also considered by the light of the European Convention on Human Rights, although at the date of the decision the Human Rights Act 1998 was not in force. Simon Brown LJ opined that there was no breach of art 6(1) because there was no dispute to be determined, the existence of which is a necessary element to be present before art 6(1) comes into play. He would also have held that the requirement of a deposit had a legitimate aim and was proportionate to that aim and therefore, if there was a restriction on the right arising under art 6(1), the restriction was justified. The suggestion that art 14 was infringed was dismissed on the basis that no convention right had been infringed.

¹   [1998] 4 All ER 764, [1999] 2 WLR 1126 (Laws J), [2000] QB 597, [1999] 4 All ER 583, CA.
²   [1998] QB 575, [1997] 2 All ER 779.

3.148 The same result would seem to obtain if the petition had been presented by a creditor. With respect to the common law right, recognised in *Ex p Witham*, a creditor in petitioning is not seeking the adjudication of his contested legal rights but something akin to execution in respect of his established right to payment of a debt¹. With respect to art 6, the requirement of the deposit, in a reasonable sum, is likely to be a justified restriction.

¹   Although see *Hornsby v Greece* (1997) 24 EHRR 250 for recognition by the European Court of Human Rights that execution proceedings must be regarded as an integral part of the trial for the purpose of art 6(1).

K COURT RECORDS AND OTHER DOCUMENTS

Court records

3.149 The court shall keep records of all insolvency proceedings, and shall cause to be entered in the records the taking of any step in the proceedings and such decisions of the court as the court thinks fit. Subject to the IR 1986, r 7.28, the court record is open to inspection by any person. The IR 1986, r 7.28(2) provides that 'if in any case of a person applying to inspect the records the registrar is not satisfied as to the propriety of the purpose for which inspection is required, he may refuse to allow it'.

3.150 The application is made in the first instance to the registrar. If the registrar refuses to allow inspection, the person seeking to inspect may apply forthwith and without notice to the judge, who may refuse the inspection or allow it on such terms as he thinks fit. His decision is final. The Court of Appeal has recognised that it may not interfere with the judge's decision¹.

¹   *Ex p Austintel Ltd* [1997] 1 WLR 616, [1997] 1 BCLC 233, CA.

3.151 It is plain that, in the ordinary course, any creditor of a bankrupt has sufficient interest to justify inspection and it may well be appropriate that inspection by a journalist should be permitted. But inspection has not been permitted where the purpose has been to seek information for commercial exploitation. In *Re an Application under the Insolvency Rules 1986*¹ the application was made by an insolvency consultant who made multiple searches against the names of all those against whom a bankruptcy petition had been presented. His plan was to offer them advisory services. Millett J held that this was not a legitimate purpose for which inspection might be permitted. He defined the legitimate purpose as being to enable persons who have a legitimate interest in particular insolvency proceedings to discover what has taken place. This test was applied by Jonathan Parker J in *Re Credit-net Ltd*[2] in which a number of organisations supplied their customers with information about companies' creditworthiness. They made multiple applications for the purpose of gathering information about the presentation of winding-up petitions and the conduct of proceedings under such petitions. These applications also failed. The principal objection to permitting the applications was that the effect of granting them would be to enable the applicant organisations to establish a secondary set of records, reflecting what was contained in the court records, but outside the control of the court. As was pointed out by Ward LJ in obiter comments following the dismissal of the appeal from Jonathan Parker J's decision for lack of jurisdiction[3], this may be a good reason for prohibiting multiple applications, or regulating the use to which such applicants may put the information they gather from inspecting the records, but it does not address whether the purpose of inspection is legitimate or not. For example, the customer of a credit agency may legitimately wish to know what is recorded with respect to an individual, or a company, because it is going to enter into a trading relationship with that individual or company and it would not appear to be objectionable for such a customer to appoint the credit agency as his agent to inspect the court records. Permission was given to a firm of accountants and insolvency practitioners to conduct multiple searches on behalf of local authorities by whom they were retained. The permission was subject to restrictions contained in undertakings given to the court that the searches would be conducted by reference to the area administered by an authority and disclosed only to that authority[4].

[1] [1996] 1 WLR 1291, [1994] 2 BCLC 104.
[2] [1996] 2 BCLC 133.
[3] *Re Austintel Ltd* [1997] 1 BCLC 233, CA.
[4] *Re Haines Watts* [2005] BPIR 798.

Court's file

3.152 In addition to the record, the court must open and maintain a file for each case in respect of all insolvency proceedings and, subject to directions of the registrar, all documents relating to the relevant proceedings must be placed on the file[1]. No insolvency proceedings shall be filed in the Central Office of the High Court[2].

[1] IR 1986, r 7.30(1).
[2] IR 1986, r 7.30(2).

3.153 The right to inspect at all reasonable times the court file relating to any insolvency proceedings is given to:

(a) the person who is the responsible insolvency practitioner in relation to the proceedings;

(b) any duly authorised officer of the Department of Trade and Industry;

(c)   any person stating himself in writing to be a creditor of the individual to whom the proceedings relate[1];

(d)   in proceedings relating to an IVA, the debtor[2];

(e)   the bankrupt;

(f)   any person against whom or by whom a bankruptcy petition has been presented;

(g)   any person who has been served with a statutory demand[3].

[1]   IR 1986, r 7.31(1).
[2]   IR 1986, r 7.31(2)(b).
[3]   IR 1986, r 7.31(2)(c).

3.154 Any other person may inspect the file with the leave of the court[1].

[1]   IR 1986, r 7.31(4).

3.155 The right of inspection is not exercisable in the case of documents or parts of documents as to which the court directs that they are not to be open to inspection without the leave of the court. An application for leave may be made by the official receiver, the responsible insolvency practitioner, or by any party appearing to the court to have an interest[1]. This is a useful provision where, for example, it is sought to keep a business plan or other commercially sensitive document confidential.

[1]   IR 1986, r 7.31(5).

3.156 The court must comply with a request by the Secretary of State, the Department or the official receiver for the transmission of the file in order to inspect it for the purpose of exercising a power under the IA 1986 or the IR 1986[1].

[1]   IR 1986, r 7.31(6).

3.157 As with the inspection of the court records the registrar is entitled to refuse to allow a person to inspect if he is not satisfied as to the propriety of his purpose. That person may apply forthwith and without notice to the judge, whose decision is final[1].

[1]   IR 1986, r 7.31(7) referring to r 7.28(2), (3).

Confidential documents

3.158 Where, in insolvency proceedings, the responsible insolvency practitioner considers (in the case of a document forming part of the records of the insolvency, except for any proof or proxy) that it should be treated as confidential or that it is of such nature that its disclosure would be calculated to be injurious to the interests of the insolvent's creditors, he may decline to allow it to be inspected by a person who would otherwise be entitled to inspect it. The responsible insolvency practitioner may refuse to allow a document to be seen by a member of the creditors' committee. A person refused inspection on this basis may apply to the court to overrule the responsible insolvency practitioner's determination[1].

[1] IR 1986, r 12.13.

Right to copy documents

3.159 Where a person is entitled to inspect documents he may also take copies of those documents on payment of the appropriate fee[1]. Where the responsible insolvency practitioner or official receiver is asked to supply copies of documents to a creditor or member of the creditors' committee he is entitled to require payment of the appropriate fee of 15 pence per A4 or A5 page and 30 pence per A3 page[2].

[1] IR 1986, r 12.15.
[2] IR 1986, rr 12.15A and 13.11.

L PERSONS INCAPABLE OF MANAGING THEIR OWN AFFAIRS

Persons incapable of managing their own affairs

3.160 It may occur that a person affected by insolvency proceedings is someone who is incapable of managing and administering his property and affairs either by reason of mental disorder within the meaning of the Mental Health Act 1983 or due to physical affliction or disability[1]. In such a case the court may appoint such person as it thinks fit to appear for, represent or act for the incapacitated person and the appointment may be general or for a specific purpose[2].

[1] IR 1986, r 7.43.
[2] IR 1986, r 7.44(1), (2).

3.161 The court may make such an appointment either of its own motion or on application by:

(a) a person who has been appointed by a court in the United Kingdom or elsewhere to manage the affairs of, or represent, the incapacitated person;
(b) any relative or friend of the incapacitated person who appears to the court to be a proper person to make the application;
(c) the official receiver; or
(d) the person who is the responsible insolvency practitioner in relation to the proceedings[1].

[1] IR 1986, r 7.44(3).

3.162 The application may be made without notice but the court may require notice of it to be given to the person alleged to be incapacitated or others and may adjourn the application for notice to be given[1].

[1] IR 1986, r 7.44(4).

3.163 An application must be supported by an affidavit of a registered medical practitioner as to the mental or physical condition of the incapacitated person. Such evidence is not required when the application is made by the official receiver, in which case a report by the official receiver is said by the IA 1986 to be sufficient[1]. Given the need to establish a mental disorder within the meaning of the Mental Health Act 1983 or physical affliction or disability, it is perhaps unlikely that such a report could in fact be sufficient unless it at least exhibits a further report by a registered medical practitioner.

1   IR 1986, r 7.45.

3.164 Where the court has appointed a person to act for the incapacitated person, any notice served on, or sent to, the appointed person has the same effect as if it had been served on, or given to, the incapacitated person[1]. Although this rule is drafted in general terms, presumably if the terms of the appointment were limited to a particular application or proceeding, the effect of the rule would be similarly limited.

1   IR 1986, r 7.46.

M ENFORCEMENT PROCEDURES

3.165 In any insolvency proceedings, orders of the court may be enforced in the same manner as a judgment to the same effect[1]. Where an order in insolvency proceedings is made or any process is issued by one county court, the order or process may be enforced, executed and dealt with by any other county court, as if it had been made or issued for the enforcement of a judgment or order to the same effect made by that other county court. This rule applies whether or not the second county court has jurisdiction to take insolvency proceedings[2].

1   IR 1986, r 7.19(1).
2   IR 1986, r 7.19(2).

Warrants

3.166 A warrant issued by the court under any provision of the IA 1986 must be addressed to such officer of the High Court or of a county court as the warrant specifies[1]. The court may in certain circumstances[2] issue warrants for the arrest of a debtor or a bankrupt, for the seizure of his property or for the purpose of bringing him or his documents before the court. Such warrants may only be issued to a constable or to a prescribed officer of the court. These prescribed officers are, in the High Court, the tipstaff and his assistants of the court and, in a county court, the district judge[3] and the bailiffs.

1   IR 1986, r 7.21(1).
2   IA 1986, ss 364(1), 365(3) and 366(3).
3   See the Courts and Legal Services Act 1990, s 74.

Property seized under a warrant

3.167 Where a warrant issued under the IA 1986 authorises the person to whom it is addressed to seize property, that property must be (a) lodged with, or otherwise dealt with as instructed by, whoever is specified in the warrant as authorised to receive it, or (b) kept by the officer seizing it pending the receipt of written orders from the court as to its disposal. The court should direct in the warrant in which of these ways the property should be dealt with[1]. Property for these purposes includes books, papers and records[2].

[1]   IR 1986, rr 7.22(b), 7.23(5) and 7.25(2).
[2]   IR 1986, r 7.21(3).

Person arrested under a warrant

3.168 Where a person is arrested under a warrant issued under the IA 1986, s 364, the officer apprehending him must give him into the custody of the governor of the prison named in the warrant. The governor of that prison must keep the arrested person until such time as the court otherwise directs and shall produce him before the court as it may from time to time direct[1].

[1]   IR 1986, r 7.22.

3.169 Where a bankrupt is arrested for the purpose of bringing him before the court for examination, the officer arresting him must bring him before the court issuing the warrant so that he may be examined. If that is not possible, the bankrupt should be delivered into the custody of the governor of the prison named in the warrant, who must keep him in custody and produce him before the court as it may from time to time direct. The officer who made the arrest must report forthwith to the court the arrest or delivery into custody and apply to the court to fix a venue for the bankrupt's examination. The court must appoint the earliest practicable time for the examination and direct the governor of the prison to produce the bankrupt for examination at the time and place appointed, and forthwith give notice to the person who applied for the warrant[1].

[1]   IR 1986, r 7.23.

3.170 If one county court ('the primary court') issues in insolvency proceedings a warrant for a person's arrest which is addressed to another county court ('the secondary court') for execution in its district, the secondary court may send the warrant to the district judge of any other county court in whose district the person to be arrested is, or is believed to be, with a notice to the effect that the warrant is transmitted to that court for execution in its district at the request of the primary court. The court receiving the warrant from the secondary court must apply its seal to the warrant and secure that all such steps are taken for its execution as would be appropriate in the case of a warrant issued by itself[1].

[1]   IR 1986, r 7.24.

3.171 The Criminal Law Act 1977, s 38 applies to a warrant which, in the exercise of any jurisdiction in relation to insolvency law, is issued in any part of the United Kingdom for the arrest of any person as it applies to a warrant issued in that part of the United Kingdom for the arrest of a person charged with an offence[1].

1   IA 1986, s 426(7).

N THE INDIVIDUAL INSOLVENCY REGISTER; THE BANKRUPTCY RESTRICTIONS REGISTER

3.172 The Secretary of State is under an obligation to create and maintain a register of matters relating to bankruptcies and individual voluntary arrangements, called 'the individual insolvency register'[1] and to maintain a register of bankruptcy restrictions orders, interim bankruptcy restrictions orders and bankruptcy restrictions undertakings called 'the bankruptcy restrictions register'[2]. These registers are to be open to public inspection on any business day between the hours of 9.00 am and 5.00 pm[3]. The individual insolvency register consolidates the two registers previously kept, namely the register of individual voluntary arrangements and the register of bankruptcy orders. These were kept under IR 1986, r 5.28 and rr 6.223(A)–(C), which were revoked with effect from 1 April 2004 and replaced by the rules contained in IR 1986, rr 6A.1–6A.8. The obligation to maintain the bankruptcy restrictions register arises under IA 1986, s 281A, Sch 4A, para 12 but it is to be maintained in accordance with IR 1986, Pt 6A.

1   IR 1986, r 6A.1(1).
2   IA 1986, s 281A, Sch 4A, para 12.
3   IR 1986, r 6A.1(4).

3.173 Where an obligation to enter information onto, or delete information from, the registers arises under IA 1986, Pt 6A, that obligation must be performed as soon as is reasonably practicable after it arises[1].

1   IR 1986, r 6A.1(5).

Individual voluntary arrangements

3.174 The Secretary of State must enter onto the individual insolvency register:

(a)   as regards any voluntary arrangement other than a voluntary arrangement under IA 1986, s 263A any information that was required to be held on the register of individual voluntary arrangements maintained by the Secretary of State immediately before 1 April 2004 and which relates to a voluntary arrangement which has not been completed or has not terminated on or before 1 April 2004[1]; or that is sent to him in pursuance of IR 1986, r 5.29 or IR 1986, r 5.34; and

(b)   as regards any voluntary arrangement under IA 1986, s 263A of which notice is given to him pursuant to IR 1986, r 5.45:
   (i)   the name and address of the debtor;

(ii) the date on which the arrangement was approved by the creditors; and

(iii) the court in which the official receiver's report has been filed; and,

(c) in the circumstances set out in (a) and (b) above, the debtor's gender, date of birth and any name by which he was known, not being the name in which he has entered into the voluntary arrangement[2].

1 See the revoked rule contained in IR 1986, r 5.28.
2 IR 1986, r 6A.2.

3.175 The Secretary of State must delete from the individual insolvency register all information concerning an individual voluntary arrangement where:

(a) he receives notice under IR 1986, r 5.30(5) or IR 1986, r 5.46(4) of the making of a revocation order in respect of the arrangement; or

(b) he receives notice under IR 1986, r 5.34(3) or IR 1986, r 5.50(3) of the full implementation or termination of the arrangement[1].

1 IR 1986, r 6A.3.

Bankruptcy orders

3.176 The Secretary of State must enter onto the individual insolvency register any information that was required to be held on the register of bankruptcy orders maintained by the Secretary of State immediately before 1 April 2004 and which relates to a bankrupt who:

(a) has not received his discharge on or before 1 April 2004; or

(b) was discharged in the period of three months immediately before 1 April 2004[1].

1 For the relevant information, see IR 1986, r 6.223(A) and (B) now revoked.

3.177 Where the official receiver receives pursuant to IR 1986, r 6.34 or IR 1986, r 6.46 a copy of a bankruptcy order from the court, he must cause to be entered onto the individual insolvency register:

(a) the matters listed in IR 1986, rr 6.7 and 6.38 with respect to the debtor as they are stated in the bankruptcy petition;

(b) the date of the making of the bankruptcy order;

(c) the name of the court that made the order; and

(d) the court reference number as stated on the order.

3.178 The official receiver must cause to be entered onto the individual insolvency register as soon as reasonably practicable after receipt by him, the following information:

(a) the name, gender, occupation (if any) and date of birth of the bankrupt;

(b) the bankrupt's last known address;

(c)   the date of any bankruptcy order (or if more than one the latest of them) made in the period of six years immediately prior to the date of the latest bankruptcy order made against the bankrupt (excluding for these purposes any order that was annulled);

(d)   any name by which the bankrupt was known, not being the name in which he was adjudged bankrupt;

(e)   the address of any business carried on by the bankrupt and the name in which that business was carried on if carried on in a name other than the name in which the bankrupt was adjudged bankrupt;

(f)   the name and address of any insolvency practitioner appointed to act as trustee in bankruptcy;

(g)   the address at which the official receiver may be contacted; and

(h)   the automatic discharge date under IA 1986, s 279.

3.179 Where pursuant to IR 1986, r 6.176(5) or IR 1986, r 6.215(8) the official receiver receives a copy of an order suspending the bankrupt's discharge he must cause to be entered onto the individual insolvency register:

(a)   the fact that such an order has been made; and

(b)   the period for which the discharge has been suspended or that the relevant period has ceased to run until the fulfilment of conditions specified in the order.

3.180 Where pursuant to IR 1986, r 6.216(7) a copy of a certificate certifying the discharge of an order under IA 1986, s 279(3) is received by the official receiver, he must cause to be entered onto the individual insolvency register:

(a)   that the court has discharged the order made under IA 1986, s 279(3); and

(b)   the new date of discharge of the bankrupt,

but where the order discharging the order under IA 1986, s 279(3) is subsequently rescinded by the court, the official receiver must cause the register to be amended accordingly.

3.181 Where a bankrupt is discharged from bankruptcy under IA 1986, s 279(1) or s 279(2), the official receiver must cause the fact and date of such discharge to be entered in the individual insolvency register[1].

1   IR 1986, r 6A.4.

3.182 The Secretary of State shall delete from the individual insolvency register all information concerning a bankruptcy where:

(a)   the bankruptcy order has been annulled pursuant to IA 1986, ss 261(2)(a), 261(2)(b), 263D(3) or 282(1)(b);

(b)   the bankrupt has been discharged from the bankruptcy and a period of three months has elapsed from the date of discharge;

(c)   the bankruptcy order is annulled pursuant to IA 1986, s 282(1)(a) and he has received notice of the annulment under IR 1986, r 6.213(2); or

(d)   the bankruptcy order is rescinded by the court under IA 1986, s 375 and the Secretary of State has received a copy of the order made by the court[1].

[1]   IR 1986, r 6A.5.

Bankruptcy restrictions orders and undertakings

3.183 Where an interim bankruptcy restrictions order or a bankruptcy restrictions order is made against a bankrupt, the Secretary of State must enter onto the bankruptcy restrictions register:

(a)   the name, gender, occupation (if any) and date of birth of the bankrupt;
(b)   the bankrupt's last known address;
(c)   a statement that an interim bankruptcy restrictions order or, as the case may be, a bankruptcy restrictions order has been made against him;
(d)   the date of the making of the order, the court and the court reference number; and
(e)   the duration of the order.

3.184 Where a bankruptcy restrictions undertaking is given by a bankrupt, the Secretary of State must enter onto the bankruptcy restrictions register:

(a)   the name, gender, occupation (if any) and date of birth of the bankrupt;
(b)   the bankrupt's last known address;
(c)   a statement that a bankruptcy restrictions undertaking has been given;
(d)   the date of the acceptance of the bankruptcy restrictions undertaking by the Secretary of State; and
(e)   the duration of the bankruptcy restrictions undertaking[1].

[1]   IR 1986, r 6A.6.

3.185 In any case where an interim bankruptcy restrictions order or a bankruptcy restrictions order is made or a bankruptcy restrictions undertaking has been accepted, the Secretary of State must remove from the bankruptcy restrictions register all information regarding that order or, as the case may be, undertaking after:

(a)   receipt of notification that the order or, as the case may be, the undertaking has ceased to have effect; or
(b)   the expiry of the order or, as the case may be, undertaking[1].

[1]   IR 1986, r 6A.7.

Rectification of the registers

3.186 Where the Secretary of State becomes aware that there is any inaccuracy in any information maintained on the registers he must rectify the inaccuracy as soon as reasonably practicable.

3.187 Where the Secretary of State receives notice of the date of the death of a bankrupt in respect of whom information is held on the register, he must cause the fact and date of the bankrupt's death to be entered onto the individual insolvency register and bankruptcy restrictions register[1].

1   IR 1986, r 6A.8.

Debt relief orders, etc

3.188 The Secretary of State will, when the regime relating to debt relief orders is brought into force, be under a duty to maintain a register of debt relief orders and debt relief restrictions orders and undertakings[1]. Power is conferred to amalgamate this register with another register; so it may be expected that it will form part of the individual insolvency register[2].

1   IA 1986, s 251W (inserted by TCEA 2007, s 108(1) and Sch 17).
2   IA 1986, s 412, Sch 9, para 7E (inserted by TCEA 2007, s 108(3) and Sch 20, para 14(5)).

Chapter 4

THE EC INSOLVENCY REGULATION

A INTRODUCTION

Introduction

4.1 The purpose of this chapter is to provide a distilled account of the EC Council Regulation of 29 May 2000 on insolvency proceedings[1], referred to here as the EC Insolvency Regulation. The EC Insolvency Regulation came into force on 31 May 2002[2].

[1] 1346/2000/EC.
[2] EC Insolvency Regulation, art 47.

B APPLICATION AND INTERPRETATION

4.2 The EC Insolvency Regulation, where it applies, contains a set of rules which, looking from the perspective of the English court, provide solutions to the questions whether that court has jurisdiction over a debtor; whether it should recognise judgments or orders, including foreign bankruptcy orders, made with respect to a debtor or his assets by the court of another Member State or steps taken by a liquidator appointed in foreign proceedings; and what law is to be applied to issues arising in bankruptcy proceedings. From the perspective of the court of another Member State, the Regulation provides solutions to the converse questions when they arise. If the process of interpretation proceeds consistently, the same solutions should obtain wherever the questions arise. Thus, the EC Insolvency Regulation is the starting point in determining whether the English court has jurisdiction to make a bankruptcy order against an individual. But where it does not apply, because the centre of the debtor's main interests is located outside the EC (or in Denmark), the English court must determine whether it has jurisdiction by reference to the criteria otherwise applicable, principally those set out in IA 1986, s 265(1). These jurisdictional topics are addressed in **Chapter 8**[1]. Further, where the EC Insolvency Regulation does not apply, it does not govern either (1) the recognition or effect of a foreign bankruptcy order or the recognition of and provision of assistance to a foreign office-holder to be afforded by the English court, or (2) the recognition or effect of an English bankruptcy order or the recognition of and provision of assistance to an English trustee in bankruptcy to be afforded by the foreign court. The latter set of questions is primarily a matter for the foreign court, but it should be noted that, as a matter of English law, the purported effect of the bankruptcy order embraces all the bankrupt's property wherever located[2]. The approach of the English court to the first set of questions will, since 4 April 2006, be governed by the Cross-Border Insolvency Regulations 2006 which are discussed in **Chapter 5**.

[1] See para **8.9ff**.
[2] See para **14.17**.

4.2A As a council regulation, the EC Insolvency Regulation has direct effect and so has the force of law in England and Wales, and elsewhere in the United Kingdom, without further legislative implementation. A principle of interpretation applicable to EC legislation is that the instrument in question should be given a uniform interpretation throughout the Community. Consequently words and concepts used in EC legislation are to be interpreted autonomously, not by reference to the concepts of the national law but by reference to concepts emergent or defined at the level of EC law.

The preamble to the EC Insolvency Regulation

4.3 As important as the operative articles of the EC Insolvency Regulation are the paragraphs of its preamble. For example, even to determine when the EC Insolvency Regulation applies, it is necessary to supplement the provisions in art 1 with the statement in paragraph (14) of the preamble which explains that the regulation applies only to proceedings where the centre of the debtor's main interests is located in the Community.

Virgós-Schmit report

4.4 The EC Insolvency Regulation is closely modelled on the European Convention on Insolvency Proceedings put forward for adoption in 1995. That Convention was not in the event adopted. But because of the similarity of the provisions, the report prepared to assist in the interpretation of this Convention by Professors Miguel Virgós and Mr Etienne Schmit also provides useful help in the interpretation of the EC Insolvency Regulation although it has no authoritative force[1].

¹   *Re Eurofoods IFSC Ltd (Case C-341/04)* [2006] 3 WLR 309, see the opinion of Jacobs AG at para 2.

Role of the European Court of Justice

4.5 The ultimate arbiter of the interpretation of the EC Insolvency Regulation is the European Court of Justice. Any question regarding the interpretation of the regulation raised before a court of a Member State may, where that court considers it necessary to enable it to give judgment, be referred to the European Court for a preliminary ruling[1].

¹   Treaty establishing the European Community, art 234.

Denmark

4.6 Although Denmark is a Member State of the Community, it has not participated in the adoption of the regulation and so is not bound by or subject to its application. References to Member States in the regulation are therefore to be read as references to Member States other than Denmark[1].

¹   EC Insolvency Regulation, preamble para (33).

Subsequent accessions

4.7 Ten states have joined the Community since the EC Insolvency Regulation came into force. The regulation has been amended by the Council, pursuant to its power contained in art 45, to reflect their accession.

Applicability in time

4.8 The provisions of the EC Insolvency Regulation only apply to proceedings begun after the regulation came into force on 31 May 2002[1].

¹   EC Insolvency Regulation, art 43.

Relevant insolvency proceedings

4.9 The regulation applies to collective insolvency proceedings which entail the partial or total divestment of a debtor and the appointment of a liquidator[1]. There are four elements to such insolvency proceedings: (1) the proceedings must be collective; (2) the debtor must be insolvent; (3) there must be partial or total divestment of the debtor; and (4) a liquidator must be appointed. The insolvency proceedings in question are listed by reference to each Member State in Annex A to the regulation[2]. In relation to the United Kingdom, bankruptcy and individual arrangements are included. The regulation also defines a sub-category of collective insolvency proceedings: winding-up proceedings. These are collective insolvency proceedings which involve realising the assets of the debtor, including where the proceedings have been closed by a composition or other measure terminating the insolvency, or closed by reason of the insufficiency of the assets. These are listed in Annex B to the regulation. The relevance of this distinction is that while main proceedings may be of any type listed in Annex A, secondary proceedings must be of a kind listed in Annex B.

[1] EC Insolvency Regulation, art 1(1).
[2] EC Insolvency Regulation, art 2(a).

Debtors to whom the regulation applies

4.10 Apart from the exceptional cases mentioned below, the EC Insolvency Regulation applies to all corporate and individual insolvents, whether the debtor is a natural or legal person, a trader or an individual[1]. In this book the focus is, of course, on individual insolvency.

[1] EC Insolvency Regulation, preamble para (9).

Basic jurisdictional condition: the centre of the debtor's main interests must be within the Community

4.11 The fundamental jurisdictional concept employed by the EC Insolvency Regulation is the centre of the debtor's main interests. As discussed below, the location of the centre of the debtor's main interests is the primary determinant of the allocation of jurisdiction between Member States. But the concept is also important at an even more basic level. For, the regulation only applies where the centre of the debtor's main interests is located in a Member State[1]. This essential feature has to be gathered from the preamble to the regulation.

[1] EC Insolvency Regulation, preamble para (14).

Exceptional cases to which the EC Insolvency Regulation is not applicable: insurance, credit and certain investment undertakings

4.12 Certain types of undertakings are excepted from the scope of the EC Insolvency Regulation because the nature of their business requires special treatment in insolvency. These are insurance undertakings, credit institutions, investment undertakings which provide services involving the holding of funds or securities for third persons and collective investment undertakings[1]. The regimes applicable to these undertakings are not discussed in this book.

[1] EC Insolvency Regulation, art 1(2) and preamble para (9).

Liquidator

4.13 'Liquidator' is defined as meaning any person or body whose function is to administer or liquidate assets of which the debtor has been divested or to supervise and the relevant persons and bodies are listed in Annex C[1]. A liquidator for the purpose of the regulation includes the official receiver, a trustee in bankruptcy and a supervisor of an individual voluntary arrangement. In the context of bankruptcy, the question arises whether the appointment of an interim receiver under IA 1986, s 286 is an appointment of an EC Insolvency Regulation liquidator and therefore a judgment opening insolvency proceedings[2] or is the appointment of a temporary administrator as a preliminary measure to preserve the debtor's assets[3]. In *Re Eurofoods IFSC Ltd*[4], the European Court of Justice answered that the appointment of a provisional liquidator under Irish insolvency law constituted the appointment of a liquidator within the meaning of the EC Insolvency Regulation because a provisional liquidator was included in Annex C as a relevant office-holder in Ireland. An interim receiver appointed under IA 1986, s 286 is not included in Annex C as a relevant office-holder in the United Kingdom, but, subject to one exception, the interim receiver must be the official receiver. Since the official receiver is listed in Annex C, his appointment will constitute the appointment of a liquidator for the purpose of the EC Insolvency Regulation, and therefore a judgment opening insolvency proceedings, even though it is an interim appointment. However, where the court has appointed an insolvency practitioner to report on the debtor's affairs under IA 1986, s 273, such an appointment would seem not to involve the appointment of a liquidator for the purpose of the EC Insolvency Regulation.

[1]   EC Insolvency Regulation, art 2(b).
[2]   EC Insolvency Regulation, art 16 and art 2(e).
[3]   EC Insolvency Regulation, art 38.
[4]   *(Case C-341/04)* [2006] 3 WLR 309.

Court and judgment

4.14 'Court' is defined as meaning the judicial body or any other competent body of a Member State empowered to open insolvency proceedings or to take decisions in the course of such proceedings[1]. Thus where the creditors in meeting are empowered to open insolvency proceedings, for example by approving a voluntary arrangement, the creditors' meeting is a court for the purpose of the EC Insolvency Regulation. And, in relation to the opening of insolvency proceedings or the appointment of a liquidator, 'judgment' includes the decision of any such court[2].

[1]   EC Insolvency Regulation, art 2(d).
[2]   EC Insolvency Regulation, art 2(e).

C JURISDICTION AND OPENING OF INSOLVENCY PROCEEDINGS

Main proceedings, territorial proceedings and secondary proceedings

4.15 In the terminology of the regulation 'main insolvency proceedings' are insolvency proceedings opened in the courts of the Member State in whose territory the centre of the debtor's main interests are situated[1]; 'territorial insolvency proceedings' are insolvency proceedings opened, where available, in a Member State other than that Member State[2]. Insolvency proceedings opened in another Member State after main insolvency proceedings have been opened in the Member State in whose territory the centre of the debtor's main interests are situated are called 'secondary proceedings'[3]. Territorial proceedings, opened at a time when no main proceedings have been opened are referred to as independent territorial proceedings and are not secondary proceedings. But when independent territorial proceedings have been opened in one Member State and main proceedings are later opened in another Member State, the territorial proceedings become secondary proceedings[4].

1   EC Insolvency Regulation, preamble para (12). Main proceedings are not defined in the articles of the regulation and the phrase is not used in art 3, though it is throughout chapter III (arts 27–38) which address secondary insolvency proceedings. The regulation uses the phrases 'main insolvency proceedings' and 'main proceedings' interchangeably; that practice is followed in this book. The usage is the same as regards territorial and secondary proceedings.
2   EC Insolvency Regulation, art 3(2) and (4).
3   EC Insolvency Regulation, art 3(3).
4   EC Insolvency Regulation, preamble para (17).

General principle

4.16 The basic principle informing the EC Insolvency Regulation is that insolvency proceedings should be opened in the courts of the Member State where the debtor has the centre of his main interests and that the ensuing proceedings should have universal scope and encompass all the debtor's assets[1]. But this principle is not absolute.

1   EC Insolvency Regulation, preamble para (12).

Qualification of the principle

4.17 The possibility is recognised that in certain circumstances insolvency proceedings may be opened against a debtor in the courts of a Member State other than that in whose territory the centre of the debtor's main interests is situated. The situations in which the EC Insolvency Regulation permits the courts of such a Member State to open proceedings are where the debtor has an establishment in the territory of the Member[1] State in question and:

(1)   main proceedings have already been opened against him in the Member State where the centre of his main interests is located[2]; or
(2)   where main proceedings have not been opened against him in that Member State, either:
    (i)   main proceedings cannot be opened against him in that Member State because of conditions laid down by the law of that state; or
    (ii)   the proceedings are requested by a creditor who has his domicile, habitual residence or registered office in the Member State within the territory of which the debtor's establishment is located or whose claim arises from the operation of that establishment[3].

¹   EC Insolvency Regulation, art 3(2).
²   EC Insolvency Regulation, arts 3(2) and 29; and see preamble para (18).
³   EC Insolvency Regulation, art 3(4)(a) and (b); and see preamble para (17).

Community jurisdiction and national jurisdiction

4.18 The operation of the EC Insolvency Regulation in regulating jurisdiction between the courts of Member States is in part negative: only the courts of a Member State to which jurisdiction is allowed by the EC Insolvency Regulation may open insolvency proceedings. But the EC Insolvency Regulation does not positively confer jurisdiction at a national level: where, by designating the courts of a Member State as having jurisdiction at the community level, it permits those courts to open insolvency proceedings, but territorial jurisdiction must also be established at the national level by the national law of the Member State concerned¹. In other words, where the EC Insolvency Regulation applies, that a court opening insolvency proceedings has jurisdiction at a community level is a necessary, but not a sufficient, condition to be fulfilled before it may open the insolvency proceedings.

¹   EC Insolvency Regulation, preamble para (15).

National jurisdiction within the United Kingdom

4.19 The jurisdictional rules of the EC Insolvency Regulation determine at the community level when a court within the United Kingdom may open insolvency proceedings against a debtor. But, first, as mentioned the EC rules do not exhaust the jurisdictional conditions which need to be fulfilled to establish territorial jurisdiction. Secondly, the EC rules do not allocate jurisdiction between the legal systems within the United Kingdom. Hence for these two reasons it is necessary, having established that the courts of the United Kingdom have jurisdiction at the community level, then to consider the national conditions relevant to establishing bankruptcy jurisdiction within the relevant part of the United Kingdom. No legislative rules have been established within the United Kingdom for the purpose of allocating jurisdiction between the component United Kingdom jurisdictions of England and Wales, Scotland and Northern Ireland. But since a person may only have one centre of his main interests, that centre will be located within one of those jurisdictions and so can operate without more to allocate jurisdiction as between the legal systems within the United Kingdom. Once the relevant system within the United Kingdom has thereby been identified, the national rules applicable within it to establish bankruptcy jurisdiction or its equivalent must be fulfilled.

English jurisdictional conditions

4.20 For the purpose of bringing bankruptcy proceedings on a creditor's or debtor's petition in England and Wales, territorial jurisdiction is established by fulfilling the conditions laid down in IA 1986, s 265(1). Territorial jurisdiction to conclude an individual voluntary arrangement is dependent on those same conditions being fulfilled because in order to propose such an arrangement the debtor must either be an undischarged bankrupt or able to petition for his own bankruptcy[1].

1   Cf IA 1986, s 256(3).

Opening insolvency proceedings

4.21 Insolvency proceedings are opened where the court hands down an effective judgment to that effect. 'Court' and 'judgment' here bear the extended meanings mentioned above[1]. Article 2(f) defines 'the time of the opening of proceedings' as the time at which the judgment opening proceedings becomes effective, whether it is a final judgment or not.

1   See para **4.14**.

D APPLICABLE LAW

General principle

4.22 The general principle adopted in the EC Insolvency Regulation is that the law of the Member State in whose courts the insolvency proceedings are opened, the *lex concursus*, shall apply to questions arising in or pursuant to those proceedings whether relating to their opening, conduct or closure and whether substantive or procedural[1]. This principle also applies to secondary proceedings[2].

1   EC Insolvency Regulation, art 4(1) and preamble para (23).
2   EC Insolvency Regulation, art 28.

4.23 Where the EC Insolvency Regulation provides that the law of the State of the opening of proceedings should be applicable, what is thereby caused to apply is the law of that State not including its rules as to the conflicts of laws; in other words, *renvoi* is excluded. Nothing in the regulation itself makes this clear, but it is to be gathered from the Virgós-Schmit report[1]. But the exclusion of *renvoi* only extends to the matters covered by the regulation. It does not apply where a conflict arises between the law of the State where the insolvency proceedings have been opened and the law of a non-Member State.

1   Virgós-Schmit report para 87.

Time factor

4.24 The rules contained in the regulation do not apply to acts done by the debtor before the regulation came into force on 31 May 2002. Such acts continue to be governed by the law applicable to them when they were done[1].

1   EC Insolvency Regulation, art 43.

Express instances in which the lex concursus applies

4.25 Article 4(2) sets out a list of matters which will, by application of this principle, be determined by the law of the State of the opening of the proceedings. These are:

(a)   against which debtors insolvency proceedings may be brought on account of their capacity;

(b)   the assets which form part of the estate and the treatment of assets acquired by or devolving on the debtor after the opening of insolvency proceedings;

(c)   the respective powers of the debtor and the liquidator;

(d)   the conditions under which set-offs may be invoked;

(e)   the effects of insolvency proceedings on current contracts to which the debtor is party;

(f)   the effects of the insolvency proceedings on proceedings brought by individual creditors, with the exception of lawsuits pending;

(g)   the claims which are to be lodged against the debtor's estate and the treatment of claims arising after the opening of insolvency proceedings;

(h)   the rules governing the lodging, verification and admission of claims;

(i)   the rules governing the distribution of proceeds from the realisation of assets, the ranking of claims and the rights of creditors who have obtained partial satisfactions after the opening of insolvency proceedings by virtue of a right in rem or through a set-off;

(j)   the conditions for and the effects of closure of insolvency proceedings, especially by composition;

(k)   creditors' rights after closure of insolvency proceedings;

(l)   who is to bear the costs and expenses incurred in the insolvency proceedings;

(m)   the rules relating to the voidness, voidability or unenforceability of legal acts detrimental to the creditors.

Exceptions

4.26 Although the general rule is that the law of the State of the opening of proceedings should govern questions arising in those proceedings, a number of exceptions are made so as to fulfil the legitimate expectations of creditors and so as to promote certainty in commercial transactions made in other Member States with the insolvent debtor before the insolvency proceedings were opened. These are set out in the following paragraphs of this section.

Rights in rem over assets in another Member State

4.27 The opening of insolvency proceedings do not affect the rights in rem of creditors or third parties in respect of tangible or intangible, moveable or immoveable assets belonging to the debtor which are situated within the territory of another Member State at the time of the opening of the proceedings[1].

---

[1]   EC Insolvency Regulation, art 5(1).

4.28 This provision is only relevant to main proceedings because territorial proceedings only affect assets located within the territory of the Member State in which they are opened. By contrast main insolvency proceedings have universal scope and aim at encompassing all the debtor's assets. So the reach of main insolvency proceedings extends to (1) assets located in the State where the proceedings are opened; (2) assets in other Member States (other than Denmark); and (3) assets located elsewhere.

4.29 But if the law of the State where the main proceedings were opened governed the effect of the insolvency on creditors' or third parties' rights in rem, this would disrupt too intrusively the basis on which credit had been granted to the debtor. So art 5(1) provides negatively that the opening of the insolvency proceedings does not affect rights in rem held by creditors or third parties over the debtor's assets situated in another Member State. Thus nothing positive is said as to what law will govern those rights although, in the preamble, it is recognised that normally it will be the law of the place where the asset is situated, the *lex situs*, which determines the basis, validity and extent of a right in rem over the asset in question[1]. Nor does art 5(1) make any provision as to assets located outside any Member State (or in Denmark).

1   EC Insolvency Regulation, preamble para (25).

4.30 But the liquidator appointed in the Member State where the main proceedings were opened should be able to apply open secondary proceedings in the Member State where the assets are located so long as the debtor has an establishment there[1]. Alternatively, if and when the secured creditor realises the security, he must pay the surplus to the liquidator in the main proceedings. The secured creditor's obligation to do this arises because the surplus will no longer be subject to the right in rem and so will form part of the assets within the reach of the main proceedings[2].

1   EC Insolvency Regulation, art 29(a).
2   EC Insolvency Regulation, preamble para (25).

4.31 Creditors' and third parties' rights in rem in respect of assets include:

(a)   the right to dispose of assets or have them disposed of and to obtain satisfaction from the proceeds of or income from those assets, in particular by virtue of a lien or a mortgage;

(b)   the exclusive right to have a claim met, in particular a right guaranteed by a lien in respect of the claim or by an assignment of the claim by way of guarantee;

(c)   the right to demand the assets from, and/or to require restitution by, anyone having possession or use of them contrary to the wishes of the party so entitled; and

(d)   a right in rem to the beneficial use of assets[1].

1   EC Insolvency Regulation, art 5(2).

4.32 The right, recorded in a public register and enforceable against third parties, under which a right in rem in the relevant sense may be obtained, shall be considered a right in rem[1].

[1]   EC Insolvency Regulation, art 5(3).

4.33 Article 5(1) does not preclude actions for voidness, voidability or unenforceability being brought pursuant to the law of the State of the opening of proceedings[1].

[1]   EC Insolvency Regulation, art 5(4).

Rights of set-off

4.34 The general rule is that the conditions under which set-offs may be invoked will be determined by the *lex concursus*. Article 4(2)(d) expressly so provides. But, the opening of insolvency proceedings shall not affect the right of creditors to demand the set-off of their claims against the claims of the debtor, where such set-off is permitted by the law applicable to the insolvent debtor's claim. Again this does not preclude actions for voidness, voidability or unenforceability being brought pursuant to the law of the State of the opening of proceedings[1].

[1]   EC Insolvency Regulation, art 6.

Reservation of title

4.35 Article 4(2)(b) applies the law of the State of the opening of proceedings to the determination of which assets form part of the estate. But art 7 provides differently where an asset which is subject to rights reserving title in a contract of sale is situated in the territory of a different Member State.

4.36 First, if it is the purchaser against whom insolvency proceedings have been opened, then, so long as the asset is situated in a different Member State, the opening of the proceedings will not affect the seller's rights based on the reservation of title[1].

[1]   EC Insolvency Regulation, art 7(1).

4.37 Secondly, if it is the seller against whom the insolvency proceedings have been opened and the asset is situated in a different Member State, the opening of the proceedings does not constitute grounds for rescinding or terminating the sale and does not prevent the purchaser from acquiring title. This rule does not render the law of any individual Member State applicable in the event of the seller's becoming subject to insolvency proceedings; instead it applies a positive rule of law applicable without regard to the law of any individual State which might otherwise be applicable[1].

[1]   EC Insolvency Regulation, art 7(2).

4.38 But, an action for voidness, voidability or unenforceability may nonetheless be brought pursuant to the law of the State of the opening of proceedings[1].

1 EC Insolvency Regulation, art 7(3).

Contracts relating to immoveable property

4.39 Article 8 provides that the effects of insolvency proceedings on a contract conferring the right to acquire or make use of immoveable property shall be governed solely by the law of the Member State within the territory of which the immoveable property is situated. Relevant contracts will include leases as well as contracts for sale[1].

1 Virgós-Schmit report para 119.

Payment systems and financial markets

4.40 The EC Insolvency Regulation recognises the need for special protection in the case of payment systems and financial markets[1]. To achieve this the rule applied is that only the law of the Member State applicable to the system or market in question shall govern the effects of insolvency proceedings on the rights and obligations of the parties to a payment or settlement system or to the financial market. Exceptionally any actions for voidness, voidability or unenforceability are also to be subject to the law applicable to the relevant payment system or financial market[2].

1 EC Insolvency Regulation, preamble para (27).
2 EC Insolvency Regulation, art 9.

Contracts of employment

4.41 The effects of insolvency proceedings on employment contracts and relationships are to be governed solely by the law of the Member State applicable to the contract of employment[1]. The purpose of this rule is to protect the rights and preserve the expectations of employees from the application of a foreign law. The law applicable to the employment contract will be determined by arts 6 and 7 of the Rome Convention. But the rule is restricted to questions relating to the impact on the employment contract or relationship of the fact that insolvency proceedings have been opened. The law of the Member State of the opening of the insolvency proceedings will still cover such questions as whether employees' claims in the insolvency have any preferential ranking in distribution of the estate. Where an employee is guaranteed a payment under a state scheme in the event of the employer's insolvency, the payments will be governed by the law of the State which governs the scheme[2].

1 EC Insolvency Regulation, art 10.
2 Virgós-Schmit report para 128.

Rights subject to registration

4.42 The effects of insolvency proceedings on the rights of the debtor in immoveable property, a ship or an aircraft subject to registration in a public register shall be determined by the law of the Member State under the authority of which the register is kept[1]. Significantly, this rule does not provide that the effects of the proceedings are to be determined solely by the law of the State governing the register. As is explained in the Virgós-Schmit report, the purpose of the rule is not to interfere with the system of registration[2]. But the rule does not prevent rights registered on the register from being acquired by the liquidator; it preserves the applicability of the law governing the register to what steps need to be taken to make entries on the register to take due note of the effect of the insolvency proceedings. So, what is described in the report as a sort of cumulative application of both laws is required: the law of the Member State of the opening of proceedings will determine whether the assets to which the registered rights relate form part of the estate and the law of the Member State under whose authority the register is kept will determine what the liquidator must do to protect the rights for the benefit of the debtor's creditors.

[1]   EC Insolvency Regulation, art 11.
[2]   Virgós-Schmit report para 130.

Community patents and trademarks

4.43 For the purposes of the EC Insolvency Regulation, a Community patent, a Community trademark or any other similar right established by Community law may be included only in main insolvency proceedings. This rule overrides rules contained in the Conventions relating to these rights that they would be included in the first insolvency proceedings to be opened against the debtor[1].

[1]   EC Insolvency Regulation, art 12.

Detrimental acts

4.44 Actions for voidness, voidability or unenforceability are governed by the law of the Member State of the opening of the proceedings[1]. But a defence is provided in such proceedings to a person who has benefited from an act detrimental to all the creditors if he provides proof (1) that the act in question is subject to the law of a Member State other than that of the opening of the proceedings, and (2) that that law does not allow any means of challenging that act in the relevant case[2]. As regards the second limb of this defence, the Virgós-Schmit report states that the act should not be capable of being challenged by rules applicable in the event of insolvency or under the general rules of national law applicable under the law of the State governing the act in question[3]. The reference to the relevant case imports a requirement that the challenge should be possible upon the actual facts of the case in question. The defence is only available with respect to acts done before the insolvency proceedings were opened.

[1]   EC Insolvency Regulation, art 4(2)(m).

Protection of third party purchasers

4.45 Where, by an act concluded after the opening of insolvency proceedings, the debtor disposes, for valuable consideration, of an immoveable asset, a ship or an aircraft subject to registration in a public register or securities whose existence presupposes registration in a register laid down by law, the validity of that act shall be governed by the law of the State within the territory of which the immoveable asset is situated or under the authority of which the register is kept[1].

1   EC Insolvency Regulation, art 14.

4.46 In general the effect of opening insolvency proceedings is to divest the debtor of his title to his assets and transfer title to the liquidator. Thereafter an attempt by the debtor to pass title to a third party will be a hollow act and, even if he gives value, the third party will not obtain good title. But it would undermine confidence in public registers if a third party, having checked the register, found that he failed to obtain good title contrary to what his check had led him to expect. As is explained in the Virgós-Schmit report[1], the provision protecting third party purchasers contained in art 14 was originally intended to protect such confidence in registers, but the ambit of the rule was extended so as to include immoveable property generally. The rule does not refer to the law of another Member State and so might be taken to include reference to non-Member States. The Virgós-Schmit report proceeds on the assumption that Member State is meant.

1   Virgós-Schmit report para 140.

Effects of insolvency proceedings on lawsuits pending

4.47 The effects of insolvency proceedings on a lawsuit pending concerning an asset or a right of which the debtor has been divested shall be governed solely by the law of the Member State in which that lawsuit is pending[1]. This rule needs to be read in conjunction with art 4(2)(f): that article provides that the effects of the insolvency proceedings on proceedings brought by individual creditors are to be determined according to the law of the State of the opening of proceedings. But art 15 excepts pending lawsuits from the ambit of the general rule. The distinction is between the enforcement of established rights against the debtor which are subject to the general rule and the pursuit of unresolved claims, including claims by the debtor, to which the exception applies. In the latter case the procedural rules of the law of the Member State where the lawsuit is pending will determine the effect of the opening of the insolvency proceedings on the lawsuit, for example on whether the lawsuit should be stayed or the liquidator substituted as party in place of the debtor and so forth.

1   EC Insolvency Regulation, art 15.

E RECOGNITION OF JUDGMENTS OPENING INSOLVENCY PROCEEDINGS

General principle: judgments opening insolvency proceedings

4.48 Where a court of a Member State having jurisdiction under the EC Insolvency Regulation to open such proceedings hands down a judgment opening insolvency proceedings, the judgment must be recognised in all the other Member States from the time that it becomes effective in the State where the proceedings were opened[1].

[1]   EC Insolvency Regulation, art 16(1).

Non-recognition on grounds of public policy

4.49 Recognition may be refused where the effect of recognition would be manifestly contrary to public policy in the State where recognition is sought, in particular to the fundamental principles of that State or the constitutional rights and liberties of the individual[1].

[1]   EC Insolvency Regulation, art 26.

Challenging a judgment opening insolvency proceedings

4.50 Save where justified by the exceptional ground of infringement of public policy allowed by art 26, it is not competent for the court of a second Member State to challenge or go behind the judgment of the court of the Member State which opened insolvency proceedings. So a court opening main proceedings bears a duty to check that it has jurisdiction to do so. If a challenge is to be made to that court's decision to open proceedings, the challenge must be made in that court or by the applicable appellate procedure available in the legal system of which it forms part[1].

[1]   *Re Eurofoods IFSC Ltd (Case C-341/04)* [2006] 3 WLR 309.

Judgments refusing to open proceedings

4.51 Equally the decision of a court of a Member State refusing to open insolvency proceedings must be recognised by the courts of other Member States. For, the court's refusal to open proceedings may be based on a decision that the centre of the relevant debtor's main interests is not located within the territory of that Member State but is instead located within another Member State; if the court in that other Member State were to form a different view, then it might become impossible to open main proceedings in any Member State.

Courts and judgments

4.52 A broad interpretation is given to the meaning of 'court' and 'judgment' in the EC Insolvency Regulation[1]. 'Court' means the judicial body or any other competent body of a Member State empowered to open insolvency proceedings or to take decisions in the course of such proceedings[2]. A creditors' meeting may therefore constitute a court for this purpose. 'Judgment' has a correspondingly extended sense and includes, in relation to the opening of insolvency proceedings or the appointment of a liquidator, the decision of any court empowered to open such proceedings or to appoint a liquidator[3].

[1] EC Insolvency Regulation, preamble para (10). Cf para **4.14** above.
[2] EC Insolvency Regulation, art 2(d).
[3] EC Insolvency Regulation, art 2(e).

The time of the opening of insolvency proceedings

4.53 The time of the opening of insolvency proceedings means the time at which the judgment opening proceedings becomes effective, whether it is a final judgment or not[1].

[1] EC Insolvency Regulation, art 2(f).

Debtor's capacity to be the subject of insolvency proceedings

4.54 The courts of a Member State must recognise a judgment handed down in another Member State opening insolvency proceedings against a debtor even where, on account of his capacity, insolvency proceedings could not be brought against him in the courts of the Member State required to recognise the judgment[1]. Thus capacity to be subjected to insolvency proceedings is to be determined according to the law of the Member State where jurisdiction lies to open insolvency proceedings.

[1] EC Insolvency Regulation, art 16(1).

Recognition of main proceedings does not preclude opening secondary proceedings

4.55 Where main proceedings have been opened in one Member State, they must be recognised in all other Member States, but such recognition does not, where appropriate, preclude the subsequent opening of territorial, secondary proceedings in a second Member State[1].

[1] EC Insolvency Regulation, art 16(2).

Effects of recognition: main proceedings

4.56 The judgment opening main insolvency proceedings is to have the same effect in any other Member State, with no further formalities, as it does in the Member State where the main proceedings were opened unless either:

(1)   the EC Insolvency Regulation provides otherwise; or

(2)   any territorial proceedings are opened in the other Member State[1].

[1]   EC Insolvency Regulation, art 17(1).

Effects of recognition: territorial proceedings

4.57 When territorial proceedings have been opened in a Member State, their effects may not be challenged in another Member State[1]. But the effects of territorial proceedings are restricted to the assets of the debtor situated in the territory of the Member State where the territorial proceedings are opened[2] and any restriction of the creditors' rights, for example a stay or discharge, will only produce effects vis-à-vis assets situated within the territory of another Member State in the case of those creditors who have given their consent.

[1]   EC Insolvency Regulation, art 17(2).
[2]   EC Insolvency Regulation, art 3(2) and preamble para (12).

F RECOGNITION AND ENFORCEMENT OF OTHER JUDGMENTS

Relationship with the EC Judgments Regulation

4.58 The Brussels Convention on Jurisdiction and Judgments in Civil and Commercial Matters does not apply to bankruptcy, proceedings relating to the winding up of insolvent companies or other legal persons, compositions and other analogous proceedings. The EC Insolvency Regulation governs the field of those excluded proceedings. Article 25 of the EC Insolvency Regulation is crafted so that the scope of the two regimes neither overlap nor omit any relevant matter. So, all relevant judgments are governed by one or other of the two regimes, but not both.

4.59 For most purposes the Brussels Convention has been replaced by the EC Judgments Regulation[1] and therefore references to the Brussels Convention in the EC Insolvency Regulation should presumably be read as references to the relevant provisions of the EC Judgments Regulation. Thus the reference in art 25(1) of the EC Insolvency Regulation to arts 31 to 51, with the exception of art 34(2) of the Brussels Convention should be read as referring to arts 38 to 58, with the exception of art 45(1) of the EC Judgments Regulation.

[1]   EC Regulation 44/2001.

Judgments concerning the course and closure of insolvency proceedings and compositions

4.60 Like judgments opening insolvency proceedings, judgments handed down by a court whose judgment opening proceedings is recognised which concern the course and closure of the insolvency proceedings and compositions approved by that court are to be recognised in other Member States without further formalities[1].

[1]   EC Insolvency Regulation, art 25(1), sub-paragraph 1.

Judgments deriving directly from the insolvency proceedings

4.61 Judgments deriving directly from the insolvency proceedings and which are closely linked with them even though handed down by a different court must also be recognised. Recognition of judgments in this category is governed by the EC Insolvency Regulation because they do not fall within the ambit of the EC Judgments Regulation which for most purposes replaces it. The scope of that Convention and Regulation does not extend to the field of bankruptcy and winding up. In *Gourdain v Nadler*[1] the European Court held that actions having their legal basis in the excluded fields of bankruptcy or insolvent winding up and being closely linked with the insolvency proceedings were outside the scope of the EC Judgments Regulation. The second sub-paragraph of art 25(1) ensures that they are brought within the EC Insolvency Regulation[2].

[1]   [1979] ECR 733.
[2]   Virgós-Schmit report para 195.

Judgments relating to preservation measures

4.62 Judgments relating to preservation measures taken after the request for the opening of insolvency proceedings must likewise be recognised without further formalities[1]. Judgments relating to preservation measures are to be recognised even if handed down before the insolvency proceedings are opened. Again the reason for the inclusion of this provision is that provisional orders and protective measures which serve to protect insolvency proceedings are excluded from the scope of the EC Judgments Regulation by reason of the nature of the rights which they seek to protect[2]. The court competent to make provisional orders and impose protective measures is the court competent to open main proceedings pursuant to art 3(1).

[1]   EC Insolvency Regulation, art 25(1), sub-paragraph 3.
[2]   *De Cavel v De Cavel* [1979] ECR 1055; Virgós-Schmit report para 198.

Other judgments

4.63 Recognition of judgments other than those just mentioned are governed by the EC Judgments Regulation. Thus where a trustee in bankruptcy brings an action against a third party based on the private law rights of the bankrupt which have vested in him by virtue of the bankruptcy, the question whether the judgment resulting from that action is to be recognised in another Member State will be governed by the EC Judgments Regulation[1].

1   EC Insolvency Regulation, art 25(2).

Enforcement

4.64   Judgments which are to be recognised in other Member States by virtue of art 25(1) are to be enforced in accordance with arts 38 to 58, with the exception of art 45(1) of the EC Judgments Regulation[1].

1   EC Insolvency Regulation, art 25(1) with the substitution of references to the EC Judgments Regulation for references to the Brussels Convention.

Grounds for non-recognition

4.65   In addition to power to refuse to recognise or enforce judgments on grounds of public policy[1], Member States are not obliged to recognise or enforce a judgment which might result in a limitation of personal freedom or postal secrecy[2].

1   EC Insolvency Regulation, art 26.
2   EC Insolvency Regulation, art 25(3).

G LIQUIDATOR'S POWERS

Liquidator appointed in main proceedings

4.66   In general, main proceedings have universal scope through all Member States. So a liquidator appointed in main proceedings may exercise all the powers conferred on him by the law of the State of the opening of proceedings in any other Member State[1]. In particular, subject to any rights in rem protected by art 5 or rights arising from reservation of title protected by art 7, he may remove any of the debtor's assets which are situated in another Member State. If his powers include coercive measures or the right to rule on legal proceedings and disputes, those powers cannot be exercised in another Member State[2].

1   EC Insolvency Regulation, art 18(1).
2   EC Insolvency Regulation, art 18(3).

Obligation to observe local law

4.67   In exercising his powers, he must observe the laws of the State in which he intends to act[1].

1   EC Insolvency Regulation, art 18(3).

Powers curtailed where other insolvency proceedings have been opened or preservation implemented

4.68 Since territorial proceedings may be proceeding at the same time as the main proceedings, conflict between the two liquidators is avoided by curtailing the power of the liquidator in the main proceedings to act in a Member State where other insolvency proceedings have been opened[1]. In such a case the liquidator appointed in the territorial proceedings holds sway within the territory in which he has been appointed[2]. Similarly, where any preservation measure has been taken in another Member State further to a request for the opening of insolvency proceedings in that state, that preservation measure will displace the power of the liquidator in the main proceedings[3].

1   EC Insolvency Regulation, art 18(1).
2   Virgós-Schmit report para 163.
3   EC Insolvency Regulation, art 18(1).

Liquidator appointed in territorial proceedings

4.69 Where a liquidator has been appointed in territorial proceedings, his principal efforts will be concentrated within the territory of the State in which he has been appointed. But he is given specific powers to act in other jurisdictions for the purposes of (1) recovering assets which have been moved out of the jurisdiction after the opening of proceedings, and (2) bringing actions to set aside which are in the interests of the creditors[1].

1   EC Insolvency Regulation, art 18(2).

Opposing steps taken by the liquidator

4.70 It is observed in the Virgós-Schmit report that no rule is included regarding opposition to the exercise of the liquidator's powers and that therefore general rules are applicable[1].

1   Virgós-Schmit report para 166.

Proof of the liquidator's appointment

4.71 A certified copy of the original decision appointing the liquidator or some other certificate issued by the court having jurisdiction is sufficient proof of the liquidator's appointment without further formality although a translation may be required[1].

1   EC Insolvency Regulation, art 19.

Publication and registration of the liquidator's appointment

4.72 The liquidator may request that the judgment opening the insolvency proceedings and his appointment be published in other Member States in accordance with publications procedures. A Member State is entitled to require this in cases where the debtor has an establishment within the territory of that State and, if so, the liquidator must take steps to ensure that publication is achieved[1]. Similarly the liquidator may request that the judgment opening the insolvency proceedings be registered in the land register, trade register or any other public register kept in another Member State. Again such registration may be mandatory and, if so, the liquidator must take steps to ensure it is done[2]. The costs of publication and registration are to be regarded as costs incurred in the proceedings[3].

[1]   EC Insolvency Regulation, art 21.
[2]   EC Insolvency Regulation, art 22.
[3]   EC Insolvency Regulation, art 23.

Protection of persons who honour obligations to the debtor without knowledge of the insolvency proceedings

4.73   A general consequence of insolvency proceedings being opened against a debtor is that he cannot thereafter give a good receipt to a person who honours an obligation owed to the debtor; only the liquidator of his assets has the authority to do so. Article 24 provides protection to a person who honours an obligation by paying the debtor when he should have paid the liquidator: he is deemed to have discharged his obligation if he was unaware of the opening of the proceedings. Whether notice of the judgment opening the proceedings or of the appointment of the liquidator has been published pursuant to art 21 determines where the burden of proof lies. If the obligation is honoured before publication, then the payer is presumed not to have knowledge of the proceedings and so the burden lies on the person, likely to be the liquidator, claiming that the payer was aware of the proceedings. If the obligation is honoured after publication, the position is reversed: the payer is presumed to be aware of the proceedings in the absence of proof to the contrary[1].

[1]   EC Insolvency Regulation, art 24(2).

H EQUAL TREATMENT OF CREDITORS

Return of assets obtained after main insolvency proceedings opened

4.74   As the preamble declares, main proceedings have universal scope and aim at encompassing all the debtor's assets[1]. So, if an unsecured creditor garners for himself any of the debtor's assets after main proceedings have been opened, his keeping those assets would run counter to the scheme inherent in insolvency proceedings whereby all the debtor's assets are collected, realised and their value distributed *pari passu* amongst the debtor's unsecured creditors. The EC Insolvency Regulation provides a rule governing this problem where the creditor who obtains the asset contrary to the insolvency scheme obtains an asset of the debtor which is situated in the territory of a different Member State from that in which the insolvency proceedings were opened. Unless he is entitled to retain the asset because he holds rights in rem over it protected under art 5 or has reserved or obtained title to the assets protected under art 7, the creditor must return what he has obtained to the liquidator appointed in the main proceedings[2]. This rule does not apply with respect to territorial proceedings because the liquidator in those proceedings does not have any claim, apart from the special recovery or avoidance actions permitted under art 18(2), to assets outside the territory of the Member State to which the territorial proceedings relate.

[1] Paragraph (12).
[2] EC Insolvency Regulation, art 20(1).

Hotchpot

4.75 Although the principle underpinning the structure of the EC Insolvency Regulation is that there should be one set of main proceedings against any one insolvent with universal scope, this principle is qualified by the possibility that secondary proceedings with only territorial scope may also be opened. Indeed it is possible that only territorial proceedings may be opened against a debtor in a number of different Member States without any main proceedings being opened at all. Where this happens, a creditor may obtain a dividend in one set of proceedings before creditors elsewhere have obtained a dividend in the proceedings pending in another Member State[1]. Article 20(2) seeks to ensure equal treatment between the creditors proving in the different proceedings by requiring the creditor who has obtained a dividend in proceedings in one Member State to bring that dividend into account if he proves in proceedings in another Member State. He may only obtain a dividend in those other proceedings where creditors of the same ranking or category have, in those other proceedings, obtained an equivalent dividend. He is not obliged to give up the dividend which he obtained in the first proceedings. So, this provision only tends towards achieving equal treatment in that it may be that the dividend paid in the second proceedings never reaches an equivalent proportion of the debts. If so, the creditor will retain his advantage, though it may be reduced and he will not be permitted to obtain any dividend in the second proceedings.

[1] Any creditor with his habitual residence, domicile or registered office in a Member State other than the State of the opening of the proceedings may prove in the proceedings; see art 39.

I SECONDARY PROCEEDINGS

Introduction

4.76 Chapter III of the EC Insolvency Regulation makes special provision for the regulation of secondary insolvency proceedings. As mentioned in connection with jurisdiction, the primary place in which to open insolvency proceedings against a debtor is the courts of the Member State in the territory of which the centre of the debtor's main interests is situated. But although proceedings opened on that footing as main proceedings under art 3(1) aim at universal scope, that aim may not be fully realisable by the liquidator appointed in those proceedings acting directly in a second Member State. Accordingly it may be desirable to open secondary proceedings in that other Member State. The possibility of opening secondary proceedings caters for that requirement. Secondly, in the circumstances permitted under art 3(4), independent territorial proceedings may have been commenced before any main proceedings are opened. If main proceedings are later opened, the independent territorial proceedings become secondary proceedings.

Opening secondary proceedings after main proceedings have been opened

4.77 Where main proceedings have been opened in one Member State and have been recognised in a second Member State, then, so long as the court of that second Member State has jurisdiction to open secondary proceedings against the debtor, that court may open secondary proceedings without the debtor's insolvency being examined in that second state[1]. Thus, the court in the second State must therefore recognise the judgment, in the wide sense of judgment defined by art 2(e), opening the main proceedings; there are only limited grounds of public policy which might justify a refusal to recognise that judgment. Secondly, in order that the court in the second State should have jurisdiction, the debtor must have an establishment within the territory of that Member State. Secondary proceedings opened in these circumstances must be winding-up proceedings of a kind listed in Annex B to the regulation[2]. Annex B only includes winding-up proceedings involving the realisation of the debtor's assets. The persons with standing to request the opening of secondary proceedings are (a) the liquidator in the main proceedings, and (b) any other person or authority empowered to request the opening of insolvency proceedings under the law of the Member State within the territory of which the opening of secondary proceedings is requested[3]. Where required by the law of the Member State in which the secondary proceedings are requested, the applicant may be made to make an advance payment of costs or to provide appropriate security[4].

[1]   EC Insolvency Regulation, art 27.
[2]   EC Insolvency Regulation, arts 27 and 2(c) and 3(3).
[3]   EC Insolvency Regulation, art 29.
[4]   EC Insolvency Regulation, art 30.

Impact of opening main proceedings on existing territorial proceedings

4.78 As mentioned, where independent territorial proceedings are on foot when main proceedings are opened, the territorial proceedings become secondary proceedings[1]. But the territorial proceedings may have been opened either as insolvency proceedings of a kind listed in Annex A to the regulation or as proceedings of a kind listed in Annex B. If they are proceedings of a kind listed in Annex A, the liquidator in the main proceedings may request that they be converted into proceedings of a kind listed in Annex B. Where he does so, the court with jurisdiction over the territorial proceedings must order the conversion[2]. Articles 31 to 35 of the regulation apply to secondary proceedings which derive from independent territorial proceedings in so far as the progress of the proceedings permits[3].

1   EC Insolvency Regulation, preamble para (17).
2   EC Insolvency Regulation, art 37.
3   EC Insolvency Regulation, art 36.

Restriction on effect of secondary proceedings

4.79 The effect of secondary proceedings is restricted to the assets of the debtor within the territory of the Member State in which the secondary proceedings are opened[1]. This restricted effect applies equally to independent territorial proceedings[2].

1   EC Insolvency Regulation, art 27.
2   EC Insolvency Regulation, art 3(2).

Applicable law

4.80 Article 28 provides that, save as otherwise provided in the Regulation, the law applicable to secondary proceedings is that of the Member State within the territory of which the secondary proceedings are opened. This provision re-iterates the general rule laid down in art 4(1) and, save perhaps for its contribution towards clarity, is redundant in that art 4(1) applies to all insolvency proceedings, whether main or otherwise. The position as to the applicable law is the same for independent territorial proceedings, although art 28 does not in terms apply to them.

Communication and co-operation between liquidators in main and secondary proceedings

4.81 The liquidators in the main proceedings and the secondary proceedings are under a duty to communicate information to each other. The communication should be immediate where the information may be relevant to the other proceedings. The duty is subject to any rules, such as those protecting data. Subject to the rules applicable to the respective proceedings, they are also bound to co-operate with each other. Reflecting the subordination of the secondary proceedings to the main proceedings, the liquidator in the secondary proceedings must give the liquidator in the main proceedings an early opportunity to submit proposals on the liquidation or the use of the assets in the secondary proceedings[1].

1   EC Insolvency Regulation, art 31.

Exercise of creditors' rights

4.82 Article 39 provides that any creditor whose habitual residence, domicile or registered office is situated in a Member State other than the State of the opening of proceedings, may lodge a claim in the proceedings. This right applies to all kinds of insolvency proceedings and art 32(1) confirms that any creditor may lodge his claim in the main proceedings and in any secondary proceedings. There is no reference in art 32(1) to the creditor's need to have his habitual residence, domicile or registered office in a Member State although paragraph (21) of the preamble indicates that this is intended. The reason for this may be that, by virtue of art 4, particularly art 4(2)(h), it is a matter for the law of the State of the opening of proceedings which creditors to permit to lodge claims against the debtor's estate. But if it is a rule of that law to exclude foreign creditors, such rule is overridden by art 39 as regards creditors whose habitual residence, domicile or registered office is situated in another Member State. This leaves it unclear whether art 32(1) assists a foreign creditor who is not connected to any Member State by one of the specified connecting factors; given the operative effect of the preamble with regard to other matters, it would seem that art 32(1) should be read as attenuated by paragraph (21) of the preamble.

4.83 Subject to that qualification as to the creditors to which it applies, art 32(1) enables any creditor to lodge his claim in both the main and any secondary proceedings which may be on foot.

4.84 The liquidators in the main and any secondary proceedings also have the power to lodge in other proceedings claims which have been lodged in the proceedings for which they were appointed. But a liquidator should only exercise this power if the interests of the creditors in those latter proceedings are served by doing so. It appears to be the interests of those creditors as a whole to which the liquidator should have regard. A creditor is entitled to oppose the exercise of this power by the liquidator or to withdraw his claim where the applicable law allows. A reason suggested in the Virgós-Schmit report why he might wish to do so is that the lodgement in the further proceedings might expose him to a risk in costs[1].

[1]   Virgós-Schmit report para 239.

Participation of the liquidator in other insolvency proceedings

4.85 The liquidator in the main or secondary proceedings may participate in other proceedings on the same basis as a creditor, in particular by attending creditors' meetings[1].

[1]   EC Insolvency Regulation, art 32(3).

Stay of liquidation

4.86 The liquidator appointed in the main proceedings may request that secondary proceedings be stayed. If so, the court which opened the secondary proceedings should stay them for a period of up to three months, subject to its being continued or renewed for similar periods, although that court may require the liquidator in the main proceedings to take suitable measures to guarantee the interests of the creditors in the secondary proceedings and of individual classes of creditors. The competent court may only reject the liquidator's request if it is manifestly of no interest to the creditors in the main proceedings[1]. That court should terminate the stay (a) at the request of the liquidator in the main proceedings, or (b) of its own motion, at the request of a creditor, or at the request of the liquidator in the secondary proceedings if the stay no longer appears justified, in particular, by the interests of creditors in the main proceedings or in the secondary proceedings[2]. Thus although whether the stay should be imposed is to be determined solely by reference to the interests of the creditors in the main proceedings, wider considerations are relevant in deciding whether to lift the stay. It would seem open to the liquidator in the main proceedings immediately to request that the stay be re-imposed where it is lifted over his opposition.

1   EC Insolvency Regulation, art 33(1).
2   EC Insolvency Regulation, art 33(2).

Measures ending secondary insolvency proceedings

4.87 The law applicable to the secondary proceedings may allow for those proceedings to be closed without liquidation by a rescue plan, a composition or a comparable measure. If so, the liquidator in the main proceedings is enabled to propose such a measure in addition to those who are entitled to propose it under the applicable law[1]. While a stay imposed under art 33 is in place, only the liquidator in the main proceedings may propose such a measure and no other proposal may be put to the vote or approved[2]. But if the liquidator in the main proceedings does not consent the closure of the secondary proceedings by such measure shall not become final unless the financial interests of the creditors in the main proceedings are not affected by the measure proposed[3]. If the measure restricts creditors' rights in any way, the restriction may not affect the debtor's assets which are not covered by the proceedings without the consent of all the creditors having an interest[4].

1   EC Insolvency Regulation, art 34(1).
2   EC Insolvency Regulation, art 34(3).
3   EC Insolvency Regulation, art 34(1).
4   EC Insolvency Regulation, art 34(3).

J PRESERVATION MEASURES

Generally

4.88 Mention has already been made of the competence of the court having jurisdiction to open main proceedings to impose provisional orders and protective measures with extra-territorial effect in support of the insolvency proceedings before as well as after the proceedings are opened[1]. Such orders are to be recognised in other Member States by virtue of art 25(1). They may include injunctions, attachment of assets or the appointment of a temporary administrator[2].

1   EC Insolvency Regulation, preamble para (16).
2   Virgós-Schmit report para 78.

Temporary administrator

4.89 Where the court competent to open the main proceedings has appointed a temporary administrator in order to ensure the preservation of the debtor's assets, the temporary administrator is enabled to request any measures to secure and preserve any of the debtor's assets situated in another Member State which are provided for under the law of that state, for the period between the request for the opening of insolvency proceedings and the judgment opening the proceedings[1].

[1]   EC Insolvency Regulation, art 38.

K LODGEMENT OF CREDITORS' CLAIMS AND PROVISION OF INFORMATION FOR CREDITORS

4.90 Any rule of national law which prohibits a foreign creditor from lodging claims is abrogated with respect to any creditor who has his habitual residence, domicile or registered office in a Member State other than the State of the opening of proceedings. This includes the tax authorities and social security authorities of Member States[1]. To enable such creditors to lodge their claims, the court or the liquidator must, as soon as insolvency proceedings are opened in a Member State, immediately inform known creditors about their right to lodge claims[2]. The information must be given by individual notice and include information about time limits, penalties laid down in regard to those time limits, the body or authority empowered to accept the lodgement of claims and other relevant measures. It must also indicate whether creditors whose claims are preferential or secured in rem need to lodge their claims[3]. The information must be provided in the official language of the State of the opening of proceedings but must bear the heading '*Invitation to lodge a claim. Time limits to be observed*' in all the official languages of the institutions of the European Union[4]. When he lodges his claim, the creditor must send copies of supporting documents, if any, and indicate the nature of the claim, the date on which it arose and its amount as well as whether he alleges that it should receive preferential treatment, that he holds security in rem or a reservation of title in respect of the claim and what assets are covered by the security which he is invoking[5]. Where the creditor has his habitual residence, domicile or registered office in another Member State, he may lodge his claim in the official language of that state. But the lodgement should be headed '*Lodgement of claim*' in the official language of the State of the opening of proceedings and he may be required to provide a translation into that language[6].

[1]   EC Insolvency Regulation, art 39.
[2]   EC Insolvency Regulation, art 40(1).
[3]   EC Insolvency Regulation, art 40(2).
[4]   EC Insolvency Regulation, art 42(1).
[5]   EC Insolvency Regulation, art 41. In the regulation, 'guarantee' is used to mean security; cf art 5(2)(b).
[6]   EC Insolvency Regulation, art 42(2).

Chapter 5

THE CROSS-BORDER INSOLVENCY REGULATIONS 2006

A UNCITRAL MODEL LAW

Introduction

5.1 In an endeavour to harmonise cross-border insolvency law throughout the commercial world the United Nations Commission on International Trade

Law ('UNCITRAL') set up a working group which, after extensive discussions and final negotiations held at Vienna from 12 to 30 May 1997, produced a Model Law for this purpose. The Model Law was adopted by UNCITRAL on 30 May 1997. On 15 December 1997 the General Assembly of the United Nations passed resolution 52/158 in which it expressed its appreciation to UNCITRAL for completing and adopting the Model Law.

5.2 In the preamble to the Model Law, its purposes are described as promoting through the mechanisms which it provides the objectives of:

(a)   co-operation between the courts and other competent authorities of States involved in cases of cross-border insolvency;
(b)   greater legal certainty for trade and investment;
(c)   fair and efficient administration of cross-border insolvencies that protects the interests of all creditors and other interested persons, including the debtor;
(d)   protection and maximisation of the value of the debtor's assets; and
(e)   facilitation of the rescue of financially troubled businesses, thereby protecting investment and preserving employment.

5.3 The Model Law does not itself have legal effect. It provides a form which any State may adopt and enact as part of its law with such adaptations or omissions as it sees fit.

5.4 Like the EC Insolvency Regulation, the Model Law respects the differences among national procedural laws and does not attempt a substantive unification of insolvency law. Rather it offers solutions to problems of recognition and assistance both to foreign trustees administering insolvency proceedings with a cross-border element and to creditors wishing to prove in a 'foreign' insolvency proceeding, and provides for co-ordination of relief granted in respect of the same debtor where there are multiple insolvency proceedings in more than one jurisdiction. Unlike the EC Insolvency Regulation, it does not impose rules as to the choice of law. The adoption of the Model Law is a unilateral act by a State and is neither dependent on reciprocation by other States nor capable of imposing rules to be observed by foreign courts in foreign proceedings.

The Cross-Border Insolvency Regulations 2006

5.5 The Secretary of State has power under the IA 2000, s 14 to give effect by regulations[1] to the Model Law on cross-border insolvency with or without modifications. The power to make regulations includes power by those regulations to amend IA 1986, s 426[2] or to modify the application of insolvency law in relation to foreign proceedings or generally[3] and to apply any provision of insolvency law in relation to foreign proceedings whether begun before or after the regulations come into force[4].

[1]   Subject to the agreement of the Lord Chancellor and approval of each House of Parliament, IA 2000, s 14(5), (6).

2   This section makes provision for co-operation between insolvency courts.
3   IA 2000, s 14(1), (2)(b), (c).
4   IA 2000, s 14(2)(a).

5.6 The regulations made pursuant to that power are the Cross-Border Insolvency Regulations 2006 ('CBIR 2006')[1]. They came into force on 4 April 2006[2].

1   SI 2006/1030.
2   CBIR 2006, reg 1(1).

Nomenclature

5.7 The provisions contained in Schedule 1 to the regulations are referred to therein as 'this Law'. To refer here to those provisions as 'the Law' would lead to awkward phrasing. It would be cumbersome to follow the usage in some of the regulations where they are referred to as 'the UNCITRAL Model Law as set out in Schedule 1 to these Regulations'. Although unsatisfactory in that it connotes that the Law remains only a model, the label used in this chapter is 'the Model Law', as it is in the Schedules to the regulations.

Interpretation

5.8 In interpreting the Model Law the court should have regard as to its international origin and to the need to promote uniformity in its application and the observance of good faith. In addition to any other material properly available, account may be taken of the UNCITRAL Model Law (meaning here the version adopted by UNCITRAL), any documents of the UNCITRAL and its working group relating to the preparation of the UNCITRAL Model Law; and the Guide to Enactment of the UNCITRAL Model Law (UNCITRAL document A/CN 9/442) prepared at the request of the UNCITRAL made in May 1997. By contrast with the EC Insolvency Regulation, there is no single overarching body, like the European Court of Justice, which acts as the ultimate arbiter of the meaning of the Model Law. Nevertheless, courts of different States should strive towards harmony in their interpretation of the Model Law.

Relationship with domestic law

5.9 By reg 2(1) the Model Law is given the force of law in Great Britain, ie in England and Wales and Scotland, in the form set out in Schedule 1 to the regulations and insolvency law in both parts of Great Britain[1] now applies with such modifications as the context requires for the purpose of giving effect to the regulations[2]. In case of any conflict between any relevant provision of domestic law and the Cross-Border Insolvency Regulations 2006, the regulations prevail. As regards England and Wales, the relevant provisions of domestic law means the provision extending to England and Wales and made by or under the Insolvency Act 1986 (including, for this purpose, Part 3 of that Act) or by or under that Act as extended or applied by or under any other enactment (excluding these Regulations)[3].

[1]   'British insolvency law' is defined in Sch 1, art 2 as meaning (i) in relation to England and Wales, provision extending to England and Wales and made by or under the Insolvency Act 1986 (with the exception of Part 3 of that Act) or by or under that Act as extended or applied by or under any other enactment (excluding these Regulations); and (ii) in relation to Scotland, provision extending to Scotland and made by or under the Insolvency Act 1986 (with the exception of Part 3 of that Act), the Bankruptcy (Scotland) Act 1985 or by or under those Acts as extended or applied by or under any other enactment (excluding these Regulations). IA 1986, Part 3 concerns administrative receivership which does not count as an insolvency proceeding in this context because it is a regime serving the purposes of the secured creditor entitled to appoint the receiver rather than the collectivity of creditors.
[2]   CBIR 2006, reg 3(1).
[3]   CBIR 2006, reg 3(2).

5.10 In bankruptcy, the regulations will almost entirely eclipse the provisions contained in IA 1986, s 426. First, reg 7 deals with co-operation between the insolvency courts of England and Wales and those of Scotland so as to supersede IA 1986, s 426(1) and (2). Those provisions will only now have effect with regard to co-operation between insolvency courts in Great Britain and those in Northern Ireland. Secondly, requests for assistance emanating from foreign courts will now be governed by the regulations and the Model Law given effect by reg 3(1). IA 1986, s 426(4) will still be applicable where the insolvent entity is excluded from the ambit of the Model Law under article 2[1], but otherwise requests will be governed by the Model Law.

[1]   For an example see *Re HIH Casualty and General Insurance Ltd* [2006] EWCA Civ 732, [2007] 1 All ER 177.

Relationship with EC Insolvency Regulation

5.11 But although the regulations override any rules of domestic law with which they conflict, they yield to any obligation of the United Kingdom under the EC Insolvency Regulation[1].

[1]   CBIR 2006, reg 3(1), Sch 1, art 3.

5.12 Nothing in the Model Law limits the power of a court or a British insolvency office-holder[1] to provide additional assistance to a foreign representative under other laws of Great Britain.

[1]   Defined in CBIR 2006, reg 3(1), Sch 1, art 2(b).

5.13 Measures relating to finality and certainty in the financial markets are also protected against interference pursuant to the regulations[1].

[1]   CBIR 2006, reg 3(1), Sch 1, art 1(4).

Public policy

5.14 The Model Law does not prevent the court from refusing to take action governed by the Model Law if the action would be manifestly contrary to the public policy of Great Britain or any part of it[1].

1   CBIR 2006, reg 3(1), Sch 1, art 6.

Scope of application

5.15 The Model Law applies where (a) assistance is sought in Great Britain by a foreign court or a foreign representative in connection with a foreign proceeding; (b) assistance is sought in a foreign State in connection with a proceeding under British insolvency law; (c) a foreign proceeding and a proceeding under British insolvency law in respect of the same debtor are taking place concurrently; or (d) creditors or other interested persons in a foreign State have an interest in requesting the commencement of, or partici- pating in, a proceeding under British insolvency law[1]. Where insolvency proceedings concern an entity listed in art 1, para 2, Schedule 1 does not apply. Most of these entities are categories of incorporated bodies and so are not relevant to this book.

1   CBIR 2006, reg 3(1), Sch 1, art 1(1).

5.16 Since the Model Law now governs cases where assistance is sought in Great Britain by a foreign court or foreign representative, requests to the English court for assistance in bankruptcy cases will almost always be governed by the Model Law, rather than IA 1986, s 426[1].

1   *Re HIH Casualty and General Insurance Ltd* [2006] EWCA Civ 732, [2007] 1 All ER 177 at [21]. The CBIR 2006 were not relevant in that case because the insolvency company was an insurance company.

Foreign representative and proceedings

5.17 For the purpose of the Model Law 'foreign representative' means a person or body, including one appointed on an interim basis, authorised in a foreign proceeding to administer the reorganisation or the liquidation of the debtor's assets or affairs or to act as a representative of the foreign proceed- ing[1]. Foreign proceeding is defined as meaning a collective judicial or administrative proceeding in a foreign State, including an interim proceeding, pursuant to a law relating to insolvency in which proceeding the assets and affairs of the debtor are subject to control or supervision by a foreign court, for the purpose of reorganisation or liquidation[2]. Foreign proceedings divide into (i) foreign main proceedings which occur where the foreign proceedings take place in the State where the debtor has the centre of his main interests, and (ii) foreign non-main proceedings meaning foreign proceedings, other than a foreign main proceeding, taking place in a State where the debtor has an establishment[3]. The definition of 'establishment', like that in the EC

Insolvency Regulation, is any place of operations where the debtor carries out a non-transitory economic activity with human means and assets or services[4].

1   CBIR 2006, reg 3(1), Sch 1, art 2(j).
2   CBIR 2006, reg 3(1), Sch 1, art 2(i).
3   CBIR 2006, reg 3(1), Sch 1, art 2(g) and (h).
4   CBIR 2006, reg 3(1), Sch 1, art 2(e).

5.18 Thus a distinction is drawn between foreign main proceedings and foreign non-main proceedings in terms similar to those employed in the EC Insolvency Regulation. This has important effects, for instance on whether recognition of the proceeding results in an automatic stay of individual proceedings and of the debtor's right to dispose of his assets[1]. But, the Model Law does not, as the EC Insolvency Regulation does, specifically provide that a foreign non-main proceeding is confined in its effects to the territory of the State in which it was opened. Indeed if that were so, the question might arise why the foreign representative was concerned to have the proceeding recognised in Great Britain or to take steps here himself. All the same, it is implicit in various provisions that a foreign representative appointed in a foreign non-main proceeding has a weaker basis for intruding into Great Britain than a foreign representative appointed in a foreign main proceeding. For example, where a foreign representative appointed in a non-main proceeding seeks relief under article 21 relating to assets and where he seeks to set aside a transaction pursuant to article 23, he must satisfy the court that the assets in question should be administered in the foreign proceeding[2].

1   CBIR 2006, reg 3(1), Sch 1, art 20(1).
2   CBIR 2006, reg 3(1), Sch 1, arts 21(3) and 23(5).

5.19 However, where a British insolvency is opened after a foreign main proceeding, the British insolvency proceeding will be restricted in its territorial scope to assets located in Great Britain[1].

1   CBIR 2006, reg 3(1), Sch 1, art 28.

The competent court

5.20 In England and Wales, the functions referred to in the Model Law relating to recognition of foreign proceedings and co-operation with foreign courts are to be performed by the High Court and assigned to the Chancery Division; in Scotland, by the Court of Session[1]. Jurisdiction in relation to those functions lies over a debtor in the appropriate court in England and Wales or Scotland if (a) the debtor has (i) a place of business; or (ii) in the case of an individual, a place of residence; or (iii) assets, situated in that part of Great Britain; or (b) the court in that part of Great Britain considers for any other reason that it is the appropriate forum to consider the question or provide the assistance requested[2]. Thus there may be concurrent jurisdiction over a debtor in the courts of both parts of Great Britain. In considering, under the second limb, whether it is the appropriate forum to hear an application for recognition of a foreign proceeding in relation to a debtor, the court shall take into account the location of any court in which a proceeding under British insolvency law is taking place in relation to the debtor and the likely location of any future proceedings under British insolvency law in relation to the debtor[3]. Since the second limb is alternative to the first, it is not clear whether the court in one part of Great Britain might decline jurisdiction on the footing where one of the connecting factors listed in the first limb is established.

[1]   CBIR 2006, reg 3(1), Sch 1, art 4(1).
[2]   CBIR 2006, reg 3(1), Sch 1, art 4(2).
[3]   CBIR 2006, reg 3(1), Sch 1, art 4(3).

Supervision over foreign representatives

5.21 The court has power to examine the conduct of a person who is or has been or purports or has purported to be the foreign representative in relation to a debtor. But it may only do so on the application of a British insolvency office-holder acting in relation to the debtor, a creditor of the debtor or, with the permission of the court, any other person who appears to have an interest justifying an application. An application for the examination of a foreign representative or a person purporting to be such a representative may only be made (if justified) on the basis of allegations that that representative or person has misapplied or retained money or other property of the debtor, has become accountable for money or other property of the debtor, has breached a fiduciary or other duty in relation to the debtor, or has been guilty of misfeasance. On such an examination into a person's conduct the court may order him to repay, restore or account for money or property, to pay interest, or to contribute a sum to the debtor's property by way of compensation for breach of duty or misfeasance[1].

[1]   CBIR 2006, reg 4, Sch 2, para 29.

B DIRECT ACCESS OF FOREIGN REPRESENTATIVES AND CREDITORS TO COURTS IN GREAT BRITAIN

Foreign representative's right of direct access

5.22 Article 9 of the Model Law enables a foreign representative to apply directly to a court in Great Britain. By making an application to a court in Great Britain pursuant to the Model Law, a foreign representative does not subject himself or the foreign assets and affairs of the debtor to the jurisdiction of the courts of Great Britain or any part of it for any purpose other than the application[1].

[1]   CBIR 2006, reg 3(1), Sch 1, art 10.

Foreign representative's right to commence insolvency proceedings under British insolvency law

5.23 A foreign representative appointed in a foreign main proceeding or foreign non-main proceeding is entitled to apply to commence a proceeding under British insolvency law if the conditions for commencing such a proceeding are otherwise met[1]. In the case of bankruptcy in England and Wales, the territorial jurisdiction of the court will have to be established under IA 1986, s 265. Where the centre of the debtor's main interests is situated outside any EC Regulation Member State, the EC Insolvency Regulation will have no part to play and the only jurisdictional conditions will be those set out in IA 1986, s 265(1). But in a case where the centre of the debtor's main interests is situated within one of the EC Regulation Member States (*ex hypothesi* not the United Kingdom) and a foreign representative from a non-EC Regulation Member State applies to make the debtor bankrupt, the foreign representative will additionally have to show that the debtor has an establishment in the United Kingdom so as to found jurisdiction under the EC Insolvency Regulation. The ensuing proceedings will be either secondary proceedings or independent territorial proceedings within the meaning of the EC Insolvency Regulation, depending on whether main proceedings have also been opened in the EC Regulation Member State where the centre of the debtor's main interests is located or not. It is not necessary for the petition to be preceded by a statutory demand: the fact of the debtor's insolvency is sufficiently proved by the existence of the foreign proceedings[2]. A reason for enabling a foreign representative to commence insolvency proceedings directly is that the urgent need to preserve assets sometimes requires it; that objective would be obstructed if the debtor had first to be warned by statutory demand of the intention to start bankruptcy proceedings and then given time to respond to it.

1   CBIR 2006, reg 3(1), Sch 1, art 11.
2   CBIR 2006, reg 3(1), Sch 1, art 31.

Participation of a foreign representative in insolvency proceedings pending under British insolvency law

5.24   Where the foreign proceeding in which he has been appointed has been recognised, the foreign representative is entitled to participate in a proceeding regarding the debtor under British insolvency law[1]. The Guide to Enactment explains that the purpose of this provision is to give the foreign representative procedural standing to make petitions, requests or submissions concerning issues such as protection, realisation, or distribution of assets of the debtor or co-operation with the foreign proceedings[2]. Thus the foreign representative is given a voice, but he is not given any specific powers or rights. In particular, he is not enabled to submit proofs in an English bankruptcy on behalf of creditors who have lodged claims in the foreign proceedings in which he is appointed.

1   CBIR 2006, reg 3(1), Sch 1, art 12.
2   Guide to Enactment, para 100.

Access of foreign creditors to a proceeding under British insolvency law

5.25   Foreign creditors have the same rights regarding the commencement of, and participation in, a proceeding under British insolvency law as creditors in

Great Britain[1]. The rights of creditors to participate include the right to attend and vote at creditors' meetings and to prove. So, the right of foreign creditors to participate which is protected by this measure extends to deeper participation in the British proceedings than is allowed to the foreign representative. This measure does not affect the ranking of claims in a proceeding under British insolvency law, except that the claim of a foreign creditor shall not be given a lower priority than that of general unsecured claims solely because the holder of such a claim is a foreign creditor[2].

[1]   CBIR 2006, reg 3(1), Sch 1, art 13(1).
[2]   CBIR 2006, reg 3(1), Sch 1, art 13(2).

Grounds for rejecting claims

5.26 A claim by a creditor may be challenged (a) on the ground that it is in whole or in part a penalty, or (b) on any other ground that a claim might be rejected in a proceeding under British insolvency law[1]. Thus, if the claim was based on an award of multiple damages, it might be challenged under art 13, para 3(b). However, a claim may not be challenged solely on the grounds that it is a claim by a foreign tax or social security authority. Thus the rule that an English court will not collect the taxes of foreign States[2] is abrogated where the foreign authority claims the tax due in insolvency proceedings pending in Great Britain. Indeed, it would appear that since foreign creditors have the same right to commence insolvency proceedings in Great Britain[3], a foreign tax authority is now entitled not only to prove in pending proceedings, but itself to initiate the proceedings.

[1]   CBIR 2006, reg 3(1), Sch 1, art 13(3).
[2]   *Government of India v Taylor* [1955] AC 491, [1955] 1 All ER 292. The application of this rule is reduced within the EC by the Council Directive (76/308/EEC) on mutual assistance for the recovery of claims relating to certain levies, duties, taxes and other matters, amended by Council Directive (EC) 2001/44.
[3]   CBIR 2006, reg 3(1), Sch 1, art 13(1).

Hotchpot

5.27 Article 32 of the Model Law introduces a hotchpot rule. So, unsecured creditors who prove directly in a British proceeding, having received part payment in a foreign proceeding, may not receive payment in the British proceeding so long as the payment to other creditors of the same class is proportionately less than the payment which the creditor has already received[1].

[1]   CBIR 2006, reg 3(1), Sch 1, art 32.

Notification to foreign creditors of a proceeding under British insolvency law

5.28 Whenever under British insolvency law notification is to be given to creditors in Great Britain, such notification shall also be given to the known creditors that do not have addresses in Great Britain. The court may order that appropriate steps be taken with a view to notifying any creditor whose address is not yet known. Such notification shall be made to the foreign creditors individually, unless (a) the court considers that under the circumstances some other form of notification would be more appropriate; or (b) the notification to creditors in Great Britain is to be by advertisement only, in which case the notification to the known foreign creditors may be by advertisement in such foreign newspapers as the British insolvency office-holder considers most appropriate for ensuring that the content of the notification comes to the notice of the known foreign creditors. When notification of a right to file a claim is to be given to foreign creditors, the notification shall (a) indicate a reasonable time period for filing claims and specify the place for their filing; (b) indicate whether secured creditors need to file their secured claims; and (c) contain any other information required to be included in such a notification to creditors pursuant to the law of Great Britain and the orders of the court. References here to 'the court' are to the court which has jurisdiction in relation to the particular proceeding under British insolvency law under which notification is to be given to creditors[1].

[1]   CBIR 2006, reg 3(1), Sch 1, art 14.

C   RECOGNITION OF FOREIGN PROCEEDINGS AND EFFECTS OF RECOGNITION

Recognition orders

Foreign representative's right to obtain recognition of the foreign proceedings

5.29   A foreign representative may apply to the court for recognition of the foreign proceeding in which the foreign representative has been appointed[1]. Since the definition of foreign proceedings includes an interim proceeding, a recognition order may be sought even where the foreign proceeding is an interim proceeding so long as it is nonetheless a collective proceeding within the definition[2].

[1]   CBIR 2006, reg 3(1), Sch 1, art 15(1).
[2]   CBIR 2006, reg 3(1), Sch 1, art 2(i).

Procedure

5.30   The application must be made using Form ML1 and has to be supported by an affidavit sworn by the foreign representative complying with CBIR 2006, Sch 2, para 4[1]. The application shall state the following matters:

(a)   the name of the applicant and his address for service within England and Wales;
(b)   the name of the debtor in respect of which the foreign proceeding is taking place;
(c)   the name or names in which the debtor carries on business in the country where the foreign proceeding is taking place and in this country, if other than the name given under sub-paragraph (b);

(d)   the principal or last known place of business of the debtor in Great Britain (if any) and, in the case of an individual, his usual or last known place of residence in Great Britain (if any);

(e)   (inapplicable in bankruptcy cases) any registered number allocated to the debtor under the Companies Act 1985;

(f)   brief particulars of the foreign proceeding in respect of which recognition is applied for, including the country in which it is taking place and the nature of the proceeding;

(g)   that the foreign proceeding is a proceeding within the meaning of article 2(i) of the Model Law;

(h)   that the applicant is a foreign representative within the meaning of article 2(j) of the Model Law;

(i)   the address of the debtor's centre of main interests and, if different, the address of its registered office or habitual residence, as appropriate; and

(j)   if the debtor does not have its centre of main interests in the country where the foreign proceeding is taking place, whether the debtor has an establishment within the meaning of article 2(e) of the Model Law in that country, and if so, its address.

[1]   CBIR 2006, reg 4, Sch 2, para 2.

5.31 Reference should also be made to Schedule 2, Part 6 to the Cross-Border Insolvency Rules 2006 for the general rules of procedure governing the application. These are discussed at section G below.

Evidence

5.32 The affidavit supporting the application must contain or have exhibited to it:

(a)   a certified copy of the decision commencing the foreign proceeding and appointing the foreign representative; or a certificate from the foreign court affirming the existence of the foreign proceeding and of the appointment of the foreign representative; or in the absence of either of those two documents, any other evidence acceptable to the court of the existence of the foreign proceeding and of the appointment of the foreign representative[1]; the original certified copy of the decision or the original certificate must be filed; a photocopy will not suffice[2];

(b)   a statement identifying all foreign proceedings, proceedings under British insolvency law and IA 1986, s 426 requests in respect of the debtor that are known to the foreign representative[3];

(c)   any other evidence which in the opinion of the applicant will assist the court in deciding whether the proceeding the subject of the application is a foreign proceeding within the meaning of article 2(i) of the Model Law and whether the applicant is a foreign representative within the meaning of article 2(j) of the Model Law;

(d)   evidence that the debtor has its centre of main interests or an establishment, as the case may be, within the country where the foreign proceeding is taking place; and

(e)   any other matters which in the opinion of the applicant will assist the court in deciding whether to make a recognition order.

1   CBIR 2006, reg 3(1), Sch 1, art 15(2).
2   *Re Rajapakse* [2007] BPIR 99n.
3   CBIR 2006, reg 3(1), Sch 1, art 15(3).

5.33 The affidavit must also state whether, in the opinion of the applicant, the EC Insolvency Regulation applies to any of the proceedings identified in accordance with article 15(3) of the Model Law and, if so, whether those proceedings are main proceedings, secondary proceedings or territorial proceedings. If the foreign representative does not know of any other foreign proceedings, proceedings under British insolvency law or under IA 1986, s 426, he should state that there are no proceedings to which the EC Insolvency Regulation applies[1].

1   *Re Rajapakse* [2007] BPIR 99n.

5.34 If the foreign court has given permission to the foreign representative to apply to be recognised, the affidavit must state whether an appeal has been lodged against the ordering granting that permission and, if it has not, the time limits within which such an appeal may be made[1].

1   *Re Rajapakse* [2007] BPIR 99n.

Translations

5.35 The foreign representative must provide the court with a translation into English of documents supplied in support of the application for recognition[1] and these, certified by the translator as a correct translation, must be exhibited to the affidavit[2].

1   CBIR 2006, reg 3(1), Sch 1, art 15(4).
2   CBIR 2006, reg 4, Sch 2, para 4(3) and (4).

The hearing and powers of the court

5.36 An application for recognition of a foreign proceeding shall be decided upon at the earliest possible time[1].

1   CBIR 2006, reg 3(1), Sch 1, art 17(3).

5.37 Article 16 sets out how the court may approach the evidence which is put before it. If the decision or certificate referred to in paragraph 2 of article 15 indicates that the foreign proceeding is a proceeding within the meaning of sub-paragraph (i) of article 2 and that the foreign representative is a person or body within the meaning of sub-paragraph (j) of article 2, the court is entitled to so presume. The court is entitled to presume that documents submitted in support of the application for recognition are authentic, whether or not they have been legalised. In the absence of proof to the contrary, the debtor's registered office, or habitual residence in the case of an individual, is presumed to be the centre of the debtor's main interests.

5.38 Unless it would be manifestly contrary to public policy[1], the court should make a recognition order in respect of the foreign proceeding if:

(a)   it is a foreign proceeding within the meaning of sub-paragraph (i) of article 2;

(b)   the foreign representative applying for recognition is a person or body within the meaning of sub-paragraph (j) of article 2;

(c)   the application meets the requirements of paragraphs 2 and 3 of article 15; and

(d)   the application has been submitted to the competent court referred to in article 4[2].

[1]   CBIR 2006, reg 3(1), Sch 1, art 6.
[2]   CBIR 2006, reg 3(1), Sch 1, art 17(1).

5.39 The court should also determine whether the foreign proceedings are to be recognised as main or non-main proceedings. The foreign proceeding should be recognised as a foreign main proceeding if it is taking place in the State where the debtor has the centre of his main interests; or as a foreign non-main proceeding if the debtor has an establishment within the meaning of sub-paragraph (e) of article 2 in the foreign State[1].

[1]   CBIR 2006, reg 3(1), Sch 1, art 17(2).

5.40 In addition to its power to make a recognition order, the court has power to:

(a)   dismiss the application;
(b)   adjourn the hearing conditionally or unconditionally;
(c)   make any other order which the court thinks appropriate[1].

[1]   CBIR 2006, reg 4, Sch 2, para 5(1).

5.41 If the court makes a recognition order, it shall be in Form ML2[1].

[1]   CBIR 2006, reg 4, Sch 2, para 5(2).

Modification and termination of a recognition order

5.42 The court may modify or terminate a recognition order if appropriate. In particular it may do so, and is not prevented from doing so by any provisions in article 15 to 18, if it is shown that the grounds for granting it were fully or partially lacking or have fully or partially ceased to exist and in such a case, the court may, on the application of the foreign representative or a person affected by recognition, or of its own motion, modify or terminate recognition, either altogether or for a limited time, on such terms and conditions as the court thinks fit[1].

[1]   CBIR 2006, reg 3(1), Sch 1, art 17(4).

5.43 The procedure governing applications for modification and termination orders is set out below.

Subsequent information

Subsequent information

5.44 From the time of filing the application for recognition of the foreign proceeding, the foreign representative shall inform the court promptly of (a) any substantial change in the status of the recognised foreign proceeding or the status of the foreign representative's appointment; and (b) any other foreign proceeding, proceeding under British insolvency law or IA 1986, s 426 request regarding the same debtor that becomes known to the foreign representative[1]. The foreign representative must set out any such subsequent information in a statement which he shall attach to Form ML3 and file with the court. The statement must include details of the required information; and in the case of any proceedings which required to be notified to the court, a statement as to whether, in the opinion of the foreign representative, any of those proceedings are main proceedings, secondary proceedings or territorial proceedings under the EC Insolvency Regulation. The foreign representative must send a copy of Form ML3 and the attached statement filed with the court to the debtor and the persons referred to in CBIR 2006, Sch 2, para 26(3)[2].

[1] CBIR 2006, reg 3(1), Sch 1, art 18.
[2] CBIR 2006, reg 4, Sch 2, para 6.

Interim relief

Interim relief

5.45 From the time of filing an application for recognition until the application is decided upon, the court may, at the request of the foreign representative, where relief is urgently needed to protect the assets of the debtor or the interests of the creditors, grant relief of a provisional nature, including staying execution against the debtor's assets; entrusting the administration or realisation of all or part of the debtor's assets located in Great Britain to the foreign representative or another person designated by the court, in order to protect and preserve the value of assets that, by their nature or because of other circumstances, are perishable, susceptible to devaluation or otherwise in jeopardy; and any relief mentioned in paragraph 1(c), (d) or (g) of article 21[1].

[1] CBIR 2006, reg 3(1), Sch 1, art 19(1).

Procedure

5.46 The procedural rules set out in Schedule 2, Part 6 to the Cross-Border Insolvency Rules 2006 do not govern an application for interim relief, but they do apply to any order granting interim relief[1]. These are described in section G below. Unless the court otherwise directs, it shall not be necessary to serve the interim relief application on, or give notice of it to, any person[2].

¹   CBIR 2006, reg 4, Sch 2, para 18 in which no reference to applications under article 19 is made and para 18(1)(b)(ii) referring to an order granting relief under article 19.
²   CBIR 2006, reg 4, Sch 2, para 8.

Evidence

5.47 An interim relief application must be supported by an affidavit sworn by the foreign representative stating:

(a)   the grounds on which it is proposed that the interim relief applied for should be granted;

(b)   details of any proceeding under British insolvency law taking place in relation to the debtor;

(c)   whether, to the foreign representative's knowledge, a receiver or manager of the debtor's property is acting in relation to the debtor[1];

(d)   an estimate of the value of the assets of the debtor in England and Wales in respect of which relief is applied for;

(e)   whether, to the best of the knowledge and belief of the foreign representative, the interests of the debtor's creditors (including any secured creditors or parties to hire-purchase agreements) and any other interested parties, including if appropriate the debtor, will be adequately protected;

(f)   whether, to the best of the foreign representative's knowledge and belief, the grant of any of the relief applied for would interfere with the administration of a foreign main proceeding; and

(g)   all other matters that in the opinion of the foreign representative will assist the court in deciding whether or not it is appropriate to grant the relief applied for[2].

¹   If an administrative receiver has been appointed, this should be stated but that will not arise in bankruptcy.
²   CBIR 2006, reg 4, Sch 2, para 7.

The hearing and powers of court

5.48 On hearing an interim relief application the court may make an order for interim relief of one or more of the kinds referred to above. The court may refuse to grant interim relief if doing so would interfere with the administration of a foreign main proceeding[1]. The relief may not interfere with any financial transaction protected by the provisions of article 1(4). In granting or denying interim relief, the court must be satisfied that the interests of the creditors (including any secured creditors or parties to hire-purchase agreements) and other interested persons, including if appropriate the debtor, are adequately protected[2]. The court may impose any conditions it considers appropriate, including the provision by the foreign representative of security or caution for the proper performance of his functions[3].

¹   CBIR 2006, reg 3(1), Sch 1, art 19(3).

²   CBIR 2006, reg 3(1), Sch 1, art 22(1).
³   CBIR 2006, reg 3(1), Sch 1, art 22(2).

5.49 The court has, in addition to its power to grant interim relief, power to:

(a)   dismiss the application;
(b)   adjourn the hearing conditionally or unconditionally;
(c)   make any other order which the court thinks appropriate[1].

¹   CBIR 2006, reg 4, Sch 2, para 9.

5.50 Unless extended under paragraph 1(f) of article 21 on an application made on recognition of the foreign proceeding, any interim relief granted terminates when the application for recognition is decided upon[1].

¹   CBIR 2006, reg 3(1), Sch 1, art 19(3).

Modification and termination of interim relief

5.51 The court may, at the request of the foreign representative or a person affected by relief granted under article 19, or of its own motion, modify or terminate such relief[1].

¹   CBIR 2006, reg 3(1), Sch 1, art 22(3).

Effects of recognition

5.52 Recognition of a foreign main proceeding has the immediate and automatic effect of staying proceedings and execution against the debtor's assets and of suspending his right to dispose of his assets[1]. Recognition of any foreign proceeding, whether main or not, gives the foreign representative standing:

(1)   to seek orders for the protection of the debtor's assets (including, where it has not arisen automatically, a stay of proceedings and suspension of the debtor's power to dispose of his assets), for the investigation of his affairs and for the administration and distribution of his assets located in Great Britain[2];
(2)   to bring proceedings to set aside transactions made by the debtor[3]; and
(3)   to intervene in any proceedings in which the debtor is a party[4].

These effects are addressed in turn.

¹   CBIR 2006, reg 3(1), Sch 1, art 20.
²   CBIR 2006, reg 3(1), Sch 1, art 21.
³   CBIR 2006, reg 3(1), Sch 1, art 23.
⁴   CBIR 2006, reg 3(1), Sch 1, art 24.

Automatic stay of proceedings and execution and suspension of debtor's right to dispose of assets

Terms of the stay and suspension

5.53 Upon recognition of a foreign proceeding that is a foreign main proceeding (a) commencement or continuation of individual actions or individual proceedings concerning the debtor's assets, rights, obligations or liabilities is stayed; (b) execution against the debtor's assets is stayed; and (c) the right to transfer, encumber or otherwise dispose of any assets of the debtor is suspended. The stay and suspension just referred to shall be (a) the same in scope and effect as if, in the case of an individual debtor, he had been adjudged bankrupt in England and Wales under the Insolvency Act 1986 or in Scotland, had his estate sequestrated under the Bankruptcy (Scotland) Act 1985; and (b) subject to the same powers of the court and the same prohibitions, limitations, exceptions and conditions as would apply under the law of Great Britain in such a case and the provision imposing the stay and suspension is to be interpreted accordingly[1]. Thus, a recognition order gives rise to similar results as IA 1986, s 285 regarding the stay of proceedings and execution. Regarding the suspension of the right to dispose of assets, the position is similar to that arising under IA 1986, s 284; since the right to dispose is suspended, any purported disposition would likewise be void and the asset recoverable from the disponee.

[1]   CBIR 2006, reg 3(1), Sch 1, art 20(1) and (2).

Limits on the extent of the stay and suspension

5.54 The stay and suspension resulting from recognition of a foreign main proceeding does not affect any right:

(a)   to take any steps to enforce security over the debtor's property;

(b)   to take any steps to repossess goods in the debtor's possession under a hire-purchase agreement;

(c)   exercisable under or by virtue of or in connection with the provisions relating to finality of settlements in, and collateral employed for the purposes of, financial markets referred to in article 1(4); or

(d)   of a creditor to set off its claim against a claim of the debtor,

being a right which would have been exercisable if the debtor, in the case of an individual, had been adjudged bankrupt under the Insolvency Act 1986 or had his estate sequestrated under the Bankruptcy (Scotland) Act 1985[1].

[1]   CBIR 2006, reg 3(1), Sch 1, art 20(3).

5.55 Secondly, the stay on commencing or continuing actions does not affect the right to:

(a)   commence individual actions or proceedings to the extent necessary to preserve a claim against the debtor; or

(b)   commence or continue any criminal proceedings or any action or proceedings by a person or body having regulatory, supervisory or investigative functions of a public nature, being an action or proceedings brought in the exercise of those functions[1].

¹   CBIR 2006, reg 3(1), Sch 1, art 20(4).

5.56 Thirdly, the stay and suspension does not affect the right to request or otherwise initiate the commencement of a proceeding under British insolvency law or the right to file claims in such a proceeding[1].

¹   CBIR 2006, reg 3(1), Sch 1, art 20(5).

Modification or termination of the stay and suspension

5.57 In addition to and without prejudice to any powers of the court under or by virtue of paragraph 2 of this article (which imports the discretions available under IA 1986, ss 284 and 285), the court may, on the application of the foreign representative or a person affected by the stay and suspension resulting from the recognition order, or of its own motion, modify or terminate such stay and suspension or any part of it, either altogether or for a limited time, on such terms and conditions as the court thinks fit[1].

¹   CBIR 2006, reg 3(1), Sch 1, art 20(6).

Stay and suspension where the foreign proceeding is a non-main proceeding

5.58 It will be necessary, where the foreign proceeding is a non-main proceeding, for the foreign representative to seek a stay of proceedings and suspension of the debtor's right to dispose of his assets as relief under article 21.

Relief available on and after recognition of a foreign proceeding

Available forms of relief

5.59 Upon recognition of a foreign proceeding, whether main or non-main, where necessary to protect the assets of the debtor or the interests of the creditors, the court may, at the request of the foreign representative, grant any appropriate relief, including:

(a)   staying the commencement or continuation of individual actions or individual proceedings concerning the debtor's assets, rights, obligations or liabilities, to the extent they have not been stayed under paragraph 1(a) of article 20;

(b)   staying execution against the debtor's assets to the extent it has not been stayed under paragraph 1(b) of article 20;

(c)   suspending the right to transfer, encumber or otherwise dispose of any assets of the debtor to the extent this right has not been suspended under paragraph 1(c) of article 20;

(d)   providing for the examination of witnesses, the taking of evidence or the delivery of information concerning the debtor's assets, affairs, rights, obligations or liabilities;

(e)   entrusting the administration or realisation of all or part of the debtor's assets located in Great Britain to the foreign representative or another person designated by the court;

(f)   extending relief granted under paragraph 1 of article 19; and

(g)   granting any additional relief that may be available to a British insolvency office-holder under the law of Great Britain[1].

[1]   CBIR 2006, reg 3(1), Sch 1, art 21(1). Para (g) expressly includes any relief which may be provided under paragraph 43 of Schedule B1 to the Insolvency Act 1986; that is only directly relevant where the debtor is a company, but reference to it may assist in interpreting the provision.

5.60 No stay under paragraph 1(a) of this article shall affect the right to commence or continue any criminal proceedings or any action or proceedings by a person or body having regulatory, supervisory or investigative functions of a public nature, being an action or proceedings brought in the exercise of those functions[1].

[1]   CBIR 2006, reg 3(1), Sch 1, art 21(4).

5.61 Further, on recognition of a foreign proceeding, whether main or non-main, the court may, at the request of the foreign representative, entrust the distribution of all or part of the debtor's assets located in Great Britain to the foreign representative or another person designated by the court, provided that the court is satisfied that the interests of creditors in Great Britain are adequately protected[1].

[1]   CBIR 2006, reg 3(1), Sch 1, art 21(2).

Evidence

5.62 An application for relief under article 21 must be supported by an affidavit sworn by the foreign representative stating:

(a)   the grounds on which it is proposed that the relief applied for should be granted;

(b)   an estimate of the value of the assets of the debtor in England and Wales in respect of which relief is applied for;

(c)   in the case of an application by a foreign representative who is or believes that he is a representative of a foreign non-main proceeding, the reasons why the applicant believes that the relief relates to assets that, under the law of Great Britain, should be administered in the foreign non-main proceeding or concerns information required in that proceeding;

(d)   whether, to the best of the knowledge and belief of the foreign representative, the interests of the debtor's creditors (including any secured creditors or parties to hire-purchase agreements) and any other interested parties, including if appropriate the debtor, will be adequately protected; and

(e)   all other matters that in the opinion of the foreign representative will assist the court in deciding whether or not it is appropriate to grant the relief applied for.

5.63 If the foreign court has given permission to the foreign representative to apply for relief under article 21, the affidavit must state whether an appeal has been lodged against the ordering granting that permission and, if it has not, the time limits within which such an appeal may be made[1].

1   *Re Rajapakse* [2007] BPIR 99n.

The hearing and powers of court

5.64 On hearing an application for relief under article 21 the court may, in addition to its powers to make an order granting relief available under article 21:

(a)   dismiss the application;
(b)   adjourn the hearing conditionally or unconditionally;
(c)   make any other order which the court thinks appropriate.

5.65 If it is likely that the foreign representative will make an application for the registration of an interest to the Chief Land Registrar, the order should include a statement to the effect that the applicant is permitted by the terms of the order to apply to the Chief Land Registrar for the purpose of registering his interest in the property in question[1].

1   *Re Rajapakse* [2007] BPIR 99n.

Matters to which the court must have regard

5.66 In granting or denying any form of relief sought under article 21, the court must be satisfied that the interests of the creditors (including any secured creditors or parties to hire-purchase agreements) and other interested persons, including if appropriate the debtor, are adequately protected[1]. It may also impose any conditions it considers appropriate, including the provision by the foreign representative of security or caution for the proper performance of his functions[2]. Where the foreign representative has been appointed in a foreign non-main proceeding, the court must be satisfied that the relief relates to assets that, under the law of Great Britain, should be administered in the foreign non-main proceeding or concerns information required in that proceeding before granting the relief sought[3].

1   CBIR 2006, reg 3(1), Sch 1, art 22(1).
2   CBIR 2006, reg 3(1), Sch 1, art 22(2).
3   CBIR 2006, reg 3(1), Sch 1, art 21(3).

Modification and termination of relief

5.67 The court may, at the request of the foreign representative or a person affected by relief granted under article 21, or of its own motion, modify or terminate such relief[1].

1   CBIR 2006, reg 3(1), Sch 1, art 22(3).

Actions to avoid acts detrimental to creditors

Avoidance actions

5.68 Once the foreign proceeding has been recognised, the foreign representative has standing to make an application to the court for an order under or in connection with IA 1986, ss 339, 340, 342A, 343 and 423[1]. Although the foreign representative has his right of direct access pursuant to article 9 of the Model Law, that right of direct access would not enable him to bring proceedings under these sections because, as a matter of statutory language, he must be a person able to proceed pursuant to them.

1   CBIR 2006, reg 3(1), Sch 1, art 23(1). Where the debtor is a company actions under IA 1986, ss 238, 239, 242–245 are available, and in Scotland, if he is an individual, actions under the Bankruptcy (Scotland) Act 1985 ss 34–36, 36A and 61.

No retrospective effect

5.69 Nothing in article 23(1) applies in respect of any preference given, alienation, assignment or relevant contributions (within the meaning of the IA 1986, s 342A(5)) made or other transaction entered into before 4 April 2006 when the Model Law came into force[1]. As explained below, the relevant periods during which transactions may be vulnerable run back from the date when the foreign proceeding in which the foreign representative was appointed. But this provision will prevent those periods from running to their full extent if they run further back than 4 April 2006.

1   CBIR 2006, reg 3(1), Sch 1, art 23(9).

Status of the debtor

5.70 The foreign representative may seek to avoid relevant transactions irrespective of whether the debtor has been adjudged bankrupt in England and Wales or had his estate sequestrated in Scotland[1].

1   CBIR 2006, reg 3(1), Sch 1, art 23(2)(a).

Relevant periods and knowledge

5.71 The provisions in IA 1986 enabling a trustee in bankruptcy to avoid prior transactions of a debtor render transactions vulnerable if they were made during a defined period running back from the date of presentation of the petition on which the debtor was adjudged bankrupt. The liability of a transferee to return a benefit may depend on whether he was aware of the bankruptcy petition or order. Where the application is made by a foreign representative in consequence of the recognition of a foreign proceeding, these aspects are modified so as to base them on the foreign proceedings. Thus, where the application is made by a foreign representative pursuant to article 23:

(a)   the periods referred to in ss 341(1)(a) to (c) and 343(2) shall be periods ending with the date of the opening of the relevant foreign proceeding; and

(b)   for the purposes of IA 1986, s 342(2A)(a), a person has notice of the relevant proceedings if he has notice of the opening of the relevant foreign proceeding[1].

[1]   CBIR 2006, reg 3(1), Sch 1, art 23(2)(b) and (3).

5.72 In this context, the date of the opening of the foreign proceeding shall be determined in accordance with the law of the State in which the foreign proceeding is taking place, including any rule of law by virtue of which the foreign proceeding is deemed to have opened at an earlier time[1].

[1]   CBIR 2006, Sch 1, art 23(2)(4).

Restriction on bringing an application under article 23

5.73 At any time when a proceeding under British insolvency law is taking place regarding the debtor, the foreign representative shall not make an article 23 application except with the permission of, in the case of a proceeding under British insolvency law taking place in England and Wales, the High Court; or in the case of a proceeding under British insolvency law taking place in Scotland, the Court of Session[1]. If such proceeding is taking place, the application under article 23 must be made in that court[2].

[1]   CBIR 2006, Sch 1, art 23(2)(6)(a).
[2]   CBIR 2006, Sch 1, art 23(2)(6)(b).

Relevant assets where the foreign proceeding is a non-main proceeding

5.74 When the foreign proceeding is a non-main proceeding, the court must be satisfied that the article 23 application relates to assets that, under the law of Great Britain, should be administered in the foreign non-main proceeding[1].

[1]   CBIR 2006, Sch 1, art 23(2)(5).

Directions regarding distribution

5.75 On making an order on an article 23 application, the court may give such directions regarding the distribution of any proceeds of the claim by the foreign representative as it thinks fit to ensure that the interests of creditors in Great Britain are adequately protected[1].

[1]   CBIR 2006, Sch 1, art 23(2)(7).

Impact on powers of any English trustee in bankruptcy

5.76 Nothing in article 23 affects the right of a British insolvency office-holder to make an application under or in connection with any of the provisions referred to in article 23(1). However, although his right may not be affected, it may be that both an English trustee in bankruptcy and the foreign representative would be equally interested in setting the transaction in question aside. If so, the competition for the asset may be resolved pursuant to co-operation between the office-holders. But, if agreement could not be reached, the court would have to determine who should take precedence. It may be that the issue will depend on which office-holder has been appointed in main proceedings. But, if it is neither, then some other criterion will have to be adopted.

Intervention by a foreign representative in proceedings in Great Britain

5.77 Upon recognition of a foreign proceeding, the foreign representative may, provided the requirements of the law of Great Britain are met, intervene in any proceedings in which the debtor is a party[1]. In England and Wales, this might involve the foreign representative being required to be substituted in place of the debtor, if the basis for the intervention that the title to sue has passed to the foreign representative.

[1]   CBIR 2006, reg 3(1), Sch 1, art 24.

Modification and termination orders

Orders which may be modified or terminated

5.78 The court may modify or terminate:

(1)   a recognition order[1];
(2)   an order granting interim relief under article 19[2];
(3)   the automatic stay and suspension arising under article 20[3];
(4)   an order granting relief under article 21[4].

[1]   CBIR 2006, reg 3(1), Sch 1, art 17(4).
[2]   CBIR 2006, reg 3(1), Sch 1, art 22(3).
[3]   CBIR 2006, reg 3(1), Sch 1, art 20(6).
[4]   CBIR 2006, reg 3(1), Sch 1, art 22(3).

Standing to apply for a modification or termination order

5.79 The foreign representative or a person affected by the order or matter in question may apply for its modification or termination[1].

1   CBIR 2006, reg 3(1), Sch 1, arts 17(4), 20(6) and 22(3).

Procedure relating to modification and termination orders

5.80 The court shall not of its own motion make a modification or termination order unless the foreign representative and the debtor have either (a) had an opportunity of being heard on the question; or (b) consented in writing to such an order. Where the foreign representative or the debtor desires to be heard on the question of such an order, the court shall give all relevant parties notice of a venue at which the question will be considered and may give directions as to the issues on which it requires evidence. For this purpose, 'all relevant parties' means the foreign representative, the debtor and any other person who appears to the court to have an interest justifying his being given notice of the hearing.

Evidence

5.81 A review application must be supported by an affidavit sworn by the applicant stating:

(a)   the grounds on which it is proposed that the relief applied for should be granted;

(b)   whether, to the best of the knowledge and belief of the applicant, the interests of the debtor's creditors (including any secured creditors or parties to hire-purchase agreements) and any other interested parties, including if appropriate the debtor, will be adequately protected; and

(c)   all other matters that in the opinion of the applicant will assist the court in deciding whether or not it is appropriate to grant the relief applied for.

Hearing and powers of the court

5.82 On hearing a review application, the court may, in addition to its powers under the Model Law to make a modification or termination order, dismiss the application; adjourn the hearing conditionally or unconditionally; make an interim order; or make any other order which the court thinks appropriate, including an order making such provision as the court thinks fit with respect to matters arising in connection with the modification or termination[1].

1   CBIR 2006, reg 4, Sch 2, para 17.

5.83 Where the court modifies or terminates interim relief given under article 19 or relief given under article 21 or a stay or suspension pursuant to article 20(6), the court must be satisfied that the interests of the creditors (including any secured creditors or parties to hire-purchase agreements) and other interested persons, including if appropriate the debtor, are adequately protected[1].

1   CBIR 2006, reg 3(1), Sch 1, art 22(1).

Applications to Chief Land Registrar following court orders

5.84 Where the court makes any order in proceedings under the Cross-Border Insolvency Regulations 2006 which is capable of giving rise to an application or applications under the Land Registration Act 2002, the foreign representative must, as soon as reasonably practicable after the making of the order or at the appropriate time, make the appropriate application or applications to the Chief Land Registrar. An appropriate application is:

(a)   in any case where a recognition order in respect of a foreign main proceeding or an order suspending the right to transfer, encumber or otherwise dispose of any assets of the debtor is made, and the debtor is the registered proprietor of a registered estate or registered charge and holds it for his sole benefit, an application under the Land Registration Act 2002, s 43 for a restriction of the kind referred to in sub-paragraph (3) to be entered in the relevant registered title; and

(b)   in any other case, an application under the Land Registration Act 2002 for such an entry in the register as shall be necessary to reflect the effect of the court order under these Regulations.

5.85 The restriction referred to in the first of these cases is a restriction to the effect that no disposition of the registered estate or registered charge (as appropriate) by the registered proprietor of that estate or charge is to be completed by registration within the meaning of the Land Registration Act 2002, s 27 except under a further order of the court[1].

1   CBIR 2006, reg 4, Sch 2, para 28.

D CO-OPERATION WITH FOREIGN COURTS AND FOREIGN REPRESENTATIVES

Co-operation and direct communication between a court of Great Britain and foreign courts or foreign representatives

5.86 Article 25 of the Model Law enables a British court, in matters referred to in article 1(1), to co-operate to the maximum extent possible with foreign courts or foreign representatives, either directly or through a British insolvency office-holder. The court is entitled to communicate directly with, or to request information or assistance directly from, foreign courts or foreign representatives.

Co-operation and direct communication between the British insolvency office-holder and foreign courts or foreign representatives

5.87 A British insolvency office-holder is under a duty to co-operate. Article 26(1) of the Model Law provides that, in matters referred to in paragraph 1 of article 1, a British insolvency office-holder shall to the extent consistent with his other duties under the law of Great Britain, in the exercise of his functions and subject to the supervision of the court, co-operate to the maximum extent possible with foreign courts or foreign representatives. He is also entitled, in the exercise of his functions and subject to the supervision of the court, to communicate directly with foreign courts or foreign representatives.

Forms of co-operation

5.88 Co-operation referred to in articles 25 and 26 may be implemented by any appropriate means, including:

(a) appointment of a person to act at the direction of the court;
(b) communication of information by any means considered appropriate by the court;
(c) co-ordination of the administration and supervision of the debtor's assets and affairs;
(d) approval or implementation by the courts of agreements concerning the co-ordination of proceedings;
(e) co-ordination of concurrent proceedings regarding the same debtor.

E CO-OPERATION BETWEEN INSOLVENCY COURTS WITHIN GREAT BRITAIN

Enforcement of orders

5.89 As regards insolvency courts in Great Britain, the Cross-Border Insolvency Regulations 2006, reg 7 replaces the provisions of IA 1986, s 426 by making provision to similar effect. Thus, an order made by a court in either part of Great Britain in the exercise of jurisdiction in relation to the subject matter of the Cross-Border Insolvency Regulations 2006 must be enforced in the other part as if it were made by a court exercising the corresponding jurisdiction in that other part. But that does not require the court in one part of Great Britain to enforce, in relation to property situated in that part, an order made in the other part[1], though the court may, if appropriate, enforce the order.

[1] CBIR 2006, reg 7(1) and (2); cf IA 1986, s 426(1) and (2).

Duty to assist

5.90 The courts having insolvency jurisdiction in either part of Great Britain must assist the courts having the corresponding jurisdiction in the other part[1].

[1] CBIR 2006, reg 7(3); cf IA 1986, s 426(4).

Forms of assistance

5.91 Under IA 1986, s 426(5) a request for assistance constituted authority for the court to apply either English insolvency law or the insolvency law of the country from the courts which the request for assistance came. No similar provision is included in reg 7. Although the question would not be directly governed by article 22 of the Model Law, the test there laid down, that the court must be satisfied that the interests of the creditors, including secured creditors, and other interested persons, including the debtor, are adequately protected, would seem an appropriate touchstone[1].

1   See *Re HIH Casualty and General Insurance Ltd* [2007] 1 All ER 177 at [54].

F CONCURRENT PROCEEDINGS

Commencement of a proceeding under British insolvency law after recognition of a foreign main proceeding

5.92 Where a foreign main proceeding has been recognised, the effects of a proceeding under British insolvency law in relation to the same debtor shall, insofar as the assets of that debtor are concerned, be restricted to assets that are located in Great Britain and, to the extent necessary to implement co-operation and co-ordination under articles 25, 26 and 27, to other assets of the debtor that, under the law of Great Britain, should be administered in that proceeding[1].

1   CBIR 2006, reg 3(1), Sch 1, art 28.

Co-ordination of a proceeding under British insolvency law and a foreign proceeding

5.93 Article 29 of the Model Law regulates the co-ordination of a British proceeding with a foreign proceeding. First and generally, where a foreign proceeding and a proceeding under British insolvency law are taking place concurrently regarding the same debtor, the court may seek co-operation and co-ordination under articles 25, 26 and 27.

5.94 Secondly, when the proceeding in Great Britain is taking place at the time the application for recognition of the foreign proceeding is filed (i) any relief granted under article 19 or 21 must be consistent with the proceeding in Great Britain; and (ii) if the foreign proceeding is recognised in Great Britain as a foreign main proceeding, article 20 (imposing an automatic stay of proceedings and execution and suspension of the debtor's power to dispose of his assets) does not apply.

5.95 Thirdly, when the proceeding in Great Britain commences after the filing of the application for recognition of the foreign proceeding (i) any relief in effect under article 19 or 21 shall be reviewed by the court and shall be modified or terminated if inconsistent with the proceeding in Great Britain; (ii) if the foreign proceeding is a foreign main proceeding, the stay and suspension referred to in paragraph 1 of article 20 shall be modified or terminated pursuant to paragraph 6 of article 20, if inconsistent with the proceeding in Great Britain; and (iii) any proceedings brought by the foreign representative by virtue of paragraph 1 of article 23 before the proceeding in Great Britain commenced shall be reviewed by the court and the court may give such directions as it thinks fit regarding the continuance of those proceedings.

5.96 Fourthly, in granting, extending or modifying relief granted to a representative of a foreign non-main proceeding, the court must be satisfied that the relief relates to assets that, under the law of Great Britain, should be administered in the foreign non-main proceeding or concerns information required in that proceeding[1].

[1]   CBIR 2006, reg 3(1), Sch 1, art 29.

Co-ordination of more than one foreign proceeding

5.97 Questions of co-ordination may also arise where two or more foreign proceedings are on foot. At a general level, in matters referred to in article 1(1), in respect of more than one foreign proceeding regarding the same debtor, the court may seek co-operation and co-ordination under articles 25, 26 and 27. More particularly:

(a)   any relief granted under article 19 or 21 to a representative of a foreign non-main proceeding after recognition of a foreign main proceeding must be consistent with the foreign main proceeding;

(b)   if a foreign main proceeding is recognised after the filing of an application for recognition of a foreign non-main proceeding, any relief in effect under article 19 or 21 shall be reviewed by the court and shall be modified or terminated if inconsistent with the foreign main pro-ceeding; and

(c)   if, after recognition of a foreign non-main proceeding, another foreign non-main proceeding is recognised, the court shall grant, modify or terminate relief for the purpose of facilitating co-ordination of the proceedings[1].

[1]   CBIR 2006, reg 3(1), Sch 1, art 30.

Presumption of insolvency based on recognition of a foreign main proceeding

5.98 In the absence of evidence to the contrary, recognition of a foreign main proceeding is, for the purpose of commencing a proceeding under British insolvency law, proof that the debtor is unable to pay its debts or, in relation to Scotland, is apparently insolvent within the meaning given to those expressions under British insolvency law[1].

[1]   CBIR 2006, reg 3(1), Sch 1, art 31.

Hotchpot: rule of payment in concurrent proceedings

5.99 Article 32 applies a rule of hotchpot. It provides that, without prejudice to any secured claims or rights in rem, a creditor who has received part payment in respect of its claim in a proceeding pursuant to a law relating to insolvency in a foreign State may not receive a payment for the same claim in a proceeding under British insolvency law regarding the same debtor, so long as the payment to the other creditors of the same class is proportionately less than the payment the creditor has already received[1].

1   CBIR 2006, reg 3(1), Sch 1, art 32.

G COURT PROCEDURE AND PRACTICE

Introduction

Introduction

5.100 Applications made under the Cross-Border Insolvency Regulations 2006 are not applications made under the Insolvency Act 1986 or the Insolvency Rules 1986. So, the procedural rules contained in Part 7 of the Insolvency Rules 1986 do not apply to them. Instead, Part 9 of Schedule 2 to the Cross-Border Insolvency Regulations 2006 contains detailed provision as to the applicable court procedure and practice.

Principal court rules and practice to apply with modifications

5.101 The CPR and the practice and procedure of the High Court (including any practice direction) apply to proceedings under the Cross-Border Insolvency Regulations in the High Court with such modifications as may be necessary for the purpose of giving effect to the provisions of the regulations. In the case of any conflict between any provision of the CPR and the provisions of the Cross-Border Insolvency Regulations 2006, the latter shall prevail[1].

1   CBIR 2006, reg 4, Sch 2, para 30(1).

Allocation to the multi-track

5.102 All proceedings under the Cross-Border Insolvency Regulations 2006 are allocated to the multi-track for which CPR Pt 29 (the multi-track) makes provision. The provisions of the CPR which provide for allocation questionnaires and track allocation do not apply[1].

1   CBIR 2006, reg 4, Sch 2, para 30(2).

Court procedure applicable only to principal applications and orders

Applications and orders to which these rules apply

5.103 Detailed rules of procedure are contained in Schedule 2, Part 6 to the Cross-Border Insolvency Regulations 2006 which apply to specified applications and orders[1]. The applications to which these rules apply are:

(1)   a recognition application;
(2)   an article 21 relief application;
(3)   an application under paragraph 12(3) for an order confirming the status of a replacement foreign representative; and
(4)   a review application.

[1]   CBIR 2006, reg 4, Sch 2, para 18.

5.104 The orders to which they apply are:

(1)   a recognition order;
(2)   an order granting interim relief under article 19 of the Model Law;
(3)   an order granting relief under article 21 of the Model Law;
(4)   an order confirming the status of a replacement foreign representative; and
(5)   a modification or termination order.

Form and contents of application

5.105 Under these rules any application, other than a recognition application[1], is to be an ordinary application and must be in Form ML5[2]. The application must be in writing and state:

(a)   the names of the parties;
(b)   the nature of the relief or order applied for or the directions sought from the court;
(c)   the names and addresses of the persons (if any) on whom it is intended to serve the application;
(d)   the names and addresses of all those persons on whom these Regulations require the application to be served (so far as known to the applicant); and
(e)   the applicant's address for service[3].

[1]   For an application for a recognition order, see para **5.30ff** above.
[2]   CBIR 2006, reg 4, Sch 2, para 19(1) and (4).
[3]   CBIR 2006, reg 4, Sch 2, para 19(2).

5.106 The application must be signed by the applicant if he is acting in person, or, when he is not so acting, by or on behalf of his solicitor[1].

[1]   CBIR 2006, reg 4, Sch 2, para 19(3).

Filing of application

5.107 The application (and all supporting documents) must be filed with the court, with a sufficient number of copies for service and use. The number of copies required will depend on how many persons have to be served as mentioned in the following paragraph. Each of the copies filed must have applied to it the seal of the court and be issued to the applicant; and on each copy there is to be endorsed the date and time of filing. The court shall fix a venue for the hearing of the application and this also is to be endorsed on each copy of the application[1].

1   CBIR 2006, reg 4, Sch 2, para 20.

Service of the application

5.108 Where the application is to be served, what must be served is a sealed copy of the application issued by the court together with any affidavit in support of it and any documents exhibited to the affidavit[1]. Unless the court otherwise directs, the application shall be served on the following persons, unless they are the applicant:

(a)   on the foreign representative;
(b)   on the debtor;
(c)   if a British insolvency office-holder is acting in relation to the debtor, on him;
(d)   if any person has been appointed an administrative receiver of the debtor or, to the knowledge of the foreign representative, as a receiver or manager of the property of the debtor in England and Wales, on him;
(e)   if a Member State liquidator has been appointed in main proceedings in relation to the debtor, on him;
(f)   if to the knowledge of the foreign representative a foreign representative has been appointed in any other foreign proceeding regarding the debtor, on him;
(g)   if there is pending in England and Wales a petition for the winding up or bankruptcy of the debtor, on the petitioner;
(h)   on any person who to the knowledge of the foreign representative is or may be entitled to appoint an administrator of the debtor under paragraph 14 of Schedule B1 to the 1986 Act (appointment of administrator by holder of qualifying floating charge); and
(i)   if the debtor is a debtor who is of interest to the Financial Services Authority, on that Authority[2].

1   CBIR 2006, reg 4, Sch 2, para 21(1).
2   CBIR 2006, reg 4, Sch 2, para 21(2).

Manner in which service to be effected

5.109 Service of the application must be effected by the applicant, or his solicitor, or by a person instructed by him or his solicitor, not less than five business days before the date fixed for the hearing. Service shall be effected by delivering the documents to a person's proper address or in such other manner as the court may direct. A person's proper address is any which he has previously notified as his address for service within England and Wales; but, if he has not notified any such address or if for any reason service at such address is not practicable, service may be effected as follows:

(a)   unless not practicable, in the case of a company incorporated in England and Wales, by delivery to its registered office;

(b)   in the case of any other person, by delivery to his usual or last known address or principal place of business in Great Britain.

5.110 If delivery to a company's registered office is not practicable, service may be effected by delivery to its last known principal place of business in Great Britain. Delivery of documents to any place or address may be made by leaving them there or sending them by first-class post in accordance with the provisions of paragraphs 70 and 75(1) of CBIR 2006[1]. Where the debtor does not have an address for service in England and Wales or, being an individual, is resident outside the jurisdiction, service should be made on him at his usual or last known address outside the jurisdiction[2].

[1]   CBIR 2006, reg 4, Sch 2, para 22.
[2]   *Re Rajapakse* [2007] BPIR 99n.

Proof of service

5.111 Service of the application must be verified by an affidavit of service in Form ML6, specifying the date on which, and the manner in which, service was effected. The affidavit of service, with a sealed copy of the application exhibited to it, must be filed with the court as soon as reasonably practicable after service, and in any event not less than one business day before the hearing of the application[1].

[1]   CBIR 2006, reg 4, Sch 2, para 23.

Urgent cases

5.112 Where the case is one of urgency, the court may (without prejudice to its general power to extend or abridge time limits):

(a)   hear the application immediately, either with or without notice to, or the attendance of, other parties; or

(b)   authorise a shorter period of service than the period of five days provided for by paragraph 22(1) of CBIR 2006, Sch 2, Part 6.

5.113 Any such application may be heard on terms providing for the filing or service of documents, or the carrying out of other formalities, as the court thinks fit[1].

[1]   CBIR 2006, reg 4, Sch 2, para 24.

The hearing

5.114 At the hearing of the application, the applicant and any of the following persons (not being the applicant) may appear or be represented:

(a) the foreign representative;
(b) the debtor[1];
(c) if a British insolvency office-holder is acting in relation to the debtor, that person;
(d) if any person has been appointed as a receiver or manager of the property of the debtor in England and Wales[2], that person;
(e) if a Member State liquidator has been appointed in main proceedings in relation to the debtor, that person;
(f) if a foreign representative has been appointed in any other foreign proceeding regarding the debtor, that person;
(g) any person who has presented a petition for the bankruptcy[3] of the debtor in England and Wales;
(h) if the debtor is a debtor who is of interest to the Financial Services Authority, that Authority; and
(i) with the permission of the court, any other person who appears to have an interest justifying his appearance[4].

[1] In the case of a debtor which is a partnership, any person who is an officer of the partnership within the meaning of article 2 of the Insolvent Partnerships Order 1994. Provision is also made, but not relevant here, for the representation of a corporate debtor.
[2] Or, in the case of a company, an administrative receiver of the debtor. Also where the debtor is a company, any person who is or may be entitled to appoint an administrator of the debtor under paragraph 14 of Schedule B1 to the 1986 Act (appointment of administrator by holder of qualifying floating charge) must be served.
[3] Or winding up.
[4] CBIR 2006, reg 4, Sch 2, para 25.

5.115 A debtor who is of interest to the Financial Services Authority is a debtor who is, or has been, an authorised person within the meaning of the Financial Services and Markets Act 2000, s 31 (authorised persons); is, or has been, an appointed representative within the meaning of s 39 (exemption of appointed representatives) of that Act; or is carrying on, or has carried on, a regulated activity in contravention of the general prohibition[1].

[1] CBIR 2006, reg 4, Sch 2, para 1(6) and see para 1(7) for the references to the definitions of 'the general prohibition' and 'regulated activity' in the Financial Services and Markets Act 2000.

Notification and advertisement of order

5.116 If the court makes any of the orders listed in para **5.104** above, it shall as soon as reasonably practicable send two sealed copies of the order to the foreign representative. The foreign representative must send a sealed copy of the order as soon as reasonably practicable to the debtor. He must also, as soon as reasonably practicable after the date of the order give notice of the making of the order:

(a)   if a British insolvency office-holder is acting in relation to the debtor, to him;

(b)   if any person has been appointed, to the knowledge of the foreign representative, as a receiver or manager of the property of the debtor, to him;

(c)   if a Member State liquidator has been appointed in main proceedings in relation to the debtor, to him;

(d)   if to his knowledge a foreign representative has been appointed in any other foreign proceeding regarding the debtor, that person;

(e)   if there is pending in England and Wales a petition for the bankruptcy of the debtor, to the petitioner;

(f)   if the debtor is a debtor who is of interest to the Financial Services Authority, to that Authority;

(g)   to such other persons as the court may direct.

5.117 In the case of an order recognising a foreign proceeding in relation to the debtor as a foreign main proceeding, or an order under article 19 or 21 of the Model Law staying execution, distress or other legal process against the debtor's assets, the foreign representative must also, as soon as reasonably practicable after the date of the order give notice of the making of the order:

(a)   to any enforcement officer or other officer who to his knowledge is charged with an execution or other legal process against the debtor or its property; and

(b)   to any person who to his knowledge is distraining against the debtor or its property.

5.118 In this context, the references to property shall be taken as references to property situated within England and Wales. The foreign representative shall advertise the making of the following orders once in the Gazette and once in such newspaper as he thinks most appropriate for ensuring that the making of the order comes to the notice of the debtor's creditors:

(a)   a recognition order;

(b)   an order confirming the status of a replacement foreign representative; and

(c)   a modification or termination order which modifies or terminates recognition of a foreign proceeding,

and the advertisement shall be in Form ML8[1]. The court is not required to approve the advertisement but will give guidance; any difficulties should be reported to the court and the Insolvency Service Policy Unit[2].

[1]   CBIR 2006, reg 4, Sch 2, para 26.
[2]   *Re Rajapakse* [2007] BPIR 99n.

Adjournment of hearing; directions

5.119 In any case where the court exercises its power to adjourn the hearing of the application, it may at any time give such directions as it thinks fit as to:

(a)   service or notice of the application on or to any person, whether in connection with the venue of a resumed hearing or for any other purpose;
(b)   the procedure on the application;
(c)   the manner in which any evidence is to be adduced at a resumed hearing and in particular as to (i) the taking of evidence wholly or in part by affidavit or orally; and (ii) the cross-examination on the hearing in court or in chambers, of any deponents to affidavits;
(d)   the matters to be dealt with in evidence[1].

1   CBIR 2006, reg 4, Sch 2, para 27.

Court procedure applicable to applications other than principal applications

5.120 The following rules relate to other applications made under the regulations[1].

1   CBIR 2006, reg 4, Sch 2, para 31.

Form and contents of application

5.121 The application must be in the form appropriate to the application concerned. Forms ML4 and ML5 shall be used for an originating application and an ordinary application respectively under the Cross-Border Insolvency Regulations 2006. The application must be in writing and must state:

(a)   the names of the parties;
(b)   the nature of the relief or order applied for or the directions sought from the court;
(c)   the names and addresses of the persons (if any) on whom it is intended to serve the application or that no person is intended to be served;
(d)   where the Cross-Border Insolvency Regulations 2006 require that notice of the application is to be given to specified persons, the names and addresses of all those persons (so far as known to the applicant); and
(e)   the applicant's address for service.

5.122 An originating application must set out the grounds on which the applicant claims to be entitled to the relief or order sought. The application must be signed by the applicant if he is acting in person or, when he is not so acting, by or on behalf of his solicitor[1].

1   CBIR 2006, reg 4, Sch 2, para 32.

Filing and service of application

5.123 The application must be filed in court, accompanied by one copy and a number of additional copies equal to the number of persons who are to be served with the application. Subject to the court's power to hear the application immediately or *ex parte* or unless it otherwise orders, upon the presentation of the application and the appropriate number of copies, the court shall fix a venue for the application to be heard. The venue means the time, date and place of the hearing[1]. Unless the court otherwise directs, the applicant must serve a sealed copy of the application, endorsed with the venue of the hearing, on the respondent named in the application (or on each respondent if more than one). The court may give any of the following directions:

(a)   that the application be served upon persons other than those specified by the relevant provision of the Cross-Border Insolvency Regulations 2006;
(b)   that the giving of notice to any person may be dispensed with;
(c)   that notice be given in some other way.

[1]   CBIR 2006, reg 4, Sch 2, para 1(4).

5.124   Unless the case is urgent, the application must be served at least 10 business days before the date fixed for the hearing. Where the case is one of urgency, the court may (without prejudice to its general power to extend or abridge time limits) (a) hear the application immediately, either with or without notice to, or the attendance of, other parties; or (b) authorise a shorter period of service than the 10 business days ordinarily required. In an urgent case, the application may be heard on terms providing for the filing or service of documents, or the carrying out of other formalities, as the court thinks fit[1].

[1]   CBIR 2006, reg 4, Sch 2, para 33.

Other hearings ex parte

5.125   Where the relevant provisions of the Cross-Border Insolvency Regulations 2006 do not require service of the application on, or notice of it to be given to, any person, the court may hear the application *ex parte*. Where the application is properly made *ex parte*[1], the court may hear it forthwith, without fixing a venue as would otherwise be required. Alternatively, the court may fix a venue for the application to be heard; if so, the court may give directions as to service or giving notice as it would in an ordinary case[2].

[1]   Ex *parte* is defined at CBIR 2006, reg 4, Sch 2, para 1(5).
[2]   CBIR 2006, reg 4, Sch 2, para 34.

Use of affidavit evidence

5.126   In any proceedings evidence may be given by affidavit unless the court otherwise directs; but the court may, on the application of any party, order the attendance for cross-examination of the person making the affidavit. Where, after such an order has been made, the person in question does not attend, his affidavit shall not be used in evidence without the permission of the court[1].

[1]   CBIR 2006, reg 4, Sch 2, para 35.

Filing and service of affidavits

5.127 Unless the court otherwise allows:

(a) if the applicant intends to rely at the first hearing on affidavit evidence, he must file the affidavit or affidavits (if more than one) in court and serve a copy or copies on the respondent, not less than 10 business days before the date fixed for the hearing; and

(b) where a respondent to an application intends to oppose it and to rely for that purpose on affidavit evidence, he must file the affidavit or affidavits (if more than one) in court and serve a copy or copies on the applicant, not less than five business days before the date fixed for the hearing.

5.128 Any affidavit may be sworn by the applicant or by the respondent or by some other person possessing direct knowledge of the subject matter of the application[1].

[1] CBIR 2006, reg 4, Sch 2, para 36.

Adjournment of hearings; directions

5.129 The court may adjourn the hearing of an application on such terms (if any) as it thinks fit[1]. If the court adjourns the hearing, it may give such directions as it thinks fit as to:

(a) service or notice of the application on or to any person, whether in connection with the venue of a resumed hearing or for any other purpose;

(b) the procedure on the application;

(c) the manner in which any evidence is to be adduced at a resumed hearing and in particular as to (i) the taking of evidence wholly or in part by affidavit or orally; and (ii) the cross-examination on the hearing in court or in chambers, of any deponents to affidavits;

(d) the matters to be dealt with in evidence[2].

[1] CBIR 2006, reg 4, Sch 2, para 37.
[2] CBIR 2006, reg 4, Sch 2, para 27.

Rules of general application

Transfer of proceedings within the High Court

5.130 The High Court may, having regard to the criteria in CPR r 30.3(2), order proceedings in the Royal Courts of Justice or a district registry, or any part of such proceedings (such as an application made in the proceedings), to be transferred from the Royal Courts of Justice to a district registry or from a district registry to the Royal Courts of Justice or to another district registry. The High Court may order proceedings before a district registry for the detailed assessment of costs to be transferred to another district registry if it is satisfied that the proceedings could be more conveniently or fairly taken in that other district registry. An application for an order for such a transfer must, if the claim is proceeding in a district registry, be made to that registry. A transfer of proceedings may be ordered by the court of its own motion; or on the application of a person appearing to the court to have an interest in the proceedings. Where the court orders proceedings to be transferred, the court from which they are to be transferred must give notice of the transfer to all the parties. An order made before the transfer of the proceedings shall not be affected by the order to transfer[1].

1   CBIR 2006, reg 4, Sch 2, para 38.

Transfer of proceedings: actions to avoid acts detrimental to creditors

5.131 If in accordance with article 23(6) of the Model Law, the court grants a foreign representative permission to make an application in accordance with paragraph 1 of that article; and the relevant proceedings under British insolvency law taking place regarding the debtor are taking place in the county court, the court may also order those proceedings to be transferred to the High Court. Where the court makes an order transferring proceedings on this footing, it must send sealed copies of the order to the county court from which the proceedings are to be transferred, and to the official receivers attached to that court and the High Court respectively; and the county court shall send the file of the proceedings to the High Court. Once this has been done, if the official receiver attached to the court to which the proceedings are transferred is not already, by virtue of directions given by the Secretary of State under s 399(6)(a) of the 1986 Act, the official receiver in relation to those proceedings, he becomes, in relation to those proceedings, the official receiver in place of the official receiver attached to the other court concerned[1].

1   CBIR 2006, reg 4, Sch 2, para 39.

Shorthand writers

5.132 The judge may in writing nominate one or more persons to be official shorthand writers to the court. The court may, at any time in the course of proceedings under the Cross-Border Insolvency Regulations 2006, appoint a shorthand writer to take down the evidence of a person examined in pursuance of a court order under article 19 or 21 of the Model Law. The remuneration of a shorthand writer appointed in proceedings under the Cross-Border Insolvency Regulations 2006 shall be paid by the party at whose instance the appointment was made or otherwise as the court may direct. Any question arising as to the rates of remuneration payable under this paragraph shall be determined by the court in its discretion[1].

1   CBIR 2006, reg 4, Sch 2, para 40.

Enforcement procedures

5.133 In any proceedings under the Cross-Border Insolvency Regulations 2006, orders of the court may be enforced in the same manner as a judgment to the same effect[1].

[1]   CBIR 2006, reg 4, Sch 2, para 41.

Title of proceedings

5.134 Every proceeding under the Cross-Border Insolvency Regulations 2006 shall, with any necessary additions, be entitled 'IN THE MATTER OF ... (naming the debtor to which the proceedings relate) AND IN THE MATTER OF THE CROSS-BORDER INSOLVENCY REGULATIONS 2006'. This requirement does not apply in respect of any form prescribed under the Cross-Border Insolvency Regulations 2006[1].

[1]   CBIR 2006, reg 4, Sch 2, para 42.

Court records

5.135 The court shall keep records of all proceedings under the Cross-Border Insolvency Regulations 2006, and is to cause to be entered in the records the taking of any step in the proceedings, and such decisions of the court in relation thereto, as the court thinks fit[1].

[1]   CBIR 2006, reg 4, Sch 2, para 43.

Inspection of records

5.136 Subject as follows, the court's records of proceedings under the Cross-Border Insolvency Regulations 2006 shall be open to inspection by any person. If in the case of a person applying to inspect the records the Registrar is not satisfied as to the propriety of the purpose for which inspection is required, he may refuse to allow it. That person may then apply forthwith and *ex parte* to the judge, who may refuse the inspection or allow it on such terms as he thinks fit. The decision of the judge is final[1].

[1]   CBIR 2006, reg 4, Sch 2, para 44.

File of court proceedings

5.137 In respect of all proceedings under the Cross-Border Insolvency Regulations 2006, the court shall open and maintain a file for each case; and (subject to directions of the Registrar) all documents relating to such proceedings shall be placed on the relevant file. No proceedings under the Cross-Border Insolvency Regulations 2006 shall be filed in the Central Office of the High Court[1].

[1]   CBIR 2006, reg 4, Sch 2, para 45.

Right to inspect the file

5.138 In the case of any proceedings under the Cross-Border Insolvency Regulations 2006, the following have the right, at all reasonable times, to inspect the court's file of the proceedings:

(a)   the Secretary of State;

(b)   the person who is the foreign representative in relation to the proceedings;

(c)   if a foreign representative has been appointed in any other foreign proceeding regarding the debtor to which the proceedings under the Cross-Border Insolvency Regulations 2006 relate, that person;

(d)   if a British insolvency office-holder is acting in relation to the debtor to which the proceedings under the Cross-Border Insolvency Regulations 2006 relate, that person;

(e)   any person stating himself in writing to be a creditor of the debtor to which the proceedings under the Cross-Border Insolvency Regulations 2006 relate;

(f)   if a Member State liquidator has been appointed in relation to the debtor to which the proceedings under the Cross-Border Insolvency Regulations 2006 relate, that person; and

(g)   the debtor to which the proceedings under the Cross-Border Insolvency Regulations 2006 relate[1].

---

[1]   Or, if the debtor is a company, corporation or partnership, every person who is, or at any time has been a director or officer of the debtor, a member of the debtor; or where applicable, a person registered under Part 23 of the Companies Act 1985 as authorised to represent the debtor in respect of its business in England and Wales.

5.139 If, for the purpose of powers conferred by the 1986 Act or the Rules, the Secretary of State or the official receiver wishes to inspect the file of any proceedings under the Cross-Border Insolvency Regulations 2006, and requests the transmission of the file, the court shall comply with such request (unless the file is for the time being in use for the court's purposes).

5.140 The right of inspection conferred as above on any person may be exercised on his behalf by a person properly authorised by him.

5.141 Any person may, by leave of the court, inspect the file.

5.142 As with court records, the Registrar has power to refuse access if he is not satisfied as to the propriety of the purpose for which inspection is sought. An appeal lies to the judge against his decision, but no appeal may be made from the judge.

5.143 Where the Cross-Border Insolvency Regulations 2006 confer a right for any person to inspect documents on the court's file of proceedings, the right includes that of taking copies of those documents on payment of the fee chargeable under any order made under the Courts Act 2003, s 92[1].

[1]   CBIR 2006, reg 4, Sch 2, para 46.

Restricted documents

5.144 The right of inspection is not exercisable in the case of documents, or parts of documents, as to which the court directs (either generally or specially) that they are not to be made open to inspection without the court's permission. An application for a direction of the court to this effect may be made by the foreign representative or by any party appearing to the court to have an interest[1].

[1]   CBIR 2006, reg 4, Sch 2, para 46(4).

Copies of court orders

5.145 In any proceedings under the Cross-Border Insolvency Regulations 2006, any person who has a right to inspect documents on the court file also has the right to require the foreign representative in relation to those proceedings to furnish him with a copy of any court order in the proceedings. This does not apply if a copy of the court order has been served on that person or notice of the making of the order has been given to that person under other provisions of the Cross-Border Insolvency Regulations 2006[1].

[1]   CBIR 2006, reg 4, Sch 2, para 47.

Filing of Gazette notices and advertisements

5.146 In any court in which proceedings under the Cross-Border Insolvency Regulations 2006 are pending, an officer of the court must file a copy of every issue of the Gazette which contains an advertisement relating to those proceedings. Where there appears in a newspaper an advertisement relating to proceedings under the Cross-Border Insolvency Regulations 2006 pending in any court, the person inserting the advertisement must file a copy of it in that court. The copy of the advertisement shall be accompanied by, or have endorsed on it, such particulars as are necessary to identify the proceedings and the date of the advertisement's appearance. An officer of any court in which proceedings under the Cross-Border Insolvency Regulations 2006 are pending must from time to time file a memorandum giving the dates of, and other particulars relating to, any notice published in the Gazette, and any newspaper advertisements, which relate to proceedings so pending. The officer's memorandum is prima facie evidence that any notice or advertisement mentioned in it was duly inserted in the issue of the newspaper or the Gazette which is specified in the memorandum[1].

[1]   CBIR 2006, reg 4, Sch 2, para 48.

Persons incapable of managing their affairs

5.147 Where in proceedings under the Cross-Border Insolvency Regulations 2006 it appears to the court that a person affected by the proceedings is one who is incapable of managing and administering his property and affairs either by reason of mental disorder within the meaning of the Mental Health Act 1983 or due to physical affliction or disability, the court may appoint such person as it thinks fit to appear for, represent or act for that person. The person concerned is referred to as 'the incapacitated person'. The appointment may be made either generally or for the purpose of any particular application or proceeding, or for the exercise of particular rights or powers which the incapacitated person might have exercised but for his incapacity. The court may make the appointment either of its own motion or on application by a person who has been appointed by a court in the United Kingdom or elsewhere to manage the affairs of, or to represent, the incapacitated person, or any relative or friend of the incapacitated person who appears to the court to be a proper person to make the application, or in any case where the incapacitated person is the debtor, the foreign representative. An application to appoint someone to represent or act for an incapacitated person may be made *ex parte*; but the court may require such notice of the application as it thinks necessary to be given to the person alleged to be incapacitated, or any other person, and may adjourn the hearing of the application to enable the notice to be given. The application must be supported by an affidavit of a registered medical practitioner as to the mental or physical condition of the incapacitated person[1].

[1]   CBIR 2006, reg 4, Sch 2, paras 49–51.

Service of notices following appointment

5.148 Any notice served on, or sent to, a person appointed to represent or act for an incapacitated person has the same effect as if it had been served on, or given to, the incapacitated person[1].

[1]   CBIR 2006, reg 4, Sch 2, para 52.

Rights of audience

5.149 Rights of audience in proceedings under the Cross-Border Insolvency Regulations 2006 are the same as obtain in proceedings under British insolvency law[1].

[1]   CBIR 2006, reg 4, Sch 2, para 53.

Right of attendance

5.150 Subject as follows, in proceedings under the Cross-Border Insolvency Regulations 2006, any person stating himself in writing, in records kept by the court for that purpose, to be a creditor of the debtor to which the proceedings relate, is entitled at his own cost, to attend in court or in chambers at any stage of the proceedings. Attendance may be by the person himself, or his solicitor. A person entitled to attend may request the court in writing to give him notice of any step in the proceedings; and, subject to his paying the costs involved and keeping the court informed as to his address, the court shall comply with the request. If the court is satisfied that the exercise by a person of his rights to attend has given rise to costs for the estate of the debtor which would not otherwise have been incurred and ought not, in the circumstances, to fall on that estate, it may direct that the costs be paid by the person concerned, to an amount specified. The rights of that person under this paragraph shall be in abeyance so long as those costs are not paid[1].

[1]   CBIR 2006, reg 4, Sch 2, para 54(1)–(4).

5.151 The court may appoint one or more persons to represent the creditors of the debtor and to have the rights of attendance, instead of the rights being exercised by any or all of them individually. If two or more persons are appointed to represent the same interest, they must (if at all) instruct the same solicitor[1].

[1]   CBIR 2006, reg 4, Sch 2, para 54(5).

Right of attendance for Member State liquidator

5.152 A Member State liquidator appointed in relation to a debtor subject to proceedings under the Cross-Border Insolvency Regulations 2006 is deemed to be a creditor for the purpose of the entitlement to attend in court or in chambers[1].

[1]   CBIR 2006, reg 4, Sch 2, para 55.

British insolvency office-holder's solicitor

5.153 Where in any proceedings the attendance of the British insolvency office-holder's solicitor is required, whether in court or in chambers, the British insolvency office-holder himself need not attend, unless directed by the court[1].

[1]   CBIR 2006, reg 4, Sch 2, para 56.

Formal defects

5.154 No proceedings under the Cross-Border Insolvency Regulations 2006 shall be invalidated by any formal defect or by any irregularity, unless the court before which objection is made considers that substantial injustice has been caused by the defect or irregularity, and that the injustice cannot be remedied by any order of the court[1].

[1]   CBIR 2006, reg 4, Sch 2, para 57.

Restriction on concurrent proceedings and remedies

5.155 Where in proceedings under the Cross-Border Insolvency Regulations 2006 the court makes an order staying any action, execution or other legal process against the property of a debtor, service of the order may be effected by sending a sealed copy of the order to whatever is the address for service of the claimant or other party having the carriage of the proceedings to be stayed[1].

1   CBIR 2006, reg 4, Sch 2, para 58.

Affidavits

5.156 Where in proceedings under the Cross-Border Insolvency Regulations 2006, an affidavit is made by any British insolvency office-holder acting in relation to the debtor, he must state the capacity in which he makes it, the position which he holds and the address at which he works. Any officer of the court duly authorised in that behalf, may take affidavits and declarations. Except in the cases mentioned below, where the Cross-Border Insolvency Regulations 2006 provide for the use of an affidavit, a witness statement verified by a statement of truth may be used as an alternative. The cases where an affidavit must be made are those arising under paragraphs 4 (affidavit in support of recognition application), 7 (affidavit in support of interim relief application), 10 (affidavit in support of article 21 relief application), 13 (affidavit in support of application regarding status of replacement foreign representative) and 16 (affidavit in support of review application).

1   CBIR 2006, reg 4, Sch 2, para 59.

Security in court

5.157 Where security has to be given to the court (otherwise than in relation to costs), it may be given by guarantee, bond or the payment of money into court. A person proposing to give a bond as security shall give notice to the party in whose favour the security is required, and to the court, naming those who are to be sureties to the bond. The court must forthwith give notice to the parties concerned of a venue for the execution of the bond and the making of any objection to the sureties. The sureties must make an affidavit of their sufficiency (unless dispensed with by the party in whose favour the security is required) and must, if required by the court, attend the court to be cross-examined[1].

1   CBIR 2006, reg 4, Sch 2, para 60.

Further information and disclosure

5.158 Any party to proceedings under the Cross-Border Insolvency Regulations 2006 may apply to the court for an order:

(a)   that any other party clarify any matter which is in dispute in the proceedings or give additional information in relation to any such matter in accordance with CPR Pt 18 (further information); or

(b)   to obtain disclosure from any other party in accordance with CPR Pt 31 (disclosure and inspection of documents).

5.159 An application to obtain further information or disclosure may be made without notice being served on any other party[1].

1   CBIR 2006, reg 4, Sch 2, para 61.

Office copies of documents

5.160 Any person who has under the Cross-Border Insolvency Regulations 2006 the right to inspect the court file of proceedings may require the court to provide him with an office copy of any document from the file. A person's right under this paragraph may be exercised on his behalf by his solicitor. An office copy provided by the court under this paragraph shall be in such form as the Registrar thinks appropriate, and shall bear the court's seal[1].

1   CBIR 2006, reg 4, Sch 2, para 62.

'The court'

5.161 Anything to be done in proceedings under the Cross-Border Insolvency Regulations 2006 by, to or before the court may be done by, to or before a judge of the High Court or a Registrar. Where the Cross-Border Insolvency Regulations 2006 require or permit the court to perform an act of a formal or administrative character, that act may be performed by a court officer[1].

1   CBIR 2006, reg 4, Sch 2, para 63.

Forms for use in proceedings under the Cross-Border Insolvency Regulations 2006

5.162 The forms contained in Schedule 5 to the regulations are to be used in, and in connection with, proceedings under the Cross-Border Insolvency Regulations 2006. But they may be used with such variations, if any, as the circumstances may require[1].

1   CBIR 2006, reg 4, Sch 2, para 73.

Time limits

5.163 The provisions of CPR r 2.8 (time) apply, as regards computation of time, to anything required or authorised to be done by the Cross-Border Insolvency Regulations 2006. The provisions of CPR r 3.1(2)(a) (the court's general powers of management) apply so as to enable the court to extend or shorten the time for compliance with anything required or authorised to be done by the Cross-Border Insolvency Regulations 2006[1].

[1]   CBIR 2006, reg 4, Sch 2, para 74.

False claim of status as creditor

5.164 IR 1986, r 12.18 (false claim of status as creditor, etc) applies with any necessary modifications in any case where a person falsely claims the status of a creditor of a debtor, with the intention of obtaining a sight of documents whether on the court's file or in the hands of the foreign representative or other person, which he has not under the Cross-Border Insolvency Regulations 2006 any right to inspect. IR 1986, r 12.21 and Schedule 5 to IR 1986 apply to an offence under IR 1986, r 12.18[1].

[1]   CBIR 2006, reg 4, Sch 2, para 78.

Costs

Costs and detailed assessment

5.165 In any proceedings before the court, the court may order costs to be decided by detailed assessment[1].

[1]   CBIR 2006, reg 4, Sch 2, para 64.

Costs of officers charged with execution of writs or other process

5.166 Where by virtue of article 20 of the Model Law or a court order under article 19 or 21 of the Model Law an enforcement officer, or other officer, charged with execution of the writ or other process:

(a)   is required to deliver up goods or money; or
(b)   has deducted costs from the proceeds of an execution or money paid to him,

the foreign representative may require in writing that the amount of the enforcement officer's or other officer's bill of costs be decided by detailed assessment. Where such a requirement is made, if the enforcement officer or other officer does not commence detailed assessment proceedings within three months of the requirement, or within such further time as the court, on application, may permit, any claim by the enforcement officer or other officer in respect of his costs is forfeited by such failure to commence proceedings. Where, in the case of a deduction of costs by the enforcement officer or other officer, any amount deducted is disallowed at the conclusion of the detailed assessment proceedings, the enforcement officer or other officer shall forthwith pay a sum equal to that disallowed to the foreign representative for the benefit of the debtor[1].

[1]   CBIR 2006, reg 4, Sch 2, para 65.

Final costs certificate

5.167 A final costs certificate of the costs officer is final and conclusive as to all matters which have not been objected to in the manner provided for under the rules of the court. Where it is proved to the satisfaction of a costs officer that a final costs certificate has been lost or destroyed, he may issue a duplicate[1].

1   CBIR 2006, reg 4, Sch 2, para 66.

Appeals

Appeals from court orders

5.168 An appeal from a decision of a Registrar of the High Court in proceedings under the Cross-Border Insolvency Regulations 2006 lies to a single judge of the High Court; and an appeal from a decision of that judge on such an appeal lies, with the permission of the Court of Appeal, to the Court of Appeal[1]. The reference to the Registrar includes the district judge where the case is proceeding in a district registry[2]. An appeal from a decision of a judge of the High Court in proceedings under the regulations which is not a decision on an appeal made to him from a Registrar lies, with the permission of that judge or the Court of Appeal, to the Court of Appeal[3].

1   CBIR 2006, reg 4, Sch 2, para 67(1).
2   CBIR 2006, reg 4, Sch 2, para 1(3).
3   CBIR 2006, reg 4, Sch 2, para 67(2).

Procedure on appeals

5.169 Subject as follows, CPR Pt 52 (appeals to the Court of Appeal) and its practice direction apply to appeals in proceedings under the Cross-Border Insolvency Regulations 2006. The provisions of Part 4 of the practice direction on Insolvency Proceedings supporting CPR Pt 49 relating to first appeals (as defined in that Part) apply in relation to any appeal to a single judge of the High Court from a Registrar, with any necessary modifications. In proceedings under the regulations, the procedure under CPR Pt 52 is by ordinary application and not by appeal notice[1].

1   CBIR 2006, reg 4, Sch 2, para 68.

Notices and service

Notices

5.170 All notices required or authorised by or under the Cross-Border Insolvency Regulations 2006 to be given must be in writing, unless it is otherwise provided, or the court allows the notice to be given in some other way. Where in proceedings under the regulations a notice is required to be sent or given by any person, the sending or giving of it may be proved by means of a certificate by that person that he posted the notice, or instructed another person (naming him) to do so. A certificate under this paragraph may be endorsed on a copy or specimen of the notice to which it relates[1].

[1]   CBIR 2006, reg 4, Sch 2, para 69.

'Give notice', etc

5.171 A reference in the Cross-Border Insolvency Regulations 2006 to giving notice, or to delivering, sending or serving any document, means that the notice or document may be sent by post[1]. Where service is not required, any form of post may be used[2].

[1]   CBIR 2006, reg 4, Sch 2, para 70(1).
[2]   CBIR 2006, reg 4, Sch 2, para 70(2).

Service by post

5.172 For a document to be properly served by post, it must be contained in an envelope addressed to the person on whom service is to be effected, and pre-paid for first-class post. A document to be served by post may be sent to the last known address of the person to be served. Where first-class post is used, the document is treated as served on the second business day after the date of posting, unless the contrary is shown. The date of posting is presumed, unless the contrary is shown, to be the date shown in the postmark on the envelope in which the document is contained[1].

[1]   CBIR 2006, reg 4, Sch 2, para 75.

Personal service

5.173 Personal service of a document is permissible in all cases[1].

[1]   CBIR 2006, reg 4, Sch 2, para 70(3).

General provisions as to service and notice

5.174 Subject to the rules governing service of principal applications, service by post and service outside the jurisdiction[1], CPR Pt 6 (service of documents) applies as regards any matter relating to the service of documents and the giving of notice in proceedings under the Cross-Border Insolvency Regulations 2006[2].

[1]   CBIR 2006, reg 4, Sch 2, paras 22, 75 and 77 respectively.
[2]   CBIR 2006, reg 4, Sch 2, para 76.

Service outside the jurisdiction

5.175 Sections III and IV of CPR Pt 6 (service out of the jurisdiction and service of process of foreign court) do not apply in proceedings under the

Cross-Border Insolvency Regulations 2006. Where for the purposes of proceedings under the Cross-Border Insolvency Regulations 2006 any process or order of the court, or other document, is required to be served on a person who is not in England and Wales, the court may order service to be effected within such time, on such person, at such place and in such manner as it thinks fit, and may also require such proof of service as it thinks fit. An application under this paragraph shall be supported by an affidavit stating:

(a)   the grounds on which the application is made; and
(b)   in what place or country the person to be served is, or probably may be found[1].

[1]   CBIR 2006, reg 4, Sch 2, para 77.

5.176 Where the debtor does not have an address for service in England and Wales or, being an individual, is resident outside the jurisdiction, service should be made on him at his usual or last known address outside the jurisdiction[1].

[1]   *Re Rajapakse* [2007] BPIR 99n.

Notice of the venue for an application

5.177 Notice of the venue fixed for an application may be given by service of the sealed copy of the application on which the venue has been endorsed[1].

[1]   CBIR 2006, reg 4, Sch 2, para 70(4).

Notice, etc to solicitors

5.178 Where in proceedings under the Cross-Border Insolvency Regulations 2006 a notice or other document is required or authorised to be given to a person, it may, if he has indicated that his solicitor is authorised to accept service on his behalf, be given instead to the solicitor[1].

[1]   CBIR 2006, reg 4, Sch 2, para 71.

Notice to joint British insolvency office-holders

5.179 Where two or more persons are acting jointly as the British insolvency office-holder in proceedings under British insolvency law, delivery of a document to one of them is to be treated as delivery to them all[1].

[1]   CBIR 2006, reg 4, Sch 2, para 72.

The Gazette

5.180 A copy of the Gazette containing any notice required by the Cross-Border Insolvency Regulations 2006 to be gazetted is evidence of any fact stated in the notice. In the case of an order of the court notice of which is required by the Cross-Border Insolvency Regulations 2006 to be gazetted, a copy of the Gazette containing the notice may in any proceedings be produced as conclusive evidence that the order was made on the date specified in the notice[1].

[1]   CBIR 2006, reg 4, Sch 2, para 79.

Part II

VOLUNTARY ARRANGEMENTS AND COMPOSITIONS OUTSIDE BANKRUPTCY

Chapter 6

INDIVIDUAL VOLUNTARY ARRANGEMENTS

A INTRODUCTION

General background

6.1 The individual voluntary arrangement was introduced by the Insolvency Act 1986 ('IA 1986') with the aim of introducing a procedure whereby a debtor facing financial difficulties could enter into binding arrangements with creditors and avoid bankruptcy. The Deeds of Arrangement Act 1914 had failed to provide a satisfactory mechanism for this purpose essentially because an arrangement under the 1914 Act cannot bind non-assenting creditors who remain free to petition for the debtor's bankruptcy. The essential element of the voluntary arrangement under the IA 1986 is the provision that a three-quarters' majority of the creditors[1] voting together at the creditors' meeting may bind minority creditors to an arrangement against their wishes. This element was strengthened by the amendment to the original 1986 scheme introduced by the Insolvency Act 2000 ('IA 2000')[2], which provided that every creditor of the debtor who would have been entitled to vote at the creditors' meeting had he been given notice of it is bound by a voluntary arrangement once approved whether or not he did in fact have notice of the meeting[3]. The IA 2000 introduced other, more technical, changes which are discussed in the text. It is no longer necessary for an individual voluntary arrangement to be preceded by, and implemented under the protection of, an interim order. And where an interim order is in force, or an application for an interim order is pending, distress may not be levied on the debtor's goods nor may a right of forfeiture by peaceful re-entry be exercised without the leave of the court[4].

1   Provided they are not creditors associated with the debtor, see paras **6.174–6.175**.
2   Which came into force on 1 January 2003.
3   Previously only creditors who did in fact have notice of the creditors' meeting were bound to the voluntary arrangement if approved.
4   See IA 1986, ss 252(2), 254(1) and para **6.47**.

6.2 Further changes were introduced by the Enterprise Act 2002 ('EA 2002'). The most important was the abolition of the Crown's preferential status as a creditor in order to improve unsecured creditors' prospects of recovery against insolvent estates. The loss of preferential status for Crown debts will have its impact on individual voluntary arrangements, primarily because HM Revenue and Customs are so frequently substantial creditors. In seeking further to reduce the number of bankruptcies the EA 2002 introduced a new 'fast-track' procedure for an IVA for debtors who are undischarged bankrupts[1], and provided that on the approval of an IVA proposed by an undischarged bankrupt either the bankrupt or the official receiver may apply for the bankruptcy order to be annulled[2].

1   IA 1986, ss 263A–263G inserted by EA 2002, s 264 and Sch 22.
2   IA 1986, s 261 as amended by EA 2002, s 264 and Sch 22.

Company voluntary arrangements

6.3 The Insolvency Act 1986 also introduced the concept of the company voluntary arrangement. The regimes for individual voluntary arrangements and company voluntary arrangements are similar in many respects. Decisions of the courts made under one regime are frequently relevant to the other, and many of the cases cited in the text are decisions made in company voluntary arrangement cases.

The statutory scheme

6.4 The essential element of a voluntary arrangement is the creditors' meeting. The debtor makes a proposal to the creditors who consider its terms, sometimes agreeing modifications with the debtor, and who then vote on the proposal in accordance with the rules. In essence, provided that (1) at least 75% of the creditors by value approve the proposal and (2) the proposal is not opposed by more than 50% of the creditors who are not associates[1] of the debtor, then the voluntary arrangement is approved[2]. Once approved the voluntary arrangement binds all the creditors of the debtor entitled to vote at the creditors' meeting as from the time of the meeting, whether they voted in favour of the proposal and whether they attended the meeting or not. Since 1 January 2003 even creditors who were unaware of the proposal and the holding of the creditors' meeting are bound by the voluntary arrangement once it has been approved at the creditors' meeting[3].

1   For the definition of 'associate' see IA 1986, s 435, **Appendix 2**.
2   See paras **6.174–6.176**.
3   IA 1986, s 260(2) as amended by IA 2000, see para **6.251** et seq.

6.5 The legal analysis of the approved arrangement is that there is a consensual agreement between the debtor and all the creditors entitled to vote at the creditors' meeting; all these creditors are treated as consenting parties to the arrangement under the statutory hypothesis[1] whichever way they voted, if at all, and whatever their attitude to the voluntary arrangement[2]. As all creditors are treated as having consented to the voluntary arrangement, questions as to the consequences of the arrangement on the rights of creditors and third parties are to be determined on a proper construction of the terms of the arrangement[3].

1   Imposed by IA 1986, s 260(2).
2   See *Johnson v Davies* [1999] Ch 117 at 138, CA approved in *Raja v Rubin* [2000] Ch 274, [1999] 3 All ER 73, CA. As both these cases pre-date the changes introduced by the IA 2000 the principle is there framed in terms that there is a consensual agreement between the debtor and all the creditors who *had notice of and* were entitled to vote at the meeting. The words in italics now need to be deleted.
3   See paras **6.251–6.261**.

6.6 Time is often of the essence in the establishment of a voluntary arrangement. A debtor who needs to make an arrangement with his creditors will usually have to act with expedition. An interim order affords protection to the debtor from legal process and execution while the proposal is formulated and put to the creditors[1]. This protection is, however, available only for a short time. The procedure cannot be used, or misused, to stay the hands of creditors for any lengthy period. Equally important is the time available to creditors to challenge an approved arrangement. All parties bound by a voluntary arrangement need to know where they stand as soon as possible, free from the uncertainty which results from there being a right to challenge the arrangement in court. Once a voluntary arrangement is approved the chairman of the creditors' meeting has four days to report to the court[2]. Any application to challenge the approval of the arrangement or the conduct of the creditors' meeting which approved it must be brought within 28 days of this report to the court. There is power to extend this 28-day period in individual voluntary arrangements[3] but it is sparingly used[4]. To protect creditors who were not given notice of the meeting such a creditor has 28 days to challenge the voluntary arrangement from the date on which he became aware of it[5]. It follows that to the extent that there may be one or more creditors who were not given notice of the meeting the parties to the arrangement cannot be certain that it will continue undisturbed once 28 days after the chairman's report to the court has passed. It is to be hoped that the existence of such creditors will only occasionally be encountered in practice.

1   See paras **6.46–6.49**.
2   IR 1986, r 5.22(3) – the report to the court must be made whatever the outcome of the creditors' meeting.
3   The 28-day time period cannot be extended in CVA.

The nature of voluntary arrangements: compositions or schemes of arrangement

6.7 The IA 1986 provides that an individual voluntary arrangement may comprise either a composition with creditors or a scheme of arrangement[1]. An arrangement can, and not infrequently does, involve both a composition and a scheme of arrangement. Both compositions and schemes of arrangement are treated equally under the Insolvency Act 1986. There is no distinction either as to procedure or effect of approval. Where a composition or scheme is approved in accordance with the provisions of the statute it is legally binding on all the debtor's creditors[2]. The provisions of the IA 1986 do not impose the arrangement directly on a dissenting creditor. Rather he is bound to the arrangement by virtue of a statutory hypothesis which requires him to be treated as though he had consented to it[3]. Voluntary arrangements are to be treated as, and have the same consequences as, consensual deeds of arrangement. The same consequences therefore follow as if the dissenting creditor had agreed to be bound by the arrangement[4].

[1]   IA 1986, s 253(1).
[2]   IA 1986, s 260(2).
[3]   *Johnson v Davies* [1999] Ch 117, [1998] 2 All ER 649; *Raja v Rubin* [2000] Ch 274, [1999] 3 All ER 73, CA.
[4]   So where, as in *Johnson v Davies*, the issue whether a co-debtor was discharged by the arrangement fell to be determined by construction of the terms of the arrangement. In the event the terms of the arrangement in that case did not have the effect of releasing co-debtors who remained liable to the creditor on the joint debt.

6.8 A proposal for a voluntary arrangement by a debtor constitutes an offer to all the creditors as a class, and does not comprise an offer to each creditor individually[1].

[1]   *Re a Debtor (No 2389 of 1989)* [1991] Ch 326, [1990] 3 All ER 984.

Composition and scheme of arrangement

6.9 A 'composition' is an agreement between the debtor and his creditors whereby the compounding creditors agree with the debtor and between themselves to accept from the debtor payment of less than the respective amounts due to them in full satisfaction of the whole of their claim[1]. Outside statutory provision the consideration which would support the agreement by each creditor to accept part payment as a discharge of the whole debt is the mutual agreement of the other creditors to do likewise[2]. It is essential however that a money payment is made or some other consideration is provided by the debtor. Accordingly a proposal which provides for a nil dividend to unsecured creditors (a dividend being payable to secured creditors) is not capable of being a composition[3], although it may be a scheme of arrangement.

1   See e g *Irish Land Commission v Grant* (1884) 10 App Cas 14, 30 and see *Re Griffith* (1886) 3 Morr 111, 116 per Cave J 'Where the debtor makes over his assets to be administered by a trustee there is no doubt that that is a scheme. Where the debtor keeps his assets and undertakes to pay over the creditors a certain sum, that is a composition'.

2   *Good v Cheesman* (1831) 2 B & Ad 328; *Boyd v Hind* (1857) 1 H & N 938; and see *West Yorkshire Darracq Agency Ltd v Coleridge* [1911] 2 KB 326 and *Snelling v John G Snelling* [1973] 1 QB 87, [1972] 1 All ER 79.

3   *IRC v Adam & Partners Ltd* [2001] 1 BCLC 222, CA overruling the judge on this point, reported at [1999] 2 BCLC 730. On a proper construction the proposal constituted a moratorium and was therefore a scheme of arrangement. See also *IRC v Bland* [2003] EWHC 1068 (Ch), [2003] BPIR 1274.

6.10   A 'scheme of arrangement' may take any form acceptable to the parties[1]. The usual method is an assignment by the debtor of his property or a specified part of his property to a trustee (the supervisor) for realisation and distribution of the proceeds of sale amongst the creditors rateably or in such proportions as they agree. The trusts under which the supervisor holds the debtor's property will be agreed by the creditors and specified in the deed of assignment. Such deeds have in the past appointed a committee of inspection to control the trustee's administration of the estate. Such provision is not necessary with an arrangement under the IA 1986, as the court may control the supervisor on the application of any creditor, the debtor or other person dissatisfied by any act, omission or decision of the supervisor[2]. Other forms of scheme of arrangement involve a moratorium, often coupled with the payment of a dividend at the end of the moratorium period. However, a moratorium by itself may comprise a valid scheme of arrangement[3]. Whether or not the terms of the voluntary arrangement expressly so state, where a voluntary arrangement provides for monies or other assets to be paid to or transferred or held for the benefit of the arrangement creditors, a trust is created of those monies and assets for the benefit of the creditors[4]. While the precise status of money subject to an individual voluntary arrangement may become the subject of debate, the court will not be slow to find that a voluntary arrangement has created a trust[5].

1   And see the comments of Lightman J in *March Estates v Gunmark Ltd* [1996] 2 BCLC 1 at 5; although at 5b the learned judge states that 'a scheme of arrangement (a scheme) is plainly something different from a composition and involves something less than the release or discharge of creditors' debts, e g a moratorium', a scheme may involve something *more* than release or release; at 5e the learned judge states 'A scheme does not, or does not necessarily, involve any compromise or release'. There was no compromise or release in the case before him, but schemes have been implemented involving both a moratorium and the release and discharge of debts.

2   IA 1986, s 263(3).

3   See, for example, *IRC v Adam & Partners Ltd* [2001] 1 BCLC 222, CA where the proposal anticipated no payment of dividend to unsecured creditors during a three-year period during which it was thought that the bank as secured creditor would receive a better return. The proposal also provided that if the creditors received distributions these were to be accepted in full and final settlement of all sums due from the debtor at the start of the voluntary arrangement. If however no distributions were made the creditors were entitled to assert such contractual rights as they had at the end of the moratorium period.

4   *Re N T Gallagher & Son Ltd (in liq)* [2002] EWCA Civ 404, [2002] 3 All ER 474 at [28]–[30].

5   *Welburn v Dibb Lupton Broomhead (a firm)* [2002] EWCA Civ 1601 at [20].

6.11 *Individual voluntary arrangements*

Standard forms of arrangement

6.11 Even today it remains the case that many of the standard forms of arrangement in use do not actually spell out the consequences of the composition or scheme on the creditors' debts. In some instances this is of little consequence. Where there is a composition the debts will be compromised and no longer exist in their original form. But with a scheme of arrangement it may be necessary in the absence of express provision for the court to imply a term that creditors bound by the arrangement may not take any steps to enforce their debts against the debtor while the debtor is complying, or has complied, with his obligations under the scheme[1].

---

[1] See *Johnson v Davies* [1999] Ch 114, at p 128F; note that the precise ambit of the implied term may well depend upon the precise terms of the individual scheme. See also paras 6.287–6.290.

6.12 Time does not run for the purposes of limitation during the currency of a voluntary arrangement, unless specific provision is made for this in a particular arrangement, an unlikely occurrence. It is agreed by implication that the limitation period does not run so as to bar the creditors' debts while the voluntary arrangement is in force and prevents a creditor from suing[1].

---

[1] *Tanner v Everitt* [2004] EWHC 1130 (Ch), [2004] BPIR 1026 at [72]–[76].

The involvement of third parties

6.13 There is no limit to the potential flexibility of a scheme of arrangement. The intention is that it should be tailored to suit the circumstances of the individual debtor. A scheme may comprise no more than a short-term moratorium on the enforcement of the creditor's debts, perhaps coupled with the payment of dividends during the period of the moratorium[1], or it may require the active involvement of a third party who is prepared to give assistance to the debtor on certain terms. The involvement of third parties is envisaged by the IR 1986[2], but there is no statutory mechanism whereby a third party may incur rights and obligations under the arrangement. Neither is there any provision restrictive of such participation. In Australia it has been held that someone other than the debtor or his creditors may become a party to a scheme of arrangement[3], and there is no obvious reason why this approach should not be followed in England. Certainly if the scheme depends upon monetary contributions or other benefits being supplied by a third party it is important that the party in question is bound to the creditors either by joining the scheme or by entering into a contract with the nominee which the supervisor may then enforce on behalf of the creditors. Thus, for example, where a third party agrees to provide one or more payments if an arrangement is carried into effect the nominee should ensure that there is an enforceable contract with the third party for the benefit of the arrangement. Furthermore, it would be advisable for the nominee to ensure that the third party binds himself to the relevant proposal, conditional upon its acceptance by the creditors, before it is voted on in the creditors' meeting. A voluntary arrangement may expressly or by necessary implication regulate the rights inter se of a creditor of a debtor and of third parties liable for the same debt[4], and there is no obvious reason why the third party should not become a party to the arrangement if, exceptionally, the third party, the debtor and the creditors wish this to be so.

1   See eg the CVA in *March Estates plc v Gunmark Ltd* [1996] 2 BCLC 1.
2   See IR 1986, r 5.3(2)(b)(j).
3   See *Re Glendale Land Development Ltd* (1982) 1 ACLC 540; Supreme Court of New South Wales.
4   *Johnson v Davies* [1999] Ch 117, [1998] 2 All ER 649, CA; *March Estates plc v Gunmark* [1996] 2 BCLC 1, 6d; *Burford Midland Properties Ltd v Marley Extrusions Ltd* [1995] 1 BCLC 102.

6.14 The statutory sanction for default in connection with an IVA, namely the making of a bankruptcy order against the debtor, arises only where the debtor himself fails to honour his obligations[1]. In cases where the involvement of a third party is essential to the arrangement therefore the nominee and the creditors should consider what sanction if any there should be on the debtor in the event that the third party defaults on his obligations. The more usual practice is to draft the terms of the arrangement so that there is an obligation on the debtor to ensure that the benefits due from the third party do accrue to the arrangement. The debtor will therefore be in default if the third party fails to honour his commitment to the arrangement leaving the creditors free to petition for the debtor's bankruptcy.

1   IA 1986, s 264(1)(c), s 276(1)(a)(c).

The court for voluntary arrangement proceedings

6.15 In the majority of cases the debtor proposing a voluntary arrangement will be domiciled or habitually resident in England and Wales, or will be carrying on business solely within England and Wales, in which case the appropriate court for any particular voluntary arrangement will be governed by IA 1986 and determined by the rules allocating business between the various courts of England and Wales. Where the debtor's trading or residence is in more than one jurisdiction including England and Wales, the question whether the English courts have jurisdiction is governed by the EC Insolvency Regulation or the Cross-Border Insolvency Regulations 2006 where either applies[1] and the IA 1986 and rules of private international law where they do not.

1   As to which see **Chapters 4** and **5**.

6.16 Both in the case of the EC Insolvency Regulation and the Cross-Border Insolvency Regulations 2006 jurisdiction for insolvency proceedings is determined primarily by the debtor's Centre of Main Interests ('CoMI')[1]. Proceedings commenced in the jurisdiction where the debtor has his CoMI are 'main' proceedings. Proceedings which are instituted in a jurisdiction other than that in which the debtor has his CoMI will, where they are permitted, be 'secondary' or 'non-main' proceedings and will be subservient to any main proceedings when they are issued. Voluntary arrangements, being 'rescue proceedings' (ie proceedings not designed to liquidate and realise all the debtor's assets) may not be secondary proceedings under the EC Insolvency

Regulation, although they may be 'territorial proceedings' and commence and continue until such time, if ever, as main proceedings are commenced[2]. Voluntary arrangement proceedings may be 'non-main' proceedings under the Cross-Border Insolvency Regulations 2006 but in the vast majority of cases it is unrealistic to suppose that they will be able to continue after main proceedings to liquidate or bankrupt the debtor have been commenced in a foreign jurisdiction. In all but the most exceptional of cases therefore it will be the case that voluntary arrangement proceedings will only proceed with any prospect of success in England and Wales where the debtor has his CoMI in this jurisdiction.

[1]   See **Chapter 4.**
[2]   See **Chapter 4.**

The court within England and Wales

6.17   The appropriate court for an individual voluntary arrangement will be the court having jurisdiction in bankruptcy. The High Court has jurisdiction over cases where the debtor has resided or carried on business within the London Insolvency District for the greater part of the six months immediately preceding the commencement of the IVA proceedings, and where the debtor is not resident in England and Wales[1]. Jurisdiction over insolvency districts outside London is vested in designated county courts[2].

[1]   IA 1986, s 373(1)(3)(a) and IR 1986, r 6.9.
[2]   IA 1986, s 373(1)(3)(b); for the individual districts see County Courts Directory (HMSO).

The nominee

6.18   A debtor may not proceed to an individual voluntary arrangement on his own. The assistance of an authorised practitioner, styled for these purposes as 'the nominee', is required. He must report to the court, and thus to the creditors, on the merits of the proposal. This practitioner must either be an insolvency practitioner[1] or a person who has been authorised to act as a nominee or supervisor of the voluntary arrangement[2].

[1]   Licensed for the purposes of IA 1986, s 389 and see the Insolvency Practitioners (Recognised Professional Bodies) Order 1986, SI 1986/1764, and the Insolvency Practitioners Regulations 1990, SI 1990/439.
[2]   Under IA 1986, s 389A, added by IA 2000, s 4 which introduced the possibility that a nominee or supervisor need not be a qualified insolvency practitioner provided he is a member of a body recognised by the Secretary of State for the express purpose of acting in relation to voluntary arrangements. Security will be required for the proper performance of the nominee/supervisor's functions (IA 1986, s 389A(2)(b)) which may be exercised in respect of CVAs, PVAs or IVAs. It is very unlikely that these provisions will be utilised.

6.19   Where the proposal is approved by the creditors, the nominee, now called the 'supervisor', implements the composition or scheme subject to the control of the court. The IA 1986[1] provides that the supervisor should act 'either as trustee or otherwise' no other capacity being specified. There is no restriction on the powers the supervisor may have under an arrangement, but there are no statutory powers afforded the supervisor in the carrying out of the arrangement. The court may exercise control over the supervisor in his implementation of the arrangement, and in doing so may make any order it thinks fit with respect to any act, omission or decision of the supervisor[2].

1   IA 1986, s 253(2).
2   See paras **6.293–6.294**.

6.20 As nominee and chairman of the creditors' meeting, the insolvency practitioner will be called upon to exercise a quasi judicial rôle in admitting or rejecting claims or in valuing debts. It is of course essential that an insolvency practitioner who may have worked closely with an individual debtor and who might be tempted to make common cause with the debtor against creditors who oppose a voluntary arrangement, preserves his 'utter independence' from any party, either the debtor or any creditor[1].

1   See *Smurthwaite v Simpson-Smith* [2006] EWCA Civ 1183, [2006] BPIR 1504, per Jacob LJ at [33].

Fast-track procedure for undischarged bankrupt

6.21 This procedure is introduced by the Enterprise Act 2002 in order to encourage the greater use of individual voluntary arrangements and reduce the number of debtors in bankruptcy. It is available only to undischarged bankrupts where the official receiver is the proposed nominee and there is no application for an interim order[1], and any IVA which may be approved is restricted to bankruptcy creditors[2]. Once the fast-track procedure is underway however it will be possible for a bankrupt with post-bankruptcy debts to make a further proposal to his post-bankruptcy creditors under the protection of an interim order[3]. The fast-track scheme is that a proposal will be agreed between the bankrupt and the official receiver. It is then filed with the court. No meeting of creditors will be called and it will not be possible to modify the proposal. The official receiver will simply send out the details of the proposal to the creditors on a 'take it or leave it' basis, and the creditors will either agree to or disagree with the proposal by correspondence. Now that the period for automatic discharge has been reduced to 12 months it is unlikely that this procedure will be much used[4].

1   IA 1986, s 263A; note that a bankruptcy order has no effect on debts arising after the date on which it is made, so that this procedure (which applied only to bankruptcy creditors) may be difficult to utilise in the relatively rare cases where the bankrupt continues to trade and incur debts shortly after becoming bankrupt.
2   IA 1986, s 263B(3).
3   See IA 1986, s 263B(5).
4   The details of the fast-track voluntary arrangement 'FTVA' are covered at paras **6.354–6.382**.

B INTERIM ORDER

Introduction

6.22 As the scheme for individual voluntary arrangements was originally enacted under IA 1986, obtaining an interim order was an essential step for an individual debtor wishing to propose an IVA to his creditors, even where the debtor was a bankrupt[1]. The statute assumed that all debtors would require the protection against proceedings and execution afforded by an interim order. An interim order protects the debtor from all proceedings and execution while his proposal is prepared and put before his creditors[2]. It has been the case that the overwhelming proportion of IVAs are proposed and considered by the creditors' meeting under an interim order. Since 1 January 2003 it has been possible however to proceed to an approved arrangement without an interim order being obtained[3]. This procedure may be used by a debtor proposing to a small group of creditors who are aware of his position and supportive of a proposal, a debtor who wishes to make a further proposal to creditors within 12 months of applying for an interim order, a debtor who has an IVA in place who wishes to amend the terms of an IVA which makes no provision for amendment, or an undischarged bankrupt seeking to have his bankruptcy order annulled. It is envisaged that the interim order will remain the preferred route for a substantial majority of creditors; certainly for those creditors who have not been made bankrupt. Where a debtor is bankrupt he may of course have accrued further debts since the commencement of his bankruptcy, but in most cases he is unlikely to need the protection from creditors that the interim order provides.

[1]   IA 1986, s 253(1); and see *Fletcher v Vooght* [2000] BPIR 435, where the court concluded that on the wording of the legislation a 'report to the court' in a case where no interim order has been made cannot be a report under IA 1986, s 256 and cannot lead to a creditors' meeting being summoned under IA 1986, s 257 nor, therefore, to a voluntary arrangement with binding force under IA 1986, s 260.
[2]   See paras **6.46–6.49**.
[3]   IA 1986, s 256A inserted by IA 2000, s 3, Sch 3, para 7.

Pending hearing of application for an interim order

6.23 While an application for an interim order is pending no right of forfeiture by peaceable re-entry of premises let to the debtor may be exercised without leave of the court[1], and the court has a discretionary power to stay any action, execution or other legal process[2] against the debtor or his property[3]. This power is exercisable by the bankruptcy court[4] or by any other court in which proceedings against the debtor are pending and covers the levying of distress on the debtor's property or its subsequent sale[5]. Any court may stay the proceedings or allow them to continue on such terms as the court considers fit[6]. Similar powers in the court to protect the assets of insolvent companies are intended to be exercised widely to enable the proper implementation of insolvency principles[7], and the court should similarly protect the assets of debtors proposing to enter into IVAs under the provisions of IA 1986.

[1]   IA 1986, s 254(1).
[2]   See *Smith (a bankrupt) v Braintree District Council* [1990] 2 AC 215 where the House of Lords held that the equivalent provision in bankruptcy proceedings covered a warrant of committal for non-payment of rates in Magistrates' Court proceedings.
[3]   IA 1986, s 254(1).

4   IA 1986, s 254(1). If an application for a stay is made to a court other than that in which the proceedings are pending, it is necessary to adduce proof that the application for an interim order has been made. The IA 1986 does not specify any form of proof. Ideally this will be by a sealed copy of the application formally produced by affidavit or witness statement.
5   IA 1986, s 254(2).
6   IA 1986, s 254(2).
7   See *Bristol Airport Plc v Powdrill* [1990] Ch 744, [1990] 2 All ER 493, CA.

Applicant for interim order

6.24 An application for an interim order may be made personally by a debtor, or where the debtor is an undischarged bankrupt, by the debtor, the trustee of his estate, or the official receiver[1]. A debtor who wishes to enter into an individual voluntary arrangement with his creditors must formulate a proposal for a composition or scheme of arrangement[2]. The proposal must provide for a qualified practitioner[3] to act in relation to the individual voluntary arrangement either as trustee or otherwise for the purpose of supervising its implementation[4].

1   IA 1986, s 253(3). An application may not be made by a debtor who is an undischarged bankrupt unless he has given notice of the proposal he intends to make to his creditors to the official receiver and any trustee who has been appointed to this estate; IA 1986, s 253(4).
2   IA 1986, s 253. The Rules effectively require the proposal to be in writing as IR 1986, r 5.4(2) provides that the debtor must give his intended nominee written notice of his proposal, this notice 'accompanied by a copy of the proposal' to be delivered to the nominee or to a person authorised to take delivery of documents on his behalf. For what constitutes a composition or scheme of arrangement see paras **6.9–6.10**.
3   The supervisor may be a qualified insolvency practitioner or an authorised practitioner under the provisions of IA 1986, s 389A, see para **6.18**.
4   IA 1986, s 253(2).

6.25 Both the Act and the Rules proceed upon the basis that the debtor himself applies for the interim order and makes the proposal, which he then delivers to the intended nominee who, if he agrees to act, endorses the written notice of the proposal to this effect[1]. In practice the debtor will usually engage an insolvency practitioner to prepare the proposal for him and this will be done before the application is made for an interim order[2]. The practical effect is that the nominee can present both the proposal and his report upon it[3] when applying for the interim order, and the court can make a 'concertina order' under which both an interim order and an order for a meeting of the creditors are made with the effective period of the interim order extended beyond the date of the creditors' meeting. This cuts out one stage of what is envisaged by the Insolvency Act 1986 to be a two-stage procedure. In suitable cases a concertina order may be made without the attendance of any party[4].

1   See IR 1986, r 5.4(3).
2   The argument that an IVA was invalid because the proposal had been prepared by the nominee's solicitors on behalf of the nominee and been signed by the debtor without independent legal advice was rejected in *Tanner v Everitt* [2004] EWHC 1130 (Ch), [2004] BPIR 1026.
3   See paras **6.106–6.107**.
4   *Practice Direction: Insolvency Proceedings*, para 16.1(3), see **Appendix 1**.

6.26 *Individual voluntary arrangements*

Pending bankruptcy petition

6.26 An application for an interim order may not be made while a bankruptcy petition presented by the debtor is pending where the court has decided to appoint an insolvency practitioner to prepare a report on the feasibility of the debtor entering into a voluntary arrangement. In that event the court may, if appropriate, proceed to make an interim order without there being a formal application by the debtor[1].

1   IA 1986, ss 253(5) and 273(2).

Restraint order under Proceeds of Crime Act 2002

6.27 An application for an interim order may not be made where the proposal which the debtor intends to make to his creditors involves realisable property which is the subject of a restraint order under the Proceeds of Crime Act 2002, s 41[1].

1   *Re M* [1992] QB 377 at 382; previously the Drugs Trafficking Offences Act 1986, s 8.

Procedure on application for interim order

6.28 A debtor who is not bankrupt should present an originating application[1] for an interim order to a court in which the debtor would be entitled to present his own petition in bankruptcy[2]. The general rule is that a bankruptcy petition is to be presented to the county court for the insolvency district in which the debtor has resided or carried on business for the longest period during the six months immediately before the presentation of the petition[3]. Should the debtor's place of business be situated in a different insolvency district from his place of residence, it is the place of business which is decisive[4]. If the debtor has carried on business in more than one insolvency district, the correct court is that for the insolvency district in which the debtor's principle place of business is situated or has been for the longest period during the six months immediately before presentation of the petition[5]. The High Court is the insolvency court for the London Insolvency District, and it is to the High Court that petitions should be presented where the debtor is not resident in England or Wales[6]. In the case of an undischarged bankrupt the application should be made to the court having the conduct of the bankruptcy[7].

1   Ie in Form 7.1, see IR 1986, r 7.2(1), Sch 4.
2   IR 1986, r 5.8(1) see IR 1986, r 6.40; the application must contain sufficient information to establish that it is brought in the appropriate court, IR 1986, r 5.8(2).
3   IR 1986, r 6.9(2).
4   IR 1986, r 6.9(3).
5   IR 1986, r 6.9(4).
6   IR 1986, r 6.9(1).
7   IR 1986, r 5.8(3) which provides that the application must be filed with the bankruptcy proceedings.

6.29 The application must be accompanied by an affidavit[1] dealing with the following matters:

(a)   the reasons for making the application;

(b)   particulars of any execution or other legal process which, to the debtor's knowledge, has been commenced against him;

(c)   that he is an undischarged bankrupt or is able to petition for his own bankruptcy, as appropriate;

(d)   that no previous application for an interim order has been made by or in respect of the debtor in the period of 12 months ending with the date of the affidavit; and

(e)   naming the nominee under the proposal, and stating that he is qualified to act as an insolvency practitioner in relation to the debtor and is willing to act[2] in relation to the proposal[3].

[1]   Following the provisions of IA 1986, s 253(3) where the application is made by or in respect of an undischarged bankrupt the affidavit may presumably be sworn by the debtor, the trustee of his estate or the official receiver. Where the debtor has not been adjudicated bankrupt he should swear the affidavit.

[2]   A copy of the notice to the intended nominee under IR 1986, r 5.4, see para **6.68**, endorsed to the effect that he agrees to act, together with a copy of the debtor's proposal given to the nominee under IR 1986, r 5.4, must be exhibited to the affidavit, IR 1986, r 5.7(2). In some courts proof of the nominee's certification is required.

[3]   IR 1986, r 5.7(1).

6.30 On receiving the application and affidavit the court fixes a venue[1] for the hearing[2]. The applicant must give at least two days' notice[3] of the hearing (i) to the nominee who has agreed to act, and (ii) to any creditor who to the debtor's knowledge has presented a bankruptcy petition against him, or, where the application is made by or on behalf of an undischarged bankrupt, to whoever of the bankrupt, his trustee or the official receiver is not the applicant[4]. Any person to whom notice has been given may appear or be represented at the hearing of the application[5].

[1]   Under the Insolvency Rules 'venue' means not only the place but also the time and date for the hearing, IR 1986, r 13.6.

[2]   IR 1986, r 5.7(3).

[3]   The provisions of CPR r 2.8 (time) apply, and accordingly Saturdays, Sundays, Bank Holidays, Christmas Day and Good Friday are excluded from the computation of time where the specified period is five days or less, IR 1986, r 12.9.

[4]   IR 1986, r 5.7(4).

[5]   IR 1986, r 5.9(1).

6.31 In suitable cases the bankruptcy registrar or district judge will make a 14-day interim order with the application adjourned 14 days for consideration of the nominee's report without the attendance of the parties[1]. The papers must be in order and the nominee's signed consent to act must include a waiver of notice of the application or a consent by the nominee to the making of an interim order without attendance[2].

[1]   See *Practice Direction: Insolvency Proceedings*, para 16.1(1), see **Appendix 1**.

[2]   An interim order made without a hearing under the Practice Direction may be combined with a standard order made on consideration of the nominee's report to the court, para **6.25**, a 'concertina' order.

Representations at hearing for interim order

6.32 In deciding whether to make an interim order the court is required to take into account any representations made by or on behalf of any person who is entitled to notice of the hearing[1]. In particular, where the application relates to an undischarged bankrupt the court must consider any representations made as to the exercise of the court's power[2]:

(a)   to make provision in the interim order for the conduct of the bankruptcy and the administration of the estate during the period for which the interim order is in force; and

(b)   to include in such provision a stay of the bankruptcy proceedings or the modification of any provision in the Insolvency Act 1986 or the Insolvency Rules 1986 in their application to the debtor's bankruptcy[3].

[1]   IR 1986, r 5.9(2).
[2]   Under IA 1986, s 255(3)(4).
[3]   IR 1986, r 5.9(2).

6.33 This potentially wide discretion in the court to modify provisions of the Act or the Rules may only be exercised where the court is satisfied that the modification proposed is unlikely to result in any significant diminution in, or in the value of, the debtor's estate for the purposes of the bankruptcy[1].

[1]   IA 1986, s 255(5).

6.34 Where a High Court judge allows an appeal against a refusal by a district judge to make an interim order, the matter can be dealt with by the judge who may make an interim order in the High Court to save incurring further costs on a remission back to the county court[1].

[1]   *Knowles v Coutts & Co* [1998] BPIR 9.

The making of an interim order

6.35 On the hearing of the application the court may make an interim order if it considers that it would be appropriate to do so for the purpose of facilitating consideration and implementation of the debtor's proposals for a voluntary arrangement[1], provided that it is satisfied as to four conditions:

(a)   the debtor intends to make a proposal for an individual voluntary arrangement;

(b)   on the day of the making of the application the debtor was an undischarged bankrupt or was able to petition for his own bankruptcy[2];

(c)   no previous application has been made by the debtor for an interim order during the 12 months preceding the date of the application[3]; and

(d)   the nominee under the debtor's proposal is authorised[4] and is willing to act in relation to the proposal[5].

[1]   IA 1986, s 255(2).

2   The only ground on which a debtor may present his own petition is that he is unable to pay his debts, ie pay his debts as they fall due, *Re Coney (a bankrupt)* [1998] BPIR 333, CA. The requirement that a debtor must be either an undischarged bankrupt or able to present his own petition is clear. It follows that a discharged bankrupt cannot enter into an IVA as a means of paying her creditors in full when it transpires that because of a significant increase in property values the assets in her estate become worth rather more than was at first thought to be the case, see *Wright v Official Receiver* [2001] BPIR 196, a decision of the Medway County Court district judge. It is surprising that an interim order was ever made in this case, but it does perhaps demonstrate that interim orders are readily obtained. A discharged bankrupt will be able to propose an IVA only in respect of (a) debts which are not released on his discharge, as to which see IR 1986, r 12.3(2)(2A), or (b) post-bankruptcy debts.

3   The fact that a proposal was not properly formulated and there was no nominee (the insolvency practitioner having refused to act further) did not prevent it being an application for an interim order on which the court made a decision to dismiss. Accordingly when an application was made a month later with a different proposal and a new nominee it failed under the 12-month rule, *Hurst v Bennett (No 2)* [2001] EWCA Civ 1398, [2002] BPIR 102.

4   See paras **6.18–6.20.**

5   IA 1986, s 255(1).

6.36 Conditions (a) and (d) reflect the procedure envisaged when the voluntary arrangement scheme was originally enacted, namely that the debtor would himself apply for the interim order before the nominee is involved in the detailed preparation of the proposal. In practice the nominee is almost invariably the effective applicant for the interim order and will be able to put a detailed proposal before the court even though it may not yet be finalised.

6.37 Condition (b) enables an undischarged bankrupt to obtain an interim order with a view to making a voluntary arrangement with his creditors and so secure an annulment of the bankruptcy order. The undischarged bankrupt will face this difficulty. He may only make a voluntary arrangement with his 'creditors', and by operation of IA 1986, s 281 his discharge from bankruptcy releases him from his bankruptcy debts. In other words his creditors cease to be creditors. The undischarged bankrupt has therefore to act swiftly, for even if he obtains his interim order before discharge, when he obtains his discharge he will not be able to enter into a valid IVA with his (former) bankruptcy creditors[1]. He will then be precluded from obtaining an annulment. Since 1 April 2004[2] a bankrupt obtains an automatic discharge after one year from the commencement of the bankruptcy[3], so his discharge will soon be upon him. An application to suspend discharge may only be made by the official receiver or the trustee in bankruptcy and then the court may suspend discharge only if satisfied that the bankrupt has failed or is failing to comply with an obligation in his bankruptcy. Subject therefore to some arranged failure with the connivance of the official receiver or trustee, of which the court is hardly likely to approve, the bankrupt is unable to extend the period at the end of which he is discharged. Neither may the bankrupt obtain an annulment in anticipation of his creditors approving an IVA[4]. Discharge from bankruptcy debts will not of course prevent the former bankrupt entering into an IVA in respect of pre-bankruptcy debts from which he is not released by IA 1986, s 281.

6.37 *Individual voluntary arrangements*

1   See eg *Re Ravichandran* [2004] BPIR 814, *Wright v Official Receiver* [2001] BPIR 196, *Shah v Cooper* [2003] BPIR 1018, and *Demarco v Perkins* [2006] EWCA Civ 188, [2006] BPIR 645, a professional negligence action where the court found that the insolvency practitioner was in breach of duty in not warning his client that he needed to ensure that the creditors' meeting took place before automatic discharge (these decisions all pre-date the shortening of the period of automatic discharge from three years to 12 months). Provided the voluntary arrangement is approved before discharge it does not matter that the application to annul is made after discharge, *Re Johnson* [2006] BPIR 987.

2   Ie the date from which IA 1986, s 279(1) was amended by EA 2002, s 256(1).

3   The period may be even shorter where the official receiver files a notice stating that investigation of the conduct and affairs of the bankrupt is unnecessary or concluded, IA 1986, s 279(2).

4   IA 1986, s 282(1) provides that a court may annul a bankruptcy order if the bankruptcy debts and expenses 'have all ... been either paid or secured for'. Once an application for an annulment has been made the court may make an interim order staying any proceedings which it thinks it ought (IR 1986, r 6.208) but the period at the end of which the bankrupt obtains his discharge is not 'proceedings' for this purpose.

6.38 Condition (c) above prevents excessive resort to the voluntary arrangement procedure. It is a condition that has been strictly enforced by the court. In *Hurst v Bennett (No 2)*[1] the debtor, facing a bankruptcy petition, made an application for an interim order on 15 March. A bankruptcy order was made on the petition on 12 April, against which the debtor applied for a review on 11 May. The registrar refused both a review and to grant an interim order on 11 July, and on 30 July the appeal against the registrar's refusal was dismissed by the judge inter alia on the grounds that the registrar had no jurisdiction to hear what was in effect a fresh application for an interim order within 12 months of the application of 15 March. The Court of Appeal dismissed the debtor's application for permission to appeal on the basis that the judge was correct to treat the application for a review as a further application for an interim order prohibited by IA 1986, s 255(1)(c)[2].

1   [2001] EWCA Civ 1398, [2002] BPIR 102.

2   See the summary of this litigation in *Hurst v Kroll Buchler Phillips Ltd* [2003] BPIR 872.

Appropriate to make an order

6.39 The court 'may' make an order 'if it thinks it would be appropriate to do so for the purpose of facilitating the consideration and implementation of the debtor's proposal'[1]. There is no statutory guidance as to when it will be 'appropriate' for the court to make an interim order. As envisaged by the IA 1986 the debtor is at this stage of the procedure asking for an interim order preparatory to the nominee considering its details and reporting back to the court[2]. It is likely to be very difficult for the court to reach any firm conclusion as to the bona fides of the proposal or the practicability of the proposal's terms. In practice however most proposals will have been prepared by or with the assistance of the nominee and this will usually give the court confidence to grant an interim order to allow the proposal to proceed.

1   IA 1986, s 255(2).

2   See paras **6.106–6.107**.

6.40 The statutory wording, quoted above, gives the court a full discretion to decide whether, in all the circumstances of the case, it should make or decline to make an interim order[1]. The court should be satisfied that the proposal is one which can be described as 'serious and viable'[2] being careful not to allow applications for interim orders simply to become a means of postponing the making of a bankruptcy order in circumstances where there is no apparent likelihood of benefit to the creditors from such postponement[3]. The court will also be conscious that one of the reasons for it having a discretion as to the making of an interim order is to act as a filter to avoid the unnecessary and wasteful convening of creditors' meetings where the proposal is not serious and viable. The consideration of a proposal by creditors involves time, effort and expense, and the court should not expose creditors to the cost and expense of a meeting which has no real prospect of being productive[4]. Nevertheless in considering whether the proposal is serious and viable the court should keep in mind that it is for the creditors to decide whether the proposal produces a sufficient level of return to make it acceptable. The court should ordinarily leave it to the creditors where it is purely a question of quantum[5], or where the paramount question for the creditors is one of delay in payment[6]. It is important to note that the creditors may propose a modification of the voluntary arrangement terms before agreeing to approve them, and accordingly any view taken by the court that the terms will be unacceptable may be premature. The court should also keep in mind that any creditors who wish to avoid the cost and expense of attending the meeting may always vote by proxy. Nonetheless the court will act in clear cases, and refused to make an interim order on an opposed application where it appeared that the debtor's assessment of the value of proposed inventions not yet patented and the likely fruits of litigation not yet commenced which were to fund the proposed voluntary arrangement could not possibly be sustained[7].

1   See *Hook v Jewson Ltd* [1997] BPIR 100 at 104–105 where Scott V-C rejected the suggestion that the court had only a limited discretion to refuse an application for an interim order. See also *Greystoke v Hamilton-Smith, Re a Debtor (No 140 IO of 1995)* [1996] 2 BCLC 429, and *Hurst v Kroll Buchler Phillips Ltd* [2003] BPIR 872 at [58].
2   *Cooper v Fearnley, Re a Debtor (No 103 of 1994)* [1997] BPIR 20, 21. When the nominee reports to the court as to the holding of a creditors' meeting he must now express an opinion whether or not the proposals have a reasonable prospect of being approved and implemented, IA 1986, s 256(1)(a) as amended by IA 2000, see para **6.80**.
3   *Hook v Jewson Ltd* [1997] 1 BCLC 664, 669, [1997] BPIR 100.
4   *Fletcher v Vooght* [2000] BPIR 435; *Davidson v Stanley* [2005] BPIR 279 at [42].
5   *Knowles v Coutts & Co* [1998] BPIR 96, at 99: while a small return to the creditors from the proposed arrangement is a factor the court may take into consideration it is not by itself a proper reason for refusing to make an interim order; that is matter for the creditors to consider.
6   In *Re O'Sullivan* [2001] BPIR 534 the court suggested that a postponement of dividend by 18 months would be insufficient to justify a refusal of an interim order. Cf *Hook v Jewson* [1997] BPIR 100 where an important factor in the court's refusal of an interim order was the fact that payment to the creditors would be postponed by some four years.
7   *Davidson v Stanley* [2005] BPIR 279.

Matters relevant to the exercise of discretion

6.41 The court should ordinarily look to matters other than the quantum of the return to creditors and the length of any period of postponement when considering whether or not the proposal is serious and viable, quantum and postponement being essentially matters for the creditors. Plainly however there may be cases where the quantum is so low, or postponement so long, that these become important factors for the court. If the court concludes that there is no reasonable prospect of the proposal being complied with were it to be approved an interim order should be refused[1]. In considering the viability of the proposal the court is entitled to take into account the debtor's previous conduct and litigation history. Where the debtor showed a propensity for relentless and misconceived litigation and the court concluded that an individual voluntary arrangement was unlikely to proceed in good faith or lead to finality between the debtor and his creditors an interim order could properly be refused[2]. The court may also take into account the size of the nominee's fee and, in exceptional cases, the remuneration which it is proposed should be paid to the supervisor if the proposal is approved. The level of remuneration might affect the validity of the proposal; it will (almost invariably) take priority over distributions to creditors and will thus both reduce the amount of any dividend and postpone the time of payment. Whether or not the level of remuneration may affect the viability of the proposal the court may refuse an interim order on the ground that the remuneration in itself is excessive, particularly in respect of payments to the nominee over which there can be no direct control by the creditors[3]. However, the court should only intervene by refusing to allow the proposal to proceed in a plain case of overcharging, and only after affording the nominee the opportunity to justify his proposed remuneration[4]. It is understandable that the court should adopt this approach, and there will be many instances of individual debtors requiring a measure of protection from insolvency practitioners on the question of fees. On this basis it may be justifiable that a different practice develops in IVA than in CVA where the court has no real opportunity to intervene as it does in IVA on the application for an interim order.

[1] *Greystoke v Hamilton-Smith, Re a Debtor (No 140 IO of 1995)* [1996] 2 BCLC 429 where the court refers to a 'realistic' prospect of acceptance. The amendments to IA 1986, s 256(1)(a) introduced by IA 2000 now require 'reasonable' prospect of acceptance and implementation: there should be no difference in practice.

[2] *Hurst v Kroll Buchler Phillips Ltd* [2002] EWHC 2885, [2003] BPIR 872.

[3] *Re O'Sullivan* [2001] BPIR 534, 538 where the court rejected the argument that the amount of the remuneration to be paid to the nominee or supervisor was a matter for the debtor and creditors alone and beyond the scope of any proper intervention by the court in the exercise of its discretion whether to make an interim order.

[4] *Re O'Sullivan* [2001] BPIR 534. The district judge had taken the view that for a relatively simple IVA the nominee's fee of £2,500 was excessive; he was not prepared to allow more than £1,000. The High Court judge deferred to his experience.

6.42 Where the debtor is an undischarged bankrupt the court may include provisions in the interim order regulating the conduct of the bankruptcy and the administration of the estate while the order is in force[1]. Such provisions may stay proceedings in the bankruptcy or modify any provision in the IA 1986 or the IR 1986 relating to the bankruptcy[2] provided that the court is satisfied that no significant diminution in, or in the value of, the debtor's estate will result[3].

[1] IA 1986, s 255(3).

[2] Ie any provision in the 'second group of parts', IA 1986, ss 252–385.

[3] IA 1986, s 255(4)(5).

Procedure where interim order made

6.43 Where an interim order is made the court must send at least two sealed copies of the order to the applicant who must then (i) serve one of the copies on the nominee under the proposal[1], and (ii) give notice forthwith of the making of the order to any person who was given notice of the hearing[2] but was not present or represented at it[3].

1   IR 1986, r 5.10(1), for the form of interim order see IR 1986, Sch 4, Form 5.2.
2   Under IR 1986, r 5.7(4), see para **6.30**.
3   IR 1986, r 5.10(2).

6.44 On making an interim order the court must fix a time and place for consideration of the nominee's report[1], unless the report has been filed on the making or hearing of the application for an interim order[2]. The consideration of the nominee's report must take place within the 14-day life of the interim order[3], though where the nominee is granted an extension of time for filing his report[4] the court should order a corresponding extension to the period for which the interim order has effect unless there appears to be good reasons against doing so[5]. An interim order may not be made retrospectively so as to validate an otherwise invalid voluntary arrangement[6].

1   IR 1986, r 5.9(3).
2   See paras **6.28–6.31**.
3   See IA 1986, s 255(6) and para **6.50**.
4   Under IA 1986, s 256(4) and see para **6.50**.
5   IR 1986, r 5.9(4); the court may direct that the interim order should continue for such further period as it may specify where the debtor applies for the replacement of the nominee on the ground that he has failed to submit his report, see IA 1986, s 256(3).
6   *Fletcher v Vooght* [2000] BPIR 435.

6.45 Within the period during which the interim order is valid the nominee must submit a report to the court stating whether, in his opinion, a meeting of the debtor's creditors should be summoned to consider the debtor's proposal, and if so the date, time and place where the meeting should take place[1].

1   IA 1986, s 256(1). The court must fix a date for the consideration of the nominee's report when making the interim order: IR 1986, r 5.9(3). The nominee's report must be delivered to the court not less than two days before the interim order ceases to have effect, IR 1986, r 5.11(1).

Effect of interim order

6.46 The interim order has the effect of preventing a bankruptcy petition being presented or proceeded with against the debtor[1], neither may any other proceedings or execution or other legal process[2] be commenced or continued against the person or property of the debtor without the leave of the court[3]. This means that secured creditors require the leave of the court to commence or continue proceedings to enforce their security. For example, a bank would need leave before seeking an order for possession and sale of property charged as security for a debt. In the normal course of events a secured creditor will be granted the leave he requires, but he should not neglect to obtain it before enforcing his security. Retrospective leave can be given, even after the expiry of the limitation period[4]. However, leave is mandatory and if not obtained, and in the absence of an application for retrospective leave, the security will be set aside[5]. Any court may give leave, not just the court making the interim order[6].

1 IA 1986, s 252(2)(a).
2 Which will include the bankruptcy administration itself where the applicant for an interim order is a bankrupt.
3 IA 1986, s 252(2)(b).
4 *Re Saunders (a bankrupt)* [1997] Ch 60, [1997] 3 All ER 992 approved by implication in *Coutts & Co v Clarke* [2002] EWCA Civ 943, [2002] BPIR 916 see paras 44, 45.
5 *Coutts & Co v Clarke* [2002] EWCA Civ 943, [2002] BPIR 916; a charging order nisi is not a completed execution and therefore leave is required to make the order absolute if the debtor chargor obtains an interim order after charging order nisi.
6 *Coutts & Co v Clarke* [2002] EWCA Civ 943, [2002] BPIR 916 see para 50.

6.47 'Execution or other legal process' means a process of a judicial, adjudicative or quasi-judicative nature[1]. As a result both the levying of distress[2] and peaceable re-entry under the forfeiture clause of a lease[3] were permitted despite an interim order. These decisions were reversed by the IA 2000, and now a landlord requires the leave of the court before he can either levy distress or exercise a right of re-entry[4].

1 See *Smith (a bankrupt) v Braintree District Council* [1990] 2 AC 214, [1989] 3 All ER 897, HL; *Re Paramount Airways Ltd, Bristol Airport plc v Powdrill* [1990] Ch 744; *Exchange Travel Agency Ltd v Triton Property Trust plc* [1991] BCLC 396, [1991] BCC 341; *Re Olympia & York Canary Wharf Ltd* [1993] BCLC 453, [1993] BCC 154.
2 *McMullen & Sons Ltd v Cerrone* [1994] BCLC 152, [1994] BCC 25; where however the court noted that distress was precluded without leave of the court in company administration, IA 1986, s 11(3).
3 *Re Debtors (Nos 13A IO and 14A IO of 1994)* [1996] BCC 57, [1996] BPIR 43, but see *Re Naeem* [1990] 1 WLR 48, at p 50E.
4 IA 1986, s IA 1986, s 252(2)(aa) (peaceable re-entry), s 252(2)(b) (distress), as amended by IA 2000, Sch 3, para 2.

6.48 Any court in which proceedings are pending against an individual may, on proof that an application has been made for an interim order in respect of that individual, either stay the proceedings or allow them to continue on such terms as it thinks fit[1]. The interim order has a short initial life. It ceases to have effect at the end of 14 days beginning with the day after the order is made[2]. The period for which the interim order has effect may, however, be extended by the court on the application of the nominee[3] in order to give the nominee more time to prepare his report to the court[4].

1 IA 1986, s 254(2).
2 IA 1986, s 255(6) where the interim order is made after the presentation of a debtor's petition for bankruptcy the court has power to determine the length of its validity, IA 1986, s 274(4).
3 See para **6.50**.
4 IA 1986, s 256(4): for the nominee's report to the court see paras **6.106–6.107**.

6.49 A secured creditor will not need leave to appoint a receiver under a charge or a statutory power because such an appointment does not involve any court process. An interim order does not preclude the appointment of a receiver by the court under the Proceeds of Crime Act 2002, s 41(7)[1], nor does it prevent the enforcement either of a fine for a criminal offence or a criminal compensation order[2].

1   *Re M* [1992] QB 377, [1992] 1 All ER 537. The Proceeds of Crime Act 2002 replaces the Drugs Trafficking Offences Act 1986 which was in force in 1992.
2   *R v Barnet Justices, ex p Phillippou* [1997] BPIR 134.

Duration of interim order

6.50 Unless extended an interim order ceases to have effect at the end of a period of 14 days beginning with the day after it is made[1]. Should the nominee fail to submit a report to the court[2] the debtor may apply to the court for a direction that the interim order shall continue, or if it has ceased to have effect shall be renewed, for such period as the court may specify in the direction[3]. On the application of the nominee, the court may extend the period for which the interim order has effect so as to enable the nominee to have more time to prepare his report[4].

1   IA 1986, s 255(6).
2   IA 1986, s 256(3), as to the obligation of the nominee to submit a report see paras 6.106–6.107.
3   IA 1986, s 256(3).
4   IA 1986, s 256(4).

6.51 If satisfied on receiving the nominee's report that a meeting of the debtor's creditors should be summoned to consider the debtor's proposal, the court should then extend the period for which the interim order has effect for such further period as is necessary for the purpose of enabling the debtor's proposal to be considered by his creditors[1].

1   IA 1986, s 256(5); the court extends the interim order by direction.

6.52 In practice interim orders are often extended to enable the nominee either to obtain further instructions or to discuss amendments to the proposal with major creditors. 14 days is a short time in which to consider the debtor's proposals and formulate an effective proposal for a voluntary arrangement. Additionally interim orders are extended because it does not prove possible to hold the creditors' meeting on the date anticipated, not least because the proposal has to be amended by the nominee in the light of further information received from the debtor or creditors. A further difficulty which is not infrequently encountered is that major creditors will be represented at the creditors' meeting by junior staff who do not have the authority to vote on any significant amendment to the proposal which may be raised during the course of the meeting. When considering applications to extend the interim order the court should consider whether there remains a sufficient likelihood that arrangements will be approved by the creditors to justify the continuance of an order which restricts creditors' legal rights and remedies against the debtor. Where there is evidence that the meeting will not approve the proposal, and in particular where creditors holding 25% in value of the debtor's debts adamantly oppose it, the court should not continue the interim order even if directions have been given for the holding of a creditors' meeting which has not yet taken place[1].

1   *Re Cove (a debtor)* [1990] 1 All ER 949.

6.53 An interim order which is in force immediately before the end of the period of 28 days beginning with the day on which the decision of the creditors' meeting was reported to the court[1] ceases to have effect at the end of that period[2], unless the court continues or renews the order in the course of an application to challenge the decision of the creditors' meeting[3]. Where the creditors' meeting has declined to approve the debtor's proposal the court may discharge any interim order then in force[4].

1   See paras **6.183–6.185**.
2   IA 1986, s 260(4).
3   Under IA 1986, s 262, see IA 1986, s 260(4).
4   IA 1986, s 259(2).

6.54 The court may discharge an interim order if it is satisfied, on the application of the nominee, that the debtor has failed to comply with his obligation[1] to submit to the nominee a proposal and statement of affairs or that for any other reason it would be inappropriate for a meeting of the debtor's creditors to be summoned to consider the debtor's proposal[2].

1   Under IA 1986, s 256(2).
2   IA 1986, s 256(6).

Proceeding without interim order

6.55 A debtor, whether or not he is an undischarged bankrupt, may propose a voluntary arrangement without an interim order first being in place[1]. This is plainly appropriate where a proposal is being made by an undischarged bankrupt. A debtor who is an undischarged bankrupt must first give notice of his proposal to the official receiver and his trustee, if one has been appointed, before he may proceed[2]. Before bankruptcy an interim order will not be necessary where the debtor has only a few creditors who are prepared to stay their hands pending a proposal for a voluntary arrangement. Proceeding without the protection afforded by an interim order may also be useful in the rare case where a debtor who has a voluntary arrangement in place wishes to amend the terms of the arrangement and has no procedure available to him to do so within the terms of the arrangement[3].

1   IA 1986, s 256A(1), a provision introduced by the IA 2000.
2   IA 1986, s 256A(1)(b); notice has to be given of the proposal not merely the intention to propose.
3   As an interim order may not be made within 12 months of a previous application for an interim order (IA 1986, s 255(1)(c)) it was not previously possible for a new voluntary arrangement to vary an existing arrangement to be made in the first 12 months of that arrangement.

6.56 The statutory scheme[1] envisages the debtor providing the nominee with a document setting out the terms of his proposed voluntary arrangement together with a statement of affairs containing the prescribed information[2]. Provided the nominee is satisfied that the debtor is either an undischarged bankrupt or is able to petition for his own bankruptcy, he has 14 days after receiving the debtor's documentation to submit a report to the court stating his opinion whether the proposed arrangement has a reasonable prospect of being approved and implemented, whether a meeting of creditors should be summoned, and the date, time and place of the creditors' meeting if this is being proposed[3]. The court is not to consider the report unless an application is made under the IA 1986 or the IR 1986 in respect of the debtor's proposal[4]. It is therefore accepted by the IR 1986 that no useful purpose is served by the court considering the nominee's report as a matter of course; the court is to assume that all is well unless and until an application is made by a creditor or a debtor in respect of any aspect of the procedure or the proposal itself. With his report the nominee must deliver to the court:

(a)   a copy of the debtor's proposal (with any amendments authorised by the nominee[5]);

(b)   a copy or summary of any statement of affairs provided by the debtor; and

(c)   a copy of the nominee's consent to act[6].

[1]   IA 1986, s 256A(2).
[2]   See paras **6.69–6.82**.
[3]   IA 1986, s 256A(3); the court may allow a longer period than 14 days for the nominee to submit his report on the nominee's own application, IA 1986, s 256A(5) and also IR 1986, r 5.14(1).
[4]   IR 1986, r 5.14(1).
[5]   IR 1986, r 5.3(3) permits amendments at any time up to the delivery of the nominee's report to the court with the written consent of the nominee.
[6]   IR 1986, r 5.14(2); with these documents must be served two copies of Form 5.5 listing the various documents delivered by the nominee together with a statement that no interim order is to be made. On receipt of the report and Form 5.5 the court is to endorse one copy with the date of filing in court and return it to the nominee, IR 1986, r 5.14(4).

6.57 If the nominee expresses the opinion that the debtor's proposal has a reasonable prospect of being approved and implemented, and that a meeting of the debtor's creditors should be summoned, his report must annex his comments on the proposal[1]. If his opinion is against the proposal proceeding he must give reasons[2]. These documents must also be sent to the official receiver and any trustee in cases where the debtor is an undischarged bankrupt[3], and where he is not a bankrupt the documents must be sent to any person who has presented a bankruptcy petition[4]. Where the debtor is an undischarged bankrupt the nominee's report must be filed in the court having the conduct of the bankruptcy proceedings and must be filed with those proceedings[5]. In all other cases the nominee files his report in the court in which the debtor would be entitled to present his own bankruptcy petition[6]. Any creditor of the debtor is entitled to inspect the file, at all reasonable times on any business day[7].

[1]   IR 1986, r 5.14(3).
[2]   IR 1986, r 5.14(3).
[3]   IR 1986, r 5.14(6).
[4]   IR 1986, r 5.14(7).
[5]   IR 1986, r 5.15(3).

6 Under IR 1986, r 6.40, IR 1986, r 5.15(1), see para **6.28**. The report must contain
   sufficient information to establish that it is filed in the appropriate court, IR 1986,
   r 5.15(2).
7 IR 1986, r 5.14(5); express provision is made by IR 1986, r 5.14(8) that the service of the
   report under IA 1986, s 256A constitutes an insolvency proceeding for the purpose of the
   rules requiring the court to keep records of insolvency proceedings (IR 1986, r 7.27) with
   a file opened and maintained for each case in which all documents relating to the relevant
   proceedings are to be placed, IR 1986, r 7.30.

Applications to the court where no interim order

6.58 Any application in relation to any matter relating to a voluntary
arrangement or a proposal for a voluntary arrangement where there is no
interim order is to be made to the court in which the nominee's report was
filed[1].

1 IR 1986, r 5.16(1); as to this court see para **6.28**.

Replacement of nominee

6.59 The court may replace the nominee with another practitioner authorised
to act in relation to a voluntary arrangement either on the application of the
debtor where the nominee has failed to submit his report or has died, or on
the application of the nominee or the debtor where it is impracticable or
inappropriate for the nominee to continue acting on behalf of the debtor[1]. A
debtor who wishes to apply for the nominee to be replaced must give at least
seven days' notice of his application to the nominee[2]. A nominee must also
give seven days' notice of any application he wishes to make to be replaced by
the court[3]. Before any order is made replacing a nominee there must be filed in
court a statement from the replacement indicating his consent to act as
nominee[4].

1 IA 1986, s 256A(4).
2 IR 1986, r 5.16(2).
3 IR 1986, r 5.16(3).
4 IR 1986, r 5.16(4).

C THE PROPOSAL

Proposal for IVA by debtor

6.60 To make a proposal for an individual voluntary arrangement a debtor
must be either an undischarged bankrupt, or be able to petition for his own
bankruptcy. As originally enacted the IA 1986 permitted an IVA only after an
interim order had been made, providing that an interim order may be applied
for only by an undischarged bankrupt or a debtor who 'on the day of the
making of the application [for an interim order] was able to petition for his
own bankruptcy'[1]. As amended by IA 2000 it is now possible for a debtor to
make a proposal for an IVA without an interim order first being made[2]. In
such cases the debtor simply instructs a practitioner prepared to act as

nominee[3], and the nominee submits a report to the court if he is 'of the opinion that the debtor is an undischarged bankrupt or is able to petition for his own bankruptcy'[4].

1   IA 1986, s 255(1)(b).
2   IA 1986, s 256A (introduced by IA 2000, Sch 3, para 7) as from 1 January 2003.
3   See para **6.18**.
4   IA 1986, s 256A(3).

6.61 A debtor may present a petition for his own bankruptcy only on the ground that he is unable to pay his debts[1]. An inability to pay debts is determined on a liquidity basis, that is whether the debtor is able to pay his debts as they fall due, irrespective of whether he is insolvent on a balance sheet basis, namely a comparison of his assets and his liabilities[2].

1   IA 1986, s 272.
2   *Re Coney (a bankrupt)* [1998] BPIR 333, CA.

6.62 An undischarged bankrupt who makes a proposal for an IVA should be conscious of the fact that his ability to make a binding arrangement with his bankruptcy creditors will cease when he obtains his discharge. He is then released from his bankruptcy debts and no longer has any pre-bankruptcy creditors save for those restricted classes of creditors whose debts are not released on discharge[1]. The undischarged bankrupt will have to move quickly to prepare his voluntary arrangement now that he is automatically discharged after one year from the commencement of the bankruptcy[2].

1   See IA 1986, s 281.
2   Ie the date on which the bankruptcy order is made, IA 1986, s 278(a).

Proposal by undischarged bankrupt

6.63 A trustee in bankruptcy may not make a proposal for an IVA[1]; that is a matter for the individual debtor himself. Should an undischarged bankrupt wish to propose an IVA he himself, his trustee in bankruptcy or the official receiver may make an application for an interim order[2], should it be thought advisable to obtain such an order[3]. An interim order may be required when the bankrupt has incurred post-bankruptcy debts and the post-bankruptcy creditors are threatening proceedings.

1   This is in contrast to the position in CVA or PVA.
2   IA 1986, s 253(3).
3   Note that since the implementation of the amendments introduced by IA 2000 it is not essential to obtain an interim order before proceeding with a proposal for an IVA, see IA 1986, s 256A.

6.64 Notice of the application must be given to whichever of the three (debtor, official receiver, trustee in bankruptcy) is not the applicant for the interim order[1], and the court hearing the application may include in any interim order directions as to the conduct of the bankruptcy or the administration of the estate while the order remains in force[2]. The undischarged bankrupt makes his proposal as would any other debtor[3], although he need not prepare a statement of affairs if he has already delivered one in the bankruptcy unless expressly required to do so by the nominee for the purpose of supplementing or amplifying the existing statement[4]. If there has been post-bankruptcy trading a further statement of affairs is likely to be necessary. There is no need for the bankrupt's nominee to be the trustee in bankruptcy; there may indeed be a dispute between the bankrupt, supported by his nominee, and the trustee in bankruptcy as to the appropriateness of a proposal going forward to the creditors. It will be important for an undischarged bankrupt that his proposal includes creditors whose debts have arisen since the date of the bankruptcy order. This is achieved through IA 1986, s 257(3) which provides that the creditors of an undischarged bankrupt to be summoned to the creditors' meeting include both the bankruptcy debt creditors and 'every person who would be such a creditor if the bankruptcy had commenced on the day on which notice of the meeting is given'.

[1]   IR 1986, r 5.5(4)(a).
[2]   IA 1986, s 255(3).
[3]   See paras **6.69–6.73**.
[4]   IR 1986, r 5.8(1).

No proposal after discharge

6.65   Once a bankrupt debtor has been discharged it is no longer possible for the debtor to seek an IVA in respect of his bankruptcy debts[1]; he may of course propose for an IVA in respect of debts arising after the commencement of his bankruptcy or indeed for debts which are not provable in the bankruptcy and from which the debtor is not released on his discharge[2]. It may seem surprising that any debtor should wish to propose for an IVA in respect of debts from which he has been discharged by his bankruptcy. However, the recovery of the housing market from its low point in the early 1990s gave rise to a number of problematic cases where trustees who had long since finished actively administering the estate but had not held final meetings or sought their release discovered that matrimonial homes which had negative equity at the date of the bankruptcy had risen in value far faster than the loans to which they had been charged. Whatever routes may be available to the discharged bankrupt debtor in such circumstances, an IVA is not one of them[3].

[1]   Under the IA 1986 as originally enacted an IVA could only be sought after obtaining an interim order, and such an order could only be obtained by an undischarged bankrupt or a debtor who was able to petition for his own bankruptcy. The only ground on which a debtor may petition for his own bankruptcy is that he is unable to pay his debts. Once debts have been discharged under IA 1986, s 281 they are no longer debts. Under the IA 1986 as amended by IA 2000 it is no longer necessary to obtain an interim order. However, an IVA cannot proceed without the nominee first reporting to the court, and by IA 1986, s 256A(3) the nominee may only report to the court if he is of the opinion that the debtor is an undischarged bankrupt or is able to petition for his own bankruptcy. An IVA may be sought where there are debts accruing after the bankruptcy, but the original (bankruptcy) 'creditors' cannot become parties to the IVA under the provisions of IA 1986, s 260(2); they are no longer creditors.
[2]   See IA 1986, s 281 and IR 1986, r 12.3(2) which specifies the debts not provable in a bankruptcy.
[3]   For an example in the law reports see *Wright v Official Receiver* [2001] BPIR 196.

6.66 It is the case that significant numbers of debtors made bankrupt in the early 1990s discovered years later, long after their discharge, the harsh reality of the law which automatically transfers the bankrupt's property to the trustee and leaves it with him even if he takes no steps to realise it. Long after the bankrupt and the creditors thought it was all over the trustee discovered that the bankrupt's home had increased in value faster than the mortgage debt. The trustee was then in a position to realise the asset. Provisions designed to prevent this happening in the future were introduced by EA 2002[1], and from 1 May 2004, any interest in the bankrupt's sole or principal residence automatically re-vests in the bankrupt after three years from the date of the bankruptcy if the trustee has not within that period applied for an order to realise the asset for the estate. Further, an additional new provision[2] protects a 'low value home', that is an interest of the bankrupt in his sole or principal residence the value of which is less than a prescribed amount[3]. Any application to realise a low value home must be dismissed by the court.

---

[1] EA 2002, s 261, adding IA 1986, s 283A.
[2] IA 1986, s 313A.
[3] The prescribed amount is currently £1,000, see Insolvency Proceedings (Monetary Limits) (Amendment) Order 2004, SI 2004/547.

The preparation of the proposal

6.67 The scheme envisaged by the IA 1986 and IR 1986 is that the debtor prepares 'a document setting out the terms of the proposed voluntary arrangement'[1] or 'proposal'[2] which is passed to the intended nominee and on which the nominee then makes his report to the court[3]. This proposal may be amended at any time up to the delivery of the nominee's report to the court, with the agreement in writing of the nominee[4]. The detail required for the proposal demands both time and legal knowledge, and thus in practice the proposal will almost invariably be prepared by the insolvency practitioner who it is intended should act as nominee[5]. In *Tanner v Everitt*[6] the debtors argued that because their proposals had in fact been drafted by solicitors acting for the nominee and had been signed by them without their receiving independent legal advice, there was a failure to comply with the rules which made their voluntary arrangements invalid. This argument was rejected. The court stated that provided a debtor was content to sign the proposal, make it his own, and place it before the nominee (ie submit it for the purpose of the rules) then there is due compliance with the IR 1986 whoever in fact drafted the proposal.

---

[1] The wording of IA 1986, s 256(2) (IVA with interim order), s 256A(2) (IVA without interim order).
[2] The wording of IR 1986, r 5.2.
[3] For the duty to report to the court under IA 1986, s 256(1) (IVA with interim order), s 256A(2) (IVA without interim order) see para **6.106**.
[4] IR 1986, r 5.3(3).
[5] If the Secretary of State ever implements the IA 2000 amendment which permits members of business rescue bodies to act as nominees and supervisors it will be interesting to see how this aspect of their work will be managed.
[6] [2004] EWHC 1130 (Ch), [2004] BPIR 1026.

Notice to nominee

6.68 The formal requirement of the IR 1986 is that written notice of the proposal must be given to the intended nominee by delivery of such notice, together with a copy of the proposal, either to the nominee himself or his authorised agent for the purpose[1]. If the intended nominee agrees to act he must endorse a copy of the notice to the effect that it has been received by him on a specified date, and return a copy of the endorsed notice to the debtor at the address specified in the notice for that purpose[2]. In practice the nominee will have helped prepare the proposal, and will be ready to report to the court. Where the debtor is an undischarged bankrupt, the notice he is required to give the official receiver and any trustee of his estate[3] must contain the name and address of the insolvency practitioner who has agreed to act as his nominee[4].

[1] IR 1986, r 5.4(1)(2).
[2] IR 1986, r 5.4(3)(4).
[3] Under IA 1986, s 253(4).
[4] IR 1986, r 5.4(5).

The contents of the proposal

6.69 The proposal must:

(a) provide a short explanation why in the debtor's opinion, a voluntary arrangement is desirable, and give reasons why the creditors may be expected to concur with such an arrangement[1];

(b) state, or deal with, the various matters specified in the Rules. There are 17 heads of matters to be dealt with[2].

[1] IR 1986, r 5.3(1).
[2] IR 1986, r 5.3(2).

6.70 The desirability of the arrangement will often be indicated by a comparison of the dividends to be received under the arrangement with the dividends which might be anticipated in liquidation or bankruptcy[1]. An effective voluntary arrangement will usually require a wider range of matters to be covered than the 17 heads of matters which must be dealt with in order to comply with the Rules. In practice the terms which relate specifically to the particular arrangement are usually prepared with some care. As for the remaining terms there are a number of standard forms of voluntary arrangement in general circulation.

[1] Ideally this comparison will be shown in schedule form with all appropriate calculations.

6.71 First and foremost the proposal must identify the debtor's assets and liabilities specifying the extent to which assets have been charged. An estimate of the value of each asset must be given, and if any particular asset is to be excluded from the voluntary arrangement that fact must be specifically stated. The nature and amount of the debtor's liabilities must be stated together with an explanation as to how it is proposed that these liabilities will be dealt with under the arrangement. The proposal must identify any preferential creditors[1] or associates[2] and state how their debts are to be dealt with. It must state whether to the debtor's knowledge there are circumstances giving rise to the possibility of claims to set aside transactions as being at an undervalue, or preferences or extortionate credit transactions[3], and whether and if so how it is proposed to indemnify the debtor's estate, either wholly or in part, in respect of such claims. These provisions are aimed at ensuring that creditors are informed as to their position should the debtor become bankrupt, or, in the case of a proposal by an undischarged bankrupt, should the bankruptcy continue[4]. Insofar as the creditors may be looking to provision being made to maximise the assets available to them under the arrangement, the difficulty arises that the jurisdiction of the court to set aside transactions at an undervalue or preferences only arises in formal insolvency[5]. The debtor, with the assistance of the nominee, may be prepared to assess the prospects of a successful application to the court to set aside such transactions in the event of formal insolvency. It has to be recognised however that in many instances this will be, or may be made to seem to be, an extremely difficult exercise. It will not be in the debtor's interests to suggest that applications made after formal insolvency may increase the assets available to creditors. In all but rare cases effective indemnification of the debtor's assets for the purposes of a voluntary arrangement in respect of perceived undervalue transactions or preferences will require the co-operation of the relevant third party which may not be forthcoming.

1   IR 1986, r 5.3(2)(c)(i), as defined by IA 1986, s 386. Note that EA 2002 s 251 abolishes Crown preference leaving employee's remuneration (as limited under IA 1986, Sch 6), occupational pension scheme contributions, and ECSC levies as the only remaining preferential debts.
2   IR 1986, r 5.3(2)(c)(ii).
3   IR 1986, r 5.3(2)(c)(iii).
4   In cases where the debtor is an undischarged bankrupt the interim order may not make provision relaxing or removing any of the requirements of the Insolvency Act or Rules in relation to bankruptcy unless the court is satisfied that any particular provision relaxed or removed is unlikely to result in any significant diminution in, or in the value of, the debtor's estate for the purposes of the bankruptcy, IA 1986, s 255(5).
5   See IA 1986, ss 339–342C.

6.72 The debtor must also state whether or not guarantees are being offered for the purposes of the arrangement by third parties. An explanation must be given as to how any business of the debtor will be conducted during the course of the arrangement. The proposed duration of the voluntary arrangement must be given. The proposed supervisor of the arrangement, usually the nominee, must be identified with an explanation of his functions under the arrangement and details of his proposed remuneration.

6.73 In preparing his proposal the debtor must not only be honest in making assertions but should take care to put all relevant facts before the creditors[1]. The duty of the proposer under the IR 1986 to give details of assets, charges and liabilities is qualified by the phrase 'so far as within the [proposer's] immediate knowledge'. Accordingly while painstaking research into old matters need not be undertaken, the proposer cannot avoid checking matters readily available to him in documentary material. The debtor should bear in mind that the making of any false representation or the commission of any other fraud for the purpose of obtaining the approval of his creditors to a proposal for an arrangement is a criminal offence[2]. An agreement between a debtor and a creditor behind the arrangement whereby the debtor agrees to pay to the creditor a sum additional to that to which the creditor is entitled under the arrangement is fraudulent and unenforceable by the creditor[3]. The information provided by the debtor must be complete in all material particulars[4] and the obligation to provide such particulars to all the creditors continues up to the date of and during the meeting of the creditors itself[5].

1 *Re a Debtor (No 2389 of 1989)* [1991] 2 WLR 578, 586.
2 IA 1986, s 262A (as inserted by IA 2000, Schs 2 and 3). These provisions extend the criminal offence previously contained in IR 1986, r 5.30(1); a person guilty of an offence under either provision is liable to imprisonment or a fine or both. It has been customary to include a statement signed by the debtor setting out IR 1986, r 5.30, as appropriate, or stating that the rule has been brought to the proposer's attention. This statement should now refer to IA 1986, s 6A or s 262A as appropriate.
3 *Mallalieu v Hodgson* (1851) 16 QB 689.
4 A particular, or its omission, is material if, objectively assessed, it would be likely to have made a material difference to the way in which the creditors would have considered and assessed the terms of the proposed IVA, *Cadbury Schweppes plc v Somji* [2001] 1 WLR 615, para 25, CA.
5 *Cadbury Schweppes plc v Somji* [2001] 1 WLR 615, para 43, CA.

Information to nominee; statement of affairs

6.74 In addition to the document setting out the terms of the arrangement[1] the debtor is required[2] to submit to the nominee a statement of affairs containing the following prescribed particulars of his creditors, debts, other liabilities, assets and other information[3]:

(a)   a list of assets, divided into such categories as are appropriate for easy identification, with estimated values assigned to each category;
(b)   in the case of any property on which a claim against the debtor is wholly or partly secured, particulars of the claim and its amount, and of how and when the security was created;
(c)   the names and addresses of the debtor's preferential creditors[4] with the amounts of their respective claims;
(d)   the names and addresses of the debtor's unsecured creditors, with the amounts of their respective claims;
(e)   particulars of any debts owed by or to the debtor to or by persons or companies who are associates of the debtor;
(f)   such other particulars, if any, as the nominee may in writing require to be furnished for the purposes of making his report to the court on the debtor's proposal.

1 The 'document setting out the terms of the proposed voluntary arrangement' IA 1986, s 256(2) (IVA with interim order), s 256A(2) (IVA without interim order) is called 'the proposal' in the IR 1986, and see paras **6.69–6.73**.
2 IA 1986, s 256(2) (IVA with interim order), s 256A (IVA without interim order).
3 The particulars which are to be contained in the statement of affairs are prescribed by IR 1986, r 5.3(3). The statement must be certified as correct to the best of his knowledge and belief by the individual debtor, IR 1986, r 5.3(5).

4   See IA 1986, Sch 6. Note that Crown preference is abolished by EA 2002, s 251 leaving as preferential debts only outstanding employee's remuneration (limited to four months' pay and a statutory maximum), sums owed by way of contribution to an occupational pension scheme and, theoretically, outstanding levies on coal and steel production under the ECSC treaty.

6.75 All these above particulars relate to matters which are required to be in the proposal. The purpose of the statement of affairs is to 'supplement or amplify, so far as is necessary for clarifying the state of the debtor's affairs, the particulars already given in the proposal'[1]. The Insolvency Rules do not prescribe forms to be used for the debtor's statement of affairs in IVA as is the case in bankruptcy (Form 6.33), but there is no good reason why this form should not be used, if convenient, provided all the prescribed particulars, set out above, are included.

1   IR 1986, r 5.5(3).

6.76 The statement of affairs must be made up to a date not earlier than two weeks before the date on which the debtor gives notice of the proposal to the intended nominee[1], though the nominee may allow an extension of that period to the nearest practicable date (not earlier than two months before the date of notice) and if he does so he must give his reasons in his report to the court on the debtor's proposal[2]. The use in the rules of the word 'practicable' indicates that it is for reasons of practicality, and those alone, that a nominee may extend the period.

1   See para **6.68**.
2   IR 1986, r 5.5(4).

6.77 A debtor who is an undischarged bankrupt and who has already delivered a statement of affairs[1] need not deliver a further one unless required to do so by the nominee in order to supplement or amplify the earlier one[2]. The debtor who is not an undischarged bankrupt, has seven days after delivery of the proposal to the nominee to deliver the statement of affairs, or such longer period as the nominee shall allow[3].

1   Under IA 1986, s 272 (debtor's petition) or s 288 (creditor's petition).
2   IR 1986, r 5.5(1); there is no limit to the extension of time permitted under this rule.
3   IR 1986, r 5.5(2).

6.78 If it appears to the nominee that he cannot properly prepare his report on the basis of the details given in the debtor's proposal and statement of affairs, he may call on the debtor to provide him with further information[1] and allow him access to the debtor's accounts and records[2]. The nominee may also call on a debtor to inform him whether the debtor has been concerned with the affairs of any company, wherever incorporated, which has become insolvent or whether the debtor has previously been adjudged bankrupt or entered into an arrangement with his creditors[3].

1   IR 1986, r 5.6(1) which gives the nominee extremely wide authority to call for:
    (a) further and better particulars as to the circumstances in which, and the reasons why, the debtor is insolvent or is threatened with insolvency;

(b) particulars of any previous proposals the debtor may have made for voluntary arrangements; and
(c) further information with respect to the debtor's affairs which the nominee thinks necessary for the purposes of his report.

²   IR 1986, r 5.6(3).
³   IR 1986, r 5.6(2).

Investigation by nominee

6.79 While the nominee has wide powers to investigate the debtor's proposals and statement of affairs there is no duty on him to do so imposed by statute. Undoubtedly nominees can find themselves in a difficult position. They have to prepare or consider a debtor's proposal in a relatively short time. They have to do so with no real prospect of being paid to carry out any detailed investigation of the full extent of the debtor's assets or liabilities, or check whether any of the debts disclosed on the statement of affairs are in fact shams in the names of confederates who the debtor can count on to vote in favour of the proposal, and who will then improperly take a share of the assets made available to creditors under the arrangements if approved[1].

¹   Furthermore, having prepared the proposal the nominee can face the risk of having the role of supervisor taken from him by another insolvency practitioner acting in conjunction with one or more of the substantial creditors.

6.80 Difficult though an independent investigation may be the nominee is nevertheless in the position of an officer of the court and, subject to the limitations of his position, must be satisfied that the proposal is properly carried forward and that the statement of affairs may be relied on by creditors. He must do more than simply act as a post-box, accepting without query what he is told by the debtor[1]. It is fundamental to the intended operation of voluntary arrangements that what the creditors vote on is not the debtor's raw material but a proposal that has survived scrutiny and to that extent at least has commended itself to an independent professional practitioner[2] as being proper to put before the creditors[3]. The nominee's duty is to report his *opinion*[4] as to whether the proposals have a reasonable prospect of being approved and implemented, and whether a meeting of creditors should be summoned[5]. The nominee must be satisfied that the proposal is 'serious and viable'[6]. In *Greystoke v Hamilton-Smith*[7] Lindsay J considered what is to be expected of a nominee before he reaches a conclusion whether or not a meeting should be summoned to consider a proposed voluntary arrangement[8]. He concluded that, at least in those cases where the fullness or candour of the debtor's information has properly come into question, the nominee must take such steps as are in all the circumstances reasonable to satisfy himself on three counts:

(1)   that the debtor's true position as to assets and liabilities does not appear to him in any material respect to differ substantially from that which it is to be represented to the creditors to be[9];
(2)   that the debtor's proposal as put to the creditors' meeting has a real prospect[10] of being implemented in the way it is represented it will be.

A measure of modification to proposals is possible under IA 1986, s 258 so this question is to be approached broadly;

(3)   that the information that the nominee has provides a basis such that (within the broad limits inescapably applicable to what have to be the speedy and robust functions of admitting or rejecting claims to vote and agreeing values for voting purposes) no already manifest yet unavoidable prospective unfairness in relation to those functions is present[11].

[1]   See the Department of Trade Guidance Notes to Insolvency Practitioners of March 1995 quoted by Lindsay J in *Greystoke v Hamilton-Smith, Re a Debtor (No 140 IO of 1995)* [1997] BPIR 24, 27.

[2]   See para **6.18**.

[3]   See *Greystoke v Hamilton-Smith, Re a Debtor (No 140 IO of 1995)* [1997] BPIR 24 at p 29B.

[4]   Stressed by the Insolvency Service's 'Dear IP' letter Millennium Edition, chapter 24(1) (appendix 7) which continues 'The clear implication is that as nominee you will consider the proposal, and make such enquiries as you consider necessary to satisfy yourself that the proposal ought to be put to creditors'.

[5]   As laid down in IA 1986, s 256(1) (IVA with interim order), s 256A(3) (IVA without interim order). The requirement of an opinion as to the proposed arrangement having a reasonable prospect of being approved and implemented was introduced by IA 2000.

[6]   See para **6.40**.

[7]   [1997] BPIR 24.

[8]   The learned judge, at p 27C, stated that 'where doubts reasonably arise as to the accuracy and reliability of information provided by the debtor the nominee will have to satisfy himself as to the amount and quality of such information to such degree that from it is able to arrive at what seems to him to be a fair prime facie or provisional view as to whether a particular claimant should be admitted or rejected in respect of his claim for voting purposes, and as to what figure, if any, an 'agreement' should be reached in order to attribute a minimum value for voting purposes to an unliquidated debt'; for an application of Lindsay J's principles see *Shah v Cooper* [2003] BPIR 1018.

[9]   Plainly there must be proper disclosure and due compliance with any requests by the nominee for further information by the debtor, without which due consideration cannot be given to the proposal, which cannot then be said to be one which is serious and viable, *Hook v Jewson Ltd* [1997] BPIR 100, at 105–106.

[10]   With the amendments introduced by the IA 2000 this is now, by statute, a 'reasonable prospect', see IA 1986, s 256(1)(a). There is no difference in substance, it is suggested, between a 'real prospect' and a 'reasonable prospect'.

[11]   The Society of Insolvency Practitioners have advised members that if a nominee cannot satisfy himself that these three conditions are met but still wishes to recommend that a meeting be held, he should explain in his comments to the court the basis on which he is making the recommendation and qualify his comments so that the fact that the three conditions are not met is 'conspicuously' brought to the court's attention, see Statement of Insolvency Practice 3, November 1997. The nominee must now explain how it is that he is able to hold the opinion required of him by IA 1986, s 256(1)(a) that there is a reasonable prospect of approval and implementation.

6.81   The court considered whether there should be a fourth count, namely that the proposed arrangement must appear to offer a reasonable prospect of a better recovery for the creditors, in financial terms, than would bankruptcy (or liquidation). While noting that this would almost invariably be a highly relevant consideration, this was not seen as a necessary condition[1].

[1]   The point was made that Parliament could so easily have specified as a necessary condition something analogous to IA 1986, s 8(3)(d) (administration orders) ('a more advantageous realisation of the company's assets that would be effected on a winding up') that it must be taken to have decided against such a provision. Note that IA 1986, s 8 is repealed by EA 2002, s 248 and replaced by the provisions of EA 2002, Sch 18, ie IA 1986, Sch B1.

6.82 It is particularly important that nominees should ensure that if further information does come to light the details are circulated to all creditors, and in particular those who have given him as chairman of the meeting proxy votes in favour of the proposal without being aware of such further information[1]. Creditors at the meeting who find that the details of the statement of affairs or proposal are revised after the nominee's report to the court are well advised to check the date of any proxy votes held by the chairman in favour of the proposal and object to the proposal being put to the vote until the creditors who have given proxies which antedate the revisions have been fully appraised of all developments.

[1] See *Cadbury Schweppes v Somji* [2001] 1 WLR 615 at para 43.

HM Revenue and Customs

6.83 The view of the proposal taken by HM Revenue and Customs will often be decisive to the prospects of it obtaining the approval of creditors. Although the Revenue and Customs are no longer preferential creditors[1] they are frequently sizeable creditors. Additionally, the Revenue and Customs' representative at the creditors' meeting will often be influential because he will usually have more information on the debtor than will other creditors.

[1] The removal of preferential status for all Crown debts, whether due to the Inland Revenue, Customs & Excise or by way of Social Security contributions was effected by EA 2002, s 251 as from 15 September 2003. Transitional provisions are contained in SI 2003/2093, art 4.

Voluntary Arrangements Service

6.84 Since before their amalgamation, from 1 April 2001, the Revenue and Customs & Excise operated a joint single unit to handle voluntary arrangements, called the Voluntary Arrangements Service (VAS)[1]. VAS continues under the new HM Revenue and Customs regime. VAS has pledged itself to assist in the development of a rescue culture by supporting businesses which are seen to be viable but experiencing temporary financial difficulties. More importantly VAS is prepared to discuss proposals with nominees or the proposer in an effort to arrive at a proposal which is acceptable and can be supported at the creditors' meeting[2]. To assist practitioners VAS has published a leaflet explaining how it approaches proposals for voluntary arrangements[3]. Understandably nominees are expected to do their job properly. VAS looks to nominees to confirm to creditors (a) the proposer's true position as to assets and liabilities, (b) that the open market value of assets is not materially different from that in the proposal, (c) that the value being placed upon liabilities is not materially different from that in the proposal, and (d) that the proposal has a real prospect of working. VAS will also compare its knowledge of the debtor's financial position with that in the proposal, raising any difficulties. It will also review projected income and expenditure to ensure that all expenditure is reasonable and necessary and that unacceptable expenditure is eliminated, and require that achievable provision is made for payment of statutory liabilities as they fall due within the lifetime of the arrangement. If this is done conscientiously in all cases where the debtor is in trade or business VAS will be performing a useful service not simply for the Crown but for the other creditors. VAS will discuss relevant matters with the other creditors. It will of course hold confidential material on the debtor, but VAS have indicated that they will divulge such material to the nominee if it may influence their decision on voting on the proposal. To this end VAS requests that proposals sent to it are accompanied by the proposer's signed authority to disclose to the nominee or supervisor information held in Revenue and Customs files.

[1] VAS took over from existing units with the aim of centralising and co-ordinating voting on and monitoring voluntary arrangements.

[2] The address is Voluntary Arrangements Service, Durrington Bridge House, Barrington Road, Worthing, West Sussex, BN12 4SE. Nominees are urged to send proposals direct to this address as soon as possible, quoting clearly the NIC number(s), PAYE/Tax reference(s) and VAT registration number.

[3] HMRC Notice 'Working with insolvency practitioners' see also Reference Notice 700/56 and Guidance leaflet INS 10100 and the 11 leaflets to which it refers.

Modifications

6.85 VAS expects the 'optimum offer' to be put forward to creditors after due provision for necessary business expenses including all statutory liabilities as they fall due. If it appears that the offer may be improved this will be discussed and if the proposal is not improved voluntarily VAS are likely to insist that modifications designed to improve the return to creditors are approved before it agrees to support the proposal. It will also put forward technical amendments where these are considered necessary.

Opposition to the proposal

6.86 VAS will not support a proposal unless satisfied that there has been full and honest disclosure of (a) a detailed business cash flow forecast, (b) reliable or professional valuations, (c) a statement of business assets and liabilities; and in the case of individual debtors, (d) a statement of personal assets and liabilities and (e) a statement of the proposer's current personal income and expenditure and a projection for the period of the proposed arrangement. Where the information shows that the return offered in the proposal may be improved upon this will be discussed. VAS also makes clear that there may be overriding reasons why it considers that it has no choice but to vote against the proposal. So far as confidentiality allows it will inform the nominee of the reasons. Examples given are (i) deliberate default or evasion of statutory liabilities or past association with contrived insolvency; (ii) operating a policy of withholding payment of Crown money; (iii) any proposal that required sale of HMRC debt or does not provide cash; (iv) failure to meet any obligations under a prior voluntary arrangement; (v) exclusion of creditors who are entitled to receive the same treatment as all others within their class; (vi) a purchaser assuming responsibility for payment of some of the debtor's debts in consideration for the purchase of the debtor's assets; (vii) any proposal by any member of any organisation that requires debts owed to its members[1] to be paid in full, whether inside or outside of the arrangement or before or after the completion of the arrangement when all other unsecured creditors will become bound to accept a compromise of their debt.

¹ 'Members' includes any prescribed associate or other creditors specified by the organisation.

Bad debt relief

6.87 Bad debt relief is available to any creditor involved in a voluntary arrangement where he has written off the whole or any part of the consideration for the relevant supply in his accounts as a bad debt, and a period of six months has elapsed, beginning with the date of supply[1]. VAT becomes due at the time of supply[2] and therefore VAT due on supplies which have taken place by the date of the creditors' meeting will comprise a debt covered by the arrangement even if the debtor was not then liable to account for the VAT[3].

¹ Value Added Tax Act 1994, s 36.
² Value Added Tax Act 1994, s 1(2).
³ *Re KG Hoare* [1997] BPIR 683.

Outstanding tax and value added tax returns

6.88 While no specific reference is made in the VAS guidance leaflet to outstanding accounts and returns where the nominee finds that the debtor's outstanding tax liabilities are uncertain he will usually have to agree outstanding accounts and assessments if VAS is not to oppose the proposed arrangement. A nominee who is not an accountant should normally seek the assistance of the debtor's accountants. The nominee must also bear in mind that realising assets of the debtor for an arrangement may attract capital gains tax. As this liability will arise after the approval of the arrangement the nominee should consider whether VAS may be persuaded to agree in advance to this liability coming within the terms of the arrangement and be both postponed and subject to any composition alongside other Crown liabilities and liabilities to other creditors generally. Other taxation implications may well result from the implementation of an arrangement, particularly as regards reliefs where the debtor continues to trade, and should not be overlooked by the nominee[1]. Once the arrangement has been approved any liability for corporation or income tax on subsequent profits or earnings will remain with the debtor, and this future liability should be taken into account when formulating the proposal. Future PAYE liabilities in respect of employees will also remain the debtor's liability, although VAS may require the proposal to contain provisions designed to ensure that such liabilities are met, if necessary through the intervention of the supervisor.

¹ Taxation aspects of the IVA are outside the scope of this work. The Institute of Chartered Accountants have issued a technical release (TR 799) entitled 'Tax aspects of the Insolvency Act 1986' which deals with items of importance to practitioners. It is available free of charge.

6.89 In the case of VAT the nominee will almost certainly have to ensure that all outstanding VAT returns are completed within a relatively short period following the creditors' meeting if the support of VAS is to be secured. The debtor's registration for VAT will not be affected by his becoming bound to an arrangement, and the debtor rather than the supervisor will be responsible for VAT on any continuing trading even where this trading forms an integral part of the arrangement. The nominee should however check in each case with the relevant HM Revenue and Customs office what provisions, if any, may be required to be inserted in the proposal with regard to maintaining proper VAT records and paying VAT as it accrues due. On the realisation of assets the supervisor rather than the debtor will usually find himself responsible for accounting for any VAT which arises.

6.90 The approval of an individual voluntary arrangement does not automatically result in the debtor's de-registration for VAT. A formal request to be de-registered must be made, otherwise on resumption of trading even below the registration threshold the debtor will be liable to pay VAT on his receipts[1].

[1] *Bedford v Customs & Excise Comrs (No 17085 of 2001)* (8 February 2001, unreported). De-registration cannot be retrospective.

The debtor's wife

6.91 Where the debtor is married the nominee must take care to consider the position of his wife[1] under the proposal. It has to be borne in mind that the financial problems which have resulted in the debtor having to propose an IVA could have precipitated or be consequent upon matrimonial problems giving rise to the possibility of matrimonial proceedings. It may be noted that although an order made in matrimonial proceedings is not a debt provable in bankruptcy[2], the definition of debt for the purposes of presenting a bankruptcy petition[3] is wide enough to include debts arising from matrimonial orders. Accordingly a wife may petition for her husband's bankruptcy based on his failure to pay sums due under a matrimonial order, even though the wife may not then prove in the consequent bankruptcy[4]. The bankruptcy of the husband will not preclude the making of a lump sum or property adjustment order against him[5] although no such orders may be made against assets which have become vested in the trustee[6].

[1] For convenience it is here assumed that the debtor is a husband. In the interests of correctness it is noted that the principles are the same where the debtor is a wife.
[2] IR 1986, r 12.3(2).
[3] See IA 1986, s 382(1).
[4] See e g *Russell v Russell* [1998] BPIR 259 where the court stressed that as a matter of discretion a bankruptcy order would not usually be made. In that case however it was considered that there were special circumstances justifying the making of a bankruptcy order, namely the husband's failure to give full disclosure of his financial position in the family proceedings, his failure to pay the wife's costs of those proceedings (which was a provable debt in the bankruptcy), and his failure to pay costs to another creditor. See also *Re a Debtor (No 488 IO of 1996), JP v Debtor* [1999] 2 BCLC 571, [1999] BPIR 206.
[5] *Hellyer v Hellyer* [1997] BPIR 85, *Re X (a bankrupt)* [1996] BPIR 494.
[6] *Hellyer v Hellyer* [1997] BPIR 85, *McGladdery v McGladdery* [2000] 1 FLR 315.

6.92 Where the wife is a creditor of the debtor (other than by order in matrimonial proceedings) the nominee should take into account that as a creditor in her husband's bankruptcy the wife is postponed to all other debts and interest on those debts[1]. In an IVA her debts should similarly be postponed.

[1]   IA 1986, s 329.

6.93 Where the debtor's wife is standing by him she may wish to help promote the arrangement by enabling the realisation of jointly-owned assets. There will often be pressure on her to co-operate with the nominee so as to avoid the stigma of bankruptcy falling on her husband. It is important that the nominee assures himself that any assertions by the debtor as to his wife's willingness to help and perhaps sacrifice her interest in jointly-owned assets may properly be relied upon. In most cases the debtor's wife should be advised to seek independent legal advice. The nominee must bear in mind that the wife may be in a position to prevent an arrangement proceeding if she has not in fact agreed to her interest in jointly-held assets being realised, whether or not for the benefit of the scheme. Even where her agreement has been obtained the nominee should be aware that an agreement obtained by misrepresentation or undue influence may be set aside. The case law relating to the wife's execution of bank guarantees or charges should be noted[1]. In particular if the nominee arranges or even allows the debtor to obtain his wife's consent to the realisation of her assets or her vacating the matrimonial home the husband is likely to be treated by the court as the nominee's agent for this purpose[2]. In this event the nominee would be liable for any fraudulent misrepresentation or undue influence practised on his wife by the debtor and could find that an essential ingredient of the arrangement was set aside by reason of deceit or pressure applied to his wife by the debtor of which the nominee was completely unaware.

[1]   See *Royal Bank of Scotland plc v Etridge (No 2)* [2001] UKHL 44, [2002] 2 AC 773; *Barclays Bank v O'Brien* [1994] 1 AC 180, [1993] 4 All ER 417; *Barclays Bank v Boulter* [1997] 2 All ER 1002; *National Westminster Bank v Morgan* [1985] AC 686; *Bank of Baroda v Shah* [1988] 3 All ER 24; *Bank of Credit and Commerce International SA v Aboody* [1990] 1 QB 923, [1992] 4 All ER 955.
[2]   See *Barclays Bank v O'Brien* [1994] 1 AC 180, [1993] 4 All ER 417 and *Kingsnorth Trust Ltd v Bell* [1986] 1 All ER 423, [1986] 1 WLR 119, CA.

Matrimonial proceedings

6.94 Where the debtor's wife is not standing by the debtor the nominee may well face the prospect of an order made in matrimonial proceedings depleting the debtor's assets. The proposal for an IVA will not restrict the exercise of the discretion of the matrimonial court to make lump sum or periodical awards in favour of the wife, though the nominee should take steps to ensure that a matrimonial court before which a wife's application is pending is fully appraised of the husband's liabilities and the terms of the proposal for an IVA. The making of an interim order will operate as a stay in respect of any matrimonial proceedings which affect the debtor's property, although the leave of the court to continue such proceedings will readily be given.

[1]   IA 1986, s 252(2)(b).

6.95 Any obligation of the debtor to his wife in consequence of an order in family or domestic proceedings is not a debt provable in a bankruptcy and is not therefore a debt which is postponed to the debts held by preferential and ordinary creditors[1]. The effect of this rule may be to disadvantage the wife. For while she is not bound to accept a dividend in her husband's bankruptcy, her husband's assets will pass to his trustee and will be distributed to the proving creditors ahead of the wife's claim; in effect she will rank behind them all[2]. The suggestion that in consequence IR 1986, r 12.3(2)(a) was ultra vires was rejected by the Court of Appeal in *Woodley v Woodley (No 2)*[3]. In many of the standard conditions incorporated into a proposal for an IVA there is express provision to the effect that any creditor whose claim falls within IR1986, r 12.3(2) will not be bound by the arrangement or entitled to vote in connection with or prove in the arrangement. In such a case it follows that in respect of a liability owed to her under a matrimonial order the wife is not a 'creditor'[4] and so will not be eligible to challenge the meeting's decision[5] on the grounds of unfair prejudice should she consider that the IVA adversely affects her interests. However, where there is no express exclusion of the wife as a creditor entitled to prove and vote in respect of the proposal, she is a creditor so entitled and she will be bound by the arrangement[6]. Furthermore, where the proposal expressly provided for the (former) wife, who had a lump sum order in her favour, to receive a dividend and she proved in and voted on the proposal it was held that she was a creditor bound by the IVA, the standard condition to the contrary being impliedly excluded by the express terms of the proposal[7].

[1] IR 1986, r 12.3(2)(a) which defines domestic and family proceedings by reference to the Magistrates' Courts Act 1980 and the Matrimonial and Family Proceedings Act 1984.
[2] 'She would receive the crumbs from her husband's table left unconsumed by his other creditors', per Sir Donald Nicholls V-C in *Re Mordant, Mordant v Halls* [1996] BPIR 30, at 307.
[3] [1993] 4 All ER 1010, [1994] 1 WLR 1167.
[4] For the purposes of the 'second group of parts' of the Insolvency Act 1986 (which include IVAs) creditor is defined in IA 1986, s 383 by reference to 'bankruptcy debts': 'Creditor, *in relation to a bankrupt,* means a person to whom any of the bankruptcy debts is owed'. Sums due to the wife under a matrimonial order are not such debts, IR 1986, r 12.3(2). But where the debtor husband is not a bankrupt it may be objected that this definition does not apply.
[5] Under IA 1986, s 262; see paras **6.195–6.199**.
[6] *Re Bradley-Hole (a bankrupt)* [1995] 4 All ER 865, [1995] 2 BCLC 163.
[7] *Re a Debtor (No 488 IO of 1996), JP v Debtor* [1999] BPIR 206.

The position of the wife in an arrangement

6.96 While the wife (or former wife) may be a creditor bound by the arrangement she is in a special position, for her matrimonial debt is not released on the discharge of a bankrupt. This distinguishes her position from that of the creditors generally, and to the extent that she is compelled by the terms of an arrangement to accept a dividend in satisfaction of the matrimonial debt her right to enforce her matrimonial debt irrespective of bankruptcy is overridden. This may result in unfair prejudice entitling her to mount a successful challenge to an approval of an IVA[1]. Equally other creditors may be prejudiced if a wife with no right to prove in the bankruptcy is able either to frustrate a voluntary arrangement against the creditors' wishes or use her voting rights to force them to accept an arrangement which would otherwise be rejected[2]. It is essential therefore that the special position of the wife or former wife who has obtained an order in matrimonial proceedings in her favour is recognised. If the wife is not simply excluded from the IVA, as will usually be the case, the nominee must consider how her position is to be safeguarded. At the least it will probably be necessary expressly to provide that the wife's debt will not be compromised by a dividend less than 100p in the £, even though she will not receive more than other creditors before all the dividends due under the arrangement have been paid. Depending upon the exact circumstances an IVA which provides for the postponement in the payment of the wife's debt may not be unfairly prejudicial towards her.

[1]   See *Re a Debtor, JP v Debtor* [1999] BPIR 206, 219.
[2]   See *Re a Debtor, JP v Debtor* [1999] BPIR 206.

6.97 The wife may be able to prevent the debtor parting with his assets for an IVA or have disposals of assets set aside under the provisions of the Matrimonial Causes Act 1973[1]. Where proceedings for financial relief are brought by his wife against the debtor the court may restrain any proposed disposition or dealing with property ('disposition') where it is satisfied that the debtor is acting with the intention of defeating the claim for financial relief. The court may also set aside any completed disposition if satisfied that (a) the disposition was made with the intention of defeating the wife's claim and (b) if the order is made financial relief (which otherwise would not be granted) or different financial relief would be granted to the wife[2]. The wife must establish the necessary intention on the part of the debtor to defeat her claim. However, where any disposition took place within three years of the wife's application for financial relief there is a statutory presumption that the debtor had the intention of defeating the wife's claim unless the contrary is shown[3]. The nominee must therefore be aware that where the debtor proposes to dispose of or assign the bulk of his assets for the benefit of the IVA there is a risk that the debtor's wife may seek to have the disposition set aside. The fact that the debtor is concerned to avoid bankruptcy and is making the disposition for this purpose may well be sufficient to satisfy the court that the relevant disposition was not made with the requisite intention, even against the presumption in favour of the intention during the three years following the disposition. But it will be a question of fact in each case.

[1]   Matrimonial Causes Act 1973, s 37.
[2]   Matrimonial Causes Act 1973, s 37(2).
[3]   Matrimonial Causes Act 1973, s 37(5).

6.98 Where the disposition is made for valuable consideration to the supervisor or other trustee on behalf of the IVA who acted in good faith and without notice of any intention on the part of the debtor to defeat the wife's claim it cannot be set aside by the court[1]. A lack of good faith for these purposes amounts to something akin to fraud and should at the very least involve a lack of honesty[2].

[1]   Matrimonial Causes Act 1973, s 37(4).
[2]   *Whittingham v Whittingham* [1979] Fam 9, [1978] 3 All ER 805, CA.

The matrimonial home

6.99 In most cases the matrimonial home will constitute the debtor's largest single asset, and creditors will be concerned to see how it is dealt with in the proposal. The debtor's wife may well have or claim to have an interest in this asset. When considering how to deal with the matrimonial home in the proposal the nominee will need first to ascertain whether the debtor's wife has a legal or beneficial interest in the property, and the extent of any beneficial interest. Even if she has no beneficial interest in the property the wife will have rights of occupation in the matrimonial home, and these may affect the supervisor's ability to realise the home as an asset for the IVA[1]. In the majority of cases the creditors will wish to be assured before approving a proposed IVA that all the assets which would be readily realised in a bankruptcy will be brought into account to fund the IVA. The nominee will therefore have to have regard to the bankruptcy provisions relating to the realisation of the matrimonial home[2]. The debtor's spouse, having taken independent advice, may wish to encourage the creditors to vote for the IVA by contributing her share or part of her share of the beneficial interest to the IVA, waiving her rights of exoneration[3], or agreeing to vacate the home to enable an earlier sale than might be possible in the event of her husband's bankruptcy bearing in mind the 12 months she is given under the IA 1986 before the interest of the husband's creditors outweigh her interests[4]. The nominee should have in mind that giving up the matrimonial home may be emotionally very difficult and should ensure that a clear agreement to vacate the property and authorise a sale is reached, after independent advice for the spouse, before the proposal is put to the creditors. It may become necessary to institute proceedings for possession and sale[5], and it will assist the eventual supervisor if the proposal includes the debtor's agreement to proceedings being brought in his name for this purpose. Where the supervisor holds what was the debtor's interest in the matrimonial home on behalf of the creditors he will be able to bring proceedings under the Trusts of Land and Appointment of Trustees Act 1996, s 14 in his own name[6]. If, however, the terms of the IVA provide simply for the realisation of the home and other assets by the debtor with the proceeds being paid to the supervisor, it will not be possible for the supervisor to bring proceedings in his own name, as he will have no proprietary interest in the property[7].

[1] See the Family Law Act 1996, s 30 which defines a spouse's 'matrimonial homes rights' as:
'(a) if in occupation, a right not to be evicted or excluded from the dwelling-house or any part of it by the other spouse except with the leave of the court given by an order under s 33 [Family Law Act 1996];
(b) if not in occupation, a right with the leave of the court so given to enter into and occupy the dwelling-house'.

[2] In this regard the amendments to the IA 1986 which are introduced by the Enterprise Act 2002, s 261 should be noted.

[3] See *Re Pittortou* [1985] 1 WLR 58 at 61, and see generally *Personal Insolvency: Berry, Bailey and Schaw Miller* 3rd Edn (2001) paras 18.29 and following.

[4] IA 1986, s 336(5).

[5] Under the Trusts of Land and Appointment of Trustees Act 1996, s 14 (replacing the Law of Property Act 1925, s 30).

[6] Cf *Re Solomon, ex p Trustee of Property of Bankrupt v Solomon* [1967] Ch 573, and *Re McCarthy, ex p Trustee v McCarthy* [1975] 2 All ER 857, [1975] 1 WLR 807, CA, cases where the trustee in bankruptcy was held to be a 'person interested' for the purposes of the Trusts of Land and Appointment of Trustees Act 1996, s 14 (replacing the Law of Property

6.99 *Individual voluntary arrangements*

Act 1925, s 30(1)) and *Levermore v Levermore* [1980] 1 All ER 1, [1979] 1 WLR 1277
where a receiver appointed by way of equitable execution was able to bring proceedings.
7   See *Stevens v Hutchinson* [1953] Ch 299.

Foreign assets and liabilities

6.100 No distinction is drawn under the IA 1986 between the debtor's assets
and liabilities within and outside the jurisdiction. Assets held abroad must be
disclosed together with an estimate of their value and details of any charges on
such assets[1]. Equally details of any foreign liabilities must be included in the
proposal together with details of how it is proposed that such liabilities are to
be met, modified, postponed or otherwise dealt with under the arrangement[2].
There is no express requirement in the IR 1986 that the proposal explain how
assets are to be realised. Unless foreign assets are to be excluded from the
voluntary arrangement however it is sensible that the proposal addresses the
realisation of foreign assets, both as to cost and time, and in the absence of
such information a creditor should seek it. Obtaining the information may
often itself take some time; if foreign assets form a significant part of the estate
issues as to realisation should be raised early.

1   IR 1986, r 5.3(2)(a)(i).
2   IR 1986, r 5.3(2)(c).

6.101 A particular point of difficulty may be the existence of so-called
'bankruptcy havens' where local rules provide that assets situated within the
foreign jurisdiction must first be realised to meet local tax liabilities and even
local creditors before the assets or their proceeds may be utilised to meet
claims of creditors outside the local jurisdiction. This is one of the matters
dealt with by the EU Regulation, but there remain many jurisdictions, with a
number in the USA, which operate a rigid policy in this respect.

Foreign creditors

6.102 Foreign creditors have to be given notice of the creditors' meeting and
be sent a form of proxy, as with any creditor[1]. They will be bound by the
voluntary arrangement, at least in England. Enforcement abroad, especially
where the creditor has voted against the proposal may be another matter. It is
still the law that the UK courts will not enforce claims by foreign revenue
authorities[2], although in the case of Member States of the EU[3], claims of the
tax authorities and social security authorities must now be admitted[4]. It would
in any event be inappropriate to extend the law so as to prevent foreign
revenue claims being the subject of a voluntary arrangement. For it is of the
essence of voluntary arrangements that there is a consensual agreement
between the debtor and the creditors. It cannot be said that the court enforces
a creditor's claim when imposing the statutory hypothesis that all creditors are
bound to the voluntary arrangement irrespective of whether and if so how
they voted.

226

1   Creditors who are habitually resident, domiciled or have a registered office in another EU member state are entitled to information as to lodging claims, and in particular any time limits applying, and may lodge their claim in their own state's official language.
2   *Government of India v Taylor* [1955] AC 491, [1955] 1 All ER 292, HL.
3   Other than Denmark which exercised its opt-out from the EC Insolvency Regulation.
4   EC Insolvency Regulation, art 39.

D PROPOSAL TO CREDITORS' MEETING

The procedure through to the creditors' meeting

6.103 Experience has shown that the procedures laid down in the 1986 legislation were unnecessarily formal. The scheme as envisaged is that the debtor would himself prepare a proposal. The debtor would himself apply to the court for an interim order. The proposal would then be passed to the intended nominee. The nominee would consider it against a statement of affairs provided by the debtor and would, if he thought appropriate, seek further information from the debtor. With all the information in hand the nominee would then make a report to the court stating whether or not in his opinion a meeting of creditors should be summoned to consider the proposal. At this point the debtor's interim order would be about to expire, and the court would hold a hearing to consider the nominee's report and decide whether to extend the interim hearing. In cases where the nominee had expressed an opinion in favour of the proposal being considered by the creditors, notices would then be sent to those entitled to attend and the meeting(s) would take place as suggested by the nominee.

6.104 For a procedure where time is usually of the essence this is unnecessarily cumbersome, and where money is scarce, unnecessarily expensive. Furthermore it has the unrealistic starting point that the debtor will be able to formulate a proposal which both complies with the rules and is likely to meet the expectations of creditors. In practice the first step any debtor will take is to seek the advice of an insolvency practitioner as to whether or not a voluntary arrangement is a realistic proposition. By the time an insolvency practitioner is in a position to give confident advice he will have sufficient knowledge of the debtor's affairs to formulate a proposal, at least in draft, and except in unusual cases it will be sensible to complete the proposal before taking any further steps. Accordingly when an application for an interim order is made it is almost invariably made by an insolvency practitioner who has already prepared, or almost prepared, the proposal and there is no real need for a formal report to the court. The nominee's report to the court[1] is a good discipline; the report is available to any interested party[2] but only rarely is it an important document for creditors deciding how to vote at the creditors' meeting. Under the amendments introduced by IA 2000 the report to the court is used to require the nominee to state publicly that he is of the opinion that the proposed voluntary arrangement has a reasonable prospect of being approved and implemented[3]. There is however no compelling reason why the court should take time to consider the report even when the need for extension of the interim order arises[4]. Indeed the court is unlikely to be in any position to give informed consideration to the report without requiring a great deal of information from the nominee and spending an appreciable amount of time on the report, time which can be better spent on other matters. The best assurance for the court that the proposal for voluntary arrangement is being properly pursued, and that an interim order should be extended in IVA, is in the fact that it is being handled by an insolvency practitioner whose licence to practise is at risk if he does not conduct himself properly[5].

1   Required by IA 1986, s 256(1) (IVA with interim order), s 256A(2) (IVA without interim order).
2   IR 1986, r 5.10(4): the report is put on the court file and any creditor, or director or shareholder of a corporate debtor may inspect the file 'at all reasonable times on any business day'.
3   IA 1986, s 256(2)(a).
4   In CVA there is no express provision for the court to consider the nominee's report; in IVA IR 1986, r 5.12 provides for a hearing with notice to be given to any creditor who has presented a bankruptcy petition against the debtor.
5   In many instances the insolvency practitioner will be known personally by the district judge or registrar at the court in which the voluntary arrangement is proceeding.

6.105 It is not surprising therefore that practice has run ahead of the legislation. The *Practice Direction*[1] provides that in the absence of a bankruptcy order or pending petition the court will 'normally be prepared to make orders ... without the attendance of either party' which take the procedure through to the meeting of creditors, and indeed to a final order after the chairman of the meeting has reported its decision to the court. An individual voluntary arrangement may therefore be put in place without any formal court hearing. If a creditor considers that the proposal for a voluntary arrangement is improper, or merely a device to delay inevitable insolvency, he may issue a petition for winding up or bankruptcy and bring his complaint to the court.

1   Ie *Practice Direction: Insolvency Proceedings*, para 16, see **Appendix 1**.

Nominee's report to the court

6.106 The purpose of the nominee's report is to state whether, in the nominee's opinion, (a) the voluntary arrangement being proposed has a reasonable prospect of being approved and implemented[1], (b) whether a meeting of the debtor's creditors should be summoned to consider the debtor's proposal and, if a meeting should be summoned, when and where the creditors' meeting should be[2]. The statutory scheme is that the nominee should deliver his report to the court together with a copy of the proposal and any statement of affairs provided by the debtor to the court not less than two days before the interim order ceases to have effect[3]. In practice the application for an interim order is frequently made on the basis of a report which has already been prepared. If the nominee expresses an opinion that a creditors' meeting should be summoned to consider the proposals his report should have annexed to it his comments on the proposal, and if he expresses an adverse opinion he must give his reasons[4]. The court endorses the report with the date on which it is filed and any creditor is entitled to inspect the file[5]. In IVA the documents which are delivered to the court together with a copy of the nominee's report and any comments he has made upon it must also be sent by the nominee to any person who has presented a bankruptcy petition against the debtor[6], or, where the debtor is an undischarged bankrupt, to the official receiver and any trustee in bankruptcy[7].

[1]   IA 1986, s 256(1)(a) (IVA with interim order), s 256A(3) (IVA without interim order), this
        requirement being added by IA 2000.
[2]   IA 1986, s 256(1)(aa)(b) (IVA with interim order), s 256A(3)(b)(c) (IVA without interim
        order).
[3]   IR 1986, r 5.11(1)(2). With the report to the court is to be delivered a copy of the proposal
        incorporating any amendments authorised by the nominee under IR 1986, r 5.3(3); a
        summary of the statement of affairs may be provided rather than the full statement if the
        nominee prefers.
[4]   IR 1986, r 5.11(3).
[5]   IR 1986, r 5.11(4)(5) inspection may be at all reasonable times on any business day,
        r 1.7(3), r 5.11(5).
[6]   IR 1986, r 5.11(7).
[7]   IR 1986, r 5.11(6).

6.107 In practice[1] the court rarely holds a hearing to consider the nominee's report. Nevertheless, as was pointed out by the court in *Fletcher v Vooght*[2], the terms in which the IA 1986 has been drafted make the nominee's report a pre-requisite to the valid summoning of the creditors' meeting. On receiving the report the court may consider it inappropriate to proceed further with the proposal in its existing form. It may then, presumably only after holding a hearing at which its concerns are raised with the nominee and, where necessary, the proposer, direct that a creditors' meeting should not be held[3].

[1]   See paras **6.103–6.105**.
[2]   [2000] BPIR 435; in this case through an error no interim order had been made. However,
        the IVA proceeded as if it had been made, both to approval and implementation for some
        three years before the debtor was in breach of its requirements and the error was noted.
        The court held that in the absence of an interim order there could not be a valid report to
        the court because of the wording of IA 1986, s 256(1), 'where an interim order has been
        made ... the nominee ... shall submit a report to the court'. As there had been no valid
        report to the court there could be no valid creditors' meeting and therefore no valid IVA.
        When the error was discovered the IVA had to be declared invalid although it had been
        partly executed. Since 1 January 2003 a report may be made to the court without an
        interim order being made, IA 1986, s 256A. There must however be a report to the court.
[3]   See IA 1986, s 257(1).

Content of nominee's report

6.108 There is no specific duty imposed on the nominee in the Act or the Rules in relation to the preparation of the report. The report should be as thorough as it can be on the information available to the nominee, taking into account his powers to seek further information from the debtor[1]. Insolvency practitioners have been rightly criticised for providing short and uninformative reports appearing simply to rubber stamp the proposal which they themselves have helped to formulate[2].

[1]   See para **6.68**. IR 1986, r 5.6(3) requires the debtor to give the nominee access to his
        accounts and records in order that the nominee may prepare his report to the court. The
        implication therefore is that the nominee will be expected to have examined the debtor's
        financial records before reporting to the court.

² Severe criticism of the nominee for a 'deplorably low quality' report was made by the court in *Re a Debtor (No 222 of 1990), ex p Bank of Ireland* [1992] BCLC 137, at 140 but it is fair to say that standards have rarely, if ever, fallen to this standard in more recent times.

6.109 The Insolvency Service of the DTI, in stressing that nominees should exercise their professional judgment when considering proposals and making their reports to the court, have expressed the view[1] that, at the least, the following questions should be considered in relation to each and every arrangement:

(1)   Is it feasible?
(2)   Is it fair to creditors?
(3)   Is it an acceptable alternative to formal insolvency?
(4)   Is it fit to be considered by the creditors?
(5)   Is it fair to the debtor?
(6)   Where a previous proposal has been put forward and rejected are there good reasons why the creditors should be asked to consider a further proposal?

¹ See 'Dear IP' letter, Millennium Edition, Chapter 24 voluntary arrangements, see appendix 7.

6.110 There is plainly a good degree of overlap with these questions, but they serve to remind the nominee that 'any old' arrangement which can be put together to stave off bankruptcy is not necessarily in the debtor's interests, and no arrangement should be put before the creditors that does not have a reasonable prospect of acceptance by the creditors or of working in practice. It is now indeed a statutory requirement that the nominee express his opinion in his report to the court that the proposed voluntary arrangement has a reasonable prospect of being approved and implemented before a creditors' meeting is summoned[1].

¹ IA 1986, s 256(1)(a).

Guidance notes from R3

6.111 In April 2007 R3, the Association of Business Rescue Professionals (Technical Committee) revised its guidance notes[1] to nominees for the preparation of their reports to the court with regard to proposed voluntary arrangements, stating that the matters upon which the nominee will wish to comment, although varying from case to case should include:

(a)   the extent to which the nominee has investigated the debtor's circumstances;
(b)   the basis upon which assets have been valued;
(c)   the extent to which the nominee considers that reliance can be placed upon the debtor's estimate of the liabilities to be included in the VA;
(d)   information on the attitude adopted by the debtor with particular reference to instances of failure to co-operate with the nominee;

(e)   the result of any discussions between the nominee and secured creditors or other interested parties upon whose co-operation the performance of the VA will depend;

(f)   information on the attitude of any major unsecured creditor which may affect the approval of the arrangement by creditors;

(g)   details of any previous history of failures in which the debtor has been involved in so far as they are known to the nominee;

(h)   an estimate of the result for the creditors if the VA is approved, explaining why it is more beneficial for creditors than any alternative insolvency proceeding;

(i)   the likely effect of the proposal's rejection by the creditors;

(j)   details of any claims which have come to his attention which might be capable of being pursued by a liquidator, administrator, or trustee in bankruptcy if one were appointed;

(k)   where the conditions set out in *Greystoke v Hamilton-Smith*[2] have not been met, the basis on which the nominee is recommending that a meeting be held.

[1]   Reproduced by kind permission of R3, the Association of Business Rescue Professionals.
[2]   [1996] 2 BCLC 429, [1997] BPIR 24, see paras **6.80–6.81**.

6.112 The nominee must now explain how it is that he is able to hold the opinion required of him by statute[1] that there is a reasonable prospect of approval and implementation.

[1]   IA 1986, s 256(1)(a).

Replacement of nominee

6.113 As the procedure for a voluntary arrangement requires the nominee to report to the court, the debtor will be unable to proceed if the nominee fails to make such a report, whatever may be the reason. In the event that the nominee does fail to report to the court, due to his death or for any other reason, an application may be made to the court by the debtor intending to make a proposal for a direction that the nominee be replaced by another person qualified to act as an insolvency practitioner or authorised to act as nominee in relation to the voluntary arrangement[1]. Where a nominee finds that it is impracticable or inappropriate to continue to act for the debtor he or the debtor may apply to the court for a replacement nominee to be appointed[2].

[1]   IA 1986, s 256(3)(a) (IVA with interim order), s 256A(4)(a) (IVA without interim order). For a person other than a qualified insolvency practitioner authorised to act as nominee, see para **6.18**.
[2]   IA 1986, s 256(3)(b) (IVA with interim order), s 256A(4)(b) (IVA without interim order).

6.114 In an individual voluntary arrangement with an interim order it will usually be necessary to seek a direction that the interim order shall continue or be renewed for a further period[1]. The debtor is required to give the nominee at least seven days' notice of the application to replace him as nominee[2]. Accordingly if the debtor is not to wait for the interim order to expire, with the serious consequences that such expiry may entail, and if he is not in a position to give notice at least five days before the last date allowed by the rules to the nominee to submit his report, which is unlikely, the debtor should on making his application to replace the nominee apply immediately to the court for the continuation of the interim order pending the hearing of his application.

¹   IA 1986, s 256(3A).
²   IR 1986, r 5.11.

The court's consideration of the nominee's report

6.115 For the reasons given in para **6.104** above the court rarely holds a hearing to consider the nominee's report[1]. Nevertheless the Rules envisage a court hearing to consider the nominee's report as a matter of course[2]. If the proposal on which the nominee has given a favourable report to the court is in fact invalid, it is not possible to the debtor to retrieve the situation with the consent of the creditors and amend the proposal so that it becomes a valid composition or scheme of arrangement when voted on at the creditors' meeting[3]. It is particularly important therefore that the nominee ensures that the proposal on which he reports to the court is valid, for once the proposal proceeds to the creditors' meeting it may be modified but not validated and the debtor will be unable to make a further proposal to his creditors for 12 months[4].

¹   A hearing will be necessary however in IVA where there is a pending bankruptcy petition against the debtor; see *Practice Direction: Insolvency Proceedings*, para 16.1, see **Appendix 1**.
²   IR 1986, r 5.13. It is essential that there be a report to the court and a hearing if required, see *Fletcher v Vooght* [2000] BPIR 435, see para **6.107**.
³   *IRC v Bland* [2003] EWHC 1068 (Ch), [2003] BPIR 1274. The original proposal made no offer of dividend to creditors and was therefore not a composition, and indeed proposed nothing but a payment to the supervisor and the exclusion of the debtor's estate from the arrangement. It could not therefore be a scheme of arrangement. After the report to the court amendments were proposed allowing for the payment of a small dividend of 0.5p in the £. The court held that the whole procedure was a nullity.
⁴   Although it is difficult to argue with the logic behind the decision in *IRC v Bland* [2003] EWHC 1068 (Ch), [2003] BPIR 1274 (the facts of which were most unusual) it could be very unfortunate that, perhaps by some oversight or clerical error, a proposal which is rendered valid by modification in the meeting of creditors has to be declared invalid with potentially dire consequences for the debtor. A debtor may make a further proposal within 12 months but not with the benefit of an interim order.

6.116 At any hearing by the court to consider the nominee's report any of the persons who were given notice of the application for an interim order[1] may appear or be represented[2]. This includes any creditor petitioning for bankruptcy[3], who may presumably request the court to direct that a creditors' meeting should not be held despite the nominee's opinion to the contrary. In practice where an application is made for an interim order or for the consideration of a nominee's report where a petition has been issued, the application is usually stood over to the date fixed for the hearing of the petition to be heard immediately before the hearing of the petition.

1   See IR 1986, r 5.7(4), see paras **6.24–6.27**, ie the nominee, any creditor who to the debtor's knowledge has presented a bankruptcy petition, or in applications by undischarged bankrupts, the trustee or official receiver.
2   IR 1986, r 5.13(1).
3   IR 1986, r 5.7(4).

6.117 Where a creditor appears at the court's consideration of a nominee's report which expresses the opinion that a meeting should be held, he will have to show that more than 25% in value of the debtor's creditors are implacably opposed to the proposal[1], or that the proposal has no reasonable prospect of being approved and implemented[2] if he is successfully to oppose a direction that a creditors' meeting be held to consider the proposal. Provided that the proposal appears to have a reasonable prospect of success it will only be in exceptional circumstances that the court will prevent the creditors' meeting considering the proposal. Whatever doubts the court may have as to its eventual approval by the creditors it is the creditors who are concerned with the payment or compromise of their debts; without a compelling reason to the contrary the clear scheme of the Act is to leave the decision on the proposal with them[3]. The court should however delay the holding of a creditors' meeting in the event that a creditor is able to establish that the debtor has not been completely frank with his nominee as to the extent of his liabilities or assets, or that the nominee has not taken proper steps to verify the accuracy of the debtor's statement of affairs. In this event it would be inappropriate if not futile to proceed to the creditors' meeting until the nominee has had an opportunity to consider any deficiencies in the debtor's statement of affairs and amend the proposal accordingly.

1   See eg *Re Cove (a debtor)* [1990] 1 All ER 949, [1990] 1 WLR 708; note the court should always be aware that creditors may change their minds, and that at the creditors' meeting the debtor or other creditors will have an opportunity to persuade dissentients to alter their position; and see *Re Symes (a debtor), Kent Carpets Ltd v Symes* [1995] 2 BCLC 651, [1996] BCC 137.
2   The nominee must express the opinion that the voluntary arrangement has this reasonable prospect, IA 1986, s 256(1) (as amended by IA 2000). Previously the court had developed a 'serious and viable' test, see *Cooper v Fearnley, Re a Debtor (No 103 of 1994)* [1997] BPIR 20 and *Greystoke v Hamilton-Smith, Re a Debtor (No 140 IO of 1955)* [1996] 2 BCLC 429, [1997] BPIR 24.
3   Both IA 1986, s 257(1) and IR 1986, r 5.17 proceed upon the basis that the nominee's opinion in favour of a creditors' meeting will be acted upon. IR 1986, r 5.13(2) applies r 5.10 to any 'order' made by the court at the hearing, ie two sealed copies of the order are sent by the court to the applicant one of which is to be served on the nominee. Notice of any order made, which includes a direction that the meeting should not be held or should be held at a time and place other than that proposed by the nominee, must be given to anyone given notice of the hearing but who was not present or represented at it.

6.118 If, having considered the nominee's report, the court is satisfied that the proposal should be put before the creditors' meeting it will direct that the interim order be extended for such further period as it may specify for the purpose of enabling the creditors' meeting to be held[1].

1   IA 1986, s 256(5); usually 49 days.

6.119 Where there is no bankruptcy order in existence, and so far is known, no pending petition for the debtor's bankruptcy, the court will normally be prepared to make a 'standard order' on consideration of the nominee's report without the need for the parties' attendance[1]. The standard order extends the interim order to a date seven weeks after the date of the proposed meeting, directing the meeting to be summoned and adjourning to a date about three weeks after the meeting. Before this order will be made the nominee's report must be delivered to the court and the date proposed for the creditors' meeting must be not less than 14 nor more than 28 days after the date of the order[2].

[1] *Practice Direction: Insolvency Proceedings*, para 16.1(2), see **Appendix 1**.
[2] This order may be made in conjunction with an interim order made without the parties' attendance, see para **6.25**, a 'concertina' order.

Presentation of petition for insolvency before creditors' meeting is held

6.120 The court will not make a bankruptcy order where it is satisfied that the debtor will be able to come to terms with the creditors such that there will be no debt to support the petition. The aim of insolvency law is to treat all ordinary creditors alike. It would plainly be inappropriate were one or more creditors with debts amounting to less than 25% of the debtor's total liabilities are able to thwart a voluntary arrangement by presenting a petition for bankruptcy[1]. Were a bankruptcy petition to be presented while the debtor was preparing to put proposals for a voluntary arrangement before the creditors the court might readily stay proceedings on the petition until after the creditors' meeting had considered the proposals. Indeed in an appropriate case the court may review and set aside a bankruptcy order so as to enable the debtor to propose a voluntary arrangement[2]. However, before granting a stay the court would have to be satisfied not only that there was a reasonable prospect of the voluntary arrangement being approved and implemented but that it was in all the circumstances a proper case in which to refuse a bankruptcy order[3].

[1] And see para **6.117**.
[2] See eg *Re Dollar Land (Feltham) Ltd* [1995] 2 BCLC 370, [1995] BCC 740.
[3] *Re Piccadilly Property Management Ltd* [1999] 2 BCLC 145 where the court refused to rescind a winding-up order even though it was apparent that a CVA would be supported by a creditor with more than 75% of the vote. A previous CVA had failed and the operation of the company required investigation.

E CONSIDERATION OF THE PROPOSAL

The creditors' meeting

6.121 The creditors' meeting is the centrepiece of the voluntary arrangement procedure. The statutory scheme is that in open meeting, with all relevant information before them, the creditors decide whether or not to accept the debtor's proposals for a voluntary arrangement or, in effect, put the debtor into bankruptcy. In many cases the reality is rather different. Many creditors have neither the time nor the will to consider the detail of a proposed arrangement, investigate the completeness of the debtor's information, and form a considered view as to the appropriateness of the proposals. In revising the criminal offence of fraud in connection with a voluntary arrangement[1] and in imposing an obligation on the nominee or supervisor to report criminal conduct to the Secretary of State[2], Parliament has acknowledged that improper advantage has been taken by many debtors of the availability of statutory voluntary arrangements. Few insolvency offences reach the criminal courts however, and without more careful monitoring of voluntary arrangements it seems unlikely that these new provisions will result in any significant improvement in conduct on the part of those debtors who are prepared to 'play the system' and those insolvency practitioners who acquiesce in such behaviour by their clients.

1   Previously IR 1986, r 5.30, now IA 1986, s 262A.
2   IA 1986, s 262B.

6.122 The creditors' meeting will be under the control of the chairman who will be the nominee[1] unless he is unable to attend. In this event the nominee may nominate another person to chair the meeting in his place, provided that person is authorised to act in relation to the voluntary arrangement or is an employee of the nominee or his firm who is experienced in insolvency matters[2].

1   IR 1986, r 5.19(1).
2   IR 1986, r 5.19(2).

Summoning the creditors' meeting

6.123 On receiving the nominee's report the court considers whether a meeting of the debtor's creditors should be summoned to consider the debtor's proposal, and if satisfied that a creditors' meeting should be called the court must direct that the interim order should be extended for such further period as may be necessary for the debtor's proposals to be considered[1].

1   IA 1986, s 256(5).

6.124 Both the IA 1986[1] and the IR 1986[2] proceed upon the assumption that the nominee's opinion in the matter will be followed, and it is fair to say that in very many cases the court follows the nominee's recommendation that a meeting be held after a very brief consideration of the matter. Where a competent insolvency practitioner is acting as nominee, and district judges will tend to know the insolvency practitioners in their locality, the court may have some confidence in the recommendation. Technical compliance with the IR 1986 will be checked, but rarely will the court become involved in the substance of the proposal. Where there are no complications it is indeed possible for the court to make an order carrying the procedure forward to the holding of the creditors' meeting without the need for hearing. Provided the nominee's report has been delivered to the court, complies with the Act and the Rules[3], and proposes a date for the creditors' meeting which complies with the Rules, a 'standard order' may be made on consideration of the nominee's report. This order extends the interim order to a date seven weeks after the date of the proposed meeting, directs the meeting to be summoned and adjourns the application to the court to a date about three weeks after the meeting, and may be made without attendance of any party[4].

¹   IA 1986, s 257(1).
²   IR 1986, r 5.17(1).
³   Ie IA 1986, s 256(1) and IR 1986, r 5.11(2)(3).
⁴   See *Practice Direction: Insolvency Proceedings*, para 16.1(2), see **Appendix 1**. IR 1986,
    r 5.17(1) requires the meeting to be held not less than 14 days from that on which the
    nominee's report is filed in court nor more than 28 days from that on which the report is
    considered by the court.

6.125 Nevertheless the court does have a duty¹ to consider whether the
debtor's proposals are viable so that they are fit to be put to a meeting of
creditors². The point was made in *Fletcher v Vooght*³ that while scrutiny of
the proposals is the more important where, but for the interim order, the
creditors would be taking proceedings against the debtor, it is still required if
only to avoid the unnecessary and wasteful convening of creditors' meetings⁴.

¹   Arising under the terms of IA 1986, s 256(5).
²   *Greystoke v Hamilton-Smith, Re a Debtor (No 140 IO of 1995)* [1996] 2 BCLC 429,
    [1997] BPIR 24; *Re a Debtor (No 103 of 1994)* [1997] BPIR 20; *Hook v Jewson Ltd*
    [1997] 1 BCLC 664, [1997] BPIR 100.
³   [2000] BPIR 435.
⁴   And see para **6.40**.

6.126 It is very important that nominees and debtors appreciate that the
validity of an approval of a voluntary arrangement obtained at a creditors'
meeting is dependent upon the statutory provisions governing the summoning
of the meeting being strictly complied with. The informality surrounding the
obtaining of an interim order and the nominee's report to the court, and the
apparent ease with which the procedure proceeds to a creditors' meeting has
on occasion led to nominees forgetting that they are involved in a statutory
procedure governed by clear rules. In the standard case where an interim order
is in force, the nominee must ensure that the court is indeed satisfied on
receiving his report that a meeting should be summoned and has extended the
interim order for this purpose, before proceeding to summon the meeting. In
*Vlieland-Boddy v Dexter Ltd*¹ the nominee filed on 6 March a report to the
court which provided for the summoning of a creditors' meeting on
14 March². The registrar had made an interim order on 13 February, extended
on 27 February to 13 March requiring the nominee to clarify the position
under the EC Regulation³. There was no attendance at court on 13 March and
the nominee proceeded to hold a creditors' meeting on 14 March at which a
resolution approving the voluntary arrangement was passed. The court held
that the meeting was invalid, and the approval a nullity, because the court had
not decided that it was satisfied that a meeting should be held, as required by
IA 1986, s 265(5)⁴.

¹   [2003] EWHC 2592 (Ch), [2004] BPIR 235.
²   The nominee was thereby in breach of IR 1986, r 5.17(1), see para **6.124**, footnote 4
    above, but the case turned on another point.
³   The debtor's witness statement in support of his application for an interim order had given
    an address in Spain, describing it as his main residence.
⁴   [2004] BPIR 235 at [39]. Furthermore because no valid meeting had been held it was not
    possible to invoke the provisions of IA 1986, s 262 and revoke the approval and give
    directions for a further meeting.

6.127 The creditors' meeting must be summoned for at the time, date and place proposed by the nominee unless the court directs otherwise[1]. This meeting is to be held not less than 14 days from that on which the nominee's report is filed in court nor more than 28 days after the date on which the report is considered by the court[2]. It is essential that the nominee summons the meeting in accordance with his report to the court, or the court's direction if made. It is not open to the nominee to hold a valid meeting other than in accordance with his report or the court's direction. In *Re N (a debtor)*[3] the nominee's report to the court proposed that a meeting of creditors be held on 27th June at 12 noon. The meeting was in fact held on 11th July at 3.30pm[4]. The court held that on a true construction of IA 1986, s 257(1) a valid approval of a voluntary arrangement could only be given at a meeting held in accordance with the nominee's report to the court or other direction of the court[5].

1   IA 1986, s 257(1). In fixing the venue for the creditors' meeting, the nominee must have regard to the convenience of creditors, IR 1986, r 5.18(1), and must summon the meeting to start between 10.00 and 16.00 hours on a business day, r 5.18(2).
2   IR 1986, r 5.17(1)(b) where there is an interim order in force. Where no interim order has been obtained the meeting is to be held not less than 14 days and not more than 28 days from that on which the report is considered by the court, r 5.17(1)(a).
3   [2002] BPIR 1024.
4   This discrepancy was picked up when it was noted that the report to the court was not in proper form as it failed to deal with the EC Insolvency Regulation.
5   The court considered that the chairman should apply under IA 1986, s 262 to revoke the IVA and seek a further meeting of creditors, and on that application being made ordered a further meeting, extending the interim order for that purpose, and ordered the nominee to bear all the costs personally without recourse to any of the assets available in the voluntary arrangement.

6.128 The nominee must summon every creditor of the debtor of whose existence he is aware[1], giving at least 14 days' notice of the meeting[2]. The notice given to the creditors must (1) explain the rules governing the majorities required to approve the IVA[3], and (2) be accompanied by (a) a copy of the proposal, (b) the debtor's statement of affairs or a summary of it (at the nominee's discretion), and (c) the nominee's comments on the proposal[4]. It is plainly important that once the meeting has been convened the venue should not be changed without giving all creditors reasonable notice of the change[5].

1   Ie all creditors of whom the nominee is aware whether or not they have been listed in the debtor's statement of affairs, IR 1986, r 5.17(2). It should be noted that IA 1986, s 257(2) specifies that the nominee needs to be aware both of the creditor's claim and of his address. In the case of a debtor who is an undischarged bankrupt creditors who must be given notice include (a) every person who is a creditor of the bankrupt in respect of a bankruptcy debt, and (b) every person who would be a creditor in respect of a bankruptcy debt if the bankruptcy had commenced on the day on which notice of the meeting is given, IA 1986, s 257(3).
2   IR 1986, r 5.17(2).
3   Ie the provisions of IR 1986, r 5.23(1)(3)(4).
4   IR 1986, r 5.17(3).
5   Cf *Re High Spirits Cellars Pty Ltd* (1988) 6 ACLC 644, Supreme Court of New South Wales, where a scheme of arrangement was set aside after approval at a meeting held at a changed time not notified to a number of creditors whose addresses were not traced even though their votes would not have altered the outcome. In England this case would probably have been differently decided, since to form the basis of a successful challenge the irregularity must be material, ie the number of missing votes may have altered the

outcome, see e g *Doorbar v Alltime Securities Ltd* [1996] 1 BCLC 487; *Re a Debtor (No 259 of 1990)* [1992] 1 WLR 226, at 229, *Cadbury Schweppes v Somji* [2001] 1 WLR 615 para 25.

6.129 The nominee is to act as chairman of the meeting[1], but should he be unable to attend he may nominate another person to act as chairman in his place provided that person is either an insolvency practitioner or is an employee of the nominee's firm who is experienced in insolvency matters[2].

[1] IR 1986, r 5.19(1); as chairman of the meeting the nominee may cast proxy votes but may not use such votes to increase or reduce the amount of the remuneration or expenses of the nominee or the supervisor of the proposed arrangement unless the proxy specifically directs him to vote that way, IR 1986, r 5.20. Should the chairman use a proxy vote contrary to this rule, it does not count towards any requisite majority as defined in IR 1986, r 5.23(1) or (2), r 5.23(6).

[2] IR 1986, r 5.19(2); for 'experience in insolvency matters' note the provisions of the Insolvency Practitioners Regulations 2005, SI 2005/524, regs 7 and 8. These lay down the experience required of an applicant for authorisation as an insolvency practitioner. Presumably less experience will be required of the employee who stands in for the nominee who is unable to attend the creditors' meeting.

Power of creditors' meeting to modify the proposal

6.130 It is open to the creditors' meeting to modify the proposal put forward by the debtor and his nominee. The power to modify is just that. The creditors' meeting may not by modification validate a proposal which is invalid, in the sense that it is neither a composition nor a scheme of arrangement[1]. Once the nominee has reported to the court[2] that a meeting of creditors should be summoned to consider what is in fact an invalid proposal and a meeting has been convened in accordance with the report to the court[3], then the whole procedure has become a nullity and the situation cannot be retrieved by modification at the creditors' meeting[4]. In practice modifications are often made with creditors pressing for more advantageous terms. The meeting may therefore approve the proposal with modifications, but:

(a)   the debtor must consent to each modification[5];

(b)   no modification may be approved which has the effect of causing the proposal to cease to be a composition or scheme of arrangement[6];

(c)   no proposal or modification may be approved which affects the right of a secured creditor of the debtor to enforce his security unless that creditor concurs with the relevant provision[7];

(d)   no proposal or modification may be approved which prejudices the rights of a preferential creditor[8] whether by interfering with his right to priority in payment or by paying him a smaller proportion of his debt than that paid in respect of another preferential debt, except with the concurrence of the preferential creditor involved[9].

[1] As required by IA 1986, s 253(1).
[2] Under IA 1986, s 256(1).
[3] IA 1986, s 257(1).
[4] *IRC v Bland* [2003] EWHC 1068 (Ch), [2003] BPIR 1274. This decision involves a very strict approach to the relevant statutory provisions and may be open to review in cases where a clear intention to propose a voluntary arrangement appears on the proposal document. It is particularly important that the nominee ensures that the proposal on which

he reports to the court is valid for if it is not the debtor will find that he is caught by the rule that he cannot apply for another interim order for 12 months from the date of his first interim order, IA 1986, s 255(1)(a), and see *IRC v Bland* at [50]. It should be a rare case where the proposal does not set out either a valid composition or scheme of arrangement; the facts in *IRC v Bland* were most unusual the creditors being asked to receive a nil dividend in what would otherwise have been a composition.

5   IA 1986, s 258(2).
6   IA 1986, s 258(3).
7   IA 1986, s 258(4).
8   'Preferential debt' is defined as in IA 1986, s 386 and 'preferential creditor' is to be construed accordingly, IA 1986, s 258(7). Crown preference was abolished by EA 2002, s 251.
9   IA 1986, s 258(5).

6.131 A modification may be approved which has the effect of replacing the nominee with another insolvency practitioner or practitioner authorised to act as nominee qualified to act in relation to the voluntary arrangement[1], provided the replacement signifies his consent in person at the meeting or in writing produced to the chairman of the meeting[2]. It is permissible for there to be more than one practitioner (whether a qualified insolvency practitioner or other authorised person) responsible for implementing the approved arrangements[3]. Subject to the above there are no further statutory provisions qualifying the meetings' power to modify the proposed arrangement.

1   IA 1986, s 258(3). With voluntary arrangements involving substantial debtors it is not unknown for a major creditor to agree to vote for the proposal only on the basis that an insolvency practitioner of his choice replaces the nominee.
2   IR 1986, r 5.20(2).
3   See the provisions of IR 1986, r 5.25(1).

6.132 Not only must the debtor consent to any modification, it is essential that the debtor's consent is obtained at the time of the meeting, which if necessary will have to be adjourned[1]. Where the meeting approved a modified voluntary arrangement in the absence of the debtor's consent, and her consent was obtained only some weeks after the chairman had reported to the court indicating the proposal had been approved with modifications, the voluntary arrangement was held to be a nullity[2].

1   The statutory requirement is clear and mandatory. An IVA cannot be valid if the debtor has not approved the modifications for there is no consensual agreement between him and his creditors. In *Reid v Hamblin* [2001] BPIR 929 (Milton Keynes County Court) a nominee (who subsequently lost his licence) wrote to the debtors after the creditors' meeting, which no creditor had attended and at which the nominee used a proxy vote without informing the creditor concerned that modifications had been required by the bank (a major creditor), stating 'I am pleased to confirm that your IVAs have been approved by your creditors, subject to you formally consenting to the 4 modifications [sought by the bank]'. Documents for signature were enclosed which the debtors would not sign. The debtors then made payments apparently under the impression that the original proposal was in force. In due course the IVA was held to be a nullity and an order made for payments made under it to be returned. If nothing else the reporting of this case serves as a useful reminder of quite how bad things can be in the hands of a minority of insolvency practitioners.
2   *Re Plummer* [2004] BPIR 767 (Mr Registrar Baister). Accordingly, the supervisor was not entitled to present a bankruptcy petition when the arrangement unravelled some two years later.

6.133 Care needs to be taken by the chairman of the meeting to ensure that modifications are not so radical as to result in what is effectively a different proposal. Not only is this a matter of interpretation of 'modification' but there is the practical consideration that all creditors and members will have received a copy of the proposal and have determined whether or not to attend the meeting or given proxy votes on their assessment of the proposal in its original form. Although the necessary majorities may be obtained for a radically altered proposal from those creditors who attend the meeting, creditors who voted by proxy may have voted differently had they been aware of the proposed modifications and the presence at the meeting of other creditors who decided not to attend and voted by proxy may have given a different result. In cases where the creditors attending the meeting wish to make radical alterations to the proposal the chairman should adjourn the meeting and inform the creditors who have given proxy votes as to the nature of the proposal now before the creditors.

Entitlement to vote at creditors' meeting

6.134 A creditor's entitlement to vote at the creditors' meeting is a critical consideration for it is on this entitlement that the question whether or not he is bound to the voluntary arrangement if approved is determined[1]. The IA 1986 provides that where the creditors' meeting approves the proposed voluntary arrangement it:

(a)   takes effect as if made by the debtor at the meeting, and
(b)   binds every person who in accordance with the rules:
        (i)   was entitled to vote at the meeting (whether or not he was present or represented at it), or
        (ii)   would have been so entitled if he had had notice of it, as if he were a party to the arrangement[2].

[1]   See paras **6.251–6.254**.
[2]   IA 1986, s 260(2).

6.135 A person is entitled to vote at the creditors' meeting if he has notice of the meeting[1], and notice of the meeting is to be given to every creditor of the debtor of whose claim and address the person summoning the meeting is aware[2]. While notice of the meeting is therefore the criterion for a creditor to be entitled to vote at the meeting, in order to deal with the real problem of the creditor who for whatever reason is not given notice of the meeting the IA 1986 binds creditors who were not given notice. As a drafting exercise this may seem somewhat strange, for the aim is simple enough: to bind all the debtor's creditors to the arrangement whether or not they have notice of the creditors' meeting. However, the original scheme of the IA 1986 was to bind only those creditors who had notice of the meeting, and when the problem of the 'omitted creditor'[3] was tackled in the amendments introduced by IA 2000 the approach adopted was to maintain entitlement to vote as the criterion for a creditor being bound, keep notice as the criterion for entitlement to vote and then statutorily bind creditors who would have been entitled to vote if they had had notice of the meeting. The Rules provide for the giving of notice[4] but this still leaves the creditor who is not given notice of the meeting but who learns of it before the meeting takes place and decides to attend. Such a creditor may vote, provided he can satisfy the chairman that he is indeed a creditor[5].

1   IR 1986, r 5.21.
2   IA 1986, s 257(2).
3   That is a debtor who was not given notice of the meeting and was therefore not bound to any approved arrangement.
4   See IR 1986, r 5.17.
5   *Re a Debtor (No 400 IO of 1996)* [1997] 2 BCLC 144, [1997] BPIR 431 Rimer J at 153 held that the wording of IR 1986, r 5.21(1) (the same as r 1.17(1)) meant 'every creditor who was given notice of the creditors' meeting by the nominee', but that, nevertheless, all the debtor's creditors were entitled to attend and vote at the creditors' meeting regardless of whether they learnt of the meeting from the nominee or some other source. Note also that IR 1986, r 5.23(3)(a) envisages that written notice of the creditor's claim may be given to the chairman or convener of the meeting at the creditors' meeting as well as before it. See also *Beverley Group plc v McClue* [1995] BCC 751, 759.

Creditors of the debtor

6.136 There is no provision in either the IA 1986 or the IR 1986 which defines 'creditor' specifically for the purposes of a voluntary arrangement[1]. There are statutory definitions[2] for both 'debt' and 'liability' which would give a wide interpretation to 'creditor'. Debt and liability includes 'debts or liabilities which are present or future, certain or contingent, or in respect of an amount which is fixed or liquidated or is capable of being ascertained by fixed rules or as a matter of opinion'. The provisions of the Rules relating to voting rights[3] cover a creditor with a 'debt for an unliquidated amount' or any 'debt whose value is not ascertained'. While accepting that it was possible in certain contexts for the word 'creditor' to include only those with present and enforceable claims and not to encompass those with future or contingent claims, the court in *Re Cancol Ltd*[4] rejected this construction as applying in a CVA, making the point that it would be highly anomalous if company voluntary arrangements under IA 1986, which are intended to be alternatives to liquidation and CA 1985, s 425 compromises or arrangements did not have the same potential ambit[5]. A similar observation could be made with respect to individual voluntary arrangements as an alternative to bankruptcy. The person to whom future rent under a lease, or any future payment under an existing valid instrument, will become due is a creditor entitled to vote at the creditors' meeting, and the future claim will be subject to any approved voluntary arrangement[6].

1   In the case of a proposal by an undischarged bankrupt IA 1986, s 257(3) provides that creditors 'include' (a) every person who is a creditor of the bankrupt in respect of a bankruptcy debt, and (b) every person who would be such a creditor if the bankruptcy had commenced on the day on which notice of the meeting is given.
2   See IA 1986, s 382(3).
3   See IR 1986, r 5.21(3) and see paras **6.174–6.176**.
4   [1996] 1 BCLC 100, p 110, [1996] BPIR 252.
5   [1996] 1 BCLC 100, p 110, [1996] BPIR 252, at 259.
6   *Re Cancol Ltd* [1996] 1 BCLC 100; *Re T&N Ltd* [2005] EWHC 2870 (Ch), [2006] 2 BCLC 374, [2006] BPIR 532 at [43].

Debt for unliquidated amount or whose value is not ascertained

6.137 The Rules[1] provide that a creditor may vote in respect of 'a debt for an unliquidated amount or any debt whose value is not ascertained', although unless the chairman agrees to put a higher value on the debt such a debt is to be valued at £1[2]. The reference to unliquidated and unascertained debts continues the use of expressions which have a long history in insolvency law. By virtue of the Bankruptcy Act 1869, s 16(3) a creditor could not vote at a meeting of creditors in respect of 'any unliquidated or contingent debt, or any debt the value of which is not ascertained'. While noting that this long history has resulted in the expressions carrying with them a lot of 'intellectual freight' the court in *Tager v Westpac Banking Corpn*[3] quoted the words of Mellish LJ in *Re Dummelow, ex parte Ruffle*[4]:

> 'The question really is what is meant by an "unliquidated debt" in the 3rd subsection. The fair construction of the clause seems to me this: a "contingent" debt refers to a case where there is a doubt if there will be any debt at all; a "debt the value of which is not ascertained" means a debt the amount of which cannot be estimated until the happening of some future event, and an "unliquidated debt" includes not only all cases of damages to be ascertained by a jury, but beyond that, extends to any debt where the creditor fairly admits that he cannot state the amount. In that case there must be some further inquiry before he can vote.'

[1]   IR 1986, r 5.17(3).
[2]   See paras **6.143–6.145** and **6.147–6.153**.
[3]   [1997] 1 BCLC 313 at 325–6.
[4]   (1873) 8 Ch App 997, 1001.

6.138 A claim by a landlord for future rent and for damages for breach of covenant comprise debts or claims[1] which are both unliquidated and unascertained[2].

[1]   Under most leases claims arising for breach of covenant, e g the covenant to keep in repair, may arise in debt or damages.
[2]   See e g *Chittenden v Pepper, Re Newlands (Seaford) Educational Trust* [2006] EWHC 1511 (Ch), [2006] BPIR 1230 at [24].

Contingent creditors

6.139 A 'contingent claim' or 'contingent liability' is not a term of art and its precise meaning will depend on its context. Although a contingent liability has been defined as a liability which depends for its existence upon an event which may or may not happen[1], a voluntary arrangement is a commercial contract which should be construed in a practical fashion[2]. Accordingly where the debtor's liability to pay a creditor was technically contingent on the creditor raising invoices, as the creditor had an immediate or vested or unrestricted right to raise invoices on outstanding instalments under a contract, the court refused to construe these debts as contingent liabilities[3].

[1]   See *Winter v IRC* [1963] AC 235, per Lord Guest at p 253, a case where there was a divergence of view in the House of Lords as to whether there had to be an existing underlying obligation. The majority considered that this was too narrow a view. Either the liability itself or payment due under it might arise on the happening of a future event. See

also *Glenister v Rowe* [2000] Ch 76, [1999] 3 All ER 452 where the Court of Appeal considered *Winter v IRC* and other authorities in point.
2   *Re Brelec Installations* [2001] BPIR 210, at 218D–G, *County Bookshops v Grove* [2002] EWHC 1160 (Ch), [2002] BPIR 772 at [35].
3   *County Bookshops v Grove* [2002] EWHC 1160 (Ch), [2002] BPIR 772 at [47], [49].

6.140 In *Re T&N Ltd*[1] David Richards J considered the position in a CVA of potential claimants for damages for asbestos-related injuries who had been carelessly exposed to asbestos but who had not suffered any compensatable loss at the date of the creditors' meeting. Having reviewed the authorities the learned judge concluded that (i) the holder of a contingent claim was a creditor for the purposes of a CVA, and (ii) the holder of the contingent claim was still a creditor even if the claim was not a provable debt in any insolvency[2]. He acknowledged the distinction between a contingent claim based on an existing contractual obligation, for example a person with the benefit of a guarantee, and a person who may in the future suffer loss and so acquire a cause of action in tort. Noting that it was well established that it made no difference whether the source of the liability was contract, statute, or tort[3], the learned judge concluded that both types of contingent creditor came within the scope of voluntary arrangements and that potential claimants for asbestos-related injuries were creditors for the purposes of a CVA[4].

1   [2005] EWHC 2870 (Ch), [2006] 2 BCLC 374, [2006] BPIR 532.
2   [2005] EWHC 2870 (Ch), [2006] 2 BCLC 374, [2006] BPIR 532 at [46].
3   *Winter v IRC* [1963] AC 235; *Re West End Networks Ltd (in liq), Secretary of State for Trade and Industry v Frid* [2004] UKHL 24, [2004] 2 AC 506.
4   The learned judge stressed that his conclusion covered cases where the relevant acts or omissions of the tortfeasor had been committed and the contingency was whether the claim in tort was completed by the development of the relevant asbestos condition. He had not considered the position where other events essential to a cause of action had not occurred, for example, where the company had negligently made a product but the putative claimant had not acquired or used it.

6.141 By way of contrast to the contingent claims in *Re T&N Ltd* there is the case where liability arises from events before the relevant date, but is only created by the subsequent exercise of independent discretion. A party to litigation against the bankrupt could not prove for costs incurred in the litigation prior to the bankruptcy where the order of costs was made after the bankruptcy[1]. The discretionary nature of the court's power to order costs indicated that there was no liability, contingent or otherwise, in the absence of a court order. A liability to repay benefit which was determined to have been a recoverable overpayment subsequent to the bankruptcy of the person liable to repay, was not a contingent liability as at the date of the bankruptcy[2]. This was because the power to make the determination[3] required the Secretary of State to be satisfied that there was a misrepresentation of a material fact. It was therefore impossible to treat the determination as a mere formality. As the determination was made after the commencement of the bankruptcy it could not be said at the date of the bankruptcy that the risk of there being a recoverable overpayment was a contingent liability in the bankruptcy[4]. A liability to pay interest on a debt existing at the relevant time[5] which was determined after that time by the court exercising its discretion under the Supreme Court Act 1981, s 35A is not a contingent debt[6].

1   *Glenister v Rowe* [2000] Ch 76, [1999] 3 All ER 452, CA.
2   *R (on the application of Steele) v Birmingham City Council* [2005] EWCA Civ 1824, [2007] 1 All ER 73.
3   Under the Social Security Administration Act 1992, s 71.
4   *R (on the application of Steele) v Birmingham City Council* [2005] EWCA Civ 1824, [2007] 1 All ER 73 at [14].
5   Ie the time at which the arrangement debts are determined in IVA (or the date of the order in a bankruptcy).
6   *El Ajou v Stern* [2006] EWHC 3067 (Ch) at [68]: '... the discretionary nature of the power to award interest under s 35A indicates that there is no liability, contingent or otherwise, under s 35A in the absence of a court order'. In the event although the creditor's claim for interest (which amounted to some £602,000) was not an arrangement debt, Kitchin J held that the existence of an IVA constituted a special circumstance for the purposes of CPR Sch 1 RSC Ord 47 r 1 which rendered it unjust (and therefore inexpedient) to allow the order for interest to be enforced against the debtor for so long as the IVA subsisted.

Creditors' votes: the role of the chairman

6.142 The chairman of the creditors' meeting will be the nominee, but if for any reason he is unable to attend the nominee may nominate another person to act as chairman in his place[1]. With respect to voting, the chairman has two overlapping but distinct duties to perform[2]. First he must decide whether a claim should be admitted or rejected. Secondly he must decide what value to put on claims which he admits or which are admitted subject to objection. These are plainly important tasks for votes cast at the creditors' meeting are calculated in accordance with the amount of the creditor's debt as assessed by the chairman. On his decisions as to voting the proposed voluntary arrangement may stand or fall.

1   Such a person must either be an insolvency practitioner qualified in relation to the debtor, or an employee of the nominee who is experienced in insolvency matters, IR 1986, r 5.19(2).
2   IR 1986, r 5.22(1).

Admission or rejection of claims

6.143 The chairman has the task of adjudicating on any dispute as to the right of anyone claiming to be a creditor to vote. This is a quasi-judicial task which must be undertaken accordingly. Where the chairman is in real doubt whether a claim should be admitted or rejected the IR 1986[1] provide that he should mark the claim as objected to and allow votes to be cast in respect of it, subject to such votes being subsequently declared invalid if the objection to the claim is sustained. Any decision which the chairman makes with respect to the admission or rejection of claims may be appealed to the court by any creditor or the debtor (or member of the company in CVA)[2]. The chairman does therefore have this fallback position where he is in doubt as to what decision to make, but he should consider the merits of the debt first; there is no reason for the chairman to abdicate his responsibility to make a decision as to admissibility.

1   IR 1986, r 5.22(4). It is important to keep the distinction between admissibility and valuation clear. The chairman may have doubts about admissibility and he may also or alternatively have doubts about valuation. As described in this paragraph where the chairman has doubts about admissibility the Rules require him to allow the claim for

voting purposes marking it as objected to, but where the chairman has doubts as to the valuation of a claim which is unliquidated or unascertained he should ascribe a value of £1 to it. In some case he may, of course, need to do both.

2   IR 1986, r 5.22(3).

6.144 In practice the nominee will have considered the claims of many of the debtor's creditors well in advance of the meeting, when preparing the proposal or considering the debtor's statement of affairs. It will be open to the nominee to decide that any particular claimant is not in fact a creditor, and if so he need not, on a strict application of the Rules, give that claimant notice of the meeting. However, where there is a dispute as to whether any person is in fact a creditor of the debtor it should only be in the clearest of cases that the chairman decides not to treat the person in question as a creditor and so omit him from the list of creditors to whom notice of the meeting is sent. As the Rules provide that if the chairman of the creditors' meeting is in doubt whether a creditor's claim should be admitted or rejected he should mark it as objected to and allow the creditor to vote[1]. There is a presumption that a person claiming to be a creditor is entitled to vote, although the chairman will plainly have a discretion to ignore claims which are clearly invalid. In appropriate cases the chairman may seek legal advice[2]. The assertion of a set-off of doubtful validity which, if good, would have extinguished the claim, was no justification for the nominee's omission to give the relevant creditor notice of the meeting[3].

1   IR 1986, r 5.22(4), subject to his vote subsequently being declared invalid if an objection is taken to court, and see *National Westminster Bank v Scher* [1998] BCLC 124, [1998] BPIR 224.
2   The court in *Re Cranley Mansions Ltd* [1994] 1 WLR 1610 concluded that the chairman had made no real attempt to value the claim or even to arrive at a minimum value for the claim. He merely put a value of £1 on what the creditor asserted was a claim for over £900,000. In the circumstances the court found the £1 valuation 'deeply suspect'. It is suggested that the chairman should make a reasonable attempt to value the claim, perhaps with legal assistance if time permits, before he allows doubt to take over, places a nominal value on the claim and, in effect, passes the task to the court with the inevitable delay and cost that entails. The Rules (IR 1986, r 5.21(3)) now provide that an unliquidated or unascertained debt be valued at £1 'unless the chairman agrees to put a higher value on it'. That is not however an excuse for a chairman to leave a debt at £1 because a proper valuation is not straightforward, especially where the creditor is understood to be hostile to the proposal.
3   *Re a Debtor (No 400 IO of 1996)* [1997] 1 WLR 1319, [1997] 2 BCLC 144.

Valuation of claims

6.145 The chairman must assess the value of all admitted debts (including those of which he has doubt and has marked 'objected to') for the purposes of voting. This assessment is as to the value of the debt at the date of the meeting[1]. The assessment of the creditor's debt will usually be a straightforward task where the debt is present and ascertained, though various issues as to the proper valuation of the debt, particularly as to set-off, may arise on occasion. Where the debt is for an unliquidated amount or its value cannot be ascertained it is to be valued at £1 unless the chairman agrees to put a higher value on it[2]. A valuation at £1 or any valuation placed on a debt by the chairman is only for the purposes of voting. If a voluntary arrangement is approved the supervisor may place a different value on the debt for the purpose of any dividend.

¹ IR 1986, r 5.21(2); but where a debtor is bankrupt, the calculation of votes is as at the date of the bankruptcy order, IR 1986, r 5.21(2).
² IR 1986, r 5.21.

Creditor to supply information

6.146 It is incumbent on a creditor who wishes to vote in respect of his debt to state to the best of his ability the total amount that he states is owing to him, and, if the value of his debt or of some part of it is not ascertained, to state that fact and to supply the chairman of the creditors' meeting with as much information as is available to enable the chairman to put an estimated minimum value on the debt¹. Where the chairman has sufficient information to ascertain the value of a creditor's debt he may not rely on the failure of the creditor to provide details in rejecting the debt for the purposes of voting².

¹ *Re K G Hoare* [1997] BPIR 683, 695. The deputy judge continued: 'Just as it does not lie in the mouth of a creditor who stays away to say that the chairman has not agreed to minimum value for his debt and that he is therefore not bound by the IVA, so in my judgment it does not lie in the mouth of a creditor who has put a figure on his debt, albeit one that he says is subject to verification and possible amendment at a later date, to claim later that he is owed some other debt which he has not included in the figure he has stated and in respect of which he has not voted, and that he is therefore not bound in respect of that other debt.'
² *Roberts v Pinnacle Entertainment Ltd* [2003] EWHC 2394 (Ch), [2004] BPIR 208, where the debtor had himself admitted the debt in a specified sum, which amounted to more than 25% of the total debt, in his statement of affairs.

Valuing unliquidated and contingent debts

6.147 Entitlement to vote is dependent upon being a creditor with a debt of certain value for voting purposes. The IR 1986 provide that an unliquidated or unascertained debt must be valued at £1, unless the chairman 'agrees' to put a higher value on it¹. This 'agreement' required by the rules is merely the preparedness of the chairman to estimate a minimum value; there is no need for the chairman to reach an agreement with the creditor as to the proper value for the debt². The chairman may estimate the value of a debt at the meeting itself; there is no need for him to notify the creditor of the value that he will put on the debt before the meeting, although it is plainly good practice that he should do so if possible³. Neither need the creditor be in agreement with the chairman. The creditor will be bound by the chairman's valuation of his debt even where he is unaware of that valuation⁴. The fact that the debtor has a counterclaim against the creditor or has objected to the quantum of the creditor's claim does not render the debt in question either unliquidated or unascertained for the purposes of voting⁵.

¹ IR 1986, r 5.21(3) (as amended from 1 January 2003). The £1 value is 'for the purposes of voting (but not otherwise)' and so the creditor will not be prejudiced by the valuation on the payment of dividends.

² *Doorbar v Alltime Securities Ltd* [1996] 1 WLR 456, 465C (overruling *Re Cranley Mansions Ltd* [1994] 1 WLR 1610); see also *Beverley Group plc v McClue* [1995] 2 BCLC 407, 417–418, and *Re Cancol Ltd* [1996] 1 BCLC 100. This avoids the unsatisfactory situation which would arise if a creditor refused to reach any sensible agreement with the chairman in order not to be bound to the arrangement. These decisions all pre-date the change in the IR 1986 as from 1 January 2003. Sir Andrew Morritt C considered the point afresh under the new rules in *Chittenden v Pepper, Re Newlands (Seaford) Educational Trust* [2006] EWHC 1511 (Ch), [2006] BPIR 1230 and held (at [27]) that the phrase 'unless the chairman agrees' in the new rules should be interpreted in a similar manner.
³ *Re Cancol Ltd* [1996] 1 BCLC 100; also reported as *Cazaly Irving Holdings v Cancol Ltd* [1996] BPIR 252, where the creditor had corresponded with the chairman before the meeting but did not attend the meeting itself.
⁴ See *Beverley Group plc v McClue* [1995] 2 BCLC 407, [1995] 2 BCLC 407 where the company proposing the arrangement had put an estimated value on the creditor's unliquidated claim but the creditor, who knew about the meeting, did not attend on the ground that he had not received formal notice. The court held that as the creditor knew about the meeting and that notice had been duly sent to, albeit not apparently received by, the creditor was bound by the arrangement.
⁵ *Re a Debtor (No 222 of 1990) ex p Bank of Ireland* [1992] BCLC 137.

6.148 Not infrequently the chairman of a creditors' meeting faces difficult decisions in the calculation of unliquidated and contingent claims. The requirement of the Rules that an unliquidated or unascertained debt must be valued at £1 unless the chairman agrees to put a higher value on it was introduced on 1 January 2003. Under the previous Rules a creditor with an unliquidated or unascertained debt could not vote unless the chairman agreed to put an estimated minimum value for the purpose of entitlement to vote. The amendment to the Rules ensures that the creditor is bound to any approved arrangement. Nevertheless, the need for careful consideration by the chairman of the value of such a debt remains, particularly where it is clear that the value put on the debt may affect the outcome of the vote at the creditors' meeting[1]. The chairman should bear well in mind that, whatever concerns he may have as to the approval of an arrangement with which he has been involved and where he may become the supervisor, it is important that he approach the task of valuing debts in an independent manner without regard to the likely way in which the creditor holding the debt may vote. It is always open to a creditor to apply to the court to alter the outcome of the vote whichever way it goes on the basis that the chairman was wrong not to put a higher, or indeed a lower, value on any debt including unliquidated or unascertained debts. Failure on the part of the chairman to act properly in valuing debts may only lead to a waste of time and expense. The chairman does not have a completely unfettered discretion in placing values on debts, and placing a value on a debt which cannot be justified demonstrates a serious falling short of the standards to be expected of a competent insolvency practitioner[2]. As to the duty of the chairman when considering an unascertained or unliquidated claim Sir Andrew Morritt C said in *Re Newlands (Seaford) Educational Trust*[3]:

'The chairman should not speculate. Nor is he obliged to investigate the creditor's claim. But he must examine such evidence, and I do not use that word in any technical sense, as the creditor puts forward and any relevant evidence provided by any other creditor or the debtor. If the totality of that evidence lead him to the conclusion that he can safely attribute to the claim a minimum value higher than £1 then he should do so.'

1   In *Chittenden v Pepper, Re Newlands (Seaford) Educational Trust* [2006] EWHC 1511
     (Ch), [2006] BPIR 1230 Sir Andrew Morritt C noted (at [28]) that the issue of 'higher
     value' is literally different to the issue of 'an estimated minimum value' but stated that the
     context remains one of an unliquidated or unascertained claim for which a minimum value
     is now prescribed by the rules. Thus the comparator implicit in the word 'higher' is the
     minimum value of £1.
2   *Fender v IRC* [2003] BPIR 1304 at [18].
3   [2006] EWHC 1511 (Ch), [2006] BPIR 1230 at [28].

6.149 In *Re Cranley Mansions Ltd*[1] the chairman put a value of £1 on an
uncertain counterclaim estimated at £900,000 and costs. The court considered
the valuation to be deeply suspect[2], but found it impossible to say that the
chairman ought to have valued the claim at some other, much higher figure. In
valuing a debt arising under a continuing contract as at the date of the meeting
the chairman may have to take into account the possibility that either the
debtor or the creditor may act in breach of contract at some later date. In *Re
Millwall Football Club & Athletic Co (1985) plc*[3] the debtor, a company,
entered voluntary arrangements after it had been the subject of an administration order. The holders of all debts incurred before the date of the administration order ('the record date') were to be paid a small dividend under the CVA.
Following their appointment the administrators had dismissed various
employees including the respondent. After voting for the CVA he then claimed
that he was not bound by the arrangements because his claim for premature
termination of his contract of employment arose on his dismissal after the
record date. The court rejected his claim holding that it was based on a
liability incurred by the debtor before the record date. The debtor's liability to
make payments to its employee under his contract of employment was one
which was in existence at the record date and it was one which was destined
to give rise in the future to the damages claim. Although the events which gave
rise to the claim had not happened at the record date when they did happen
they were founded on an obligation or liability incurred before the record
date. The debtor's liability could properly be characterised as a future,
prospective or contingent liability before the relevant date. This decision,
understandable in its context[4], and straightforward to assess because the
events giving rise to the liability occurred before the making of the CVA could
give rise to extremely difficult questions of valuation if taken to its logical
extremes.

1   [1994] 1 WLR 1610.
2   Had any valuation above £1,722 been ascribed to the debt the creditor could have
     prevented approval of the arrangement. Note that the decision in this case turned on the
     holding that it was necessary under the Rules for the chairman to reach agreement with the
     creditor as to the value of the debt, a view overruled by the Court of Appeal in *Doorbar v
     Alltime Securities Ltd* [1996] 2 All ER 948, [1996] 1 WLR 456.
3   [1998] 2 BCLC 272, [1999] BCC 455.
4   The company had a strong secondary argument in estoppel, as the court found.

6.150 In *Lombard North Central plc v Brook*[1] the proof submitted by the
applicant in respect of lease purchase agreements with the debtor company
included both arrears and a specific sum by way of agreed damages payable in
the event of termination of the agreement. The court held that the chairman
had been wrong to admit the proof only as to the arrears. The term in the

agreement for the payment of agreed damages was not a penalty. It represented a contractual obligation to pay a certain sum on the happening of a specified event and was therefore properly included in the applicant's proof of debt. A litigant in ongoing proceedings against the debtor where no order for costs has been made may not vote in respect of potential liability to costs on the part of the debtor[2]. In *Chittenden v Pepper, Re Newlands (Seaford) Educational Trust*[3] the landlords opposed to a CVA designed to allow a school to continue in existence had a claim for two years' future rent at £300,000 and a claim for dilapidations in the sum of £875,000. Had the chairman allowed the landlords' claim at any figure above £443,000 the CVA would not have been approved. The schedule of dilapidations did not quantify individual items, but, as the court pointed out, even if it had, this would be neither a measure of the cost of repairs actually incurred by the landlords for a claim under the lease nor would it indicate the amount, if any, by which the value of the landlords' reversion was diminished by the want of repair[4]. The company's surveyors disagreed with the landlord's surveyors' schedule. In these circumstances while the court noted that the landlord might very well have a claim exceeding £1 it accepted that there was no evidence on which the chairman could 'conclude with any degree of confidence' that any specific value could be put on the claim and concluded that the chairman had no option but refuse to put any higher value on it.

[1] [1999] BPIR 701.
[2] *Re Wisepark Ltd* [1994] BCC 221.
[3] [2006] EWHC 1511 (Ch), [2006] BPIR 1230.
[4] Referring to the provisions of the Landlord and Tenant Act 1927, s 18.

6.151 Perhaps the most frequently encountered situation in which the chairman has to put a minimum value on the debtor's future liabilities is in the case of future rent for leasehold property. An important factor to be taken into account in such an assessment will be the state of the property market and thus the value of the landlord's right to forfeit the tenancy and re-let the premises. In two reported decisions[1] the court has accepted the chairman's assessment of one year's rent to cover all future rent liabilities, and it is understood that this is an approach adopted by several chairmen where no other assessment is plainly more appropriate in the circumstances.

[1] *Doorbar v Alltime Securities Ltd* [1996] 2 All ER 948, [1996] 1 WLR 456 (7½ years to run); *Re Sweatfield Ltd* [1997] BCC 744 (7 years to run to break clause).

6.152 The submission that the holder of a guarantee was entitled to vote in respect of the debtor's maximum exposure under it even though no sum was payable at the date of the creditors' meeting and the actual sum that might ultimately be payable could not be ascertained was firmly rejected in *Fender v IRC*[1]. As with any contingent claim the value of a claim under a guarantee has to be valued in its particular circumstances, and given a value of £1 if it is not reasonably possible to ascribe a higher value to it.

[1] [2003] BPIR 1304 at [15].

Right of appeal

6.153 There is a right of appeal against any decision of the chairman as to the rights of any one claiming to be entitled to vote, by the debtor, or member of the company in CVA, or any creditor[1]. This applies both as to questions of admissibility and of valuation. As with issues of admissibility, the chairman should make a reasonable attempt to value the claim, perhaps with legal assistance if time permits, in the light of the information before him from the debtor, the claimant or any other creditor, before he allows doubt to take over and passes the task to the courts[2].

1 IR 1986, r 5.22(3), see para **6.154**.
2 *Re Cranley Mansions Ltd* [1994] 1 WLR 1610 at 1625C.

Appeal from chairman's decision on entitlement to vote

6.154 The chairman's decision on a creditor's entitlement to vote at the creditors' meeting is subject to appeal to the court by any creditor or the debtor[1]. An appeal to the court may be 'on any matter' relating to the creditor's voting rights and cover both questions of admissibility and valuation[2]. A decision of the chairman as to entitlement to vote may also result in an irregularity on which the meeting's decision may be challenged if it is material, that is if the votes involved would have altered the outcome of the vote. Both the chairman's decision on voting rights and the meeting's decision to approve or reject the proposal may be the subject of one appeal[3]. Any application to the court by way of appeal against the chairman's decision must be made within the period of 28 days from the day on which the chairman makes his report to the court[4], although this 28-day time limit may be extended under the court's general discretionary power to disregard time limits[5]. Where the creditors' approval of voluntary arrangements was successfully challenged by creditors on the ground that a supporting creditor ought not to have voted, the court allowed the debtor to challenge out of time the entitlement to vote of an approving creditor[6]. In exercising the discretion to extend the time limits the court relied on the guidelines suggested in *C M Van Stillevolt BV v E L Carriers Inc*[7], the relevant factors being:

(i)   length of delay;
(ii)   reasons for delay;
(iii) the apparent merits of the underlying application; and
(iv)   the prejudice to each side other than the inevitable prejudice inherent in reopening the matter.

1 IR 1986, r 5.22(3).
2 IR 1986, r 5.22(4); and see *Re a Debtor (No 222 of 1990) ex p Bank of Ireland* [1992] BCLC 137; *National Westminster Bank v Scher* [1998] BPIR 224 but note *Re Cranley Mansions Ltd* [1994] 1 WLR 1610 and *Doorbar v Alltime Securities Ltd* [1996] 2 All ER 948, [1996] 1 WLR 456, and see paras **6.143–6.145** and **6.147–6.153**.
3 See eg *Ex p Bank of Ireland* [1992] BCLC 137. As to challenge of the meeting's decision to approve the voluntary arrangement see paras **6.195–6.199**.
4 IR 1986, r 5.22(6). The chairman reports to the court under IA 1986, s 259(1), see paras **6.183–6.185**. Any challenge of whatever nature to any decision of the creditors' meeting must be brought within 28 days, see paras **6.232–6.235**.

⁵ Under IA 1986, s 376. The Rules also contain a general power to extend time limits. IR 1986, r 12.9(2) imports the CPR into the Insolvency Rules and by CPR r 3.1(2)(a) there is power 'so as to enable the court to extend or shorten the time for compliance with anything required or authorised to be done by the Rules'.

⁶ *Tager v Westpac Banking Corpn* [1997] 1 BCLC 313, [1997] BPIR 543 (Judge Weeks QC).

⁷ [1983] 1 WLR 207, CA per Griffiths LJ.

6.155 At the hearing of the appeal the court will have to decide the merits of the dispute over the debt, and in so doing will not be confined to such evidence as was before the chairman of the meeting. The court is entitled to consider whatever evidence the parties to the appeal decide to put before the court[1]. The court does not however have to try fully what might be a complex claim. Rather it should come to a conclusion whether, on balance, the claim of the creditor has been established and, if so, in what amount[2].

¹ *Re a Company (No 4539 of 1993)* [1995] 1 BCLC 459 (a decision on the equivalent wording in IR 1986, r 4.70 – liquidation); *National Westminster Bank v Scher* [1998] BPIR 224.

² *Re a Company (No 4539 of 1993)* [1995] 1 BCLC 459.

6.156 On appeal the court may reverse or vary the chairman's decision, or declare a vote to be invalid, but only if the court considers the matter is such as to give rise to unfair prejudice or a material irregularity[1]. It has been said that the test for unfair prejudice or material irregularity on an appeal against the chairman's decision on an entitlement to vote is the same as on a challenge to the decision of the creditors' meeting[2]. This must however be seen in the respective contexts of these appeals. An appeal against a chairman's decision on entitlement to vote is just that. It is the decision on voting which must give rise to the unfair prejudice. It is only on an appeal against the meeting's decision that the court will consider whether the terms of the arrangement itself give rise to unfair prejudice. It follows that an appeal solely under the IR 1986 will be restricted to a complaint as to the chairman's decision to allow or disallow a vote[3], and where a creditor also wishes to complain about other decisions of the chairman and their implication on the fairness of the arrangement as a whole it will be necessary to couple the appeal under IR 1986, r 5.17 with an appeal under IA 1986, s 262.

¹ IR 1986, r 5.22(5).

² *Re Sweatfield Ltd* [1998] BPIR 276; as to the meaning of unfair prejudice or material irregularity, see paras **6.204–6.213, 6.222–6.226**.

³ Which will include a decision on a proxy.

6.157 On upholding an appeal the court may order another meeting to be summoned, or make such order as it thinks just[1]. The Rules provide that the chairman may not be personally liable for any costs incurred by any person in respect of an appeal against his decision as to a creditor's right to vote[2], but he is not necessarily protected against an order for costs if there are successful appeals both against his decision on voting and against the meeting's decision on the basis that there was a material irregularity at the meeting by reason of the chairman's decision on a creditor's entitlement to vote[3].

¹ IR 1986, r 5.22(5).

² IR 1986, r 5.22(7).

3   *Ex p Bank of Ireland* [1992] BCLC 137, and as to costs *Ex p Bank of Ireland (No 2)* [1993] BCLC 233.

6.158 If a creditors' claim is not admitted for voting purposes by the chairman of the meeting the creditor will not be bound by the voluntary arrangement. The creditor cannot later be compelled to participate in the voluntary arrangement when it is shown that his claim has been wrongly rejected. However, in cases where the whole or the bulk of the debtor's realisable assets have been put into the voluntary arrangement it will be in the interests of the creditor whose claim has been wrongly rejected to join in the voluntary arrangement. He will not be able to claim against the fund which is transferred to the supervisor which is impressed with a trust in favour of the participants in the voluntary arrangement. Once a creditor has established his claim against the debtor, having previously been rejected by the chairman, the creditor will be entitled to join in the voluntary arrangement on the same basis as other creditors (in his class if appropriate), and where dividends have already been paid, no further payment will be made to other creditors until the previously omitted creditor has been put into the same position as existing creditors[1].

1   *Re TBL Realisations, Oakley-Smith v Greenberg* [2002] EWCA Civ 1217, [2003] BPIR 709. The previously omitted creditor should neither be adversely affected by the approval of the voluntary arrangement nor should he be able to seek an advantage over the voluntary arrangement creditors by enforcing the entirety of his claim.

Conduct of the creditors' meeting

6.159 The nominee takes the chair at the creditors' meeting[1]. If for any reason the nominee is unable to attend he may nominate as chairman in his place either another insolvency practitioner qualified to act or an authorised person in relation to the debtor or an employee of the nominee or his firm who is experienced in insolvency matters[2]. The chairman has overall control of the meeting.

1   IR 1986, r 5.19(1).
2   IR 1986, r 5.19(2).

6.160 The IA 1986 expressly provides that the creditors' meeting must be conducted in accordance with the IR 1986[1]. The first task of the chairman will usually be to determine who is entitled to vote and in what amounts. The chairman, as nominee, will then normally explain the reasons for the proposal and why it has been formulated in the manner which is being put to the creditors. The debtor, or its officers where the debtor is a company, should usually be present to answer questions from the creditors where these cannot properly be dealt with by the nominee or his representative. Any modifications to or amendments of the proposal put forward by creditors will need to be debated and even where acceptable to the debtor may require voting on by the creditors. Once the proposal is in its final form the chairman may proceed to putting it to the vote, subject to the need to adjourn should there be significant alterations to the proposal which ought to be put before creditors who have not attended the meeting.

1   IA 1986, s 258(6) expressly provides that the meeting shall be conducted in accordance
     with the rules. The relevant rules are IR 1986, rr 5.17–5.24.

Casting a vote

6.161 A creditor must have a debt of certain value, if necessary estimated by
the chairman, and must attend the meeting in person or by proxy to cast his
vote[1].

1   *Beverley Group plc v McClue* [1995] 2 BCLC 407.

Proxy voting

6.162 In practice many votes are cast by proxy[1]. Provided that the form of
proxy is with the chairman before the vote is taken it is validly lodged for
voting purposes even if it was not presented before the meeting started[2]. A
creditor is free to withdraw a proxy and replace it with a new one at any time
before the vote is taken[3]. A proxy which is sent by fax is valid for voting
purposes[4]. It is advisable that a creditor submitting a form of proxy sets out
clearly on the form, or in an accompanying document, how his claim is
calculated. There may be questions at the meeting as to the validity or
quantum of his claim, and if he had not made his claim clear the chairman
may determine any challenge against the creditor, or, indeed, decide himself
not to admit the claim or to admit it at a lower value than that for which the
creditor contends[5]. Inevitably proxies are given before the meeting, often some
time before the meeting. The creditor concerned will therefore have given his
proxy without knowledge of any information which is given to the meeting or
which becomes available shortly before the meeting. Where new information
of significance becomes available the nominee, or chairman of the creditors'
meeting if this is someone other than the nominee, should consider whether he
ought to adjourn the meeting and report the new information to all creditors
including those for whom he holds proxies, even if this means that he may
have to obtain an extension of the interim order or an extension of time of
moratorium to hold the meeting[6]. This is unlikely to be necessary where the
debtor, perhaps under pressure from the creditors at the meeting, has
improved the proposal from the creditors' point of view. There have been
cases however where the chairman has used proxy votes to support a proposal
where the dividend forecast to the creditors has been reduced. To use proxy
votes in such a situation may well amount to a material irregularity leaving the
approval of the voluntary arrangements open to challenge[7].

1   A form of proxy must be sent out with every notice summoning the creditors' meeting, IR
     1986, r 5.18(3). For the rules of general applicability covering proxy voting see IR 1986,
     Pt 8.
2   *Re Philip Alexander Securities & Futures Ltd* [1999] 1 BCLC 124 (company administra-
     tion) and *Re a Company (No 4539 of 1993)* [1995] 1 BCLC 459 (liquidation).
3   *Re Cardona* [1997] BPIR 604 where the terms of the proxy were altered between the first
     and the adjourned meeting.
4   *Re a Debtor (No 2021 of 1995), ex p IRC v Debtor* [1996] 2 All ER 345 also reported at
     IRC v Conbeer [1996] BPIR 398.
5   See generally *Roberts v Pinnacle Entertainment Ltd* [2003] EWHC 2394 (Ch), [2004]
     BPIR 208.

6.162 *Individual voluntary arrangements*

6   *Cadbury Schweppes plc v Somji* [2001] 1 WLR 615, 626 para 25; in all bankruptcy matters an extension of time may be obtained under IA 1986, s 376 either before or after the original period of time has expired. In CVA reliance must be had to IR 1986, r 12.9(2) which imports CPR r 3.1(2)(a) into the IR 1986 and enables the court to extend (or shorten) the time for compliance with anything required or authorised to be done by the rules.
7   See paras **6.222–6.226**.

Remuneration and expenses of nominee or supervisor

6.163 The chairman of the creditors' meeting may not use any proxy held by him to increase or reduce the amount of the remuneration or expenses of the nominee or the supervisor of the proposed arrangement without specific authorisation by the proxy[1]. If he does so the vote does not count towards any majority on such a resolution[2].

1   Which will be contrary to IR 1986, r 5.20.
2   IR 1986, r 5.23(6).

Quorum

6.164 The meeting is competent to act if a quorum of at least one creditor entitled to vote is present in person or by proxy[1]. The chairman must delay the start of the meeting from its appointed time by at least 15 minutes where there is a quorum comprised of the chairman alone (ie a chairman with a proxy) or the chairman and one other person and the chairman is aware that there are other persons entitled to vote[2].

1   IR 1986, r 12.4A; this rule governs any meeting in 'insolvency proceedings' which by IR 1986, r 13.7 means any proceedings under the IA 1986 or the IR 1986. Although it is arguable on the precise wording of the rule that a creditor may not attend by his authorised representative it is anticipated that the court will hold that such a representative fulfils the requirement of the rule.
2   IR 1986, r 12.4A(4).

Modifications

6.165 See paras **6.130–6.133**.

Adjournment of meeting

6.166 The chairman may adjourn a creditors' meeting from time to time, and he must do so if the meeting resolves to adjourn[1]. It is assumed that in fixing the time and place of the adjourned meeting the chairman must comply with the provisions of the Rules governing the summoning of the initial meeting[2]. The final adjournment may not be to a date later than 14 days after the original day on which the meeting is held[3]. The chairman may however apply to the court for an extension of time, either before or after the 14 days has expired, under the general power vested in the court to extend time limits[4].

Should a proposal fail to obtain the agreement of creditors on the final adjournment it is deemed to be rejected[5].

1   IR 1986, r 5.24(1).
2   Ie in accordance with IR 1986, r 5.18 which provide that (1) the nominee must 'have regard to the convenience of creditors' when fixing the venue; (2) the meeting must be summoned to commence between 10.00 and 16.00 hours on a business day. Presumably it will not be necessary for the chairman to send a further form of proxy which is required when summoning the initial meeting.
3   IR 1986, r 5.24(3). Such adjournment may take place even if the requisite majority has not been obtained after a vote, and indeed if the meeting resolves to adjourn the chairman must abide by this decision, IR 1986, r 5.24(2). Notice of any adjournment which follows a failed vote to approve the proposal must be given to the court, IR 1986, r 5.24(4).
4   IA 1986, s 376 or by IR 1986, r 12.9(2) which imports CPR r 3.1(2)(a) into the IR 1986 'so as to enable the court to extend or shorten the time for compliance with anything required or authorised to be done by the Rules'. Either under IA 1986, s 376 or IR 1986, r 12.9(2) and CPR r 3.1(2) an application to extend time may be made after the time limit in question has expired.
5   IR 1986, r 5.24(5).

Calculation of votes

6.167 Votes are calculated according to the amount of the creditor's debt as at the date of the meeting or, in the case of an arrangement proposed by a company in administration or liquidation or an undischarged bankrupt, the amount of the debt as at the date of the relevant insolvency order[1].

1   IR 1986, r 5.21(2).

Recording of votes

6.168 The chairman must take care to record how each creditor votes on each resolution taken at the meeting for he is required to include this information in his report to the court[1]. It follows that creditors' votes cannot be confidential.

1   IR 1986, r 5.27(2)(c).

Voting subject to objection

6.169 If in doubt whether to admit or reject a claim, or leave a vote out of account[1], the chairman should mark it as objected to and allow the creditor to vote subject to the vote being subsequently declared invalid if the objection to the claim is sustained[2]. See generally paras **6.143–6.145** above.

1   IR 1986, r 5.23(7) provides that the provisions of IR 1986, r 5.22 which grants and governs an appeal against the chairman's decision on entitlement to vote applies equally in relation to an appeal against the chairman's decision on whether a vote is to be left out of account or on whether a person is an associate of the debtor.
2   IR 1986, r 5.22(4), and see *Re a Debtor (No 222 of 1990) ex p Bank of Ireland* [1992] BCLC 137; *National Westminster Bank v Scher* [1998] BCLC 124, [1998] BPIR 224. But note *Re Cranley Mansions Ltd* [1994] 1 WLR 1610; the chairman should make a reasonable attempt to value the claim, perhaps with legal assistance if time permits, before he allows doubt to take over and passes the task to the courts.

Appeal from chairman's decision

6.170 Any creditor may appeal to the court against the chairman's decision on a creditor's entitlement to vote or on any value he puts on an unliquidated or unascertained debt[1], or any decision made by him whether or not to leave a vote out of account, see above, or to declare a resolution invalid[2].

[1]   IR 1986, r 5.22(3).
[2]   IR 1986, r 5.23(7).

Time for appeal

6.171 No appeal may be made to the court against the chairman's decision after the end of the period of 28 days from the first day on which each of the chairman's reports[1] is submitted to the court[2]. This time period may be extended under the court's general power to extend time limits[3].

[1]   The chairman is required by IA 1986, s 259(1) to report to the court at the conclusion of the creditors' meeting.
[2]   IR 1986, r 5.22(6). The scheme of the legislation is to restrict all appeals to this 28-day period but it is open to the court to extend the time for appealing, see paras **6.232–6.235**.
[3]   See para **6.154**, footnote 5.

Where chairman's decision is reversed

6.172 If on appeal the court reverses or varies the chairman's decision, or declares a creditor's vote invalid, the court may order another meeting to be summoned, or make such other order as it thinks just[1]. Before making such an order however, the court must first be satisfied that the matter is such as to give rise to unfair prejudice or a material irregularity[2].

[1]   IR 1986, r 5.22(5).
[2]   IR 1986, r 5.22(5); as to unfair prejudice and material irregularity see paras **6.204–6.213**, **6.222–6.226**.

Costs of appeal

6.173 The chairman may not be made personally liable for any costs incurred by any person in respect of an appeal against his decisions on voting rights, leaving votes out of account or the validity of resolutions[1]. He may become liable for costs however where on appeal his decision on voting is coupled with a challenge to the arrangement[2].

[1]   IR 1986, r 5.22(7), and as to leaving votes out of account or the validity of resolutions, IR 1986, r 5.23(7) which applies IR 1986, r 5.22(9) to an appeal against a chairman's decision as to leaving a vote out of account.
[2]   See para **6.157**.

Creditors' meeting: required majorities

6.174 In making provision for the majority required to approve the proposal for voluntary arrangement, the rules are concerned to ensure that minority creditors should not be forced into an acceptance by majority creditors who are closely associated in some way with the debtor[1]. Accordingly in order to secure approval the voluntary arrangements must pass what is in effect a two-stage process. First, any resolution to approve the proposal or any modification of the proposal must pass with a majority in excess of three-quarters in value of the creditors present in person (or by representative) or by proxy and voting on the resolution[2]. Secondly, notwithstanding the obtaining of this three-quarters majority, the resolution is nevertheless invalid if those voting against it include more than half in value of the creditors, counting only those:

(a)   to whom notice of the meeting was sent;
(b)   whose votes are not to be left out of account[3]; and
(c)   who are not associates[4] of the debtor, to the best of the chairman's belief[5].

[1]   That is IR 1986, r 5.23(1)(4).
[2]   IR 1986, r 5.23(1).
[3]   See paras **6.177–6.179**.
[4]   For 'associate' see IA 1986, s 435 set out in **Appendix 2**.
[5]   IR 1986, r 5.23(4).

6.175 It is for the chairman to decide whether a person is an associate of the debtor[1], subject to an appeal to the court[2].

[1]   IR 1986, r 5.23(5)(b), and for these purposes the chairman is entitled to rely on the information provided by the debtor's statement of affairs and on any further information given to the nominee, see paras **6.74–6.78**.
[2]   IR 1986, r 5.23(7), applying the provisions of IR 1986, r 5.22 to decisions by the chairman as to whether a person is an associate of the debtor.

6.176 In order to carry any resolution proposed at the creditors' meeting other than one to approve or modify the proposal a majority in excess of one-half in value of the creditors present in person or by proxy and voting on the resolution is required[1]. Any resolution which amends any essential term of the proposed composition or scheme of arrangement will be a resolution to modify the proposal and a three-quarters majority will be required. In order to determine whether any particular resolution is one which modifies the proposal regard may be had to the matters which must be dealt with in the proposal under IR 1986, r 5.3(2)[2]. As it is mandatory that these various matters should be stated or otherwise dealt with in the proposal it is hard to resist the conclusion that alteration of any these matters constitutes a modification of the proposal for the purpose of determining the majority required to pass the relevant resolution.

[1]   IR 1986, r 5.23(2).
[2]   See paras **6.69–6.70**.

Votes to be left out of account

6.177 A creditor's vote is to be left out of account where, in respect of any claim or part of a claim:

(a)   written notice of the claim was not given either at the meeting or before it, to the chairman or convener of the meeting;

(b)   the claim or part of a claim is secured[1];

(c)   the claim is in respect of a debt wholly or partly on, or secured by, a current bill of exchange or promissory note. However, where the creditor is willing to treat the liability to him on the bill or note of every person who is liable on it antecedently to the debtor, and against whom a bankruptcy order or winding-up order has not been made, as a security in his hands, and having estimated the value of this security, deduct it from his claim, the balance may be voted and the vote taken into account[2].

[1]   Where part only of a creditor's claim is secured only the secured part is to be discounted for the purpose of voting, *Re a Debtor (No 31/32/33 of 1993) ex p Calor Gas Ltd v Piercy* [1994] 2 BCLC 321, [1994] BCC 69.

[2]   IR 1986, r 5.23(3); with respect to sub rule (c) it is provided in the rule that the estimating of the value of the security provided by antecedent holders of the bill or promissory note is for the purpose of entitlement to vote only and not in respect of any distribution under the arrangement.

6.178 The chairman determines whether a vote should be left out of account under one of these heads[1]. It should be noted that creditors whose votes are left out of account are nevertheless creditors entitled to vote at the meeting, and will therefore be bound by the arrangement should it be approved.

[1]   IR 1986, r 5.23(5)(a).

6.179 The rule requiring written notice of the claim to be given to the chairman or convener of the meeting either at or before the meeting (para **6.177**(a) above) requires written notice to be given by the creditor seeking to vote, but does not require the giving of details of the claim[1]. However, the chairman is required by the IR 1986[2] to ascertain the entitlement of persons wishing to vote and for this purpose it may be necessary for the creditor to specify how his claim arises and how it is made up. In *Roberts v Pinnacle Entertainment Ltd*[3] the nominee wrongly rejected the proxy vote of a creditor whose claim was for more than 25% of the total, and who wished to vote against the voluntary arrangement, on the basis that his form of proxy did not specify the amount of his claim. The court held that as the debtor had admitted the claim in its full amount the chairman had sufficient evidence of the claim for the purposes of the Rules.

[1]   *Roberts v Pinnacle Entertainment Ltd* [2003] EWHC 2394 (Ch), [2004] BPIR 208 at [16]. Submitting a form of proxy gives the necessary notice.

[2]   IR 1986, r 5.22(1).

[3]   [2004] BPIR 208.

Approval of arrangements

6.180 The voluntary arrangement is approved if it secures the necessary majority, calculated as required by the Rules, in the creditors' meeting[1]. The voluntary arrangement then takes effect, duly approved, as if made by the debtor at the creditors' meeting on the necessary majority being secured[2].

Appointment of supervisor

6.181 On approving a proposal the creditors' meeting may pass a resolution providing that an authorised practitioner[1] other than the nominee be appointed supervisor of the voluntary arrangement, or that two or more authorised practitioners be appointed to act as supervisor[2].

1   See para **6.18**, an 'authorised practitioner' is an insolvency practitioner or a practitioner who is a member of a body authorised by the Secretary of State under IA 1986, s 389A to act in relation to voluntary arrangements.
2   See IR 1986, r 5.25(1).

6.182 It is usual for the nominee to be appointed supervisor, but it is not unknown for substantial creditors to make it a condition of supporting an arrangement that their preferred candidate becomes the supervisor. Where a resolution is moved to make an alternative appointment there must first be produced to the chairman at or before the creditors' meeting the written consent of the proposed supervisor to act and his written confirmation that he is qualified or authorised to act as a practitioner in relation to the debtor's voluntary arrangement[1]. Should two or more insolvency practitioners be appointed joint supervisors the creditors' meeting may resolve whether acts to be done in connection with the arrangement may be done by any one of them or must be done by both or all of them[2].

1   IR 1986, r 5.25(2).
2   IR 1986, r 5.25(1).

Chairman's report to the court

6.183 The chairman must prepare a report of the creditors' meeting for the court. No form is prescribed under IR 1986, but the report must contain the following information:

(a)   whether the proposed voluntary arrangement was approved, if appropriate specifying any modifications made, or rejected;

(b)   each resolution taken at the meeting, setting them out, and the decision in each case;

(c)   a list of all the creditors present or represented with the value of the debts, and how they voted on each resolution;

(d)   whether the EC Insolvency Regulation applies to the voluntary arrangement and, if so, whether the proceedings are main proceedings or territorial proceedings[1]; and

(e)   such further information as the chairman considers appropriate to make known to the court[2].

1   See **Chapter 4**. Strictly speaking the EC Insolvency Regulation always applies. The report to the court should presumably be concerned with the possibility that EC Regulation cross border issues might arise. The debtor might have a 'centre of main interests' in another EU

state, in which event the voluntary arrangement will be territorial proceedings. Alternatively the debtor has a 'centre of main interests' in the UK but has an 'establishment' in another EU state in respect of which there are territorial proceedings to which the voluntary arrangement will be main proceedings.

2 IR 1986, r 5.27(1)(2).

6.184 A copy of the chairman's report must be filed in court within four days of the meeting being held[1], and notice of the result of the meeting must be given to all those who were sent notice of the meeting immediately after the copy report is filed in court[2]. Where the debtor is a bankrupt, notice of the result of the creditors' meeting must be sent to the official receiver and any trustee[3].

1 IA 1986, s 259(1) requires the chairman to report; the time limit of four days is provided for by IR 1986, r 5.27(3) which further specifies that the court must endorse the filed copy with the date of filing.
2 IR 1986, r 5.27(4); r 5.27(4) further provides that the chairman must send notice of the result of the creditors' meeting to any other creditor of whom the chairman is aware who was not sent notice of the creditors' meeting.
3 IR 1986, r 5.27(4); the notice to creditors, the official receiver and any trustee must be sent immediately after the report is filed in court.

6.185 Where the report is that the meeting has declined to approve the debtor's proposal the court may, and in practice will, discharge any interim order which is in force in relation to the debtor[1]. A final order on consideration of the chairman's report may be made without the attendance of the parties provided the chairman's report has been filed and complies with the Rules[2]. The order records the effect of the chairman's report and discharges the interim order[3]. Where no interim order was obtained the court does not consider the chairman's report unless an application is made in relation to it[4].

1 IA 1986, s 259(2).
2 Ie IR 1986, r 5.27(1).
3 *Practice Direction: Insolvency Proceedings*, para 16.1(4), see **Appendix 1**.
4 IR 1986, r 5.27(5).

Register of individual voluntary arrangements

6.186 The Secretary of State is required to keep a register of individual voluntary arrangements[1]. Immediately after the chairman of the creditors' meeting has filed in court his report that the meeting has approved the individual voluntary arrangement, he must report the prescribed details[2] to the Secretary of State. This register is open to public inspection[3]. The supervisor of the individual voluntary arrangement is also required to give notice of his appointment as supervisor to the Secretary of State[4]. The IR 1986 now provide for old arrangements to be deleted from the register. IVAs in which a revocation order[5] was made before 22 March 1999 or where the final completion or termination of the arrangement occurred more than two years prior to 22 March 1999 have now been deleted from the register[6]. In future all entries in the register in respect of an IVA are deleted when the Secretary of State receives notice of a making of a revocation order[7], and after two years of receipt of notice of the full implementation or termination of an IVA[8] all entries in the register relating to that arrangement will be deleted[9].

1   IR 1986, r 5.28(1).
2   Namely (a) the name and address of the debtor, (b) the date on which the arrangement was approved by the creditors, (c) the name and address of the supervisor, and (d) the court in which the chairman's report has been filed, see IR 1986, r 5.29(1).
3   IR 1986, r 5.28(5). An application to inspect the Register of Voluntary Arrangements should be made to the General Services Team, 5th Floor, West Wing, Ladywood House, 45–46 Stephenson Street, Birmingham B2 4UP; Tel: 0121 698 4000, Fax 0121 698 4406. A request for a search may be made by post or fax but not by telephone. It is not unknown for practitioners to fail to make the required report, so it is not possible to obtain a complete picture of the number of Voluntary Arrangements by consulting the Register, neither can a negative search be relied on in any particular case.
4   IR 1986, r 5.29(2).
5   Under IA 1986, s 262.
6   IR 1986, r 5.28(2).
7   IR 1986, r 5.28(3); notice of a revocation order is given under IR 1986, r 5.30; see para 6.250.
8   Under IR 1986, r 5.34(3).
9   IR 1986, r 5.28(4).

Secured creditors

6.187 The scheme of the Insolvency Act is to leave any secured creditor outside the arrangement free to enforce his security as the law allows, unless he is prepared to join the arrangement despite any interference with his rights over his security that this may entail. Accordingly any vote which a secured creditor may cast at the creditors' meeting is to be left out of account to the extent that it relates to a claim or part of a claim which is secured[1]. The creditors' meeting may not approve any proposal or modification which affects the rights of a secured creditor of the debtor to enforce his security, except with the secured creditor's concurrence[2]. A secured creditor is, of course, entitled to vote in respect of any unsecured part of his claim[3].

1   IR 1986, r 5.23(3)(b).
2   IA 1986, s 258(4).
3   *Re a Debtor (Nos 31/32/33 of 1993) ex p Calor Gas Ltd v Piercy* [1994] 2 BCLC 321, [1994] BCC 69.

6.188 It is always possible that the terms of a voluntary arrangement may be so drawn as to interfere with the secured creditor's ability to enforce his security, but such terms will only prevent a secured creditor from enforcing his security when the secured creditor has clearly assented to them. The court will require clear language before interpreting the terms of the arrangement as interfering with a secured creditor's rights. Where an approved arrangement provided that creditors were not entitled 'to commence or continue any proceedings, execution or other legal process in respect of the [IVA] debts', the court held that while this language was apt to preclude proceedings to enforce the personal liability of the debtor it was not apt to preclude a secured creditor from enforcing his security even where to do so required recourse to the court. It therefore remained open to a secured creditor to enforce his security by action[1].

¹   *Rey v FNCB Ltd* [2006] EWHC 1386 (Ch), [2006] BPIR 1260, refusing permission to
    appeal the decision of His Honour Judge Peter Cowell. The court also drew attention to
    the fact that the terms of the arrangement incorporated IR 1986, r 6.115(1) (which permits
    a secured creditor to revalue his security, although only with the leave of the court if he has
    voted in respect of the unsecured balance), and held that the express inclusion of this rule
    is consistent only with the provision quoted in the text having no effect on security.

The position of the underlying debt

6.189   The distinction is to be drawn between the underlying debt owed to the
creditor and the security the creditor holds to enforce the discharge of the
debt. The language of IA 1986¹, protecting as it does 'the right of a secured
creditor of the debtor to enforce his security' without reference to the debt in
respect of which the creditor holds his security, lends itself to the argument
that an arrangement may adversely affect the creditors' underlying debt while
leaving untouched his right to enforce his security. Were this the case the
secured creditor would find himself in a worse position in a voluntary
arrangement than he would be in a liquidation or bankruptcy, where he would
be entitled to enforce his security to the full extent of the debt. This despite the
fact that the secured creditor cannot vote on the proposal or any modification
to the extent that his debt is secured. This can hardly have been intended by
Parliament². However, in *Re Naeem*³ the court, having stated that a landlord's
right of re-entry provides him with security for payment of the rent and that
the effect of the arrangement was to modify the landlord's claim for arrears of
rent in the same way as other creditors' claims were modified, stated that 'it
does not appear ... to be unfairly prejudicial that after such modification the
right to forfeit should only stand as security for the recovery of the modified
debt rather than the original one'. It is now clear that a landlord's right of
re-entry is not a security for the purposes of the Insolvency Act 1986⁴, and it
is suggested that for established forms of security the reasoning that the
security may be divorced from the debt secured and permitted to stand only
for the modified debt will not be followed.

¹   IA 1986, s 258(4).
²   Although it may be noted that Parliament did not take the opportunity presented by the
    passage of the bill which became the IA 2000 to amend IA 1986, s 258(4).
³   [1990] 1 WLR 48.
⁴   *Christopher Moran Holdings Ltd v Bairstow* [2000] 2 AC 172, HL at p 186; this is a
    decision on IA 1986, s 248 (corporate insolvency); see *Razzaq v Pala* [1997] 1 WLR 1336
    (Lightman J on IA 1986, s 383(2) – bankruptcy) and *Re Lomax Leisure Ltd* [2000]
    Ch 502, [1999] 2 BCLC 126 (Neuberger J on IA 1986, s 10(1)(b), company administration
    – previous regime).

Secured creditor voting in respect of secured debt

6.190   The primary rule is that where a secured creditor votes in respect of his
secured debt his vote is to be left out of account, and the fact that he has voted
has no bearing on his security¹. But voluntary arrangements are contractual,
and occasions may arise where, on the terms of the particular arrangement, a
secured creditor may impliedly if not expressly surrender his rights as a
secured creditor either by voting for the arrangement, or, more likely, by
accepting dividends under an approved arrangement. The appropriate

approach would be to ask whether, in the particular circumstances, the secured creditor is to be taken to have agreed to be treated as an unsecured creditor. If this is the case, and particularly if he has received dividends as if an unsecured creditor, it would be quite inappropriate for the creditor then to seek to enforce his security for the original debt or even the balance of that debt after deducting the dividends he has received[2].

[1]   IR 1986, r 5.23(3)(b).
[2]   See *Khan v Permayer* [2001] BPIR 95, CA; the security here was a second charge on a lease which at the time of the proposal was worth less than the sum secured by the first charge.

Date for valuation of security

6.191 Difficulties may arise where the value of the secured creditor's security fluctuates, especially where the secured creditor's vote as to the unsecured part of his debt may determine the outcome of the creditors' meeting whether or not to approve the arrangement. The relevant date for valuing the creditor's security will be the date of the creditors' meeting[1]. In cases of dispute the chairman will have to assess the value of the unsecured part of the secured creditor's claim by reference to the value of the security and allow the creditor to vote on this amount subject to any subsequent appeal.

[1]   IR 1986, r 5.21(2) except where the debtor is in formal insolvency in which event the date for valuing the security will be the date of the relevant insolvency order, whether administration, liquidation or bankruptcy.

Dividends payable on the unsecured balance

6.192 After approval and implementation of a voluntary arrangement the value of the security will affect the secured creditor's right to dividends in respect of the unsecured balance of his claim. The secured creditor is not bound by his original valuation[1]. He may realise his security for what it is worth at the time of realisation notwithstanding the fact that he has claimed and received dividends on the basis of a lower valuation[2]. Many voluntary arrangements deal with the potential difficulties which follow a fluctuating value to the security by importing the provisions of the IR 1986 as to revaluation, redemption and realisation of the security[3]. A secured creditor may claim in the arrangement in respect of any anticipated shortfall on a provisional basis (absent any express term to the contrary) without having to surrender the right to apply the proceeds of sale of its security towards the satisfaction of the whole of the unpaid balance of its debt[4]. Acceptance of a dividend will of course compromise any claim in respect of the unsecured portion of the debt. In the absence of a provision importing the IR 1986 as to security into the arrangement, or of any express terms governing the position, it is suggested that neither the supervisor nor the secured creditor will be bound by any value the chairman put on the security for the purposes of voting, even where the creditor has agreed the valuation, provided always that there are reasonable grounds for belief that the value of the security has changed by a significant margin. The supervisor will be well advised to adopt a generous valuation[5] for the purpose of paying dividends, while retaining sufficient reserves to pay more in the event that the creditor mounts a successful application to the court complaining of the valuation adopted[6]. Once a supervisor has paid dividend money away to a secured creditor he will have a restitutionary remedy to recover any excess as money paid under a mistake, but the costs involved may well be substantial and may fall on the supervisor[7].

[1] Unless there is an express provision in the voluntary arrangement to this effect to which he has assented.
[2] *Khan v Mortgage Express (No 2)* [2000] BPIR 473.
[3] IR 1986, rr 6.115–6.119.
[4] *Whitehead v Household Mortgage Corpn plc* [2002] EWCA Civ 1657, [2003] 1 All ER 319 para [26], where a mortgagee with a debt of £102,110 valued its security at £65,000 and accepted dividends on an unsecured balance of £37,110. The property was eventually sold for £137,000 when the mortgage debt had reached £118,000. As the mortgagee had not abandoned its security it was entitled to insist that the security be redeemed for the full amount of the mortgage debt. The court pointed out that in bankruptcy (and the position is the same in liquidation) the secured creditor is entitled to participate in a distribution of assets on a provisional basis. If it transpires that he has been paid too much he must repay the overpayment. In the absence of an express term in the voluntary arrangement the court should be slow to imply a term that would lead to a different result from that which would apply in the bankruptcy for which the voluntary arrangement was proposed as a substitute.
[5] Ie a valuation at the top of the bracket of realistic valuations.
[6] The creditor will be able to apply under IA 1986, s 263(3), see para **6.295**.
[7] *Whitehead v Household Mortgage Corpn plc* [2002] EWCA Civ 1657, [2003] 1 All ER 319, see para [24].

6.193 A tenant (as with the case of any debtor) has the right to apportion any payments he makes to a particular debt. Accordingly it is not open to a landlord to apply payments made in respect of rent which is not subject to a voluntary arrangement to rent which would be so subject. Having accepted payments apportioned to particular rental periods the landlord was fixed with the consequences of the payments in an action for forfeiture[1].

[1] *Thomas v Ken Thomas Ltd* [2006] EWCA Civ 1504, [2007] Bus LR 429, [2007] L&TR 21.

6.194 An execution creditor on whose behalf goods are seized under a writ of fieri facias[1] is a secured creditor for the purposes of voluntary arrangements despite the fact that the goods have not yet been sold[2].

[1] As to the nature of the security right derived from the writ of fieri facias, see *Re Davies, ex p Williams* (1872) LR 7 Ch App 314.
[2] *Peck v Craighead* [1995] 1 BCLC 337. NB compare the position in bankruptcy where an execution creditor who has not completed his execution or attachment at the date of the bankruptcy order is not entitled to retain the benefit of the execution or attachment as against the trustee, IA 1986, s 346(1) (bankruptcy).

F CHALLENGE TO ARRANGEMENTS

Grounds of challenge

6.195 The IA 1986[1] permits an application to be made to challenge the decision of the creditors' meeting on one or both of two grounds, namely:

(a)   that the arrangement as approved unfairly prejudices the interests of a creditor of the debtor;

(b)   that there has been some material irregularity at or in relation to the meeting[2].

1   IA 1986, s 262.
2   IA 1986, s 262(1).

6.196 It is not open to a creditor or anyone else to assert that the meeting's decision is invalid other than by a challenge under IA 1986[1]. The scheme of the Act is to provide a short time period, 28 days[2], within which an application may be made to challenge the meeting's decision after which the arrangement may proceed without fear of subsequent challenge even if it subsequently transpires that there was an irregularity at or in relation to the meeting or that one or more creditors' interests are prejudiced by the arrangement. Before the amendments introduced by the IA 2000 a creditor who had no notice of the creditors' meeting was not bound by any voluntary arrangement which was approved by the creditors. From 1 January 2003 however every creditor of the debtor is bound by a voluntary arrangement which has been approved by the creditors whether or not he received notice of the creditors' meeting or was otherwise aware of the proposal for a voluntary arrangement[3]. A creditor who was ignorant of the proposal and the summoning of the creditors' meeting is given a right of challenge on either of the above grounds, but he must issue his application to challenge within 28 days of becoming aware of the arrangement[4].

1   IA 1986, s 262(8).
2   See paras **6.232–6.235** as to this time limit, which may be extended.
3   IA 1986, s 260(2).
4   IA 1986, s 262(3)(b) as amended by IA 2000.

6.197 It is important to note the precise extent of these two grounds. Ground (a), that the arrangement as approved unfairly prejudices the interests of a creditor, relates only to unfairness brought about by the terms of the arrangement itself[1]. It does not cover the situation where a creditor is concerned that the proposal is in some way improper and unfair on creditors because, for example, the debtor's statement of affairs is not accurate and includes debts which are a sham or does not disclose all the debtor's assets.

1   *Re A Debtor (No 259 of 1990)* [1992] 1 All ER 641, [1992] 1 WLR 226; Hoffmann J, and see *Cadbury Schweppes plc v Somji* [2001] 1 WLR 615, CA para 37.

6.198 Ground (b) covers any material irregularity at or in relation to the creditors' meeting including irregularities involving voting in respect of which there may also be an appeal under the Rules[1]. Under this ground an application may be made to challenge a refusal of the creditors' meeting to approve the arrangements, as well as to an approval of the arrangements. The court has, however, no power to declare the arrangements approved. If satisfied that there was a material irregularity at or in relation to a meeting which rejected the proposed arrangements the court may give a direction for the summoning of a further meeting to reconsider the proposal with or without amendment[2].

¹   IR 1986, r 5.22(3) and see para **6.154**.
²   IA 1986, s 262(4) and see para **6.239**.

6.199 Where a creditor believes that the creditors' approval has been obtained under false pretences he may challenge the voluntary arrangement under ground (b) above or by presenting a petition for the insolvency of the debtor. In *Re A Debtor (87 of 1993) (No 2)*[1] the court decided that the provision of false or misleading information was information provided 'in relation to' the meeting, as this phrase covered documentation supplied in connection with the meeting. It was therefore open to a creditor to challenge the creditors' decision on the basis that there had been a material irregularity at or in relation to the meeting[2], ie ground (b) above. This approach does have the considerable advantage of flexibility. The court can exercise its powers[3] to give directions for a further meeting to consider revised proposals or reconsider the original proposal, and if the creditors so wish insolvency may be avoided.

¹   [1996] 1 BCLC 63.
²   See [1996] 1 BCLC 63 at 94–95.
³   Under IA 1986, s 262(4).

Petitioning for bankruptcy

6.200 The alternative to the statutory challenge to the voluntary arrangement is to petition for the debtor's bankruptcy. The IA 1986 expressly permits a creditor bound by an approved individual voluntary arrangement to present a petition where he can show that information which was false or misleading in any material particular or which contained misleading omissions was (i) contained in the debtor's statement of affairs or any other document supplied by the debtor to any person in the course of the approval of the IVA, or (ii) was in some way made available by the debtor to his creditors at or in connection with the creditors' meeting[1].

¹   IA 1986, s 264(1)(c), s 276(1)(b).

6.201 Where a creditor wishes to challenge a debt as a sham he must do so by way of appeal against the chairman's decision to allow the claim for the purposes of voting[1], and not by way of challenge under the IA 1986[2].

¹   Under IR 1986, rr 5.21, 5.22; see paras **6.154–6.158**.
²   *Re a Debtor (No 259 of 1990)* [1992] 1 WLR 226, 229; the challenge would be under IA 1986, s 262.

6.202 It should be emphasised that the statutory scheme for voluntary arrangements is that once an arrangement has been approved by the creditors' meeting the only routes to challenge or circumvent that approval are by direct challenge under IA 1986, s 262[1] or by indirect challenge by bankruptcy petition under IA 1986, s 264(1)(c), s 276(1)[2]. The Court of Appeal therefore refused to order that the approval of a voluntary arrangement was void when the debtor had failed to disclose that some only of the creditors had been given secret inducements to support the arrangement[3]. At first instance[4] the court had held, by reference to pre-1986 authorities, that there was a strict duty of good faith on the part of the debtor as between all competing unsecured creditors. Finding a breach of that duty the court held that the approval of the arrangements at the creditors' meeting was void. While overturning the declaration that the approval was void, the Court of Appeal effectively endorsed the existence of the strict duty of good faith on the part of the debtor[5], and made a bankruptcy order on the basis that information provided by the debtor was false and misleading in a material particular.

1   With its strict time limits, see paras **6.232–6.235**.
2   And see paras **6.332–6.338**.
3   *Cadbury Schweppes plc v Somji* [2001] 1 WLR 615.
4   [2001] 1 BCLC 498.
5   [2001] 1 WLR 615 at para 25 'The deputy judge's impressive survey of the old law shows that in relation to compositions and arrangements with creditors the court did impose a strict requirement of good faith as between competing unsecured creditors, and prohibited any secret inducement to one creditor even if that inducement did not come from the debtor's own estate. There is no strong presumption that a similar principle must be found in the new regime set out in Part VIII of the 1986 Act, but (to put it at its lowest) it would be no great surprise to find it there in one form or another' per Robert Walker LJ.

Challenge coupled with appeal from chairman's decision on voting

6.203 A challenge to the meeting's decision with respect to a proposed arrangement may be brought together with an appeal against the chairman's decision as to a creditor's entitlement to vote[1].

1   See eg *Re A Debtor (No 222 of 1990) ex p Bank of Ireland* [1992] BCLC 137, and many other cases where both applications have been brought together. See paras **6.154–6.158** for appeal against the chairman's decision as to voting.

Ground (a): unfair prejudice

6.204 To constitute a good ground of challenge under this head the unfair prejudice complained of must result from the terms of the arrangement itself, and not the fact of the individual voluntary arrangement or some extraneous matter, such as the status of any of the debts or the conduct of other creditors. Whether a voluntary arrangement unfairly prejudices the interests of a creditor is to be judged on the information available at the time that the voluntary arrangement was approved[1].

1   *Prudential Assurance Co Ltd v PRG Powerhouse Ltd* [2007] EWHC 1002 (Ch), [2007] 19 EG 164 (CS).

6.205 A creditor applicant must show that the prejudice is to his interests as a creditor and not in some other capacity[1]. Accordingly a scheme which proposed a 10% dividend to all creditors could not be unfairly prejudicial on the basis that the debts of certain of the supporting creditors were suspicious[2]. It is not unfair prejudice that by entry into voluntary arrangement the debtor escapes the investigation into past business dealings, assets and debts, and third party transactions that would follow bankruptcy. Any challenge to the voluntary arrangement should demonstrate that the scheme has been framed in a manner which prejudices a creditor or class of creditor in a way which is unfair compared to what would have been the position if the scheme had been framed in a different way[3].

1   *Re a Debtor (No 259 of 1990)* [1992] 1 WLR 226; *Re a Debtor (No 87 of 1993) (No 2)* [1996] 1 BCLC 63, 86; *Doorbar v Alltime Securities Ltd* [1996] 2 All ER 948; *Re a Debtor (No 574 of 1995)* [1998] 2 BCLC 124; and see *Cadbury Schweppes v Somji* [2001] 1 WLR 615, at para 37 per Robert Walker LJ: 'It is sufficient to say that there is a fairly strong line of first-instance authority, starting with the decision of Hoffmann J in *Re a Debtor (No 259 of 1990)*, which is uniformly in favour of limiting the effect of the provision to unfairness brought about by the terms of the IVA itself. As Hoffmann J pointed out in that case, at p 229, section 276(1) provides an alternative remedy in many cases of unfairness brought about by other causes.'
2   *Re a Debtor (No 259 of 1990)* [1992] 1 All ER 641, [1992] 1 WLR 226; there might however have been a material irregularity at or in relation to the meeting, see paras **6.222–6.226**.
3   *Re a Debtor (No 259 of 1990)* [1992] 1 All ER 641, [1992] 1 WLR 226; *Re a Debtor (No 574 of 1995)* [1998] 2 BCLC 124, sub nom *National Westminster Bank v Scher* [1998] BPIR 225.

6.206 Neither the IA 1986 nor the IR 1986 attempt a definition of 'unfair prejudice'. It is not a term which has been used in previous insolvency legislation. 'Prejudice' denotes something detrimental to existing rights[1]. All creditors who do not receive 100p in the £ will to that extent be prejudiced by the arrangement. A creditor's rights can however go beyond the actual amount of his debt; the date of payment, the right to require further transactions at existing rates, restrictions on other dealings, the availability of other remedies, and the ability to exploit licences all being examples. The concept of 'unfairness' suggests a differential treatment as between creditors. As was stated in *Doorbar v Alltime Securities Ltd (No 2)*[2]:

'Unfair prejudice ... is a reference to the degree of prejudice to one creditor or class of creditors as compared with other creditors or class of creditors. It involves an assessment of any imbalance between possible prejudices to one or the other ... The concept of unfair prejudice is aimed at disproportionate prejudice on one side or the other.'

1   See e g *Re a Company (No 4475 of 1982)* [1983] Ch 178, 188.
2   [1995] 2 BCLC 513, at 518, Knox J.

6.207 Differential treatment may more obviously appear where one creditor is expected to receive a lower dividend under the arrangement than other creditors who have no better security for their debts. It is also possible however that prejudice is suffered by a particular creditor even where the dividends payable under the arrangement are equal. Where one creditor had rights under the Third Party (Rights against Insurers) Act 1930 he was unfairly prejudiced by an arrangement which might have prevented him proceeding to judgment for the full amount of his claim against the assured, thus prejudicing his statutory rights against the assured's insurers[1]. Other examples of prejudice being suffered by a creditor despite receiving an equal dividend under the arrangement would include a creditor who is bound to pay a proportion of the original monies due from the debtor to a subcontractor or agent who is not bound by the arrangement, or a creditor who is prevented by the arrangement from completing an execution[2]. The fact that the majority creditors have collateral benefits through eg friendship or the continued provision of specialist services, might result in unfair prejudice to the minority creditors who receive no such benefits even though all creditors receive an equal dividend[3]. Where the terms of the arrangement provide for the release from liability of a co-debtor or surety, a creditor who loses his additional rights of recourse against a co-debtor or surety may be unfairly prejudiced[4]. A voluntary arrangement does not affect proprietary rights such as the right of a landlord to forfeit a debtor's lease[5], although the terms of an arrangement might be drawn so as to restrict such a right with the consent of the landlord.

[1] Sea *Voyager Maritime Inc v Bielecki* [1999]1 All ER 628.
[2] Although if it could be shown that the creditor would not have been able to complete his execution before the date on which, but for the voluntary arrangement, the debtor would have been made insolvent he will not have been prejudiced, see IA 1986, s 183 (liquidation), s 346 (bankruptcy).
[3] See eg *Re a Debtor (No 101 of 1999) (No 2)* [2001] BPIR 996, where the court refused to direct a further meeting to consider revised proposals after a successful challenge. Although all the creditors were to receive an equal dividend under the new proposal the court considered that a 75% majority of creditors could only be achieved through the votes of friends or creditors motivated by a desire that the debtor, a racehorse trainer, could continue to train their horses. Such collateral benefits were not available to the minority creditors, the Inland Revenue and Customs & Excise (now HM Revenue & Customs).
[4] *Johnson v Davies* [1998] 2 BCLC 252, 270.
[5] *Re Naeem (a bankrupt) (No 18 of 1988)* [1990] 1 WLR 48.

6.208 In some circumstances however it may not be unfair to treat creditors differently, certainly in respect of different classes of debt. It may be necessary for example to pay suppliers in full in order to ensure that the debtor can continue to trade and so earn the funds which underpin the voluntary arrangement[1]. Indeed in appropriate circumstances there may be unfair prejudice where the terms of the arrangement fail to discriminate in favour of a particular creditor or class of creditors[2]. There was unfair prejudice to a creditor where the effect of the voluntary arrangement could have been to prevent him pursuing his claim against the debtor for the purpose of making a claim against the debtor's insurers[3] even though under the terms of the arrangement all unsecured creditors were treated the same[4].

[1] *Sea Assets Ltd v PT Garuda Indonesia* [2001] EWCA Civ 1696, [2000] 4 All ER 371 at [45]–[46]; *IRC v Wimbledon Football Club Ltd* [2004] EWCA Civ 655, [2005] 1 BCLC 66 at [18]; *Sisu Capital Fund Ltd v Tucker* [2005] EWHC 2170 (Ch), [2006] BCC 463; *Prudential Assurance Co Ltd v PRG Powerhouse Ltd* [2007] EWHC 1002 (Ch), [2007] 19 EG 164.
[2] See eg *Re Primlaks (UK) Ltd (No 2)* [1990] BCLC 234, 236–7; *Sea Voyager Maritime Inc v Bielecki* [1999] 1 All ER 628, 642.
[3] Under the Third Parties (Rights against Insurers) Act 1930.
[4] See *Sea Voyager Maritime Inc v Bielecki* [1999] 1 All ER 628. In the event, at a further meeting of creditors, a modification was approved permitting the relevant creditor to sue the debtor provided he undertook not to enforce any judgment obtained against the debtor's personal assets.

6.209 When considering the question of prejudice the court may wish to compare the position of dissenting creditors under the arrangement with that in the event of liquidation, but such a comparison is not determinative[1]. Where the proposal provided for the Inland Revenue and the Customs & Excise to be paid a dividend of about 19% in priority to the remaining creditors whose debts were, however, not compounded, the proposal was held to be unfair. The result of the proposed arrangement would have been that the remaining creditors (all friends of the debtor) would have succeeded in removing £77,000 of competing debt at a cost of £15,000 against the wishes of the Crown creditors whose debts were eliminated. It was not rendered fair by the fact that the Crown creditors were likely to receive less in the event of the debtor's bankruptcy or the fact that the debtor had no assets immediately available with which to pay the remaining creditors[2].

1   See *Re a Debtor (No 222 of 1990) ex p Bank of Ireland* [1992] BCLC 137, 145; *Re a Debtor (No 87 of 1993) (No 2)* [1996] 1 BCLC 63, 86.
2   *Re a Debtor (No 101 of 1999)* [2001] 1 BCLC 54. A further, inappropriate, proposal was then made, see *Re a Debtor (No 101 of 1999) (No 2)* [2001] BPIR 996.

6.210 In considering whether or not there has been unfairness the court should have regard to all the circumstances, including the alternatives available to the debtor and to the creditors together with the practical consequences of a decision either to approve or reject the proposed voluntary arrangement, but unfair prejudice must necessarily be demonstrated on the terms of the arrangement itself[1]. In *Sisu Capital Fund Ltd v Tucker*[2] the court had to consider a challenge to company voluntary arrangements approved in respect of two subsidiary companies, one in administration and one in liquidation, the position being the more complex because of dealings between companies in the group and the allocation of payments made to the holding company between the subsidiaries. The court considered the duty of the respective office-holders, whose interests were in conflict, in seeking to structure voluntary arrangements which would achieve the required statutory majorities without unfairly prejudicing any particular creditor. The fact that an office-holder faced a conflict of interest and was in breach of his own professional rules was not itself enough to establish unfair prejudice. The court had to look at the terms of the company voluntary arrangement to decide whether a creditor was prejudiced and it mattered not that criticism could be made of the process by which the final proposal was arrived at. Neither could it be suggested by any creditor or class of creditor that they were unfairly prejudiced by a company voluntary arrangement because had the office-holders proceeded by way of scheme of arrangement[3] they would have been able to block the scheme as a separate class. Furthermore, in the circumstances, the fact that the company voluntary arrangements contained a release of the office-holders with regard to the manner in which they had performed their functions did not unfairly prejudice the applicants because their claims against the office-holders were fraught with difficulty.

1   *Sisu Capital Fund Ltd v Tucker* [2005] EWHC 2170 (Ch), [2006] BCC 463.
2   [2005] EWHC 2170 (Ch), [2006] BCC 463.
3   Under CA 1985, s 425, CA 2006, ss 895ff.

6.211 Any proposal which infringes the provisions of the IA 1986 requiring the payment of preferential debts in priority to non-preferential debts[1] must unfairly prejudice the interests of that creditor[2].

1   Ie IA 1986, s 258(5)(a).

2   *IRC v Wimbledon Football Club Ltd* [2004] EWCA Civ 655, [2005] 1 BCLC 66 at [36].
     From 15 September 2003 Crown debts no longer have priority. The three remaining
     categories of preferential debt are (a) contributions to occupational pension schemes, (b)
     employee remuneration up to a prescribed limit, and (c) levies on coal and steel production
     under the ECSC Treaty.

6.212 There is little prospect that a successful challenge to an arrangement
may be mounted solely on the ground that it is unfairly weighted toward the
debtor. That is a matter for the creditors. Indeed, an arrangement which
provides for a nil dividend to unsecured creditors is capable of being a valid
scheme of arrangement under the IA 1986[1]. It follows that the court will not
speculate whether the terms of the proposal are the best which could have
been obtained; when considering unfair prejudice the comparison to be made
(in the absence of bad faith by debtor or nominee) is between the proposed
arrangement and no arrangement at all[2].

1   *IRC v Adam & Partners Ltd* [2001] 1 BCLC 222, CA. Where there is a nil dividend there
     cannot be a composition. See also *IRC v Bland* [2003] EWHC 1068, [2003] BPIR 1274.
2   *Re Greenhaven Motors Ltd* [1999] 1 BCLC 635, at 643d; *Sisu Capital Fund Ltd v Tucker*
     [2005] EWHC 2170 (Ch), [2006] BCC 463.

6.213 The term 'unfairly prejudicial' is used in sections 994–999 of the
Companies Act 2006, the provisions designed to give protection to minority
shareholders, but it is unlikely that assistance may be had from decisions
under these provisions[1]. However, in voluntary arrangements as with minority
protection cases the test of unfairness is an objective one[2]. Where members of
the same class are not treated equally it will not be difficult to establish
prejudice[3]. Equal treatment however does not preclude unfair prejudice, as
noted above, and in rare cases it may be shown that an intention to
discriminate did not in fact give rise to unfairness[4].

1   Note the comments of Peter Gibson LJ in *Doorbar v Alltime Securities Ltd* [1996] 1 BCLC
     487, at 498h, and Robert Walker LJ in *Cadbury Schweppes plc v Somji* [2001] 1 WLR 615
     para 37.
2   *Re R A Noble & Sons (Clothing) Ltd* [1983] BCLC 273, 290.
3   *Re Carrington Viyella plc* (1983) 1 BCC 98, 951; *Re A Company (No 2612 of 1984)*
     [1985] BCLC 800, but it does not necessarily follow that different treatment amounts to
     unfair prejudice, see *Re Cancol Ltd* [1996] 1 All ER 37, [1996] 1 BCLC 100.
4   See *Re Cumana Ltd* [1986] BCLC 430, CA; *Re a Company* [1986] BCLC 362.

Prejudice in practice

6.214 The court looks to see whether the applicant has suffered practical
prejudice; it is not sufficient that prejudice can be demonstrated in theory on
an academic approach to the terms of the arrangement. Thus where the terms
of a voluntary arrangement appeared to discriminate against two banks who
alone of the unsecured creditors were required to forgo their rights against the
debtor's wife, because the wife had no assets of her own and no separate
income the banks were held not to have suffered unfair prejudice in being
prevented from suing her[1]. Neither was it unfairly prejudicial for the arrangement to allow for future creditors whose co-operation for the continuation of
the business was essential to be paid in full whereas other creditors would

merely receive a dividend[2]. The court expressed the view that the distinction proposed between the categories of future creditors was a 'realistic and commercially sensible' distinction, and on this basis rejected the argument that the different treatment which the terms of the arrangement afforded these creditors amounted to unfair prejudice.

[1]   *Re a Debtor (No 574 of 1995)* [1998] 2 BCLC 124, 131 (sub nom *National Westminster Bank v Scher* [1998] BPIR 224, 230 (it would appear that the banks would have been better advised to cross-examine the debtor in this case and perhaps sought disclosure against the wife, CPR Pt 34.2), see also *Re a Debtor (No 259 of 1990)* [1992] 1 All ER 641, [1992] 1 WLR 226; it is not a material irregularity to fail to notify the debtor's ex-wife who as an associate could not effectively vote against the IVA.

[2]   *Re Cancol Ltd* [1996] 1 BCLC 100 sub nom *Cazaly Irving Holdings v Cancol* [1996] BPIR 252.

6.215   In *Swindon Town Properties Ltd v Swindon Town Football Co Ltd*[1] the applicant complained that a company voluntary arrangement entered into while the company was in administration unfairly prejudiced his rights as a debenture holder because under the company voluntary arrangement implemented funds would be channelled to the creditors participating in the arrangement rather than be paid to the applicant under its debenture. The company voluntary arrangement (as was to be expected) contemplated the discharge of the administration order. This would leave the debenture holder free to enforce its security. The debenture-holder did not wish to do so (football club cases have more than purely commercial considerations in play), but, as the court observed, the applicant could not have its cake and eat it. There was no basis for holding that the creditor was unfairly prejudiced by the fact that the company intended to trade for the purposes of the arrangement and pay the proceeds of its trading to the participating creditors.

[1]   [2003] BPIR 253, [2002] All ER (D) 85.

Third party funding

6.216   Difficulties may arise in cases where money made available by a third party is used to pay some creditors but not others in apparent prejudice to those not paid. Where those monies do not and will never belong to the debtor, and have in no way been contributed to by the debtor, it will be a matter for the third party which creditors receive the benefit of his money and a disappointed creditor cannot complain that he is prejudiced by non-payment[1]. It will however be an unusual case where the third party payments do not impact in some way on the debtors' assets, for example by a reduction in the purchase price otherwise payable for assets of the debtor. In such cases there will be prejudice to the creditors who do not receive payments from the third party and they will be able successfully to challenge the proposal's approval.

[1]   See *IRC v Wimbledon Football Club Ltd* [2004] EWCA Civ 655, [2004] BPIR 700 at [54] where the disappointed creditor was a preferential creditor who complained that the result of the payments to the 'football creditors' (whose support was essential to the viability of the CVA) was a breach of IA 1986, s 4(4)(a) which prohibits the approval of any proposal which provides for the payment of the debtor's preferential debts otherwise than in priority to the debts of the ordinary creditors.

Unfair prejudice: position of debtor's landlord

6.217 Unless expressly agreed otherwise, the debtor's future liability to pay rent will be subject to the terms of the arrangement. The landlord will be bound to an approved arrangement in respect of future rent because, as a creditor with a future debt, he will be entitled to vote at the creditors' meeting. The chairman should make a proper assessment of the value of the landlord's prospective claim, but even if, for whatever reason, the chairman is unable to or fails to value this claim the Rules now provide that the claim is to be valued at £1 if no higher value is put upon it[1]. In addition to his right in debt to the rent, the landlord will have additional rights against his tenant under the lease in the nature of security. In particular the right to distrain for unpaid rent, and the right to re-enter and forfeit the lease in the event of non-payment of rent and, usually, in the case of insolvency of the tenant[2]. In *March Estates plc v Gunmark Ltd*[3] the court confirmed that the landlord's right to re-enter and the right to forfeit are security rights for the purposes of the IA 1986. To the extent that he is a secured creditor the approval of an arrangement by the tenant's creditors may not affect the landlord's rights against his wishes[4]. Any attempt to do so without the landlord's consent will amount to unfair prejudice, assuming that the relevant provisions in the arrangement are valid and bind the landlord at all[5]. An arrangement which provided that the lease should be sold as soon as possible was not unfairly prejudicial to the landlord however, as on a proper construction of the arrangement it was only intended to bind the landlord in his capacity as creditor and did not affect his right to forfeit the lease[6]. As regards rent however the landlord is in no different position than other unsecured creditors. An arrangement may postpone, modify or even extinguish the landlord's rights both to arrears and future rent, without this being of itself unfair prejudice[7]. Although the landlord's right to recover future rent as a debt may be modified by the arrangement it would seem that the better view is that where the landlord seeks to forfeit the lease the debtor would only be entitled to relief against forfeiture by paying the reserved rent in full[8]. In valuing the landlord's claim for future rent for voting purposes the chairman is entitled to take into account the degree of likelihood that the landlord will exercise his right of re-entry. It was not a material irregularity therefore where the chairman restricted the landlord's future claim to one year's rent[9]. In *Doorbar v Alltime Securities Ltd (No 2)*[10] the landlord had a right to require the surety to take a new lease in the event that the tenant became bankrupt and the trustee disclaimed the lease. The landlord claimed that it was unfairly prejudiced by the arrangement as it would prevent the right to require the surety to take a new lease from coming into effect. Both at first instance and in the Court of Appeal it was held that the interest of the landlord in enforcing his right against the surety fell outside the scope of IA 1986, s 262, as it was a right exercisable against a person other than the debtor and which arose through disclaimer by the debtor's trustee. It was therefore a substitute for rather than a constituent part of the debtor's indebtedness[11].

---

1   IR 1986, r 5.21(3), see paras **6.143–6.144**. Before 1 January 2003 it was necessary for the chairman to put a value on the claim if the landlord was to be bound to the arrangement, see *Doorbar v Alltime Securities (No 2)* [1995] 2 BCLC 513 overruling *Burford Midland Properties Ltd v Marley Extensions* [1995] 1 BCLC 102, [1994] BCC 604.

2   Note however that a landlord's right of re-entry is not a security for the purposes of the IA 1986, *Christopher Moran Holdings Ltd v Bristow* [2000] 2 AC 172, HL; *Razzaq v Pala* [1997] 1 WLR 1336; *Re Lomax Leisure Ltd* [2000] Ch 502, [1999] 2 BCLC 126. See also in connection with Rent Act tenancies, *Cadogan Estates Ltd v McMahon* [2001] 1 AC 378.
3   [1996] 2 BCLC 1.
4   IA 1986, s 258(4); *Doorbar v Alltime Securities Ltd (No 2)* [1995] 2 BCLC 513.
5   While the landlord may assert that any such provision must be invalid by reason of IA 1986, s 258(4), he must be careful not to act so as to give implied consent.
6   *Re Naeem (a bankrupt) (No 18 of 1988)* [1990] 1 WLR 48.
7   *Re Cancol Ltd* [1996] 1 All ER 37, [1996] BPIR 252; *March Estates v Gunmark* [1996] 2 BCLC 1.
8   In *Re Naeem (a bankrupt) (No 18 of 1988)* [1990] 1 WLR 48 the court expressed the view that relief from forfeiture would be given on payment of the modified not reserved rent. This was doubted in *March Estates v Gunmark* [1996] 2 BCLC 1 where the court considered that the basis on which the Court of Appeal had decided *Doorbar v Alltime Securities Ltd* [1996] 2 All ER 948 was that the reserved rent would have to be paid to secure relief.
9   *Doorbar v Alltime Securities Ltd (No 2)* [1995] 2 BCLC 513, 527, upheld on appeal, see footnote 10 below.
10   [1995] 2 BCLC 513 (Knox J), CA.
11   See [1996] 1 BCLC 487 at 499.

6.218 The assignee of the reversion will be bound to a voluntary arrangement to the same extent as a landlord[1].

1   *Burford Midland Properties Ltd v Marley Extrusions Ltd* [1995] 1 BCLC 102.

6.219 Where the tenant's interest under the lease has been assigned the original tenant and any intermediate assignor will usually remain liable on their covenants to the landlord in respect of rent for periods covered by the voluntary arrangement. The statutory binding which operates on creditors' claims is not the equivalent to a release by accord or satisfaction or a release under seal. Accordingly the making of a voluntary arrangement by the assignee tenant does not operate to release the original tenant or subsequent assignors from liability to the landlord under their covenants[1]. If a tenant by assignment enters into a voluntary arrangement the original and any subsequent assignor tenants face the difficulty that there is no provision in the IA 1986 to enable a vesting order to be made. The original and any subsequent assignor tenants should be given notice of the creditors' meeting as they will be contingent if not actual creditors[2]. The possibility may be canvassed at the creditors' meeting that the voluntary arrangement contain a provision for the re-vesting of the lease in the original or one of the subsequent assignor tenants[3].

1   *R A Securities Ltd v Mercantile Credit Co Ltd* [1995] 3 All ER 581; *Mytre Investments Ltd v Reynolds* [1995] 3 All ER 588.
2   *Mytre Investments Ltd v Reynolds* [1995] 3 All ER 588.
3   *Mytre Investments Ltd v Reynolds* [1995] 3 All ER 588.

Unfair prejudice: IVA: position of spouse or dependent child

6.220 A spouse, former spouse or dependent child may be in a different position from other creditors in that any obligation arising under an order made in family proceedings or under a maintenance assessment made under the Child Support Act 1991 (a 'matrimonial debt') does not give rise to a debt provable in a bankruptcy[1] neither will a matrimonial debt be released on the bankrupt's discharge[2]. Although a matrimonial debt is not provable in bankruptcy it is nevertheless a debt on which a bankruptcy petition may be founded; it will only be in rare cases however that a bankruptcy order is made on such a petition[3]. A spouse with a matrimonial debt is a creditor to whom notice must be given of the creditors' meeting[4], and is a creditor capable of being bound by an IVA[5]. As a spouse has a right to assert a matrimonial debt notwithstanding the release of debts which accompanies the bankrupt's discharge, he or she has a right which is not enjoyed by creditors generally. That right is overridden by the terms of any arrangement which compels acceptance of a dividend in satisfaction of a matrimonial debt, and the spouse is unfairly prejudiced as a consequence[6]. The appropriate course is for the IVA to provide that the matrimonial debt is not extinguished at the end of the arrangement[7].

1 IR 1986, r 12.3(2).
2 IA 1986, s 281(5)(b).
3 *Russell v Russell* [1999] 2 FCR 137, [1998] BPIR 259.
4 *Re Bradley-Hole (a bankrupt)* [1995] 4 All ER 865, [1995] BCC 418; the point was conceded but Rimer J considered the concession to be well founded.
5 *Re a Debtor, JP v Debtor* [1999] BPIR 206; *Re Bradley-Hole (a bankrupt)* [1995] 4 All ER 865, [1995] BCC 418.
6 *Re a Debtor (No 488 I0 of 1996), JP v Debtor* [1999] BPIR 206.
7 See *Re Timothy* [2005] EWHC 1885 (Ch), [2006] BPIR 329 where the CSA was not permitted to challenge an IVA which extinguished the debtor's obligation to pay mainte-nance for his 10 year old daughter where the application was made some nine months' out of time. And see paras **6.232–6.235**.

6.221 It is a standard term in many arrangements that a creditor whose claim falls within the definition in the Insolvency Rules of those debts which are not provable[1] is not entitled to vote in connection with or prove in the arrange-ment, and will not be a creditor entitled to make an application for the purposes of IA 1986, s 262. The aim of this standard term is to keep the IVA separate from matrimonial claims. However, in *Re a Debtor (No 488 I0 of 1996), JP v Debtor*[2] the proposal included the matrimonial debt as a liability in the statement of affairs. Sir John Vinelott held that the standard condition was by implication excluded by this inclusion of the debt in the proposal.

1 Ie IR 1986, r 12.3(2) (matrimonial debts, criminal fines, drugs trafficking confiscation order obligations).
2 [1999] BPIR 206, at 217.

Ground (b): material irregularity

6.222 The second ground for an application to challenge the approval of a voluntary arrangement is that there has been 'some material irregularity at or in relation to' the creditors' meeting. There is no statutory definition either of 'material' or 'irregularity'.

6.223 *Irregularity at the meeting:* The IA 1986 imposes three requirements on the meeting(s) namely that (1) no modification may be agreed which causes the proposal to cease to be either a composition or scheme of arrangement[1], (2) no proposal or modification may be agreed which affects the right of a secured creditor except with his consent[2], (3) no proposal or modification may be agreed which removes the priority of a preferential debt or which provides for a smaller dividend to be payable in respect of preferential debts except with the consent of the preferential creditor[3]. Subject to these requirements the meetings must be conducted in accordance with the Rules[4]. Accordingly any failure of the chairman to comply with the Rules whether as to voting or otherwise will be an irregularity[5]. It follows that an incorrect decision of the chairman as to the voting entitlement of a creditor will give rise to an appeal both under the IR 1986, by way of appeal from the decision itself, and under IA 1986 as a material irregularity at the meeting[6].

1   IA 1986, s 258(3); the debtor must consent to each modification, IA 1986, s 258(2).
2   IA 1986, s 258(4).
3   IA 1986, s 258(5).
4   IA 1986, s 258(6).
5   See paras **6.142–6.174.**
6   *Re Cranley Mansions Ltd* [1994] 1 WLR 1610, where the chairman's arbitrary reduction of a creditor's claim from, an admittedly excessive, £900,000 to a nominal £1 without the creditors' agreement was held to be a breach of IR 1986, r 1.17(3) (r 1.49(3) where a moratorium is in force) and a material irregularity. Ferris J held that the creditor had no entitlement to vote at all and was therefore not bound by the arrangement. Equally this meant that she could not challenge the meeting's decision, as she was not ' a person entitled in accordance with the rules to vote at the [creditors'] meeting', see IA 1986, s 262(2); but see *Doorbar v Alltime Securities Ltd (Nos 1 and 2)* [1996] 1 WLR 456, CA. Also *Re Wisepark Ltd* [1994] BCC 221 at 223; *Re a Debtor (No 400 IO 1996), JP v Debtor* [1997] 1 WLR 1319, *Re a Debtor (No 574 of 1995)* [1998] 2 BCLC 124 at 127, and see paras **6.217–6.219.** See also *Re Sweatfield Ltd* [1998] BPIR 276 where the chairman's decision on the value of the claim for voting purposes was held not to be an irregularity at all.

6.224 Many creditors can afford neither the time nor the expense of attending the creditors' meeting and take advantage of the form of proxy which must be sent out with the notice summoning the meeting[1]. A proxy which is faxed to the chairman is valid for the purposes of voting, and the refusal of the chairman to admit it for voting is an irregularity[2]. A creditor is entitled to alter the terms of the authority given by proxy, and the refusal of the chairman to admit the altered proxy for voting is an irregularity[3]. It is not unusual for further information to become available after the proposal has been sent to creditors, often only at the meeting itself on questioning the debtor. This can cause difficulties with proxy votes sent in without the benefit of the further information. A nominee who obtains proxy votes in favour of the proposal should assess the possible impact of further information on the creditors and not cast the proxies without further reference to the creditors involved unless confident that it is proper to do so. When the new information is significant the nominee is duty bound to adjourn the meeting and report the new information to all creditors even if this means having to seek an extension of time for the holding of the meeting and any moratorium[4].

1   IR 1986, r 5.18(3).
2   *IRC v Conbeer* [1996] BPIR 398; the point taken was that a form of proxy had to be signed, see IR 1986, r 8.2. Laddie J held the faxed signature should be treated as authentic unless there are surrounding circumstances which indicate otherwise, and see 404–5, where the learned judge considered that other forms of electronically generated signatures would be sufficient for the purposes of the rules.

³   *Re Cardona* [1997] BPIR 604.
⁴   *Cadbury Schweppes plc v Somji* [2001] 1 WLR 615, para 25.

6.225 Where a creditor attended the meeting although he had not been given notice of it he was entitled to vote; failure to allow the creditor to vote would have amounted to an irregularity¹. An error as to a proxy vote on the chairman's schedule of creditors might be suggestive of other mistakes, but where the complainant failed to take up the chairman's offer to allow him to inspect the proxies the court summarily dismissed the complaint of irregularity².

¹   See eg *Re a Debtor (No 400 IO of 1996)* [1997] 1 WLR 1319, [1997] 2 BCLC 144 a case decided under what was IR 1986, r 5.17 (now r 5.21) not IA 1986, s 262.
²   *Swindon Town Properties Ltd v Swindon Town Football Co Ltd* [2003] BPIR 253, 257D.

6.226 When considering a potential irregularity which does not itself constitute a breach of the Rules, such as decisions by the chairman as to what information to put before creditors, the chairman has a margin of appreciation. The court will only find that there has been an irregularity and interfere if a judgment made by the chairman about the material to be placed before creditors is one to which no reasonable insolvency practitioner could come; and the court will make that decision on the basis of the material available to the chairman at the time and not with the benefit of hindsight¹. But the reasonable chairman is conscious of the fact that the purpose of the creditors' meeting is to enable the creditors to decide what is the best way forward for themselves and not have that decision pre-empted by the chairman². A misrepresentation to the creditors will be an irregularity. An insolvency practitioner who chooses to explain must give a fair and balanced explanation, and questions must be answered fairly and not in a manner which might mislead the creditors³.

¹   *Re Trident Fashions plc, Anderson v Kroll Ltd* [2004] 2 BCLC 35 at [39].
²   *Re Trident Fashions plc, Anderson v Kroll Ltd* [2004] 2 BCLC 35 at [42].
³   *Re Trident Fashions plc, Anderson v Kroll Ltd* [2004] 2 BCLC 35 at [43]. The essential issue here was the failure of the chairman, the administrator of the company proposing a CVA, to inform the creditors of two offers for the company's assets while telling them of a third. There were reasons for the chairman not mentioning the other two offers but he stated at the meeting that there was only one 'formal offer' for the business. The learned judge held that this was a distortion of the truth in the absence of further explanation. Accordingly there was an irregularity. Thus far the analysis is impeccable. However, it is at the very least arguable that the learned judge then became too involved in speculating as to what might have happened had the full information been put before the creditors, and in deciding that the irregularity was not material was guilty of pre-empting the creditors' decision, the sin which should not have been committed by the chairman.

Irregularity in relation to the meeting

6.227 The courts have interpreted 'in relation to the meeting' as covering any part of the voluntary arrangement process which leads to the meeting. An irregularity may occur in the giving of false or misleading information in the proposal, or the statement of affairs, or the preparation of a nominee's report to the court¹ and there is no reason in principle why it should not cover the giving of further information following the nominee's request or any other information given to creditors for them to rely on[2]. Questions of culpability are irrelevant; if the creditors are given false or misleading information that is an irregularity whether the debtor proposing the voluntary arrangement intended it or not[3]. Neither is an irregularity to be restricted to false and misleading information. There is no limit to the scope of possible irregularity. Possible irregularities include the failure of the nominee to notify one or more creditors of the meeting, or the full details of the proposal, or a change of venue without due notice. If, through oversight (or for any other reason) notice is not sent to a creditor whose claim, name and address is know to the nominee or convener, there is an irregularity in relation to the meeting. But if the creditor or his address is unknown there is no obligation or ability to send notice to him and there is no irregularity in not sending him notice[4]. Failure properly to identify creditors, or the creditor who was to purchase an asset of the debtor in settlement of his claim, was an irregularity which in the circumstances was sufficiently material to justify revoking the arrangement[5]. Giving an inaccurate assessment of the possibility that the debtor's assets available to creditors might be increased in an insolvency by setting aside a transaction as being at an undervalue is an irregularity[6]. It was an irregularity where the nominee allowed the co-habitee of the debtor both to vote in respect of a debt stated to arise on giving up a claim to part of the beneficial interest in the debtor's residence and also to reserve the right to claim such an interest after a voluntary arrangement had been approved[7]. If the nominee takes the view, reasonably, that particular shares have no value, failure to disclose the existence of the shares to creditors is not an irregularity[8].

[1]   *Fender v IRC* [2003] BPIR 1304 at [11].
[2]   *Re a Debtor (87 of 1993) (No 2)* [1996] 1 BCLC 63, where at 88–95 Rimer J considered the earlier cases.
[3]   *Re Keenan* [1998] BPIR 205; *Bradburn v Kaye* [2006] BPIR 605 at [27]–[39]. Culpability is unlikely to be relevant to questions of materiality either, although in some cases the court may take the view that the creditors would be more forgiving where there is no culpability and this may influence their voting. Questions of false or misleading information will arise in cases where a bankruptcy petition is presented under IA 1986, s 264(1)(c) and culpability may then be relevant to the making of a bankruptcy order.
[4]   *Re T&N Ltd* [2006] EWHC 842 (Ch), [2006] 1 WLR 2831 at [17]. Note also IR 1986, r 12.16 which provides that a meeting is presumed to have been duly summoned and held notwithstanding that not everyone to whom notice was to be given has received it.
[5]   *IRC v Duce* [1999] BPIR 189.
[6]   *Fender v IRC* [2003] BPIR 1304 at [24].
[7]   *Smurthwaite v Simpson-Smith* [2006] EWCA Civ 1183, [2006] BPIR 1504. A rather serious irregularity indeed, and, as Jacob LJ observed at [33], the insolvency practitioner had made common cause with the debtor and had failed to preserve the 'utter independence from any party' which was to be required of the nominee and chairman of the creditors' meeting.
[8]   *Fender v IRC* [2003] BPIR 1304 at [27]. Plainly if the shares had no value any irregularity could not be material.

Materiality

6.228 The court takes a practical approach. To be 'material' the irregularity must be one which, objectively assessed, would be likely to have made a material difference to the way in which the creditors would have considered and assessed the terms of the proposed voluntary arrangement[1]. The fact that a creditor who is not notified of the meeting would not himself have had sufficient voting strength to alter the outcome of the vote which was taken at the meeting should not of itself necessarily render immaterial the irregularity in failing to give him notice. It will depend on the circumstances whether the creditor in question might be able to show that he may have been able to persuade other voters to vote differently. But many creditors adopt positions in advance, and submit proxy votes, and it will take strong evidence to establish that a creditor would have had a reasonable prospect of persuading other creditors to change their minds. The courts have tended to look at the size of any disputed debt and decide the issue of materiality as a matter of simple mathematics[2]. But this is not necessarily the whole story, and in an appropriate case the court should look to see the nature of the objection and consider whether creditors who voted for or against the proposal might have been influenced sufficiently to vote differently had they been aware of the full facts. The court does not have to second guess the creditors' reactions. It is always open to the court to give a direction for the summoning of a further meeting to reconsider the original proposal in the light of the true facts[3]. It should be borne in mind that it is only rarely that creditors' meetings are 'take it or leave it' affairs. A debtor proposing a voluntary arrangement must not only be honest, but should take care to put all relevant facts before creditors[4]. With all relevant facts available the creditors may be in a position to negotiate modifications of advantage to the creditors.

[1] *Cadbury Schweppes plc v Somji* [2001] 1 WLR 615, per Robert Walker LJ at 626.
[2] See, for example, *Doorbar v Alltime Securities Ltd (Nos 1 and 2)* [1996] 1 BCLC 487, see 498, CA; *Re a Debtor (No 259 of 1990)* [1992] 1 WLR 226, 229 where notice was not given to a creditor whose vote could not have altered the result. In *Re Cancol Ltd* [1996] 1 All ER 37, [1996] BPIR 252 where the complaint was that one creditor's representative had persuaded the chairman of the meeting to increase the value of the creditor's debt for voting purposes to a remarkable extent. Knox J stated that had the increase in voting rights been capable of affecting the outcome of the vote he would have stood the matter over for evidence as to how the debt was valued.
[3] See para **6.239–6.243**.
[4] *Re a Debtor (No 2389 of 1989)* [1991] Ch 326, at 337.

6.229 Where the chairman of the meeting is guilty of conduct which prejudices creditors this may constitute a material irregularity as well as constituting unfair prejudice[1].

[1] *Re A Debtor (No 222 of 1990) ex p Bank of Ireland* [1992] BCLC 137, and note the judgment on costs at [1993] BCLC 233.

Applicant for relief

6.230 The persons entitled to apply to challenge the decision of the creditors' meeting are:

(1) the debtor;
(2) any person entitled, in accordance with the rules[1], to vote at the creditors' meeting;
(3) any person who would have been entitled to vote at the creditors' meeting if he had been given notice of it[2];
(4) the nominee or any authorised practitioner who has replaced him[3];

(5)   where the debtor is an undischarged bankrupt, the trustee or the official
        receiver, as appropriate[4].

¹   See paras **6.134–6.153**.
²   IA 1986, s 262(2)(b)(ii) as introduced by IA 2000.
³   See paras **6.113–6.114**.
⁴   IA 1986, s 262(2).

6.231 The positions of the debtor and the creditor seem clear enough. The
former may wish to challenge the refusal of the proposed arrangement, or a
modification voted through by the creditors[1]. A creditor may be concerned to
challenge a decision which binds him to an arrangement which unfairly
prejudices him; he may wish to overturn a refusal of an arrangement on the
ground of material irregularity where he is concerned that a bankruptcy may
follow under which he will receive less than under the proposed arrangement.
The interest of the nominee in applying is not so clear. He may be concerned
that a modification was approved without the consent of the debtor. He may
indeed be concerned that the failure of the proposal will deprive him of the
administration of the arrangement, but if this interest is primarily financial it
will be unattractive. A trustee in bankruptcy may consider that the arrangements as approved might prejudice his administration of the estate or the
interests of one or more creditors in the insolvency. Why the official receiver in
his capacity other than trustee might wish to apply for relief is far from
obvious, and he receives no assistance from the Act or the Rules should he
wish to do so. Neither he (nor a trustee in bankruptcy) has any right to be
given notice of the meeting under the Rules, nor do they have a right to attend
the meeting.

¹   See para **6.130** et seq.

Time for making application

6.232 The application may not be made 'after the end of the period of 28
days beginning with the day on which the report of the creditors' meeting was
made to the court'[1]. The wording is to be noted. The first day is part of the
28-day period which therefore ends on the 28th day counting the day of the
report, and not on the following day which would be the case with most time
limits[2]. This short time limit for bringing challenges to approved arrangements
follows the recommendation of the Cork Committee[3] that there should be
only a short period within which a challenge could be brought in order that
finality should be reached speedily. However, there is no provision in IA 1986,
Pt VIII (which deals with IVAs) disapplying the general provision in the IA
1986 covering the law relating to individuals giving the court power to extend
time, either before or after it has expired, on any terms it thinks fit to impose[4].
In consequence it is open to an applicant to bring an application to challenge
the meeting's decision on an IVA after the expiry of the 28-day limit[5].

¹   IA 1986, s 262(3); as to the report of the meeting to the court see IA 1986, s 259(1) and
      paras **6.183–6.185**.
²   See *Re Bournemouth & Boscombe Athletic Football Club Co Ltd* [1998] BPIR 183 where
      it was noted that the same formula is used in IA 1986, s 5(4)(a) (CVA) which provides that
      the court should not make an order consequent upon an approval of a CVA at any time

before the end of the period of 28 days beginning with the first day on which each of the chairman's reports are made to the court, although this is to tie this provision in with the time limit for launching a challenge to the CVA. The court extended time in *UK Hydroslides Ltd v Stern* (9 July 2004) where the application was made one day late, an 'honest mistake as to time limits', the Deputy High Court Judge stating that it was wrong of the district judge to have struck out the application on a 15-minute appointment without a proper consideration of the authorities.

3   The Review Committee on Insolvency Law and Practice Cmnd 8558 published June 1982.
4   IA 1986, s 376 note that this power enables the court to extend the 28-day time limit imposed by IR 1986, r 5.22(6) against the chairman's decision on entitlement to vote at the creditors' meeting.
5   *Tager v Westpac Banking Corpn* [1997] 1 BCLC 313; *Plant v Plant* [1998] 1 BCLC 38, and *Warley Continental Services Ltd v Johal* [2002] All ER (D) 224 (Oct).

6.233 There is a great merit in having certainty for all concerned with a voluntary arrangement, and in many instances it will be important to the success of the arrangement that it is implemented without delay. It is anticipated that the court will be slow to extend the time limit; an extension will require special circumstances[1]. In *Tager v Westpac Banking Corpn*[2] an approved arrangement was challenged by dissenting creditors on the ground that one of the supporting creditors should not have voted. The application was not served on the debtor until after the 28-day time limit had expired, and was upheld by the court some six weeks after the date of the report to the court. The debtor then discovered that one of the dissenting creditors had been allowed to vote for more than his true debt, and issued an application three weeks later, ie some nine weeks after the expiry of the 28-day time limit. In exercising its discretion to extend time the court considered the relevant factors to be (a) the length of the delay, (b) the reasons for the delay, (c) the apparent merits of the underlying application, and (d) the prejudice to each side other than the inevitable prejudice inherent in reopening the matter[3]. In *Re A Debtor (No 488 IO of 1996); JP v Debtor*[4] the time for making an application was extended 10 months where the court was satisfied that the applicant wife was not responsible for the delay and where the debtor husband had not suffered any significant prejudice. In *Warley Continental Services Ltd v Johal*[5] the court noted the width of the power conferred by IA 1986, s 376 which led to the conclusion that any circumstance might be of potential relevance in any particular case. This would include the conduct of the parties. For instance, on the applicant's side, any warning given of the application[6], and on the supervisor/debtor's side the promptness and openness shown in addressing concerns raised by potential applicants; this particularly bearing in mind the status of the supervisor as an independent professional responsible to the court. In the event an application to revoke or suspend the voluntary arrangement was issued some six weeks two days out of time, and although the court considered that the merits of the case counted strongly in favour of the applicant this was outweighed by the significant delay for which there was no real justification[7].

1   See the observations of Carnwath J in *Plant v Plant* [1998] 1 BCLC 38 at 54 where he refused to say that the decision in *Tager v Westpac Banking Corpn* [1997] 1 BCLC 313 was 'plainly wrong' while noting the policy arguments for treating the time limit as absolute. In *Tanner v Everitt* [2004] EWHC 1130 (Ch), [2004] BPIR 1026, an extraordinary case in many ways, the debtors made an application some 13 years out of time. It was given short shrift.
2   [1997] BPIR 543.

3   [1997] BPIR 543 at 555; the guidelines are those suggested in *C M Van Stillevoldt BV v El Carriers Inc* [1983] 1 All ER 699, [1983] 1 WLR 207, CA.
4   [1999] BPIR 206.
5   [2002] All ER (D) 224 (Oct).
6   Although it cannot count for much that a warning is given within 28 days but no application is made within that time; it is of the essence of the short time period that all parties may treat a decision on a proposed voluntary arrangement as final 28 days after the chairman's report to the court.
7   The decision in *Warley Continental Services Ltd v Johal* [2002] All ER (D) 224 (Oct) was referred to with apparent approval in *Re Timothy* [2005] EWHC 1885 (Ch), [2006] BPIR 329. In this case the CSA declined to take part in the creditors' meeting on the basis that it was not bound to any voluntary arrangement. As the second largest creditor the CSA could, had it voted against the proposal, have prevented its approval. Form the start of the IVA the supervisor maintained that the CSA was bound, and some nine months after its approval the CSA issued an application to challenge the meeting's decision. Warren J carefully considered the competing interests of the CSA, the debtor's 10 year old daughter, the supervisor and the other creditors and in dismissing the challenge on the grounds of delay concluded that the significant and unjustified delay in bringing the application outweighed a 'not very great' prejudice to the daughter.

6.234 The fact that there is uncertainty as to whether a creditor is bound by a voluntary arrangement is no justification for delay in challenging the meetings' approval of the arrangement. Such a creditor should issue a protective application within the 28-day period[1]. The court suggested that if necessary the creditor unsure of his position in a voluntary arrangement could make an application under CPR Pt 8, but plainly inclined to the view that it was open to such a creditor to bring a challenge in the voluntary arrangement proceedings[2].

1   *Re Timothy* [2005] EWHC 1885 (Ch), [2006] BPIR 329 at [47].
2   If only on a purely practical level this must be right. If the creditor is indeed a creditor bound by the voluntary arrangement he will have locus standi to bring a challenge under IA 1986, s 262. If he is not a creditor bound by the arrangement the court will make a sufficient finding (if not a declaration) for the creditor's purposes in adjudicating on the application.

6.235 It is always open to seek a review of a decision of the court under IA 1986, s 375(1), but this is not a mechanism for a late appeal[1].

1   *Re Debtors (Nos VA7 and 8 of 1990), ex p Stevens* [1996] BPIR 101.

Creditors without notice of the meeting

6.236 Following the amendments introduced by IA 2000, a creditor who should have been but was not given notice of the creditors' meeting may make an application to challenge the decision within 28 days of his becoming aware that the creditors' meeting has taken place[1]. It is no bar to his making an application (within 28 days of his becoming aware of the meeting) that the arrangement has ceased to have effect, unless it came to an end prematurely[2]. The exclusion of arrangements which come to a premature end appears to arise from the view that a premature end must mean a resolution of the debtor's position, and hence that of the creditors, by bankruptcy or solvency. But there is no magic in a premature end. Coming to an end prematurely may have very different effects in different arrangements. The trusts on which the funds are held by the supervisor under an arrangement may or may not fail on the premature end of that arrangement depending upon the terms of the trust and nature of the end. The applicant creditor who had no notice of the arrangement may still be prejudiced therefore despite the premature end to the arrangement, and it is suggested ought to have the right to apply to set aside the arrangement.

1   IA 1986, s 262(3)(b).
2   IA 1986, s 262(3). A voluntary arrangement comes to an end prematurely if, when it ceases to have effect, it has not been fully implemented in respect of all persons bound by the arrangement, IA 1986, s 262C as added by IA 2000.

6.237 The aim of the amendments to the IA 1986 by the IA 2000, which bind creditors to the arrangement who have had no notice of the creditors' meeting, is to strengthen the statutory scheme for voluntary arrangements and keep debtors out of insolvency. Plainly the creditors who are bound without their knowledge must be given an opportunity to appeal when they learn that an arrangement has been approved and implemented. The IA 1986 as amended gives no thought however as to the original creditors. In most cases their position will be adversely affected by the inclusion of one or more new creditors of whose debts, almost certainly, the original creditors were unaware when approving the arrangement. The new creditors will now be entitled to share in the available funds. If the new creditors' debts are substantial in value the position may be reached where original creditors will say that had they known the true position they would not have voted for the arrangement. Failure by the debtor to inform the creditors of the true extent of his indebtedness by any significant degree is on its face a material irregularity at or in relation to the meeting. Should the court extend the time limit to allow the original creditors to challenge the approval of the arrangement? In any particular case the court may well feel that it should incline to supporting the arrangement and reject late applications to challenge. But for this to become general practice may have a serious impact on institutional creditors who may respond by opposing other debtor's proposals. To avoid such difficulties creditors would be well advised to consider a provision in the arrangement that it be reconsidered by the whole body of creditors should it transpire that additional creditors with debts of a value exceeding, say, 10% of the debts listed on the debtor's statement of affairs were in fact entitled to, but were not given, notice of the creditors' meeting.

6.238 The 28-day time limit applies to an application to challenge the decision of the creditors' meeting. It will not prevent an application being made at any time to declare the voluntary arrangement invalid[1].

1   See eg *Re Plummer* [2004] BPIR 767.

Powers of the court on an application

6.239 Where the court is satisfied that either of the two grounds on which a challenge may be brought[1] is established it may do one or both of the following:

6.239 *Individual voluntary arrangements*

(a)   revoke or suspend any approval given by the meeting;
(b)   give a direction to any person for the summoning of a further meeting
       of the debtor's creditors to consider any revised proposal the debtor
       may make or, in a case of material irregularity, to reconsider the
       original proposal[2].

¹   See para **6.195**.
²   IA 1986, s 262(4).

6.240 Although satisfied that one or both grounds of the application are
made out, the court may conclude that no good purpose is served in
summoning another meeting, eg because of the implacable attitude of sufficient creditors, and refuse to give a direction under para **6.239**(b) above[1]. In
considering whether or not to summon a further meeting the court should
carry out a balancing exercise between the seriousness and the heinousness of
the irregularity and the likely attitude of the other creditors[2]. Where the
debtor wishes to put forward a revised proposal similar principles apply as
with the original proposal; the court should not direct a further meeting unless
there will be a serious and viable proposal, that is one with a reasonable
prospect of approval and implementation, to put before the creditors[3]. In an
appropriate case the court may direct that the applicant is not bound by the
arrangement[4]. Where the court makes a direction under **6.239**(b) above, it
may also give a direction continuing or, as appropriate, renewing the interim
order relating to the debtor[5]. In most cases it will be advisable, if not essential,
to renew the interim order pending the holding of the further meeting.

¹   *Re Cove (a debtor)* [1990] 1 All ER 949, [1990] 1 WLR 707.
²   *IRC v Duce* [1999] BPIR 189, 201.
³   *Re a Debtor (No 101 of 1999) (No 2)* [2001] BPIR 996, where the debtor whose IVA had
    been set aside on the application of the Crown debtors (see para **6.209**) then proposed that
    the original fund, which after depletion had fallen to £3,100 should be shared equally
    among the creditors whose debts amounted to £541,000. The court refused to direct a
    further meeting assuming that a vote in favour could only be achieved by friends voting
    through motives of friendship or through a wish that the debtor, a racehorse trainer, would
    continue to train their horses; i e a collateral matter which would not apply to the minority
    (Crown) creditors.
⁴   *Re Cranley Mansions Ltd* [1994] 1 WLR 1610 (no entitlement to vote).
⁵   IA 1986, s 262(6) 'for such period as may be specified in the direction'. The court has
    therefore a complete discretion as to how long the moratorium or interim order will be
    extended. It will doubtless wish to set a tight timetable.

6.241 In the event that the court is satisfied that there is no intention on the
part of the debtor to submit a revised proposal, or resubmit the original
proposal, it must revoke the direction summoning a further meeting and
revoke or suspend any approval given at the previous meeting[1].

¹   IA 1986, s 262(5).

6.242 The court has power to give supplemental directions as it may think fit
in any case where it revokes or suspends an approval[1] or gives a direction
under **6.239**(b) above. In particular such directions may relate to (i) things
done under the voluntary arrangement since it took effect[2], and (ii) things
done since the voluntary arrangement took effect as could not have been done

284

if an interim order had been in force in relation to the debtor when they were done[3]. This power enables the court by direction to validate acts carried out under the voluntary arrangement, particularly by the supervisor, which when the arrangement is revoked or suspended may leave the supervisor or other person exposed to a civil suit who reasonably thought at the time that he acted that he had the necessary authority. Similarly, the court may reinstate the original position where the supervisor has acted in a manner which would not have been permitted under the interim order. In either case third parties may be involved. There is no express provision in the rules requiring third parties who may be affected by any directions made to be given notice of the hearing, but the court will presumably wish to hear any third parties involved, especially where the effect of the directions may be final. An applicant who intends to seek such directions would be well advised to notify any potentially interested third party.

[1]   Whether under IA 1986, s 262(4)(a) or (5).
[2]   'Things done since the meeting under any voluntary arrangement approved by the meeting', IA 1986, s 262(7)(a).
[3]   IA 1986, s 262(7).

6.243 The power of the court to summon a further meeting or give supplemental directions only arises on a successful challenge to the decision of the creditors' meeting. The court cannot use this power to enable the remedying of an otherwise invalid voluntary arrangement procedure where for any reason the proposal or procedure leading to the creditors' meeting is improper in any way. Accordingly it is not possible to rescue an arrangement where the proposal is a nullity[1], or where the creditors' meeting is invalidly held because it was not properly summoned[2]. Neither the IA 1986 nor the IR 1986 provide the court with any general power to control the voluntary arrangement procedure before approval and if things do go wrong, even without fault on the part of the debtor, there is nothing the court can do to assist. The debtor finds himself in the invidious position of having to start over again, with the additional problem that there can be no interim order within 12 months of a previous application for an interim order[3]. The debtor may only therefore make a second attempt at a voluntary arrangement without the benefit of protection from any creditors who may wish to petition for the debtor's insolvency[4].

[1]   *IRC v Bland* [2003] EWHC 1068 (Ch), [2003] BPIR 1274 at [54].
[2]   *Vlieland-Boddy v Dexter Ltd* [2003] EWHC 2592 (Ch), [2004] BPIR 235.
[3]   IA 1986, s 255(1)(c).
[4]   Ie by IVA without interim order under IA 1986, s 256A.

Challenge to decisions of subsequent meetings

6.244 The Insolvency Act 1986 is drafted so as to give a right of challenge to a voluntary arrangement approved by the original creditors' meeting[1]. On a strict interpretation a further meeting of creditors summoned on the court's direction would not come within this wording. A decision of this further meeting might therefore not be susceptible to challenge under IA 1986, s 262. It would be advisable for the court when directing a further meeting to give a general liberty to apply which would enable the debtor, nominee, or any creditor entitled to vote at the meeting to challenge any decision of the further meeting on either of the grounds specified in IA 1986, s 262.

1   IA 1986, s 262(1) which refers to 'a creditors' meeting summoned under section 257'. In a CVA without moratorium different wording is used; the challenge permitted by IA 1986, s 6(1) is to a voluntary arrangement 'which has effect under section s 4A' and so this drafting difficulty does not arise.

Procedure on application

6.245 An application to challenge the approval of the arrangement or any decision of the creditors' meeting is made by ordinary application in Form 7.2[1]. Where the application is on the grounds that the arrangement unfairly prejudices the interests of the applicant creditor, the nominee and other creditors should not ordinarily[2] be made respondents to the application (although it is advisable to give the nominee notice) and they should not be ordered to pay the costs[3]. The application is heard by the registrar or district judge in chambers, although in difficult cases it may be adjourned to the judge in open court.

1   IR 1986, r 7.2(1). This is the usual procedure. It is however arguable that at this stage there are no pending proceedings before the court, and so the application should be made by originating application in Form 7.1, IR 1986, r 7.2(1).
2   It is a different matter if misconduct is alleged against the nominee or another creditor.
3   *Re Naeem (A bankrupt) (No 18 of 1988)* [1990] 1 WLR 48, 51 where Hoffmann J observed that it was convenient that the nominee be given notice of the application but that it was not necessary for that purpose that he be made a respondent.

6.246 Evidence is given on affidavit, subject to the court's direction that deponents attend for cross examination[1]. It should be borne in mind that in the absence of cross examination of the deponent the court may feel bound to accept the affidavit evidence of the witness[2]. The practice and procedure of the High Court applies with regard to the form, contents and procedure governing the use of affidavits[3]. Accordingly affidavits may contain hearsay evidence[4], and service of the affidavit will constitute compliance with the notice requirements of the Civil Evidence Act 1995, s 2(1)[5].

1   See e g *Re a Debtor (No 87 of 1993) (No 2)* [1996] 1 BCLC 63, 73.
2   See e g *National Westminster Bank plc v Scher* [1998] BCLC 124, sub nom *Re a Debtor (No 574) of 1995* [1998] BPIR 224.
3   IR 1986, r 7.57, which has not been amended to allow witness statements.
4   Note that the decision in *Re A Debtor (No 87 of 1993)* [1996] 1 BCLC 55, [1996] BPIR 56 (hearsay not permitted as the court's decision on an application under IA 1986, s 262 is a final one and not an interlocutory one) was reached before the passing of the Civil Evidence Act 1995.
5   CPR Pt 33.2(1); the CPR, save where inconsistent with the Insolvency Rules, apply to insolvency proceedings by virtue of IR 1986, r 7.51.

6.247 An applicant may seek orders for further information[1] and disclosure[2]. Full disclosure may be essential to enable the court properly to assess merits of an application, and in the appropriate case both standard and specific disclosure will be ordered[3]. Where the creditors had various complaints about the conduct of the chairman of the meeting (an administrator) including one that he had misrepresented the position as to offers received for the company debtor's assets, the court ordered disclosure of all documentation relating to such offers together with documents relating to the validity of a floating charge granted to a creditor. The court refused however to order disclosure of documents passing between the administrator and one of the company's suppliers because these were sought in an endeavour to find evidence of fraud, an allegation for which the applicants had no evidential basis[4]. An order was made for the disclosure of documents showing the policy or attitude of VAS (the Voluntary Arrangement Service of the Inland Revenue and Customs) towards CVAs by football clubs. Such CVAs throw up the difficulty of the 'football creditors' rule imposed by the sport's governing bodies. This requires the football creditors to be paid in full if the club is to maintain its position in its relevant league. The court was informed that there had been some 20–30 cases of football clubs seeking CVAs and the court ruled that the attitude taken by VAS to other clubs might well be relevant to a consideration whether or not the approach of the instant club to its CVA creditors was fair[5]. The fact that documents have been released to the supervisor did not mean that the documents were in the public domain and accordingly available to applicants seeking to challenge the arrangements[6].

1   IR 1986, r 7.60, 'in accordance with CPR Part 18'.
2   IR 1986, r 7.60, and see *Re Primlaks (UK) Ltd (No 2)* [1990] BCLC 234, 240–1 where disclosure was ordered so as to enable the creditor to know the facts of the transactions which he asserted were unfairly prejudicial toward him, the onus being on him to demonstrate that he had suffered prejudice, and that this was unfair to him individually.
3   See CPR Pt 31.
4   *Re Trident Fashions plc (in administration), Anderson v Knoll Ltd* [2004] EWHC 351 (Ch), [2004] 2 BCLC 28.
5   *IRC v Exeter City Association Football Club Ltd* [2004] BCC 519.
6   *Plant v Plant* [1998] BPIR 243.

6.248 In determining disputes concerning the decisions of the chairman of the creditors' meeting the court is not confined to the evidence that was before the chairman at the meeting, but is entitled to consider whatever evidence on the issue the parties to the appeal choose to place before the court[1].

1   *Re a Company (No 4539 of 1993)* [1995] 1 BCLC 459, [1995] BCC 116; *National Westminster Bank plc v Scher* [1998] BCLC 124, sub nom *Re a Debtor (No 574) of 1995* [1998] BPIR 224.

6.249 The nominee acts as agent for the debtor and the costs of a successful application will be paid out of the debtor's estate unless there has been some personal conduct on the part of the nominee which would justify an order for costs against him[1]. Where the ground of application is that there was a material irregularity at the meeting for which the nominee as chairman was responsible and the application is brought together with an appeal against his decision on a creditor's entitlement to vote[2], the chairman is not protected from an order for costs by reason of the provision in the rules that an order for costs cannot be made against the chairman's decision on voting rights[3]. Where the chairman acts in good faith, albeit in error, no order for costs will be made against him[4].

1   *Re Naeem (A Bankrupt) (No 18 of 1988)* [1990] 1 WLR 48.
2   Under IR 1986, rr 5.21, 5.22, see paras **6.154–6.158**.

3   See IR 1986, r 5.22(7) and *Re a Debtor (No 222 of 1990), ex p Bank of Ireland* [1992] BCLC 137, and, on costs *Re a Debtor (No 222 of 1990) (No 2), ex p Bank of Ireland* [1993] BCLC 233 where the chairman, whose refusal to allow substantial creditors to vote was the cause of the appeals, was ordered to pay one-half of the standard costs of the appellants, the balance falling on the debtor who had resisted the appeals.
4   *Re Cranley Mansions Ltd* [1995] 1 BCLC 290, 314–5.

6.250 Where a court makes an order revoking or suspending the voluntary arrangement the applicant is required to serve sealed copies of the order on (i) the debtor, and, if the debtor is an undischarged bankrupt, the trustee and official receiver, and (ii) the supervisor of the voluntary arrangement[1]. The applicant must also serve notice of the order, if the court directs that a further creditors' meeting be held, (iii) on the person required to summon that meeting[2], and (iv) within seven days, on the Secretary of State[3]. The debtor[4] is responsible for notifying all persons who were sent notice of the creditors' meeting which approved the arrangement or who appear to be affected by the order[5]. The debtor must also within seven days of receiving the order (or within such longer period as the court may allow) give notice to the court whether it is intended to make a revised proposal to creditors or to invite reconsideration of the original proposal[6].

1   IR 1986, r 5.30(2).
2   IR 1986, r 5.30(3).
3   IR 1986, r 5.30(5).
4   Or in the case of an undischarged bankrupt the trustee or official receiver where no trustee.
5   IR 1986, r 5.30(4)(a).
6   IR 1986, r 5.30(4)(b).

G EFFECT OF APPROVAL OF VOLUNTARY ARRANGEMENT

The binding of creditors: the statutory hypothesis

6.251 The voluntary arrangement, as approved by the creditors' meeting, (a) takes effect as if made by the debtor at the meeting[1], and (b) binds every person who in accordance with the Rules[2] (i) was entitled to vote at the creditors' meeting, whether or not he was present or represented at it, or (ii) would have been entitled to vote if he had had notice of the meeting, as if he were a party to the arrangement[3]. Prior to the amendments introduced by the IA 2000 the creditor had actually to have had notice of the meeting in order to be bound by the arrangement[4], although so long as the notice was sent according to the rules and the creditor was in fact aware of the notice before the meeting, even if he learnt of the meeting by other means, he was treated as having had notice of the meeting[5]. The IR 1986[6] require notices to be sent to creditors at least 14 days before the meeting[7]. Although a creditor is now bound to a voluntary arrangement even if he did not receive notice of the creditors' meeting, it remains of considerable importance that the debtor and his nominee ensure that all persons who have a claim against the debtor do receive the requisite notice. A creditor who discovers late that he was entitled to but did not receive notice has 28 days to challenge the meetings' decision from learning of it[8], and he may be able to upset an otherwise successful arrangement. Solicitors do not have implied authority to accept service of notices[9].

1   IA 1986, s 260(2)(a).
2   See para **6.135**.
3   IA 1986, s 260(2)(b).
4   IA 1986, s 260(2) (prior to amendment); *Re a Debtor (No 64 of 1992)* [1994] 2 All ER
    177, [1994] BCC 55; *Skipton Building Society v Collins* [1998] BPIR 267.
5   *Beverly Group Plc v McClue* [1996] BPIR 25.
6   IR 1986, r 5.17(2).
7   Accordingly it was not enough before the amendment to the IA 1986 to bind the creditor
    to the arrangement that the creditor had some but insufficient notice, *Mytre Invest-
    ments Ltd v Reynolds (No 2)* [1996] BPIR 464, where Blackburne J rejected the suggestion
    that 'substantial compliance' was sufficient or that the period of notice could be computed
    back from the date of an adjourned meeting. Where a creditor satisfied the court that he
    had not received the notice, although there was evidence of posting, he was not bound to
    the IVA, *Re a Debtor (No 64 of 1992)* [1994] 2 All ER 177, [1994] BCC 55.
8   IA 1986, s 262(3)(b).
9   *Re Munro and Rowe, Singer v Trustee in Bankruptcy* [1981] 1 WLR 1358, 1361.

6.252 The legal analysis of the approved arrangement is that there is a
consensual agreement between the debtor and all the creditors who were
entitled to vote at the meeting; these creditors must be treated as consenting
parties to the arrangement under the statutory hypothesis imposed by the IA
1986[1] however they voted, if at all, and whatever their attitude to the
arrangement[2]. As it forms an agreement between the debtor and the creditor
questions as to any further consequences of the voluntary arrangement beyond
it binding the debtor's creditors are to be determined on a construction of its
particular terms. Thus, for example, co-debtors or sureties may or may not be
discharged from liability to the principal creditor depending upon the precise
terms of the arrangement[3]. The terms of the arrangement will also determine
whether or not the creditor's claim against the debtor is extinguished. An
investor who is bound by an IVA made by a financial adviser will lose his right
to make a claim against the Investors Compensation Scheme[4] where the
arrangement extinguishes the claim, as in a composition[5]. In a scheme of
arrangement the terms of the scheme may be drawn so as not to extinguish the
claim against the financial adviser in which event the investor may pursue his
ICS claim, subject to the relevant rules.

1   IA 1986, s 260(2).
2   See *Johnson v Davies* [1999] Ch 117, CA at p 138, approved in *Raja v Rubin* [2000]
    Ch 270, CA. As these cases pre-date the changes introduced by IA 2000 the principle is
    there framed in terms that there is a consensual agreement between the debtor and all the
    creditors who *had notice of and* were entitled to vote at the meeting.
3   *Johnson v Davies* [1999] Ch 117, CA where on a proper construction of the IVA's terms
    the co-debtor and sureties were not released.
4   Operated by the Securities and Investment Board under the Financial Services Act 1986,
    s 14.
5   See the Financial Services (Compensation of Investors) Rules 1994, r 2.04(2).

Secured creditor

6.253 Unless the voluntary arrangement is unusually drafted the effect of
approval on a secured creditor is that he will not be able to sue the debtor for
payment under his covenant. The secured creditor will of course be able to
enforce his security if he has not abandoned it[1]. While the notice of the
meeting may set out the debt or debts owed to the creditor at the date of the

proposal or statement of affairs, it is the creditor who has to receive notice not the holder of each particular debt. Accordingly where a further debt becomes due between the date of the interim order and the approval of the arrangement, the further debt should be included in the creditor's claim and will become subject to the arrangement[2].

1   See *Whitehead v Household Mortgage Corpn plc* [2002] EWCA Civ 1657, [2003] 1 All ER 319 and generally see paras **6.187–6.188**.
2   *Re KG Hoare* [1997] BPIR 683, where the deputy judge, at 694, suggested that IA 1986, s 260 did not prevent the splitting of a creditor's overall debt so that a creditor might be bound to an arrangement in respect of one debt, but not bound in respect of another. Such a result could only arise in unusual circumstances even before the amendments introduced by the IA 2000 binding creditors to the arrangement regardless of whether they had notice.

Future claims

6.254   It is open to a creditor who is aware that he will or may have a claim against the debtor in the future to agree to be bound to a voluntary arrangement in respect of that claim if and when it becomes a liquidated debt. If he lodges a proof he will be deemed to have agreed and will be bound to the arrangement when his debt is liquidated[1].

1   *Re Goldspan Ltd* [2003] BPIR 93, where the creditor (the Legal Services Commission) had referred to two claims but not a third. The court held that on the facts it was to be inferred that all the LSC claims would fall under the IVA.

The debtor

6.255   The debtor is of course bound to the arrangement and its legal consequences. In *Welburn v Dibb Lupton Broomhead (a firm)*[1] the debtor obtained an interim award in his favour in an arbitration against certain contractors. The debtor later entered into a voluntary arrangement and on discovering that his solicitors had failed to enforce the interim award against the contractors before they had gone into liquidation issued proceedings against the solicitors for professional negligence. The debtor's claim was struck out. Although the debtor held nominal legal title to the claim, the benefit of the claim was held on trust by the supervisor for the voluntary arrangement creditors. The debtor had therefore suffered no loss[2].

1   [2002] EWCA Civ 1601, [2003] BPIR 768.
2   The position might have been different if the amount of the claim against the contractors would have left a surplus for the debtor after payment of the voluntary arrangement debts. He would still however have faced the further difficulty that on the approval of the voluntary arrangement it was for the supervisor and not the debtor to give instructions to the solicitors, and on the facts the supervisor had given no instructions to the solicitors to enforce the award.

6.256   The Deeds of Arrangement Act 1914 does not apply to the approved individual voluntary arrangement[1].

1   IA 1986, s 260(3).

The position of the omitted creditor

6.257 A creditor who is not given notice of the creditors' meeting (an 'omitted creditor') may discover that he is bound to an arrangement which has been in place for some time. The arrangement may even have been implemented completely. Where the arrangement is ongoing an omitted creditor should be entitled to such dividends or other payments as are due to other creditors in the same class, and, subject always to the terms of the voluntary arrangement, all outstanding dividends should be paid to the omitted creditor before further payments are made to existing creditors[1]. If the supervisor refuses to accept an omitted creditor, or the amount of his debt, or his entitlement to be paid all outstanding dividends, the omitted creditor may apply to the court for appropriate directions[2]. Where the arrangement has 'ceased to have any effect' the debtor becomes liable, as at the date that the arrangement so ceased, to pay 'the amount payable under the arrangement' to the omitted creditor[3]. This will be a debt recoverable by the omitted creditor in place of his original debt. Although the words used, 'ceased to have any effect', are very wide, they necessarily mean fully implemented according to the terms of the arrangement in respect of all the creditors who had notice of the meeting. This is because where the arrangement has not been fully implemented in respect of all persons bound by the arrangement who had notice of the creditors' meeting it has 'ended prematurely'[4] and in such cases no liability to pay a dividend to an omitted creditor arises. In this event the statute is silent as to the omitted creditor's position, and his rights to recover monies which may be held by the supervisor, or petition for bankruptcy will depend on the terms of the arrangement and the reasons for its failure. The omitted creditor who discovers that he is bound by an arrangement which has ended prematurely will not be able to challenge the validity of the arrangement[5] and he is unlikely to be able to challenge any act, omission or decision of the former supervisor[6]. He may be able to bring proceedings against the debtor for breach of duty of good faith in connection with the proposal and his exclusion from the list of creditors to be given notice of the creditors' meeting[7], but in most cases the premature end of the voluntary arrangement will lead to bankruptcy. Whether the omitted creditor is prejudiced by his not having had notice will then depend on the terms of the arrangement; if he has missed the opportunity to be paid dividends from a trust which has survived the insolvency and in which most of the debtor's assets have been placed the omitted creditor will be prejudiced and may well find there is nothing that he can do to recover the position[8].

1   See, for example, *Re TBL Realisations, Oakley-Smith v Greenberg* [2002] EWCA Civ 1217, [2005] BCLC 74.
2   IA 1986, s 263(3).
3   IA 1986, s 260(2A)(b).
4   See IA 1986, s 262C.
5   He is expressly precluded from doing so by the terms of IA 1986, s 262(3).
6   See paras **6.295–6.301.**
7   *Cadbury Schweppes plc v Somji* [2001] 1 WLR 615, CA also [2001] 1 BCLC 498 where the judgment at first instance is reported. At para 24 Robert Walker LJ noted that the deputy judge's 'impressive survey of the old law shows that in relation to compositions and arrangements with creditors the court did impose a strict requirement of good faith as between competing unsecured creditors ... There is no strong presumption that a similar principle must be found in the new regime [for voluntary arrangements] but (to put it at its lowest) it would be no great surprise to find it there in one form or another'. Good faith

was owed not only between competing creditors but between the debtor and the creditors, and if the court does import these principles into IVAs an action may lie where a lack of good faith can be shown by a creditor in respect of his omission from the creditors listed on the statement of affairs or of whom notice was given to the nominee.

8 It is suggested that the legislature should give further thought to the position of the omitted creditor. It should be straightforward enough to provide that the omitted creditor should be put into the position he would have been in, so far as may be practicable, had he been given the notice of the creditors' meeting to which he was entitled whether or not the voluntary arrangement ends prematurely. At the least he should be able to apply to the court for directions to do justice to his position whatever the eventual outcome for the debtor.

Effect of approval on third parties

6.258 In most cases the approval of a voluntary arrangement will have no effect on persons who are not parties to it. Approval may however have an effect on third parties where they have joint liability on a debt with the debtor. Depending upon the terms of the original liability and the terms of the arrangement the compromise or discharge agreed with the debtor under the voluntary arrangement may discharge a third party liable on the same debt. In *Johnson v Davies*[1] the Court of Appeal considered whether co-debtors and sureties should be excluded from the operation of the general law relating to joint liability in cases of voluntary arrangements, in a manner similar to that in formal insolvency. The court concluded that the drafting of the IA 1986 indicated that Parliament intended that the general law should have effect: 'It is up to the debtor to propose, and for the creditors to accept or reject, proposals which either do or do not have the effect of releasing co-debtors and sureties. A creditor who is prejudiced by the decision of the majority to approve proposals which have the effect of releasing a co-debtor against whom he could otherwise have recourse can apply to the court under IA 1986, s 262 for the approval of the meeting to be revoked'[2]. No fetter on the right of the creditor to pursue a co-debtor is to be implied[3]. For there to be a release of a joint obligor that discharges another joint obligor, whether the liability be joint or joint and several, the release must either be immediate or have become operative and it must be without reservation of rights against the other joint obligor[4].

1 [1999] Ch 117.
2 Per Chadwick LJ on *Johnson v Davies* [1999] Ch 117 at p 138.
3 *Johnson v Davies* [1999] Ch 117 at p 128G–129A; and see *Re Goldspan Ltd* [2003] BPIR 93.
4 *Johnson v Davies* [1999] Ch 117; *Koutrouzas v Lombard Natwest Factors Ltd* [2002] EWHC 1084 (QB), [2003] BPIR 444.

6.259 A creditor may nevertheless wish to make matters certain and reserve his rights against co-debtors and sureties at the time when approval is given to the voluntary arrangement. It is not necessary that there is a provision in the contract of surety permitting a reservation of rights, neither is it necessary for the reservation to be included as a term of the voluntary arrangement[1]. Plainly it would be preferable for a creditor who has reasonable concerns about his position to seek the addition of an appropriate provision in the terms of the arrangement but the other creditors may not be agreeable. In determining whether there has been a reservation the court should look at all the circumstances including the dealings and correspondence between the parties[2].

1   *Greene King plc v Stanley* [2001] EWCA Civ 1966, [2002] BPIR 491 at 72 (no need for provision in contract of surety) and 83 (no need for provision in terms of arrangement).
2   *Greene King plc v Stanley* [2001] EWCA Civ 1966, [2002] BPIR 491 at 83.

6.260 As the Court of Appeal stated in *Lloyds Bank plc v Ellicott*[1], in the case where the terms of a voluntary arrangement are silent as to the rights of co-debtors there is no fetter on the creditor's right to pursue the co-debtor and, in turn, the co-debtor's right to pursue the debtor who has made the voluntary arrangement for a contribution, or, on the facts of *Lloyds Bank plc v Ellicott* a complete indemnity. The standard position was summed up by Chadwick LJ[2]:

> '... it is to be borne in mind, .., that IVAs – in what is, I think, a standard or conventional form used in this case – do not have the effect of preventing the creditor from proceeding against the co-debtor, or the effect of preventing the co-debtor from claiming contribution and indemnity against the assets which are the subject of the voluntary arrangement[3]. If that object is desired, then it needs to be spelt out in the arrangement. But, of course, if it is spelt out in the arrangement, it will be unlikely that any creditor who has a debt which he can hope to enforce against a co-debtor will agree to the arrangement. A court faced with an application to set aside the arrangement might well be persuaded to do so.

1   [2002] EWCA Civ 1333, [2003] BPIR 632.
2   [2002] EWCA Civ 1333 at [59].
3   The co-debtor will presumably be a creditor bound by the arrangement having been a contingent creditor until such time as the claim is enforced against him.

6.261 On a procedural note the Court of Appeal stressed that where the creditor brings proceedings against one co-debtor alone that co-debtor should bring his claim against the other co-debtor under CPR Pt 20[1].

1   [2002] EWCA Civ 1333 at [54].

End of interim order

6.262 An interim order is no longer required after the approval of an individual voluntary arrangement. Any interim order in force covering the debtor immediately before the end of the period of 28 days beginning with the day on which the report of the creditors' meeting was made to the court ceases to have effect at the end of that period[1]. Where bankruptcy proceedings have been stayed by an interim order which ceases to have effect following the approval of the arrangement the bankruptcy petition is deemed to be dismissed unless the court otherwise orders[2].

1   IA 1986, s 260(4).
2   IA 1986, s 260(5). The rules make no provision as to any costs incurred by the petitioning creditor on the deemed dismissal of the petition. The petitioning creditor would be advised to request that the payment of these costs be a term of the debtor's proposal for a voluntary arrangement.

Effect on bankruptcy

6.263 Where the approved voluntary arrangement relates to a debtor who is an undischarged bankrupt, the court must annul the bankruptcy order on an application by the bankrupt, or, where he does not make the application within the prescribed period[1], by the official receiver[2]. The making of an annulment order lifts from the debtor the status of a bankrupt for such matters as disqualification and his position on any future bankruptcy[3]. It does not however invalidate any sale or other disposition of property, payment made or any other act duly performed in the bankruptcy before annulment by or under the authority of the official receiver or the bankrupt's trustee or the court[4]. In the event that any part of the bankrupt's estate is vested in the trustee at the date of the annulment the court may vest it in the supervisor or any other person it may appoint[5]. The court must not annul a bankruptcy order under this power before the end of the period of 28 days beginning with the day on which the report of the creditors' meeting was made to the court[6] or at any time while an application is pending to challenge the meeting's decision[7] or, after such an application has been heard, the period for an appeal has not expired or an appeal is pending[8].

[1]   14 days after the time for challenging the decision of the creditors' meeting, or the conclusion of any appeal against such a challenge.
[2]   IA 1986, s 261(1)(2) (as amended by IA 2000).
[3]   Which, for example, will affect the date on which he obtains his discharge.
[4]   IA 1986, s 282(4)(a).
[5]   IA 1986, s 282(4)(b), in default of any appointment the property concerned reverts to the bankrupt on such terms (if any) as the court may direct.
[6]   Under IA 1986, s 259; the amendment introduced by IA 2000 refers to 'the period specified in s 262(3)(a) during which the decision of the creditors' meeting can be challenged' in place of 'the period of 28 days beginning with the day on which the report of the creditors' meeting was made to the court under s 259'. The words replaced are those used in IA 1986, s 262(3)(a).
[7]   Under IA 1986, s 262.
[8]   IA 1986, s 261(3); as to time limits for appealing see paras **6.232–6.235**.

Application by bankrupt to annul bankruptcy order

6.264 On the approval of an IVA the court must annul any bankruptcy order made against the bankrupt on his application[1]. The application may not be made during the 28-day period allowed for a challenge to the voluntary arrangement, or while an application to challenge is pending, or while an appeal in respect of an application may be brought or is pending[2]. The IA 1986 refers specifically to 'the bankrupt' but now that a bankrupt receives his automatic discharge after one year[3] it will frequently be the case that by the time the voluntary arrangement is in place, and the 28 days for challenge has passed, the debtor is no longer a bankrupt. In *Re Johnson*[4] the court held that a purposive interpretation of the statutory provision was permissible and that the term 'the bankrupt' could include a former bankrupt.

[1]   IA 1986, s 261(2)(a); the procedure governing the application is provided for in IR 1986, Part 5 Chapter 8, IR 1986, r 5.51. These provisions were inserted into the IR 1986 by the Insolvency (Amendment) Rules 2003, SI 2003/1730.
[2]   IA 1986, s 261(3).

3   IA 1986, s 279(1).
4   [2006] BPIR 987.

6.265 The application to the court to annul a bankruptcy order must specify the section under which it is made[1]. The application must be supported by an affidavit stating:

(a)   that the voluntary arrangement has been approved at a meeting of creditors;

(b)   the date of the approval by the creditors; and

(c)   that the 28-day period allowed for challenges to the decision of the creditors' meeting[2] has expired and no applications or appeal remain to be disposed of[3].

1   IR 1986, r 5.52(1).
2   See IA 1986, s 262(3)(a).
3   IR 1986, r 5.52(2).

6.266 The application and supporting affidavit are be filed in court, and the court gives the bankrupt notice of the venue[1] fixed for the hearing[2]. The bankrupt must give notice of the venue, accompanied by copies of the application and affidavit to the official receiver, any trustee who is not the official receiver, and the supervisor of the voluntary arrangement not less than seven days before the date of the hearing[3]. The official receiver, the supervisor of the voluntary arrangement, and any trustee who is not the official receiver may attend the hearing or be represented and call to the attention of the court any matters which seem to be relevant[4]. This is plainly a sensible requirement, and is designed to assist the court to consider whether it should give directions as to the conduct of the bankruptcy or the administration of the estate in order to facilitate the implementation of the individual voluntary arrangement[5]. On annulling the bankruptcy order, the court sends sealed copies of the order of annulment in the prescribed form[6] to the bankrupt, the official receiver, the supervisor of the voluntary arrangement and any trustee who is not the official receiver[7]. In the annulment order the court must include provision permitting vacation of the registration of the bankruptcy petition as a pending action, and of the bankruptcy order, in the register of writs and orders affecting land[8].

1   That is the time, date and place for the hearing, IR 1986, r 13.6.
2   IR 1986, r 5.52(3).
3   IR 1986, r 5.52(4).
4   IR 1986, r 5.52(5).
5   Under IA 1986, s 261(4).
6   IR 1986, Sch 4, Form 5.7.
7   IR 1986, r 5.52(6).
8   IR 1986, r 5.60(1).

6.267 The court must as soon as reasonably practicable give notice of the making of the annulment order to the Secretary of State[1]. The former bankrupt may, in writing within 28 days of the date of the order, require the Secretary of State to give notice of the making of the order:

(a)   in the Gazette;

(b)   in any newspaper in which the bankruptcy order was advertised; or
(c)   in both[2].

1   IR 1986, r 5.60(2).
2   IR 1986, r 5.60(3); the original provision that the Secretary of State could require the former bankrupt to pay the cost of advertising the annulment order, r 5.60(4), was deleted by the Insolvency (Amendment) Rules 2004, SI 2004/584. Where the former bankrupt has died, or is a person incapable of managing his affairs (within the meaning of IR 1986, r 7.43), the references to him in r 5.60(3) are to be read as referring to his personal representative or, as the case may be, a person appointed by the court to represent or act for him, r 5.60(5).

6.268 Where the official receiver has notified creditors of the debtor's bankruptcy, and the bankruptcy order is annulled, he must notify them of the annulment as soon as reasonably practicable[1]. Any expenses incurred by the official receiver in giving notice to the creditors are a charge in his favour on the property of the former bankrupt, whether or not actually in the official receiver's hands[2]. Where any property is in the hands of a trustee or any person other than the former bankrupt himself, the official receiver's charge is valid subject only to any costs that may be incurred by the trustee or that other person in effecting realisation of the property for the purpose of satisfying the charge[3].

1   IR 1986, r 5.53(1).
2   IR 1986, r 5.53(2).
3   IR 1986, r 5.53(3).

6.269 The annulment of a bankruptcy order does not of itself release the trustee from any duty or obligation imposed on him by or under the IA 1986 or the IR 1986 to account for all his transactions in connection with the former bankrupt's estate[1]. The trustee must submit a copy of his final account to the Secretary of State as soon as reasonably practicable after the court's order annulling the bankruptcy order; and he shall file a copy of the final account in court[2]. The final account must include a summary of the trustee's receipts and payments in the administration, and contain a statement to the effect that he has reconciled his account with that held by the Secretary of State in respect of the bankruptcy[3]. The trustee is released from such time as the court may determine, having regard to whether he has complied with the requirement to submit a copy of his final account to the Secretary of State, and file that account in court[4].

1   IR 1986, r 5.61(1).
2   IR 1986, r 5.61(2).
3   IR 1986, r 5.61(3).
4   IR 1986, r 5.61(4).

Application by official receiver to annul bankruptcy order

6.270 Where the bankrupt has not made an application to annul his bankruptcy order within the prescribed period, 14 days, the application may be made by the official receiver[1]. An application to the court to annul a bankruptcy order by the official receiver must specify the section under which it is made[2], and no application may be brought before the expiry of 14 days from the date that the 28-day period allowed for challenges to the decision of the creditors' meeting has expired[3]. The application must be supported by a report stating the grounds on which it is made, and must also state that:

(a)   the time period for the application has expired; and
(b)   the official receiver is not aware that any application or appeal remains to be disposed of[4].

---

1   IA 1986, s 261(2)(b); the procedure governing the application is provided for in IR 1986, Part 5 Chapter 9, IR 1986, r 5.54. These provisions were inserted into the IR 1986 by the Insolvency (Amendment) Rules 2003, SI 2003/1730.
2   IR 1986, r 5.55(1).
3   IR 1986, r 5.55(2).
4   IR 1986, r 5.55(3)

6.271 On the application and the report being filed in court, the court gives the official receiver notice of the venue fixed for the hearing[1]. The official receiver must give notice of the venue, accompanied by copies of the application and the report, to the bankrupt not less than seven days before the date of the hearing[2]. On annulling the bankruptcy order, the court sends sealed copies of the order of annulment in the prescribed form[3] to the official receiver, any trustee who is not the official receiver, the supervisor of the voluntary arrangement and the bankrupt[4]. In the annulment order the court must include provision permitting vacation of the registration of the bankruptcy petition as a pending action, and of the bankruptcy order, in the register of writs and orders affecting land[5].

---

1   IR 1986, r 5.55(4).
2   IR 1986, r 5.55(5).
3   IR 1986, Sch 4, Form 5.7.
4   IR 1986, r 5.55(6).
5   IR 1986, r 5.60(1).

6.272 The court must as soon as reasonably practicable give notice of the making of the annulment order to the Secretary of State[1]. The former bankrupt may, in writing within 28 days of the date of the order, require the Secretary of State to give notice of the making of the order:

(a)   in the Gazette;
(b)   in any newspaper in which the bankruptcy order was advertised; or
(c)   in both[2].

---

1   IR 1986, r 5.60(2).
2   IR 1986, r 5.60(3); the original provision that the Secretary of State could require the former bankrupt to pay the cost of advertising the annulment order, IR 1986, r 5.60(4), was deleted by the Insolvency (Amendment) Rules 2004, SI 2004/584. Where the former bankrupt has died, or is a person incapable of managing his affairs (within the meaning of IR 1986, r 7.43), the references to him in IR 1986, r 5.60(3) are to be read as referring to his personal representative or, as the case may be, a person appointed by the court to represent or act for him, IR 1986, r 5.60(5).

6.273 Where the bankruptcy order is annulled, the official receiver must notify all creditors of whom he is aware of the annulment[1]. Any expenses incurred by the official receiver in giving notice to the creditors are a charge in his favour on the property of the former bankrupt, whether or not actually in the official receiver's hands[2]. Where any property is in the hands of a trustee or any person other than the former bankrupt himself, the official receiver's charge is valid subject only to any costs that may be incurred by the trustee or that other person in effecting realisation of the property for the purpose of satisfying the charge[3].

1   IR 1986, r 5.56(1).
2   IR 1986, r 5.56(2).
3   IR 1986, r 5.56(3).

Foreign creditors

6.274 Within England and Wales foreign creditors will be treated as any other creditor. They will be bound to the arrangement whether or not they voted and irrespective of how they voted. Within the foreign creditors' own jurisdiction local rules will apply and it may not be possible for the supervisor to prevent a foreign creditor enforcing his debt in full against local assets particularly if he voted against the proposal. Foreign creditors who are habitually resident, domiciled or have a registered office within another Member State of the EU, except Denmark, will be subject to the rights and obligations imposed on creditors under the EC Insolvency Regulation[1]. All EU claims may be lodged (the wording is aimed at claims against insolvent estates) including claims from the tax and social security authorities of Member States[2]. EU creditors are entitled to be told of the start of insolvency proceedings, which include voluntary arrangements, and to be given information as to the lodging of claims, and any applicable time limit[3]. In lodging a claim the creditor must give full details of the claim, its nature, amount and date on which it arose, and provide copies of any supporting documents. Any preference, security in rem or reservation of title asserted by the creditor must be specified[4]. Information provided to a foreign creditor may be in English, but the form used must be headed '*Invitation to lodge a claim. Time limits to be observed*' in all the official languages of the EU[5]. A creditor may lodge a claim in the official language of his State, but may be required to provide a translation into English[6].

1   Ie Council Regulation (EC) No 1346/2000 of May 29 2000 on Insolvency Proceedings which came into force on 31 May 2002. Denmark is the sole EU State to which the EC Insolvency Regulation does not apply.
2   EC Insolvency Regulation, art 39.
3   EC Insolvency Regulation, art 40.
4   EC Insolvency Regulation, art 41.
5   EC Insolvency Regulation, art 42(1).
6   EC Insolvency Regulation, art 42(2).

H VARIATION OF VOLUNTARY ARRANGEMENT

Express provision to vary arrangement

6.275 Many voluntary arrangements are approved on the basis that the debtor will make periodical contributions over a lengthy period, often five years. The chances that the debtor's situation will change during that period are significant and the ability to vary the arrangements as approved is often welcome. Many arrangements contain express provision for variation, usually on a 75% vote of the creditors in accordance with the provisions of the Insolvency Rules[1]. Such express provisions for variation are valid. In *Horrocks v Broome*[2] the court rejected the argument that the scheme of the Insolvency Act precluded a variation in an individual voluntary arrangement. Various matters were raised in support of the argument, including the points that:

(a)   the detailed safeguards in the Insolvency Act which applied to the implementation of the voluntary arrangement would be absent at the time of variation, and a dissentient creditor would not be able to challenge the arrangement at the time of its implementation because ex hypothesi he would not know at that stage whether the power to vary would be used so as to prejudice his interests;

(b)   if the arrangement was indeed subsequently varied in a manner prejudicial to the creditor he might have no remedy under s 263(3)[3] since the court would not normally entertain any challenge to the exercise of his discretion by the supervisor unless satisfied that it had been exercised improperly[4];

(c)   there was nothing in the IA 1986 or the IR 1986 which suggested that Parliament had conceived of the possibility of variation, but rather the statute contemplated only a fresh proposal to the creditors which the debtor could not make within 12 months of the initial interim order[5]. Furthermore the court had no power to sanction a variation[6];

(d)   the criminal sanction[7] on the debtor in respect of false information supplied to the supervisor would not be available on a variation; and

(e)   the power to vary was ex facie bad since it would potentially permit provisions to be introduced into the arrangement which would not have been permissible in the original proposal, for example varying the rights of a secured or preferential creditor.

---

[1]   Ie IR 1986, r 5.23(3)–(6), see paras **6.174–6.176**.
[2]   [1999] BPIR 66.
[3]   See para **6.295**.
[4]   Cf *Re Edennote Ltd* [1996] 2 BCLC 389, CA.
[5]   By virtue of IA 1986, s 255(1)(c); note that with the implementation of the amendments introduced by the IA 2000 it will be possible for a debtor to propose a new IVA within 12 months of an existing IVA because he no longer needs to obtain an interim order before making his proposal to creditors, IA 1986, s 256A.
[6]   *Re Alpa Lighting* [1997] BPIR 341, and see para **6.301**.
[7]   Previously IR 1986, r 5.30, now repealed and re-enacted in wider terms in IA 1986, s 262A, inserted by IA 2000.

6.276 While accepting that a variation might adversely affect the interests of a particular creditor the court directed that the arrangement could be varied under the procedure contained in its terms, with the requisite 75% majority. The variation clause had to be construed as permitting only variations or modifications which could have been validly included in the original proposal. It was recognised that a challenge might be brought against an approved arrangement under IA 1986, s 262[1] on the grounds of potential substantial prejudice, and the court cautioned debtors and nominees to exercise care before including variation clauses to ensure that they were drafted to meet any objections that were likely to be taken.

¹   See paras **6.204–6.213**.

6.277 In *Re Circuit Leisure Ltd, Larchstone Ltd v Eric Stonham*[1] the voluntary arrangement contained a provision that the supervisor might convene a meeting of creditors to consider whether amendments should be made to the arrangements if it appeared that there was no reasonable prospect of the voluntary arrangement being successfully completed. The court implied a term that the creditors' meeting so convened might vary the arrangements on a 75% majority vote in accordance with IR 1986, r 1.19[2].

¹   24 March 1999, unreported (Miss E Gloster QC). Lawtel Doc No C9200093.
²   IR 1986, r 5.23 for individual voluntary arrangements.

Sanctions on debtor with respect to variation

6.278 One of the arguments before the court in *Horrocks v Broome*[1] was that the criminal sanction on a debtor who supplies false information to his creditors is so worded that it applies only in connection with the approval of the original arrangement, and not in connection with a variation[2]. A debtor may propose a variation to gain an ancillary advantage. He might learn of a substantial bequest which is likely to come to him shortly, or he may wish to bring an arrangement to an earlier end than originally approved so as to avoid paying the fruits of a new business venture to the creditors. In proposing a variation the debtor will be subject to the general law as to misrepresentation and deceit, but it is uncertain to what extent he is obliged to disclose information without a specific request to do so. There is a strong case to be made on historical grounds that the debtor owes creditors a strict duty of good faith[3], but the courts can sometimes be strangely reluctant to impose duties of good faith within a quasi commercial context. It would be advisable for creditors to ensure that the arrangement as approved imposes such a duty or for the supervisor or creditors to require disclosure before a proposal to vary the arrangement is put before the creditors.

¹   [1999] BPIR 66.
²   A debtor commits an offence if he makes any fraudulent representation or fraudulently does, or omits to do, anything 'for the purpose of obtaining the approval of his creditors to a proposal for a voluntary arrangement', IA 1986, s 262A. At the time of the decision in *Horrocks v Broome* [1999] 1 BCLC 356 the criminal sanction was in IR 1986, r 5.30: 'The debtor commits an offence if he makes any fraudulent representation or commits any other fraud for the purpose of obtaining the approval of his creditors to a proposal for a voluntary arrangement'.
³   The essential principles are considered with some care by the deputy judge at first instance in *Cadbury Schweppes plc v Somji* [2001] 1 WLR 615, CA §25, reported with the decision at first instance at [2001] 1 BCLC 498.

Variation where no express power

6.279 In the absence of express authorisation a term will not be implied into an arrangement permitting a variation by 75% of the creditors[1]. However, the

Court of Appeal decided in *Raja v Rubin*[2] that it is permissible for all the creditors, or all the creditors of a distinct class, to reach a consensual variation to the arrangement with the debtor which would be binding upon them all. Such a consensual arrangement would not have the effect of altering the original arrangement which would continue to have statutory force. If all the creditors and the debtor consent to the variation in the arrangement it proceeds as a binding agreement between them. If only a class of creditors agree to a variation as between themselves and the debtor, this variation not affecting the rights of creditors outside the class, the voluntary arrangement continues in its original form as between the debtor and any creditor not in the relevant class, but in its varied form as between the class creditors and the debtor. The court appreciated that this approach might give rise to uncertainty, in that no creditor at the start of the arrangement could be sure how the arrangement might develop through future amendment. But this consideration is outweighed by the advantages of allowing variation to which all affected creditors agree. The present law as to variation of voluntary arrangements may therefore be summarised as follows:

(1) it is legitimate for a voluntary arrangement to contain an express provision for variation[3];

(2) the fact that an arrangement as approved contains a variation provision might in appropriate (albeit, it is suggested, unusual) circumstances form the basis of a challenge under IA 1986[4];

(3) where a variation takes place pursuant to an express power the varied arrangement continues as if it were the arrangement approved in the creditors' meeting, subject always to rights accrued before the variation;

(4) in the absence of an express power of variation the creditors as a whole, or any distinct class of creditors, may unanimously vary the terms of the arrangement provided that the rights of creditors not in the relevant class are not affected[5]. For the creditors outside the class the arrangement continues as originally approved;

(5) where there is a consensual variation in the absence of an express power, any party who is affected by the variation may apply to the court to complain of the relevant act or decision of the supervisor which permitted the variation to proceed[6]. The court will then have power to disallow the variation;

(6) where there is any variation, whether under express power or otherwise, any person affected by its terms, even if not a party to the arrangement[7], may apply to the court to complain of the relevant act or decision of the supervisor which permitted the variation to proceed[8]. The court will then have power to disallow the variation.

[1] *Raja v Rubin* [1998] BPIR 647 (at first instance; there was no appeal on this point).

[2] [2000] Ch 274.

[3] If there is express provision for variation but no provision as to how the variation is to be agreed the court will imply the provisions of IR 1986, r 5.23, *Re Circuit Leisure Ltd* (24 March 1999, unreported). Lawtel Doc No C9200093. See paras **6.275–6.277**.

[4] IA 1986, s 262, see para **6.204**.

[5] And see *Tanner v Everitt* [2004] EWHC 1130, [2004] BPIR 1026 at [47]–[57] where the court rejected any notion of implied consent or estoppel on the part of creditors who had not expressly agreed to the variations.

[6] Under the provisions of IA 1986, s 263(3), see para **6.295**.

[7] See IA 1986, s 263(3), which permits *any* person dissatisfied by an act or decision of the supervisor to apply to the court.
[8] See previous footnote.

I IMPLEMENTATION OF ARRANGEMENT

The supervisor

6.280 Where an arrangement is approved by the creditors' meeting, the person who is for the time being carrying out in relation to the arrangement the functions conferred by virtue of that approval on the nominee or his replacement is known as the supervisor of the arrangement[1]. The supervisor must be authorised to act as supervisor in relation to the arrangement[2]. The supervisor will usually have been the nominee, but it is open to the creditors' meeting to appoint one or more other persons to replace or in addition to the practitioner who has acted as nominee provided the practitioner or practitioners concerned are qualified insolvency practitioners or are authorised to act as supervisor in relation to the arrangement[3]. The rôle of supervisor may be undertaken by two or more practitioners. In such a case the creditors may resolve whether acts to be done in connection with the arrangement may be done by any one of them, or must be done by both or all the relevant practitioners[4].

[1] IA 1986, s 263(1)(2).
[2] Whether as a qualified insolvency practitioner or a member of a body specifically recognised for the purpose of its members acting as nominees or supervisors by the Secretary of State, IA 1986, s 388(1)(b), s 389A, as amended and added by IA 2000, s 4, see para **6.18**.
[3] IA 1986, s 258(3) and IR 1986, r 5.25; It is the rules that permit more than one supervisor, the statute envisages only one.
[4] IR 1986, r 5.25(1).

6.281 The supervisor implements the arrangement, and the terms of the arrangement will dictate what activities the supervisor undertakes in connection with it. Whether assets subject to a voluntary arrangement are held by the supervisor and if so on what terms will ultimately depend on the terms of the arrangement. The court should not be slow to find that the supervisor holds assets under the arrangement on trust[1]. The supervisor holds any funds which have been passed to him by or on behalf of the debtor for distribution under the arrangement on trust for the creditors whether or not he is formally constituted a trustee under the terms of the arrangement[2]. In *Welburn v Dibb Lupton Broomhead (a firm)*[3] the debtor's entire estate, apart from his dwelling house, was included in his IVA. A major asset of the estate was an arbitration claim against a third party. The terms of the IVA required the supervisor to oversee the progress of the arbitration with the debtor providing assistance in the prosecution of the claim. The Court of Appeal held that the supervisor held the chose in action representing the claim on trust for the creditors[4], and it fell to the supervisor to give instructions to the solicitors acting on the claim, not the debtor in whose name was the nominal legal title to the claim.

[1] *Welburn v Dibb Lupton Broomhead (a firm)* [2002] EWCA Civ 1601, [2003] BPIR 768.

[2]   *Re Leisure Study Group Ltd* [1994] 2 BCLC 65; *Re Bradley-Hole (a bankrupt)* [1995] 4 All ER 865, [1995] 1 WLR 1097, see also *Re N T Gallagher & Sons Ltd* [2002] EWCA Civ 404, [2002] 1 WLR 2380 para 29.
[3]   [2002] EWCA Civ 1601, [2003] BPIR 768.
[4]   It followed that the debtor could not claim damages for loss resulting from the failure of his solicitors to recover an interim award before the insolvency of the respondent company against whom the award had been made. It was the creditors not the debtor who had suffered any loss.

6.282   As soon as the arrangement is approved by the creditors' meeting, the debtor, or where the debtor is bankrupt, his trustee in bankruptcy, must do all that is required for putting the supervisor into possession of the assets included in the arrangement[1]. The supervisor becomes responsible for the discharge of any balance due to the relevant office-holder by way of remuneration on account of fees, costs, charges or expenses properly incurred in the insolvency, and any advances made in respect of the insolvent estate together with interest at judgement rate[2]. The supervisor may either discharge such sums as may be owing or give a written undertaking to do so out of the first realisation of assets. Until such sums are discharged the office-holder has a charge over the assets included in the arrangement[3]. The supervisor must also discharge any guarantees properly given by the office-holder for the benefit of the estate out of the realisation of the assets included in the arrangement[4].

[1]   IR 1986, r 5.26(1).
[2]   IR 1986, r 5.26(2).
[3]   IR 1986, r 5.26(3)(4). Any sums due to the official receiver take priority over those due to a trustee, r 5.26(4).
[4]   IR 1986, r 5.21(5).

Fees and expenses

6.283   The fees, costs, charges and expenses that may be incurred for any purposes of the arrangement are (1) any disbursements made by the nominee prior to the approval of the arrangement, and any remuneration for his services as such agreed between himself and the debtor or, where appropriate, the office-holder[1]; (2) any fees, costs, charges and expenses which are sanctioned by the terms of the arrangement or would be payable, or correspond to those which would be payable, in the debtor's liquidation or bankruptcy[2]. The priority in respect of the trustee's fees, charges and expenses extends to the date on which the supervisor takes possession of the assets, but not to fees, charges and expenses incurred after that date[3].

[1]   Ie the official receiver or the trustee.
[2]   IR 1986, r 5.33; as to the fees, etc payable in bankruptcy see IR 1986, r 6.224.
[3]   *Rooney v Cardona and Judd* [1999] BPIR 954.

No statutory protection when carrying on debtor's business

6.284   There is no statutory protection for a supervisor who carries on the debtor's business or who trades within the context of the arrangement. He will be liable under the general law in respect of any business dealings, or the administration or disposal of assets. If there is to be further trading in the debtor's business the supervisor is well advised to ensure that he does not become liable for trade liabilities, tax, business rates and other such liabilities. A voluntary arrangement does not of itself terminate contracts of employment where the debtor is employer or employee. There may however be express provisions covering contracts of employment when the voluntary arrangement takes effect in the terms of the arrangement or, exceptionally, in the contract of employment. Where a supervisor obtains an interest in land under the terms of the arrangement he may register it as a caution against first registration in respect of unregistered land[1], or a notice where the land is registered[2]. The supervisor may seek the assistance of the court and apply for directions in relation to any particular matter arising under the arrangement[3].

[1] See the Land Registration Act 2002, s 15.
[2] See the Land Registration Act 2002, s 32 previously a class C(iv) land charge under the Land Registration Act 1925, s 54.
[3] IA 1986, s 263(4). As to the supervisor's power to present a petition for a bankruptcy order see paras **6.327**–**6.331**.

Resignation or replacement

6.285 There is no provision in the IA 1986 or the IR 1986 for the resignation or replacement of the supervisor. Such provision may be made within the terms of the arrangement or arranged with the consent of the debtor and the creditors provided, where there is no express power to replace a supervisor, the debtor and all the creditors agree[1]. A supervisor who wishes to resign and who is unable to do so by agreement may apply to the court for an order to appoint a replacement[2]. In IVAs any supervisor who vacates office, and any new appointee as supervisor, must give notice to the Secretary of State of his vacation of office or appointment as the case may be[3].

[1] This must be a positive unanimous agreement; there is no place for implied consent, *Tanner v Everitt* [2004] EWHC 1130 (Ch), [2004] BPIR 1026 at [58]–[63].
[2] Under IA 1986, s 263(5), see para **6.323**.
[3] IR 1986, r 5.29(2).

Powers and responsibilities of the supervisor

6.286 The supervisor will have such powers, and only such powers, as are vested in him by the arrangement. In the rare case where the voluntary arrangement comprises territorial proceedings[1] for the purposes of the EC Insolvency Regulation the supervisor must be conscious that his powers are restricted to assets situated in the UK, whatever provision may be made about them in the terms of the arrangement[2]. No powers are implied by the IA 1986 or IR 1986[3]. It is important therefore that the arrangement contains sufficient powers to enable the supervisor to implement the arrangement, e g powers to collect in assets, bring proceedings, etc. This is an obligation falling primarily on the nominee when preparing the proposal. Should the supervisor find that he does not have any necessary power he should in the first instance refer the matter to the creditors. Provided all the creditors, or all the creditors who are affected, agree, or the terms of any express provision in the arrangement as to variation are complied with, it will be possible to amend the arrangement as necessary[4]. The supervisor may apply to the court for directions to assist him on any matter[5], but the court may not make any order which amounts to a variation of the arrangement which has been approved by the creditors[6].

1   See **Chapter 4**.
2   EC Insolvency Regulation, art 3(2).
3   There is no power in the supervisor to disclaim leases or other onerous contracts, and no such power can, of course, be vested in the supervisor by a provision in the arrangement.
4   *Raja v Rubin* [2000] Ch 274.
5   IA 1986, s 263(4).
6   *Re Alpa Lighting Ltd* [1997] BPIR 341; the creditors' consent has to be obtained, under the express terms of the voluntary arrangement if this is possible, and in the absence of appropriate provision in the arrangement itself, by unanimous agreement.

Implying terms into the arrangement

6.287 As with any consensual agreement the court will only imply terms when it is necessary to do so for the efficacy of the voluntary arrangement[1]. A strict approach is generally adopted on the question of necessity for the implication of a term into a voluntary arrangement[2]. Many standard forms of voluntary arrangement do not spell out the effect that the voluntary arrangement is to have on the creditors' debts. This is basic, and perhaps so obvious that it is missed, but plainly if there is no express term to this effect a term will have to be implied that the creditors bound by the arrangement will take no steps to enforce their debts against the debtor while the debtor is complying, or has complied with his obligations under the arrangement[3]. Faced with standard conditions that made no express provision to compromise the debts of creditors in the arrangement the court in *El Ajou v Stern*[4] held that to give the IVA business efficacy the following were implied terms:

(1)   that creditors with debts subject to the IVA would take no steps to enforce their debts against the debtor so long as the IVA subsisted;

(2)   that if the IVA was duly completed, and was not deemed to have failed, creditors would accept what, if anything, was distributed to them under the IVA in full and final settlement of their debts.

1   *Liverpool City Council v Irwin* [1977] AC 239.
2   See eg *Johnson v Davies* [1999] Ch 117 at 128.
3   *Johnson v Davies* [1999] Ch 117 at 128F.
4   [2006] EWHC 3067 (Ch), [2006] All ER (D) 11 (Dec), [2007] BPIR 693 at [31].

6.288 The court will, it is suggested, readily imply a term in the arrangement to the effect that the debtor should do all such acts as are necessary to enable the supervisor to carry the arrangement into effect. Such a term will enable the court, for example, to direct the debtor to execute a power of attorney to enable the supervisor to bring proceedings against the third party where this is necessary for the implementation of the arrangement. In *Alman v Approach Housing Ltd*[1] a creditor with a small admitted claim wished to establish by action in the High Court a much larger claim for unliquidated damages which had been given only a nominal value for voting purposes by the chairman of the creditors' meeting. The corporate debtor contended that it was implicit that the pursuit of legal proceedings was prohibited by the terms of the CVA.

The remedy for any creditor who could not persuade the supervisor to agree his debt was to apply to the court as a person dissatisfied with a decision of the supervisor[2]. The court held that it was not necessary to imply a term which prohibited the bringing of legal proceedings against the company. There was no express provision in the voluntary arrangement for dealing with claims nor was a machinery provided for determining disputed claims. The creditor was therefore permitted, albeit with some hesitation on the part of the court, to proceed with his action against the debtor.

[1] [2001] 1 BCLC 530.
[2] See paras **6.295–6.301**.

6.289 A term was implied into the voluntary arrangement in *Re Hellard and Goldfarb, Joint Supervisors of Pinson Wholesale Ltd*[1]. The approved arrangement, a CVA which followed an administration, provided for the supervisor to be paid on a time basis, subject to a cap, with provision for an additional fee if approved by a general meeting of creditors. The administrator became the supervisor. Concerns arose as to the supervisor's conduct both in the CVA and as administrator. He was replaced by joint supervisors who recovered a considerable sum from the original supervisor on grounds of improper conduct of the CVA and misappropriation of company assets in the administration. Time-costing of the work carried out by the joint supervisors took them well above the agreed cap. When the joint supervisors summoned a creditors' meeting to consider their claim for additional fees, not a single creditor responded. The court implied a term into the voluntary arrangement that where a meeting was summoned under the agreed procedure but was inquorate the supervisor could set his remuneration within the context of the voluntary arrangement subject to the right of any creditor or other person dissatisfied to apply to the court[2].

[1] 23 July 2007, unreported (HHJ Norris QC). Lawtel Doc No AC0114832.
[2] See paras **6.295–6.301**.

6.290 Where the proposal put before creditors is that the equity in specified properties would be available to meet good any shortfall in the event that trading over the period of the arrangement proved insufficient to generate enough funds to pay the promised dividend, it is implicit that the equity in the properties is maintained and not eroded by further charges or by allowing the sums due under existing charges to increase[1]. A term in a voluntary arrangement precluding all creditors, secured or otherwise, from commencing or continuing proceedings against the debtor prohibits such proceedings to enforce the personal liability of the debtor, but does not prevent a secured creditor from enforcing his security[2].

[1] *Harris v Gross* [2001] BPIR 586, 598.
[2] *Rey v FNCB Ltd* [2006] EWHC 1386 (Ch), [2006] BPIR 1260.

Claims by creditors and against third parties

6.291 The supervisor will have to determine claims made by creditors for the purpose of dividend in the voluntary arrangement, particularly where a nominal or minimum value was placed on the claim for voting purposes at the creditors' meeting. The supervisor may make a decision as to whether or not a person is a creditor, and that decision may be challenged[1] by the creditor concerned or any other creditor[2]. Depending upon the terms of the arrangement any creditor may seek to revalue or add to his claim for the purpose of dividend. There are no express provisions in the IR 1986 governing proofs of debt in voluntary arrangements, and it is common for the terms of arrangements to incorporate the winding-up or bankruptcy rules as to proof. In *Meisels v Martin*[3] the question arose whether a creditor was restricted to only one proof, which had to be varied if a further claim was made, or could submit a second or further proofs. The court considered, but did not decide, that where a single claim was submitted that claim could only be increased by variation of the original proof. Where however the creditor has two completely independent claims it might be possible for them to form the subject matter of separate proofs.

1   See paras **6.295–6.301.**
2   *Re Timothy* [2005] EWHC 1885 (Ch), [2006] BPIR 329 at [48].
3   [2005] EWHC 845 (Ch), [2005] BPIR 1151.

6.292 In the ordinary course proceedings to recover or protect assets will be brought or defended by the debtor. Even if all the proceeds of the litigation will go to the creditors in the arrangement, it is unlikely that the debtor will be held to be a nominal claimant for the purposes of security for costs[1]. In *Envis v Thakkar*[2] the Court of Appeal held that the debtor had a genuine personal interest in such litigation. In the absence of any element of duplicity the definition of nominal claimant did not extend to the debtor even though his interest may not be directly in the proceeds of the litigation but indirectly in the payment of his creditors through the proper implementation of the arrangement. There is no reason in principle why an individual debtor should not be entitled to funding from the Legal Services Commission[3] to bring or defend proceedings which benefit the arrangement; whether he will receive it is quite another matter. Where the terms of a voluntary arrangement provided an ADR mechanism for the determination of claims which was not final and binding between the parties, and also expressly provided that the right of the supervisor to seek directions should not be affected or restricted, the court directed that the claims should be determined by the court rather than by ADR including as they did issues of construction which applied substantially to all creditor claimants[4].

1   For the power to award security for costs see CPR Pt 25.12, which applies to insolvency proceedings by virtue of IR 1986, r 7.51.
2   [1997] BPIR 189.
3   The successor to the Legal Aid Board.
4   *Re Enron Direct Ltd* [2003] EWHC 1437 (Ch), [2003] BPIR 1132.

Liability of supervisor

6.293 In carrying out his duties as nominee, convener or chairman of the creditors' meeting and supervisor of the arrangement, the relevant insolvency practitioner (or other person authorised to act as supervisor in relation to the arrangement[1]) should ensure that he complies with good practice and in particular the guidance given by:

(a)   the Statement of Insolvency Practice 3, produced by R3, the Association of Business Recovery Professionals[2];

(b)   the Guide to Professional Conduct and Ethics, issued by the Insolvency Practitioners Association; and

(c)   the 'Dear IP' notices issued by the Insolvency Service[3].

---

[1]   See para **6.18**.
[2]   Previously called the Society of Practitioners of Insolvency.
[3]   These are now collected together in the Dear IP Millennium Edition. Chapter 24 covers voluntary arrangements.

6.294   The supervisor's decisions may well impact on a number of people; the debtor, the creditors and a range of third parties who have or have had dealings with the debtor. It has been held that no private law right of action exists in the debtor, creditor or third party against the supervisor for breach of statutory duty. In *King v Anthony*[1] the Court of Appeal noted that Part VIII of the Insolvency Act 1986 comprised a self-contained scheme including express powers in the court to give appropriate directions if complaint is made to the court of the conduct of the supervisor. Since the Insolvency Act 1986 provides an effective means of enforcing the duty of a supervisor, this indicates that the statutory right was intended to be enforceable by application under IA 1986, s 263 and not by private right of action[2]. Funds held by the supervisor for distribution to the creditors under the arrangement will be held by him as trustee, whether or not the supervisor is formally constituted a trustee under the arrangement[3], and the liabilities of a trustee will therefore attach to the supervisor with regard to such funds.

---

[1]   [1998] 2 BCLC 517, [1999] BPIR 73.
[2]   See 78–79. To the extent that the supervisor is performing private functions this decision survives the Human Rights Act 1998. However, in complying with the directions of the court the supervisor is a public authority for the purposes of the Human Rights Act 1998, s 6 and a complaint arising out of his acts or omissions in this regard may be the subject matter of a private right of action at the suit of a victim, Human Rights Act 1998, s 7.
[3]   *Re Leisure Study Group Ltd* [1994] 2 BCLC 65.

Control by the court: who may apply

6.295   The court may exercise control over the arrangement by giving directions or by removing the supervisor or appointing a further supervisor to assist in the implementation of the arrangement[1]. The IA 1986 gives the court a complete discretion to give directions in relation to any matter arising under the arrangement on the application of the supervisor[2]. An application to challenge any act, omission, or decision of the supervisor may be made by the debtor, any of his creditors, or any other person who is dissatisfied by the relevant act, omission or decision. On such an application the court may (a) confirm, reverse or modify any act or decision of the supervisor, (b) give him directions, or (c) make such other order as it thinks fit[3]. The existence of this summary remedy on the part of any dissatisfied applicant will preclude private rights of action against the supervisor by any claimant who may bring such an application[4].

1   IA 1986, s 263(4)(5).
2   IA 1986, s 263(3).
3   IA 1986, s 263(3).
4   See *King v Anthony* [1998] 2 BCLC 517.

6.296 'Dissatisfied' is not a word used in previous insolvency legislation. It replaces 'aggrieved' in earlier legislation. In *Re Sidebotham, ex p Sidebotham*[1] James LJ said that:

> 'A person aggrieved must be a man who has suffered a legal grievance, a man against whom a decision has been pronounced which has wrongfully deprived him of something, or wrongfully refused him something or wrongfully affected his title to something.'

1   (1880) 14 Ch D 458 at 465.

6.297 To this Lord Denning added:

> 'But the definition of James LJ is not to be regarded as exhaustive. The words "person aggrieved" are of wide import and should not be subjected to a restrictive interpretation. They do not include, of course, a mere busybody who is interfering in things which do not concern him; but they do include a person who has a genuine grievance because an order has been made which prejudicially affects his interests'[1].

1   *A-G of Gambia v N'Jie* [1961] AC 617 per Lord Denning at 634.

6.298 It is not clear whether 'dissatisfied' is used as a more modern equivalent of 'aggrieved' or whether it was intended to alter the scope of possible applicant. The likelihood is that the change in wording brings no change in substance[1]. It would be unrealistic to suppose that the court will entertain an application by a person whose dissatisfaction arose merely through general concern at the manner in which the supervisor was implementing the proposal rather than through his being prejudicially affected by a particular act, omission or decision of the supervisor. There must be a limit to the class of persons who can make such an application. But any person who is directly affected by any act, omission or decision is likely to come within the class of potential applicant[2].

1   ' "Dissatisfied" is certainly no narrower than "aggrieved", and is arguably wider', per Stanley Burnton QC in *Re Dennis Michael Cook* [1999] BPIR 881 at p 883.
2   A former solicitor of the bankrupt who had received a letter from the trustee authorising him to assist the SFO in enquiries into the affairs of the bankrupt and who faced prosecution by the SFO if he refused to answer questions and proceedings by the bankrupt for breach of professional privilege if he did was a person dissatisfied by the trustee's letter of authority for the purposes of IA 1986, s 303, *Re Dennis Michael Cook* [1999] BPIR 881.

6.299 Within the context of formal insolvency, the equivalent provisions by which the court may exercise control over liquidators have been interpreted restrictively[1]. In compulsory liquidation IA 1986, s 168(5) entitles 'any person' aggrieved by an act or decision of the liquidator to apply to the court. This may be compared with the entitlement in IA 1986, s 167(3) of 'any creditor or contributory' to apply to the court with respect to the exercise or purported exercise by the liquidator of any of his powers. The courts recognise that the class of potential applicant under s 168(5) is wider than that under s 167(3), but nevertheless have stated that no 'outsider' to the liquidation has locus standi to make an application[2]. Accordingly a person denied an opportunity to purchase an asset of a company in compulsory liquidation sold by the liquidator may not apply[3], neither may a surety bring an application in respect of acts or decisions affecting the assets of the company when his subrogation rights do not in any way depend on the company being in liquidation[4]:

> 'It could not have been the intention of Parliament that any outsider to the liquidation, dissatisfied with some act or decision of the liquidator, could attack that act or decision by the special procedure of s 168(5). However, I would accept that someone, like the landlord in *Re Hans Place Ltd*[5], who is directly affected by the exercise of a power given specifically to liquidators, and who would not otherwise have any right to challenge the exercise of that power, can utilise s 168(5). It may be that other persons can properly bring themselves within the subsection.'[6]

[1] The draftsman of the Insolvency Act 1986 has not been consistent. In bankruptcy an application may be made to the court by the bankrupt, any of his creditors or any other person who is 'dissatisfied' with any act, omission or decision of the trustee, IA 1986, s 303(1).

[2] 'In the latter capacity alone, like any other outsider to the liquidation, they would not have the locus standi to apply under s 168(5)', per Nourse LJ in *Re Edennote Ltd* [1996] 2 BCLC 389 at 393 quoted by Peter Gibson LJ in *Mahomed v Morris* [2000] 2 BCLC 536 at para [24].

[3] *Re Edennote Ltd* [1996] 2 BCLC 389.

[4] *Mahomed v Morris* [2000] 2 BCLC 536.

[5] [1993] BCLC 768.

[6] Per Peter Gibson LJ in *Mahomed v Morris* [2000] 2 BCLC 536 at para 26.

6.300 It is suggested that these authorities do not bear directly on applications in respect of acts, omissions and decisions of supervisors while implementing the voluntary arrangement, at least when the context is very different. In a composition where assets are assigned to the supervisor to realise and distribute the proceeds the supervisor's task will be little different to that of a liquidator or trustee in bankruptcy. But in 'trading out' voluntary arrangements and other schemes of arrangement the supervisor may have a more commercial rôle and may have to deal with a wide variety of third parties over a range of matters. It would be inappropriate to deny a third party the opportunity to complain to the court about the supervisor simply on the basis that he is 'an outsider' to the voluntary arrangement, particularly as he is unable to challenge the supervisor by private right of action. Any person who (a) is directly affected by the acts, omissions or decisions of the supervisor in undertaking his rôle in the voluntary arrangement, and (b) has no other right of challenge, should be able to apply to the court for relief[1].

[1] See the passage quoted in the text (at para **6.299**) from Peter Gibson LJ's judgment in *Mahomed v Morris* [2000] 2 BCLC 536.

6.301 Although the court has a wide discretion on an application in respect of a supervisor's acts, omissions or decisions, it has no power to vary the terms of the arrangement[1]. Extending the duration of the arrangement amounts to a variation[2]. Subject to this important limitation the court's jurisdiction is extensive[3]. Nevertheless the court should be careful not to allow the width of the jurisdiction to control the supervisor to be used as a means for allowing the expensive and time consuming ventilation of claims which are likely to be fruitless[4].

1   *Re Alpa Lighting Ltd* [1997] BPIR 341, CA, impliedly overruling *Re FMS Financial Management Services Ltd* (1988) 5 BCC 191 where the court ordered that creditors who had been excluded from voting should be included in the voluntary arrangement and share in the sums paid as dividends.
2   *Re Alpa Lighting Ltd* [1997] BPIR 341, CA.
3   *King v Anthony* [1999] BPIR 73, see 78–79.
4   *Holdenhurst Securities plc v Cohen* [2001] 1 BCLC 460, quoting *Port v Auger* [1994] 1 WLR 862 at 874, but holding in the circumstances that there was a reasonable claim to be pursued.

Circumstances in which court will act on application

6.302 With so many voluntary arrangements in place it is not surprising that there have been a steady flow of applications to challenge acts and decisions of the supervisor and by supervisors seeking directions from the court when disputes arise with or between creditors bound by the arrangement. Most applications turn on their facts, and no points of principle emerge. There is a natural and proper reluctance on the part of the courts to go against the course proposed by a supervisor where he appears to be acting in accordance with the terms of the arrangement and is doing so in good faith. A few points which may be worthy of note:

(1)   It is important that the supervisor acquaints himself with all the terms of the voluntary arrangement he is implementing and ensures that he acts in accordance with those terms[1]. Arrangements do tend to be very lengthy documents, and insolvency practitioners are practical men not lawyers, but as in most cases the supervisor was the nominee who advised on the proposal it is not asking a great deal that he familiarises himself with it and is conscious when important decisions arise that he should keep to its terms. Where a supervisor proceeds on an erroneous view of the requirements of the arrangement neither he nor his successor is likely to be criticised as a result from enforcing the true terms of the arrangement; no estoppel will arise where the supervisor and the debtor have proceeded on a common but erroneous view of the arrangement where there is no evidence that the creditors ever shared or acted on that view[2].

(2)   The court will not however require the supervisor to follow the terms of the arrangement if there is a more convenient course which may be taken for the benefit of creditors which is not inconsistent with the arrangement terms. In *Re Enron Direct Ltd*[3] where four out of nine consultant creditors wanted the supervisor to exhaust the dispute resolution mechanism written into the voluntary arrangement before he had recourse to the High Court to determine how their claims should

be resolved, the court gave directions for the claims to be resolved by the court. This on the basis that all the claims raised matters of construction which, on determination, would apply across the board, and were the claimants to proceed with ADR there could still be a referral to the court on substantive issues.

(3) Where a creditor wishes to add to his claim for the purpose of dividend or other benefit under the arrangement the better view is that if he has a single claim he should add to his claim by varying his existing proof of debt, which will require the agreement of the supervisor if the relevant bankruptcy rules have been applied to the arrangement[4] but that if he has a new claim that may be made the subject of further proof of debt[5].

(4) Although most supervisors will act with relative informality in receiving and dealing with claims it is important for creditors to be in a position to prove their claims strictly. Where foreign claims are being advanced creditors should bear in mind that matters of foreign law must be proved where foreign law differs from English law. As do the courts the supervisor must apply English law to any foreign claim in the absence of evidence of the relevant foreign law[6].

(5) It is essential to join the debtor to the application if the supervisor or a creditor wishes the court to make a declaration as to the status of the voluntary arrangement[7].

(6) It should be possible for a creditor who suffers loss as a result of a wrongful decision or act of the supervisor to claim compensation in an application under the IA 1986[8]. Indeed it is likely that this is the only procedural route by which compensation may be claimed[9].

[1] In *Timmins v Conn* [2004] EWCA Civ 761, [2005] BPIR 647 at [26] the supervisor in evidence frankly admitted that he had never directed his mind to the relevant clause (which allowed him in effect to disclaim onerous property) and did not know that it was in the arrangement although he thought some provision of the nature probably was.
[2] *Stanley v Phillips* [2003] EWHC 720 (Ch), [2004] BPIR 632.
[3] [2003] EWHC 1437, [2003] BPIR 1132.
[4] See IR 1986, r 6.106.
[5] *Meisels v Martin* [2005] EWHC 845 (Ch), [2005] BPIR 1151 at [35]. In the normal case this is most unlikely to matter.
[6] *Meisels v Martin* [2005] EWHC 845 (Ch), [2005] BPIR 1151 at [28], [29].
[7] *Timmins v Conn* [2004] EWCA Civ 761, [2005] BPIR 647 at [33].
[8] Ie IA 1986, s 263(3).
[9] *King v Anthony* [1998] 2 BCLC 517; *Timmins v Conn* [2004] EWCA Civ 761, [2005] BPIR 647 at [34] where no compensation was considered because, having released the debtor from the proceedings, the court was not in a position to make a declaration that the voluntary arrangement was still continuing notwithstanding the supervisor's notice to creditors that he had completed its administration.

Commercial decisions of the supervisor

6.303 There is yet to be a case reported where the court has given detailed consideration to the principles on which it should interfere with commercial aspects of the supervisor's implementation of a voluntary arrangement which involves trading either with a view to more beneficial realisation of the debtor's assets or with the aim of rescuing the whole or part of the debtor's business. In general terms it may be expected that similar principles will be applied as apply to the control of other office-holders by the court[1], having due regard to the fact that the supervisor will be implementing an arrangement which is designed to enable the debtor to keep out of formal insolvency to the advantage of his creditors as opposed to administering an insolvent estate for the benefit of creditors in accordance with the general principles applicable to liquidation or bankruptcy. In formal insolvency cases the court has been slow to act, being concerned to allow office-holders to exercise their powers and their discretion without 'undue fetters'[2]. It may be noted that although bankruptcy and then company liquidation legislation has enabled 'any person ... aggrieved by an act or decision of an [officer-holder]' to apply to the court for summary relief since 1869[3] there have been relatively few applications; certainly few reported decisions.

1   See IA 1986, s 168(5) (control of liquidator in winding up by the court), s 303(1) (control of trustee in bankruptcy).
2   *Harold M Pitman & Co v Top Business Systems (Nottingham) Ltd* [1984] BCLC 593, 597b.
3   Bankruptcy Act 1869, s 20 introduced the jurisdiction.

6.304 In *Re Peters, ex p Lloyd*[1] the trustee decided not to sell a contingent reversionary interest. The creditor applicant argued that a refusal to sell an asset of the estate was an absurd exercise of the discretion of the trustee but the Court of Appeal disagreed, stating that the court would not interfere unless the trustee is doing that which is so utterly unreasonable and absurd that no reasonable man would so act. It was the bankrupt who applied in *Re a Debtor (No 400 of 1940) ex p Debtor v Dodwell*[2]. On the debtor's bankruptcy the trustee found himself with a very substantial property portfolio in London, extremely difficult to realise and almost as difficult to manage because of the ongoing hostilities. The bankrupt made general complaints that the estate had been mismanaged by the trustee who had decided against making use of the bankrupt's offers of assistance, and he sought to restrain a sale of one property on the basis that it was a bad time of year to sell. Harman J noted that there must be circumstances in which the court would interfere but, without attempting to define what such circumstances were, stated that they could not '(in the absence of fraud) justify interference in the day to day administration of the estate, nor can they entitle the bankrupt to question the exercise by the trustee in good faith of his discretion, nor to hold him accountable for an error of judgment'. The court pointed out that the bankrupt had had ample time to put forward his own scheme for realising the portfolio and dismissed the application.

1   (1882) 47 LT 64 (the whole of the very short judgment is set out by Plowman J in his judgment in *Leon v York-O-Matic Ltd* [1966] 3 All ER 277, [1966] 1 WLR 1450).
2   [1949] Ch 236.

6.305 These bankruptcy decisions have been relied on by the court when considering decisions taken by a liquidator[1]. In *Leon v York-O-Matic Ltd*[2] the company had operated a chain of launderettes. The liquidator contracted to sell all its properties in December 1965 for £47,000 having rejected an offer of £40,000 for some only of the properties from one of the former directors. The director commenced proceedings in March 1966 seeking to restrain completion of the sale, asserting that the properties were being sold at a gross undervalue. The court was not satisfied that the allegation of undervalue was made out, and expressed concern as to the delay in seeking relief. There was no question of fraud. In refusing the application the court stated that it was not satisfied either that the liquidator had not exercised his discretion bona fide or that he had acted in a way in which no reasonable liquidator could have acted. This decision was followed in *Harold M Pitman & Co v Top Business Systems (Nottingham) Ltd*[3], an application to strike out the statement of claim as disclosing no reasonable cause of action. The material allegation was that the liquidator had entered into a contract to sell intellectual property rights without a proper valuation of those rights and without the approval of the creditors. There was no allegation of fraud and no pleading that the liquidator had not exercised his discretion bona fide or that he was proposing to do something which was so utterly unreasonable and absurd that no reasonable man would do it. The court accepted that such a pleading was necessary, expressly making the point that it would not be enough to establish negligence[4], and struck out the pleading. The applicants in *Re Hans Place Ltd (in liquidation)*[5] were lessees of property which had been sub-let. The liquidator disclaimed the underlease thereby releasing the sureties[6] and the applicant sought an order setting the disclaimer aside. Counsel for the applicants argued that the previous authorities were all examples of a challenge being made to a commercial decision of the office-holder. While it was understandable that the court would not allow the routine challenge of such decisions, he argued that there should be no requirement of mala fides or perversity where the applicant could demonstrate that, as a landlord, he would be seriously affected by the decision to disclaim. The deputy judge disagreed and refused to interfere with the liquidator's decision.

[1]   See *Leon v York-O-Matic Ltd* [1966] 3 All ER 277, [1966] 1 WLR 1450.
[2]   [1966] 3 All ER 277, [1966] 1 WLR 1450.
[3]   [1984] BCLC 593.
[4]   [1984] BCLC 593, at 597d.
[5]   [1993] BCLC 768.
[6]   But see now *Hindcastle v Barbara Attenborough Associates Ltd* [1997] AC 70, [1996] 1 All ER 737.

6.306 A test which requires the court to find, before interfering, that the office-holder's actions were 'so utterly unreasonable and absurd that no reasonable man would have done it' is, conventionally expressed, the test for perversity. It suggests a test of such rigour that few challenges, absent fraud or bad faith, can hope to succeed. Success did however attend the application in *Re Edennote Ltd*[1]. The application concerned the assignment by the liquidator of the company's cause of action in existing proceedings concerning a football club over which various parties were wrangling. The applicant creditors of the company, effectively one of the competing parties, complained that the assignment was made to the other main competitor without an approach being made to them. They might well have made a more valuable offer for the assignment which would have been to the benefit of the creditors as a whole. The Court of Appeal affirmed the judge's view that the correct test was one of perversity[2] and held that it was perverse for the liquidator to assign the cause of action to one side of the dispute without enquiring whether a better offer might be obtained from the other side. If this is utterly unreasonable and absurd it is a less rigorous approach to perversity than might commonly be supposed would be applied by the court, and one to be welcomed. In this connection it is interesting to note two passages from the judgment. Counsel for the assignee had made the point that the possibility of a better offer for the cause of action had not been obvious to others. The learned judge referred to this and continued:

> 'While [counsel for the assignee] accepted that [the liquidator's] action must be judged objectively, he said, correctly, that the question was how a reasonable liquidator would have acted in the circumstances prevailing at the time, a question the court must answer eschewing the wisdom of hindsight'[3].

1   [1996] 2 BCLC 389, CA, affirming on this point [1995] 2 BCLC 248.
2   The judge below applied a perversity test, and also referred to the administrative law principle of *Wednesbury* unreasonableness (see *Associated Provincial Picture Houses Ltd v Wednesbury Corpn* [1948] 1 KB 223). Nourse LJ, with whom Millett LJ agreed, suggested that this reference was unnecessary and possibly confusing. The learned judge made the point that office-holders had to act as prudent businessmen in most of what they do, and added: 'In general there seems to be something unrealistic in judging the propriety of the acts and decisions of a businessman by asking whether he took into account something he ought not to have taken into account or failed to take into account something he ought to have taken into account'.
3   [1996] 2 BCLC 389 at 396b.

6.307 The learned judge continued:

> 'I have felt the force of [counsel's] submissions on this question. But they overlook an important point. A reasonable liquidator must be taken to be one who is properly advised. If support be needed for that proposition it can be found in *Re Hans Place Ltd* [1993] BCLC 768 at 778 … where [counsel] is recorded as having submitted that the court can only reverse a decision of a liquidator under s 168(5) where it is satisfied that it was taken in some way mala fide or "was so perverse as to demonstrate that no liquidator properly advised could have taken it". Although [the deputy Judge's] acceptance of [counsel's] submissions (at 779) was a general one and not specifically directed to the need for proper advice, it nevertheless confirms the view that a reasonable liquidator must be taken to be one who has such advice where he needs it. Very often a liquidator will not need advice before he acts. Here he clearly did. If [the liquidator] had been properly advised, he would have been told that the applicants, once apprised of the possibility of an assignment to Mr Venables, would see that their application for security was likely to avail them nothing and, as the judge observed, that Mr Venables would acquire a very considerable nuisance value in the settlement of the action as a whole. Thus it would have become obvious to a liquidator in [this liquidator]'s position, properly advised, that an approach should be made to the applicants.'

6.308 It is difficult to disagree with the outcome of this case, but not so easy to analyse it in terms of perversity. As appears from the passage cited it was not a straightforward matter. Once appropriate advice was taken the matter would have become obvious, but how is the liquidator to know when he does and when he does not need advice? He should not lightly incur the cost of obtaining professional advice. In *Re Edennote Ltd* the liquidator was presumably rather pleased to receive £7,000 (and a promise of 10% of the proceeds) for assigning a cause of an action of no obvious interest to him or the company. Certainly, in the circumstances, it was unreasonable for the liquidator not to appreciate that he should seek an alternative offer from the applicants or at least obtain advice, even at some cost to the liquidation, as to the better realisation of the asset. But was it perverse?

6.309 In *Mitchell v Buckingham International plc*[1] the Court of Appeal was concerned with cross-border issues and the liquidator's decision as to restraining orders in America, the effect of which was to prevent judgment creditors obtaining priority over other unsecured creditors. The court drew a distinction between liquidators exercising their administrative powers to realise assets 'where the court will be very slow to substitute its judgment for the liquidators' on what is essentially a businessman's decision[2]' and liquidators seeking, in effect, anti-execution relief from the court to prevent one creditor obtaining an advantage over others:

> 'That is eminently a matter for the Companies Court, or for liquidators acting under the control of the Companies Court. It is not a matter for the liquidators to decide at their own discretion in the way in which they might take decisions as to the disposal of their company's assets'.

[1]   [1998] 2 BCLC 369.
[2]   Per Robert Walker LJ (giving the judgment of the court) at 391f.

6.310 This has been referred to as 'the exception recognised in *Mitchell v Buckingham International plc* ... to the perversity test which the court in *Re Edennote Ltd* ... said was the appropriate test for justifying interference with the decisions of the liquidator'[1]. In *Mahomed v Morris*[2] the court on an application to strike out found that the issue was a decision by the liquidators on the realisation of assets of the company where a rival claim to the assets had been made. The compromise reached was a commercial decision to be decided by the liquidators at their own discretion. The court also rejected the submission that the liquidators should have consulted persons affected by their decision or obtain the approval of the Companies Court:

> 'I have never heard it suggested that a secured creditor who is contemplating realising the charged assets is under some duty to consult the debtor or the surety of the debtor, even if he is aware that the price he obtains on realisation may mean that the debt is not discharged and so there are no surplus proceeds which the surety may claim by subrogation ... [Counsel for the applicants] could point to no authority in support of the alleged duty to consult. In my judgment to impose such an obligation on a secured creditor would impose a serious fetter on the freedom of the secured creditor to exercise his power of sale over the charged property at the time and in the manner he chooses ... The fact that the secured creditor happens to be in liquidation cannot alter the position. The same must apply to rival claims to such property. Nor could [counsel] point to any authority directly in point in support of the alleged duty to obtain the sanction of the court.'[3]

[1]   Per Peter Gibson LJ in *Mahomed v Morris* [2000] 2 BCLC 536 at para 31.
[2]   [2000] 2 BCLC 536.
[3]   [2000] 2 BCLC 536 at paras 33, 35.

6.311 Another example of a successful application is that in *Hamilton v Official Receiver*[1]. In this case a contributory offered the liquidator £1,000 for the assignment of a speculative claim in negligence against solicitors which had been valued 'more in hope than through scientific analysis' at £500,000. His first offer was on the basis that the liquidator would receive 50% of the proceeds but with an indemnity against an adverse costs order of £3,000. This was rejected by the liquidator on the basis that he required a complete indemnity as to costs and 100% of the proceeds; 'a counter-offer which, on its face, could not have been accepted by any reasonable person'[2]. However, the learned judge suggested that it would have been legitimate for the contributory's offer to be turned down because of the limited nature of the indemnity. The contributory then offered to purchase the claim outright for £1,000. The liquidator refused this offer, concerned that to sell for £1,000 an asset which might eventually prove to be worth £500,000 would expose him to proceedings for creditors. It was however quite plain that the liquidator had no interest whatsoever in pursuing the negligence claim for reasons not only of substance but of limitation. The court took the view that:

> 'the refusal to accept a reasonable and indeed the only offer on the table for an asset which the [liquidator] has no interest now in realising is, within the meaning of the words as used in the *Re Hans Place* decision, perverse and in my view it is right that I should make an order under the provisions of s 168(5) requiring him to assign the cause of action for £1,000'[3].

It appears that the decision in *Re Peters, ex p Lloyd* was not cited to the court.

[1]   [1998] BPIR 602.
[2]   Per Laddie J at 604C.
[3]   Per Laddie J at 605H.

6.312 The approach therefore in applications against the commercial decisions of office-holders in liquidation or bankruptcy is one of non-interference except in cases of fraud, mala fides, or perversity, although it may be that the courts will construe perversity in a purposive manner giving due consideration to the commercial realities of the situation that the officer-holder finds himself in at the material time. In decisions relating to the formal conduct of the relevant insolvency procedure the court will interfere readily if necessary to ensure that the insolvency process duly complies with general principle. While a similar approach is to be anticipated in voluntary arrangement cases, it is to be hoped that the court will view the actions of the supervisor in commercial context and will not apply a perversity test with the utmost rigour.

6.313 Finally it should be noted that there is no room for private rights of action against the supervisor, whether for breach of statutory duty or duty of care or otherwise, in carrying out his tasks under an approved voluntary arrangement. Any complaint about his acts, omissions or decisions, must be brought under the 'self-contained statutory scheme' which precludes the existence of private rights of action against a supervisor[1].

[1]   *King v Anthony* [1998] 2 BCLC 517.

The unco-operative debtor

6.314 Should the supervisor or creditors find that the debtor is not giving the co-operation that is required to ensure the proper functioning of the arrangement the supervisor can bring that failure on the part of the debtor to the attention of the court by seeking directions[1]. Failure to comply with the court's directions will constitute contempt and can be punished by imprisonment or a fine. If the supervisor fails to act to seek appropriate directions one or more creditors may apply to the court as persons dissatisfied[2] with the supervisor's omission to seek directions from the court to remedy the debtor's default. Apart from seeking directions from the court the sanction available to the creditors against the unco-operative debtor is bankruptcy. A bankruptcy order may be made against the debtor, despite the existence of an individual voluntary arrangement, on a petition by the supervisor or any creditor bound by the arrangements where the court is satisfied that the debtor has failed to do all such things for the purposes of the arrangement as have been reasonably required of him by the supervisor[3]. Apart from this draconian step the supervisor and creditors may ensure the compliance of the debtor with the arrangement by enforcing its terms as may be appropriate, seeking directions or other appropriate order from the court[4]. The terms of the voluntary arrangement will constitute a contract between the debtor and the creditors, and also the supervisor if the arrangements are so framed. The contract may be enforced by proceedings, subject to its terms, but the more convenient way to control the debtor will usually be by application to the insolvency court for directions.

[1]   Under IA 1986, s 263(4).
[2]   See paras **6.295–6.301**.
[3]   IA 1986, s 276(1)(c).
[4]   And see paras **6.295–6.301** above; the supervisor may apply for appropriate directions under IA 1986, s 263(4).

Access to essential supplies

6.315   A supervisor of a voluntary arrangement is given power under the IA 1986 to require the continuation of supplies by public utilities notwithstanding unpaid accounts due to the utility concerned by the debtor[1]. This power applies from the 'relevant day' which is the day on which the arrangement is approved by the creditors[2]. The utilities subject to these provisions are (a) those providing a supply of gas[3], (b) a public supply of electricity[4], (c) water supplied by a water undertaker[5], and (d) a supply of telecommunication services by a public telecommunications operator[6].

[1]   See IA 1986, s 372(2)(b).
[2]   IA 1986, s 372(1)(b).
[3]   By a gas supplier within the meaning of Part I of the Gas Act 1986, IA 1986, s 372(4).
[4]   Within the meaning of Part I of the Electricity Act 1989.
[5]   IA 1986, s 372(4)(c) as amended by the Water Act 1989, Sch 25, para 78.
[6]   IA 1986, s 372(4)(d); 'telecommunication services' and 'public telecommunications operator' mean the same as in the Telecommunications Act 1984, except that the former does not include local delivery services within the meaning of Part II of the Broadcasting Act 1990, IA 1986, s 374(5).

6.316   A request for a supply of any of these services may be made by or with the concurrence of the supervisor for the purposes of any business which is or has been carried on by the individual debtor, by a firm or partnership of which the individual is or was a member, or by an agent or manager for the individual or for such firm or partnership[1].

1   IA 1986, s 372(3).

Supervisor's accounts and reports

6.317 Where the arrangement authorises or requires the supervisor (1) to carry on the debtor's business or to trade on his behalf or in his name, (2) to realise the assets of the debtor[1], or (3) otherwise to administer or dispose of any funds of the debtor or the estate, the supervisor must keep accounts and records of his acts and dealings in and in connection with the arrangement, including in particular records of all receipts and payment of money[2]. At least once every 12 months beginning with the date of his appointment the supervisor must prepare an abstract of these receipts and payments and send copies, accompanied by his comments on the progress and efficacy of the arrangement to the court, the debtor, and all creditors bound by the arrangement[3]. The abstract must be sent out within two months of the end of the period to which it relates[4]. In the rare cases where the arrangement does not authorise the supervisor to trade, realise assets or administer or dispose of funds, the supervisor must send out a report on the progress and efficacy of the arrangement not less often than once in every 12 months[5]. On the application of the supervisor the court may vary the dates on which the obligation to send abstracts or reports arises[6].

1   Or the assets belonging to the estate where the individual debtor is an undischarged bankrupt, IR 1986, r 5.31(1)(b).
2   IR 1986, r 5.31(1).
3   IR 1986, r 5.31(2). If during any period of 12 months no payments are made and there have been no receipts a statement must be sent to this effect, IR 1986, r 5.31(2).
4   IR 1986, r 5.31(3).
5   IR 1986, r 5.31(4), the report to be sent to the court, the debtor, and all creditors bound by the arrangement.
6   IR 1986, r 5.31(5).

6.318 At any time during the course of the arrangement or after its completion the Secretary of State may require the supervisor to produce for inspection (a) his records and accounts relating to the arrangement and (b) copies of his abstracts and reports[1]. Any accounts and records produced to the Secretary of State may be audited and the supervisor must give any further information and assistance as may be needed for the purposes of the audit[2].

1   IR 1986, r 5.32(1). Production may be required either at the supervisor's premises or elsewhere, IR 1986, r 5.32(2).
2   IR 1986, r 5.32(3).

6.319 The fees, costs, charges and expenses that may be incurred for any purposes of the arrangement are those which are sanctioned by its terms or which would or would correspond to those which would be payable in the debtor's bankruptcy[1]. Additionally any disbursements made by the nominee prior to the arrangement's approval, and any remuneration for his services agreed between the nominee and the debtor, the liquidator or administrator, the official receiver or the trustee are also chargeable to the arrangement[2].

1   IR 1986, r 5.33(b); as to fees, etc payable in bankruptcy see IR 1986, r 6.224.
2   IR 1986, r 5.33(1).

Supervisor's duties on completion or termination of arrangement

6.320 Within 28 days of the final completion or termination[1] of the arrangement the supervisor must send to all creditors bound by the arrangement and the members of the corporate debtor or the individual debtor (a) a notice that the arrangement has been fully implemented or terminated as the case may be, and (b) a report summarising all receipts and payments made in the administration of the arrangement explaining any difference in the actual implementation of it as compared with the voluntary arrangement as approved, or, in the case of termination, explaining the reasons why the arrangement was not duly completed[2]. Should the debtor or any creditor be dissatisfied with the supervisor's summary the fact of or his explanation of any difference in the actual implementation of the arrangement from that envisaged, an application may be made to the court for an appropriate order or directions[3]. Also within this 28-day period the supervisor must send copies of the notice and report to the Secretary of State and to the court, and until he does so he may not vacate his office[4].

1   Or 'come to an end prematurely' ie ceases to have effect before it has been fully implemented in respect of all persons bound to the arrangement, IA 1986, s 262C.
2   IR 1986, r 5.34(1)(2).
3   See IA 1986, s 263(3). See eg *Stanley v Phillips* [2003] EWHC 720 (Ch), [2003] All ER (D) 101 (Feb) where the supervisor successfully appealed the declaration by the deputy district judge that the debtors had complied with all their obligations and that their failure to realise the equity in their domestic property and disclose the fact that they owned property in Spain were not material omissions.
4   IR 1986, r 5.34(3).

6.321 The period of 28 days allowed for the notice and summary may be extended by the court on the supervisor's application[1].

1   IR 1986, r 5.34(4).

Removal of supervisor

6.322 In the absence of an express power in the terms of the arrangement there is no power in the debtor and creditors to remove a supervisor and replace him with another, although if the debtor and every creditor agreed to such a course it would be possible for the arrangement to be varied accordingly[1].

1   *Tanner v Everitt* [2004] EWHC 1130 (Ch), [2004] BPIR 1026 at [61], and see paras **6.279–6.279**; a change of identity of the supervisor is as much a variation as any other.

6.323 There is a general power in the court to make an order appointing as supervisor a person who is qualified to act as an insolvency practitioner or who is authorised to act as supervisor in relation to the arrangement whenever (a) it is expedient to make such an appointment, and (b) it is inexpedient, difficult or impracticable for an appointment to be made without the assistance of the court[1]. The appointment may be either to replace an existing supervisor or to fill a vacancy[2], and may be used so as to increase the number of supervisors implementing the arrangement[3]. The condition that a court appointment should be made only where it is inexpedient, difficult or impracticable for the appointment to be made without the court's assistance recognises that many arrangements will make provision for the creditors to replace the supervisor within the terms of the arrangement.

1   IA 1986, s 263(5).
2   IA 1986, s 263(5); the power is expressly without prejudice to the Trustee Act 1925, s 41(2) (power of court to appoint trustees of deeds of arrangement).
3   IA 1986, s 263(6); a sole appointee cannot be replaced by a joint appointment, *Re A & C Supplies Ltd* [1998] 1 BCLC 603, [1998] BPIR 303.

6.324 Any interested person may apply for an order, the application being made in the first instance to the registrar or district judge[1]. The former partners of an insolvency practitioner were entitled to apply to remove the insolvency practitioner from offices he held jointly with other former partners and where he was a sole appointee. Although the appointments were personal, the reality was that the work was carried out by various members of the firm's staff, and it was impracticable for the practitioner to fulfil the obligations of the offices following his departure from the firm[2]. Unless the court so directs it will not be necessary to serve notice of the application on all creditors of the arrangement, but the possibility of substituting a new insolvency practitioner[3] for the existing supervisor should first be put to the creditors before any application is made[4]. Where a supervisor wishes to resign he may presumably make the application himself, and in other cases the debtor, or a representative or dissatisfied creditor will make the application[5]. In situations where the supervisor wishes to retire from practice, or loses his qualification to act as an insolvency practitioner or authorisation to act as supervisor, it may be necessary for him, or the Secretary of State or relevant recognised professional body, to bring a block application to remove the insolvency practitioner from all his appointments and substitute him with one or more qualified insolvency practitioners. Such an application may be made to the High Court, to which all proceedings before county courts may be transferred pursuant to the IR 1986 and the County Courts Act 1984[6]. Where the matter is contested the High Court may order an insolvency practitioner who is substituted by a new supervisor to deliver up all documents and records relating to the arrangement[7]. It is helpful when a block application for substitution of an insolvency practitioner is made for the court to be provided with a table detailing the appointments in question and the powers available to the court in each of the various insolvency cases[8].

1   *Re John Abbot* [1998] BPIR 171, 176.
2   *Re A & C Supplies Ltd* [1998] 1 BCLC 603, [1998] BPIR 303.
3   Or other person authorised to act as supervisor in relation to the arrangement, see para **6.18**.
4   *Re Sankey Furniture Ltd* [1995] 2 BCLC 594: this decision can however give rise to a great deal of cost and might not necessarily be followed in every case depending upon the precise circumstances.

⁵   Strictly, by the time that an application is made to replace or add a further supervisor it is likely that there will be no 'pending proceedings before the court' for the purposes of IR 1986, r 7.1 and accordingly the application should be by originating application in Form 7.1, see **Appendix 3**. However, the court will usually entertain an application by 'ordinary application' under IR 1986, r 7.2, see Form 7.2, as there will by then have been relevant proceedings before the court.

⁶   IR 1986, r 7.11(4) and the County Courts Act 1984, s 41(1); and see *Re Bullard and Taplin Ltd* [1996] BPIR 526; *Re John Abbot* [1998] BPIR 171, but cf *Re Bridgend Goldsmiths Ltd* [1995] BCC 266: note in *Re A & C Supplies Ltd* [1998] BPIR 303 Blackburne J, at 308, stated that the provisions of the County Courts Act 1984, s 41 had not been drawn to his attention in *Re Bridgend Goldsmiths Ltd*.

⁷   *Re Stella Metals Ltd* [1997] BPIR 293, where the original insolvency practitioner was ordered to pay the costs.

⁸   *Re Supperstone v Auger* [1999] BPIR 152; a suggested form of table, and notes is at 155–156.

J FAILURE OF VOLUNTARY ARRANGEMENT

When arrangement has failed

6.325   Whether and if so when a voluntary arrangement has failed will be a matter of construction of the terms of the arrangement. Neither culpability on the part of the debtor nor the views of the creditors are matters relevant to the proper construction of the terms[1]. Unless the terms have been drawn unusually it will be open to any creditor to petition for insolvency or otherwise proceed to enforce his debt on the failure of the arrangement. 'Failure' of an arrangement will often be important in cases where the debtor, whether in trade or professional practice, has agreed to make periodic payments out of income to the supervisor for distribution among the creditors. Such arrangements are more common in company voluntary arrangements and are referred to as 'trading out' CVAs. Where a debtor in such an arrangement fails to make his promised payments there may be uncertainty and differing views among the arrangement creditors as to whether it will more advantageous to permit the arrangement to continue in the hope that payments will be made in the future or to bring the arrangement to an end and put the debtor into formal insolvency. The standard conditions of many arrangements provide that there is a failure of the arrangement on the happening of any one of a number of events; in particular where there is a breach of the debtor's obligations under the arrangement, or when it becomes possible for any person not bound by the arrangement to petition for the debtor's bankruptcy, or something happens which renders it impossible for the supervisor to continue implementing the arrangement. Where an event of failure occurs such standard conditions usually require the supervisor to report the fact to the creditors and distribute any funds in his possession under the terms of the arrangement, and further provide that individual creditors cease to be bound by the arrangement. Two connected questions arise for consideration. First whether the happening of an event of failure automatically brings the voluntary arrangement to an end irrespective of whether the supervisor is aware of the event and acts on it. Secondly whether a requirement that the supervisor petitions for insolvency on learning that the debtor has failed to comply with the obligations of the arrangement is permissive or mandatory.

[1]   *Re Keenan* [1998] BPIR 205.

6.326 In considering the standard conditions of the arrangement applying to the company in CVA in *Welsby v Brelec Installations Ltd*[1] the court construed the condition specifying the events of failure as a threshold requirement to be satisfied before the supervisor took steps to bring the arrangement to an end, and not as a provision which automatically terminated the arrangement. Accordingly it was only if the relevant event came to the notice of the supervisor and he then proceeded to take any unequivocal step to that end that the voluntary arrangement would terminate and the consequences of the arrangement failing would come into play. It was not to be supposed that the creditors in approving the voluntary arrangement had contemplated that any default, however trivial, might bring the arrangement to an end, and indeed do so without the supervisor or the creditors being aware of the fact. The decision in *Welsby v Brelec Installations Ltd* may be contrasted with that in *Re Maple Environmental Services Ltd*[2] where it had been suggested that where a company was involved in a 'trading out' arrangement any failure by the company to comply with its ongoing obligations would represent a failure of the voluntary arrangement. Much may depend in any particular case on the precise wording of the voluntary arrangement.

[1]   [2000] 2 BCLC 576.
[2]   [2000] BCC 93.

Presentation of petition by supervisor

6.327 While the question of automatic termination can present difficulties it might be thought that the terms of the voluntary arrangement would be conclusive one way or the other on the second question raised above, namely whether the supervisor is or is not obliged to present a petition for winding up or bankruptcy in the event of failure of the debtor to meet obligations under the arrangement. The terms of an arrangement may indeed be drawn to as to make the presentation of a petition obligatory for breach of certain terms, but discretionary in the case of breach of other terms. In *Re Maple Environmental Services Ltd* the point was stressed that in circumstances where the company was not meeting its ongoing trading obligations continued payments to the CVA creditors could only be made to the prejudice of the post-arrangement creditors, who may well be unaware that the company was in CVA. In these circumstances it was suggested that it could not be open to the supervisor to maintain that it is a matter for him to determine whether or not there has been a failure of the arrangement. In *Welsby* however the court considered that the fact that an arrangement had continued to function at the expense of the company's post-arrangement creditors did not of itself constitute some special circumstance which necessitated the termination of the arrangement and the revocation of the trusts under which the supervisor held the funds paid over by the company in favour of the CVA creditors. It was pointed out[1] that if the liquidator subsequently considered that the company was wrong to continue making payments to the CVA he could invoke the antecedent provisions of the IA 1986[2] to seek to recover money which should not have been paid away[3]. Accordingly, although in apparently obligatory terms the requirements of the arrangements' conditions that the supervisor take steps to terminate the arrangement were held to be permissive not mandatory.

¹   [2000] 2 BCLC 576 at 589c.

²   That is the provisions enabling a liquidator to seek an order restoring the position to what it would have been had the company not made a transaction at undervalue, IA 1986, s 238, or given a preference, IA 1986, s 239.

³   Or seek to render the directors personally accountable under IA 1986, s 214 for any wrongful trading which may have occurred. This plainly does not arise in personal insolvency. It is suggested that it is by no means clear that sums paid to the voluntary arrangement creditors would be recoverable by the trustee or liquidator as transactions at an undervalue or preferences, and while the decision is likely to be followed this aspect of the reasoning will in many cases be inapplicable.

6.328 It is suggested that such a view should be treated with caution. The supervisor is as bound by the terms of the voluntary arrangement as is the debtor and any creditor. If on a true construction of those terms a failure of obligation on the part of the debtor results in the failure of the voluntary arrangement and a requirement that a petition for formal insolvency be presented then that is what should happen. In *Re N T Gallagher & Son Ltd*[1] the CVA was subject to the following term:

'The joint supervisors shall petition for the winding up of the company immediately it fails in any of its obligations under the arrangement, the supervisors to retain sufficient funds at all times to do so.'

¹   [2002] 1 WLR 2380.

6.329 In due course the company fell into arrears with its contributions such that under the terms of the arrangement it was deemed to have failed. Notwithstanding, the supervisors, with the consent of the creditors' committee, allowed the CVA to continue on condition that the company complied with a revised contribution arrangement. The view was taken that the supervisors had a discretion whether to petition for the winding up of the company despite its failure to comply with its obligation to make contributions. The Court of Appeal[1] described the correctness of this view as 'dubious' but noted that it was not an issue in the appeal.

¹   [2002] 1 WLR 2380, para 20.

6.330 It may well be that if a supervisor allows a voluntary arrangement to continue and accepts further contributions from the debtor after the debtor is in breach of obligation despite a requirement to petition for insolvency, creditors whose debts post-date the voluntary arrangement are likely to be prejudiced in an eventual insolvency where the trusts on which the voluntary arrangement contributions are held survive the insolvency. It should be open to such creditors to apply to the court as persons dissatisfied with the acts of the supervisor[1] in the expectation that the court would order that all 'post failure' contributions should be held for the benefit of all the debtors' creditors and not just those creditors who are bound to the voluntary arrangement.

¹   See para **6.295** et seq.

6.331 If the terms of a voluntary arrangement provide that it should last for a fixed period of time subject to extension with the consent of the creditors in a creditors' meeting it is not open to the creditors to extend the voluntary arrangement after the expiry of its fixed period. The creditors cannot extend a voluntary arrangement which has ceased to exist[1].

¹   *Strongmaster Ltd v Stephen Kaye* [2002] EWHC 444 (Ch), [2002] BPIR 1259.

Bankruptcy order despite IVA

6.332 There are two circumstances in which the existence of an arrangement does not protect the debtor against the presentation of a bankruptcy petition or the making of a bankruptcy order[1]. First, a creditor whose debt arose after the arrangement will not be affected by it and may present a petition against the debtor in the normal way. Secondly, a petition may be presented by the supervisor or any creditor bound by the arrangement where the debtor is in default[2].

¹   Before the implementation of the amendments introduced by IA 2000 there was a third. A creditor whose debt ante-dated the arrangement was not bound by the arrangement if he was not given notice of the creditors' meeting. If he was unwilling or unable to join the arrangement he could present a petition against the debtor.
²   IA 1986, ss 264(1)(c), 276.

6.333 A petitioner who presents a petition in connection with an IVA must satisfy one of three grounds, namely that:

(a)   the debtor has failed to comply with his obligations under the arrangement;
(b)   information which was false or misleading in any material particular or which contained material omissions:
   (i)   was contained in any statement of affairs or other document supplied by the debtor to any person in connection with the arrangement, or
   (ii)   was otherwise made available by the debtor to his creditors at or in connection with a creditors' meeting; or
(c)   the debtor has failed to do all such things as may for the purposes of the voluntary arrangement have been reasonably required of him by the supervisor[1].

¹   IA 1986, s 276(1).

6.334 For the purposes of (a) (para **6.333** above), it is not necessary to show any degree of culpability on the part of the debtor with regard to the failure; failure is to be considered objectively[1]. The court is not bound to make a bankruptcy order however, and in cases where the failure is not serious and there is no culpability on the part of the debtor may refuse to do so[2]. Where there is a significant default by the debtor, and the underlying scheme of the voluntary arrangement is that if it is not properly carried out by the debtor bankruptcy will follow, then the court will only refuse a bankruptcy order in exceptional cases whatever the view of the creditors[3]. The requirement of IA 1986, s 276(1)(a) is that the court is satisfied that the debtor 'has failed' to comply with his obligation. There is no requirement that this failure persist at the date of the bankruptcy order[4], and accordingly a bankruptcy order may be made in respect of a past failure remedied before the date of the hearing of the petition[5].

1   *Re Keenan* [1998] BPIR 205; *Stanley v Phillips* [2003] EWHC 720 (Ch), [2004] BPIR 632.
2   See *Re Keenan* [1998] BPIR 205 and *Vadher v Weisgard* [1998] BPIR 295.
3   *Harris v Gross* [2001] BPIR 586; where at a meeting called by the supervisor to consider the position 69% in value of the creditors voted against bankruptcy.
4   This is in contrast with the provisions of IA 1986, s 271(1)(a) 'the court shall not make a bankruptcy order on a creditors' petition unless it is satisfied that one or more of the petition debts ... has neither been paid or compounded for'.
5   *Carter Knight v Peat* [2000] BPIR 968, the court rejecting the argument that the effect of IR 1986 rr 6.6 and 6.25 was that there must be an outstanding default under the IVA on the date of the hearing before a bankruptcy order could be made. The case was however remitted for rehearing because the judge below had not given sufficient reasons for making the order to demonstrate the basis on which he had proceeded.

6.335 For the purposes of (b) (para **6.333** above), an omission is 'material' if it would be likely to have made a material difference to the way in which the creditors would have considered and assessed the terms of the proposed arrangement[1]. The court should apply this as an objective test[2]. Whether the debtor acted deliberately or was otherwise culpable is immaterial. It should also be borne in mind that where new information of a significant nature comes to light a nominee who holds proxies should adjourn the creditors' meeting so that the new information may be reported to all creditors[3]. Failure to do so on the part of the nominee would constitute a material omission, or result in information before creditors becoming misleading or even false. It is a material omission not to inform all creditors that some creditors had been offered an inducement by a third party to vote for the debtor's arrangement[4]. A similar approach will be applied to a consideration as to whether information was materially false or materially misleading.

1   *Apton New Homes v Tack* [2000] BPIR 164, referred to in *Cadbury Schweppes plc v Somji* [2001] 1 WLR 615 at para 25; and see paras **6.222–6.226**.
2   *Cadbury Schweppes plc v Somji* [2001] 1 WLR 615 at para 25.
3   *Cadbury Schweppes plc v Somji* [2001] 1 WLR 615 at para 25.
4   *Cadbury Schweppes plc v Somji* [2001] 1 WLR 615.

6.336 There remains a discretion in the court as to whether it is appropriate to make a bankruptcy order. In exercising this discretion the court will have regard to the principle that a creditor is entitled to payment of his debt; if it is not paid in full by the hearing of the petition, the petition should not be adjourned except on the basis that there was a reasonable prospect of payment within a reasonable time[1]. Nevertheless the interests of the voluntary arrangement creditors as a whole are of the greatest significance. Even where the debtor has behaved badly if it is in the interests of the voluntary arrangement creditors to maintain the arrangement the court may refuse a bankruptcy order[2].

1   *Judd v Williams* [1998] BPIR 88. Lloyd J made the point that the granting of repeated adjournments of the petition thereby allowing the debtor to make payment by instalments imposed an ad hoc voluntary arrangement on the creditor without his consent and without the protection afforded by a true IVA. If a bankruptcy order was made on another creditor's petition the sums paid under the initial petition might have to be returned.
2   *Re Bourne, Kaye v Bourne* [2004] EWHC 3236 (Ch), [2005] BPIR 590.

6.337 It is open to a supervisor to petition for bankruptcy even after the expiry of the period for which the IVA was to run, or, indeed, after the expiry of the IVA[1]. If there is unjustified delay in the presentation of the petition that would be a factor which would be taken into account by the court when considering whether or not to make a bankruptcy order[2]. An appeal against an order of the registrar or district judge making or refusing a bankruptcy order is a true appeal and the judge will not interfere with the decision unless satisfied that there was a wrongful exercise of discretion[3]. Where a voluntary arrangement is so flawed that it is a nullity the insolvency practitioner acting as supervisor has no locus standi to present a bankruptcy petition[4].

[1]   *Re Arthur Rathbone Kitchens Ltd* [1998] BPIR 1; *Stanley v Phillips* [2004] BPIR 632 at [45].
[2]   *Harris v Gross* [2001] BPIR 586.
[3]   *Vadher v Weisgard* [1998] BPIR 295.
[4]   *Re Plummer* [2004] BPIR 767 at [28].

6.338 Where the debtor has been in breach of the terms of his voluntary arrangement he is likely to have to pay the costs of the proceedings on the petition even where the court does not make a bankruptcy order[1].

[1]   *Re Bourne, Kaye v Bourne* [2004] EWHC 3236 (Ch), [2005] BPIR 590.

Supervisor as trustee

6.339 Where a bankruptcy order is made at a time when there is a voluntary arrangement in force[1] there is a presumption that the court will appoint the supervisor as trustee in bankruptcy[2]. The court has a discretion as to the appointment, which has to be exercised judicially, and where there were no reasonable grounds for complaint against the supervisor he was appointed trustee[3].

[1]   Whether or not the order is made on a petition presented under IA 1986, s 264(1)(c).
[2]   On making the order the court 'if it thinks fit' may appoint the supervisor as trustee, IA 1986, s 297(5).
[3]   *Landsman v De Concilio* [2005] EWHC 267 (Ch), [2005] BPIR 829. Here the debtor objected to the appointment of the supervisor (who had been appointed as supervisor by the court as a replacement) but no creditor objected. In allowing the appeal against the district judge, the High Court judge noted that there was likely to be a considerable advantage in time and cost to having the insolvency practitioner already in the saddle to handle the bankruptcy.

The effect of a bankruptcy order on a voluntary arrangement

6.340 A voluntary arrangement does not protect the debtor from bankruptcy either at the petition of a creditor not bound to the arrangement[1], or at the petition of the supervisor or a creditor in respect of a breach by the debtor of obligations arising under the arrangement. If an order is made on the petition the vexed question arises as to the effect the order has on the existing voluntary arrangement. No assistance on this question may be found in the IA 1986 or the IR 1986. Although the IA 1986 envisages that a bankruptcy order may be made against a debtor who is subject to an arrangement it makes no provision with respect to the arrangement on the making of such an order[2]. It would not appear to be open to the supervisor to apply to the court for directions to determine the arrangement solely on the basis that a bankruptcy order has been made, as this is not a matter 'arising under the arrangement'[3]. It may be possible to seek directions however where the arrangement requires the debtor to make continuing payments to the creditors and he is prevented from doing so by his bankruptcy.

[1]   As all pre-voluntary arrangement creditors are now bound whether or not they receive notice of the creditors' meeting such a petition will now come only from a post-voluntary arrangement creditor.
[2]   The draftsman of the Act evidently proceeded upon the basis that the IVA would come to an end on the making of a bankruptcy order on a petition by a supervisor or creditor subject to an IVA for default, for provision is made that in this event any expenses properly incurred in the administration of the IVA should be a first charge on the bankrupt's estate, IA 1986, s 276(2) and see *Davis v Martin-Sklan* [1995] 2 BCLC 483, 486–7. It would presumably be open to the court on an application by the supervisor under IA 1986, s 263(4) to direct that the IVA should be wound up and the assets transferred to the trustee.
[3]   See IA 1986, s 263(4).

6.341 Where a voluntary arrangement comprises a composition, the amount for which the voluntary arrangement creditors will be able to prove will depend on the terms of the arrangement. It is standard practice for the terms to provide that the debtor is released from the creditors' debts only when he has completed his payments due under the arrangement. Creditors are well advised to ensure that a term of this nature is included in the arrangement, for otherwise they may find that they are only able to prove for such amounts as are due from the debtor under the voluntary arrangement at the commencement of the liquidation or bankruptcy, as opposed to their full pre-voluntary arrangement debt. In cases where the voluntary arrangement comprises a scheme of arrangement involving no more than a moratorium, the bankruptcy of the debtor is unlikely to be of any particular consequence. The moratorium will end and the creditors will participate in the payment of dividends in the bankruptcy. There may be more important considerations at stake where the arrangement comprises a scheme of arrangement involving the debtor creating a trust over assets[1], or assigning assets to the supervisor, for realisation and distribution to the creditors. The likelihood is that the voluntary arrangement creditors will require a substantial proportion of the debtors' assets to be transferred to the voluntary arrangement. On the debtor becoming bankrupt shortly afterwards the cupboard could be largely bare. If the trust over or assignment of assets to the supervisor is unimpeachable by the trustee the voluntary arrangement creditors are likely to have a distinct advantage over the non-voluntary arrangement creditors in terms of dividend. This may be a real matter of concern on the part of a creditor whose debt arose after the arrangement, and who was unaware of the arrangement or its terms[2]. The prospects of the trustee in bankruptcy being able to set aside the transfer of assets under the arrangement as a transaction at an undervalue, or a transaction in fraud of creditors[3], will be minimal. Neither will there normally be any realistic prospect of a successful challenge to the arrangement as a preference.

[1]   A supervisor who holds money or other assets for the purpose of implementing the IVA will do so as a trustee, *Re Leisure Study Group Ltd* [1994] 2 BCLC 65.

² Before the IA 2000 amendments a creditor whose debt was antecedent to the IVA but who was not given notice of the arrangement could find himself in a particularly unfortunate position. Making the debtor bankrupt would have no financial advantage. His best course was to apply to the supervisor to join the arrangement and if he was refused then apply to the court as a person dissatisfied with a decision of the supervisor for an appropriate direction or order to enable him to join the arrangement, subject always to the terms of the relevant arrangements.

³ See IA 1986, ss 339–342C.

6.342 The critical question thus arises whether the trusts on which the voluntary arrangement assets are held survive the bankruptcy. This issue has arisen not infrequently and, in differing circumstances, some 12 decisions[1] of the courts at first instance had been reported before the Court of Appeal considered the matter in *Re N T Gallagher & Son Ltd*[2]. These decisions showed a divergence of approach, and could be reconciled, if at all, only by drawing careful distinctions between the identity of the petitioner in both IVA and CVA cases and the forms of liquidation in CVA cases.

¹ *Re McKeen (a debtor)* [1995] BCC 412; *Re Bradley-Hole (a bankrupt)* [1995] 4 All ER 865, [1995] 1 WLR 1097; *Davis v Martin-Sklan* [1995] 2 BCLC 483; *Re Halson Packaging Ltd* [1997] BPIR 194; *Re Arthur Rathbone Kitchens Ltd* [1997] 2 BCLC 280; *Re Excalibur Airways Ltd* [1998] 1 BCLC 436; *Kings v Cleghorn* [1998] BPIR 463; *Re Maple Environmental Services Ltd* [2000] BCC 93; *Welsby v Brelec Installations Ltd* [2000] 2 BCLC 576; *Re Kudos Glass Ltd* [2001] 1 BCLC 390 and *Re N T Gallagher & Son Ltd* at first instance reported at [2002] 1 BCLC 224.

² [2002] 1 WLR 2380.

6.343 The Court of Appeal in *Re N T Gallagher & Son Ltd* considered all these cases and concluded that such distinctions were misplaced. The court noted that the starting point for the determination of the question whether the voluntary arrangement trusts survived the liquidation or bankruptcy had to be the terms of the arrangement itself. The court went on to state that, as a matter of policy, in the absence of any provision in the voluntary arrangement as to what should happen to trust assets on liquidation or bankruptcy the court should prefer a default rule which furthers rather than hinders what might be taken to be the statutory purpose of the IA 1986. Parliament plainly intended to encourage debtors and creditors to enter into voluntary arrangements so as to provide creditors with a means of recovering what they are owed without recourse to the more expensive means provided by formal insolvency, thereby giving some debtors the opportunity to trade[1]. The rescue aspects of these observations are only heightened by the amendments to the voluntary arrangement regime introduced by the IA 2000 and the EA 2002. As for the rights of the voluntary arrangement creditors to prove in the liquidation or bankruptcy if, on the facts of a particular case, the voluntary arrangement should fail, the Court of Appeal could see no substantial basis for the analysis of the court at first instance in *Re N T Gallagher & Son Ltd* that the voluntary arrangement creditors' rights were analogous to the rights of secured creditors who are only entitled to prove if they abandon their security. Accordingly, if the terms of the arrangement are appropriately drafted, the voluntary arrangement creditors both retain the benefit of the assets transferred to the arrangement and may also prove for any sums remaining due to them on the failure of the voluntary arrangement should, on the facts, the arrangement have failed. Careful drafting of voluntary arrangements will ensure that the voluntary arrangement creditors should have both the benefits of the assets transferred to the voluntary arrangement and the ability to prove for the full amount of their voluntary arrangement debts. The result is that a post-voluntary arrangement creditor may be hard hit on a bankruptcy. The Court of Appeal met this head on:

> 'Whilst we acknowledge the possibility that there will be post-CVA creditors who are unaware of the CVA and its terms, in practice there is likely to be a considerable overlap between the CVA creditors and the post-CVA creditors. Further, save for the Crown and local authorities in respect of fiscal liabilities (and they are likely to be CVA creditors), no one is forced to become a creditor of a company without making such inquiries as are thought appropriate to ascertain the financial position of the company. We do not therefore accept that to treat a trust created by a CVA as continuing notwithstanding the liquidation of the company is productive of such unfairness that the court should conclude that liquidation brings the trust to an end. Such a conclusion would run counter to the general law which leaves trusts of assets not held for a company unaffected by its liquidation.'[2]

[1] [2002] 1 WLR 2380 at para 50. This being a CVA case the court here refers to the position of companies and their creditors, but similar considerations must also apply to individual debtors even though they will not always be traders.
[2] [2002] 1 WLR 2380 at para 49.

6.344 It is understandable that the court should have resolved the questions thrown up by the formal insolvency of voluntary arrangement debtors in this way. There is however always the possibility that potential trading partners will in future be careful to avoid giving credit to any individual trader known to be in IVA, and this will impede, perhaps prevent, the opportunities for rescuing his business. But, as the court pointed out, in most cases there will be a considerable overlap between the pre- and post-voluntary arrangement creditors.

6.345 The Court of Appeal in *Re N T Gallagher & Son Ltd* provided a helpful summary of its conclusions as follows[1]:

(1)   Where an IVA provides for moneys or other assets to be paid to or transferred or held for the benefit of IVA creditors, this will create a trust of those moneys or assets for those creditors.
(2)   The effect of the bankruptcy of the debtor on a trust created by the IVA will depend on the relevant provisions of the IVA.
(3)   If the IVA provides what is to happen on bankruptcy (or the failure of the IVA), effect must be given thereto[2].
(4)   If the IVA does not so provide, the trust will continue notwithstanding the bankruptcy or failure and must take effect according to its terms.
(5)   The IVA creditors can prove in the bankruptcy for so much of their debt as remains after payment of what has been or will be recovered under the trust.

[1]   [2002] 1 WLR 2380 at para 54.
[2]   In *Re Zebra Industrial Projects Ltd* [2004] EWHC 549 (Ch), [2005] BPIR 1022, the voluntary arrangement contained conditions in common use including condition 23.6: 'Any funds or assets held by the supervisor are held on trust for the benefit of creditors

bound by the arrangement until the arrangement has been terminated in terms of condition 23.1'. The court, construing the terms as a whole, rejected the arrangement that on the termination of the arrangement within the provisions of condition 23.1 the voluntary arrangement trusts failed and any funds or assets held by the supervisor were thenceforth held for the benefit of the general creditors. It was evident from other provisions in the standard conditions that there was a general intention that the CVA assets should remain applicable for the benefit of the CVA creditors after the arrangement had failed.

Third party funds

6.346 In cases where a third party has provided funds to support the voluntary arrangement the destination of those funds on the failure of the voluntary arrangement and the making of an insolvency order will depend upon the terms on which the funds were provided. In *Cooper v Official Receiver*[1] the father of the debtor promised substantial payments to creditors under the proposed arrangement and paid a significant first instalment when the proposal was approved. The voluntary arrangement was successfully challenged by a creditor[2]. The father had made the payment in order to avoid his son's bankruptcy, but had not said so expressly nor was there any provision in the terms of the arrangement for any of the father's funds in the hands of the supervisor on the failure of the arrangement to be returned to the father. The court rejected the father's argument that there was a trust under *Quistclose* principles[3] and ordered that the funds be paid over to the official receiver as trustee in bankruptcy for the benefit of the bankruptcy creditors[4].

[1] [2003] BPIR 55.
[2] See *Cadbury Schweppes plc v Somji* [2001] 1 WLR 615.
[3] See *Barclays Bank Ltd v Quistclose Investments Ltd* [1970] AC 567.
[4] The court noted, at [2003] BPIR 55, p 59B, that the bankruptcy creditors 'are for all practical purposes the same as the IVA creditors' and so did not have to consider competing interests between the IVA and bankruptcy creditors. The better view is that the money was held for the IVA creditors.

K DEATH OF DEBTOR

Insolvency administration order

6.347 A debtor who is involved with voluntary arrangements will presumably be insolvent in the event of his death, that is his estate when realised will be insufficient to meet in full all debts and other liabilities to which it is subject[1]. Where an estate is found to be or is likely to be insolvent after an individual's death it has to be administered for the benefit of the deceased's creditors and not for those entitled under a will or on intestacy until all the debts are paid. Insolvent estates are regulated by the Administration of Insolvent Estates of Deceased Persons Order 1986 ('DPO 1986')[2] and in the case of any conflict between the provisions of the IA 1986 and those of the DPO 1986 the latter prevail[3].

[1] IA 1986, s 421(4).

[2] The DPO is SI 1986/1999 made by the Lord Chancellor, with the concurrence of the Secretary of State by virtue of the provisions of IA 1986, s 421. These provisions enable the statutory instrument to apply those provisions of the IA 1986 which are considered relevant to the administration of the insolvent estates with any modifications which are considered appropriate.

[3] DPO 1986, art 3(2).

6.348 An insolvency administration order under DPO 1986 may be made on the petition of any of the deceased debtor's creditors or by the supervisor or any person who is bound by an IVA[1]. Once an order is made the estate is administered and distributions made in the same way as any bankrupt's estate. The administration will be subject to the control of the bankruptcy court which will have the same powers and the same procedures as in bankruptcy[2]. The trustee of the estate will stand in the same position toward the supervisor of an IVA as would a trustee of a living bankrupt.

[1] IA 1986, s 264 modified by DPO 1986, art 3, Sch 1, Pt II, para 2.
[2] DPO 1986, art 3, Sch1, Pt II, para 30.

6.349 An insolvent estate does not have to be administered under an insolvency administration order. An executor or administrator may if he wishes administer the estate outside formal bankruptcy for so long as no insolvency administration order is made[1]. If he does, he must comply with the bankruptcy rules as to the administration of the estate, the rights of secured and unsecured creditors, proof of debts, priority of debts and payments and all other rules applicable to the particular administration[2]. It is open to the personal representative to present a petition for an insolvency administration order if he does not wish to administer or continue with the administration of the estate, and provided the estate is indeed insolvent the court must make an insolvency administration order on the personal representative's petition[3].

[1] DPO 1986, art 4(1).
[2] DPO 1986, art 4(1).
[3] IA 1986, s 273, substituted by DPO 1986, art 3, Sch 1, Pt II, para 7.

Death of debtor before IVA is approved

6.350 The DPO 1986 brings a proposal for an individual voluntary arrangement to an end if the arrangements have not been approved by the creditors before the death of the debtor. Thus where an interim order has been made but the debtor dies before he has submitted his proposal the nominee must give notice to the court of the death of the debtor[1], and on receiving this notice the court must discharge the interim order[2]. Where an interim order has been made and the court has been satisfied by the nominee's report that a creditors' meeting should be held to consider the debtor's proposal, but the debtor dies before the creditors' meeting can be held, the meeting is cancelled[3]. If at the date of his death the debtor was an undischarged bankrupt, the personal representative shall give notice of the death to the trustee of his estate and the official receiver[4].

[1] IA 1986, s 256(1A) added by the DPO 1986, art 3, Sch 1, Pt III, para 1.
[2] IA 1986, s 256(1B) added by the DPO 1986, art 3, Sch 1, Pt III, para 1.

3 IA 1986, s 257 added by the DPO 1986, art 3, Sch 1, Pt III, para 2.
4 IA 1986, s 257 added by the DPO 1986, art 3, Sch 1, Pt III, para 2.

Death after approval of voluntary arrangement

6.351 Where the creditors' meeting summoned to consider the proposals has approved them, and the chairman of the meeting has reported the result to the court, the voluntary arrangement takes effect. Subject to any provision in the arrangement to the effect that the death of the debtor brings the arrangement to an end, the IVA is then implemented by the supervisor notwithstanding the subsequent death of the debtor[1]. It would appear however that if the debtor dies after the approval by the creditors' meeting, but before the report to the court, then the voluntary arrangement cannot be enforced as a valid and binding arrangement. This is because IA 1986, ss 260–262 are disapplied on the death of the debtor[2]. The court may not act on the basis of the approval[3], and the approval cannot be challenged by any of the interested parties[4]. It is somewhat strange that the DPO 1986 should apparently permit an IVA to continue after approval by creditors but only if the chairman has reported the meeting's decision to the court. The report to the court would seem to be merely an administrative function so that, if appropriate, the court may discharge the interim order. It is not for the court to review or interfere with the creditors' decision. In the ordinary course the IVA takes effect as if made by the debtor at the meeting[5], not when the result of the meeting is reported to the court.

1 IA 1986, s 263 modified by the DPO 1986, art 3, Sch 1, Pt III, para 5.
2 DPO 1986, art 3, Sch 1, Pt III, para 4.
3 Under IA 1986, s 261 (disapplied, as above).
4 Under IA 1986, s 262 (disapplied, as above).
5 See IA 1986, s 260(2).

6.352 Provided therefore that the chairman has reported the approval of the IVA by the creditors' meeting to the court there is no statutory reason why the IVA should not continue. Whether it does or not will depend on the terms of the arrangement, and in particular any term which makes specific provision in the event of the debtor's death[1]. Where the IVA involves a scheme under which the debtor assigns specific property to the supervisor as trustee to realise and distribute among the creditors the death of the debtor will have little impact. The position is clearly otherwise where the debtor has committed himself to make periodic payments throughout the life of the IVA. These payments will be debts enforceable against the estate but in the normal case it is unlikely that the estate will be able to meet these obligations. Many debtors will have life assurance policies with significant sums payable on death. Nominees preparing proposals, and creditors considering the implications of any proposal, would be well advised to ensure that the proposal has an after-acquired assets clause which expressly includes (or excludes) the proceeds of any life or term assurance policies under which benefits accrue during the currency of the IVA. A further point for nominees and creditors to consider is whether insurance might be obtained to cover the continuing payments covenanted by a debtor under an IVA in the event of death or incapacity.

¹   See generally the cases on failure of a voluntary arrangement after bankruptcy order, see paras **6.340–6.345**, and in particular *Re N T Gallagher & Son Ltd* [2002] 2 BCLC 133.

6.353 On the death of the debtor after the arrangement has been approved, the personal representative succeeds to the deceased debtor's rights to challenge any act or decision of the supervisor in the course of his implementation of the IVA¹. The supervisor must give notice to the court that the debtor has died².

¹   IA 1986, s 263 modified by the DPO 1986, art 3, Sch 1, Pt III, para 5(a).
²   IA 1986, s 263 modified by the DPO 1986, art 3, Sch 1, Pt III, para 5(b).

L FAST-TRACK VOLUNTARY ARRANGEMENTS

A procedure for bankrupts

6.354 Introduced by the Enterprise Act 2002¹ as from 1 April 2004 the fast-track voluntary arrangement ('FTVA') is a procedure whereby a debtor who has been made bankrupt may enter into a voluntary arrangement and have his bankruptcy annulled. It is a procedure available only to bankrupts. In an FTVA the official receiver acts as nominee, assists the debtor prepare a proposal to the creditors, and acts as supervisor if the proposal is accepted. It is a procedure suitable only for straightforward cases, and the official receiver will only be prepared to act as nominee and supervisor where there is to be a relatively simple disposal of assets or collection of regular payments in order to fund the voluntary arrangement. There have been very few FTVAs since their introduction. This may well be because at the same time as they were introduced the government also reduced the period before automatic discharge to bankruptcy from three years to twelve months. This removed what was probably going to be the main incentive for many debtors to enter into an FTVA, now that the stigma attached to bankruptcy has been much reduced.

¹   EA 2002, s 264(1), Sch 22, para 2.

6.355 The FTVA is available where:

(a)   the debtor is an undischarged bankrupt;
(b)   the official receiver is specified in the proposal as the nominee in relation to the voluntary arrangement; and
(c)   there is no application for an interim order¹.

¹   IA 1986, s 263A.

6.356 FTVAs have their own section in the Insolvency Rules 1986, at Part 5, Chapter 7¹. It is a proposal made only to the bankruptcy creditors², the aim being to turn an uncomplicated bankruptcy into a voluntary arrangement with the minimum of administration. The proposal is put to the creditors on a take it or leave it basis, no modifications being permitted³.

¹   IR 1986, r 5.35, with 'voluntary arrangement' and 'proposal' interpreted by reference solely to this chapter of the rules, IR 1986, r 5.36.

²   IA 1986, s 263B(2), creditor being defined in s 263B(3) as a creditor of the debtor in respect of a bankruptcy debt where the official receiver is aware both of the claim and of the creditor's address.
³   IA 1986, s 263B(4)(c).

The fast-track proposal

6.357 The debtor is required to submit his proposal, a 'document setting out the terms of the voluntary arrangement which the debtor is proposing' together with a statement of his affairs to the official receiver[1]. The debtor's proposal must:

(a)   be accompanied by the fee payable to the official receiver for acting as nominee[2]; and

(b)   contain:
    (i)   a statement that the debtor is eligible to propose a voluntary arrangement;
    (ii)   a short explanation why, in his opinion, a voluntary arrangement is desirable, and give reasons why his creditors may be expected to concur with such an arrangement; and
    (iii)   a statement that the debtor is aware that he commits an offence[3] if, for the purpose of obtaining the approval of his creditors to his proposal, he makes any false representation, or fraudulently does, or omits to do, anything.

¹   IA 1986, s 263B(1).
²   This is a fixed fee of £300.
³   Under IA 1986, s 262A.

6.358 The proposal must cover a long list of matters set out at IR 1986, r 5.37(2) which are essentially the same matters as must be in a proposal for an IVA where the debtor is not a bankrupt[1].

¹   See IR 1986, rr 5.3(2), 5.30. The debtor must include a correspondence address for the official receiver, which the official receiver will supply on request, IR 1986, r 5.37(3).

6.359 The expectation is that, in practice, FTVAs will be led by the official receiver's department. A bankrupt in what appears to be a straightforward case will be given information about an FTVA by the official receiver involved in his case, usually as part of the bankruptcy interview. If the debtor expresses an interest and the basis of a workable voluntary arrangement can be agreed, the debtor will be sent forms which, when completed, will constitute the proposal.

Official receiver's involvement

6.360 It is essential that the official receiver agrees to act as nominee for otherwise there cannot be an FTVA. The official receiver is not obliged to agree but may do so if he considers that the proposed voluntary arrangement has a reasonable prospect of being approved and implemented[1]. He will not agree to act if the bankrupt's affairs are complicated[2].

¹   IA 1986, s 263B(2).
²   The Insolvency Service Guidance Note URN04–1700.

6.361 Where the official receiver receives the debtor's proposal for a voluntary arrangement he must, within 28 days of its receipt, serve a notice on the debtor stating that:

(a)   he agrees to act as nominee in relation to the proposal;
(b)   he declines to act as nominee in relation to the proposal and specifying reasons for his decision; or
(c)   on the basis of the information supplied to him he is unable to reach a decision as to whether to act and specifying what further information he requires[1].

¹   IR 1986, r 5.38(1).

6.362 It is for the debtor to decide whether he provides the further information requested and so enable the proposal to proceed. If the debtor does provide the information the official receiver then has a further 28 days to serve a notice stating whether he does or does not agree to act as nominee[1].

¹   IR 1986, r 5.38(2).

Notification to creditors

6.363 Only creditors with bankruptcy debts of whose claim and address the official receiver is aware will be notified of and invited to vote on the proposal[1]. The debtor who does not notify the official receiver of the claims and addresses of all his creditors faces the possibility of a challenge from any bankruptcy creditor who is not notified of the proposal if made within 28 days of the creditor learning of the approved arrangement[2]. As soon as reasonably practicable after the official receiver agrees to act as nominee, he must send to the creditors and any trustee who is not the official receiver:

(a)   a copy of the proposal;
(b)   a notice inviting creditors to vote to approve or reject the debtor's proposal; and
(c)   a voting form.

¹   IA 1986, s 263B(2)(3), see para **6.356**.
²   IR 1986, r 5.39(1)(b)(ii)(bb).

6.364 The notice must explain that:

(i)   no modifications to the proposal may be put forward;
(ii)   if a majority in excess of three-quarters in value of creditors who vote approve the proposal, the official receiver will report to the court that the proposal has been approved (at which time the voluntary arrangement will then come into effect); and
(iii)   that if the proposal is approved it may be challenged on the ground of unfair prejudice or material irregularity[1].

¹   IR 1986, r 5.39(1).

6.365 The notice must include a date specified by the official receiver as the final date on which he will accept votes from creditors, being a date not less than 14 days and not more than 28 days from the date of the notice[1].

1   IR 1986, r 5.39(2).

Voting on the proposal

6.366 A creditor's entitlement to vote is determined by the official receiver on the basis of the information given to him by the bankrupt, and by sending a notice[1] to a creditor the official receiver is treating him as being entitled to vote on the proposal[2]. A creditor's entitlement to vote is calculated by reference to the amount of the creditor's debt at the date of the bankruptcy order[3]. A creditor may vote in respect of a debt for an unliquidated amount or any debt whose value is not ascertained, and for the purposes only of voting his debt is to be valued at £1 unless the official receiver agrees to put a higher value on it[4].

1   See para **6.363**, at (b).
2   IR 1986, r 5.41(1).
3   IR 1986, r 5.41(2).
4   IR 1986, r 5.41(3).

6.367 The official receiver has the power to admit or reject the whole or part of a creditor's claim for the purpose of voting[1], subject to appeal to the court by any creditor or the debtor[2]. On an appeal the official receiver's decision may be reversed or varied, or votes may be declared invalid, but only if the court considers that the circumstances giving rise to the appeal are such as give rise to unfair prejudice or material irregularity. The court may order another vote to be held, or make such order as it thinks just[3]. An application to the court by way of appeal against the official receiver's decision may not be made after the end of the period of 28 days beginning with the day on which the official receiver makes his report to the court[4].

1   IR 1986, r 5.42(1).
2   IR 1986, r 5.42(2).
3   IR 1986, r 5.42(3).
4   IR 1986, r 5.42(4); the official receiver is not personally liable for any costs incurred by any person in respect of an appeal against his decision on voting entitlement, IR 1986, r 5.42(5).

6.368 All creditors who wish to vote must do so on the form provided sent to the official receiver at the address specified in the notice[1]. Votes may be signed by a representative of a creditor[2], provided they are accompanied by written authority for that representation signed and dated by the creditor[3].

1   IR 1986, r 5.40(1); the voting form is Form 5.6.
2   IR 1986, r 5.40(2).
3   IR 1986, r 5.40(3).

Approval of arrangement

6.369 A proposal is approved by the creditors if a majority in excess of three-quarters in value of the voting creditors vote for the proposal[1]. A creditor's vote in respect of any claim or part of a claim is to be left out of account:

(a)   where the claim or part is secured;
(b)   where the claim is in respect of a debt wholly or partly on, or secured by, a current bill of exchange or promissory note, unless the creditor is willing:

  (i)   to treat the liability to him on the bill or note of every person who is liable on it antecedently to the debtor, and against whom a bankruptcy order has not been made (or in the case of a company, which has not gone into liquidation), as a security in his hands; and
  (ii) to estimate the value of the security and (for the purpose of entitlement to vote, but not of any distribution under the arrangement) to deduct it from his claim[2].

[1]   IR 1986, r 5.43(1).
[2]   IR 1986, r 5.43(2).

Notification to the court

6.370 The official receiver is required to report to the court as soon as practicable after the vote to inform the court whether the proposal has been approved or rejected[1]. In his report the official receiver must include a statement whether, in his opinion, the EC Regulation applies to the voluntary arrangement; and, if so, whether the proceedings are main proceedings or territorial proceedings[2].

[1]   IA 1986, s 263C.
[2]   IR 1986, r 5.44.

6.371 On the official receiver's report to the court that the proposal has been approved, the voluntary arrangement takes effect and binds the debtor and every person who was entitled to participate in the arrangements, namely all bankruptcy creditors of whose claims and addresses the official receiver was aware[1]. An FTVA does not therefore bind 'omitted creditors'[2] nor does it bind any creditor whose debt arose after the making of the bankruptcy order against the debtor.

[1]   IA 1986, ss 263D(1)(2), and 263B(2).
[2]   See para **6.135**.

6.372 On learning that the proposal has been approved the court may give directions on the conduct of the bankruptcy and the administrations of the bankrupt's estate as it considers appropriate for facilitating the implementation of the approved voluntary arrangement[1].

> 1   IA 1986, s 263D(5); the Deeds of Arrangement Act 1914 does not apply to an FTVA, IA 1986, s 263D(6).

Application to annul bankruptcy order

6.373 Once the voluntary arrangement has been approved the court is required to annul the bankruptcy order on an application by the official receiver[1]. Such an application may not be made until the 28-day period allowed to challenge the approved arrangement has elapsed, or while a challenge is pending or while the time allowed to bring an appeal is running or an appeal is pending[2].

> 1   IA 1986, s 263D(3).
> 2   IA 1986, s 263D(4); see para **6.232** for the time allowed for an appeal.

6.374 An application to the court to annul a bankruptcy order after the approval of an FTVA under IA 1986, s 263D(3) must specify that it is made under IA 1986, s 263D(3)[1]. It is to be made within 21 days of the expiry of the relevant period[2], and must be supported by a report stating the grounds on which it is made and a statement by the official receiver that he is not aware that any application or appeal against the approval of the FTVA remains outstanding[3]. The report must be accompanied by a copy of the proposal for the voluntary arrangement and a copy of the report to the court notifying it of the result of the vote[4]. The application, together with the report and the documents in support, is filed in court and the court gives the official receiver notice of the venue fixed for the hearing[5]. The official receiver must then give not less than seven days' notice to the bankrupt of the venue, at the same time sending him copies of the application and the report[6].

> 1   IR 1986, rr 5.57, 5.58(1).
> 2   IR 1986, r 5.58(2).
> 3   IR 1986, r 5.58(3).
> 4   IR 1986, r 5.58(4).
> 5   IR 1986, r 5.58(5).
> 6   IR 1986, r 5.58(6).

6.375 On annulling the bankruptcy order, the court sends sealed copies of the order of annulment[1] to the official receiver and the bankrupt[2].

> 1   In Form 5.8.
> 2   IR 1986, r 5.58(7).

6.376 The official receiver must notify all creditors of the debtor to whom he gave notice of his bankruptcy that the bankruptcy order has been annulled[1].

> 1   IR 1986, r 5.59(1); expenses incurred by the official receiver in giving notice to the creditors are a charge in his favour on the property of the former bankrupt, whether or not actually in his hands, IR 1986, r 5.59(2). Where any property is in the hands of a trustee or any person other than the former bankrupt himself, the official receiver's charge is valid subject only to any costs that may be incurred by the trustee or that other person in effecting realisation of the property for the purpose of satisfying the charge, IR 1986, r 5.59(3).

Implementation of arrangement

6.377 The provisions of IA 1986, s 263 apply to an FTVA[1]. The official receiver will be appointed to act as supervisor of the FTVA and he must, as soon as reasonably practicable, give written notice of his appointment to the Secretary of State, all creditors of whom he is aware, and any trustee in bankruptcy[2]. For acting as supervisor the official receiver will charge 15% of the amount raised from the sales of assets or collected from the debtor by way of payments to support an FTVA[3]. As the FTVA is subject to the provisions of IA 1986, s 263 it will be possible for a replacement supervisor to be appointed, although as FTVAs will only be proposed where the debtor's affairs are not complex it is most unlikely that a replacement supervisor will be required. Should the official receiver vacate office as supervisor he must give written notice of that fact to the Secretary of State[4]. The supervisor is given express power to employ agents in connection with the realisation of any assets which are subject to the FTVA provided that the use of agents is not inconsistent with the terms of the FTVA[5].

[1] IA 1986, s 263E.
[2] IR 1986, r 5.45(1).
[3] The Insolvency Service Guidance Note URN04–1700.
[4] IR 1986, r 5.45(2).
[5] IR 1986, r 5.49, any costs incurred in connection with the employment of agents will be costs for which the official receiver as supervisor has a charge over the assets realised in the voluntary arrangement, IR 1986, r 5.48.

6.378 The supervisor must keep accounts and records of his various acts and dealings in and in connection with the arrangement, including in particular records of all receipts and payments of money[1]. Not less often than once in every 12 months beginning with the date of his appointment the supervisor must prepare a report on the progress of the voluntary arrangement, including a summary of receipts and payments, and send copies of it to the debtor and all of the debtor's creditors of whom he is aware[2]. These reports must begin with the date of the supervisor's appointment, must be sequential, and must be sent within the two months following the end of the period to which they relate[3].

[1] IR 1986, r 5.47(1).
[2] IR 1986, r 5.47(2). If in any 12-month period the supervisor has made no payments and has had no receipts, he must send a statement to that effect.
[3] IR 1986, r 5.47(3).

6.379 The fees, costs and expenses in respect of the performance by the official receiver of his functions in relation to the bankruptcy and those of any trustee in bankruptcy who is not the official receiver are a first charge on any sums realised under the terms of the voluntary arrangement, and those of the official receiver in relation to the voluntary arrangement, are a second charge[1].

[1] IR 1986, r 5.48.

6.380 Within 28 days after the final completion or termination of the voluntary arrangement, or such longer period as the court may allow[1], the supervisor must send a notice to that effect to the debtor, all creditors of the debtor who are bound by the arrangement, and the Secretary of State[2]. With each notice must be sent a copy of a report by the supervisor summarising all receipts and payments made by him in pursuance of the voluntary arrangement, and explaining any difference in the actual implementation of it compared with the proposal as approved by the creditors[3]. The supervisor may not vacate office until after he has sent the various notices as required[4].

[1]   IR 1986, r 5.50(4).
[2]   IR 1986, r 5.50(1).
[3]   IR 1986, r 5.50(2)(3).
[4]   IR 1986, r 5.50(3).

Revocation of arrangement

6.381 The court may make an order revoking an FTVA on either or both of the grounds of unfair prejudice and material irregularity in relation to the arrangements[1]. Such an order may be made only on the application of the debtor, a creditor entitled to participate in the arrangements, the trustee of the bankrupt's estate or the official receiver[2], and may not be made after the end of the period of 28 days beginning with the date on which the official receiver makes his report to the court[3].

[1]   IA 1986, s 263F(1), and see paras **6.195–6.229**.
[2]   IA 1986, s 263F(2).
[3]   IA 1986, s 263F(3), see paras **6.370–6.372**.

6.382 Where the court makes an order of revocation the person who applied for the order must serve it on the Secretary of State and any person who could have applied for it other than the creditors, or the other creditors, where appropriate[1]. It is the duty of the supervisor to serve copies of the order on the creditors and on all other persons who are affected by the order[2].

[1]   IR 1986, r 5.46(1)(2)(4).
[2]   IR 1986, r 5.46(3).

Chapter 7

DEEDS OF ARRANGEMENT

A   General
B   Registration of deeds of arrangement
C   Trustees under deeds of arrangement
D   Creditors under deeds of arrangement
E   Enforcement of deeds of arrangement

A GENERAL

Introduction

7.1 Independently of bankruptcy, an insolvent debtor may enter into a valid arrangement with the general body of his creditors, or with some of his creditors, by which he obtains either a release from the claims of the arranging creditors, or temporary protection from legal proceedings for the recovery of the debts due to them without paying his debts in full[1]. Such an arrangement will constitute a contract between the debtor and his creditors and will usually take the form either of a composition with creditors, or an assignment of the arranging debtor's property to a trustee for their benefit. There are, however, other forms of arrangement permitted by the Deeds of Arrangement Act 1914[2]. To be valid the deed must benefit creditors. Each deed must be considered as a whole, to determine whether it is what it appears to be, namely a deed for the benefit of creditors generally, rather than a deed for the debtor's benefit. If it is the latter, the deed may be declared void as being in fraud of the creditors or being a transaction defrauding creditors[3] in spite of being in form a deed for the creditors' benefit[4].

[1]   As to the effect of a covenant not to sue see *Bateson v Gosling* (1871) LR 7 CP 9.
[2]   See para **7.4** below.
[3]   Therefore impeachable under the IA 1986, ss 423–425 (see **Chapter 21**).
[4]   See *Maskelyne and Cooke v Smith* [1903] 1 KB 671 at 676, CA per Vaughan Williams LJ; *Alton v Harrison* (1869) 4 Ch App 622; *Evans v Jones* (1864) 3 H & C 423; *Spencer v Slater* (1878) 4 QBD 13; *Boldero v London and Westminster Loan and Discount Co* (1879) 5 Ex D 47.

7.2 Deeds of arrangement have been seldom used[1]. Under the Bankruptcy Act 1914 not only the execution of the deed of arrangement but also several of the preliminary procedural steps[2] prior to its execution constituted an act of bankruptcy on which any dissenting creditor could found a bankruptcy petition. Creditors who did not assent to the deed were not bound by it and remained free to pursue any remedies available to them. This effectively made such deeds unworkable. The provisions in the Insolvency Act 1986 ('IA 1986') relating to personal insolvency do not re-enact the concept of the act of bankruptcy and to this extent deeds of arrangement are now a more satisfactory method for a debtor to compromise with his creditors. An individual voluntary arrangement under the IA 1986, Pt VII[3] or one of the procedures introduced by the Tribunals, Courts and Enforcement Act 2007[4] is, however, likely to prove a far more satisfactory procedure for the debtor who wishes to compound with his creditors. A deed of arrangement has a number of advantages over the individual voluntary arrangement. It requires only a simple majority of the creditors in number and value to bring it into effect, it is not necessary to call a meeting of creditors and the administration costs are likely to be lower, and there is no need for a nominee. However, these advantages are likely to be outweighed by the fact that a dissenting creditor may pursue all his remedies against the debtor. A few deeds of arrangement are still being registered however[5]. While such deeds have provided a possible alternative to other insolvency procedures where the debtor's assets are small and there are only a few creditors who have no particular interest in taking proceedings to enforce their remedies, the procedures aimed at such debtors which are discussed in **Chapter 30** are likely, when brought into force, to form a better method of arranging the debtor's affairs.

1   See the report of the Review Committee into Insolvency Law and Practice (Cmnd 8558) which in fact recommended the repeal of the Deeds of Arrangement Act 1914.
2   Eg the issue and service of the notice summoning the required meeting of creditors, statements made in the notice, and statements made at the meeting by or on behalf of the debtor.
3   See **Chapter 6** above.
4   See **Chapter 30** below.
5   11 between 1994 and 2000 to be precise.

Application of the Deeds of Arrangement Act 1914

7.3 A deed of arrangement to which the Deeds of Arrangement Act 1914 applies includes any 'instrument', ie written agreement[1], of a designated class made by, for or in respect of the affairs of a debtor (a) for the benefit of his creditors generally[2], or (b) for the benefit of any three or more of his creditors[3], where the debtor is insolvent at the date of the execution of the instrument[4]. It follows that if at the date of execution the debtor was solvent, the deed must be for the benefit of creditors generally. This is a question of fact[5]. Such a deed is revocable right up to the time that the fact of execution is communicated to a creditor[6] including a creditor who is also trustee[7]. 'Creditors generally' includes all creditors who may assent to, or take the benefit of, a deed of arrangement[8].

1   The Deeds of Arrangement Act 1914 does not apply to oral agreements, and a receipt stating the terms of an oral agreement for a composition is not a deed of arrangement within the 1914 Act so as to require registration: *Hughes and Falconer v Newton* [1939] 3 All ER 869.
2   Deeds of Arrangement Act 1914, s 1(1)(a).

7.3 Deeds of arrangement

3   Deeds of Arrangement Act 1914, s 1(1)(b). For the purpose of determining the number of creditors for whose benefit a deed is made, any two or more joint creditors are to be treated as a single creditor: Deeds of Arrangement Act 1914, s 30(2).
4   Deeds of Arrangement Act 1914, s 1(1). The deed must be made 'otherwise than in pursuance of the law for the time being in force relating to bankruptcy'. The Deeds of Arrangement Act 1914 does not apply to a voluntary arrangement approved under the IA 1986, s 260(3).
5   *Re Hobbins, ex p Official Receiver* (1899) 6 Mans 212.
6   *Ellis & Co v Cross* [1915] 2 KB 654.
7   *Beebee & Co v Turner's Successors* (1931) 48 TLR 61.
8   Deeds of Arrangement Act 1914, s 30(1). See *Re Rileys Ltd, Harper v Rileys* [1903] 2 Ch 590; *Re Allix, ex p Trustee* [1914] 2 KB 77 (where a deed signed by 13 out of 20 creditors described as 'hereinafter called the creditors' was held to be a deed for the benefit of creditors generally); *Huddersfield Fine Worsteds Ltd v Todd* (1925) 134 LT 82.

7.4 The designated classes of deed, which do not have to be under seal, are:

(a)   an assignment of property[1];

(b)   a deed of or agreement for a composition[2];

(c)   in cases where creditors of the debtor obtain any control over his property or business, a deed of inspectorship[3] entered into for the purpose of carrying on or winding up a business[4];

(d)   a letter of licence authorising the debtor or any other person to manage, carry on, realise or dispose of a business with a view to the payment of debts[5]; and

(e)   any agreement or instrument entered into for the purpose of carrying on or winding up the debtor's business, or authorising the debtor or any other person to manage, carry on, realise or dispose of the debtor's business with a view to the payment of his debts[6].

1   Deeds of Arrangement Act 1914, s 1(2)(a). 'Property' has the same meaning as that in the IA 1986, s 436, Deeds of Arrangement Act 1914, s 30(1) (amended by the IA 1986, s 439(2), Sch 14. As to whether an instrument is an assignment of property see *Re Halstead, ex p Richardson* [1917] 1 KB 695, CA; *Re Lee, ex p Grunwaldt* [1920] 2 KB 200; *Landsberg v Mendel* [1924] WN 46 (where there was an arrangement by way of assignment of property and also a lump sum composition); *B Lipton Ltd v Bell* [1924] 1 KB 701, CA, where an authority to realise the debtor's property, coupled with a declaration of trust for the application of the proceeds, was held not to be an assignment of property.
2   Deeds of Arrangement Act 1914, s 1(2)(b). See *Re Lee, ex p Grunwaldt* [1920] 2 KB 200.
3   See *Marconi's Wireless Telegraph Co Ltd v Newman* [1930] 2 KB 292, where it was held that a deed of inspectorship did not constitute a partnership between the debtor and either his creditors or the inspector and the committee, and that the debtor did not become the agent of the inspector or of the committee to carry on the business, but it remained the business of the debtor.
4   Deeds of Arrangement Act 1914, s 1(2)(c).
5   Deeds of Arrangement Act 1914, s 1(2)(d).
6   Deeds of Arrangement Act 1914, s 1(2)(e).

7.5 A power of attorney given by the debtor authorising a third party to execute a deed of arrangement under the Deeds of Arrangement Act 1914 is not in itself a deed of arrangement[1]. An assignment of a stockbroker's assets on default to the official assignee of the London Stock Exchange is a registrable instrument[2]. A deed of arrangement by a limited joint stock company is not registrable under the 1914 Act[3].

1   Under the Deeds of Arrangement Act 1914, s 1(2)(e); *Re Wilson* [1916] 1 KB 382 at 398, CA.
2   *Re Halstead, ex p Richardson* [1916] 2 KB 902; affd [1917] 1 KB 695, CA.
3   *Re Rileys Ltd, Harper v Rileys* [1903] 2 Ch 590.

Deed of assignment

7.6 A deed of assignment will usually involve the debtor assigning all, or substantially all, of his property to a trustee upon trusts declared in the deed, by which the assigned property is to be held and applied for the benefit of the creditors. A deed of arrangement may be executed by the donee of a power of attorney given by the debtor for that purpose[1]. The deed may provide for the exercise by the creditors, or by a committee appointed by them, of some control over the trustee's administration of the trust estate, and for the release of the debtor from, or the suspension of, legal proceedings for the recovery of the debts due to the assenting creditors. A trustee of a deed of arrangement is a trust corporation[2] and may therefore give a valid receipt on the sale of land[3].

1   *Re Wilson* [1916] 1 KB 382, DC.
2   Law of Property (Amendment) Act 1926, s 3.
3   See the Law of Property Act 1925, s 27(2) and the Trustee Act 1925, s 14(2).

7.7 The assignment of the debtor's property to a trustee is the voluntary act of the arranging creditor[1], and the trusts to which the assignment is subject are those which the debtor himself creates on the vesting by him of the property comprised in the assignment in the trustee[2]. The effect of the deed is to release or suspend the operation of creditors' claims by virtue of the creditors' assent to it, and it binds only those creditors who, in writing or otherwise, expressly or impliedly assent to it[3]. Until a deed of assignment to a trustee has been executed by the creditors or has come to their knowledge, the trustee is only an agent for the debtor under a revocable authority to deal with the estate[4]. The fact that a deed of assignment has been executed in pursuance of previous resolutions or at the request of the creditors does not, in the absence of its execution being communicated to them, make the deed irrevocable[5]. The bankruptcy of the debtor before the deed has become operative by virtue of the creditors' assents so as to create a binding trust, revokes and invalidates the trusts of the deed[6].

1   *Wallwyn v Coutts* (1815) 3 Mer 707; *Gibbs v Glamis* (1841) 11 Sim 584.
2   *Johns v James* (1878) 8 Ch D 744, CA. Cf *Re LG Clarke, ex p Debtor v S Aston & Son Ltd* [1967] Ch 1121, [1966] 3 All ER 622, DC.
3   *Ilderton v Jewell* (1864) 16 CBNS 142; *Benham v Broadhurst* (1864) 3 H & C 472.
4   *Acton v Woodgate* (1833) 2 MY & K 492; *Harland v Binks* (1850) 15 QB 713; *Re Douglas, ex p Snowball* (1872) 7 Ch App 534; *Re Ashby, ex p Wreford* [1892] 1 QB 872.
5   *Ellis & Co v Cross* [1915] 2 KB 654.
6   See *Smith v Dresser* (1866) LR 1 Eq 651 at 655; *Johns v James* (1878) 8 Ch D 744, CA; *R v Humphris* [1904] 2 KB 89 at 97; See also *Siggers v Evans* (1855) 5 E & B 367, where the trustee was also a beneficiary under the deed, and it was held that assent on his part was not necessary to perfect his title.

7.8 In construing a deed of assignment, a special limited condition overrides any general implied condition in the deed[1]. Similarly, general words of assignment are controlled by a recital in the deed showing that the assignment was confined to the contents of the schedule[2].

1   See *Re Clement, ex p Goas* (1886) 3 Morr 153, CA.
2   See *Re Moon, ex p Dawes* (1886) 17 QBD 275, CA.

7.9 Arrangements by means of the assignment of a debtor's property to a trustee for the benefit of his creditors are usually effected in one of two ways, either (1) where the insolvent debtor, before communicating with his creditors, assigns his property to a trustee selected by himself on trust for their benefit, and then obtains the assent of all or some of his creditors to the arrangement[1]; or (2) where, before making any assignment, the debtor calls his creditors together to a meeting, or the creditors themselves meet, and the creditors agree to forbear from enforcing their claims, on condition that the debtor assigns his property to a trustee chosen at the meeting, and on trusts of which the creditors approve. Whichever of these methods is adopted, the assignment becomes operative to create a valid title in the trustee, and validly enforceable trusts for the benefit of the creditors, as soon as the deed has been executed and creditors have assented to it, but subject to the requirements as to registration[2].

1   See e g *Re Woodroff, ex p Woodroff* (1897) 4 Mans 46. As to revocation of assent before execution of the deed see *Re Jones Bros, ex p Associated Newspapers Ltd* [1912] 3 KB 234, and as to when assents can no longer be revoked see *Re LG Clarke, ex p Debtor v S Aston & Son Ltd* [1967] Ch 1121, DC.
2   See para **7.13** and section B below.

Compositions

7.10   A composition is an agreement between the compounding debtor and all or some of his creditors by which the compounding creditors agree with the debtor, and, expressly or impliedly, with each other, to accept from the debtor payment of less than the amounts due to them in full satisfaction of the whole of their claims[1]. A composition agreement may be made orally or in writing, or partly orally and partly in writing. The consideration supporting the agreement which enables the acceptance of part of a debt to operate as a discharge of the whole debt is the mutual agreement of the creditors to forgo part of their claims[2].

1   *Re Hatton* (1872) 7 Ch App 723 at 726; *Slater v Jones, Capes v Ball* (1873) LR 8 Exch 186 at 193, 194; *Re Griffith* (1886) 3 Morr 111 at 116.
2   *Norman v Thompson* (1850) 4 Exch 755 at 759: 'it is a good consideration for one to give up part of his claim that another should do the same'; *Carey v Barrett* (1879) 4 CPD 379. See also *Couldery v Bartrum* (1881) 19 Ch D 394 at 399, CA. If a deed is executed the question of consideration is immaterial.

7.11   The effect of any particular agreement for a composition depends on its terms. Sometimes the payment of instalments under a composition is secured by an assignment by the debtor of his property on trust, if the instalments are not paid, to realise the property and to apply it towards the satisfaction of the composition. The deed of composition normally contains a release by the creditors of the debts due to them, or an agreement by the creditors not to enforce their claims by legal proceedings, so long as the instalments are duly paid and the provisions of the agreement are observed by the debtor. There will further be a condition that, on payment of the entire composition, the debtor is released from the whole of the creditors' respective claims. There may also be a proviso that the composition is to be at an end and that the creditors are to regain their original rights if the composition or any instalment is not duly paid or if bankruptcy proceedings are taken against the debtor. In cases where bills of exchange or promissory notes for the amounts payable under the composition are given to the creditors, or a trustee on their behalf, the agreement to pay the composition should not be under seal because the obligation of the debtor and sureties on the negotiable instruments might merge in the agreement under seal[1].

[1]   *Owen v Homan* (1851) 3 Mac & G 378; affd (1853) 4 HL Cas 997.

7.12   Subject to express provision to the contrary, the effect of the composition is that the creditors accept it as compromising their debts, although failure by the debtor to comply with his obligations under the composition will usually entitle the creditors to sue him for the whole of the balance of their debts[1]. Time runs against a creditor in respect of his right to sue on the debt only from the date of the debtor's default[2]. It appears, however, that where the terms of the composition are that the creditors accept the debtor's promise in satisfaction, as opposed to compromise, of their debts, on the debtor's default the creditors may sue only for the balance of the amount of the composition[3].

[1]   *Re Hatton* (1872) 7 Ch App 723; cf *Couldery v Bartrum* (1881) 19 Ch D 394, CA.
[2]   *Re Stock, ex p Amos* (1896) 3 Mans 324; following *Irving v Veitch* (1837) 7 LJ Ex 25.
[3]   *Re Hatton* (1872) 7 Ch App 723 at 726. It is irrelevant whether or not the debtor has given a surety.

Requirement for registration

7.13   A deed of arrangement is void unless (1) it is registered within seven clear days[1] after the first execution thereof by the debtor or any creditor, or if it is executed in any place out of England[2], then within seven clear days after the time at which it would arrive in England in the ordinary course of post, if posted within one week after its execution; and (2) it bears such stamp as is provided by the Deeds of Arrangement Act 1914[3].

[1]   This time may be extended: see para **7.23** below. Where the time for registering a deed of arrangement expires on a Sunday, or other day on which the registration office is closed, the registration is valid if made on the next following day on which the office is open: Deeds of Arrangement Act 1914, s 8.
[2]   A deed executed in Scotland under Scots law by a debtor domiciled in England does not require registration in Scotland and is valid in England: *Re Pilkington's Will Trusts* [1937] Ch 574, [1937] 3 All ER 213.
[3]   Deeds of Arrangement Act 1914, s 2 (amended by the Finance Act 1949, s 52, Sch 11, Pt V).

7.14   The deed of arrangement must be registered with the registrar appointed for the purpose by the Department of Trade and Industry[1]. If a deed of arrangement is declared void for want of registration, the money in the hands of the trustee under the instrument passes to any trustee in bankruptcy and, if the instrument is declared void, the release it contains is also void[2].

1 Deeds of Arrangement Act 1914, s 2 and see the Administration of Justice Act 1925, s 22 which replaced the Registrar of Bills of Sale as the registering authority. The address for registration is: The Insolvency Service, Insolvency Practitioners Control Unit, 2nd Floor Ladywood House, 45/46 Stephenson Street, Birmingham B2 4UZ, telephone: 0121 698 4098.
2 *Re Lee, ex p Grunwaldt* [1920] 2 KB 200. As to the recovery of moneys expended by the trustee see *Re Zakon, ex p Trustee v Bushell* [1940] Ch 253, [1940] 1 All ER 263.

Requirement for creditors' assent

7.15 A deed of arrangement which either is expressed to be or is in fact for the benefit of a debtor's creditors generally is void unless assented to by a majority of creditors in number and value either before or within 28 days after its registration[1], or within such extended time as may be allowed by the court[2]. The assent of a creditor for these purposes is established by his executing the deed of arrangement or sending to the trustee his assent in writing attested by a witness, and in no other way[3]. In calculating the majority of creditors, a creditor holding security upon the property of the debtor is to be reckoned as a creditor only in respect of any balance due to him after deducting the value of such security, and creditors whose debts amount to sums not exceeding £10 are to be reckoned in the majority in value but not in the majority in number[4]. The list of creditors annexed to the affidavit of the debtor filed on registration of the deed of arrangement is prima facie evidence of the names of the creditors and the amounts of their claims[5].

1 Deeds of Arrangement Act 1914, s 3(1). For the prescribed form of assent see the Deeds of Arrangement Rules 1925, r 4(1), Appendix, Form 2.
2 Ie by the High Court or the court having bankruptcy jurisdiction in respect of the debtor at the date of the execution of the deed: Deeds of Arrangement Act 1914, s 3.
3 Deeds of Arrangement Act 1914, s 3(3).
4 Deeds of Arrangement Act 1914, s 3(5) and see *Re Wilson* [1916] 1 KB 382.
5 Deeds of Arrangement Act 1914, s 3(2).

7.16 The trustee must file at the time of the registration of a deed of arrangement, or in the case of a deed of arrangement assented to after 28 days of registration, within 28 days after registration or within such extended time as may be allowed, a statutory declaration by the trustee that the requisite majority of the creditors of the debtor have assented to the deed of arrangement. This declaration is, in favour of a purchaser for value, conclusive evidence, and, in other cases, prima facie evidence, of the fact declared[1].

1 Deeds of Arrangement Act 1914, s 3(4). The form of statutory declaration is prescribed, see the Deeds of Arrangement Rules 1925, Appendix, Form 3.

B REGISTRATION OF DEEDS OF ARRANGEMENT

Mode of registration

7.17 The registration of a deed of arrangement under the Deeds of Arrangement Act 1914 is effected by presenting and filing, within seven clear days of the deed's execution:

(1)   the original deed, and of every schedule or inventory annexed to it or referred to in it, with the applicable stamp duty[1], together with a sworn 'A' copy and two further copies, signed by the debtor and the trustee duly witnessed[2];

(2)   an affidavit of execution verifying the time of execution, and containing a description of the residence and occupation of the debtor, and of the place or places where his business is carried on[3];

(3)   the debtor's affidavit[4] stating the total estimated amount of property and liabilities included under the deed, the total amount of the composition, if any, payable thereunder, and the names and addresses of his creditors[5]; and

(4)   a certificate by the debtor's solicitor or the presenter that the copy of the deed is correct.

[1]   This is 50p.
[2]   The additional copies are required by the registrar for filing with the court and HMRC. If copies are not provided the registrar will make photocopies and a fee will be charged to the person who is seeking to register the deed.
[3]   In Form DA4.
[4]   In Form DA6. As to when the debtor's affidavit will be dispensed with see *Re X (an arranging Debtor)* (1910) 44 ILT 167.
[5]   Deeds of Arrangement Act 1914, s 5(1).

7.18 The Deeds of Arrangement Rules 1925 make provision for the indorsement of the deed and the form of affidavits[1]. These affidavits may not be sworn before the solicitor to the trustee of the deed, or the deed, although registered, will be void[2]. The deed will be void if the debtor's affidavit is sworn by a donee of his power of attorney instead of by the debtor personally[3]. The affidavit need not include the names and addresses of secured creditors[4] and, if, without fraud, the names and addresses of some of the creditors that should be included are omitted, the registration is not rendered void[5].

[1]   See the Deeds of Arrangement Rules 1925, rr 4–8.
[2]   *Re Bagley* [1911] 1 KB 317.
[3]   *Re Wilson* [1916] 1 KB 382.
[4]   *Chaplin v Daly* (1894) 71 LT 569.
[5]   *Maskelyne and Cooke v Smith* [1903] 1 KB 671.

7.19 There are fees payable on registration: a judicature fee of £1.50 on the original deed, an affidavit fee of £1.10 on both the execution affidavit and debtor's affidavit, and a scale fee based on the total value of the property recorded in the deed[1].

[1]   The following scale applies: Nil value = £11.00; Nil to £1,000 = £8.25; £1,000 to £2,500 = £14.00; £2,500 to £5,000 = £22.00; over £5,000 = £27.50. Cheques for fees are payable to 'The Insolvency Service'.

Procedure on registration

7.20 The registrar seals the original deed and stamps it with the date of registration before returning it to the presenter[1]. Copies are sent to the court and HMRC, and the registrar enters the following details on the register:

7.20 *Deeds of arrangement*

(1) the date of the deed;
(2) the name, address and description of the debtor, and the place or places where his business was carried on at the date of the execution of the deed, and the title of the firm or firms under which the debtor carried on business, and the name and address of the trustee, if any, under the deed;
(3) the date of registration;
(4) the amount of property and liabilities included under the deed, as estimated by the debtor[2].

[1] Deeds of Arrangement Rules 1925, r 8.
[2] Deeds of Arrangement Act 1914, s 6.

7.21 Where the place of business or residence of the debtor is situated outside the London insolvency district, the registrar must transmit a copy of the deed to the registrar of the debtor's local county court within three clear days after registration[1].

[1] Deeds of Arrangement Act 1914, s 10; Deeds of Arrangement Rules 1925, r 10.

7.22 Where unregistered land is affected by a deed of arrangement, the deed should be registered in the name of the debtor under the Land Charges Act 1972[1]. If the deed is not so registered it is void as against a purchaser of any land comprised in it or affected by it[2]. A deed of arrangement affecting registered land or a registered charge on land is an interest affecting an estate or, as the case may by, a charge[3]. No notice may be entered in the register in respect of it but it must, instead, be protected by a restriction[4]. If not protected by a restriction, a disposition for valuable consideration of the estate or charge will take priority over it[5].

[1] See the Land Charges Act 1972, s 7(1). Registration may be made on the application of the trustee of the deed or a creditor assenting to or taking the benefit of the deed: Land Charges Act 1972, s 7.
[2] Land Charges Act 1972, s 7(2).
[3] Land Registration Act 2002, s 87(1).
[4] Land Registration Act 2002, s 87(2).
[5] Land Registration Act 2002, ss 29(1) and 30(1).

Rectification of the register

7.23 Upon being satisfied that the omission to register a deed of arrangement within the time required[1] or that the omission or misstatement of the name, residence or description of any person was accidental, or due to inadvertence, or to some cause beyond the control of the debtor and without there being negligence on his part, the High Court may extend the time for registration on such terms and conditions as are just and expedient or order the omission or misstatement to be supplied or rectified by the insertion in the register of the true name, residence or description on the application of any party interested[2].

[1] See para **7.13** above.
[2] Deeds of Arrangement Act 1914, s 7.

7.24 The application may be made to a master of the Queen's Bench Division without notice being served on any other party. The application is made by witness statement or affidavit setting out particulars of the deed of arrangement and of the omission or misstatement in question and stating the grounds of the application[1].

¹ CPR Sch 1 RSC Ord 94 r 4.

Searches

7.25 Any person is entitled to search the register on payment of the prescribed fee, and to take office copies of, or extracts from, any registered deed of arrangement as to the extent permitted by the rules[1]. The register is open for inspection by the public between 10 am and 4 pm[2]. Similarly, the index kept by the county court district judge may be searched and office copies taken of extracts made from any instrument filed at the county court[3]. An office copy of or extract from a registered instrument is prima facie evidence of the instrument and of the fact and date of registration in all courts and before all arbitrators and other persons[4].

¹ Deeds of Arrangement Act 1914, ss 9, 26(1); Deeds of Arrangement Rules 1925, rr 9, 16. For the prescribed fees see the Deeds of Arrangement Fees Order 1984, SI 1984/887, art 3, Schedule, Fee 8.
² The register is kept at Ladywood House (2nd Floor), 45/46 Stephenson Street, Birmingham B2 4UZ, telephone: 0121 698 4098.
³ Deeds of Arrangement Act 1914, ss 10, 25; Deeds of Arrangement Rules 1925, rr 10, 16.
⁴ Deeds of Arrangement Act 1914, s 25; Deeds of Arrangement Rules 1925, r 16.

C TRUSTEES UNDER DEEDS OF ARRANGEMENT

The trustee

7.26 A person who acts as trustee under a deed which is a deed of arrangement made for the benefit of an individual's creditors must be qualified to act as an insolvency practitioner in relation to that individual[1]. The trustee must give the prescribed security within seven days[2] from the date of filing the statutory declaration certifying the creditors' assent[3], in a sum equal to the estimated assets available for distribution amongst the unsecured creditors as shown by the affidavit filed on registration. The security is in respect of the trustee's obligation to administer the deed properly and account fully for the assets which come into his hands. The security is given to the district judge of the county court having bankruptcy jurisdiction in relation to the district in which the debtor resided or carried on business as at the date of the execution of the deed, or, if he then resided or carried on business in the London insolvency district, to the senior bankruptcy registrar of the High Court[4]. The giving of security may be dispensed with if a majority in number and value of the creditors[5] so resolve either by a resolution passed at a meeting convened by notice to all the creditors, or in writing addressed to the trustee[6]. A trustee who has been excused giving security must forthwith file with the registrar a statutory declaration to that effect[7].

1   IA 1986, s 388(2)(b); see generally **Chapter 2** above.
2   The court cannot extend the seven days' limit: *Re Early, Smith and Pavey, ex p Trustee* (1928) 98 LJ Ch 34.
3   See the Deeds of Arrangement Rules 1925, rr 24–26, Appendix, Forms 9–11. For the prescribed fee on applying to give security see the Deeds of Arrangement Fees Order 1984, 1984/887, art 3, Schedule, Fee 1.
4   Deeds of Arrangement Act 1914, s 11(1) (amended by the IA 1985, s 235(1), Sch 8, para 2(3); the IA 1986, s 439(2), Sch 14).
5   In calculating a majority of creditors for these purposes a secured creditor is to be reckoned as a creditor only in respect of any balance due to him after deducting the value of his security, and creditors whose debts amount to sums not exceeding £10 are to be reckoned in the majority in value but not in the majority in number: Deeds of Arrangement Act 1914, s 11(5).
6   Deeds of Arrangement Act 1914, s 11(1).
7   Deeds of Arrangement Act 1914, s 11(1).

7.27 If the trustee fails to comply with these requirements, the court may declare the deed void or may make an order appointing another trustee on the application of any creditor and after hearing such persons as it thinks fit[1]. A certificate that the required security has been given, signed by the registrar of the court and filed with the registrar of deeds of arrangement, is conclusive evidence of the fact[2].

1   Deeds of Arrangement Act 1914, s 11(2).
2   Deeds of Arrangement Act 1914, s 11(3).

Trustee's duty to keep accounts

7.28 All money received by the trustee must be banked by him to an account to be opened in the name of the debtor's estate[1]. The form of the accounts kept by the trustee are governed by the rules[2], and where the trustee carries on a business, he must keep a separate trading account[3]. In the case of a partnership, separate accounts must be kept of the joint and separate estates[4].

1   Deeds of Arrangement Act 1914, s 11(4).
2   Deeds of Arrangement Rules 1925, rr 31–42.
3   Deeds of Arrangement Rules 1925, r 33.
4   Deeds of Arrangement Rules 1925, r 37.

7.29 The trustee must send accounts, duly stamped, to the Department of Trade and Industry at the prescribed times[1] and in the prescribed form[2]. The department may require a trustee to complete or amend an account which appears to the department imperfect, or to furnish an explanation of an account[3]. If, since becoming trustee or transmitting his last account, a trustee has not received or paid out any money on account of the estate he must, at the period when he is required to transmit his account, send to the department an affidavit of no receipts or payments[4].

1   The first account must be sent within 30 days from the expiration of 12 months from the date of registration of the deed, and must commence at the date of its execution and be brought down to the end of 12 months from the date of registration; subsequent accounts must be sent at intervals of 12 months and must be brought down to the end of the 12-month period for which they are sent: Deeds of Arrangement Rules 1925, r 31.

²   Deeds of Arrangement Act 1914, s 13(1); Deeds of Arrangement Rules 1925, rr 31–37, Appendix, Form 15. As to the affidavit verifying the accounts, see the Deeds of Arrangement Rules 1925, r 42, Appendix, Form 17. As to the submission of a summary or modified statement of accounts, see Deeds of Arrangement Rules 1925, r 41.
³   Deeds of Arrangement Rules 1925, r 38.
⁴   Deeds of Arrangement Rules 1925, r 39. Even if there are no assets, the trustee must stamp the account: *Re Hertage* (1896) 3 Mans 297.

7.30 As soon as the trustee has realised all the property included in the deed or so much as can probably be realised, and has distributed a final dividend or final instalment of composition, or in any other case as soon as the trusts of the deed and the trustee's obligations have been completely fulfilled, he must transmit his final account and a verifying affidavit[1].

¹   Deeds of Arrangement Rules 1925, r 40, Appendix, Form 20.

7.31 Where dividends or instalments of composition are distributed to creditors, the total amount of each dividend or instalment must be entered in the account as one sum, but the trustee must forward to the Department of Trade and Industry a statement showing the amount of each creditor's claim and the amount of dividend or composition payable to each creditor, distinguishing in the statement the dividends or instalments paid and those remaining unpaid[1]. With his final account the trustee must forward a complete statement showing the amount of the claim and the full amount of the dividend or composition paid to or reserved for each creditor[2].

¹   Deeds of Arrangement Rules 1925, r 36.
²   Deeds of Arrangement Rules 1925, r 36, and Appendix, Form 19.

Trustee's duties towards creditors[1]

7.32 When an assignment for the benefit of creditors has become operative and valid, the creditors become the beneficiaries, and the trustee under the deed must be treated as a trust corporation[2] with the powers provided under the Trustee Act 1925[3]. The trustee may therefore compromise and treat a creditor as a preferential creditor even where not specifically authorised by the deed[4].

¹   Where the deed of arrangement is made for the benefit of creditors generally, but not where the deed is for the benefit of only three or more creditors and not the creditors generally; Deeds of Arrangement Act 1914, s 22.
²   Law of Property (Amendment) Act 1926, s 3.
³   See the Trustee Act 1925, s 15.
⁴   *Re Shenton* [1935] Ch 651.

7.33 The trustee's duty is to ascertain all the persons entitled to the benefit of the trusts, assess the validity of their claims, and to administer the trust estate in accordance with the trusts declared in the deed. If out of the assigning debtor's property he pays to any creditor a sum larger in proportion to the creditor's claim than that paid to other creditors entitled to the benefit of the deed, then, unless the deed authorises him to do so, or unless such payments are either made to a creditor entitled to enforce his claim by distress or are such as would be lawful in a bankruptcy, he is guilty of an offence[1]. A trustee who fails to give priority to preferential creditors according to express trusts in the deed acts in breach of trust[2]. A trustee who desires to contract on behalf of the arrangement without personal liability must clearly express such a limitation; a mere description of him as 'trustee' is insufficient[3].

[1] Deeds of Arrangement Act 1914, s 17.
[2] *Re Moss, Westminster Corpn v Reubens* [1935] WN 171.
[3] *Hunt Bros (a firm) v Colwell* [1939] 4 All ER 406, CA.

7.34 Questions arising in the administration of the trust estate are determined by the court having jurisdiction in the district in which the debtor resided or carried on business at the date of the execution of the deed[1].

[1] Deeds of Arrangement Act 1914, s 23.

7.35 At the expiration of six months from the date of the registration of a deed of arrangement, and at the expiration of every subsequent period of six months until the estate has been finally wound up, the trustee must send to each creditor who has assented to the deed a statement in the prescribed form of his accounts and of the proceedings under the deed down to the date of the statement[1]. In his affidavit verifying his accounts he must state whether or not he has duly sent such statements, and the dates on which they were sent; and, if a trustee fails to comply with any of the above provisions, he is guilty of contempt of court and liable to be punished accordingly[2].

[1] Deeds of Arrangement Act 1914, s 14; Forms are prescribed by the Deeds of Arrangement Rules 1925, r 4(1), see the Appendix, Form 13 (statement of accounts to be sent to creditors), Form 17 (affidavit verifying trustee's accounts).
[2] Deeds of Arrangement Act 1914, s 14 (amended by the Insolvency Act 1985, s 235(1), Sch 8, para 2(5)).

7.36 On the written application by a majority in number and value of the creditors who have assented to the deed for an official audit of the trustee's accounts, the Department of Trade and Industry may order the audit of the trustee's accounts[1]. Such an audit takes place under the same rules as apply to the audit of a trustee in bankruptcy's accounts under the IA 1986[2]. Within seven days of the department's order being served on him the trustee must deliver to the department both copies of all his previous accounts and a further account from the final date of the last account to the date of the order, and an affidavit verifying the copies and account[3]. The audited accounts and the auditor's certificate or observations must be filed, and are open to inspection by creditors or the trustee[4].

[1] Deeds of Arrangement Act 1914, s 15(1) (amended by the Insolvency Act 1985, s 235(1), Sch 8, para 2(6); IA 1986, s 439(2), Sch 14).
[2] Deeds of Arrangement Act 1914, s 15(1).
[3] Deeds of Arrangement Rules 1925, r 29 (amended by SI 1962/297).
[4] Deeds of Arrangement Rules 1925, r 30.

7.37 The Department of Trade and Industry may determine how and by what parties the fees, costs and expenses of, and incidental to, the audit are to be borne, whether by the applicants or by the trustee or out of the estate. Before granting an application for an audit the applicants may be required to give security for the costs[1].

[1]   Deeds of Arrangement Act 1914, s 15(2).

Payment of undistributed money in court

7.38 At any time after the expiration of two years from the date of registration of a deed of arrangement, the court having insolvency jurisdiction in relation to the district in which the debtor resided or carried on business at the date the deed was executed may, on the application of the trustee, a creditor, or of the debtor, order that all money representing unclaimed dividends and undistributed funds then in the trustee's hands or under his control be paid into the Supreme Court or any county court having jurisdiction in the matter[1].

[1]   Deeds of Arrangement Act 1914, s 16 (amended by the Administration of Justice Act 1965, s 17(1), Sch 1; the Insolvency Act 1985, s 235(1), Sch 8, para 2(7); IA 1986, s 439(2), Sch 14).

Appointment of new deed trustee

7.39 Whenever it is necessary to appoint a new deed trustee, and it is found inexpedient, difficult or impracticable to do so without the court's assistance, the court[1] may appoint a new trustee, either in substitution for or in addition to an existing trustee, or even where there is no existing trustee[2]. For example the court may appoint a new trustee in substitution for a trustee who is incapable by reason of mental disorder of exercising his functions as trustee, or who is a bankrupt, or who is a corporation which is in liquidation or has been dissolved[3].

[1]   Ie the High Court, or the court having insolvency jurisdiction in the district in which the debtor resided or carried on business at the date of the execution of the deed.
[2]   Trustee Act 1925, s 41(1), (2).
[3]   Trustee Act 1925, s 41(1).

7.40 If a trustee has failed to comply with the requirements as to the giving of security to administer the deed properly and account fully for the assets, the court having insolvency jurisdiction in the district in which the debtor resided or carried on business at the date of the execution of the deed may, on the application of any creditor and after hearing such persons as it may think fit, appoint another trustee in place of the trustee appointed by the deed[1].

[1]   Deeds of Arrangement Act 1914, s 11(2). Where an application to appoint a new trustee is made under the Deeds of Arrangement Act 1914, s 11(2), notice of the application must be served on the existing trustee not less than eight days before the day appointed for the hearing: Deeds of Arrangement Rules 1925, r 22.

7.41 On his appointment a new trustee must forthwith send the registrar for deeds of arrangement notice of his appointment[1].

[1]   Deeds of Arrangement Rules 1925, r 27.

Power to ensure continuation of essential supplies

7.42 A trustee under a deed of arrangement has the same rights as the supervisor of a voluntary arrangement, the official receiver, an interim receiver and a trustee in bankruptcy for ensuring continued supplies of gas, electricity, water and telecommunication services for the benefit of an individual's creditors[1].

[1]   IA 1986, s 372(1)(c).

Position of trustee where deed void

7.43 Where a deed of arrangement is void by reason that the requisite majority of creditors have not assented to it, or, in the case of a deed for the benefit of three or more creditors, by reason that the debtor was insolvent at the time of the execution of the deed and that the deed was not registered as required by the Deeds of Arrangement Act 1914, but is not void for any other reason, and a bankruptcy order is made against the debtor upon a petition presented after the lapse of three months[1] from the execution of the deed, the trustee under the deed is not liable to account to the trustee in the bankruptcy for any dealings with or payments made out of the debtor's property which would have been proper if the deed had been valid, if he proves that, at the time of such dealings or payments, he did not know, and had no reason to suspect, that the deed was void[2].

[1]   The period of three months has no significance under the IA 1986 but derives from the doctrine of relation back under the Bankruptcy Act 1914.
[2]   Deeds of Arrangement Act 1914, s 19(1).

7.44 If a trustee acts under a deed of arrangement (1) after it has, to his knowledge, become void by reason of non-compliance with any of the requirements of the Deeds of Arrangement Act 1914; or (2) after he has failed to give security within the time and in the manner provided by the 1914 Act, he is liable to a criminal penalty[1]. As soon as practicable after a trustee has become aware that a deed is void by virtue of the 1914 Act for any reason other than that, being for the benefit of creditors generally, it has not been registered in time, he must give written notice to each creditor known to him[2].

[1]   This takes the form, on summary conviction, of a fine not exceeding £5 for every day between the date on which the deed became void, and the last day on which he is proved to have acted as trustee, unless he satisfies the court that his contravention of the law was due to inadvertence, or that his action was confined to taking such steps as were necessary for the protection of the estate: Deeds of Arrangement Act 1914, s 12.
[2]   Deeds of Arrangement Act 1914, s 20; failure to give notice to creditors is a criminal offence.

7.45 Where a deed of arrangement is avoided by reason of the bankruptcy of the debtor, any expenses properly incurred[1] by the trustee under the deed in the performance of any of the duties imposed on him by the Deeds of Arrangement Act 1914 must be allowed or paid to him by the trustee in the bankruptcy as a first charge on the estate[2]. Where, however, the deed has never become effective because the necessary majority of creditors has not assented, the trustee's expenses may be allowed only by the court, and then only if there has been real benefit to the creditors[3].

1   See *Re Geen, ex p Parker* [1917] 1 KB 183.
2   Deeds of Arrangement Act 1914, s 21.
3   *Re Zakon, ex p Trustee v Bushell* [1940] Ch 253.

D CREDITORS UNDER DEEDS OF ARRANGEMENT

Creditors entitled to benefit

7.46 Where a deed of arrangement by a debtor is expressed to be with his creditors generally, or with all creditors who assent to it, any creditor who assents to it expressly or by conduct and elects to take the benefit of it within the time limit for assent fixed by the instrument is entitled to share in the benefits of the arrangement, even if he has not signed the instrument[1]. In the exercise of its equitable jurisdiction the court may permit a creditor who has not assented to an arrangement to come in under it and share in its benefits, notwithstanding that the time limited by the instrument for assent has elapsed[2]. The arrangement by the debtor may be expressed to be subject to the rules of bankruptcy. The words 'according to the law of bankruptcy' in a deed of arrangement have been held to be descriptive only of a rateable payment without prejudice or priority and by a series of instalments or dividends, and not sufficient to import into the distribution of the money the obligation of mutual set-off under the statutory provisions[3] with a person who had not signified his assent to the deed[4]. In a case where the deed does not incorporate the bankruptcy rules a person having only a contingent or future claim against the debtor cannot benefit under the deed[5].

1   *Re Chambers, ex p Jerrard* (1837) 3 Deac 1 at 7; *Re Baber's Trusts* (1870) LR 10 Eq 554.
2   *Watson v Knight* (1845) 19 Beav 369; *Raworth v Parker* (1855) 2 K & J 163; *Brandling v Plummer* (1857) 27 LJ Ch 188; and cf *Re Pilet, ex p Toursier & Co and Berkeley* [1915] 3 KB 519, DC, where creditors whose debts were provable under a previous composition which had been discharged were not allowed to come in under a subsequent arrangement as creditors in respect of those debts.
3   Pursuant to IA 1986, s 323.
4   *Baker v Adam* (1910) 102 LT 248.
5   *Re Casse, ex p Robinson v Trustee* [1937] Ch 405.

7.47 A creditor entitled to the benefit of an arrangement must perform fairly all the conditions of the arrangement which apply to the creditors. If he takes any step which is inconsistent with or opposed to those conditions, for example by bringing an action against the debtor to recover his debt, he will be liable to be excluded from the benefit of the arrangement[1]. A creditor who makes any underhand or secret bargain with the debtor, by which he is to receive some payment or advantage in which the other creditors do not share, may be excluded from all the benefits of the arrangement[2].

1   *Field v Lord Donoughmore* (1841) 1 Dr & War 227.
2   *Wood v Barker* (1865) LR 1 Eq 139; *Re Milner, ex p Milner* (1885) 15 QBD 605, CA; *Dauglish v Tennent* (1866) LR 2 QB 49; *Re EAB* [1902] 1 KB 457.

7.48   Deeds of arrangement

7.48 Where there is no fraud and no inequality among creditors, the court will not interfere to judge the reasonableness of the arrangement[1].

[1]   *Re Richmond Hill Hotel Co, ex p King* (1867) 3 Ch App 10; *Bailey v Bowen* (1868) LR 3 QB 133 at 140.

Creditors bound by arrangements

7.49 A composition is binding on creditors who execute it, or who assent to it expressly or by conduct[1]. The principle is that a creditor who puts himself in the situation where he benefits under the deed must bear its obligations even though he has not literally executed the deed[2]. An assent by one branch of a company, followed by dissent by another branch, was held to bind the company in respect of all the debts due to the branches from the debtor[3]. A creditor may execute a deed of arrangement after its registration without impairing its validity[4]. However, where creditors have attempted to defeat a deed and have failed they may not claim to come in subsequently and execute it[5].

[1]   *Victor Weston (Fabrics) Ltd v Morgensterns (a firm)* [1937] 3 All ER 769, CA.
[2]   *Forbes v Limond* (1854) 4 De GM & G 298 at 315 per Lord Cranworth LC.
[3]   *Dunlop Rubber Co v WB Haigh & Son* [1937] 1 KB 347, [1936] 3 All ER 381.
[4]   *Re Batten, ex p Milne* (1889) 6 Morr 110, CA.
[5]   *Re Meredith, Meredith v Facey* (1885) 33 WR 778.

7.50 As with any other agreement if a creditor's assent has been obtained by misrepresentation he may avoid being bound by it[1]. Neither will creditors be bound to arrangements if the debtor or some third person acting with his knowledge and on his behalf makes a secret bargain with some of the creditors with a view to securing them an advantage over others[2], and they will be able to enforce their debts by legal proceedings[3]. Where the composition agreement provides that the release contained in it is to be void if the instalments are not duly paid, a creditor who has fraudulently obtained a secret advantage over the other creditors will be bound by the agreement, and his debt will be released, even though the debtor defaults in paying the instalments[4].

[1]   *Lewis v Jones* (1825) 4 B & C 506; *Sier v Bullen* (1915) 84 LJKB 1288, DC.
[2]   *Dauglish v Tennent* (1866) LR 2 QB 49; *Re Milner, ex p Milner* (1885) 15 QBD 605, CA.
[3]   *Re Milner, ex p Milner* (1885) 15 QBD 605, CA.
[4]   *Re Hodgson, ex p Oliver* (1851) 4 De G & Sm 354. As to the recovery of money paid under a secret bargain see *Atkinson v Denby* (1862) 7 H & N 934.

Creditors' rights under the arrangements

7.51 In the event of the deed being avoided by the debtor becoming bankrupt, creditors who are parties to the deed will not be debarred from proving for their debts in the bankruptcy, unless it is clear from the terms of the deed that they intended to release their debts, whether or not bankruptcy should supervene[1]. Where a composition deed or agreement reserves to creditors their rights in respect of any securities held by them over the debtor's property, a general release contained in the deed or agreement will not prevent them from realising or dealing with and obtaining the benefit of their securities in reduction of the debts due to them[2].

1   See *Re Stephenson, ex p Official Receiver* (1888) 20 QBD 540, DC.
2   *Cullingworth v Loyd* (1840) 2 Beav 385; *Mawson v Stock* (1801) 6 Ves 300.

7.52 If there is a surplus in the hands of the trustee after payment of the debts and expenses, the creditors are not entitled to interest on their debts, unless the deed contains an express or implied provision for payment of interest[1].

1   *Re Rissik* [1936] Ch 68.

7.53 The debtor or any creditor or other person interested is entitled, on payment of the prescribed fees, to inspect the trustee's accounts and to be furnished with copies of or extracts from them[1].

1   Deeds of Arrangement Act 1914, s 13(3). For the prescribed fees see the Deeds of Arrangement Fees Order 1984, 1984/887, art 3, Schedule, Fees 10, 13.

Rights against persons liable jointly or as sureties

7.54 A debtor's creditors may hold rights against sureties as security for their debts, or hold securities over parts of the compounding debtor's property. If a general release in a composition deed or agreement contains also a reservation of the creditors' rights against all persons who are liable to them jointly with or as sureties for the debtor, the release operates only as an obligation not to sue the debtor; it does not operate to prejudice the creditors' rights against persons liable to them jointly with the debtor or as sureties for him[1]. The reservation by creditors of their rights against sureties imports the continuance of the sureties' rights of indemnity against the debtor[2].

1   *Kearsley v Cole* (1846) 16 M & W 128; *Ex p Gifford* (1802) 6 Ves 805; *Bateson v Gosling* (1871) LR 7 CP 9.
2   *Cole v Lynn* [1942] 1 KB 142, [1941] 3 All ER 502, CA.

E ENFORCEMENT OF DEEDS OF ARRANGEMENT

Courts having jurisdiction

7.55 Any application by the trustee under a deed of arrangement which is in fact or is expressed to be for the benefit of the debtor's creditors generally, or by the debtor or by any creditor entitled to the benefit of such a deed of arrangement, for the enforcement of the trusts or the determination of questions under it, must be made to the court having insolvency jurisdiction[1] in relation to the district in which the debtor resided or carried on business at the date of its execution[2]. An application by the debtor for a declaration that a deed of arrangement is void for non-compliance with the provisions of the Deeds of Arrangement Act 1914 is not an application for the enforcement of the trusts or the determination of questions 'under' it, and therefore a judge in the county court having insolvency jurisdiction has no jurisdiction to entertain such an application, unless it would otherwise come before that court[3]. A trustee under a deed of arrangement for the benefit of creditors generally is entitled to obtain a declaration[4] that certain persons named in a schedule to the deed are not in fact creditors of the assignor, notwithstanding that the trustee is himself a party to the deed[5]. The object of the section is to provide a trustee or beneficiary under a deed of arrangement with a summary means of obtaining a determination of questions arising in the administration of the trusts of the deed and accordingly a creditor who has not assented to the deed cannot avail himself of the summary jurisdiction contained in the section[6].

[1] See IA 1986, s 373 and para **1.18**ff above.
[2] Deeds of Arrangement Act 1914, s 23 (amended by the Insolvency Act 1985, s 235(1), Sch 8, para 2(9); IA 1986, s 439(2), Sch 14).
[3] *Re Wilson* [1916] 1 KB 382 at 398, CA.
[4] Under the Deeds of Arrangement Act 1914, s 23.
[5] *Re Pilet, ex p Toursier & Co and Berkeley* [1915] 3 KB 519, DC.
[6] *Re Ellis* [1925] Ch 564, CA.

7.56 Any question as to whether any person claiming to be a creditor entitled to the benefit of a deed of arrangement is so entitled may be decided either by the court having insolvency jurisdiction or by the High Court[1].

[1] Deeds of Arrangement Act 1914, s 23 proviso, expressly subject to rules made for the purposes of the Deeds of Arrangement Act 1914, see ss 17–23.

Applications

7.57 All applications, other than applications for rectification of the register[1], may be made to the High Court or the county court having insolvency jurisdiction in the district in which the debtor resided or carried on business at the date of the execution of the deed and are deemed to be proceedings in bankruptcy. They are accordingly to be conducted under the Insolvency Rules 1986 with such variations as the circumstances may require[2].

[1] Applications are made to a master of the Queen's Bench Division of the High Court, see para **7.24** above.
[2] Deeds of Arrangement Rules 1925, r 17 (amended by SI 1986/2001).

7.58 All applications must be supported by witness statement or affidavit[1], save for applications for extension of time for procuring the assent of creditors to a deed or for filing the prescribed statutory declaration which may be made without notice to other parties and without affidavit unless the court orders otherwise[2].

[1] Deeds of Arrangement Rules 1925, r 17.
[2] Deeds of Arrangement Rules 1925, r 17 proviso.

7.59 Applications are heard by the bankruptcy registrar or district judge of the court in chambers, but he may in any case, and must at the request of any party, adjourn the application to be heard and determined by the judge of the court[1].

[1] Deeds of Arrangement Rules 1925, r 21.

7.60 Unless the court otherwise orders, the evidence to be used on the application must be given by witness statement or affidavit, but any opposite party may require the attendance of any deponent for cross-examination by notice in writing addressed to any deponent or his solicitor[1]. Witness statements or affidavits must be filed in the court, and copies served on the applicant not less than four days before the day appointed for the hearing of the application[2].

1   Deeds of Arrangement Rules 1925, r 19.
2   Deeds of Arrangement Rules 1925, r 20.

Part III
BANKRUPTCY

Chapter 8

BANKRUPTCY PETITIONS

A INTRODUCTION

General

8.1 The proceedings in which the court may determine whether a bankruptcy order should be made are commenced by bankruptcy petition. This chapter discusses the circumstances in which a bankruptcy petition may be presented and the procedure applicable to proceedings on a bankruptcy petition.

Types of petition

8.2 In this introductory section the various types of petition are enumerated.

Creditor's petition

8.3 A creditor may present a petition against a debtor who owes him a debt for a liquidated sum in excess of the minimum sum, at present £750. Before a creditor may present a petition he must justify doing so either (1) by serving a statutory demand on the debtor which the debtor neither complies with nor sets aside, or (2) by obtaining a judgment in respect of which execution is returned unsatisfied. In either case the debtor will have had the opportunity to dispute the debt: either where a statutory demand is served, by applying to set the demand aside, or where a judgment has been obtained, in the proceedings in which the judgment was given[1].

[1]   See further para **8.41**ff on judgments.

Petitions presented by the Financial Services Authority

8.4 The Financial Services Authority is empowered to present a petition against an individual but only on the ground that he appears to be unable to pay a debt arising from a regulated activity or that he appears to have no reasonable prospect of being able to pay such a debt[1]. Although the Financial Services Authority will not usually itself be a creditor, the form of the petition and the procedure relating to it is a modified version of the form and procedure applicable to a creditor's petition.

[1]   Financial Services and Markets Act 2000, s 372.

Debtor's petition

8.5 A debtor may present a petition against himself where he is unable to pay his debts. In this case, since the insolvency proceedings are initiated voluntarily, the presentation of the petition may be followed swiftly, even immediately, by a bankruptcy order.

Petition in connection with an IVA

8.6 Where a debtor has entered into an IVA, the supervisor of the IVA or any person apart from the debtor who is bound by the IVA may present a petition where the debtor has defaulted or provided false information in respect of the IVA. In the case of this third category of petition, although the basis for the petition is a default or the provision of false information in respect of the IVA, it will still be the case that the debtor is unable to pay his debts since otherwise the IVA would not have been required.

Petition presented in connection with insolvency proceedings against a debtor in another EU State

8.7 The EC Insolvency Regulation enables the office-holder in insolvency proceedings pertaining to an individual which are pending in or intended to be opened in the courts of another Member State to present an English bankruptcy petition against that individual. There are two situations in which the office-holder appointed in another Member State may present a petition to the English court. First, where main proceedings have been commenced in another Member State against the debtor, the office-holder appointed in those proceedings is entitled, in defined circumstances[1], to present a petition against the debtor in the English court. Secondly, where in anticipation of main insolvency proceedings being commenced in the court of another Member State, a temporary administrator has been appointed by that court so as to protect the debtor's estate, that temporary administrator is also entitled, again in defined circumstances, to petition for the debtor's bankruptcy in England.

¹ EC Insolvency Regulation, arts 29(a) and 3(2) and IA 1986, s 264(1)(bb).
² EC Insolvency Regulation, arts 38 and 3(2) and IA 1986, s 264(1)(ba).

Where the petitioner could present different types of petition

8.8 Where a person is entitled to present a petition in more than one of those categories the petition is to be treated as a petition presented by him in the capacity specified in the petition¹.

¹ IA 1986, s 266(1).

B JURISDICTION

General

8.9 Bankruptcy petitions may only be presented against individuals¹ who fall within the bankruptcy jurisdiction of the English court. Since 31 May 2002, the rules as to the bankruptcy jurisdiction of the English court are to be found in the jurisdictional provisions of Council Regulation (EC) No 1346/2000 of 29 May 2000 on insolvency proceedings and, subject to those provisions, the jurisdictional provisions of the Insolvency Act 1986. In this book Council Regulation (EC) No 1346/2000 is referred to as the EC Insolvency Regulation.

¹ 'Individual' may include a partnership; see IA 1986, s 388(3).

Summary

8.10 In summary, the English bankruptcy court will have jurisdiction over a debtor in the following circumstances:

(a) where the centre of his main interests, as defined in the EC Insolvency Regulation, is located in England and Wales and at least one of the domestic jurisdictional conditions set out in IA 1986, s 265(1) is fulfilled;

(b) where the centre of his main interests is located in a Member State other than the United Kingdom, apart from Denmark, but he possesses an establishment in England and Wales; if no main proceedings in another Member State have been opened, certain other conditions must also be satisfied; and in any case at least one of the domestic jurisdictional conditions set out in IA 1986, s 265(1) must be fulfilled;

(c) where the centre of his main interests is located in Denmark or outside the EC and at least one of the domestic jurisdictional conditions set out in IA 1986, s 265(1) is fulfilled.

8.11 Bankruptcy petitions

Jurisdiction where the centre of the debtor's main interests is in England and Wales

8.11 A bankruptcy petition may be presented against an individual the centre of whose main interests is situated in England and Wales and with respect to whom at least one of the domestic jurisdictional conditions set out in IA 1986, s 265(1) is fulfilled.

The centre of a debtor's main interests

8.12 Paragraph (13) of the recital to the EC Insolvency Regulation states that the centre of a debtor's main interests should correspond to the place where the debtor conducts the administration of his interests on a regular basis and is therefore ascertainable by third parties. The requirement that the location of the centre of the debtor's main interests be overt is a key factor. As explained in the Virgos-Schmit report, the rationale is to enable creditors to foresee what insolvency regime would be likely to apply if the debtor were to become insolvent. 'In principle,' it is stated in that report, 'the centre of main interests will in the case of professionals be the place of their professional domicile and for natural persons in general, the place of their habitual residence'. Relevant interests are economic interests. These include commercial, industrial and professional interests, but also the economic activities of a consumer. The burden is on the party contending that the English court has jurisdiction[1]. Although the approach indicated in the Virgos-Schmit report indicates a straightforward test, determining the question can involve a more detailed inquiry into where the debtor conducts the activities comprehended in the administration of his relevant interests[2]. The activities of a debtor as the representative of a company in administering the company's affairs should not be confused with the administration of his own interests[3].

[1] *Shierson v Vlieland-Boddy* [2005] EWCA Civ 974, [2005] 1 WLR 3966; but the question as to the standard of proof remains open: it may suffice to establish a good arguable case as opposed to proof on the balance of probabilities; see the judgment of Longmore LJ.
[2] For examples concerning individuals, see *Skjevesland v Geveren Trading Co Ltd* [2002] EWHC 2898 (Ch), [2003] BPIR 924; *Shierson v Vlieland-Boddy* [2005] EWCA Civ 974, [2005] 1 WLR 3966; *Cross Construction Sussex Ltd v Tseliki* [2006] All ER (D) 334 (Mar); *Stojevic v Official Receiver* [2007] BPIR 141.
[3] *Cross-Construction Sussex Ltd v Tseliki* [2006] All ER (D) 334 (Mar); *Stojevic v Official Receiver* [2007] BPIR 141.

Time for determining where the centre of main interests is situated

8.13 The material time for assessing where the centre of the debtor's main interests is situated is the time when the request that insolvency proceedings be opened is made. In *Re Staubitz-Schreiber (Case C-1/04)*[1] the individual insolvent had requested that insolvency proceedings be commenced against herself in Germany. Before her request was heard by the court, she moved to Spain in order to live and work there. When the German court then heard her request, it declined to open insolvency proceedings on the basis that the centre of the applicant's main interests was no longer situated in Germany. The European Court of Justice held that the material time for determining where the centre of main interests was situated was the time when the debtor made her request that insolvency proceedings be opened and that, even if she moved the centre before the request was acted on, the courts of the territory where it was located at the time of the request retained jurisdiction.

¹   [2006] ECR I-701, [2006] BPIR 510.

8.14 In England and Wales, the question would be unlikely to arise on a debtor's petition because the practice is that bankruptcy orders are made on the same day as a debtor's petition is presented. But clearly time will elapse between the date of when a creditor's petition is presented and the date when it is heard. Following the approach in *Re Staubitz-Schreiber (Case C-1/04)*¹, the material date will be the date of presentation². This will not eliminate the problem since a creditor's petition will usually be preceded by a statutory demand and it will remain possible for a debtor to move the centre of his main interests during the period between the service of the statutory demand and the presentation of the petition upon it.

¹   [2006] ECR I-701, [2006] BPIR 510.
²   In *Shierson v Vlieland-Boddy* [2005] EWCA Civ 974, [2005] 1 WLR 3966 the Court of Appeal has earlier ruled that the relevant date was the date when the petition is heard.

Jurisdiction where the debtor has an establishment in England and Wales

8.15 Where the centre of the debtor's main interests is situated in another Member State apart from Denmark, then a petition may only be presented against him in England and Wales if he has an establishment in England and Wales and *either*:

(a)   main insolvency proceedings have been opened in the Member State where the centre of his main interests is situated¹; *or*

(b)   insolvency proceedings cannot be opened in the Member State where the centre of his main interests is situated because of conditions laid down by the law of that State²; *or*

(c)   the bankruptcy petition is presented by a creditor who has his domicile, habitual residence or registered office in England and Wales or whose claim arises from the operation of the debtor's establishment in England and Wales³.

¹   EC Insolvency Regulation, arts 3(2) and 27.
²   EC Insolvency Regulation, art 3(2) and (4)(a).
³   EC Insolvency Regulation, art 3(2) and (4)(b).

8.16 Further, at least one of the domestic jurisdictional conditions set out in IA 1986, s 265(1) must also be fulfilled.

Establishment

8.17 An 'establishment' means any place of operations where the debtor carries out a non-transitory economic activity with human means and goods.

Merely owning assets within the jurisdiction does not suffice. In the Virgos-Schmit report it is said, 'The emphasis on an economic activity having to be carried out using human resources shows the need for a minimum level of organisation. A purely occasional place of operations cannot be classified as an "establishment". A certain stability is required. The negative formula ("non-transitory") aims to avoid minimum time requirements. The decisive factor is how the activity appears externally, and not the intention of the debtor'. As an example of an establishment, owning a unit in a business park and carrying on the business of letting to multiple occupiers sufficed in *Shierson v Vlieland-Boddy*[1].

[1]   [2005] EWCA Civ 974, [2005] 1 WLR 3966.

Jurisdiction where the centre of the debtor's main interests is situated outside any Member State (or in Denmark)

8.18 Where the centre of an individual debtor's main interests is not situated in any Member State (or is situated in Denmark), a creditor's bankruptcy petition may be presented against him in England and Wales or he may himself present a debtor's bankruptcy petition so long as he fulfils at least one of the domestic jurisdictional conditions set out in IA 1986, s 265(1).

The domestic jurisdictional conditions: IA 1986, s 265(1)

8.19 The domestic jurisdictional conditions which must be fulfilled with respect to a debtor if the English courts are to have bankruptcy jurisdiction over him are that:

(1)   he is domiciled in England and Wales; or
(2)   he is personally present in England and Wales on the day on which the petition is presented; or
(3)   at any time in the period of three years ending with that day:
     (i)   he has been ordinarily resident, or has had a place of residence, in England and Wales, or
     (ii)   he has carried on business in England and Wales[1].

[1]   IA 1986, s 265(1).

Domicile[1]

8.20 In this context, 'domicile' refers to the common law concept of domicile, not the concept introduced by the Civil Jurisdiction and Judgments Act 1982[2]; for the Brussels Convention does not apply to insolvency matters[3].

[1]   See Dicey and Morris *Conflict of Laws* 14th edn, ch 6, Cheshire and North *Private International Law* 14th edn, ch 9.
[2]   Civil Jurisdiction and Judgments Act 1982, s 41.
[3]   Article 1. See *Gourdain v Nadler Case* 133/78 [1979] ECR 733, ECJ.

8.21 The concept of domicile in English law, although essentially based on the idea of an individual's permanent home[1], is complicated by technicality, particularly of the rules relating to change of domicile. There are two categories of domicile: domicile of origin and domicile of choice. In broad terms domicile of origin is determined as follows: in the case of a legitimate child, by the father's domicile[2], in the case of an illegitimate child, by the mother's domicile[3] and in the case of a foundling by the place where he is found.

[1] *Whicker v Hume* (1858) 7 HL Cas 124.
[2] *Udny v Udny* (1869) LR 1 Sc & Div 441, HL.
[3] *Udny v Udny* (1869) LR 1 Sc & Div 441, HL; *Urquhart v Butterfield* (1887) 37 Ch D 357.

8.22 A person cannot be without a domicile and will retain his domicile of origin unless and until he acquires a different domicile by exercise of choice. The burden of proving that a person's domicile has changed lies on the party asserting that such charge has occurred. However, it should be noted that where an individual who has changed his domicile by choice, loses that domicile of choice without acquiring a further domicile of choice, his domicile of origin will, under English law, revive and remain his domicile until, if he does, he acquires a further domicile of choice[1].

[1] *Udny v Udny* (1869) LR 1 Sc & Div 441, HL; *Tee v Tee* [1973] 3 All ER 1105, [1974] 1 WLR 213, CA.

8.23 To acquire a domicile of choice an individual must voluntarily establish his residence in a territory with the intention to reside there permanently[1]. In *Henwood v Barlow Clowes International Ltd*[2] the debtor had abandoned his domicile of choice in the Isle of Man; the issue was whether his domicile of origin in England had revived or whether he had acquired a further domicile of choice in Mauritius. The judge held in favour of the latter. The case contains a useful review of the authorities and analysis of the multifarious factors, arising over the full extent of the debtor's life, which impinge on the question.

[1] *Udny v Udny* (1869) LR 1 Sc & Div 441, HL; *Re Fuld's Estate (No 3)* [1968] P 675, [1965] 3 All ER 776; *Agulian v Cyganik* [2006] EWCA Civ 129, [2006] 1 FCR 406.
[2] [2007] EWHC 1579 (Ch), [2007] All ER (D) 25 (Jul).

Personal presence

8.24 Personal presence is a question of physical fact. In relation to the service of proceedings, no matter how short the presence is, it still renders the person subject to the jurisdiction[1]. However, again in the context of the service of proceedings, service has been set aside where the defendant was improperly or fraudulently persuaded into the jurisdiction[2].

[1] *Re Thulin (a debtor)* [1995] 1 WLR 165.
[2] *Colt Industries Inc v Sarlie* [1966] 1 All ER 673, [1966] 1 WLR 440.

Ordinary residence and place of residence

8.25 An individual resides where he lives. 'Ordinarily resident' refers to a man's abode in a particular place or country which he has adopted voluntarily and for settled purposes as part of the regular order of his life for the time being, whether of short or of long duration[1]. A degree of permanence is required but it is possible to reside in two places at the same time[2]. In *Mark v Mark*[3] the question was whether a wife was habitually resident in England so as to found matrimonial jurisdiction under s 5(2) of the Domicile and Matrimonial Proceedings Act 1973. The overt facts were such as to justify finding that she was, but her presence in England was unlawful under immigration law and so the issue was whether the residence had also to be lawful. The House of Lords decided that, as a matter of statutory interpretation, there was no need to imply into the section a requirement that the wife's residence was lawful. In the context of bankruptcy, the proper interpretation would seem to be the same in that it would be odd if a debtor were immune from bankruptcy because his presence within the jurisdiction was unlawful. But in any event having a place of residence in England and Wales is sufficient and it would be difficult, as a matter of ordinary interpretation, to imply any additional requirement as to the lawfulness of the debtor's presence within the United Kingdom in relation to that limb of the section.

[1] *Levene v IRC* [1928] AC 217, HL; *IRC v Lysaght* [1928] AC 234, HL; *Shah v Barnet London Borough Council* [1983] 2 AC 309, HL.
[2] *Levene v IRC* [1928] AC 217, HL.
[3] [2005] UKHL 42, [2006] 1 AC 98.

Carrying on business

8.26 The Act states that the reference to a person carrying business includes (a) the carrying on of business by a firm or partnership of which the individual is a member, and (b) the carrying on of business by an agent or manager for the individual or for such a firm or partnership[1]. In order to be carrying on business the relevant activity must have some continuity and involve some degree of management and control[2]. An isolated transaction would not ordinarily suffice.

[1] IA 1986, s 265(2).
[2] *Graham v Lewis* (1888) 22 QBD 1, CA; *Re Brauch (A Debtor), ex p Britannic Securities and Investments Ltd* [1978] Ch 316, [1978] 1 All ER 1004, CA; *Re Sarflax Ltd* [1979] Ch 592.

8.27 It may be that the substance of a person's business is carried out through the machinery of companies set up for the purpose. However, the individual may still himself be carrying on business personally by his activity in promoting those companies and acquiring them as shell companies[1].

[1] *Re Brauch (A Debtor), ex p Britannic Securities and Investments Ltd* [1978] Ch 316, [1978] 1 All ER 1004, CA.

8.28 A person continues to carry on business until all the debts of the business have been paid, including any liability for tax, even though all other activity connected with the business has ceased[1]. But an outstanding assessment to tax which has not been challenged by the taxpayer does not by itself establish that the taxpayer had carried on business in the jurisdiction. The fact that he was carrying on business in the jurisdiction, and that therefore the assessment to tax was justified, needs to be independently proved[2].

[1]   *Re A Debtor (No 784 of 1991), ex p Debtor v IRC* [1992] Ch 554, [1992] 3 All ER 376 applying the decision of the House of Lords in *Theophile v Solicitor-General* [1950] AC 186, [1950] 1 All ER 405.
[2]   *Debtor v IRC* (1994) 68 TC 157.

Jurisdiction where the petition is presented in connection with an IVA

8.29 These conditions do not apply directly in respect of petitions presented by the supervisor of an IVA or a creditor bound by such arrangement. However an IVA can only be initiated by an undischarged bankrupt or, if the debtor is not bankrupt where an insolvency practitioner is of the view that the debtor proposing the arrangement is susceptible to a bankruptcy petition. In the latter case, it is further arguable that the debtor submits to the jurisdiction.

C GROUNDS FOR PRESENTING A CREDITOR'S PETITION

8.30 Where a person seeks, as a creditor, to present a bankruptcy petition against an individual, it is fundamental that he must be owed at least one debt by that individual. Thus, for example, where a judgment creditor has obtained a garnishee order against a third party individual who owes a debt to the judgment debtor, the judgment creditor may not present a petition against that third party[1].

[1]   *Re Combined Weighing and Advertising Machine Co* (1889) 43 Ch D 99, CA.

8.31 The Act provides that there must be one or more debts owed by the debtor and that the petitioning creditor or each of the petitioning creditors must be a person to whom the debt or (as the case may be) at least one of the debts is owed[1]. Thus petitions may be presented by two or more creditors jointly, either on the basis of a single debt owed to them all as joint creditors or on the basis of distinct debts owed to each of them severally.

[1]   IA 1986, s 267(1).

8.32 Further, a creditor's petition may only be presented if[1]:

(a)   the amount of the debt, or the aggregate amount of the debts, is equal to or exceeds the bankruptcy level[2];

(b)   the debt, or each of the debts, is for a liquidated sum payable to the petitioning creditor, or one or more of the petitioning creditors, either immediately or at some certain, future time, and is unsecured;

(c)   the debt, or each of the debts, is a debt which the debtor appears either to be unable to pay or to have no reasonable prospect of being able to pay; and

(d)   there is no outstanding application to set aside a statutory demand
       served in respect of the debt or any of the debts[3].

1   IA 1986, s 267(2).
2   Presently £750; see para **8.51**.
3   The application to set aside the statutory demand must be a valid application in order to
     prevent the presentation of the petition. An application made out of time was not a valid
     application: *Chohan v Times Newspapers Ltd* [2001] 1 WLR 184, [2001] BPIR 187.

8.33 There are two ways in which a debtor's inability to pay a debt can be
established so as to justify the presentation of the petition[1]. First, the creditor
may present a petition where he has served a statutory demand based on the
debt which the debtor fails to comply with or to apply to set aside.
Alternatively, he may present a petition where he has obtained a judgment in
respect of which execution is returned unsatisfied in whole or part. Where the
debt is payable in the future only the first method may be used. Where the
creditor has obtained judgment, he can choose whether to issue execution and
see whether the judgment can be enforced or to serve a statutory demand
based on the judgment and to pursue bankruptcy proceedings immediately[2].

1   IA 1986, s 268.
2   See IR 1986, Sch 4, Form 6.2.

Petition barred by other debt management arrangements

8.33A The Tribunals, Courts and Enforcement Act 2007 introduces four new
regimes whereby debtors who, in broad terms, have no substantial assets and
no surplus income, can obtain relief from their debts without going into
bankruptcy. These regimes, which are not yet in force, are discussed in
Chapter 30. If one of them is in force with respect to a debtor, then a creditor,
if the debt owed to him is governed by the relevant arrangement, may not
petition for the debtor's bankruptcy without the permission of the court
whether the arrangement is a county court administration order[1], an enforcement restrictions order[2], a debt relief order[3], or a debt repayment plan[4].

1   County Courts Act 1984, s 112F, inserted by TCEA 2007, s 106(1) (not yet in force).
2   County Courts Act 1984, s 117C, inserted by TCEA 2007, s 107(1) (not yet in force).
3   IA 1986, s 251G(2), inserted by TCEA 2007, s 108(1) and Sch 17 (not yet in force).
4   TCEA 2007, s 115 (not yet in force).

The debt

8.34 The basic element of a creditor's petition is the debt. In general terms
this means an obligation owed by one person, referred to as the debtor, to pay
a liquidated sum of money immediately or at some future but certain time to
another person, the creditor. However, in the context of the Insolvency
Act 1986, a debt may be present or future, certain or contingent and its
amount may be fixed or liquidated or capable of being ascertained by fixed
rules or as a matter of opinion[1]. Out of this wide category of debts, only debts
for a liquidated sum can form a good petitioning debt[2].

1   IA 1986, ss 385(1) and 382(3).
2   IA 1986, s 267(2)(b).

Claim for liquidated sum

8.35 To be liquidated the sum of money must be a specific amount which has been fully and finally ascertained. Thus in *Re Broadhurst ex p Broadhurst*[1], under an agreement whereby the petitioning creditor agreed to join a partnership, the alleged debtor had covenanted with the petitioning creditor to pay into that partnership the amount by which the partnership's debts exceeded the sums owed to it. The petitioning creditor became a partner but the promisor failed to honour the covenant. Although the sum due to the partnership was liquidated, that sum was not directly due to the petitioning creditor; what was due to him was the difference in value to him of his share of the partnership by reason of the promisor's default. Hence the petitioning creditor's true claim was unliquidated and required an account to be taken before the amount of the debt due could be ascertained. In the same way one partner may not present a petition against his co-partner in respect of sums due between them if the amount of the sum can only be ascertained by taking an account as to the partnership assets and such accounts have not been taken[2].

1   (1852) 22 LJ Bcy 21.
2   *Re Notley, ex p Notley* (1833) 1 Mont & A 46; *Windham (Assignee of Fletcher) v Paterson* (1815) 1 Stark 144; *Re Palmer, ex p Richardson & Son* (1833) 3 Deac & Ch 244.

8.36 A further illustration of what is meant by a liquidated sum arises in the context of the right of a surety, A, to a contribution from his co-surety, B, when A has paid more than his due proportion of the sum guaranteed[1]. In order for A to be entitled to petition against B, the amount due to A from B as B's contribution must be ascertained. Ordinarily that cannot be done until a final account of all sums paid under the guarantee has been taken. However, where the debt guaranteed is payable by instalments and the guarantee is expressed to be in respect of the instalments, an account can be taken of payments made in respect of each instalment as it falls due and if A has paid more than B, the amount due as contribution in respect of the instalment can be ascertained and form a good petitioning debt, on which A may petition for B's bankruptcy[2].

1   *Wolmershausen v Gullick* [1893] 2 Ch 514.
2   *Re Macdonald, ex p Grant* [1888] WN 130, CA.

8.37 A claim for an account is not a claim for a liquidated sum[1], but it is possible that the steps which would be necessary in order to take the account are so obvious and the result so easily seen that it cannot be disputed.

1   *Portman Building Society v Hamlyn Taylor Neck* [1998] 4 All ER 202 at 205d.

8.38 Where a secured creditor estimates the value of his security and deducts the estimated value of the security from the total amount of the debt, the resulting balance is a liquidated sum for the purpose of a petition[1]. It remains open to the debtor to dispute the estimated value of the security where this would be material, for example because it would reduce the unsecured balance to below the bankruptcy level or because of a counterclaim or set-off.

¹ In *Re a Debtor (No 64 of 1992)* [1994] 2 All ER 177, [1994] 1 WLR 264.

Claim for damages or liquidated damages

8.39 A claim for damages will not ordinarily form a good petitioning debt because the sum claimed is unliquidated¹. Thus in *Re Miller*² where the Court of Appeal found that the claim was in fact for damages, it was held that the claimant did not have the right to petition. However, certain types of contracts frequently include clauses setting out how, in the event of breach, damages may be calculated and thereby liquidated. Where the sum claimed can be quantified under such a clause, it is possible to present a petition based on that sum. However such clauses are vulnerable to being held void as penalty clauses. If the clause is held void, the claimant is left to a claim for unliquidated damages. Where the party in breach can successfully argue that the clause is a penalty clause, the petition must be dismissed.

¹ *Hope v Premierspace (Europe) Ltd* [1999] BPIR 695.
² [1901] 1 KB 51, CA.

Tax and other imposts

8.40 A petition may be based on a liability to pay tax based on an assessment, so long as all the statutory requirements to render the tax payable have been complied with¹. In *Re D & D Marketing (UK) Ltd and D & D Marketing (a firm)*² it was held that where a VAT assessment had been made the sum remained due under the assessment until successfully appealed. The fact that an appeal was pending did not affect HM Customs and Excise's right to enforce the unpaid assessment. The court would take into consideration the prospects of the appeal when exercising its discretion to grant a winding-up order. In *Worby v IRC*³ an appeal against the making of a bankruptcy order on the basis of unpaid tax and penalties was dismissed. The court was of the view that it was not for a bankruptcy court to entertain complaints about tax assessments which should be dealt with via the appropriate tax appeals procedures. A petition may be based on unpaid arrears of rates⁴.

¹ *Sinclair v IRC* (1992) 65 TC 94 (case remitted for further evidence on service of assessment); *Re a Debtor (No 383/SD/92), Neely v IRC* (1992) 66 TC 131 (statutory demand based, in part, on assessments which were unappealed); *Re a Debtor (No 960/SD/92), Debtor v IRC* (1993) 66 TC 268 (statutory demand based on an assessment under appeal upheld by reason of Taxes Management Act 1970, s 56(9) which provided that tax should be paid on the assessment, despite the appeal and refunded if the appeal succeeded).
² [2002] EWHC 660 (Ch), [2003] BPIR 539.
³ [2005] EWHC 835 (Ch), [2005] BPIR 1249.
⁴ *Re McGreavy, ex p McGreavy v Benfleet UDC* [1950] Ch 269, [1950] 1 All ER 442, CA; *Re a Debtor (No 48 of 1952), ex p Ampthill RDC v Debtor* [1953] Ch 335, [1953] 1 All ER 545, CA.

Judgments and orders

8.41 Where an unconditional order for the payment to the petitioning creditor of a sum of money has been made and that sum has not been paid, the sum will ordinarily form a good petitioning debt. Under the Insolvency Act 1986 there is no need for such a debt to be created by a final judgment. Thus an order that a defendant make an interim payment to the plaintiff under RSC Ord 29 r 10[1] created a debt on the basis of which a statutory demand could be served and a petition presented[2].

[1] See CPR 25.1(1)(k) and r 25.6 for interim payments.
[2] *Maxwell v Bishopsgate Investment Management Ltd (in liquidation)* [1993] TLR 67.

Power of bankruptcy court to investigate a judgment debt

8.42 It has long been established that the bankruptcy court has power to ensure that a bankruptcy is not instituted in circumstances which amount to injustice and has exercised a power to inquire into the consideration for the petitioning debt even to the extent of going behind judgments[1]. James LJ in *Re Onslow, ex p Kibble*[2], stated:

'It is the settled rule of the court of bankruptcy, on which we have always acted, that the court can inquire into the consideration for a judgment debt. There are obviously strong reasons for this, because the object of the bankruptcy laws is to procure the distribution of a debtor's goods among his just creditors. If a judgment were conclusive, a man might allow any number of judgments to be obtained by default against him by his friends or relations without any debt being due on them at all; it is, therefore, necessary that the consideration of the judgment should be liable to investigation.'

[1] *Eberhardt & Co Ltd v Mair* [1995] 3 All ER 963, [1995] 1 WLR 1180.
[2] (1875) 10 Ch App 373, 376.

8.43 Similarly in *Re Van Laun*[1] Bigham J said:

'No judgment recovered against the bankrupt, no covenant given by or account stated with him, can deprive the trustee of this right. He is entitled to go behind such forms to get at the truth, and the estoppel to which the bankrupt may have subjected himself will not prevail against him.'

[1] [1907] 1 KB 155, 163 (concerning the rejection by the trustee in bankruptcy of a proof of debt; this passage was approved by the Court of Appeal [1907] 2 KB 23, [1904–7] All ER Rep 157).

8.44 Thus, the court exercising the bankruptcy jurisdiction has power to go behind a judgment in order to investigate the circumstances in which the judgment was obtained and if appropriate treat the debt as unenforceable in bankruptcy, either as a debt which may found a petition or as a debt which may be proved in bankruptcy. But this is a power which will not lightly be exercised. In *Dawodu v American Express Bank*[1] Etherton J reviewed the authorities and concluded that where the judgment debt was not the subject of a pending appeal, there must be some fraud, collusion or miscarriage of justice before the court would investigate the debt.

8.44 *Bankruptcy petitions*

¹ [2001] BPIR 983. For another useful summary see *McCourt Ltd v Baron Meats* [1997] BPIR 114; a decision of the Divisional Court in Bankruptcy given on 17 December 1984 on hearing an appeal by the debtor against a receiving order made under the Bankruptcy Act 1914.

8.45 In *Re Exchange Securities and Commodities Ltd*¹ the question was whether a liquidator was bound by an estoppel by representation. Harman J observed that judgments raise estoppels *per rem judicatam* and thereby become conclusive, but judgments are not conclusive in bankruptcy. Deciding that, in general, estoppels are not conclusive either in liquidations or in bankruptcies, Harman J explained the underlying principle:

'The reason in all cases is the same: that the person sought to be estopped is not the person who made the representation and is therefore not bound by it, that is that the trustee or liquidator is not the person who suffered the judgment or made the representations, and is not the person who gave the covenant, to use the instances from the other earlier cases. Thus in all these cases there is nothing which binds the liquidator or trustee in bankruptcy.'

¹ [1998] Ch 46, [1987] BCLC 425.

8.46 Examples of cases where the bankruptcy court have gone behind a judgment include a judgment in default founded on a bill of exchange drawn by an infant¹; a judgment giving effect to a compromise of an action brought by one party to a fraud against the other party to it for the fruits of the fraud²; a judgment based on a penalty clause³.

¹ *Re Onslow, ex p Kibble* (1875) 10 Ch App 373, 376.
² *Re Blythe, ex p Banner* (1881) 17 Ch D 480 and see also *Re Lennox, ex p Lennox* (1885) 16 QBD 315.
³ *Re a Debtor, ex p Berkshire Finance Co Ltd* (1962) 106 Sol Jo 468.

Orders for costs

8.47 Costs are not liquidated until they have been assessed¹.

¹ *Re a Debtor (No 20 of 1953), ex p Debtor v Scott* [1954] 3 All ER 74, [1954] 1 WLR 1190, CA; *Chohan v Times Newspapers Ltd* [2001] 1 WLR 184; *Klamer v Kyriakides and Braier (a firm)* [2005] BPIR 1142.

Orders in family proceedings

8.48 An obligation to pay money which arises under an order made in family proceedings or under a maintenance assessment order made under the Child Support Act 1991 forms a special case. Under the Insolvency Rules 1986 as originally promulgated, no obligation of this sort could be proved in bankruptcy because the definition of provable debt in IR 1986, r 12.3(2)(a) excluded it. But, although not provable, such a debt was recognised as still being capable of forming the basis of a petition. Even so, the court would not normally exercise its jurisdiction to make a bankruptcy order on such a petition unless there are special circumstances¹. Examples of special circumstances have included a failure on the part of a husband to be frank about his assets and to pay costs[2]; a failure to comply with orders in the family proceedings, in respect of which failures the husband had been committed for contempt[3].

1   *Russell v Russell* [1999] 2 FCR 137; *Wheatley v Wheatley* [1999] BPIR 431.
2   *Russell v Russell* [1999] 2 FCR 137.
3   *Wheatley v Wheatley* [1999] BPIR 431.

8.49 However, the inability to prove debts arising from orders to pay lump sums was thought to be unfair[1] and in consequence the definition of provable debt was amended so as to render obligations arising in family proceedings to pay lump sums and costs provable. For present purposes the relevance of this change is that there is no longer to be any reason to require special circumstances in order to justify a petition based on an order in family proceedings to pay a lump sum or costs.

1   *Woodley v Woodley (No 2)* [1993] 4 All ER 1010, [1994] 1 WLR 1167, CA.

Foreign currency debt

8.50 A petition may be based on an undisputed debt owed in a foreign currency. At the hearing, evidence will be necessary of the exchange rate at the date of the hearing in order to show that the debt exceeds the minimum[1].

1   IR 1986, r 6.111(1). Cf *Re A Debtor (No 51-SD-1991), ex p Ritchie Bros Auctioneers v Debtor* [1993] 2 All ER 40, [1992] 1 WLR 1294.

Minimum debt

8.51 A creditor's petition may only be presented on a total debt which exceeds the bankruptcy level, presently set at £750[1], but more than one debt may be relied upon for the purpose of petitioning[2]. Accordingly, so long as the total sum owed amounts to £750 or more, debts of any size may be added together in order to form the basis of a statutory demand.

1   IA 1986, s 267(4).
2   IA 1986, s 267(2)(a).

8.52 The total debt of at least £750 must remain due at the date of presentation of the petition[1]. Accordingly, the debtor may pay the debt or reduce it to less than £750 at any time before the petition is presented. Where a part payment reduces the outstanding balance to below £750, a bankruptcy petition may not be presented in respect of that debt[2]. But if such part payment is made after presentation, the court retains a discretion to make a bankruptcy order on the petition[3].

1   *Re Riley* (1988) Independent, 14 March, CA.
2   *Re Patel (a debtor)* [1986] 1 All ER 522, [1986] 1 WLR 221.
3   *Lilley v American Express Europe Ltd* [2000] BPIR 70.

Security

8.53 Where a debt is secured the creditor has a means of recovering his money from the debtor without needing to invoke the bankruptcy jurisdiction. Reflecting this, a debt on which a bankruptcy petition is based must ordinarily be unsecured[1]. In only two instances may a secured debt form the basis of a bankruptcy petition: first, where the secured creditor is prepared to give up his security, in the event of a bankruptcy order, being made for the benefit of all the bankrupt's creditors; and secondly, where the amount of the debt is greater than the value of the security, in which case the partially secured creditor may rely on the unsecured part of the debt to found bankruptcy proceedings[2]. If a secured creditor has stated his willingness to give up his security in the petition and a bankruptcy order is subsequently made on it, he is thereupon deemed to have given up the specified security for the purposes of the Act insofar as it relates to individual insolvency[3]. The effect of this deeming provision is to render the security valueless to the creditor where the debtor is made bankrupt. However, the security would recover its value if the bankruptcy order were annulled.

1   IA 1986, s 267(2)(b).
2   IA 1986, s 269(1).
3   IA 1986, s 383(3).

8.54 IA 1986 defines a debt as secured to the extent that the person to whom the debt is owed holds any security for the debt (whether a mortgage, charge, lien or other security) over any property of the person by whom the debt is owed[1]. The reference to a security does not include a lien on books, papers or other records, except to the extent that they consist of documents which give a title to property and are held as such[2].

1   IA 1986, s 383(2). Under IA 1986, s 385(1) it is provided that 'secured' and related
     expressions are to be construed in accordance with IA 1986, s 383.
2   IA 1986, s 383(4).

8.55 The statutory definition excludes security provided by persons other than the debtor. The fact that the debt is guaranteed by a third party does not cause it to be secured[1].

1   *Re A Debtor (No 310 of 1988) ex p Debtor v Arab Bank Ltd* [1989] 2 All ER 42, [1989]
     1 WLR 452 per Knox J.

8.56 Where the debt is secured in part or in full, the petitioning creditor must ensure that he includes such statements in the petition and in the statutory demand as are required by the Act or the Rules[1]. The failure by a secured creditor to comply with IA 1986, s 269, although a serious flaw, does not lead to the automatic dismissal of the petition. The court has a discretion to permit amendment of the petition[2]. A partly secured creditor who wishes to petition on the basis of the unsecured balance of the debt should be careful to put a realistic value on the security in the petition; for he may only revalue it for the purpose of proof with the leave of the court[3] and the trustee is entitled to redeem the security at the valuation put on it in the creditor's proof[4].

1   IA 1986, s 269(1) sets out the requirement in respect of the petition; IR 1986, r 6.1(5), in respect of the statutory demand. See further para **8.77**.
2   *Barclays Bank plc v Mogg* [2003] EWHC 2645 (Ch), [2004] BPIR 259.
3   IR 1986, r 6.115(2)(a).
4   IR 1986, r 6.117.

Limitation

8.57 A bankruptcy petition founded on a judgment debt is not an action upon a judgment within the meaning of the Limitation Act 1980, s 24(1)[1]. Accordingly, a judgment creditor is not barred from petitioning on his judgment debt even though six years have elapsed since the judgment. The position is said to be different where the debt, not being the subject of a judgment, is statute-barred. This result occurs because once the debt is statute-barred, the person previously entitled to enforce it ceases to have the status of 'creditor' with respect to it and so may not present a petition based on it. This analysis might seem to be open to question on the basis that the limitation statute bars the remedy but does, in respect of a personal claim for a debt, extinguish the right.

1   *Ridgeway Motors (Isleworth) Ltd v ALTS Ltd* [2005] EWCA Civ 92, [2005] 2 All ER 304 concerning a winding-up petition but expressed to apply equally to a bankruptcy petition and holding that *Re a Debtor (No 50A-SD-1995)* [1997] Ch 310, [1997] 2 All ER 789 was wrongly decided.

The debtor

8.58 The Insolvency Act 1986 does not impose any limit on the kinds of individuals who may be made bankrupt.

Foreigners and debtors residing abroad

8.59 Provided that the conditions relating to domicile, presence or residence can be met (see above), a foreign national or a British subject residing abroad may be made bankrupt in England and Wales. There is no requirement that the bankruptcy debt be incurred in the jurisdiction, nor need the petitioning creditor have any territorial connection with England or Wales[1]. A bankruptcy petition may be served out of the jurisdiction with the leave of the court[2].

1   See eg *Re Myer, ex p Pascal* (1876) 1 Ch D 509, CA; and *Cooke v Charles A Vogeler Co* [1901] AC 102, HL.
2   IR 1986, r 12.12(2).

Minors

8.60 A minor was amenable to bankruptcy under the Bankruptcy Act 1914 so long as the debt on which the petition was presented was enforceable[1]. Nothing indicates that the position should be different under the Insolvency Act 1986.

[1]   *R v Newmarket Income Tax Comrs, ex p Huxley* [1916] 1 KB 788, CA; *Re a Debtor (No 564 of 1949)* [1950] Ch 282, [1950] 1 All ER 308, CA where earlier decisions concerning minors were reviewed; *Re Davenport, ex p Bankrupt v Eric Street Properties Ltd* [1963] 2 All ER 850, [1963] 1 WLR 817, CA.

Persons incapable of managing their affairs

8.61   Incapacity is no bar to being made bankrupt. The Insolvency Rules make specific provision for proceedings in bankruptcy against a person incapacitated by reason of mental or physical infirmity[1].

[1]   IR 1986, rr 7.43–7.46.

Members of Parliament

8.62   Bankruptcy proceedings may be issued against a member of either House of Parliament, and if adjudged bankrupt the individual member is disqualified from sitting or voting in the House of Lords or House of Commons, or a committee of either House[1].

[1]   IA 1986, s 427.

Diplomats

8.63   An ambassador, a minister or a consul accredited by a foreign government is exempt from local jurisdiction, and may claim privilege from bankruptcy law even though a British subject[1]. The privilege will not apply to a British subject whose appointment had been obtained for the purpose of defeating creditors[2]. Diplomatic privileges and immunities, which now extend to senior representatives of many international organisations, are generally regulated by statute[3]. The Attorney General's statement on the instructions of the Foreign and Commonwealth Office as to the status of a person claiming immunity from judicial process on the ground of diplomatic privilege is conclusive[4].

[1]   *Macartney v Garbutt* (1890) 24 QBD 368.
[2]   *Re Cloete, ex p Cloete* (1891) 8 Morr 195, CA.
[3]   See eg Diplomatic Privileges Act 1964, International Organisations Act 1968.
[4]   *Engelke v Musmann* [1928] AC 433, HL.

Undischarged bankrupts

8.64   A bankrupt may be made the subject of a second or subsequent bankruptcy order, in respect of liabilities incurred after the commencement of the earlier bankruptcy. The Insolvency Rules contain specific provision as to the duties of an existing trustee where the bankrupt is adjudged bankrupt for a second time[1], and the Insolvency Act 1986 provides for the existing trustee to stay any distribution of after-acquired property or post-commencement income on being given the prescribed notice of the presentation of a further bankruptcy petition against the bankrupt[2].

¹   IR 1986, rr 6.225–6.228.
²   IA 1986, s 334.

The creditor

8.65 In general any creditor may petition who is owed a good petitioning debt by the debtor. However, a creditor may not present a creditor's petition if he is bound by an IVA established under IA 1986, Pt VIII¹ nor may he petition while there is in force in respect of the debtor an interim order made under IA 1986, s 252². As discussed above, a creditor whose debt is wholly secured by rights of security which the creditor continues to assert does not have a good petitioning debt³.

¹   Under IA 1986, s 260(2)(b). Such a creditor may present a petition under IA 1986, s 264(1)(c); see further para **8.250**.
²   IA 1986, s 252(2)(a).
³   See para **8.53**.

Companies

8.66 A company may present a petition as the petitioning creditor in the company's name. Where the company petitioning is in liquidation it, rather than its liquidator, remains the petitioning creditor and it should style itself in the petition as 'the AB Company Limited in Liquidation by CD its Liquidator'¹.

¹   *Re A Debtor (No 41 of 1951), ex p the Debtor v Hunter (Liquidator of Marvel Paper Products Ltd)* [1952] Ch 192, [1952] 1 All ER 107.

Partnerships

8.67 Partnerships may petition as creditors in the name of the firm provided that the partnership is carrying on business within the jurisdiction¹. As between partners, a petition may not be presented against one partner by another in a case where partnership accounts would be necessary to ascertain whether the sum was due or what the size of the sum due was. In the latter case there could not be a liquidated sum due².

¹   CPR Sch 1 RSC Ord 81 r 1.
²   See para **8.35**.

Receivers

8.68 A receiver appointed by the court may not present a petition in his own name unless he is specifically authorised to do so or he is entitled to be paid the debt in some other capacity, for example as the holder of a bill of exchange¹. A receiver appointed out of court under the terms of a charge will ordinarily thereby be appointed the agent of the chargor whose property he is authorised to receive for the benefit of the chargee; accordingly, where a debt

383

is owed to the chargor, a petition based on it must be presented in the chargor's name, not that of the receiver.

1   *Re Sacker, ex p Sacker* (1888) 22 QBD 179, CA; *Re Macoun* [1904] 2 KB 700, CA.

Assignees

8.69 Where a debt has been legally assigned under the Law of Property Act 1925, s 136 the assignee may petition without joining the assignor. Further, it has been held that an equitable assignee may petition without joining the assignor as co-petitioner because a debt to which the creditor is entitled in equity but not in law may form a good petitioning debt[1]. However, it is submitted that this decision ought not to be followed since in an action the debtor would have a defence to a claim brought by the equitable assignee alone[2]. Further, it seems that an equitable assignee cannot serve an effective statutory demand[3].

1   *Re Baillie, ex p Cooper* (1875) LR 20 Eq 762. This case was decided under the Bankruptcy Act 1869 which referred to a debt as a liquidated sum due at law or in equity; the Insolvency Act 1986 does not include such words.
2   *William Brandt's Sons & Co v Dunlop Rubber Co Ltd* [1905] AC 454, HL.
3   *Re Steel Wing Co Ltd* [1921] 1 Ch 349 (relating to demands under the Companies (Consolidation) Act 1908, s 130(1)).

Judgment creditors

8.70 A judgment creditor may petition against the judgment debtor, but a judgment creditor who has obtained a garnishee order against a third party who owes a debt to the judgment debtor may not petition against that third party[1].

1   *Re Combined Weighing and Advertising Machine Co* (1889) 43 Ch D 99, CA.

Trustees

8.71 Where the debt is trust property, all the trustees must be joined in presenting the petition.

Trustee in bankruptcy

8.72 A trustee in bankruptcy may present a petition in respect of a debt due to the bankrupt which forms part of the bankrupt's estate. He requires the permission of the creditors' committee or the court to do so[1].

1   IA 1986, s 314(1), Sch 5, para 2.

Persons under a disability

8.73 Persons under a disability may petition in the same manner as they may bring actions: a minor by his next friend; a mentally disordered person by his duly qualified representative[1].

1   CPR 21.2.

Inability to pay

Current debts

8.74 A petitioning creditor must show that the debtor appears to be unable to pay the relevant debt. Where the debt is payable immediately the debtor's inability to pay may be established by one of two sets of facts:

(1)   the petitioning creditor to whom the debt is owed may serve on the debtor a demand (known as 'the statutory demand') in the prescribed form requiring him to pay the debt or to secure or compound for it to the satisfaction of the creditor and at least three weeks must elapse from the date when the demand was served without its being complied with or set aside in accordance with the rules[1]; alternatively

(2)   where a judgment or order of any court has been made in favour of the creditor and execution or other process has been issued in respect of that judgment debt, that execution or other process must be returned unsatisfied in whole or part[2].

1   IA 1986, s 268(1)(a).
2   IA 1986, s 268(1)(b).

Future debts

8.75 In addition, the Insolvency Act 1986 provides a method of showing that the debtor appears to have no reasonable prospects of paying a debt which falls due in the future. To establish inability to pay in such a case, three conditions must be fulfilled:

(1)   the petitioning creditor to whom the debt is owed must have served on the debtor a demand (also known as the 'statutory demand') in the prescribed form requiring him to establish to the satisfaction of the creditor that there is a reasonable prospect that the debtor will be able to pay the debt when it falls due;

(2)   at least three weeks have elapsed since the demand was served; and

(3)   the demand has been neither complied with nor set aside in accordance with the rules[1].

1   IA 1986, s 268(2).

8.76 A future, contingent debt does not form a good petitioning debt against a company[1] and the position will be the same in bankruptcy because if the debt is contingent it will not be possible to know whether the debt will fall due.

¹   *JSF Finance and Currency Exchange Co Ltd v Akma Solutions Inc* [2001] 2 BCLC 307. See also *O'Driscoll v Manchester Insurance Committee* [1915] 3 KB 499 at 516–517.

The statutory demand

Form and content

8.77 The Insolvency Rules make detailed requirements as to the form and content of statutory demands[1]. There are statutory forms which must be used[2]. The requirements are as follows[3]:

(1)   the demand must be dated;

(2)   it must be signed either by the creditor[4] or by a person stating himself to be authorised to make the demand on the creditor's behalf;

(3)   it must specify whether it is made in respect of a debt payable immediately or a debt payable in the future;

(4)   it must state the amount of the debt;

(5)   it must state the consideration given for the debt or, if there is no consideration, the way in which the debt arises;

(6)   if the demand is founded on a judgment or order of a court, it must give details of the judgment or order;

(7)   if the demand is made in respect of a debt which is not payable immediately, it must state the grounds on which it is alleged that the debtor appears to have no reasonable prospect of paying the debt. Where the sum claimed in the demand is in a foreign currency, the demand need not state a sterling equivalent[5].

¹   IR 1986, rr 6.1 and 6.2.
²   IR 1986, Sch 4, Forms 6.1, 6.2 and 6.3. As a transitional measure IR 1986, r 6.36 provides that in certain circumstances bankruptcy notices served under the Bankruptcy Act 1914 will count as statutory demands for purposes of founding a petition under the new law.
³   IR 1986, r 6.1(1)–(3).
⁴   The creditor's name may be signed by another person authorised so to sign the demand. In such a case it is good practice to write 'per procurationem' or 'pp' after the signature: *Re Horne (a bankrupt)* [2000] 4 All ER 550, CA.
⁵   *Re A Debtor (No 51-SD-1991) ex p Ritchie Bros Auctioneers v Debtor* [1993] 2 All ER 40, [1992] 1 WLR 1294.

Interest or other charges

8.78 If the amount claimed in the demand includes (a) any charge by way of interest not previously notified to the debtor as a liability of his, or (b) any other charge accruing from time to time, the amount or rate of the charge must be separately identified, and the grounds on which payment of it is claimed must be stated. In either case the amount claimed must be limited to that which has accrued due at the date of the demand[1].

¹   IR 1986, r 6.1(4).

Secured debts

8.79 If the creditor holds any security in respect of the debt, the full amount of the debt must be specified in the demand, but (a) there must also be specified the nature of the security and the value which the creditor puts upon it as at the date of the demand, and (b) the amount payment of which is claimed by the demand must be the amount of payment obtained by reducing the full debt by the amount specified as the value of the security[1]. Failure to comply with this rule may lead to the demand being set aside[2]. Security which must be disclosed in the demand is security according to the statutory definition given in the IA 1986, s 383. Thus there is no requirement to disclose a guarantee given by a third party[3].

1   IR 1986, r 6.1(5).
2   IR 1986, r 6.5(4)(c).
3   *Re A Debtor (No 310 of 1988), ex p Debtor v Arab Bank Ltd* [1989] 2 All ER 42, [1989] 1 WLR 452.

Legal explanation

8.80 The demand must carry an explanation of its legal effect. In particular it must explain:

(a)   the purpose of the demand, and the fact that, if the debtor does not comply with the demand, bankruptcy proceedings may be commenced against him;
(b)   the time within which the demand must be complied with, if that consequence is to be avoided;
(c)   the methods of compliance which are open to the debtor; and
(d)   his right to apply to the court for the statutory demand to be set aside[1].

1   IR 1986, r 6.2(1).

8.81 To assist the debtor to comply with the demand it must specify one or more named individuals with whom the debtor may, if he wishes, enter into communication with a view to securing or compounding for the debt to the satisfaction of the creditor or (as the case may be) establishing to the creditor's satisfaction that there is a reasonable prospect that the debt will be paid when it falls due. The address and telephone number (if any) of such a named individual must also be given[1].

1   IR 1986, r 6.2(2).

Nature of a statutory demand

8.82–8.83 A statutory demand is not issued by the court and has been described as an extra-judicial document[1] and a non-legal process[2]. To serve a statutory demand is not to bring an action. Thus a statutory demand may be served before the expiration of one month from the date on which a solicitor's bill of costs is delivered by him to his client, during which period the solicitor is prohibited by the Solicitors Act 1974, s 69(1) from bringing an action to recover the costs claimed in the bill[3]. Nor does the service of a statutory demand relating to a debt under an agreement regulated by the Consumer Credit Act 1974 constitute an action to enforce that agreement[4].

[1]   *Re a Debtor (No 190 of 1987)* (1988) Times, 21 May.
[2]   *Re a Debtor (No 88 of 1991)* [1993] Ch 286, [1992] 4 All ER 301.
[3]   *Re a Debtor (No 88 of 1991)* [1993] Ch 286, [1992] 4 All ER 301.
[4]   *Mills v Grove Securities Ltd* [1997] BPIR 243, CA.

8.84 Leave is not required to serve a statutory demand out of the jurisdiction because of its extra-judicial character[1].

[1]   *Re a Debtor (No 190 of 1987)* (1988) Times, 21 May; CPR *Practice Direction: Insolvency Proceedings*, para 10.1; see further para **8.89**.

Service of the statutory demand

8.85 The creditor should do all that is reasonable for the purpose of bringing the statutory demand to the debtor's attention and, if practicable in the particular circumstances, to cause personal service of the demand to be effected[1].

[1]   IR 1986, r 6.3(2). See *Regional Collection Services v Heald* [2000] BPIR 661, CA.

8.86 Various forms of substituted service may be employed, but before using them, the creditor must take all those steps which would justify the making of an order for the substituted service of a petition. Those steps are set out in para **8.154** below. If the creditor has purported to effect substituted service but those steps have not been taken (or there is no evidence that they have been taken), then the court may decline to file the petition or, when the petition is heard, the court may dismiss it[1]. In *Andrews v Bohm*[2] it was held even though an order made in other proceedings which provided for substituted service in bankruptcy proceedings was made without jurisdiction, service of the statutory demand effected in accordance with that order constituted good service of the statutory demand but service by the same method of the petition was not effective under IR 1986, r 6.14.

[1]   CPR *Practice Direction: Insolvency Proceedings*, para 11.3.
[2]   [2005] EWHC 3520 (Ch), [2005] All ER (D) 161 (Jul).

8.87 Where it is not possible to effect prompt personal service, service may be effected by other means such as first-class post or by insertion through a letter box[1]. The address for such service will be the debtor's usual or last known residence or, if he is the proprietor of a business, his usual or last known place of business[2]. But there must be doubt that a statutory demand posted to, or left at, the debtor's last known address will be effective where there is doubt that the debtor retains any connection with that address.

[1]   CPR *Practice Direction: Insolvency Proceedings*, para 11.1.
[2]   CPR r 6.5(6) which applies by virtue of IR 1986, r 12.11.

8.88 Service of a statutory demand by publishing an advertisement in one or more newspapers may only be used where (1) the demand is based on a judgment or order of any court, (2) the debtor has absconded or is keeping out of the way with a view to avoiding service, and (3) there is no real prospect of the sum due being recovered by execution or other process[1]. In the second of these conditions, the word 'absconded' is used as meaning that the debtor has left the place where he formerly resided without leaving a forwarding address or other means of discovering his present address so that he cannot be found by any reasonable endeavour; it is not therefore necessary to adduce evidence of the debtor's state of mind in order to show that the condition is satisfied[2]. The purpose of the advertisement as a form of service is to try to bring the statutory demand to the debtor's attention. If, therefore, at the hearing of the petition when the petitioner must show that the statutory demand has been served, the petitioner adduces evidence which shows that the advertisement is, on the balance of probabilities, likely to have brought the statutory demand to the debtor's attention, that will suffice. It is wrong to require proof, in such a case, that the demand has actually come to the debtor's attention. Thus, where a judgment debtor, formerly living in Wales, was thought to be living in the London area, advertisement in a London evening paper and a national paper was held sufficient[3]. The Practice Direction sets out a form of advertisement to be used[4]. Time for compliance with the demand runs from the date of the advertisement's appearance, or its first appearance if published more than once[5].

[1] IR 1986, r 6.3(3); CPR *Practice Direction: Insolvency Proceedings*, para 11.2.
[2] *Lilly v Davison* [1999] BPIR 81.
[3] *Lilly v Davison* [1999] BPIR 81.
[4] CPR *Practice Direction: Insolvency Proceedings*, para 11.2.
[5] IR 1986, r 6.3(3).

8.89 A statutory demand may be served abroad and, because it is not a document issued by the court, leave (or permission) to serve out of the jurisdiction is not required[1]. The same obligation to bring the demand to the debtor's attention, by personal service if practicable, applies[2]. A creditor who wishes to serve a statutory demand in a foreign country with which a civil procedure convention has been made (including the Hague Convention[3]) may and, if the assistance of a British Consul is required, must adopt the procedure prescribed by CPR 6.25[4]. In all other cases, service of the statutory demand must be effected by private arrangement in accordance with IR 1986, r 6.3(2) and local foreign law[5]. When a statutory demand is to be served out of the jurisdiction, the time limits of 21 days and 18 days respectively referred to in the demand must be amended by reference to the table set out in the practice direction supplementing CPR Pt 6[6]. For the period of 18 days there should be substituted the appropriate number of days set out in the table plus four days; and for the period of 21 days, the appropriate number of days in the table plus seven days[7]. A debtor wishing to maximise the period for complying with a demand should take himself to the New Zealand Island Territories: the number of days in the table is 50 and so the substitutions to be made in the demand are 54 days in place of 18 days and 57 in place of 21. The practice direction draws attention to the fact that in all forms of statutory demand the figure 18 and the figure 21 (in connection with periods of time measured in days) occurs in more than one place.

8.89 *Bankruptcy petitions*

1   *Re a Debtor (No 190 of 1987)* (1988) Times, 21 May; CPR *Practice Direction: Insolvency Proceedings*, para 10.1.
2   CPR *Practice Direction: Insolvency Proceedings*, para 10.2.
3   The Convention on the service abroad of judicial and extra-judicial documents in civil or commercial matters signed at the Hague on 15 November 1965; Cmnd 3986 (1969).
4   CPR *Practice Direction: Insolvency Proceedings*, para 10.3. RSC Ord 11 r 6 is contained in CPR Sch 1. In the case of any doubt whether a country is a 'convention country', enquiries should be made of the Queen's Bench Masters' Secretary Department, Room E216, Royal Courts of Justice.
5   CPR *Practice Direction: Insolvency Proceedings*, para 10.4.
6   CPR *Practice Direction: Insolvency Proceedings*, para 10.5.
7   CPR *Practice Direction: Insolvency Proceedings*, para 10.6.

Compliance with the demand

8.90 Where the demand is made on the basis of a debt which is due at the time the demand is made, the debtor must pay the debt in full[1], unless the debt is disputed in which case he should apply to set it aside. If the debt is admitted in part but the balance is disputed, the debtor should pay the debt in so far as it is undisputed and, if the demand is not withdrawn, apply to set it aside as to the disputed part[2].

1   Or at least reduce it to below the minimum debt, presently £750.
2   IR 1986, r 6.25(3); *Re A Debtor (No 490-SD-1991), ex p Debtor v Printline (Offset) Ltd* [1992] 2 All ER 664, [1992] 1 WLR 507.

8.91 In the case of a demand made on a future debt which the creditor alleges that the debtor will not be able to pay when it falls due, the debtor is required, within three weeks of the demand being served, to establish to the creditor's satisfaction that there is a reasonable prospect that he will be able to pay on the due date[1].

1   IA 1986, s 267(2).

Setting the statutory demand aside

Outline of grounds on which a statutory demand may be set aside

8.92 On hearing the debtor's application, the court may set a statutory demand aside if:

(a)   the debtor appears to have a counterclaim, set-off or cross demand which equals or exceeds the amount of the debt or debts specified in the statutory demand;

(b)   the debt is disputed on grounds which appear to the court to be substantial;

(c)   it appears that the creditor holds some security in respect of the debt claimed by the demand, and either IR 1986, r 6.1(5)[1] is not complied with in respect of it, or the court is satisfied that the value of the security equals or exceeds the full amount of the debt; or

(d)   the court is satisfied, on other grounds, that the demand ought to be set aside[2].

1   IR 1986, r 6.1(5) requires the demand to specify any security held and to put a value on it; see para **8.79**.
2   IR 1986, r 6.5(4). As a summary procedure, disclosure is not appropriate: *Worrall v Landau* [2003] EWHC 3111 (Ch), [2004] BPIR 370.

Counterclaim, set-off or cross demand

8.93   Ground (a) concerns the case where the debt on which the demand is based is itself undisputed but the debtor contends that he has a counterclaim, set-off or cross demand against the creditor the value of which equals or exceeds the creditor's claim on him[1].

1   IR 1986, r 6.5(4)(a).

Types of cross claim which the debtor may rely on

8.94   'Cross demand' has a wider meaning than counterclaim or set-off. Thus, even where the creditor's demand is based on a debt arising from a cheque or bill of exchange, the debtor may raise a counterclaim for the purpose of seeking to set aside the demand, even though he would not be able to do so for the purpose of resisting summary judgment in an action[1]. Similarly a cross claim may provide an answer in insolvency proceedings to a demand for payment of freight[2]. Equally, a debtor may rely on a cross demand where the demand is based on a judgment or order and, according to the *Practice Direction: Insolvency Proceedings*, he may do so, whether or not he could have raised the cross demand in the action in which the judgment or order was obtained[3]. Where a litigant has obtained an order for costs against his adversary, that adversary may rely on the value of his pending claim in the litigation to defeat a statutory demand based on the costs order[4].

1   *Hofer v Strawson* [1999] BPIR 501.
2   *Re Bayoil SA, Seawind Tankers Corpn v Bayoil SA* [1999] 1 All ER 374, [1999] 1 BCLC 62 (winding-up petition based on claim for freight).
3   CPR *Practice Direction: Insolvency Proceedings*, para 12.4.
4   *Popeley v Popeley* [2004] BPIR 778.

Mutuality

8.95   The debtor's cross claim must be one which is capable of liquidating the debt on which the statutory demand is made[1]. It may be that in appropriate circumstances the debtor may raise a cross claim in a different capacity from that under which he is himself pursued[2]. But where the demand was made on one partner by trustees, themselves being some of the partners in a firm, holding partnership property on trust for all the partners pursuant to the trustees' entitlement to an indemnity, the debtor could not raise as a cross claim his claim against all the other partners for his share of the partnership assets.

1   *Hurst v Bennett* [2001] EWCA Civ 182, [2001] 2 BCLC 290. See also *Southward v Banham* [2002] BPIR 1253 where *Hurst v Bennett* was followed.
2   *Re a Debtor (No 87 of 1999)* [2000] BPIR 589.

No requirement that debtor has been unable previously to litigate the cross claim

8.96   In the context of a winding-up petition presented against a company, it has been suggested that the company seeking to resist the petition on the footing of a cross demand should have been unable earlier to have litigated the cross demand[1]. In relation to statutory demands in bankruptcy, such a requirement is at odds with the terms of the Practice Direction noted in the last paragraph. In *Garrow v Society of Lloyds* the Court of Appeal held that no such requirement applies in relation to applications under IR 1986, r 6.5(4)(a)[2]. In any event it is doubtful whether it applies with respect to companies[3].

1   *Re Bayoil SA, Seawind Tankers Corpn v Bayoil SA* [1999] 1 All ER 374, [1999] 1 BCLC 62; *Popeley v Popeley* [2004] BPIR 778.
2   [1999] BPIR 885; see also *Re a Debtor (No 87 of 1999)* [2000] BPIR 589.
3   *Montgomery v Wanda Modes Ltd* [2001] 1 BCLC 289.

Standard

8.97   Clearly it does not suffice simply that the debtor asserts that he has a cross claim. The standard to which the debtor must establish his cross claim is not specified in IR 1986, r 6.5(4); by contrast, the rule requires in paragraph (b) that, where a debt is disputed, it must be disputed on substantial grounds. The standard relating to cross claims is similar and various phrases have been used to define or describe it. The court will normally set aside the statutory demand if, in its opinion, on the evidence there is a genuine triable issue in respect of the counterclaim, set-off or cross demand relied on by the debtor[1]. This formulation of the test was applied by the Court of Appeal in *TSB Bank plc v Platts*[2] and in *Garrow v Society of Lloyds*[3]. In *Hofer v Strawson*[4] Neuberger J (as he then was) suggested that the test was not dissimilar from that which applies under CPR Pt 24, namely that it requires the debtor to show that he has a real prospect of succeeding on the cross demand[5]. In *Lloyd's v Bowman*[6] the Court of Appeal observed that where a judge of the High Court had already decided that the debtor's counterclaims had no prospect of success and had refused permission to appeal, a judge sitting in the bankruptcy court should be slow to hold that IR 1986, r 6.5(4)(a) had been satisfied. Whether the debtor has established that he has a sufficiently strong cross claim is a matter for the bankruptcy court. The fact that the debtor has issued proceedings based on his cross claim does not prevent an application for the statutory demand to be set aside from being determined by the court[7].

1   CPR *Practice Direction: Insolvency Proceedings*, para 12.4.
2   [1998] 2 BCLC 1. And see also *McAllister v Society of Lloyds* [1999] BPIR 548 (Carnwath J); *Garrow v Society of Lloyds* [1999] BPIR 668 (Jacob J) and [1999] BPIR 885, CA and *Gustavii v Moore* [2003] EWHC 2390 (Ch), [2004] BPIR 268.
3   [1999] BPIR 885, CA.
4   [1999] 2 BCLC 336, [1999] BPIR 501. He expressed a similar view in *Guinan v Caldwell Associates Ltd* [2003] EWHC 3348 (Ch), [2004] BPIR 531 at 538, doubting the utility in distinguishing between different types of test.

5   For other examples of cases where the standard has been discussed see *BBR Graphics Engineering (Yorkshire) Ltd v Kellar* [2003] EWHC 858 (QB), [2002] BPIR 544; *Martin v Lanesborough Management Ltd* [2005] All ER (D) 260 (Jun) and *Wilson v Edwards* [2006] BPIR 367.
6   [2004] BPIR 324.
7   *Jens Hills & Co v Byrd* [2003] All ER (D) 97 (May).

Amount

8.98 It is sufficient to show, to the court's satisfaction, that the value of the cross demand equals or exceeds the amount of the debt, or at least that it reduces it below the statutory minimum[1]. However, it is not necessary that the cross demand be precisely quantified[2].

1   *AIB Finance Ltd v Debtors* [1997] 4 All ER 677, [1997] 2 BCLC 354 (Carnwath J).
2   *Garrow v Society of Lloyds* [1999] BPIR 668 (Jacob J) and [1999] BPIR 885.

Creditor's defence to the cross claim

8.99 In evaluating the cross-demand, the court may take into account any equitable set-off on which the creditor may rely as a defence to the cross demand, even though the claim on which such set-off is based does not form part of the debt on which the statutory demand is based[1]. Where appropriate the debtor's cross claim may be defeated by a reverse cross claim available to the creditor[2].

1   *TSB Bank plc v Platts (No 2)* [1998] BPIR 284, CA.
2   *Montgomery v Wanda Modes Ltd* [2001] 1 BCLC 289.

Contractual exclusion of right to raise a cross claim to a statutory demand

8.100 It is an open question whether it is possible by contract validly to exclude a person's right to rely on a cross demand under IR 1986, r 6.5(4)(a)[1].

1   *Garrow v Society of Lloyds* [1999] BPIR 885, CA in which the argument failed because the court found as a matter of construction that the contract did not have that effect and so the question of the validity of such a contractual term did not arise.

Disputed debt

8.101 The court may set aside the statutory demand if the debt on which it is based is disputed on grounds which appear to the court to be substantial[1].

1   IR 1986, r 6.5(4)(b). For a recent example of what does not constitute 'substantial' see *Williamson v Governor and Co of the Bank of Scotland* [2006] EWHC 1289 (Ch), [2006] All ER (D) 323 (Mar).

Judgment debts

8.102 In practice, a distinction is drawn between judgment debts[1] and other debts. Where the debt is a judgment debt, the court will not at the stage of the statutory demand go behind the judgment and inquire into the validity of the debt, nor, as a general rule, will it adjourn the application to set the demand aside to await the result of an application to set the judgment aside[2]. These questions will be addressed at the hearing of the petition[3]. The advantage to the creditor of allowing matters to proceed is that he can present a petition at an earlier date, even if the hearing of that petition is subsequently adjourned. The date of presentation is important, if a bankruptcy order is later made, for the purpose of preventing dispositions of assets and of recovering assets disposed of at an undervalue or by way of preference[4].

[1] By 'judgment debt' is meant any judgment or order of the court to pay money.
[2] *Practice Direction: Insolvency Proceedings*, para 12.3. *Morley v IRC* [1996] BPIR 452. Cf *Re a Debtor (No 383/SD/92)*, *Neely v IRC* (1992) 66 TC 131; *Coverdale v Inland Revenue* [2006] EWHC 2244.
[3] See IR 1986, r 6.25(2).
[4] See IA 1986, ss 284(3) and 341(1) and eg *Neely v IRC* [1996] BPIR 662. The far-reaching effects of these sections militate against allowing a petition to be presented and then be adjourned for a long period where the statutory demand is of doubtful validity; see *Garrow v Society of Lloyd's* [1999] BPIR 885, CA (cross-demand case).

Debts other than judgment debts

8.103 Where the debt is not a judgment debt, the court will normally set a demand aside if, in its opinion, on the evidence there is a genuine triable issue as to the validity of the debt[1]. In the context of winding up, presentation of a winding-up petition has been described as a high-risk strategy where the dispute has already emerged[2]. If the defence giving rise to the dispute is based on a pure point of law, the court hearing the application to set the demand aside is entitled to decide that dispute[3].

[1] *Re a Debtor (Nos 49 and 50 of 1992)* [1995] Ch 66, CA; *Practice Direction: Insolvency Proceedings*, para 12.4. See also para **8.101** above concerning the test to be applied.
[2] *Re a Company (No 0012209 of 1991)* [1992] 2 All ER 797, [1992] 1 WLR 351 (Hoffmann J).
[3] *Cale v Assiuodoman KPS (Harrow) Ltd* [1996] BPIR 245.

Date by reference to which the dispute is to be assessed

8.104 In *Sullivan v Samuel Montagu & Co Ltd*[1] the judge, founding himself on the use of the present tense in IR 1986, r 6.5(4)(b), opined in *obiter dicta* that the issue whether a debt is disputed is to be resolved with reference to the position at the time of the hearing, not the time of the demand. A result to similar effect occurred in *Coulter v Chief Constable of Dorset Police*[2] where a statutory demand was served by the current chief constable in respect of a judgment debt obtained by the previous chief constable, but the judgment debt was assigned to the current chief constable by the former chief constable before the debtor's application to set the demand aside came on for hearing. The Court of Appeal held that the district judge had rightly dismissed the application: there was in the circumstances no injustice to the debtor.

[1] [1999] BPIR 316.
[2] [2004] EWCA Civ 1259, [2005] 1 WLR 130.

Dispute as to part of the debt

8.105 The demand will not be set aside if the dispute only relates to part of the debt[1]. Thus an overstatement of the level of debt in the statutory demand is not a ground on which it can be set aside and was no defence to the petition, provided that the amount actually due exceeds the bankruptcy limit[2]. But the court will set the demand aside under ground (d) if the undisputed part is less than the bankruptcy minimum of £750[3].

1   *Re a Debtor (No 1 of 1987, Lancaster), ex p Debtor v Royal Bank of Scotland plc* [1989] 2 All ER 46, [1989] 1 WLR 271, CA and *Re a Debtor (No 490-SD-1991), ex p Debtor v Printline (Offset) Ltd* [1992] 2 All ER 664, [1992] 1 WLR 507 (Hoffmann J) in which the judge recognised that his earlier decision in *Re a Debtor (No 10 of 1988, Aylesbury) ex p Lovell Construction (Southern) Ltd v Debtor* [1989] 2 All ER 39, [1989] 1 WLR 405 had been implied overruled by the Court of Appeal in *Re a Debtor (No 1 of 1987, Lancaster), ex p Debtor v Royal Bank of Scotland plc* [1989] 2 All ER 46, [1989] 1 WLR 271, CA.
2   *Takavarasha v Newham London Borough Council* [2006] BPIR 311 and *Southwark London Borough Council v Mohammed* [2006] EWHC 305 (Ch), [2006] BPIR 782.
3   *Re a Debtor (Nos 49 and 50 of 1992)* [1995] Ch 66, CA and see further para **8.112** below.

Security

8.106 What is meant by 'security' has been discussed at para **8.53** above. IR 1986, r 6.5(4)(c) provides that the court may grant the application to set the demand aside if the creditor holds some security in respect of his debt and either the security is not properly specified in the demand or the court is satisfied that its value equals or exceeds the debt. An offer of security does not amount to security[1]. Such an offer would fall to be considered at the hearing of the petition[2].

1   *King v IRC* [1996] BPIR 414 (Mummery J).
2   IA 1986, s 271(3).

Burden on debtor to show value of the security

8.107 In *Khan v Breezevale SARL*[1] the debt comprised the unpaid price of shares in a company which the creditor was entitled by an option contract to require the debtor to buy. The security was the creditor's lien over the shares as an unpaid vendor. No reference was made to this lien in the statutory demand. However, the shares were shares in a company of which the debtor was the controlling director. His application to set the demand aside failed because he did not establish that he had suffered any prejudice by reason of the defect in the demand. It would have been easy for him in the circumstances to show what the value of the lien was but he did not adduce any valuation evidence in respect of the shares or any evidence of ability to pay the difference between the admitted debt and whatever value the lien might have.

1   [1996] BPIR 190.

Valuing the security

8.108 Where the value of the security is disputed, the court may determine the dispute on the hearing of the application to set aside and it may receive oral evidence for that purpose. A direction for the cross-examination of any valuers whose evidence is disputed should be sought at an early stage. The question for the court is whether it is satisfied that the value of the security equals or exceeds the debt; this imposes a higher test than under grounds (a) and (b). However, the court may act within the scope of its powers by considering the evidence available to it at the hearing[1], even where that evidence is incomplete. In *Platts v Western Trust & Savings Ltd*[2] the Court of Appeal upheld a decision not to set the demand aside where the district judge exercising the original jurisdiction had simply read the valuation reports tendered by either side and decided that she could not be satisfied by the debtor's valuation evidence that the value to be put on the security equalled or exceeded the debt. The dismissal of the appeal was reinforced by the fact that the question would have to be revisited on the hearing of the petition[3]. But it should be noted that the Court of Appeal expressly recognised that other cases might well arise where the court hearing the application to set the demand aside would properly take the view that justice would best be served by determining the issue of valuation on full evidence before the petition was presented. The result in *Platts v Western Trust & Savings Ltd*[4] is perhaps best viewed as depending on the fact that the debtor had not sought or complied with such directions, including a direction for cross-examination, as would have been appropriate to ensure that complete evidence was before the court on the application to set the demand aside.

1   IR 1986, r 6.5(3).
2   [1996] BPIR 339, CA.
3   See IA 1986, s 271(1)(a).
4   [1996] BPIR 339, CA.

Costs of enforcing security not included

8.109 In *Owo-Samson v Barclays Bank plc*[1] the Court of Appeal held that the creditor was not entitled to add estimated costs of future enforcement to the debt so as to contend that it was not fully secured.

1   [2003] EWCA Civ 714, [2003] 28 LS Gaz R 30.

Other grounds

8.110 The court may set the demand aside if satisfied, on other grounds, that it ought to be. The circumstances which normally will be required for the court to set aside a demand under this residual power are circumstances which would make it unjust in the particular case to allow the statutory demand to stand and form the basis of a bankruptcy petition[1]. Various examples follow but obviously the category is an open one.

1   *Re a Debtor (No 1 of 1987, Lancaster), ex p Debtor v Royal Bank of Scotland plc* [1989]
    1 WLR 271, 276, CA; *Re a Debtor (No 490-SD-1991) ex p Debtor v Printline
    (Offset) Ltd* [1992] 2 All ER 664, [1992] 1 WLR 507. Cf *Morley v IRC* [1996] BPIR 452
    (Ferris J) overstatement of the debt, without more, does not justify setting the demand
    aside whether by reference to ground (b) or ground (d).

Misleading demand

8.111 The fact that a demand contains mistakes, in particular an overstatement of the amount of the debt, or other defects will not necessarily lead
to its being set aside but it may be if it is so confusing and misleading that,
having regard to all the circumstances, justice requires that it should be; a
particularly important point would be whether the debtor had in fact been
misled or otherwise prejudiced[1].

1   *Re a Debtor (No 1 of 1987, Lancaster), ex p Debtor v Royal Bank of Scotland plc* [1989]
    1 WLR 271, 276, CA.

Debt below statutory level

8.112 A statutory demand will be set aside if there is no good purpose to be
served in allowing it to stand. Thus in *Re a Debtor (Nos 49 and 50 of 1992)*[1]
the Court of Appeal held that a statutory demand should be set aside under
ground (d) where the balance of indebtedness was less than the bankruptcy
level[2]. In *City Electrical Factors Ltd v Hardinham*[3] the decision of a district
judge to set aside a demand based on an undisputed debt of £756.96 was
upheld on appeal, where the debtor had shown that he was making good
efforts to pay the debt, which was the reduced balance of a higher debt, and
where, at the suggestion of the district judge, the debtor paid £10 at the
hearing of the application to set aside thereby reducing the undisputed part
below the bankruptcy minimum.

1   [1995] Ch 66.
2   £750 by virtue of IA 1986, s 267(4).
3   [1996] BPIR 541.

Time-barred debt

8.113 Although a bankruptcy petition cannot be statute-barred under the
Limitation Act 1980, s 24(1) where it is based on a judgment debt, a petition
will, it appears, be statute-barred where the debt is not a judgment debt and
an action to enforce the debt would be barred[1]. Accordingly, it would still
seem to be right to set aside a statutory demand based on a debt other than a
judgment debt where enforcement of the debt was statute-barred[2].

1   *Ridgeway Motors (Isleworth) Ltd v ALTS Ltd* [2005] EWCA Civ 92, [2005] 2 All ER 304.
2   See *Re a debtor (No 50A-SD-1995)* [1997] Ch 310, [1997] 2 All ER 789 where this was
    the course taken with respect to a statutory demand based on a judgment debt; this
    decision has been held to be wrongly decided in so far as it was based on the proposition
    that a petition based on a judgment debt may be time-barred under the Limitation

Act 1980, s 24(1), but it appears that petitions may not be presented which are based on non-judgment debts which have become time-barred; see *Ridgeway Motors (Isleworth) Ltd v ALTS Ltd.*

Cases where the court has declined to set aside a demand under the residual ground

8.114 The fact that the debtor has made an offer to compound is not a reason for setting aside the demand; the time to consider such an offer is at the hearing of the petition pursuant to IA 1986, s 271[1].

[1]   *Re a Debtor (No 415/SD/93), ex p Debtor v IRC* [1994] 2 All ER 168.

8.115 In *Turner v Turner*[1] a registrar's decision to set aside a statutory demand on the basis that the making of a bankruptcy order would stifle a probate claim to challenge the validity of a will was overturned on appeal. Peter Smith J held that the probate claim was made by the debtor in a representative capacity and therefore would not fall into the bankrupt's estate and could be continued by the debtor after a bankruptcy order had been made. Therefore this was not a good reason upon which the statutory demand should be set aside under ground (d). In *Shuttari v Solicitors' Indemnity Fund Ltd*[2] an application to set aside the statutory demand under IR 1986, r 6.5(4)(d), on the basis that a bankruptcy petition would sterilise the debtor's ability to bring proceedings in the European Court of Human Rights and create a risk of inconsistent findings in parallel proceedings, was unsuccessful.

[1]   [2006] EWHC 2023 (Ch), [2006] All ER (D) 63 (Jul).
[2]   [2005] BPIR 1004.

8.116 In *TS & S Global Ltd v Fithian-Franks*[1] the creditor served a statutory demand on a guarantor without first serving demands under the guarantee. Although the guarantee was expressed to be on demand, the guarantor's liability was expressed to be a primary liability and so was presently due even if no demand was made. But in *obiter dicta* the court opined that on the facts of the case, where it was apparent that the debtor would not in any event have complied with the demand, it would still not have been appropriate, in the exercise of the court's discretion, to have set aside the demand.

[1]   [2007] EWHC 1401 (Ch), [2007] All ER (D) 171 (Jun).

Future debts

8.117 Where the demand has been made on the basis of a future debt, the debtor may rely on the grounds provided by IR 1986, r 6.5(4)(a)–(c) if applicable but where the debtor's case is that there is a reasonable prospect that he will be able to pay the debt when it falls due he will have to rely on the residual discretion to set aside under IR 1986, r 6.5(4)(d). Although the provisions of the Insolvency Act 1986 directed towards cases involving future debts may be taken to indicate that the draughtsman envisaged that the dispute would arise at the hearing of the petition[1], it would be unwise for a debtor to wait for that hearing since when the petition is filed notice of it will be sent to the Chief Land Registrar for registration[2].

1   See eg the provision for security for the debtor's costs of the petition; IR 1986, r 6.17 discussed at para **8.150**.
2   IR 1986, r 6.13.

Applicable test in connection with a future debt

8.118 Compliance with a demand by a creditor in respect of a future debt means establishing to the creditor's satisfaction that there is a reasonable prospect that the debt will be paid when it falls due[1]. That means that where the debtor has attempted to do this but the creditor has not been satisfied by the attempt the court has a choice as to the test it should apply on an application to set aside the demand by the debtor, either:

(1)   did the creditor act reasonably in refusing to accept the information provided by the debtor as showing a reasonable prospect of payment? or

(2)   is there, in the court's own view, no reasonable prospect of payment?

1   IA 1986, s 268(2)(a).

8.119 It is submitted that the second of these tests is the one which should be adopted. First, it is the test which applies on the hearing of the petition based on a future debt[1]. Secondly, consideration of whether the creditor's view is reasonable is a distraction from what ought to be the central issue which is whether the debtor is insolvent in the sense that he is or will be unable to pay his debts when they fall due. Thirdly, the second test ought to favour the debtor and it is appropriate that the applicable test should favour the debtor given that the debt has not yet fallen due.

1   IA 1986, s 271(1)(b).

8.120 In applying the test the assumption which applies on the hearing of the petition that the prospect given by the facts and matters known to the creditor at the time he entered into the transaction resulting in the debt was a reasonable prospect[1] ought to apply.

1   IA 1986, s 271(4).

8.121 If the second test is the correct one, it follows that the court should set aside the demand where the debtor shows on the application to set aside that there is a reasonable prospect of payment, even though he has made no attempt to establish this to the creditor's satisfaction before the hearing of the application to set aside. Perhaps, in such case, if the debtor has acted unreasonably in failing to attempt to show the creditor that there is a reasonable prospect of payment before making the application, an order for costs might be made against the debtor despite the application succeeding.

Procedure for applications to set aside a statutory demand

Time for making the application

8.122   The application to set the demand aside must be made within 18 days from the date of service on the debtor of the demand[1]. If the application is late the debtor must add to the witness statement or affidavit in support of the application paragraphs deposing (1) that to the best of the debtor's knowledge and belief the creditor has not presented a petition against him; (2) what the reasons for the failure to apply in time are; and (3), if appropriate, a statement that the creditor may present a petition against the debtor unless restrained by injunction[2]. An injunction restraining presentation of the petition is necessary because an application made out of time is not effective to prevent the presentation of a petition[3]. The balance of convenience would almost always justify the granting of an injunction in such a case unless the application to set aside was made on grounds which would entitle the court to dismiss the application without a hearing[4].

[1]   IR 1986, r 6.4(1).
[2]   *Practice Direction: Insolvency Proceedings*, para 12.5; note that the application should now be made to the Registrar.
[3]   *Chohan v Times Newspapers Ltd* [2001] BPIR 187.
[4]   See IR 1986, r 6.5(1) and paragraph below.

Court to which the application should be made

8.123   The appropriate court to which the application should be made is that to which a debtor would present his own bankruptcy petition[1]. The exception is where the creditor is a Minister of the Crown or a Government Department and (a) the debt is the subject of a judgment or order of any court, and (b) the statutory demand specifies the date of the judgment or order and the court in which it was obtained, but indicates the creditor's intention to present a bankruptcy petition against the debtor in the High Court[2]. The application must be supported by a witness statement or an affidavit, which must specify the date on which the statutory demand came into the hands of the debtor and state the grounds on which he claims that it should be set aside[3].

[1]   See para **8.131**.
[2]   IR 1986, r 6.4(2). IR 1986, r 6.40(1)–(3) set out which is the appropriate court for a debtor's petition.
[3]   IR 1986, r 6.4(4).

Disposal without hearing

8.124   If the application to set the demand aside obviously does not disclose sufficient cause, the court may dismiss it without giving notice to the creditor[1]. If the application is not dismissed without a hearing, the court will fix a venue for it to be heard. Seven days' notice of the hearing must be given to (a) the debtor or his solicitor, (b) the creditor, and (c) any individual named in the demand as the person with whom the debtor may communicate with reference to the demand[2]. On consideration of the evidence available at the hearing, the court may either determine the application summarily or adjourn it with such directions as it thinks appropriate[3].

1   IR 1986, r 6.5(1).
2   IR 1986, r 6.5(2).
3   IR 1986, r 6.5(3).

Suspension of time to comply with the statutory demand

8.125 Time for compliance with the demand ceases to run when the application is filed at court[1]. If the application to set the demand aside is dismissed, time will begin to run again from the date of that dismissal[2]. However, the date on which the petition is to be presented will be affected by the order which, on dismissing the application, the court must make authorising the creditor to present the petition either forthwith or on or after a date specified in that order[3].

1   IR 1986, r 6.4(3).
2   IR 1986, r 6.5(1).
3   IR 1986, r 6.5(6).

Costs of application to set aside statutory demand

8.126 An application to set a statutory demand aside is a set of proceedings in which the question for determination is whether the demand should be upheld or set aside. Thus where a creditor agrees that a demand should be set aside after the debtor has issued his application to set it aside, the creditor will ordinarily be liable to pay the debtor's costs[1]. In *McLinden v Redbond*[2] despite the successful defence of a set aside application and an allegation that that application had been made dishonestly, the court refused to make an order for costs on an indemnity basis against the debtor.

1   *Liveras v a Debtor (No 620 of 1997)* [1999] BPIR 89 (Hart J). Cf *Re Cannon Screen Entertainment Ltd* [1989] BCLC 660; *Re Fernforest* Ltd [1990] BCLC 693; *GlaxoSmith-Kline Export Ltd v UK (Aid) Ltd* [2004] BPIR 528.
2   [2006] EWHC 234 (Ch), [2006] All ER (D) 320 (Feb).

Appeals from applications to set statutory demands aside

8.127 Neither party requires leave to appeal from the decision on an application to set a statutory demand aside[1]. The appeal lies to a single judge of the High Court.

1   *Practice Direction: Insolvency Proceedings*, para 17.2(3).

8.128 On hearing the appeal the court may determine the matter or, if appropriate, remit the matter to the court below[1]. Guidance on the admission of new evidence on appeal can be found in *Sadrolashrafi v Marvel International Food Logistics Ltd*[2].

8.128   *Bankruptcy petitions*

1   See, for an example of remission, *Sinclair v IRC* [1996] BPIR 482 where the case was
    remitted to allow evidence to be adduced of the service of a notice, which was a
    pre-condition of the liability to pay tax on which the demand was based.
2   [2004] BPIR 834.

8.129   Under the rules governing appeals which were in force before 2 May
2000 it was a vexed question whether fresh evidence might be received by the
court on an appeal from the determination of an application to set aside a
statutory demand. The difficulty arose because it was unclear whether the
hearing of the application was a hearing of the proceedings on the merits.
However, the new rules governing appeals do not give rise to the same
question[1]. The court hearing the appeal will exercise its power to receive
evidence that was not before the lower court in accordance with the
overriding objective of dealing with cases justly. The criteria in *Ladd v
Marshall*[2] will be referred to as principles rather than applied as rules[3].

1   The relevant provision now in force is *Practice Direction: Insolvency Proceedings*,
    para 17.18(2)(b).
2   [1954] 3 All ER 745, [1954] 1 WLR 1489, CA.
3   *Hertfordshire Investments Ltd v Bubb* [2000] 1 WLR 2318, CA. See further para **3.116**.

Execution returned unsatisfied

8.130   Where the creditor has a judgment debt he may present a petition
without serving a statutory demand if execution or other process has been
issued in respect of the judgment debt and has been returned unsatisfied in
whole or in part[1]. The court should look at the return indorsed on the writ
and conclude whether, when properly read, it returns that execution has been
unsatisfied. That requires there to be execution and no adequate satisfaction[2].
In *Skarzynski v Chalford Property Co Ltd*[3] it was held that 'returned' does
not have a technical meaning and merely requires proof that the execution or
other process failed to satisfy the debt. The fact that the Sheriff had failed to
endorse a statement on the writ did not impair the writ's validity.

1   IA 1986, s 268(1)(b).
2   *Re a debtor (No 340 of 1992), Debtor v First National Commercial Bank plc* [1994]
    3 All ER 269.
3   [2001] BPIR 673.

D   PROCEDURE ON CREDITOR'S PETITION

Where to present

8.131   The general rule is that the petition should be presented to the county
court for the insolvency district in which the debtor has resided or carried on
business for the longest period during the six months immediately before the
presentation of the petition[1]. The main exception to this rule is where the
debtor has resided or carried on business in the London insolvency district for
the greater part of that six-month period or for a longer period there than in

any other insolvency district, in which case the petition should be presented to the High Court[2]. The other cases in which the High Court is the correct forum are:

(a)   where the petition is presented by a Minister of the Crown or a Government Department and either the creditor has indicated an intention to present the petition to the High Court in the statutory demand or the petition is based on a judgment;

(b)   where the debtor is not resident in England or Wales;

(c)   where the petitioner is unable to ascertain the place of residence of the debtor or his place of business[3]; and

(d)   where the demand was made by the Financial Services Authority and in it the Authority indicated that its intention was to present a bankruptcy petition to the High Court[4].

[1]   IR 1986, r 6.9(2).
[2]   IR 1986, r 6.9(1)(b).
[3]   IR 1986, r 6.9(1).
[4]   Bankruptcy (Financial Services and Markets Act 2000) Rules 2001, SI 2001/3634, rr 1, 3 and 8.

8.132 If the debtor's place of business is situated in a different insolvency district from his place of residence, then it is the place of business which is decisive[1]. If he has carried on business in more than one insolvency district, the correct court is that for the insolvency district in which his principal place of business is situated or has been for the longest period during the six months immediately before presentation of the petition[2].

[1]   IR 1986, r 6.9(3).
[2]   IR 1986, r 6.9(4).

8.133 Where there is an IVA in force for the debtor, the petition must be presented to the court to which the nominee's report under IA 1986, s 256, s 256A or s 263C was submitted. This rule overrides any other provision concerning to which court the petition should be presented[1].

[1]   IR 1986, r 6.9(4A).

8.134 The petition must contain sufficient information to establish that it is presented to the right court[1]. Where an IVA is in force in respect of the debtor the petition must be presented to the court to which the nominee's report in respect of that arrangement was presented[2]. This will ordinarily be the court to which the debtor would be entitled to present his own petition in bankruptcy[3].

[1]   IR 1986, r 6.9(5).
[2]   IR 1986, r 6.9(4A).
[3]   IR 1986, r 5.5A; see also IR 1986, r 6.40.

Content of creditor's petition

8.135 The petition must state, in so far as the creditor knows:

8.135 *Bankruptcy petitions*

(a)   the debtor's name, place of residence and occupation (if any);
(b)   the name or names in which he carries on business, if other than his true name, and whether, in the case of any business of a specified nature, he carries it on alone or with others;
(c)   the nature of his business, and the address or addresses at which he carries it on;
(d)   any name or names, other than his true name, in which he has carried on business at or after the time when the debt was incurred, and whether he has done so alone or with others;
(e)   any address or addresses at which he has resided or carried on business at or after that time, and the nature of that business; and
(f)   whether the debtor has his centre of main interests or an establishment in another Member State[1].

[1]   IR 1986, r 6.7(1).

8.136 If the debtor has used any other name which is known to the petitioning creditor, that fact is to be included in the petition[1]. The particulars of the debtor constitute the full title of the proceedings[2].

[1]   IR 1986, r 6.7(3).
[2]   IR 1986, r 6.7(2).

8.137 The petition must identify the debt. To do so it must state:

(a)   the amount of the debt, the consideration for it (or, if there is no consideration, the way in which it arises) and the fact that it is owed to the petitioner;
(b)   when the debt was incurred or became due;
(c)   if the amount of the debt includes any charge by way of interest not previously notified to the debtor as a liability of his, or any other charge accruing from time to time, the amount or rate of the charge and the grounds on which it is claimed as part of the debt[1].

[1]   IR 1986, r 6.8(a)–(c).

8.138 The petition must include a statement (whichever is appropriate) either:

(1)   that the debt is for a liquidated sum payable immediately and that the debtor appears to be unable to pay it; or
(2)   that the debt is for a liquidated sum payable at some certain, future and specified time and that the debtor appears to have no reasonable prospect of being able to pay it.

8.139 In either case the petition must also state that the debt is unsecured or contains such statement as the Act requires where the creditor holds some security over all or part of the debt[1].

[1]   IR 1986, r 6.8(1) and IA 1986, s 269.

8.140 Guidance on completing the form of a creditor's bankruptcy petition is given in the *Practice Direction: Insolvency Proceedings*, para 15.

When to present the petition

8.141 Bankruptcy petitions must not, ordinarily, be presented until three weeks have elapsed since the date on which the demand was served[1]. However, where a creditor's petition is based wholly or partly on a debt which is the subject of a statutory demand, that petition may be presented before the end of those three weeks if there is a serious possibility that the debtor's property or the value of any of his property will be significantly diminished during that period[2]. The petition must state that such a possibility exists. Such an expedited petition may be presented even where the debtor has made an application to set aside the statutory demand on which it is based and the application remains outstanding[3].

1 IA 1986, s 268.
2 IA 1986, s 270.
3 *Re a Debtor (No 22 of 1993)* [1994] 2 All ER 105, [1994] 1 WLR 46.

8.142 Where a petitioning creditor fails to present the petition within four months of serving the statutory demand, he must explain this delay in the affidavit verifying the petition[1].

1 IR 1986, r 6.12(7).

Presentation of the petition

8.143 To present the petition means to file it in court together with an affidavit verifying the statements in the petition[1] and, if appropriate, with an affidavit proving service of the statutory demand[2]. Before the petition is presented the petitioning creditor must pay a deposit to the court[3]. The petition cannot be filed unless there is produced with it the receipt for the deposit payable on presentation[4] or the Secretary of State has given written notice to the court that the petitioner has made suitable alternative arrangements for the payment of the deposit to the official receiver and that notice has not been revoked[5]. Copies must be delivered to the court with the petition: one for service on the debtor, one to be exhibited to the affidavit of verification, and one for the supervisor of any IVA in force for the debtor, if that supervisor is not the petitioner[6]. Each copy will be sealed and issued to the petitioner (save for the copy exhibited to the verifying affidavit which will remain in the court file) endorsed with the date and time of filing and of the venue fixed for the hearing of the petition[7].

1 IR 1986, r 6.10(1).
2 IR 1986, r 6.11(1).
3 Insolvency Proceedings (Fees) Order 2004, SI 2004/593, art 6.
4 IR 1986, r 6.10(2).
5 IR 1986, r 6.10(2A).
6 IR 1986, r 6.10(3).
7 IR 1986, r 6.10(5).

8.144 Where a petition contains a request for the appointment of the supervisor of an IVA as the trustee in bankruptcy[1] that supervisor must file in court a report including particulars of (a) the date on which he gave written notification to creditors bound by the arrangement of the intention to seek his appointment as trustee (this date must be at least 10 days before the filing of the report) and (b) details of any response to that notice from the creditors including any objection to his appointment[2]. His report must be filed not less than two days before the day appointed for the hearing of the petition[3].

[1]   See IA 1986, s 297.
[2]   IR 1986, r 6.10(6).
[3]   IR 1986, r 6.10(6).

8.145 When the petition is filed notice of it must be sent by the court to the Chief Land Registrar together with a request that it be entered in the register of pending actions[1]. Where the land is registered, the further step of entering a creditors' notice against the debtor's title will be taken as soon as practicable by the registrar[2]. If the petition is dismissed or withdrawn, the debtor should ensure that the notice on the register of pending actions is vacated or, where the land is registered, that the creditors' notice is cancelled[3].

[1]   IR 1986, r 6.13. For the prescribed form of the notice see IR 1986, Sch 4, Form 6.14 (substituted by SI 1987/1919). See in the case of unregistered land, the Land Charges Act 1972, s 5 and, in the case of registered land, the Land Registration Act 2002, s 86.
[2]   Land Registration Act 1925, ss 59 and 61(1), (2).
[3]   See IR 1986, r 6.27.

Witness statement or affidavit verifying the petition

8.146 The affidavit verifying the statements in the petition must do so expressly by stating that they are true or are true to the best of the deponent's knowledge, information and belief[1]. If the petition is based on debts owed to different creditors, the debts owed to each creditor must be separately verified[2]. The person who should make the affidavit is the petitioner, or one of them if they are plural, or some other person who has been concerned in the matters giving rise to the presentation of the petition (eg a director, company secretary, similar company officer or a solicitor) or by some responsible person duly authorised to make the affidavit and having the requisite knowledge[3]. If the deponent is not the petitioner he must identify himself and state the capacity in which, and the authority by which, he makes the affidavit and the means of his knowledge of the matters sworn to in the affidavit[4]. The petition may be verified by a witness statement containing a statement of truth[5].

[1]   IR 1986, r 6.12(1).
[2]   IR 1986, r 6.12(2).
[3]   IR 1986, r 6.12(4).
[4]   IR 1986, r 6.12(5).
[5]   IR 1986, r 7.57(5).

8.147 If the petition is based on a statutory demand and more than four months have elapsed between service of that demand and the presentation of the petition, the affidavit must explain the delay[1].

[1]   IR 1986, r 6.12(7).

Proof of service of statutory demand

8.148 If the petition has been preceded by a statutory demand, a second affidavit proving service of the demand must also be filed in court[1]. The affidavit must exhibit the demand[2] and it must be made by the person who effected service if the demand was served personally on the debtor[3], or, if service has been acknowledged, it must be made by the creditor or by some other person acting on his behalf and the acknowledgement must be exhibited[4]. In any other case the affidavit must be made by some person having direct personal knowledge of the means adopted to serve the demand and must:

(a)   give particulars of the steps taken to serve the demand personally;

(b)   state the means (those steps having been ineffective) whereby it was sought to bring the demand to the debtor's attention; and

(c)   specify a date by which, to the best of the deponent's knowledge, information and belief, the demand will have come to the debtor's attention[5].

[1]   IR 1986, r 6.11(1).
[2]   IR 1986, r 6.11(2).
[3]   IR 1986, r 6.11(3).
[4]   IR 1986, r 6.11(4).
[5]   IR 1986, r 6.11(6).

8.149 The steps taken to serve the debtor with the demand personally must have been such as would have sufficed to justify an order for substituted service[1].

[1]   IR 1986, r 6.11(6). For examples of cases where the court has considered whether the steps taken to effect service were sufficient, see *Regional Collection Services v Heald* [2000] BPIR 661; *Anderson v KAS Bank NV* [2004] EWHC 532 (Ch), [2004] BPIR 685; *Dickins v Inland Revenue* [2004] BPIR 718.

Security for costs

8.150 Where the debt on which the petition is based is payable on a future date and the petitioner alleges that there is no reasonable prospect of its being paid[1] the debtor may apply for security for his costs[2]. The court has a discretion as to the nature and amount of the security to be ordered[3]. The circumstances in which the court will order security are not clear. The provision relates only to petitions presented in relation to debts payable in the future. Thus it does not cover an application to set aside a statutory demand even where the demand is for a future debt. Since a petition based on a future debt must be preceded by a statutory demand and the better way for the debtor to contest bankruptcy proceedings is by applying to set aside the demand, the bulk of the costs which he will incur will be the costs of applying to set aside. If the debtor fails to set aside the demand, then it is unlikely that there will be much prospect of his successfully disputing the petition. Hence if a factor in the exercise of the discretion to order security is the petitioner's likelihood of success on the petition, orders for security will rarely be made.

[1]   Under IA 1986, s 268(2).

8.151 It is, therefore, submitted that the rule might be improved by amendment so as to give the court power to order the creditor to lodge security for the debtor's costs in applying to set aside the demand.

8.152 If an order that the creditor pay security is made, then no hearing of the petition may take place until the whole amount of the security has been given. Where the creditor fails to provide the security the debtor ought to apply for the dismissal of the petition under the court's general power to do so[1] since otherwise the petition will remain registered against him[2]. Once the petition is dismissed, the registration may be vacated[3].

1   IA 1986, s 266(3).
2   IR 1986, r 6.13.
3   IR 1986, r 6.27.

Service of the petition

8.153 The petition must be served personally on the debtor unless an order is made for substituted service[1]. Personal service is effected by the delivery of a sealed copy of the petition to the debtor by an officer of the court, the petitioning creditor or his solicitor or by a person instructed for that purpose by the petitioning creditor or his solicitor[2].

1   IR 1986, r 6.14(1).
2   IR 1986, r 6.14(1).

8.154 Substituted service may be ordered if the court is satisfied by affidavit or other evidence that prompt personal service cannot be effected because the debtor is keeping out of the way to avoid service or other legal process or for any cause[1]. Before applying for an order for substituted service a petitioner should observe the following practice as set out in the *Practice Direction: Insolvency Proceedings*[2]:

(1)   a personal call should be made at each known residential or business address of the debtor;
(2)   if service is not effected, a letter should be sent by first-class post:
    (a)   referring to the calls and why they were made,
    (b)   giving at least two business days' notice of a time and place at which a further call will be made,
    (c)   asking the debtor to name some other time and place if the suggested appointment is not convenient, and
    (d)   stating that an application for substituted service will be made if the debtor fails to keep the appointment made;
(3)   in attending any appointment made by letter, inquiry should be made whether the debtor has received all letters left for him. If the debtor is away, inquiry should be made whether letters are being forwarded to an address in England and Wales or elsewhere;

(4)   if the debtor is represented by a solicitor an attempt should be made to arrange an appointment for personal service through that solicitor.

¹   IR 1986, r 6.14(2).
²   *Practice Direction: Insolvency Proceedings*, paras 11.44–11.45.

8.155 The application for an order for substituted service should be supported by an affidavit setting out the steps taken in attempting to effect service, all relevant facts as to the debtor's whereabouts and whether any of the appointment letters have been returned.

8.156 If an order for substituted service is made, the petition will be deemed served when the order has been complied with¹. Where service is ordered to be by ordinary first-class post, the order will normally provide that service will be deemed to be effected on the seventh day after posting². A defect in the service of a bankruptcy petition cannot be cured by application of the IR 1986, r 7.55³.

¹   IR 1986, r 6.14(2).
²   *Practice Direction: Insolvency Proceedings*, para 11.5.
³   *Re Awan* [2000] BPIR 241.

Service out of the jurisdiction

8.156A A bankruptcy petition may, with the leave of the court, be served outside England and Wales in such manner as the court may direct¹. An application must be supported by a witness statement verified by a statement of truth stating the grounds on which the application is made and in what place or country the debtor is or may probably be found².

¹   IR 1986, r 12.12(2).
²   IR 1986, r 12.12(4) and r 7.57(5).

Service on supervisor of an IVA

8.157 If the petitioner is aware that the debtor is the subject of an IVA currently in force and the petitioner is not the supervisor of that arrangement, a copy of the petition must be sent by the petitioner to the supervisor¹.

¹   IR 1986, r 6.14(4).

Death of debtor

8.158 If the debtor dies before the petition is served, the court may order service to be effected on his personal representatives or on such other persons as it thinks fit¹.

¹   IR 1986, r 6.16.

Extension of time for hearing

8.159 If the petitioning creditor has not been able to serve the petition, he may, by ordinary application stating the reasons why the petition has not been served, request the court to appoint another venue for the hearing[1]. No costs occasioned by the application shall be allowed in the proceedings except by order of the court[2]. Where the application is made less than two clear working days before the hearing date, the costs of the application will not be allowed[3].

1   IR 1986, r 6.28(1), (2).
2   IR 1986, r 6.28(3).
3   *Practice Direction: Insolvency Proceedings*, para 14.1(1).

8.160 Where an application for an extension is made, it should state the date currently fixed for the hearing of the petition. The petitioning creditor must attend the court on or before the hearing date in order to check that the extension has been given and should not assume that the extension will be given as a matter of course[1].

1   *Practice Direction: Insolvency Proceedings*, paras 14.2 and 14.3.

8.161 If the court does appoint another date for the hearing, the petitioning creditor shall forthwith notify any creditor who has given notice of an intention to appear.

E HEARING OF CREDITOR'S PETITION

8.162 The petition may not be heard until at least 14 days after it was served on the debtor[1]. This period may be shortened if it appears that the debtor has absconded, if the court is satisfied that it is a proper case for an expedited hearing, or if the debtor consents, in any of which cases the court may hear the petition on an earlier date on such terms as it thinks fit[2].

1   IR 1986, r 6.18(1).
2   IR 1986, r 6.18(2).

Appearances

8.163 The persons who may appear and be heard at the hearing are the petitioning creditor, the debtor and any creditor who has given notice of his intention to appear[1]. Where the debtor intends to oppose the petition, he must give notice of the grounds on which he objects to the making of a bankruptcy order[2]. Copies of that notice must be filed in court and sent to the petitioning creditor not less than seven days before the hearing.

1   IR 1986, r 6.18(3) and see IR 1986, r 6.23.
2   IR 1986, r 6.21.

8.164 The notice of intention to appear by a creditor must specify:

(1)   the name and address of the person giving it, and any telephone number and reference which may be required for communication with him or any other person specified in the notice to be authorised to speak or act on his behalf;

(2)   whether he intends to support or oppose the petition; and

(3)   the amount and nature of his debt[1].

¹   IR 1986, r 6.23(2).

8.165 The notice must be sent so as to reach the petitioning creditor not later than 4 pm on the business day before the day appointed for the hearing (or where the hearing has been adjourned, for the adjourned hearing)[1]. If a creditor wishes to appear but fails to give proper notice he may only appear with the leave of the court[2]. The petitioning creditor must prepare a list of the creditors (if any) who intend to appear specifying their names and addresses and (if known) their solicitors with a statement against the name of each creditor as to whether he intends to support or oppose the petition[3]. On the day of the hearing a copy of the list should be handed to the court before the commencement of the hearing[4]. If leave to appear is given to a creditor who has not given notice, his particulars must be added to the list by the petitioner[5].

¹   IR 1986, r 6.23(1), (3).
²   IR 1986, r 6.23(4).
³   IR 1986, r 6.24(1), (2).
⁴   IR 1986, r 6.24(3).
⁵   IR 1986, r 6.24(4).

Failure to attend by petitioning creditor

8.166 If the petitioning creditor fails to appear on the hearing of the petition, no subsequent petition against the same debtor, either alone or jointly with any other person, shall be presented by the same creditor in respect of the same debt, without the leave of the court to which the previous petition was presented[1]. In such circumstances it is possible for a second creditor who does appear at the hearing, having given notice of his intention to do so, to apply at the hearing for an order giving him the carriage of the petition in place of the petitioning creditor but without amendment of the petition[2].

¹   IR 1986, r 6.26.
²   IR 1986, r 6.31; see further para **8.175** below.

8.167 Where the petition has not been served and no extension of the hearing date has been given, then, if the petitioning creditor fails to attend the hearing, the court will relist the petition for hearing about 21 days later. Notice of the new date will be given by the court to the petitioning creditor's solicitors or, if acting in person, the petitioning creditor and any known supporting or opposing creditors. The obligation to serve the debtor will remain the petitioning creditor's. Written evidence should then be filed on behalf of the petitioning creditor explaining fully the reasons for the failure to apply for an extension or to appear at the hearing, and, if appropriate, giving reasons why the petition should not be dismissed[1].

1   *Practice Direction: Insolvency Proceedings*, para 4.1(2).

Adjournment

8.168 The court has power to adjourn the hearing of the petition. The grounds on which an adjournment may be granted cannot be listed comprehensively. For example an adjournment may be justified because evidence has been adduced late or for some other reason which arises as an ordinary incident of litigation. One situation in which the court ought to adjourn the hearing is where the petition is based on a judgment or order to pay money which is the subject of an appeal which appears to be made in good faith[1]. The Court of Appeal granted an adjournment in circumstances where the debtors had been taken unaware of the hearing of the bankruptcy petitions and were without legal representation[2]. It was thought in that case that given the complexity of the matter and the severity of the consequences of a bankruptcy order, an adjournment should be granted in accordance with the overriding objective to do justice between the parties.

1   IR 1986, r 6.25(2); *Re Yeatman, ex p Yeatman* (1880) 16 Ch D 283; *Re Noble, ex p Bankrupt v Official Receiver* [1965] Ch 129, [1964] 2 All ER 522; *Heath v Tang* [1993] 4 All ER 694, [1993] 1 WLR 1421, CA.
2   *Henry Butcher International Ltd v KG Engineering (a partnership)* [2006] BPIR 60.

Adjournment to facilitate payment

8.169 There are circumstances in which the court's power to adjourn is restricted by principle. Where a debtor seeks an adjournment because he wishes to pay the debt on which the petition is based, the proper test appears to be whether, in the circumstances of the case, there is a reasonable prospect that the debt will be paid in full within a reasonable time[1]. There must be credible evidence before the court that the petition debt can be paid. In *Dickins v Inland Revenue*[2] no evidence supported the request for a 14-day adjournment to allow the debtor to pay. The court should not grant a series of adjournments in order that the debtor may, by paying instalments, seek to extinguish the debt[3]. In *Harrison v Seggar*[4] it was held that an adjournment for payment by instalments which would take four years for the petition debt to be paid was not for a reasonable time. Nor should payments be made into court in support of some form of trust[5].

1   *Re Gilmartin* [1989] 1 WLR 513, 516 (Harman J). In *Anderson v KAS Bank NV* [2004] EWHC 3520 (Ch), [2004] BPIR 685 it was reiterated that the debtor has no right to an adjournment in order to pay the debt in issue.
2   [2004] BPIR 718.
3   *Judd v Williams* [1998] BPIR 88 (Lloyd J).
4   [2005] BPIR 583.
5   *Re a Debtor (No 72 of 1982)* [1984] 2 All ER 257, [1984] 1 WLR 1143, 1165 (Megarry J).

8.170 Where the debt is to be paid from money belonging to the debtor, the disposition of property thereby involved will need to be approved by the court and the position of other creditors considered before the petition is withdrawn, which will require the court's permission[1].

1   See IA 1986, s 284(1), IR 1986, r 6.32 and *Smith v Ian Simpson & Co* [2001] Ch 239, [2000] 3 All ER 434 discussed at para **8.181**.

Notice of adjournment

8.171 If the court adjourns the hearing of the petition, the petitioning creditor must, unless the court otherwise directs, forthwith send notice of the adjournment to the debtor and to any creditor who has given notice of intention to appear but was not present at the hearing. The notice must state the venue for the adjourned hearing[1]. If there are no such creditors and the debtor is present, it is sensible to seek a direction that such notice be dispensed with.

1   IR 1986, r 6.29.

Substitution of petitioner

8.172 The court may order that another creditor be substituted for the petitioning creditor where the petitioning creditor is found not to be entitled to petition, or where the petitioning creditor consents to withdraw his petition or to allow it to be dismissed, or consents to an adjournment, or fails to appear in support of his petition at the original or an adjourned hearing, or where the petitioning creditor appears but does not apply for an order in the terms of the prayer of his petition[1].

1   IR 1986, r 6.30(1).

8.173 The creditor who is to be substituted must be a creditor who has given notice of intention to appear, wishes to prosecute the petition and was, on the date on which the petition was presented, in such a position as would have entitled him on that date to present a bankruptcy petition in respect of a debt or debts owed to him by the debtor[1]. Entitlement to present a petition requires that there be a good petitioning debt owed to the creditor by the debtor which the debtor appears to be unable to pay by reason of his failure to comply with a statutory demand[2].

1   IR 1986, r 6.30(2).
2   By virtue of the statutory definition of 'inability to pay' in IA 1986, s 268 a statutory demand is required in all cases save that in which execution of a judgment has been returned unsatisfied.

8.174 Where a creditor is substituted the petition will have to be amended and re-verified.

Change of carriage of the petition

8.175 Any creditor who appears at the hearing having given notice of his intention to do so[1] may apply to the court for an order giving him carriage of the petition in place of the petitioning creditor, but without requiring any amendment of the petition[2]. The effect of the order, if made, is to put the applicant into the shoes of the previously petitioning creditor rather than to allow the applicant to proceed in reliance upon a debt owed to him. A formal amendment of the petition is not required. Accordingly the person given the carriage by such order is entitled to rely on all evidence previously adduced in the proceedings[3]. The court may make the order on such terms as it thinks just if satisfied that the applicant is an unpaid and unsecured creditor of the debtor and that the petitioning creditor either (i) intends by any means to secure the postponement, adjournment or withdrawal of the petition, or (ii) does not intend to prosecute the petition, either diligently or at all[4]. But the court cannot make the order if satisfied that the petitioning creditor's debt has been paid, secured or compounded for by means of a disposition of property made by some person other than the debtor or a disposition of the debtor's own property made with the approval of, or ratified by, the court[5].

[1]   Under IR 1986, r 6.23. *Re Purvis* [1997] 3 All ER 663.
[2]   IR 1986, r 6.31(1).
[3]   IR 1986, r 6.31(5).
[4]   IR 1986, r 6.31(2).
[5]   IR 1986, r 6.31(3).

8.176 An order changing the carriage of the petition may be made whether the petitioning creditor is present at the hearing or not[1].

[1]   IR 1986, r 6.31(4).

Leave to withdraw

8.177 No petition may be withdrawn without leave of the court[1]. Nor may an order be made giving leave to withdraw a creditor's petition before the petition is heard[2]. Where a petitioning creditor seeks the dismissal or withdrawal, such leave must be obtained by an application to the court supported by an affidavit[3] setting out the reasons for the application[4]. If the petition debt has been paid or some arrangement has been made to secure it or compound for it, the affidavit must state:

(a)   what dispositions of property have been made for the purpose of the settlement or arrangement;
(b)   whether, in the case of any disposition, it was the property of the debtor or of someone else; and
(c)   whether, if it was the debtor's property, the disposition was made with the approval of, or has been ratified by, the court and if so, specifying the relevant court order[5].

[1]   IA 1986, s 266(2).
[2]   IR 1986, r 6.32(3).
[3]   Or witness statement under IR 1986, r 7.57(5).

8.178 By their reference[1] to the court's consent to, or ratification of, a disposition of the debtor's own property, the Insolvency Act 1986 and the Insolvency Rules 1986 envisage applications being made to the court before or after such dispositions are made[2]. Such applications are essential where any disposition of the debtor's property is to be made during the period between the presentation of the petition and its hearing to a person who knows that the petition has been presented. For although bankruptcy commences on the making of the bankruptcy order[3], a disposition by a person who is adjudged bankrupt during the period from the presentation of the petition and ending with the vesting of the estate in the trustee is void unless made with the consent of, or ratified by, the court[4].

1   See IA 1986, s 284(1) and IR 1986, r 6.32.
2   See para **16.28** in respect of such applications.
3   IA 1986, s 278(a). Contrast the compulsory winding up of a company which commences on the presentation of a petition; see IA 1986, s 129(2).
4   IA 1986, s 284(1), (4).

8.179 This provision effectively means that if a petitioning creditor decides after presenting the petition to accept payment directly from the debtor, he must abandon the opportunity to make the debtor bankrupt, at least on the basis of the petition debt. For it is unlikely to be appropriate for the court both to consent to a disposition of the debtor's own property to the petitioning creditor and to make a bankruptcy order on the basis of the balance of the debt, since that would almost certainly give the petitioning creditor an undeserved advantage over other creditors. It should be noted that where a disposition has been ratified or approved, that will not render it invulnerable to attack as a preference if a bankruptcy order is subsequently made on another petition[1].

1   IA 1986, s 340(6).

8.180 If the petition is withdrawn by leave of the court, an order shall be made at the same time permitting vacation of the registration of the petition as a pending action[1]. Two copies of the order must be sent by the court to the debtor[2].

1   IR 1986, r 6.27.
2   IR 1986, r 6.27.

Bankruptcy order

8.181 No bankruptcy order may be made on a creditor's petition unless the court is satisfied that there is a debt in respect of which the petition was presented and either (a) the debt was payable at the date of the petition or has since become payable and has not been paid, secured or compounded for, or (b) the debt is a future debt which the debtor has no reasonable prospect of being able to pay when it becomes due[1]. In *Smith (a bankrupt) v Ian Simpson*

& Co[2] the Court of Appeal, by a majority, construed the reference in the IA 1986, s 271(1)(a) to payment of the petition debt as a reference to unconditional payment, that is to say to payment which is not liable to be avoided under IA 1986, s 284(1) as a disposition of the debtor's property made after presentation of the petition. Hence, the court retains power to make a bankruptcy order on a petition despite the payment of the debt, if the payment has been made from funds belonging to the debtor. The petitioning creditor would not have an interest in seeking such an order, but where there are creditors who support the petition yet have not got standing to be substituted as petitioner, the court may order that one such supporting creditor have the carriage of the petition. Where there is no supporting creditor who wishes to pursue the petition, the petition should be dismissed even if the payment of the petition debt was made out of the debtor's own funds[3].

[1] IA 1986, s 271(1). In *Re a Debtor* [2005] All ER (D) 174 (Apr) the bankruptcy order was set aside on appeal and a rehearing ordered. Although the debtor had failed to prove that the debt was disputed to the extent necessary to justify the dismissal of the bankruptcy petition, the quality of the evidence advanced by the petitioning creditor was such that it was impossible to say whether or not the bankruptcy order should be allowed to stand.
[2] [2001] Ch 239, [2000] 3 All ER 434.
[3] *Re Marr (a bankrupt)* [1990] 2 All ER 880, [1990] Ch 773, CA.

8.182 Where the debt is payable in the future, the court must assume that the prospect of payment given by the facts and other matters known to the creditor at the time when he entered into the transaction resulting in the debt constituted a reasonable prospect[1]. This means that the creditor must show that some new fact has arisen or come to his knowledge since the transaction and that that fact detrimentally affects the prospect of payment.

[1] IA 1986, s 271(4).

8.183 If the petition has been expedited pursuant to IA 1986, s 270, no bankruptcy order may be made until three weeks have elapsed from the service of the statutory demand[1].

[1] IA 1986, s 271(2).

Repetition of arguments which failed on an application to set aside the statutory demand on which the petition is based

8.184 Where the petition is preceded by a statutory demand, the primary method by which a debtor should dispute the debt on which the petition is based is by application to set aside the statutory demand. But, since the court must be satisfied as to the debt on hearing the petition, the possibility arises that a debtor may raise the same arguments on the petition as have already been raised and dismissed on the application to set aside the demand. How courts have approached such attempts has varied. One view was that the outcome of an application to set aside a statutory demand did not bind the court when it came to hear the petition and so the debtor was entitled to dispute the debt again at the hearing of the petition[1].

[1] *Eberhardt & Co Ltd v Mair* [1995] 3 All ER 963, [1995] 1 WLR 1180.

8.185 But a more restrictive view has come to prevail. Repetition at the hearing of the petition of arguments raised on an application to set aside will not ordinarily be permitted. Different tests have been adopted. The Court of Appeal has held that a subsequent and real change of circumstances will justify re-opening at the hearing of the petition an argument which had been determined at the set aside application[1]. In *Atherton v Ogulende*[2] the court considered that exceptional circumstances would be required.

1   *Turner v Royal Bank of Scotland plc* [2000] BPIR 683.
2   [2003] BPIR 21.

8.186 A debtor may face a similar obstacle if he tries to raise an argument at the hearing of the petition which was not raised on the application to set aside but could have been. Thus, in *Adams v Mason Bullock (a firm)*[1] the debtor claimed that the court was not prevented from considering at the hearing of the petition a point which had been raised on a set aside application but upon which there had been no adjudication. On appeal it was held that the question whether an issue could be raised by a debtor on the hearing of the petition would ordinarily depend on whether there had been an earlier hearing of the merits at which the debtor could, but did not, raise the issue. A fortiori where there had been a hearing at which an argument raised on paper had not been raised in oral argument as this suggested that the argument had been abandoned.

1   [2005] BPIR 241.

8.187 However, as explained in *IRC v Lee-Phipps*[1], on hearing the petition, the court still has the duty to decide whether a bankruptcy order should be made on the material then before it. In discharge of that duty the court will ask itself whether the arguments have already been run and failed, and why arguments run before it have not been run before. And, where no application to set aside a statutory demand has been made, the jurisdiction remains, where appropriate, to hear on the petition matters which could or should have been raised on an application to set aside because the court has to satisfy itself that there is a debt due before making a bankruptcy order[2].

1   [2003] BPIR 803.
2   *Barnes v Whitehead* [2004] BPIR 693.

8.188 The doctrine underlying the approach is pragmatic. As Chadwick LJ explained in *Coulter v Chief Constable of Dorset Police (No 2)*[1], the principle is not based on res judicata or abuse of process and goes no further than that repetition of arguments wastes the court's time and the parties' money and that if arguments have not been run at the stage of applying to set aside the demand, the court will inquire why not.

1   [2006] BPIR 10.

The court's duty to check that it has jurisdiction

8.189 The European Court of Justice has said that the court itself has a duty to check that it has jurisdiction to open insolvency proceedings against the debtor. The justification for imposing such an obligation on the court lies in the fact that, if the EC Insolvency Regulation applies and the court makes a bankruptcy order, the courts of other Member States cannot go behind the judgment of the court opening the insolvency proceedings but must recognise the judgment even if there are grounds for thinking that the jurisdiction of the English court was not properly established[1]. But, in the English adversarial system, the court can only discharge this duty by assessing the material put before the court by the petitioner or, in a disputed case, by the parties[2].

1   *Re Eurofoods IFSC Ltd (Case C-341/04)* [2006] 3 WLR 309.
2   *Stojevic v Official Receiver* [2007] BPIR 141 at para 24.

Power to dismiss where debtor can pay all his debts

8.190 The court may dismiss the petition if it is satisfied that the debtor is able to pay all his debts, taking into account his contingent and prospective liabilities[1].

1   IA 1986, s 271(3).

Power to dismiss where debtor makes an offer to secure or compound which is unreasonably refused

8.191 The court may dismiss the petition if it is satisfied that:

(a)   the debtor has made an offer to secure or compound for a debt in respect of which the petition is presented;
(b)   the acceptance of that offer would have required the dismissal of the petition; and
(c)   that the offer has been unreasonably refused[1].

1   IA 1986, s 271(3).

8.192 A proposal for an IVA does not constitute an offer for the purpose of this provision because it is an offer made to the creditors as a class. Each of the creditors acting alone cannot either accept or refuse because acceptance depends on there being a relevant majority in favour[1]. But it is open to a debtor to make an offer, outside the provisions of the IA 1986 relating to IVAs, to all his creditors on terms that the offer is conditional on all of them accepting it. If only the petitioning creditor refused to accept the offer, it seems that the court would have jurisdiction under IA 1986, s 271(3) to consider whether his refusal was unreasonable, because the offer would have been one which was capable of acceptance or refusal by each creditor and each creditor's response would not be capable of being overruled by there being a relevant majority in favour of the proposed IVA[2].

1   *Re a Debtor (No 2389 of 1989)* [1991] Ch 326.
2   The possibility was suggested by Vinelott J in *Re a Debtor (No 2389 of 1989)* [1991] Ch 326.

8.193 Where the creditor has refused an offer, the question whether his refusal was reasonable is to be determined objectively. The refusal will only be unreasonable if no reasonable creditor would have refused the offer in the light of the history as disclosed to the court[1]. By way of example, in *John Lewis plc v Pearson Burton* the refusal of an offer of payment which would have taken seven years to complete the payment of the debt was held not to be unreasonable[2]. When making the offer, the debtor must be full, frank and open and provide the creditor with all the information necessary to enable him to make an informed decision[3].

1   *Re a Debtor (No 32 of 1993)* [1995] 1 All ER 638, [1994] 1 WLR 899; *Re a Debtor (No 6349 of 1994), IRC v Debtor* [1996] BPIR 271; *HM Customs & Excise v Dougall* [2001] BPIR 269.
2   [2004] BPIR 70.
3   *HM Customs & Excise v Dougall* [2001] BPIR 269.

General power to dismiss petition

8.194 The court has a general power, if it appears to it appropriate to do so on the ground that there has been a contravention of the rules or for any other reason, to dismiss a bankruptcy petition or to stay proceedings on it[1]. Abuse of process, discussed below, is one basis on which this power might be exercised so as to dismiss a petition, but the power is a general one. In *Re Ross (a bankrupt) (No 2)*[2] the effect of the bankruptcy order was to stifle a claim, with a real prospect of success, which the bankrupt might otherwise have been able to pursue against the petitioning and only creditor to which he was indebted under a judgment. The Court of Appeal held that the decision to make the bankruptcy order was vitiated by a failure to consider whether it was appropriate, in the circumstances, to dismiss the petition because of its consequential effect on the bankrupt's claim, and expressed the opinion[3] that, even though the presentation of the petition was not an abuse of process, it must be dismissed. Lack of assets, or lack of assets within the jurisdiction are capable of forming reasons why a bankruptcy order should not be made but the onus of proof is very difficult for a debtor to shift and lack of assets is certainly not a bar to an order[4].

1   IA 1986, s 266(3). It was held in *Re Micklethwait* [2002] EWHC 1123 (Ch), [2003] BPIR 101 that this power was unfettered and would be exercised in favour of a debtor if the making of the bankruptcy order would cause injustice. Neither an adjournment nor a dismissal was granted in that case as the petition debts were undisputed, unpaid and long-standing.
2   [2000] BPIR 636.
3   Procedurally, the issue before the court was an appeal against a decision refusing to extend time to appeal. The conclusion reached by the court was given effect by an order made by consent.
4   *Re Thulin* [1995] 1 WLR 165; *Shepherd v Legal Services Commission* [2003] BPIR 140. For a case where a bankruptcy order was annulled because the bankrupt had no assets and so the bankruptcy was pointless, see *Amihayia v Official Receiver* [2005] BPIR 264.

Power to stay petition

8.195 The court may stay the petition on such terms and conditions as it thinks fit[1]. It may be appropriate to stay a petition because it is based on a judgment which is subject to challenge by way of application to set it aside or appeal in another court[2].

1   IA 1986, s 266(3).
2   Cf *Practice Direction: Insolvency Proceedings*, para 12.3 and para **8.102** above.

Abuse of process

8.196 A bankruptcy petition may be dismissed on the ground that it is, or has been tainted by, an abuse of process[1].

1   A recent case concerning abuse of process is *Bank of Scotland v Bennett* [2004] EWCA Civ 988, (2004) Times, 4 August.

Petition based on a debt known to be disputed

8.197 It is an abuse of process to present a winding-up petition against a solvent company in respect of a debt which the petitioner knows is disputed on substantial grounds[1]. The consequence is that an injunction will be granted to stay advertisement of the petition (or an order made dismissing it) and the petitioner may be ordered to pay costs on the indemnity basis. Bankruptcy proceedings against individuals differ from winding-up proceedings against companies because a bankruptcy petition must be preceded by a statutory demand served on the debtor, whereas a winding-up petition may be presented without any preliminary step. So, in bankruptcy, a precisely analogous situation ought not to arise for the debtor has an opportunity to dispute the debt before the petition is presented[2] and the proof of his insolvency is that he has failed to comply with or set aside the statutory demand.

1   *Re a company (No 12209 of 1991)* [1992] 2 All ER 797, [1992] 1 WLR 351.
2   As was the case in *Re Ebert* [2002] All ER (D) 116 (Jul) where the statutory demand was set aside as an abuse of process.

Attempts to extract additional payment

8.198 The abuse of process which has arisen in bankruptcy is that which occurs where the petitioning creditor extracts, or attempts to extract, from the debtor some additional sum or benefit beyond the debt on which the petition is based and the costs properly payable in respect of the petition as the price of the petitioning creditor's agreement either to adjourn[1] or to withdraw the petition or to consent to its dismissal. An agreement not to present a petition on similar terms is equally offensive. Extracting, or seeking to extract, such collateral benefit may constitute extortion[2]. It may be abuse even though the collateral benefit is trifling in comparison with the amount of the debt[3].

1   *Re Atkinson* (1892) 9 Morr 193; *Re Otway* [1895] 1 QB 812.
2   *Re Shaw, ex p Gill* (1901) 83 LT 754; *Re a Debtor (883 of 1927)* [1928] Ch 199.
3   *Re a Judgment Summons (No 25 of 1952), ex p Henlys Ltd* [1953] 1 Ch 195, 213–214.

8.199 However, it is not an absolute rule that any agreement or agreement between the creditor and debtor whereby the creditor receives more than he would have recovered at law when the bankruptcy proceedings commenced or were threatened amounts to an abuse. There are circumstances in which the fact that a creditor has received more than he was entitled to receive has not amounted to extortion. Thus in *Re Bebro*[1], the debtor offered on his own initiative and without any pressure by the creditor to deliver to the creditor a new bill of exchange for some £15 more than the petition debt in return for the creditor's agreement to dismiss the petition; when the bill was dishonoured and a second petition presented, the debtor's argument that the second petition should be dismissed on the ground of extortion failed. What was lacking was conduct on the part of the creditor amounting to pressure on the debtor to provide a collateral benefit. So, the fact alone that a creditor has obtained a collateral benefit may not be sufficient to show extortion. But the court will look strictly at the conduct of a creditor who uses or threatens bankruptcy proceedings and if it finds that he has done so oppressively, in order to obtain a collateral benefit, it will not allow him to make use of the bankruptcy proceedings[2].

[1]   [1900] 2 QB 316.
[2]   *Re Majory, ex p the Debtor v FA Dumont Ltd* [1955] Ch 600, 623–624.

8.200 Where there has been extortion the court will dismiss the petition which has been used as the means of obtaining, or seeking to obtain, the collateral benefit. Further, if the collateral benefit comprises a promise to make a payment over and above the debt due and the debtor fails to make that extra payment, a petition based on that failure will also be dismissed[1].

[1]   *Re a Debtor (883 of 1927)* [1928] Ch 199.

8.201 Where a bankruptcy petition founded on a judgment debt had been dismissed on the ground of extortion, the judgment debt was not extinguished and the creditor, though disqualified from presenting a bankruptcy petition based on it, was entitled to use other means of lawfully enforcing the debt[1].

[1]   *Re a Judgment Summons (No 25 of 1952), ex p Henlys Ltd* [1953] Ch 195.

Second petition on same debt as founded prior petition which has been dismissed

8.202 It would be an abuse of process for a petitioner to present a second petition on the basis of sums which had been included in an earlier petition, that petition having been dismissed after a full hearing[1].

[1]   *IRC v Verrall* [2003] EWHC 3083 (Ch), [2004] BPIR 456.

Collateral purpose

8.203 So long as the petition is properly based on a debt owed by the debtor to the creditor, it is not an abuse of process for a creditor to present a petition with the collateral purpose of obtaining some advantage which will result from the debtor's being made bankrupt[1]. For example, it may well be a proper concern of a creditor that the debtor ought not to be spending money on an action without any prospect of success[2].

¹ *Strongmaster Ltd v Kaye* [2004] BPIR 335; *Mahmood v Penrose* [2005] BPIR 170.
² *Hicks v Gulliver* [2002] BPIR 518.

Vacation of registration of petition

8.204 Where the court dismisses the petition, it should also make an order vacating registration of the petition as a pending action and should send two copies of the order to the debtor¹.

¹ IR 1986, r 6.27.

Malicious presentation of bankruptcy petition

8.205 Where a petition is presented maliciously and without reasonable and probable cause, an action may lie against the petitioner¹, provided that the claimant can establish that the proceedings in which the petition is brought have been determined in his favour². A distinction is drawn between traders and non-traders: traders do not need to prove special damage whereas non-traders do.

¹ *Quartz Hill Consolidated Gold Mining Co v Eyre* (1883) 11 QBD 674, CA; *Gregory v Portsmouth City Council* [2000] 1 AC 419 at 427; *Jacob v Vockrodt* [2007] EWHC 2403 (QB).
² *Metropolitan Bank Ltd v Pooley* (1885) 10 App Cas 210, HL. In *Tibbs v Islington London Borough Council* [2002] EWCA Civ 1682, [2003] BPIR 743 a claim for malicious prosecution failed as it could not be said that the bankruptcy proceedings had been determined in the debtor's favour where the petitioner had recovered a significant amount, if not the entirety of the sum claimed.

8.206 The need to show a favourable outcome effectively requires the claimant, if made bankrupt, to apply immediately to annul the bankruptcy order on the basis that it ought not to have been made¹. In *Beechey v William Hill (Park Lane) Ltd*² the petition was based on a judgment founded on a debt which was unenforceable at law. A receiving order was made and the bankruptcy proceedings took their ordinary course until after about two years the bankruptcy was annulled on the basis that all the debts had been paid in full. As well as finding that there was no malice on the part of the petitioning creditor, the court held that the proceedings had not determined in the favour of the plaintiff in that the bankruptcy had run its ordinary course and was annulled on the basis that all the debts were paid in full.

¹ Ie under IA 1986, s 282(1)(a).
² [1956] CLY 5442.

8.207 A person who institutes legal process, including bankruptcy proceedings, does not owe a duty of care to the respondent as to the manner in which the litigation is conducted, whether in regard to the service of process or in regard to any other step. Thus where a winding-up order was made against a company when by mistake it had not been served at the company's registered office but rather at the registered office of another company, a claim made in negligence by the company against the petitioner was struck out¹.

¹   *Business Computers International Ltd v Registrar of Companies* [1988] Ch 229, [1987] 3 All ER 465.

F PETITION PRESENTED BY THE FINANCIAL SERVICES AUTHORITY

Grounds on which petition may be presented

8.208 The Financial Services and Markets Act 2000, s 372 confers power on the Financial Services Authority ('the Authority') to present a bankruptcy petition against an individual who is or has been an authorised person¹ or who is carrying on or has carried on a regulated activity in contravention of the general prohibition on carrying on a regulated activity unless authorised or exempt². The Authority may present a petition against such an individual if, but only if, either:

(a)   the individual appears to be unable to pay a regulated activity³ debt; or
(b)   the individual appears to have no reasonable prospect of being able to pay a regulated activity debt.

¹   For the definition of 'authorised person' see the Financial Services and Markets Act 2000, s 31.
²   The general prohibition is set out and defined in the Financial Services and Markets Act 2000, s 19.
³   For the definition of 'regulated activity' see the Financial Services and Markets Act 2000, s 22.

Inability to pay a current regulated activity debt

8.209 An individual appears to be unable to pay a regulated activity debt if he is in default on an obligation to pay a sum due and payable under an agreement the making or performance of which constitutes or is part of a regulated activity carried on by the individual concerned¹. Thus the Authority is entitled to present the petition not on the basis of a debt owed to it but on the basis of the individual's default with regard to his counterparty to an agreement made or to be performed as part of his regulated activity. Secondly, the Authority is not required to serve any form of demand before presenting the petition. If there is a dispute about whether the individual is in default of a relevant agreement, that dispute must be resolved on the hearing of the petition.

¹   Financial Services and Markets Act 2000, s 372(3) and (8).

Inability to pay a future regulated activity debt

8.210 An individual appears to have no reasonable prospect of being able to pay a regulated activity debt if:

(a)   the Authority has served on him a demand requiring him to establish to the satisfaction of the Authority that there is a reasonable prospect that he will be able to pay a sum payable under an agreement made or to be performed as part of his regulated activity;

(b)   at least three weeks have elapsed since the demand was served; and

(c)   the demand has been neither complied with nor set aside in accordance with the applicable rules.

Statutory demand in connection with a future regulated activity debt

8.211 Special rules apply to the form and content of, and information to be given in, the demand in substitution for the ordinary rules[1]. The demand must be dated and signed by a member of the Authority's staff authorised by the Authority for that purpose. It must specify that it is made under the Financial Services and Markets Act 2000 and must state the amount of the debt, to whom it is owed and the consideration for it, or, if there is no consideration, the way in which it arises. If the person to whom it is owed holds any security in respect of the debt of which the Authority is aware, the demand must specify the nature of the security and the value which the Authority puts on it as at the date of the demand, and the amount of which payment is claimed by the demand must be the full amount of the debt less the amount specified as the value of the security. The demand must state the grounds on which it is alleged that the individual appears to have no reasonable prospect of paying the debt. The demand must include an explanation of the following matters:

(a)   the purpose of the demand and the fact that, if the individual does not comply with the demand, bankruptcy proceedings may be commenced against him;

(b)   the time within which the demand must be complied with, if that consequence is to be avoided;

(c)   the methods of compliance which are open to the individual; and

(d)   the individual's right to apply to the court for the demand to be set aside.

[1]   Bankruptcy (Financial Services and Markets Act 2000) Rules 2001, SI 2001/3634, rr 4 and 5.

8.212 The demand must specify the name and address and telephone number, if any, of one or more persons with whom the individual may, if he wishes, enter into communication with a view to establishing to the Authority's satisfaction that there is a reasonable prospect that the debt will be paid when it falls due or (as the case may be) that the debt will be secured or compounded.

Compliance with the demand

8.213 The clearest form of compliance would be for the individual to establish that there is a reasonable prospect of the debt being paid in full. The reference to discussions with the Authority about the debt's being secured or compounded raises questions. There is no suggestion in s 372 of the Financial Services and Markets Act 2000 that it would suffice either to secure or to compound the debt, though in the case of security, the provision of security may well provide grounds for concluding that there is a reasonable prospect that the debt will be paid. But, compounding the debt would mean paying less than the full amount due; so, it is difficult to see how establishing that the debt will be compounded could constitute a reason for concluding that there was a reasonable prospect that the debt will be paid when it falls due.

Applications to set the demand aside

8.214 IR 1986, r 6.4 applies in a modified form to applications to set aside demands made under the Financial Services and Markets Act 2000, s 372(4)(a). First, references in IR 1986, r 6.4 to the debtor are to be read as references to an individual. Secondly, as regards the court to which the application is to be made, IR 1986, r 6.4(2) is to be read as providing, in effect, that where the debt is the subject of a judgment or order of any court and the statutory demand specifies the date of the judgment or order and the court in which it was made but indicates the Authority's intention to present a bankruptcy petition against the individual in the High Court, then the application should be made in the High Court, but otherwise it should be made to the court to which the individual would present his own petition in accordance with IR 1986, r 6.40[1]. As mentioned below, the Authority is entitled to present the petition to the High Court even where the debt is not the subject of a judgment or order so long as the Authority indicates its intention to do so in the demand. In such a case it appears that the application to set the demand aside should nonetheless be made in the court to which the individual would present his own petition. IR 1986, r 6.5 is to be read as if references to the debtor were references to an individual and as if references to the creditor were references to the Authority, except in r 6.5(2) where the reference to the creditor is to be read as a reference both to the person to whom the debt is owed and to the Authority and in IR 1986, r 6.5(4)(c) where the reference to the creditor is to be read as a reference to the person to whom the debt is owed. The modification to IR 1986, r 6.5(2) has the effect that notice of the hearing to set aside the demand must be given to the individual, the Authority, the person to whom the debt is owed and anyone named in the demand as a person with whom the individual may communicate with reference to the demand. IR 1986, r 6.5(5) is disapplied and in its stead is substituted a provision so that the Authority may be required to amend the petition where the security held by the person to whom the debt is owed has been undervalued in the petition[2].

[1] Bankruptcy (Financial Services and Markets Act 2000) Rules 2001, SI 2001/3634, r 7.
[2] Bankruptcy (Financial Services and Markets Act 2000) Rules 2001, SI 2001/3634, r 6.

Where to present

8.215 The petition should be presented to the High Court where the demand was made by the Financial Services Authority and in it the Authority indicated that its intention was to present a bankruptcy petition to the High Court[1]. If the Authority omits to indicate that intention, the petition should be presented to the court which would ordinarily have bankruptcy jurisdiction with respect to the individual concerned[2].

1 Bankruptcy (Financial Services and Markets Act 2000) Rules 2001, SI 2001/3634, rr 1, 3 and 8.
2 See the definition of 'the court' in the Financial Services and Markets Act 2000, s 355(1)(a).

Other procedural modifications

8.216 IR 1986, r 6.3 as to service of the petition, IR 1986, r 6.11 as to proof of service of the statutory demand and IR 1986, r 6.25 as to the decision on the hearing of the petition apply as if references to the debtor were references to an individual and references to the creditor were references to the Authority[1].

1 Bankruptcy (Financial Services and Markets Act 2000) Rules 2001, SI 2001/3634, r 6(1).

G GROUND FOR PRESENTING A DEBTOR'S PETITION

Ground for debtor's petition

8.217 There is only one ground on which a debtor may present his own petition. That is that he is unable to pay his debts[1]. In order to show this a statement of the debtor's affairs must be prepared containing:

(a) such particulars of the debtor's creditors and of his debts and other liabilities and of his assets; and
(b) such other information as the Insolvency Rules require[2].

1 IA 1986, s 272(1).
2 IA 1986, s 272(2). See para **8.226** below.

8.218 Inability to pay debts is not statutorily defined for the purpose of a debtor's petition. In general, for the purpose of determining insolvency, the question is whether the person concerned can pay his debts as they fall due. That test has been applied in the case of a debtor's petition[1]. But it is likely, since the statement of affairs to be filed with the petition takes the form of a list of debts and liabilities set against a list of assets, that the test, whether the amount of the liabilities exceeds the value of the assets, will ordinarily be applied. By virtue of the meaning of 'debt' in the context of the Insolvency Act 1986[2], future and contingent liabilities must be included.

1 *Re Coney* [1998] BPIR 333, CA.
2 IA 1986, s 385(1) referring to IA 1986, s 382(3).

H PROCEDURE ON DEBTOR'S PETITION

Where to present

8.219 A debtor's petition must be presented to the High Court if the debtor has resided or carried on business in the London insolvency district for the greater part of the six months immediately preceding the presentation of the petition, or for a longer period in those six months than in any other insolvency district, or if the debtor is not resident in England and Wales[1]. In any other case the debtor must present the petition to his own county court which is either:

(a) the county court for the insolvency district in which he has resided or carried on business for the longest period in the six months immediately preceding the presentation of the petition;

(b) if he has for the greater part of those six months carried on business in one insolvency district and resided in another, the county court for the district in which he carried on business; or

(c) if he has during those six months carried on business in more than one insolvency district, the county court for the district which is, or has been for the longest period in those six months, his principal place of business[2].

[1]   IR 1986, r 6.40(1).
[2]   IR 1986, r 6.40(2).

8.220 In relation to those county courts with limited insolvency facilities there are alternative county courts to which a debtor who is not bound to present his petition to the High Court may present his petition if it will be more expedient for him with a view to expediting the petition[1]. The alternative county courts, described in the Insolvency Rules 1986 as full-time, are listed in IR 1986, Sch 2. Also, if more expedient from the point of view of speed, a debtor who is not bound to present his petition to the High Court and who has carried on business in one insolvency district but resided in another, may as an alternative present his petition in the county court for the district in which he has resided[2].

[1]   IR 1986, r 6.40(3)(a).
[2]   IR 1986, r 6.40(3)(b).

8.221 Where there is an IVA in force for the debtor, the petition must be presented to the court to which the nominee's report under IA 1986, s 256, s 256A or s 263C was submitted. This rule overrides any other provision concerning to which court the petition should be presented[1].

[1]   IR 1986, r 6.40(3A).

Content of the petition

8.222 The petition must state:

(a) the debtor's name, place of residence and his occupation if he has one;

(b)   the name or names in which he carries on business if these are different from his true name and must state whether, in the case of a business of a specified nature, he carries it on alone or with others;

(c)   the nature of his business and the address or addresses at which he carries it on;

(d)   any name or names, other than his true name, in which he has carried on business in the period in which any of his bankruptcy debts were incurred and, in the case of any such business, whether he has carried it on alone or with others; and

(e)   any address or addresses at which he has resided or carried on business during that period and the nature of that business[1].

[1]   IR 1986, r 6.38(1).

8.223 If the debtor has at any time used a name other than that given as his current name[1] the petition must state this fact[2] and, presumably, identify the name. The petition must contain sufficient information to establish that it has been presented to the appropriate court[3]. The particulars of the debtor determine the full title of the proceedings[4].

[1]   Under IR 1986, r 6.38(1)(a).
[2]   IR 1986, r 6.38(3).
[3]   IR 1986, r 6.40(4).
[4]   IR 1986, r 6.38(2).

8.224 The petition must contain the statement that the debtor is unable to pay his debts, and request that a bankruptcy order be made against him[1]. Particulars must be given in the petition if the debtor has, within the period of five years ending with the date of the petition, been adjudged bankrupt, made a composition with his creditors in satisfaction of his debts or a scheme of arrangement of his affairs, entered into any IVA or been subject to an administration order under the County Courts Act 1984, Pt VI[2].

[1]   IR 1986, r 6.39(1).
[2]   IR 1986, r 6.39(2).

8.225 If there is in force at the date of the petition an IVA, then the particulars must include a statement that the arrangement is in force and must give the name and address of the supervisor of the arrangement[1].

[1]   IR 1986, r 6.39(3).

Statement of affairs

8.226 A statement of the debtor's affairs, verified by affidavit, must accompany the petition[1]. The statement must be in the statutory form[2] and contain all the particulars required by that form[3]. The affidavit verifying the debtor's statement of affairs may be sworn before an officer of the court duly authorised in that regard[4].

[1]   IR 1986, r 6.41(1).
[2]   Form 6.28.

3   IR 1986, r 6.68 which applies by virtue of IR 1986, r 6.41(2).
4   IR 1986, r 6.42(5).

Presentation of the petition

8.227 Presentation means filing the petition and the statement of affairs in court, together with three copies of the petition and one copy of the statement. The petition cannot be filed unless there is produced with it the receipt for the deposit payable on presentation[1].

1   IR 1986, r 6.42(1).

8.228 The petition may be heard forthwith unless it contains particulars of an IVA in force for the debtor[1]. If the petition is not heard forthwith then the court must fix a venue for the hearing of the petition and, if it contains particulars of an IVA in force for the debtor, give 14 days' notice of the venue to the supervisor of the arrangement[2].

1   IR 1986, r 6.42(2).
2   IR 1986, r 6.42(2A).

8.229 One of the copies of the petition will be returned to the debtor, endorsed with any venue fixed for its hearing; the second, also endorsed with the venue, will be sent by the court to the official receiver together with the copy of the statement of affairs[1]; and the third will be retained by the court together with the second copy of the statement of affairs to be sent to an insolvency practitioner if the court decides to appoint one[2] to consider the appropriateness of an IVA[3]. Where the court hears the petition forthwith, or where the court thinks it will expedite delivery of any document to the official receiver, the court may direct the debtor to deliver the document to the official receiver[4].

1   IR 1986, r 6.42(4).
2   Under IA 1986, s 273(2); see further below para **8.238**.
3   IR 1986, r 6.42(3), (4).
4   IR 1986, r 6.42(6).

8.230 Where there is an IVA in force for the debtor, it is possible for the petition to include a request for the supervisor of that arrangement to be appointed as trustee under the IA 1986, s 297(5).

8.231 Where the petition includes such a request the proposed trustee must give written notification of the request to all the creditors bound by the arrangement and, not less than ten days later, he must file in court stating the date on which he notified the creditors bound by the arrangement and what response they gave including any objections to his appointment. That report must be filed in court not less than two clear days before the day appointed for the hearing of the petition[1].

1   IR 1986, r 6.42(7).

8.232 When the petition is filed notice of it must be sent forthwith by the court to the Chief Land Registrar together with a request that it be entered in the register of pending actions[1].

[1]   IR 1986, r 6.43. See Land Charges Act 1972, s 5 and Land Registration Act 2002, s 86.

Proceedings on the petition

8.233 Unless there is an IVA in force for the debtor, it will be possible for the court to make a bankruptcy order forthwith on the basis of the petition and the statement of affairs. In such circumstances the only appearance will be by the debtor.

8.234 The alternative course of appointing an insolvency practitioner to consider the possibility of an IVA is considered in the following chapter.

General power to dismiss petition

8.235 As in the case of a creditor's petition, the court to which a debtor's petition has been presented has a general power to dismiss it or to stay proceedings on it, if it appears to the court appropriate to do so on the grounds that there has been a contravention of the Insolvency Rules or for any other reason[1]. If the proceedings on a petition are stayed, the court may impose the stay on such terms and conditions as it thinks fit[2].

[1]   IA 1986, s 266(3).
[2]   IA 1986, s 266(3).

I HEARING OF DEBTOR'S PETITION

The court's duty to check that it has jurisdiction

8.236 As mentioned above with regard to a creditor's petition, the court itself has a duty to check that it has jurisdiction to open insolvency proceedings against the debtor[1].

[1]   *Re Eurofoods IFSC Ltd (Case C-341/04)* [2006] 3 WLR 309.

Making a bankruptcy order

8.237 On hearing a debtor's petition the court may make a bankruptcy order if it is satisfied that the debtor is unable to pay his debts. This is not expressly stated in the Insolvency Act 1896 but follows from the fact that inability to pay one's debts is the only legitimate ground on which a debtor may present his own petition[1].

[1]   IA 1986, s 272. See para **8.218** above on the meaning of inability to pay debts.

8.238 However, even where a debtor is unable to pay his debts, the court is prohibited from making a bankruptcy order on a debtor's petition if four matters appear to it to be present:

(a)   that if a bankruptcy order was made the aggregate amount of the bankruptcy debts[1], so far as unsecured, would be less than the small bankruptcies level[2];

(b)   that if a bankruptcy order was made, the value of the bankrupt's estate would be equal to or more than the minimum amount[3];

(c)   that within the period of five years ending with the presentation of the petition the debtor has neither been adjudged bankrupt nor made a composition with his creditors in satisfaction of his debts or a scheme of arrangement of his affairs; and

(d)   that it would be appropriate to appoint a person to prepare a report as to whether it would be possible to make an IVA[4].

[1]   Defined in IA 1986, s 382.
[2]   Presently prescribed by the Insolvency Proceedings (Monetary Limits) (Amendment) Order 2004, SI 2004/547 as £40,000.
[3]   Presently prescribed in that order as £4,000.
[4]   IA 1986, s 273(1).

8.239 Although the use of the phrase 'appears to the court' suggests a lower standard of proof in respect of these four matters, it is not clear that this distinction is justified in view of the fact that the same phrase is used in relation to applications for annulment[1].

[1]   See IA 1986, s 282(1), which is, however, qualified in respect of subsection (1)(b) by IR 1986, r 6.211(1) which requires satisfaction.

8.240 If it does appear to the court on hearing the petition that the four matters set out in the last paragraph are present, it must appoint a person who is qualified to act as an insolvency practitioner in relation to the debtor to report in the first instance on whether an IVA is practicable and then, if an arrangement is established, to act in relation to it either as trustee or otherwise for the purpose of supervising its implementation[1].

[1]   IA 1986, s 273(2). The power to modify any proposal for a voluntary arrangement by conferring the functions proposed to be conferred on the person nominated by the court under IA 1986, s 273 on another person under IA 1986, s 258(3) is reserved.

8.241 Where the court makes such an appointment it must send forthwith to the person appointed a sealed copy of the order of appointment and copies of the petition and statement of affairs. It must also forthwith fix a venue for considering the report and send notice of the venue to the insolvency practitioner and to the debtor[1].

[1]   IR 1986, r 6.44(1).

Reference for purpose of applying for a debt relief order

8.241A The Tribunals, Courts and Enforcement Act 2007 introduces a new insolvency regime for individuals who do not have any substantial assets or income. Such persons may be made the subject of a debt relief order. This form of relief is discussed in **Chapter 30**. On hearing a debtor's own petition, the court can suggest that the debtor seek a debt relief order instead of becoming bankrupt. The court can take that step if, on hearing the debtor's petition, it appears to the court that a debt relief order would be made in relation to the debtor if, instead of presenting the petition, he had made an application for such an order; and the court does not appoint an insolvency practitioner under IA 1986, s 273. If the court thinks it would be in the debtor's interests to apply for a debt relief order instead of proceeding on the petition, the court may refer the debtor to an approved intermediary for the purposes of making an application for a debt relief order. The reason for referring the debtor to an approved intermediary is that a debtor may only apply for a debt relief order through an approved intermediary. Where the court takes that course, it must stay proceedings on the petition on such terms and conditions as it thinks fit; but if following the reference a debt relief order is made in relation to the debtor the court shall dismiss the petition[1].

[1]   IA 1986, s 274A, inserted by TCEA 2007, s 108(3), Sch 20, para 3 (not yet in force).

The insolvency practitioner's report

8.242 The appointed insolvency practitioner must inquire into the debtor's affairs and, within such period as the court directs, submit a report stating whether the debtor is willing to make a proposal for an IVA[1]. Where the report states that the debtor is willing to make such a proposal, it should also state whether, in the opinion of the person making the report, a meeting of the debtor's creditors should be called to consider the proposal and, if so, the date on which, and time and place at which, the insolvency practitioner proposes the meeting should be held[2]. The insolvency practitioner must file the report in court and send one copy of it to the debtor not less than three days before the date fixed for consideration of the report[3].

[1]   IA 1986, s 274(1).
[2]   IA 1986, s 274(2).
[3]   IR 1986, r 6.44(2).

Consideration of the report

8.243 When it considers the report under this section the court may without an application being made, if it thinks that it is appropriate to do so for the purpose of facilitating the consideration and implementation of the debtor's proposal, make an interim order under the IA 1986, s 252[1]. In the event that the court makes an interim order, that order will cease to have effect at the end of such period as the court may specify for the purpose of enabling the debtor's proposal to be considered by his creditors in accordance with the provisions of Part VIII of the Act[2]. Alternatively if the court thinks that it would be inappropriate to make an interim order, it may make a bankruptcy order[3]. The effect of an interim order is, inter alia, that no bankruptcy petition relating to the debtor may be proceeded with[4]. Accordingly where an interim order is made the court cannot proceed on the debtor's own petition to make a bankruptcy order.

1   IA 1986, s 274(3)(a).
2   IA 1986, s 274(4).
3   IA 1986, s 274(3)(b).
4   IA 1986, s 252(2)(a).

8.244 The structure of the provision leaves it open to the court on considering the report to take a third course of neither making an interim order nor making a bankruptcy order. Such a course might be appropriate where in preparing his report the insolvency practitioner discovered that in truth the debtor was able to pay his debts.

8.245 The debtor is entitled to attend the hearing at which the report is considered and must do so if so directed by the court. If he attends, the court must hear any representations which the debtor makes with respect to any of the matters dealt with in the report[1].

1   IR 1986, r 6.44(3).

The creditors' meeting

8.246 Where it has been reported to the court that a meeting of the debtor's creditors should be summoned and the court accepts that recommendation, the person making the report must summon the meeting for the time, date and place proposed in his report, unless the court directs otherwise. The meeting is then deemed to have been summoned under the relevant provision[1] of the Part of the Act governing voluntary arrangements and the provisions[2] of that Part applicable to creditors' meetings to consider proposals for IVAs apply[3].

1   IA 1986, s 257.
2   IA 1986, ss 258–263.
3   IA 1986, s 274(4).

Abuse of process

8.247 The court may refuse to make a bankruptcy order on a debtor's petition where the presentation of the petition is an abuse of process. It is not an abuse of process for a debtor to present his own petition in order to avoid the effect of a committal order or a judgment summons, since the purpose of bankruptcy legislation is to give debtors such protection[1]. However it is an abuse of process for a debtor to present his own petition where he has already obtained the protection of an instalment order[2].

1   *Re Painter, ex p Painter* [1895] 1 QB 85; *Re Hancock, ex p Hillearys* [1904] 1 KB 585, CA.
2   *Re a Debtor (No 17 of 1966), ex p Debtor v Allen* [1967] Ch 590, [1967] 1 All ER 668.

8.248 It was an abuse of process for a husband and wife to present a joint petition where they had no joint assets or liabilities and did so for the purpose of avoiding the payment of two sets of court fees[1]. In such a case the name of one of the petitioners should be struck out.

1   *Re Bond* (1888) 21 QBD 17.

8.249 A party to matrimonial proceedings, usually the wife, may contend that the husband has presented a petition for his own bankruptcy in order to disrupt the wife's claims in the matrimonial proceedings and that the petition therefore represents an abuse of process. The cases in which this has occurred have been cases where the wife, after the bankruptcy order has been made, has sought to have it annulled and they are discussed in the section on annulment of bankruptcy orders in **Chapter 9**.

J PETITIONS IN CONNECTION WITH INDIVIDUAL VOLUNTARY ARRANGEMENTS

8.250 Where an IVA is in force for a debtor, no petition may be proceeded with by any creditor bound by the arrangement. However in three cases where the IVA is vitiated by the conduct of the debtor the court may make a bankruptcy order on a petition presented by the supervisor of the arrangement or by a person, other than the debtor, who is bound by it. The court shall not make a bankruptcy order on such a petition unless it is satisfied either:

(a)   that the debtor has failed to comply with his obligations under the IVA;
(b)   that information which was false or misleading in any material particular or which contained material omissions was contained in any statement of affairs or other document supplied by the debtor under Part VIII to any person or was otherwise made available to his creditors at or in connection with a meeting summoned under that Part; or
(c)   that the debtor has failed to do all such things as may for the purposes of the IVA have been reasonably required of him by the supervisor of the arrangement[1].

1   IA 1986, s 276(1).

8.251 Where the petition is based on the debtor's failure to comply with his obligations under the IVA, there is no requirement to show culpability on the part of the debtor[1].

1   *Re Keenan* [1998] BPIR 205.

8.252 The form of the provision, prohibiting the making of an order unless one of the grounds is made out, leaves the court with a discretion to dismiss the petition notwithstanding that it was satisfied that a ground was made out. An occasion where that discretion might be exercised is where the petition, although justifiably presented, was opposed by the majority in value of the creditors.

Procedure

8.253 The same rules apply to a petition presented by the supervisor of, or a person bound by, an IVA as apply to creditor's petitions with any necessary modifications[1]. There is a specific statutory form for the petition[2]. The petitioner must include particulars in sufficient detail of the ground on which the court may be satisfied that it may make a bankruptcy order.

[1]   IR 1986, r 6.6.
[2]   Form 6.10.

Expenses of the IVA

8.254 Where a bankruptcy order is made on a petition presented by the supervisor of, or a person bound by, an IVA, any expenses properly incurred as expenses of the administration of the IVA form a first charge on the bankrupt's estate[1]. For other consequences of the bankruptcy order on the IVA, see paras **6.340ff**.

[1]   IA 1986, s 276(2).

Supervisor becoming the trustee in bankruptcy

8.255 The court has a discretion whether to permit the supervisor of the failed voluntary arrangement to become the trustee[1].

[1]   *Landsman v De Concilio* [2005] EWHC 267 (Ch), [2005] BPIR 829.

K PETITIONS PRESENTED BY OFFICE-HOLDERS IN ANOTHER MEMBER STATE

8.256 A petition may be presented by a temporary administrator within the meaning of the EC Insolvency Regulation, art 38 or by a liquidator within the meaning of the EC Insolvency Regulation, art 2(2)[1]. There is no prescribed form of petition for such cases. Nor do the rules deeming a member state liquidator to be a creditor apply with respect to the presentation of petitions[2]. It would seem that such office-holders should be able to present petitions directly without first serving any statutory demand.

[1]   IA 1986, s 264(1)(ba) and (bb).
[2]   IR 1986, rr 6.238 and 6.239.

Chapter 9

BANKRUPTCY ORDERS

A	Commencement of bankruptcy
B	Procedural steps following a bankruptcy order made on a creditor's petition
C	Debtor's petition
D	Annulment of bankruptcy orders
E	Procedure on annulment
F	Effect of annulment

A COMMENCEMENT OF BANKRUPTCY

Bankruptcy order

9.1 A bankruptcy order is an order that the debtor be adjudged bankrupt.

Commencement of bankruptcy

9.2 The bankruptcy of an individual against whom a bankruptcy order has been made commences with the day on which the order is made, and continues until the individual is discharged under the relevant provisions of the Insolvency Act 1986 ('IA 1986')[1].

[1] IA 1986, s 278. The relevant provisions are contained in IA 1986, ss 279–282.

B PROCEDURAL STEPS FOLLOWING A BANKRUPTCY ORDER MADE ON A CREDITOR'S PETITION

Settlement and content of the bankruptcy order

9.3 The bankruptcy order shall be settled by the court[1] and must:

(a) state the date of the presentation of the petition on which the order is made and the date and time of the making of the order; and

436

(b)   contain a notice requiring the bankrupt, forthwith after service of the order on him, to attend on the official receiver at the place stated in the order[2].

[1]   See Form 6.25.
[2]   IR 1986, r 6.33(1), (2).

9.4 Subject to the effect of the bankruptcy on enforcement proceedings by virtue of the IA 1986, s 346, the order may stay any action or proceeding against the bankrupt[1].

[1]   IR 1986, r 6.33(3).

9.5 The order should give details of the petitioning creditor's solicitor if the petitioning creditor has been represented, including name, address, telephone number and reference[1].

[1]   IR 1986, r 6.33(4).

Action to follow the order and registration of bankruptcy order

9.6 Following the making of the order, at least two sealed copies must be sent forthwith by the court to the official receiver, who must in turn send one forthwith to the bankrupt[1]. The official receiver must then:

(a)   send notice of the making of the order to the Chief Land Registrar, for registration in the register of writs and orders affecting land[2];
(b)   cause the order to be advertised in such newspaper as he thinks fit;
(c)   cause the order to be gazetted[3]; and
(d)   cause to be entered on to the individual insolvency register the information contained in the petition as to the identity of the bankrupt, the date of the making of the bankruptcy order, the name of the court which made it and the court reference number stated on the order[4].

[1]   IR 1986, r 6.34(1).
[2]   See the Land Charges Act 1972, s 6 and also, in the case of registered land, the Land Registration Act 1925, ss 59 and 61.
[3]   IR 1986, r 6.34(2).
[4]   IR 1986, r 6A.4(2).

9.7 However, the official receiver may be ordered to suspend such action, including registration in the individual insolvency register, by the court pending further order on the application of the bankrupt or a creditor. Where such an application is made it must be supported by an affidavit stating the grounds on which it is made[1]. An instance where such a stay would be appropriate is where the debtor intends to seek to annul the bankruptcy order on the ground that it ought not to have been made[2]. If an order staying action by the official receiver to promulgate the bankruptcy order is made, the applicant must deliver forthwith a copy of the order granting the stay to the official receiver[3].

[1]   IR 1986, r 6.34(3).

Bankruptcy of solicitors

9.8 Where a bankruptcy order is made against a solicitor, the court must give notice of the order forthwith to the Secretary of the Law Society[1].

1   IR 1986, r 6.235.

Amendment of title of proceedings

9.9 At any time after the making of a bankruptcy order, the official receiver or the trustee may apply to the court for an order amending the full title of the proceedings[1]. A reason for doing so would be to add further names under which the bankrupt had carried on business[2]. Where such an order is made, the official receiver shall forthwith send notice of it to the Chief Land Registrar for corresponding amendment of the register; and if the court so directs he shall also cause notice of the order to be gazetted and to be advertised in such local newspaper as the official receiver thinks fit[3].

1   IR 1986, r 6.35(1). For the full title see IR 1986, r 6.7 and para **8.136** above.
2   *Yee Fun Cho v Price* [2004] BPIR 603.
3   IR 1986, r 6.35(2).

C DEBTOR'S PETITION

Bankruptcy order

9.10 The various orders which a court may make on the hearing of a debtor's petition have been discussed in the previous chapter. As described there the court may make a bankruptcy order if it is satisfied that the debtor is unable to pay his debts. Despite the measures laid down[1], where the amount of the liabilities and the size of estate are low, for the appointment of an insolvency practitioner to report and, if appropriate, to hold a creditors' meeting for the purpose of attempting to establish an IVA, a bankruptcy order may still be made in such a case; for the report may be unfavourable or the creditors may reject the proposal.

1   IA 1986, ss 273, 274.

Settlement and content of the bankruptcy order

9.11 As with a bankruptcy order made on a creditor's petition, the order shall be settled by the court[1] and must:

(a)   state the date of the presentation of the petition on which the order is made and the date and time of the making of the order; and

438

(b)   contain a notice requiring the bankrupt, forthwith after service of the order on him, to attend on the official receiver at the place stated in the order[2].

1   There is a different statutory form: Form 6.30.
2   IR 1986, r 6.45(1), (2).

9.12 Subject to the effect of the bankruptcy on enforcement proceedings by virtue of the IA 1986, s 346, the order may stay any action or proceeding against the bankrupt[1].

1   IR 1986, r 6.45(3).

9.13 The order should give details of the bankrupt's solicitor if he has been represented, including name, address, telephone number and reference[1].

1   IR 1986, r 6.45(4).

Action to follow the order

9.14 Following the making of the order, at least two sealed copies must be sent forthwith by the court to the official receiver, who must in turn send one forthwith to the bankrupt[1]. The official receiver is then obliged:

(a)   to send notice of the making of the order to the Chief Land Registrar, for registration in the register of writs and orders affecting land[2];
(b)   to cause the order to be advertised in such newspaper as he thinks fit;
(c)   to cause the order to be gazetted[3]; and
(d)   to cause to be entered on to the individual insolvency register the information contained in the petition as to the identity of the bankrupt, the date of the making of the bankruptcy order, the name of the court which made it and the court reference number stated on the order[4].

1   IR 1986, r 6.46(1).
2   See the Land Charges Act 1972, s 6 and also, in the case of registered land, the Land Registration Act 1925, ss 59 and 61.
3   IR 1986, r 6.46(2).
4   IR 1986, r 6A.4(2).

9.15 However, the official receiver may be ordered to suspend such action, including registration in the individual insolvency register, by the court pending further order on the application of the bankrupt or a creditor.

9.16 Where such an application is made it must be supported by an affidavit stating the grounds on which it is made[1]. If an order is made staying action by the official receiver to promulgate the bankruptcy order, the applicant must deliver forthwith a copy of the order granting the stay to the official receiver[2].

1   IR 1986, r 6.46(3).
2   IR 1986, r 6.46(4).

Amendment of title of proceedings

9.17 At any time after the making of a bankruptcy order, the official receiver or the trustee may apply to the court for an order amending the full title of the proceedings[1]. Where such an order is made, the official receiver shall forthwith send notice of it to the Chief Land Registrar for corresponding amendment of the register; and if the court so directs the official receiver shall also cause notice of the order to be gazetted and to be advertised in such local newspaper as he thinks appropriate[2].

[1]   IR 1986, r 6.47(1). For the full title see IR 1986, r 6.38 and cf para **8.223**.
[2]   IR 1986, r 6.47(2).

Repeal of summary administration

9.18 Before 1 April 2004 the court, on making a bankruptcy order on a debtor's petition, was obliged, if certain conditions were satisfied and it appeared appropriate to do so, to issue a certificate for the summary administration of the bankrupt's estate. But the provisions relating to summary administration were repealed with effect from 1 April 2004[1]. Transitional provisions apply to bankruptcies where a certificate of summary administration was in force on 1 April 2004[2].

[1]   Enterprise Act 2002, s 269 and Sch 23.
[2]   Enterprise Act 2002 (Commencement No 4 and Transitional Provisions and Savings) Order 2003, SI 2003/2093, art 8.

Registration of bankruptcy orders received by the official receiver on or after 1 April 2004

9.19 When the official receiver receives the copy of the bankruptcy order which is sent to him by the court, he must cause to be registered in the individual insolvency register the following information as stated in the bankruptcy petition:

(a)   the bankrupt's name, place of business and occupation (if any);
(b)   the name or names in which the bankrupt carries on business, if other than his true name, and whether, in the case of any business of a specified nature, he carries it on alone or with others;
(c)   the nature of the bankrupt's business, and the address or addresses at which he carries it on;
(d)   any name or names, other than his true name, in which he has carried on business in the period during which any of his bankruptcy debts were incurred and, in the case of any such business, whether he has carried it on alone or with others;
(e)   any address or addresses at which he has resided or carried on business during that period and the nature of that business;
(f)   where the bankruptcy order was made on a creditor's petition whether the bankrupt has his centre of main interests or an establishment in another Member State; and

(g)   any name which the bankrupt has used other than that first-mentioned above[1].

1   IR 1986, r 6A.4(2)(a).

9.20 At the same time the official receiver must cause to be registered the date of the bankruptcy order, the court which made it and the court reference number[1]. He must register further information when he receives it[2].

1   IR 1986, r 6A.4(2)(b)–(d).
2   IR 1986, r 6A.4(3), see para **3.178**.

9.21

The individual insolvency register is described more fully at para **3.172**.

D ANNULMENT OF BANKRUPTCY ORDERS

Overview

9.22 An order of annulment restores the bankrupt to his pre-bankruptcy status and he remains liable in full for all his bankruptcy debts. It is to be contrasted with discharge, whether automatic or by order, which releases the bankrupt from almost all his bankruptcy debts.

9.23 There are three situations in which an order of annulment may be made:

(1)   if it appears to the court that, on any grounds existing at the time when the bankruptcy order was made, the order ought not to have been made[1];
(2)   if it appears to the court that, to the extent required by the rules, the bankruptcy debts and the expenses of the bankruptcy have all, since the making of the bankruptcy order, been either paid or secured for to the satisfaction of the court[2]; and
(3)   where an undischarged bankrupt makes an IVA with his creditors.

The third case is discussed in **Chapter 6**[3].

1   IA 1986, s 282(1)(a).
2   IA 1986, s 282(1)(b).
3   See para **6.264**.

9.24 The jurisdiction to order annulment is discretionary and even if one of the grounds on which an order may be made is established, the court may still refuse to order annulment[1].

1   *Gill v Quinn* [2004] EWHC 883 (Ch), [2005] BPIR 129.

Persons who may apply

9.25 The Insolvency Act 1986 does not limit the class of persons who may apply to annul a bankruptcy order. Usually it will be the bankrupt who wishes to annul the order, but others who are affected by the order are entitled to apply: for example, a divorcing wife who considers that her husband's bankruptcy has been wrongly contrived in order to thwart her claim for ancillary relief[1].

1   *F v F (S Intervenor)* [2002] EWCA Civ 1527 at para 10.

No time limit

9.26 An application to annul may be made after the bankrupt's discharge[1] and no period is prescribed within which an application must be made. But, the consequences of a long lapse of time between the making of the bankruptcy order and the application to annul it will be relevant to the exercise of discretion and may lead the court to refuse to annul[2].

1   IA 1986, s 282(3).
2   *Gill v Quinn* [2004] EWHC 883 (Ch), [2005] BPIR 129.

Orders which ought not to have been made

9.27 The grounds showing why the order ought not to have been made must be grounds existing at the time when the order was made. The court may not take into account events which occurred after the time when the bankruptcy order was made. But evidence setting out the facts obtaining at the time of the bankruptcy order may be adduced on the application to annul even though it was not before the court which made the bankruptcy order. For example, the applicant may give an explanation why he or his representative was not present at the hearing of the petition[1]. Evidence of matters arising after the bankruptcy may be adduced to show that the debt on which the petition is based did not in fact exist. Such evidence is admissible even where the petition is based on a default judgment which had not been set aside when the bankruptcy order was made[2].

1   *Hope v Premierspace (Europe) Ltd* [1999] BPIR 695 (Rimer J).
2   *Royal Bank of Scotland v Farley* [1996] BPIR 638, CA; see 639H–640D where Hoffmann LJ disagreed with the approach taken on this point by Harman J whose decision is reported at [1996] BPIR 511. If the bankruptcy order is made, the bankrupt will not have standing to pursue the application to set aside the judgment while the bankruptcy subsists; he must therefore seek annulment of the bankruptcy order before proceeding with the application to set aside the judgment. If the court decides to annul the bankruptcy order, it need not dismiss the petition which can be adjourned to be reheard after the application to set aside the judgment has been made. If the bankruptcy order stands, what to do with the proceedings, and any cause of action to which they relate, is a matter for the trustee to decide. See also *Heath v Tang* [1993] 4 All ER 694, [1993] 1 WLR 1421, CA.

9.28 In *Re Coney*[1] the bankrupt sought to set aside an order made on his own petition on the basis that it was not true that he was unable to pay his debts at the time the order was made. He sought to show that he was able to pay his debts by recreating a balance sheet of his assets and liabilities with a view to show that assets exceeded liabilities. He failed to establish this on the evidence, but in any event the judge held that the correct test was whether he could pay his debts as they fell due.

¹   [1998] BPIR 333, CA.

Examples under the Bankruptcy Act 1914

9.29 Examples of circumstances in which the court annulled bankruptcy orders under the old law are where the bankruptcy order was made on a petition, presentation of which was an abuse of process[1]; where the order was made on the basis of evidence which turned out to be untrue[2]; where the debtor was dead at the time when bankruptcy proceedings were commenced[3]; where the debtor was a minor and the debt was not legally enforceable against him[4]. Failure to serve the petition ought to be sufficient ground.

¹   *Re Painter, ex p Painter* [1895] 1 QB 85; *Re a Debtor (No 17 of 1966), ex p Debtor v Allen* [1967] Ch 590, [1967] 1 All E 668.
²   *Re Bright, ex p Wingfield and Blew* [1903] 1 KB 735.
³   *Re Stanger, ex p Geisel* (1882) 22 Ch D 436, CA.
⁴   *Re Davenport, ex p Bankrupt v Eric Street Properties Ltd* [1963] 2 All ER 850, [1963] 1 WLR 817, CA as explained in *Re Noble, ex p Bankrupt v Official Receiver* [1965] Ch 129, [1964] 2 All ER 522, CA.

Abuse of process

9.30 A line of cases illustrate that the possibility that a spouse, usually the husband against whom the other spouse seeks financial relief in matrimonial proceedings may cause himself to be adjudged bankrupt with the purpose of thereby thwarting or obstructing the wife's application for financial relief. If the wife then applies to annul the bankruptcy order, it may be appropriate to transfer her application to the court seised of the matrimonial proceedings[1]. The advantages are first, that, since full disclosure of assets should be made to the matrimonial court, the evidence available to the matrimonial court as to the bankrupt's financial affairs is likely to be as good as can be achieved; secondly, that it ensures consistency between the decisions in the matrimonial and bankruptcy proceedings; and thirdly, that duplication of costs will be avoided.

¹   *F v F (S Intervenor)* [2002] EWCA Civ 1527 where the wife applied in the Family Division to annul the bankruptcy order; the judge decided to stand the application over until he had heard the wife's application for ancillary relief; the Court of Appeal dismissed the husband's appeal against that decision on the ground that it was an appropriate exercise of the judge's power to manage the proceedings with which it would not interfere.

9.31 But whatever the forensic context the issues remain (1) whether the bankruptcy order ought not to have been made on grounds existing at the time when it was made, and (2) whether in the circumstances the court should annul the bankruptcy order. Thus in *F v F (divorce: insolvency)*[1] Thorpe J held that, since the bankruptcy order, made on the husband's own petition, had been obtained on the basis of the husband's false statement as to his financial circumstances, the bankruptcy order was the result of an abuse of the bankruptcy process and should be set aside. It is important to observe that the abuse of process was comprised in the false statement of the husband's affairs made by him in support of his petition; the abuse was not comprised in the fact that the husband's purpose was to intensify the wife's difficulties in the matrimonial proceedings. Further, it is clearly implicit that the court was satisfied that the value of the husband's assets exceeded the amount of his liabilities[2]. Similarly in *Couvaras v Wolf*[3], where the petition was presented by someone who untruly and with the husband's connivance claimed to be a creditor, Wilson J annulled the ensuing bankruptcy order on the ground that the bankruptcy proceedings were an abuse of the process of the bankruptcy court. It is clearly correct that the order should not have been made where a creditor's petition is founded on non-existent debts. The court also found that the husband was solvent in the sense that the value of his assets exceeded that of his liabilities[4].

[1] [1994] 1 FLR 359.
[2] See [1994] 1 FLR 359 at 366E.
[3] [2002] 2 FLR 107.
[4] See [2002] 2 FLR 107 at 112H.

9.32 There does not appear to have been any need in the two cases just mentioned to consider whether it was right to assess the bankrupt's solvency by balancing the value of the assets against the amount of the liabilities. As a general rule, the better test is whether a debtor is able to pay his debts when they fall due. In *F v F (S intervening)*[1] the husband owed substantial and genuine debts which were unpaid when he presented his own petition and was adjudged bankrupt on it. But his assets, which well exceeded his liabilities in value, included property capable of being used to satisfy his creditors' claims. Accordingly Coleridge J found that the husband had, when the bankruptcy order was made, 'some tangible and immediate prospect of being able' to meet his liabilities and that hence 'there was no basis for his filing a bankruptcy petition on that date'. Since there was money held in court, the judge was able to order that the genuine debts be paid out of that money and thereby ensure prompt payment. It is interesting to speculate what the result would have been had the bankruptcy order been made on a petition presented by one of the genuine creditors whom the husband in his intransigence had refused to pay. It would seem impossible in that case for the court to find that the bankruptcy order ought not to have been made[2], but on the facts all the bankruptcy debts and expenses could be paid in full; so, perhaps, pursuant to its general control of the bankruptcy[3], the court could, on the wife's application, direct the trustee to pay or, where appropriate, secure all the bankruptcy debts so as to enable the court to order an annulment under the IA 1986, s 282(1)(b).

[1] [2003] 1 FLR 911.
[2] Compare *Artman v Artman* [1996] BPIR 511 where the petition was presented by a creditor and, in addition, the bankrupt was insolvent on a balance sheet basis.
[3] IA 1986, s 363(1).

Payment of all bankruptcy debts

9.33 The second situation in which a bankruptcy order may be annulled is where it appears to the court that, to the extent required by the rules, the bankruptcy debts and the expenses of the bankruptcy have all, since the making of the bankruptcy order, been either paid or secured to the satisfaction of the court. The requirements imposed by the rules are contained in IR 1986, r 6.211. The circumstances in which the bankrupt may provide security for his debts are limited.

9.34 The principal requirement is that all bankruptcy debts[1] which have been proved must have been paid in full[2]. This does not mean that the bankrupt need only pay those bankruptcy debts which have been proved before the application to annul is heard; if there are known creditors who have not proved, steps to find them may be taken and the application adjourned for the purpose of enabling them to prove[3]. The court's current practice is not to order annulment on the basis of an undertaking, even by a solicitor, to pay the debts. In *IRC v Khan*[4] annulment was ordered on the basis of an accountant's undertaking. The accountant absconded without fulfilling his undertaking.

1   IA 1986, s 382.
2   IR 1986, r 6.211(2).
3   *Re Robertson (a bankrupt)* [1989] 1 WLR 1139 (Warner J); IR 1986, r 6.209.
4   [2005] BPIR 409.

9.35 But where a debt is disputed or a creditor who has proved can no longer be traced, the bankrupt must give such security as the court considers adequate to satisfy any sum that may subsequently be proved to be due to the creditors concerned and, if the court thinks fit, costs. The security may be given in the form of money paid into court or a bond entered into with approved sureties[1]. Where security has been given in the case of an untraced creditor, the court may direct that particulars of the debt and the security be advertised; if no claim has been made within 12 months, the court shall, on an application, order the release of the security[2]. Presumably where the security was in the form of a bond supported by sureties, any one of those sureties would have sufficient standing to apply for the release of the security.

1   IR 1986, r 6.211(3).
2   IR 1986, r 6.211(4).

9.36 Interest on the bankruptcy debts is not referred to in IA 1986, s 282(1)(b) and it has been held that payment of interest is not required in order to fulfil the condition set by that subsection which when fulfilled empowers the court to order annulment[1]. But, where the condition is fulfilled, the court has still to exercise a discretion whether to exercise that power[2]. In general, the court will require interest to be paid. Where the debts are being paid out by third party funds, then the court may by concession consider whether annulment may be granted without payment of interest. But the concession is only likely to be made where the creditor has expressly waived the interest. The trustee should make enquiries of the creditors and include their responses in his report[3].

1   *Harper v Buchler* [2004] BPIR 724.
2   *Harper v Buchler* [2004] BPIR 724 and *Harper v Buchler (No 2)* [2005] BPIR 577.
3   *Wilcock v Duckworth* [2005] BPIR 682.

The court's discretion

9.37 If the applicant establishes the primary ground for an annulment, the court has power to annul. But exercise of the power is discretionary[1]. The Insolvency Act 1986 does not lay down any particular matters to be taken into account and the court may take all the circumstances into account in deciding whether to exercise the power or not. Relevant factors include the likely effect of the annulment on the applicant, on the bankrupt where he is not the applicant and on the bankrupt's creditors. Any abuse of process in the obtaining or making of the bankruptcy order may also be taken into account[2]. Abuse of process is more likely to be present where the application is made under the IA 1986, s 282(1)(a) and the applicant for the annulment order is someone other than the bankrupt; it would militate in favour of annulment. It has been suggested in *obiter dicta* that special circumstances would be required for the court to uphold the bankruptcy order where it has been established that, because the petition debt was on proper analysis disputed, the order should not have been made[3].

1   *Owo-Samson v Barclays Bank plc (No 3)* [2004] BPIR 303.
2   *Artman v Artman* [1996] BPIR 511 (Robert Walker J).
3   *Guinan v Caldwell Associates Ltd* [2003] EWHC 3348 (Ch), [2004] BPIR 531.

9.38 By way of example, in *Askew v Peter Dominic Ltd*[1] the Court of Appeal refused leave to appeal in a case where the single judge hearing the appeal from the original application for annulment had refused to annul a bankruptcy order although it was clear that there were grounds, existing at the time when the order was made, establishing that it ought not to have been made. The grounds were that the statutory demand and the petition did not name the bankrupt but her husband. Nevertheless the district judge exercising the original jurisdiction refused to order an annulment; that decision was upheld on appeal to the single judge, on the basis that the applicant was, in truth, the debtor and had no defence to the claim; and leave to appeal was refused by the Court of Appeal.

1   [1997] BPIR 163, CA; cf *Re Taylor, ex p Taylor* [1901] 1 KB 744; *Re Keet, ex p Official Receiver* [1905] 2 KB 666, CA; and *Re a Debtor (No 37 of 1976), ex p Taylor v Debtor* [1980] Ch 565, [1980] 1 All ER 129.

9.39 In *Gill v Quinn*[1] sufficient and satisfactory security was available to cover liabilities to creditors who had not proved. But the length of time which had elapsed since the bankruptcy order made it improbable that those creditors who had not proved would do so and the number of them made them too substantial a body to overlook. Hence, although the requirements of IA 1986, s 282(1)(b) were satisfied, Mann J declined to order annulment.

1   [2004] EWHC 883 (Ch), [2005] BPIR 129.

9.40 The court ought not to annul a bankruptcy order by consent and without investigation because bankruptcy is a class remedy and not simply a matter between the bankrupt and the petitioning creditor[1].

1   *Housiaux (t/a Harpers of Weybridge) v HM Customs and Excise* [2003] BPIR 858.

Form of order

9.41 If an order is made in conditional terms, there may be doubt later whether the conditions have been satisfied and the annulment taken effect. So, the practice is not to make conditional orders but a similar effect may be achieved by the court's making an unconditional order but directing that it lie on the court file and only be perfected on completion of the further steps. There will then be no doubt after the order is made that it has taken effect[1].

1   *Engel v Peri* [2002] BPIR 961, [2002] All ER (D) 285 (Apr).

Costs

9.42 In a case where the court annulled a bankruptcy order under this ground on the basis that no liquidated debt was disclosed by the petition, it ordered the petitioner to pay the official receiver's costs because the petition ought not to have been presented[1]. Although the bankruptcy order may have been made through no fault of the bankrupt, the trustee will, in general, still be entitled to his costs out of the estate because it would be unfair to impose on him the need to pursue some other party for his costs[2].

1   *Hope v Premierspace (Europe) Ltd* [1999] BPIR 695 (Rimer J).
2   *Thornhill v Atherton* [2004] EWCA Civ 1853, [2005] BPIR 437.

Relationship between applications for annulment and applications to review

9.43 Where a bankrupt seeks to impeach a bankruptcy order on grounds which fall within IA 1986, s 282, the primary method of setting the bankruptcy order aside is by way of application to annul. In exceptional circumstances, it may also be open to the bankrupt to seek to rescind the order under IA 1986, s 375. In *IRC v Robinson*[1] the bankrupt sought to rescind the bankruptcy order which had been made against him by arranging for the petition debt, but no others, to be paid with third party funds. The deputy judge held that it was clear that a bankrupt should not be able to escape from his bankruptcy simply by paying the petition debt: IA 1986, s 282(1)(b) requires all the bankruptcy debts to be paid before the bankruptcy order may be annulled.

1   [1999] BPIR 329.

Relationship between applications to annul and appeals

9.44 Where it is open to a bankrupt to seek to annul the bankruptcy order because it ought not to have been made, he ought to apply to annul rather than seek to appeal. The application to annul will be heard more promptly and his ability to adduce further evidence is less restricted.

447

Annulment following implementation of a voluntary arrangement

9.45 It is open to a debtor, after a bankruptcy order has been made, to make a proposal for a voluntary arrangement within the meaning of the IA 1986, Pt VIII. How to make such a proposal is explained in **Chapter 6** and the rules relating to making a proposal apply where the debtor is an undischarged bankrupt[1].

1   IR 1986, r 5.1(2).

9.46 Where the creditors' meeting summoned[1] to consider a proposal made by an undischarged bankrupt approves it, with or without modifications, the court must annul the bankruptcy order on the bankrupt's application or on the application of the official receiver, if the bankrupt fails to apply within the prescribed period[2]. The court may also give such directions about the conduct of the bankruptcy and the administration of the bankrupt's estate as it thinks appropriate for facilitating the implementation of the approved voluntary arrangement[3]. The power to annul may not be exercised at any time before the end of the period of 28 days beginning with the day on which the report of the creditors' meeting was made to the court[4], or while an application to challenge the decision to approve the proposal[5], or while an appeal in respect of such application, is pending or at any time in the period within which such an appeal may be brought[6]. Thus the bankruptcy order may not be annulled at any time when the voluntary arrangement is liable to be upset on the application of a creditor.

1   Under IA 1986, s 257.
2   IA 1986, s 261(2).
3   IA 1986, s 261(4).
4   Under IA 1986, s 259.
5   Under IA 1986, s 262.
6   IA 1986, s 261(3).

Stay of advertisement

9.47 If the application to annul is made before the official receiver advertises the bankruptcy order or registers it in the register of bankruptcy orders, the applicant may seek an order staying the advertisement and the registration[1] until after the hearing of the application to annul. The application to stay the advertisement should be made immediately when it is decided to apply to annul, if necessary without notice at first, since the official receiver is obliged to advertise forthwith and may not hold his hand until the hearing of the application to annul.

1   Under IR 1986, r 6.34(3) in the case of a creditor's petition or IR 1986, r 6.46(3) in the case of a debtor's petition.

E PROCEDURE OF ANNULMENT

9.48 An application to annul made under the IA 1986, s 282(1) must specify under which paragraph of that subsection it is made and must be supported by a witness statement or affidavit stating the grounds on which it is made[1]. If the application is made on the basis that all the bankruptcy debts which have been proved have been paid in full there must be set out in the affidavit all the facts of which the court must be satisfied before annulling the bankruptcy order[2]. Where the application is made under the IA 1986, s 261, the same rules of procedure apply as do to an application made on the ground that the bankruptcy order was wrongly made[3].

1   IR 1986, r 6.206(1), (2).
2   IR 1986, r 6.206(2). Those matters are set out in IR 1986, r 6.211; see further para **9.33** above.
3   IR 1986, r 6.212A.

9.49 A copy of the application and the supporting affidavit must be filed in court and the court shall give to the applicant notice of the venue fixed for the hearing[1]. The applicant must give the official receiver and, if different, the trustee, notice of the venue, accompanied by copies of the application and the supporting affidavit. Where the application is made on the basis of full payment, the applicant must give them notice not less than 28 days before the hearing; where it is made on the basis that the bankruptcy order ought not to have been made or on the basis of an accepted voluntary arrangement, the applicant must give them and the person on whose petition the order was made notice in sufficient time to enable them to be present at the hearing[2].

1   IR 1986, r 6.206(3).
2   IR 1986, r 6.206(4), (5).

Trustee's report

9.50 Where the application is made on the basis that all the bankruptcy debts and expenses are paid or secured[1], the trustee or, if no trustee has been appointed, the official receiver must file in court a report with respect to:

(a)   the circumstances leading to the bankruptcy;
(b)   (in summarised form) the extent of the bankrupt's assets and liabilities at the date of the bankruptcy order and at the date of the present application;
(c)   details of any creditors known to him to have claims, but who have not proved; and
(d)   such other matters as the person making the report considers to be, in the circumstances, necessary for the information of the court[2].

1   Under IA 1986, s 282(1)(b).
2   IR 1986, r 6.207(1), (2).

9.51 The report must be filed not less than 21 days before the date fixed for the hearing[1]. The report must include particulars of the extent, if any, to which the debts and expenses of the bankruptcy have been paid or secured. Insofar as debts are unpaid but secured, the person making the report must state in it whether and to what extent he considers the security to be satisfactory[2].

1   IR 1986, r 6.207(2).
2   IR 1986, r 6.207(3).

9.52 A copy of the report must be sent to the applicant at least 14 days before the hearing date and he may, if he wishes, file further affidavits in answer to any statements made in the report; copies of such affidavits must be sent by the applicant to the official receiver and, if different, the trustee[1]. If the trustee is different from the official receiver, a copy of his report must be sent to the official receiver at least 21 days before the hearing. The official receiver may then file an additional report, a copy of which shall be sent to the applicant at least seven days before the hearing[2].

1   IR 1986, r 6.207(4).
2   IR 1986, r 6.207(5).

9.53 If the trustee's report states that there are known creditors of the bankrupt who have not proved, the court may direct the trustee to send notice of the application to such of the creditors as the court thinks ought to be informed of it, with a view to their proving their debts within 21 days, and direct the trustee to advertise the fact that the application has been made, so that creditors who have not proved may do so within a specified time, and adjourn the application meanwhile, for any period not less than 35 days[1]. Where no trustee has been appointed, the court's directions will be made to the official receiver.

1   IR 1986, r 6.209.

Interim order

9.54 In advance of the hearing of the application to annul the bankruptcy order the court may make an interim order staying any proceedings which it thinks ought, in the circumstances of the application, to be stayed[1]. This would not necessarily have the same effect as an interim order within the meaning of the IA 1986, s 252, in that it may not amount to a blanket stay. An application for an order staying proceedings may be made without notice unless it is made for an order staying all or any part of the proceedings in the bankruptcy; in the latter case the applicant must send copies of the application to the official receiver and, if different, the trustee in sufficient time to enable them to be present at the hearing and, if they wish, to make representations[2]. If the court makes an order staying all or part of the proceedings in the bankruptcy, the relevant Insolvency Rules[3] continue to apply to any application for, or other matters in connection with, the annulment of the bankruptcy order[4].

1   IR 1986, r 6.208(1).
2   IR 1986, r 6.208(2), (3).
3   Ie IR 1986, rr 6.206–6.214.
4   IR 1986, r 6.208(4).

Attendances

9.55 At the hearing of the application to annul the bankruptcy order, the trustee must attend[1]. The official receiver is not required to attend unless he is the trustee or he has filed a report under IR 1986, r 6.207[2]. If the court makes an order on the application, it must send copies to the applicant, the official receiver and, if different, the trustee[3].

[1]   IR 1986, r 6.210(1).
[2]   IR 1986, r 6.210(2).
[3]   IR 1986, r 6.210(3).

The order of annulment

9.56 The form of the order of annulment is that the bankruptcy petition on which the order was made is dismissed and the bankruptcy order is annulled. The court must include in the order provision permitting vacation of the registration of the bankruptcy petition as a pending action, and of the bankruptcy order, in the register of writs and orders affecting land[1]. Where further steps need to be taken such as a payment into court to secure debts or the payment of costs, the court has power to make the order of annulment conditional upon those steps being taken. But the better technique is to make an unconditional order but direct that it lie on the court file and only be perfected on completion of the further steps. There will then be no doubt after the order is made that it has taken effect[2].

[1]   IR 1986, r 6.213(1).
[2]   *Engel v Peri* [2002] BPIR 961.

9.57 If the court makes an order, it must send copies of the order to the applicant, the official receiver and, if different, the trustee[1].

[1]   IR 1986, r 6.208(5).

Notice of annulment

9.58 If the court annuls the bankruptcy order, it must forthwith give notice to the Secretary of State that the order has been made[1]. To publicise the annulment the former bankrupt may then require the Secretary of State to publish a notice stating that the annulment order has been made in the Gazette, or in any newspaper in which the bankruptcy order was advertised, or in both[2]. The requirement must be made in writing addressed to the Secretary of State; on receipt of the requirement the Secretary of State must inform the bankrupt of the cost of the advertisement and need not advertise until the cost has been paid by the bankrupt[3]. The rules provide for the requirement to be made by a personal representative where the bankrupt is dead or, where he is incapable of managing his affairs[4], by a person appointed by the court[5] to represent or act for him[6].

[1]   IR 1986, r 6.213(2).
[2]   IR 1986, r 6.213(3).

3   IR 1986, r 6.213(4).
4   Ie a person who is incapable of managing and administering his property and affairs either
     by reason of a mental disorder within the meaning of the Mental Health Act 1983 or due
     to physical affliction or disability; see IR 1986, r 7.43(1).
5   See IR 1986, r 7.44.
6   IR 1986, r 6.213(5).

9.59 If the official receiver has notified creditors of the bankruptcy and the order is annulled, then he must notify them forthwith of the annulment[1]. If he incurs expense in notifying creditors, a charge arises in his favour on the property of the former bankrupt, whether that property is in the official receiver's hands or not[2]. Where the property is held by a trustee or any person other than the former bankrupt himself, the charge is valid subject only to any costs that may be incurred by the person holding the property in realising the property for the purpose of satisfying the charge[3].

1   IR 1986, r 6.212(1).
2   IR 1986, r 6.212(2).
3   IR 1986, r 6.212(3).

9.60 Where the bankruptcy order is annulled and, in the case where the annulment is on the ground that the order ought not to have been made the Secretary of State has received notice of the annulment, the Secretary of State should delete from the individual insolvency register all information concerning the bankruptcy[1].

1   IR 1986, r 6A.5(a) and (b).

9.61 Where a bankruptcy order made against a solicitor is annulled or rescinded, the court must forthwith give notice to the Secretary of the Law Society of the order which it has made[1].

1   IR 1986, r 6.235.

Costs

9.62 If a bankruptcy order is annulled on the basis that it ought not to have been made and the court orders a person other than the former bankrupt to bear the costs, it is important that the order for costs should, if justified, include any costs and expenses incurred by the official receiver and, if different, the trustee, since these will otherwise come out of the estate.

Dispute as to the amount of the costs

9.63 Where there is a dispute as to the amount of the costs of the administration, security for the amount sought should be provided and the costs assessed following the annulment[1].

1   *Hirani v Rendle* [2003] EWHC 2538 (Ch), [2004] BPIR 274.

F EFFECT OF ANNULMENT

9.64 The principal effect of annulment has been said to be to remit the party whose bankruptcy is set aside to his original position or situation[1]. This is correct in that the individual concerned will revert to his former status and, for certain purposes, the bankruptcy will be treated as though it had not occurred.

[1]   *Bailey v Johnson* (1872) LR 7 Exch 263.

9.65 However, there are some consequences from which the individual concerned will not escape. Any sale or other disposition of property, payment made, or other thing done, under any provision of the Insolvency Act 1986 relating to insolvent individuals[1], by or under the authority of the official receiver or a trustee of the bankrupt's estate or by the court, is valid. But if any of the bankrupt's estate is vested by reason of any such provision in a trustee of the estate, that property shall vest in such person as the court may appoint or, in default of such an appointment, it shall revert to the bankrupt on such terms, if any, as the court may direct[2]. In its order the court may include such supplemental provisions as may be authorised by the Insolvency Rules.

[1]   Ie IA 1986, ss 252–385.
[2]   IA 1986, s 282(4).

9.66 The fact that a bankruptcy order has been made, even though it has been subsequently annulled, may operate harshly where rights have become forfeit by reason of the order. Thus if a lease contains a proviso for forfeiture on the bankruptcy of the tenant, the landlord's entitlement to forfeit the lease is not lost by the annulment of the bankruptcy order relating to the tenant. However, where the right to relief had not been lost by the bankruptcy[1], the annulment of the order would lend strong support to an application for relief from forfeiture.

[1]   Law of Property Act 1925, s 146(9), (10).

9.67 Under a settlement or a will, an entitlement to a payment of income may be defeasible on the payment becoming due to some person other than the original donee. Forfeiture of such an entitlement will be effective, despite annulment, where a payment under the settlement falls due before the annulment is made[1].

[1]   *Re Forder, Forder v Forder* [1927] 2 Ch 291, CA.

Bankruptcy offences

9.68 The provisions of the Insolvency Act 1986 relating to bankruptcy offences[1] apply whether or not the bankruptcy order is annulled but proceedings for such an offence may not be instituted after the annulment[2].

[1]   Ie IA 1986, ss 350–362.
[2]   IA 1986, s 350(2).

Trustee's continuing duties

9.69 Annulment of the bankruptcy order does not release the trustee from the duties and obligations imposed on him by the Insolvency Act 1986 and the Insolvency Rules, to account for all his transactions in connection with the former bankrupt's estate[1]. In particular, he must submit a copy of his final account to the Secretary of State as soon as practicable after the order of annulment is made; and he must file a copy of that final account in court[2]. In it he must include a summary of the receipts and payments in the administration and he must state that he has reconciled his account with that which is held by the Secretary of State in respect of the bankruptcy[3]. The trustee will be released at such time as the court may determine. When considering whether to release the trustee, the court must have regard to whether the trustee has submitted copies of his final account to the Secretary of State and to the court, and whether any security given in respect of a disputed debt or an untraced creditor[4] has been, or will be, released[5].

[1]   IR 1986, r 6.214(1).
[2]   IR 1986, r 6.214(2).
[3]   IR 1986, r 6.214(3).
[4]   Under IR 1986, r 6.211(3).
[5]   IR 1986, r 6.214(4).

Chapter 10

EFFECT OF BANKRUPTCY ON THE BANKRUPT'S CAPACITY

A INTRODUCTION

10.1 A consequence of bankruptcy used to be to disqualify the bankrupt, until he is discharged, from holding a variety of offices. The most conspicuous disqualification was the disqualification from participating in Parliament as an MP or as a peer. Underlying this approach used to be the thought 'that he who has made shipwreck of his own fortunes is not fit to be trusted to guide and care for the interests of others'[1]. The Enterprise Act 2002 has made a substantial change. Bankruptcy no longer automatically entails many of the disqualifications which previously attended it. Instead, in those cases, disqualification will only result if a bankruptcy restrictions order or undertaking is made or given. The signal exception is the office of director of a company; an undischarged bankrupt may not be a director without the permission of the court. Bankruptcy restrictions orders are discussed in **Chapter 11**.

[1]   *Re Lord Colin Campbell* (1888) 20 QBD 816. Cf for similar remarks *Re Barker's Trust* (1875) 1 Ch D 43.

10.2 When the provisions relating to debt relief orders[1] are brought into force, they will include provision for making debt relief restrictions orders. Such orders will cause disqualification in the same way as bankruptcy restrictions orders. For example, the provision relating to Parliamentary disqualification has been amended to arise also on the making of a debt relief restrictions order[2].

[1]   IA 1986, Part 7A and Sch 4ZA and Sch 4ZB, inserted by TCEA 2007, s 108 and Schs 17–19 (not yet in force).
[2]   IA 1986, s 426A(1).

455

B PROHIBITION ON ACTING AS A COMPANY DIRECTOR

Prohibition on acting as director

10.3 A bankrupt may not act as director of, or directly or indirectly take part in or be concerned in the promotion, formation or management of a company without leave of the court[1]. If an individual acts as a director without leave when he needs it, he commits an offence[2]. Subsequent annulment of the bankruptcy order does not expunge the criminal liability[3]. The company may enforce contracts made on its behalf while the bankrupt was unlawfully managing its affairs[4].

[1]   Company Directors Disqualification Act 1986, s 11(1).
[2]   Company Directors Disqualification Act 1986, s 13; punishable on indictment with two years' imprisonment or a fine; and summarily to a term of six months' imprisonment or the maximum magistrates' court fine.
[3]   *IRC v McEntaggart* [2004] EWHC 3431 (Ch), [2006] 1 BCLC 476.
[4]   *Hill v Secretary of State for the Environment, Food and Rural Affairs* [2005] EWHC 696 (Ch), [2006] 1 BCLC 601.

Application for leave to act as director

10.4 The court may not give leave to an undischarged bankrupt to act as a director, unless he first gives notice of his intention to apply to the official receiver[1]. Should the official receiver consider that it is contrary to the public interest that the application be granted he is under a duty to attend the hearing and oppose the application[2]. The court from which leave may be sought is the court which made the bankruptcy order[3]. An application for leave to act as a director or otherwise be concerned with a company must be supported by an affidavit which identifies the company in respect of which leave to act is being sought and specifies:

(1)   the nature and place of the company's business or intended business;
(2)   whether the company is or is to be a private or public company;
(3)   the persons who are, or who are to be, principally responsible for the conduct of the company's affairs, whether as directors, shadow directors, managers or otherwise;
(4)   the manner or capacity in which the applicant proposes to take part or be concerned in the promotion or formation of the company or its management; and
(5)   the emoluments and other benefits to be obtained from the directorship[4].

[1]   Company Directors Disqualification Act 1986, s 11(3).
[2]   Company Directors Disqualification Act 1986, s 11(3).
[3]   Company Directors Disqualification Act 1986, s 11(2).
[4]   IR 1986, r 6.203(1), (2).

10.5 If the company is already in existence the affidavit must give details of its date of incorporation and share capital, and if it is not in existence the affidavit must state what the proposed share capital is for the company and the sources from which that capital will be obtained[1]. Where the bankrupt intends to be concerned in the promotion of a company he must undertake in the affidavit to file a copy of the memorandum of association and certificate of incorporation in court within seven days of the company's incorporation[2].

1 IR 1986, r 6.203(3).
2 IR 1986, r 6.203(4).

10.6 Not less than 28 days before the day fixed by the court for the hearing of the application[1], the bankrupt must give notice to the official receiver and his trustee, together with copies of his affidavit[2]. The official receiver may file in court a report of any matters which he considers ought to be drawn to the court's attention at least 14 days before the hearing[3]. A copy of the official receiver's report must be served on the bankrupt and the trustee, and the bankrupt has seven days to reply stating which statements in the report he intends to deny or dispute[4]. The official receiver and the trustee may appear on the hearing of the application both to make representation and to question the applicant as the court may allow[5].

1 IR 1986, r 6.203(5).
2 IR 1986, r 6.204(1).
3 IR 1986, r 6.204(2).
4 IR 1986, r 6.204(3); this report must be served on the official receiver at least four days before the hearing.
5 IR 1986, r 6.204(4).

Order on application

10.7 If the court grants the bankrupt's application for leave to act as a director, the order must specify precisely what the bankrupt has leave to do[1]. If the trustee makes representations at the hearing the court may include in the order a provision making an income payments order, or varying an existing order for income payments by the bankrupt to the estate[2]. Whatever the outcome of the application the court must send copies of the order to the bankrupt, the official receiver and the trustee[3].

1 IR 1986, r 6.205(1).
2 IR 1986, r 6.205(2).
3 IR 1986, r 6.205(3).

C OTHER PROHIBITIONS AND DISQUALIFICATIONS

Parliament

10.8 An enactment about insolvency applies in relation to a member of the House of Commons or the House of Lords irrespective of any Parliamentary privilege[1]. But the making of a bankruptcy order against an individual no longer disqualifies him from membership of the House of Commons or sitting in the House of Lords. Disqualification only ensues if a bankruptcy restrictions order or undertaking is made or given[2].

1 IA 1986, s 426C.
2 IA 1986, s 426A(1).

Devolved institutions

10.9 There is no longer a requirement on the court to give any notification to the presiding officer of the Scottish Parliament, Northern Irish Assembly or National Assembly for Wales with respect to bankruptcy orders. But a court making a bankruptcy restrictions order or interim order in respect of a member of one of these bodies must notify the relevant presiding officer[1].

[1] IA 1986, s 426B.

Greater London Authority

10.10 A person is no longer disqualified from being elected or being the Mayor or a member of the London Assembly if he has been adjudged bankrupt. But disqualification ensues from a bankruptcy restrictions order or interim order[1].

[1] Greater London Authority Act 1999, s 21(1)(c).

Local government disqualification

10.11 Bankruptcy no longer disqualifies a person from being elected or remaining a member of a local authority. Disqualification only results if a bankruptcy restrictions order or interim order is made[1].

[1] Local Government Act 1972, s 80(1)(b).

Miscellaneous

10.12 An undischarged bankrupt may be removed from various positions within the Nuclear Decommissioning Authority[1], the Civil Nuclear Police Authority[2], and the Serious Organised Crime Agency[3].

[1] Energy Act 2004, Sch 1, para 1(6) and (7)(b).
[2] Energy Act 2004, Sch 1, paras 2(5) and 6(b).
[3] Serious Organised Crime and Police Act 2005, Sch 1, para 4(e).

Prohibition on acting as receiver or manager or insolvency practitioner

10.13 An undischarged bankrupt is not qualified to act as an insolvency practitioner[1], neither may he act as receiver or manager of the property of a company on behalf of debenture holders[2], and commits an offence by doing so[3]. This disqualification does not extend to appointments by the court to act as a receiver or manager[4].

[1] IA 1986, s 390(4)(a).
[2] IA 1986, s 31.
[3] For penalties see the IA 1986, s 430, Sch 10: on indictment, two years' imprisonment or a fine; on summary conviction, six months' imprisonment or a fine not exceeding the statutory maximum.
[4] IA 1986, s 31.

Trustees

10.14 Save in the case of charitable trusts, a trustee is not disqualified from continuing to hold office on his being adjudged bankrupt. But the bankruptcy or the circumstances surrounding it of a trustee may render him unfit to act as a trustee and, thereby, afford grounds for exercising a power of appointing a new trustee in his place[1]. The person entitled to exercise that power, where it is appropriate to do so, is the person[2] nominated for the purpose of appointing new trustees by the instrument, if any, creating the trust, or, if there is no such person or no such person able and willing to act, then the surviving trustees or trustee for the time being or the personal representatives of the last surviving or continuing trustee. Further, the bankruptcy of a trustee is a ground on which the court may make an order appointing a new trustee in substitution for the bankrupt trustee[3]. Although the court retains a discretion, the general rule is that the court will remove a bankrupt trustee where, as will ordinarily be the case, he has trust money to receive or deal with[4].

[1] Trustee Act 1925, s 36(1).
[2] Or persons.
[3] Trustee Act 1925, s 40(1).
[4] *Re Barker's Trusts* (1875) 1 Ch D 43; *Re Adam's Trust* (1879) 12 Ch D 634.

Pensions and investments

10.15 An undischarged bankrupt is disqualified from acting as trustee of a pension trust scheme[1], as a plan manager of personal equity plans[2] or as an account manager of individual savings accounts[3].

[1] Pensions Act 1995, s 29(1)(b).
[2] Personal Equity Plan Regulations 1989, SI 1989/469, reg 15(1)(b).
[3] Individual Savings Account Regulations 1998, SI 1998/1870, reg 20(1)(b).

Charitable trusts and charities

10.16 A person is disqualified from being a charity trustee or a trustee for a charity if he has been adjudged bankrupt and has not been discharged[1]. It is an offence to act as a charity trustee or a trustee for a charity while disqualified[2]. In this context, 'charity' means, subject to certain exceptions, any institution, corporate or not, which is established for charitable purposes and is subject to the control of the High Court in the exercise of the court's jurisdiction with respect to charities[3]. 'Charity trustees' means the persons having the general control and management of the administration of a charity[4]. Thus, for example, where a charity has been incorporated, the persons who have general control and management of its administration are the charity trustees in respect of it, even though they may not be trustees in the ordinary sense of holding property subject to a trust. If the charity is a company and the charity trustee is a director, he would be disqualified from continuing to hold office in any event by virtue of the prohibition on bankrupts acting as directors[5].

1   Charities Act 1993, s 72(1)(b). The disqualification also applies where a person has made a composition or arrangement with, or granted a trust deed for, his creditors and has not been discharged in respect of it; Charities Act 1993, s 72(1)(c).
2   Charities Act 1993, s 73(1). Section 73(1) does not apply where the charity concerned is a company and the disqualified person is disqualified by reason of being an undischarged bankrupt; see Charities Act 1993, s 73(2). But that is not because such activity is not criminal but because so to act, without the leave of the court, would be an offence under the Company Directors Disqualification Act 1986, s 11(1).
3   Charities Act 1993, s 96(1); for the exceptions alluded to in the text, which comprise certain ecclesiastical bodies, see Charities Act 1993, s 96(2).
4   Charities Act 1993, s 97(1).
5   Company Directors Disqualification Act 1986, s 11(1).

Leave to act as charity trustee or trustee of a charity

10.17 Where a person is disqualified by virtue of his bankruptcy from being a charity trustee or a trustee for any charity by reason of his being an undischarged bankrupt, his disqualification is lifted if leave has been granted under the Company Directors Disqualification Act 1986, s 11 for him to act as director of the charity[1].

1   Charities Act 1993, s 72(3).

Enduring and lasting powers of attorney

10.18 On 1 October 2007[1] a new regime was introduced by the Mental Capacity Act 2005 whereby an individual could grant a power of attorney which would continue to have effect even though the individual subsequently ceased to have mental capacity. Such powers of attorney are called lasting powers of attorney and may enable the donee to make decisions both about the donor's personal welfare and about his property and affairs[2]. A bankrupt may not be appointed as donee of a lasting power of attorney in relation to the donor's property and affairs[3]. If the donor becomes bankrupt, the lasting power of attorney is revoked in so far as it relates to his property and affairs[4]. Save as regards authority to make decisions about the donor's personal welfare, if the donee becomes bankrupt, his appointment is terminated and the power is revoked unless the bankrupt donee is replaced under the terms of the instrument or he is one of two or more persons appointed to act as donees jointly and severally and another donee remains[5]. The donee's bankruptcy does not terminate his appointment or revoke the power in so far as the donee's authority relates to the donor's personal welfare[6]. In this context, reference to the bankruptcy of an individual includes a case where a bankruptcy restrictions order has effect in respect of him[7].

1   Mental Capacity Act 2005 (Commencement No 2) Order 2007, SI 2007/1897, art 2.
2   Mental Capacity Act 2005, s 9(1).
3   Mental Capacity Act 2005, s 10(2).
4   Mental Capacity Act 2005, s 13(3).
5   Mental Capacity Act 2005, s 13(5), (6)(b) and (7).
6   Mental Capacity Act 2005, s 13(8).
7   Mental Capacity Act 2005, s 64(3). See further at **11.44** as regards bankruptcy restrictions orders.

10.19 Under the previous regime which obtained under the Enduring Powers of Attorney Act 1985, a bankrupt could not be appointed as an attorney under an enduring power of attorney[1]. But that Act ceased to have effect on 1 October 2007[2] and no new enduring powers of attorney may be granted. But, Schedule 4 to the Mental Capacity Act 2005 contains provisions governing enduring powers of attorney created before 1 October 2007[3]. By virtue of Sch 4, para 2(7) an enduring power of attorney is revoked by the bankruptcy of the donor or the attorney.

[1]   Enduring Powers of Attorney Act 1985, s 2(7)(a).
[2]   Mental Capacity Act 2005, s 66(1)(b).
[3]   Mental Capacity Act 2005, s 66(3).

Secretary of State's power to change disqualification provisions

10.20 The Enterprise Act 2002, s 268 empowers the Secretary of State to repeal or revoke statutory provisions relating to disqualifications imposed on bankrupts[1]. The Secretary of State has made a statutory instrument pursuant to this power affecting a miscellany of disqualifications[2].

[1]   EA 2002, s 268(1), (2) and (3).
[2]   The Enterprise Act 2002 (Disqualification from Office: General) Order 2006, SI 2006/1722.

Bankruptcy of professionals

Barristers

10.21 A practising barrister must report promptly to the Bar Council if a bankruptcy order or director's disqualification order is made against him or if he enters into an individual voluntary arrangement with his creditors[1]. In the context of this professional rule 'bankruptcy order' includes a bankruptcy order made pursuant to the IA 1986 and any similar order in any jurisdiction in the world[2].

[1]   Bar Code of Conduct, Eighth Edition, para 905(c).
[2]   Bar Code of Conduct, Eighth Edition, para 1001.

Certified accountants

10.22 A member of the Association of Chartered Certified Accountants must notify the Admissions and Licensing Committee of the Association within one month of being made bankrupt[1] and satisfy it that he is still eligible to be a member. The Association's rules provide for a hearing before the committee for the purpose of determining whether the member remains eligible. Failure to notify the Committee within one month of the bankruptcy order will result in automatic termination of membership[2].

[1]   Or becoming subject to a bankruptcy restrictions order or undertaking or an order analogous to a bankruptcy order in another jurisdiction.
[2]   The Chartered Certified Accountants Regulations 1996, reg 12.

Chartered accountants

10.23 An accountant's membership of the Institute of Chartered Accountants ceases on bankruptcy[1].

1   ICAEW, Principal Bye-law 7(a).

Chartered surveyors

10.24 A member of the Royal Institution of Chartered Surveyors is under a duty to conduct his business and personal financial affairs so as to ensure that he is not adjudicated bankrupt (or made subject to a similar order in another jurisdiction or enter into an arrangement or composition with his creditors)[1]. If he is in breach of this duty the Institute must expel him from membership unless satisfied either that the breach was not the result of fault on the member's part or that it would be unreasonable to expel him; if so satisfied some other disciplinary sanction may be imposed[2].

1   RICS, Bye-law 19(9)(b).
2   RICS, Bye-law 21(4).

Solicitors

10.25 The making of a bankruptcy order of a solicitor immediately suspends any practising certificate of that solicitor for the time being in force[1]. The Law Society may, however, in its discretion grant an application for a practising certificate by a solicitor who is an undischarged bankrupt, who has been bankrupt and discharged, or who has made a composition or arrangement with his creditors, if appropriate, subject to such conditions as the Society thinks fit[2]. A court making a bankruptcy order, or annulling such order against a solicitor, must forthwith give notice to the Secretary of the Law Society[3]. The Law Society is entitled to inspect the file of any bankruptcy proceedings against a solicitor without payment of any fee, though it must pay the usual charge for any office copies it requests[4].

1   Solicitors Act 1974, s 15(1).
2   Solicitors Act 1974, s 12(1)(h), (i) and (4).
3   IR 1986, r 6.235.
4   Solicitors Act 1974, s 83.

Estate agents

10.26 A bankrupt may not engage in estate agency work of any description except as an employee of another person[1].

1   Estate Agents Act 1979, s 23(1); see s 1(1) for the definition of 'estate agency work'.

D RESTRICTIONS AFFECTING A BANKRUPT'S ABILITY TO TRADE

Restriction on obtaining credit

10.27 A bankrupt may not obtain credit of £250 or more, alone or jointly with any other person, without informing the person from whom he obtains credit that he is an undischarged bankrupt[1]. Failure so to inform the person giving credit is an offence. Obtaining credit includes obtaining possession of goods under a hire-purchase agreement or agreeing to buy goods under a conditional sale agreement and receiving payments (where in money or otherwise) in advance for the supply of goods and services[2].

[1]   IA 1986, s 360(1)(a).
[2]   IA 1986, s 360(2).

Restriction on trading under a different name

10.28 A bankrupt may not engage, directly or indirectly, in any business under a name other than that in which he was adjudged bankrupt without disclosing to all persons with whom he enters into any business transaction the name in which he was adjudged bankrupt[1]. The requirement seems to be to provide the relevant name, not the information that the bankrupt is an undischarged bankrupt. This gives the person with whom the bankrupt seeks to transact business the same information as a person would have where the bankrupt is operating under the name in which he was adjudged bankrupt. Knowledge of that name will enable the other party to make an effective search of the register of writs and orders affecting land[2] and of the individual insolvency register[3].

[1]   IA 1986, s 360(1)(b).
[2]   This register is maintained under the Land Charges Act 1972; see Land Charges Act 1972, ss 1(1)(c) and 6(1)(c). See paras **9.6** and **9.14** above for the court's duty to inform the Chief Land Registrar that a bankruptcy order has been made under the IR 1986, r 6.34 (creditor's petition) and the IR 1986, r 6.46 (debtor's petition).
[3]   See the IR 1986, Pt 6A and para **3.172**ff.

Chapter 11

BANKRUPTCY RESTRICTIONS ORDERS

A   Bankruptcy restrictions orders
B   Procedure
C   Bankruptcy restrictions undertakings
D   Registration
E   Effect of orders

A BANKRUPTCY RESTRICTIONS ORDERS

Introduction

11.1 Since 1 April 2004 a bankrupt will, generally, be discharged from bankruptcy one year after his bankruptcy commenced. On discharge the disqualifications and restrictions which apply to an undischarged bankrupt will lapse. The reduction in the period before discharge reflects Parliament's recognition that often mere misfortune, not turpitude, brings on bankruptcy and that the unlucky should obtain their commercial rehabilitation after one year. But some bankruptcies are not simply the result of misfortune and reflect adversely on the bankrupt's conduct; in those cases it may be appropriate to ensure that the disqualifications and restrictions attendant on bankruptcy are maintained for a longer period than one year. The court's power to make a bankruptcy restrictions order against the bankrupt, or to accept a bankruptcy restrictions undertaking from him, provides a method of dealing with such cases. By this means, although the bankrupt may obtain his discharge from bankruptcy after only one year, he will remain subject to restrictions on what he may lawfully do for a period of between two and fifteen years.

11.2 The provisions relating to bankruptcy restrictions orders and undertakings are contained in Schedule 4A to the Insolvency Act 1986 ('IA 1986')[1].

[1]   Schedule 4A has effect by virtue of IA 1986, s 281A.

11.3 The bankruptcy restrictions regime came into force on 1 April 2004[1]. The court cannot take into account when considering whether to make an interim or final bankruptcy restrictions order any conduct of the bankrupt that took place before 1 April 2004[2].

464

1   Enterprise Act 2002, s 257(2), Sch 20; Enterprise Act 2002 (Commencement No 4 and Transitional Provisions and Savings) Order 2003, SI 2003/2093, art 2.
2   Enterprise Act 2002 (Commencement No 4 and Transitional Provisions and Savings) Order 2003, SI 2003/2093, art 7.

Similarity to the Company Directors Disqualification Act 1986

11.4 The jurisdiction to impose bankruptcy restrictions orders is similar to that which empowers the court to impose disqualification orders on directors of companies under the Company Directors Disqualification Act 1986[1]. Where the correspondence is close, cases decided under that Act are likely to provide guidance as to how the court should deal with issues arising with regard to bankruptcy restrictions orders.

1   On the similarities between the two regimes, see the judgment of Launcelot Henderson QC in *Randhawa v Official Receiver* [2006] EWHC 2946 (Ch), [2007] 1 All ER 755, [2007] 1 WLR 1700 at [62] and [70] et seq.

Persons who may apply

11.5 A bankruptcy restrictions order may only be made on the application of the Secretary of State or an official receiver acting on a direction of the Secretary of State[1].

1   IA 1986, s 281A, Sch 4A, para 1(2).

Time limit

11.6 The general rule is that the application must be made within one year of the commencement of the bankruptcy[1].

1   IA 1986, s 281A, Sch 4A, para 3(1)(a).

Suspension of time running

11.7 While the period set for the bankrupt's discharge is suspended under IA 1986, s 279(3), time also ceases to run for the purpose of calculating the one year period during which an application for a bankruptcy restrictions order may be made[1]. Thus if the moment when discharge will occur is postponed by suspension of time for that purpose, the period during which an application for a bankruptcy restrictions order may be made is extended to the same extent.

1   IA 1986, s 281A, Sch 4A, para 3(2).

Extension of time

11.8 However, the time limit is not absolute and an application may be made after the expiry of the primary one-year period if the court grants permission

11.8 *Bankruptcy restrictions orders*

to make the application[1]. In determining whether that primary period has expired, any period during which the period set for the bankrupt's discharge is suspended should be left out of account by virtue of IA 1986, Sch 4A, para 3(2), discussed at para **11.7**.

[1] IA 1986, s 281A, Sch 4A, para 3(1)(b).

Permission to make a late application

11.9 Nothing is specified as to the circumstances which might justify granting permission to make a late application. But it is safe to say that the applicant will have to show some good reason[1]. An example might be that the bankrupt had concealed the relevant facts which only came to light at a late stage. The primary period for making the application is shorter than the two years allowed under the Company Directors Disqualification Act 1986, s 7(2). But the approach to granting permission to make late applications under that Act would seem likely to be followed. On that basis the onus to show good reason will lie on the applicant; while the court's discretion is unfettered, the relevant considerations may be summarised, though not exhaustively, as comprising the length of the delay, the reasons for the delay, the strength of the applicant's case and the degree of any prejudice to the respondent[2] and the public interest[3].

[1] *Secretary of State v Davies* [1997] 2 BCLC 317 at 324.
[2] [1997] 2 BCLC 317 at 324–5.
[3] [1997] 2 BCLC 317 at 332.

11.10 Applying the practice followed in respect of applications for disqualification orders against directors, the application for permission should be made by a separate application[1] and cannot be granted retrospectively[2].

[1] *Re Crestjoy Products Limited* [1990] BCLC 677.
[2] *Secretary of State v Cleland* [1997] 1 BCLC 437 at 440–441.

Conduct which justifies making a bankruptcy restrictions order

11.11 The basic question for the court on hearing an application for a bankruptcy restrictions order is whether it thinks that the order is appropriate having regard to the conduct of the bankrupt[1]. Although conduct which led to the bankrupt's becoming unable to pay his debts is an obvious focus for the court's attention, the court is entitled to take any conduct which it regards as relevant into account whether it occurred before or after the bankruptcy[2]. But the court must take into account any of a series of listed kinds of behaviour on the part of the bankrupt[3].

(a) failing to keep records which account for a loss of property by him or by a business carried on by him, where the loss occurred in the period beginning two years before the presentation of the petition on which he was made bankrupt and ending with the date of the application for a bankruptcy restrictions order[4];

(b)   failing to produce records of that kind on demand by the official receiver or the trustee;

(c)   entering into a transaction at an undervalue;

(d)   giving a preference;

(e)   making an excessive pension contribution;

(f)   a failure to supply goods or services which were wholly or partly paid for which gave rise to a claim provable in the bankruptcy;

(g)   trading at a time before commencement of the bankruptcy when the bankrupt knew or ought to have known that he was himself to be unable to pay his debts;

(h)   incurring, before commencement of the bankruptcy, a debt which the bankrupt had no reasonable expectation of being able pay;

(i)   failing to account satisfactorily to the court, the official receiver or the trustee for a loss of property or for an insufficiency of property to meet bankruptcy debts;

(j)   carrying on any gambling, rash or hazardous speculation or unreasonable extravagance which may have materially contributed to or increased the extent of the bankruptcy or which took place between presentation of the petition and commencement of the bankruptcy[5];

(k)   neglect of business affairs which may have materially contributed to or increased the extent of the bankruptcy;

(l)   fraud or fraudulent breach of trust;

(m)   failing to co-operate with the official receiver or trustee.

[1]   IA 1986, s 281A, Sch 4A, para 2(1).
[2]   IA 1986, s 281A, Sch 4A, para 2(1). See further para [66] of the judgment of Launcelot Henderson QC in *Randhawa v Official Receiver* [2006] EWHC 2946, [2007] 1 All ER 755, [2007] 1 WLR 1700.
[3]   IA 1986, s 281A, Sch 4A, para 2(2).
[4]   Before 1 April 2004, a bankrupt who had been engaged in business was guilty of an offence under IA 1986, s 361 if he had not kept and preserved proper accounting records during the period starting two years before presentation of the petition and ending with the commencement of the bankruptcy. That offence has been repealed with effect from 1 April 2004: Enterprise Act 2002, ss 263(b), 278(2), and Sch 26.
[5]   This type of conduct could, before 1 April 2004, constitute an offence under IA 1986, s 362. That section has been repealed with effect from 1 April 2004: Enterprise Act 2002, ss 263(b), 278(2), and Sch 26.

Previous bankruptcy

11.12 The court must also consider whether the bankrupt was an undischarged bankrupt at some time during the period of six years ending with the date of the bankruptcy to which the application relates[1].

[1]   This factor is found in IA 1986, s 281A, Sch 4A, para 2(3).

Matters that the court cannot consider

11.13 The court cannot take into account, in considering whether or not to make a bankruptcy restrictions order, any conduct that took place before 1 April 2004[1].

11.13   Bankruptcy restrictions orders

1   See the Enterprise Act 2002 (Commencement No 4 and Transitional Provisions and Savings) Order 2003, SI 2003/2093, arts 2 and 7.

Material obtained on private examination

11.14 It is permissible to use the powers conferred by IA 1986, s 236 principally or solely for the purpose of gathering evidence for use in disqualification proceedings brought under the Company Directors Disqualification Act 1986[1]. So similar use of the analogous powers in bankruptcy should be available to gather information for the purpose of seeking a bankruptcy restrictions order.

1   *Re Pantmaenog Timber Co Ltd (in liq), Official Receiver v Meade-King (a firm)* [2003] UKHL 49, [2004] 1 AC 158, [2003] 2 BCLC 257.

The approach of the court to determining whether to make a bankruptcy restrictions order

11.15 A number of principles were elucidated in *Randhawa v Official Receiver*[1] where the bankrupt had borrowed £9,500 on his wife's credit card and given various differing explanations of what he had done with the money, finally that he had lent it to an employee to gamble with.

1   [2006] EWHC 2946 (Ch), [2007] 1 All ER 755.

11.16 First, on hearing an application for a bankruptcy restrictions order, the role of the court is to consider whether it is appropriate to make the order having regard to the bankrupt's conduct. This does not confer a general discretion on the court. If the court concludes that it does, then the court is obliged to make a bankruptcy restrictions order for at least the minimum period of two years[1].

1   IA 1986, s 281A, Sch 4A, para 1(1); *Randhawa v Official Receiver* [2006] EWHC 2946 (Ch), [2007] 1 All ER 755 at [65].

11.17 Secondly, the court observed that the policy underlying the bankruptcy restrictions order regime is both to protect the public against irresponsible financial conduct[1] and to deter other persons from engaging in similar conduct. In consequence, although the bankrupt in question may persuade the court that he no longer represents a danger to the public, that fact will not avail to avoid a bankruptcy restrictions order if his conduct justifies making an order[2].

1   *Randhawa v Official Receiver* [2006] EWHC 2946 (Ch), [2007] 1 All ER 755 at [69].
2   *Randhawa v Official Receiver* [2006] EWHC 2946 (Ch), [2007] 1 All ER 755 at [75].

11.18 Thirdly, with regard to the question when conduct will be of sufficient gravity to merit the making of a bankruptcy restrictions order, it was said that the threshold would be met when a bankrupt's conduct exhibits 'a failure in some significant respect to live up to proper standards of competence or probity in the conduct of one's financial affairs. An element of culpability or irresponsibility will usually, if not always, need to be present. Mitigating factors may of course be taken into account, and need not be confined either to matters directly related to the allegations of misconduct or to events after 1 April 2004'[1].

[1]   *Randhawa v Official Receiver* [2006] EWHC 2946 (Ch), [2007] 1 All ER 755 at [68].

Impact of annulment

11.18A The fact that the bankruptcy order has been annulled does not prevent a bankruptcy restrictions order from being made in relation to the bankrupt's conduct while the bankruptcy was on foot. Thus where annulment was obtained by payment of the debt in full, a bankruptcy restrictions order was nevertheless made where the bankrupt had continued to act as a director and cited company funds as if they were his own[1].

[1]   *Jenkins v Official Receiver* [2007] EWHC 1402 (Civ).

The duration of a bankruptcy restrictions order

11.19 Where no interim order has been made, a bankruptcy restrictions order comes into effect on the date on which an order is made and ceases to have effect on the date specified in the order[1]. The date on which the order ceases to have effect must be between two and fifteen years from the date on which the order is made[2]. The court cannot impose a bankruptcy restrictions order for a period of less than two years[3].

[1]   IA 1986, s 281A, Sch 4A, para 4(1).
[2]   IA 1986, s 281A, Sch 4A, para 4(2).
[3]   See *Randhawa v Official Receiver* [2006] EWHC 2946 (Ch), [2007] 1 All ER 755 at [69].

11.20 In *Randhawa v Official Receiver* it was suggested that the approach to be adopted by the court in setting the period for which the bankruptcy restrictions order should endure should correspond to the approach taken to disqualifying directors: in particular the exercise should not be unduly refined or technical and the same brackets routinely used in directors' disqualification cases as guidance for the appropriate period of restriction[1]. Thus, 'the most serious cases, attracting a period of disqualification within the suggested top bracket of 10 to 15 years, will include cases of deceit and fraud. To draw the line between cases which should fall in the suggested bottom bracket (two to five or six years) and the middle bracket (five to six to ten years) is more difficult. However, possible areas of distinction are (a) whether the serious failures came about deliberately or with knowledge of their potential result and harm they would cause, or innocently and through lack of knowledge or incompetence, and (b) whether the failures were "one off" or part of a pattern'[2].

[1]   *Randhawa v Official Receiver* [2006] EWHC 2946 (Ch), [2007] 1 All ER 755 at [88].
[2]   *Re Sevenoaks Stationers (Retail) Ltd* [1991] Ch 164 at 171 per Dillon LJ.

11.21 *Bankruptcy restrictions orders*

Interim bankruptcy restrictions orders

11.21 At any time between the institution of an application for a bankruptcy restrictions order and the determination of that application, the Secretary of State or the official receiver may apply for an interim bankruptcy restrictions order to be made[1]. An interim bankruptcy restrictions order comes into force when it is made and has the same effect as a bankruptcy restrictions order[2]. In order to make an interim bankruptcy restrictions order, the court must be satisfied that (a) there are prima facie grounds to suggest that a bankruptcy restrictions order will ultimately be granted, and (b) that it is in the public interest to make an interim order[3]. Presumably, then, the interim bankruptcy restrictions order procedure is aimed at drastic cases where the public would be at risk if a bankrupt were to be automatically discharged from his bankruptcy without the protection of a bankruptcy restrictions order being in place.

[1] IA 1986, s 281A, Sch 4A, paras 5(1) and 5(3). The rules for evidence are similar to those that apply for applications for full bankruptcy restrictions orders, save that the evidence in support of an interim bankruptcy restrictions order application must explicitly address the public interest in making the order: see IR 1986, r 6.246.
[2] IA 1986, s 281A, Sch 4A, para 5(4). It will cease to have effect when the bankruptcy restrictions order application has been determined, if a bankruptcy restrictions undertaking is accepted by the bankrupt, or if it is discharged by the court: see IA 1986, s 281A, Sch 4A, para 5(5).
[3] IA 1986, s 281A, Sch 4A, para 5(2).

11.22 A bankrupt must be given two clear business days' notice of an application for an interim bankruptcy restrictions order[1], and has the opportunity to file evidence in opposition to, and attend at the hearing of, any such application[2]. Specific provision is also made for the bankrupt to apply to set aside an interim bankruptcy restrictions order[3]. When the making of an interim bankruptcy restrictions order is followed by the making of a full bankruptcy restrictions order, the full bankruptcy restrictions order is to have effect from the date on which the interim bankruptcy restrictions order is made[4].

[1] IR 1986, r 6.245(2).
[2] IR 1986, r 6.247.
[3] IR 1986, r 6.248.
[4] IA 1986, s 281A, Sch 4A, para 6(2).

Effect of annulment of bankruptcy on bankruptcy restrictions orders and bankruptcy restrictions undertakings

11.23 The effect of the annulment of an individual's bankruptcy on any existing interim or final bankruptcy restrictions order, bankruptcy restrictions undertaking or pending or future application for a restrictions order depends upon the basis on which an annulment is granted.

11.24 If an annulment is granted on the basis that the bankruptcy order ought not to have been made (under IA 1986, s 282(1)(a)), or where a criminal bankruptcy has been rescinded as the result of a successful appeal (under IA 1986, s 282(2)), any existing interim or final bankruptcy restrictions order or bankruptcy restrictions undertaking shall be annulled, no new interim or final bankruptcy restrictions order can be made, and no new bankruptcy restrictions undertaking can be accepted[1].

¹   IA 1986, s 281A, Sch 4A, para 10.

11.25 If, on the other hand, the bankruptcy is annulled on the basis that the bankrupt has entered into a regular or fast-track IVA (under IA 1986, ss 261 or 263D) or on the basis that the bankrupt has paid or secured to the satisfaction of the court his bankruptcy debts and expenses (under IA 1986, s 282(1)(b)), then any extant interim or final bankruptcy restrictions order or any bankruptcy restrictions undertaking shall not be affected[1]. Furthermore, the court may make a bankruptcy restrictions order on an application instituted, and the Secretary of State may accept an undertaking offered, before these types of annulment take effect[2]. However, no new application for an interim or final bankruptcy restrictions order can be instituted after the annulment[3].

¹   IA 1986, s 281A, Sch 4A, para 11.
²   IA 1986, s 281A, Sch 4A, para 11(b) and (c).
³   IA 1986, s 281A, Sch 4A, para 11(d).

B PROCEDURE

11.26 The procedure for applying for, and resisting the making of, bankruptcy restrictions orders is prescribed by IR 1986, rr 6.240 to 6.241. Paragraph 16A of the Practice Direction on Insolvency Proceedings summarises and supplements these rules.

Application

11.27 An ordinary application should be used[1].

¹   See *Practice Direction: Insolvency Proceedings*, para 16A.1.

Supporting documents

11.28 The application should also be supported by a report prepared by the Secretary of State or official receiver[1] which includes (a) a statement of conduct by reference to which it is alleged that it is appropriate for a bankruptcy restrictions order to be made, and (b) the evidence upon which the Secretary of State or official receiver relies upon in support of their application (such as the bankrupt's statement of affairs, transcripts of examinations or interviews that have been conducted, etc). Evidence in support of an application should be adduced by way of affidavit, unless the evidence is given by the Secretary of State[2].

11.28 *Bankruptcy restrictions orders*

1   IR 1986, r 6.241(1). References to Secretary of State are to be interpreted as also being references to the official receiver: see IR 1986, r 6.240.
2   IR 1986, r 6.241(3).

Hearing date

11.29 Upon receipt of an application, the Court shall list the matter for a date at least eight weeks in the future[1].

1   IR 1986, r 6.241(4).

Service on bankrupt

11.30 Within 14 days of making an application to court[1], the Secretary of State must serve the following documents on the bankrupt:

(i)   the application;
(ii)   the Secretary of State or official receiver's report;
(iii)   the evidence in support of the application;
(iv)   a form for acknowledging service; and
(v)   the court's listing notice[2].

1   IR 1986, r 6.242(1).
2   IR 1986, r 6.242(2).

Acknowledgement of service

11.31 Within 14 days of service of these documents, the bankrupt must file an acknowledgement of service indicating whether or not he consents to the application[1]. If the bankrupt fails to file an acknowledgement of service within the appropriate time frame, he may still attend the hearing of the application but may only take part with the court's permission[2].

1   IR 1986, r 6.242(3).
2   IR 1986, r 6.242(4).

The bankrupt's evidence

11.32 If the bankrupt chooses to defend the application, he must file the evidence upon which he wishes to rely within 28 days of the date on which he was served with the application[1]. He must also serve a copy of the evidence on which he will rely on to the Secretary of State or official receiver within three days of filing it at court[2].

1   IR 1986, r 6.243(1).
2   IR 1986, r 6.243(1).

Evidence in reply

11.33 If the Secretary of State or official receiver wishes to rely upon any further evidence, such evidence must be filed at court within 14 days of receipt of the bankrupt's evidence, and served on the bankrupt as soon as is reasonably practicable thereafter[1].

[1] IR 1986, r 6.243(2).

The hearing

11.34 An application for a bankruptcy restrictions order shall be heard in public[1]. No other express rules are set down for conduct of the hearing. In practice, however, the judge dealing with a bankruptcy restrictions application will usually want to hear oral evidence from the bankrupt. The Secretary of State or official receiver will normally wish to cross-examine the bankrupt in relation to their oral evidence. The necessity of cross-examining the official receiver on the content of their affidavit in support should be afforded to the bankrupt or his representative.

[1] IR 1986, r 6.241(5).

Making an order

11.35 As might be expected, the court can make a bankruptcy restrictions order against a bankrupt whether or not the bankrupt attends the hearing of the application and whether or not the bankrupt files evidence[1]. When the court makes a bankruptcy restrictions order, it must send two sealed copies to the Secretary of State who must, in turn, send a sealed copy of the Order to the bankrupt as soon as reasonably practicable[2].

[1] IR 1986, r 6.244(1).
[2] IR 1986, r 6.244(2) and (3).

C BANKRUPTCY RESTRICTIONS UNDERTAKINGS

11.36 As an alternative to defending a proposed bankruptcy restrictions order application, a bankrupt may offer bankruptcy restrictions undertakings to the Secretary of State[1]. In determining whether to accept such undertakings, the Secretary of State must consider the factors listed in IA 1986, Sch A4, para 2(2) and (3)[2]. A bankruptcy restrictions undertaking comes into effect on the date that the offer is accepted by the Secretary of State[3]; it will cease to have effect at the end of a date specified in the undertaking, being between two and fifteen years after the date of acceptance of the undertaking[4]. Specific provision is made for the bankrupt to make an application to annul a bankruptcy restrictions undertaking or an application for a reduction in the duration of a bankruptcy restrictions undertaking[5].

[1] IA 1986, s 281A, Sch 4A, para 7(1).
[2] IA 1986, s 281A, Sch 4A, para 7(2).

[3] An undertaking is deemed to be accepted when signed by the Secretary of State: see IR 1986, r 6.249.

[4] IA 1986, s 281A, Sch 4A, para 9.

[5] IA 1986, s 281A, Sch 4A, para 9(3). Such an application must be supported by an affidavit setting out the grounds on which it is made (IR 1986, r 6.251(1)). The Secretary of State must be given at least 28 days' notice of any such hearing. Further, the Secretary of State has the right to attend the hearing of any such application and to make submissions and give and call evidence (IR 1986, r 6.251(2) and (3)). A person subject to a bankruptcy restrictions order can achieve the same result by applying for the variation or rescission of his bankruptcy restrictions order under IA 1986, s 375(1).

11.37 The Secretary of State must file a copy of any bankruptcy restrictions undertaking that it accepts at court as soon as is reasonably practicable. A copy must also be sent to the bankrupt and the official receiver[1].

[1] See IR 1986, r 6.250.

D REGISTRATION

11.38 The Secretary of State is required to maintain a register recording bankruptcy restrictions orders, interim bankruptcy restrictions orders, and bankruptcy restrictions undertakings[1]. The register, known as the 'bankruptcy restrictions register'[2], is open to the public for inspection during business hours[3]. Details of those individuals that are subject to bankruptcy restrictions orders or bankruptcy restrictions undertakings are also available on the online individual insolvency register.

[1] IA 1986, s 281A, Sch 4A, para 12.
[2] See IR 1986, r 6A.1(2).
[3] See IR 1986, r 6A.1(4).

11.39 The register must contain the following details: the name, gender, occupation (if any) and date of birth of the bankrupt; the bankrupt's last known address; a statement that a bankruptcy restrictions order, interim bankruptcy restrictions order or bankruptcy restrictions undertaking has been made in respect of that person; a statement of the date on which the relevant order was made or undertaking given; and a record of the duration of the order[1]. All details must be removed from the register as soon as reasonably practicable after the relevant order or undertaking has ceased to have effect or has expired[2].

[1] See IR 1986, r 6A.6(1) and (2).
[2] See IR 1986, rr 6A.1(5) and 6A.7.

E EFFECT OF ORDERS

11.40 A bankruptcy restrictions order or a bankruptcy restrictions undertaking has a similar effect on an individual to his being an undischarged bankrupt. In particular, the making of a bankruptcy restrictions order or a bankruptcy restrictions undertaking has the following consequences.

Disqualification from being a director of a limited liability company or a member of a limited liability partnership

11.41 It is a criminal offence for a person subject to bankruptcy restrictions to act as a director of a company or to take part or be concerned in, whether directly or indirectly, the promotion, formation or management of a company[1]. Similar prohibitions apply in respect of a person subject to bankruptcy restrictions acting as a member or being involved in the promotion, formation or management of a limited liability partnership[2].

[1] Company Directors Disqualification Act 1986, s 11(1)(b). The court can nevertheless consent for a person subject to bankruptcy restrictions to act in an otherwise prohibited manner, upon the application of any such person. Company Directors Disqualification Act 1986, s 13 sets out the penalties that can be imposed for acting in breach of s 11.
[2] See the Limited Liability Partnerships Regulations 2001, SI 2001/1090, reg 4(2).

Obtaining credit and engaging in business under a different name

11.42 A person subject to bankruptcy restrictions remains under the same obligations as an undischarged bankrupt in respect of obtaining credit and in respect of engaging in business in a name other than that in which he was adjudged bankrupt[1].

[1] IA 1986, s 360(5).

Public office

11.43 A person subject to bankruptcy restrictions is precluded from holding high public office. In particular, such a person cannot:

  (i)   be a member of the House of Commons[1];
  (ii)   sit or vote in the House of Lords or on a House of Lords committee or a joint committee of both Houses[2];
  (iii) be a member of a local authority or an elected mayor[3]; or
  (iv)   be the Mayor of London or a member of the London Assembly[4].

In addition, when a court imposes bankruptcy restrictions on a member of the Scottish Parliament, the Northern Ireland Assembly or the National Assembly for Wales, it must notify the presiding officer of the relevant body[5].

[1] IA 1986, s 426A(1)(a).
[2] IA 1986, s 426A(1)(b) and (c).
[3] Local Government Act 1972, s 80(1)(b).
[4] Greater London Authority Act 1999, s 21(1)(c).
[5] IA 1986, s 426B.

Enduring and lasting powers of attorney

11.44 The impact of bankruptcy on enduring powers of attorney created under the Enduring Powers of Attorney Act 1985 and on lasting powers of attorney created under the Mental Capacity Act 2005 has been discussed in

11.44 *Bankruptcy restrictions orders*

Chapter 10[1]. As mentioned there, an individual who is the subject of a bankruptcy restrictions order is treated as being bankrupt[2]. In consequence an individual who is subject to a bankruptcy restrictions order may not be appointed as the donee of a lasting power of attorney[3]. In almost all cases where a bankruptcy restrictions order is made against the donee of a lasting power, it will not be that order which determines his appointment but the preceding bankruptcy order which rendered him bankrupt. But it is possible to imagine that an individual might be appointed as the donee of a lasting power shortly after his discharge from bankruptcy but while an application for a bankruptcy restrictions order is pending against him. There would be no bar to his appointment at that time, but on the bankruptcy restrictions order being made, the appointment would determine. Although in this context bankruptcy restrictions orders include interim bankruptcy restrictions orders[4], the making of an interim bankruptcy restrictions order does not terminate the appointment but, if it is the only reason why the donee is to be considered bankrupt, the interim order merely suspends the appointment[5].

[1]   See para **10.19**.
[2]   Mental Capacity Act 2005, s 64(3).
[3]   Mental Capacity Act 2005, s 10(2).
[4]   Mental Capacity Act 2005, s 64(4).
[5]   Mental Capacity Act 2005, s 13(9).

11.45 Enduring powers of attorney are revoked by the bankruptcy of either the donor or the attorney[1]. The making of a bankruptcy restrictions order is therefore capable of causing the revocation of an enduring power of attorney, but, since no new enduring power of attorney may now be created, it is likely that in fact any such power will have been revoked by the relevant preceding bankruptcy order[2].

[1]   Mental Capacity Act 2005, s 66(3), Sch 4, para 2(7).
[2]   It is difficult, therefore, to imagine cases on which the provision for interim bankruptcy restrictions orders only to have suspensory effect (contained in Mental Capacity Act 2005, Sch 4, para 2(8)) will bite.

Matters relating to insolvency of others

11.46 He cannot be a manager or receiver of property on behalf of a debenture holder[1]; cannot be an insolvency practitioner[2], cannot be a member of a creditors' committee appointed in a company administration[3], receivership[4], liquidation[5], or bankruptcy[6].

[1]   IA 1986, s 31(1)(b).
[2]   IA 1986, s 390(5).
[3]   IR 1986, r 2.55(4).
[4]   IR 1986, r 3.21(4).
[5]   IR 1986, r 4.159(4).
[6]   IR 1986, r 6.156(4).

Charity trustee

11.47 He cannot be a trustee for a charity or a charity trustee[1].

[1]   Charities Act 1993, s 72(1)(b).

Pensions and investments

11.48   He cannot be the trustee of a pension trust scheme[1]; cannot be a plan manager of personal equity plans[2] or an account manager of individual savings accounts[3].

[1]   Pensions Act 1995, s 29(1)(b).
[2]   Personal Equity Plan Regulations 1989, SI 1989/469, reg 15(1)(b).
[3]   Individual Savings Account Regulations 1998, SI 1998/1870, reg 20(1)(b).

Miscellaneous public offices

11.49   Furthermore, a person subject to bankruptcy restrictions: can be removed from various positions within the Nuclear Decommissioning Authority[1], the Civil Nuclear Police Authority[2], the Office of Rail Regulation[3], the Serious Organised Crime Agency[4]; cannot be a member of an arbitration panel established under the Industry Act 1975[5]; cannot be a member of the Valuation Tribunal Service[6]; cannot be appointed to be a member of the British Transport Police Authority[7]; cannot be a director of Associated British Ports[8]; cannot be a registrar of births, deaths or marriages[9]; cannot be a member of a community charge valuation tribunal[10]; is disqualified from holding numerous positions in NHS-related and educational organisations[11]; cannot act as the chairman or as a non-executive member of the Appointments Commission[12]; and cannot be a fiscal representative of an aircraft operator[13].

[1]   Energy Act 2004, Sch 1, para 1(6) and (7)(b).
[2]   Energy Act 2004, Sch 10, para 2(5) and (6)(b).
[3]   Railways and Transport Safety Act 2003, Sch 1, para 2(c).
[4]   Serious Organised Crime and Police Act 2005, Sch 1, para 4(e).
[5]   Industry Act 1975, Sch 3, para 6(1)(c).
[6]   Local Government Act 2003, Sch 4, para 2(1)(b).
[7]   Railways and Transport Safety Act 2003, Sch 4, para 7(3)(a).
[8]   Transport Act 1981, Sch 2, para 3(2)(a).
[9]   Registration of Births, Deaths and Marriages Regulations 1968, SI 1968/2049, reg 5(a)(i).
[10]   Valuation and Community Charge Tribunals Regulations 1989, SI 1989/439, reg 9(1)(a).
[11]   See, for instance, the National Institute for Clinical Excellence Regulations 1999, SI 1999/260, reg 5(1)(b) and the Education (Foundation Body) (England) Regulations 2000, SI 2000/2872, Sch 4, para 2(b).
[12]   Appointments Commission Regulations 2006, SI 2006/2380, reg 5(1)(b).
[13]   Air Passenger Duty Regulations 1994, SI 1994/1738, reg 7(1)(d).

Chapter 12

DISCHARGE FROM BANKRUPTCY

A   Duration of bankruptcy
B   Postponement of discharge
C   Application for discharge
D   Effect of discharge

A DURATION OF BANKRUPTCY

Introduction

12.1 A bankruptcy order effects a change of status in the person against whom it is made. For example, while a person is an undischarged bankrupt, he may not act as a director of a company without the leave of the court[1]; he may not obtain credit of £250 or more without disclosing that he is an undischarged bankrupt[2]; he is disqualified from being elected to, or sitting or voting in the House of Commons[3]. Although debtors are not made bankrupt in punishment for their failure to pay their debts, the disadvantages which bankruptcy brings is, or historically was, intended to discourage debtors from lightly submitting to bankruptcy so to avoid their debts and, perhaps, to provide some moral compensation to their disappointed creditors. But, even under the Bankruptcy Acts in force before the Insolvency Act 1986 ('IA 1986'), the legislative intention was that the bankrupt, having given up all his property for the benefit of his creditors, should ordinarily at some time become 'a free man again, able to earn his livelihood and having the ordinary inducements to industry'[4]. Modern bankruptcy law has reduced the length of time that in general the bankrupt must endure that reduction in status. Automatic discharge after three years was introduced by the IA 1986; and, where the bankruptcy commenced on or after 1 April 2004, a bankrupt is discharged at the end of one year from the commencement of his bankruptcy[5]. But the period may be extended where the bankrupt fails to comply with his obligations under the IA 1986[6]. And, where his conduct warrants it, the bankrupt may be subjected to a bankruptcy restrictions order, the effect of which is to impose restrictions on him akin to those affecting undischarged bankrupts[7]. The jurisdiction to make bankruptcy restriction orders, which may last from between two to fifteen years, provides a check against debtors

478

taking advantage of the shorter period before discharge. One of the matters which the court must take into account, when considering an application for such an order, is whether the bankrupt has been an undischarged bankrupt at any time during the six years ending with the commencement of the then current bankruptcy[8].

[1] Company Directors Disqualification Act 1986, s 11(1).
[2] IA 1986, s 360(1)(a).
[3] IA 1986, s 427(1)(b).
[4] *Re Gaskell* [1904] 2 KB 478, CA per Vaughan Williams LJ (a case involving a captain in the Indian Army who had been adjudged bankrupt on his own petition following judgment being given against him in an action for breach of promise).
[5] IA 1986, s 279(1) as amended by the Enterprise Act 2002, s 256 and brought into effect by the Enterprise Act 2002 (Commencement No 4 and Transitional Provisions and Savings) Order 2003, SI 2003/2093, art 2(1).
[6] IA 1986, s 279(3).
[7] Bankruptcy restriction orders are discussed in **Chapter 11**.
[8] IA 1986, s 281A, Sch 4A, para 2(3).

Duration of bankruptcy

12.2 The bankruptcy of an individual against whom a bankruptcy order has been made commences with the day on which the order is made and continues until the individual is discharged from bankruptcy under the appropriate provision of the IA 1986[1].

[1] IA 1986, s 278.

Continuing administration

12.3 Although the bankruptcy of an individual comes to an end when he is discharged[1], the bankrupt's discharge does not mark the end of the administration of his estate. In many, if not most, bankruptcies, the trustee will not have completed the administration by the date of discharge. Discharge has no effect on the functions of the trustee so far as they remain to be carried out or on the operation of the IA 1986 for the purpose of carrying out those functions[2]. Consequently, the bankrupt remains under a duty to assist in the administration after his discharge[3]. Nor does discharge affect the right of any creditor to prove in the bankruptcy for a provable debt[4].

[1] IA 1986, s 278(b).
[2] IA 1986, s 281(1).
[3] IA 1986, s 333(1) and (3).
[4] IA 1986, s 281(1).

Automatic discharge

12.4 Subject to one exception, where the bankruptcy order is made on or after 1 April 2004 the bankrupt is discharged from his bankruptcy at the end of the period of one year beginning with the commencement of the bankruptcy[1]. The discharge is called 'automatic' because it occurs solely by reason of the lapse of the relevant period. The exception mentioned is the case where the bankrupt was made bankrupt on a petition presented pursuant to a criminal bankruptcy order[2].

1   IA 1986, s 279(1).
2   The power to make criminal bankruptcy orders has been abolished; see the Criminal Justice Act 1988, s 101. But there remain persons adjudged bankrupt upon petitions presented under IA 1986, s 164(1)(d) pursuant to criminal bankruptcy orders. How such persons may obtain their discharge is discussed below at paras **12.7** and **12.22**.

Early discharge

12.5   A bankrupt may be discharged after a period shorter even than one year. IA 1986, s 289 imposes a duty on the official receiver to investigate the conduct and affairs of the bankrupt, unless he thinks that such investigation is unnecessary, and to make such report, if any, as he thinks fit to the court. If, during the period of the first year after the commencement of the bankruptcy, the official receiver files with the court a notice stating that the investigation of the conduct and affairs of the bankrupt under IA 1986, s 289 is either unnecessary or concluded, then the bankrupt will be discharged when the notice is filed[1]. It would seem that the possibility of early discharge is to be available where either there is no conduct which requires investigation or that the investigation has been straightforward and quickly concluded. It is possible to say that no investigation is necessary where the bankrupt's bad conduct is so overt that it does not require investigation to uncover it; equally, where such conduct was overt, the investigation might be quickly concluded. It seems unlikely that early discharge should be available in such cases.

1   IA 1986, s 279(2).

Postponing automatic discharge

12.6   The only method of delaying the moment when discharge occurs is a court order, made on the application of the official receiver or the trustee, which suspends the running of time[1]. This is discussed in section B below.

1   IA 1986, s 279(3).

Where an order of discharge is required: criminal bankruptcy orders

12.7   If the bankrupt was adjudged bankrupt on a petition presented pursuant to a criminal bankruptcy order under the IA 1986, s 264(1)(d), he may only be discharged by an order of the court[1]. Applications for orders of discharge are discussed in section C below.

1   IA 1986, s 279(6).

B POSTPONEMENT OF DISCHARGE

Court's power to postpone discharge

12.8 The court has power to order that the one-year period during which the bankrupt is undischarged shall cease to run. This has, obviously, the effect of postponing the discharge. The order may not provide that the period shall cease to run indefinitely or without qualification but must specify either a period during which time shall not run or a condition upon the fulfilment of which time will run again[1]. The court may only exercise this power if it is satisfied that the bankrupt has failed or is failing to comply with an obligation under the IA 1986, Pt IX[2]. In *Shierson v Rastogi*[3] discharge was suspended because the bankrupt had not provided clear information concerning his affairs to his trustee: discharge was postponed until one year after the bankrupt's trial on charges of conspiracy to defraud. The court opined that although postponement might provide an incentive for the bankrupt to comply with his obligations to his trustee, the primary purpose was to maintain the disabilities that being an undischarged bankrupt imposes.

1 IA 1986, s 279(3).
2 IA 1986, s 279(4). IA 1986, Pt IX comprises ss 264–371.
3 [2007] EWHC 1266 (Ch), [2007] All ER (D) 446 (May).

Persons who may apply

12.9 The application to suspend time may now be made by the official receiver or the trustee[1]. This avoids the delay which previously was caused by the need for the trustee to ask the official receiver to make the application. But a creditor cannot bring the application[2]. His recourse, if any, would be to complain about the failure of the trustee or, perhaps, the official receiver to apply[3].

1 IA 1986, s 279(3).
2 *Hardy v Focus Insurance Co Ltd* [1997] BPIR 77.
3 Pursuant to IA 1986, s 303(1).

Court's power to suspend discharge on interim basis

12.10 Where the application is filed at court shortly before the expiry of the relevant period, there may be insufficient time for the court fully to hear the application, particularly where it is contested. But the court has power, where there is evidence before it which shows reasonable grounds that postponement would be ordered on the substantive hearing, to make an order suspending discharge on an interim basis[1]. The full hearing, at which the bankrupt may adduce whatever evidence is appropriate in answer to the application, may then take place after the expiry of the relevant period from the commencement of the bankruptcy. At that hearing the court must decide, after consideration of all the admissible evidence, whether or not to continue the suspension.

1 *Bagnall v Official Receiver* [2003] EWCA Civ 1925, [2004] BPIR 445 decided under IA 1986, s 279(3) before its amendment by the Enterprise Act 2002 and over-ruling the more stringent test in *Re Jacobs (a Bankrupt)* [1999] 1 WLR 619.

12.11 *Discharge from bankruptcy*

Terms of the order

12.11 The order may provide that the period shall cease to run for a specified period or until some specified condition is fulfilled. Although IA 1986, s 279(3) mentions 'a specified condition' in the singular, there does not seem to be any reason why this should not be read as including the plural. The order should specify the period or the conditions[1].

[1] IA 1986, s 279(3).

Procedure

12.12 The following procedure applies except where the application is made by the official receiver pursuant to IR 1986, r 6.176(4) on the adjournment of the public examination of the bankrupt. The application should be made by ordinary application. When the official receiver or the trustee, as the case may be, files his application he must file with it evidence in support setting out the reasons why it appears to him that the order should be made[1]. The official receiver may give his evidence by way of a report[2] but the trustee will need to make a witness statement. The court will fix a date for the hearing of the application, giving notice to the official receiver, the trustee (if he is different) and the bankrupt[3]. Where the application is made by the official receiver, copies of his report must be sent by him to the trustee and the bankrupt so as to reach them at least 21 days before the date fixed for the hearing[4]. And, similarly, where the application is made by the trustee, he must send his evidence to the official receiver and the bankrupt so as to reach them at least 21 days before the date fixed for the hearing[5].

[1] IR 1986, r 6.215(2).
[2] IR 1986, r 7.9(1)(a).
[3] IR 1986, r 6.215(3).
[4] IR 1986, r 6.215(4).
[5] IR 1986, r 6.215(5).

12.13 If the bankrupt intends to contest any points made against him in the evidence filed in support of the application, he should, not later than seven days before the hearing, file in court a notice specifying the statements in the official receiver's or the trustee's evidence which he intends to deny or dispute. If he does give such notice he must send copies of it to the official receiver and the trustee not less than four days before the hearing date[1]. Where the bankrupt needs to adduce evidence in order to show why he disputes the official receiver's report, he ought to do so by witness statement or affidavit unless the court directs that he may give his evidence orally[2].

[1] IR 1986, r 6.215(5).
[2] See the IR 1986, r 7.7.

12.14 If the court makes an order suspending the bankrupt's discharge, it must send copies of the order to the official receiver, the trustee and the bankrupt[1].

[1] IR 1986, r 6.216(6).

Application on the adjournment of a public examination

12.15 Where the public examination of the bankrupt is adjourned by the court, the official receiver may there and then apply for an order suspending the bankrupt's discharge if the bankrupt would otherwise be automatically discharged[1]. If the court makes an order suspending the discharge on such an application, copies of the order must be sent by the court to the official receiver, the trustee and the bankrupt[2]. In a case where a public examination had by consent been converted into a private examination, the official receiver had to apply to reinstate the public examination before making his application to suspend the discharge. The court permitted him to do so at short notice[3].

1 IR 1986, r 6.176(4).
2 IR 1986, r 6.176(5).
3 *Holmes v Official Receiver* [1996] BCC 246 sub nom *Re a Debtor (No 26 of 1991)* [1996] BPIR 279.

Lifting an order suspending discharge

12.16 Where an order suspending discharge has been made the bankrupt may apply to have it lifted[1]. The court must fix a date for the hearing of the application but it is the bankrupt who must give notice, not less than 28 days before the date fixed for the hearing, to the official receiver and the trustee[2]. The notice must in both cases be accompanied by a copy of the application.

1 IR 1986, r 6.216(1).
2 IR 1986, r 6.216(2).

12.17 The official receiver and the trustee may appear and be heard at the hearing of the application, and whether or not he appears the official receiver may file in court a report of any matters which he considers ought to be drawn to the court's attention[1]. If the order suspending discharge was made to have effect until the fulfilment of specified conditions, the court may request the official receiver to make a report as to whether or not those conditions have been fulfilled[2]. If the official receiver does file a report either at his own or the court's behest, he must send copies of it to the bankrupt and the trustee not later than 14 days before the hearing[3]. The bankrupt may file in court not later than seven days before the date of the hearing a notice identifying statements in the official receiver's report which he denies or disputes, and if he does so, the bankrupt must send copies of that notice to the official receiver and to the trustee not less than four days before the hearing date[4].

1 IR 1986, r 6.216(3).
2 IR 1986, r 6.216(4).
3 IR 1986, r 6.216(5).
4 IR 1986, r 6.216(6).

Grounds for lifting the order suspending discharge

12.18 Where the order suspending discharge was made on terms that the relevant period of bankruptcy should cease to run until the fulfilment of

483

specified conditions, the bankrupt will still have to apply to lift the order where it included a term requiring the court to be satisfied that the bankrupt has complied with the conditions imposed on him.

12.19 Where the order for suspension is for a fixed period which has not expired or is to last until specified conditions are fulfilled which have not been fulfilled, it is unclear when a court will lift the suspension unless, on the application to lift it, some matter is raised which was not raised when the order was made but which, had it been raised, would have dissuaded the court from making the suspension order. It would be no answer in such a case that the bankrupt should have appealed the suspension order since an insolvency court may review, rescind or vary any order made by it in the exercise of its jurisdiction[1].

[1] IA 1986, s 375(1).

12.20 If the court discharges the order suspending automatic discharge, it must issue a certificate to the bankrupt stating that it has done so with effect from a specified date[1].

[1] IR 1986, r 6.216(7).

Costs

12.21 In no circumstances may any costs or expenses arising by reason of the bankrupt's application for an order suspending automatic discharge to be lifted fall on the official receiver[1].

[1] IR 1986, r 6.223.

C APPLICATION FOR DISCHARGE

Right to apply to be discharged

12.22 The only class of bankrupts in respect of which an order of discharge is required is the obsolescent class of bankrupts who were made bankrupt by a criminal bankruptcy order. A bankrupt within this class may apply to the court for an order discharging him from bankruptcy at any time after the end of the period of five years beginning with the commencement of his bankruptcy[1].

[1] IA 1986, s 280(1).

Procedure

12.23 When a bankrupt applies for an order discharging him from bankruptcy, he must give the official receiver notice of the application and deposit with him such sum as the official receiver may require to cover his costs of the application[1]. If the court is satisfied that the bankrupt has given that notice and deposit, it must fix a date for the hearing of the application and give at least 42 days' notice of it to the official receiver and the bankrupt[2]. The official receiver must then give notice of the application, not later than 14 days before the date fixed for the hearing, to the trustee and to every creditor who, to the official receiver's knowledge, has a claim outstanding against the estate which has not been satisfied[3].

1 IR 1986, r 6.217(1).
2 IR 1986, r 6.217(2).
3 IR 1986, r 6.217(3), (4).

The official receiver's report

12.24 The official receiver must also, at least 21 days before the date fixed for the hearing of the application, file in court a report. In it must be contained the following information with respect to the bankrupt:

(a) any failure by him to comply with his obligations under the provisions[1] of the IA 1986 relating to individual insolvency;
(b) the circumstances surrounding the present bankruptcy and those surrounding any previous bankruptcy of his;
(c) the extent to which, in the present and in any previous bankruptcy, his liabilities exceeded his assets; and
(d) particulars of any distribution which has been, or is expected to be, made to creditors in the present bankruptcy, or, if such is the case, that there has been and is to be no distribution.

1 Ie the IA 1986, ss 252–385.

12.25 The official receiver must include in the report any other matters which in his opinion ought to be brought to the court's attention[1]. The rule does not restrict relevant previous bankruptcies to any specified period; accordingly the official receiver must report on all previous bankruptcies and not only on any previous bankruptcy which brought the bankrupt within the IA 1986, s 279(1)(a). The official receiver's report is absolutely privileged from proceedings in defamation[2].

1 IR 1986, r 6.218(1).
2 *Bottomly v Brougham* [1908] 1 KB 584; *Mond v Hyde* [1999] QB 1097, [1998] 3 All ER 883, CA.

Service of official receiver's report and objections to it

12.26 The official receiver must send a copy of the report to the bankrupt and to the trustee so as to reach them at least 14 days before the date fixed for the hearing[1]. In response the bankrupt may file in court not later than seven days before the date of the hearing a notice identifying statements in the report which he denies or disputes, and if he does so, the bankrupt must send copies of that notice to the official receiver and to the trustee not less than four days before the hearing date[2].

¹ IR 1986, r 6.218(2).
² IR 1986, r 6.218(4).

The hearing

12.27 At the hearing the official receiver, the trustee and any creditor may appear and may make such representations and put such questions to the bankrupt as the court may allow[1]. The requirement that a creditor obtain permission before putting questions to the bankrupt continues the practice which obtained under the Bankruptcy Act 1914. The rationale for that practice was to avoid the waste of money and unfairness which might result if an opposing creditor possibly unaffected by the outcome and activated by malice was entitled to cross-examine as of right[2]. The court is likely to give permission under the current rule on a similar basis.

¹ IR 1986, r 6.218(4).
² *Re Stern, ex p Keyser Ullmann Ltd v The Bankrupt* [1982] 2 All ER 600, [1982] 1 WLR 860, CA.

12.28 Although there is no obligation on any creditor to attend the hearing, no creditor may enter into a contract with the bankrupt by virtue of which he agrees not to oppose the bankrupt's application for a discharge[1]. If he purports to do so, the contract will be void for illegality[2]. Similarly no such agreement should be made with the bankrupt by the trustee[3].

¹ *Kearley v Thomson* (1890) 24 QBD 742, CA.
² *Hall v Dyson* (1852) 17 QB 785.
³ *Re Shaw* [1917] 2 KB 734, CA.

Court's power on hearing the application

12.29 On hearing the application, the court may:

(a)   refuse to discharge the bankrupt from bankruptcy;
(b)   make an order discharging him absolutely; or
(c)   make an order discharging him subject to such conditions with respect to any income which may subsequently become due to him or with respect to property devolving on him or acquired by him after his discharge as may be specified in the order[1].

¹ IA 1986, s 280(2).

12.30 If the court makes an order discharging the bankrupt, whether absolutely or subject to conditions, it may provide that the order has immediate effect or that its effect is suspended for such period or until the fulfilment of such conditions (including a condition requiring the court to be satisfied as to any matter) as may be specified in the order[1].

¹ IA 1986, s 280(3).

Exercise of the court's discretion

12.31 The court's discretion whether to order that the bankrupt be discharged is at large. The matters on which the official receiver is required to report provides a clear indication of the sort of matters which are relevant to the court's decision. But, since the official receiver must report on the prescribed matters whenever the application is made, the weight which the court will attach to them will no doubt differ depending on how distant in time they are from the date of the application. The protection of the public from the repetition of any reprehensible activity on the part of the bankrupt must remain an important objective[1].

1   *Re Smith* [1947] 1 All ER 769, CA.

Order of discharge

12.32 An order of the court discharging the bankrupt either absolutely[1] or subject to conditions with respect to income or property[2] must bear the date on which it was made; but it will not take effect until such time as it is drawn up by the court[3]. When drawn up the order has effect retrospectively from the date on which it was made[4].

1   Under the IA 1986, s 280(2)(b).
2   Under the IA 1986, s 280(2)(c).
3   IR 1986, r 6.219(1).
4   IR 1986, r 6.219(2).

12.33 Copies of any order made by the court on a bankrupt's application for discharge under the IA 1986, s 280 must be sent by the court to the bankrupt, the trustee and the official receiver[1]. However, no order made by the court on such an application shall be issued or gazetted until the time allowed for appealing has expired or, if an appeal is entered, until the appeal has been determined[2].

1   IR 1986, r 6.219(3).
2   IR 1986, r 6.221.

Costs

12.34 In no circumstances may any costs or expenses arising by reason of the bankrupt's application to be discharged fall on the official receiver[1].

1   IR 1986, r 6.223.

D EFFECT OF DISCHARGE

Relief of the bankrupt from bankruptcy debts

12.35 At the core of the bankruptcy scheme is the idea that in return for surrendering his estate for the benefit of his creditors and accepting the disqualifications which are inherent to the status of a bankrupt, the bankrupt should be protected against and relieved from the claims of his creditors. Protection against the seizure of the bankrupt's property or person is achieved after the making of the bankruptcy order by the provision that no creditor of the bankrupt in respect of a debt provable in the bankruptcy has any remedy against the property or person of the bankrupt in respect of that debt[1]; subject to certain restricted exceptions in respect of executions and distress[2], such a creditor is restricted to his right of proving in the bankruptcy. But removing the creditor's right to seize the property or person of the bankrupt does not, by itself, affect the existence of the creditor's claim or of the possibility of his bringing proceedings in respect of that claim. During the bankruptcy, the bankrupt is protected against proceedings to the extent that no claims may be brought by a creditor to whom a provable debt is owed without the leave of the court[3]. That protection ceases on the bankrupt's discharge. But by his discharge the bankrupt is released from all the bankruptcy debts save for certain specified bankruptcy debts, liability for which is preserved[4]. Thus, except for those bankruptcy debts which are specifically preserved, the bankrupt's discharge releases him from liability for his bankruptcy debts and, subject to that exception, he is entitled to plead his discharge as an absolute defence to any claim subsequently brought against him in respect of a bankruptcy debt.

[1]   IA 1986, s 285(3)(a).
[2]   See the IA 1986, ss 346 and 347.
[3]   IA 1986, s 285(3)(b).
[4]   IA 1986, s 281(1).

General release from bankruptcy debts

12.36 Subject to those bankruptcy debts which are expressly preserved and those other matters expressly stated not to be affected by the discharge, where a bankrupt is discharged, the discharge releases him from all the bankruptcy debts[1]. The bankruptcy debts are:

(a)   any debt or liability to which the bankrupt is subject at the commencement of the bankruptcy;

(b)   any debt or liability to which he may become subject after the commencement of the bankruptcy (including after his discharge) by reason of any obligation incurred before the commencement of the bankruptcy;

(c)   any amount specified in pursuance of the Powers of Criminal Courts Act 1973, s 39(3)(c) in any criminal bankruptcy order made against him before the commencement of the bankruptcy[2]; and

(d)   any interest which a bankruptcy debt bears and which is provable in the bankruptcy under the IA 1986, s 322(2)[3].

[1]   IA 1986, s 281(1).
[2]   Repealed from a date to be specified; see the Criminal Justice Act 1988, s 170(2), Sch 16.
[3]   IA 1986, s 382(1).

12.37 'Liability' means a liability to pay money or money's worth, including any liability under an enactment, any liability for breach of trust, any liability in contract, tort or bailment and any liability arising out of an obligation to make restitution[1]. It is immaterial whether the amount of the debt or liability is fixed or liquidated, or is capable of being ascertained by fixed rules or as a matter of opinion[2].

[1] IA 1986, s 382(4).
[2] IA 1986, s 382(3).

When liability arises in tort

12.38 In determining whether any liability in tort is a bankruptcy debt, the bankrupt is deemed to become subject to that liability by reason of an obligation incurred at the time when the cause of action accrued[1].

[1] IA 1986, s 382(2).

Future and contingent liabilities

12.39 A debt or liability which is payable in the future or on the occurrence of a contingency is included so long as the obligation which gives rise to the debt or the liability is an existing obligation which has been incurred before the commencement of the bankruptcy[1]. The possibility that liability for the opposing party's costs may be imposed in the course of litigation commenced before the commencement of the bankruptcy is not a contingent liability in the required sense because costs are in the discretion of the court and no obligation to pay them exists until an order is made[2].

[1] IA 1986, s 382(1)(b) and (3). See *Re Bradley-Hole (a bankrupt)* [1995] 4 All ER 865, [1995] 1 WLR 1097.
[2] *Glenister v Rowe* [2000] Ch 76, [1999] 3 All ER 452, CA.

Liability under an enactment

12.40 Where a decision has been made before a debtor becomes bankrupt to recover from him overpayments of social security benefits, he will be released from the debt by his discharge[1].

[1] *R (on the application of Balding) v Secretary of State for Work and Pensions* [2007] EWHC 759 (Admin), [2007] 4 All ER 422.

Foreign aspect

12.41 On his discharge from an English bankruptcy, the bankrupt is released from all his bankruptcy debts. That means that he may not be sued in respect of them before an English court[1]. It appears that this is so even where the law applicable to the contract giving rising to the debt is a foreign law. The position is the same under the EC Insolvency Regulation because English law will govern the effect of the bankruptcy on creditors' rights (subject to excepted cases)[2].

12.41 *Discharge from bankruptcy*

1   *Ellis v M'Henry* (1871) LR 6 CP 228.
2   EC Insolvency Regulation, art 4(1) and (2)(e), (j) and (k).

12.42 Where the English bankruptcy is a main proceeding, the release ought also to be recognised by a court in another Member State to which the regulation applies[1]; but if the English bankruptcy is a territorial or secondary proceeding within the meaning of the EC Insolvency Regulation, although the bankrupt will be released from his debts[2], the effect of the release will not extend to assets which are situated outside the United Kingdom and belonged to him at the commencement of the bankruptcy[3].

1   EC Insolvency Regulation, art 17(1).
2   EC Insolvency Regulation, arts 4(1) and 28.
3   EC Insolvency Regulation, art 17(2) and Virgós-Schmit report, para 157.

Bankruptcy debts from which the bankrupt is not released by his discharge

12.43 In the following paragraphs are listed the bankruptcy debts from which the bankrupt is not released by his discharge. Since he is not released from these debts, the creditors to whom they are owed may sue the bankrupt in respect of them. After discharge such creditors do not require the leave of the court to bring such proceedings. Before discharge, they do need such leave[1] but, because the bankrupt is not discharged from the liability to which the claim relates, leave is likely to be given[2]. Some, but not all, of the bankruptcy debts liability for which is preserved are provable in the bankruptcy[3]. Where the debt has been proved and a dividend paid, the creditor would have to give credit in any action for what he has received by way of dividend in the bankruptcy.

1   IA 1986, s 285(3)(b).
2   *Polly Peck International plc v Nadir* [1992] BCLC 746.
3   See the IR 1986, r 12.3 for the definition of provable debts.

Fraud

12.44 Discharge does not release the bankrupt from any debt which he incurred in respect of, or forbearance in respect of which was secured by means of, any fraud or fraudulent breach of trust to which he was a party[1]. Fraud, in this context, means actual fraud; constructive fraud, such as may be said to found a claim to repay money obtained by undue influence, does not suffice[2]. A creditor who alleges that the debt was incurred in respect of any fraud, carries the burden of proving that this is the case. A default judgment of a foreign court on a cause of action alleging fraud is insufficient evidence for this purpose[3]. Dishonesty is an essential element of a fraudulent breach of trust[4]. The reference to forbearance is somewhat cryptic. The provision might be taken to mean that a debt incurred, without fraud, in the ordinary course of the bankrupt's business might be converted into a debt from which he is not released because, by a fraudulent representation, he persuaded the creditor to forbear, even for some short time, from pursuing the debt. This would encompass a case where, shortly before the commencement of the bankruptcy, the bankrupt represented to a creditor that he would shortly be paid from funds which the bankrupt was about to receive and, induced by that statement, the creditor agreed not to pursue the matter for some period. If the bankrupt made the representation that he was soon to receive the funds knowing that it was false, then it could be said that the creditor's forbearance was secured by means of a fraud. Although the bankrupt's conduct is reprehensible, it does not seem to justify the conversion of an ordinary bankruptcy debt from which he would be released on discharge into one which survives his bankruptcy. That result would only seem justified where, but for the fraudulently obtained forbearance, the creditor would have been paid in full. In many cases, where the forbearance was obtained only shortly before the commencement of the bankruptcy, this may not be so. For if the creditor had pursued the debt, the result would have been that the bankruptcy would have commenced at some earlier date than it did. Nevertheless, the provision (if known to debtors) may provide a salutary discouragement to their making dishonest representations to their creditors in order to induce the creditors to stop pressing for payment.

1   IA 1986, s 281(3). See *Polly Peck International plc v Nadir* [1992] BCLC 746.
2   *Mander v Evans* [2001] 28 LS Gaz R 42 (Ferris J).
3   *Masters v Leaver* [2000] BPIR 284, CA.
4   *Woodland-Ferrari v UCL Group Retirement Benefits Scheme* [2002] EWHC 1354 (Ch), [2002] BPIR 1270.

Fines and recognisances

12.45 Discharge does not release the bankrupt from any liability in respect of a fine imposed for an offence or from any liability under a recognisance except, in the case of a penalty imposed for an offence under an enactment relating to the public revenue or of a recognisance, with the consent of the Treasury[1]. Liability in respect of a fine imposed for an offence is not provable[2]. A fine includes any pecuniary penalty or pecuniary forfeiture or pecuniary compensation payable under a conviction[3]. A confiscation order made under Parts 2, 3 or 4 of the Proceeds of Crime Act 2002 counts as a fine in this context[4]. A recognisance is the liability accepted by a person who stands surety for an accused who is released on bail or by a parent or guardian who agrees to ensure that proper care is taken of a juvenile offender on terms that if he re-offends a sum of money, the recognisance, will be forfeit.

1   IA 1986, s 281(4).
2   IR 1986, r 12.3(2)(a).
3   IA 1986, s 281(8) and Magistrates' Courts Act 1980, s 150(1).
4   IA 1986, s 281(4A).

Liability to pay damages for personal injury

12.46 Discharge does not, except to such extent and on such conditions as the court may direct, release the bankrupt from any bankruptcy debt which consists of a liability to pay damages for negligence, nuisance or a breach of statutory, contractual or other duty or to pay damages by virtue of the

Consumer Protection Act 1987, Pt I where such damages are payable in respect of personal injuries to any person[1].

1   IA 1986, s 281(5)(a).

Liability arising in family proceedings or under a maintenance assessment

12.47 Discharge does not, except to such extent and on such conditions as the court may direct, release the bankrupt from any bankruptcy debt which arises under any order made in family proceedings or under any assessment made under the Child Support Act 1991[1]. 'Family proceedings' means (a) family proceedings within the meaning of the Magistrates' Courts Act 1980 and any proceedings which would be such proceedings but for s 65(1)(ii) of that Act, and (b) family proceedings within the meaning of the Matrimonial and Family Proceedings Act 1984, Pt V. Debts that arise under any order made in family proceedings or under any assessment made under the Child Support Act 1991 are not provable[2].

1   IA 1986, s 281(5)(b).
2   IR 1986, r 12.3(2)(a). See *Woodley v Woodley (No 2)* [1993] 4 All ER 1010, [1994] 1 WLR 1167, CA.

Liability under confiscation order

12.48 As mentioned above, a confiscation order under Parts 2, 3 or 4 of the Proceeds of Crime Act 2002 is treated as a fine and so not released by discharge[1]. The same result is achieved in respect of confiscation orders made under the Drug Trafficking Offences Act 1986, s 1, the Criminal Justice (Scotland) Act 1987, s 1 or the Criminal Justice Act 1988, s 71. Discharge does not release the bankrupt from such other bankruptcy debts, not being debts provable in his bankruptcy, as are prescribed[2]. Confiscation orders made under these enactments are prescribed in the Insolvency Rules as not being released on discharge[3].

1   IA 1986, s 281(4A).
2   IA 1986, s 281(6).
3   IR 1986, r 6.223.

Student loans

12.49 A person's bankruptcy debts do not include any debt or liability to which he is or may become subject in respect of any sum payable to an eligible student by way of a loan and which he receives or is entitled to receive (i) if the bankruptcy commenced before 1 September 2004, after the commencement of the bankruptcy, or (ii) if the bankruptcy commenced on or after 1 September 2004, before or after the commencement of the bankruptcy[1]. Since these liabilities are excluded from being bankruptcy debts, the bankrupt is not released from them on his discharge.

1   Education (Student Support) Regulations 2007, SI 2007/176, reg 91(1).

Matters which are not affected by discharge

12.50 It is expressly provided that the bankrupt's discharge does not affect the continuing administration of his estate, the right of any creditor to prove in the bankruptcy for a debt from which the bankrupt is released[1], the rights of his secured creditors[2] and the liabilities of other persons jointly liable for any bankruptcy debt or liable as surety for the bankrupt[3].

[1]   IA 1986, s 281(1).
[2]   IA 1986, s 281(2).
[3]   IA 1986, s 281(7).

Residual administration of the estate

12.51 The discharge has no effect on the functions of the trustee, in so far as they remain to be carried out or on the operation of the IA 1986, Pt IX[1] for the purpose of carrying out those functions[2]. Thus the discharged bankrupt continues to owe his duty to the trustee to provide information, attend on the trustee and to do all such things as the trustee may reasonably require of him[3]. The right of any creditor to prove in the bankruptcy for any debt from which the bankrupt is released is not affected by the bankrupt's discharge[4]. The trustee retains his responsibility to the creditors for the proper administration of the estate.

[1]   Ie the IA 1986, ss 264–371.
[2]   IA 1986, s 281(1).
[3]   IA 1986, s 333(1), (3).
[4]   IA 1986, s 281(1).

Continuing right of proof

12.52 The discharge of the bankrupt does not affect the right of any creditor of his to prove in the bankruptcy for any debt from which the bankrupt is released[1].

[1]   IA 1986, s 281(1).

Rights of secured creditors

12.53 The rights of any secured creditor of the bankrupt to enforce his security for the payment of a debt from which the bankrupt is released are not affected by the bankrupt's discharge[1].

[1]   IA 1986, s 281(2).

Persons jointly liable with the bankrupt or liable as surety for the bankrupt

12.54 The bankrupt's discharge does not release any person other than the bankrupt from any liability, whether as partner or co-trustee of the bankrupt or otherwise, from which the bankrupt is released by the discharge, or from any liability as surety for the bankrupt or as a person in the nature of such a surety[1]. Thus, by virtue of the relevant definition of debt[2], persons jointly liable with the bankrupt, or sureties for his liabilities, may remain liable after his discharge for present, future and contingent liabilities incurred jointly with him, or on his behalf, under obligations entered into before the commencement of the bankruptcy.

1 IA 1986, s 281(7).
2 IA 1986, ss 382(3), 385(1).

After-acquired property and income payments orders

12.55 The trustee may not claim for the estate property which is acquired by or devolves on the bankrupt after his discharge, unless, where the bankrupt requires an order of discharge, the order discharging him contains a condition with respect to such property[1]. An income payments order may not be made after the discharge of the bankrupt and, if made before, shall not have effect after his discharge except (a) in the case of a discharge by order of the court, by virtue of a condition contained in the order of discharge[2], or (b) where discharge occurs automatically on the expiry of the relevant period[3], by virtue of an express provision in the order requiring it to continue for a period ending after the discharge but no later than three years after the making of the order[4]. Accordingly the bankrupt's duty to inform his trustee about his acquiring property or about increases in his income does not continue after his discharge[5].

1 IA 1986, ss 307(2)(c) and 280(2)(c) (concerning the court's power to impose such condition).
2 See the IA 1986, ss 279(1)(a) and 280(2)(c).
3 See the IA 1986, s 279(1)(b).
4 IA 1986, s 310(6).
5 See the IA 1986, s 333(2) for the duty. That it does not continue after discharge is apparent from IA 1986, s 333(3) which expressly provides that IA 1986, s 333(1), imposing the duty to assist the trustee, applies after discharge but makes no mention of IA 1986, s 333(2).

Bankruptcy offences

12.56 The former bankrupt cannot be guilty of a bankruptcy offence[1] in respect of anything done after his discharge, but proceedings may be instituted against a discharged bankrupt for an offence committed before his discharge[2].

1 Ie an offence created under the IA 1986, ss 350–365.
2 IA 1986, s 350(3).

Disqualification from offices

12.57 The bankrupt's discharge will lift the disqualification which being an undischarged bankrupt imposes on him from holding certain offices[1], but a bankruptcy restrictions order or undertaking, if one has been made or given, will continue to have effect after discharge.

1 See **Chapter 10** for the relevant offices and positions.

Certificate of discharge

12.58 Once an individual has been discharged from bankruptcy, it may help him to make a fresh start in business to have clear evidence that he is no longer bankrupt. He can obtain a certificate of discharge by applying to the court for one. The application should be supported by an affidavit setting out how the discharge has occurred. On that application, where it appears to the court that the applicant has been discharged, whether by expiration of time or otherwise, it must issue a certificate of his discharge on which is stated the date from which it is effective[1].

[1] IR 1986, r 6.220(1).

12.59 The discharged bankrupt may also require the Secretary of State to give notice of the discharge in the Gazette, or in any newspaper in which the bankruptcy was advertised, or in both[1]. The requirement must be made in writing addressed to the Secretary of State. The Secretary of State must notify the discharged bankrupt forthwith as to the cost of the advertisement and is under no obligation to advertise until that sum has been paid[2].

[1] IR 1986, r 6.220(2).
[2] IR 1986, r 6.220(3).

12.60 Where the former bankrupt has died or is a person incapable of managing his own affairs[1], his personal representative or, as the case may be, a person appointed by the court to represent or act for him[2] may require the Secretary of State to give notice of the discharge subject to the same conditions[3].

[1] Ie a person who is incapable of managing and administering his property and affairs either by reason of a mental disorder within the meaning of the Mental Health Act 1983 or due to physical affliction or disability; see the IR 1986, r 7.43(1).
[2] See the IR 1986, r 7.44.
[3] IR 1986, r 6.220(4).

Deletion of registration on discharge

12.61 The Secretary of State must delete all information on the individual insolvency register concerning the bankrupt when the bankrupt has been discharged and a period of three months has elapsed from the date of discharge[1].

[1] IR 1986, r 6A.5(b).

Chapter 13

TRUSTEE IN BANKRUPTCY

A INTRODUCTION

13.1 The function of the trustee is to get in, realise and distribute the bankrupt's estate in accordance with the Insolvency Act 1986 ('IA 1986'), ss 305–335. What is involved in those activities is described in later chapters. In this chapter are discussed various general matters pertaining to the office of the trustee: who may be a trustee in bankruptcy; how he is appointed; his remuneration; how he ceases to hold office; his release and the summary procedure for making claims against him for misappropriation of assets or other breach of duty in the conduct of his trusteeship. Then certain general duties incumbent on a trustee in bankruptcy are described concerning duties to provide information to the official receiver and the Financial Services Authority, the banking of funds, and keeping records and providing accounts. The duties concerning the banking of funds received in the course of administering the estate and of keeping records and providing accounts apply to the official receiver, not only when he acts as trustee but also when he acts as receiver and manager of the estate pending the appointment of a trustee.

496

Officer of the court

13.2 In *Re Condon, ex p James*[1] James LJ stated, 'I am of opinion that a trustee in bankruptcy is an officer of the Court. He has inquisitorial powers given him by the Court, and the Court regards himself as its officer, and he is to hold money in his hands upon trust for its equitable distribution among the creditors.' Although expressed there as an opinion, the trustee's status as an officer of the court is clearly established[2]. In consequence the court expects the trustee to apply the highest standards in the discharge of his functions[3].

[1]   (1874) 9 Ch App 609, 614. For a discussion of the application of the rule in *Ex p James*, see para **18.271**.
[2]   See *Re Carnac, ex p Simmonds* (1885) 16 QBD 308; *Re Tyler, ex p Official Receiver* [1907] 1 KB 865.
[3]   See, for a more recent expression of the court's expectations, *Re Ng (a Bankrupt), Ng v Ng* [1997] BPIR 267.

Official name

13.3 The official name of the trustee is 'the trustee of the estate of … a bankrupt' (inserting the name of the bankrupt); but he may be referred to as 'the trustee in bankruptcy' of the particular bankrupt[1].

[1]   IA 1986, s 305(4).

B PERSONS QUALIFIED TO BE THE TRUSTEE

13.4 Except where the official receiver is the trustee, no person may be appointed as trustee of a bankrupt's estate unless he is, at the time of the appointment, qualified to act as an insolvency practitioner in relation to the bankrupt[1]. This requirement involves two components. First, to be qualified to act as an insolvency practitioner a person must be authorised so to act by virtue of membership of a recognised professional body and he must hold an authorisation granted by a competent authority[2]. Secondly, for an insolvency practitioner to be qualified to act as an insolvency practitioner in relation to another person, there must be in force security for the performance of the insolvency practitioner's functions and the security must meet the prescribed requirements with respect to the insolvency practitioner's so acting in relation to that other person[3].

[1]   IA 1986, s 292(2) and (5). For the definition of 'act as an insolvency practitioner,' see IA 1986, s 388.
[2]   IA 1986, s 390(2). For the recognised professional bodies see IA 1986, s 391 and the Insolvency Practitioners (Recognised Professional Bodies) Order 1986, SI 1986/1764. For the authorities competent to grant authorisation and the granting of authorisations, see the IA 1986, ss 392–394 and the Insolvency Practitioners Regulations 2005, SI 2005/524, regs 5–11.
[3]   IA 1986, s 390(3). For the prescribed requirements as to the insolvency practitioner's security, see the Insolvency Practitioners Regulations 2005, SI 2005/524, reg 12 and Sch 2.

13.5 The trustee must be an individual because only an individual may act as an insolvency practitioner[1]. The following categories of individuals cannot act as a trustee in bankruptcy because they may not be insolvency practitioners:

13.5 *Trustee in bankruptcy*

(a)   a person who has been adjudged bankrupt or sequestration of whose estate has been awarded and (in either case) he has not been discharged;

(b)   a person who is subject to a disqualification order made or a disqualification undertaking accepted under the Company Directors Disqualification Act 1986 or to a disqualification order made under Part II of the Companies (Northern Ireland) Order 1989;

(c)   he is a patient within the meaning of the Mental Health (Scotland) Act 1984, s 125(1) or has had a guardian appointed to him under the Adults with Incapacity (Scotland) Act 2000; or

(d)   he lacks capacity (within the meaning of the Mental Capacity Act 2005) to act as an insolvency practitioner[2].

[1]   IA 1986, s 390(1).
[2]   IA 1986, s 390(4).

13.6 A person may not act as an insolvency practitioner while a bankruptcy restrictions order is in force in respect of him[1].

[1]   IA 1986, s 390(5).

13.7 It is an offence to act as trustee in bankruptcy to an individual or a partnership (or otherwise to act as an insolvency practitioner in relation to an individual, partnership or company) when not qualified to do so[1].

[1]   IA 1986, s 389.

13.8 A trustee must vacate office if he ceases to be a person who is for the time being qualified to act as an insolvency practitioner in relation to the bankrupt[1]. The trustee would cease to be so qualified either if he ceased to be an insolvency practitioner or if his security ceased to be effective. The official receiver will be the trustee while the office is otherwise vacant[2].

[1]   IA 1986, s 298(6).
[2]   IA 1986, s 300(1) and (2).

C APPOINTMENT OF THE TRUSTEE

Power to appoint trustee

13.9 A person may be appointed as trustee of a bankrupt's estate[1]:

(1)   by a general meeting of the bankrupt's creditors;
(2)   by the Secretary of State[2]; or
(3)   by the court[3].

[1]   IA 1986, s 292(1).
[2]   Under the IA 1986, s 295(2), s 296(2) or s 300(6) (see para **13.25** below).
[3]   Under the IA 1986, s 297.

13.10 The provision to appoint the trustee operates without prejudice to the various provisions under which the official receiver is, in certain circumstances, to be trustee of the estate[1].

[1]   IA 1986, s 292(5). As to such circumstances see para **13.32** below.

13.11 The appointment will normally be made by the creditors in general meeting summoned by the official receiver, with appointment by the Secretary of State or the court taking place only in certain restricted circumstances.

13.12 Two or more persons may be appointed as joint trustees, but such an appointment must make provision as to the circumstances in which the trustees must act together and the circumstances in which one or more of them may act for the others[1].

1   IA 1986, s 297(3).

13.13 Provided the appointee accepts the appointment in accordance with the Insolvency Rules 1986[1], it takes effect at the time specified in the certificate of appointment[2].

1   IA 1986, s 292(4).
2   IA 1986, s 292(4).

Summoning of meeting to appoint first trustee

13.14 Once a bankruptcy order has been made, the official receiver must, subject to the exceptions mentioned below, decide whether to summon a general meeting of the bankrupt's creditors for the purpose of appointing a trustee of the bankrupt's estate[1]. He must do this as soon as practicable in the 12 weeks after the making of the order. If he decides not to summon a meeting, he must, before the end of the 12-week period, give notice of his decision to the court and to all those creditors who are known to him or who are identified in the bankrupt's statement of affairs[2].

1   IA 1986, s 293(1).
2   IA 1986, s 293(2).

13.15 The first exception is that the obligation to decide whether to call a meeting is removed where the court appoints as trustee either, following the presentation of a debtor's petition, the insolvency practitioner who was ordered to make a report on the debtor's affairs or, where there is a supervisor of a voluntary arrangement, that supervisor[1].

1   IA 1986, s 297(4)–(6).

13.16 Secondly, any creditor may request the official receiver to summon a meeting to appoint a trustee[1]. If such a request is made with the concurrence of not less than one-quarter, in value, of the creditors, including the creditor making the request, the official receiver must summon the requested meeting[2] and this obligation to call a meeting overrides the trustee's duty to decide whether to call a meeting or not[3].

1   IA 1986, s 294(1).
2   IA 1986, s 294(2).
3   IA 1986, ss 293(1) and 294(3).

Procedure for calling first meeting of creditors

13.17 If under the IA 1986, s 293(1) the official receiver decides to summon a meeting of creditors, he must fix a venue for the meeting, not more that four months from the date of a bankruptcy order[1]. The venue for the meeting means the time, date and place for the meeting[2]. When the venue has been fixed, notice of the meeting must be given to the court and to every creditor of the bankrupt who is known to the official receiver or is identified in the bankrupt's statement of affairs[3]. Notice to the court must be given forthwith and the notice to the creditors must be given at least 21 days before the date fixed for the meeting[4]. The notice to the creditors must specify a time and date, not more that four days before the date fixed for the meeting, by which they must lodge proofs and (if applicable) proxies, in order to be entitled to vote at the meeting[5]. Notice must also be given by public advertisement[6].

[1]   IR 1986, r 6.79(1).
[2]   IR 1986, r 13.6.
[3]   IR 1986, r 6.79(2).
[4]   IR 1986, r 6.79(3).
[5]   IR 1986, r 6.79(4).
[6]   IR 1986, r 6.79(5).

Procedure where creditor requires a meeting

13.18 Where the official receiver receives a request by a creditor for a meeting of creditors to be summoned, and it appears to him that the request is properly made in accordance with the IA 1986, he must withdraw any notice which he has already given to the effect that he has decided not to summon such a meeting, fix the venue for the meeting not more than three months from his receipt of the request and follow the same procedure for giving notice of the meeting as is set out in the preceding paragraph[1].

[1]   IR 1986, r 6.79(6).

Business at the first meeting of creditors

13.19 At the first meeting of creditors, no resolutions shall be taken other than:

(a)   a resolution to appoint a named insolvency practitioner to be trustee in bankruptcy or two or more named insolvency practitioners as joint trustees;

(b)   a resolution to establish a creditors' committee;

(c)   (unless it has been resolved to establish a creditors' committee) a resolution specifying the terms on which the trustee is to be remunerated, or to defer consideration of that matter;

(d)   (if and only if two or more persons are appointed to act jointly as trustee) a resolution specifying whether acts are to be done by both or all of them, or only by one;

(e)   (where the meeting has been requisitioned by a creditor) a resolution authorising payment out of the estate, as an expense of the bankruptcy, of the cost of summoning and holding the meeting;

(f)   a resolution to adjourn the meeting for not more than three weeks;
(g)   any other resolution which the chairman thinks it right to allow for special reasons[1].

[1]   IR 1986, r 6.80(1).

13.20 No resolution may be proposed which has for its object the appointment of the official receiver as trustee[1]. The entitlement to vote at the meeting and other matters of procedure at the meeting are the same as at subsequent creditors' meetings, the procedure relating to which is discussed in **Chapter 18**[2].

[1]   IR 1986, r 6.80(2).
[2]   See para **18.72ff**.

Appointment by creditors' meeting

13.21 If, at the creditors' meeting, a resolution is passed appointing a trustee, then once the appointee has provided a written statement to the effect that he is a qualified insolvency practitioner, and that he consents to act, the chairman of the meeting must certify the appointment[1]. The trustee's appointment is effective from the date on which the appointment is certified, and that date is indorsed on the certificate[2].

[1]   IR 1986, r 6.120(1), (2). For the prescribed forms of appointment see rr 6.120, 12.5, Sch 4, Forms 6.40 (certificate of appointment of trustee by creditors' meeting), 6.41 (certificate of appointment of two or more trustees by creditors' meeting).
[2]   IR 1986, r 6.120(1), (3).

13.22 The chairman of the meeting must send the certificate to the official receiver[1], who in turn must send it to the trustee and file a copy of it in court[2].

[1]   IR 1986, r 6.120(1), (4).
[2]   IR 1986, r 6.120(1), (5).

Rule against solicitation

13.23 Where the court is satisfied that any improper solicitation has been used by or on behalf of the trustee in obtaining proxies or procuring his appointment, it may order that no remuneration out of the estate shall be allowed to any person by whom, or on whose behalf, the solicitation was exercised[1].

[1]   IR 1986, r 6.148(1).

13.24 An order of the court under the above provisions takes precedence over any resolution of the creditors' committee or the creditors, or any other provision in the IR 1986 relating to the trustee's remuneration[1].

[1]   IR 1986, r 6.148(2).

13.25 *Trustee in bankruptcy*

Appointment by the Secretary of State

13.25 The Secretary of State is given the power to appoint a trustee in three sets of circumstances[1]:

(a) If at the creditors' meeting[2] no appointment of a trustee is made, the official receiver must decide whether to refer the need for an appointment to the Secretary of State[3]. On such a reference, the Secretary of State may then make an appointment[4].

(b) At any time when the official receiver is the trustee of a bankrupt's estate by virtue of any provision of the IA 1986[5], he may apply to the Secretary of State for the appointment of a trustee in his stead[6]. On such an application the Secretary of State may then make an appointment[7].

(c) In certain circumstances, where there is a vacancy in the office of trustee[8].

[1] IA 1986, s 292(1)(b).
[2] Ie the meeting called pursuant to the IA 1986, s 293 or s 294.
[3] IA 1986, s 295(1).
[4] IA 1986, s 295(2).
[5] Ie by virtue of any provision in the IA 1986, Pt IX, Ch III (ss 292–304).
[6] IA 1986, s 296(1).
[7] IA 1986, s 296(2). Such an application may be made notwithstanding that the Secretary of State has declined to make an appointment either on a previous application under s 296(1) or on a reference under s 295 or s 300(4): IA 1986, s 296(3).
[8] As to vacancies, see paras **13.98ff** below.

13.26 If the creditors' meeting fails to appoint a trustee, and either the official receiver decides not to refer the need for an appointment to the Secretary of State, or on such a reference the Secretary of State declines to make an appointment, the official receiver must give notice of the decision to the court[1]. As from the giving of such notice, the official receiver is the trustee of the bankrupt's estate[2].

[1] IA 1986, s 295(3).
[2] IA 1986, s 295(4).

13.27 A trustee appointed by the Secretary of State[1] must give notice to the creditors of his appointment or, if the court so allows, must advertise his appointment in accordance with the court's directions[2]. The notice or advertisement must:

(1) state whether the trustee proposes to summon a general meeting of the creditors for the purpose of establishing a creditors' committee[3]; and

(2) if he does not propose to summon such a meeting, set out the power of the creditors to require him to do so[4].

[1] Ie whether under the IA 1986, s 296 or otherwise.
[2] IA 1986, s 296(4).
[3] Ie under the IA 1986, s 301.
[4] IA 1986, s 296(5).

13.28 Where the Secretary of State makes an appointment under the powers set out above, he must send two copies of the certificate of appointment to the official receiver, who sends one to the person appointed, and files the other in court. The certificate must specify the date from which the trustee's appointment is effective[1].

1   IR 1986, r 6.122(1), (2).

Appointment by the court

13.29 The court is given the power to appoint a trustee in the following circumstances:

(a)   Where a bankruptcy order is made in a case in which an insolvency practitioner's report has been submitted to the court[1], the court may, on making the order, appoint the person who made the report as trustee[2].

(b)   Where a bankruptcy order is made at a time when there is a supervisor of a voluntary arrangement approved in relation to the bankrupt, the court may on making the order, appoint the supervisor of the arrangement as trustee[3]. This power is available whether or not the bankruptcy order is made on a petition by the supervisor.

1   Ie under the IA 1986, s 274.
2   IA 1986, s 297(4). Where an appointment is made under s 297(4) or (5), the official receiver is not under the duty imposed by s 293(1) to decide whether or not to summon a meeting of creditors: IA 1986, s 297(6).
3   IA 1986, s 297(5). See also note 2 above.

13.30 Where the trustee of a bankrupt's estate has been appointed by the court, the trustee must give notice to the bankrupt's creditors of his appointment or, if the court so allows, must advertise his appointment in accordance with the directions of the court[1]. The notice must give the same information as that required where the trustee has been appointed by the Secretary of State[2].

1   IA 1986, s 297(7).
2   IA 1986, s 297(8); and see s 296(5) and para **13.27** above.

13.31 Where the court appoints the trustee[1], the court's order may not issue unless and until the person appointed has filed in court a statement of the effect that he is a qualified insolvency practitioner and that he consents to act[2]. Thereafter, the court must send two copies of the order to the official receiver. One of those copies must be sealed, and this must be sent by him to the person appointed as trustee[3]. The trustee's appointment takes effect from the date of the order[4].

1   Ie under the IA 1986, s 297(3), (4) or (5): see above.
2   IR 1986, r 6.121(1), (2). For the prescribed forms of orders of court see rr 6.121, 12.7, Sch 4, Forms 6.42 (order of court appointing trustee), 6.43 (order of court appointing two or more trustees).
3   IR 1986, r 6.121(1), (3).
4   IR 1986, r 6.121(1), (4).

13.32   *Trustee in bankruptcy*

Official receiver as trustee

13.32   In certain circumstances, the official receiver becomes the trustee of the estate by operation of law.

13.33   If the official receiver decides not to summon a creditors' meeting[1] and gives notice of such decision, he is, as from the giving of such notice to the court, the trustee of the bankrupt's estate[2].

[1]   Ie under the IA 1986, s 293.
[2]   IA 1986, s 293(2), (3).

13.34   If a creditors' meeting is held[1], but no trustee is appointed, then as from the giving of notice by the official receiver of his decision not to refer the need for an appointment to the Secretary of State, or, on such a reference, of the Secretary of State's decision to decline to make an appointment[2], the official receiver is the trustee of the bankrupt's estate[3].

[1]   Ie under the IA 1986, s 293 or s 294.
[2]   Ie from the date of a notice given under the IA 1986, s 295(3).
[3]   IA 1986, s 295(4).

13.35   Where the court issues a certificate for the summary administration of a bankrupt's estate[1], the official receiver is, as from the issue of that certificate, the trustee[2]. However, where such a certificate is issued or is in force, the court may, if it thinks fit, appoint a person other than the official receiver as trustee[3].

[1]   Ie under the IA 1986, s 295(3).
[2]   IA 1986, s 297(2).
[3]   IA 1986, s 297(3).

13.36   Where, prior to the abolition of criminal bankruptcy, a bankruptcy order was made in a case of criminal bankruptcy[1], the official receiver was and remains the trustee of the bankrupt's estate[2].

[1]   Ie under the IA 1986, s 264(1)(d). The power to make criminal bankruptcy orders was abolished by the Criminal Justice Act 1988, s 101, with effect from 14 October 1991, but by s 101(2), this is without prejudice to orders already made.
[2]   IA 1986, s 297(1).

Proof of trustee's status

13.37   Where a trustee has been appointed, a sealed copy of the order of appointment or, as the case may be, a copy of the certificate of appointment may in any proceedings be adduced as proof that he is duly authorised to exercise the powers and perform the duties of trustee of the bankrupt's estate[1].

[1]   IR 1986, r 6.123.

Notice of appointment

13.38 Immediately after receiving his certificate of appointment, the trustee must give notice of his appointment in such newspaper as he thinks most appropriate for ensuring that it comes to the notice of the bankrupt's creditors[1].

[1]   IR 1986, r 6.124(1).

13.39 The expense of giving the notice must be borne in the first instance by the trustee; but he is entitled to be reimbursed by the estate, as an expense of the bankruptcy[1].

[1]   IR 1986, r 6.124(2). IR 1986, r 6.124(2) applies also in the case of the notice or advertisement under IA 1986, s 296(4) and of the notice or advertisement under IA 1986, s 297(7): IR 1986, r 6.124(2).

D REMUNERATION OF THE TRUSTEE

Source of remuneration

13.40 The trustee ordinarily looks to the estate for his remuneration. It is an expense of the bankruptcy[1] and is payable out of the estate before any distribution is made to any creditor[2]. Where the estate is insufficient to cover the trustee's remuneration and he has expended skill and labour on assets held by the bankrupt on trust for others, he may be entitled to recoup remuneration for that activity from those assets[3]. But the entitlement must be justified and the trustee will not be permitted to take remuneration from the proceeds of sale of an asset claimed by third parties simply because they form a ready source of money[4].

[1]   IR 1986, r 12.2.
[2]   IA 1986, s 328(2). For the order in which the expenses rank amongst themselves, see IR 1986, r 6.224(1); the trustee's remuneration features at IR 1986, r 6.224(1)(o).
[3]   *Re Berkeley Applegate (Investment Consultants) Ltd, Harris v Conway* [1989] Ch 32, [1989] BCLC 28.
[4]   *Re Local London Residential Ltd* [2004] EWHC 114 (Ch), [2004] 2 BCLC 72.

Fixing of remuneration by the creditors' committee or the creditors generally

13.41 The trustee is entitled to receive remuneration for his services, decided either:

(1)   as a percentage of the value of the assets in the bankrupt's estate which are realised or distributed, or of the one value and the other in combination; or
(2)   by reference to the time properly given by the trustee, and his staff, in attending to matters arising in the bankruptcy[1].

[1]   IR 1986, r 6.138(1), (2).

13.42 *Trustee in bankruptcy*

13.42 Where the trustee is other than the official receiver, it is for the creditors' committee, if there is one, to determine whether his remuneration is to be fixed under heads (1) or (2) above (para **13.41**) and, if under head (1) above, to determine any percentage to be applied[1].

1   IR 1986, r 6.138(3).

13.43 In arriving at that determination, the committee must have regard to the following matters:

(a)   the complexity, or otherwise, of the case;
(b)   any exceptional responsibility involved;
(c)   the effectiveness with which the trustee appears to be carrying out, or to have carried out, his duties; and
(d)   the value and nature of the assets in the estate[1].

1   IR 1986, r 6.138(4).

13.44 If there is no creditors' committee, or the committee does not make the requisite determination, the trustee's remuneration may be fixed, in accordance with heads (1) and (2) above (para **13.41**), by a resolution of a meeting of creditors, made with regard to the same matters[1].

1   IR 1986, r 6.138(5).

Remuneration when not fixed by the creditors' committee or the creditors generally

13.45 If the trustee's remuneration has not been fixed by the creditors' committee or a resolution of a meeting of the creditors, then the trustee, unless he is the official receiver, is entitled to remuneration calculated in accordance with IR 1986, r 6.138A[1]. In summary, the amount of the remuneration is the sum of (1) a capped proportion of the monies realised by the trustee (the first element) and (2) a proportion of the value of the assets distributed by the trustee (the second element). The rule provides a formula for calculating the amount of the remuneration; it does not give the trustee any proprietary right to share in or security over the monies or assets referred to. In detail the amount of the remuneration is determined as follows:

The first element

(1)   There must be ascertained the amount of the monies received by the trustee from the realisation of the assets of the bankrupt. VAT on the amount realised should be included. But from the total received should be deducted (a) any sums paid to secured creditors in respect of their securities, and (b) any sums spent out of money received in carrying on the business of the bankrupt.
(2)   To the resulting total should be applied the realisation scale set out in IR 1986, Schedule 6. This scale sets out a percentage to be applied to the amount realised as follows:

(i)	on the first £5,000 or fraction thereof	20%
(ii)	on the next £5,000 or fraction thereof	15%
(iii)	on the next £90,000 or fraction thereof	10%
(iv)	on all further sums realised	5%

(3)   The figure reached by the application of that scale of percentages forms the first of the two elements constituting the amount of the remuneration[2]. But this element is subject to a cap.

(4)   Calculating the cap involves first adding the following amounts:

    (a)   the bankruptcy debts including any interest payable by virtue of IA 1986, s 328(4) to the extent that such debts are required to be paid by IR 1986 but ignoring any bankruptcy debts paid otherwise than out of the proceeds of realisation of the bankrupt's assets or which have been secured to the satisfaction of the court;

    (b)   the expenses of the bankruptcy other than (i) fees or the remuneration of the official receiver, and (ii) any sums spent out of money received in carrying on the business of the bankrupt;

    (c)   fees payable by virtue of any order made under IA 1986, s 415;

    (d)   the remuneration of the official receiver.

Then the same realisation scale is to be applied to the resulting total in order to calculate the amount of the cap[3].

(5)   So, the first element of the remuneration calculation will be the amount referred to at point (3) above or, if lower, the amount of the cap.

The second element

(6)   Then, in order to calculate the second element, there must be ascertained the value of assets distributed to the creditors of the bankrupt, including sums paid in respect of preferential debts.

(7)   To the resulting total should be applied the distribution scale set out in IR 1986, Sch 6. This scale sets out a percentage to be applied to the amount realised as follows:

(i)	on the first £5,000 or fraction thereof	10%
(ii)	on the next £5,000 or fraction thereof	7.5%
(iii)	on the next £90,000 or fraction thereof	5%
(iv)	on all further sums realised	2.5%

(8)   The figure reached by the application of that scale of percentages forms the second element of the remuneration calculation[4].

Total amount of remuneration

(9)   Finally, the total amount of remuneration to which the trustee is entitled on this basis is obtained by adding together the first element, as capped if applicable, and the second element.

---

[1]   IR 1986, r 6.138(6). 'General regulations' means regulations made by the Secretary of State under r 12.1: IR 1986, rr 13.1, 13.13(5).

2   IR 1986, r 6.138A(2)(a).
3   IR 1986, r 6.138A(3) and (4).
4   IR 1986, r 6.138A(2)(b).

Other matters affecting remuneration

13.46 Where the trustee (not being the official receiver) sells assets on behalf of a secured creditor, he is entitled to such sum by way of remuneration as is arrived at by applying the realisation scale set out in IR 1986, Sch 6 to the monies received by him in respect of the assets realised, including any VAT thereon[1].

1   IR 1986, r 6.139(1).

13.47 Where there are joint trustees, it is for them to agree between themselves as to how the remuneration payable should be apportioned; and any dispute between them may be referred to the court for settlement by order, or to the creditors' committee or a meeting of creditors for settlement by resolution[1].

1   IR 1986, r 6.139(2).

13.48 If the trustee is a solicitor and employs his own firm, or any partner in it, to act on behalf of the estate, profit costs may not be paid unless this is authorised by the creditors' committee, the creditors or the court[1].

1   IR 1986, r 6.139(3).

Recourse of trustee to creditors' meeting or the court

13.49 If the trustee considers the rate or amount of his remuneration as determined by the creditors' committee to be insufficient, he may request that it be increased by resolution of the creditors[1].

1   IR 1986, r 6.140.

13.50 If he considers that the remuneration fixed for him by the committee, or by resolution of the creditors, or pursuant to the method set out in IR 1986, r 6.138A[1], is insufficient, he may apply to the court for an order increasing its amount or rate[2].

1   See para **13.45** above.
2   IR 1986, r 6.141(1).

13.51 The trustee must give at least 14 days' notice of his application to the members of the creditors' committee, and the committee may nominate one or more members to appear or be represented, and to be heard, on the application[1]. If there is no creditors' committee, the trustee's notice of his application must be sent to such one or more of the bankrupt's creditors as the court may direct, which creditors may nominate one or more of their number to appear or be represented[2].

1   IR 1986, r 6.141(2).
2   IR 1986, r 6.141(3).

13.52 In a proper case, the court may order the costs of the trustee's application, including the costs of any member of the creditors' committee appearing or being represented on it, or any creditor so appearing or being represented, to be paid out of the estate[1].

1   IR 1986, r 6.141(4).

Creditors' claim that remuneration is excessive

13.53 A similar right of recourse in respect of remuneration is provided to the creditors. Any creditor of the bankrupt may, with the concurrence of at least 25% in value of the creditors, including himself, apply to the court for an order that the trustee's remuneration be reduced, on the grounds that it is, in all the circumstances, excessive[1].

1   IR 1986, r 6.142(1).

13.54 If the court thinks that no sufficient cause is shown for the application, it may dismiss it; but not before the applicant has had an opportunity to attend the court for an *ex parte* hearing, of which he has been given at least seven days' notice; and, if the application is not dismissed, the court must fix a venue for it to be heard[1].

1   IR 1986, r 6.142(2).

13.55 At least 14 days before the hearing, the applicant must send to the trustee a notice stating the venue so fixed; and the notice must be accompanied by a copy of the application, and of any evidence which the applicant intends to adduce in support of it[1]. If the court considers the application to be well-founded, it must make an order fixing the remuneration at a reduced amount or rate[2].

1   IR 1986, r 6.142(3).
2   IR 1986, r 6.142(4).

13.56 Unless the court orders otherwise, the costs of the application must be paid by the applicant, and do not fall on the estate[1].

1   IR 1986, r 6.142(5).

Trustee's duty to provide information about the time spent

13.57 The bankrupt or any creditor is entitled to require the trustee to provide a statement setting out:

(a)   the total number of hours spent on the case by the trustee and any staff assigned to it during the relevant period;

(b) for each grade of individual so engaged, the average hourly rate at which any work carried out by individuals in that grade is charged; and

(c) the number of hours spent by each grade of staff during the relevant period[1].

1   Insolvency Regulations 1994, SI 1994/2507, reg 36A(1), (2).

13.58 The relevant period is the period between the date of the trustee's appointment and either the date next before the date of the making of the request on which the trustee has completed any period in office which is a multiple of six months or, if he has vacated office, the date that he vacated office[1].

1   Insolvency Regulations 1994, SI 1994/2507, reg 36A(3).

13.59 The request must be made in writing[1]. If the request is not made within two years of the date when the trustee vacated office, he is not obliged to answer it[2]. The information must be supplied free of charge[3] within 28 days of the receipt of the request[4].

1   Insolvency Regulations 1994, SI 1994/2507, reg 36A(1).
2   Insolvency Regulations 1994, SI 1994/2507, reg 36A(5).
3   Insolvency Regulations 1994, SI 1994/2507, reg 36A(1).
4   Insolvency Regulations 1994, SI 1994/2507, reg 36A(6).

Hearing of application to fix fees

13.60 Applications for the fixing and approval of the trustee's fees should be heard in the first instance by a registrar or district judge in the appropriate District Registry where the court is the High Court or a district judge where it is a county court[1]. The court hearing the application should consider the evidence then available to it and may either summarily determine the application or give directions, including if appropriate that an assessor or costs judge prepare a report to the court in respect of the remuneration which it sought to be fixed or approved and/or that the application be heard by the registrar or district judge sitting with or without an assessor or costs judge or by a judge sitting with or without any assessor or costs judge. Usually the registrar or district judge should determine the application sitting without an assessor or costs judge and without requiring any report. Where an assessor is engaged, his reasonable costs will be paid from the assets under the control of the trustee in bankruptcy.

1   Practice Statement: The Fixing and Approval of the Remuneration of Appointees (2004), para 4.1.

Information to be provided by the trustee

13.61 The trustee must provide extensive details of the work which he has carried out in order to enable the court to determine the application[1].

1   Practice Statement: The Fixing and Approval of the Remuneration of Appointees (2004), para 5.2.

Criteria

13.62 The Practice Statement sets out eight guiding principles by reference to which applications are to be determined[1]. For an example of the application of these principle, see *Simion v Brown*[2].

[1]   Practice Statement: The Fixing and Approval of the Remuneration of Appointees (2004), paras 3.3–3.4.
[2]   [2007] EWHC 511 (Ch), [2007] All ER (D) 237 (Mon).

E RESIGNATION, REMOVAL OF THE TRUSTEE AND VACANCY IN HIS OFFICE

Resignation of the trustee

13.63 In the case where the trustee suffers ill health, or where he intends ceasing to practise as an insolvency practitioner, or where there is some conflict of interest or change of personal circumstances which precludes or makes impracticable the further discharge of his duties[1], the trustee may resign his office by giving notice to the court[2].

[1]   IR 1986, r 6.126(3).
[2]   IA 1986, s 298(7).

13.64 Before resigning, the trustee must call a meeting of creditors for the purpose of receiving his resignation. Notice of the meeting must be sent to the official receiver at the same time as it is sent to creditors[1]. The notice to creditors must be accompanied by an account of the trustee's administration of the estate, including a summary of his receipts and payments, and a statement by him that he has reconciled his account with that held by the Secretary of State in respect of the bankruptcy[2].

[1]   IR 1986, r 6.126(1).
[2]   IR 1986, r 6.126(2).

13.65 However, where two or more persons are acting as trustee jointly, any one of them may proceed under these provisions, without prejudice to the continuation in office of the other or others, on the ground that, in his opinion and that of the others, it is no longer expedient that there should continue to be the present number of joint trustees[1].

[1]   IR 1986, r 6.126(4).

13.66 If there is no quorum present at the meeting summoned to receive the trustee's resignation, the meeting is deemed to have been held, a resolution is deemed passed that the trustee's resignation be accepted and the creditors are deemed not to have resolved against the trustee having his release[1].

[1]   IR 1986, r 6.126(5).

Action to follow acceptance of resignation

13.67 Where a meeting is summoned to receive the trustee's resignation, the notice summoning it must indicate this purpose, and must draw the attention of creditors to the statutory provisions[1] with respect to the trustee's release[2]. A copy of the notice must at the same time also be sent to the official receiver[3].

1   Ie IA 1986, s 299(4): see para **13.124** below.
2   IR 1986, r 6.127(1). For the prescribed form of notice to creditors see IR 1986, rr 6.127, 12.7, Sch 4, Form 6.35.
3   IR 1986, r 6.127(2).

13.68 Where the chairman of the meeting is other than the official receiver, and there is passed at the meeting any of the following resolutions:

(1)   that the trustee's resignation be accepted;
(2)   that a new trustee be appointed;
(3)   that the resigning trustee not be given his release,

the chairman must, within three days, send to the official receiver a copy of the resolution[1]. If it has been resolved to accept the trustee's resignation, the chairman must send to the official receiver a certificate to that effect[2].

1   IR 1986, r 6.127(3).
2   IR 1986, r 6.127(3). For the prescribed form of certificate see IR 1986, rr 6.127, 12.7, Sch 4, Form 6.44.

13.69 If the creditors have resolved to appoint a new trustee, the certificate of his appointment must also be sent to the official receiver within that time; and the statutory provisions applicable to such an appointment[1] must be complied with[2].

1   Ie IR 1986, r 6.120: see para **13.21** above.
2   IR 1986, r 6.127(4).

13.70 If the trustee's resignation is accepted, the notice of it[1] must be given by him forthwith after the meeting; and he must send a copy of the notice to the official receiver[2]. The notice must be accompanied by a copy of the account sent to creditors[3]; and the official receiver must file a copy of the notice in court[4]. The trustee's resignation is effective from the date on which the official receiver files the copy notice in court, that date to be indorsed on the copy notice[5].

1   Ie the notice required by the IA 1986, s 298(7).
2   IR 1986, r 6.127(5).
3   Ie the account sent to creditors under the IR 1986, r 6.126(2).
4   IR 1986, r 6.127(6).
5   IR 1986, r 6.127(7).

Leave to resign granted by court

13.71 If the creditors' meeting resolves not to accept the trustee's resignation, the court may, on the trustee's application, make an order giving him leave to resign[1].

1   IR 1986, r 6.128(1). For the prescribed form of order see IR 1986, rr 6.128, 12.7, Sch 4, Form 6.45.

13.72 The court's order may make provision for any matters arising in connection with the resignation, and must determine the date from which the trustee's release is effective[1].

1   IR 1986, r 6.128(2).

13.73 The court must send two sealed copies of the order to the trustee, who must send one of the copies forthwith to the official receiver[1]. On sending notice of his resignation to the court[2], the trustee must send a copy of it to the official receiver[3].

1   IR 1986, r 6.128(3).
2   Ie as required by the IA 1986, s 298(7). For the prescribed form of notice see the IR 1986, rr 6.128, 12.7, Sch 4, Form 6.46.
3   IR 1986, r 6.128(4).

Advertisement

13.74 Where a new trustee is appointed in place of one who has resigned, the new trustee must, in the advertisement of his appointment, state that his predecessor has resigned and, if it be the case, that he has been given his release[1].

1   IR 1986, r 6.134.

Removal of trustee

13.75 The trustee of a bankrupt's estate may be removed from office by an order of the court or by a general meeting of creditors summoned specially for that purpose[1] or, if he has been appointed by the Secretary of State, by a direction given by the Secretary of State[2].

1   IA 1986, s 298(1). However, where the official receiver is trustee on a criminal bankruptcy order, he may not be so removed from office: IA 1986, s 298(2). The Criminal Justice Act 1988, s 101 abolishes the power to make criminal bankruptcy orders as from 14 October 1991, but without prejudice to orders already in force.
2   IA 1986, s 298(5).

13.76 A general meeting of the bankrupt's creditors may not be held for the purpose of removing the trustee at any time when a certificate for the summary administration of the estate is in force[1].

1   Ie under the IA 1986, s 275.

13.77 Where the official receiver is trustee[1], or a trustee is appointed by the Secretary of State or by the court[2], a general meeting of the bankrupt's creditors may be summoned for the purpose of replacing the trustee only if:

(1)   the trustee thinks fit;

(2)   the court so directs; or
(3)   the meeting is requested by one of the bankrupt's creditors with the concurrence of not less than one-quarter, in value, of the creditors, including the creditor making the request[3].

1   Ie by virtue of the IA 1986, s 293(3) or s 295(4).
2   Ie otherwise than under the IA 1986, s 297(5): see IA 1986, s 298(4).
3   IA 1986, s 298(3).

Meeting of creditors to remove trustee

13.78 Where a meeting of creditors is summoned for the purpose of removing the trustee, the notice summoning it must indicate that this is the purpose, or one of the purposes, of the meeting, and must draw attention to the statutory provisions[1] with respect to the trustee's release[2]. A copy of the notice must at the same time also be sent to the official receiver[3].

1   Ie the IA 1986, s 299(3).
2   IR 1986, r 6.129(1). For the prescribed form of notice see IR 1986, rr 6.129, 12.7, Sch 4, Form 6.35.
3   IR 1986, r 6.129(2).

13.79 At the meeting, a person other than the trustee or his nominee may be elected as chairman; but, if the trustee or his nominee is chairman and a resolution has been proposed for the trustee's removal, the chairman may not adjourn the meeting without the consent of at least one-half, in value, of the creditors present, in person or by proxy, and entitled to vote[1].

1   IR 1986, r 6.129(3).

13.80 Where the chairman of the meeting is other then the official receiver, and there is passed at the meeting any of the following resolutions:

(1)   that the trustee be removed;
(2)   that a new trustee be appointed;
(3)   that the removed trustee not be given his release,

the chairman must, within three days, send to the official receiver a copy of the resolution[1]. If it has been resolved to remove the trustee, the chairman must send to the official receiver a certificate to that effect[2].

1   IR 1986, r 6.129(4).
2   IR 1986, r 6.129(4). For the prescribed form of certificate see IR 1986, rr 6.129, 12.7, Sch 4, Form 6.47.

13.81 If the creditors have resolved to appoint a new trustee, the certificate of his appointment must also be sent to the official receiver within that time; and the statutory provisions applicable where a trustee has been appointed by a creditors' meeting[1] must be complied with in respect of it[1].

1   IR 1986, r 6.129(5).

13.82 Where a meeting[1] of creditors to remove the trustee is to be held, or is proposed to be summoned, the court may, on the application of any creditor, give directions as to any aspect of it which appears to require regulation or control[2].

1   Ie under the IR 1986, r 6.129.
2   IR 1986, r 6.130.

Procedure on removal

13.83 Where the creditors have resolved that the trustee be removed, the official receiver must file the certificate of removal in court[1]. The resolution is effective as from the date of filing, and that date must be indorsed on the certificate[2]. A copy of the certificate, so indorsed, must be sent by the official receiver to the trustee who has been removed and, if a new trustee has been appointed, to him[3].

1   IR 1986, r 6.131(1).
2   IR 1986, r 6.131(2).
3   IR 1986, r 6.131(3).

13.84 The official receiver may not file the certificate in court until the Secretary of State has certified to him that the removed trustee has reconciled his account with that held by the Secretary of State in respect of the bankruptcy[1].

1   IR 1986, r 6.131(4).

Advertisement of removal

13.85 Where a new trustee is appointed in place of one who has been removed, the new trustee must, in the advertisement of his appointment, state that his predecessor has been removed and, if it be the case, that he has been given his release[1].

1   IR 1986, r 6.134.

Removal of trustee by the court

13.86 Where application is made to the court for the removal of the trustee[1], or for an order directing the trustee to summon a meeting of creditors for the purpose of removing him[2], the court may, if it thinks that no sufficient cause is shown for the application, dismiss it; but it may not do so unless the applicant has had an opportunity to attend the court for an *ex parte* hearing, of which he has been given at least seven days' notice[3]. If the application is not so dismissed, the court must fix a venue for it to be heard[4]. At least 14 days before the hearing, the applicant must send to the trustee and the official receiver notice stating the venue so fixed; and the notice must be accompanied by a copy of the application, and of any evidence which the applicant intends to adduce in support of it[5].

13.86 *Trustee in bankruptcy*

1   Under the IA 1986, s 298(1).
2   Under the IA 1986, s 298(4)(b).
3   IR 1986, r 6.132(1), (2). For the prescribed form of order see IR 1986, rr 6.132, 12.7, Sch 4, Form 6.48.
4   IR 1986, r 6.132(1), (2).
5   IR 1986, r 6.132(1), (3).

13.87 The court has a wide discretion whether to order removal and, while there must be good reason to do so, that need not involve misconduct on the part of the trustee[1].

1   *Re Edennote* [1996] 2 BCLC 389; *AMP Enterprises Ltd v Hoffman* [2002] EWHC 1899 (Ch), [2003] 1 BCLC 319; *Re Buildlead Ltd, Quickson (South and West) Ltd v Katz* [2004] EWHC 2443 (Ch), [2004] BPIR 1139 esp para [161].

13.88 Subject to any contrary order of the court, the costs of the application do not fall on the estate[1].

1   IR 1986, r 6.132(1), (4).

13.89 Where the court removes the trustee:

(1)   it must send copies of the order of removal to him and to the official receiver;
(2)   the order may include such provision as the court thinks fit with respect to the matters arising in connection with the removal; and
(3)   if the court appoints a new trustee, the statutory provisions relating to appointment of a trustee by the court apply[1].

1   IR 1986, r 6.132(1), (5).

Multiple orders for removal and replacement

13.90 It is now well established that the High Court has jurisdiction to remove insolvency practitioners from multiple offices in a single application and, where appropriate, to appoint replacements for them[1]. These types of orders are also discussed in para **2.70**, where more detail on the procedure is given[2]. As regards trustees in bankruptcy appointed under the IA 1986, the steps involved are:

(1)   in the case of a bankruptcy proceeding in a county court, to order the transfer of the proceedings into the High Court pursuant to the IR 1986, r 7.11(4)[3] for the purpose only of making the order for the removal of the outgoing trustee and the appointment of the new trustee; since the transfer is only for that limited purpose, no further order is required to transfer the matter back to the relevant county court;
(2)   to order the removal of the outgoing trustee pursuant to the IA 1986, s 298(1); and
(3)   to appoint the new trustee pursuant to the IA 1986, s 303(2).

1   *Re Equity Nominees Ltd* [1999] 2 BCLC 19.
2   For the procedure see the *Practice Direction: Insolvency Proceedings*, para 1.6.

516

3   This rule enables a judge of the High Court to order any bankruptcy proceedings which are pending in a county court to be transferred to the High Court. The County Courts Act 1984, s 41(1) provides an overlapping power to order transfer.

13.91 The application should be made to a judge of the High Court because an order under the IR 1986, r 7.11(4) may only be made by such a judge. Similar steps may be taken in relation to any bankruptcy under the Bankruptcy Act 1914 still pending[1]. It should not be made without notice to the existing trustee, though in an urgent case an additional trustee may be appointed where appropriate[2]. Interested parties may apply to review a block transfer order[3].

1   *Supperstone v Auger* [1999] BPIR 152. Annexed to this decision is a helpful table prepared by Park J setting out the relevant provisions for the making of orders for the removal and replacement of all relevant permutations of office-holders.
2   *Clements v Udal* [2002] 2 BCLC 606.
3   *HM Customs and Excise v Allen* [2003] BPIR 830.

Protection of creditors

13.92 Orders for the removal and replacement of office-holders bypass the need to hold creditors' meetings at which the creditors may consider whether to accept the office-holder's resignation. Given the expense of holding such meetings, it is in the interest of the creditors, as well as the office-holder, that a shortcut be taken. But the courts have been concerned to ensure that the creditors are properly protected. Firstly, making the orders involves an exercise of discretion. Before exercising the discretion, the court must consider whether holding a creditors' meeting would serve any useful purpose. If the court is satisfied that holding the meeting would not or is unlikely to serve any useful purpose, it will be willing to make the orders sought. Addressing this question in the case of a multiple application involves some consideration of each of the offices in respect of which orders are sought. Secondly, the courts have imposed conditions in various terms enabling creditors to re-open the question whether the orders should have been made. Differing approaches have been adopted. In *Re Sankey Furniture Ltd, ex p Harding, Re Calorifique Ltd, ex p Betts*[1], Chadwick J imposed three conditions:

(1)   that each creditor should have liberty to apply within a defined period;
(2)   that the office-holder should send to creditors copies of his receipts and payments accounts stating that such accounts had been reconciled with the account held by the Secretary of State[2];
(3)   that the office-holder should notify creditors that he would have his release from the date on which his resignation becomes effective under the order.

1   [1995] 2 BCLC 594.
2   Cf the IR 1986, r 6.126(2).

13.93 In *Re Equity Nominees Ltd*[1] Neuberger J imposed the first of these conditions but not the second and third. In place of the second he directed that a letter be sent to all the creditors explaining the effect of the order. In a bankruptcy, in the event of a creditors' committee, where there is one, calling for the applicant to comply with the requirements of the IR 1986, r 6.126(2), or, where there is no such committee, in the event of a creditor applying to the court for an order to that effect and the court granting the application, the outgoing trustee must make such compliance as soon as reasonably practicable. He did not impose the third condition because the order would not result automatically in the outgoing trustee's being released. The outgoing trustee would have to apply to the Secretary of State under the IR 1986, r 6.135(3) to obtain his release and therefore no special measure was required with regard to it.

1   [1999] 2 BCLC 19.

Costs of the application

13.94 The order made in *Re Equity Nominees Ltd*[1] was that the remuneration, costs and expenses in relation to the application in so far as referable to a particular insolvency should be fixed and paid in the ordinary way as remuneration or as costs and expenses of such insolvency. This did not preclude the creditors' committee or the registrar from taking steps subsequently to challenge or disallow the costs. If the retirement was unreasonable or there were special circumstances, such an order might not be justified. In so far as the costs were not referable to any particular insolvency it was ordered that they be apportioned equally between all the insolvencies, subject to the proviso that in no circumstances should the costs payable in relation to an insolvency exceed 10% of the value of the realised assets in that insolvency.

1   [1999] 2 BCLC 19.

Removal by the Secretary of State

13.95 A trustee appointed by the Secretary of State may be removed by a direction of the Secretary of State[1].

1   IA 1986, s 298(5).

13.96 If the Secretary of State decides to remove the trustee, he must before doing so notify the trustee and the official receiver of his decision and the grounds of it, and specify a period within which the trustee may make representations against implementation of the decision[1].

1   IR 1986, r 6.133(1).

13.97 If the Secretary of State directs the removal of the trustee, he must forthwith file notice of his decision in court, and send notice to the trustee and the official receiver[1]. If the trustee is removed in this manner, the court may make any such order in his case as it would have power to make if he had been removed by the court itself[2].

1   IR 1986, r 6.133(2).
2   IR 1986, r 6.133(3).

Vacancies

13.98 Where there is a vacancy[1] in the office of trustee, the official receiver is trustee until the vacancy is filled[2].

[1]   References in IA 1986, s 300 to a vacancy include a case where it is necessary, in relation to any property which is or may be comprised in a bankrupt's estate, to revive the trusteeship of that estate after the holding of a final meeting summoned under IA 1986, s 331 (see para **13.120** below) or the giving by the official receiver of notice under IA 1986, s 299(2) (see para **13.118** below): IA 1986, s 300(1), (8).
[2]   IA 1986, s 300(1), (2).

13.99 The official receiver may summon a general meeting of the bankrupt's creditors for the purpose of filling the vacancy and must summon such a meeting if required to do so[1] on a creditors' requisition[2].

[1]   Ie in pursuance of IA 1986, s 314(7).
[2]   IA 1986, s 300(1), (3).

13.100 If, 28 days after the vacancy first came to the official receiver's attention, he has not summoned, and is not proposing to summon, a general meeting of creditors for the purpose of filling the vacancy, he must refer the need for an appointment to the Secretary of State[1].

[1]   IA 1986, s 300(1), (4).

13.101 Where a certificate for the summary administration of the estate is for the time being in force[1], the official receiver may refer the need to fill any vacancy to the court or, if the vacancy arises because a person appointed by the Secretary of State has ceased to hold office, to the court or the Secretary of State. The above provisions[2] relating to the official receiver's power or duty to summon a general meeting of the bankrupt's creditors and his referring the need for an appointment to the Secretary of State do not then apply[3]. On such a reference, the Secretary of State must either make an appointment or decline to make one[4]; and, if on a reference to the Secretary of State no appointment is made, the official receiver continues to be trustee of the bankrupt's estate, but without prejudice to his power to make a further reference[5].

[1]   See IA 1986, s 275.
[2]   Ie IA 1986, s 300(3), (4).
[3]   IA 1986, s 300(1), (5).
[4]   IA 1986, s 300(1), (6).
[5]   IA 1986, s 300(1), (7).

Loss of qualification

13.102 If he ceases to be qualified to act as an insolvency practitioner in relation to the bankrupt, the trustee must vacate office[1]. He must forthwith give notice of his doing so to the official receiver, who must give notice to the Secretary of State[2]. The official receiver must file in court a copy of his notice[3].

[1]   IA 1986, s 298(6).

2   IR 1986, r 6.144(1), (2). For the prescribed form of notice see IR 1986, rr 6.144, 12.7,
     Sch 4, Form 6.51. IR 1986, r 6.135 applies as regards the trustee obtaining his release, as
     if he had been removed by the court: IR 1986, r 6.144(1), (3).
3   IR 1986, r 6.144(1), (2).

Final meeting or annulment

13.103 The trustee must vacate office on giving notice to the court that a
final meeting has been held[1] and of the decision, if any, of that meeting[2].

1   Ie under IA 1986, s 331: see para **13.120** below.
2   IA 1986, s 298(8).

13.104 The trustee must also vacate office if the bankruptcy order is
annulled[1].

1   IA 1986, s 298(9).

Death of trustee

13.105 If the trustee should die, it is the duty of his personal representatives
to give notice of the fact to the official receiver, specifying the date of the
death[1]. This provision does not, however, apply if notice has been given under
any of the following provisions[2].

1   IR 1986, r 6.143(1).
2   IR 1986, r 6.143(1).

13.106 If the deceased trustee was a partner in a firm, notice may be given to
the official receiver by a partner in the firm who is qualified to act as an
insolvency practitioner, or is a member of any body recognised by the
Secretary of State[1] for the authorisation of insolvency practitioners[2].

1   As to the bodies recognised by the Secretary of State see para **2.18** above.
2   IR 1986, r 6.143(2).

13.107 Notice of the death may be given by any person producing to the
official receiver the relevant death certificate or a copy of it[1].

1   IR 1986, r 6.143(3).

13.108 The official receiver must give notice to the court, for the purpose of
fixing the date of the deceased trustee's release[1].

1   IR 1986, r 6.143(4). The date of the trustee's release is fixed in accordance with IA 1986,
     s 299(3)(a).

Notice of intention to vacate office

13.109 If the trustee intends to vacate office, by resignation or otherwise, he
must give notice of this to the official receiver, together with notice of any

creditors' meeting to be held in respect of his vacation of office, including any meeting to receive his resignation[1]. The notice must be given at least 21 days before the meeting[2].

¹   IR 1986, r 6.145(1).
²   IR 1986, r 6.145(2).

13.110 Where there remains in the estate any property which has not been realised, applied, distributed or otherwise fully dealt with in the bankruptcy, the trustee must include in his notice to the official receiver details of the property, its value if any, its location, any action taken by the trustee to deal with that property or any reason for his not dealing with it, and the current position in relation to it[1].

¹   IR 1986, r 6.145(3).

Trustee's duties on vacating office

13.111 The trustee, when he vacates office, must forthwith deliver up to the person succeeding him as trustee the assets of the estate, after deduction of any expenses properly incurred, and distributions made, by him, and further he must deliver up:

(1)   the records of the bankruptcy, including correspondence, proofs and other related papers appertaining to the bankruptcy while it was within his responsibility; and
(2)   the bankrupt's books, papers and other records[1].

¹   IR 1986, r 6.146(1).

13.112 The trustee is no longer required to file in court all proofs remaining with him in the proceedings[1]. The trustee must also, on vacating office, send accounts to the Secretary of State[2].

¹   The requirement to do so previously contained in IR 1986, r 6.146(2) was removed by the Insolvency (Amendment) Rules 2004, SI 2004/584.
²   Insolvency Regulations 1994, SI 1994/2507, reg 28; see para **13.148**.

F RELEASE OF THE OFFICIAL RECEIVER AND THE TRUSTEE

In the course of administration

Release of official receiver

13.113 Where the official receiver is replaced as trustee by a person appointed by a general meeting of the bankrupt's creditors or by the Secretary of State, he has his release with effect from the time when he gives notice to the court that he has been replaced. Where his replacement is appointed by the court, the official receiver has his release at such time as the court may determine[1].

¹   IA 1986, s 299(1).

13.114 *Trustee in bankruptcy*

Release of trustee

13.114 A trustee who has died, or who has been removed from office by a general meeting of the bankrupt's creditors that has not resolved against his release, has his release at the time at which notice is given to the court that he has ceased to hold office[1]. Where the trustee is removed by a meeting of creditors which has not resolved against his release, the fact of his release must be stated in the certificate of removal[2].

1   IA 1986, s 299(3)(a); IR 1986, r 6.135(1).
2   IR 1986, r 6.135(2).

13.115 A trustee who has been removed from office by the court, or by the Secretary of State, or who has vacated office on ceasing to be qualified to act as an insolvency practitioner in relation to the bankrupt[1], has his release at such time as the Secretary of State may, on application by that person, determine[2].

1   Ie under IA 1986, s 298(6).
2   IA 1986, s 299(3)(b).

13.116 A trustee who has resigned has his release from the date when his resignation is effective[1].

1   IA 1986, s 299(3)(c) and the IR 1986, r 6.165(1).

13.117 Where the trustee resigns and the creditors' meeting called to receive his resignation has resolved against his release[1], or where he has been removed from office by a general meeting of the bankrupt's creditors that has resolved against his release, the trustee must apply to the Secretary of State for his release[2]. Where the Secretary of State gives the release, he must certify it accordingly, and must send the certificate to the official receiver to be filed in court[3]. A copy of the certificate must be sent by the Secretary of State to the former trustee, whose release is effective from the date of the certificate[4].

1   IR 1986, r 6.135(3)(a).
2   IR 1986, r 6.135(3)(b). For the prescribed form of application to the Secretary of State see
      IR 1986, rr 6.135, 12.7, Sch 4, Form 6.49.
3   IR 1986, r 6.135(4).
4   IR 1986, r 6.135(5).

On completion of administration

Release of official receiver

13.118 If the official receiver, while he is the trustee, gives notice to the Secretary of State that the administration of the bankrupt's estate is for practical purposes complete, he has his release with effect from such time as the Secretary of State may determine[1]. However, before giving such notice, he must send out notice of his intention to do so to all creditors who have proved their debts, and to the bankrupt[2]. The notice in each case must be accompanied by a summary of the official receiver's receipts and payments as trustee[3].

The court may relieve the official receiver of the duty to send notices to the creditors. To obtain the relief, the official receiver must apply to the court which may either relieve him from the duty or authorise him to carry out the duty in some other way. The court must have regard to the cost of carrying out the duty, the amounts of funds available in the estate and the extent of the interest of creditors or any particular class of them[4].

1   IA 1986, s 299(2).
2   IR 1986, r 6.136(1).
3   IR 1986, r 6.136(2).
4   IR 1986, r 6.137A.

13.119 When the Secretary of State has determined the date from which the official receiver is to have his release, he must give notice to the court that he has done so; and the notice must be accompanied by the summary of the official receiver's receipts and payments as trustee[1].

1   IR 1986, r 6.136(3).

Final meeting of creditors and release of trustee other than the official receiver

13.120 In any other case, the trustee must give at least 28 days' notice of the final meeting of creditors[1]. The notice must be sent to all creditors who have proved their debts, and to the bankrupt[2]. The trustee's report laid before the meeting must include a summary of his receipts and payments, and a statement by him that he has reconciled his account with that which is held by the Secretary of State in respect of the bankruptcy[3].

1   Ie the meeting to be held under IA 1986, s 331.
2   IR 1986, r 6.137(1).
3   IR 1986, r 6.137(2).

13.121 At the final meeting, the creditors may question the trustee with respect to any matter contained in his report, and may resolve against his having his release[1]. The trustee must give notice to the court that the final meeting has been held; and the notice must state whether or not he has been given his release, and must be accompanied by a copy of the report laid before the final meeting; and a copy of the notice must be sent by the trustee to the official receiver[2].

1   IR 1986, r 6.137(3).
2   IR 1986, r 6.137(4). For the prescribed form of notice to the court of the final meeting of creditors see IR 1986, rr 6.137, 12.7, Sch 4, Form 6.50.

13.122 If there is no quorum at the final meeting, the trustee must report this to the court, and the final meeting is then deemed to have been held, and the creditors not to have resolved against the trustee having his release[1]. Unless the creditors resolve otherwise, the trustee is released when the notice to the court that the final meeting has been held[2] is filed in court. If they have so resolved, the trustee must obtain his release from the Secretary of State[3].

1   IR 1986, r 6.137(5); IA 1986, s 299(3)(d)(ii).

13.122 *Trustee in bankruptcy*

Ie the notice under the IR 1986, r 6.137(4): see above.
IR 1986, r 6.137(6); IA 1986, s 299(3)(d)(i). The release is obtained from the Secretary of State as provided by the IR 1986, r 6.135: see para **13.117** above.

13.123 The court may relieve the trustee of any of the duties imposed on him by IR 1986, r 6.137. If the trustee wishes to be relieved of any of these duties, he must apply to the court which may either relieve him from the duty or authorise him to carry out the duty in some other way. The court must have regard to the cost of carrying out the duty, the amounts of funds available in the estate and the extent of the interest of creditors or any particular class of them[1].

IR 1986, r 6.137A.

On annulment of bankruptcy order

Release on annulment

13.124 Where a bankruptcy order is annulled[1], the trustee has his release with effect from such time as the court may determine[2]. In determining when the release should take effect, the court should have regard to whether the trustee has submitted his final account to the Secretary of State and whether any security given in respect of disputed debts or of creditors who have proved but cannot be traced has been or will be released[3].

As to annulment of bankruptcy orders see para **9.22**ff above.
IA 1986, s 299(4).
IR 1986, r 6.214(4).

Effect of release

Effect of release

13.125 Where the official receiver or the trustee has his release[1], he is, with effect from the time of the release, discharged from all liability both in respect of acts or omissions of his in the administration of the estate and otherwise in relation to his conduct as trustee, save for the exercise of the court's statutory power under IA 1986, s 304[2].

Under IA 1986, s 299.
IA 1986, s 299(5).

G SUMMARY PROCEDURE FOR PURSUING CLAIMS AGAINST THE DELINQUENT TRUSTEE

13.126 Where, on application under IA 1986, s 304, the court is satisfied:

(1) that the trustee has misapplied or retained, or become accountable for, any money or other property comprised in the estate; or

(2)   that an estate has suffered any loss in consequence of any misfeasance
       or breach of fiduciary or other duty by the trustee in the carrying out of
       his functions,

the court may order the trustee, for the benefit of the estate, to repay, restore
or account for money or other property, together with interest at such rate as
the court thinks just, or, as the case may be, to pay such sum by way of
compensation as the court thinks just. The above provisions are in addition to
and not in substitution for, any other liability arising[1].

[1]   IA 1986, s 304(1). Cf IA 1986, s 212 (summary remedy against delinquent directors,
       liquidators etc).

13.127 Such an application may be made by the official receiver, the
Secretary of State, a creditor of the bankrupt or, whether or not there is, or is
likely to be, a surplus on final distribution[1], the bankrupt himself. However,
the leave of the court is required for the making of an application if it is to be
made by the bankrupt or if it is to be made after the trustee has had his
release[2].

[1]   Ie a surplus for the purposes of IA 1986, s 330(5): see para **23.25** below.
[2]   IA 1986, s 304(2).

13.128 The IA 1986, s 304(1) is expressed in similar terms to IA 1986, s 212
which provides a summary procedure for obtaining remedies against delinquent directors and liquidators and other company officers. Like s 212,
s 304(1) is a procedural measure providing a means whereby the court's
process may be invoked. It does not create any cause of action which does not
otherwise exist.

13.129 In the context of the IA 1986, s 212 breach of duty has been held to
include liability for negligence[1] and there seems no good reason why IA 1986,
s 304(1) should not be similarly interpreted.

[1]   *Re D'Jan of London Ltd* [1994] 1 BCLC 561.

H DUTY TO PROVIDE INFORMATION TO THE OFFICIAL RECEIVER

Duty to provide information to the official receiver

13.130 Unless the trustee is the official receiver, he is under a duty:

(a)   to furnish the official receiver with such information;
(b)   to produce to the official receiver, and permit inspection by the official
       receiver of, such books, papers and other records; and
(c)   to give the official receiver such other assistance

as the official receiver may reasonably require for the purpose of enabling him
to carry out his functions in relation to the bankruptcy[1].

[1]   IA 1986, s 305(3).

Enforcement of trustee's obligations

13.131 On the application of the official receiver, the court may make whatever orders it thinks necessary for enforcement of the trustee's duty[1] to give information and assistance and to produce and allow inspection of books and records relating to the bankruptcy[2]. Such an order of the court may provide that all costs of and incidental to the official receiver's application shall be borne by the trustee[3].

[1] Ie under the IA 1986, s 305(3).
[2] IR 1986, r 6.149(1).
[3] IR 1986, r 6.149(2).

I DUTY TO REPORT TO THE FINANCIAL SERVICES AUTHORITY

13.132 If, while a bankruptcy order is in force by virtue of a petition presented by someone other than the Financial Services Authority, it appears to the trustee in bankruptcy that the bankrupt is carrying on or has carried on an activity regulated under the Financial Services and Markets Act 2000 in contravention of the prohibition against doing so without authorisation, the trustee must report this without delay to the Financial Services Authority[1].

[1] Financial Services and Markets Act 2000, s 373.

J DUTIES CONCERNING BANKING OF FUNDS

Application to official receiver

13.133 The provisions described in this section set out the trustee's duties concerning banking of funds received in virtue of his trusteeship but they also apply to the official receiver whether acting as trustee or as receiver and manager under the IA 1986, s 287[1].

[1] Insolvency Regulations 1994, SI 1994/2507, reg 19.

Payments into the Insolvency Services Account

13.134 Subject to the provisions relating to local bank accounts applicable where the trustee exercises the power to carry on the business of the bankrupt[1], the trustee must pay all money received by him in the course of his functions, without any deduction, into the Insolvency Services Account kept by the Secretary of State with the Bank of England[2]. He must remit the money so received by him once every 14 days, or forthwith if £5,000 or more has been received. Every remittance must be paid in through the Bank Giro System or sent direct to the Bank of England, Threadneedle Street, London EC2R 8AH, by cheque drawn in favour of the 'Insolvency Services Account' and a receipt must be given on request[3]. Every remittance must be accompanied by the appropriate form[4].

[1] See the IA 1986, s 314(1)(a) and Sch 5, para 1.
[2] Insolvency Regulations 1994, SI 1994/2507, reg 20(1).

3   Insolvency Regulations 1994, SI 1994/2507, reg 20(2).
4   Insolvency Regulations 1994, SI 1994/2507, reg 20(3).

Payments out of the Insolvency Services Account

13.135 Upon his application to the Department of Trade and Industry on the appropriate form, the trustee shall be repaid all necessary disbursements made by him, and expenses properly incurred by him, in the course of his administration to the date of his vacation of office, out of any moneys standing to the credit of the bankrupt in the Insolvency Services Account[1].

1   Insolvency Regulations 1994, SI 1994/2507, reg 22(1).

13.136 If a trustee vacates office, he must be repaid by any succeeding trustee out of any funds available for the purpose, any necessary disbursements made by him and any expenses properly incurred by him which remain outstanding to him[1].

1   Insolvency Regulations 1994, SI 1994/2507, reg 22(4).

13.137 The trustee must obtain payment instruments to the order of the payee for sums which become payable on account of the bankrupt, and send them to those to whom the payments are to be made[1].

1   Insolvency Regulations 1994, SI 1994/2507, reg 22(2).

Local bank accounts

13.138 Any trustee who intends to exercise his power to carry on the business of the bankrupt may apply to the Secretary of State for authorisation to open a local bank account[1]. A local bank account means a current account opened with a bank in, or in the neighbourhood of, the insolvency district in which the proceedings are taken, or in the locality in which any business of the insolvent is carried on[2]. The Secretary of State may authorise the trustee to make his payments into and out of a specified bank, subject to a limit, instead of into and out of the Insolvency Services Account, if satisfied that an administrative advantage will be derived from having such an account[3]. Money received by the trustee relating to the purpose for which the account was opened may be paid into the local bank account to the credit of the bankrupt to whom the account relates[4]. Where the trustee opens a local bank account pursuant to an authorisation granted by the Secretary of State, he must open and maintain the account in the name of the bankrupt[5]. Where money which does not form part of the bankrupt's estate is provided to the trustee for a specific purpose, it must be clearly identifiable in a separate account[6]. The trustee must keep proper records including documentary evidence of all money paid into and out of every local bank account opened and maintained under these provisions[7], and he must obtain and keep bank statements relating to any local bank account in the name of the bankrupt[8]. He must pay without deduction any surplus over any authorised limit into the Insolvency Services Account[9]. As soon as he ceases to carry on the business of the bankrupt, or vacates office, or an authorisation given by the Secretary of State is withdrawn, he must close the account and remit any balance to the Insolvency Services Account[10].

1   Insolvency Regulations 1994, SI 1994/2507, reg 21(1).
2   Insolvency Regulations 1994, SI 1994/2507, reg 3(1) which also contains a definition of 'bank'.
3   Insolvency Regulations 1994, SI 1994/2507, reg 21(1).
4   Insolvency Regulations 1994, SI 1994/2507, reg 22(2).
5   Insolvency Regulations 1994, SI 1994/2507, reg 21(3).
6   Insolvency Regulations 1994, SI 1994/2507, reg 21(4).
7   Insolvency Regulations 1994, SI 1994/2507, reg 21(5).
8   Insolvency Regulations 1994, SI 1994/2507, reg 24(2).
9   Insolvency Regulations 1994, SI 1994/2507, reg 21(6).
10   Insolvency Regulations 1994, SI 1994/2507, reg 21(7).

Claiming money paid into the Insolvency Services Account

13.139 Any person claiming to be entitled to any moneys paid into the Insolvency Services Account may apply to the Secretary of State for payment, supported by such evidence of the claim as the Secretary of State may require[1].

1   Insolvency Regulations 1994, SI 1994/2507, reg 32(1).

13.140 Any person dissatisfied with the decision of the Secretary of State in respect of his claim made under this provision may appeal to the court[1].

1   Insolvency Regulations 1994, SI 1994/2507, reg 32(2). As to the procedure on appeal see para **3.122** above.

K DUTIES CONCERNING RECORDS AND ACCOUNTS

Introduction

13.141 Under the Insolvency Regulations 1986[1] a trustee in bankruptcy was required to keep extensive administrative, as well as financial, records and was required each year during his tenure of office to send an account of receipts and payments to the Secretary of State[2]. This regime was relaxed by the Insolvency Regulations 1994[3]. Under these regulations the trustee does not have to keep the same administrative records and he need only account if required to do so by the Secretary of State and at the end of his term of office. But the creditors' committee is given an increased role in scrutinising the financial records kept by the trustee and may complain to the Secretary of State if not satisfied with their contents. The Secretary of State has a discretion how to respond but his powers to require an account, further information or documents or an audit are described below.

1   SI 1986/1994.
2   See Insolvency Regulations 1986, SI 1986/1994, regs 8 and 12.
3   SI 1994/2507.

Application to official receiver

13.142 The provisions described in this section also apply to the official receiver whether acting as trustee or as receiver and manager under the IA 1986, s 287[1].

[1]   Insolvency Regulations 1994, SI 1994/2507, reg 19.

Financial records

13.143 The trustee must prepare and keep (a) separate financial records in respect of each bankrupt; and (b) such other financial records as are required to explain the receipts and payments entered in those records or, where the trustee carries on any business of the bankrupt, any trading accounts, including an explanation of the source of any receipts and the destination of any payments. He must, subject to the following special provision in the case of trading accounts, from day to day enter in the financial records all the receipts and payments made by him[1]. Where the trustee carries on any business of the bankrupt, he shall (a) keep a separate and distinct account of the trading, including, where appropriate, particulars of all local bank account transactions; and (b) incorporate in the financial records above the total weekly amounts of the receipts and payments made by him in relation to the account kept under paragraph (a) above[2]. The trustee shall obtain and keep bank statements relating to any local bank account in the name of the bankrupt[3].

[1]   Insolvency Regulations 1994, SI 1994/2507, reg 24(1).
[2]   Insolvency Regulations 1994, SI 1994/2507, reg 26.
[3]   Insolvency Regulations 1994, SI 1994/2507, reg 24(2).

Power of creditors' committee to scrutinise records

13.144 The trustee shall submit financial records to the creditors' committee when required for inspection[1]. If the creditors' committee is not satisfied with the contents of the financial records submitted pursuant to such requirement, it may so inform the Secretary of State, giving the reasons for its dissatisfaction and the Secretary of State may take such action as he thinks fit[2].

[1]   Insolvency Regulations 1994, SI 1994/2507, reg 24(3).
[2]   Insolvency Regulations 1994, SI 1994/2507, reg 24(4).

Provision of information to creditor or bankrupt

13.145 The trustee shall, within 14 days of the receipt of a request from any creditor or the bankrupt for a statement of his receipts and payments as trustee, supply free of charge to the person making the request, a statement of his receipts and payments as trustee during the period of one year ending on the most recent anniversary of his becoming trustee which preceded the request[1].

[1]   Insolvency Regulations 1994, SI 1994/2507, reg 25.

Retention and delivery of records

13.146 All financial records and trading accounts kept by the trustee and any such records received by him from a predecessor in that office shall be retained by him for a period of six years following (a) his vacation of office, or (b) in the case of the official receiver, his release as trustee under the IA 1986, s 299, unless he delivers them to another trustee who succeeds him in office[1]. Where one trustee is succeeded in office by another trustee, all financial records and trading accounts kept by the out-going trustee and any such records received by him from any predecessor in that office shall be delivered to the out-going trustee's successor forthwith, unless the bankruptcy is for practical purposes complete and the successor is the official receiver, in which case the records are only to be delivered to the official receiver if the latter so requests[2].

[1]   Insolvency Regulations 1994, SI 1994/2507, reg 27(1).
[2]   Insolvency Regulations 1994, SI 1994/2507, reg 27(2).

Secretary of State's power to require an account

13.147 The trustee must, if required by the Secretary of State at any time, send to the Secretary of State an account of his receipts and payments as trustee of the bankrupt covering such period as the Secretary of State may direct and such account must, if so required by the Secretary of State, be certified by the trustee[1].

[1]   Insolvency Regulations 1994, SI 1994/2507, reg 28(1).

Mandatory accounts

13.148 Where the trustee vacates office before the final general meeting of creditors is held under the IA 1986, s 331, the trustee must within 14 days of vacating office send to the Secretary of State an account of his receipts and payments as trustee for any period not covered by an account previously so sent by him, or if no such account has been sent, an account of his receipts and payments in respect of the whole period of his office[1].

[1]   Insolvency Regulations 1994, SI 1994/2507, reg 28(2).

13.149 Where (a) a final general meeting of creditors has been held pursuant to the IA 1986, s 331, or (b) a final general meeting is deemed to have been held by virtue of the IR 1986, r 6.137(5), the trustee must send to the Secretary of State, in case (a), within 14 days of the holding of the final general meeting of creditors and, in case (b), within 14 days of his report to the court pursuant to the IR 1986, r 6.137(5), an account of his receipts and payments as trustee which are not covered by any previous account so sent by him, or if no such account has been sent, an account of his receipts and payments in respect of the whole period of his office[1].

[1]   Insolvency Regulations 1994, SI 1994/2507, reg 28(3).

Summary of statement of affairs or of known assets

13.150 Where a statement of affairs has been submitted under the IA 1986, any account sent to the Secretary of State must be accompanied by a summary of that statement of affairs and shall show the amount of any assets realised and explain the reasons for any non-realisation of any assets not realised[1]. Where a statement of affairs has not been submitted under the IA 1986, any account sent under this regulation shall be accompanied by a summary of all known assets and their estimated values and shall show the amounts actually realised and explain the reasons for any non-realisation of any assets[2].

1   Insolvency Regulations 1994, SI 1994/2507, reg 28(4).
2   Insolvency Regulations 1994, SI 1994/2507, reg 28(5).

Secretary of State's power to require audit or further information

13.151 Any account sent to the Secretary of State shall, if he so requires, be audited, but whether or not the Secretary of State requires the account to be audited, the trustee shall send to the Secretary of State on demand any documents (including vouchers and bank statements) and any information relating to the account[1].

1   Insolvency Regulations 1994, SI 1994/2507, reg 28(6).

Production and inspection of records

13.152 The trustee must produce on demand to the Secretary of State, and allow him to inspect, any accounts, books and other records kept by him (including any passed to him by a predecessor in office), and this duty to produce and allow inspection shall extend (a) to producing and allowing inspection at the premises of the trustee, and (b) to producing and allowing inspection of any financial records explaining receipts and payments prepared by the trustee before 24 October 1994 and kept by him. Whether or not the Secretary of State requires the account to be audited, any such demand may require the trustee to produce any such accounts, books or other records to the Secretary of State, and allow him to inspect them either at the same time as any account is sent to the Secretary of State under reg 28, or at any time after such account is sent to the Secretary of State. Alternatively, where the demand is made for the purpose of ascertaining whether the provisions of these regulations relating to the handling of money received by the trustee in the course of carrying out his functions have been or are likely to be complied with, the demand may be made at any time, whether or not an account has been sent or should have been sent to the Secretary of State and whether or not the Secretary of State has required any account to be audited. The trustee shall allow the Secretary of State on demand to remove and take copies of any accounts, books and other records kept by the trustee (including any passed to him by a predecessor in office), whether or not they are kept at the premises of the trustee[1].

1   Insolvency Regulations 1994, SI 1994/2507, reg 29.

Chapter 14

THE BANKRUPT'S ESTATE

A INTRODUCTION

Introduction

14.1 A cardinal principle of bankruptcy law is that the bankrupt should transfer what he owns to his trustee for division amongst his creditors. 'The plain spirit of the bankruptcy laws is that every beneficial interest which the bankrupt has shall be disposed of for the benefit of the estate'[1]. The body of assets owned by the bankrupt are called his estate. The primary category of assets within the estate comprises, subject to various qualifications discussed below, all property belonging to or vested in the bankrupt at the commencement of his bankruptcy, that is to say on the date when the bankruptcy order was made against him. But, there may also be brought into the estate:

(i)   property which belonged to the bankrupt before the commencement of the bankruptcy but which no longer belongs to him, where the trustee may impugn the disposal of the property by the bankrupt and recover the property or its value for the estate[2];

(ii)   property which the bankrupt acquires after the commencement of the bankruptcy, where the trustee may claim the property as part of the estate[3];

(iii)   property which belongs to the bankrupt at the commencement of the bankruptcy but which is excluded from the estate, where the trustee is empowered to override the exclusion either wholly or in part and claim the property or part of it for the estate[4].

[1]   *Smith v Coffin* (1795) 2 Hy Bl 444, 462.
[2]   The trustee's powers to apply to recover such property is discussed in **Chapter 20**.
[3]   See sections N and O below on after-acquired property and income payments orders.
[4]   See section G.

14.2 In each of these categories, relevant property is property which at some time belonged or belongs to the bankrupt or in which he had or has title. Property belonging to third parties may not be claimed for the estate unless the property previously belonged to the bankrupt and the third party's title may be impeached be reason of the circumstances in which the property was transferred from the bankrupt to the third party. Further, for an interest to fall within the estate and to be available for his creditors, it must belong beneficially to the bankrupt: property which the bankrupt holds on trust for others does not fall within his estate[1].

[1]   See section I.

Scope of this chapter

14.3 In this chapter, after setting out the statutory definition of the estate, the principal focus is on the primary category of assets belonging to the bankrupt, namely those which belong to him at the commencement of the bankruptcy and the boundary between the property which falls into the estate and that which falls outside it. But how the trustee may claim property subsequently acquired by the bankrupt is discussed in the last two sections of the chapter. Property formerly belonging to the bankrupt which may be claimed for the estate is discussed in **Chapter 20**.

B STATUTORY DEFINITION OF THE ESTATE

Statutory definition of the estate

14.4 The basic statutory definition of the bankrupt's estate is that, subject to the elaborations and qualifications made in the Insolvency Act 1986 ('IA 1986'), it comprises:

'(a)   all property belonging to or vested in the bankrupt at the commencement of his bankruptcy; and

(b)   all property which by virtue of any of the following provisions of this Part is comprised in that estate or is treated as falling within the preceding paragraph.'[1]

[1]   IA 1986, s 283(1).

14.5   The bankrupt's estate

Property

14.5 The word 'property' carries at least two relevant meanings, the distinction between which is not observed in the drafting of the IA 1986 (or in this book) any more than it was in previous Bankruptcy Acts.

(i)   'Property' may be used to refer to things capable of being owned.

(ii)   Alternatively, 'property' may refer to the title which the owner of the thing owned holds in the thing.

14.6 Although this does not often impede the practical application of the IA 1986, it is capable of causing ambiguity. An example, observed and discussed by Lindley LJ in *Re Finley, ex p Clothworkers Co*[1], is the use of the word in the IA 1986, s 321 concerning vesting orders of disclaimed property of a leasehold nature.

[1]   (1888) 21 QBD 475, 484. Lindley LJ was discussing the Bankruptcy Act 1883, s 55 which contains provisions governing vesting orders following disclaimer materially in the same terms as those which now appear in the IA 1986, s 321 to which his comments remain applicable.

Statutory elaboration of 'property'

14.7 No proper definition of 'property' is provided in the IA 1986, but a list is enumerated, descriptive of what is embraced by it, and the word itself is elaborated: 'property' includes money, goods, things in action, land and every description of property wherever situated and also obligations and every description of interest, whether present or future or vested or contingent, arising out of, or incidental to, property[1]. Most obviously from the range of the list is that for the purpose of the IA 1986, the widest meaning is to be adopted in deciding whether some asset or interest counts as property[2]. For example, an obligation might not ordinarily be conceived as an item of property. The wide meaning adopted reflects the principle of public policy 'that in bankruptcy the entire property of the bankrupt, of whatever kind or nature it may be, whether alienable or inalienable, subject to being taken in execution, legal or equitable, or not so subject, shall, with the exception of some compassionate allowances for his maintenance, be appropriated and made available for the payment of his creditors'[3]. Despite the reference to inalienable property in that statement of principle, it will ordinarily be an identifying characteristic of some items having the status of property that it is transferable, even though in fact it may have little prospect of being realised for value[4]. Indeed it is because some property may, so far from having any value, be onerous that the trustee is empowered to disclaim it[5].

[1]   IA 1986, s 436.
[2]   *Bristol Airport plc v Powdrill* [1990] Ch 744, 759.
[3]   *Hollinshead v Hazleton* [1916] 1 AC 428, 436 (Lord Atkinson) and for similar statements see note below.
[4]   *De Rothschild v Bell* [2000] 1 QB 33, [1999] 2 All ER 722, CA; *Re Celtic Extraction Ltd* [2001] Ch 475, [1999] 4 All ER 684.
[5]   See IA 1986, s 315.

14.8 Although the statutory enumeration of 'property' may appear, at first blush, to be a list assembled in no particular order, it reflects the orthodox division between personal property, subdivided into things in possession, ie money and goods, and things in action[1], and real property[2]. Perhaps, it is appropriate that personal property should be listed first since, until the passing of the Bankruptcy Act 1861, bankruptcy law applied only to traders whose estates primarily tended to comprise personal property. The examples of property mentioned in the following section follows the same order as the statutory list.

[1]   See per Fry LJ in *Colonial Bank v Whinney* (1885) 30 Ch D 261 at 285 (dissenting but approved in the House of Lords (1886) 11 App Cas 426).
[2]   Similar words were used in the Bankruptcy Act 1883, s 168(1) and the Bankruptcy Act 1914, s 167.

Powers

14.9 Powers which the bankrupt may exercise over property are made capable of falling into the bankrupt's estate, if held by him at the commencement of his bankruptcy[1]. The provision bringing powers within the ambit of property does so by way of what is, in effect, a deeming provision: 'References to property ... include references to any power exercisable by him.' This is because, statute apart, as it was put by Fry LJ in *Re Armstrong, ex p Gilchrist*[2], 'a "power" is an individual personal capacity of the donee of the power to do something. That it may result in property becoming vested in him is immaterial; the general nature of the power does not make it property. The power of a person to appoint an estate to himself is, in my judgment, no more his "property" than the power to write a book or to sing a song'. The person on whom a power is conferred is referred to as the donee. A power of appointment is a power entitling the donee to create or dispose of a beneficial interest in property. Such powers are classified, non-exhaustively, as general powers, where there is no restriction on the class of persons in whose favour the donee may exercise the power, and special powers, where that class is restricted.

[1]   IA 1986, s 283(4).
[2]   (1886) 17 QBD 521, 531. And see *Clarkson v Clarkson* [1994] BCC 921, CA.

Powers not within the ambit of the statutory provision

14.10 A power exercisable by the bankrupt over property does not itself amount to property, for the purposes of bankruptcy, if it is exercisable over or in respect of property not for the time being comprised in the bankrupt's estate and either:

(a)   is so exercisable at a time after either: (i) the official receiver has had his release in respect of that estate on giving notice that the administration of an estate administered by him as trustee is for practical purposes complete; or (ii) a final meeting has been held which was summoned by the trustee (other than the official receiver) when he considered the administration complete for practical purposes; or

(b)   cannot be exercised for the benefit of the bankrupt[1].

[1]   IA 1986, s 283(4).

14.11 By virtue of (b), if the class of person in whose favour a special power exercisable by the bankrupt over property not within his estate does not include the bankrupt, the power is not capable of being property for the purposes of bankruptcy.

14.12 In the context of the provisions in the IA 1986 relating to the insolvency of individuals, a power exercisable over or in respect of property is deemed to vest in the person entitled to exercise it at the time of the transaction or event by virtue of which it is exercisable by that person, whether or not it becomes exercisable at that time[1]. This deeming provision, awkwardly expressed, appears to be intended to distinguish between the date when a power is created and the date when any exercise of it by the donee may become effective. These may differ because a power may be expressed to be exercisable at some future date or on the happening of some contingency. But the expression is awkward because a contingent power presently given to a designated person may be exercised before the contingency happens, in which case the exercise of the power takes effect when the contingency subsequently occurs[2]. The deeming provision establishes that it is the date of creation, rather than the date of any later event, which is the date when the power is to be taken to vest in the donee.

[1]   IA 1986, s 283(4).
[2]   *Hanbury v Bateman* [1920] 1 Ch 313, 320.

Rights of others

14.13 Property comprised in a bankrupt's estate is so comprised subject to the rights of any other person other than the bankrupt, whether as a secured creditor or otherwise, in relation to that property[1]. But the rights of another person in property which forms part of the estate are to be disregarded if: (a) the rights comprise security, the person holding them was the petitioning creditor and in the petition he stated that, in the event of a bankruptcy order being made, he would give up the security for the benefit of all the bankrupt's creditors[2]; or (b) the rights have otherwise been given up in accordance with the Insolvency Rules 1986 ('IR 1986')[3].

[1]   IA 1986, s 283(5). See also *Kassam v Toohey* [2005] BPIR 1370.
[2]   See the IA 1986, s 269(1)(a).
[3]   See the IR 1986, r 6.116.

Belonging to or vested in the bankrupt

14.14 To fall within the estate the property in question must belong to or be vested in the bankrupt. Property which the bankrupt holds on trust for any other person is not comprised in the estate[1].

[1]   IA 1986, s 283(3)(a).

The commencement of the bankruptcy

14.15 The bankruptcy commences on the day on which the bankruptcy order is made[1].

[1] IA 1986, s 278(a).

Provisions referred to in the IA 1986, s 283(1)(b)

14.16 The relevant provisions relating to property which previously belonged to the bankrupt are the IA 1986, ss 339–347 and ss 423–425 and those relating to property subsequently acquired by the bankrupt are the IA 1986, ss 307 and 309–310.

C TERRITORIAL AMBIT

Domestic law

14.17 The definition of 'property' contained in IA 1986, s 436 extends to property wherever situated. As a matter of English domestic law, the property which forms the estate of a bankrupt comprises all property held by him at the commencement of his bankruptcy wherever situated. That does not, of course, mean that property located outside the jurisdiction will vest automatically in the trustee or that the courts of the State in whose territory the property is located will recognise the trustee's claim to the property. But it does mean that as a matter of English domestic law, the bankrupt's foreign property falls within his estate and his trustee is entitled to gather that property in for the benefit of the bankrupt's creditors if and when he can.

Impact of the EC Insolvency Regulation

14.18 Where the bankruptcy forms territorial or secondary insolvency proceedings within the meaning of the EC Insolvency Regulation, the scope of the proceedings is restricted and the effect of the proceedings only reaches to the assets, or property, of the debtor situated in the Member State where the proceedings are opened[1]. The possibility that the ambit of the estate may be reduced in that manner is recognised in the provision contained in IA 1986, s 436A that reference to property in the context of proceedings where the English court's jurisdiction depends on the EC Insolvency Regulation, art 3 is a reference to property which may be dealt with in the proceedings. Since the EC Insolvency Regulation operates at Community level, the territory which determines the relevant territorial scope is the territory of the United Kingdom, not the territory of England and Wales.

[1] Exceptionally a liquidator within the meaning of the EC Insolvency Regulation who is appointed in territorial or secondary proceedings may bring actions in other States to recover moveable property which was removed from the territory of the State where the proceedings were opened after they were opened or to set aside transactions; see EC Insolvency Regulation, art 18(2).

14.19 By contrast, where the proceedings are main proceedings, their scope is universal and so no territorial restriction is applicable. Equally where the EC Insolvency Regulation is inapplicable, because the centre of the debtor's main interests is not located in any Member State, no territorial restriction will apply and property will mean property wherever situated.

Rules for determining where assets are situated

14.20 The EC Insolvency Regulation establishes rules for identifying where assets are situated[1]. Given the direct effect of the EC Insolvency Regulation, these rules will override any rules of domestic law regarding where property is to be regarded as situated where they conflict with such domestic rules.

1   EC Insolvency Regulation, art 2(g).

14.21 First, tangible property is situated in the territory of the Member State where the tangible property is situated. Secondly, property and rights, the ownership of or the entitlement to which must be registered in a public register, are situated in the Member State under the authority of which the register is kept. Where tangible property must be registered, this second rule overrides the first. Thirdly, claims are situated in the territory of the Member State of which the person who is required to meet the claim has the centre of his main interests. So, where the debtor has a bank account in credit at a bank which has its centre of main interests in another Member State, territorial proceedings will not ordinarily extend to include the chose in action which the debt owed by the bank to the debtor comprises. This appears to be so even where the bank has a branch in the State where the territorial proceedings are opened.

D EXAMPLES OF PROPERTY

Money

14.22 Money includes currency[1], that is, coins issued by the Crown under common law powers, now regulated by statute and banknotes issued by the Bank of England under its statutory powers[2]. In the context of a statute concerned with the payment of money into court[3], Brandon J said that he thought that 'it is right to say that the word "money", in its ordinary and natural meaning, includes money in foreign currency as well as money in sterling'[4]. But in the context 'money' may be construed in a popular sense[5] to include eg money at the bank held in a deposit or current account.

1   For a definition of which see *Moss v Hancock* [1899] 2 QB 111.
2   See 32 *Halsbury's Laws* (2005 Reissue) para 158.
3   The Administration of Justice Act 1965, s 4(1) now repealed and replaced by the Administration of Justice Act 1982, s 38(1).
4   *The Halcyon the Great* [1975] 1 All ER 882, [1975] 1 WLR 515.
5   See *Re Sale Hotel and Botanical Gardens Ltd, ex p Hesketh* (1898) 78 LT 368, CA construing 'money or other property of the company' in the Companies Winding-Up Act 1890, s 10(1).

Goods

14.23 Goods beneficially owned by the bankrupt at the commencement of his bankruptcy fall into his estate.

Sale of goods

14.24 More usually, perhaps, in bankruptcy, the question who has title to goods under a contract of sale in the course of performance arises where the bankrupt is the buyer of goods for which he has not paid but of which he has gained possession. Is his trustee entitled to keep the goods and leave the unpaid seller to prove in the bankruptcy for the price? Or, where title but not possession has passed to the bankrupt buyer, can the unpaid seller keep the goods and, if so, can he sell them to another buyer?

Passing of title

14.25 Subject to the rules relating to goods which form part of a bulk, where the contract of sale concerns unascertained goods, property cannot pass before the goods are ascertained[1]. Where the contract of sale concerns specific goods, or where it concerns unascertained goods but the goods to be sold have been ascertained, property passes at such time as the parties to the contract intend it to be transferred[2]. The Sale of Goods Act 1979, s 18 sets out a series of rules, displaceable by agreement to other effect, for ascertaining the intention of the parties. Particularly important in the context of insolvency is the fact that transfer of title does not necessarily depend on payment having been made. If both title and possession have passed to the bankrupt before the commencement of the bankruptcy, the goods will fall into his estate and the unpaid seller will be restricted to proving in the bankruptcy for his debt[3].

[1] Sale of Goods Act 1979, s 16. Section 20A governs the passing of title in goods forming part of a bulk.
[2] Sale of Goods Act 1979, s 17.
[3] Sale of Goods Act 1979, s 49(1) (action for the price) subject to IA 1986, s 285(3) (no remedy, save proof, for a provable debt).

Rights of unpaid seller

14.26 However, in some situations, an unpaid seller may be in a better position, even though property in the goods has passed.

(1)   Where the unpaid seller is in possession of the goods, the seller has a lien on the goods and, if the buyer becomes insolvent, he is entitled to retain possession of them until payment or tender of the price. The unpaid seller is also entitled to exercise his lien where the goods have been sold without any stipulation as to credit or where goods have been sold on credit but the term of credit has expired. If the unpaid seller

retains the goods in exercise of his lien, the trustee of the bankrupt buyer is not entitled to claim the goods for the estate unless he pays or tenders the price[1].

(2)   Where the unpaid seller has parted with possession of the goods but they remain in transit and the buyer becomes insolvent, the seller has a right of stopping the goods in transit[2].

[1]   Sale of Goods Act 1979, ss 39(1)(a) and 41.
[2]   Sale of Goods Act 1979, ss 39(1)(b) and 44 to 46.

14.27 A person is deemed to be insolvent for the purpose of the Sale of Goods Act 1979 if he has either ceased to pay his debts in the ordinary course of business or he cannot pay his debts when they fall due[1]. Where property in the goods has not passed from the seller to the buyer, the unpaid seller is entitled to exercise a right of withholding delivery co-extensive with his rights of lien or of stoppage in transit exercisable where property has passed[2].

[1]   Sale of Goods Act 1979, s 61(4).
[2]   Sale of Goods Act 1979, s 39(2).

Rescission and resale

14.28 The contract of sale is not rescinded by the unpaid seller's exercise of his right of lien or stoppage in transit[1]. In order to be able to resell the goods the unpaid seller must take the further step of rescinding the contract. If the contract expressly provides for a right of resale in case the buyer should default, the seller's exercise of that right of resale will rescind the contract[2]. If the goods are of a perishable nature or the unpaid seller gives notice of his intention to resell to the buyer and the buyer does not pay or tender the price within a reasonable time[3], the unpaid seller may resell the goods and prove for any loss occasioned[4]. The unpaid seller is entitled to determine the contract if the buyer repudiates by declaring that he is unable or unwilling to complete the contract, but the mere fact that the buyer is insolvent does not constitute a repudiation[5]. Good title passes to the new buyer under the contract of resale[6].

[1]   Sale of Goods Act 1979, s 48(1).
[2]   Sale of Goods Act 1979, s 48(4).
[3]   What is a reasonable time is a question of fact; s 59.
[4]   Sale of Goods Act 1979, s 48(3) subject to the IA 1986, s 285(3).
[5]   *Re Nathan, ex p Stapleton* (1879) 10 Ch D 586; *Mess v Duffus & Co* (1901) 6 Com Cas 165.
[6]   Sale of Goods Act 1979, s 48(2).

Retention of title

14.29 Contracts for the sale of goods commonly include clauses retaining title to the goods in the seller until the buyer has made payment for them. In essence, this involves an agreement between the parties concerning the stage in the transaction at which property is to pass. The possibility of the seller's reserving a right to dispose of the goods until certain conditions are fulfilled and the consequence that the property in the goods shall not pass until those conditions are fulfilled is expressly recognised in the Sale of Goods Act 1979[1]. Under the Bankruptcy Act 1914 property which was in the reputed ownership of the bankrupt would pass to his trustee in bankruptcy[2]. The effect of that provision prevented suppliers of goods from relying on clauses the object of which was to prevent title passing. But, the doctrine of reputed ownership plays no part under the Insolvency Act 1986. Whether property falls into the bankrupt's estate depends on whether it actually belongs to the bankrupt at the commencement of the bankruptcy[3]. Hence retention of title clauses and the line of cases relating to their effect in sales of goods to companies which began with *Aluminium Industrie Vaassen BV v Romalpa Aluminium Ltd*[4] are now relevant to individual insolvency.

[1]   Sale of Goods Act 1979, s 19.
[2]   Bankruptcy Act 1914, s 38.
[3]   See now the IA 1986, s 283 for the definition of the bankrupt's estate.
[4]   [1976] 2 All ER 552, [1976] 1 WLR 676.

14.30 A common problem regarding terms which purport to reserve title in the seller is that their true effect is to create a security interest or charge for the benefit of the seller in the property which has passed to the buyer. Where the buyer is a company, the charge must be registered under the Companies Act 1985 or, when it comes into force, the Companies Act 2006. Where the buyer is an individual, the equivalent question is whether the effect of the clause renders the contract a bill of sale or, where proceeds of sale are concerned, a general assignment of book debts[1] such as to require registration under the Bills of Sale Acts[2]. If the contract should be registered as a bill of sale but is not, it will be void against the creditors.

[1]   See the IA 1986, s 344, discussed further below.
[2]   Bills of Sale Act 1878 and Bills of Sale Act (1878) Amendment Act 1882. These do not apply in respect of charges created by companies; see *Slavenburg's Bank NV v Intercontinental Natural Resources Limited* [1980] 1 All ER 955, [1980] 1 WLR 1076.

Simple retention of title

14.31 Most simply a contract of sale may provide that title to the goods agreed to be sold will pass on payment by the buyer of the price of the goods themselves. By agreeing this, the parties to the contract do no more than displace the general rule that title passes on delivery[1]. In *Clough Mill Ltd v Martin*[2] the Court of Appeal upheld a clause in this form as being a retention of title by the seller rather than a transfer of title followed by a regrant by the buyer for the purpose of securing the price.

[1]   Sale of Goods Act 1979, ss 17 and 19(1).
[2]   [1984] 3 All ER 982, [1985] 1 WLR 111.

14.32 A provision which aims to retain title must provide that legal title to the goods is to be retained. For a purported retention of equitable title will be construed as operating in two stages: a transfer of title from the seller to the buyer followed by the creation by the buyer of an equitable interest vested in the seller[1].

[1]   *Re Bond Worth Ltd* [1980] Ch 228, [1979] 3 All ER 919.

14.33 The bankrupt's estate

14.33 So long as the goods which are the subject matter of the contract can be identified, the unpaid seller will be able to enforce a claim for delivery up of the goods. If a period of credit has been agreed, the seller will not be entitled to reclaim the goods until that period has expired. However, if the buyer's insolvency has intervened, the seller may be able to rely on that as an anticipatory breach[1]. If title to the goods has not passed the contract will not constitute a bill of sale[2].

1 See para **18.196**.
2 *McEntire v Crossley Bros* [1895] AC 457.

14.34 An extension of this form of clause is where the contract provides that title to the goods supplied under the current contract will not pass until all sums due to the seller from the buyer have been paid by the seller. This provision too is an example of the parties' freedom to stipulate the point at which title will pass, albeit that the event on which title passes is defined in terms of the fulfilment of obligations arising under other contracts than the present one. In *Clough Mill Ltd v Martin*[1] the Court of Appeal indicated that this form of clause validly retains the seller's title, and in *Armour v Thyssen Edelstahlwerke AG*, on appeal from the Court of Session, the House of Lords upheld as valid a clause retaining title to goods in the seller 'until all debts owed to [the seller]' were paid[2]. Scottish law does not differ from English law on this point.

1 [1984] 3 All ER 982, [1985] 1 WLR 111.
2 [1991] 2 AC 339, [1990] 3 All ER 481.

Mixed goods

14.35 In order to be able to reclaim goods, the seller must be able to identify the particular goods which he delivered. Where fungible goods have been mixed into a greater bulk of goods of the same nature, this identification will no longer be possible. However, if the seller is able to show that his goods are included in the bulk, then he may be able to claim that he is a co-owner of the bulk to the extent that it is made up of his goods. Whether he can do this will depend on whether the buyer who caused the goods to be commingled was entitled to do so under the contract or not. If not, the seller will be entitled to claim a share in the ownership of the bulk[1]. Hence the claim may depend on whether the contract includes an obligation to store the goods separately until paid for by the buyer.

1 *Indian Oil Corpn Ltd v Greenstone Shipping SA* [1988] QB 345, [1987] 2 Lloyd's Rep 286.

14.36 Where goods are supplied to a manufacturer, it is likely that the seller knows that they will be mixed with other goods in a process of production. An attempt has been made in a case where the seller had purported to retain title in the goods supplied to trace that title into the new goods into which the seller's goods had been incorporated[1]. The goods supplied were resin for use in the manufacture of chipboard by the buyer. The Court of Appeal rejected the seller's claim on the basis that once the resin had been incorporated with other goods in such a way as to make it impossible for the resin to be recovered, the seller's title was extinguished. By contrast in *Hendy Lennox Ltd v Grahame Puttick Ltd*[2] where the goods in question, being engines, retained their identity despite being attached to generator sets, the seller's title was not extinguished.

1   *Borden (UK) Ltd v Scottish Timber Products Ltd* [1981] Ch 25, [1979] 3 All ER 961, CA.
2   [1984] 2 All ER 152, [1984] 1 WLR 485.

14.37 If the seller's title has been extinguished by reason of the incorporation of the goods into a new product, the contract may provide that title to the new goods will vest in the seller. The possibility that a clause in this form may be effective has been recognised by the Court of Appeal[1]. To achieve this end the parties must have intended that the seller would obtain the windfall of the value to his goods added to his goods by the work done by the buyer and by the addition of other materials into the goods. For, unless the seller is to take the benefit of this added value absolutely, the effect of the provision will be to create a charge. The intention was absent in *Re Peachdart Ltd*[2] where leather was supplied to a manufacturer of handbags and the seller claimed title in the partly and fully manufactured handbags. Similarly in *Clough Mill Ltd v Martin*[3], the Court of Appeal opined[4] that there was a lack of the relevant intention in a contract for the sale of yarn to a carpet manufacturer. A factor which influenced the court in that case was the fact that other materials supplied to the manufacturer would also be subject to retention of title clauses, thus giving rise to the difficulty of resolving the conflicting claims of two suppliers of ingredients in the new product[5]. Since this factor is likely to be present in almost all cases, presumably the parties' intention will have to be expressed in such a way as to take into account the existence of competing claims to the new products.

1   *Clough Mill Ltd v Martin* [1985] 1 WLR 111 per Robert Goff LJ at 119, per Oliver LJ at 123–4.
2   [1984] Ch 131, [1983] 3 All ER 204.
3   [1984] 3 All ER 982, [1985] 1 WLR 111.
4   This part of the decision is *obiter*.
5   Per Robert Goff LJ at 124.

Proceeds of sale

14.38 Where goods have been delivered but title has been retained by the seller, the buyer may nonetheless be permitted to sell the goods on to a sub-buyer. By that sub-sale the sub-buyer will obtain good title by virtue of the Sale of Goods Act 1979, s 25 and any claim by the seller to the goods themselves will be lost. However the seller may be entitled to claim from the buyer the proceeds of the sub-sale. The claim in the *Romalpa*[1] case itself was a claim of this nature. The essential issue was whether the buyer owed a fiduciary duty to the seller in respect of the proceeds of sale. The Court of Appeal held that the buyer did. Perhaps less clear is the source of that duty. It was conceded on behalf of the buyer that the buyer held the goods as bailee. At first instance this concession led directly to the conclusion that a fiduciary duty existed[2]. However, the Court of Appeal's decision rested on different grounds[3]. Roskill LJ identified the critical question as whether there was a fiduciary duty entitling the seller to claim the proceeds of sale. In determining that issue his inquiry was directed to the provisions of the contract in order to ascertain whether there should be implied into them a power vested in the buyer to sell the goods before title passed and an obligation owed by the buyer to account for the proceeds of sale. The conclusion was that both the power and the obligation should be implied and that hence the buyer's obligation under the contract coincided with that ordinarily owed by a bailee[4].

[1]   *Aluminium Industrie Vaassen BV v Romalpa Aluminium Ltd* [1976] 2 All ER 552, [1976] 1 WLR 676.
[2]   *Aluminium Industrie Vaassen BV v Romalpa Aluminium Ltd* [1976] 1 WLR 676 per Mocatta J at 82A quoting Sir G Jessell MR in *Re Hallett's Estate* (1879) 13 Ch D 696 at 709.
[3]   See *Hendy Lennox Ltd v Grahame Puttick Ltd* [1984] 1 WLR 485 at 498 per Staughton J.
[4]   *Hendy Lennox Ltd v Grahame Puttick Ltd* [1984] 1 WLR 485 at 687F–690G.

14.39 Subsequent cases have cast doubt on whether the concession that the buyers were bailees of the goods was correct. For example, in *Borden (UK) Ltd v Scottish Timber Products Ltd*[1] where resin was supplied for the manufacture of chipboard, Bridge LJ held that so long as the business transacted between the parties continued in the ordinary way and the resin was delivered for use in a manufacturing process which would render it irrecoverable, the contract was essentially one of sale and purchase not of bailment[2]. However, since in *Romalpa* in the Court of Appeal the mere proposition that the buyer held the goods as bailee did not lead immediately to the conclusion that it owed a fiduciary duty, whether the concept of bailment provides the correct approach may not be a fruitful topic of speculation. For (to adapt the words of Staughton J in *Hendy Lennox*) although there may be a presumption that bailees owe a fiduciary duty, some bailees do not occupy a fiduciary position and one has to examine the relationship in each case to see whether it is of a fiduciary nature[3].

[1]   [1981] Ch 25, [1979] 3 All ER 961.
[2]   *Borden (UK) Ld v Scottish Timber Products Ltd* [1981] Ch 25 at 35. See also *Pfeiffer Weinkellerei-Weineinkauf GmbH & Co v Arbuthnot Factors Ltd* [1988] 1 WLR 150 at 159 per Phillips J.
[3]   *Hendy Lennox Ltd v Grahame Puttick Ltd* [1984] 1 WLR 485 at 498.

14.40 The problem, then, is to identify the sorts of circumstances in which the implication should be drawn. It should be noted that, both in *Hendy Lennox* and in *Re Andrabell Ltd*[1], where sellers argued in favour of implying an obligation to account, the proposed implication failed because it was not necessary in order that the contract should have business efficacy. In *Pfeiffer GmbH v Arbuthnot Factors Ltd*[2] Phillips J considered that the normal implication that arose from the relationship of buyer and seller was that if the buyer was permitted to sub-sell in the normal course of his business, he would do so for his own account without, therefore, any duty to account. In the light of those decisions it must be unlikely that the implication that a buyer should account for the proceeds of a sub-sale will be made where the sole basis for making the implication is that the seller has purported to retain title.

[1]   [1984] 3 All ER 407.
[2]   [1988] 1 WLR 150.

14.41 However, where the contract provides that the buyer must store the goods separately and pay all proceeds of sale into an account used only for that purpose, the implication might well be made[1]. The difficulty with a clause in this form is that it may be construed as a charge created by the buyer in favour of the seller[2]. This conclusion need not follow if it can be established that the buyer is not to have any interest in the proceeds of sale but must pass them in their totality to the seller. However, where the conclusion is that the clause creates a charge, this will lead, if the buyer is an individual, to the requirement of registration under the Bills of Sale Acts as a general assignment of a class of book debts[3].

[1] *Hendy Lennox Ltd v Grahame Puttick Ltd* [1984] 1 WLR 485 at 499; *Re Andrabell Ltd* [1984] 3 All ER 407 at 415.
[2] *Tatung (UK) Ltd v Galex Telesure Ltd* (1988) 5 BCC 325.
[3] See para **14.47**.

Bills of sale

14.42 The Bills of Sale Acts[1] apply to every bill of sale 'whereby the holder or grantee has power to seize or take possession of any personal chattels comprised in or made subject to such bill of sale'[2]. Bills of sale include:

(1) bills of sale, assignments, transfers, declarations of trust without transfer, inventories of goods with receipt attached thereto, or receipts for purchase moneys of goods and other assurances of personal chattels;
(2) powers of attorney, authorities or licences to take possession of personal chattels as security for any debt;
(3) any agreement whereby a right in equity to any personal chattels or to any charge or security thereon is conferred[3].

[1] Bills of Sale Act 1878 and Bills of Sale Act (1878) Amendment Act 1882.
[2] Bills of Sale Act 1878, s 3.
[3] Bills of Sale Act 1878, s 4.

14.43 A transfer of goods in the ordinary course of business of any trade or calling is not a bill of sale[1].

[1] Bills of Sale Act 1878, s 4.

14.44 'Personal chattels' means goods, furniture and other articles capable of complete transfer by delivery and does not include choses in action[1].

[1] Bills of Sale Act 1878, s 4.

14.45 The Bills of Sale Acts distinguish between security and absolute bills of sale[1]. Security bills of sale are bills of sale given as security for the payment of money[2]. These are governed by both the 1878 and the 1882 Acts and must be registered in the statutory form, otherwise they are void both against the grantor's creditors and the grantee[3]. Absolute bills of sale[4] are governed only by the 1878 Act and if not registered are void against the creditors of the owner of the goods affected by the bill but will not be void between the parties[5].

1   Bills of Sale 1878 (Amendment) Act 1882, s 3.
2   See the Bills of Sale Act 1878 (Amendment) Act 1882, s 3.
3   Bills of Sale Act 1878 (Amendment) Act 1882, ss 8 and 9.
4   Being bills of sale given otherwise than as security for the payment of money.
5   Bills of Sale Act 1878, s 8.

14.46 In relation to a contract for the sale of goods to an individual buyer which includes a retention of title clause the need for compliance with the Bills of Sale Acts arises where, on the true construction of the clause, title to the goods passes to the buyer but he, as the owner of the goods, retransfers a security interest to the seller. Accordingly the questions whether title has passed by virtue of a particular contractual provision and whether, therefore, any rights to take possession of the goods which the seller seeks to enforce are rights which the buyer has conferred on the seller rather than retained by him are equally germane in the context of sale to an individual buyer as to a company[1].

1   *McEntire v Crossley Bros Ltd* [1895] AC 457, HL.

Assignments of book debts

14.47 The IA 1986, s 344 brings assignments of book debts into the ambit of the Bills of Sale Acts. It does so by providing that an assignment of book debts is to be treated for the purpose of registration under the Bills of Sale Act 1878 as if it were a bill of sale given otherwise than as security for the payment of a sum of money[1]. Hence, where a person engaged in any business makes a general assignment to another person of his existing or future debts, or any class of them, that assignment will be void against his trustee in bankruptcy if it is not registered under the Bills of Sale Act 1878. In the context of a clause by which a seller of goods claims title to the proceeds of their sale by the buyer, the initial question is whether the provisions agreed between the parties constitute an assignment. If the buyer agrees to receive the proceeds of sale on behalf of the seller, in the sense that all the proceeds of sale are the seller's irrespective of the amount owed by the buyer to the seller, then the agreement contained in the contract of sale would appear not to form an assignment. If, by contrast, the buyer is entitled to make sub-sales and use the proceeds as his own, save that he is liable to account to the extent of the price, the agreement would constitute an assignment of a class of future debts[2] and so would have to be registered under the Bills of Sale Acts. Probably this group would form a class of debts within the meaning of the Insolvency Act 1986 in that all the debts included would share a characteristic, namely that they arise from the sub-sale of goods supplied to the buyer under one contract of sale, or perhaps from the same seller under a series of contracts. Hence, effectively, the issue in the case of an individual buyer would be the same as in the case of a corporate buyer: does the agreement to account constitute a charge on property, book debts, belonging to the buyer or does a liability to account arise because the debts concerned at all times belong to the seller? If the agreement constitutes a charge, it will be void unless registered.

1   IA 1986, s 344(4).
2   *Pfeiffer Weinkellerei-Weineinkauf GmbH & Co v Arbuthnot Factors Ltd* [1988] 1 WLR 150 at 161.

Goods supplied on hire-purchase or similar contract of supply

14.48 The bankrupt may have possession of goods which have been bailed to him under a hire-purchase contract or other contract for the supply of goods pursuant to which possession but not title passes to the bailee. Since title does not pass during the currency of such agreements, the goods will not form part of the bankrupt's estate. Usually such contracts make express provision for termination on the bankruptcy of the bailee. If, unusually, no express provision for termination is made in the contract, then the trustee may, if he wishes, continue to perform the contract by making whatever payments are due under it. Conceivably, this would be worthwhile where, for example under the terms of a hire purchase contract, title could be obtained to goods which would have a greater realisable value than the sum required to be paid in order to obtain title. Alternatively, if the trustee did not wish to perform the contract, he could disclaim it.

Gifts of chattels

14.49 A gift of chattels made *inter vivos* must be completed either by delivery or deed. In *Re Cole, ex p Trustee of Property of Bankrupt v Cole*[1] a husband who told his wife that all the furniture in the house where they both continued to live was a gift to her had not perfected the gift by adequate delivery. Gifts made by the bankrupt within the period of five years before the presentation of the petition on which the bankruptcy order was made or for the purpose of putting assets beyond the reach of actual or potential creditors may be set aside[2].

1   [1964] Ch 175, [1963] 3 All ER 433, CA.
2   See the IA 1986, ss 339 and 423.

Things in action

14.50 Personal property comprises things in possession and things in action. Originally, things in action were rights of property which could only be enforced by being claimed in an action, but some things in action, now recognised as such, are not capable of being enforced that way, such as shares in a company[1]. Examples include debts, benefits under contracts, stocks and shares[2], equitable rights to property, legacies, and causes of action[3]. A thing in action need not be immediately recoverable[4].

1   *Colonial Bank v Whinney* (1885) 30 Ch D 261 at 285, CA (Fry LJ dissenting), (1886) 11 App Cas 426 (HL overruling CA).

14.50   *The bankrupt's estate*

2   *Gemshore Investments plc v Stewart* [2002] All ER (D) (Jan) a company in which the
    bankrupt had a 100% shareholding and over which he exercised sole control was
    considered to be the bankrupt's alter ego so that the company and its underlying assets
    formed part of the bankrupt's estate.
3   Recent examples include *Re Landau (a bankrupt), Pointer v Landau* [1998] Ch 223,
    [1997] 3 All ER 322 (retirement annuity contract); *Morris v Morgan* [1998] BPIR 764, CA
    (rights under a contract); *Performing Rights Society Ltd v Rowland* [1997] 3 All ER 336,
    [1998] BPIR 128 (rights to distributions under the performing rights scheme). In *Shepherd
    v Legal Services Commission* [2003] BPIR 140 the court held that the trustee had a duty to
    consider how best to realise a claim which formed part of the bankrupt's estate such that
    the claim would not be stifled by a bankruptcy order being made.
4   *Kwok v Comr of Estate Duty* [1988] 1 WLR 1035, 1040.

Life assurance

14.51   Where a bankrupt has effected life assurance on his own life expressed
to be for the benefit of a third party, the policy money, in the absence of a
declaration of trust, belongs to his estate. But where such life assurance is for
the benefit of the bankrupt's spouse and/or children, a trust is created in their
favour, and so long as the spouse or any of the children remains alive, the
money paid under the policy does not form part of the bankrupt's estate or
become subject to his debts[1].

1   Married Women's Property Act 1882, s 11.

14.52   However, where the trustee is able to prove that the policy was effected
and the premiums paid with the intent to defraud creditors, he may seek an
order for restitution[1]. Even in the absence of such proof, the trustee will
normally be able to impeach the contract of insurance as an undervalue
transaction within the two- or five-year period allowed for in the IA 1986[2]
and obtain a return of the premiums paid together, possibly, with a further
sum in respect of any accrued benefits where the premiums were paid to an
endowment fund[3].

1   Either under the Married Women's Property Act 1882, s 11 (a sum equal to premiums paid
    only) or the IA 1986, s 423 (any order the court thinks fit).
2   IA 1986, s 339.
3   See the IA 1986, s 342(1).

14.53   In *Cork v Rawlins*[1] the Court of Appeal held that the right to a
payment due under a contract of insurance by virtue of an event defined by
reference to the bodily disablement of the insured was a thing in action falling
within the estate. For the right to the payment is a contractual right, hence an
asset, and the bodily disablement is the event determining if and when it
became payable. The Court of Appeal did not consider that there was any
analogy between such a contractual claim and the tortious claim for damages
for pain and suffering. But, it is submitted, the conclusion cannot be justified
solely by reference to the difference between claims arising under a contract
and those arising in tort. For, damages for pain and suffering are not excluded
from the estate because the cause of action under which they arise is not
capable of forming part of the estate but because reasons are admitted
justifying their exclusion. Similar reasons could be admitted to justify the

exclusion of payments under a policy of insurance calculated to enable the bankrupt to provide for his and his family's basic domestic needs. In *Cork v Rawlins* the payment was a single sum, but if the payments arising were periodical payments calculated to replace the income of a person who has become disabled, they would still form part of the estate given that they are contractual rights which, as part of a bundle of contractual rights created before bankruptcy, form part of the estate[2]. The further question, which is a question of policy, is whether they ought to be excluded. An argument for permitting a bankrupt to retain the part of such periodical payments as was necessary to satisfy his and his family's basis domestic needs might seem to have some worth by analogy with the policy permitting the bankrupt to keep sufficient income for his and his family's maintainance[3]. But the creation of such a rule, if thought appropriate, requires legislative intervention.

[1]   *Cork v Rawlins* [2001] EWCA Civ 197, [2001] 3 WLR 300.
[2]   See *Re Landau (a bankrupt), Pointer v Landau* [1998] Ch 223, [1997] 3 All ER 322 and *Krasner v Dennison* [2000] Ch 76, [2000] 3 All ER 234 in relation to retirement annuity contracts, both approved by *Rowe v Sanders* [2002] BPIR 847. The validity of those decisions in respect of the contractual analysis on the current point contained in them is unaffected by the legislative changes made by the Welfare Reform and Pensions Act 1999.
[3]   See paras **14.79** and **14.174** below.

Pensions

14.54 Whether rights to a pension fall within the estate is discussed in paras **14.129**ff below.

Causes of action

14.55 Save for causes of action 'where the damages are solely to be estimated by immediate reference to pain felt by the bankrupt in respect of his body, mind or character, and without immediate reference to his rights of property'[1], causes of action pursuable by an individual which have accrued before the commencement of his bankruptcy form part of his estate as items of property and vest in his trustee[2]. The bankrupt's lack of standing is unaffected by a grant of LSC funding to him in respect of the claim[3]. Where the damages include heads of loss referable to the bankrupt's body, mind or character, such as general damages for pain and suffering, as well as heads of loss forming part of the estate, such as a claim for past loss of earnings, the trustee will hold such part of any judgment or settlement as relates to the heads of loss referable to the bankrupt's body, mind or character on a trust for the bankrupt[4]. The right to resist possession proceedings is part of the bankrupt's estate although the bankrupt is the proper defendant to the possession proceedings and does have standing to argue that procedural requirements have not been observed[5].

[1]   *Beckham v Drake* (1849) 2 HL Cas 579; *Ord v Upton* [2000] Ch 352, [2000] 1 All ER 193, CA; *Kaberry v Freethcartright* [2003] EWCA Civ 1077, [2003] BPIR 1144. The quotation is from the opinion of Erle J in *Beckham v Drake* with the word 'solely' added to reflect the decision in *Ord v Upton*.

2   *Heath v Tang* [1993] 4 All ER 694, [1993] 1 WLR 1421, CA. The principle also applies to tax appeals as they directly concern the estate vested in the trustee in bankruptcy: *Ahajot v Waller* [2005] BPIR 82.
3   *James v Rutherford-Hodge* [2005] EWCA Civ 1580, [2006] BPIR 973.
4   *Ord v Upton* [2000] Ch 352, CA. See para **19.5** for further discussion of this topic.
5   *Seven Eight Six Properties Ltd v Ghafoor* [1997] BPIR 519.

Interest in a partnership

14.56 If the bankrupt has carried on business in partnership with others, then, subject to any agreement between the partners, the partnership is dissolved by the bankruptcy[1], unless it is a limited partnership[2]. The trustee is entitled to the value of the bankrupt partner's share and to an account[3]. If, after the bankruptcy, the other partner continues to carry on the business with the capital as constituted at the time of the bankruptcy, the bankrupt partner's trustee is entitled to participate in the subsequent profits[4].

1   Partnership Act 1890, s 33(1).
2   A limited partnership is not dissolved by the bankruptcy of a partner: Limited Partnerships Act 1907, s 6(2).
3   See *Wilson v Greenwood* (1818) 1 Swan 471; *Whitmore v Mason* (1861) 2 John & H 204; *Re Williams, ex p Warden* (1872) 21 WR 51.
4   *Crawshay v Collins* (1808) 15 Ves 218.

14.57 A proviso in a partnership deed that, in the event of the bankruptcy of one of the partners, his share shall go over to his co-partners, is void as being in fraud of the bankruptcy laws[1]. This is no more than an example of the application of the rule set out at para **14.110ff** below that an owner of property may not, by contract or otherwise, qualify his own interest in it by a condition to take effect in the event of his own bankruptcy. The same applies to a proviso that the bankrupt partner should, in the event of his bankruptcy, receive for his share a smaller sum than its real value[2]. Such arrangements between partners do not bind creditors. The trustee in bankruptcy of the bankrupt partner is entitled, in spite of such arrangements, to an account of the estate and profit of the partnership[3].

1   *Whitmore v Mason* (1861) 2 John & H 204.
2   *Wilson v Greenwood* (1818) 1 Swan 471; *Re Williams, ex p Warden* (1872) 21 WR 51.
3   *Re Williams, ex p Warden* (1872) 21 WR 51 at 52.

Goodwill in a business

14.58 If the bankrupt has carried on a business, the goodwill of the business passes to his trustee[1], except:

(1)   where the business premises have been mortgaged and the goodwill is attached to the premises, in which case the goodwill is comprised in the security[2]; and
(2)   where the goodwill is personal to the bankrupt, as in the case of a professional man, in which case, it seems, it does not pass[3].

1   As to the rights of a trustee to the goodwill of a bankrupt's business see *Re Thomas, ex p Thomas* (1841) 2 Mont D & De G 294; revsd on another point (1842) 3 Mont D & De G 40; *Hudson v Osborne* (1869) 39 LJ Ch 79; *Walker v Mottram* (1881) 19 Ch D 355, CA.
2   *Re Kitchin, ex p Punnett* (1880) 16 Ch D 226.
3   See *Farr v Pearce* (1818) 3 Madd 74.

14.59 Compensation which is given by statute to a bankrupt for the destruction of his business is analogous to goodwill and passes to the trustee[1]. Secret unwritten formulae used by the debtor in the manufacture of goods must be disclosed to the trustee as part of the goodwill of the business[2].

1   See *Chandler v Gardiner* (undated) (cited in *Cruttwell (or Crutwell) v Lye* (1810) 17 Ves 335 at 338, 343), where compensation to the proprietors of quays for the loss of their exclusive trade by the establishment of the East India Docks was held on bankruptcy to pass to their creditors.
2   See *Re Keene* [1922] 2 Ch 475, CA; cf *Cotton v Gillard* (1874) 44 LJ Ch 90.

Expectancies and contingent interests

14.60 The statutory definition of property includes future and contingent interests. Where such interests arise under an existing settlement of property, they will fall within the estate. Thus, where property is settled on trust for a tenant for life, and on his death to be divided amongst such of his children as should be living at his death, and one of the children becomes bankrupt during the life tenant's lifetime, that child's interest in remainder will pass to his trustee in bankruptcy[1]. Equally where a benefactor settled property so as to provide income for life to a person then bankrupt, but imposed a condition that the income was to be paid to him on his obtaining his discharge, the bankrupt obtained a contingent interest which vested in his trustee and on the bankrupt obtaining his discharge (which at the relevant period was a contingent event since discharge could not be obtained as of right), the interest fell into the trustee's possession. To be contrasted with the foregoing cases is the hope which an expectant beneficiary has under another person's will during that other person's lifetime.

1   See *Higden v Williamson* (1732) 3 P Wms 132.

14.61 In *Re Vizard's Trust*[1] property was settled on a life tenant and after her death to such of a limited class of persons as she might appoint or in default of appointment to all of the members of that class in equal shares. It was held that the possibility which a member had of acquiring an interest was not an asset forming part of his estate for the purpose of an assignment under the Bankruptcy Act 1861. It is submitted that the outcome would be different under the present legislation because the interest held by each member of the class from the outset was a future interest, albeit defeasible by the exercise of the power of appointment in favour of other members[2]. But the bankrupt would not have held even a contingent interest if he had not been a member of the class which took the property in equal shares in default of appointment.

1   (1866) 1 Ch App 588.
2   See *Re Brooks' Settlement Estates, Lloyds Bank v Tillard* [1939] Ch 993, 997.

14.62 Future property, including future things in action such as future book debts, possibilities and expectancies are capable of being assigned in equity for value[1]. But an assignment relating to a future interest takes effect (when supported by valuable consideration[2]) as an agreement to assign which may be specifically enforced by the equitable assignee when the interest falls into the possession of the equitable assignor. An equitable assignment may be effected of an expectancy which in the events which subsequently occur is never realised, and, because an equitable assignment may be made of both a future or contingent interest currently held by a person and mere possibilities which might accrue to him, whether some future thing is capable of being assigned in equity is no test of whether it is an item of property belonging to the bankrupt at the commencement of his bankruptcy and falling within his estate.

1   *Tailby v Official Receiver* (1888) 13 App Cas 523; *Re Ellenborough, Towry Law v Burne* [1903] 1 Ch 697, 700; *Glegg v Bromley* [1912] 3 KB 474; *Cotton v Heyl* [1930] 1 Ch 510.
2   The consideration must be valuable; so the fact that the assignment is made by deed will not suffice, for equity will not assist a volunteer.

14.63 It appears to be settled that, if a bankruptcy is annulled between the time when a future interest is vested in a bankrupt and the time when it falls into possession, the bankrupt is in the same position as if he had never been bankrupt, and is entitled to receive the fund. But the annulment will not have this effect if the fund has become payable and been intercepted, by a forfeiture, in the meantime. Thus in *Ancona v Waddell*[1], it was held that no forfeiture had taken place because the income had not been payable before the annulment of the bankruptcy. On the other hand, in *Re Broughton, Peat v Broughton*[2]; *Metcalfe v Metcalfe*[3], and *Re Forder, Forder v Forder*[4], it was held that a forfeiture had taken place because the income became payable before the annulment[5].

1   (1878) 10 Ch D 157.
2   (1887) 57 LT 8.
3   [1891] 3 Ch 1, CA.
4   [1927] 2 Ch 291.
5   See also *Samuel v Samuel* (1879) 12 Ch D 152; *Re James, Clutterbuck v James* (1890) 62 LT 545.

14.64 In *Re Campbell (a bankrupt)*[1] Knox J held that the hope that an individual entertains of receiving an award from the Criminal Injuries Compensation Board in respect of injuries suffered as the result of a criminal assault is not a thing in action because the realisation of the hope depended on the Board's future exercise of discretion in favour of the bankrupt. It was not an existing item of property but something which might possibly come into existence on some uncertain event in the future and was, therefore, distinct from a future and contingent interest in property because, although contingent on a future event, there was no existing item of property to which the interest, before the event occurred, related. Knox J gave as possible examples of similar situations the hope which the holder of a lottery ticket has in winning the prize or which an entrant in the football pools has that he will have filled his coupon in successfully. But in these cases, it is submitted, the trustee might establish that there is an item of property, if the prize is payable to whoever holds the ticket, which itself, as a chattel, could be claimed for the estate[2].

¹   [1997] Ch 14, [1996] 2 All ER 537.
²   See *Abrahams v Abraham's Trustee in Bankruptcy* [1999] BPIR 637.

Land

14.65 Where the bankrupt holds an interest in land at the commencement of his bankruptcy, his estate will include that interest.

Interest in bankrupt's residence

14.66 Where an interest in a dwelling house which was, at the date of the commencement of the bankruptcy, the sole or principal residence of the bankrupt, his spouse or civil partner or his former spouse or former civil partner, then that interest will form part of his estate; but at the end of three years beginning with the date of the bankruptcy the interest will automatically cease to be included within the estate and will revert to the bankrupt¹. This is discussed in the following chapter.

¹   IA 1986, s 283A.

Settled land

14.67 For the purposes of determining, where the estate owner of any settled land¹ is bankrupt, whether the legal estate in the settled land is comprised in, or is capable of being claimed for, the bankrupt's estate, the legal estate in the settled land is deemed not to vest in the estate owner², unless and until the estate owner becomes absolutely and beneficially entitled to the settled land free from all limitations, powers and charges taking effect under the settlement³.

¹   For the meaning of 'settled land' see the Settled Land Act 1925, ss 2, 117(1)(xxiv).
²   For the meaning of 'estate owner' see the Settled Land Act 1925, s 117(1)(xi); Law of Property Act 1925, s 1(4).
³   Settled Land Act 1925, s 103 (amended by the IA 1985, s 235(1), Sch 8, para 3). As to the trustee in bankruptcy's power to apply under the Settled Land Act 1925, s 24 for the exercise of the powers under the Act see *Re Thornhill's Settlement* [1941] Ch 24, [1940] 4 All ER 249, CA.

Land owned jointly by the bankrupt and another person

14.68 Where the legal interest in land is vested jointly in the bankrupt and another person, the legal interest will not form part of the bankrupt's estate. But any equitable (or beneficial) interest in the land belonging to the bankrupt will form part of his estate.

Leaseholds

14.69 Unless disclaimed by the trustee¹, the bankrupt's leasehold property passes to the trustee subject to the landlord's rights as to rent and to the enforcement of the covenants[2] which bind assignees, except those which are not enforceable against a lessee's trustee in bankruptcy, such as the covenant not to assign without the landlord's consent. The bankrupt's property is also subject to rights of distress and to any rights of seizure which have been validly created in respect of it[3]. The interrelationship between bankruptcy and leasehold interests in land, and in particular the power of the trustee to claim the benefit of certain statutory tenancies not otherwise forming part of the estate, is mentioned further below at paras **14.80** and **14.98**.

1   See para **18.204** below.
2   See *Re Solomon, ex p Dressler* (1878) 9 Ch D 252, CA; *Wilson v Wallani* (1880) 5 Ex D 155; *Titterton v Cooper* (1882) 9 QBD 473, CA.
3   *Krehl v Great Central Gas Co* (1870) LR 5 Exch 289; *Re Garrud, ex p Newitt* (1881) 16 Ch D 522, CA; *Leman v Yorkshire Rly Waggon Co* (1881) 50 LJ Ch 293.

14.70 A proviso in a lease of land that the lease should be forfeited on the lessee's bankruptcy[1] is valid subject to the availability of relief; where there is such a proviso and the lessee becomes bankrupt, no interest in the demised premises is divisible among the creditors[2]. A proviso of this kind, however, applies only to the bankruptcy of the person in possession of the term created by the lease; if a lessee assigns his term and after the assignment becomes bankrupt, his bankruptcy does not operate to determine the lease[3]. The landlord's right to forfeit is subject to statutory conditions[4].

1   Where a lease contains a condition as to forfeiture on the tenant's bankruptcy and, on his assigning without licence, and after the tenant's bankruptcy, the landlord accepts rent from the trustee and treats him as tenant, the condition is gone; it is not clear whether in such a case the landlord can insist on the condition as to forfeiture for assigning without licence: see *Dyke v Taylor* (1861) 30 LJ Ch 281.
2   *Roe d Hunter v Galliers* (1787) 2 Term Rep 133. If the landlord enters for forfeiture on a tenant's bankruptcy, any growing crops on the land belong to the landlord, and not to the tenant's creditors: *Davis v Eyton* (1820) 7 Bing 154. A provision in a lease giving the tenant a right to compensation for certain crops 'at the expiration of the term' has no application when the landlord enters for a forfeiture on the tenant's bankruptcy: *Silcock v Farmer* (1882) 46 LT 404, CA; but see *Re Morrish, ex p Hart Dyke* (1882) 22 Ch D 410, CA, applied in *Re ABC Coupler and Engineering Co Ltd (No 3)* [1970] 1 All ER 650, [1970] 1 WLR 702.
3   *Smith v Gronow* [1891] 2 QB 394. The proviso runs with the land: *Horsey Estate Ltd v Steiger* [1899] 2 QB 79, CA.
4   See the Law of Property Act 1925, s 146.

14.71 A tenancy, arising under a lease or contract for a lease is an item of property, but the statutory right to remain in possession arising under the Rent Acts, or their successor Housing Acts, does not have the status of property because it is personal to the tenant (or his statutory successor)[1]. Since the bankrupt tenant under such a tenancy whose contractual tenancy had determined before he became bankrupt would be put in a better position than the tenant under a contractual tenancy which had not been determined, because the contractual tenancy, not being a matter of merely personal status, formed part of his estate[2], such contractual tenancies were expressly excluded from the estate[3]. As a consequence, a possession order granted in respect of a secure tenancy just before a bankruptcy order is made does not offend IA 1986, s 285 as there is no enforcement against property of the bankrupt[4]. But, a continuation tenancy under the Landlord and Tenant Act 1954, Pt I is property and falls within the estate[5]. The right to a new business tenancy under Pt II of that Act is also property and with it is included the right to continue proceedings to enforce the right[6].

[1]   *Sutton v Dorf* [1932] 2 KB 304. For the position under the Housing Act 1985 in respect of secure tenancies in the public sector, see *City of London Corpn v Bown* (1989) 60 P & CR 42 (secure tenancy not part of the estate).
[2]   *Smalley v Quarrier* [1975] 2 All ER 688, [1975] 1 WLR 938.
[3]   IA 1986, s 283(3A).
[4]   *Harlow District Council v Hall* [2006] EWCA Civ 156, [2006] 1 WLR 2116, [2006] BPIR 712.
[5]   *De Rothschild v Bell* [2000] 1 QB 33, [1999] 2 All ER 722, CA.
[6]   *Saini v Petroform* [1997] BPIR 515, CA.

Contracts for the sale of land

14.72 Where the bankrupt has contracted before the presentation of the petition on which he was made bankrupt to sell an interest in land but completion has not occurred at the commencement of the bankruptcy, the interest remains part of his estate but it is subject to the obligation comprised in the contract and, on the estate vesting in him, the trustee becomes bound by that obligation. For, the legal estate in the property vests in the trustee subject to the equitable interest of the purchaser to have the estate conveyed to him on payment of the purchase price[1]. Where the bankrupt made the contract after the presentation of the petition on which he was made bankrupt, it is arguable that the contract will be void unless it was made with the consent of the court or is subsequently ratified by the court or the purchaser can bring himself within the protection afforded by the IA 1986, s 284(4)(a) to bona fide purchasers for value without notice of the bankruptcy, because it has the effect of transferring the beneficial ownership to the purchaser[2]. Although the contract is void, rather than voidable, the trustee, if he wished, could abide by its terms, without seeking the court's approval, by selling the property on the same terms in exercise of his power of sale over property comprised in the estate[3].

[1]   IA 1986, s 283(5); *Re Scheibler, ex p Holthausen* (1874) 9 Ch App 722, 276; *Lysaght v Edwards* (1876) 2 Ch D 499; *Re Pooley, ex p Rabbidge* (1878) 8 Ch D 367, 370, CA.
[2]   IA 1986, s 284(1).
[3]   IA 1986, s 314(1)(b), Sch 5, para 9.

14.73 A trustee may not disclaim a contract for the sale of real property, including a lease, unless he disclaims the interest in the land as well[1]. For, a contract for the sale of real estate operates so as to pass an equitable interest to the purchaser and the right to disclaim does not enable the trustee to take back from a person the equitable interest which has so passed to him and thereby free the trustee from the equity created by the bankrupt[2].

[1]   Under the power of disclaimer conferred by the IA 1986, s 315. It is possible to disclaim freehold interests in land; see *Re Mercer and Moore* (1880) 14 Ch D 287; *Re Nottingham General Cemetery Co* [1955] Ch 683, [1955] 2 All ER 504; *Scmlla Properties Ltd v Gesso Properties BVI Ltd* [1995] BCC 793.
[2]   *Pearce v Bastable's Trustee in Bankruptcy* [1901] 2 Ch 122 (Cozens-Hardy J); *Re Bastable, ex p the Trustee* [1901] 2 KB 518, CA; *Capital Prime Properties plc v Worthgate Ltd (in liq)* [2000] 1 BCLC 647.

Specific performance

14.74 Specific performance is mentioned here since it is a remedy usually sought in respect of contracts for the sale and purchase of land, but where it is available in respect of other contracts, the principles are likely to be the same. The right to enforce a contract which has been entered into by the bankrupt forms part of his estate and therefore may be exercised by his trustee. Hence, whether the contract is to sell or purchase land, unless the performance of the contract involves an exercise of some skill or discretion that is personal to the bankrupt, the trustee will be entitled, subject to the defences generally available, to specific performance of the contract[1]. Where the contract made by the bankrupt of which the trustee seeks specific performance is a contract for the grant of a lease to the bankrupt, the trustee may be required to enter into the covenants of the lease personally as a condition of specific performance being decreed[2]. But specific performance of a contract to purchase land will not generally be ordered against the trustee[3].

[1]   *Jennings' Trustee v King* [1952] Ch 899, [1952] 2 All ER 608.
[2]   See *Powell v Lloyd* (1827) 1 Y & J 427; *on appeal* (1828) 2 Y & J 372 and *Crosbie v Tooke* (1833) 1 My & K 431. As to the form of such a lease to the trustee, see *Page v Broom* (1842) 6 Jur 308. The trustee is not entitled to specific performance of a lease entered into for the bankrupt's personal accommodation: *Flood v Finlay* (1811) 2 Ball & B 9.
[3]   *Holloway v York* (1877) 25 WR 627.

Pre-emption right

14.75 An assignable right of pre-emption relating to a parcel of land, being both a thing in action and a future, contingent interest incidental to property, is property within the meaning of the IA 1986, s 436[1].

[1]   *Dear v Reeves* [2001] EWCA Civ 277, [2001] 1 BCLC 643.

Licences or similar rights conferred by statutory or other authority

14.76 Where a right to carry on an activity has been conferred on the bankrupt by licence granted pursuant to statutory or other authority, the licence may constitute an item of property which falls within his estate. In the usual case a licence is granted in order to permit the recipient to carry on an activity which is otherwise prohibited. It may therefore be seen as an exemption from that prohibition. As a matter of intuition an exemption might not seem to be an item of property, but licences of this type have been recognised as property within the meaning of the IA 1986. Examples are a licence granted under the Sea Fish (Conservation) Act 1967 in respect of a fishing vessel[1] and a waste management licence granted under the Environmental Protection Act 1990[2]. In *Re Celtic Extraction Ltd* Morritt LJ set out the following features as indicative of when a licence conferring an exemption from some wider statutory prohibition has the status of property: (1) there must be a statutory framework conferring an entitlement on a person who satisfies certain conditions, even though there may be some element of discretion exercisable within that framework; (2) the licence or exemption must be transferable; and (3) the licence or exemption will have some value. But the terms of the statute under which a licence is granted may show that the licence in question does not pass to the licensee's trustee in bankruptcy. Thus in *Re Celtic Extraction Ltd* the Court of Appeal accepted the submission that a liquor licence does not pass to the licensee's trustee in bankruptcy because of the provisions of the Licensing Act 1964, ss 8(1)(c) and 10(5)[3]. For milk quota, see *Swift v Dairywise Farms Ltd*[4].

[1] *Re Rae* [1995] BCC 102.
[2] *Re Celtic Extraction Ltd* [2001] Ch 475, [1999] 4 All ER 684, CA.
[3] See also the Licensing Act 2003, ss 27 and 50.
[4] [2001] 1 BCLC 672.

E PROPERTY EXCLUDED FROM THE ESTATE BY EXPRESS STATUTORY PROVISION

Principles underlying the exclusions

14.77 Although the various forms of property which are excluded from the estate are excluded by specific statutory provision or by implication from the statutory scheme, underlying and justifying the choice of most excluded items is a set of identifiable principles.

(1)   The bankrupt should not by the surrender of his estate to his creditors or by his status as a bankrupt be reduced to a condition below an acceptable standard of living[1]. Hence equipment which he needs in his employment, business or vocation, so he may continue to earn a living, and items necessary to satisfy his basic domestic needs are excluded[2]. Under the old law the bankrupt was entitled to keep from his post-bankruptcy earnings such amount as was sufficient for the maintenance of himself and his family[3]. Similarly, under the IA 1986, income payments orders may not be made which reduce the bankrupt's income below what appears to the court to be necessary for meeting the reasonable domestic needs of the bankrupt and his family[4]. The principle is now being better reflected in relation to pensions by the Welfare Reform and Pensions Act 1999 discussed in paras **14.129**ff below. Another manifestation is the exclusion of student loans.

(2)   A second principle, of closely restricted ambit[5], recognises that certain items of property are so closely personal to the bankrupt that they should not be available to his creditors, such as claims for damages referable to the bankrupt's body, mind or character and not referable to any property and his personal correspondence[6].

(3)   Less a distinct principle than a reflection of the cardinal principle mentioned at the outset of this chapter, that it is the bankrupt's own property which he must surrender to his creditors, property to which the bankrupt holds only the legal, but not the beneficial, title does not fall into the estate.

[1] See *Re Rae* [1995] BCC 102, 111.
[2] IA 1986, s 283(2).
[3] *Re Roberts* [1900] 1 QB 122, CA and see, for a case under the old law reflecting the principle in relation to payments received under a settlement, *Re Ashby, ex p Wreford* [1892] 1 QB 872.

4   IA 1986, s 310(2). See *Re Rayatt* [1998] BPIR 495.
5   See *Cork v Rawlins* [2001] EWCA Civ 197, [2001] 3 WLR 300.
6   *Haig v Aitken* [2001] Ch 110, [2000] 3 All ER 80.

Tools of the bankrupt's trade

14.78 Such tools, books, vehicles and other items of equipment as are necessary to the bankrupt for use personally by him in his employment, business or vocation are excluded from the estate[1]. The same exclusion is made in the Law of Distress Amendment Act 1888, s 4. Examples under that Act of relevant equipment include a cab driver's cab[2] and a piano teacher's piano used for teaching[3]. Where the equipment is no longer in the possession of the bankrupt, it is questionable whether he holds the right to sue for its delivery up or whether that right forms part of his estate[4]. It is submitted that in principle the right to sue should remain in the bankrupt, but as a matter of fact it may be difficult for him to establish the required degree of necessity where the equipment has been out of his possession for any length of time.

1   IA 1986, s 283(2)(a).
2   *Lavell v Richings* [1906] 1 KB 480.
3   *Boyd Ltd v Bilham* [1909] 1 KB 14.
4   *Church of Scientology Advanced Organisation Saint Hill Europe and South Africa v Scott* [1997] BPIR 418, CA, in which the bankrupt failed to establish that the property he claimed, comprising various documents, was necessary for his use in his vocation of counselling.

Necessary domestic items

14.79 Such clothing, bedding[1], furniture, household equipment and provisions as are necessary for satisfying the basic domestic needs of the bankrupt and his family are excluded from the estate[2].

1   *Davis v Harris* [1900] 1 QB 729.
2   IA 1986, s 283(2)(b).

Residential tenancies with statutory security of tenure

14.80 Various contractual tenancies having security of tenure under the Housing Act 1988, the Rent Act 1977, the Rent (Agriculture) Act 1976 and the Housing Act 1985 are excluded from the estate[1]. They are tenancies which, when determined, give rise to a security of tenure personal to the tenant or his statutory successor. The right arising on their termination to that statutory security of tenure does not form part of the estate, because it is not property, and the prior contractual tenancies are excluded in order that the tenant should be in the same position before termination of the contractual tenancy as he is in afterwards[2].

1   IA 1986, s 283(3A).
2   See para **14.71** above.

Pensions

14.81 The bankrupt's entitlement to pension arrangements are or may be excluded from the bankrupt's estate where the bankruptcy commenced after 29 May 2000[1]. The law governing such rights before and after that date is set out in para **14.129**ff below.

[1]   Welfare Reform and Pensions Act 1999, s 11.

Proceeds of Crime Act 2002: restraint orders

14.82 The Proceeds of Crime Act 2002 provides powers for restraining the use of property which is or is suspected of being the proceeds of crime and for confiscating such property. Where, at the time when an individual is made bankrupt, any property is subject to a restraint order made pursuant to ss 41, 120 or 190 of that Act, then that property is excluded from his estate[1]. But if the restraint order is discharged without any order having been made under ss 50, 52, 198 or 200 of that Act, then (save for the proceeds of property realised to meet the receiver's remuneration and expenses) the property excluded from the estate by reason of the restraint order will vest in the trustee as part of the estate[2]. Equally, if property is excluded from the estate because it is subject to a restraint order and then a confiscation order is made which is later discharged or quashed, then (again save for the proceeds of property realised to meet the receiver's or administrator's remuneration and expenses) any property in the hands of the receiver or administrator appointed under the Proceeds of Crime Act 2002 will vest in the trustee in bankruptcy as part of the bankrupt's estate[3].

[1]   Proceeds of Crime Act 2002, s 417(2)(a).
[2]   IA 1986, s 306A.
[3]   IA 1986, s 306C.

Other orders under the Proceeds of Crime Act 2002

14.83 Secondly, if an order is made in respect of any property under a number of other sections of the Proceeds of Crime Act 2002, then that property is also excluded from the bankrupt's estate. Specifically property is excluded from the estate where, in respect of that property:

(a)   an order under ss 50 or 52 is in force;
(b)   an order under s 128(3) is in force; or
(c)   an order under ss 198 or 200 is in force[1].

[1]   Proceeds of Crime Act 2002, s 417(2)(b)–(d).

14.84 A distinction appears to be drawn between property in respect of which an order under one of these sections is in force and property in respect of which a restraint order is made since in the case of restraint orders it is specified that the property is excluded from the estate if the restraint order was made before the bankruptcy order, but no similar condition is applied in relation to the other orders. That would appear to have the effect that if one of those other orders were made after the bankruptcy order, the property to which it related would cease to form part of the estate. However, the following section of the Act, s 418, provides that various powers conferred on the court, including the powers to make orders under all the sections mentioned above, must not be exercised in relation to property which is for the time being comprised in the bankrupt's estate[1]. So, although if such an order were made, it would have the effect of taking the property to which it relates out of the estate, no such order should be made.

[1]   Proceeds of Crime Act 2002, s 418(1), (2) and (3)(a).

14.85   Where property is excluded from the estate because an order under one of these sections is in force in respect of it and a confiscation order is made and then fully paid, any property remaining in the hands of a receiver or administrator appointed under the Proceeds of Crime Act 2002 will vest in the trustee as part of the bankrupt's estate[1]. And, if property is excluded from the estate because one of those orders in force in respect of it and then a confiscation order is made which is later discharged or quashed, then (save for the proceeds of property realised to meet the receiver's or administrator's remuneration and expenses) any property in the hands of the receiver or administrator appointed under the Proceeds of Crime Act 2002 will vest in the trustee in bankruptcy as part of the bankrupt's estate[2].

[1]   IA 1986, s 306B.
[2]   IA 1986, s 306C.

14.86   Similarly, a charging or restraint order made under the Criminal Justice Act 1988 before the commencement of bankruptcy removes the property or the proceeds of realisation from the bankrupt's estate[1].

[1]   Criminal Justice Act 1988, s 84.

Student loans

14.87   Any sum payable to an eligible student by way of a loan and which he receives or is entitled to receive after the commencement of his bankruptcy, whether his entitlement arises before or after the commencement of his bankruptcy, does not form part of his estate and may not be claimed as after-acquired property or made the subject of an income payments order[1].

[1]   Education (Student Support) Regulations 2007, SI 2007/176, reg 91(1)(a).

Property held by the bankrupt on trust for others

14.88   Such property does not fall within the estate[1] since the bankrupt has no beneficial interest in it. This provision is discussed further below at para **14.104ff**.

[1]   IA 1986, s 283(3)(a).

The right of nomination to a vacant ecclesiastical benefice

14.89 This right is excluded from the estate[1].

[1] IA 1986, s 283(3)(b).

F PROPERTY OTHERWISE EXCLUDED FROM THE ESTATE

Personal causes of action and heads of loss

14.90 Certain causes of action do not form part of the estate because they relate to the body, mind or character of the bankrupt and not to his property. These are discussed further at para **19.4ff**. However, if one cause of action gives rise to different heads of loss, some of which are referable to the bankrupt's person such as general damages for pain and suffering in a personal injuries action, but others do not, such as past loss of earnings, the cause of action will vest in the trustee who will hold such part of the judgment or settlement as relates to the head of personal loss on trust for the bankrupt[1]. Such claims are referred to as 'hybrid claims'.

[1] *Ord v Upton* [2000] Ch 352, [2000] 1 All ER 193, CA.

Private letters

14.91 In *Haig v Aitken*[1] the trustee of a former cabinet minister sought directions from the court as to whether he might sell for the benefit of the creditors the bankrupt's personal correspondence. Rattee J held that, on a proper construction of the IA 1986, the bankrupt's estate did not include the bankrupt's personal correspondence which 'like a right of action for libel, is of a nature peculiarly personal to him and his life as a human being'.

[1] [2001] Ch 110, [2000] 3 All ER 80.

Personal goodwill

14.92 Mentioned above is the goodwill of a professional man as a form of property which has been recognised as not falling into the estate[1]. Whether this decision would continue to apply under contemporary conditions must be dubious. But there may be circumstances in which the goodwill or value in a name is so closely related to the person of the bankrupt that it would be impossible to realise either at all or without such co-operation by the bankrupt himself that it should be recognised as something so personal to him that it is excluded from the estate.

[1] *Farr v Pearce* (1818) 3 Madd 74.

Contracts for personal service

14.93 Unexecuted contracts for personal services have been recognised as not passing to the bankrupt's trustee, although, if a sum of money is due in respect of such a contract, it falls within the estate and the trustee is entitled to the money[1].

[1]   *Bailey v Thurston & Co Ltd* [1903] 1 KB 137, CA.

G THE TRUSTEE'S POWER TO CLAIM CERTAIN EXCLUDED PROPERTY FOR THE ESTATE

Claiming certain items of excess value

14.94 Where property is excluded from the estate because it is equipment necessary to the bankrupt for use personally by him in his employment, business or vocation or because it is household equipment or provisions necessary for satisfying the basic domestic needs of the bankrupt and his family[1], but it appears to the trustee that the realisable value of the whole or any part of that property exceeds the cost of a reasonable replacement for that property or that part of it, the trustee may by notice in writing claim that property or that part of it for the bankrupt's estate[2]. Since the trustee has to be aware of what the difference between the value of the property and the cost of its replacement is, he will have to investigate this before serving a notice. Although the phrase 'where ... it appears to the trustee that ...' might indicate a lower standard of investigation than would have been imported by a phrase such as 'if the trustee is satisfied that ...', the trustee ought to be able to justify his opinion[3]. Except with the leave of the court, the notice may not be served after the end of the period of 42 days beginning with the day on which the property in question first came to the knowledge of the trustee[4].

[1]   Such property is excluded by the IA 1986, s 283(2).
[2]   IA 1986, s 308(1).
[3]   See *Re Rayatt* [1998] 2 FLR 264, [1998] BPIR 495, 506.
[4]   IA 1986, s 309(1)(b).

Effect of the notice

14.95 The effect of the notice's being served on the bankrupt is that the property to which it relates vests in the trustee as part of the bankrupt's estate. Except against a purchaser in good faith, for value and without notice of the bankruptcy, the trustee's title to the property relates back to the commencement of the bankruptcy[1]. Such a purchaser takes free of the trustee's claim[2].

[1]   Ie the day on which the bankruptcy order was made: IA 1986, s 278.
[2]   IA 1986, s 308(2).

Third party funds in lieu of claim

14.96 Where a third party proposes to the trustee that the third party should provide the estate with a sum of money enabling the bankrupt to be left in possession of property which would otherwise vest in the trustee by his claiming it for the estate, the trustee may accept the proposal, if he is satisfied that it is a reasonable one and that the estate will benefit to the extent of the value of the property in question less the cost of a reasonable replacement[1].

¹   IR 1986, r 6.188.

Trustee's duty to buy reasonable replacement

14.97 The trustee must apply funds comprised in the estate, ie whatever funds are so comprised, not just those realised by selling the property claimed for the estate, to the purchase by or on behalf of the bankrupt of a reasonable replacement for any property claimed for the estate in this way[1], but he is under no obligation to apply funds to the purchase of a replacement for the property vested in him, unless and until he has sufficient funds in the estate for that purpose[2]. If he has the funds, he may not set off against the sum which he is obliged to spend on buying a replacement item sums otherwise payable by the bankrupt, eg under an income payments order, nor can he retain it in order to recoup expenditure on legal costs[3]. He may purchase the replacement property either before or after realising the value of the property claimed for the estate[4]. This duty on the trustee has priority over his obligation to distribute the estate[5]. Property is a reasonable replacement if it is reasonably adequate for meeting the needs met by the property which has been claimed for the estate[6].

¹   IA 1986, s 308(3).
²   IR 1986, r 6.187(2).
³   *Re Rayatt* [1998] 2 FLR 264, [1998] BPIR 495.
⁴   IR 1986, r 6.187(1).
⁵   IA 1986, s 308(3).
⁶   IA 1986, s 308(4).

Claiming excluded tenancies

14.98 The trustee may claim for the estate any tenancy which is excluded from the estate by virtue of the IA 1986, s 283(3A) and to which the notice relates by serving a notice in writing on the bankrupt[1]. Except with the leave of the court, a notice shall not be served after the end of the period of 42 days beginning with the day on which the tenancy in question first came to the knowledge of the trustee[2].

¹   IA 1986, s 308A.
²   IA 1986, s 309(1)(b).

Effect of the notice

14.99 The effect of the notice's being served on the bankrupt is that the tenancy to which it relates vests in the trustee as part of the bankrupt's estate. Except against a purchaser in good faith, for value and without notice of the bankruptcy, the trustee's title to the tenancy relates back to the commencement of the bankruptcy[1]. Such a purchaser takes free of the trustee's claim[2].

¹   Ie the day on which the bankruptcy order was made, IA 1986, s 278.
²   IA 1986, s 308A.

Realisation

14.100   Once the property or tenancy in question forms part of the estate, the trustee may sell it pursuant to his general power to sell property comprised in the estate.

H PROPERTY WHICH MAY BECOME EXCLUDED FROM THE ESTATE

14.101   Certain categories of property which form part of the estate at the commencement of the bankruptcy may cease to be included within the estate unless steps are taken to ensure that they remain within the estate or if steps are taken to exclude them. These are discussed elsewhere and are mentioned here only by way of cross-reference.

The bankrupt's home

14.102   A dwelling house which at the commencement of the bankruptcy is the sole or principal residence of the bankrupt, his present or former spouse, or his present or former civil partner will automatically cease to be part of the estate at the end of the period of three years beginning with the date of the bankruptcy unless the trustee takes steps within that period to realise or claim the property for the estate¹. This provision is discussed in more detail in the following chapter.

¹   IA 1986, s 283A.

Unapproved pension arrangements

14.103   Unapproved pension arrangements are not excluded from the bankrupt's estate but may become excluded if an exclusion order or qualifying agreement is made with respect to the arrangement in question¹. This topic is discussed in the section on pensions at para **14.129** below.

¹   Welfare Reform and Pensions Act 1999, s 12 and the Occupational and Personal Pension Schemes (Bankruptcy) (No 2) Regulations 2002, SI 2002/836, regs 4–6.

I PROPERTY HELD ON TRUST BY THE BANKRUPT FOR OTHERS

14.104   Any property which the bankrupt holds on trust for another person or persons does not fall within his estate¹. For, since the beneficial interest does not belong to the bankrupt, it is not property which, according to the general principles of bankruptcy law, could be divisible amongst his creditors². The principle applies to any type of trust whether express, resulting, implied or constructive. For example, moneys held on a solicitor's client account do not fall within his estate on his bankruptcy[3], and where, in a commercial context, an individual agrees to hold funds separately for another, then, unless the arrangement constitutes an assignment of book debts void against the individual's trustee, a valid trust of the funds will be established[4].

1   IA 1986, s 283(3)(a). See *Roberts v Nunn* [2004] BPIR 623.
2   See *Boddington v Castelli* (1853) 1 E & B 879.
3   *Re a Solicitor* [1952] Ch 328, [1952] 1 All ER 33.
4   See *Re Chelsea Cloisters Ltd* (1980) 41 PC & R 98, CA; *Re Kayford Ltd* [1975] 1 All ER 604, [1975] 1 WLR 279; *Re Multi Guarantee Co Ltd* [1987] BCLC 257, CA; *Re Branston & Gothard Ltd* [1999] 1 All ER (Comm) 289, [1999] BPIR 466.

14.105 Where a bankrupt holds property on trust for himself and for other persons, his own beneficial interest falls within his estate[1].

1   See *Carvalho v Burn* (1833) 4 B & Ad 382 at 393; *affd sub nom Burn v Carvalho* (1834) 1 Ad & El 883.

The bankrupt as a personal representative

14.106 Property held by the bankrupt as executor or administrator is property held on trust within the meaning of the bankruptcy legislation. Thus an executor who carries on the trade of his testator under testamentary directions is personally liable for debts so incurred, but has a right to be indemnified out of the testator's assets[1]. He has a lien on the assets of the business, which lien passes on bankruptcy to his trustee[2]. If the executor is in default, he is not entitled to an indemnity, except on the terms of making good his default, and his creditors will be in no better position[3]. If one of several executors is in default, the executors who are not in default are entitled to an indemnity[4].

1   *Dowse v Gorton* [1891] AC 190, HL.
2   *Jennings v Mather* [1902] 1 KB 1, CA (trustee under creditors' deed).
3   *Re Johnson, Shearman v Robinson* (1880) 15 Ch D 548.
4   *Re Frith, Newton v Rolfe* [1902] 1 Ch 342.

Funds advanced for a special purpose

14.107 Where money is advanced to the bankrupt for a special purpose, he holds the funds clothed with a specific trust and title to the money does not pass to his trustee. The funds are held on a primary trust under which they must be applied for the purpose for which they have been advanced or, if they cannot be so applied, the beneficial interest in them reverts, under a secondary, resulting trust to the person who advanced them to the bankrupt[1]. The secondary trust is a resulting trust because it arises on the failure of the primary trust in circumstances in which there is no provision for what should happen to the beneficial interest in the relevant funds. Funds may be impressed with such a trust where they are advanced to the bankrupt for the purpose of paying one or more creditors[2]. If the purpose has not failed, the person who advanced the funds may enforce the carrying out of the special purpose under the primary trust against the trustee[3].

1   *Toovey v Milne* (1819) 2 B & Ald 683; *Barclays Bank Ltd v Quistclose Investments Ltd* [1970] AC 567, [1968] 3 All ER 651, HL; *Re EVTR, Gilbert v Barber* [1987] BCLC 646, CA.

2   *Re Angerstein, ex p Angerstein* (1874) 9 Ch App 479; *Re Rogers, ex p Holland v Hannen* (1891) 8 Morr 243, CA; *Re Drucker, ex p Basden* [1902] 2 KB 237; *Re Gothenburg Commercial Co* (1881) 44 LT 166, CA; *Re Watson, ex p Schipper* (1912) 107 LT 783, CA; *Bank of Scotland v Macleod* [1914] AC 311 (debenture, agreed to be assigned by company, held not to be treated as trust property but part of insolvent company's assets); *Re Hooley, ex p Trustee* (1915) 84 LJKB 1415.

3   *Carreras Rothmans Ltd v Freeman Mathews Treasure Ltd* [1985] Ch 207, [1985] 1 All ER 155.

Funds held by an agent on behalf of his principal

14.108 Where an agent holds funds on behalf of his principal which he is obliged to hold separately from his own funds, then such funds are held on trust for his principal[1]. If, on the agent's bankruptcy, the funds remain separate from the bankrupt's agent's other funds, they will not form part of his estate. The difficult question which usually arises in a commercial context is whether there is such an obligation or not[2].

1   *Henry v Hammond* [1913] 2 KB 515.

2   *Neste Oy v Lloyds Bank (The Tiiskeri, Nestegas and Enskeri)* [1983] 2 Lloyd's Rep 658; *Re Japan Leasing (Europe) Ltd* [1999] BPIR 911.

Funds received by an individual on the brink of bankruptcy

14.109 Where an individual receives funds when he knows that he is unable to pay his debts and that, in consequence of his immediate and inevitable bankruptcy, there will be a total failure of consideration in respect of the payment of those funds or that they otherwise represent a windfall, then, if he retains the funds at the commencement of the bankruptcy, they will be held subject to a constructive trust in favour of the person who transferred the funds to him and therefore will not fall within the estate[1]. The cases in which this principle has been recognised and applied have involved corporate insolvencies in which the point at which the insolvent company decides that it is insolvent will tend to be more clear-cut because the decision that the company is insolvent may be taken by the board and the time of such an explicit decision is easier to identify. But, in appropriate circumstances the principle would seem equally applicable to individuals.

1   *Neste Oy v Lloyds Bank (The Tiiskeri, Nestegas and Enskeri)* [1983] 2 Lloyd's Rep 658; *Re Japan Leasing (Europe) Ltd* [1999] BPIR 911.

J ATTEMPTS TO EXCLUDE PROPERTY FROM THE ESTATE

An individual cannot prevent property held by him from falling into his estate

14.110 'The owner of property cannot by contract or otherwise, qualify his own interest in property by a condition determining or controlling it in the event of his own bankruptcy to the disappointment or delay of his creditors', wrote Mr Swanston in a note to *Wilson v Greenwood*[1] in which he collected some of the principal authorities then applicable to the point. Such conditions are void against the trustee in bankruptcy.

[1]   (1818) 1 Swan 471 at 481. Phillimore J uses the same language to express the principle in *Re Johnson Johnson, ex p Matthews & Wilkinson v Johnson Johnson* [1904] 1 KB 134.

The intention of the parties

14.111   Although the fact that the parties, when agreeing the deprivation provision, did not intend to disadvantage creditors on bankruptcy is not a factor which will validate the provision, the presence of such an intention may lead the court to find void a deprivation which would otherwise have been valid[1].

[1]   *British Eagle International Airlines Ltd v Cie Nationale Air France* [1975] 2 All ER 390, [1975] 1 WLR 758, 780; *Money Markets International Stockbrokers Ltd v London Stock Exchange Ltd* [2002] 1 WLR 1151, para 101.

Contract

14.112   As a general rule, parties cannot agree by contract that in the event of the bankruptcy of one of them, property belonging to him will pass to or become secured in favour of the other[1]. Such an agreement is void because the parties attempt by it to take out of the estate of the bankrupt property which should be available as part of that estate for the general body of his unsecured creditors. Thus, in *Re Jeavons, ex p Brown, Re Jeavons, ex p Mackay*[2] Jeavons sold a patent to Brown & Co in respect of which Brown & Co agreed to pay royalties to Jeavons. At the same time Jeavons borrowed £12,500 from Brown & Co which was to be repaid by Brown & Co's retaining one-half of the royalties and such sums as might become due from Brown & Co for work done for them by Jeavons. However, it was further agreed that if Jeavons became bankrupt, the whole of the royalties might be retained by Brown & Co. On Jeavons' insolvency Brown & Co claimed a charge on the whole of the royalties but were challenged by Jeavons' trustee, Mackay. The Court of Appeal in Chancery held that Brown & Co were only entitled to a charge on half of the royalties and the further agreement as to their taking the other half on Jeavons' bankruptcy was ineffective. Sir George Mellish LJ expressed the rule in these terms: 'A person cannot make it part of his contract that, in the event of bankruptcy, he is then to get some additional advantage which prevents the property being distributed under the bankruptcy laws'[3]. Similarly a provision in articles of association that a bankrupt member of a company should sell his shares at a price lower than that which would obtain if he were selling when solvent will be void as repugnant to the bankruptcy laws[4]. A provision providing for sale at a fair price would be valid. This, in the context of a partnership, was the question which fell to be decided by Lord Eldon in *Wilson v Greenwood*[5]. He upheld a clause in the partnership deed providing that on a member of the firm's becoming bankrupt, that member's share would be sold to the remaining members. Since the insolvent member had contracted to receive a proper price, the argument that the clause was void and that there should be a general dissolution failed.

1   *Re Harrison, ex p Jay* (1880) 14 Ch D 19.
2   (1873) 8 Ch App 643.
3   For further examples, see *Re Johns, Worrell v Johns* [1928] 1 Ch 737; *British Eagle International Airlines Ltd v Air France* [1975] 2 All ER 390, [1975] 1 WLR 758, HL.
4   *Borland's Trustee v Steel Bros & Co Ltd* [1901] 1 Ch 279.
5   (1818) 1 Swan 471.

14.113 There are further grounds on which a contractual provision depriving the debtor of an asset on his bankruptcy may be found valid. Thus, in *Money Markets International Stockbrokers Ltd v London Stock Exchange Ltd*[1] the claimant company was deprived of its share in the defendant on going into liquidation pursuant to the defendant's articles of association. The deprivation was held to be valid on the basis that the share was not capable of uncontrolled transfer and was linked to a right, membership of the exchange, which was legitimately determined on insolvency.

1   [2001] 4 All ER 223, [2002] 1 WLR 1151.

Leases

14.114 A clause in a lease providing for forfeiture on bankruptcy is valid[1].

1   *Money Markets International Stockbrokers Ltd v London Stock Exchange Ltd* [2001] 4 All ER 223, [2002] 1 WLR 1151, para 90.

Settlements

14.115 Equally, a person cannot settle his own property on himself with a gift over on his bankruptcy. An attempt to do so is void against his trustee, who will take the property free from the gift over[1]. Thus a person may not settle his own property on himself as the principal beneficiary under a statutory protective trust[2] but a person may settle his own property on a discretionary trust under which he is one among a plurality of beneficiaries. Unless the settlement may be impugned as a transaction at an undervalue or a sham or for some other reason over and above the mere fact of the settlement, it is valid against the settlor's trustee in bankruptcy[3].

1   *Higginbotham v Holme* (1803) 19 Ves 88; *Lester v Garland* (1832) 5 Sim 205; *Re Moon, ex p Danes* (1886) 17 QBD 275; *Re Detmold, Detmold v Detmold* (1889) 40 Ch D 585. An exception was made under the old law relating to married women's property to the effect that if the husband and wife both brought property into a marriage settlement, a trust of the income arising from the wife's property in favour of the husband until his bankruptcy was effective, but a similar trust of the husband's own property was bad; see *Mackintosh v Pogose* [1895] 1 Ch 505.
2   See the Trustee Act 1925, s 33(3).
3   *Holmes v Penney* (1856) 3 K & J 90. And see *Twopeny v Peyton* (1840) 10 Sim 487 and *Re Gulbenkian's Settlement Trusts (No 2), Stevens v Maun* [1970] Ch 408, [1969] 2 All ER 1173.

Validity of conditions against alienation outside bankruptcy

14.116 However, bankruptcy apart, a condition determining an interest in property on an attempted alienation is not void as between the individual and the person who takes on the determination. So, if an event determining the interest under the condition has occurred before the bankruptcy, the gift over will take effect and this prevents the relevant interest from forming part of the estate on the subsequent bankruptcy of the individual whose interest was forfeit, whether the effect is to vest the property in some other person absolutely[1] or in trustees on discretionary trusts[2]. This would appear simply to reflect the fact that if, before bankruptcy, the bankrupt has disposed of an interest in property, it will no longer form part of his estate (subject to the trustee's power to apply to set aside transactions at an undervalue). But if the clause providing for the determination provides for determination on the happening of a number of different events and the first to occur is the bankruptcy of the settlor holding the defeasible interest, his trustee will take that interest on the basis that it is incapable of further forfeiture because it will be considered as having been forfeited against the settlor and so the condition will be treated as having no further operation[3].

1   *Re Detmold, Detmold v Detmold* (1889) 40 Ch D 585.
2   *Re Johnson Johnson, ex p Matthews & Wilkinson v Johnson Johnson* [1904] 1 KB 134.
3   *Re Burroughs-Fowler, Trustee of the Property of Burroughs-Fowler (a bankrupt) v Burroughs-Fowler* [1916] 2 Ch 251.

Rule against spendthrift trusts or similar arrangements

14.117 'Trusts in which the interest of a beneficiary cannot be assigned by him or reached by his creditors have come to be known as "spendthrift trusts" '[1]. In English law, an owner of property cannot settle property on another on terms that the property is inalienable, even though the beneficiary is an individual and the purpose of the trust is to provide for his maintenance. For it is contrary to the policy of the law that property should be settled so as to continue in the enjoyment of the bankrupt notwithstanding his bankruptcy[2].

1   *Scott on Trusts* (4th edn), para 151.
2   *Brandon v Robinson* (1811) 1 Rose 197; *Graves v Dolphin* (1826) 1 Sim 66; *Davidson v Chalmers* (1864) 33 LJ Ch 622; *Re Fitzgerald, Surman v Fitzgerald* [1904] 1 Ch 573, CA.

Circumvention by choice of foreign law?

14.118 Under art 6 of the Convention on the Law Applicable to Trusts and Their Recognition[1], a trust is to be governed by the law chosen by the settlor. Since trusts under which the beneficiary's interest is inalienable are recognised in various foreign jurisdictions, in particular various of the United States[2], this appears to open the possibility of a settlor choosing a system of law which permits property to be settled on terms preventing its being reached by creditors. But this is likely to fail either because art 6 goes on to provide that where the law chosen does not provide for the category of trust involved, the choice shall not be effective or because art 18 provides that the provisions of the Convention may be disregarded when their application would be manifestly incompatible with public order.

¹ Which, save for certain articles, is given the force of law by the Recognition of Trusts Act 1987.
² *Scott on Trusts* (4th edn), paras 151 and 152; *Nichols v Eaton* 91 US 716 (1875); *Broadway National Bank v Adams* (1882) 133 Mass 170.

Determinable interests

14.119 One person, A, may settle his property on another person, B, on terms that the interest should determine on B's bankruptcy or B's attempted alienation of the property and that there be a gift over to another or other persons in such event¹. So long as the terms on which the property is settled are construed as conferring on the bankrupt an interest which determines on the occurrence of the relevant event they will be valid and, on his bankruptcy or other attempt to alienate the interest, the bankrupt's interest will determine and whatever gift over or further disposition was made by the settlement will take effect. But, if a particular interest, for example a life interest, is settled on the bankrupt subject to a condition or proviso for forfeiture on bankruptcy or alienation, the condition will be void against his trustee and on his bankruptcy the life interest will form part of his estate. The reason for the distinction is that 'property cannot be given for life any more than absolutely, without the power of alienation being incident to the gift; and that any mere attempt to restrict the power of alienation, whether applied to an absolute interest or to a life-estate, is void, as being inconsistent with the interest given.'

¹ *Brandon v Robinson* (1811) 18 Ves 429; *Rochford v Hackman* (1852) 9 Hare 475; *Re Ashby, ex p Wreford* [1892] 1 QB 872; *Re Leach, Leach v Leach* [1912] 2 Ch 422; *Kemble v Hicks* [1998] PLR 141 (Rattee J).

Forfeiture of future interests

14.120 However, where a future interest is settled on an individual subject to a condition that it be forfeit if, before it falls into possession, the beneficiary should attempt to alienate it or become bankrupt, the condition will be valid¹. But if a forfeiture clause purports to apply both to interests in possession (whether the relevant such interest is an absolute interest or a life interest or other limited interest) and to future interests, it will be wholly void, even with respect to its application to future interests (as to which it would have been valid) if it had been expressed as being applicable solely to such interests². As discussed below in connection with pensions, forfeiture clauses have been used to prevent an individual's interest in a pension scheme from falling into his estate, but statute has now rendered such clauses no longer effective for that purpose³.

¹ *Churchill v Marks* (1844) 1 Coll 441; *Re Porter, Coulson v Capper* [1892] 3 Ch 481; *Re Forder, Forder v Forder* [1927] 2 Ch 291; *Kemble v Hicks* [1998] PLR 141; *Re Walker, Public Trustee v Walker* [1939] Ch 974, [1939] 3 All ER 902. Where there is no gift over, a proviso for forfeiture may be rendered ineffective; *Bird v Johnson* (1854) 18 Jur 976.

2   *Re Smith, Smith v Smith* [1916] 1 Ch 369; *Kemble v Hicks* [1998] PLR 141.
3   See para **14.138**.

Shams

14.121 An act done or a document executed is a sham if it is done or executed by the parties to the 'sham' with the intention of giving to third parties or the court the appearance of creating between the parties legal rights and obligations different from the actual legal rights and obligations (if any) which the parties intended to create[1]. A settlement, apparently valid, may in truth be a sham because both the settlor and the trustee subjectively intended at the time the settlement was established (or later came to share the intention) that the deed was not to have effect[2]. If the settlement is a sham, the assets apparently subject to it will remain the settlor's and so form part of his estate.

1   *Snook v London and West Ridings Investments Ltd* [1967] 2 QB 786, 802 (Diplock LJ). See also *Vooght v Hoath* [2002] BPIR 1047 and *Re Yates* [2005] BPIR 476.
2   *Shalson v Russo* [2003] EWHC 1637 (Ch), [2005] Ch 281, [2005] 2 WLR 1213.

K DISCRETIONARY AND PROTECTIVE TRUSTS

14.122 Where the bankrupt is beneficially interested under a trust, his interest will vest in his trustee, whether it is a present or future interest or vested or contingent. However, save that a person cannot settle property of his own on protective trusts where he is the principal beneficiary[1], it is possible to use discretionary trusts and protective trusts to settle assets so that they may be or become available to a person while remaining shielded from his creditors.

1   As defined in the statutory protective trusts provided for by the Trustee Act 1925, s 33.

Discretionary trusts

14.123 Where the trust is a discretionary trust, meaning that the property is held on trust by the trustees to be applied for the benefit of the members of a class of beneficiaries as the trustees think fit, the beneficiary does not have a proprietary interest under the trust[1]. He merely has the right to ensure that the trustees exercise their discretion, even though that exercise may not result in any distribution to him. Thus, unless the trustees choose to make a distribution to him, there is no interest which may pass to his trustee in bankruptcy. This is so even where the settlor has settled property on a discretionary trust under which he is a member of the class of beneficiaries[2].

1   *Gartside v IRC* [1968] AC 553, [1967] 2 All ER 173, HL.
2   *Twopeny v Peyton* (1840) 10 Sim 487; *Holmes v Penney* (1856) 3 K & J 90; *Re Coleman, Henry v Strong* (1888) 39 Ch D 443, CA, and see *Re Gulbenkian's Settlement Trusts (No 2), Stevens v Maun* [1970] Ch 408, [1969] 2 All ER 1173.

14.124 If a distribution is made to the bankrupt, it may be that the nature of the payment is such that it would constitute income within the meaning of the

IA 1986, s 310 and so the trustee would only be able to claim it for the estate by seeking an income payments order, in which case if the bankrupt had no other income he would retain such part of the payment as the court considered necessary for meeting his and his family's reasonable domestic needs. Under the old law, when after-acquired property was vested automatically in the trustee, a bankrupt beneficiary receiving such payments under a trust was only required to account to his trustee for the excess over what he required for his maintenance[1].

1   *Re Ashby, ex p Wreford* [1892] 1 QB 872.

14.125 Where the class of possible beneficiaries consists only of the bankrupt, his trustee in bankruptcy may require the property held under the trust to be transferred to him in full[1].

1   *Re Smith, Public Trustee v Aspinall* [1928] Ch 915. Contrast *Twopeny v Peyton* (1840) 10 Sim 487 where there was a sole beneficiary entitled to receive income during his life, but the trustees had a discretion whether to pay him the whole or part of the income.

Protective trusts

14.126 A more sophisticated device to prevent trust property from passing to a trustee in bankruptcy is the protective trust. The protective trust takes advantage of the validity of determinable interests in order to protect the trust property against the creditors of the beneficiary. It does so by establishing an interest vested in the beneficiary, determinable upon his death or after some earlier fixed period or upon an attempted alienation, which is followed in the event of its determination, by a discretionary trust. Thus there is never any interest which can vest in the original beneficiary's trustee in bankruptcy.

14.127 An instrument may create a protective trust by directing that income be held on protective trusts for the benefit of a beneficiary for his life or a lesser period, in which case the income will be held on the statutory protective trusts set out in the Trustee Act 1925, s 33(1). The form of trust provided there is based on the trusts which had previously been expressly provided for by conveyances. In summary, by the Trustee Act 1925, s 33(1), it is implied that:

(a)   the property is held for the beneficiary on trust for the trust period or until he does or attempts to do or suffers any act or thing whereby he would be deprived of the trust income;

(b)   if the trust fails or determines during the subsistence of the trust period, the income is held on trust to be applied as the trustees think fit for the maintenance or support of:

   (i)   the beneficiary, his spouse, children or more remote issue, or

   (ii)   where he has no spouse or issue, the beneficiary and those persons who would be entitled if he were actually dead.

14.128 The rule that a settlor cannot create by his own settlement an interest in favour of himself determinable on his bankruptcy is not affected by this provision[1].

1   Trustee Act 1925, s 33(3).

L PENSIONS

14.129 Whether a bankrupt's pension rights should form part of his estate or are or should be excluded from it has been an area of debate and the subject of statutory intervention. The debate has been resolved in favour of excluding a bankrupt's pension from his bankruptcy estate and thereby protecting his pension from the impact of his bankruptcy. But, first, his trustee may be able to claim for the estate, by an income payments order, income payments made to the bankrupt pursuant to the pension arrangement or, by a claim for after-acquired property any lump sum so paid and secondly, if the contributions to the pension arrangement made before the bankruptcy were excessive, then they may be claimed for the benefit of the estate.

14.130 In this section is discussed, first the general position as to the impact of bankruptcy on pension rights, secondly the impact of the Welfare Reform and Pensions Act 1999 on that position and finally applications for income payments orders relating to payments made under a pension scheme.

Outline of varieties of pension arrangements

14.131 Provision for old age may be made by a variety of arrangements[1]. For present purposes, three categories may be identified:

(1)   occupational pension schemes which are established by an employer for the purpose of providing pensions for its employees[2]; under such schemes an employee for whose benefit the pension is provided is usually referred to as an active member of the scheme;

(2)   personal pension arrangements made by individuals with pension providers; the principal examples of which are: personal pension schemes under which employees make arrangements with a pension provider; personal pensions schemes under which self-employed persons may make similar arrangements; and retirement annuity contracts; in such cases the pension provider will ordinarily be an institution such as a life office[3];

(3)   statutory schemes for public service employees and other state pensions.

This section is concerned with pensions in the first and second categories.

1   For the purposes of the Finance Act 2004 which deals with registration of pension schemes s 152 of that Act defines the meaning of 'arrangement'.
2   The Finance Act 2004, s 150 defines the main concepts for Part 4 of that Act. An occupational pension scheme is defined as 'a pension scheme established by an employer or employers and having or capable of having effect so as to provide benefits to or in respect of any or all of the employees of (a) that employer or those employers, or (b) any other

employer (whether or not it also has or is capable of having effect so as to provide benefits to or in respect of other persons)'; see Finance Act 2004, s 150(5).

3   For a statutory definition see the Pension Schemes Act 1993, s 1 (as amended) defining a personal pension scheme as: 'any scheme or arrangement which is comprised in one or more instruments or agreements and which has, or is capable of having, effect so as to provide benefits, in the form of pensions or otherwise, payable on death or retirement to or in respect of earners (whether employed or self-employed) who have made arrangements with the trustees or managers of the scheme for them to become members of it'.

Questions arising in the context of bankruptcy

14.132 Two main questions arise where an individual who has made pension arrangements is made bankrupt:

(1)   Does the pension arrangement constitute property which falls within his estate?[1]

(2)   Can payments arising pursuant to such pension arrangement be claimed for the estate under an income payments order or in the case of lump sum payments as after-acquired property?[2]

1   See paras **14.134–14.156.**
2   See paras **14.157–14.159.**

14.133 The second question only arises where the answer to the first is No, since if the rights fall into the estate, they will carry with them the right to receive any payment accruing in respect of the pension.

The first question: do an individual's pension arrangements fall within his estate?

14.134 Before the measures made by the Welfare Reform and Pensions Act 1999 came into force, the position had been reached that, in general, pension arrangements did fall within the bankrupt's estate. It was held, in the case of retirement annuity contracts and personal pension schemes for the self-employed, that the rights to a pension under the arrangement had the status of property and were therefore capable of falling within the estate. In *Re Landau (a bankrupt), Pointer v Landau*[1] Ferris J held that a bankrupt solicitor's retirement annuity contract was a thing in action capable of falling within the estate. And in *Krasner v Dennison*[2] in the Court of Appeal, that ruling was not challenged and was regarded as applicable also to personal pension schemes entered into by the two bankrupts concerned who had been self-employed. There seems no reason to think that the position would be different in the case of personal pension schemes entered into by employees.

1   [1998] Ch 223, [1997] 3 All ER 322.
2   [2001] Ch 76, [2000] 3 All ER 234, CA.

14.135 As to occupational pension schemes, it was sometimes suggested that members did not have any property interest under such schemes. A possible ground for this suggestion was the rights held by a member depended on the terms of the scheme and those terms might be such as to provide the member with something less than an enforceable right. But where the scheme conferred enforceable rights on a member, then those rights would form a chose in action with the status of property within the wide meaning of that word which applies in bankruptcy. Thus in *Jones v Patel*[1] the bankrupt's rights under an occupational pension scheme operated by a local authority by whom he had formerly been employed were held to constitute property. It may be that, where it was said that the bankrupt member had no property under such a scheme which fell into his estate, the point being made was not that the member's rights under the scheme did not, considered in isolation, have the status of property but that, although they did have such status, nevertheless under the terms usual to such schemes they were subject to forfeiture by reference to the member's bankruptcy or other attempted alienation occurring where that occurred before any payment or benefit became payable under the scheme. Accordingly the important question was whether such rights may legitimately be forfeited, before the payments or benefits to which the rights relate become payable. As is discussed below, statute has intervened to prohibit such forfeiture.

[1] [1999] BPIR 509, upheld on appeal [2002] BPIR 919. Also *Rowe v Saunders* [2003] BPIR 847, a non-assignable annuity arising in respect of an occupational pension automatically vested in the bankrupt's estate and could not be subject to the income payments order regime.

14.136 An attempt to argue that the difference between the treatment formerly accorded to personal pension schemes and that accorded to occupational pension schemes breached art 14 of the European Convention on Human Rights failed before the Court of Appeal[1].

[1] *Malcolm v Benedict Mackenzie (a firm)* [2004] EWCA Civ 1748, [2005] ICR 611, [2005] BPIR 176.

Guaranteed minimum pension and protected rights payments

14.137 A person may be entitled under an occupational pension scheme to a guaranteed minimum pension or to payments giving effect to protected rights under such a scheme. Where his entitlement is in respect of his or another person's service in employment which was contracted-out by reference to the scheme, then any assignment of or charge on, or agreement to assign or charge, that pension or those payments is void[1]. On the bankruptcy of a person entitled to such a pension or payments, nothing passes to his trustee the assignment of which is rendered void by the foregoing provision[2]. Nor may the trustee obtain an income payments order in respect of payments by way of guaranteed minimum pension or giving effect to a bankrupt's protected rights[3]. This exclusion is unaffected by the Welfare Reform and Pensions Act 1999.

[1] Pension Schemes Act 1993, s 159(1).
[2] Pension Schemes Act 1993, s 159(5)(a).
[3] IA 1986, s 310(7)–(9).

Forfeiture of pension rights on alienation or bankruptcy

14.138 As a matter of general law, a future interest may be forfeited by bankruptcy or an attempted alienation before it falls into possession. Until the time when they fall due to be paid or fulfilled, the rights to the payments or benefits which active members hold under an occupational pension scheme are future interests and so provision could be made that these rights be forfeit on bankruptcy and in such case the trustees of the scheme have a discretion to make payments to the bankrupt member. So long as the provision related only to future interests, it used to be effective[1]. However, the prohibition on forfeiture of rights under an occupational pension scheme imposed by the Pensions Act 1995, s 92(1) now applies so as to prevent forfeiture on bankruptcy[2].

1   *Kemble v Hicks* [1998] PLR 141.
2   Before 6 April 2002, the Pensions Act 1995, s 92(2)(b) exempted from that prohibition forfeitures which occurred by reference to the bankruptcy of the person entitled to the pension. That exemption was repealed by the Welfare Reform and Pensions Act 1999, s 14(3) with effect from 6 April 2002: see the Welfare Reform and Pensions Act 1999 (Commencement No 13) Order 2002, SI 2002/153.

14.139 Where the forfeiture occurred before 6 April 2002, any pension which was or would but for the forfeiture have become payable may, if the trustees or managers of the scheme so determine, be paid to all or any of the following:

(a)   the member of the scheme to or in respect of whom the pension was or would have become payable;
(b)   the spouse, widow or widower of the member;
(c)   any dependant of the member; and
(d)   any other person falling within a class prescribed by regulations[1].

1   Pensions Act 1995, s 92(3).

14.140 Draftsmen have included similar provisions in personal pension schemes and retirement annuity contracts. In part their purpose in doing so was to ensure that the relevant contract complied with the requirement of the applicable Taxes Act that the contract should not be assignable[1]. However, in relation to retirement annuity contracts and personal pensions schemes, such clauses have been found by the courts to be ineffective against the trustee in bankruptcy of the individual with rights under them. In *Re Landau (a bankrupt), Pointer v Landau*[2] Ferris J held, as a matter of construction, that a clause providing for forfeiture on assignment did not take effect in relation to the statutory vesting of property in the trustee in bankruptcy on his appointment. Chadwick LJ, in *Krasner v Dennison*[3], concerned with personal pension schemes for the self-employed as well as retirement annuity contracts, did not overrule Ferris J's reasons but preferred to put the point on the wider footing 'that an attempt to provide, by contract, that benefits will be inalienable on a bankruptcy must fail on grounds of public policy'[4].

1   See the Income and Corporation Taxes Act 1970, s 226 and the Income and Corporation Taxes Act 1988, s 620(2), the latter having been repealed as of 6 April 2006 by the Finance Act 2004, s 326.
2   [1998] Ch 223, [1997] 3 All ER 322.

3   [2001] Ch 76, [2000] 3 WLR 720
4   [2000] 3 WLR 720 at para 49.

14.141 In the case of *Malcolm v Benedict Mackenzie (a firm)*[1], where the bankruptcy had commenced in December 1996 and so the provisions of the Welfare Reform and Pensions Act 1999 were not in play, it was argued that the different approach to forfeiture provisions between those contained in occupational pension schemes available to employees and those contained in the contractually founded pension arrangement made by a bankrupt who was formerly self-employed breached the bankrupt's Convention rights. The contention was that there was an unjustified differentiation between the two cases thereby breaching art 14. The Court of Appeal held that the differential treatment was not a difference of treatment based on discrimination on the ground of status or any other ground, but arose because contractual pension rights fell within the description of property for the purposes of IA 1986 and the rights of a beneficiary under an occupational pension scheme, after forfeiture on bankruptcy, did not fall within that description.

1   [2004] EWCA Civ 1748, [2005] ICR 611, [2005] BPIR 176.

The impact of the Welfare Reform and Pensions Act 1999

14.142 In summary the changes made by the Welfare Reform and Pensions Act 1999 are as follows:

(1)   If a pension arrangement is an approved pension arrangement, it is excluded from the bankrupt's estate. In relation to personal pension arrangements, this overturns the effect of the decisions in *Re Landau* and *Krasner v Dennison* and, in the case of occupational pension schemes renders it unnecessary to rely on any forfeiture provision (were it still possible to do so)[1].

(2)   If a pension arrangement is an unapproved pension arrangement and certain other conditions are met, then the bankrupt may apply for an order that it be excluded from his estate or may make an agreement to that effect with his trustee[2].

(3)   Where the pension arrangement is excluded from the estate, the trustee may recover for the estate payments made into the arrangement by the bankrupt where those payments have unfairly prejudiced his creditors[3]. The trustee's power to seek recovery of excessive payments is not discussed in this chapter but in **Chapter 20**.

1   Welfare Reform and Pensions Act 1999, s 11.
2   Welfare Reform and Pensions Act 1999, s 12 and Occupational and Personal Pension Schemes (Bankruptcy) (No 2) Regulations 2002, SI 2002/836.
3   IA 1986, s 342A.

Pension arrangements which are automatically excluded from the estate

14.143 Where a bankruptcy order is made against a person on a petition presented on or after 29 May 2000, any rights of his under an approved pension arrangement are excluded from his estate.

Approved pension arrangements

14.144 The Welfare Reform and Pensions Act 1999, s 11(2) defines 'approved pension arrangement' as follows:

(a)   a pension scheme registered under the Finance Act 2004, s 153;
(b)   an occupational pension scheme set up by a government outside the United Kingdom for the benefit, or primary benefit, of its employees[1];
(c)   an annuity purchased for the purpose of giving effect to rights under a scheme falling within any of paragraph (a) including an annuity in payment before 6 April 2006, giving effect to rights under any scheme approved (i) before that date under Chapters 1, 3 or 4 of Part 14 of the Income and Corporation Taxes Act 1988; or (ii) any relevant statutory scheme, as defined in s 611 of that Act;
(d)   any pension arrangements of any description which may be prescribed by regulations made by the Secretary of State.

[1]   'Occupational pension scheme' has the meaning given in the Finance Act 2004, s 150(5): Welfare Reform and Pensions Act 1999, s 11(11)(a).

14.145 The Secretary of State has prescribed that certain other pension arrangements should be approved by the Occupational and Personal Pension Schemes (Bankruptcy) (No 2) Regulations 2002, reg 2.

Provisions relating to changes to the registration of schemes

14.146 Provision is made to cover the case where the Revenue have declined to register a pension scheme but an appeal against that decision is pending. In such a case, if the appeal fails and so the scheme remains unregistered, the rights of the bankrupt under the scheme vest in his trustee immediately on the decision of the General or Special Commissioners or, if later, on the appointment of the trustee[1]. If the appeal succeeds, then the scheme will be registered and so will be an approved scheme within the Welfare Reform and Pensions Act 1999, s 11(2)(a) and thereby excluded from the estate.

[1]   Welfare Reform and Pensions Act 1999, s 11(4) and (5).

14.147 It is possible for the registration of a scheme to be revoked and provision is also made to cover this situation. In this case, the bankrupt's rights under the scheme vest in his trustee immediately on the Revenue's giving notice withdrawing the registration of the scheme or, if later, the appointment of the trustee[1].

[1]   Welfare Reform and Pensions Act 1999, s 11(6) and (7).

14.148 Where any rights vest in a person's trustee in bankruptcy either because an appeal against the Revenue's decision not to register a scheme fails or because the Revenue give notice that registration has been withdrawn, the trustee's title to those rights has relation back to the commencement of that person's bankruptcy. But where any transaction is entered into by the trustees or managers of the scheme in question in good faith and without notice of the decision on the appeal by the General or Special Commissioners or, as the case may be, of the notice of withdrawal of the registration, the trustee in bankruptcy is not entitled by virtue of the provision relating his title back to the commencement of the bankruptcy to any remedy against them or any person whose title to any property derives from them[1].

1   Welfare Reform and Pensions Act 1999, s 11(9).

14.149 If the bankrupt's rights under a pension scheme have vested in his trustee because the Commissioners have decided not to register the scheme or have withdrawn registration, it may be that the bankrupt will be able to seek an order, or make an agreement with his trustee, that the rights should not form part of his estate under the provisions to be made by regulations in respect of unapproved pension arrangements, reference to which is made in the next paragraph

Pension arrangements which may be excluded from the estate by order or agreement

14.150 By the Welfare Reform and Pensions Act 1999, s 12[1] the Secretary of State may make regulations providing for, or in connection with, enabling rights of a person under an unapproved pension arrangement to be excluded, in the event of a bankruptcy order being made against that person, from his estate for the purposes of the IA 1986, Pts VIII–XI. Those regulations are contained in the Occupational and Personal Pension Schemes (Bankruptcy) (No 2) Regulations 2002[2].

1   Brought into force on 6 April 2002.
2   SI 2002/836.

Unapproved pension arrangement

14.151 An unapproved pension arrangement is not simply a residual category of pension arrangements which are not approved. To be an unapproved pension arrangement, the arrangement in question must first fall within (i) the Finance Act 2004, s 157, (ii) paragraphs 52 to 57 of Sch 36 to that Act, or (iii) the Income Tax (Earnings and Pensions) Act 2003, s 393A. Secondly, it must be (1) established under an irrevocable trust or a contract, agreement or arrangement made with the bankrupt; (2) have as its sole primary purpose the provision of relevant benefits; and (3) be the bankrupt's sole pension arrangements or his main means of pension provision (other than a pension under Part II of the Social Security Contributions and Benefits Act 1992 or the equivalent Act for Northern Ireland)[1].

1   Occupational and Personal Pension Schemes (Bankruptcy) (No 2) Regulations 2002, SI 2002/836, reg 3(2).

Exclusion order

14.152 A bankrupt may apply to the court for an order excluding an unapproved pension arrangement from his estate. The bankrupt's application to the court for an exclusion order must be made either (i) within 13 weeks of the date of the estate vesting in the trustee under IA 1986, s 306 or, if later, the date when the bankrupt's rights under the scheme vested in his trustee in bankruptcy on the deregistration of the pension scheme, or (ii) within 30 days of the revocation of a qualifying agreement which the bankrupt has made with his trustee. These time periods may be extended before or after expiry upon good cause being shown. Upon such an application the court must consider the future likely needs of the bankrupt and his family and any benefits which are likely to be received by virtue of rights of the bankrupt which have already accrued under any pension arrangements at the date of the application for the exclusion order and the extent to which those benefits appear likely to be adequate for meeting the bankrupt's future likely needs and those of his family[1].

[1] Occupational and Personal Pension Schemes (Bankruptcy) (No 2) Regulations 2002, SI 2002/836, regs 4(a) and 5.

Qualifying agreement

14.153 A qualifying agreement is an agreement made between the bankrupt and his trustee for the purpose of excluding the bankrupt's rights under an unapproved pension arrangement from his estate[1]. It must be made by deed and must incorporate all the terms which have been expressly agreed[2]. The trustee must inform the person responsible for the pension arrangement that the qualifying agreement has been made within the period of 30 days beginning with the date on which the agreement was made[3]. The person responsible means the trustees, managers or provider of the arrangement or the persons having functions in relation to the arrangement corresponding to those of a trustee, manager or provider.

[1] Occupational and Personal Pension Schemes (Bankruptcy) (No 2) Regulations 2002, SI 2002/836, reg 4(b).
[2] Occupational and Personal Pension Schemes (Bankruptcy) (No 2) Regulations 2002, SI 2002/836, reg 6(2).
[3] Occupational and Personal Pension Schemes (Bankruptcy) (No 2) Regulations 2002, SI 2002/836, reg 6(5) and see IA 1986, s 342C(6) for the definition of the person responsible for the pension arrangement.

14.154 The time limit within which a qualifying agreement must be made is nine weeks from the date when the estate vested in the trustee under IA 1986, s 306 or, if later, the date when the bankrupt's rights under the scheme vested in his trustee in bankruptcy on the deregistration of the pension scheme[1]. No provision is made for the extension of the nine-week period; so if the agreement is not made by the end of that period, the bankrupt must apply for an exclusion order within the four weeks remaining of the 13-week period in which such application may be made. It would appear that the application will have to be pursued to a hearing because a compromise would be in effect a qualifying agreement and since the time to make such an agreement would have expired, none could be made.

¹   Occupational and Personal Pension Schemes (Bankruptcy) (No 2) Regulations 2002, SI 2002/836, reg 6(1).

Revocation of a qualifying agreement

14.155   The trustee in bankruptcy is able to revoke the qualifying agreement if the bankrupt has failed to make full disclosure of all material facts and has failed to do so in order to obtain an exclusion of pension rights which would not otherwise be excluded. The notice of revocation must (a) be dated, (b) be in writing, (c) specify the reasons for revocation of the qualifying agreement, (d) specify the date on which the agreement shall be revoked, not before 30 days after the date of the notice has expired, and (e) inform the bankrupt that he has a right to apply for an exclusion order within 30 days from the date of the notice[1]. The trustee must also notify the responsible person that the qualifying agreement has been revoked within the period of 30 days beginning with the date of the notice of revocation[2].

¹   Occupational and Personal Pension Schemes (Bankruptcy) (No 2) Regulations 2002, SI 2002/836, reg 6(3) and (4).
²   Occupational and Personal Pension Schemes (Bankruptcy) (No 2) Regulations 2002, SI 2002/836, reg 6(5) and see IA 1986, s 342C(6) for the definition of the person responsible for the pension arrangement.

Right to information from the person responsible for the pension arrangement

14.156   The trustee in bankruptcy may request information from the person responsible for a pension arrangement in connection with the making of an exclusion order and the bankrupt may request information from that person either in connection with the making of an exclusion order or for or in connection with the making of a qualifying agreement. The request must be complied with within a period of nine weeks beginning with the date on which it is received or such later period as the court may, for good cause, allow[1]. Since there is only a nine-week period within which a qualifying agreement may be made, this right to obtain information may be provided too late to assist a bankrupt.

¹   Occupational and Personal Pension Schemes (Bankruptcy) (No 2) Regulations 2002, SI 2002/836, reg 10 and IA 1986, s 342C(6) for the definition of the person responsible for the pension arrangement.

Income payments order

14.157   An income payments order may not be made unless the bankrupt's income exceeds a level which appears to the court to be necessary for meeting the reasonable needs of the bankrupt and his family. In deciding whether to make such an order the court has to make an assessment of what the bankrupt's income is in order to see whether it exceeds the relevant level. For this purpose, the bankrupt's income includes any payment under a pension scheme notwithstanding anything in the Welfare Reform and Pensions Act 1999, ss 11 and 12[1] subject to the exclusion, discussed below, of certain protected minimum payments. So, even if the pension arrangement is or could be excluded from the estate, payments arising under it will be taken into account by the court when assessing the bankrupt's income for the purpose of deciding whether to make an income payments order. Like the answer to the first question, save for certain minimum payments mentioned in the following paragraph, the law governing the question whether payments arising pursuant to pension arrangements can be claimed for the estate under an income payments order depends on whether the bankruptcy commenced before 29 May 2000 or on or after that date.

[1]   IA 1986, s 310(7).

Guaranteed minimum pension and protected rights payments

14.158   As mentioned above, a person may be entitled under an occupational pension scheme to a guaranteed minimum pension or to payments giving effect to protected rights under such a scheme. Such sums are excluded from the definition of income in the IA 1986, s 310[1]. So these payments may not be taken into account by the court for the purpose of assessing the bankrupt's income when it is considering whether to make an income payments order.

[1]   IA 1986, s 310(7)–(9).

Lump sums

14.159   The definition of income for the purposes of the trustee's power to seek income payments orders was amended by the Pensions Act 1995[1] to include 'any payment under a pension scheme' except for the minimum payments mentioned in para **14.158** above. Read literally, those words would seem to encompass any payment of a lump sum which may be payable under the pension scheme either at the election of the person entitled to the pension rights or otherwise. On that basis a trustee should claim such sum, if it becomes payable to the bankrupt, by seeking an income payments order. But it may be better to read the phrase as meaning 'any payment in the nature of income under a pension scheme'. On that basis, if a lump sum is paid, it should be claimed as after-acquired property.

[1]   Pensions Act 1995, s 122 and Sch 3, para 15 with effect from 6 April 1997.

M PROPERTY BELONGING TO THE BANKRUPT HELD AS SECURITY FOR DEBTS

Trustee takes subject to security interest

14.160   Where an individual has validly created a security interest over property which is comprised in his estate, his trustee in bankruptcy takes the property on its vesting in him subject to the rights of the secured creditor[1]. The trustee should consider whether by creating the security, the individual gave a preference to the secured creditor[2].

[1] IA 1986, s 283(5). *Re Caine's Mortgage Trusts* [1918] WN 370.
[2] Under the IA 1986, s 340.

N AFTER-ACQUIRED PROPERTY

Trustee's power to claim after-acquired property

14.161 Property may be acquired by or be devolved upon the bankrupt after the commencement of his bankruptcy. Subject to certain exclusions, the trustee may by notice in writing claim such property for the estate[1]. Except with the leave of the court, a notice claiming after-acquired property for the estate may not be served after the end of the period of 42 days beginning with the day on which it first came to the knowledge of the trustee that the property in question had been acquired by or had devolved upon the bankrupt[2]. Good reason is required if the court is to extend time[3].

[1] IA 1986, s 307(1).
[2] IA 1986, s 309(1)(a). After offering guidelines on an application by a trustee for permission to serve a notice out of time, the court refused to permit a s 307 notice to be served out of time in *Solomons v Williams* [2001] BPIR 1123.
[3] *Franses v Oomerjee* [2005] BPIR 1320.

Excluded property

14.162 The trustee may not serve a notice claiming for the estate in respect of:

(a) any property falling within the IA 1986, s 283(2) and (3), ie equipment necessary to the bankrupt for use personally by him in his employment, business or vocation; household equipment and provisions necessary for satisfying the basic domestic needs of the bankrupt and his family; property held by the bankrupt on trust for any other person; or the right of nomination to a vacant ecclesiastical benefice;

(b) any interest in a dwelling house which has vested in the bankrupt by virtue of IA 1986, s 283A;

(c) any property which by virtue of any other enactment is excluded from the estate; examples include property excluded because of orders made under the Proceeds of Crime Act 2002[1], student loans[2], approved pension arrangements and unapproved pension arrangements which are the subject of an exclusion order or a qualifying agreement[3];

(d) save under a condition imposed in a conditional order of discharge made under the IA 1986, s 280(2)(c), any property which is acquired by or devolves upon the bankrupt after his discharge[4];

(e) any property which may be the subject of an income payments order under the IA 1986, s 310[5].

[1] See paras **14.82–14.86**.
[2] See para **14.87**.

14.163 As mentioned above[1], some property is excluded from the estate although no express exclusion is provided for by the IA 1986 or any other enactment, eg damages referable solely to the bankrupt's mind, body or character and not referable to any property belonging to him. It is submitted that, since such property is excluded from the estate if it belongs to the bankrupt at the commencement of the bankruptcy, it ought also to be exempt from being claimed as after-acquired property. For example, the money awarded in respect of his injuries to the bankrupt by the Criminal Injuries Compensation Board after the commencement of the bankruptcy ought not to be claimable as after-acquired property[2].

1   See para **14.90**ff above.
2   Cf *Re Campbell (a bankrupt)* [1997] Ch 14, [1996] 2 All ER 537.

Bankrupt's duty of disclosure

14.164 Where at any time after the commencement of the bankruptcy any property is acquired by or devolves upon the bankrupt or there is an increase in his income, the bankrupt must give the trustee notice of the property or, as the case may be of the increase[1]. The notice must be given within 21 days of the bankrupt's becoming aware of the relevant facts[2]. The property to which this duty relates is not confined to property which the trustee may claim for the estate. Hence the bankrupt must disclose any property he acquires and the trustee will then be able to decide whether he is entitled to claim the property. If the bankrupt disagrees with the trustee's decision, he may apply to the court under the IA 1986, s 303(1), unless the trustee makes an application for an income payments order, in which case the bankrupt may seek to resist that application. Failure by a bankrupt without reasonable excuse to comply with the duty of disclosure is a contempt of court and may be punished accordingly (in addition to any other punishment to which he may be subject).

1   IA 1986, s 333(2).
2   IR 1986, r 6.200.

Limited duty in respect of business activity

14.165 Where the bankrupt carries on a business, he remains under the duty[1] to inform the trustee that he has acquired property after the commencement of his bankruptcy, but the duty to inform the trustee by notice within 21 days of acquisition and the restrictions on disposal, mentioned below, do not apply to property acquired by the bankrupt in the ordinary course of a business carried on by him[2]. Instead, a bankrupt who carries on a business must, not less often than six-monthly, furnish to the trustee information with respect to it, showing the total of goods bought and sold (or, as the case may be, services supplied) and the profit or loss arising from the business[3].

1   Imposed by the IA 1986, s 333(2).

2   IR 1986, r 6.200(4).
3   IR 1986, r 6.200(5).

Effect of the trustee's notice

14.166 The effect of service on the bankrupt of the trustee's notice claiming the property for the estate is that the property to which it relates vests in the trustee as part of the bankrupt's estate. Subject to the protection afforded to purchasers and bankers acting in good faith mentioned below, the trustee's title to the property relates back to the date when the property was acquired by or devolved upon the bankrupt[1].

1   IA 1986, s 307(3).

Restriction on disposal of after-acquired property by the bankrupt

14.167 The bankrupt may not dispose of any after-acquired property of which he has given notice to the trustee within the period of 42 days beginning with the date of the notice unless the trustee consents[1]. It is implicit that the bankrupt should not dispose of any after-acquired property before informing the trustee that he has acquired it.

1   IR 1986, r 6.200(2).

Consequences of wrongful disposal

14.168 If the bankrupt does dispose of property before giving notice of its acquisition to the trustee or, without the trustee's consent, before the end of the 42-day period just mentioned, a duty is imposed on the bankrupt forthwith to disclose to the trustee the name and address of the disponee and to provide any other information which may be necessary to enable the trustee to trace the property and recover it for the estate[1]. Where the bankrupt has wrongfully disposed of property, the trustee may serve a notice on the disponee claiming the property as part of the estate by virtue of the IA 1986, s 307(3)[2]. Service of the notice will have the effect of causing title to the property to vest in the trustee with effect from the date when the property was acquired by or devolved upon the bankrupt. The trustee must serve the notice within 28 days of becoming aware of the disponee's identity and an address at which he can be served[3]. The trustee may have to bring proceedings in order to recover the property disposed of from the disponee, but it would appear that it is necessary for him to have served a notice on the disponee within the period just mentioned as a preliminary step. This is implicit from the mandatory requirement that the notice be served within that period. There is no specific provision enabling the court to extend time for the service of such a notice, but the trustee will be able to rely on the general provision contained in the IA 1986, s 376.

1   IR 1986, r 6.200(3).
2   IR 1986, r 6.201(1).
3   IR 1986, r 6.201(2).

Purchasers and bankers acting in good faith

14.169 Where, before or after the trustee serves a notice claiming after-acquired property for the estate, a person acquires property in good faith, for value and without notice of the bankruptcy or a banker enters into a transaction in good faith and with such notice, the trustee is not in respect of that property entitled, by virtue of his right to claim after-acquired property, to any remedy against that person or banker or against any person whose title derives from that person or banker[1].

[1]   IA 1986, s 307(4).

Expenses

14.170 Any expenses incurred by the trustee in acquiring title to after-acquired property shall be paid out of the estate in the prescribed order of priority[1].

[1]   IR 1986, r 6.202.

O INCOME RECEIVED BY THE BANKRUPT AND INCOME PAYMENT ORDERS AND AGREEMENTS

Trustee's power to apply for an income payments order

14.171 The trustee may apply to the court for an order claiming for the bankrupt's estate so much of the bankrupt's income during the period for which the order is in force as may be specified in the order[1]. Such an order is referred to as an income payments order. Sums received by the trustee under an income payments order form part of the estate.

[1]   IA 1986, s 310(1) and (1A)(a).

Bankrupt's duty to disclose an increase in income

14.172 Where at any time after the commencement of the bankruptcy there is an increase in his income, the bankrupt must give the trustee notice of the increase[1]. The notice must be given within 21 days of the bankrupt's becoming aware of the relevant facts[2]. Whether there has been an increase depends on a comparison with some earlier level of income which must be the level of income which the bankrupt was receiving at the commencement of the bankruptcy. That should have been disclosed in the statement of affairs which, in the case of a bankruptcy order made on a creditor's petition, would have been submitted within 21 days after the commencement of the bankruptcy[3] and, in the case of an order on a debtor's petition, would have accompanied the petition[4].

[1]   IA 1986, s 333(2).
[2]   IR 1986, r 6.200.
[3]   IA 1986, s 288(1) and IR 1986, r 6.59.
[4]   IA 1986, s 272(2) and IR 1986, r 6.41 and r 6.68.

Income

14.173 For the purposes of an application for an income payments order, the bankrupt's income comprises every payment in the nature of income which is from time to time made to him or to which he from time to time becomes entitled, including any payment in respect of the carrying on of any business[1] or in respect of any office or employment and any payment under a pension scheme except payments by way of guaranteed minimum pension and payments giving effect to the bankrupt's protected rights as a member of a pension scheme[2]. Under the Bankruptcy Acts income has been held to mean income of the same genus as a salary[3]. This should be taken as an indicative, rather, than exhaustive, definition although it is submitted that the cases under the old law are of some assistance in exemplifying what may count as income. 'Income' in the IA 1986, s 310 does not have the same meaning as the word bears in distinguishing income from capital in the context of a trust under which a life tenant is to receive the income; nor does it have the same meaning as it bears in tax law[4]. In *Supperstone v Lloyd's Names Working Party*[5] Evans-Lombe J held, obiter, that the phrase 'from time to time' meant the same as 'at any time' and that a single payment might be income.

[1] In *Papanicola v Humphreys* [2005] EWHC 335 (Ch), [2005] 2 All ER 418 it was held that the income generated by a restaurant run by the bankrupt had always belonged to the estate and never to the bankrupt as the bankrupt had merely been acting as an agent when running the business.
[2] See paras **14.157** and **14.158**.
[3] *Re Huggins, ex p Huggins* (1882) 21 Ch D 85, CA; *Re Hutton, ex p Benwell* (1884) 14 QBD 301, CA; *Re Shine, ex p Shine* [1892] 1 QB 522, CA; *Hollinshead v Hazleton* [1916] 1 AC 428, HL; *Re Landau, ex p Trustee* [1934] Ch 549, CA; *Re Tennant's Application* [1956] 1 All ER 425, [1956] 1 WLR 128, CA; affd [1956] 1 WLR 874.
[4] *Re Cohen (a Bankrupt), ex p the Bankrupt v the Trustee of the Property of the Bankrupt* [1961] 1 All ER 646, [1961] Ch 246, CA.
[5] [1999] BPIR 832.

Bankrupt's reasonable domestic needs

14.174 The court shall not make an income payments order the effect of which would be to reduce the income of the bankrupt below what appears to the court to be necessary for meeting the reasonable domestic needs of the bankrupt and his family[1]. This reflects the principle mentioned at para **14.77** above in relation to the exclusion from his estate of the equipment necessary to his work, that a bankrupt should not be reduced by the surrender of his assets and his status to below an acceptable basic standard of living. What that standard should be depends on all the circumstances of the case. In *Re Rayatt*[2] where the question arose whether expenditure on the bankrupt's daughter's education was necessary to meet the reasonable needs of the bankrupt or his family, the deputy judge held that it was, taking particular account of the evidence given by the girl's headmistress. In *Boyden v Watson*[3] the court refused to make an income payments order in a case where the bankrupt's reasonable expenditure exceeded his income and only a nominal payment could be made, which, in any event, would not benefit creditors in any way.

[1] IA 1986, s 310(2).

2   [1988] 2 FLR 264, [1998] BPIR 495. Followed in *Scott v Davis* [2003] BPIR 1009.
3   [2004] BPIR 1131 (a decision of a district judge).

14.175 In assessing the amount of the bankrupt's income, the court must take into account any payments which the bankrupt is receiving by way of guaranteed minimum pension or such as give effect to his protected rights as a member of a pension scheme. These forms of payment are defined by reference to the Pension Schemes Act 1993 and have been mentioned at para **14.157** and **14.158** above.

Liability to tax

14.176 A bankrupt will be liable to tax on his income. Provision should be made in the income payments order to ensure that sufficient sum is kept aside to pay such tax[1].

1   See *Green v Satsangi* [1998] BPIR 55 where such provision was not made.

Time limit

14.177 An application for an income payments order must be instituted before the discharge of the bankrupt[1]. Unless extended because of the bankrupt's failure to comply with his obligations under the Insolvency Act 1986, the discharge will occur at the end of one year beginning with the date of the bankruptcy order[2]. So ordinarily the trustee must make any application within one year of the bankruptcy order.

1   IA 1986, s 310(1A)(b).
2   IA 1986, s 279(1), (3) and (4).

Period to which an income payments order may relate

14.178 An income payments order must specify the period during which it is to have effect. Although that period may extend beyond the discharge of the bankrupt, it may not end after the period of three years beginning with the date on which the order is made[1].

1   IA 1986, s 310(6).

Content of the order

14.179 An income payments order shall, in respect of any payment of income to which it is to apply, either (a) require the bankrupt to pay to the trustee an amount equal to so much of that payment as is claimed by the order, or (b) require the person making the payment to pay so much of it as is so claimed to the trustee, instead of the bankrupt. The court may, where it makes an income payments order, discharge or vary any attachment of earnings order that is for the time being in force to secure payments by the bankrupt[1].

1   IA 1986, s 310(4).

Procedure

14.180 Where the trustee applies for an income payments order, the court must fix a venue for the hearing. Notice of the application and venue must be sent by the trustee to the bankrupt at least 28 days before the day fixed for the hearing, together with a copy of the trustee's application and a short statement of the grounds on which it is made. The notice must inform the bankrupt that, unless at least seven days before the day fixed for the hearing he sends to the court and to the trustee written consent to an order being made in the terms sought, he is required to attend the hearing and that if he attends he will be given an opportunity to show cause why the order should not be made or, if made, not in the terms sought by the trustee[1]. If the trustee seeks an order against a person making the payments to the bankrupt, the trustee should not serve the notice of application on that person. For the person making the payments has no interest in the question whether an income payments order should be made and, if the order that he should make any payments to the trustee is inappropriate, he is given an opportunity to raise this after the order is made[2].

1   IR 1986, r 6.189.
2   IR 1986, r 6.192(3).

Implementation of the order

14.181 If an order is made by the court, the trustee must forthwith send a sealed copy to the bankrupt and, if an order is made in terms that the person paying the income should pay it to the trustee, the trustee must also send a copy to that person[1]. Where a person receives notice that an income payments order has been made requiring him to make payments specified in the order to the bankrupt's trustee instead of the bankrupt, he must make the arrangements requisite for immediate compliance with the order[2]. He may deduct the appropriate fee, set at 50 pence[3], towards the clerical and administrative costs of complying with the order and he must give a statement to the bankrupt of any amount deducted by him in that respect[4]. If a person receives notice of an income payments order imposing on him a requirement to make payments to the trustee of sums otherwise payable or said to be payable to the bankrupt and he is then no longer liable to make to the bankrupt any payment of income or having made payments in compliance with the order, he ceases to be so liable, he must forthwith give notice of that fact to the trustee[5]. Although it is not expressly provided for, if he has never been liable to make such payments and is not at the time of receiving notice of the order, it seems sensible that he should likewise inform the trustee immediately.

1   IR 1986, r 6.190.
2   IR 1986, r 6.192(1).
3   IR 1986, r 13.11.

⁴   IR 1986, r 6.192(2).
⁵   IR 1986, r 6.192(3).

14.182   An income payments order made in terms that the bankrupt pay the required sums to the trustee may be varied, if the bankrupt does not comply with it, so as to require the person paying the income to the bankrupt to pay the required amount to the trustee[1].

¹   IR 1986, r 6.191.

Variation or discharge of order

14.183   Where an income payments order is in force, either the trustee or the bankrupt may apply to the court for the order to be varied or discharged[1]. A variation cannot extend the period during which the order is to remain effective beyond the period of three years beginning with the date on which the original order was made[2]. Where the bankrupt makes the application he must accompany it with a short statement of the grounds on which it is made[3].

¹   IA 1986, s 310(6A) and IR 1986, r 6.193(1).
²   IA 1986, s 310(6A).
³   IR 1986, r 6.193(3).

Income payments agreements

14.184   IA 1986, s 310A enables income payments agreements to be made between the bankrupt and his trustee or between the bankrupt and the official receiver thereby avoiding the need to apply to the court. Such agreements must be in writing and may provide that the bankrupt should pay to the trustee or official receiver a specified part or proportion of his income for a specified period or that a third person is to pay to the trustee or the official receiver a specified proportion of money due to the bankrupt by way of income for a specified period[1]. Income has the same meaning in this context as it does for the purpose of income payments orders. Sums received pursuant to the agreement form part of the bankrupt's estate[2].

¹   IA 1986, s 310A(1).
²   IA 1986, s 310A(4).

Time limit

14.185   Like income payments orders, income payments agreements may only be made before the bankrupt is discharged[1].

¹   IR 1986, r 6.193A(1).

Period to which an income payments order may relate

14.186 An income payments agreement must specify the period during which it is to have effect. Although that period may extend beyond the discharge of the bankrupt, it may not end after the period of three years beginning with the date on which the order is made[1].

[1]   IA 1986, s 310A(5).

Making an income payments agreement

14.187 Income payments agreements must be made in writing. The trustee or official receiver should prepare the draft agreement and provide it to the bankrupt for his approval. The bankrupt must respond within 14 days from the date when the draft agreement was sent or such longer period as may have been specified by the trustee or official receiver, either, if he has decided to approve the draft agreement, by signing and returning it or, if he has decided not to approve it, by notifying the trustee or official receiver in writing of his decision. Where the bankrupt has signed and returned the draft agreement, the trustee or official receiver should on receiving it, sign and date it and send a copy to the bankrupt. The agreement comes into force when the trustee or official receiver signs and dates it. Where the agreement requires a third party to make payments to the trustee or official receiver, the trustee or official receiver should send notice of the agreement to the third party containing the prescribed information. The third party is entitled to deduct the appropriate fee of 50 pence towards his clerical and administrative costs of compliance[1].

[1]   IR 1986, r 6.193B; r 13.11 specifies the amount of the third party's fee.

Variation

14.188 An income payments agreement may be varied by agreement in writing between the parties or by the court on an application made by the trustee, official receiver or the bankrupt. The court cannot vary the agreement so as to include a provision which could not be contained in an income payments order but must grant an application to vary the agreement where it considers it necessary to avoid the result that the income of the bankrupt is reduced below what appears to the court to be necessary for meeting the reasonable domestic needs of the bankrupt and his family[1].

[1]   IA 1986, s 310A(6) and (7). IR 1986, r 6.193C provides for the procedure to be followed on applications for orders varying the terms of an income payments agreement.

Enforcement

14.189 A provision of an income payments agreement may be enforced as if it were a provision of an income payments order.

Chapter 15

THE BANKRUPT'S HOME

A Introduction
B Ascertaining the bankrupt's beneficial interest
C Property adjustment orders in family proceedings
D Gifts and other voidable transactions
E Orders for sale
F Orders for possession
G Charge on the dwelling house
H Period within which the trustee must claim the home for the estate
I Property abroad

A INTRODUCTION

15.1 In many bankruptcies the house that provides the bankrupt with his home will be the principal asset in the estate available for realisation and distribution among the creditors. In recognition of the special nature of a person's home, a number of provisions in the Insolvency Act 1986 ('IA 1986') restrict the trustee's ability to take possession of and sell the property which forms that home. This chapter focuses on those provisions. In various ways, they impose rules limiting the power of the trustee to realise the bankrupt's proprietary interest in his home or requiring the court to address the interests of others whose home the property also is. Before discussing these provisions, two other topics are considered: first, what beneficial interest does the bankrupt hold in the property? This question is primarily one within the field of the law of property and the approach to it is discussed here only in outline. Secondly, where the relationship between the bankrupt and his spouse or civil partner has broken down, a property adjustment order may have been made in the ensuing proceedings for financial relief; how do such orders impinge on the trustee's ability to claim the property for the estate?

Definitions of the bankrupt's home

15.2 Various definitions are employed in the Insolvency Act 1986 for the purpose of defining the bankrupt's home[1]. The central elements are that the

592

property should be a dwelling house and that it should be occupied at the relevant time by the bankrupt or certain members of his family as a residence.

1   See IA 1986, ss 283A(1), 313, 335A(2)(b) and 337(1).

B ASCERTAINING THE BANKRUPT'S BENEFICIAL INTEREST

15.3 Any property belonging to the bankrupt at the commencement of the bankruptcy falls into the bankrupt's estate. But, since property which the bankrupt holds on trust for another person does not fall within his estate, the important question is, what is the beneficial interest held by the bankrupt in his home? This is easily answered where an express declaration of trust has been made evidenced in writing and signed by the person or persons able to declare it but frequently the parties may only have made an informal arrangement or no clear arrangement at all. Since the decisions of the House of Lords in *Pettit v Pettit*[1] and *Gissing v Gissing*[2], a complicated jurisprudence has burgeoned, regulating such arrangements by use of constructive and resulting trusts. The following paragraphs seek only to summarise the current law. Ascertaining what the bankrupt's share is involves the same process of analysis of property rights whether the bankrupt is married, party to a civil partnership or cohabiting outside marriage or civil partnership.

1   [1970] AC 777, [1969] 2 All ER 385, HL.
2   [1971] AC 886, [1970] 2 All ER 780, HL.

Sole ownership

15.4 In the simplest case, the property occupied by the bankrupt as his home is owned solely by him at law and in equity. In such a case, the whole property falls into the estate; the legal title to it will vest in the trustee and an entry may be made in the proprietorship register at the Land Registry to reflect this. Although ownership may thus be acquired by the trustee, there may still be rights of occupation held by a spouse or civil partner who has no proprietary interest in the property and the court must take those rights of occupation into account before giving the trustee possession of the property so as to be able to realise it. Those rights of occupation are discussed later.

15.5 Where the bankrupt is the sole legal owner, he may nonetheless hold the property on trust for himself and his spouse, civil partner or partner (or, indeed, some other person). If that trust is established by writing signed by the bankrupt in fulfilment of the requirements of form imposed by the Law of Property Act 1925, s 53(1)(b), then, absent any question of fraud or mistake, there will be no further issue as to the existence of the trust or the rights established under it[1]. Since the trust may involve an element of bounty from the bankrupt to the other beneficiary, the trustee should consider whether he may set the trust aside as a transaction at an undervalue under IA 1986, ss 339 or 423.

1   *Goodman v Gallant* [1986] Fam 106, [1986] 1 All ER 311, CA.

15.6   The bankrupt's home

15.6 Even where there is no formally effective express trust, the spouse, civil partner or partner of the bankrupt may be able to establish that he or she has acquired a beneficial interest under a constructive trust to which the requirement of writing does not apply[1]. The circumstances in which a trust of this sort may arise are discussed below.

[1]   Law of Property Act 1925, s 53(2).

Co-ownership

15.7 Frequently the bankrupt's spouse, civil partner or partner will not only share the occupation of the property bought for the purpose of forming their home but also its ownership. Where the legal ownership is shared, the co-owners will hold the property as legal joint tenants[1]. As legal joint tenants, they necessarily hold the property on trust, almost invariably in the case of a jointly occupied home, for themselves. Where the terms of the trust have been established expressly in writing signed by both parties, then, absent fraud or mistake, those terms will govern the matter. But, if there is no express trust satisfying the requirement of writing, then, although the existence of the trust and the identity of the beneficiaries may be clear by virtue of the joint legal ownership, dispute may yet break out over the quantification of the shares held by those beneficiaries.

[1]   Law of Property Act 1925, ss 1(6), 34 and 36.

Determining the beneficial ownership where there is no express declaration of trust: onus on claimant seeking to show that beneficial ownership differs from legal ownership

15.8 Where there is no express declaration of trust, the starting point is that the equitable or beneficial interests in the property will follow the legal title. So, if the legal title is held solely by the bankrupt, then the starting point is that he holds the entire beneficial interest. Equally if the legal title is vested jointly in the bankrupt and his spouse, civil partner or partner, then the starting point is that they hold as beneficial joint tenants and, on severance, as beneficial tenants in common in equal shares. The onus lies on the spouse, civil partner or partner to establish that the beneficial interest is held on terms which differ from the legal ownership[1].

[1]   *Stack v Dowden* [2007] UKHL 17, [2007] 2 All ER 929, [2007] 2 WLR 831 at [56].

Where the legal title is held solely by one party: establishing that the beneficial interest is to be shared

15.9 Since the decision of the House of Lords in *Lloyds Bank v Rosset*[1], cases where the legal title is held solely by one party but the other party claims a beneficial interest have been divided into two classes. The first class comprises those cases where, at any time before acquisition or exceptionally at some later date, there has been an agreement, arrangement or understanding reached between the parties that the property is to be shared beneficially. Such understanding must be based on express discussion. Once it is found that there was such agreement, arrangement or understanding, then the party claiming the beneficial interest against the party holding the legal title need only show that he or she has acted to his or her detriment or significantly altered his or her position in reliance on the agreement in order to give rise to a constructive trust. Payment by the claiming party of money towards the purchase of the property will clearly suffice; but so will substantial contributions of money towards the general household expenditure[2] and physical work undertaken to improve the property[3].

1   [1991] 1 AC 107, HL at 132–133.
2   *Grant v Edwards* [1986] Ch 638, CA.
3   *Eves v Eves* [1975] 1 WLR 1338, CA.

15.10 The second class embraces those cases where there is no evidence to support a finding of an agreement or arrangement to share the beneficial interest. The approach to cases of this sort is bedevilled by the necessary judicial insistence that the court is not simply imposing a fair solution but is vindicating subsisting property rights. In *Lloyds Bank v Rosset*[1] Lord Bridge said that in this situation direct contributions to the purchase price by the claiming party, whether initially or by payment of mortgage instalments, would readily justify the inference necessary to the creation of a constructive trust but that it was extremely doubtful whether anything less would do. The inference he was referring to enfolded both elements of such a trust in this context: that the parties intended to share the beneficial interest and that the party claiming an interest against the party entitled to the legal title had acted to his or her detriment in reliance on that common intention. Lord Bridge's approach has been criticised as unduly restrictive, particularly so in cases where the parties in a long-term relationship have both contributed to the family expenditure but only the party entitled to the legal title has made direct financial contributions to the purchase of the family home. A more relaxed view has been signalled in *Stack v Dowden*[2] but without describing what sort of steps taken by the claiming party would fall within the envisaged wider range and thereby suffice to draw the required inferences.

1   [1991] 1 AC 107, [1990] 1 All ER 1111, HL.
2   [2007] UKHL 17, [2007] 2 All ER 929, [2007] 2 WLR 831 at [26] and [63].

Where the legal title is held solely by one party: quantifying the other party's beneficial interest

15.11 Once it is established that the parties intended that both should have a beneficial share in the property even though legal title was transferred only to one of them, the second question to be answered is what the extent is of the parties' respective beneficial interests in the property[1]. Where there is an express agreement or arrangement which, having been sufficiently acted on, forms the basis of the constructive trust, that agreement or arrangement may provide the answer. But it may not; nor, where there is no such agreement or arrangement, will anything have been agreed or arranged which supplies the quantification. In such cases, the answer must be gathered by undertaking a survey of the whole course of dealing between the parties and taking account of all conduct which throws light on the question what shares were intended.

¹   *Oxley v Hiscock* [2004] EWCA Civ 546, [2005] Fam 211, [2004] 3 All ER 703 at [69].

Where the legal title is held jointly by both parties: establishing that the beneficial interest is shared

15.12 Since equity follows the law, where two parties are entitled to the property as legal joint tenants, the normal inference will be they hold the beneficial interest as beneficial joint tenants. Thus in such a case, the common intention to share the beneficial interest will be readily inferred.

Where the legal title is held jointly by both parties: quantifying the other party's beneficial interest

15.13 In *Stack v Dowden*¹ it was held that the usual inference to be drawn from a transfer of a property into the parties' joint names will be that the parties intended that they should hold as beneficial joint tenants even where their contributions to the purchase are unequal; that the burden will lie on the party claiming that the intention was to hold in unequal shares; and that cases where joint legal owners are to be taken to have intended that their beneficial interests should differ from their legal interests will be very unusual. As it happened, on its facts, *Stack v Dowden* was one of those unusual cases. The principal feature identified as being unusual was that the unmarried parties, over a long relationship during which they had four children together, maintained a rigid separation between their finances. In consequence, it could be inferred that they did not intend their shares to be equal and that since Ms Dowden was the higher earner and had contributed more to the purchase, the decision of the Court of Appeal to divide the proceeds of sale in the ratio 65% to Ms Dowden and 35% to Mr Stack was upheld by the House of Lords.

¹   [2007] UKHL 17, [2007] 2 All ER 929, [2007] 2 WLR 831.

Severance

15.14 Where the parties hold as beneficial joint tenants, the beneficial joint tenancy will be severed on the bankruptcy of one of them and they will thereafter hold as beneficial tenants in common in equal shares, the share of the bankrupt party falling into his bankruptcy estate.

When does severance occur?

15.15 There is some uncertainty about when severance occurs. The possibilities are that it happens on the bankruptcy order being made or that it occurs on the bankrupt's interest vesting in the trustee on the first appointment of a trustee. In *Re Pavlou*¹ it was common ground that the effect of the bankruptcy order was to sever the beneficial joint tenancy, although it was not until three days later that the trustee was appointed and the bankrupt's estate vested in him.

¹   [1993] 3 All ER 955, [1993] 1 WLR 1046.

15.16 The question in *Re Palmer, dec'd (a debtor)*¹ was whether an insolvency administration order made on a petition presented after the debtor had died had the effect of severing, before his death, his interest in property which he and his wife had held as joint tenants. Although the insolvency administration order was made after the debtor's death, it was deemed to have been made on the date of his death. Unless the order had retrospective effect so as to sever the joint tenancy before the moment of the debtor's death, the debtor's entire interest would pass on his death to his widow by survivorship. The Court of Appeal, reversing the decision at first instance, held that the insolvency administration order did not have retrospective effect. Their reasons are discussed elsewhere² but they proceeded on the footing that the date which was material was the date, or the deemed date, on which the insolvency administration order took effect, as opposed to the date on which the estate vested in the trustee.

¹   [1994] Ch 316.
²   See para **26.17** where the IA 1986, s 421A, inserted by the Insolvency Act 2000, reversing the effect of *Re Palmer, dec'd (a debtor)* is also discussed.

Resulting trusts

15.17 No reference has been required in this summary to resulting trusts, that is, in this context, to the presumption that where the parties have contributed in unequal shares to the purchase of property, without stipulating what their respective beneficial shares are to be, they should hold the beneficial interest in proportion to their contributions because neither is to be taken to have intended to make a gift to the other. Since the approach to quantification outlined above seems to govern every situation in which the presumption of resulting trust might formerly apply, there is no scope left for the application of that presumption. The opinions subscribed to by the majority of the members of the House of Lords in *Stack v Dowden*¹ favoured the abandonment of resulting trusts in this area².

¹   [2007] UKHL 17, [2007] 2 All ER 929, [2007] 2 WLR 831.
²   Contrast the dissenting opinion of Lord Neuberger.

Future development

15.18 There seem two points on which further development by case law is likely. First, it seems that, where one party is the sole legal owner but there is no express, albeit informal, agreement or arrangement that the beneficial interest should be shared, a range of acts beyond direct financial contributions to the purchase of the property on the part of the other party claiming an interest will suffice to ground a constructive trust. What sort of conduct will lie within that range will need to be defined. Secondly, in cases where the property is held in joint names without stipulating what the parties' beneficial interests are, only unusual circumstances will lead to a conclusion other than that the parties intended to hold as beneficial joint tenants. Parties are likely to debate about what counts as being unusual for this purpose.

Ancillary matters

15.19 Where the parties' beneficial interests are either clear or if disputed, have been established, there may be further adjustments to be made between the parties. Bases on which such adjustments may be made are:

(1)   pursuant to the Matrimonial Proceedings and Property Act 1970, s 37, where a spouse has made improvements to the property;

(2)   by way of equitable accounting, where one party has contributed more than his due proportion to the value of the property;

(3)   by payment of an occupation 'rent', where one party has been in occupation to the exclusion of the other;

(4)   by operation of the equity of exoneration, where money jointly borrowed and secured over the entire property has been applied to the sole benefit of one party.

15.20 Only the first of these matters can affect the size of the parties' shares in the property; the others make purely financial adjustments between the parties, but since these adjustments affect the distribution of the proceeds, they nevertheless make a real difference, even where one party is bankrupt, to the amount to be received by the parties on distribution following sale or to the amount which the solvent party needs to pay to buy the trustee's interest.

Improvement by a spouse

15.21 Where the parties are married, statutory provision[1] is made to create or increase the beneficial interest of a spouse who has made a substantial contribution in money or money's worth to the improvement of any property, real or personal, in which either or both spouses have a beneficial interest. This rule also applies, where an agreement to marry is determined, to any property in which either or both of the parties to the agreement had a beneficial interest[2].

[1]   Matrimonial Proceedings and Property Act 1970, s 37.
[2]   Law Reform (Miscellaneous Provisions) Act 1970, s 2(1).

15.22 The provision is subject to any express or implied agreement made between the parties. The existence and size of any interest so created or the extent to which an existing interest is increased may be determined by the court if not agreed between the parties. In either case the trustee in bankruptcy of the improver takes the interest so arising or increased.

Equitable accounting

15.23 Whether the parties were beneficial joint tenants or tenants in common, the court may take an account for the purpose of establishing that one party has contributed more than his due proportion towards the value of the property[1]. The purpose of the account is not to adjust the size of the parties' respective interests but to identify sums of money for which one party ought to give credit to the other. The due proportion is to be determined by reference to the size of the parties' beneficial interests. In the case of a beneficial joint tenancy, they will be equal.

[1]   *Re Gorman (a bankrupt)* [1990] 1 All ER 717, [1990] 1 WLR 616; *Re Pavlou* [1993] 3 All ER 955, [1993] 1 WLR 1046.

15.24 Such contributions might be made by way of expenditure on works which improve the value of the property. In that case the party who has contributed beyond his due proportion is entitled to credit in respect of an appropriate share of the increase in the value of the property. The same principle applies in respect of payments, made during the period when the non-paying party is not living in the property, of the mortgage instalments, both capital and interest, which inure to the benefit of the non-paying party by increasing the value of the equity of redemption.

Occupation 'rent'

15.25 But on the other side of the account, the party in occupation may have to make a payment by way of compensation to the other party if that other party's entitlement to occupy the property has been excluded or restricted[1]. An argument by the wife of a bankrupt who remained in possession, together with the bankrupt husband, that she should not pay an occupation rent because the trustee had delayed in making an application to realise the bankrupt's interest failed in *Byford v Butler*[2]. It may be that the only basis on which an occupation rent may now be sought between beneficiaries is pursuant to the statutory provisions contained in the Trusts of Land and Appointment of Trustees Act 1996[3]. It may appear dubious whether a trustee in bankruptcy can contend that he had an entitlement to occupy which has been excluded or restricted so as to bring himself within the Trusts of Land and Appointment of Trustees Act 1996, s 13(6) and thereby to complain hat the trustees of the land ought to have imposed on the occupying beneficiary a requirement to pay rent by way of compensation.

[1]   *Suttill v Graham* [1977] 3 All ER 1117, [1977] 1 WLR 819, CA; *Dennis v McDonald* [1982] Fam 63, [1982] 1 All ER 590, CA.
[2]   [2003] EWHC 1267 (Ch), [2004] 1 P & CR 159.
[3]   *Stack v Dowden* [2007] UKHL 17, [2007] 2 All ER 929, [2007] 2 WLR 831 at 93–94.

Payments made by the bankrupt

15.26 If the bankrupt occupies any premises on condition that he makes payments towards satisfying any liability arising under a mortgage of the premises or otherwise towards the outgoings of the premises, the bankrupt does not, by virtue of those payments, acquire any interest in the premises[1].

¹   IA 1986, s 338.

The equity of exoneration

15.27 Where a husband has borrowed money for his own purposes which is secured against the entirety of the co-owned property, the wife may require that the secured debt be borne first by the beneficial share of the husband. Equity exonerates the wife's beneficial share, to the extent possible, on the basis of what it presumes to be the parties' intention. Thus in *Re Pittortou*[1] Scott J approved the following statement of principle taken from *Halsbury's Laws*[2]:

> 'If the property of a married woman is mortgaged or charged in order to raise money for the payment of her husband's debts, or otherwise for his benefit, it is presumed, in the absence of evidence showing an intention to the contrary, that she meant to charge her property merely by way of surety, and is entitled to be indemnified by the husband, and to throw the debt primarily on his estate to the exoneration of her own.'

¹   [1985] 1 WLR 58 at 61.
²   Taken from (4th edn) Vol 22, para 1071.

15.28 The effect of the equity is that on the sale of the property, the proceeds of sale will first be divided according to the respective shares of the co-owners, thereafter the whole of the relevant charge or charges will be deducted from the first co-owner's share, and only if that share is insufficient to discharge the full debt, will any of the debt be repaid out of the second co-owner's share. The equity cannot be exercised so as to increase the proprietary share of the non-bankrupt co-owner[1].

¹   *Re Debtor (No 24 of 1971), ex p Marley v Trustee* [1976] 2 All ER 1010, [1976] 1 WLR 952.

15.29 In the context of bankruptcy the further right to be indemnified will be of little value, being a right to prove in the bankruptcy for the relevant amount. In general, where the parties are married or are civil partners, the right to prove is likely to be worthless because no distribution may be made until after all unsecured debts have been paid with interest[1], but where the bankrupt's spouse or civil partner as surety meets the claim of the bankrupt's creditor, he or she may claim in the bankruptcy with the same priority as that creditor would have had.

¹   IA 1986, s 329.

Operation of the equity of exoneration

15.30 The equity of exoneration is only a presumptive right. It depends on the intention of the parties being that the wife should stand in the position of surety for her husband. No intention need be expressed; it is to be ascertained from all the relevant circumstances in any individual case[1]. And while the cases describe the right as presumptive, there is no evidential burden on the husband or trustee to disprove it. In the words of Lindley MR:

> 'To say that in all such cases there is a presumption in favour of the wife, and that it is for the husband to rebut it, is, in our opinion, to go too far and to use language calculated to mislead. The circumstances of each case must all be weighed to see what inference ought to be drawn; and until an inference in favour of the wife arises there is no presumption for the husband to rebut. If this is forgotten, error may creep in'.[2]

1   *Paget v Paget* [1898] 1 Ch 470 at 474 per Lindley MR; *Clinton v Hooper* (1791) 1 Ves 173; see also other cases cited at 27(1) *The Digest* (*3rd Reissue*) 278–283.
2   *Paget v Paget* [1898] 1 Ch 470 at 475.

15.31 No inference has been drawn in favour of the wife in the following circumstances:

(1)   The evidence showed that the wife intended to make a gift to the husband[1].

(2)   The money was raised to pay debts of the husband incurred to maintain an extravagant style of living on the part of both husband and wife[2].

(3)   The money was raised in part to discharge the wife's debts and the husband had the benefit of the surplus. The court here inferred that as there was only one primary transaction there was a uniform intention that the wife's interest should be primarily liable[3]. This case must be compared with the position where the wife's interest is charged partly for the husband's benefit and partly for hers for the discharge of their respective obligations or to raise money for their individual purposes. In this event the wife may be entitled to exoneration to the extent of her husband's interest[4].

(4)   The money was borrowed for the wife's benefit either wholly or jointly with her husband. Into this latter category will fall money which is used for general household and family living expenses[5].

1   *Clinton v Hooper* (1791) 3 Bro CC 201.
2   *Paget v Paget* [1898] 1 Ch 470.
3   *Lewis v Nangle* (1752) 1 Cox Eq Cas 240.
4   *Gee v Smart* (1857) 8 E & B 313.
5   *Hudson v Carmichael* (1854) Kay 613; *Gray v Dowman* (1858) 27 LJ Ch 702; *Re Pittortou* [1985] 1 All ER 285, [1985] 1 WLR 58.

15.32 There is authority which suggests that a presumption does arise that the money was for the husband's benefit and that the wife was simply a surety for it where the husband covenants to repay the money raised on the wife's property or where the mortgage deed states that the money was paid only to the husband[1]. Perhaps today the better approach is to treat such matters as strong indications of the intention of the parties without dealing in presumptions. The money raised may after all go to a number of different purposes, particularly where the charge on the family home secures an overdraft or other bank facilities. It is not necessary to treat the whole of the money secured as being either subject to the equity or not. The court may order an inquiry as to which sums forming part of the money raised under the charge went solely to the husband and in respect of which the wife's interest in the property may be exonerated, and which went for the benefit of the wife, either solely or jointly with her husband, children or third parties. In respect of these latter sums the wife has no right of exoneration.

1   *Hudson v Carmichael* (1854) Kay 613; *Hall v Hall* [1911] 1 Ch 487.

In whose favour can the equity of exoneration arise?

15.33 In many cases the equity of exoneration has been applied in favour of wives, but it has also been applied in favour of a husband who has charged his property as surety for the benefit of his wife[1]. So it would seem equally applicable to civil partners.

1   *Bagot v Oughton* (1717) 1 P Wms 347; *Gray v Dowman* (1858) 27 LJ Ch 702.

Modern application of the equity of exoneration

15.34 Doubt has been expressed as to the contemporary applicability of the equity[1]. However this doubt is unjustified. In *Re Pittortou, ex p Trustee of Property of The Bankrupt v Bankrupt*[2] Scott J applied the equity as follows. The bankrupt husband ran a restaurant business on his own account. The matrimonial home was in joint names and the husband and wife executed a second charge in favour of a bank to secure borrowings on the husband's bank account. The husband used the money borrowed for various purposes which Scott J divided into three broad categories:

(a)   payments made 'for the joint benefit of the household', eg mortgage instalments and other payments made for the purposes of the occupation of the property by the husband, the wife and their daughter together with their living expenses;
(b)   the debts of the restaurant business; and
(c)   debts incurred by the husband when he left his family and set up a separate home with another woman.

1   See *Re Woodstock* [1980] CLY 148.
2   [1985] 1 All ER 285, [1985] 1 WLR 58.

15.35 The judge held that money paid from the secured bank account to pay debts falling within categories (b) and (c) should fall on the bankrupt's share of the matrimonial home, while debts within category (a) should be shared. An inquiry was directed as to which payments fell within the respective categories. Although an order for the sale of the property was made, that order was not to take effect until the inquiry was complete in order that the wife could make an informed offer to the trustee to purchase his interest in the property.

C PROPERTY ADJUSTMENT ORDERS IN FAMILY PROCEEDINGS

Property adjustment orders

15.36 In a variety of types of family law proceedings, the court has power to order a party to transfer assets to another person. Thus, in matrimonial proceedings, the court has power to make property adjustment orders under the Matrimonial Causes Act 1973, s 24 whereby a party is required to transfer specified property to another party. Similar orders may be made under the Children Act 1989 and under the Civil Partnership Act 2004. Such an order effects an immediate transfer of the asset to which it relates[1]. Under the order the party whose property is thereby transferred is the person making the disposal, because it is his property which is disposed of by the order[2].

[1]   *Mountney v Treharne* [2002] EWA Civ 1174, [2003] Ch 135, [2002] 3 WLR 1760, disapproving *Burton v Burton* [1986] 2 FLR 419 and *Beer v Higham* [1997] BPIR 349.
[2]   *Treharne v Forrester* [2003] EWHC 2784 (Ch), [2004] 1 FLR 1173.

Property adjustment orders made before the presentation of the bankruptcy petition

15.37 A settlement or transfer of property made in compliance with a property adjustment order remains subject to avoidance as a transaction at an undervalue or a preference pursuant to an order made under IA 1986, s 339 or s 340[1].

[1]   Matrimonial Causes Act 1973, s 39.

15.38 Whether the transfer pursuant to the court order might be set aside as a transaction at an undervalue depends on whether consideration was given by the transferee. In *Hill v Haines*[1] the Court of Appeal held that the transferee, in a standard case, did give good consideration for a transfer made pursuant to a court order made in matrimonial proceedings. For, the claimant in matrimonial proceedings has a statutory entitlement to financial provision which is capable of forming consideration for the transfer of property. Thus the position under IA 1986 is the same as that under the Bankruptcy Act 1914 (and its predecessors)[2].

[1]   [2007] EWCA Civ 1284. It is understood that an appeal to the House of Lords may be pursued from this decision.
[2]   *Re Pope, ex p Dicksee* [1908] 2 KB 169; *Re Abbott, ex p Trustee of Property of the Bankrupt v Abbott* [1983] Ch 45.

15.39 Where the order is made in contested proceedings, the court will put a value on the claimant's entitlement and the transfer made in vindication of that entitlement will therefore be matched to its value. Where the order is made to give effect to an agreement made out of court by the parties, here the position will be the same, so long as the match between the value of the entitlement and the property to be transferred remains truly commensurate. The possibility in any case remains that the match will not be commensurate, because of collusion or some other vitiating factor, and in such cases the transfer will be open to challenge even though it is made pursuant to a court order[1].

¹ *Hill v Haines* [2007] EWCA Civ 1284 at 35–36; Matrimonial Causes Act 1973, s 39.

Property adjustment order made after presentation of the petition but before estate vests in the trustee in bankruptcy

15.40 If the property adjustment order is made between the presentation of the petition and the first vesting of the estate in the trustee, the order comprises a disposition by the debtor of property belonging to him and so is rendered void by IA 1986, s 284(1), unless approved or ratified by the court[1]. The competent court is the appropriate bankruptcy court having bankruptcy jurisdiction over the debtor or bankrupt whose property is to be transferred[2].

¹ *Treharne v Forrester* [2003] EWHC 2784 (Ch), [2004] 1 FLR 1173.
² IA 1986, ss 385(1) and 373 and IR 1986, rr 6.9 and 6.40.

After the estate has vested in the trustee in bankruptcy

15.41 The final period to consider is the period after the estate has first vested in the trustee. After the estate has so vested, the relevant asset will belong to the trustee. The court having jurisdiction in the family proceedings in which property adjustment orders may be made does not have jurisdiction to make a property adjustment order against the trustee[1]. Nor does the possibility that the bankrupt might receive some surplus enable the court to make a property adjustment order against him[2]. So no property adjustment order may be made at this stage and if, perhaps in ignorance of the bankruptcy, the court seised of the family proceedings purports to make one, the trustee should apply to have it set aside.

¹ *Re Holliday (a bankrupt)* [1981] Ch 405, [1980] 3 All ER 385 and *McGladdery v McGladdery* [1999] 2 FLR 1102.
² *Ram v Ram (No 2)* [2004] EWCA Civ 1452, [2004] 3 FCR 425, [2005] 2 BCLC 476.

D GIFTS AND OTHER VOIDABLE TRANSACTIONS

15.42 A transfer of an interest in the family home may be made in other circumstances than matrimonial proceedings discussed in the preceding section. The trustee will be concerned to see whether an interest in the home has been transferred to or acquired by the bankrupt's spouse in circumstances where the relevant transaction may be set aside as a transaction at an undervalue[1], a preference[2] or as a transaction to defraud creditors[3]. Such circumstances would include the case of a straightforward transfer of the property out of the husband's name into joint names or the wife's name, or the acquisition in joint names or the wife's sole name from funds supplied by the husband. In this context, it should be noted that a transaction will have been made at an undervalue if it was made in consideration of marriage[4]. Property may be recovered which represents the proceeds of sale of other property or of money which was transferred under a transaction liable to be set aside under either IA 1986, s 339 or s 340.

1   IA 1986, s 339.
2   IA 1986, s 340.
3   IA 1986, s 423.
4   IA 1986, s 339(3)(b).

15.43 Where the transfer of property is vulnerable as a preference because at the time it was made the wife was one of the husband's creditors, her husband's trustee may take advantage of the provision that a wife is an associate of her husband[1]. This has the effect that the period during which the preference is vulnerable is extended from six months to two years[2] and the husband will be presumed to have been influenced by the desire to prefer the wife[3]. In this context references to a husband or wife include a former husband or wife and a reputed husband or wife[4]. The definition of 'associate' has been extended so as to embrace civil partners to the same extent.

1   IA 1986, s 435(2).
2   IA 1986, s 341(1)(b).
3   IA 1986, s 340(5).
4   IA 1986, s 341(8).

E ORDERS FOR SALE

15.44 The trustee's aim must be to realise the value of the bankrupt's interest in his home for his creditors. Usually that will require the sale of the property or of the bankrupt's interest in it. Achieving a sale may involve two stages: first, where the property is jointly owned, establishing that there should be a sale, and secondly, obtaining possession in order to achieve a sale with vacant possession. The matters which the court should take into account in determining in the first case, whether to make an order for sale in a case of co-ownership and in the second, whether to make an order for possession are similar, but they are nonetheless distinct exercises. In this section is discussed the approach to making an order for sale in cases of co-ownership; in the next are discussed the measures relating to the protection of occupation which must be considered before making orders for possession.

Trusts of land

15.45 If two or more persons are beneficially interested in land, the legal title is held by the proprietor or proprietors on a trust of land. In general, it is the trustee or trustees of the land who has or have the power to decide whether or not to sell, but in the event that either a person having an interest in the property which is subject to the trust or being a trustee of the land wishes to sell but the trustees or the other trustees will not consent to the sale, that person may make an application to the court for an order under the Trusts of Land and Appointment of Trustees Act 1996, s 14 directing that there should be a sale. Such an application may also be made by a person holding security over the interest of a beneficiary. The court's jurisdiction to make an order pursuant to s 14 of the 1996 Act is not removed by an earlier property adjustment order in matrimonial proceedings limiting the situations in which the trustees of the land should sell it because such an order cannot remove the trustees' competence to sell in situations other than those mentioned in the property adjustment order or the court's competence to direct that they should sell, even where one of them does not consent, under s 14(2)(a)[1].

[1] *Turner v Avis* [2007] EWCA Civ 748, [2007] 4 All ER 1103.

Applications by the trustee in bankruptcy of a beneficiary

15.46 Where the bankrupt held a beneficial interest under a trust of land at the commencement of his bankruptcy and the trustee wishes to realise that interest, the trustee in bankruptcy must apply to the court for an order under the Trusts of Land and Appointment of Trustees Act 1996, s 14 for an order of sale. The court to which the application should be made is the court having jurisdiction in relation to the bankruptcy[1].

[1] IA 1986, s 335A(1).

Matters to which the court must have regard

15.47 Where the application is made otherwise than by a trustee in bankruptcy, the court must have regard to the matters set out in the Trusts of Land and Appointment of Trustees Act 1996, s 15. However, that section does not apply where the application for an order for the sale of the property is made by the trustee in bankruptcy of a person interested under the trust[1]. Instead the matters which are to be taken into consideration are those set in IA 1986, s 335A.

[1] Trusts of Land and Appointment of Trustees Act 1996, s 15(4).

Where the application is made during the first year after the estate vested in the trustee in bankruptcy

15.48 If less than one year has elapsed since the date of the first vesting of the estate in the trustee in bankruptcy[1] and the application relates to land which includes a dwelling house which is or has been the home of the bankrupt or his present or former spouse or civil partner, the court must make such order as it thinks just and reasonable having regard to:

(a)   the interests of the bankrupt's creditors;
(b)   the conduct of the present or former spouse or civil partner, so far as contributing to the bankruptcy;
(c)   the needs and financial resources of the present or former spouse or civil partner;
(d)   the needs of any children; and
(e)   all the circumstances of the case other than the needs of the bankrupt[2].

1   The estate vests in the trustee on the appointment of the first trustee in bankruptcy; see IA 1986, s 306(1).
2   IA 1986, s 335A(2).

15.49 The balancing exercise which consideration of these matters entails appears to conform with the right to respect for the home and family life of those affected required by art 8 of the European Convention on Human Rights and to respect for their property rights required by art 1 of the First Protocol.

15.50 If the application does not relate to land including a dwelling house so used as a home, then the court is directed to have regard to the interests of the bankrupt's creditors and all the circumstances of the case other than the needs of the bankrupt.

15.51 A feature of the drafting is that in a case where the application relates to a dwelling house which the bankrupt occupied as his home in cohabitation with a woman who is not his wife, the court is not (expressly) directed to have regard either to her conduct in so far as it contributed to the bankruptcy or her needs or financial resources, but if there were any children of the relationship, their needs would have to be considered. But since the court must in any event have regard to all the circumstances of the case apart from the needs of the bankrupt, it is likely that this will not give rise to any injustice in practice.

Where the application is made after the end of the first year

15.52 Where the application is made after the end of one year beginning with the date on which the bankrupt's estate first vested in a trustee, the court must assume, unless the circumstances of the case are exceptional, that the interests of the creditors outweigh all other considerations[1]. This provision puts the burden of showing that there are exceptional circumstances on the spouse, or other person, seeking to prevent or, more usually, delay the making of an order of sale. Where exceptional circumstances are found, the court cannot assume that the creditors' interests predominate, but must instead consider the matters to which it is to have regard had the application been made within the first year following the first vesting of the estate in a trustee[2]. Where exceptional circumstances have been found, the usual consequence is that consideration of the circumstances more generally leads to some postponement of the sale.

1   IA 1986, s 335A(3).
2   *Nicholls v Lan* [2006] EWHC 1255 (Ch), [2007] 1 FLR 744.

Exceptional circumstances

15.53 Some hardship will almost always fall on a family following bankruptcy. 'As the cases show, it is not uncommon for a wife with young children to be faced with eviction in circumstances where the realisation of her beneficial interest will not produce enough to buy a comparable home in the same neighbourhood, or indeed elsewhere; and, if she has to move elsewhere, there may be problems over schooling and so forth. Such circumstances, while engendering a natural sympathy in all who hear of them, cannot be described as exceptional. They are the melancholy consequences of debt and improvidence with which every civilised society has been familiar'[1]. Exceptional circumstances mean circumstances which take the case out of the ordinary and general run[2].

[1]   *Re Citro (a bankrupt)* [1991] Ch 142, [1990] 3 All ER 952, CA; *Judd v Brown* [1999] BPIR 517.
[2]   *Harrington v Bennett* [2000] BPIR 630; *Dean v Stout* [2005] EWHC 3315 (Ch), [2005] BPIR 1113; *Foyle v Turner* [2007] BPIR 43.

15.54   The fact that the proceeds of sale will be swallowed up by the expenses of the bankruptcy is not an exceptional circumstance[1]. But an order for sale has been postponed for the purpose of ensuring that there be sufficient time for the local authority to provide suitable alternative accommodation where the bankrupt's wife suffered from serious mental illness[2] and an appeal against a circuit judge's finding of exceptional circumstances was dismissed in a case where the bankrupt's wife was in a state of acute ill health[3]. The interests of the children in postponing sale prevailed in *Martin-Sklan v White*[4] where their home was of special importance in maintaining their welfare in a testing family situation.

[1]   *Bowe (a bankrupt) (trustee) v Bowe* [1997] BPIR 747.
[2]   *Re Raval (a bankrupt)* [1998] 2 FLR 718, [1998] BPIR 389.
[3]   *Cloughton v Charalambous* [1998] BPIR 558. *Re Bremner* [1999] BPIR 185 is a similar example.
[4]   [2006] EWHC 3313 (Ch), [2007] BPIR 76.

15.55   Doubt has been expressed whether the narrow approach adopted in *Re Citro*[1] to the ambit of exceptional circumstances is consistent with giving due respect to the family life and home of members of the bankrupt's family which is required by art 8 of the European Convention on Human Rights[2]. The suggested construction to be adopted was that circumstances would be exceptional if, though in themselves routine consequences of bankruptcy, they were exceptionally severe or where if the circumstances were of the usual kind but the creditors would suffer relatively slight loss in the event that sale was postponed. However, it would seem that the better view is that the exercise involved in considering the circumstances required by IA 1986, s 335A(2) and (3) represents the assessment which art 8 requires; the priority given to the interests of the creditors where the application is made more than a year after the estate has vested in the trustee unless there are exceptional circumstances is a compatible determination by Parliament of how the conflicting interests of the creditors and the bankrupt should be resolved[3].

[1]   [1991] Ch 142, [1990] 3 All ER 952, CA.
[2]   *Barca v Mears* [2004] EWHC 2170 (Ch), [2005] 2 FLR 1. See *Donohoe v Ingram* [2006] 2 FLR 1084, [2006] All ER (D) 132 (Jan) for similar comments.
[3]   *Nicholls v Lan* [2006] EWHC 1255 (Ch), [2007] 1 FLR 744; *Foyle v Turner* [2007] BPIR 43.

Time limit

15.56 The application must be made within three years beginning with the date of the bankruptcy otherwise the trustee will lose the right to make it because the bankrupt's interest in the dwelling house will cease to form part of the estate[1]. It is important to note that, since this three-year period begins with the date when the bankruptcy order was made, it runs from an earlier date than the one-year period mentioned in the preceding paragraphs (which begins on the date when the estate first vests in a trustee).

1   IA 1986, s 283A, discussed further below.

Order for possession ancillary to an order for sale

15.57 Where the court makes an order for sale pursuant to an application made by the trustee in bankruptcy under the Trusts of Land and Appointment of Trustees Act 1996, the order will usually also include an order that the respondents give possession of the property to the trustee in bankruptcy. The trustee will require possession in order to be able to sell with vacant possession. But although the facts will usually justify making an order for possession and obviously it would increase costs if the trustee were put to the trouble of having to make a further application in order to obtain possession, the court may consider whether or not to include an order for possession. In *Re McCarthy, ex p the trustee v McCarthy*[1], a decision under the Law of Property Act 1925, s 30, Goff J said: 'bearing in mind that an order for possession, as opposed to an order to concur in a sale, is a more onerous order on respondents in possession of the property, such an order should not be made unless the facts before the court justify it'. Hence if the persons in occupation, whether the bankrupt or his spouse, credibly make clear that they are willing to co-operate in a sale with vacant possession, the court need not make an order for possession at the time of ordering the sale, but, if it does not, the order ought to include a liberty to apply for an order for possession in case it is later required.

1   [1975] 2 All ER 857, [1975] 1 WLR 807.

Is separate consideration of rights of occupation required?

15.58 The regimes for the protection of a co-owner holding a share of the beneficial interest and of an occupier with rights of occupation may be intended to be mutually exclusive[1]. But, in some cases, it appears that there may be an overlap. Those cases are first, where the spouse or civil partner has an equitable interest in a dwelling house or its proceeds of sale but is not a legal proprietor[2] and so has statutory home rights to occupy the dwelling house which must be addressed pursuant to IA 1986, s 336 and secondly, where children under 18 occupy the dwelling house with the bankrupt both when the petition was presented and the commencement of the bankruptcy, in which case the bankrupt has rights of occupation to be considered by the court pursuant to IA 1986, s 337. These rights have to be considered by the court before making a possession order because such an order interferes with the applicable right of occupation. But the matters to which the court must have regard in relation to these rights are the same as the matters to which it is to have regard in deciding whether or not to make an order under the Trusts of Land and Appointment of Trustees Act 1996, s 14. So separate consideration of them for the purpose of deciding whether to order possession would seem likely to be repetitive. Further, since in determining whether to order a sale, the court usually considers when the sale is to occur, there may well be no practical difference between the purposes of the two exercises even though there is a conceptual difference between deciding that there should be a sale and ordering that those in occupation give up possession.

[1] See *Turner v Avis* [2007] EWCA Civ 748, [2007] 4 All ER 1103 at [12].
[2] A spouse having only an equitable interest in the property holds statutory home rights because by virtue of the Family Law Act 1996, s 30(9) she is deemed not to be entitled to occupy the house by virtue of that interest. It is to some extent anomalous that such a spouse should have an additional right of occupation which a spouse who shares in both the legal and beneficial interests in the property does not.

Protection where the bankrupt's interest is of low value

15.59 Where the trustee applies for an order for the sale of a dwelling house which at the date of the bankruptcy was the sole or principal residence of the bankrupt, or his present or former spouse or civil partner, and value of the interest in the property which is comprised in the bankrupt's estate is below £1,000, the court must dismiss the application[1]. In determining that value the court must disregard that part of the value of the property in which the bankrupt's interest subsists which is equal to the value of any loans secured by mortgage or other charge against the property, any other third party interest and the reasonable costs of sale[2].

[1] IA 1986, s 313A(1) and (2) and the Insolvency Proceedings (Monetary Limits) Order 1986, SI 1986/1996, art 3 and Schedule.
[2] IA 1986, ss 313A(3), 313(2B) and IR 1986, r 6.237D(10).

F ORDERS FOR POSSESSION

Trustee in bankruptcy's power of sale where the bankrupt was the sole legal and beneficial owner

15.60 An individual may be the sole legal and beneficial owner of a dwelling house which he nonetheless shares with his spouse or civil partner as their home. On that individual's bankruptcy, the entire property will vest in his trustee and the trustee will be entitled to sell without making any application under the Trusts of Land and Appointment of Trustees Act 1996, s 14. The trustee's power to sell arises from his power to sell any part of the property comprised within the estate[1]. But although the trustee in bankruptcy may have power to sell, his ability to obtain possession of the property is restricted by the rights of occupation which may be afforded to the bankrupt's spouse or civil partner and indeed, where there are children living in the house, to the bankrupt himself. If those rights are asserted against the trustee, by virtue of IA 1986, ss 336 and 337, he must apply for an order of possession.

[1] IA 1986, s 314(1) and Sch 5, para 9.

Time limit

15.61 Where the trustee must obtain an order for possession in order to realise the property for the benefit of the creditors, his application must be made within three years beginning with the date of the bankruptcy otherwise the trustee will lose the right to make it because the bankrupt's interest in the dwelling house will cease to form part of the estate[1]. It is important to note that, since this three-year period begins with the date when the bankruptcy order was made, it runs from an earlier date than the one-year period mentioned in the preceding paragraphs (which begins on the date when the estate first vests in a trustee).

[1] IA 1986, s 283A, discussed further in para **15.88ff** below.

Protection where the bankrupt's interest is of low value

15.62 An application by a trustee for an order for possession of a dwelling house which at the date of the bankruptcy was the sole or principal residence of the bankrupt, or his present or former spouse or civil partner must be dismissed in the same circumstances as an application for an order for sale must be[1].

[1] IA 1986, s 313A discussed in para **15.85** below.

The rights of occupation of the bankrupt's spouse or civil partner

15.63 Where the dwelling house occupied by the parties to a marriage or civil partnership is owned solely by one of the spouses or civil partners and the other has no interest in the property, the Family Law Act 1996 confers rights to occupy the dwelling house on the party without any interest in it. These rights, called 'home rights', comprise (a) if in occupation, a right not to be evicted or excluded from the dwelling house or any part of it by the other party except with the leave of the court given by an order under the Family Law Act 1996, s 33, and (b) if not in occupation, a right with the leave of the court, again given by order under s 33, to enter into and occupy the dwelling house[1]. The rights are, therefore, only concerned with use and occupation of the dwelling house, not its ownership.

[1] Family Law Act 1996, s 30(2).

15.64 The rights are also conferred on a spouse or civil partner who holds an equitable interest in the dwelling house or its proceeds of sale but in whom the legal title is not vested[1].

[1] Family Law Act 1996, s 30(9).

Charge on the dwelling house

15.65 If, at any time during a marriage or civil partnership, one party is entitled to occupy a dwelling house by virtue of a beneficial estate or interest, the other party's home rights are a charge on the first party's estate or interest[1]. The charge comprised by the home rights should, if it is a charge on a legal estate, be registered either by notice if the relevant legal estate is registered under the Land Registration Act 2002[2] or as a Class F land charge if it is not[3]. But whether it is appropriately registered or not, the charge is binding on a trustee in bankruptcy and persons deriving title under him[4].

1   Family Law Act 1996, s 31(1) and (2).
2   Family Law Act 1996, s 31(10).
3   Land Charges Act 1972, s 2; Family Law Act 1996, s 31(12).
4   IA 1986, s 336(2)(a).

Effect of presentation of a bankruptcy petition

15.66 Home rights cannot arise in relation to a dwelling house comprised in a bankrupt's estate by virtue of anything occurring between the presentation of the petition on which the bankruptcy order against the bankrupt was made and the vesting of his estate in his trustee[1].

1   IA 1986, s 336(1).

Impact on trustee in bankruptcy's power to realise the bankrupt's interest in the dwelling house

15.67 Where the bankrupt's spouse's or civil partner's home rights form a charge on the property and the spouse or civil partner does not agree to give up possession to enable the property to be sold, the trustee in bankruptcy may only obtain possession by applying for an order under the Family Law Act 1996, s 33[1]. The application must be made to the court having jurisdiction in relation to the bankruptcy.

1   IA 1986, s 336(2)(b).

Where the application is made during the first year after the estate vested in the trustee in bankruptcy

15.68 If the application is made within one year of the estate's first vesting in the trustee, the court shall make such order under the Family Law Act 1996, s 33 as it thinks just and reasonable having regard to:

(a)   the interests of the bankrupt's creditors;
(b)   the conduct of the spouse or former spouse, so far as contributing to the bankruptcy;
(c)   the needs and financial resources of the present or former spouse or civil partner;
(d)   the needs of any children; and

(e)   all the circumstances of the case other than the needs of the bankrupt[1].

¹   IA 1986, s 336(4).

15.69 The order which a trustee will usually require is an order under the Family Law Act 1996, s 33(3)(e) terminating the other spouse's or civil partner's home rights.

Where the application is made after the end of the first year

15.70 Where the application is made after the end of one year after the estate first vested in the trustee, the court shall assume, unless the circumstances are exceptional[1], that the interests of the creditors outweigh all other considerations[2].

¹   See para **15.53** on exceptional circumstances.
²   IA 1986, s 336(5).

Overlap with application for order of sale

15.71 It appears that it is necessary to obtain an order terminating the home rights under the Family Law Act 1996, s 33 as well as an order for sale under the Trusts of Land and Appointment of Trustees Act 1996, s 14 in a case where the bankrupt as one spouse or civil partner is the sole legal owner but he holds the property on trust for himself and the other spouse and the spouse holding the legal title is adjudged bankrupt, his trustee in bankruptcy, in order to make a sale with vacant possession, will need to apply for both and an order terminating the other spouse's matrimonial home rights. Although the matters to be taken into account in respect of both applications will be the same, because the property to which the applications relate will comprise a dwelling house which is or has been the home of the bankrupt or the spouse, the two applications need to be distinguished since the fact that an order for sale should be made may not necessarily entail that an order terminating the matrimonial home rights should also be made, at least, with immediate effect.

Bankrupt's right of occupation

15.72 Where a person who is entitled to occupy a dwelling house by virtue of a beneficial estate or interest[1] is adjudged bankrupt and any person under the age of 18 with whom that person had at some time occupied that dwelling house had their home with him at the time when the bankruptcy petition was presented and at the commencement of the bankruptcy, the bankrupt has rights similar to the home rights conferred under the Family Law Act 1996. That is to say, the bankrupt has the following rights as against his trustee in bankruptcy: (i) if in occupation of the dwelling house, the right not to be evicted or excluded from it or any part of it, except with the leave of the court; and (ii) if not in occupation, the right with the leave of the court to enter into and occupy the dwelling house[2]. These rights are a charge, having the like

15.72 *The bankrupt's home*

priority as an equitable interest created immediately before the commencement of the bankruptcy on so much of his estate or interest in the dwelling house as vests in the trustee[3]. The Family Law Act 1996 has effect, with the necessary modifications, as if (1) the rights were matrimonial home rights, (2) any application for leave with respect to the exercise of those rights were an application for an order under the Family Law Act 1996, s 33, and (3) any charge on the estate or interest of the trustee were a charge under that Act on the estate or interest of a spouse[4]. Any application for leave must be made to the court having jurisdiction in relation to the bankruptcy[5].

1 There is, of course, no need for protection where the bankrupt does not own any beneficial interest.
2 IA 1986, s 337(1) and (2)(a).
3 IA 1986, s 337(2)(b).
4 IA 1986, s 337(3).
5 IA 1986, s 337(4).

15.73 Again, a distinction is drawn between applications made within a year of the estate's first vesting in the trustee and applications made after that period has expired. During the first year the court shall make such order under the Family Law Act 1996, s 33 as it thinks just and reasonable having regard to the interests of the creditors, to the bankrupt's financial resources, to the needs of the children and to all the circumstances of the case other than the needs of the bankrupt[1]. Where the application is made after the end of one year after the estate first vested in the trustee, the court shall assume, unless the circumstances are exceptional[2], that the interests of the creditors outweigh all other considerations[3].

1 IA 1986, s 337(5).
2 See para **15.53** on what may count as exceptional circumstances.
3 IA 1986, s 337(6).

G CHARGE ON THE DWELLING HOUSE

15.74 The trustee in bankruptcy has power to apply to the court for an order that a charge be imposed on any property comprised in the bankrupt's estate which is occupied by the bankrupt, his present or former spouse or civil partner and which, for any reason, the trustee is unable to realise[1]. The purpose of introducing the power into the Insolvency Act was to enable the trustee, in circumstances where he was not able to dispose of the bankrupt's interest in a dwelling house by the time he had completed the remainder of the administration of the estate, to obtain his release without leaving the property vested in the official receiver, possibly for many years.

1 IA 1986, s 313(1).

The charged value

15.75 In the charging order it must be specified what the value of the bankrupt's interest in the property is at the date of the order[1]. In determining the value of the bankrupt's interest, the court must disregard that part of the value of the property in which the bankrupt's interest subsists which is equal to the value of any loans secured by mortgage or other charge against the property, any other third party interest and the reasonable costs of sale[2]. The amount of the value of the bankrupt's interest together with interest on it accruing at the prescribed rate constitute the charged value[3]. The applicable rate of interest is the rate specified in the Judgments Act 1838, s 17 on the day when the charge is imposed[4]. Where the court imposes a charge under IA 1986, s 313, the benefit of the charge is comprised in the bankrupt's estate and is enforceable up to the charged value for any amount which is payable otherwise than to the bankrupt out of the estate and of interest on that amount at the prescribed rate[5]. So, where the property is later sold either voluntarily or pursuant to an order sought by the trustee, the charged value forms a cap on the amount which must be paid into the estate.

1   IA 1986, s 313(2A)(a).
2   IA 1986, s 313(2B) and IR 1986, r 6.237D(10).
3   IA 1986, s 313(2A).
4   IR 1986, r 6.237(5).
5   IA 1986, s 313(2).

15.76 A charging order made under IA 1986, s 313 is subject to the provisions of the Charging Orders Act 1979, s 3[1] and accordingly the court has a general power to impose conditions, *inter alia*, as to when the charge is to become enforceable. But the court cannot vary the charged value[2].

1   Except for sub-s (3); IA 1986, s 313(4).
2   IA 1986, s 313(5).

Procedure

15.77 The trustee should apply by originating application. The respondents must include any present or former spouse or civil partner of the bankrupt having or claiming an interest in the property, any other person appearing to have an interest in the property and such other persons as the court may direct[1]. It will ordinarily be appropriate to join the bankrupt.

1   IR 1986, r 6.237D(2).

15.78 The trustee must make a report to the court containing the following particulars:

(a)   the extent of the bankrupt's interest in the property;
(b)   the amount which at the date of the application remains owing to the unsecured creditors of the bankrupt; and
(c)   an estimate of the cost of realising the interest[1].

1   IR 1986, r 6.237D(3).

15.79 The terms of the charge to be imposed should be agreed between the trustee and the bankrupt; failing such agreement they will be settled by the court[1].

1   IR 1986, r 6.237D(4).

15.80 *The bankrupt's home*

The order

15.80 Where an order imposing a charge is made, it should:

(a)   describe the property to be charged;
(b)   state whether the title to the property is registered and, if it is, specify the title number;
(c)   set out the extent of the bankrupt's interest in the property which has vested in the trustee;
(d)   indicate, by reference to any, or the total, amount which is payable otherwise than to the bankrupt out of the estate and of interest on that amount, how the amount of the charge to be imposed is to be ascertained;
(e)   set out the conditions, if any, imposed by the court under the Charging Orders Act 1979, s 3(1);
(f)   identify when any property charged under IA 1986, s 313 shall cease to be comprised in the bankrupt's estate and, subject to the charge (and any prior charge), vest in the bankrupt[1].

[1]   IR 1986, r 6.237D(6).

15.81 The order must also state the applicable rate of interest, being the rate specified in the Judgments Act 1838, s 17, on the date on which the charge is imposed[1].

[1]   IR 1986, r 6.237D(5).

15.82 Unless the court thinks that a different date is appropriate, the date on which the property should ordinarily vest in the bankrupt is the date on which the charge is registered in accordance with the Charging Orders Act 1979, s 3(2)[1].

[1]   IR 1986, r 6.237D(7).

15.83 If the order is made, the trustee must as soon as reasonably practicable after the order is made make appropriate application to register the charge pursuant to the Land Charges Act 1972 or the Land Registration Act 2002[1].

[1]   IR 1986, r 6.237D(8) and (9).

Time limit

15.84 The application must be made within three years beginning with the date of the bankruptcy otherwise the trustee will lose the right to make it because the bankrupt's interest in the dwelling house will cease to form part of the estate[1]. It is important to note that, since this three-year period begins with the date when the bankruptcy order was made, it runs from an earlier date than the one-year period mentioned in the preceding paragraphs (which begins on the date when the estate first vests in a trustee).

[1]   IA 1986, s 283A, discussed further in para **15.88**ff below.

Protection where the bankrupt's interest is of low value

15.85 Where the trustee applies for a charging order over a dwelling house which at the date of the bankruptcy was the sole or principal residence of the bankrupt, or his present or former spouse or civil partner, and value of the interest in the property which is comprised in the bankrupt's estate is below £1,000, the court must dismiss the application[1]. In determining that value the court must disregard that part of the value of the property in which the bankrupt's interest subsists which is equal to the value of any loans secured by mortgage or other charge against the property, any other third party interest and the reasonable costs of sale[2].

[1]   IA 1986, s 313A(1) and (2) and the Insolvency Proceedings (Monetary Limits) Order 1986, SI 1986/1996, art 3 and Schedule.
[2]   IA 1986, ss 313A(3), 313(2B) and IR 1986, r 6.237D(10).

Effect and enforcement of the charge

15.86 The order imposing the charge must also provide for the transfer of the ownership of the property charged from the trustee to the bankrupt, who will thereafter hold the property subject to the charge. The charge takes effect as having like effect and being enforceable in the same courts and in the same manner as an equitable charge created by the debtor by writing under his hand[1]. The charge may therefore be enforced by application for an order for sale[2].

[1]   Charging Orders Act 1979, s 3(1).
[2]   See CPR r 73.10.

15.87 The charge will remain extant after the bankrupt's discharge, unless enforced by then[1]. Further, for the purpose of the Limitation Act 1980, s 20(1) time cannot begin to run before an order is made for the sale of the property because it is only then that the right to receive the principal charged arises[2].

[1]   Cf IA 1986, s 281(2).
[2]   *Gotham v Doodes* [2006] EWCA Civ 1080, [2007] 1 All ER 527, [2007] 1 WLR 86.

H PERIOD WITHIN WHICH THE TRUSTEE MUST CLAIM THE HOME FOR THE ESTATE

15.88 Where the bankrupt is adjudged bankrupt on a petition presented on or after 1 April 2004[1], the trustee must take steps to realise the bankrupt's interest in his home or the home of his present or former spouse or civil partner within three years from the date of the commencement of the bankruptcy[2]. If the trustee does not act within this period, the bankrupt's interest will cease to form part of his bankruptcy estate and will automatically vest in the bankrupt. This time limit was introduced because of the long delays of many years which could occur between the bankrupt being adjudged bankrupt and an order being sought for the sale of his home. The problem was pronounced where, at the commencement of the bankruptcy, the property was charged with a debt which exceeded the property's value, but where, over time the value of the property came to exceed the amount of the secured debt, in part because of rising property values and in part because of the payments made to the mortgagee by the bankrupt's spouse, civil partner or cohabitee or by the bankrupt himself. In such cases of protracted realisation, many years might have passed between the bankruptcy order and the eventual application for an order for sale.

¹   In cases where the bankruptcy order was made on a petition presented before 1 April 2004, transitional provisions contained in the Enterprise Act 2002, s 261 required the trustee to take the required steps within the period of three years beginning with 1 April 2004.
²   IA 1986, s 283A.

Property to which the time limit applies

15.89 The three-year period applies where the bankrupt's estate includes an interest in a dwelling house which at the date of the bankruptcy was the sole or principal residence of the bankrupt, his spouse or civil partner, or his former spouse or civil partner[1]. In the following paragraphs this interest is referred to as the relevant interest. The date of the bankruptcy must mean the date of the commencement of the bankruptcy[2].

¹   IA 1986, s 283A(1).
²   See IA 1986, s 278(a): the bankruptcy commences with the day on which the bankruptcy order is made.

15.90 The requirement that the dwelling house be the sole or principal residence of the bankrupt or other relevant person also borrows language from statutes concerned with amongst other matters, local taxation and the security of tenure of residential tenants[1]. There the question whether one or other of the properties owned by an individual is his main or principal or most important residence[2] is addressed objectively in the light of all the circumstances: 'Usually, however, a person's main residence will be the dwelling that a reasonable onlooker, with knowledge of the material facts, would regard as that person's home at the material time'[3].

¹   See eg the Housing Act 1988, s 1.
²   See *Frost (Inspector of Taxes) v Feltham* [1981] 1 WLR 452 where these expressions were treated as being synonymous.
³   *R (on the application of) v Horsham District Council* [2004] EWCA Civ 39, [2004] 1 WLR 1137, CA, concerning council tax under the Local Government Finance Act 1992, s 6.

Notice to be given by the trustee

15.91 Where it appears to the trustee that there is a relevant interest in a dwelling house to which the three-year rule applies, he must give notice of this as soon as reasonably practicable to the bankrupt, his spouse or civil partner and his former spouse or civil partner as may be appropriate[1]. The notice must contain the name of the bankrupt, the address of the dwelling house and if it is registered land, the title number. The trustee should not give the notice any later than 14 days before the applicable three-year period is due to expire. It is not clear what consequences, if any, follow on a failure by the trustee to give notice or on late notice being given because the power to make rules providing for such consequences has not been exercised[2].

1 IR 1986, r 6.237.
2 IA 1986, s 283A(8)(b) and (9).

The applicable period

15.92 In general the period during which the trustee must act is the period of three years beginning with the date of the bankruptcy[1]. But this period may be extended or shortened.

1 IA 1986, s 283A(2).

15.93 First, if the bankrupt does not inform the trustee or the official receiver of his interest in a property before the end of the period of three months beginning with the date of the bankruptcy, then the three-year period will not begin until the date on which the trustee or official receiver becomes aware of the bankrupt's interest[1].

1 IA 1986, s 283A(5).

15.94 Secondly, power is given to the court to extend the period by substituting such longer period as the court thinks just and reasonable in all the circumstances of the case[1].

1 IA 1986, s 283A(6), IR 1986, r 6.237C.

15.95 The trustee has power to shorten the period by giving notice to the bankrupt that he considers that the continued vesting of the property in the bankrupt's estate is of no benefit to creditors or that the re-vesting to the bankrupt will facilitate a more efficient administration of the bankrupt's estate[1]. Where such a notice is given, the period will end one month from the date of the notice.

1 IA 1986, s 283A(7); IR 1986, r 6.237CA.

Steps necessary to retain the relevant interest in the bankruptcy estate

15.96 In order to retain the relevant interest for the benefit of his creditors, the trustee must take one of the following steps within the applicable period:

(a) the trustee may realise the interest;
(b) the trustee may apply for an order for sale in respect of the dwelling house;
(c) the trustee may apply for an order for possession of the dwelling house;
(d) the trustee may apply for a charging order under IA 1986, s 313; or
(e) the trustee and the bankrupt may agree that the bankrupt shall incur a specified liability to his estate, with or without the addition of interest

from the date of the agreement, in consideration of which the relevant interest shall cease to form part of the estate[1].

1   IA 1986, s 283A(3).

15.97 If the trustee makes an application for an order for sale, an order for possession or for a charging order under IA 1986, s 313 and the application is dismissed during the applicable period, the relevant interest will cease to be comprised in the bankrupt's estate and vest in the bankrupt without conveyance, assignment or transfer[1].

1   IA 1986, s 283A(4).

Effect of lapse of the applicable period

15.98 If the period of three years from the date of the bankruptcy, or any substituted period, elapses without the trustee's having taken any of the steps just mentioned, the relevant interest will cease to be comprised in the bankrupt's estate and will vest in the bankrupt without any conveyance, assignment or transfer[1].

1   IA 1986, s 283A(2).

Registration and proof of title

15.99 Where the relevant interest is in registered land and has re-vested in the bankrupt, the trustee must apply to the Chief Land Registrar to vacate any entries made on the register relating to the bankruptcy and to show that the relevant interest has vested in the bankrupt. The trustee must notify the bankrupt's present or former spouse or civil partner, where the dwelling house was that person's sole or principal residence, and any other person claiming an interest in it or being under any liability with respect to it that the application has been made[1]. Where the land in question is unregistered, the trustee must issue the bankrupt with a certificate in a prescribed form[2] that the interest has vested in the bankrupt. It appears that the trustee must notify the same interested persons that the certificate has been issued[3].

1   IR 1986, r 6.247A.
2   Form 6.84.
3   IR 1986, r 6.237B, paras (3) and (4) in apparent error refer to an application.

I PROPERTY ABROAD

15.100 Where the bankruptcy comprises main insolvency proceedings or the EC Insolvency Regulation does not apply because the centre of the bankrupt's main interests lies outside any Member State other than Denmark, the estate will include all the bankrupt's property wherever situated. The English court may have jurisdiction to make orders in personam against the bankrupt and any co-owner, if they are amenable to service within the jurisdiction, so as to enable the trustee to bring effective proceedings in England for the purpose of realising the foreign property.

15.101 The first question is whether the intended defendant is domiciled, within the meaning of the EC Judgments Regulation[1], in the United Kingdom and, within the United Kingdom, in England. If the intended defendant is domiciled in England, then he may be sued in England unless the claim is one in respect of which the English court must cede jurisdiction to a foreign court[2]. Where the proceedings have as their object rights in rem in immoveable property or tenancies of immoveable property and the property in question is situated in another Member State, then the courts of that state have exclusive jurisdiction under art 22(1) of the EC Judgments Regulation and the English court must decline to entertain the proceedings[3]. Thus in *Re Hayward*[4] the trustee in bankruptcy's claim against the registered owner of property in Spain for a half-share in that property could not be heard in the English court because in substance it was a claim to the legal ownership of part of the property itself. However, where there is no claim as to the ownership of the property as such, but a claim in personam against the defendants, then the English court is not precluded from hearing the case. Hence where the trustee in bankruptcy of a husband who jointly owned property with his wife in Portugal sought an order for sale against the bankrupt and his wife, the English court retained jurisdiction because the object of the proceedings was not a right in rem over the property but based on the relationship between the parties[5].

1   Council Regulation (EC) No 44/2001, art 59 and the Civil Jurisdiction and Judgments Act 1982, s 41.
2   Council Regulation (EC) No 44/2001, art 2(1).
3   Council Regulation (EC) No 44/2001, art 22(1).
4   [1997] Ch 45, [1997] 1 All ER 32.
5   *Ashurst v Pollard* [2001] Ch 595, [2001] 2 All ER 75, applying *Webb v Webb (Case C-294/92)* [1994] QB 696, [1994] 3 All ER 911.

15.102 If the defendant is not domiciled in the relevant sense in any Member State, then the English court will have personal jurisdiction over him if he is within the jurisdiction but if the property is situated in another Member State, then art 22(1) will still restrict the extent to which the English court can exercise jurisdiction[1].

1   Council Regulation (EC) No 44/2001, art 4(1) importing reference to art 22.

15.103 If the property is not situated in another Member State, then art 22(1) will have no application and the defendant may be sued in England if he is domiciled in England for the purpose of the EC Judgments Regulation so long as the English court will exercise jurisdiction over the subject matter of the proceedings.

15.104 Equally where the defendant is not domiciled in the same sense in any Member State and the property is not situated in any Member State, whether the English court will exercise jurisdiction will depend on the subject matter of the claim[1]. The English court will not exercise jurisdiction where the claim involves determining the title to the foreign land[2]. But where the claim is based on contract or equity between the parties, the English court will exercise jurisdiction. Hence in *Massey v Glover*[3] the English court accepted that it had jurisdiction to resolve a dispute between the two legal co-owners of property in South Africa as to what their respective shares were under the trust on which they held the property and whether there should be an order for sale. The result should be the same if the same relief were sought by the trustee in bankruptcy of one of the co-owners.

1   Council Regulation (EC) No 44/2001, art 4(1).
2   *British South Africa Co v Companhia de Mocambique* [1893] AC 603.
3   [2006] EWHC 2323 (Ch), [2006] All ER (D) 303 (Jul).

Chapter 16

PROTECTION OF THE BANKRUPT'S ESTATE

A INTRODUCTION

16.1 Central to the scheme of bankruptcy is the surrender of the bankrupt's estate in order that it be rateably distributed amongst his unsecured creditors. To protect the collective interest of the unsecured creditors, a basic element in the scheme is that the estate should be received by the trustee, as far as it can be, in the state that it was in when bankruptcy was invoked by the presentation of a petition. In this chapter are described the measures which realise that policy and prevent the depletion of the estate, innocently or otherwise, by the bankrupt or by unsecured creditors seeking to advance their individual interest before the collective interest of the unsecured creditors as a class. In section C are set out the emergency measures which be employed,

623

some of them available as soon as a bankruptcy petition is presented. Between the making of the bankruptcy order, when the bankruptcy commences, and the appointment of the trustee, title to the estate and its components remains vested in the bankrupt but the official receiver is the receiver and manager of the estate during that period. His receivership is described in section D. The protection of the estate from deliberate dissipation by the bankrupt is reinforced by the criminal law, in particular those bankruptcy offences mentioned in section E.

B PROTECTION OF THE ESTATE

Restriction on dispositions of property made after presentation of petition

The restriction on post-petition dispositions

16.2–16.3 Where a person is adjudged bankrupt, any disposition of property made by him during the period beginning with the day of the presentation of the petition for the order on which he was made bankrupt and ending with the vesting of his estate in a trustee, is void except to the extent that it was made with the consent of the court or is or was subsequently ratified by the court[1].

1   IA 1986, s 284(1) and (3).

16.4 This measure affects dispositions of property and payments[1] made by the bankrupt during the period between the presentation of the petition and the vesting of the estate in the trustee. But where such dispositions or payments are made after presentation but before the bankruptcy order is made, whether they are void depends on whether a bankruptcy order is made after they take place. The more natural reading of the statute indicates that the disposition or payment is valid at the time when it is made but rendered void when the bankruptcy order is made, rather than void at the time when made but rendered valid if the petition is dismissed[2]. It may be that there is little practical difference in that in either case the disponee or payee holds a vulnerable title which remains vulnerable in the hands of a subsequent disponee (though it will be unlikely that money will be traceable into the hands of a subsequent payee[3]). But if an interim receiver is appointed with a duty to take immediate possession of the debtor's property, he will not be entitled to get in property which for the time being has been validly disposed of.

1   See IA 1986, s 284(2).
2   Cf the 'ambulatory' title which a transferee obtained under a transfer made after the transferor's act of bankruptcy on which he was subsequently adjudged bankrupt: *Re Dennis (a bankrupt)* [1996] Ch 80, [1995] 3 All ER 171, CA and *Trustee of the property of FC Jones & Sons (a firm) v Jones* [1997] Ch 159, [1996] 4 All ER 721.
3   Cf the second payment in *Re J Leslie Engineers Co Ltd* [1976] 2 All ER 85, [1976] 1 WLR 292.

16.5 The provision contained in the Insolvency Act 1986 ('IA 1986'), s 284 restricting post-petition dispositions in relation to individual insolvents was a new provision, which, save for the protection given to purchasers for value acting in good faith and for bankers, is not derived from anything contained in the Bankruptcy Acts[1] but based on a similar provision which relates to companies against which a winding-up petition has been presented now contained in the IA 1986, s 127. So it is appropriate to regard cases on s 127 and its predecessors as relevant to the interpretation of s 284.

1   Under the Bankruptcy Acts the same purpose of protecting the estate was fulfilled by the doctrine of relation back under which the trustee's title to the bankrupt's estate related back to the first act of bankruptcy committed within three months before the receiving order; see the Bankruptcy Act 1914, ss 37 and 38.

Dispositions of property

16.6   By 'disposition' is meant any method of alienating an asset[1]. 'Disposition of property' expressly includes payments whether made in cash or otherwise[2]. Payments made in cash seem clearly to be dispositions of property without any special provision declaring that they are[3]. Payments made otherwise than in cash might not involve a disposition of property belonging to the debtor. For a payment to a creditor made by cheque drawn on an overdrawn account but honoured by the banker on whom it is drawn might not otherwise count as a disposition of property, since the bankrupt's overall indebtedness remains the same, one new creditor, the banker, being substituted for another, the paid creditor. But the IA 1986, s 284(1) does not refer to 'dispositions of property belonging to the debtor' but to 'dispositions of property made by [the debtor]'. So even if the disposition was of property belonging to a banker it might still be caught.

1   *Re Mersey Steel & Iron Co v Naylor, Benzon & Co* (1884) 9 App Cas 434, HL.
2   IA 1986, s 284(2).
3   See the IA 1986, s 436 where 'property' is defined as including money.

Assignments and releases of things in action

16.7   If a debtor assigns a thing in action owed to him by another, it seems clear that he thereby makes a disposition of property[1]. It is submitted that a debtor equally disposes of property if he releases the person against whom his claim to the thing in action lies. It may seem inappropriate to speak of a thing in action being alienated in such a case. But the question is whether the IA 1986, s 284(1) should be construed as embracing such transaction and it is submitted that such a release should nonetheless count as a disposition of property by the bankrupt within the IA 1986, s 284. For otherwise if, between the presentation of the bankruptcy petition and the bankruptcy order, an individual released a person against whom he was entitled to enforce the thing in action, the release of the thing in action would not be caught by the IA 1986, s 284 and the policy which that section promotes of protecting the assets for the benefit of the creditors would be thwarted if the release was made without any commensurate benefit being received by the debtor. This point is discussed further in connection with the decision of the Court of Appeal in *Hollicourt (Contracts) Ltd v Bank of Ireland*[2] which is discussed below at para **16.15**.

16.7 *Protection of the bankrupt's estate*

1   See the IA 1986, s 436 again where 'property' is defined as including things in action.
2   [2001] Ch 555, [2001] 1 All ER 289, CA. On payment to an agent with knowledge of the petition, see *Pettit v Novakovic* (unreported) 22 January 2007 where the bankrupt's solicitors paid the proceeds of sale of property belonging to the bankrupt to his accountant after the petition had been presented but before it was heard. Although there was no disposition of the beneficial interest in the funds involved because the accountant received them as bare trustee, there was nonetheless a payment to him which IA 1986, s 284(1) caught.

Grant of security

16.8 The creation of security over property has been assumed to be a disposition of property within the IA 1986, s 127 or its statutory predecessors[1]. It is correct that it should be; for, although it may be right that the creation of a security over an asset may be said not to deplete the total of the assets of the person granting the security or to diminish their value, the availability of the asset over which the security is granted is lost as far as the unsecured creditors are concerned[2]. Since the principle which the IA 1986, ss 127 and 284 embody is that the unsecured creditors should be collectively protected against the depletion of the assets available for *pari passu* distribution to them, to treat the creation of a security over an asset as not involving a disposition would breach that principle.

1   *Re Park Ward & Co Ltd* [1926] Ch 828; *Re Steane's (Bournemouth) Ltd* [1950] 1 All ER 21; *Site Preparations Ltd v Buchan Development Co Ltd* [1983] SLT 317.
2   Cf *Re MC Bacon Ltd* [1990] BCLC 324, 340 where the issue was the different question whether the creation of a security could be characterised as a transaction at an undervalue; Millett J held that it could not. The focus in that context is a comparison of the value of the asset and the price or other consideration for which it was transferred and therefore does not bear on the meaning of 'disposition' in the IA 1986, ss 127 and 284.

Orders concerning property in matrimonial proceedings

16.9 In cases where the bankruptcy of one of the parties to a marriage has collided with matrimonial proceedings concerning their property, the question has arisen whether a property transfer order made under the Matrimonial Causes Act 1973, s 24 constitutes a disposition of property where what is ordered is that one party transfer property to the other, in other words an order requiring further steps to be taken to complete it. In *Mountney v Treharne*[1], where the question was whether the property had been effectively transferred by the bankrupt to his former spouse before he presented his own petition, the Court of Appeal held that a property transfer order itself constituted an effective disposition in equity of the property to which it related even though further steps were necessary to complete the transfer at law. Thus, where the property transfer order is made after the presentation of the petition, the order will constitute a disposition which, unless ratified by the bankruptcy court, will be void[2]. Property adjustment orders may also be made which have immediate effect, for example to vary an ante-nuptial or post-nuptial settlement. In such a case, or where the order in question may be construed as effecting an immediate disposition, the time when the disposition occurs will be when the order is made[3]. The same principles will apply to property adjustment orders made under the Children Act 1989 and the Civil Partnerships Act 2004.

1   [2002] EWCA Civ 1174, [2003] Ch 135.
2   *Treharne v Forrester* [2003] EWHC 2784 (Ch), [2004] 1 FLR 1173.
3   *Re Harper (a bankrupt), Harper v O'Reilly* [1997] BPIR 656.

Specifically enforceable contracts

16.10 Where an unconditional contract for the sale of land has been made before the petition is presented, the completion of the sale does not involve a disposition of property, but it may nonetheless be prudent to seek the court's approval[1]. The same principles should apply in relation to any contract of sale which, because it is specifically enforceable, creates an equitable interest in the purchaser in the subject matter of the sale[2].

1   *Re French's (Wine Bar) Ltd* [1987] BCLC 499; *Re Tramway Building and Construction Co Ltd* [1987] BCLC 632.
2   See *Lysaght v Edwards* (1876) 2 Ch D 499.

Property affected

16.11 In relation to the restriction on post-petition dispositions it does not matter whether the property disposed of falls within the estate or not. For a disposition of property is void notwithstanding that the property is not or, as the case may be, would not be comprised in the bankrupt's estate[1]. The only exception is that the IA 1986, s 284 does not affect any disposition made by a person of property held by him on trust for any other person.

1   IA 1986, s 284(6).

Payments made by the bankrupt in settlement of the petition debt

16.12 The restriction on post-petition dispositions affects the ability of the debtor after the presentation of the petition to settle with his own funds any debt which he owes to the petitioning creditor. For a petitioning creditor who accepts payment of the debtor's own funds in settlement of the debt before the hearing of the petition risks having to repay the money to the trustee, unless the payment has been approved or ratified by the court. For another creditor may be substituted as the petitioner[1] or may be given the carriage of the petition[2] and, in either case, a bankruptcy order may be made on it thereby rendering the payment by the debtor void if not approved or ratified by the court. In consequence, a creditor is not obliged under the IA 1986, s 271 to accept the payment tendered by a debtor where the funds are the debtor's own and there are other creditors wishing to prosecute the bankruptcy proceedings[3].

1   Insolvency Rules 1986 ('IR 1986'), r 6.3.

16.12 *Protection of the bankrupt's estate*

2   IR 1986, r 6.31. The court cannot make an order changing the carriage of the petition if the debt has been paid, secured or compounded for by means of a disposition of the debtor's own property made with the approval of, or ratified by, the court; IR 1986, r 6.31(3)(a).
3   *Smith (a bankrupt) v Ian Simpson & Co* [2001] Ch 239, [2000] 3 All ER 434, CA. The majority held that the IA 1986, s 271 was to be construed as referring to payments which were not vulnerable to being avoided if a bankruptcy order was made. *Re Purvis* [1997] 3 All ER 663 was disapproved.

16.13 In order that the court may supervise the settlement of petitions in the interest of the general body of creditors a petitioner who wishes to withdraw his petition because payment has been made by way of settlement since the petition was filed must file an affidavit stating what dispositions of property have been made for the purposes of the settlement, whether, in the case of any disposition, it was the property of the debtor himself or some other person and whether, if it was the property of the debtor, the disposition has been approved or ratified by the court[1].

1   IR 1986, r 6.32(1) and (2).

Payments out of bank accounts: (a) accounts which are in credit

16.14 As explained above, a payment made otherwise than in cash is a disposition of property. Such a payment will ordinarily be a payment made by cheque drawn on a banker or made by direct debit[1]. Under the cases governing the operation of the equivalent provision in the winding up of companies[2], the rule applied was that if a banker permitted payments to be made out of the company's bank account after the advertisement of the petition, he would be liable to restore the position of that account to that which it would have been in had those payments not been made. Despite criticisms, the rule applied, or was taken to apply, to payments made whether the company's account was in credit (in which case it is apparent that something of value was disposed of, namely the debt owed by the banker to the company) or not (in which case one creditor, the banker, was substituted for another, the paid creditor)[3]. In *Hollicourt (Contracts) Ltd v Bank of Ireland*[4] the Court of Appeal has imposed certainty on the law. In that case the company drew a cheque on its account which was in credit and the company's bank honoured the cheque although a winding-up petition had been presented and advertised. The transfer of funds thereby made to the payee represented a disposition of an asset belonging to the company and there is no doubt that the liquidator was entitled to recover the payment from the payee. But the issue was whether the bank was also liable to restore the account to the state it would have been in had payment from it not been made. The Court of Appeal held that the bank was not liable to do so. Central to the decision is the Court of Appeal's view that the policy of preserving the company's assets for the benefit of the general body of creditors does not require that both the payee and the bank be rendered liable to make restitution of the void payment. The judge at first instance had analysed the transaction as involving two dispositions: first, the disposition comprised in the transfer of funds to the payee and second, the disposition comprised in the corresponding reduction of the bank's indebtedness to the company as its customer[5]. That analysis accords with the general principles of banking law[6]. For as well as acting as the company's agent in honouring the cheque, the bank acts as principal in so far as it reduces its own debt to the company as its customer. But the Court of Appeal described the bank's role in honouring the cheque as an intermediate step which was merely part of the process by which the disposition of the company's asset to the payee was made. Also, basing itself on the policy of the IA 1986, s 127, the court held that s 127 should not be construed as applying to such disposition, if any, as might have been comprised in the reduction of the bank's liability to its customer. Thus, it is clear that a bank which makes payments out of a bank account which is in credit is not thereby rendered liable to restore the position to what it would have been if the payments had not been made. It is the payee who received the payment and only the payee who is liable to repay what he has received.

[1]   *Esso Petroleum Co Ltd v Milton* [1997] 2 All ER 593, [1997] 1 WLR 938, CA.
[2]   IA 1986, s 127.
[3]   This rule derived from the interpretation put on a passage of the judgment in *Re Gray's Inn Construction Co Ltd* [1980] 1 All ER 814, [1980] 1 WLR 711. For an example of its application, see *Re McGuinness Bros (UK) Ltd* (1987) BCC 571.
[4]   [2001] Ch 555, [2001] 1 All ER 289, CA.
[5]   [2000] 2 All ER 45, [2000] 1 WLR 895.
[6]   See Goode, *Commercial Law* (2nd edn), p 595 (and c f 1st edn, p 494 for slightly different emphasis). The relevant focus is on the proceeds of the cheque, not the question whether the bank has become a holder in due course of the cheque.

Payments out of bank accounts: (b) accounts which are overdrawn

16.15 In *Hollicourt (Contractors) Ltd v Bank of Ireland*[1] the payments were made out of a bank account which was in credit. However the Court of Appeal approved the decision of Lightman J in *Coutts & Co v Stock*[2] which concerned an overdrawn account. The bank had continued after the presentation and advertisement of a winding-up petition to honour cheques drawn on the company's account which at the date of advertisement was overdrawn in the sum of £121,875 but by the date of the winding-up order was overdrawn in excess of £190,000. The argument that the payments made by the bank were void was pursued by a director of the company who had provided a guarantee to the bank in respect of the account. The unpromising ground from which this argument was launched was not enhanced by the fact that much of the drawing on the account had been in favour of other companies owned or controlled by that director. Lightman J analysed the honouring of a cheque by the bank when the account was overdrawn as involving two steps: (i) a loan of the sum drawn by the cheque to the company; and (ii) the payment of the sum so loaned to the payee. In making the loan comprised in step (i) the bank was making a disposition but it was a disposition of its own money and therefore not caught by the IA 1986, s 127. Neither would it be a disposition of property by the bankrupt within the IA 1986, s 284. In making the payment comprised in step (ii), the bank was acting as agent for the company; hence it was the company's property which the payee received under a disposition which was capable of being avoided under the IA 1986, s 127 (or s 284) if made during the period to which that provision applies. It may be noted that in contrast to the situation where the bank account is in credit, the bank was not simultaneously taking any benefit for itself (save insofar as it became entitled in the future to charge interest on the sum lent). This analysis demonstrates why, where a bank makes a payment out of an overdrawn account, there is no disposition to the bank of any property belonging to the company (or the bankrupt) without needing the reinforcement of any considerations of policy.

1   [2001] Ch 555, [2001] 1 All ER 289, CA.
2   [2000] 2 All ER 56, [2000] 1 WLR 906.

Payments into bank accounts: (a) accounts which are overdrawn

16.16 In *Re Gray's Inn Construction Co Ltd*[1] the company's bank account was overdrawn throughout the material period. In respect of the payments made into the account, Buckley LJ said:

> 'when a customer's account with his banker is overdrawn he is debtor to his banker for the amount of the overdraft. When he pays a sum of money into the account, whether in cash or by payment in of a third party's cheque, he discharges his indebtedness to the bank pro tanto. There is clearly in these circumstances, in my judgment, a disposition by the company to the bank of the amount of the cash or of the cheque. It may well be the case, as counsel for the bank has submitted, that in clearing a third party's cheque and collecting the amount due on it, the bank acts as the customer's agent, but as soon as it credits the amount collected in reduction of the customer's overdraft, as in the ordinary course of banking business it has authority to do in the absence of any contrary instruction from the customer, it makes a disposition on the customer's behalf in its own favour discharging pro tanto the customer's liability on the overdraft.'

1   [1980] 1 All ER 814, [1980] 1 WLR 711, CA.

16.17 Although in any event, being part of the *ratio* of *Re Gray's Inn Construction Co Ltd*[1] this rule was binding on the courts which decided *Hollicourt (Contracts) Ltd v Bank of Ireland*[2], the result is consistent with the Court of Appeal's decision in *Hollicourt* because, where the account is overdrawn and a payment is made into the account, the bank and only the bank is the person who obtains the beneficial ownership of the funds which the cheque represents. Payments into an overdrawn account were treated as dispositions and avoided in *Re Tain Construction Limited*[3].

1   [1980] 1 All ER 814, [1980] 1 WLR 711, CA.
2   [2001] Ch 555, [2001] 1 All ER 289, CA.
3   [2003] EWHC 1737 (Ch), [2003] 1 WLR 2791, [2003] BPIR 1188.

Payments into bank accounts: (b) accounts which are in credit

16.18 Where payments in the form of cheques drawn by third parties are made into a bank account which is in credit, it appears that there is no disposition of property belonging to the bankrupt. In *Re Barn Crown Ltd*[1] the deputy judge analysed such a transaction as follows:

> 'In collecting payment upon a cheque the bank credits the customer's account with the amount of the cheque. If the account is already in credit, no

disposition of the property of the customer takes place in favour of the bank. The amount standing to the credit of a customer's account is increased in return for the surrender of the cheque which becomes a voucher for payment. It is the drawer of the cheque whose property is disposed of. All that happens between the customer and the banker is an adjustment of entries in the statement recording the accounts between them.'

1   [1994] 4 All ER 42, [1995] 1 WLR 147.

16.19 This analysis seems open to question. For in collecting the money which is payable on the cheque, the collecting bank acts as agent for its customer who is the payee of the cheque. If the bank retains the funds on the account, it ceases to hold them as agent for the customer but becomes, as principal, indebted to its customer in the amount credited to the account[1]. Thus, as a mirror image of Lightman J's analysis of the two steps involved in the honouring by a bank of a cheque drawn on an overdrawn account, there are likewise two steps involved in the collection of a cheque and the crediting of the amount collected to the customer's account: (i) the activities involved in presenting the cheque to the paying bank and receiving the funds; and (ii) the loan of those funds by the customer to the bank comprised in the crediting of the funds to the customer's account. In carrying out the activities comprised in step (i), the bank acts as agent; in making the credit comprised in step (ii) it acts as principal. In the ordinary case, this may not matter, because if there are funds to the credit of the bankrupt, his trustee will be able to call on the bank to make payment. But if the bank were insolvent, the difference is acute: for if, as submitted, there is a disposition of the customer's property to the bank, in bankruptcy, by reason of the IA 1986, s 284(2), the bank holds the sum paid for the bankrupt as part of his estate. The trustee would therefore be entitled to recover the sum paid into the account in its entirety, instead of having to prove for a dividend in the bank's insolvency. Nor is this result inconsistent with the Court of Appeal's decision in *Hollicourt (Contracts) Ltd v Bank of Ireland*[2] because where the bank credits the funds to an account in credit, it is the bank who, bankruptcy law apart, obtains the beneficial ownership of the proceeds. For, as is long established, the relationship of banker holding funds for his customer is that of a debtor to his creditor, not that of trustee to beneficiary[3].

1   See *Joachimson v Swiss Bank Corpn* [1921] 3 KB 110, CA; *AL Underwood Ltd v Bank of Liverpool* [1924] 1 KB 775.
2   [2001] Ch 555, [2001] 1 All ER 289, CA.
3   *Foley v Hill* (1848) 2 HL Cas 28.

The decision in Hollicourt (Contracts) Ltd v Bank of Ireland

16.20 The question whether a bank which continues to operate an account which is in credit is obliged to make restitution in respect of payments drawn on the account is capable of being broken down into the issues: (i) whether a payment out of the account holder's bank account which is in credit constitutes (a) a disposition of his property to the payee, and (b) a disposition of his property to the bank, and (ii) whether the bank is liable to make good the second (or both) of these dispositions[1]. The Court of Appeal, disagreeing with the judge at first instance, did not accept that there was any disposition of the company's property from the company to the bank. For, having referred to the bank's role as agent in honouring the cheque, the Court of Appeal stated that 'the beneficial ownership of the property represented by the cheque was never transferred to the bank, to which no alienation of the company's property was made'. In holding that there was no disposition at all of property from the company to the bank, the Court of Appeal's decision might seem to cast in doubt whether a release of a claim could amount to a disposition of property as it submitted to be above. For, it may be argued that the property represented by the cheque was part of the funds on the customer's current account at the bank. The current account, while in credit, is a thing in action, namely a debt, owed by the bank to the company as its customer. Such a thing in action amounts to property for the purpose of the IA 1986[2]. The cheque represented a direction by the customer to transfer the beneficial ownership of that part of that debt to the payee. By honouring the cheque, the bank caused payment of part of the debt which it owed to its customer, the company, to be made not to that customer but to the payee of the cheque. To the extent of the amount of the cheque, the debt or thing in action owed by the bank to its customer was released[3]. It might therefore be contended that such release is incapable of being a relevant disposition.

[1] See the approach of Lightman J in *Coutts & Co v Stock* [2000] 1 WLR 906, 911–912 in considering an overdrawn account.
[2] See the definition of 'property' in the IA 1986, s 436.
[3] This was the analysis accepted by the judge at first instance.

16.21 However, this conclusion is not justified since the Court of Appeal's decision does not entail that all releases of claims are incapable of being dispositions for the purpose of the IA 1986, s 127 or s 284. For the question whether the beneficial ownership of the relevant property passes to the person in whose favour the release is made enables a distinction to be made between a simple release of a thing in action by a debtor in favour of the person by whom it is owed and a release of the thing in action in return for its payment to a third person. In the former case the person to whom the release is given obtains the beneficial ownership of the property which the thing in action represents. Thus had Hollicourt (Contracts) Ltd directed the bank, by a cheque drawn in favour of the bank or otherwise, to draw funds in favour of itself, the bank would have been liable to restore the disposition because it was the person who received the beneficial ownership of the property represented by the cheque or other form of direction. Thus, suppose A, has a claim in respect of a debt against B and the events described occur after the presentation of a petition against A on which a bankruptcy order is made:

(1) if A simply releases B from that claim, the disposition represented by the release is void and A's liquidator or trustee in bankruptcy may still make a claim against B in respect of the thing in action because the net value of the assets beneficially owned by B is increased by the amount of the release; but

(2) if A causes B to pay the debt to C[1], the disposition thereby effected of A's interest in the debt to C would be void and A's liquidator or trustee in bankruptcy may claim from C the sum which he has received but the release by A of his claim against B in respect of the debt would not be

avoided because the net value of the assets beneficially owned by B is unaffected by whether he has paid the debt to A or to C.

In other words, in example (1) B is the person to whom the relevant disposition is made but in example (2) C is the disponee and B merely an intermediary. Hence B, in the second case, is not exposed to the unfairness of having to pay twice.

[1]   A would ordinarily cause such transfer by assigning the thing in action to C and C would take into possession the asset, to which the thing in action related, by enforcing the claim which the thing in action represented. There is therefore an intermediate stage between A's assigning the thing in action to C and C's bringing the asset which the thing in action represents into possession. If C has not brought the thing into possession by enforcing the thing in action, then B has not been released and the only disposition which has occurred is the assignment. There is no difficulty in applying the IA 1986, s 284(1) to the assignment from A to C. It therefore is void, leaving A's claim against B intact and enforceable by A's liquidator or trustee in bankruptcy.

Effect of void dispositions

16.22 Where the disposition in question comprises a payment in cash or otherwise, the IA 1986, s 284(2) provides that where a payment is made which is void, the person to whom the payment was made shall hold the sum paid for the bankrupt as part of his estate. If the disposition concerns some other form of property, then the person to whom the property has been transferred will similarly hold it as part of the bankrupt's estate. On his appointment the trustee may claim the property from the transferee, or any person to whom the transferee has subsequently transferred the property[1], unless the protection given to purchasers in good faith and those whose interests derive from such purchasers applies.

[1]   Compare, in the context of winding up, *Re J Leslie Engineers Co Ltd* [1976] 2 All ER 85, [1976] 1 WLR 292.

Defence of change of position

16.23 The possibility has been recognised that change of position may be available as a defence to a claim for repayment of money paid under a void disposition[1].

[1]   *Re Tain Construction Ltd* [2003] EWHC 1737 (Ch), [2003] 1 WLR 2791, [2003] BPIR 1188.

Protection of purchasers in good faith

16.24 No remedy lies against any person in respect of any property or payment which he received before the commencement of the bankruptcy in good faith, for value and without notice that the petition had been presented[1]. Nor does any remedy lie against any other person in respect of any interest in property which derives from an interest in such property[2]. This provision is modelled on the protection provided by the Bankruptcy Act 1914, s 46 which

was discussed by the Divisional Court in *Re Dalton, ex p Herrington &
Carmichael (a firm) v the Trustee*[3]. The court[4] held that the requirement of
good faith connoted that some duty was owed and that in the context of
bankruptcy that the duty was owed to the general body of creditors. In
showing good faith to that general body, what was involved:

> 'goes beyond mere personal honesty: it requires more than absence of dishon-
> esty, more than absence of conscious attempt to defraud. If Mr Bennett[5] had
> made the payments with the knowledge that the process would result in some
> creditors being paid in full and others whistling for their money, we do not
> consider that the payments would have been made bona fide ... It might well be
> that if a person in Mr Bennett's position had a strong suspicion that the process
> of his payments would have the result mentioned above, but took pains to
> avoid finding out the truth, he could not be said to make them bona fide.'

[1] IA 1986, s 284(4)(a).
[2] IA 1986, s 284(4)(b).
[3] [1963] Ch 336, [1962] 2 All ER 499.
[4] Russell and Cross JJ.
[5] Mr Bennett was a solicitor acting for the debtor who applied the proceeds of the sale of the
    debtor's business in payment of some but not all of his debts and who sought, successfully
    in the event, the protection of the Bankruptcy Act 1914.

16.25 If this test is applied to the situation of a person receiving the
payments, it would appear that if a person, A, suspects that his debtor, B, from
whom A is receiving payment cannot satisfy all of his, B's, other creditors but
A turns a blind eye to that possibility, then A may not be acting in good faith
and, if a petition has been presented at the time of the payment, A will not be
entitled to rely on the protection of the IA 1986, s 284(4). The question then
is how strong the suspicion must be and what circumstances would give rise to
it. If the test as stated in *Re Dalton*[1] remains the law, the strength of the
suspicion would have to be at the high end of the spectrum. What might
justify such suspicion will be a matter of fact, but the possibilities might
include cases where A was aware of unsatisfied judgments or of the service of
an uncontested statutory demand.

[1] [1963] Ch 336, [1962] 2 All ER 499.

Limited protection of bankers

16.26 Where after the commencement of the bankruptcy, the bankrupt has
incurred a debt to a banker or other person by reason of the making of a
payment which is void by virtue of the IA 1986, s 284(1), that debt is deemed
to have been incurred before the commencement of the bankruptcy unless
either (a) that banker or other person had notice of the bankruptcy before the
debt was incurred, or (b) it is not reasonably practicable for the amount of the
payment to be recovered from the person to whom it was made[1]. The
protection which this provision affords is limited in that all it does is to enable
the banker or other person to whom the bankrupt has incurred a debt to
which it applies to prove in the bankruptcy for that debt. The prime example
of the operation of this provision arises where, between the presentation of the
petition and the vesting of the estate in the trustee, the bankrupt draws a
cheque on his banker which the banker honours. If the payment on the cheque

is collected from the banker after the commencement of the bankruptcy and at that time the bankrupt's account is overdrawn, the payee will be paid and the bankrupt incurs a debt to the banker corresponding to the amount of the payment. Without the deeming provision under discussion, that debt would not be a bankruptcy debt because it is not a debt to which the bankrupt was subject at the commencement of the bankruptcy nor one to which he became liable by reason of any obligation incurred before the commencement of the bankruptcy[2], since the banker could have dishonoured the cheque. Since the debt would not have been a bankruptcy debt it would not have been a provable debt[3]. But the IA 1986, s 284(5) renders the debt provable.

[1]   IA 1986, s 284(5).
[2]   See the IA 1986, s 382(1).
[3]   See the IA 1986, s 322 (proof of bankruptcy debts) and the IR 1986, r 12.3 (definition of provable debts).

Market contracts

16.27   IA 1986, s 284 does not apply to a market contract or any disposition of property pursuant to such a contract; the provision of margin in relation to a market contract; a contract effected by an exchange or clearing house for the purpose of realising property provided as margin in relation to a market contract, or any disposition pursuant to such a contract; or any disposition of property in accordance with the rules of the exchange or clearing house as to the application of property provided as margin. But the profit gained from a market contract by a person who entered it with notice that a bankruptcy petition had been presented may be recovered from him[1].

[1]   Companies Act 1989, s 164(3)–(6).

Circumstances in which the court will grant approval

16.28   The primary objective in considering whether to approve or ratify a disposition of property is to ensure that the interests of the unsecured creditors will not be prejudiced. For the principle or policy that underlies the avoidance of post-petition dispositions is that the assets belonging to the bankrupt at the date of presentation of the petition should be available for rateable distribution amongst the general body of unsecured creditors in the event that a bankruptcy order is made[1]. There are two situations in which validation of a disposition or dispositions may be required during the period between presentation of the petition and its being heard: first, that the individual against whom the petition has been presented is solvent and able to pay his debts but has somehow become the subject of a petition; secondly, that the proposed disposition will not prejudice or even will benefit the debtor's unsecured creditors even if a bankruptcy order is made[2]. In bankruptcy, the first type of case may be unusual given the requirement that a petition be preceded by a statutory demand (unless based on the unsatisfied execution of a judgment). But where it does arise, the court must be satisfied by credible evidence that the debtor is solvent and able to pay his debts. In the second type of case the court must be satisfied that the transaction or series of transactions will be beneficial to or not prejudice the interests of all the creditors.

1   *Re Civil Service and General Store Ltd* (1887) 57 LJ Ch 119; *Re J Leslie Engineers Co Ltd* [1976] 1 WLR 292, 304; *Re Gray's Inn Construction Co Ltd* [1980] 1 WLR 711, 717–719; *Re Fairway Graphics Ltd* [1991] BCLC 468; *Denney v John Hudson & Co* [1992] BCLC 901, 904.
2   *Re Fairway Graphics Ltd* [1991] BCLC 468.

16.29 The evidence supporting any application must address the matters listed in the *Practice Note: Validation Orders (Sections 127 and 284 of the Insolvency Act 1986)*[1].

1   [2007] BPIR 94, para 16ff.

16.30 In *Re Gray's Inn Construction Co Ltd*[1] having referred to that policy, Buckley LJ said:

'it is, in my opinion, clear that the court should not validate any transaction or series of transactions which might result in one or more pre-liquidation creditors being paid in full at the expense of other creditors, who will only receive a dividend, in the absence of special circumstances making such a course desirable in the interests of the unsecured creditors as a body. If for example it were in the interests of the creditors generally that the company's business should be carried on and this could only be achieved by paying for goods already supplied to the company when the petition is presented but not yet paid for, the court might think fit in the exercise of its discretion to validate payment for those goods ... But, although that policy might disincline the court to ratify any transaction which involved preferring a pre-liquidation creditor, it has no relevance to a transaction which is entirely post-liquidation, as for instance a sale of an asset at its full market value after presentation of a petition. Such a transaction involves no dissipation of the company's assets, for it does not reduce the value of those assets. It cannot harm the creditors and there would seem to be no reason why the court should not in the exercise of its discretion validate it. A fortiori the court would be inclined to validate a transaction which would increase, or has increased, the value of the company's assets, or which would preserve, or has preserved, the value of the company's assets from harm which would result from the company's business being paralysed (*Re Wiltshire Iron Co*[2], *Re Park Ward & Co Ltd*[3], where the business of the company was eventually sold as a going concern presumably to the advantage of the creditors, and *Re Clifton Place Garage Ltd*[4]). In *Re AI Levy (Holdings) Ltd*[5] the court validated a sale of a lease which was liable to forfeiture in the event of the tenant company being wound up, and also validated, as part of the transaction, payment out of the proceeds of sale of arrears of rent which had accrued before the presentation of the petition for the compulsory liquidation of the company. If that case was rightly decided, as I trust that it was, the court can in appropriate circumstances validate payment in full of an unsecured pre-liquidation debt which constitutes a necessary part of a transaction which as a whole is beneficial to the general body of unsecured creditors. But we have been referred to no case in which the court has validated payment in full of an unsecured pre-liquidation debt where there was no such special circumstance, and in my opinion it would not normally be right to do so, because such a payment would prefer the creditor whose debt is paid over the other creditors of equal degree.'

1   [1980] 1 All ER 814, [1980] 1 WLR 711.
2   (1868) 3 Ch App 443.
3   [1926] Ch 828.
4   [1970] Ch 477, [1969] 3 All ER 892.
5   [1964] Ch 19, [1963] 2 All ER 556.

16.31 These principles apply with equal force to the exercise of the court's power to approve dispositions by an individual. Where the petitioning creditor opposed the application for the prospective validation of the sale of property by a company against which a winding-up petition was pending on the ground that the sale was at an undervalue, the court refused to validate the transaction because it was persuaded that the property might not have been properly marketed[1]. The suggestion that the petitioning creditor did not have standing to oppose the application was not accepted.

1   *Re Rescupine Ltd* [2003] EWHC 216 (Ch), [2003] 1 BCLC 661.

Procedure

16.32 An application seeking the court's approval of a disposition should ordinarily be made to a registrar or district judge. Notice should ordinarily be given to the petitioning creditor, any creditor who has given notice of intention to appear at the hearing of the petition, any creditor who has been substituted as petitioning creditor or to whom carriage of the petition has been given. The application must be supported by an affidavit or witness statement, which should ordinarily be made by the debtor. A draft order should be attached to the application[1].

1   *Practice Note: Validation Orders* [2007] BPIR 94.

Stay of proceedings

Court's power to stay proceedings

16.33 At any time when proceedings on a bankruptcy petition are pending or an individual has been adjudged bankrupt, the court, ie the court having bankruptcy jurisdiction over the debtor, may stay any action, execution or other legal process against the property or person of the debtor[1]. Further, any court in which proceedings are pending against an individual may, on proof that a bankruptcy petition has been presented in respect of that individual or that he is an undischarged bankrupt, either stay the proceedings or allow them to continue on such terms as it thinks fit[2].

1   IA 1986, s 285(1).
2   IA 1986, s 285(2).

Relevant property

16.34 In the IA 1986, s 285(6) it is provided that references to the property of the bankrupt are to any of his property whether or not comprised in his estate.

16.34 *Protection of the bankrupt's estate*

Where the court is imposing a stay before the bankruptcy order has been made, this provision seems to have no application, firstly because the property is the property of the debtor, not the bankrupt and secondly, because the estate as a subset of the property vested in and belonging to the bankrupt is not yet identifiable since the estate is primarily defined in terms of what property is vested in and belongs to the bankrupt at the commencement of the bankruptcy. Further, any court in which proceedings are pending against an individual may, on proof that a bankruptcy petition has been present against him, either stay the proceedings or allow them to continue on such terms as it thinks fit[1]. These powers to stay proceedings may also be exercised after a bankruptcy order has been made.

[1]   IA 1986, s 285(2).

Relevant proceedings

16.35 The power enabling proceedings to be stayed was conferred in terms similar to the IA 1986, s 285 by the Bankruptcy Act 1869, s 13. But in s 13 of the 1869 Act the power to stay was only exercisable to 'restrain further proceedings in any action, suit, execution or other legal process against the debtor in respect of any debt provable in the bankruptcy'. The power was extended to embrace any action, execution or other legal process against the property or person of the debtor by the Bankruptcy Act 1883, s 10(2)[1]. However, although the power may be exercised whatever the subject matter of the action, execution or other legal process, the purpose remains 'to protect the estate for the whole body of creditors and to prevent unsecured creditors, after the initiation of bankruptcy proceedings, from taking steps by putting pressure on the debtor to obtain advantages over other creditors'[2] and thereby obtain payment in full participation in the *pari passu* distribution of the estate[3].

[1]   It may seem inappropriate to refer to the Bankruptcy Acts in this context since in *Smith (a bankrupt) v Braintree District Council* [1990] 2 AC 215, [1989] 3 All ER 897, HL, Lord Jauncey of Tullichettle gave as the second of his reasons for not following a case determined under the Bankruptcy Act 1883 that the IA 1986 was a new code of insolvency law. Courts have since been more inclined to take into account the 'intellectual freight', as Hoffmann J called it in *Re a Debtor (No 784 of 1991)* [1992] Ch 554, which is carried by those actions of the IA 1986 which reproduce provisions contained in former Bankruptcy Acts.
[2]   *Smith (a bankrupt) v Braintree District Council* [1990] 2 AC 215, [1989] 3 All ER 897, HL.
[3]   Cf *Re Commercial Bank Corpn of India and the East* (1866) 1 Ch App 538.

'Other legal process'

16.36 In *Smith (a bankrupt) v Braintree District Council*[1] the House of Lords determined that a warrant of commitment issued by a magistrates' court against a bankrupt who had failed to pay his rates is a form of legal process to which the IA 1986, s 285(1) applies because, although an element of punishment might be comprehended within the order of committal, at least part of the purpose was to coerce the bankrupt into paying and the purpose of the court's power to stay proceedings was to avert such pressure being put on the bankrupt to put one creditor's interests before others. This reasoning has, perhaps, more force in relation to the need to stay proceedings during the period before the estate vests in the trustee. Indeed it indicates that a stay should be imposed until the trustee is appointed in any proceedings which might result in a transfer of property or funds out of the estate.

¹   [1990] 2 AC 215, [1989] 3 All ER 897, HL.

Proceedings in which a stay may be inappropriate

16.37 Proceedings which would ordinarily be permitted to continue include:

(1)   proceedings brought by a secured creditor to enforce his security, because the property subject to the security will not form part of the estate available for distribution to the general body of unsecured creditors;

(2)   proceedings relating to claims from which the bankrupt will not be released by his discharge, for example a claim in respect of a fraudulent breach of trust will be permitted to continue¹, because such a claim will establish a personal liability to which the bankrupt's discharge will be no defence²;

(3)   proceedings relating to claims for remedies other than money claims; for example a claim for specific performance³ or an injunction⁴; proceedings relating to money claims which do not give rise to provable debts, for example, claims for maintenance in matrimonial proceedings, because there is no means of enforcing such claims in bankruptcy⁵;

(4)   proceedings where the purpose of obtaining judgment is to pursue a claim against the bankrupt's insurers under the Third Parties (Rights against Insurers) Act 1930, because such claims bypass the estate⁶;

(5)   proceedings where liability is in issue and it is more appropriate to permit the pending proceedings to continue than to make the claimant submit a proof and resolve such dispute as arises when the trustee rejects the proof⁷.

¹   *Polly Peck International plc v Nadir* [1992] BCLC 746.
²   *Re Blake, ex p Coker* (1875) 10 Ch App 652.
³   *Re Coregrange Ltd* [1984] BCLC 453.
⁴   *Borneman v Wilson* (1884) 28 Ch D 53.
⁵   See eg *Albert v Albert* [1996] BPIR 232, CA where the proceedings continued after bankruptcy though note that no property adjustment order may be made after bankruptcy; *Re Holliday (a Bankrupt), ex p Trustee of the Property of the Bankrupt v Bankrupt* [1981] Ch 405, 419.
⁶   *Post Office v Norwich Union Fire Insurance Society Ltd* [1967] 2 QB 363, 375, 377–378; cf *Re Davies (a bankrupt)* [1997] BPIR 619.
⁷   Cf *Re Horder, ex p the Trustee* [1936] Ch 744, [1936] 2 All ER 1479; *Re Hutton (a bankrupt), Mediterranean Machine Operations Ltd v Haigh* [1969] 2 Ch 201, [1969] 1 All ER 936.

Joinder of trustee

16.38 In cases where the result is capable of affecting the estate, the claimant may be required to join the trustee as a party¹. Examples include cases where the debt is provable, although the bankrupt will not be released by his discharge[2] or where the purpose is to ascertain the amount of the liability and the proceedings are the more convenient way of doing so[3].

[1]   *Watson v Holliday* (1882) 20 Ch D 780 (a claim for an account).
[2]   *Re Blake, ex p Coker* (1875) 10 Ch App 652.
[3]   *Watson v Holliday* (1882) 20 Ch D 780.

Protection from suit and other remedies

General bar on remedies and legal proceedings

16.39   After the making of a bankruptcy order no person who is a creditor of the bankrupt in respect of a debt provable in the bankruptcy shall:

(a)   have any remedy against the property or person of the bankrupt in respect of that debt; or

(b)   before the discharge of the bankrupt, commence any action or other legal proceedings against the bankrupt except with the leave of the court and on such terms as the court may impose[1].

[1]   IA 1986, s 285(3).

16.40   The absolute bar on remedies contained in paragraph (a) (para **16.39**) applies in respect of provable debts. The qualified bar in paragraph (b) (para **16.39**) does not only apply in respect of provable debts but also in respect of claims which are not provable.

Relevant property

16.41   The property of the bankrupt for this purpose includes property which is not comprised in his estate[1]. This protects the bankrupt from a creditor seeking to enforce his claim against, for example, the bankrupt's tools of his trade which do not form part of his estate.

[1]   IA 1986, s 285(6).

Landlord's right of re-entry and distress

16.42   The landlord's right of re-entry is not a remedy against the property or person of the bankrupt within the IA 1986, s 285(3)(a). But if the right is to be exercised by issuing and serving forfeiture proceedings, leave will be required under s 285(3)(b)[1]. Similarly distress is not a remedy within the meaning of this provision[2].

[1]   *Ezekiel v Orakpo* [1977] QB 260, [1976] 3 All ER 659; *Razzaq v Pala* [1997] 1 WLR 1336. See also *Re Lomax Leisure Ltd* [2000] Ch 502, [1999] 3 All ER 22 on whether the right of re-entry is a security within the IA 1986, ss 10(1)(b) and 248(b).
[2]   *Re Fanshaw and Yorston, ex p Birmingham and Staffordshire Gas Light Co* (1871) LR 11 Eq 615; *Re Olympia and York Canary Wharf Ltd, American Express Europe Ltd v Adamson* [1993] BCLC 453.

Limited exceptions for execution, attachments and distress

16.43 The general bar on remedies and legal proceedings is subject to the provisions relating to enforcement procedures and distress[1]. The provisions relating to enforcement procedures are discussed at para **16.50** and those relating to distress at para **16.57**.

1   IA 1986, s 285(3). See IA 1986, ss 346 and 347 respectively.

Exception for secured creditors

16.44 Save that the official receiver can block the sale of any goods of an undischarged bankrupt held by way of pledge, pawn or other security[1], the general bar on remedies and legal proceedings does not affect the right of a secured creditor to enforce his security[2].

1   IA 1986, s 285(5).
2   IA 1986, s 285(4).

Proceedings for which leave will be given

16.45 Leave to commence proceedings will be given in the same cases as would be permitted to continue if begun before the commencement of the bankruptcy. Further, leave to commence proceedings would ordinarily be given where the proceedings relate to a claim arising after the commencement of the bankruptcy otherwise than by reason of an obligation incurred before the commencement of the bankruptcy[1].

1   See further para **19.43** and cf para **16.37** above.

Leave sought retrospectively

16.46 Whether the court may retrospectively grant leave to continue proceedings which have been issued without leave has been the subject of a series of first instance decisions to contrary effect. The most recent decision is that leave cannot be granted retrospectively in essence because the words of IA 1986, s 285(3) cannot be construed so as to enable the court to give such permission[1]. As matters stand, the better view and safer course is to obtain leave before commencing proceedings.

1   *Re Taylor (a bankrupt), Davenham Trust plc (t/a Booker Montagu Leasing) v CV Distribution (UK) Ltd* [2006] EWHC 3029 (Ch), [2007] 3 All ER 638, not following *Re Saunders (a bankrupt)* [1997] Ch 60.

Procedure

16.47 An application for leave to commence proceedings should be made by originating application to the court with jurisdiction over the bankruptcy. The trustee should be served with the application[1].

1   *Western and Brazilian Telegraph Co v Bibby* (1880) 42 LT 821.

16.48 *Protection of the bankrupt's estate*

Notice preventing sale of pledged goods

Realisation of goods held on pledge by pledgee

16.48 Where goods have been pledged in order to raise money, they may well have been pledged for a sum lower than their value. If that is so it will be better for the creditors for the goods to be reclaimed on payment of the debt against which they were pledged and then realised for their true value.

16.49 Thus where any goods of an undischarged bankrupt are held by any person by way of pledge, pawn or other security, the official receiver may, after giving notice in writing of his intention to do so, inspect the goods. Where such a notice has been given to any person, that person is not entitled, without leave of the court, to realise his security unless he has given the trustee of the bankrupt's estate a reasonable opportunity of inspecting the goods and of exercising the bankrupt's right of redemption[1].

[1] IA 1986, s 285(5). See further on redemption of pledged goods at para **18.166**.

Restrictions on execution

Enforcement procedures

16.50 The IA 1986[1] provides that where a creditor has effected execution against the bankrupt, he may in certain circumstances be entitled to retain the benefit of that execution.

[1] IA 1986, s 346.

COMPLETED EXECUTION OR ATTACHMENT

16.51 The IA 1986 provides that a creditor who has issued execution against, or attached a debt of, the debtor before the commencement of the bankruptcy may retain the benefit of the execution or attachment against the official receiver or trustee but only if the execution or attachment was completed before the bankruptcy order was made[1]. In this context completion means:

(a)   in the case of execution against goods, seizure and sale or the making of a charging order under the Charging Orders Act 1979, s 1;
(b)   in the case of land, seizure, the appointment of a receiver or the making of a charging order;
(c)   in the case of an attachment of a debt, by receipt of the debt[2].

[1] IA 1986, s 346(1).
[2] IA 1986, s 346(5).

16.52 The court is, however, given power to allow the creditor to retain the benefit of his execution or attachment, albeit incomplete at the commencement of the bankruptcy, to such extent and on such terms as it thinks fit[1]. It will, however, be rare that the court will exercise this discretion since to do so will involve a breach of the rule that the bankrupt's assets be distributed *pari passu*[2].

1   IA 1986, s 346(6).
2   Cf *Re Redman (Builders) Ltd* [1964] 1 All ER 851, [1964] 1 WLR 541; *Re Caribbean Products Ltd, Tickler v Swains Packaging Ltd* [1966] Ch 331, [1966] 1 All ER 181, CA.

INCOMPLETE EXECUTION AGAINST GOODS TAKEN BY ENFORCEMENT OFFICER

16.53 Where goods are taken in execution but the execution is not completed, the goods may be recovered from the enforcement officer or other officer charged with the execution by giving him notice that the debtor has been adjudged bankrupt. In the event that the notice is given, the enforcement officer or officer charged must deliver to the official receiver or trustee the goods and any money seized or recovered in part satisfaction of the execution, but the costs of the execution are a first charge on the goods or money and the official receiver or trustee may sell the goods or sufficient part of them for the purpose of satisfying the charge[1]. The right conferred on the official receiver and trustee may be set aside on such terms as the court thinks fit[2].

1   IA 1986, s 346(2).
2   IA 1986, s 346(6).

COMPLETED EXECUTION AGAINST GOODS BY ENFORCEMENT OFFICER

16.54 Further, even where execution against goods has been completed by a sale, there is a 14-day period before the enforcement officer or other officer charged with the execution is free to pass the proceeds of the sale to the execution creditor. For where under an execution in respect of a judgment for a sum in excess of the prescribed sum, being £1,000 since 1 April 2004[1], the goods of any person are sold or money is paid to avoid a sale, and before the end of 14 days beginning with the day of the sale of payment the enforcement officer or other officer charged with the execution is given notice that a bankruptcy petition has been presented in relation to the judgment debtor and a bankruptcy order is made on that petition, the balance of the proceeds of sale or money paid shall comprise part of the bankrupt's estate in priority to the claim of the execution creditor[2]. If the money is passed to the execution creditor in breach of this provision, the trustee may seek to reclaim the sum paid from the enforcement officer or the execution creditor. This right may be set aside on such terms as the court thinks fit[3].

1   Insolvency Proceedings (Monetary Limits) (Amendment) Order 2004, SI 2004/547.
2   IA 1986, s 346(3).
3   IA 1986, s 346(6).

16.55 In the case of execution against goods by an enforcement officer or other officer charged with the execution, these provisions will not apply if the execution is against goods which have been acquired by or have devolved on the bankrupt since the commencement of the bankruptcy, unless, at the time the execution is issued or before it is completed (a) the property has been or is claimed for the bankrupt's estate as after-acquired property[1], and (b) a copy of the notice given claiming the property for the estate has been served on the enforcement officer or other officer charged with the execution[2].

[1] Under the IA 1986, s 307.
[2] IA 1986, s 346(8).

16.56 In any of these cases the trustee will not be entitled to claim goods from a person who has acquired them in good faith under a sale by an enforcement officer or other officer charged with the execution[1].

[1] IA 1986, s 346(7).

Restrictions on distress

Right to distrain otherwise than for rent

16.57 The Tribunals, Courts and Enforcement Act 2007, s 71 will, when it comes into force, abolish the common law right to distrain for rent. The landlord under a lease of commercial premises will obtain a like power under statute which is referred to as 'commercial rent arrears recovery' for which the acronym CRAR is to be used[1]. The exercise of this power will be restricted in bankruptcy in the same way as distress is at present and IA 1986, s 347 will be amended accordingly.

[1] TCEA 2007, s 72 and Sch 12.

16.57A No distress may be levied against a debtor while an interim order is in effect with respect to him and while an application for an interim order is pending, the court may forbid the levying of any distress[1]. But subject to those exceptions, the provisions of the IA 1986 do not affect the right to distrain otherwise than for rent, though in the circumstances discussed below a charge is imposed on the goods distrained or their proceeds. Any other right to distrain may be exercised at any time without restriction against property comprised in the bankrupt's estate. This is so even if that right is expressed by any enactment to be exercisable in like manner as a right to distrain for rent[2]. Rating authorities have a right to distrain for rates and the Revenue has a power of distraint[3]. But a statutory charge is imposed on the proceeds of a distraint levied within three months before the making of a bankruptcy order whether the person who levied the distraint is a landlord or person entitled to rent or not[4]. Presumably the imposition of this statutory charge may be said not to affect the right to distrain because the activity of carrying out the distress may be completed without impediment, but since the proceeds are subjected to a statutory charge, it seems strained to say that the right of distress in such a case is unaffected.

[1] IA 1986, ss 252(2)(b) and 254(1)(b).
[2] IA 1986, s 347(8).

³   Cf *Re Modern Jet Support Centre Ltd* [2005] EWHC 1611 (Ch), [2006] 1 BCLC 703. The question in that case was whether, in the context of a voluntary liquidation, statutory distraint carried out by the Revenue was execution within IA 1986, s 183; it was held not. In bankruptcy such distraint would be subject to IA 1986, s 347(3) as in a winding up by the court it is subject to IA 1986, s 176.
⁴   IA 1986, s 347(3), discussed below.

Person entitled to distrain for rent

16.58 In the IA 1986, s 346 are set out a number of restrictions on the rights of a landlord or other person to whom rent is payable to distrain for rent. Such persons are referred to in these paragraphs compendiously as 'the landlord'.

Continuing right to prove

16.59 The restrictions on the landlord's right to distrain do not affect his right to prove in the bankruptcy for any bankruptcy debt. Thus, although he may only distrain after bankruptcy for six months' rent accrued before the commencement of the bankruptcy, if there is a longer period in respect of which rent arrears have accrued, he may prove for the whole sum outstanding (giving credit for the proceeds of any permitted distress).

Restricted right to distrain on the goods of an undischarged bankrupt

16.60 After the commencement of a bankruptcy a landlord may distrain on the goods and effects of an undischarged bankrupt which are comprised in his estate for rent due to the landlord, but the landlord may only levy such distress for six months' rent accrued before the commencement of the bankruptcy[1]. A landlord may levy such distress on any goods comprised in the estate at any time before the discharge of the bankrupt but not afterwards[2]. The right to levy such distress against goods and effects comprised in the estate may be exercised even though those goods and effects have vested in the trustee[3].

¹   IA 1986, s 347(1).
²   IA 1986, s 347(5).
³   IA 1986, s 347(9).

Distress levied between petition and bankruptcy order

16.61 Where a landlord levies distress during the period between the presentation of a bankruptcy petition against the individual on whose goods and effects the distress is levied and the making of a bankruptcy order, the amount of the proceeds which he is entitled to retain is restricted. He may not retain for himself any amount recovered by way of that distress which:

(a)   is in excess of the amount which he could have recovered after the commencement of the bankruptcy, ie six months' rent; or

(b)   is in respect of rent for a period or part of a period after the distress was levied.

16.62 Where the amount recovered exceeds what the landlord may retain for himself, he holds the excess for the bankrupt as part of the bankrupt's estate[1].

1   IA 1986, s 347(2).

Charge on amounts recovered under distress levied within three months before the bankruptcy order

16.63 The IA 1986, s 347(3) provides:

'Where any person (whether or not a landlord or person entitled to rent) has distrained upon the goods or effects of an individual who is adjudged bankrupt before the end of the period of three months beginning with the distraint, so much of those goods or effects, or of the proceeds of their sale, as is not held for the bankrupt under subsection (2) shall be charged for the benefit of the bankrupt's estate with the preferential debts of the bankrupt to the extent that the bankrupt's estate is for the time being insufficient for meeting those debts.'

16.64 The difficulty of squaring this provision with the IA 1986, s 347(8) is mentioned above. Where the person who levied the distraint during the relevant period levied it otherwise than for rent, the charge will be imposed on the whole of the proceeds of the distraint. The same position will obtain where a landlord levies the distress for rent during the relevant period but before the presentation of the petition on which the bankruptcy order is made. But, where the person levying the distress is a landlord and he has levied the distress between the presentation of the petition and the making of the bankruptcy order, the statutory charge will still bite on that part of the proceeds which the landlord does not hold for the bankrupt's estate under the IA 1986, s 347(2) discussed above.

16.65 The statutory charge is imposed on the proceeds of the distraint as a security for the preferential debts of the bankrupt. Where a person surrenders any goods or effects or makes a payment to the trustee, that person ranks, in respect of the amount of the proceeds of sale of the goods or effects or of the amount of the payment, as a preferential creditor of the bankrupt, except as against so much of the bankrupt's estate as is available for the payment of preferential creditors by virtue of the surrender or payment[1]. By way of example, suppose in a bankruptcy the position was:

Assets:	£1,000
Liabilities:	
preferential creditors	£2,000
general creditors	£8,000

and a person had levied distress worth £500 which was subject to the statutory charge. The £500 should be recovered for the estate and used to pay the existing preferential creditors. But the person who had levied the distress should then be substituted as a preferential creditor himself, so the position will then be:

Assets:	£1,000
Liabilities:	
original preferential creditors	£1,500
distrainor	£500
general creditors	£8,000

Since the distrainor and the original preferential creditors now rank equally, the £1,000 will be divided between them and, in the example, they will receive a dividend of 50p in the pound.

[1]   IA 1986, s 347(4).

16.66 If the distrainor does not surrender the goods and effects or their proceeds which are subject to the charge, the trustee must be the person entitled to enforce it; for it is to him that surrender or payment is to be made[1].

[1]   Cf *Re Caidan, ex p Official Receiver v Regis Property Co Ltd* [1942] Ch 90, [1941] 3 All ER 491 (concerning the Bankruptcy Act 1914, s 33(4) which made provision to similar effect).

16.67 Where goods are seized in execution by another creditor over which a landlord is entitled to levy distress in respect of unpaid rent and the landlord brings his claim to the notice of the sheriff or other officer conducting the execution, they may not be sold unless the landlord is paid the rent outstanding up to a maximum of one year's rent[1]. If a landlord is entitled to claim to be paid rent from the proceeds of sale of such goods and the person against whom the execution was levied is adjudged bankrupt before the notice of the landlord's claim is served on the sheriff or other officer charged with the execution, the right of the landlord is restricted to a claim for an amount not exceeding six months' rent and does not extend to any rent payable in respect of a period after the notice of claim is served.

[1]   The Landlord and Tenant Act 1709, s 1 (concerning executions in the High Court) and the County Courts Act 1984, s 102 (concerning executions in a county court). See *Re Mackenzie, ex p the Sheriff of Hertfordshire* [1899] 2 QB 566, CA.

16.68 If the landlord's notice is served before the bankruptcy order is made against the person whose goods have been seized, the landlord may be liable to account for what he has received to the trustee. The ground on which the landlord may be liable is not spelt out. It is possible that the seizure may have involved a disposition which was void because made after the presentation of the petition; but to fall within the IA 1986, s 284(1) a disposition has to be made by the person against whom the petition has been presented and where there has been a seizure under compulsion, it seems unlikely that the debtor will himself have been party to any disposition which has occurred. The sheriff is not under any liability to account to the official receiver or trustee for making the payment if it was made before the sheriff was served with notice of the bankruptcy[1].

1   IA 1986, s 347(7).

Distress for rent falling due after the commencement of the bankruptcy

16.69   It has been held with respect to the statutory predecessors of IA 1986, s 347(1), that the restriction imposed on the landlord's right to distress applies only to arrears of rent which have accrued before the commencement of the bankruptcy. In *Re Binns, ex p Hale*[1] the bankrupt was a woollen manufacturer who was the tenant of the top floor of a mill where he kept and operated machinery for the purpose of his business. On his bankruptcy, his trustee took possession of the demised premises for the purpose of winding up the estate. The trustee did not disclaim the lease, but failed to pay rent falling due after the bankruptcy. The landlord levied distress over the machinery. The trustee applied to restrain the landlord from proceeding with the distress, arguing that the Bank Act 1869, s 34 precluded the landlord from distraining for rent falling due after the commencement of the bankruptcy. His application failed. Bacon CJ held that, if the trustee's arguments were right, the consequence would be that a trustee might make use of a man's property without paying any rent for it, and might snap his fingers at him; and that the Bank Act 1869, s 34 was limited in its effect to distress for rent arrears which had accrued before the bankruptcy. This reasoning is open to the criticism that where the trustee does not disclaim, he is personally liable to pay the rent. It is true that he may not disclaim immediately he is appointed and if he disclaims the effect is to release him from personal liability which accrued before as well as after the disclaimer. But the landlord can, under the IA 1986, s 316, press the trustee to decide whether or not to disclaim[2]. This decision was followed by Romer J in *Re Wells*[3] as being equally determinative of the meaning of the Bankruptcy Act 1914, s 35(1). There is some difference between IA 1986, s 347(1) and the provisions which are its predecessors, but the difference does not appear to be such as to make clear that Parliament intended the effect to be different. Accordingly, although it is somewhat forced to read IA 1986, s 347(1) as applying only to rent arrears which have accrued before the commencement of the bankruptcy, it is probably correct to do so.

1   (1875) 1 Ch D 285.
2   The landlord, as a person interested in the property, had the same right to force the trustee to an election under the Bankruptcy Act 1869, s 24.
3   [1929] 2 Ch 269.

Determination of right to distrain

16.70   Initially it is open to a landlord to pursue his right to distrain and to prove in the bankruptcy simultaneously. However, once a dividend has been declared the landlord must elect which remedy he wishes to pursue[1]. Any right to distrain against property comprised in the bankrupt's estate is lost on the bankrupt's obtaining his discharge[2].

Setting distress aside

16.71 The trustee may set aside any distress levied in respect of a sham rent or an increase in rent designed to improve the landlord's position in the bankruptcy¹. The right to distrain attaches only to the goods and chattels involved so that if the landlord acts too slowly and the goods have been sold by the trustee and removed from the premises, he has no right to follow the proceeds of sale².

¹   *Re Knight, ex p Voisey* (1882) 21 Ch D 442, CA.
²   *Bradyll v Ball* (1785) 1 Bro CC 427.

Registration in register of pending actions

16.72 When a petition is filed, the court must forthwith send notice of it to the Chief Land Registrar with a request that it may be registered in the register of pending actions¹. If notice of the petition is not registered, then a purchaser in good faith of a legal estate in unregistered land for money or money's worth will not be bound by the petition².

¹   IR 1986, r 6.13 (creditor's petition) and r 6.43 (debtor's petition).
²   Land Charges Act 1972, s 5(8).

Registration of bankruptcy notice against registered land

16.73 As soon as practicable after the registration of a petition in bankruptcy as a pending action under the Land Charges Act 1972, the registrar is under a duty to register a notice in respect of the pending action in the register in relation to any registered estate or charge which appears to him to be affected¹. The registrar must give notice of the entry of the bankruptcy notice to the proprietor of the registered estate or charge to which it relates². Such notice, unless cancelled by the registrar in the prescribed manner, shall remain in force until a restriction is entered in the register following the registration of a bankruptcy order pursuant to the Land Charges Act 1972 or the trustee in bankruptcy is registered as proprietor³.

¹   Land Registration Act 2002, s 86(2). For the form of the notice, see Land Registration Rules 2003, SI 2003/1417, r 165(1).
²   Land Registration Rules 2003, SI 2003/1417, r 165(2).
³   Land Registration Act 2002, s 86(3).

Protection of purchasers

16.74 Where the proprietor of a registered estate or charge is adjudged bankrupt, the title of his trustee is void against a person to whom a registrable disposition of the estate or charge was made if it was made for valuable consideration, the disponee acted in good faith and at the time of the disposition no notice or restriction was entered under the Land Registration Act 2002, s 86 in relation to the estate or charge and the disponee has no notice of the bankruptcy petition[1]. This protection applies during the period when dispositions are avoided by IA 1986, s 284, ie the period between presentation of the petition and, following the bankruptcy order, the appointment of the first trustee, and reflects the protection given to purchasers in good, for value and without notice of the petition afforded by IA 1986, s 284(4)(a). Nothing in the Land Registration Act 2002, s 86 requires a person to whom a registrable disposition is made to make a search under the Land Charges Act 1972[2].

1   Land Registration Act 2002, s 86(5).
2   Land Registration Act 2002, s 86(7).

Registration in register of writs and orders affecting land

16.75 When a bankruptcy order is made, the court must forthwith send notice of it to the Chief Land Registrar with a request that it may be registered in the register of writs and orders affecting land[1]. Subject to notice of the petition being registered, if notice of the bankruptcy order is not registered, then the trustee's title to the land will be void against a purchaser of a legal estate in good faith for money or money's worth[2]. If notice of the petition is registered and its registration is in force at the date of the conveyance, the purchaser claiming under that conveyance will be bound by the trustee's title[3].

1   IR 1986, r 6.34(2) (creditor's petition) and r 6.46(2) (debtor's petition).
2   Land Charges Act 1972, s 6(5).
3   Land Charges Act 1972, s 6(6).

Registration of bankruptcy restriction against registered land

16.76–16.78 As soon as practicable after the registration of a bankruptcy order under the Land Charges Act 1972, the registrar is under a duty to register a restriction reflecting the effect of the Insolvency Act 1986 in relation to any registered estate or charge which appears to be affected by the order[1]. If no creditors' notice or bankruptcy inhibition is registered, a purchaser in good faith for money or money's worth obtains good title against the trustee. But a purchaser will not be treated as acting in good faith if he has notice of the petition. This does not impose a liability on a purchaser to make a search under the Land Charges Act 1972[2].

1   Land Registration Act 2002, s 86(4). See the Land Registration Rules 2003, SI 2003/1417, reg 166 for the form of the restriction.
2   Land Registration Act 2002, s 86(7).

C   EMERGENCY MEASURES AVAILABLE TO PREVENT DEPLETION OF THE ESTATE

Expedited petitions

16.79 The IA 1986, s 270 enables a petitioning creditor to present his petition before the three-week period which must otherwise elapse following the service of a statutory demand if there is a serious possibility that the debtor's property or the value of any of his property will be significantly diminished during that period[1]. The advantage obtained by early presentation of the petition is that the court has jurisdiction after presentation but not before to appoint an interim receiver under the IA 1986, s 286 and to issue a warrant for the debtor's arrest under the IA 1986, s 364. But although the presentation of the petition is expedited, the debtor is protected against a bankruptcy order being made before the expiry of the statutory demand because a bankruptcy order may not be made on the petition until at least three weeks have elapsed since the service of the statutory demand[2].

1   See para **8.141**.
2   IA 1986, s 271(2).

Court's power to appoint an interim receiver

16.80 In some cases the circumstances may require actively interventionist steps to protect the debtor's property following the presentation of a bankruptcy petition but before a bankruptcy order is made.

16.81 For this purpose the court has power to appoint an interim receiver of the debtor's property at any time after the presentation of the petition and before the bankruptcy order is made where it is shown that the appointment is necessary for the protection of the debtor's property[1]. In this context, the relevant property includes all the debtor's property, whether it would form part of his estate if he were adjudged bankrupt or not[2]. The court may appoint as interim receiver the official receiver pursuant to IA 1986, s 286 or any other suitable person pursuant to the Supreme Court Act 1981, s 37(1)[3]. If the appointment is made following the presentation of debtor's petition on which the court has appointed an insolvency practitioner to report[4], that insolvency practitioner may be appointed.

1   IA 1986, s 286.
2   IA 1986, s 286(8).
3   *Gibson Dunn & Crutcher (a firm) v Rio Properties Inc* [2004] EWCA Civ 998, [2004] 1 WLR 2702, [2004] BPIR 1203.
4   Under the IA 1986, s 273.

16.82 Unless the interim receiver's powers are expressly limited by the court he has the same rights, powers, duties and immunities as the official receiver does in his capacity as receiver and manager of the bankrupt's estate between the making of a bankruptcy order and the time at which the estate vests in the trustee[1]. An interim receiver may ensure that the supply of gas, electricity, water and telecommunications services is continued for the purpose of any business which has been carried on by the individual over whose property the interim receiver has been appointed. But the supplier may insist that the interim receiver personally guarantee the payment of future supplies[2].

1   As to which see para **18.3** below.
2   IA 1986, s 372.

16.83 The appointment of the interim receiver has the same effect as the making of a bankruptcy order as a bar to legal proceedings or execution against the person or property of the debtor, save for the enforcement procedures and landlord's distress discussed above[1].

1   IA 1986, s 286(6).

16.84 An application to the court for the appointment of an interim receiver may be made by a creditor, the debtor or, in the case where an insolvency practitioner has been appointed to report following the presentation of a debtor's petition[1], that insolvency practitioner[2].

1   Under the IA 1986, s 273(2).
2   IR 1986, r 6.51(1).

Procedure

16.85 The application must be supported by an affidavit[1] stating:

(1)   the grounds on which it is proposed that the interim receiver should be appointed;
(2)   whether the official receiver has been informed of the application and, if so, has been furnished with a copy of it;
(3)   whether, to the applicant's knowledge, there has been proposed or is in force a voluntary arrangement under the IA 1986, Pt VIII[2]; and
(4)   the estimated value of the property or business in respect of which the interim receiver is to be appointed.

1   IR 1986, r 6.51(2).
2   Ie under the IA 1986, ss 252–263.

16.86 Where it is sought to appoint the insolvency practitioner to report on a debtor's petition but the application is not made by that practitioner, the affidavit must state that he has consented to act[1].

1   IR 1986, r 6.61(3).

16.87 The official receiver and any insolvency practitioner appointed to report on a debtor's petition must be sent copies of the application and the affidavit in support of the applicant; where this is not practicable sufficient notice of the application must be given to enable them to attend[1]. The official receiver and, where an insolvency practitioner has been appointed on a debtor's petition, that insolvency practitioner may attend and make representations[2].

1   IR 1986, r 6.51(4).
2   IR 1986, r 6.51(3)–(6). A qualified insolvency practitioner may be appointed interim receiver. If such an appointment is sought, the affidavit under IR 1986, r 6.51(3) must state that he has consented to act.

The order

16.88 If satisfied that sufficient grounds are shown for the application the court may make the appointment on such terms as it thinks fit[1]. The court order appointing any person to be an interim receiver must require that person to take immediate possession of all the debtor's property, or that part of it to which his powers are limited[2]. The order must state the nature and a short description of the property of which the person appointed is to take possession and the duties to be performed by him in relation to the debtor's affairs[3].

1   IR 1986, r 6.51(6).
2   IA 1986, s 286(4).
3   IR 1986, r 6.52(1).

16.89 The court shall forthwith after the order is made send two sealed copies of it to the person appointed as interim receiver, one of which must then be sent forthwith by that person to the debtor[1].

1   IR 1986, r 6.52(2).

16.90 Where the interim receiver is appointed, the debtor must give him such inventory of his property and such other information and must attend upon him to provide such information as the interim receiver requires for the purpose of carrying out his function[1].

1   IA 1986, s 286(5).

16.91 Since the appointment is over all the debtor's property, the court may permit him to spend reasonable sums on legal representation and on his living expenses[1].

1   *Re Baars* [2003] BPIR 523.

Deposit for fees

16.92 Before an order appointing the official receiver is issued, the applicant must deposit with the official receiver or otherwise secure to his satisfaction such sum as the court directs to cover his fees and expenses[1]. Should the sum deposited subsequently prove insufficient the court may order an additional deposit on the application of the official receiver. Where this further deposit is not made within two working days of the service of the order, the court may discharge the order appointing the interim receiver[2]. If a bankruptcy order is made after an interim receiver has been appointed, any money deposited will be returned to the person who deposited it out of the bankrupt's estate in the prescribed order of priority, unless it is required by reason of the insufficiency of assets for payment of the fees and expenses of the interim receiver or it was made by the debtor out of his own estate[3].

1   IR 1986, r 6.53(1).
2   IR 1986, r 6.53(2).
3   IR 1986, r 6.61(3).

Insolvency practitioner's security

16.93 A person is not qualified to act as an insolvency practitioner in relation to another person, unless there is in force security in accordance with the prescribed requirements for the proper receiver; an insolvency practitioner is required to give security before he is appointed[1]. The cost of providing the security must in the first instance be paid by the insolvency practitioner but, (a) if a bankruptcy order is not made, the person so appointed is entitled to be reimbursed out of the property of the debtor and the court may make an order against the debtor accordingly; alternatively (b) if a bankruptcy order is made, he is entitled to be reimbursed out of the estate in the prescribed order of priority[2].

[1]   IA 1986, s 390(3); the prescribed requirements are currently set out in the Insolvency Practitioners Regulations 1990, SI 1990/439.
[2]   IR 1986, r 6.64.

16.94 An interim receiver may be removed if he fails to give or keep up his security[1]. Where the court makes an order removing an interim receiver or discharging his appointment for failure to give or keep up his security, the court shall give directions as to whether any, and if so what, steps should be taken for the appointment of another person in his place[2].

[1]   IR 1986, r 6.55(1), and see also the IA 1986, s 390(3).
[2]   IR 1986, r 6.55(2).

Termination of interim receivership

16.95 The interim receivership comes to an end automatically if the bankruptcy petition against the debtor is dismissed or a bankruptcy order is made[1]. However, the court may, at any time, terminate the appointment on the application of the interim receiver, official receiver, the debtor or any creditors[2].

[1]   IA 1986, s 286(7).
[2]   IR 1986, r 6.57.

16.96 If the interim receiver's appointment terminates, in consequence of the dismissal of the bankruptcy petition or otherwise, the court may give such directions as it thinks fit with respect to the accounts of his administration and any other matters which it thinks appropriate[1].

[1]   IR 1986, r 6.57(2).

Remuneration

16.97 The interim receiver's remuneration is fixed by the court from time to time on his application, unless the official receiver is the interim receiver[1].

[1]   IR 1986, r 6.56.

16.98 If no bankruptcy order is made, the fees should be paid out of the property of the debtor and the interim receiver may retain such sums or property out of the debtor's property as may be required for meeting his fees[1]. If a bankruptcy order is made, the fees should be paid out of the bankrupt's estate in the prescribed order of priority. In either case, if the relevant funds are insufficient, the fees may be paid out of the deposit described above[2].

1   IR 1986, r 6.55(3)(a) and (4).
2   IR 1986, r 6.56(3).

Interim receiver's duty to provide information about the time spent

16.99 The bankrupt or any creditor is entitled to require the interim receiver to provide a statement setting out:

(a)   the total number of hours spent on the case by the interim receiver and any staff assigned to it during the relevant period;

(b)   for each grade of individual so engaged, the average hourly rate at which any work carried out by individuals in that grade is charged; and

(c)   the number of hours spent by each grade of staff during the relevant period[1].

1   Insolvency Regulations 1994, SI 1994/2507, reg 36A(1), (2).

16.100 The relevant period is the period between the date of the interim receiver's appointment and either the date next before the date of the making of the request on which the interim receiver has completed any period in office which is a multiple of six months or, if he has vacated office, the date that he vacated office[1].

1   Insolvency Regulations 1994, SI 1994/2507, reg 36A(3).

16.101 The request must be made in writing[1]. If the request is not made within two years of the date when the interim receiver vacated office, he is not obliged to answer it[2]. The information must be supplied free of charge[3] within 28 days of the receipt of the request[4].

1   Insolvency Regulations 1994, SI 1994/2507, reg 36A(1).
2   Insolvency Regulations 1994, SI 1994/2507, reg 36A(5).
3   Insolvency Regulations 1994, SI 1994/2507, reg 36A(1).
4   Insolvency Regulations 1994, SI 1994/2507, reg 36A(6).

Power of arrest

16.102 The court may cause a warrant to be issued to a constable or prescribed officer of the court:

(1)   for the arrest of a debtor to whom a bankruptcy petition relates or of an undischarged bankrupt whose estate is still being administered; and

(2)   for the seizure of any books, papers, records, money or goods in the possession of a person arrested under the warrant[1].

1   IA 1986, s 364(1). As to the execution of warrants of arrest in other parts of the United Kingdom see IA 1986, s 426(7); and as to the execution of warrants outside the court's district see the IR 1986, r 7.24. As to the execution of warrants generally see the IR 1986, r 7.21.

16.103 Such powers are exercisable if, at any time after the presentation of the bankruptcy petition or the making of the bankruptcy order, it appears to the court:

(a)   that there are reasonable grounds for believing that the debtor or bankrupt has absconded, or is about to abscond, with a view to avoiding or delaying the payment of any of his debts or his appearance to a bankruptcy petition or to avoiding, delaying or disrupting any proceedings in bankruptcy against him or any examination of his affairs;

(b)   that he is about to remove his goods with a view to preventing or delaying possession being taken of them by the official receiver or the trustee of his estate;

(c)   that there are reasonable grounds for believing that he has concealed or destroyed, or is about to conceal or destroy, any of his goods or any books, papers or records which might be of use to his creditors in the courts of his bankruptcy or in connection with the administration of his estate;

(d)   that he has, without the leave of the official receiver or the trustee of his estate, removed any goods in his possession which exceed in value the prescribed sum[1]; or

(e)   that he failed, without reasonable excuse, to attend any examination ordered by the court[2].

1   For the purposes of the IA 1986, s 364(2)(d) the prescribed sum is £500: see the Insolvency Proceedings (Monetary Limits) Order 1986, SI 1986/1996, art 3, Schedule, Pt II.
2   IA 1986, s 364(2).

16.104 When a person is arrested under a warrant issued under the above provisions:

(i)   the officer must give him into the custody of the governor of the prison named in the warrant, who must keep him in custody until such time as the court otherwise orders and must produce him[1] before the court as it may from time to time direct; and

(ii)   any property in the arrested person's possession which may be seized must be lodged with, or otherwise dealt with as instructed by, whoever is specified in the warrant as authorised to receive it, or kept by the officer seizing it pending the receipt of written orders from the court as to its disposal, as may be directed by the court in the warrant[2].

1   For the prescribed form of order for production of persons arrested under the IA 1986, s 264 see the IR 1986, rr 7.22, 12.7, Sch 4, Form 7.9.
2   IR 1986, r 7.22. For the prescribed form of warrant of arrest see IR 1986, rr 7.22, 12.7, Sch 4, Form 7.7.

16.105 Where the warrant has been issued following a hearing notice of which was not given to the bankrupt, the court must order that the arrested bankrupt be produced following his arrest to the judge hearing the applications list in the Chancery Division for directions to be given in order that he may have sufficient opportunity to meet the case against him[1]. The practice of obtaining an order on the basis of information which is not shown to the respondent which applies (in appropriate circumstances) where an order for examination under IA 1986, s 366 is sought may well not be applicable to applications for a warrant of arrest under IA 1986, s 364[2].

1 *Hickling v Baker* [2007] EWCA Civ 287, [2007] 4 All ER 390 at [47].
2 *Hickling v Baker* [2007] EWCA Civ 287, [2007] 4 All ER 390.

Power of seizure

Seizure of the bankrupt's property

16.106 At any time after a bankruptcy order has been made, the court may, on the application of the official receiver or trustee, issue a warrant authorising the person to whom it is directed to seize any property comprised in the bankrupt's estate, or any books, papers or records relating to the bankrupt's estate or affairs which may be in the possession or under the control of the bankrupt or any other person who is required to deliver them up[1].

1 IA 1986, s 365(1).

16.107 Any person executing such a warrant may break open any premises where the bankrupt, or anything that may be seized under the warrant, is or is believed to be, and any receptacle of the bankrupt which contains or is believed to contain anything that may be so seized[1].

1 IA 1986, s 365(2).

16.108 If, after a bankruptcy order has been made, the court is satisfied that any property comprised in the estate is, or any books, papers or records relating to the bankrupt's estate or affairs are, concealed in any premises not belonging to him, it may issue a warrant authorising any constable or prescribed officer[1] of the court to search those premises of the property, books, papers or records[2]. Such a warrant must authorise any person executing it to seize any property of the bankrupt found as a result of the execution of the warrant[3].

1 The person referred to in the IA 1986, s 365(3), as the prescribed officer of the court is (1) in the case of the High Court, the tipstaff and his assistants of the court; and (2) in the case of a county court, the registrar and the bailiffs: IR 1986, r 7.21(2).
2 IA 1986, s 365(3). A warrant under s 365(3) may not be executed except in the prescribed manner and in accordance with its terms: s 365(4). As to execution of warrants generally see the IR 1986, r 7.21.
3 IR 1986, r 7.25(1).

16.109 Any property seized by virtue of the above provisions must be (1) lodged with, or otherwise dealt with as instructed by, whoever is specified in the warrant as authorised to receive it; or (2) kept by the officer seizing it pending the receipt of written orders from the court as to its disposal, as may be directed by the warrant[1].

[1] IR 1986, r 7.25(2). For the prescribed forms of warrant see the IR 1986, rr 7.25, 12.7, Sch 4, Form 7.12 (warrant of seizure of property), and Form 7.13 (search warrant).

Freezing order

16.110 It appears that in exceptional circumstances a petitioning creditor may be entitled to obtain a freezing order in support of the trustee's title to the estate[1].

[1] *Revenue and Customs Comrs v Egleton* [2006] EWHC 2313 (Ch), [2007] 1 All ER 606.

D OFFICIAL RECEIVER'S RECEIVERSHIP PENDING APPOINTMENT OF TRUSTEE

Official receiver as receiver and manager

16.111 A bankrupt's estate does not vest in the trustee on the commencement of the bankruptcy but only vests when the trustee's appointment takes effect or the official receiver becomes the trustee[1]. On the making of a bankruptcy order the bankrupt must:

(a) deliver possession of his estate to the official receiver; and
(b) deliver up to the official receiver all books, papers and other records of which he has possession or control and which relate to his estate and affairs[2].

[1] IA 1986, s 306(1).
[2] IA 1986, s 291.

16.112 Between the date of the bankruptcy order and the date on which the bankrupt's estate vests in a trustee, the official receiver is the receiver and manager of the bankrupt's estate and is under a duty to act as such[1].

[1] IA 1986, s 287.

16.113 Where the court orders summary administration of the estate of the bankrupt[1], the receivership will not arise, since in that case, the official receiver becomes trustee immediately upon the court issuing a certificate for summary administration[2].

[1] IA 1986, s 275.
[2] IA 1986, ss 287(5), 297(2).

Powers and duties

16.114 The function of the official receiver as receiver and manager is to protect the estate, and for this purpose he has the same powers as a receiver or manager appointed by the High Court. He has express power to sell perishable goods or any other goods of the estate the value of which is likely to diminish if not disposed of speedily[1]. While acting he is under a duty to take all such steps as he thinks fit for protecting any property which may be claimed by the trustee of that estate but is not required to do anything which involves incurring expenditure unless directed to do so by the Secretary of State. If he thinks it appropriate, he may summon a general meeting of the bankrupt's creditors and he may be directed to do so by the court[2].

1   IA 1986, s 287(2).
2   IA 1986, s 287(3).

16.115 In exercising his functions the official receiver may inadvertently take possession of property which is not comprised in the bankrupt's estate or could not be claimed by the trustee, in which case he might be liable in an action for conversion brought by the true owner of the property. To protect him against such actions the IA 1986 provides that he will not be liable to any person in respect of loss and damage resulting from his seizure or disposal, in the course of acting as receiver and manager, of any property not comprised in the bankrupt's estate, provided that he believes, on reasonable grounds, that he is entitled to seize or dispose that particular property, unless the loss or damage is caused by his negligence[1]. In respect of property belonging to third parties which the official receiver seizes, reasonably believing it to be comprised in the bankrupt's estate, he has a lien on any property or proceeds of sale for any expenses incurred in the seizure or disposal[2].

1   IA 1986, s 287(4).
2   IA 1986, s 287(4).

Official receiver's powers to invoke the court's assistance

16.116 In connection with his receivership of the estate pending the appointment of the trustee or otherwise the official receiver may invoke the court's assistance by seeking:

(1)   the issue of a warrant of arrest under the IA 1986, s 364;
(2)   the issue of a warrant authorising the person to whom it is directed to seize any property comprised in the bankrupt's estate or books, papers or records relating to the bankrupt's estate or affairs under the IA 1986, s 365;
(3)   an order for a private examination under the IA 1986, s 366;
(4)   an order for delivery up of property or payment of a debt under the IA 1986, s 367;
(5)   an order that the HMRC produce documents under the IA 1986, s 369;
(6)   an order appointing a special manager under the IA 1986, s 370;
(7)   an order redirecting the bankrupt's post under the IA 1986, s 371.

Power to ensure supply of utilities

16.117 The official receiver may request the suppliers of gas, electricity, water and telecommunications services to continue the supply for the purpose of any business carried on by the bankrupt. The supplier may insist that the official receiver personally guarantee the payment for future supplies[1].

1   IA 1986, s 372.

Bank accounts and records

16.118 When acting as receiver and manager of the bankrupt's estate, the official receiver is under the same duties as a trustee in bankruptcy to pay all funds received by him without deduction into the Insolvency Services Account and to keep records[1]. These duties are described at para **13.333**ff.

1   Insolvency Regulations 1994, SI 1994/2507, reg 19(2).

Handover of estate to trustee

16.119 If and when a trustee is appointed, the official receiver is under a duty to do all that is required for putting the trustee into possession of the estate[1]. The official receiver must give the trustee all such information relating to the affairs of the bankrupt and the course of the bankruptcy as the official receiver considers to be reasonably required for the effective discharge by the trustee of his duties in relation to the estate[2]. The official receiver has an absolute immunity from suit in respect of the statements which he makes and therefore may speak freely in passing information to the trustee. But the immunity extends not only to protect the official receiver from suit at the instance of any third party defamed or otherwise harmed by his statement, but also from suit brought by the trustee who has acted in reliance on what he has been told by the official receiver[3].

1   IR 1986, r 6.125(2).
2   IR 1986, r 6.125(7).
3   *Mond v Hyde* [1997] BPIR 250.

Charge over the estate for official receiver's expenses

16.120 The official receiver has a charge over the estate in respect of sums due to him on account of (a) expenses properly incurred by him and payable under the IA 1986 or the IR 1986; and (b) any advances made by him in respect of the estate together with interest at the rate specified in the Judgments Act 1838, s 17 at the date of the bankruptcy order[1]. The trustee must either discharge any balance due on taking possession of the estate or, before taking office, give to the official receiver a written undertaking to discharge any such balance out of the first realisation of assets[2].

1   IR 1986, r 6.125(5).
2   IR 1986, r 6.125(3) and (4).

E CRIMINAL OFFENCES RELATING TO THE DISPOSAL OF ASSETS

16.121 The bankrupt's duties to preserve his estate are reinforced by the criminal law. Although bankruptcy offences are discussed in **Chapter 24**, it is worth listing in the context of measures aimed at preserving the estate those offences which prohibit the dissipation of assets.

Removing or disposing of property

16.122 Unless the bankrupt proves that, at the time of the conduct constituting the offence, he had no intent to defraud or to conceal the state of his affairs[1], he is guilty of an offence:

(1)   if he makes or causes to be made or has in the period of five years ending with the commencement of the bankruptcy made or caused to be made any gift or transfer of or any charge on his property[2];

(2)   if he removes or at any time before the commencement of his bankruptcy removed any part of his property after or within two months before the date on which a judgment or order for the payment of money has been obtained against him, being a judgment or order which was not satisfied before the commencement of the bankruptcy[3];

(3)   if, during the period of six months ending with the presentation of the petition or during the period between the presentation of the petition and the making of the bankruptcy order, he leaves or attempts to leave England and Wales with any property the value of which is not less than the prescribed amount, presently £500, and possession of which he would have been required to deliver up to the official receiver or trustee[4]; or

(4)   if, during the period between the presentation of the petition and the making of the bankruptcy order, he removed any property of which the value was not less than the prescribed amount, presently £500, and possession of which he would have been required to deliver up to the official receiver or trustee[5].

1   IA 1986, s 352.
2   IA 1986, s 357(1).
3   IA 1986, s 357(3).
4   IA 1986, s 358.
5   IA 1986, s 354(2).

16.123 The burden of proof lies on the bankrupt to show that he had no intent to defraud or conceal the state of his affairs. It may be arguable that imposing this burden of proof on the bankrupt defendant infringes his right to a fair trial under art 6 of the European Convention on Human Rights[1].

1   See the Human Rights Act 1998, s 1 and Sch 1, Pt I and *R v DPP, ex p Kebilene* [2000] 2 AC 326, [1999] 4 All ER 801, HL.

Gambling and engaging in rash and hazardous speculations

16.124 The bankrupt is guilty of an offence:

(1)   if he has during the two years ending with the presentation of the petition materially contributed to or increased the extent of his insolvency by gambling or by rash and hazardous speculations;

(2)   if during the period between the presentation of the petition and the making of the bankruptcy order, he has lost any part of his property by gambling or by rash and hazardous speculations[1].

[1]   IA 1986, s 362.

Chapter 17

INVESTIGATION OF THE BANKRUPT'S AFFAIRS

A   Bankrupt's duties of disclosure, delivery up of his estate and assistance
B   Official receiver's duty to investigate the bankrupt's affairs
C   Court's power to order production of documents by the Inland Revenue
D   Public examination
E   Private examination
F   Summary orders for delivery up of property and payment of debts
G   Unenforceability of liens on books
H   Criminal offences relating to the concealment of assets and failure to disclose information

A BANKRUPT'S DUTIES OF DISCLOSURE, DELIVERY UP OF HIS ESTATE AND ASSISTANCE

17.1 Gathering assets requires prior knowledge of where the assets are located. In this section is discussed the bankrupt's duties to disclose information, deliver up his estate and to assist in its administration. Section B sets out the official receiver's duty to investigate and report to the court and creditors. Since the information which is required to gather the assets within the estate or which may be claimed for the estate is not always volunteered, such information may be extracted under compulsion, in the case of the bankrupt, by his public examination and, in the case both of the bankrupt and of others persons who may have information to contribute, by their private examination. Information may be obtained from the HMRC for this purpose by the procedure described in section C. Public examinations, formerly a central and mandatory element in the bankruptcy process, now less common, are discussed in section D; private examinations, an essential tool in any complex insolvency, in section E. Summary procedures for obtaining delivery up of property and records are described in section F. And finally in section G, to demonstrate again how bankruptcy is backed by the criminal law, are listed various bankruptcy offences concerned to prohibit and punish the concealment of assets and the failure to disclose information.

Statement of affairs

17.1A In order that there should be systematic disclosure by bankrupts the Insolvency Act 1986 ('IA 1986') requires that a bankrupt should make a statement of his affairs in a prescribed form. Where a debtor has presented his own petition he will have had to prepare a statement of affairs to put before the court with the petition[1] and therefore, where the bankruptcy order was made on a debtor's petition the bankrupt will not necessarily be required to provide a further statement of affairs[2]. However, where a petition has been presented other than by the debtor himself and a bankruptcy order is made, the bankrupt has 21 days from the commencement of the bankruptcy to submit a statement of affairs to the official receiver[3].

[1] IA 1986, s 272(2).
[2] See para **17.8** below.
[3] IA 1986, s 288(1). For the requirements in relation to a debtor's petition, see para **8.226** above.

Extension of time and dispensation from making statement

17.2 The period for making the statement may be extended, or indeed the statement of affairs itself may be dispensed with, by direction of the official receiver if he thinks fit. The official receiver may decide on his own volition to dispense with a statement of affairs or he may do so at the bankrupt's request[1].

[1] IR 1986, r 6.62.

17.3 Where a request is made by the bankrupt and refused by the official receiver, the bankrupt may apply to the court to exercise the power to release the bankrupt from his duty to submit a statement of his affairs or extend the 21-day period for him to do so[1].

[1] IA 1986, s 288(3); for the procedure for the bankrupt's application see the IR 1986, r 6.62(1) (release from duty to submit statement), r 6.62(2) (extension of time).

17.4 The official receiver may not revoke his release of the bankrupt from submitting a statement of affairs but may at any time require the bankrupt to submit further information or accounts[1], to be verified by affidavit if directed[2]. The bankrupt must bear his own costs of any application he makes to the court for an order that he be released from his duty to submit a statement of affairs or that his time for submission be extended, and unless the court otherwise orders, no allowance is made for them out of the estate[3].

[1] IR 1986, r 6.66(1).
[2] IR 1986, r 6.66(2).
[3] IR 1986, r 6.62(7).

Content and verification of statement of affairs

17.5 The information to be contained in the statement of affairs is prescribed in the IR 1986[1]. The official receiver should furnish the bankrupt with instructions for preparing his statement of affairs and the necessary forms[2].

> [1]   IR 1986, rr 6.58 and 6.59 (creditor's petition), rr 6.67 and 6.68 (debtor's petition), which require the statement of affairs to be in Form 6.33 or 6.28 respectively, and to contain all the particulars required by the relevant form.
> [2]   IR 1986, r 6.60(1).

17.6 The statement of affairs must be verified by affidavit[1]. Should the bankrupt be unable to prepare a proper statement of affairs, the official receiver may employ a person to assist in the preparation at the expense of the estate[2]. The bankrupt may himself request assistance and with the authority of the official receiver, employ a person to assist him at the expense of the estate[3].

> [1]   IR 1986, r 6.60(2).
> [2]   IR 1986, r 6.63(1) (creditor's petition), r 6.71(1) (debtor's petition, preparation of accounts only).
> [3]   IR 1986, r 6.63(2) (creditor's petition). Note that r 6.63(3) provides that only a named person or firm may be authorised by the official receiver and r 6.63(4) that such authorisation may be subject to conditions. Similar provisions apply in the case of a debtor's petition, see IR 1986, r 6.71(2)–(4).

17.7 The official receiver may require the bankrupt at any time to submit an amended statement of affairs[1] or trading accounts[2]. Trading accounts may not be required for any period earlier than three years before the date of presentation of the bankruptcy petition unless the court orders accounts for any earlier period[3].

> [1]   IR 1986, r 6.66 (creditor's petition), r 6.72 (debtor's petition).
> [2]   IR 1986, r 6.64(1) (creditor's petition), r 6.69(1) (debtor's petition).
> [3]   IR 1986, r 6.64(2) (creditor's petition), r 6.69(2) (debtor's petition). Accounts should be delivered in 21 days unless the official receiver allows a longer period: IR 1986, rr 6.65, 6.70.

Debtor's petition

17.8 Where a debtor petitions for his own bankruptcy, the petition must be accompanied by a statement of affairs, verified by affidavit[1]. The same provisions apply to the making of the statement of affairs in connection with a debtor's petition as they do to the statement of affairs to be made after the making of the bankruptcy order[2]. Accordingly where the debtor made such a statement he will not automatically have to make a further statement but he might be required to make further disclosure if required to by the official receiver[3].

> [1]   IA 1986, s 272(2) and IR 1986, r 6.41(1).
> [2]   IR 1986, r 6.41(2).
> [3]   IR 1986, r 6.66.

Sanctions

17.9 A bankrupt who fails to comply with his obligation to submit a statement of affairs or does so incorrectly is guilty of a contempt of court and is liable to be punished accordingly. Further, his prospect of an automatic discharge may be affected[1]. The fact that he may receive assistance in the preparation of his statement of affairs does not relieve him of his obligations, in particular to produce a statement of affairs which he believes to be true[2].

[1]   IA 1986, s 279(3).
[2]   IR 1986, r 6.63(5) (creditor's petition), r 6.71(5) (debtor's petition).

Criminal sanction

17.10 Unless he proves that, at the time of the conduct constituting the offence, he had no intent to defraud or to conceal the state of his affairs, the bankrupt is guilty of an offence if he makes any material omission in his statement of affairs[1].

[1]   IA 1986, s 356(1).

Duty to deliver estate to the official receiver

17.11 Where a bankruptcy order has been made, the bankrupt is under a duty:

(a)   to deliver possession of his estate to the official receiver; and
(b)   to deliver up to the official receiver all books, papers and other records of which he has possession or control and which relate to his estate and affairs (including any which would be privileged from disclosure in any proceedings)[1].

[1]   IA 1986, s 291(1).

17.12 In the case of any part of the bankrupt's estate which consists of items possession of which cannot be delivered to the official receiver, and in the case of any property that may be claimed for the bankrupt's estate by the trustee, it is the bankrupt's duty to do all such things as may reasonably be required by the official receiver for the protection of those things or that property[1]. These duties are not imposed where by virtue of an order under the IA 1986, s 297 the bankrupt's estate vests in a trustee immediately on the making of a bankruptcy order[2]. In such a case there is no intervening period between the making of the bankruptcy order and the appointment of the trustee, to whom on his appointment the bankrupt owes the same duties. Material obtained by the official receiver under the analogous provision relating to companies[3] may be disclosed by him to prosecuting authorities[4]. So it would appear that similar use may be made of material produced by the bankrupt under IA 1986, s 333.

[1]   IA 1986, s 291(2).
[2]   IA 1986, s 291(3).

666

³   IA 1986, s 235.
⁴   *R v Brady* [2004] BPIR 962.

Duty to assist the official receiver

17.13 Before and after his discharge the bankrupt is under a duty to give the official receiver such inventory of his estate and such other information and to attend on the official receiver at such times as the official receiver may reasonably require for the purposes of the IA 1986, ss 283–291[1]. As in the case of the like duties which the bankrupt owes to his trustee, it is necessary for the duties to continue after discharge because the administration of the estate may well continue after the bankrupt has been discharged.

¹   IA 1986, s 291(4) and (5).

Enforcement

17.14 Failure to comply with any of these duties is a contempt of court and liable to be punished accordingly[1]. The official receiver may obtain an injunction against the bankrupt in support of enforcement[2].

¹   IA 1986, s 291(6).
²   *Morris v Murjani* [1996] 2 All ER 384, [1996] 1 WLR 848, CA (concerning the duties owed by the bankrupt to the trustee under the IA 1986, s 333 but since s 291 makes the same provision both as to the content of the duty and its breach being capable of amounting to contempt of court, the decision is equally applicable to s 291).

General duty to assist trustee

17.15 The bankrupt is under a duty before and after his discharge (a) to give to the trustee such information as to his affairs, (b) to attend on the trustee at such times, and (c) to do all such other things as the trustee may reasonably require for the purpose of carrying out his functions under any of the provisions of the IA 1986 relating to the insolvency of individuals[1]. This duty and its enforcement is discussed further in **Chapter 18**, section D.

¹   IA 1986, s 333(1) and (3).

Duty to disclose acquisition of property or increase in income

17.16 Where at any time after the commencement of the bankruptcy any property is acquired by or devolves upon the bankrupt or there is an increase of the bankrupt's income, the bankrupt shall, within the prescribed period, give the trustee notice of the property or the increase of income[1]. The duty is discussed further in **Chapter 14**, sections N and O.

¹   IA 1986, s 333(2).

B OFFICIAL RECEIVER'S DUTY TO INVESTIGATE THE BANKRUPT'S AFFAIRS

Duty to investigate

17.17 Except where a certificate for summary administration is in force, the official receiver is under a duty to investigate the conduct and affairs of every bankrupt and to make such report, if any, to the court as he thinks fit[1]. Where a certificate for summary administration is in force, the official receiver need only carry out an investigation if he thinks fit[2]. The conduct and affairs of the bankrupt include his conduct and affairs before the making of the order by which he was adjudged bankrupt[3]. Any report made by the official receiver is, in any proceedings, prima facie evidence of the facts stated in it[4].

1   IA 1986, s 289(1).
2   IA 1986, s 289(5).
3   IA 1986, s 289(4).
4   IA 1986, s 289(3).

Immunity from suit

17.18 In *Mond v Hyde*[1] the Court of Appeal held that an official receiver has an absolute immunity from suit in relation to any statement which he makes while acting in the course of bankruptcy proceedings and within the scope of his powers and duties. Although the bankruptcy in that case was governed by the Bankruptcy Act 1914, the law would appear to be the same under the IA 1986. The reason given for the immunity is the need for the official receiver to be able to state with the greatest frankness all the matters which he may have ascertained in his inquiries. In *Mond v Hyde* the immunity relieved the official receiver concerned from liability for what would otherwise have been a negligent misstatement made to the trustee appointed to administer an estate previously under the official receiver's tutelage that the official receiver had not disclaimed all interest in proceedings pursued by the bankrupt.

1   [1999] QB 1097, [1998] 3 All ER 833. For the subsequent unsuccessful attempt to challenge the immunity before the ECtHR, see *Mond v United Kingdom (App No 49606/99)* [2003] BPIR 1347.

Report to creditors

17.19 The official receiver is required[1] to send to all creditors a report relating to the bankruptcy proceedings and the state of the bankrupt's affairs at least once after the making of the bankruptcy order. Where a statement of affairs has been lodged the official receiver must send a summary of the statement together with any observations he wishes to make, unless he has already reported to creditors and he has formed the opinion that the statement discloses no further matters which ought to be brought to the creditors' attention[2]. After the official receiver has released a bankrupt from the obligation to submit a statement he should send to creditors a report summarising the bankrupt's affairs, unless he considers this to be unnecessary in the light of a previous report to creditors[3]. The court may relieve the official receiver of the duty to send reports[4], or make an order on the official receiver's application limiting the extent of disclosure[5]. For these purposes 'creditors' are creditors known to the official receiver or identified in the statement of affairs[6]. A creditor who wishes to obtain more information will have to seek it through the creditor's committee, if any, from the trustee if one is appointed, or seek an examination of the bankrupt[7].

1   IR 1986, r 6.73.
2   IR 1986, r 6.75.
3   IR 1986, r 6.76.
4   IR 1986, r 6.77.
5   IR 1986, r 6.61.
6   IR 1986, r 6.74.
7   IR 1986, rr 6.163, 6.172. As to public and private examinations of the bankrupt, see sections D and E below.

C COURT'S POWER TO ORDER PRODUCTION OF DOCUMENTS BY THE INLAND REVENUE

Information from the Inland Revenue

17.20 On the application of the official receiver or the trustee of the bankrupt's estate, the court may[1] order an Inland Revenue official[2] to produce to the court:

(1)   any return, account or accounts submitted, whether before or after the commencement of the bankruptcy, by the bankrupt to any Inland Revenue official;

(2)   any assessment or determination made, whether before or after the commencement of the bankruptcy, in relation to the bankrupt by any Inland Revenue official; or

(3)   any correspondence, whether before or after the commencement of the bankruptcy, between the bankrupt and any Inland Revenue official[3].

1   Ie for the purposes of a public examination under the IA 1986, s 290 or proceedings under IA 1986, ss 366–368. IA 1986, s 369 does not, however, apply for the purposes of an examination under IA 1986, ss 366, 367 which takes place by virtue of the IA 1986, s 368: s 369(7).
2   In the IA 1986, s 369, 'Inland Revenue official' means any inspector or collector of taxes appointed by the Commissioners of Inland Revenue or any person appointed by the commissioners to serve in any other capacity: IA 1986, s 369(6).
3   IA 1986, s 369(1). The court may not address an order under IA 1986, s 369(1) to an Inland Revenue official unless it is satisfied that that official is dealing, or has dealt, with the affairs of the bankrupt: IA 1986, s 369(3).

17.21 Any such application must specify the documents required and name the official to whom the order is to be addressed[1].

1   IR 1986, r 6.194(1).

17.22 The court must fix a venue for the hearing of the application[1], and notice of the venue, accompanied by a copy of the application, must be sent by the applicant to the Commissioner of Inland Revenue at least 28 days before the hearing[2]. The notice must require the commissioners, not later than seven days before the date fixed for the hearing of the application, to inform the court whether they consent or object to the making of an order under these provisions[3]. If the commissioners consent to the making of an order, they must inform the court of the name of the official to whom it should be addressed, if other than the one named in the application[42]; and, if the commissioners object to the making of an order, they must secure that an officer of theirs attends the hearing of the application and, not less than seven days before it, deliver to the court a statement in writing of the grounds of their objection[5]. A copy of the statement must be sent forthwith to the applicant.

[1] IR 1986, r 6.194(2).
[2] IR 1986, r 6.194(3).
[3] IR 1986, r 6.194(4).
[4] IR 1986, r 6.194(5).
[5] IR 1986, r 6.194(6).

Application to the court

17.23 If on the hearing of the application it appears to the court to be a proper case, the court may make the order applied for, with such modifications, if any as appear appropriate having regard to any representations made on behalf of the Commissioners of Inland Revenue[1].

[1] IR 1986, r 6.195(1). For the prescribed form of order see IR 1986, rr 6.195, 12.7, Sch 4, Form 6.69.

17.24 The order:

(1)   may be addressed to an Inland Revenue official other than the one named in the application;
(2)   must specify a time, not less than 28 days after service on the official to whom the order is addressed, within which compliance is required; and
(3)   may include requirements as to the manner in which documents to which the order relates are to be produced[1].

[1] IR 1986, r 6.195(2).

17.25 A sealed copy of the order must be served by the applicant on the official to whom it is addressed[1].

[1] IR 1986, r 6.195(3).

17.26 If the official is unable to comply with the order because he has not got the relevant documents in his possession, and has been unable to obtain possession of them, he must deliver to the court a statement in writing as to the reasons for his non-compliance; and a copy of the statement must be sent forthwith by the official to the applicant[1]. It is the duty of the official to take all reasonable steps to secure possession of the documents named in the order, and, if he fails to do so, to report the reasons for his failure to the court[2]; and, where any document is in the possession of an Inland Revenue official other than the one to whom the order is addressed, it is the duty of that official to deliver it to the official named in the order, at his request[3].

1   IR 1986, r 6.195(4).
2   IA 1986, s 369(4).
3   IA 1986, s 369(5).

17.27 Where the court has made such an order for the purposes of any examination or proceedings, the court may, at any time after the document to which the order relates is produced to it, by order authorise the disclosure of the document, or of any part of its contents, to the official receiver, the trustee of the bankrupt's estate or the bankrupt's creditors[1].

1   IA 1986, s 369(2).

D PUBLIC EXAMINATION

Powers of official receiver

17.28 Where a bankruptcy order has been made, the official receiver may at any time before the discharge of the bankrupt apply to the court for the public examination of the bankrupt[1]. The court should make an order for public examination where one is applied for unless the circumstances are such that it can be seen that no proper questions can be put to the bankrupt[2].

1   IA 1986, s 290(1).
2   *Re Casterbridge Properties Ltd (in liq), Jeeves v Official Receiver* [2003] EWCA Civ 1264, [2003] 4 All ER 1041, [2004] 1 BCLC 96 (concerning public examination under IA 1986, s 133).

17.29 Unless the court otherwise orders, the official receiver must make an application for a public examination if requested to do so by one of the bankrupt's creditors with the concurrence of not less than one-half, in value, of those creditors, including the creditor giving notice[1].

1   IA 1986, s 290(2).

17.30 Such a request[1] must be made in writing and be accompanied by a list of the creditors concurring and the amount of their respective claims in the bankruptcy, written confirmation of the requesting creditor's own concurrence and a statement of the reasons for the request. If, however, the requesting creditor's debt is alone sufficient, the request may be made by that creditor without the concurrence of others[2]. Before an application to the court is made on the request, the requesting creditor must deposit with the official receiver such sum as the latter may determine to be appropriate by way of security for the expenses of a public examination, if ordered[3]. The official receiver must, within 28 days of receiving the request, make the application to the court[4], unless he is of the opinion that the request is an unreasonable one in the circumstances, in which case he may apply to the court for an order relieving him from the obligation to make the application for a public examination[5]. If the court so orders, and the application for the order was made *ex parte*, notice of the order must be given forthwith by the official receiver to the requesting creditor, and, if the application for such an order is dismissed, the official receiver's application for a public examination[6] must be made forthwith on conclusion of the hearing of the application[7].

1   For the prescribed forms of request by creditors see the IR 1986, rr 6.173, 12.7, Sch 4, Form 6.56.
2   IR 1986, r 6.173(1).
3   IR 1986, r 6.173(2).
4   IR 1986, r 6.173(3).
5   IR 1986, r 6.173(4). The official receiver would otherwise be required to make the application under the IA 1986, s 290(2): see para **17.29** text to note 1 above.
6   Ie under the IA 1986, s 290(2): see text to note 1 above.
7   IR 1986, r 6.173(5).

The order

17.31 On an application made by the official receiver, the court must direct that a public examination of the bankrupt shall be held on a day appointed by the court; and the bankrupt must attend on that day and be publicly examined as to his affairs, dealings and property[1].

1   IA 1986, s 290(3).

17.32 Once an order for public examination is made, a copy[1] must be sent forthwith by the official receiver to the bankrupt[2].

1   For the prescribed form of order see the IR 1986, rr 6.172, 12.7, Sch 4, Form 6.55.
2   IR 1986, r 6.172(1).

17.33 The order must appoint a venue for the hearing and direct the bankrupt to attend[1]. The official receiver must give at least 14 days' notice[2] of the hearing to any trustee or special manager, and subject to any contrary direction of the court, to every creditor of the bankrupt who is known to the official receiver or is identified in the bankrupt's statement of affairs[3]. The official receiver may, if he thinks fit, cause notice of the order to be given, by public advertisement in one or more newspapers, at least 14 days before the day for the hearing[4].

1   IR 1986, r 6.172(2).
2   As to the mode of giving notice see the IR 1986, rr 13.3–13.5.
3   IR 1986, r 6.172(3).
4   IR 1986, r 6.172(4).

Those entitled to attend

17.34 The following may take part in the public examination of the bankrupt, and may question him concerning his affairs, dealings and property and the causes of his failure:

(1)   the official receiver and, where appropriate[1], the official petitioner;
(2)   the trustee of the bankrupt's estate, if his appointment has taken effect;
(3)   any person who has been appointed a special manager of the bankrupt's estate or business;
(4)   any creditor of the bankrupt who has tendered a proof in bankruptcy[2].

1   Ie on a petition under the IA 1986, s 264(1)(d).
2   IA 1986, s 290(4).

Disability

17.35 Should the bankrupt be suffering from any mental or physical disability which renders him unfit to be examined, the court may stay the order for examination[1]. An application for a stay or for directions may be made by the official receiver, any person appointed by the court to manage the affairs of the bankrupt, or by a relative or friend of the bankrupt where considered by the court to be a proper person to make the application. The official receiver may make the application *ex parte* supported by evidence in the form of a report. Other applications must give at least seven days' notice to the official receiver and any trustee of the bankrupt's estate and deposit with the official receiver such sum as the official receiver certifies to be necessary for the additional expenses of any examination that may be ordered on the application. Except where the bankrupt is a patient within the Mental Health Act 1983, the application must be supported by an affidavit of a registered medical practitioner as to the bankrupt's mental and physical condition.

1   IR 1986, r 6.174.

The conduct of examination

17.36 At the hearing, which is in open court[1], the bankrupt must be examined on oath, and he must answer all such questions as the court may put, or allow to be put, to him[2]. Any of the persons allowed[3] to question the bankruptcy may, with the approval of the court (made known either at the hearing or in advance of it), appear by solicitor or counsel; or a person allowed to question may in writing authorise another person to question the bankrupt on his behalf[4]. The bankrupt may at his own expense employ a solicitor, with or without counsel, who may put to him such questions as the court may allow for the purpose of enabling him to explain or qualify any answers given by him, and may make representations on his behalf[5].

1   *Practice Direction: Insolvency Proceedings*, para 9.3(1).
2   IR 1986, r 6.175(1).
3   Ie under the IA 1986, s 290(6).
4   IR 1986, r 6.175(2).
5   IR 1986, r 6.175(3).

17.37 There must be made in writing such record of the examination as the court thinks proper[1]; and the record must be read over either to or by the bankrupt, signed by him, and verified by affidavit at a venue[2] fixed by the court[3]. The written record may in any proceedings[4] be used as evidence against the bankrupt of any statement made by him in the course of his public examination[5].

1   As to shorthand writers see the IR 1986, rr 7.16–7.18.
2   For the meaning of 'venue' see the IR 1986, r 13.6.
3   IR 1986, r 6.175(4). For the prescribed form of affidavit see IR 1986, rr 6.175, 12.7, Sch 4, Form 6.58.

⁴ Ie whether under the IA 1986 or otherwise.
⁵ IR 1986, r 6.175(5).

Adjournment

17.38 The public examination may be adjourned by the court from time to time, either to a fixed date or generally[1]. If criminal proceedings have been instituted against the bankrupt, and the court is of the opinion that the continuance of the hearing would be calculated to prejudice a fair trial of those proceedings, the hearing may be adjourned[2]. Since a public examination is public, the risk of prejudicing a fair trial is different and greater than is caused by a private examination[3].

1 IR 1986, r 6.176(1). For the prescribed form of order see IR 1986, rr 6.176, 12.7, Sch 4, Form 6.59.
2 IR 1986, r 6.175(6).
3 Contrast *Re Arrows (No 2)* [1994] 1 BCLC 355, CA.

17.39 Where the examination has been adjourned generally, the court may at any time on the application of the official receiver or of the bankrupt fix a venue for the resumption of the examination[1], and give directions as to the manner in which, and the time within which, notice of the resumed public examination is to be given to persons entitled to take part in it[2].

1 For the prescribed form of order see the IR 1986, rr 6.176, 12.7, Sch 4, Form 6.60.
2 IR 1986, r 6.176(2).

17.40 Where such an application is made by the bankrupt, the court may grant it on terms that the expenses of giving the notices required be paid by him and that, before a venue for the resumed public examination is fixed, he must deposit with the official receiver such sum as the latter considers necessary to cover those expenses[1]. Where the examination is adjourned generally, the official receiver may, there and then, make application[2] for suspension of the bankrupt's automatic discharge from bankruptcy[3]. There is no power to apply for a suspension from discharge in a private examination. Where a public examination was adjourned and continued by consent as a private examination, the public examination had to be reinstated before an application to suspend could be made. In special circumstances, the court may permit the application to be made at short notice[4].

1 IR 1986, r 6.176(3).
2 Ie under the IA 1986, s 279(3).
3 IR 1986, r 6.176(4).
4 *Holmes v Official Receiver* [1996] BCC 246.

Self-incrimination

17.41 It is clear that, under the law as it was before the IA 1986, the bankrupt could not refuse to answer any questions relating to his affairs or estate which were put to him at his public examination[1]. The law does not appear to have been changed in this respect by the IA 1986. In *Bishopsgate*

Investment Management Ltd v Maxwell[2], although it was a case concerning a private examination of the officer of a company under the IA 1986, s 236, Dillon LJ said that he would conclude that a bankrupt on his public examination cannot invoke the privilege against self-incrimination.

1   *Re Atherton* [1912] 2 KB 251; *Re Paget, ex p Official Receiver* [1927] 2 Ch 85, CA.
2   [1993] Ch 1, [1992] BCLC 475, CA.

Scope of questions which may be put

17.42 In *Re Paget, ex p Official Receiver*[1] the bankrupt refused to answer at his public examination the question 'in what name did you enlist in the First Battalion of the London Fusiliers in 1916?' Although in part his refusal was based on concern that he would incriminate himself by doing so, the issue whether it was a relevant question was also raised. The Court of Appeal allowed the official receiver's appeal from Clauson J who had accepted the bankrupt's refusal. Lord Hanworth said, 'I think it may rather be said that before the question can be disallowed, the court has to be satisfied that the answer could not secure any further assets or rights to the creditors or any protection to the public'. As well as indicating the scope of relevance, this suggests that the onus is on the bankrupt in resisting a question to establish that the topic to which it is addressed is outside that scope.

1   [1927] 2 Ch 85, CA.

Use to which evidence given by the bankrupt on his public examination can be put

17.43 As mentioned above, a written record must be made of the public examination. The IR 1986, r 6.175(5) provides that the written record may be used in any proceedings, whether under the IA 1986 or otherwise, against the bankrupt as evidence of any statement made by him in the course of his public examination. But this rule must now be read together with the IA 1986, s 433 as amended by the Youth Justice and Criminal Evidence Act 1999, s 59 and Sch 3, para 7. The IA 1986, s 433 was amended in consequence of the decision of the European Court of Human Rights in *Saunders v United Kingdom*[1] in which it was held that a defendant's right to a fair trial was violated in a criminal trial by the deployment as part of the prosecution's evidence in chief of testimony obtained from the defendant under compulsory questioning by inspectors appointed under the Companies Act 1985, ss 432 and 442. By the IA 1986, s 433(2) as so amended, it is provided that where any person has made a statement in pursuance of a requirement imposed by the IA 1985 or rules made under it, no evidence relating to the statement may be adduced in criminal proceedings, except for criminal proceedings relating to certain specified offences, and no question relating to it may be asked by or on behalf of the prosecution, unless evidence relating to it is adduced, or a question relating to it is asked, in the proceedings by or on behalf of that person. The excepted cases are criminal proceedings in which the accused is charged with an offence specified in the IA 1986, s 433(3). Such specified offences include: IA 1986, s 353(1), s 354(1)(b) and (3), s 356(1), (2)(a) and (b) and Sch 7, para 4(3)(a) and offences under the Perjury Act 1911, ss 1, 2 or 5.

¹ [1998] 1 BCLC 362.

17.44 However, civil proceedings are unaffected by these changes. Hence in civil proceedings the written record of the public examination and the bankrupt's answers may be used as evidence in chief. Proceedings brought under the Company Directors Disqualification Act 1986 are civil proceedings¹, but the evidence may not be used against persons other than the bankrupt.

¹ *Re Westminster Property Management Ltd, Official Receiver v Stern* [2001] 1 All ER 633, [2000] 1 WLR 2230, CA.

17.45 If the trustee, having examined the bankrupt at a public examination, later calls the bankrupt as a witness in support of a claim which the trustee has brought, the rule that a party may not cross-examine his own witness is relaxed. 'If the debtor says anything contrary to what he said at his public examination, counsel may put to him what he did say at that examination, whether the counsel examining him has called him as a witness or is cross-examining him'¹.

¹ *Re Debtor, Jacobs v Lloyd* [1944] Ch 344.

Sanction for non-attendance

17.46 If a bankrupt without reasonable excuse fails at any time to attend his public examination, he is guilty of a contempt of court and liable to be punished accordingly, in addition to any other punishment to which he may be subject¹.

¹ IA 1986, s 290(5).

Expenses

17.47 Where a public examination of the bankrupt has been ordered by the court on a creditors' requisition¹, the court may order that the expenses of the examination are to be paid, as to a specified proportion, out of the deposit paid by the requisitionists², instead of out of the estate³. In no case do the costs and expenses of a public examination fall on the official receiver personally⁴.

¹ Ie by virtue of the IA 1986, s 290(2): see para **17.29** above.
² Ie under the IR 1986, r 6.173(2): see para **17.30** above.
³ IR 1986, r 6.177(1).
⁴ IR 1986, r 6.177(2).

E PRIVATE EXAMINATION

Court's power to order private examination

17.48 At any time after a bankruptcy order has been made, the court may, on the application of the official receiver or the trustee of the bankrupt's estate, summon to appear before it:

(a) the bankrupt or the bankrupt's spouse or former spouse;
(b) any person known or believed to have any property comprised in the bankrupt's estate in his possession or to be indebted to the bankrupt;
(c) any person appearing to the court to be able to give information concerning the bankrupt or the bankrupt's dealings, affairs or property[1].

1 IA 1986, s 366(1).

17.49 In category (b) the persons included are those 'believed' to have relevant property or to be indebted to the bankrupt. By contrast, in the IA 1986, s 236, the equivalent provision in company insolvency, the phrases used are 'suspected to have [relevant property]' and 'supposed to be indebted'[1]. Belief would seem ordinarily to require a higher degree of certainty than suspicion or supposition. In relation to category (c) the bankruptcy provision refers to 'any person appearing to the court to be able to give [relevant information]', whereas the equivalent in the IA 1986, s 236 is 'any person whom the court thinks capable of giving [relevant information].' But, despite the verbal variations, there does not seem to be any reason why the categories of persons susceptible to being ordered to attend or to produce documents should differ.

1 See *Re Mid East Trading Ltd* [1998] 1 All ER 577, [1998] 1 BCLC 240, 248.

17.50 Where the respondent is a company, the order should require it to attend or furnish documents or information by a proper officer[1]. This will usually be the secretary who should be named. But if there is doubt it may suffice to make the order against 'the Secretary or other proper officer of the company'[2].

1 *Re Murjani (a bankrupt)* [1996] 1 BCLC 272, 286.
2 Cf *Re Alexandra Palace Co* (1880) 16 Ch D 58; *A-G v North Metropolitan Tramways Co* [1892] 3 Ch 70; *Chaddock v British South Africa Co* [1896] 2 QB 153, CA.

17.51 It has been held that the IA 1986, s 236 binds the Crown by virtue of the express provision of the IA 1986, s 434(a)[1]. Since IA 1986, s 434(a) refers to remedies against companies or individuals, it is clear that IA 1986, s 366 also binds the Crown.

1 *Soden v Burns* [1996] 3 All ER 967, [1996] 2 BCLC 636.

Production of documents

17.52 The court may require any person in categories (b) and (c) (as listed above) to produce any documents in his possession or under his control relating to the bankrupt or the bankrupt's dealings, affairs or property.

17.53 Where the documents sought from the respondent are documents belonging to third parties which have been seized by the respondent itself acting under powers to compel the production of evidence or are transcripts of evidence given by third parties under compulsion, the order for production should not be made until the third parties have been notified and given an opportunity to make representations[1]. 'Third party' in this context means a person other than the person who has possession and control of the documents.

[1] *Morris v Director of the Serious Fraud Office* [1993] Ch 372, [1993] 1 All ER 788 (seized documents); *Soden v Burns* [1996] 3 All ER 967, [1996] 2 BCLC 636 (transcripts). For the report of the decision on the third parties' representations made in response to the order in *Soden v Burns*, see *Re Atlantic Computers plc* [1998] BCC 200.

17.54 The court will not order documents to be produced which are subject to legal professional privilege[1], but legal professional privilege cannot be claimed in respect of documents solely because they are in the possession of a solicitor who is ordered to produce them, if the client would be obliged to produce the documents if himself required to do so[2].

[1] See *Re Ouvaroff (a bankrupt)* [1997] BPIR 712 (where, however, the privilege had been waived).
[2] *Re Murjani (a bankrupt)* [1996] 1 BCLC 272, 279.

17.55 In *Re Galileo Group Ltd, Elles v Hambro Bank Ltd*[1], applying the decision of the House of Lords in *Rowell v Pratt*[2] the court held that it had no power to order the production of documents where their production would infringe a statutory prohibition, the prohibition in question being that imposed by the Banking Act 1987, s 82. The question whether to permit a redacted version to be disclosed was considered but refused on the basis that the material remaining after redaction would be of little use.

[1] [1999] Ch 100, [1998] 1 All ER 545.
[2] [1938] AC 101, [1937] 3 All ER 660. See also *Bank of Credit and Commerce International (Overseas) Ltd v Price Waterhouse (a firm)* [1998] Ch 84, [1997] 4 All ER 781.

Documents held outside the jurisdiction

17.56 An order to produce documents held outside the jurisdiction may be made under the IA 1986, s 236. In *Re Mid East Trading Ltd*[1] the Court of Appeal justified an order for production of such documents by reference to the fact that there is jurisdiction to wind up unregistered companies, including those incorporated overseas. Although in that case the company was an overseas company which was being wound up in England, the point was that in such a case it was obvious that documents would be held outside the jurisdiction and that, since the IA 1986, s 236 applied in such windings up, it must be taken as a matter of construction to include power to order production of documents held abroad.

¹ [1998] 1 All ER 57, [1998] 1 BCLC 240, CA.

Procedure

17.57 Any application for an order for a private examination must be made in writing and be accompanied by a brief statement of the grounds on which it is made[1]. The application[2] must sufficiently identify the respondent[3], and should also specify by which of the available means it is sought to examine him[4]. The application may be made with notice[5]. The application should not be made without notice unless there are urgent circumstances which justify doing so[6]. If there are matters which the trustee does not wish to inform the bankrupt or other respondent they may be shown to the court on the basis that they are confidential and not to be shown to the bankrupt or other respondent[7].

¹ IR 1986, r 9.2(1).
² IR 1986, r 9.2(3).
³ 'The respondent' means the person in respect of whom an order is applied for: IR 1986, r 9.1(2)(a).
⁴ IR 1986, r 9.2(3).
⁵ IR 1986, r 9.2(4). If the application is made *ex parte* there is a duty to place all material facts before the court: *Re John T Rhodes Ltd (No 2)* (1987) 3 BCC 588 (company case).
⁶ *Re Murjani (a bankrupt)* [1996] 1 All ER 65, [1996] 1 WLR 1498.
⁷ *Re Murjani (a bankrupt)* [1996] 1 All ER 65, [1996] 1 WLR 1498.

17.58 Where the respondent seeks to challenge the exercise by the court of its discretion to order his examination, he may apply, and the court may allow him, to inspect the confidential statement made by the official receiver or trustee in support of the application for examination[1].

¹ *Re British and Commonwealth Holdings plc (Nos 1 & 2)* [1992] 2 All ER 801, CA.

Exercise of discretion to order examination or production of documents

17.59 The court's discretion to order an examination or the production of documents is a general discretion:

'At the same time it is plain that this is an extraordinary power and that the discretion must be exercised after a careful balancing of the factors involved: on the one hand the reasonable requirements of the [office-holder] to carry out his task, on the other the need to avoid making an order which is wholly unreasonable, unnecessary or "oppressive" to the person concerned ... . The protection for the person called upon to produce documents lies, thus, not in a limitation by category of documents ("reconstituting the company's state of knowledge") but in the fact that the applicant must satisfy the court that, after balancing all the relevant factors, there is a proper case for such an order to be made. The proper case is one where the administrator reasonably requires to see the documents to carry out his functions and the production does not impose an unnecessary and unreasonable burden on the person required to produce them in the light of the administrator's requirements. An application is not necessarily unreasonable because it is inconvenient for the addressee of the application or causes him a lot of work or may make him vulnerable to future claims, or is addressed to a person who is not an officer or employee of or a contractor with the company in administration, but all these will be relevant factors, together no doubt with many others.'[1]

[1] *Re British and Commonwealth Holdings plc (No 2)* [1993] AC 426, [1992] 4 All ER 876, HL; *Buchler v Al-Midani (No 2)* [2006] BPIR 867.

17.60 For example, an office-holder may, before proceedings have been commenced, address questions to or seek documents from a person who is at risk of being sued in those proceedings[1]. But it is unreasonable for a liquidator to ask questions not for the purpose of eliciting further information or documents but in order to obtain admissions or explanations regarding the information already obtained[2]. The existence or fear of civil proceedings will not be a major factor in many cases, but it is oppressive to require a defendant accused of serious wrongdoing to provide what may amount to pre-trial dispositions and to prove the case against himself. But even that oppression may be outweighed by the legitimate requirements of the office-holder[3].

[1] See *Re Bank of Credit and Commerce International (SA) (No 12), Morris v Bank of America National Trust and Savings Association* [1997] 1 BCLC 526, 536 (Robert Walker J); *Cloverbay Ltd (joint administrators) v Bank of Credit and Commerce International SA* [1991] Ch 90, [1991] 1 All ER 894, CA; *Re Castle New Homes* [1979] 1 WLR 1075, 1089.
[2] *Re PFTZM Ltd, Jourdain v Paul* [1995] 2 BCLC 354; *Re Sasea Finance Ltd (in liquidation)* [1998] 1 BCLC 559.
[3] *Re RGB Resources Ltd, Shierson v Rastogi* [2002] EWCA Civ 1624, [2003] 1 WLR 586; *Long v Farrer & Co (a firm)* [2004] EWHC 1774 (Ch), [2004] BPIR 1218. For the position in Australia, see *Re Southern Equities Corpn, England v Smith* [2000] 2 BCLC 21.

17.61 In the context of examinations or orders for the production of documents relating to the affairs of an insolvent company, it was thought that the order should be limited by reference to the matters that were within the knowledge of the company before it was wound up. The House of Lords has held that no such limit on the exercise of the power to order examinations or the production of documents exists[1].

[1] *Re British & Commonwealth Holdings plc (No 2)* [1993] AC 426, [1992] 4 All ER 876.

17.62 In *Re Arrows (No 2)*[1] it was conceded, because of the House of Lords' decision in *R v Director of the Serious Fraud Office, ex p Smith*[2], that the fact that charges had been brought against the person to be examined in relation to matters to which the examination would relate was not a ground for refusing to order an examination. But the Court of Appeal held that the risk that the respondent ran of incriminating himself in the examination and that the transcript would be obtained by the prosecuting authority, although a relevant consideration in the exercise of the court's discretion whether to order an examination, was not an absolute bar against ordering an examination.

[1] [1994] 1 BCLC 355, CA.
[2] [1993] AC 1, [1992] 3 All ER 456.

17.63 An order for examination should not be made where the inquiries relate to a proof lodged in the bankruptcy. The trustee should, if appropriate, reject the proof and the dispute resolved on any appeal made by the creditor[1].

1   *Bellmex International Ltd (in liq) v British American Tobacco Ltd* [2001] 1 BCLC 91.

The order

17.64 If the court, on the hearing of the application, orders[1] the respondent to appear before it, it must specify a venue for his appearance, which must be not less than 14 days from the date of the order[2]. The court may, if it thinks fit, order that any person, who if within the jurisdiction of the court would be liable to be summoned to appear before it[3], be examined in any part of the United Kingdom where he may be for the time being, or in any place outside the United Kingdom[4]. If the respondent is ordered to submit affidavits, the order must specify the matters which are to be dealt with in them, and the time within which they are to be submitted to the court[5]. If the order is to produce books, papers or other records, the time and manner of compliance must be specified[6].

1   As to the prescribed form of order see IR 1986, r 12.7(1), Sch 4, Form 9.1.
2   IR 1986, r 9.3(2).
3   Ie under the IA 1986, s 366.
4   IA 1986, s 367(3). By analogy with provision in respect of companies, an injunction may be obtained to restrain a person from leaving the jurisdiction pending the examination: *Re A Company (No 3318 of 1987)* (1987) 3 BCC 564. Considerable difficulties may, however, be encountered in obtaining and enforcing orders for the examination of unwilling respondents outside the United Kingdom: see *Re Tucker (a bankrupt), ex p Tucker* [1990] Ch 148, [1988] 1 All ER 603, CA.
5   IR 1986, r 9.3(3).
6   IR 1986, r 9.3(4).

17.65 The order must be served forthwith on the respondent; and it must be served personally, unless the court otherwise orders[1].

1   IR 1986, r 9.3(5).

Conduct of the examination

17.66 At the examination of the respondent, the applicant may attend in person, or be represented by a solicitor with or without counsel, and may put such questions to the respondent as the court may allow[1]. The examination must be made by the applicant in person or by the solicitor or counsel acting on his behalf. Thus it may not be conducted by a US attorney. Any other person who could have applied for an order[2] in respect of the bankrupt's affairs may, with the leave of the court and if the applicant does not object, attend the examination and put questions to the respondent, but only through the applicant[3]. If the respondent is ordered to answer interrogatories, the court must direct him as to the questions which he is required to answer, and as to whether his answers, if any, are to be made on affidavit[4].

1   IR 1986, r 9.4(1).
2   Ie under the IA 1986, s 366.

³ IR 1986, r 9.4(2).
⁴ IR 1986, r 9.4(3).

17.67 Where the application has been made on information provided by a creditor of the bankrupt, the creditor may, with the leave of the court and if the applicant does not object, attend the examination and put questions to the respondent, but only through the applicant[1]. The respondent may at his own expense employ a solicitor with or without counsel, who may put to him such questions as the court may allow for the purposes of enabling him to explain or qualify any answers given by him, and may make representations on his behalf[2].

¹ IR 1986, r 9.4(4). Other creditors who may not attend the examination may put to the bankrupt at the creditors' meetings such questions as the chairman may in his discretion allow: see IR 1986, r 6.84(6).
² IR 1986, r 9.4(5).

Advance notification of questions

17.68 In *Re Arrows (No 4) sub nom Hamilton v Naviede*[1] Lord Browne-Wilkinson stated that the person to be examined is entitled to advance notice, in general terms, of the topics on which he is to be examined. The court retains a discretion whether advance notice should be given[2].

¹ [1995] 2 AC 75, [1994] 3 All ER 814.
² *Re Norton Warburg Holdings Ltd* [1983] BCLC 235 and *Re Arrows (No 2)* [1992] BCLC 1176 (on appeal [1994] 1 BCLC 355 when appeal on other grounds against order for examination under the IA 1986, s 236 dismissed).

Self-incrimination

17.69 The bankrupt is not entitled to refuse to answer questions in a private examination ordered under the IA 1986, s 366 on the ground that he may incriminate himself by doing so[1].

¹ *Bishopsgate Investment Management Ltd v Maxwell Maxwell* [1993] Ch 1, [1992] 2 All ER 856, CA.

17.70 Under the similar provisions contained in the Bankruptcy Acts, the Court of Appeal held that those other persons against whom an order for a private examination might be made were entitled to rely on the privilege and to refuse to answer questions where to do so might incriminate themselves[1]. But it is clear that witnesses may not rely on the privilege where ordered under the IA 1986, s 236 to attend in order to answer questions about the affairs of a company[2] and, since ss 236 and 366 are substantially similar, it appears that the position is the same in respect of witnesses ordered to answer questions about a bankrupt's affairs, even though the distinction between the bankrupt and witnesses has a physical clarity which does not exist between the natural persons who were acting on behalf of a company and natural persons who were mere witnesses to the activities of the company (or more accurately to the activities of those natural persons who were acting on behalf of the company).

1   *Re Firth, ex p Schofield* (1877) 6 Ch D 230 (a decision on the Bankruptcy Act 1869, s 96).
2   *Bishopsgate Investment Management Ltd v Maxwell* [1993] Ch 1, [1992] 2 All ER 856, CA. See also *Re Jeffery S Levitt Ltd* [1992] Ch 457, [1992] 2 All ER 509 (examination of a director under the IA 1986, s 236); *Bank of England v Riley* [1992] Ch 475, [1992] 1 All ER 769, CA (request for production of documents under the Banking Act 1987, s 42); *Re London United Investments plc* [1992] Ch 578, [1992] 2 All ER 842, CA (investigation by inspectors appointed under the Companies Act 1985, s 432).

Record of the examination

17.71 A written record of the examination must be made, and this must be read over either to or by the respondent and signed by him at a venue fixed by the court[1]. The written record may in any proceedings[2] be used as evidence of any statement made by him in the course of his examination[3].

1   IR 1986, r 9.4(6).
2   Ie whether under the IA 1986 or otherwise.
3   IR 1986, r 9.4(7).

17.72 Unless the court otherwise directs, the written record of the respondent's examination, and any answer given by him to interrogatories, and any affidavits submitted by him in compliance with an order of the court[1] must not be filed in court[2]. The written record, answers and affidavits must not be open to inspection, without an order, or any person who could have applied for such an order[3]. This applies also to so much of the court file as shows the grounds of the application for an order[4] and to any copy of proposed interrogatories[5]. The court may from time to time give directions as to the custody and inspection of any documents and as to the furnishing of copies of, or extracts from, such documents[6].

1   Ie under the IA 1986, s 366.
2   IR 1986, r 9.5(1).
3   IR 1986, r 9.5(2).
4   For a discussion of when and to what extent the respondent will be permitted to inspect the statement made by the applicant of the grounds for the application, see *Re British and Commonwealth Holdings plc (Nos 1 & 2)* [1992] 2 All ER 801, CA.
5   IR 1986, r 9.5(2).
6   IR 1986, r 9.5(4).

Use to which evidence given at a private examination may be put

17.73 The IR 1986, r 9.4(7) provides, in the same terms as the rule relating to the use to which the record of the bankrupt's public examination may be put, that the written record of the private examination may, in any proceeding, whether under the IA 1986 or otherwise, be used as evidence against the respondent of any statement made by him in the course of his examination. 'The respondent' means the person in respect of whom the order for the examination was made[1]. But this rule must also be read together with the IA 1986, s 433 as amended by the Youth Justice and Criminal Evidence

Act 1999[2] referred to above in relation to public examinations. The evidence cannot be used as evidence in chief in criminal proceedings.

1   IR 1986, r 9.1(2)(a).
2   Youth Justice and Criminal Evidence Act 1999, s 59 and Sch 3, para 7.

Power to disclose the record of a private examination

17.74 The written record of a private examination, any answers to interrogatories and any affidavits submitted in compliance with an order of the court under the IA 1986, s 366 by any respondent shall not be filed in court, unless the court directs. Hence such documents will not ordinarily form part of the court file and are not subject to the rights of inspection which apply to the court file. Instead, the court has power under the IR 1986, r 9.5 to permit inspection of the written record, answers and affidavits submitted in compliance with IA 1986, s 366. In *Re Arrows (No 4), Hamilton v Naviede*[1] the House of Lords considered the interaction between this rule and the Serious Fraud Office's power under the Criminal Justice Act 1987, s 2(3) to require any person to produce any specified documents which appeared to the Director of the Serious Fraud Office to relate to any matter relevant to an investigation being conducted by the Serious Fraud Office. The Director had issued a request to the liquidators of a company that they produce copies of the transcripts of the private examination of the principal director of the company. The House of Lords held that the Criminal Justice Act 1987, s 3(3) did not override the discretion conferred on the court having the insolvency jurisdiction whether to permit disclosure of the information extracted under compulsion under the IA 1986, s 236. But, where the request to produce such information comes from a prosecuting authority there are severe limitations on the way in which the discretion should be exercised. In particular, the court having insolvency jurisdiction cannot impose any condition on the use to which the prosecuting authority can put the evidence which it is allowed to receive. The court having insolvency jurisdiction could not impose such a condition because to do so would be to seek to prevent a prosecutor from using or the criminal court from admitting relevant evidence at the criminal trial. On prior authority a civil court does not have jurisdiction to do this. Whether relevant evidence should be excluded is a matter within the sole discretion of the criminal court. When *Re Arrows (No 4)* was decided the only basis on which the criminal court might exclude such evidence was by exercise of the power under the Police and Criminal Evidence Act 1984 to exclude evidence if its admission would have such an adverse effect on the fairness of the proceedings that the court ought not to admit it. Since the IA 1986, s 433 was amended by the Youth Justice and Criminal Evidence Act 1999, the admissibility of evidence extracted under compulsion is more restricted. The position now is that where any person has made a statement under the compulsion of an examination under the IA 1986, s 366, no evidence relating to the statement may be adduced in criminal proceedings, except for criminal proceedings relating to certain specified offences, and no question relating to it may be asked by or on behalf of the prosecution, unless evidence relating to it is adduced, or a question relating to it is asked, in the proceedings by or on behalf of that person.

1   [1995] 2 AC 75, [1994] 3 All ER 814.

17.75 In *Re Arrows (No 4)* the House of Lords did not expand on what circumstances might justify the court having insolvency jurisdiction in refusing to permit the written record, answers or affidavits to be disclosed to the prosecuting authority which had requested them. Examples of such refusal include the refusal in *Re Barlow Clowes Gilt Managers Ltd*[1] to order the liquidators to disclose the transcripts of examinations under the IA 1986, s 236 to the defendants prosecuted for offences alleged to have been committed in the conduct of the insolvent company's business.

[1]   [1992] Ch 208, [1991] 4 All ER 385.

Enforcement of attendance

17.76 Where a person without reasonable excuse fails to appear before the court when he is summoned to do so[1] or there are reasonable grounds for believing that a person has absconded, or is about to abscond, with a view to avoiding his appearance before the court, the court may, for the purpose of bringing that person and anything in his possession before the court, cause a warrant to be issued to a constable or prescribed officer of the court[2] for the arrest of that person, and for the seizure of any books, papers, records, money or goods in that person's possession[3]. The court may also authorise a person arrested under such a warrant to be kept in custody, and anything seized under such a warrant to be held until that person is brought before the court under the warrant or until such other time as the court may order[4].

[1]   Ie under the IA 1986, s 366(1).
[2]   The prescribed officers of the court are in the case of the High Court, the tipstaff and his assistants of the court, and in the case of a county court, the registrar and the bailiffs: IR 1986, r 7.21(2).
[3]   IA 1986, s 366(2), (3).
[4]   IA 1986, s 366(4).

17.77 When a person is arrested under such a warrant, the officer arresting him must forthwith bring him before the court issuing the warrant in order that he may be examined[1]. If he cannot immediately be brought up for examination, the officer must deliver him into the custody of the governor of the prison named in the warrant, who must keep him in custody and produce him before the court as it may from time to time direct[2]. After the arrest, the officer must forthwith report the arrest or delivery into custody to the court, and apply to the court to fix a venue[3] for the person's examination[4]. The court must appoint the earliest practicable time for the examination, and must direct the governor of the prison to produce the person for examination at the time and place appointed, and forthwith give notice of the venue to the person who applied for the warrant[5].

[1]   IR 1986, r 7.23(1). For the prescribed form of warrant see IR 1986, rr 7.23, 12.7, Sch 4, Form 7.8.
[2]   IR 1986, r 7.23(2). For the prescribed form of order of production of the person arrested under such a warrant, see IR 1986, rr 7.23, 12.7, Sch 4, Form 7.9.
[3]   For the meaning of 'venue' see the IR 1986, r 13.6.
[4]   IR 1986, r 7.23(3).
[5]   IR 1986, r 7.23(4). For the prescribed form of order for the production of a person arrested, see IR 1986, rr 7.23, 12.7, Sch 4, Form 7.9.

17.78   Any property in the arrested person's possession which may be seized must, as may be directed by the court, be lodged with, or otherwise dealt with as instructed by, whoever is specified in the warrant as authorised to receive it, or kept by the officer seizing it pending the receipt of written orders from the court as to its disposal[1].

1   IR 1986, r 7.23(5).

Costs

17.79   Where the court has ordered an examination of any person and it appears to it that the examination was made necessary because information had been unjustifiably refused by the respondent, it may order that the costs of the examination be paid by him[1].

1   IR 1986, r 9.6(1).

17.80   Where the court makes an order against a person to deliver up property in his possession which belongs to the bankrupt[1], or to pay any amount in discharge of a debt due to the bankrupt[2], the costs of the application for the order may be ordered by the court to be paid by the respondent[3]. Otherwise the applicant's costs must be paid out of the bankrupt's estate, unless the court otherwise orders[4]. A person summoned to attend for examination must be tendered a reasonable sum in respect of travelling expenses incurred in connection with his attendance; but other costs falling on him are at the court's discretion[5]. In *Re Bank of Credit and Commerce International SA (No 12)*[6] Robert Walker J, without deciding the point because there were two prior conflicting decisions of judges at first instance[7], was inclined to the view that the court had jurisdiction to order the applicant office-holder to pay the respondent's costs of producing the documents sought. Where the examination is on the application of the official receiver otherwise than in the capacity of trustee, no order may be made for the payment of costs by him[8].

1   Ie under the IA 1986, s 367(1).
2   Ie under the IA 1986, s 367(2).
3   IR 1986, r 9.6(2).
4   IR 1986, rr 9.6(3), 13.8.
5   IR 1986, r 9.6(4).
6   [1997] BCC 561.
7   *Re Aveling Barford Ltd* (1988) 4 BCC 548, 522; *Re Cloverbay Ltd* (1989) 5 BCC 732, 737–738.
8   IR 1986, r 9.6(5).

F SUMMARY ORDERS FOR DELIVERY UP OF PROPERTY AND PAYMENT OF DEBTS

Property or debts revealed by examination

17.81   If it appears to the court, on consideration of any evidence obtained under examination that any person has in his possession any property comprised in the bankrupt's estate, the court may, on the application of the official receiver or the trustee of the bankrupt's estate, order that person to deliver the whole or any part of the property to the official receiver or the trustee at such time, in such manner and on such terms as the court thinks fit[1].

¹ IA 1986, s 367(1).

17.82 If it appears to the court, on consideration of any evidence so obtained, that any person is indebted to the bankrupt, the court may, on the application of the official receiver or the trustee of the bankrupt's estate, order that person to pay him, at such time and in such manner as the court may direct, the whole or any part of the amount due, whether in full discharge of the debt or otherwise, as the court thinks fit[1].

¹ IA 1986, s 367(2).

G UNENFORCEABILITY OF LIENS ON BOOKS

17.83 A lien or other right to retain possession of any books, papers or other records of a bankrupt is unenforceable to the extent that its enforcement would deny possession of any books, papers or other records to the official receiver or the trustee of the bankrupt's estate[1]. This will include a solicitors' lien over papers and records of a client[2]. A lien on documents which give title to property and are held as such is however enforceable against the trustee or official receiver[3]. This will include the situation where the documents are being held by way of security over the property concerned, but the drafting of the statute is wide enough to cover the situation where the documents are being held by a third party as security generally.

¹ IA 1986, s 349(1).
² See *Re Aveling Barford Ltd* [1988] 3 All ER 1019, [1989] 1 WLR 360.
³ IA 1986, s 349(2); *Brereton v Nicholls* [1993] BCLC 593.

H CRIMINAL OFFENCES RELATING TO THE CONCEALMENT OF ASSETS AND FAILURE TO DISCLOSE INFORMATION

Offences concerning the disclosure of information

17.84 Unless the bankrupt proves that, at the time of the conduct constituting the offence, he had no intent to defraud or to conceal the state of his affairs, he is guilty of an offence:

(1)   if he makes or has made any material omission in any statement made under the provisions of the IA 1986 relating to the insolvency of individuals and relating to his affairs[1];

(2)   if he does not to the best of his knowledge and belief disclose all the property comprised in his estate to the official receiver or the trustee[2]; or

(3)   if he does not inform the official receiver or the trustee of any disposal of any property which but for the disposal would be comprised in his estate, stating how, when, to whom and for what consideration the

property was disposed of, save that this offence does not apply to any disposal in the ordinary course of business carried on by the bankrupt or to the payment of the ordinary expenses of the bankrupt or his family[3].

1 IA 1986, s 356(1).
2 IA 1986, s 353(1)(a).
3 IA 1986, s 353(1)(b).

17.85 The bankrupt is guilty of an offence:

(1) if he without reasonable excuse fails on being required to do so by the official receiver or the court (a) to account for the loss of any substantial part of his property incurred during the period of 12 months before the petition was presented or between the presentation of the petition and the bankruptcy order or (b) to give a satisfactory explanation of the manner in which such a loss was incurred[1];

(2) if knowing or believing that a false debt has been proved by any person, he fails to inform the trustee as soon as practicable[2]; or

(3) if he attempts to account for any part of his property by fictitious losses or expenses[3].

1 IA 1986, s 354(3).
2 IA 1986, s 356(2)(a).
3 IA 1986, s 356(2)(b).

Offences of failing to deliver possession of property and records

17.86 Unless the bankrupt proves that, at the time of the conduct constituting the offence, he had no intent to defraud or to conceal the state of his affairs, he is guilty of an offence:

(a) if he does not deliver up possession to the official receiver or trustee, or as the official receiver or trustee may direct, of such part of the property comprised in his estate as is in his possession or under his control and possession of which he is required by law so to deliver up[1]; or

(b) if he does not deliver up possession to the official receiver or trustee, or as the official receiver or trustee may direct, of all books, papers and other records of which he has possession or control and which relate to his estate or affairs[2].

1 IA 1986, s 354(1)(a).
2 IA 1986, s 355(1).

Offences of concealment

17.87 Unless the bankrupt proves that, at the time of the conduct constituting the offence, he had no intent to defraud or to conceal the state of his affairs, he is guilty of an offence:

(1)   if he conceals any debt due to or from him or conceals any property the value of which is not less than the prescribed amount, currently £500, and possession of which he is required to deliver up to the official receiver or trustee[1];

(2)   if, during the period of 12 months before the petition was presented or between the presentation of the petition and the bankruptcy order, he concealed any debt due to or from him or concealed any property the value of which was not less than the prescribed amount which it would have been an offence to conceal if the bankruptcy order had been made immediately before he did it[2]; or

(3)   if he conceals or at any time before the commencement of his bankruptcy concealed any part of his property after or within two months before the date on which a judgment or order for the payment of money has been obtained against him, being a judgment or order which was not satisfied before the commencement of the bankruptcy[3].

[1]   IA 1986, s 354(1)(b).
[2]   IA 1986, s 354(1)(c).
[3]   IA 1986, s 357(3).

Offences relating to the destruction of records

17.88   Unless the bankrupt proves that, at the time of the conduct constituting the offence, he had no intent to defraud or to conceal the state of his affairs, he is guilty of an offence:

(1)   if he prevents or between presentation of the petition and the making of the bankruptcy order prevented the production of any books, papers or records relating to his estate or affairs[1];

(2)   if he conceals, destroys, mutilates or falsifies or causes or permits any concealment, destruction, mutilation or falsification of any books, papers or other records relating to his estate or affairs[2];

(3)   if he makes, or causes or permits the making of any false entries in any document or record relating to his estate or affairs[3]; or

(4)   if in the 12 months before the petition was presented or between its presentation and the making of the bankruptcy order he did anything which would have been an offence within sub-para (2) or (3) if a bankruptcy order had been made before he did it[4].

[1]   IA 1986, s 355(2)(a).
[2]   IA 1986, s 355(2)(b).
[3]   IA 1986, s 355(2)(c).
[4]   IA 1986, s 355(2)(d).

Chapter 18

ADMINISTRATION OF THE ESTATE

A INTRODUCTION

18.1 The administration of the estate involves getting in, realising and distributing the estate in accordance with the provisions set out in the Insolvency Act 1986 ('IA 1986'), ss 305–335. In this chapter the focus is on the getting in and realisation of the estate. The distribution of the estate is discussed in **Chapter 23**. But, before the estate can be distributed the persons to whom it should be distributed, the unsecured creditors, have to be identified and their claims quantified. That process is comprised in the proving of the unsecured creditors' debts which is discussed in **Chapter 22**.

18.2 The trustee's conduct of the administration begins with the estate's vesting in him and his acquiring control over it. He will often need the co-operation of the bankrupt both at the outset of the administration and in its course. His powers are discussed, some of which require the sanction of the creditors' committee or the court. The methods by which the creditors may participate in the administration either by general meeting or through the creditors' committee are then set out. Next are described various provisions concerning the management and realisation of assets comprised in the estate, including sections on contracts made by the bankrupt before bankruptcy and disclaimer of onerous property. In the final section of this chapter the supervision and control of the court over the administration of the estate is discussed.

B VESTING OF ESTATE IN THE TRUSTEE

Estate vests on trustee's appointment

18.3 The bankrupt's estate vests in the trustee immediately on his appointment taking effect or, in the case of the official receiver, on his becoming trustee[1]. The fact that the estate automatically and invariably vests in the trustee marks a significant difference between a trustee in bankruptcy and a liquidator of an insolvent company in whom the insolvent company's property does not vest unless an application is made to the court for an order that it or some part of it should[2].

[1] IA 1986, s 306(1).
[2] IA 1986, s 145(1).

Estate vests by operation of law

18.4 Where any property which is comprised in the bankrupt's estate vests in the trustee, it vests without any conveyance, assignment or transfer[1]. But although the relevant item of property vests without any positive or formal step other than the appointment of the trustee, it may be necessary or prudent for the trustee to take some further step in order to protect or perfect his title and to enable him to deal effectively with the property in question.

[1] IA 1986, s 306(2).

Registered land

18.5 In exception to the general scheme of registration, the trustee in bankruptcy of a bankrupt who is the sole proprietor of any registered land or charge obtains legal title to the land or charge without being registered[1]. But the trustee is entitled, on production of the prescribed evidence, to be registered as proprietor of the land or charge in his place[2]. Disposing of the land will be easier if the trustee is registered because he can transfer it himself. The trustee's application to be registered must be supported by the bankruptcy order, a certificate signed by the trustee that the registered estate or registered charge forms part of the estate and an appropriate document evidencing the trustee's appointment[3].

[1] Land Registration Act 2002, s 27(5)(a).
[2] Land Registration Rules 2003, SI 2003/1417, r 168(1).
[3] Land Registration Rules 2003, SI 2003/1417, r 168(2) and (3).

18.6 Where the bankrupt is registered as one of two or more proprietors, the trustee is not entitled to be registered as a proprietor because the legal interest remains vested in the proprietors as joint tenants at law and a legal joint tenancy cannot be severed. The trustee should ensure that his interest is otherwise protected, if necessary by entering a caution against dealings.

Things in action

18.7 A thing or chose in action comprised in the estate is deemed to have been assigned to the trustee[1]. Hence there is no need for any written assignment to be made or notice to be given. Further, since a chose in action vests in the trustee without an assignment, a provision prohibiting assignment is not infringed[2]. But notice should be given by the trustee of the fact that the chose in action has been assigned from the bankrupt to him where it is necessary to do so for the purpose of protecting the trustee's priority, that is to say the trustee's priority over third parties' equitable interest[3]. The transfer of the interest in a thing in action from the bankrupt to his trustee takes effect even though the person against whom the thing in action may be enforced is unaware of the bankruptcy. Hence in a case where a wife effected a policy of assurance on her life for the benefit of her husband who became bankrupt before her death, the right to the sums arising under the policy on her death had passed to the husband's trustee and the bankrupt husband, to whom the assurance company not knowing of his bankruptcy paid the money, was not able to give a good receipt for it[4].

[1] IA 1986, s 311(4).
[2] *Re Landau (a bankrupt), Pointer v Landau* [1998] Ch 223, [1997] 3 All ER 322.
[3] IA 1986, s 311(4) and see *Weddell v JA Pearce & Major* [1988] Ch 26 at 31–32 for discussion of the position under the Bankruptcy Act 1914, which was the same, and for references to cases where it was necessary for the trustee to give notice to protect his priority.
[4] *Rooney v Cardona* [1999] 1 WLR 1388, CA.

Shares

18.8 Where the bankrupt beneficially owns shares in a company, they will form part of his estate. The trustee may take steps to have himself registered as the holder of the shares. Where Table A under the Companies Act 1985[1] has been incorporated without amendment, reg 30 provides that a person becoming entitled to a share in consequence of the bankruptcy of a member may, on such evidence being produced as the directors may properly require, elect to become the holder of the share or to have some other person nominated by him registered as the transferee[2]. So long as the bankrupt remains on the register he is entitled to vote at general meetings of the company[3]. But the trustee is entitled, under the IA 1986, s 333(1)(c) to direct him as to how he should cast his vote[4].

1   SI 1985/805, Schedule.
2   Cf *Re W Key & Son Ltd* [1902] 1 Ch 467 decided under the Companies Act 1862, Table A, art 13.
3   *Morgan v Gray* [1953] Ch 83, [1953] 1 All ER 213.
4   Cf *Wise v Lansdell* [1921] 1 Ch 420 where it was accepted that a bankrupt who, though still registered as the owner of shares, had executed a transfer of them to another by way of security and was obliged to vote at that other person's direction.

18.9 Restrictions imposed by the articles on transfers of shares will not ordinarily apply to the transmission of shares from a bankrupt to his trustee (or from a deceased person to his personal representatives)[1]. But a requirement imposed by the articles that a shareholder should, in the event of his bankruptcy, sell his shares to particular specified persons is valid if the price is fixed for all persons alike and is not less than the fair price which might be obtained for the shares. However, if the price is set so as to be reduced in the event of the member's bankruptcy, the provision will not be enforceable against the trustee because repugnant to the laws of bankruptcy[2].

1   *Re Cannock and Rugeley Colliery Co, ex p Harrison* (1885) 28 Ch D 363; *Moodie v W & J Shepherd (Bookbinders) Ltd* [1949] 2 All ER 1044; *Stothers v William Steward (Holdings) Ltd* [1994] 2 BCLC 266.
2   *Borland's Trustee v Steel Bros & Co Ltd* [1901] 1 Ch 279.

Leases

18.10 Since a lease is assigned to the trustee by operation of law, the assignment does not result in the bankrupt tenant being released from his covenants; similarly, if it is the landlord who has become bankrupt, he may not apply to be released from his covenants[1].

1   Landlord and Tenant (Covenants) Act 1995, s 11.

C ACQUISITION BY THE TRUSTEE OF CONTROL OVER THE ESTATE

Trustee's duty to take possession of books and records

18.11 The trustee is under an obligation to take possession of all books, papers and other records which relate to the bankrupt's estate or affairs and which belong to the bankrupt or are in his possession or under his control, including any which would be privileged from disclosure in any proceedings[1].

[1] IA 1986, s 311(1).

Privileged documents

18.12 The trustee's entitlement to take possession of privileged documents is implicit in his being obliged to take possession of them. But his entitlement to do so has its foundation in the trustee's taking over the bankrupt's estate and standing in the bankrupt's shoes for the purpose of administering it[1]. Thus where the bankrupt had instructed solicitors jointly with another, before the bankruptcy, the trustee was entitled to information which was privileged under the joint retainer because joint clients cannot maintain privilege against each other[2]. The trustee has power to waive the privilege in relation to matters concerning the estate and affairs of the bankrupt[3]. He may disclose privileged documents to a person making a claim against the estate in order to determine whether the claim is a good one, but in such a case it may be prudent to seek directions from the court before doing so where the bankrupt is resistant to the disclosure being made[4].

[1] IA 1986, s 311(1).
[2] *Re Konigsberg (a Bankrupt), ex p Trustee v Konigsberg* [1989] 3 All ER 289, [1989] 1 WLR 1257.
[3] *Re Cook (Dennis Michael)* [1999] BPIR 881; *R v Malloy* [1997] 2 Cr App R 283, CA.
[4] *Re Omar (a bankrupt)* [1999] BPIR 1001.

Bankrupt's duty to deliver property and records to the trustee[1]

18.13 The bankrupt must deliver up to the trustee possession of any property, books, papers or other records of which he has possession or control and of which the trustee is required to take possession[2]. This duty reflects the similar duty imposed on the bankrupt relative to the official receiver[3].

[1] See **Chapter 17**, section A for further discussion of the bankrupt's duties to deliver up and disclose his estate and to assist in its administration.
[2] IA 1986, s 312(1). This duty is without prejudice to the duties of the bankrupt under the IA 1986, s 333, ie the general duty to assist discussed below and the duty to disclose any acquisition of property or increase in income discussed in **Chapter 14**.
[3] IA 1986, s 291(1).

Relevant property

18.14 The trustee's function is to get in the bankrupt's estate[1] and therefore any property in the estate is property of which the trustee is required to take possession. Since property which does not form part of the estate at the commencement of the bankruptcy can, where appropriate, be claimed for the estate, the duty to deliver up property is not exhausted by the bankrupt's delivering up such property as is in his possession or under his control on the trustee's appointment, but is a continuing duty arising whenever the bankrupt has in his possession or control property of which the trustee is required to take possession. It is not clear whether this duty, as such, continues after discharge. If the bankrupt then recovers possession or control of property rightfully forming part of his estate, there would seem to be no good reason why he should not be obliged to deliver the property to the trustee; the bankrupt would not be entitled to retain such property for himself.

¹   IA 1986, s 305(2).

Relevant books and records

18.15 All books, papers and other records which relate to the bankrupt's estate or affairs and which belong to the bankrupt or are in his possession or under his control, including any which would be privileged from disclosure in any proceedings, must be delivered up by the bankrupt to the trustee¹.

¹   IA 1986, s 311(1).

Enforcement

18.16 Failure on the part of the bankrupt to comply with this duty without reasonable excuse is a contempt and liable to be punished accordingly¹.

¹   IA 1986, s 312(4).

Prior office-holder's duty to deliver property and records to the trustee

18.17 The official receiver, any previous trustee in bankruptcy and any person who has been the supervisor of a voluntary arrangement relating to the bankrupt, if in possession of any property, books, papers or other records of which the trustee is required to take possession¹. Failure to comply with this duty is a contempt of court².

¹   IA 1986, s 311(2).
²   IA 1986, s 311(4).

Handover of estate to trustee by official receiver

18.18 Until a trustee is appointed for the first time in respect of a bankrupt, the official receiver is the receiver and manager of the estate. When the trustee's appointment takes effect, the official receiver must forthwith do all that is required for putting the trustee into possession of the estate¹. The official receiver must also give to the trustee all such information, relating to the affairs of the bankrupt and the course of the bankruptcy, as the official receiver considers to be reasonably required for the effective discharge by the trustee of his duties in relation to the estate². The trustee must be furnished with any report which the official receiver has made to the creditors³. But, because the official receiver has an absolute immunity from suit in respect of statements made by him in carrying out his functions, the trustee has no recourse against the official receiver if statements made by the official receiver (whether in a report or in answer to inquiries made by the trustee or otherwise) are incorrect, even if they were made incorrectly by reason of negligence on the part of the official receiver[4]. A trustee should, therefore, where possible, make further checks and obtain suitable indemnities before acting on information obtained from the official receiver.

1   Insolvency Rules 1986 ('IR 1986'), r 6.125(1)(a) and (2).
2   IR 1986, r 6.125(7).
3   IR 1986, r 6.125(6). See the IR 1986, r 6. 73 for the official receiver's duty to make a report to the creditors.
4   *Mond v Hyde* [1997] BPIR 250.

18.19 The official receiver is under the same obligations if he has been the trustee and a trustee is appointed in succession to him[1].

1   IR 1986, r 6.125(1)(b).

General duty on third parties to deliver property within the estate to the trustee

18.20 Any banker or agent of the bankrupt or any other person who holds any property to the account of, or for, the bankrupt shall pay or deliver to the trustee all property in his possession or under his control which forms part of the bankrupt's estate and which he is not by law entitled to retain as against the bankrupt or trustee[1]. Failure to comply with this duty is a contempt of court[2].

1   IA 1986, s 311(3).
2   IA 1986, s 311(4).

D BANKRUPT'S DUTIES TO CO-OPERATE IN THE ADMINISTRATION OF HIS ESTATE

General duty to assist trustee

18.21 The bankrupt is under a duty before and after his discharge (a) to give to the trustee such information as to his affairs, (b) to attend on the trustee at such times, and (c) to do all such other things as the trustee may reasonably require for the purpose of carrying out his functions under any of the provisions of the IA 1986 relating to the insolvency of individuals[1]. It seems probable that before the bankrupt becomes subject to an obligation to give information to the trustee, the trustee must require the bankrupt to give the information by making a request for it. For plainly there must be such a request in relation to attendance before the trustee and what is meant by 'require' must be the same in relation to (a) and (b). The duty continues after discharge because the administration of the estate by the trustee may well continue after the bankrupt has been discharged.

1   IA 1986, s 333(1) and (3).

Enforcement

18.22 Failure to comply with this duty is a contempt of court and liable to be punished accordingly[1]. But committal for contempt is not the only method of enforcing the duty and a trustee may obtain an injunction in such terms as may be justified in support of enforcing the duty. In *Morris v Murjani*[2] an injunction was granted restraining the bankrupt from leaving the jurisdiction pending the hearing of the contempt proceedings and requiring him to deliver up his passport. The court may also direct the bankrupt to takes any steps that may be required for the purpose of his bankruptcy or the administration of his estate[3]. The direction may relate to steps to be taken by the bankrupt abroad, for example to withdraw an objection lodged without good reason in a foreign court[4].

[1]   IA 1986, s 333(4).
[2]   [1996] 2 All ER 384, CA.
[3]   IA 1986, s 363(2).
[4]   *Buchler v Al-Midani (No 3)* [2006] BPIR 881.

Cross-reference to other duties incumbent on the bankrupt

18.23 Other important duties which the bankrupt must fulfil have been discussed at the stage when they arise. But, for ease of reference, they are listed again here. Failure to fulfil any of the obligations without reasonable excuse may constitute a contempt of court.

Duty to deliver estate and records to the official receiver

18.24 When a bankruptcy order is made, the bankrupt must deliver possession of his estate to the official receiver and deliver up to the official receiver all books, papers and other records of which he has possession or control and which relate to his estate and affairs (including privileged documents)[1].

[1]   IA 1986, s 291(1). See para **17.11**.

Duty to give information to and attend on official receiver

18.25 The bankrupt must give the official receiver such inventory and other information and attend on the official receiver at such times as the official receiver may reasonably require[1]. This duty continues after discharge[2].

[1]   IA 1986, s 291(4). See para **17.13**.
[2]   IA 1986, s 291(5).

Duty to deliver property and records to the trustee

18.26 The bankrupt must deliver up to the trustee possession of any property, books, papers or other records of which he has possession or control and of which the trustee is required to take possession[1].

[1]   IA 1986, s 312(1).

Duty to disclose acquisition of property or increase in income

18.27 Where at any time after the commencement of the bankruptcy any property is acquired by or devolves upon the bankrupt or there is an increase of the bankrupt's income, the bankrupt shall, within the prescribed period, give the trustee notice of the property or the increase of income[1]. Subject to any condition imposed on an order of discharge under the IA 1986, s 280(2)(c), this duty does not continue after discharge.

[1]   IA 1986, s 333(2). See **Chapter 14**, sections N and O.

Bankruptcy restriction order

18.28 Failing to co-operate with the trustee forms one of the grounds on which the court may make a bankruptcy restriction order against the bankrupt[1]. Failing to produce business and other records when required by the trustee and failing to account satisfactorily for loss of property to the trustee also form grounds for a bankruptcy restriction order[2].

[1]   IA 1986, s 281A and Sch 4A, para 2(2)(m).
[2]   IA 1986, s 281A and Sch 4A, para 2(2)(a), (b) and (i).

Criminal sanction

18.29 Unless the bankrupt proves that, at the time of the conduct constituting the offence, he had no intent to defraud or to conceal the state of his affairs, he is guilty of an offence:

(1)   if he does not deliver up possession to the official receiver or trustee, or as the official receiver or trustee may direct, of such part of the property comprised in his estate as is in his possession or under his control and possession of which he is required by law so to deliver up[1]; or

(2)   if he does not deliver up possession to the official receiver or trustee, or as the official receiver or trustee may direct, of all books, papers and other records of which he has possession or control and which relate to his estate or affairs[2].

[1]   IA 1986, s 354(1)(a).
[2]   IA 1986, s 355(1).

E REDIRECTION OF THE BANKRUPT'S POST

Obtaining information from the bankrupt

18.30 Information, it is said, is power. The bankrupt himself will hold much of the information which a trustee will need to acquire control over the assets in the estate. The bankrupt's duties to disclose such information have been discussed in **Chapter 17**, section A and the means of compelling him to disclose information by examining him have also been discussed in that

698

chapter. A further method of obtaining information is by causing the bankrupt's post to be redirected to the trustee. The court has power to order such redirection under the IA 1986, s 371. Exercise of this power is an interference by a public authority with the bankrupt's right to respect for his correspondence conferred by the European Convention on Human Rights, art 8[1] and must be justified by the qualification contained in art 8.2.

[1]   Human Rights Act 1998, s 1 and Sch 1, Pt I, art 8.

Court's power to order redirection of post

18.31 Where a bankruptcy order has been made the court may order a postal operator within the meaning of the Postal Services Act 2000 to redirect and send or deliver to the official receiver or the trustee or otherwise any postal packet (within the meaning of the Postal Services Act 2000) which would otherwise have been sent or delivered by them to the bankrupt at such place or places as may be specified in the order[1]. An order redirecting post may only be made on the application of the official receiver or trustee. Since the purpose of the order is to read the bankrupt's post without his knowing of the surveillance, it is usual for such orders to be obtained without giving notice to the bankrupt of the application. Such an order may be made for a period not exceeding three months and the period for which the order is to be effective must be specified in the order[2].

[1]   IA 1986, s 371(1).
[2]   IA 1986, s 371(2).

Procedure

18.32 The application may only be made by the official receiver or by the trustee. It must be made without notice unless the court directs otherwise and must be supported by a report, if made by the official receiver, or by an affidavit, if made by the trustee, setting out the reasons why the order is sought. The court shall fix a venue for the hearing of the application if it thinks fit and give notice to the bankrupt of the order. The order may be made on conditions. The order should identify the person on whom it is to be served and need not be served on the bankrupt unless the court directs[1].

[1]   IR 1986, r 6.235A.

Bankrupt's right to respect for his correspondence

18.33 In *Foxley v United Kingdom*[1] the European Court of Human Rights considered whether an order redirecting Mr Foxley's post to his trustee in bankruptcy violated his right under art 8 to respect for his correspondence. The court held that there were, in the circumstances of that case, violations of the right in two respects, but the court did not hold that any exercise of the power to order the redirection of post under the IA 1986, s 371 would constitute an unjustified interference with the right. Before the court the UK Government accepted that an order made under the IA 1986, s 371 was an interference with the relevant right by a public authority. The issue was whether the interference was justified. That depended on (1) its being in accordance with law, (2) its being in pursuit of a legitimate aim, and (3) its being necessary in a democratic society. Subject to one point, the court held that the redirection was made in accordance with law since it was made pursuant to an order by a court acting under a power contained in legislation. The excepted point was that two deliveries of post were redirected to the trustee and read and copied by her after the redirection order had ceased to be effective. Reading letters in those two deliveries constituted the first violation of art 8. The court accepted that the measure pursued the legitimate aim of protecting the rights of creditors. The central issue was whether the measure was necessary in a democratic society. In considering this issue the court focused on the fact that included in the post which was redirected were communications from the bankrupt's legal advisers which were subject to professional privilege. There was no suggestion that the privilege could be overridden because, for example, the communications were in furtherance to fraud or otherwise[2]. The court found that reading and copying the privileged communications violated art 8. In reaching this conclusion the court reasoned that the notion of necessity implied that the interference had to correspond to a pressing social need and was proportionate to the legitimate aim which was being pursued. The pressing social need was the need to recover concealed assets for the benefit of creditors. In passing, the court noted that the trustee's decision to seek the interception of post was taken after she had considered her other options of seeking a warrant to seize property under the IA 1986, s 365 or examination under s 366[3]. This is relevant to the question of whether there was a need for the measure to be implemented and trustees should therefore, before seeking a redirection order, consider alternative, possibly less intrusive[4], methods of obtaining the relevant information. But more central to the reasoning was that 'the implementation of the measure must be accompanied by adequate and effective safeguards which ensure minimum impairment of the right to respect for [the bankrupt's] correspondence'[5]. The trustee should have ensured that there were safeguards preventing her (or her staff) from reading and copying privileged correspondence between the bankrupt and his legal advisers. This failure and, in consequence, her reading and copying that correspondence constituted a violation of the bankrupt's right under art 8.

---

[1]   [2000] BPIR 1009, ECtHR. For further discussion of similar issues, see *Narinen v Finland (App No 45027/98)* [2004] BPIR 914.
[2]   Since the communications related to proceedings occurring after the commencement of the bankruptcy, they would not have been among the documents which the bankrupt was obliged to deliver up to the trustee pursuant to the IA 1986, s 312(1) read with s 311(1).
[3]   Para 40 of the judgment.
[4]   Other measures such as warrants to seize property may raise other questions of interference with, eg the right to privacy and the issue of a warrant may well also require justification under art 8.2.
[5]   Para 43 of the judgment.

F TRUSTEE'S POWERS

General remarks

18.34 A wide range of powers are conferred on the trustee by the IA 1986. Many provisions of the IA 1986 enable the trustee to take steps integral to the scheme which bankruptcy comprises, for example to claim after-acquired property for the estate or to disclaim onerous property[1]. But in this section the powers under discussion are the general powers which the trustee, as a person administering an estate, requires in order to administer it effectively.

1   Reference to these powers is incorporated into the IA 1986, Sch 5 (which lists the administrative powers) at para 12.

Limits on exercise of powers

18.35 In carrying out his function of getting in, realising and distributing the estate and in managing the estate the trustee is entitled to use his discretion[1]. But, although he may exercise some of his administrative powers entirely at his own discretion, he must obtain the sanction of the creditors' committee or the court before exercising others, save in the case of urgency when he may obtain such sanction afterwards[2]. The trustee's exercise of his powers is, obviously, limited in that he may only exercise his powers for the benefit of the estate and for the purpose of fulfilling his function as trustee. His acts, omissions and decisions in exercising his powers are open to challenge by the bankrupt, any of the creditors or any other person who is dissatisfied and has sufficient interest to maintain a challenge[3].

1   IA 1986, s 305(2).
2   IA 1986, s 314(1).
3   IA 1986, s 303(1).

Exercise of powers outside England and Wales

18.36 Nothing in the IA 1986 is to be construed as restricting the capacity of the trustee to exercise any of his powers outside England and Wales[1].

1   IA 1986, s 314(8).

Ancillary powers

18.37 In addition to the powers discussed below, the trustee has the following ancillary powers exercisable for the purposes of, or in connection with, the exercise of any of his powers under the IA 1986, Pts VIII to XI, namely:

(1)   power to hold property of every description;
(2)   power to make contracts;
(3)   power to sue and be sued;
(4)   power to enter into engagements binding on himself and, in respect of the bankrupt's estate, on his successors in office;

(5)   power to employ an agent;
(6)   power to execute any power of attorney, deed or other instrument,

and he may do any other act which is necessary or expedient for the purposes of or in connection with the exercise of those powers[1].

¹   IA 1986, s 314(5) and Sch 5, Pt III, para 14.

Disposal of property to an associate of the bankrupt

18.38 Where the trustee, not being the official receiver, disposes of, in exercise of the powers conferred on him by any provision of the IA 1986 relating to individual insolvency, any property comprised in the bankrupt's estate to an associate of the bankrupt, he must, if there is for the time being a creditors' committee, give notice to the committee of that exercise of his powers[1].

¹   IA 1986, s 314(6)(a). See IA 1986, s 435 for the meaning of 'associate'.

Retainer of a solicitor

18.39 Where the trustee, not being the official receiver, employs a solicitor, he must, if there is for the time being a creditors' committee, give notice to the committee of that exercise of his powers[1]. The trustee may retain the solicitor who acted for the petitioning creditor who initiated the bankruptcy, unless there is some specific circumstance creating a conflict of interest[2].

¹   IA 1986, s 314(6)(a).
²   *Re Schuppan (a bankrupt) (No 1)* [1996] 2 All ER 664, [1997] 1 BCLC 211; *Re Recover Ltd (in liquidation), Hornan v Latif Group SL* [2003] EWHC 536 (Ch), [2003] 2 BCLC 186.

Power to summon creditors' meetings

18.40 The trustee may, if he thinks fit, at any time summon a general meeting of the bankrupt's creditors[1].

¹   IA 1986, s 314(7).

Powers exercisable without sanction

Power of sale

18.41 The trustee has power to sell any part of the property for the time being comprised in the bankrupt's estate, including the goodwill and book debts of any business[1]. But sanction will be required if the consideration is not payable at the same time as the sale is completed[2]. Thus it is only sales for cash which may be made without sanction.

¹   IA 1986, s 314(1)(b) and Sch 5, para 9.
²   IA 1986, s 314(1)(a) and Sch 5, para 3.

Causes of action

18.42 It is by virtue of his power to sell property within the estate that the trustee is entitled to assign causes of action forming part of the estate and that the common law rule against maintenance and champerty is overridden[1].

1 See *Seear v Lawson* (1880) 15 Ch D 426, CA; *Guy v Churchill* (1888) 40 Ch D 481; *Ramsay v Hartley* [1977] 2 All ER 673, [1977] 1 WLR 686, CA; *Norglen Ltd v Reeds Rain Prudential Ltd* [1999] 2 AC 1, [1998] 1 All ER 218 and the discussion in **Chapter 19**, section C of assignments of causes of action.

Sale of goodwill

18.43 On the sale by the trustee of the goodwill of the bankrupt's business[1], the bankrupt can, it seems, be compelled to join in the assignment of his business and goodwill for the benefit of his creditors by virtue of his duties under the IA 1986, s 333(1)[2]. He cannot, however, be compelled to enter into any covenant restricting him from carrying on the same business[3]. Whether the bankrupt has or has not joined in the assignment of the goodwill to the purchaser, he cannot be restrained from setting up a fresh business or from soliciting his former customers[4], except when he has agreed with the purchaser not to carry on a similar business[5]; although, even if he cannot be restrained, he cannot use the trade mark of the old business[6], or in any way represent himself as carrying on the business which has been sold[7].

1 As to the trustee's power to carry on the business see the IA 1986, s 314(1), Sch 5, para 9; see para **18.57**.
2 *Walker v Mottram* (1881) 19 Ch D 355 at 363, CA (decided under what became the Bankruptcy Act 1914, s 22(2), (3) which prescribed the bankrupt's duties in more specific terms than does the IA 1986, s 333(1)).
3 *Walker v Mottram* (1881) 19 Ch D 355 at 363, CA. See *Cruttwell v Lye* (1810) 17 Ves 335.
4 *Walker v Mottram* (1881) 19 Ch D 355, CA; and see *Trego v Hunt* [1896] AC 7 at 13, 14, 23, HL; *Jennings v Jennings* [1898] 1 Ch 378 at 383. This principle also applies where a debtor has executed a deed of assignment for the benefit of his creditors; see *Green and Sons (Northampton) Ltd v Morris* [1914] 1 Ch 562; *Farey v Cooper* [1927] 2 KB 384, CA.
5 See *Clarkson v Edge* (1863) 33 Beav 227, and *Buxton and High Peak Publishing and General Printing Co v Mitchell* (1885) Cab & El 527.
6 *Hudson v Osborne* (1869) 39 LJ Ch 79; *Hammond & Co v Malcolm Brunker & Co and Collyns* (1892) 9 RPC 301; but see *Cotton v Gillard* (1874) 44 LJ Ch 90.
7 *Hudson v Osborne* (1869) 39 LJ Ch 79.

Power to give receipts

18.44 The trustee has power to give receipts for any money received by him, being receipts which effectually discharge the person paying the money from all responsibility in respect of its application[1].

1 IA 1986, s 314(1)(b) and Sch 5, para 10.

Receipts on the sale of land

18.45 A trustee in bankruptcy is a trust corporation[1] and may therefore give a valid receipt for the sale arising under a trust of land[2].

¹   Law of Property (Amendment) Act 1926, s 3.
²   See the Law of Property Act 1925, s 27(2) and the Trustee Act 1925, s 14(2).

Power to prove for debts owed to the bankrupt

18.46 The trustee has power to prove, rank, claim and draw a dividend in respect of such debts due to the bankrupt as are comprised in his estate[1]. Although proving in a bankruptcy is sometimes akin to making a claim by way of bringing an action, merely submitting a proof in another person's bankruptcy does not expose the person submitting the proof to a potential liability in costs if the claim fails. Therefore sanction is not required. But if the other trustee to whom the proof was submitted rejected the proof, sanction would be required before the trustee who had submitted the proof could bring proceedings to challenge the rejection[2].

[1]   IA 1986, s 314(1)(b) and Sch 5, para 11.
[2]   IA 1986, s 314(1)(a) and Sch 5, para 2.

Powers conferred by the IA 1986

18.47 The trustee has power to exercise in relation to any property comprised in the bankrupt's estate any powers the capacity to exercise which is vested in him under Pts VIII to XI of the IA 1986[1].

[1]   IA 1986, s 314(1)(b) and Sch 5, para 12.

Power to transfer stock, shares and property transferable in the books of a company, office or person

18.48 The trustee has power, where any part of the bankrupt's estate consists of stock or shares in a company, shares in a ship or any other property transferable in the books of a company, office or person, to exercise the right to transfer the property to the same extent as the bankrupt might have exercised if he had not become bankrupt[1].

[1]   IA 1986, s 311(3).

Power over entailed property

18.49 The trustee has power to deal with any property comprised in the estate to which the bankrupt is beneficially entitled as tenant in tail in the same manner as the bankrupt might have dealt with it[1].

[1]   IA 1986, s 314(1)(b) and Sch 5, para 13.

Powers exercisable with sanction

Sanction

18.50 The powers set out in this section may be exercised by the trustee with the permission of the creditors' committee or the court[1]. Where the official receiver is the trustee or there is no creditors' committee, the functions of the committee are exercised by the Secretary of State[2]. Where the official receiver is trustee, he may seek permission from the Secretary of State. Where the trustee is not the official receiver or there is no creditors' committee, the trustee may seek permission from the official receiver[3].

1   IA 1986, s 314(1)(a).
2   IA 1986, s 302.
3   IR 1986, r 6.166(2).

Permission should be obtained in advance

18.51 The trustee should obtain the required permission before he exercises the power in question.

Ratification in cases of urgency

18.52 Where the trustee has done anything without obtaining permission where it is required, the court or the creditors' committee may, for the purpose of enabling him to meet his expenses out of the bankrupt's estate, ratify what the trustee has done. But the committee may not do so unless it is satisfied that the trustee has acted in a case of urgency and has sought its ratification without undue delay[1].

1   IA 1986, s 314(4).

Prohibition on general permissions

18.53 Permission to exercise a power may not be given as a general power but must relate to a particular proposed exercise of the power in question[1].

1   IA 1986, s 314(3).

Consequences of exercising power without permission

18.54 A person dealing with the trustee in good faith and for value is not to be concerned to enquire whether any required permission has been given[1]. In other cases the transaction may be liable to being set aside by the court if challenged by the bankrupt, any of the creditors or any other dissatisfied and sufficiently interested person under the IA 1986, s 303(1), but although such transaction is voidable, it is not void[2]. But, even if the step taken in exercising the power is not avoided, the trustee will not be entitled to meet the expenses of taking the step in question out of the estate (unless he is able to obtain its ratification).

1   IA 1986, s 314(3).
2   *Weddell v JA Pearce & Major* [1988] Ch 26, [1987] 3 All ER 624.

Granting sanction

18.55 Where permission is sought from the court to compromise a dispute, it is for the court to decide whether to give the permission or not. In doing so it must consider whether the creditors' best interests will be served by the compromise. The court will give considerable weight to the trustee's view that the compromise is in the creditors' interest, but, since the decision is for the court, the court must form its own view on the evidence and should not approach the question on the footing that the trustee's view should prevail unless it is shown to be unreasonable or in bad faith[1].

1   *Re Greenhaven Motors Ltd (in liquidation)* [1999] 1 BCLC 635 (concerning IA 1986, s 167, the corresponding provision relating to a liquidator's powers); *Re Barings plc (No 7)* [2002] 1 BCLC 401; *Re Williams (Don Basil)* [2003] BPIR 545.

Court's power to override creditors

18.56 The court may, in an exceptional case, exercise its power to sanction the trustee's exercise of power against the wishes of the creditors[1].

1   *Re Bank of Credit and Commerce International SA (No 3)* [1993] BCLC 1490; *Re Ridgway, ex p Hurlbatt* (1889) 6 Morr 277.

Power to carry on the bankrupt's business

18.57 The trustee has power to carry on any business of the bankrupt so far as may be necessary for winding it up beneficially and so far as the trustee is able to do so without contravening any requirement imposed by or under any enactment[1]. The power to carry on the bankrupt's business is only a temporary and limited provision; it does not entitle the trustee to carry on any contracts of the business whatever their nature, for any time, but only so far as may be necessary for winding up the estate beneficially[2].

1   IA 1986, s 314(1)(a) and Sch 5, para 1.
2   *Re Sneezum, ex p Davis* (1876) 3 Ch D 463, CA.

Power to litigate

18.58 The trustee has power to bring, institute or defend any action or legal proceedings relating to the property comprised in the bankrupt's estate[1].

1   IA 1986, s 314(1)(a) and Sch 5, para 2.

Power to reclaim assets

18.59 The trustee has power to bring legal proceedings under the IA 1986, ss 339, 340 or 423[1]. This power was introduced into Part I of Schedule 5 by the Enterprise Act 2002[2]. The change made by including this power in Part I of Schedule 5 is that it is made clear that sanction is required before bringing proceedings of this kind.

1   IA 1986, s 314(1)(a) and Sch 5, para 2A.
2   Enterprise Act 2002, s 262.

Power to accept future consideration

18.60 The trustee has power to accept as the consideration for the sale of any property comprised in the bankrupt's estate a sum of money payable at a future time subject to such stipulations as to security or otherwise as the creditors' committee or the court thinks fit[1].

1   IA 1986, s 314(1)(a) and Sch 5, para 3.

Power to mortgage

18.61 The trustee has power to mortgage or pledge any part of the property comprised in the bankrupt's estate for the purpose of raising money for the payment of his debts[1].

1   IA 1986, s 314(1)(a) and Sch 5, para 4.

Power to exercise option

18.62 The trustee has power, where any right, option or other power forms part of the bankrupt's estate, to make payments or incur liabilities with a view to obtaining for the benefit of the creditors, any property which is the subject of the right, power or option[1].

1   IA 1986, s 314(1)(a) and Sch 5, para 5.

Power to refer to arbitration or to compromise liabilities owed to the bankrupt

18.63 The trustee has power to refer to arbitration, or to compromise on such terms as may be agreed, any debts, claims or liabilities subsisting or supposed to subsist between the bankrupt and any person who may have incurred any liability to the bankrupt[1]. The trustee may only exercise this power in relation to disputes between the bankrupt and a third party who is or may be under a liability to the bankrupt. But the power encompasses a reference or compromise of any cross-claim which the third party may have or claim against the bankrupt.

1   IA 1986, s 314(1)(a) and Sch 5, para 6.

18.64   *Administration of the estate*

Power to compromise bankruptcy debts

18.64 The trustee has power to make such compromise or other arrangement as may be thought expedient with creditors, or persons claiming to be creditors, in respect of bankruptcy debts[1].

¹   IA 1986, s 314(1)(a) and Sch 5, para 7.

Power to compromise claims

18.65 The trustee has power to make such compromise or other arrangement as may be thought expedient with respect to any claim arising out of or incidental to the bankrupt's estate made or capable of being made on the trustee by any person or by the trustee on any person[1].

¹   IA 1986, s 314(1)(a) and Sch 5, para 8. See *Re Don Basil Williams* [2003] BPIR 545.

Power to appoint bankrupt to assist in administration

18.66 The trustee has power to appoint the bankrupt (a) to superintend the management of his estate or any part of it, (b) to carry on his business for the benefit of his creditors, or (c) in any other respect to assist in administering the estate in such manner and in such terms as the trustee may direct[1].

¹   IA 1986, s 314(2).

G PARTICIPATION OF CREDITORS

General remarks

18.67 The administration of the estate is conducted by the trustee in the interests of the general body of unsecured creditors. But the creditors themselves have various means of making an impact on how the administration unfolds. The collective methods whereby creditors may participate are by the holding of general meetings of creditors and via the creditors' committee.

Functions of creditors' meetings

18.68 The primary functions of general meetings of the creditors are:

(1)   to appoint the trustee at the first such meeting[1];
(2)   to establish the creditors' committee[2];
(3)   to remove members of the committee[3];
(4)   to receive the resignation of the trustee[4];
(5)   to remove the trustee[5]; and
(6)   to receive the trustee's reports at the final meeting and resolve on his release[6].

¹   IA 1986, ss 293–295 and the IR 1986, r 6.79–6.80.
²   IA 1986, s 301(1).

3   IR 1986, r 6.159.
4   IR 1986, r 6.126.
5   IA 1986, s 298(1).
6   IR 1986, r 6.137.

18.69 Some of these functions are routine; others, exceptional since most trustees retain the confidence of the creditors. But general meetings may also be held for the purpose of ascertaining the wishes of the creditors in relation to any matter relating to the bankruptcy[1].

1   IR 1986, r 6.81.

Functions of the creditors' committee

18.70 The creditors' committee has a more direct role in the administration. Its primary functions are:

(1)   to fix the trustee's remuneration[1];
(2)   to sanction the trustee in the exercise of those powers which he may only exercise with the committee's (or the court's) permission[2];
(3)   to require the trustee to submit financial records to it for inspection[3], and, if not satisfied with the contents of the financial records submitted and it thinks fit to do so, to inform the Secretary of State[4].

1   IR 1986, r 6.138(3).
2   IA 1986, s 314(1)(a) and (2).
3   Insolvency Regulations 1994, SI 1994/2507, reg 24(3).
4   Insolvency Regulations 1994, SI 1994/2507, reg 24(4).

Participation of individual creditors

18.71 Participation by general meeting or via the committee are collective methods of participating; creditors do not have individual rights to participate, although they may obviously make their views known to the trustee. But they also have the means of challenging his decisions, where appropriate, which are discussed in the final section of this chapter.

Creditors' meetings

The first creditors' meeting

18.72 In **Chapter 13** was mentioned the first creditors' meeting which may be called by the official receiver for the purpose of appointing a trustee in bankruptcy[1]. The procedure for calling that meeting and the business which may be conducted at it have been discussed in that context. But otherwise the conduct of that meeting is the same as of other creditors' meetings.

1   See para **13.21**.

18.73 *Administration of the estate*

General power to call meetings

18.73 The official receiver or the trustee may at any time summon and conduct meetings of creditors for the purpose of ascertaining their wishes in all matters relating to the bankruptcy[1]. In relation to any meeting of creditors, the person summoning it is referred to as 'the convener'[2].

1 IR 1986, r 6.81(1). See the IA 1986, s 314(7) for a concomitant power in the trustee to call creditors' meetings.
2 IR 1986, r 6.81(1).

Requisitioned meetings

18.74 Where the official receiver is the trustee or the trustee has been appointed by the Secretary of State, a creditor acting with the concurrence of not less than one-quarter in value of the creditors (including himself), may request a meeting to be held for the purpose of replacing the trustee[1]. The request should be accompanied by a list of the creditors concurring with the request and the amount of their respective claims in the bankruptcy, written confirmation of his concurrence from each creditor and a statement of the purpose of the proposed meeting[2]. If the creditor making the request holds a debt which by itself is sufficient, he need only provide a statement of the purpose of the meeting[3]. If the official receiver or trustee considers that the request is properly made, he must fix a venue for the meeting to take place not more than 35 days from the receipt of the request[4].

1 IA 1986, s 298(4).
2 IR 1986, r 6.83(1).
3 IR 1986, r 6.83(1).
4 IR 1986, r 6.83(2) and (3).

18.75 The trustee must summon a creditors' meeting if he is requested to do so by a creditor of the bankrupt and the request is made with the concurrence of not less than one-tenth, in value, of the bankrupt's creditors, including the creditor making the request[1].

1 IA 1986, s 314(7).

Expenses of summoning meetings

18.76 The expenses of summoning and holding a meeting of creditors at the instance of any person other than the official receiver or the trustee shall be paid by that person, unless, where a meeting is so summoned, it votes that the expenses of summoning the meeting shall be payable out of the estate as an expense of the bankruptcy[1]. To cover the expenses in advance, the person summoning the meeting must deposit security for the payment of the expenses with the trustee or, if no trustee has been appointed, with the official receiver[2]. The sum to be deposited shall be such as the trustee or, as the case may be, the official receiver determines to be appropriate, and neither shall act without the deposit having been made[3]. To the extent that any deposit is not required for the expenses of summoning and holding the meeting, it shall be repaid to the person who made it[4].

1   IR 1986, r 6.87(1) and (3).
2   IR 1986, r 6.87(1).
3   IR 1986, r 6.87(2).
4   IR 1986, r 6.87(4).

Venue of meetings

18.77 In fixing the venue for a meeting of creditors, the person summoning the meeting must have regard to the convenience of creditors[1]. Meetings shall in all cases be summoned for commencement between the hours of 10.00 and 16.00 on a business day, unless the court otherwise directs[2].

1   IR 1986, r 6.86(1).
2   IR 1986, r 6.86(2).

Notice of meetings

18.78 When a venue for the meeting has been fixed, notice of the meeting shall be given by the convener to every creditor who is known to him or is identified in the bankrupt's statement of affairs[1]. The notice shall be given at least 21 days before the date fixed for the meeting[2]. The notice to creditors must specify the purpose for which the meeting is summoned and a time and date (no more than four days before the meeting) by which creditors must lodge proxies and those who have not already lodged proofs must do so, in order to be entitled to vote at the meeting[3]. Additional notice may be given by public advertisement if the convener thinks fit and must be given if the court so orders[4].

1   IR 1986, r 6.81(2).
2   IR 1986, r 6.81(2).
3   IR 1986, r 6.81(3).
4   IR 1986, r 6.81(4).

Forms of proxy

18.79 With every notice summoning a creditors' meeting there shall be sent out forms of proxy[1].

1   IR 1986, r 6.86(3).

Notice by advertisement only

18.80 In the case of any meeting, the court may order that notice of it shall be given by public advertisement and not by individual notice to the persons concerned[1]. In considering whether to make such order, the court shall have regard to the cost of public advertisement, the amount of funds in the estate and to the extent of the interest of the creditors or any particular class of them[2].

[1]   IR 1986, r 6.85(1).
[2]   IR 1986, r 6.85(2).

Notice to and presence of the bankrupt

18.81 Whenever a meeting of creditors is summoned, the convener must give at least 21 days' notice of the meeting to the bankrupt[1]. The convener may, if he thinks fit, give notice to the bankrupt that he is required to be present or in attendance[2]. If the meeting is adjourned, the chairman of the meeting shall, unless for any reason it appears to him to be unnecessary or impracticable, give notice of the adjournment to the bankrupt, if he was not present at the meeting[3]. If the bankrupt is not present and it is desired to put questions to him, the chairman may adjourn the meeting with a view to obtaining his attendance[4]. Where the bankrupt is present at a creditors' meeting, only such questions may be put to him as the chairman in his discretion allows[5].

[1]   IR 1986, r 6.84(1).
[2]   IR 1986, r 6.84(3).
[3]   IR 1986, r 6.84(2).
[4]   IR 1986, r 6.84(5).
[5]   IR 1986, r 6.84(6).

Quorum

18.82 A creditors' meeting is quorate if there is present or represented by proxy at least one creditor entitled to vote[1]. But if the meeting is quorate by the attendance of the chairman alone or of one other person in addition to the chairman and the chairman is aware, by virtue of proofs and proxies received or otherwise, that one or more additional persons would, if attending be entitled to vote, the meeting may not commence until at least 15 minutes after the time appointed for its commencement[2]. The meeting is competent to act if a quorum is present.

[1]   IR 1986, r 12.4A(2)(a).
[2]   IR 1986, r 12.4A(4).

Adjournment of inquorate meetings

18.83 If a quorum is not present within 30 minutes from the time appointed for the commencement of the meeting, the chairman, or, if no person is present to act as chairman, some other person who is entitled to vote, may adjourn the meeting to such time and place as the chairman or such other person may appoint[1].

[1]   IR 1986, r 6.91(2) and (4). See para **18.100** below for the restrictions on the venue to which a meeting may be adjourned.

Resolutions

18.84 Subject to the special rules applicable in the case of resolutions for the appointment of a trustee[1] and for the purpose of discounting in certain instances of votes cast by the trustee or proposed or former trustee[2], whether as creditor or as proxy-holder, a resolution is passed when a majority in value of those present and voting, in person or by proxy, have voted in favour of the resolution[3].

[1]   IR 1986, r 6.88(2).
[2]   IR 1986, r 6.88(4).
[3]   IR 1986, r 6.88(1).

Chairman as proxy-holder

18.85 Where the chairman holds a proxy for a creditor, which requires him to vote for a particular resolution, and no other person proposes that resolution, he should himself propose it, unless he considers that there is good reason for not doing so and if he does not propose it, he shall forthwith after the meeting notify his principal of the reason why he did not[1].

[1]   IR 1986, r 6.89.

Discounting votes cast by trustee

18.86 Where a resolution is proposed which affects a person in respect of his remuneration or conduct as trustee, or as proposed or former trustee, the vote of that person, and of any partner or employee of his, may not be reckoned in the majority required for passing the resolution[1]. It is possible that the person whose vote is to be discounted may also be a creditor and would be entitled to vote as a creditor in his own right, either personally or by a proxy-holder whom he has appointed. If so, his vote as a creditor in his own right cannot be counted in the majority for passing a resolution affecting his remuneration or conduct as trustee. However, it is more likely that he would hold proxies for other creditors which he might try to use to pass the resolution. But votes cast by him as proxy-holder for another creditor may not be counted as part of the majority for passing the resolution, unless the proxy specifically directs him to vote in that way[2].

[1]   IR 1986, r 6.88(4).
[2]   IR 1986, r 8.6(1).

Entitlement to vote

18.87 The basic rule is that a person is entitled to vote as a creditor only if there has been duly lodged by the time and date stated in the notice of the meeting a proof of the debt claimed to be due to him from the bankrupt and the claim has been admitted[1] for the purpose of entitlement to vote and there has been lodged by that time and date any proxy requisite for that entitlement[2]. But this is subject to the provisions of the IR 1986', rr 6.93 and 6.94, in particular the power vested in the chairman of the meeting to admit (or reject) a creditor's proof at the meeting for purpose of his entitlement to vote[3] and, in exceptional circumstances, the court's power to declare the creditors, or any class of them, entitled to vote without being required to prove[4].

1   Under the IR 1986, r 6.94.
2   IR 1986, r 6.93(1).
3   IR 1986, r 6.94(1).
4   IR 1986, r 6.93(2).

Entitlement of Member State liquidator to vote

18.88 Where insolvency proceedings have been opened in another Member State, the liquidator appointed in those proceedings is entitled to vote as a creditor if he has duly lodged a proof of the debt claimed to be due to creditors in relation to the proceedings in relation to which he holds office and that claim has been admitted for the purpose of entitlement to vote[1].

1   IR 1986, r 6.93(1)(a)(ii).

Preventing double-counting where proceedings pending in more than one Member State

18.89 Where insolvency proceedings are pending in more than one Member State, the possibility arises that a creditor might prove for his debt both in the English bankruptcy and the other insolvency proceedings. Since the Member State liquidator appointed in relation to the other insolvency proceedings is entitled to vote in the English bankruptcy in reliance on the claims made by creditors in the proceedings in another Member State in which he has been appointed, the same claim might be used to found an entitlement to vote both on the part of the creditor and on the part of the Member State liquidator. This result is prevented by IR 1986, r 6.93(7) which provides that where the creditor is entitled to vote at a meeting but has also lodged his claim in insolvency proceedings in another Member State, only his vote shall be counted. Thus where the creditor is entitled to vote and does so, the Member State liquidator cannot vote in reliance on that creditor's claim.

18.90 A further problem is that insolvency proceedings may be pending in more than one other Member State. If so, more than one Member State liquidator might seek to rely on the same claim in order to found an entitlement to vote. This is prevented by IR 1986, r 6.93(8) which provides that in this situation the entitlement to vote may be exercised by the Member State liquidator appointed in the main proceedings, even if the creditor has not lodged his claim in those proceedings. But the Member State liquidator will not be able to exercise that entitlement by virtue of IR 1986, r 6.93(7) if the creditor himself is entitled to vote and does so.

18.91 In order that the chairman may operate these provisions, a Member State liquidator will need to specify the claims on which he relies to found his entitlement to vote. The chairman will have to be astute to compare those claims with the claims of the creditors seeking to vote at the meeting in person or by proxy.

Creditors for unliquidated sums

18.92 Since the value of a creditor's vote depends on the value of the debt which he claims, a liquidated value must be put on the claim of any creditor whose claim is unliquidated or unascertained. Accordingly a creditor may not vote in respect of a debt for an unliquidated amount or any debt whose value is not ascertained except where the chairman agrees to put upon the debt an estimated minimum value for the purpose of entitlement to vote and admits his proof for that purpose[1]. It is not necessary that there should be a bilateral agreement between the creditor and the chairman; what is required is that the chairman expresses his willingness to put, and puts, an estimated minimum value on the debt[2].

1   IR 1986, r 6.93(3).
2   *Doorbar v Alltime Securities Ltd* [1996] 2 All ER 948, [1996] 1 WLR 456 (concerning the IR 1986, r 5.17(3) which is in identical terms).

Creditors holding security or bills of exchange

18.93 Since a secured creditor is able to recover his debt by realising his security outside the bankruptcy, a secured creditor may not vote at a creditors' meeting except to the extent that any part of his debt is unsecured. Thus, a secured creditor is entitled to vote only in respect of the balance of any of his debt after deducting the value of the security as estimated by him[1]. Where a creditor holds a bill of exchange or promissory note on which the bankrupt is liable, there may be other parties to the bill or note against whom the creditor has recourse. To the extent that such recourse is available to him, a creditor is able to obtain payment of his debt outside the bankruptcy and, to that extent, is akin to a secured creditor. Therefore it is provided that a creditor may not vote in respect of a debt on, or secured by, a current bill of exchange or promissory note, unless he is willing to treat the liability to him on the bill or note of every person who is liable on it antecedently to the bankrupt and against whom a bankruptcy order has not been made (or in the case of a company, which has not gone into liquidation) as a security in his hands and to estimate the value of the security and (for the purpose of entitlement to vote, but not for dividend) to deduct it from his proof[2].

1   IR 1986, r 6.93(4).
2   IR 1986, r 6.93(5).

Chairman's power to admit or reject proofs for the purpose of voting

18.94 At any creditors' meeting the chairman has power to admit or reject a creditor's proof for the purpose of his entitlement to vote and the power is exercisable with respect to the whole of any part of the proof[1]. If the chairman is in doubt whether a proof should be admitted or rejected, he should mark it as objected to and allow the creditor to vote, subject to his vote being subsequently declared invalid if the objection to the proof is sustained[2]. Where in doubt about the value of the debt, the chairman should accept the vote at the value contended for by the creditor but mark the vote as subject to objection[3].

1   IR 1986, r 6.94(1).
2   IR 1986, r 6.94(3).
3   See *Re a Debtor (No 222 of 1990), ex p Bank of Ireland* [1992] BCLC 137 (concerning the IR 1986, r 5.17(6)).

18.95 The chairman's decision to admit or reject or in respect of any matter concerning entitlement to vote is subject to appeal to the court by any creditor or by the bankrupt[1]. If the chairman is the official receiver, an appeal must be made within 28 days of the creditor's being notified of his decision[2], subject to the court's power to extend time[3]. It appears that there is no time limit where the chairman is not the official receiver, but, since the court has a discretion whether to make any order on an appeal, it is likely that no order would be made if an appeal were not made promptly, ie within the same time limit of 28 days, unless there are grounds on which the court's discretion to extend time would have been exercised.

1   IR 1986, r 6.94(2).
2   IR 1986, r 7.50.
3   IA 1986, s 376 and see *Tager v Westpac Banking Corpn* [1997] 1 BCLC 313.

Disposal on appeal

18.96 If on an appeal the chairman's decision is reversed or varied, or a creditor's vote is declared invalid, the court may order that another meeting be summoned, or make such other order as it thinks just[1]. Neither the official receiver nor any person nominated by him to be chairman is personally liable for costs incurred by any person in respect of an application to the court; and the chairman, if other than the official receiver or a person nominated by him, is not liable for costs unless the court makes an order to that effect[2].

1   IR 1986, r 6.94(4).
2   IR 1986, r 6.94(5).

Court's power to dispense with need to prove

18.97 The court may in exceptional circumstances by order declare the creditors or any class of them entitled to vote at creditors' meetings without being required to prove their debts[1].

1   IR 1986, r 6.93(2).

Suspension of meeting

18.98 Once only in the course of any meeting, the chairman may, in his discretion and without an adjournment, declare the meeting suspended for any period up to one hour[1].

[1] IR 1986, r 6.90.

Power to adjourn

18.99 Except where the chairman is the trustee or his nominee and a resolution has been proposed for the trustee's removal, the chairman at any meeting may, in his discretion, and must, if the meeting so resolves, adjourn the meeting to such time and place as seems to him to be appropriate in the circumstances[1]. In that excepted case the chairman may not adjourn the meeting without the consent of at least one-half in value of the creditors present in person or by proxy and entitled to vote[2]. As noted above, the meeting may also be adjourned where it is inquorate[3].

[1] IR 1986, r 6.91(1).
[2] IR 1986, r 6.129(3).
[3] IR 1986, r 6.91(2).

Adjournment

18.100 An adjournment must not be for a period of more than 21 days[1]. Regard for the convenience of the creditors should be had in fixing the venue of the adjourned meeting and the adjourned meeting should be set to commence between the hours of 10.00 and 16.00 on a business day, unless the court otherwise directs[2]. Where a meeting is adjourned, proofs and proxies may be used if lodged at any time up to midday on the business day immediately before the adjourned meeting[3].

[1] IR 1986, r 6.91(3). This restriction applies where the adjournment is made under IR 1986, r 6.91. On the basis that the restriction limits the time for holding the adjourned meeting, the court could extend time under the IA 1986, s 376.
[2] IR 1986, r 6.86(1) and (2).
[3] IR 1986, r 6.91(5).

Record of proceedings

18.101 The chairman at any creditors' meeting must cause minutes of the proceedings at the meeting, signed by him, to be retained by him as part of the records of the bankruptcy[1]. The minutes must include a record of every resolution passed[2]. He must also cause a list of all the creditors who attended the meeting to be made and kept[3].

[1] IR 1986, r 6.95(1).
[2] IR 1986, r 6.95(3).
[3] IR 1986, r 6.95(2).

Evidence of proceedings at meetings

18.102 A minute of proceedings at a creditors' meeting signed by a person describing himself as, or appearing to be, the chairman of that meeting is admissible in insolvency proceedings without further proof and is *prima facie* evidence that the meeting was duly convened and held, that all resolutions passed at the meeting were duly passed and that all proceedings at the meeting duly took place[1].

[1]   IR 1986, r 12.5.

Chairman's duty to ensure resolutions filed at court

18.103 It is the chairman's duty to see to it that particulars of all resolutions passed at a creditors' meeting are filed in court not more than 21 days after the date of the meeting[1].

[1]   IR 1986, r 6.95(3).

Creditors' committee

The creditors' committee

18.104 A general meeting of the bankrupt's creditors may, provided the trustee is not the official receiver[1], establish a committee ('the creditors' committee') to exercise the functions conferred on it by the IA 1986[2]. The creditors' committee exercises a general supervisory function in relation to the course of the bankruptcy and the activities of the trustee, and some of the trustee's powers are exercisable only with the consent of the committee or the court[3].

[1]   IA 1986, s 301(2).
[2]   IA 1986, s 301(2).
[3]   See the IA 1986, s 314 and Sch 5.

Composition of the committee

18.105 The creditors' committee must consist of at least three, and not more than five, members[1]. All must be creditors of the bankrupt, and any creditor, other than one who is fully secured, may be a member so long as he has lodged a proof of his debts, and his proof has neither been wholly disallowed for voting purposes nor wholly rejected for the purposes of distribution or dividend[2]. A body corporate may be a member of the committee, but it cannot act as such otherwise than by a duly appointed representative[3].

[1]   IR 1986, r 6.150(1).
[2]   IR 1986, r 6.150(2).
[3]   IR 1986, r 6.150(3). See the IR 1986, r 6.156 for the manner of appointment.

Formalities

18.106 The creditors' committee does not come into being, and accordingly cannot act, until the trustee has issued a certificate of its due constitution[1]. If the chairman of the creditors' meeting which resolves to establish the committee is not the trustee, he must forthwith give notice of the resolution to the trustee, or as the case may be, the person appointed as trustee by that same meeting, and inform him of the names and addresses of the persons elected to be members of the committee[2].

[1]   IR 1986, r 6.151(1). For the prescribed form of certificate see IR 1986, rr 6.151, 12.7, Sch 4, Form 6.52.
[2]   IR 1986, r 6.151(2).

18.107 No person may act as a member of the committee unless and until he has agreed to do so and, unless the relevant proxy contains a statement to the contrary, such agreement may be given by his proxy-holder present at the meeting establishing the committee[1]. The trustee's certificate of the committee's due constitution may not issue before at least three persons elected to be members of the committee have agreed to act[2]. As and when the others, if any, agree to act, the trustee must issue an amended certificate[3]. The certificate, and any amended certificate, must be filed in court by the trustee[4].

[1]   IR 1986, r 6.151(3).
[2]   IR 1986, r 6.151(3A).
[3]   IR 1986, r 6.151(4). For the prescribed form of amended certificate see IR 1986, rr 6.151, 12.7, Sch 4, Form 6.22.
[4]   IR 1986, r 6.151(5).

18.108 If after the first establishment of the committee there is any change in its membership, the trustee must report the change to the court[1].

[1]   IR 1986, r 6.151(6). For the prescribed form of report see IR 1986, rr 6.151, 12.7, Sch 4, Form 6.53.

18.109 The acts of the creditors' committee established for any bankrupt are valid notwithstanding any defect in the appointment, election or qualifications of any member of the committee[1].

[1]   IA 1986, s 377.

Trustee's duty to report

18.110 It is the duty of the trustee to report to the creditors' committee anything which appears to him to be, or which they have indicated to him as being, of concern to them with respect to the bankruptcy[1]. However, the trustee need not comply with any request for information where it appears to him that:

(1)   the request is frivolous or unreasonable;
(2)   the cost of complying would be excessive, having regard to the relative importance of the information; or

(3)   the estate is without funds sufficient for enabling him to comply[2].

1   IR 1986, r 6.152(1).
2   IR 1986, r 6.152(2).

18.111 Where the committee has come into being more than 28 days after the appointment of the trustee, the latter must report to them, in summary form, what actions he has taken since his appointment, and must answer such questions as they may put to him regarding his conduct of the bankruptcy hitherto[1]. A person who joins the committee after its first establishment is not entitled to require a separate report to him otherwise than in summary form[2].

1   IR 1986, r 6.152(3).
2   IR 1986, r 6.152(4).

18.112 Nothing in the above provisions disentitles the committee, or any member of it, from having access to the trustee's records of the bankruptcy, or from seeking an explanation of any matter within the committee's responsibility[1].

1   IR 1986, r 6.152(5).

Meetings

18.113 Meetings of the creditors' committee must be held when and where determined by the trustee[1]. The trustee must, however, call a first meeting of the committee to take place within three months of his appointment or of the committee's establishment, whichever is the later; and thereafter he must call a meeting:

(1)   if so requested by a member of the committee or his representative, within 21 days of receipt of the request; and
(2)   for a specified date, if the committee has previously resolved that a meeting be held on that date[2].

1   IR 1986, r 6.153(1).
2   IR 1986, r 6.152(2).

18.114 The trustee must give seven days' notice in writing of the venue of any meeting to every member of the committee, or his representative. Any member may waive this requirement either at or before the meeting[1].

1   IR 1986, r 6.153(3).

18.115 The chairman of the meeting must be the trustee, or a person appointed by him in writing to act[1]. A person so nominated must be either:

(1)   one who is qualified to act as an insolvency practitioner in relation to the bankrupt; or
(2)   an employee of the trustee or his firm who is experienced in insolvency matters[2].

¹   IR 1986, r 6.154(1).
²   IR 1986, r 6.154(2).

18.116 A meeting of the committee is duly constituted if due notice of it has been given to all the members and at least two of the members are present or represented[1].

¹   IR 1986, r 6.155.

Proxies

18.117 A member of the creditors' committee may be represented at any meeting by another person duly authorised by him for that purpose[1], who is called a proxy.

¹   IR 1986, r 6.156(1).

18.118 A person acting as a proxy must hold a letter of authority entitling him to do so, either generally or specially, and signed by or on behalf of the committee member. Any proxy is, unless the letter contains a statement to the contrary, to be treated as having authority to act generally[1]. The chairman of the meeting may call on a person claiming to act as a committee member's representative to produce his letter of authority, and may exclude him if it appears that his authority is deficient[2].

¹   IR 1986, r 6.156(2).
²   IR 1986, r 6.156(3).

18.119 No member may be represented by a body corporate, or by a person who is an undischarged bankrupt or a disqualified director or is subject to a bankruptcy restrictions order, bankruptcy restrictions undertaking or interim bankruptcy restrictions order[1].

¹   IR 1986, r 6.156(4).

18.120 No person may:

(1)   on the same committee, act at one and the same time as representative of more than one committee member; or

(2)   act both as a member of the committee and as representative of another member[1].

¹   IR 1986, r 6.156(5).

18.121 If a representative signs any document on a committee member's behalf, the fact that he so signs must be stated below his signature[1].

¹   IR 1986, r 6.156(6).

18.122 The acts of the committee are valid notwithstanding any defect in the appointment or qualifications of any committee member's representative[1].

1   IR 1986, r 6.156(7).

Resolutions

18.123 At any meeting of the creditors' committee, each member, whether present himself or by his representative, has one vote; and a resolution is passed when a majority of the members present or represented have voted in favour of it[1].

1   IR 1986, r 6.161(1).

18.124 Every resolution passed must be recorded in writing, either separately or as part of the minutes of the meeting; and the record must be signed by the chairman and kept with the records of the bankruptcy[1].

1   IR 1986, r 6.161(2).

Passing of resolutions by post

18.125 The trustee may attempt to obtain the agreement of the creditors' committee to a resolution without the members of the committee or their representatives having to attend a meeting. This can be achieved by the trustee sending to every member, or his designated representative, a copy of the proposed resolution[1]. A trustee making use of this procedure must send out to members or their representatives a copy of the proposed resolution set out in such a way that agreement or dissent may be indicated on it[2]. Any member may, within seven business days from the date of the trustee sending out a resolution, require him to summon a meeting of the committee to consider the matters raised by the resolution[3]. In the absence of such a request, the resolution is deemed to have been carried in the committee if and when the trustee is notified in writing by a majority of the members that they concur with it[4].

1   IR 1986, r 6.162(1).
2   IR 1986, r 6.162(2).
3   IR 1986, r 6.162(3).
4   IR 1986, r 6.162(4).

18.126 A copy of every resolution passed under the above provisions, and a note that the concurrence of the committee was obtained, must be kept with the records of the bankruptcy[1].

1   IR 1986, r 6.162(5).

Trustee's report

18.127 As and when directed by the creditors' committee, but not more often than once every two months, the trustee must send a written report to every member of the committee setting out the position generally as regards the progress of the bankruptcy and matters arising in connection with it, to which he, the trustee, considers the committee's attention should be drawn[1]. In the absence of any such directions by the committee, the trustee must send such a report not less often than once in every period of six months[2].

1 IR 1986, r 6.163(1). The obligations imposed by IR 1986, r 6.163 are without prejudice to those imposed by r 6.152: IR 1986, r 6.163(3).
2 IR 1986, r 6.163(2).

Members' expenses

18.128 The trustee must defray out of the estate, in the prescribed order of priority, any reasonable travelling expenses directly incurred by members of the creditors' committee or their representatives in respect of their attendance at the committee's meetings, or otherwise on the committee's business[1].

1 IR 1986, r 6.164.

Transactions involving personal gain

18.129 No member of the creditors' committee, no member's representative, no-one who is an associate[1] of a member or of a member's representative, and no person who has been a member of the committee at any time in the last 12 months, may enter into any transaction whereby he:

(1)   receives out of the estate any payment for services given or goods supplied in connection with the estate's administration;
(2)   obtains any profit from the administration; or
(3)   acquires any asset forming part of the estate[2].

1 For the meaning of 'associate' see the IA 1986, s 435.
2 IR 1986, r 6.165(1), (2).

18.130 This prohibition is a reflection of the fact that committee members, their representatives and associates, are treated as acting in a fiduciary position[1].

1 As to the fiduciary duty of a committee member see *Re Bulmer, ex p Greaves* [1937] Ch 499, [1937] 1 All ER 323, CA; and see also *Taylor v Davies* [1920] AC 636 at 647, PC.

18.131 Such a transaction may, however, be entered into by such a person:

(a)   with the prior leave of the court;
(b)   if he does so as a matter of urgency, or by way of performance of a contract in force before the commencement of the bankruptcy, and obtains the court's leave for the transaction, having applied for it without undue delay; or
(c)   with the prior sanction of the creditors' committee, where it is satisfied, after full disclosure of the circumstances, that the person will be giving full value in the transaction[1].

18.131 *Administration of the estate*

1   IR 1986, r 6.165(3). See eg *Re Spink (No 2), ex p Slater* (1913) 108 LT 811 (sanction given to trustee to pay member of committee of inspection for goods supplied to carry on bankrupt's business).

18.132 These provisos are an attempt to alleviate possible injustice caused by the strictness of the normal rules relating to fiduciaries who act in circumstances in which their duties are capable of conflicting with their self-interest[1].

1   See eg *Regal (Hastings) Ltd v Gulliver (1942)* [1967] 2 AC 134n, [1942] 1 All ER 378, HL.

18.133 No representative of a member may vote upon a resolution to sanction such a transaction if he is to participate directly or indirectly in it[1].

1   IR 1986, r 6.165(4).

18.134 On the application of any person interested[1], the court may:

(i)   set aside a transaction on the ground that it has been entered into in contravention of the above provisions; and

(ii)   make with respect to it such order as it thinks fit, including an order requiring a person to whom the above provisions apply to account for any profit made and compensate the estate for any resultant loss[2].

1   As to the meaning of 'a person interested', cf para **18.285**.
2   IR 1986, r 6.165(5).

18.135 In the case of a person to whom these provisions apply as an associate of a member of the committee or of a committee member's representative, the court may not, however, make an order under heads (i) and (ii) above (para **18.134**) if satisfied that he entered into the relevant transaction without having any reason to suppose that in doing so he would contravene the above provisions[1]. Again, this exception is an attempt to alleviate the possible harshness of the usual rules, as demonstrated by *Re Bulmer, ex p Greaves*[2]. In that instance there was a purchase by the holder of a general proxy from a company which had been appointed a member of the committee of inspection. The purchaser was held to be in a fiduciary position, even though he did not know that the property belonged to the bankrupt's estate, and he was held liable to account for the profit made.

1   IR 1986, r 6.165(6).
2   [1937] Ch 499, [1937] 1 All ER 323, CA.

18.136 The costs of an application to the court under the above provisions do not fall on the estate, unless the court so orders[1].

1   IR 1986, r 6.165(7).

Termination of membership

18.137 A member of the creditors' committee may resign by notice in writing to the trustee[1].

1   IR 1986, r 6.157.

18.138 A person's membership of the creditors' committee is automatically terminated if:

(1)   he becomes bankrupt;

(2)   at three consecutive meetings of the committee he is neither present nor represented, unless at the third of those meetings it is resolved that these provisions are not to apply in his case; or

(3)   he ceases to be, or is found never to have been, a creditor[1].

¹   IR 1986, r 6.158(1).

18.139 However, if the cause of termination is the member's bankruptcy, his trustee in bankruptcy replaces him as a member of the committee[1].

¹   IR 1986, r 6.158(2).

18.140 A member of the creditors' committee may be removed by resolution at a meeting of creditors, at least 14 days' notice having been given of the intention to move that resolution[1].

¹   IR 1986, r 6.159.

Vacancies

18.141 If there is a vacancy in the membership of the committee, it need not be filled if the trustee and a majority of the remaining committee members so agree, provided that the number of members does not fall below the minimum of three[1].

¹   IR 1986, r 6.160(1), (2). See the IR 1986, r 6.150(1) for the minimum number of members.

18.142 The trustee may appoint any qualified creditor to fill the vacancy, if a majority of the other members of the committee agree and the creditor concerned consents[1].

¹   IR 1986, r 6.160(1), (3).

18.143 Alternatively, a meeting of the creditors may resolve that a creditor be appointed, with his consent, to fill the vacancy; and in this case at least 14 days' notice must have been given of a resolution to make such an appointment, whether or not of a person named in the notice[1].

¹   IR 1986, r 6.160(1), (4).

18.144 Where the vacancy is filled by an appointment made by a creditors' meeting at which the trustee is not present, the chairman of the meeting must report to the trustee the appointment which has been made[1].

¹   IR 1986, r 6.160(1), (5).

Secretary of State exercising committee's functions

18.145 The creditors' committee cannot carry out its functions at any time when the official receiver is trustee[1]. At any such time the functions of the committee are vested in the Secretary of State, except to the extent that the IR 1986 otherwise provide[2]. At any time when there is no creditors' committee and the trustee is not the official receiver, then, save where the IR 1986 provide otherwise, the functions of the committee are vested in the Secretary of State[3].

[1]   IA 1986, s 302(1).
[2]   IA 1986, s 302(1).
[3]   IA 1986, s 302(2).

18.146 At any such time, requirements about notices to be given, or reports to be made, to the committee by the trustee do not apply, otherwise than as enabling the committee to require a report as to any matter. Where the committee's functions are vested in the Secretary of State under the IA 1986, s 302(2), they may be exercised by the official receiver[1].

[1]   IR 1986, r 6.166.

H TRUSTEE'S DUTIES

General

18.147 As stated at the outset of **Chapter 13**, the function of the trustee is to get in, realise and distribute the bankrupt's estate in accordance with the IA 1986, ss 305–335[1]. Overarching all his activity in his capacity as trustee is an obligation that he should conduct the administration and fulfil his function in the interests of the general body of unsecured creditors in whose interest he is appointed.

[1]   IA 1986, s 305(1).

18.148 Trustees' duties regarding the estate do not cease because funds are lacking to perform them[1].

[1]   *Phillips v Symes* [2006] BPIR 1430.

Cross-reference

18.149 The trustee's specific duties (1) to provide information, records and assistance to the official receiver[1], (2) concerning the banking of funds[2], and (3) to keep records and make accounts[3] have been discussed in **Chapter 13**.

[1]   IA 1986, s 305(3).
[2]   Insolvency Regulations 1994, SI 1994/2507, regs 20–23 and 31.
[3]   Insolvency Regulations 1994, SI 1994/2507, regs 24–30.

I SPECIAL MANAGER

Court's power to appoint a special manager

18.150 The court has power to appoint any person to be the special manager (a) of the bankrupt's estate; (b) of the business of an undischarged bankrupt; or (c) of the property or business of a debtor in whose case the official receiver has been appointed interim receiver[1]. The appointment may be made on the application of the official receiver or the trustee[2]. The official receiver may apply if he has been appointed as interim receiver following the presentation of a petition but pending its hearing[3], or if he is acting as receiver and manager following the making of a bankruptcy order but pending the appointment of the trustee[4], or if he is acting as trustee. Accordingly, although the topic is discussed here, it is relevant also to the protection of the estate pending the appointment of the trustee.

[1] IA 1986, s 370(1).
[2] IA 1986, s 370(2).
[3] See the IA 1986, s 286.
[4] See the IA 1986, s 287.

Grounds on which application may be made

18.151 The official receiver or trustee may apply for a special manager to be appointed in any case where it appears to the official receiver or the trustee that the nature of the estate, property or business, or the interests of the creditors generally, require the appointment of another person to manage the estate, property or business[1]. The applicant must, therefore, persuade the court that the appointment is, in the circumstances, necessary because the official receiver or trustee cannot himself adequately protect or administer the property over which the appointment is made. Possible examples of cases where an appointment would be justified are where the property in question requires some special expertise in its management or where it is situated abroad and the official receiver or trustee cannot satisfactorily maintain immediate control over its management.

[1] IA 1986, s 370(2).

Application

18.152 The application must be supported by a report setting out the reasons for the application. The report must include the applicant's estimate of the value of the estate, property or business in respect of which the special manager is to be appointed[1]. It is important that this estimate should be as accurate as possible because the minimum amount of security which the special manager must give is set by reference to that estimate[2].

[1] IR 1986, r 6.167(1).
[2] IR 1986, r 6.168(3).

Persons who may be appointed

18.153 Save that it seems implicit that the bankrupt himself should not be appointed[1], there are no restrictions on who may be appointed as special manager. Accordingly, where appropriate, a company or other legal person might be appointed.

[1]   Cf the IA 1986, s 314(2) for the trustee's power to appoint the bankrupt to superintend the management of his estate or part of it or to carry on his business for the benefit of his creditors.

Duration of appointment

18.154 The order appointing the special manager must either specify the duration of his appointment, which may be for a period of time or until the occurrence of a specified event, or specify that the duration of the appointment is subject to a further order of the court[1]. The appointment may be renewed by order of the court. Presumably, before renewing the appointment, the court must be satisfied that the appointment continues to be required by reference to the same standard as is applicable to an appointment at the outset. The appointment will terminate in the circumstances described in para **18.163** below. Those circumstances appear to override whatever may have been specified in the order making the appointment.

[1]   IR 1986, r 6.167(2).

Requirement that special manager provide security

18.155 The order appointing the special manager does not take effect until he has provided the appropriate security[1].

[1]   IR 1986, r 6.168(1).

Powers of special manager

18.156 A special manager has such powers as are entrusted to him by the court[1]. The power of the court to entrust powers to the special manager includes power to direct that any provision in the IA 1986 relating to the insolvency of individuals which has effect in relation to the official receiver, interim receiver or trustee shall have like effect in relation to the special manager for the purposes of his carrying out any of the functions of the official receiver, interim receiver or trustee[2].

[1]   IA 1986, s 370(3).
[2]   IA 1986, s 370(4).

Security

18.157 A special manager must give the prescribed security[1], which is security of an amount not less than the value of the estate, property or business as estimated by the applicant in his report[2]. Unless the security is given by, or the court accepts an undertaking to give the security from, the special manager, his appointment does not take effect[3]. It is not necessary that security should be given for each separate bankruptcy; but it may be given either specially for a particular bankruptcy, or generally for any bankruptcy in relation to which the special manager may be employed as such[4].

[1] IA 1986, s 370(5)(a).
[2] IR 1986, r 6.168(3).
[3] IR 1986, r 6.168(1).
[4] IR 1986, r 6.168(2).

18.158 When the special manager has given security to the person applying for his appointment, that person's certificate as to the adequacy of the security must be filed in court[1]. The cost of providing the security must be paid for in the first instance by the special manager but:

(1)   where a bankruptcy order is not made, he is entitled to be reimbursed out of the property of the debtor, and the court may make an order on the debtor accordingly; and

(2)   where a bankruptcy order is made, he is entitled to be reimbursed out of the estate in the prescribed order of priority[2].

[1] IR 1986, r 6.168(4).
[2] IR 1986, r 6.168(5). As to the prescribed order of priority see IR 1986, r 6.224(1).

18.159 If the special manager fails to give the required security within the time stated for that purpose by the order appointing him, or any extension of that time that may be allowed, the official receiver or trustee, as the case may be, must report the failure to the court, which may thereupon discharge the order appointing the special manager[1].

[1] IR 1986, r 6.169(1).

18.160 If the special manager fails to keep up his security, the official receiver or trustee must report his failure to the court, which may thereupon remove the special manager, and make such order as it thinks fit as to costs[1].

[1] IR 1986, r 6.169(2).

18.161 If an order is made removing the special manager, or discharging the order appointing him, the court must give directions as to whether any, and if so what, steps should be taken for the appointment of another special manager in his place[1].

[1] IR 1986, r 6.169(3).

Accounts

18.162 The special manager must prepare and keep accounts containing details of his receipts and payments[1]. The accounts must be produced for the approval of the trustee[2]. They must be in respect of three-month periods for the duration of the special manager's appointment, or for a lesser period, if his appointment terminates less than three months from its date, or from the date to which the last accounts were made up[3]. When the accounts have been approved the special manager's receipts and payments must be added to those of the trustee[4].

1   IA 1986, s 370(5)(b). A special manager must produce those accounts in accordance with the IR 1986 to the Secretary of State or such other persons as may be prescribed: IA 1986, s 370(5)(c). IR 1986, r 6.170(1) requires production of the accounts to the trustee only: see below.
2   IR 1986, r 6.170(1).
3   IR 1986, r 6.170(2).
4   IR 1986, r 6.170(3).

Termination of appointment

18.163 The special manager's appointment terminates if the bankruptcy petition is dismissed or if, an interim receiver having been appointed, the latter is discharged without a bankruptcy order having been made[1].

1   IR 1986, r 6.171(1).

18.164 If the official receiver or the trustee considers that the employment of the special manager is no longer necessary or profitable for the estate, he must apply to the court for directions, and the court may order the special manager's appointment to be terminated[1].

1   IR 1986, r 6.171(2).

18.165 The official receiver or the trustee must make the same application if a resolution of the creditors is passed, requesting that the appointment be terminated[1].

1   IR 1986, r 6.171(3).

J MISCELLANEOUS SPECIFIC PROVISIONS RELATING TO REALISATION AND DISPOSAL OF THE BANKRUPT'S PROPERTY

Redemption of pledged goods

Trustee's power to redeem pledged goods

18.166 Where the bankrupt has pledged, pawned or otherwise transferred possession of goods to another person by way of security, the trustee may exercise the bankrupt's right of redemption[1].

1   IA 1986, s 311(5).

Notices preventing disposal by pledgee

18.167 Since goods may be pawned, pledged or given as security for debts which are much smaller than the value of the goods themselves, provision is made to prevent the person holding them as security from disposing of them without giving the trustee an opportunity to redeem the goods on behalf of the bankrupt's creditors. The official receiver, when acting as receiver and manager pending the appointment of the trustee, may give a notice to the person holding them that he wishes to inspect the goods[1]. When such a notice has been given the person holding the goods may not dispose of them unless either he obtains the leave of the court or he gives the trustee a reasonable opportunity of inspecting the goods and redeeming them. If the official receiver has not served such a notice, the trustee may and if he does so, the notice has the same effect[2].

1   IA 1986, s 285(5).
2   IA 1986, s 311(5) and (6).

Redemption of security where secured creditor proves

Trustee's right to redeem partially secured creditor's security

18.168 Where a creditor holds security for his debt, he is entitled to recover outside the bankruptcy by enforcing his security[1]. Where he enforces the security by sale, any surplus after the satisfaction of his debt is payable to the trustee for the benefit of the estate. Equally if the trustee causes the property to be sold, the secured creditor will be paid first out of the proceeds of sale. But the secured creditor may hold security which only secures part of his debt. In such a case he is an unsecured creditor in respect of the balance of his debt and, to the extent of that balance, is entitled to vote at creditors' meetings[2] and to prove in the bankruptcy[3]. Where the security has not been realised a method of determining the amount of the unsecured balance is required[4]. The primary obligation is on the creditor to put a value on his security. If he was the petitioning creditor, he must have done so in the petition[5]; if he has sought to prove in the bankruptcy he must have done so in his proof of debt[6]. The trustee may consider that the value which the creditor has put on his security is lower than the market value of the asset which comprises the security. If so, advantage would be gained for the general body of creditors by redeeming the asset at the value put on it by the secured creditor and selling it in the market. Since the secured creditor has participated in the bankruptcy by petitioning or proving on the basis of the value he has put on the security, there appears to be no or little unfairness in permitting the trustee to gain this advantage. Hence provision is made in the IR 1986 enabling him to do so.

1   IA 1986, s 285(4).
2   IR 1986, r 6.93(4).
3   IR 1986, r 6.96(1) and r 6.98(1)(g).
4   Where the secured creditor realises the security, the amount of the unsecured debt is obvious; see the IR 1986, r 6.109(1).
5   IA 1986, s 269(1)(b).
6   IR 1986, r 6.98(1)(g).

Exercise of the right to redeem

18.169 The trustee may at any time give notice to a creditor whose debt is secured that he proposes, at the expiration of 28 days from the date of the notice, to redeem the security at the value put upon it in the creditor's proof[1]. Although the rule states that such notice may be given to 'a creditor whose debt is secured' which suggests that the notice may be given to any such creditor, it is implicit that the notice may only be given to a creditor whose debt is secured and who has proved in the bankruptcy because of the reference to the value put on the security in the creditor's proof. The only exception might arise where a creditor had presented a petition claiming only to be partly secured and relying on the unsecured part of his debt to found the petition but then did not submit any proof. Although the rule does not happily embrace that possibility, it would be consistent with its purpose if it were construed as enabling the trustee to redeem the security at the value which such a creditor had put on his security in the petition.

[1] IR 1986, r 6.117(1).

Secured creditor's restricted power to alter valuation

18.170 Where the trustee has given notice of his intention to redeem, the creditor has 21 days (or such longer time as the trustee may allow) in which, if the creditor wishes, to exercise his right to re-value his security[1]. Unless, being the petitioning creditor, he put a value on the security in the petition or, whether he was the petitioning creditor or not, he has voted in respect of the unsecured balance of his debt, the secured creditor may alter the value which he put on the security in his proof of debt with the agreement of the trustee. In those excepted cases or where the trustee is not willing to agree, the value may only be altered with the leave of the court[2]. Where the security is re-valued, the trustee may only redeem it at the new value[3].

[1] IR 1986, r 6.117(2).
[2] IR 1986, r 6.115.
[3] IR 1986, r 6.117(2).

Costs of transfer

18.171 If the trustee redeems the security, the cost of transferring it is borne by the estate[1]. The costs referred to are the costs incidental to the redemption of the security. It would be unfair for the amount which the secured creditor received on the redemption of his security to be reduced by the costs which the trustee has prompted to be incurred by redeeming it.

[1] IR 1986, r 6.117(3).

Notice to elect

18.172 A secured creditor may at any time, by a notice in writing, call on the trustee to elect whether he will or will not exercise his power to redeem the security at the value then placed on it; and the trustee then has six months in which to exercise the power or determine not to exercise it[1].

[1] IR 1986, r 6.117(4).

Trustee's power to force sale

18.173 Unless the security has been re-valued and the re-valuation approved by the court, the trustee, if he is dissatisfied with the value which a secured creditor puts on his security, may require the security to be offered for sale. The terms of sale shall be such as may be agreed, or as the court may direct; and if the sale is by auction, the trustee on behalf of the estate and the creditor on his own behalf may appear and bid[1]. Although it may seem curious that the trustee should be given power to bid if the sale is by auction, this provision enables the trustee to force the secured creditor to sell his security and thereby, if the trustee's dissatisfaction, ie opinion that the value put on the security is too low, is justified, ensure that the secured creditor does not prove for an excessive (allegedly) unsecured balance. A secured creditor who considered that the trustee's action in forcing a sale was unfair would have standing to challenge the trustee's decision under the IA 1986, s 303(1).

[1]   IR 1986, r 6.118.

Trusts of land

Trusts of land and orders for sale

18.174 Where land is beneficially owned by two or more persons, it will ordinarily[1] be held under a trust of land within the meaning of the Trusts of Land and Appointment of Trustees Act 1996[2]. Any person who is a trustee of land or has an interest in property subject to a trust of land may make an application for an order under s 14 of the 1996 Act. The court may make any order relating to the exercise by the trustees of any of their functions, which includes the exercise of their power of sale, or declaring the nature or extent of a person's interest in property subject to the trust[3].

[1]   The excepted cases are where the land is settled land within the meaning of the Settled Land Act 1925 and land to which the University and College Estates Act 1925 applies. See the Trusts of Land and Appointment of Trustees Act 1996, s 1(3). No new settlement for the purposes of the Settled Land Act 1925 may be created on or after 1 January 1997; see the Trusts of Land and Appointment of Trustees Act 1996, s 2.

[2]   A trust of land means (subject to the excepted cases mentioned in the last note) any trust of property which consists of or includes land. For the relevant definition of land, see the Law of Property Act 1925, s 205(1) which is incorporated by the Trusts of Land and Appointment of Trustees Act 1996, s 23(2). It includes land of any tenure.

[3]   Trusts of Land and Appointment of Trustees Act 1996, s 14(2).

Applications for orders outside bankruptcy

18.175 Where an application for an order under the Trusts of Land and Appointment of Trustees Act 1996, s 14 is made other than by a trustee in bankruptcy, the court must have regard to the matters referred to in s 15 of the 1996 Act[1]. But where the application is made by a trustee in bankruptcy for an order for the sale of land, s 15 of the 1996 Act does not apply[2].

[1]   Trusts of Land and Appointment of Trustees Act 1996, s 15(1)–(3).
[2]   Trusts of Land and Appointment of Trustees Act 1996, s 15(4).

18.176 *Administration of the estate*

Application by trustee in bankruptcy

18.176 Where the application is made by a trustee in bankruptcy not more than one year after the bankrupt's estate first vested in a trustee in bankruptcy and the land to which the application relates does not include a dwelling house[1], the court shall make such order as it thinks just and reasonable having regard to the interests of the bankrupt's creditors and all the circumstances of the case other than the needs of the bankrupt[2]. Where the application is made by a trustee in bankruptcy after the end of the period of one year beginning with the date when the estate first vested in a trustee in bankruptcy, the court must assume, unless the circumstances of the case are exceptional, that the interests of the bankrupt's creditors outweigh all other considerations[3].

[1] Applications relating to dwelling houses are mentioned in the next section of this chapter and considered in more detail in **Chapter 15**.
[2] IA 1986, s 335A(2).
[3] IA 1986, s 335A(3).

Appropriate court

18.177 The trustee in bankruptcy must make the application to the court having jurisdiction in relation to the bankruptcy[1].

[1] IA 1986, s 335A(1).

Dwelling houses and the family home

Cross-reference

18.178 The trustee's power to realise interest held by the bankrupt in the family home, and the restrictions on the exercise of that power, are considered more fully in **Chapter 15**. The relevant provisions of the IA 1986 are mentioned here in outline only.

Trusts of land and dwelling houses

18.179 Where the trustee in bankruptcy makes an application under the Trusts of Land and Appointment of Trustees Act 1996, s 14 for an order for the sale of land including a dwelling house which is or has been the home of the bankrupt or the bankrupt's spouse or former spouse, and the application is made not more than one year after the bankrupt's estate first vested in a trustee in bankruptcy, the court shall make such order as it thinks just and reasonable having regard to:

(a)   the interests of the bankrupt's creditors;
(b)   the conduct of the spouse or former spouse, so far as contributing to the bankruptcy;
(c)   the needs and financial resources of the spouse or former spouse;
(d)   the needs of any children; and

(e)   all the circumstances of the case other than the needs of the bankrupt[1].

[1]   IA 1986, s 335A(2).

18.180 Where the application is made by a trustee in bankruptcy more than one year after the first vesting of the estate in a trustee, the court must assume, unless the circumstances of the case are exceptional, that the interests of the bankrupt's creditors outweigh all other considerations[1]. The application must be made to the court having jurisdiction over the bankruptcy[2].

[1]   IA 1986, s 335A(3).
[2]   IA 1986, s 335A(1).

Spouse's rights of occupation

18.181 Where one spouse's matrimonial home rights under the Family Law Act 1996, Pt IV are a charge on the estate or interest of the other spouse or of trustees for the other spouse, the charge continues to subsist despite the bankruptcy[1]. Where the trustee wishes to override the charge which protects the matrimonial home rights, he must apply for an order under the Family Law Act 1996, s 33 to the court having jurisdiction over the bankruptcy[2]. On such an application, the court must have regard to the same matters as when it considers an application made by a trustee in bankruptcy under the Trusts of Land and Appointment of Trustees Act 1996, s 14 for an order for the sale of land[3]. In the same way, where the application is made by the trustee in bankruptcy more than one year after the first vesting of the estate in a trustee, the court must assume, unless the circumstances of the case are exceptional, that the interests of the bankrupt's creditors outweigh all other considerations[4].

[1]   IA 1986, s 336(2)(a).
[2]   IA 1986, s 336(2)(b).
[3]   IA 1986, s 336(4).
[4]   IA 1986, s 336(5).

Bankrupt's rights of occupation

18.182 Protection is afforded to the bankrupt's right to remain in occupation, or to enter and take up occupation, of a dwelling house in which he holds a beneficial estate or interest where there are any persons under the age of 18 with whom he had at some time occupied the dwelling house and who had their home with him at the time when the petition was presented and at the commencement of the bankruptcy[1]. If the bankrupt is in occupation of the dwelling house in such a case, the trustee can only evict him with the leave of the court having jurisdiction over the bankruptcy sought on an application made under the Family Law Act 1996, s 33[2]. If the bankrupt has the right to enter and occupy the dwelling house he must first obtain the leave of the same court to do so, which the trustee may resist[3]. Where the application for leave (whether by the trustee to evict the bankrupt from, or by the bankrupt for leave to enter and occupy, the dwelling house) is made not more than one year from the date on which the estate first vested in a trustee, the court must make such order as it thinks just and reasonable having regard to:

(a)   the interests of the bankrupt's creditors;
(b)   the financial resources of the bankrupt;
(c)   the needs of any children; and
(d)   all the circumstances of the case other than the needs of the bankrupt[4].

1   IA 1986, s 337(1).
2   IA 1986, s 337(2)(a)(i), (3)(b) and (4).
3   IA 1986, s 337(2)(a)(ii), (3)(b) and (4).
4   IA 1986, s 337(5).

18.183 Although it might appear that the bankrupt would have no resources because all his assets would have been surrendered to his trustee for the benefit of his creditors, his resources would include such income as he is able to earn after the commencement of the bankruptcy and such calls as he might be able to make on the generosity of his family or other persons. Again where the application is made by the trustee in bankruptcy more than one year after the first vesting of the estate in a trustee, the court must assume, unless the circumstances of the case are exceptional, that the interests of the bankrupt's creditors outweigh all other considerations[1].

1   IA 1986, s 337(6).

Charge on bankrupt's home

Court's power to impose charge on bankrupt's home

18.184 Where any property consisting of an interest in a dwelling house which is occupied by the bankrupt or by his spouse or former spouse is comprised in the bankrupt's estate and the trustee is for any reason unable for the time being to realise that property, the trustee may apply to the court for an order imposing a charge on the property for the benefit of the bankrupt's estate[1]. This provision is discussed in more detail in **Chapter 15**.

1   IA 1986, s 313 and the IR 1986, r 6.237.

Disposal of bankrupt's books, papers and other records

Power to dispose of records

18.185 The trustee, on the authorisation of the official receiver, during his tenure of office or on vacating office, or the official receiver while acting as trustee, may at any time sell, destroy or otherwise dispose of the books, papers and other records of the bankrupt[1].

1   Insolvency Regulations 1994, SI 1994/2507, reg 30.

K SALE OF MORTGAGED PROPERTY ON THE APPLICATION OF THE MORTGAGEE

Sale of bankrupt's mortgaged property

18.186 Where the estate of the bankrupt includes land which is the subject of a mortgage, the trustee may be faced with an application by the mortgagee for the land to be sold.

18.187 Any person claiming to be the legal or equitable mortgagee of land[1] belonging to the bankrupt may apply to the court for an order directing that the land be sold[2]. If it is satisfied as to the applicant's title, the court may direct accounts to be taken and inquiries to be made to ascertain:

(1)   the principal, interest and costs due under the mortgage; and
(2)   where the mortgagee has been in possession of the land or any part of it, the rents and profits, dividends, interest, or other proceeds received by him or on his behalf,

and directions may be given by the court with respect to any other mortgage, whether prior or subsequent, on the same property[3].

1   'Land' includes any interest in, or right over, land: IR 1986, r 6.197(1).
2   IR 1986, r 6.197(1).
3   IR 1986, r 6.197(2), and also r 6.197(4).

18.188 For the purpose of those accounts and inquiries, and of making title to the purchaser, any of the parties may be examined by the court, and must produce on oath before the court all such documents in their custody or under their control relating to the estate of the bankrupt as the court may direct; and the court may authorise the service of requests for further information under CPR Pt 18[1].

1   IR 1986, r 6.197(3).

18.189 The court may order that the land, or any part of it, be sold and any party bound by the order and in possession of the land or in receipt of the rents and profits from it, may be ordered to deliver up possession or receipt to the purchaser or to such other person as the court may direct[1]. The court may permit the person having conduct of the sale to sell the land in such manner as he thinks fit, or may direct that the land be sold as directed by the order[2].

1   IR 1986, r 6.198(1).
2   IR 1986, r 6.198(2).

18.190 The court's order may contain directions:

(a)   appointing the persons to have the conduct of the sale;
(b)   fixing the manner of sale, whether by contract conditional on the court's approval, private treaty, public auction or otherwise;
(c)   settling the particulars and conditions of sale;

(d)   obtaining a valuation of the property, and fixing a reserve or minimum price;
(e)   requiring particular persons to join in the sale and conveyance;
(f)   requiring the payment of the purchase money into court, or to trustees or others;
(g)   if the sale is to be by public auction, fixing the security, if any, to be given by the auctioneer, and his remuneration[1].

1   IR 1986, r 6.198(3).

18.191 If the sale is to be by public auction, the court may direct that the mortgagee may appear and bid on his own behalf[1].

1   IR 1986, r 6.198(4).

18.192 The proceeds of sale must be applied: firstly, in payment of the expenses of the trustee of the application to the court, the sale and the taking of accounts and inquiries[1]; and secondly, in payment of the amount found due to any mortgagee, for principal, interest and costs. The balance, if any, must be retained by or paid to the trustee[2].

1   Ie as directed by the IR 1986, r 6.197. See above.
2   IR 1986, r 6.199(1).

18.193 Where the proceeds of sale are insufficient to pay in full the amount found due to any mortgagee, he is entitled to prove as a creditor for any deficiency, and to receive dividends rateably with other creditors, but not so as to disturb any dividend already declared[1].

1   IR 1986, r 6.199(2).

L CONTRACTS MADE BY THE BANKRUPT BEFORE BANKRUPTCY

Contracts are not discharged by bankruptcy

18.194 The fact that a party to a contract has become insolvent does not by itself put an end to the contract[1]. In *Re Edwards, ex p Chalmers*[2] Mellish LJ, having referred to that rule, explained that 'it certainly would be very unfair if [the insolvency of one party to a contract had the effect of discharging the contract]; for if the insolvent had any beneficial contracts remaining, it would be hard on him as well as his creditors if they could not have the benefit of the contracts[3]'. Save for contracts the performance of which requires the bankrupt's personal skill and contracts which may lawfully be determined for repudiatory breach or otherwise, the benefit of any contract which the bankrupt has made before his bankruptcy passes to and is enforceable by his trustee.

1   *Brooke v Hewitt* (1796) 3 Ves 253; *Lawrence v Knowles* (1839) 5 Bing NC 399; *Gibson v Carruthers* (1841) 8 M & W 321; *Jenning's Trustee v King* [1952] Ch 899, [1952] 2 All ER 608.
2   (1873) 8 Ch App 289.
3   (1873) 8 Ch App 289 at 293–294.

Personal contracts

18.195 'Where the motive or consideration of the solvent party was founded, wholly or in part, upon his confidence in the skill or personal ability of the bankrupt, if the bankrupt, from his circumstances, is unable to perform his part, the assignees[1] are not entitled to substitute either their own capacity, or skill, or credit, for that of the bankrupt'[2]. Thus the right to enforce an executory contract does not pass to the trustee where what remains to be performed under the contract on the bankrupt's side depends on the bankrupt's personal attributes or skills. The exception is related to the rule that specific performance will not be decreed to enforce a contract for personal services. For example, it was on the footing that specific performance would not be available that Stuart V-C refused to permit the assignees of an insolvent builder to take on his commitments under a building contract and enforce the contract against the employer[3]. However, where the contract has been executed by the bankrupt, but the other party has failed to fulfil his obligation to pay the bankrupt for his services, the trustee will be entitled to enforce the claim for whatever is due under the contract[4].

[1]   Ie the assignees of the bankrupt's estate who stood in the same position (in the context of this dictum) as the trustee does under the present law.
[2]   *Gibson v Carruthers* (1841) 8 M & W 321 per Abinger CB at 343, see also Parke B at 333.
[3]   *Knight v Burgess* (1864) 33 LJ Ch 727.
[4]   *Beckham v Drake* (1849) 2 HL Cas 579; *Ord v Upton* [2000] Ch 352, [2000] 1 All ER 193, CA.

Right to determine the contract for breach

18.196 Although the insolvency of one party does not by itself determine the contract, the other party may be entitled to determine the contract if the insolvent party is guilty of a repudiatory breach[1]. If time is of the essence and on the date for performance the insolvent party fails to perform his obligations under the contract, the other party may accept the repudiation and treat the contract as determined[2]. But where time is not of the essence, the other party is not entitled without more to treat the insolvent party's failure to perform as a breach which entitles the solvent party to determine the contract[3].

[1]   *Lawrence v Knowles* (1839) 5 Bing NC 399.
[2]   *Powell v Marshall, Parkes & Co* [1899] 1 QB 710.
[3]   *Jenning's Trustee v King* [1952] Ch 899, [1952] 2 All ER 608.

18.197 In older cases failure on the part of the bankrupt, or of those to whom on his insolvency his estate was assigned, to perform a contract might be taken by the other party as showing that the bankrupt or his assignees intended to abandon it. If the bankrupt or the assignees had abandoned the contract, the other party was entitled to determine it. For example in *Lawrence v Knowles*[1], by a contract made on 1 July 1834 the bankrupt contracted to purchase shares in a railway company on terms that the purchase be completed on 1 July 1835. The bankrupt declared his insolvency in February 1835. The Court of Common Pleas ruled that the bankrupt's assignees were 'bound in a reasonable time after 1 July 1835 at the latest to declare whether they meant to take the contract or not'. Their failure to do so over a long period of months was enough to justify the jury in finding that the contract was abandoned. In *Morgan v Bain*[2] Brett J said, in discussing the effect of the judgment in *Re Edwards, ex p Chalmers*[3], that he thought that the effect of that judgment was 'not that insolvency puts an end to the contract or alters it, but that where one contracting party gives notice to the other that he is insolvent and does nothing more, the other party has the right to assume that he intends to abandon the contract'[4]. It is submitted that caution is required in the application of this statement. What is required, in the ordinary case[5], is that the bankrupt or his trustee should be guilty of a repudiatory breach of the contract, ie a breach which entitles the other party to determine the contract. Failure to perform on the due date where time is of the essence is a repudiatory breach. But non-performance on the due date in other cases is not necessarily repudiatory[6]. Since bankruptcy does not determine the contract, notice that he is insolvent given by one party to a contract to the other will not in itself suffice to determine the contract. Hence mere inactivity by the insolvent party, where time is not of the essence, is unlikely to justify the other party in determining the contract. The other party may, however, be able to put himself in a position rightfully to determine the contract by making time of the essence. For example, where the contract involves the sale of land, he may be entitled to serve a notice to complete. Further, if he is in doubt, the solvent party may (after a bankruptcy order has been made) apply to the court for an order discharging the contract under the IA 1986, s 345.

[1] (1839) 5 Bing NC 399.
[2] (1874) LR 10 CP 15.
[3] (1873) 8 Ch App 289.
[4] (1874) LR 10 CP 15, 26.
[5] It would be exceptional for months of inactivity to pass and in such a case, the solvent party might be entitled to assume that the contract had, without any express statement, been abandoned; see *Chitty on Contracts* (29th edn), para 22–027.
[6] *Jenning's Trustee v King* [1952] Ch 899, [1952] 2 All ER 608.

18.198 Further, during the period between petition and the estate vesting in the trustee, the other party is at risk in acting on a declaration by the bankrupt as to his intentions. For a disposition by the bankrupt of whatever rights he has under the contract may be avoided by the trustee[1] and, if the bankrupt simply surrenders his right to enforce the contract, his doing so may amount to a relevant disposition. The other party must, therefore, justify his conduct in determining the contract by reference to a repudiatory breach or an express term of the contract entitling him to determine the contract in the event of insolvency or some other objective factor.

[1] IA 1986, s 284(1).

Right to rescind the contract

18.199 If the bankrupt induced the other contracting party to enter into the contract by a misrepresentation, the other party may rescind the contract and may rely on such right to rescind against the trustee as well as the bankrupt.

For the trustee acquires the bankrupt's property subject to the rights of third parties[1] and the right of a party to rescind a contract made by the bankrupt is one such right[2].

[1]   IA 1986, s 283(5).
[2]   *Re Eastgate, ex p Ward* [1905] 1 KB 465 (where the other party rescinded between the bankrupt's act of bankruptcy and the receiving order); *Tilley v Bowman Ltd* [1910] 1 KB 745 (where the other party rescinded after the receiving order had been made).

Specific performance

18.200 Similarly, if the other party is entitled to specific performance of the contract, that remedy will be available against the trustee. For example if the bankrupt has contracted to sell real property, the trustee will obtain title to that property subject to the other party's right specifically to enforce the contract. But, the trustee cannot disclaim a contract to sell property which is specifically enforceable unless he also disclaims the property[1].

[1]   *Pearce v Bastable's Trustee in Bankruptcy* [1901] 2 Ch 122; *Re Bastable, ex p Trustee* [1901] 2 KB 518.

Disclaimer[1]

18.201 Power to disclaim unprofitable contracts (amongst other forms of onerous property) was first conferred on the trustee in bankruptcy by the Bankruptcy Act 1869. Before the 1869 Act, assignees of an insolvent debtor were entitled to perform contracts previously made by the bankrupt but if they decided that they did not wish to perform, even if they had performed the contract for some period during their conduct of the insolvent's affairs after the assignment, then the non-performance consequent on their decision would comprise a breach of contract on the part of the insolvent who was then exposed to a fresh claim by the other party to the contract[2]. The Bankruptcy Act 1869 introduced two significant changes which, in substance, remain in force under the IA 1986. First, the trustee is enabled to disclaim and thereby determine an unprofitable contract[3]. If the trustee disclaims, any loss caused by the breach was recoverable only by proof in the bankruptcy. Secondly, any liability for breach of a contract that was made by the bankrupt before the commencement of the bankruptcy constitutes a debt from which he will be released on discharge[4] and for which there is no remedy other than proof in the bankruptcy and from which the bankrupt would be released on his discharge[5]. Where the bankrupt, as purchaser under a contract for the sale of land, has paid a deposit in earnest of performance, the trustee will not be entitled to recover the deposit for the estate following disclaimer[6].

[1]   Disclaimer is discussed in more detail below at para **18.204** et seq.
[2]   For the position before 1869, see *Boorman v Nash* (1829) 9 B & C 145 and *Gibson v Carruthers* (1841) 8 M & W 321 and for a comparison of the law before and after the Bankruptcy Act 1869, see *Re Sneezum* (1876) 3 Ch D 463 esp at 473 per James LJ and at 475 per Mellish LJ.
[3]   IA 1986, s 315(1) derived from the Bankruptcy Act 1869, s 23 (through the Bankruptcy Act 1883, s 55 and the Bankruptcy Act 1914, s 54).

⁴ IA 1986, ss 285(3) and 382 derived from the Bankruptcy Act 1869, ss 49 and 31 (though note that no distinction was drawn in the Bankruptcy Act 1869 between bankruptcy debts and provable debts).
⁵ Bankruptcy Act 1869, s 12.
⁶ *Re Parnell, ex p Barrell* (1875) 10 Ch App 512.

Application to discharge contract

18.202 Where a contract has been made with a person who is subsequently adjudged bankrupt, the court may, on the application of any other party to the contract, make an order discharging obligations under the contract on such terms as to payment by the applicant or the bankrupt of damages for non-performance or otherwise as appear to the court to be equitable[1]. Any damages payable by the bankrupt by virtue of such an order of the court are provable as a bankruptcy debt[2].

Joint contracts

18.203 Where an undischarged bankrupt is a contractor in respect of any contract (made before he was adjudged bankrupt) jointly with any person, that person may sue or be sued in respect of the contract without the joinder of the bankrupt[1].

M DISCLAIMER OF ONEROUS PROPERTY

Introduction

18.204 The provision enabling the trustee to disclaim onerous property is a measure which gives the trustee a means (1) of disposing of property for which no buyer can be found, (2) of limiting the exposure of the estate to accruing liability in respect of property which gives rise to continuing liability after the commencement of bankruptcy, and (3) since the trustee may have become personally liable in respect of the property on its vesting in him, of defeating any such personal liability on the trustee's part. Thus the power to disclaim assists in the tidy winding up and timely distribution of the estate. For the completion of the administration need not be delayed because the estate includes an asset which the trustee cannot sell. Secondly and perhaps more importantly, where the estate includes property which gives rise to continuing liability or may do so, the trustee is enabled by disclaiming the property to crystallise that loss once and for all. For the disclaimer operates to determine the liability and if any person suffers loss in consequence of the disclaimer, he is entitled to prove in the bankruptcy for the loss but has no other remedy. Thus the actual or potential loss to which the property might give rise is crystallised. The estate may therefore be distributed to the creditors without retaining any part as provision to cover any continuing liability of either the estate or the trustee.

Onerous property

18.205 For the purpose of disclaimer, onerous property means:

(a) any unprofitable contract; and
(b) any other property comprised in the bankrupt's estate which is unsaleable or not readily saleable, or is such that it may give rise to a liability to pay money or perform any other onerous act[1].

1   IA 1986, s 315(2).

18.206 An unprofitable contract is one which carries future obligations which will prejudice the trustee's ability to realise the estate and pay a dividend within a reasonable time[1]. 'Property' takes its meaning from the definition contained in the IA 1986, s 436[2].

1   *Re SSSL Realisations (2002) Ltd* [2006] EWCA Civ 7, [2006] Ch 610, [2007] 1 BCLC 29 at [42].
2   *Re Celtic Extraction Ltd* [2001] Ch 475, [1999] 4 All ER 684, CA (concerning the liquidator's power to disclaim under the IA 1986, s 178 which at s 178(2) contains the same definition of 'onerous property').

When power is exercisable

18.207 Subject to the restrictions on disclaiming property in respect of which a notice to elect has been served and which the trustee has not disclaimed within the permitted period[1] and on disclaiming certain property which the trustee has claimed for the estate[2], the trustee may exercise his power to disclaim onerous property at any time. He may do so even though he has taken possession of the property, endeavoured to sell it or otherwise exercised rights of ownership in relation to it[3].

1   See para **18.216** below.
2   See para **18.213** below.
3   IA 1986, s 315(1).

Lease by assignment of part of premises

18.208 Where the interest in a lease which falls within the estate is an interest obtained by the bankrupt, and hence his trustee, by one or more assignments and is an interest in only part of the premises demised by the original lease, the trustee's power of disclaimer may only be exercised in relation to the relevant part of the premises[1].

1   Landlord and Tenant (Covenants) Act 1995, s 19(2).

Market contracts

18.209 The trustee's power of disclaimer may not be exercised in relation to a market contract or a contract effected by an exchange or clearing house for the purpose of realising property provided as margin in relation to market contracts[1].

[1] Companies Act 1989, s 164(1).

Property which may not be disclaimed

18.210 Disclaimer may not be available because competence to disclaim is overridden by statutory provisions governing the property in question. Thus a waste management licence, although property for the purpose of IA 1986 because marketable, may not be disclaimed because the effect of disclaimer would be contrary to the purposes of the Environmental Protection Act 1990[1].

[1] *Re Mineral Resources Ltd* [1999] 1 All ER 746.

Identifying interested parties

18.211 The trustee needs to be able to identify interested parties in order to serve notice of disclaimer on them. If, in the case of property which the trustee has the right to disclaim, it appears to him that there is some person who claims, or may claim, to have an interest in the property, he may give notice to that person calling on him to declare within 14 days whether he claims any such interest and, if so, the nature and extent of it[1]. Failing compliance with the notice, the trustee is entitled to assume that the person concerned does not have such interest in the property as will prevent or impede its disclaimer[2].

[1] IR 1986, r 6.184(1). For the prescribed form of notice of intended disclaimer to an interested party see IR 1986, rr 6.184, 12.7, Sch 4, Form 6.63.
[2] IR 1986, r 6.184(2).

Exercise of power to disclaim

18.212 Save where leave is required for the disclaimer of certain property claimed by the trustee for the estate, the power to disclaim is exercised by the trustee's filing in court a notice in the prescribed form and giving the prescribed notice to persons interested[1]. A notice of disclaimer should be construed so as to conform with the trustee's intention to get rid of the liability as a continuing liability for onerous property[2]. Except where the property disclaimed is property of a leasehold nature or is property in a dwelling house, the disclaimer is effective on the trustee's filing the prescribed notice in court. In those excepted cases, the effect of the disclaimer is suspended until, in the first case, persons claiming under the bankrupt as underlessee or mortgagee and, in the second case, persons in occupation of, or having a right to occupy, the dwelling house have had an opportunity to apply for a vesting order in respect of the property.

¹   IA 1986, s 315(1); IR 1986, r 6.178.
²   *MEPC plc v Scottish Amicable Life Assurance Society* [1996] BPIR 447, CA.

Property which may not be disclaimed without the leave of the court

18.213 A notice of disclaimer of onerous property may not be given in respect of any property that has been claimed for the estate as after-acquired property¹ or personal property of the bankrupt exceeding reasonable replacement value², except with the leave of the court³. Where the trustee requires the leave of the court, he may apply for it without notice⁴. The application must be accompanied by a report:

(1)   giving such particulars of the property proposed to be disclaimed as enable it to be easily identified;

(2)   setting out the reasons why, the property having been claimed for the estate, the court's leave to disclaim is now applied for; and

(3)   specifying the persons, if any, who have been informed of the trustee's intention to make the application⁵.

¹   Ie under the IA 1986, s 307: see para **14.161** above.
²   Ie under the IA 1986, s 308.
³   IA 1986, s 315(4).
⁴   IR 1986, r 6.182(1).
⁵   IR 1986, r 6.182(2).

18.214 If it is stated in the report that any person's consent to the disclaimer has been signified, a copy of that consent must be annexed to the report¹.

¹   IR 1986, r 6.182(3).

18.215 On consideration of the application, the court may grant the leave applied for; and it may, before granting leave, order that notice of the application be given to all such persons who, if the property is disclaimed, will be entitled to apply for a vesting or other order¹ and fix a date for the hearing of the application².

¹   Ie under the IA 1986, s 320.
²   IR 1986, r 6.182(4).

Notice to elect

18.216 The fact that a trustee may disclaim property might give rise to uncertainty on the part of other persons who are interested in the property which is vulnerable to disclaimer. In order to end that uncertainty persons interested in the property may force the trustee to elect within a fixed period whether he will disclaim or not¹. To put the trustee to his election a person interested in the property must apply in writing to the trustee requiring him to decide whether he will disclaim or not. The application must be made in the form of a 'notice to elect', or a substantially similar form². If the trustee wishes to disclaim the property, he must do so within the period of 28 days³ beginning with the day on which the application was made. If that period expires without a notice of disclaimer having been given in respect of that property, the trustee may not disclaim the property.

1   IA 1986, s 316(1).
2   IR 1986, r 6.183(1), (2). For the prescribed form of notice to elect see IR 1986, rr 6.183, 12.7, Sch 4, Form 6.62.
3   Cf the IA 1986, s 178(5), where the period referred to in corporate insolvency is '28 days or such longer period as the court may allow'. It seems unlikely, however, that the omission of a corresponding provision in individual insolvency was intended to prevent an extension of time. IA 1986, s 376 contains a broad power to extend time limits, which is likely to be exercised in appropriate cases, as to which see *Re Jones, ex p Lovering* (1874) 9 Ch App 586; *Re Richardson, ex p Harris* (1880) 16 Ch D 613.

18.217 In a case where the property concerned cannot be disclaimed by the trustee without leave of the court[1], the trustee must, if he wishes to disclaim, apply within the period of 28 days mentioned above to the court for leave to disclaim. The court must extend the time allowed for giving notice of disclaimer to a date not earlier than the date fixed for the hearing of the application[2].

1   See para **18.213** below.
2   IR 1986, r 6.183(3).

18.218 The trustee is deemed to have adopted any contract[1] which by virtue of the above provisions he is not entitled to disclaim[2].

1   In this context it is possible that 'contract' does not include a lease: see *Re ABC Coupler and Engineering Co Ltd (No 3)* [1970] 1 All ER 650 at 669, per Plowman J.
2   IA 1986, s 316(2).

Filing notice of disclaimer in court

18.219 Where the trustee seeks to disclaim property, the notice of disclaimer must contain such particulars of the property disclaimed as enable it to be easily identified[1]. The notice must be signed by the trustee and filed in court, with a copy; and the trustee must secure that both the notice and the copy are sealed and indorsed with the date of filing[2].

1   IR 1986, r 6.178(1). For the prescribed form of notice of disclaimer under the IA 1986, s 315, see the IR 1986, rr 6.178, 12.7, Sch 4, Form 6.61.
2   IR 1986, r 6.178(2).

18.220 The copy notice must be returned by the court to the trustee as follows:

(1)   if the notice has been delivered at the offices of the court by the trustee in person, it must be handed to him;
(2)   if it has been delivered by some person acting on the trustee's behalf, it must be handed to that person, for immediate transmission to the trustee; and
(3)   otherwise, it must be sent to the trustee by first-class post[1].

1   IR 1986, r 6.178(3).

18.221 The court must indorse on the original notice or record on the file the manner in which the copy notice was returned to the trustee[1]. The date of the prescribed notice is the date which is indorsed on it, and on the copy[2].

1   IR 1986, r 6.178(4).
2   IR 1986, r 6.178(5).

Trustee's duty to serve notice on interested parties

18.222 Within seven days of the notice being returned to him by the court, the trustee must send or give copies, showing the date indorsed on it, to the following persons[1]:

(1)   where the property disclaimed is of a leasehold nature, every person who, to his knowledge, claims under the bankrupt as underlessee or mortgagee[2];

(2)   where the disclaimer is of property in a dwelling house, every person who, to his knowledge, is in occupation of, or claims a right to occupy, the house[3];

(3)   in any case, to every person who, to his knowledge, claims an interest in the disclaimed property, or is under any liability in respect of the property, not being a liability discharged by the disclaimer[4];

(4)   if the disclaimer is of an unprofitable contract, to all such persons as, to his knowledge, are parties to the contract or have interests under it[5].

1   IR 1986, r 6.179(1). For the prescribed form of notice of disclaimer and the relevant indorsements by the court and the trustee see IR 1986, rr 6.179, 12.7, Sch 4, Form 6.61.
2   IR 1986, r 6.179(2).
3   IR 1986, r 6.179(3).
4   IR 1986, r 6.179(4).
5   IR 1986, r 6.179(5).

18.223 If subsequently it comes to the trustee's knowledge that any person has such an interest in the disclaimed property as would have entitled him to receive a copy of the notice in pursuance of heads (1) to (4) above (para **18.222**), the trustee must then forthwith send or give to that person a copy of the notice. Compliance with this provision is not required if the trustee is satisfied that the person has already been made aware of the disclaimer and its date, or the court, on the trustee's application, orders that compliance is not required in that particular case[1].

1   IR 1986, r 6.179(6).

18.224 The trustee disclaiming property may, at any time, give notice of the disclaimer to any persons who in his opinion ought, in the public interest or otherwise, to be informed of it[1].

1   IR 1986, r 6.180.

18.225 The trustee must notify the court from time to time of the persons to whom he has sent copies of the notice of disclaimer, giving their names and addresses, and the nature of their respective interests[1].

1   IR 1986, r 6.181.

When the disclaimer becomes effective

18.226 IA 1986, s 315(1) provides that the trustee may disclaim onerous property by giving the prescribed notice but does not spell out who the notice is to be given to. But this can be gathered from IR 1986, r 6.179 where the persons to whom the notice is to be given or served are set out. The disclaimer will be effective on the notice being given to the persons there mentioned[1]. But in the case of disclaimer of leases and of dwelling houses a further period must elapse after the notice has been given without an application for a vesting order being made before the disclaimer takes effect.

[1] See IR 1986, r 13.3 for provision as to how notice may be given.

When the disclaimer of a lease becomes effective

18.227 The disclaimer of any property of a leasehold nature does not take effect unless a copy of the disclaimer has been served (so far as the trustee is aware of their addresses) on every person claiming under the bankrupt as underlessee or mortgagee and either no application for a vesting order is made with respect to the property before the end of the period of 14 days beginning with the day on which the last such copy of the disclaimer was served or, where such an application has been made, the court directs that the disclaimer is to have effect[1].

[1] IA 1986, s 317(1).

When the disclaimer of a dwelling house becomes effective

18.228 Without prejudice to the statutory provisions as to disclaimer of leaseholds[1], the disclaimer of a dwelling house[2] does not take effect unless a copy of the disclaimer has been served, so far as the trustee is aware of their addresses, on every person in occupation of or claiming a right to occupy the dwelling house[3] and either no application for a court order vesting disclaimed property is made with respect to the property before the end of the period of 14 days beginning with the day on which the last notice served under the above provisions was served, or where such an application has been made, the court directs that the disclaimer is to take effect[4].

[1] See the IA 1986, s 317.
[2] For the meaning of 'dwelling house' see the IA 1986, s 385(1).
[3] Ie under the IA 1986, s 320.
[4] IA 1986, s 318.

Presumption that disclaimer valid

18.229 Any disclaimer of property by the trustee is presumed valid and effective, unless it is proved that he has been in breach of his duty with respect to the giving of notice of disclaimer or otherwise under the IA 1986, ss 315–319 or the IR 1986, rr 6.178–6.186[1].

[1] IR 1986, r 6.185.

Effect of disclaimer

18.230 A disclaimer operates so as to determine, as from the date of the disclaimer, the rights, interests and liabilities of the bankrupt and his estate in or in respect of the property disclaimed and discharges the trustee from all personal liability in respect of that property from the commencement of his trusteeship, but does not, except so far as is necessary for the purpose of releasing the bankrupt, the bankrupt's estate and the trustee from any liability, affect the rights or liabilities of any other person[1]. The legislative intention underlying this provision is that the disclaimer should do the least disturbance to existing rights and liabilities as is consistent with achieving the purpose of determining the rights, interests and liabilities of the bankrupt and his estate and of discharging the trustee from personal liability[2]. Thus where a trustee disclaimed shares in respect of which the bankrupt had executed a transfer to another person by way of security, the disclaimer only operated so as to discharge the bankrupt's rights in and liabilities under the shares; it did not affect the interest in the shares of the transferee[3]. Where a consequence of the disclaimer of onerous property comprised in a waste management licence is to divest the licensee of any interest in a fund held on trust for purposes connected with the management of the waste and no other person had any interest in the fund, the money went to the Crown as bona vacantia[4].

[1] IA 1986, s 315(3); *Hindcastle Ltd v Barbara Attenborough Associates Ltd* [1997] AC 70, [1996] 1 All ER 737.
[2] See eg per Vaughan Williams LJ in *Re Carter & Ellis, ex p Savill Brothers* [1905] 1 KB 735, 742.
[3] *Wise v Lansdell* [1921] 1 Ch 420.
[4] *Environment Agency v Hillridge Ltd* [2003] EWHC 3023 (Ch), [2004] 2 BCLC 358.

Effect of disclaiming a lease

18.231 As discussed above, a disclaimer operates to determine the interests and liabilities of the bankrupt and his estate in the property disclaimed and to release the trustee from personal liability but does not affect his rights or liabilities of any other person, except so far as is necessary for the purpose of releasing the bankrupt, his estate and the trustee. Where the property disclaimed is an interest under a lease, there may be persons other than the bankrupt interested in or liable in respect of a lease and the extent to which such persons' interests or liabilities should be affected has raised difficult questions. The difficulty of the questions has been much reduced by the decision of the House of Lords in *Hindcastle Ltd v Barbara Attenborough Associates Ltd*[1]. The structure and much of the content of the following discussion is drawn from the speech of Lord Nicholls of Birkenhead in that case.

[1] [1997] AC 70, [1996] 1 All ER 737.

Where the bankrupt is the original tenant

18.232 The simplest case is that which obtains where the bankrupt is the original tenant under the lease and is in possession at the commencement of the bankruptcy without having created any further interest in the lease, whether by sub-lease, mortgage or otherwise, and for whose liability under the lease no-one stands surety. When his trustee disclaims the lease, the lease is determined and the reversion expectant on the determination of the lease is accelerated[1]. With the determination of the lease ends the bankrupt's liability to pay rent. Hence the landlord cannot prove for future rent. Instead he is given a statutory right to compensation for his loss[2]. The determination of the lease is not affected by any subsequent annulment of the bankruptcy[3].

1 *Hindcastle Ltd v Barbara Attenborough Associates Ltd* [1997] AC 70, [1996] 1 All ER 737; *Re Finley, ex p Clothmakers' Company* (1888) 21 QBD 475, 485.
2 IA 1986, s 315(5).
3 *Re Hyams, ex p Lindsay v Hyams* (1923) 93 LJ Ch 184.

Where a third party is liable concurrently with the bankrupt tenant

18.233 The next question is how far the effect of the disclaimer should reach in cases where there are other persons apart from the bankrupt tenant who have liabilities in respect of the lease which has been disclaimed. Take the case where the original tenant remained in possession at the commencement of his bankruptcy but his liabilities under the lease were guaranteed by a surety. It was plain that the surety would be liable to the lessor under the guarantee for liabilities which had accrued before any disclaimer took effect, but in *Stacey v Hill*[1] the Court of Appeal held that the surety was released from liability in respect of liabilities which would have arisen after the date when the disclaimer took effect; for after that date there was no lease under which such liabilities might accrue. That decision was overruled by the House of Lords in *Hindcastle Ltd v Barbara Attenborough*[2]. Lord Nicholls of Birkenhead explained that the statute was to be considered as a deeming provision: 'when the lease is disclaimed it is determined and the reversion accelerated but the rights and liabilities of others, such as guarantors and original tenants, are to remain *as though* the lease had continued and not been determined[3]'.

1 [1901] 1 KB 660.
2 [1997] AC 70, [1996] 1 All ER 737.
3 [1997] AC 70 at 88G.

18.234 In *Warnford Investments Ltd v Duckworth*[1] the bankrupt, whose trustees had disclaimed, was the assignee of the lease from the original tenant. The issue was whether the original tenant remained liable on his covenant to the landlord despite the disclaimer. Megarry V-C held that he was. Since *Stacey v Hill*[2] was good law at the time of this decision, it was necessary to distinguish the position of the original tenant from the position of a surety in order to reach the conclusion. The distinction identified was that whereas the guarantor's liability was always secondary to the liability of another, the original tenant was primarily liable for the period when he was in possession. In *Hindcastle v Barbara Attenborough*[3] Lord Nicholls stated that such differences as there are between an original tenant and a guarantor were not material. Thus, although the conclusion in *Warnford Investments Ltd v Duckworth* would still be reached, the reasoning needs to be treated with caution.

1   [1979] Ch 127, [1978] 2 All ER 517.
2   [1901] 1 KB 660.
3   [1997] AC 70, [1996] 1 All ER 737.

Where third parties hold interests derived from the interest of the
bankrupt tenant

18.235 Next there may be persons who have an interest which has been created out of the lease which has been disclaimed. The prime example is a sub-tenant. There are three relationships to consider. First, as between the bankrupt tenant and his lessor, the position is the same as if there were no sub-lease: that is that the bankrupt's liability, and that of his trustee, is determined from the date of disclaimer. Secondly, as between the bankrupt tenant and his sub-tenant, the bankrupt's rights, interests and liabilities are determined and the extinction of the bankrupt tenant's rights involves the extinction of the sub-tenant's liabilities on his covenants[1]. But, thirdly as between the sub-tenant and the lessor, the sub-tenant is entitled to remain in possession of the demised premises so long as he observes the terms of the lease. If he does not, the lessor will be entitled to forfeit the lease or levy distress in respect of rent due under it. In *Hindcastle Ltd v Barbara Attenborough* Lord Nicholls stated that the sub-tenant's interest is not determined but continues unaffected by the determination of the tenant's interest: 'the sub-tenant holds his estate on the same terms, and subject to the same rights and obligations, as *would* be applicable *if* the tenant's interest had continued[2]'. This statement needs some elaboration. For so long as the sub-tenant observes the obligations of the bankrupt tenant, the sub-tenant is entitled to remain in possession. But the sub-tenant does not stand precisely in the position of the bankrupt tenant. For, if no further step were taken, the lessor would not be entitled to sue the sub-tenant for any arrears of rent which accrued after the disclaimer because the sub-tenant would not be liable under any covenant to the lessor in respect of the rent. But a vesting order may be sought, either on the application of the lessor or the sub-tenant, pursuant to which the sub-tenant may be made liable to the same liabilities as the bankrupt tenant was under on the date when the petition was presented or subject to such liabilities as the sub-tenant would have been under if the lease had been assigned to him on the same date[3].

1   *Re Finley, ex p Clothworkers' Company* (1888) 21 QBD 475, 485–486.
2   [1997] AC 70 at 89G.
3   IA 1986, s 321(1).

18.236 Where the bankrupt tenant has mortgaged his interest in the lease, which is the subject of the disclaimer, the mortgagee will be in the same position as a sub-tenant.

Effect of disclaiming freehold property

18.237 Where the trustee disclaims freehold property, title to the property automatically vests in the Crown by escheat. The vesting of title by escheat in the Crown does not determine any subordinate interests but the Crown does not, by virtue of escheat alone, assume the liabilities of the freeholder to lessees or mortgagees of the freehold. In order to become subject to any liability the Crown must take possession or exercise dominion over the land[1]. Thus whether the Crown incurs liability in respect of such subordinate interests depends on the same test as is applicable in determining whether it becomes subject to personal liability in respect of rentcharges where land subject to rentcharges is disclaimed[2].

1   *Scmlla Properties Ltd v Gesso Properties (BVI) Ltd* [1995] BCC 793. This decision confirms the tentative view expressed by Jessel MR in *Re Mercer and Moore* (1880) 14 Ch D 287. See also *Re Levy, ex p Walton* (1881) 17 Ch D 746, CA and *Re Nottingham General Cemetery Co* [1955] Ch 683.
2   See para **18.238**.

Effect of disclaiming land subject to rentcharge

18.238   Where, in consequence of the disclaimer of any land subject to a rentcharge, that land vests by operation of law in the Crown or any other person ('the proprietor'), the proprietor and the proprietor's successors in title are not subject to any personal liability in respect of any sums becoming due under the rentcharge before the proprietor, or some person claiming under him, has taken possession or control of the land or has entered into occupation of it[1].

1   IA 1986, s 319.

Losses suffered in consequence of disclaimer

18.239   Any person sustaining loss or damage in consequence of the operation of a disclaimer is deemed to be a creditor of the bankrupt to the extent of the loss or damage and accordingly may prove for the loss or damage as a bankruptcy debt[1]. Thus although the relevant loss may be suffered by the party against whom the disclaimer operates after the commencement of the bankruptcy, he is enabled, for what it may be worth, to prove with the general body of unsecured creditors in the bankruptcy.

1   IA 1986, s 315(5).

Measure of the loss

18.240   The person suffering the loss is entitled to prove against the estate for the amount which he would have had a right to recover or to sue for, if he had not been deprived of that right by the disclaimer[1]. Assessing the loss which a person suffers in consequence of the disclaimer involves precisely the same exercise as has to be undertaken when assessing the damages for a breach of contract as, for example, where one party has repudiated a contract and the other party has accepted that repudiation as terminating the contract and he then exercises his secondary right to claim damages[2]. Thus where the property disclaimed was a lease and the loss suffered by the landlord is the difference between the future rent which would have been received under the lease had there been no disclaimer and the letting value of the premises over the period of the unexpired term. Further, a discount must be given for the early receipt of payment in calculating the landlord's present loss.

[1]   *Re Hide, ex p Llynvi Coal and Iron Co* (1871) 7 Ch App 28.
[2]   *Christopher Moran Holdings Ltd v Bairstow* [2000] 2 AC 172, [1999] 1 All ER 673, HL.

18.241   Where the trustee disclaimed partly paid up shares, the company was entitled to prove in respect of the whole amount which it could call on a solvent shareholder to pay for such shares[1].

[1]   *Re Hallett, ex p National Insurance Co* (1894) 1 Mans 380. Contrast *Re Hooley, ex p United Ordnance and Engineering Co Ltd* [1899] 2 QB 579 where the property disclaimed was a contract to subscribe for shares and the question was what was the loss suffered by reason of the non-performance by the bankrupt of that contract.

18.242   In assessing the loss, the effect of any vesting order must be taken into account[1].

[1]   IA 1986, s 320(5).

Vesting orders

18.243   Where a trustee has disclaimed onerous property, the court has power to make an order vesting the property which has been disclaimed in a person who has applied (and has standing to do so) for the property to be vested in him[1]. As noted above, where the property disclaimed is property of a leasehold nature or property in a dwelling house, the disclaimer does not take effect until persons entitled to apply have been notified of the disclaimer and time for their making an application for a vesting order has lapsed[2].

[1]   IA 1986, s 320.
[2]   See the IA 1986, ss 317 and 318.

Who may apply for a vesting order

18.244   A vesting order may be sought by:

(a)   any person who claims an interest in the disclaimed property;
(b)   any person who is under a liability in respect of the disclaimed property which is not discharged by the disclaimer; or
(c)   where the disclaimed property is property in a dwelling house, any person who at the time when the bankruptcy petition was presented was in occupation of or was entitled to occupy the dwelling house[1].

[1]   IA 1986, s 320(2).

18.245   Relevant interests include that of the landlord of the premises where the lease by which the premises are demised has been disclaimed or any sub-tenant or mortgagee[1], or that of a local authority holding a charge over disclaimed freehold property to secure sums expended by the authority under legislation authorising it to render the premises safe at its own expense and to recover the payment from the owner of the property[2]. The interest claimed need not be a proprietary interest. Thus the interest of a statutory tenant in a disclaimed lease suffices[3]. Where the claimant relies on a liability, the liability must arise in respect of the disclaimed property itself. Thus liabilities for past breaches of covenant under a lease disclaimed after that liability had arisen do not suffice[4]. Nor do liabilities under a guarantee given to a bank entitle the guarantors to apply for a vesting order in respect of chattels held by the bank as security for the underlying debt[5].

[1]   *Re Finley, ex p Clothmakers' Co* (1888) 21 QBD 475, CA; *Re Britton* (1889) 6 Morr 130; *Re Baker, ex p Lupton* [1901] 2 KB 628, CA; *Re AE Realisations (1985) Ltd* [1987] 3 All ER 83, [1988] 1 WLR 200. An original lessee, compelled to pay the rent, following the bankruptcy of an assignee may apply: *Re Morgan, ex p Morgan* (1889) 22 QBD 592, but this situation will now be less frequent because of the Landlord and Tenant (Covenants) Act 1995.
[2]   *Hackney London Borough Council v Crown Estate Comrs* [1996] BPIR 428.
[3]   *Re Vedmay Ltd* [1994] 1 BCLC 676.
[4]   *Re No 1 London Ltd* [1991] BCLC 501.
[5]   *Re Spirit Motorsport Ltd* [1997] BPIR 288.

In whose favour a vesting order may be made

18.246   Subject to the further restrictions applicable where the property disclaimed is of a leasehold nature, the court may make an order on such terms as it thinks fit for the vesting of the disclaimed property in, or for its delivery to:

(a)   any person entitled to the disclaimed property or a trustee[1] for such person;
(b)   where it appears to the court that it would be just to do so for the purpose of compensating him in respect of his liability[2], any person subject to a liability in respect of the disclaimed property which is not discharged by the disclaimer or a trustee for such person; or
(c)   where the disclaimed property is property in a dwelling house, any person who at the time when the bankruptcy petition was presented was in occupation of or was entitled to occupy the dwelling house[3].

[1]   For an example of an order vesting property in a trustee see *Re Holmes, ex p Ashworth* [1908] 2 KB 812.
[2]   IA 1986, s 320(3).
[3]   IA 1986, s 320(2).

18.247   Where a landlord applies for a vesting order, he is not entitled to obtain an order that the lease be vested in him (so as to enforce the sub-lease granted by the insolvent tenant against the sub-tenant) because he is not entitled to the disclaimed property[1]. That is to say that he is not entitled to possession of the premises demised under the disclaimed lease. For the sub-tenant is entitled to possession against the landlord as head-lessor so long as he, the sub-tenant, performs the terms of the head-lease and until he refuses to accept a vesting order[2], in which event he is excluded from all interest in the property[3].

[1]   *ITM Corpn Ltd, Re Sterling Estates Ltd v Pickard UK Ltd* [1998] BPIR 402.

2   *Re Cock, ex p Shilson* (1887) 20 QBD 343; *Re Finley, ex p Clothmakers' Co* (1888) 21 QBD 475, CA.
3   IA 1986, s 321(4).

Special rules relating to vesting orders of leases

18.248 In the case of a lease persons who might apply for a vesting order include a lessee who has assigned but remains liable on his covenants[1] and a surety under the original lease[2]. The court may make such order as it thinks fit for the vesting of the disclaimed property in, or its delivery to:

(a)   a person entitled to the property or his trustee;

(b)   a person subject to a liability in respect of the property which is not discharged by the disclaimer or his trustee; or

(c)   where the disclaimed property is property in a dwelling house, any person who at the time when the bankruptcy petition was presented was in occupation of, or entitled to occupy, the dwelling house[3].

1   *Re Morgan, ex p Morgan* (1889) 22 QBD 592.
2   *Re AE Realisations (1985) Ltd* [1987] 3 All ER 83, [1988] 1 WLR 200.
3   IA 1986, s 320(3).

18.249 As regards paragraph (a) (para **18.248**), the entitlement must be by virtue of some interest which was held jointly with, or derived from, the bankrupt. In the case of a dwelling house, the result of the application may be to create an interest which will vest in a person who previously had neither a legal nor an equitable interest in the property. Indeed the applicant, if in occupation when the bankruptcy petition was presented, need not even have any right of occupation entitling him to do so, such as might, for example, arise under the Family Law Act 1996.

18.250 Where following disclaimer the court makes an order vesting property of a leasehold nature in a person who has applied for a vesting order under s 320 of the Act, the order must be made on terms the purpose of which is to protect the landlord. It must make the person in whom the lease vests either:

(a)   subject to the same liabilities and obligations as the bankrupt was subject to under the lease on the day the bankruptcy petition was presented; or

(b)   if the court thinks fit, subject to the same liabilities and obligations as that person would be subject to if the lease had been assigned to him on that day[1].

1   IA 1986, s 321(1).

18.251 The main difference between the two forms of vesting order are that an assignee is only bound by covenants which run with the land and only for breaches occurring after the assignment and before the assignee assigns over and that the liability of an assignee is a liability by privity of estate not privity of contract[1]. Thus in *Re Walker, ex p Mills*[2] where the bankrupt lessee had breached covenants under the lease and the mortgagee of the bankrupt lessee's interest sought a vesting order, the court made the order on terms that the mortgagee took subject to the liabilities of the bankrupt. For, had the lessee sought to forfeit the lease against the bankrupt lessee on the basis of his breaches of covenant, payment of compensation for those breaches would have been a condition of granting the relief; it would be wrong to deprive the landlord of that benefit when the effect of the vesting order would deprive him of the right to re-enter. However, where there were no past breaches the vesting order might be made in the form of an assignment to the person seeking it since that would neither cause injustice to the landlord nor give an advantage to the person in whom the lease is to vest[3].

[1]   *Re Walker, ex p Mills* (1895) 64 LJQB 783 per Vaughan Williams J at 785.
[2]   (1895) 64 LJQB 783.
[3]   *Re Carter and Ellis, ex p Savill Bros* [1905] 1 KB 735, CA.

18.252 More specifically, under the first basis the person in whom the lease was vested would (1) become liable on the bankrupt's personal covenants as well as those which would pass on assignment, (2) become liable for breaches of covenant arising before the date of presentation of the petition, and (3) if the bankrupt is the original tenant under a tenancy granted before 1 January 1996[1], remain liable to the landlord on the covenants in the lease even after he assigns the lease. Under the second basis the person accepting the vesting order will avoid all these categories of potential liability and will only be liable on the covenants in the lease which run with the land or, in a lease granted on or after 1 January 1996, the tenant covenants by privity of estate while he is the tenant in possession[2].

[1]   Ie a tenancy granted before the Landlord and Tenant (Covenants) Act 1995 came into force.
[2]   See the Landlord and Tenant (Covenants) Act 1995, s 5.

18.253 An order may be made in relation to part of any property comprised in a lease, in which case the vesting order must still be made on terms as described above but the terms need only relate to the part of the property to which the order relates[1].

[1]   IA 1986, s 321(2).

18.254 The court shall not make an order vesting any property in a person whose application is based solely on the fact that he is subject to a liability in respect of the property unless it appears just to do so for the purpose of compensating him for the loss he suffers because of the disclaimer[1]. In *Re AE Realisations (1985) Ltd*[2] Vinelot J declined to make a vesting order on the application of a surety because such an order would not achieve any purpose which would not be achieved by the surety's taking a direct lease from the landlord as the surety was bound by covenant to the landlord to do.

[1]   IA 1986, s 320(4).
[2]   [1987] 3 All ER 83, [1988] 1 WLR 200.

Court's power to impose vesting order

18.255 It may be that no person who is entitled to apply under IA 1986, s 320 is willing to accept a vesting order on the terms required by the Act[1]. If so, the court may nevertheless make an order vesting the estate or interest of the bankrupt in any person who is liable to perform the lessee's covenants in the lease[2]. This power may be exercised whether that person is liable personally or in a representative capacity or whether solely or jointly with the bankrupt. In making such an order[3] the court may vest the bankrupt's estate or interest in such a person freed and discharged from all estates, incumbrances and interests created by the bankrupt.

1.   Ie those set out in IA 1986, s 321(1).
2.   IA 1986, s 321(3).
3.   Ie pursuant to IA 1986, s 321(3).

Effect of declining to accept vesting order

18.256 If any person declines to accept a vesting order, he is excluded from all interest in the property[1].

1.   IA 1986, s 321(4).

Effect of vesting order

18.257 An order vesting property in any person under the provisions described here need not be completed by any conveyance, assignment or transfer[1]. Where a vesting order is made following disclaimer of a lease which is registered under the Land Registration Act 2002, the disposition caused by the order must be registered and will not take effect at law until it is[2]. The vesting order must accompany the application for registration[3].

1.   IA 1986, s 320(6).
2.   Land Registration Act 2002, s 27(1) and (5).
3.   Land Registration Rules 2003, SI 2003/1417, r 161(2).

Unclaimed surplus

18.258 In *Lee v Lee*[1] a vesting order in respect of a long residential lease was made in favour of a mortgagee. Following sale of the lease by the mortgagee there was a surplus after satisfaction of the mortgage debt. The mortgagee expressed no interest in retaining the surplus but there was a dispute between the trustee and the bankrupt's wife as to its disposal. The wife claimed a half interest in the lease. The court directed that half of the surplus be made available for immediate distribution to the creditors and the other half be retained pending resolution of the wife's claim. The question whether the mortgagee was obliged to return the surplus to the trustee was not debated. Although the conduct of the mortgagee was commendably fair, it is, at least, open to question whether it was obliged to do so since once the vesting order was made, the lease vested absolutely in the mortgagee and the trustee had no equity of redemption by reference to which he might insist that the surplus be paid into the estate.

¹   [1999] BPIR 926, CA.

Procedure

18.259 An application by any person for a vesting order must be made within three months of the applicant becoming aware of the disclaimer, or of his receiving a copy of the trustee's notice of disclaimer[1], whichever is the earlier[2].

¹   Ie a notice sent under the IR 1986, r 6.179.
²   IR 1986, r 6.186(1), (2).

18.260 With his application the applicant must file in court an affidavit:

(1)   stating whether he applies as a person who claims an interest in the disclaimed property[1] or a person who is under a liability in respect of the disclaimed property, not being a liability discharged by the disclaimer[2], or as a person who, at the time when the bankruptcy petition was presented, was in occupation of or entitled to occupy the dwelling house[3];

(2)   specifying the date on which he received a copy of the trustee's notice of disclaimer, or otherwise became aware of the disclaimer; and

(3)   specifying the grounds of his application and the order which he desires the court to make[4].

¹   Ie under the IA 1986, s 320(2)(a).
²   Ie under the IA 1986, s 320(2)(b).
³   Ie under the IA 1986, s 320(2)(c).
⁴   IR 1986, r 6.186(3).

18.261 The court must fix a venue for the hearing of the application and the applicant must, not later than seven days before the date fixed, give to the trustee notice of the venue, accompanied by copies of the application and the affidavit in support[1].

¹   IR 1986, r 6.186(4).

18.262 On the hearing of the application, the court may give directions as to the other persons, if any, who should be sent or given notice of the application and the grounds on which it is made[1]; and sealed copies of any order made on the application must be sent by the court to the applicant and the trustee[2].

¹   IR 1986, r 6.186(5).
²   IR 1986, r 6.186(6).

18.263 In a case where the property disclaimed is of a leasehold nature or is property in a dwelling house, and the effect of the disclaimer is suspended[1], a direction must be included in the court's order giving effect to the disclaimer, unless at the time when the order is issued other applications for vesting orders are pending in respect of the same property[2].

1   Ie under the IA 1986, ss 317 or 318.
2   IR 1986, r 6.186(7).

N TRUSTEE'S QUALIFIED IMMUNITY FROM LIABILITY FOR WRONGFUL INTERFERENCE WITH PROPERTY OF THIRD PARTIES

Qualified immunity from wrongful interference

18.264 Where the trustee seizes or disposes of any property which is not comprised in the bankrupt's estate and at the time of the seizure or disposal the trustee believes and has reasonable grounds for believing that he is entitled, whether in pursuance of an order of the court or otherwise, to seize or dispose of that property, he is not liable to any person in respect of any loss or damage resulting therefrom, except in so far as it is caused by the negligence of the trustee[1].

1   IA 1986, s 304(3).

Relevant property

18.265 Although the potential liability is more likely to arise in connection with chattels, the context does not require 'property' to be given a more restricted meaning than is conferred on it by the definition given in the IA 1986, s 436. Land, or interests in it, may certainly be disposed of. An interest in land which the bankrupt held on trust for another person would not be comprised in the bankrupt's estate[1] but if the bankrupt was the sole registered proprietor and no-one informed the trustee of the existence of the trust, then the trustee might well be in a position to rely on the immunity to defeat the beneficiary's claim.

1   IA 1986, s 283(3)(a).

Lien

18.266 If the rightful owner makes his claim to the property or its proceeds of sale while the property or proceeds remain in the hands of the trustee, the trustee has a lien on the property or proceeds for such expenses of the bankruptcy as were incurred in connection with the seizure or disposal[1].

1   IA 1986, s 304(3).

O SUPERVISION OF THE COURT

General control

General control of the court

18.267 Every bankruptcy is under the general control of the court and, subject to the provisions of the IA 1986 relating to the insolvency of individuals, the court has full power to decide all questions of priorities and all other questions, whether of law or fact, arising in any bankruptcy[1].

1 IA 1986, s 363(1).

Court's general power to give directions to the bankrupt

18.268 Without prejudice to its other powers the court may make directions against an undischarged bankrupt or a discharged bankrupt whose estate is still being administered for the purposes of his bankruptcy or the administration of his estate[1]. Failure to comply with such directions is a contempt of court[2].

1 IA 1986, s 363(2).
2 IA 1986, s 363(4).

Trustee's power to seek directions

General power to seek directions

18.269 The trustee may apply to the court for directions in relation to any particular matter arising under the bankruptcy[1]. The proceedings in which directions are sought need not have been initiated by the trustee. What is required is that the matter is properly before the court on the application of someone with a sufficient interest to invoke the court's jurisdiction[2]. Where directions are sought, the first question is whether the proposed course of action is genuinely for the benefit of the estate. The court will tend to defer to the trustee's view on that question[3].

1 IA 1986, s 303(2).
2 *Re A & C Supplies Ltd* [1998] 1 BCLC 603, 608.
3 *Re Omar (a bankrupt)* [1999] BPIR 1001.

Power to seek directions against bankrupt

18.270 Either the trustee or the official receiver may apply to the court for directions to be made against an undischarged bankrupt or a discharged bankrupt whose estate is still being administered for the purposes of his bankruptcy or the administration of his estate[1]. For example, in *Buchler v Al-Midani (No 3)* an order was made preventing the bankrupt from taking steps in foreign proceedings[2].

1 IA 1986, s 363(2) and (3).
2 [2006] BPIR 881.

The rule in Ex p James

Nature of the rule in Ex p James[1]

18.271 In *Government of India, Ministry of Finance (Revenue Division) v Taylor* Lord Keith of Avonholm said that the rule in *Ex p James*, by which the court requires from the trustee in bankruptcy as its officer the highest standard of fair and honest behaviour, is best expressed as a discretionary power of the court[2]. Whether or not it is strictly correct to describe it in those terms, the rule arises, and applies to the trustee, because he is an officer of the court and therefore it is discussed here amongst provisions relating to the supervision of the bankruptcy by the court.

1   *Re Condon, ex p James* (1874) 9 Ch App 609.
2   [1955] AC 491 at 551.

The decision in Ex p James[1]

18.272 James was a judgment creditor who, without notice of the bankruptcy proceedings and before the presentation of a petition, had completed an execution in respect of his judgment. He was asked by the trustee of Condon's estate to pay to him the proceeds of the execution and threatened with proceedings if he did not. In response, James paid the proceeds to the trustee. Subsequently, in different proceedings, it was held that an execution creditor in such a position was entitled to keep the proceeds of execution. The question which arose was whether James was entitled to recover the money paid over from the trustee. It was held that he was, even though the money was paid over under a mistake of law (in which case at that time it was not ordinarily recoverable[2]) James LJ stated:

> 'I am of opinion that a trustee in bankruptcy is an officer of the court. He has inquisitorial powers given him by the court, and the court regards himself as its officer, and he is to hold money in his hands upon trust for its equitable distribution among the creditors. The court, then, finding that he has in his hands money which belongs to someone else, ought to set an example to the world by paying it to the person entitled to it. In my opinion the court of bankruptcy ought to be as honest as other people.'

1   (1874) 9 Ch App 609, 614.
2   See now *Kleinwort Benson Ltd v Lincoln City Council* [1999] 2 AC 349, [1998] 4 All ER 513 for the ruling by the House of Lords that money paid under a mistake of law is recoverable.

Moral basis of the rule

18.273 In speaking of money which belongs in equity to someone else, James LJ was using the words in a general sense and not the sense of money which in a court of equity would belong to someone else, ie money over which the claimant had equitable rights. 'He meant money which in point of moral justice and honest dealing belongs to someone else'[1]. Throughout all the cases runs the theme that the trustee, as an officer of the court, must act 'in an honourable and high-minded way'[2].

1   *Re Tyler, ex p the Official Receiver* [1907] 1 KB 865, 673, Buckley LJ.
2   *Re Carnac, ex p Simmonds* (1885) 16 QBD 308; *Re Thellusson, ex p Abdy* [1919] 2 KB 735; *Scranton's Trustee v Pearse* [1922] 2 Ch 87; *Re Wigzell, ex p Hart* [1921] 2 KB 835; *Re Multi Guarantee Co Ltd* [1987] BCLC 257; *Customs and Excise Comrs v TH Knitwear* [1988] Ch 275, [1998] 1 All ER 860; *Jones v Patel* [2002] BPIR 919, CA.

18.274 The required turpitude may affect the trustee because he obtained the money by some act of which the court considers it would be unfair for him to take advantage. That was the situation in *Ex p James* itself. Or, even though the trustee did not prompt the person who paid the money to do so, because it would be morally unfair for him to retain the money or to retain, without making due compensation, the benefit which has accrued in consequence of its payment. In *Re Thellusson, ex p Abdy*[1] a loan was made to the bankrupt after the bankruptcy process had commenced. The lender was unaware that the bankruptcy process had begun. The Court of Appeal held that the trustee was not entitled to retain the money lent. This case might be compared with the constructive trust which may arise in respect of payments made to a person on the brink of insolvency[2]. There is similarity in the situations in that the remedy is imposed in virtue of the presumed fact that had the person paying the money to the insolvent known of the insolvency, he would not have paid it and it is unconscionable for the trustee to retain the money for the benefit of the creditors. But, perhaps, there is a difference in that the rule in *Ex p James* will not apply where the payment has been made before the onset of insolvency[3], whereas the constructive trust may arise where the payment was made immediately before that onset. In *Re Tyler*[4] the bankrupt's wife paid premiums under a life policy which accrued for the benefit of the estate. The Court of Appeal held that the trustee must repay the premiums to the wife.

[1]   [1919] 2 KB 735.
[2]   *Neste Oy v Lloyds Bank, The Tiiskeri, Nestegas and Enskeri* [1983] 2 Lloyd's Rep 658; *Re Japan Leasing (Europe) Ltd* [1999] BPIR 911 discussed at para **14.109**.
[3]   See para **18.279** below.
[4]   [1907] 1 KB 865.

Relationship with mistake of law

18.275 Some of the cases where the rule has been successfully invoked are cases where the person who paid the money which he seeks to recover made the payment because he was mistaken about the law. Before the decision of the House of Lords in *Kleinwort Benson Ltd v Lincoln City Council*[1], the law was, or was thought to be, that (subject to various exceptions) money paid under a mistake of law was not recoverable. There will now be cases in which the claimant will be entitled as a matter of law to recover funds where previously he would have had to rely on the rule in *Ex p James*. But the operation of the rule is not dependent on there having been a mistake of law[2] and therefore it is not rendered obsolete by the decision in *Kleinwort Benson Ltd v Lincoln City Council*. It is unlikely that any mistake will have been made or acted on where the rule is relied on by way of defence to a claim by the trustee to some asset.

[1]   [1999] 2 AC 349, [1998] 4 All ER 513.
[2]   *Re Tyler, ex p the Official Receiver* [1907] 1 KB 865.

Indefinite ambit of the rule

18.276 Since the rule is set on an expressly moral basis and overrides legal rights its ambit is necessarily indefinite. 'Questions of ethical propriety have always been and will always be the subject of honest differences among honest men'[1]. As a rule based in ethical propriety, it is anomalous[2]. But some limitations may be identified.

[1] *Re Wigzell, ex p Hart* [1921] 2 KB 835, 845 (Salter J at first instance) and 853 (Lord Sterndale MR approving in the Court of Appeal).
[2] *Customs and Excise Comrs v TH Knitwear Ltd* [1988] BCLC 195, 205.

18.277 The rule does not apply simply because the trustee seeks to recover property for the estate which previously had no value to the estate because there was no unencumbered equity in the property[1].

[1] *Boorer v Trustee in Bankruptcy of Boorer* [2002] BPIR 21; *Mountney v Treharne* [2002] BPIR 556 (first instance); the point was not raised on appeal [2002] EWCA Civ 1174, [2003] Ch 135, [2002] BPIR 1126.

Need for enrichment of the estate

18.278 In the cases where the rule has been successfully invoked, the estate has been enlarged by some asset, usually money, in respect of which the claim is made[1]. In *Re Wyvern Developments Ltd*[2], Templeman J relied on the rule in *Ex p James* as an alternative ground to justify the honouring by the official receiver of a promise to join in the sale of land previously contracted to be sold to the company in liquidation whose assets he was administering. The company had not paid under the contract by which it had agreed to purchase and the vendor wished to sell to a third party. Although the vendor was not seeking the recoupment of any asset, Templeman J found that there would be enrichment of the estate because, in so far as the land was worth more than the price agreed between the vendor and the third party purchaser, if the official receiver did not honour his promise to join in and permit that sale, the company would be enriched by the difference between the value and the price at the expense of the third party purchaser.

[1] *Government of India, Ministry of Finance (Revenue Division) v Taylor* [1955] AC 491 at 551; *Re Clark (a bankrupt), ex p the Trustee v Texaco Ltd* [1975] 1 All ER 453, [1975] 1 WLR 559.
[2] [1974] 1 WLR 1097, 1105.

Unsecured creditors may not rely on the rule

18.279 'The rule is not to be used merely to confer a preference on an otherwise unsecured creditor, but to provide relief for a person who would otherwise be without any'[1]. At the root of this limitation on the ambit of the rule is a distinction noted by Younger LJ in *Re Wigzell*[2] between transactions initiated by the bankrupt and transactions initiated by the trustee. If the bankrupt tricks money out of another person, then (assuming that it is not held subject to a constructive or other trust) there is no necessary reason why the money should not be available for all the creditors who may equally have been tricked by the bankrupt. But, if the trick has been played by the trustee, then, because he acts in the interest of the general body of creditors, they are affected by the equity to which the trustee's conduct gives rise and should not

18.279 *Administration of the estate*

obtain the benefit of the asset which the trick has acquired for the estate. Similarly, in *Re Sandiford (No 2), Italo-Canadian Corpn Ltd v Sandiford*, Clauson J remarked that his attention had not been drawn to any case in which the principle of *Ex p James* had been applied so as to order a trustee in bankruptcy to return money which, before the bankruptcy began, came into and became mixed with and indistinguishable from the rest of the bankrupt's property[3].

¹ *Re Clark (a bankrupt), ex p the Trustee v Texaco Ltd* [1975] 1 WLR 559, 564. See also *Re Multi Guarantee Co Ltd* [1987] BCLC 257 where this bar to the operation of the rule is referred to though not debated.
² [1921] 2 KB 835.
³ [1935] Ch 681, 691.

18.280 Examples of creditors being left to prove in the bankruptcy include *Re Shackleton, ex p Whittaker*[1] in which the bankrupt had bought wool on credit between the filing of the petition and the receiving order being made on it. He made no misrepresentation about his ability to pay or status. Despite the hardship, the seller was left to his remedy of proving in the bankruptcy as an unsecured creditor. The court discussed whether there was any misrepresentation and found that there was none. But, if there had been a misrepresentation, that would not have brought the rule in *Ex p James* into play but would have given the seller grounds on which he could rescind the contract and the trustee would have taken title to the wool subject to the seller's equity comprised in that claim for rescission. Similarly, in *Re Gozzett, ex p Messenger & Co Ltd v Trustee*[2] a supplier of greenhouses had installed four greenhouses on the bankrupt's premises having been promised that the bankrupt would arrange security for payment of what was due to the supplier. The court held that there was no reason why it was unfair that the supplier should be restricted to proving as an unsecured creditor.

¹ (1875) 10 Ch App 446.
² [1936] 1 All ER 79, CA.

Relief available

18.281 Where the trustee holds the money which is the subject of the claim, he may be ordered to repay the money. But the claim is not limited to the money itself. If the trustee has parted with the money but there is other money which has or is going to come in from the bankruptcy, he ought to pay the compensation out of such other money[1]. But there appear to be no cases in which a trustee has incurred a personal liability to repay money. The possibility of making such an order arises where the trustee has obtained funds in circumstances in which, by application of the rule in *Ex p James*, he should not retain them but he has distributed the entire estate, including those funds.

¹ *Re Carnac, ex p Simmonds* (1885) 16 QBD 308; *Re Tyler, ex p Official Receiver* [1907] 1 KB 865, 873.

Availability as a defence

18.282 Where the trustee brings a claim, the pursuit of which offends against the rule, the defendant may raise the rule as a defence[1].

¹   *Re Clark (a bankrupt), ex p the Trustee v Texaco Ltd* [1975] 1 All ER 453, [1975] 1 WLR 559.

Summary

18.283 The rule in *Ex p James* is perhaps best expressed as imposing on the trustee, because he is an officer of the court, a duty to act in accordance with standards of fairness over and above what may be required by the strict application of law. When it applies and is relied on by a person who has enlarged the estate by transferring money or other assets into it, it operates so as to confer on him a remedy to recover money or other assets, akin to a claim for restitution, by which he may recover the money or assets or compensation in their place from the trustee where it would be inconsistent with that standard of fair dealing for the trustee to retain the money, assets or their value. But the remedy is different from any restitutionary claim at law in that its availability arises, not because the claimant holds any legal right, but because of the court's willingness to enforce, in the absence of any such legal right, the standard of fairness which it expects its officer, the trustee, to observe. The rule may also be relied on, where it applies, as a defence to a claim made by the trustee.

Challenging trustee's acts, omissions and decisions

18.284 If a bankrupt or any of his creditors or any other person is dissatisfied by any act, omission or decision of a trustee of the bankrupt's estate, he may apply to the court. On such an application the court may confirm, reverse or modify any act or decision of the trustee, may give him directions or may make such other order as it thinks fit[1].

¹   IA 1986, s 303(1). This provision corresponds with the Bankruptcy Act 1914, s 80 and the IA 1986, s 168(5) although it is not in exactly the same terms. See *Heath v Tang* [1993] 4 All ER 694, [1993] 1 WLR 1421 where Hoffmann LJ refers to the decisions of Lord Alvanley MR in *Spragg v Binkes* (1800) 5 Ves 583 and of Lord Eldon LC in *Benfield v Solomons* (1803) 9 Ves 77 as the source of the jurisdiction.

Dissatisfied person

18.285 A person with an interest which has been prejudicially affected by the trustee's act, omission or decision has standing to apply[1]. It appears that the interest does not have to be a property interest. In *Re Cook (Dennis Michael)*[2] the deputy judge accepted that a solicitor who had formerly acted for the bankrupt had standing to challenge the trustee's decision to authorise the solicitor to provide documents and information to the Serious Fraud Office thereby waiving legal professional privilege over documents and information in the solicitor's possession.

¹ Cf *A-G of Gambia v N'Jie* [1961] AC 617, 634. For other cases under the Bankruptcy Acts where the phrase was 'person aggrieved' see *Re Whelan, ex p Sadler* (1878) 48 LJ Bcy 43; *Re Sidebotham, ex p Sidebotham* (1880) 14 Ch D 458; *Re Reed, Bowen & Co, ex p Official Receiver* (1887) 19 QBD 174; *Re Baron, ex p Debtor v Official Receiver* [1943] Ch 177, [1943] 2 All ER 662. The wife of a bankrupt has standing to apply to the court under IA 1986, s 303: *Woodbridge v Smith* [2004] BPIR 247.
² [1999] BPIR 881 at 883. The challenge did not succeed.

Circumstances in which court will interfere

18.286 It is easy to describe the extreme cases in which in the one case the court will interfere and in the other it will not. The court will interfere where the trustee has acted fraudulently or in bad faith. The court will not ordinarily interfere with the day-to-day administration of the estate nor with the exercise in good faith by the trustee of a discretion¹.

¹ *Re Peters, ex p Lloyd* (1882) 47 LT 64; *Re a Debtor (No 400 of 1940), ex p the Debtor v Dodwell (the Trustee)* [1949] Ch 236, [1949] 1 All ER 510.

18.287 In the absence of fraud, the test is whether the trustee's act or omission was such that no reasonable trustee in the prevailing circumstances would have so acted or omitted to act¹. In *Osborne v Cole*² it was said that the court will only interfere if the office-holder has acted in bad faith or so perversely that no trustee properly advised or properly instructing himself could so have acted, alternatively if he has acted fraudulently or in a manner so unreasonable and absurd that no reasonable person would have acted in that way.

¹ *Re Edennote Ltd* [1996] 2 BCLC 389.
² [1999] BPIR 140, applied in *Shepherd v Official Receiver* [2006] EWHC 2902 (Ch), 2007] BPIR 101.

18.288 A challenge under IA 1986, s 303 is not an appropriate method of fixing the trustee's remuneration¹.

¹ *Engel v Peri* [2002] BPIR 961.

Challenges to trustee's decision to admit or reject proof of debt

18.289 The trustee's decision to admit or reject a creditor's proof either for the purpose of the creditor's voting at a meeting of creditors or for the purpose of receiving a dividend may be challenged. The trustee's decision may be challenged by the bankrupt or any creditor, including the creditor whose proof has given rise to the controversy, by appeal to the court¹.

¹ See the IR 1986, r 6.94(2) concerning decisions for the purpose of voting at creditors' meetings and IR 1986, r 6.105 for appeals against decisions on proofs for dividends.

Setting aside transactions between the trustee and his associates

Power of the court to set aside transactions between the trustee and his associates

18.290 If, during the course of the administration of the estate, the trustee enters into any transaction with a person who is an associate[1] of his, the court may, on the application of any person interested, set the transaction aside and order the trustee to compensate the estate for any loss suffered in consequence of it[2]. 'Person interested' was considered in *Re Beesley, ex p Beesley v Official Receiver*[3] in the context of the Bankruptcy Act 1914, s 29 as meaning a person with a proprietary or pecuniary interest; a spouse was not an interested person simply by virtue of her relationship with the bankrupt[4].

[1]   For the meaning of 'associate' see the IA 1986, s 435.
[2]   IR 1986, r 6.147(1).
[3]   [1975] 1 All ER 385, [1975] 1 WLR 568, DC.
[4]   See also *Stevens v Hutchinson* [1953] Ch 299 and *Re Roehampton Swimming Pool Ltd* [1968] 3 All ER 661, [1968] 1 WLR 1693.

18.291 The above provisions do not, however, apply if either the transaction was entered into with the prior consent of the court, or it is shown to the court's satisfaction that the transaction was for value, and that it was entered into by the trustee without knowing, or having any reason to suppose, that the person concerned was an associate[1].

[1]   IR 1986, r 6.147(2).

18.292 The above provisions do not affect the rules of law or equity with respect to a trustee's dealings with trust property, or his fiduciary obligations[1].

[1]   IR 1986, r 6.147(3).

Chapter 19

EFFECT OF BANKRUPTCY ON LITIGATION AND ARBITRATION

A CAUSES OF ACTION AND THE BANKRUPT'S ESTATE

General principle

19.1 A cause of action in which the bankrupt is interested as a claimant is a thing in action vested in him[1]. Therefore, where the cause of action has accrued before the commencement of the bankruptcy, it is an item of property which falls within the bankrupt's estate and vests in his trustee in bankruptcy on his appointment[2]. It vests without any assignment and no notice need be given to complete the assignment[3]. By reason of the assignment the bankrupt loses his standing to take further steps in any proceedings arising from the cause of action[4].

[1]   See the definition of 'property' in the Insolvency Act 1986 ('IA 1986'), s 436 and the discussion of the bankrupt's estate in **Chapter 14**.
[2]   *Beckham v Drake* (1849) 2 HL Cas 579; *Heath v Tang* [1993] 4 All ER 694, [1993] 1 WLR 1421.
[3]   IA 1986, s 306 and s 311(4).
[4]   *Heath v Tang* [1993] 4 All ER 694, [1993] 1 WLR 1421; *Boyd & Hutchinson v Foenander* [2003] EWCA Civ 1516, 2004] BPIR 20.

19.2 Where a bankrupt brings a claim in respect of a cause of action which has vested in his trustee, the defendant has a good defence and in a clear case would be entitled to strike the claim out or obtain summary judgment under CPR r 24.2(a)(i) on the basis that the bankrupt claimant had no real prospect of succeeding on the claim unless the trustee was substituted as claimant or assigned the cause of action to the bankrupt. Solicitors do not warrant that a client for whom they act has a good cause of action and therefore, in *Nelson v Nelson*[1] the Court of Appeal held that if solicitors act for an undischarged bankrupt in bringing a claim which has vested in his trustee, then, so long as the solicitors acted without knowledge of the bankruptcy, they do not automatically expose themselves to a liability for the other party's costs by their conduct in doing so. But it was left open that such liability might be imposed even where the solicitor had acted without negligence or other impropriety.

[1]   [1997] 1 All ER 970, [1997] 1 WLR 233.

Examples

19.3 Rights of action which have been held to pass to the trustee under the law before the IA 1986 came into force include actions for an indemnity[1], for commission[2], for wrongful dismissal[3], for misrepresentation[4], for fraud[5], for breach of contract to deliver[6] or to repair goods[7], for return of premiums paid on an insurance policy[8], for trespass or negligence causing injury to the bankrupt's property[9], and against forfeiture[10].

[1]   *Re Perkins, Poyser v Beyfus* [1898] 2 Ch 182, CA.
[2]   *Re Byrne, ex p Henry* (1892) 9 Morr 213.
[3]   *Beckham v Drake* (1849) 2 HL Cas 579.
[4]   *Hodgson v Sidney* (1866) LR 1 Exch 313.
[5]   *Motion v Moojen* (1872) LR 14 Eq 202.
[6]   *Stanton v Collier* (1854) 23 LJQB 116, CA.
[7]   *Gibbon v Dudgeon* (1881) 45 JP 748.
[8]   *Boddington v Castelli* (1853) 1 E & B 879, Ex Ch.
[9]   *Wilson v United Counties Bank Ltd* [1920] AC 102, HL.
[10]   *Howard v Fanshawe* [1895] 2 Ch 581.

Exceptional cases

19.4 However, there are certain causes of action personal to the bankrupt which do not vest in his trustee. The scope of the exception is often illustrated by the words of Erle J in *Beckham v Drake*[1] that 'the right of action does not pass where the damages are to be estimated by immediate reference to pain felt by the bankrupt in respect of his body, mind or character, and without immediate reference to his rights of property'. Examples of such causes of action include claims for assault, injuries to reputation[2], and damages for pain, suffering and loss of amenity[3].

[1]   (1849) 2 HL Cas 579. See *Heath v Tang* [1993] 4 All ER 694, [1993] 1 WLR 1421.
[2]   *Re Bourne, ex p Bourne* (1826) 2 Gl & J 137; *Wilson v United Counties Bank Ltd* [1920] AC 102; *Re Kavanagh, ex p Bankrupt v Jackson (Trustee)* [1949] 2 All ER 264.
[3]   *Ord v Upton* [2000] Ch 352, [2000] 1 All ER 193.

Hybrid claims: Ord v Upton

19.5 In many, if not most, claims there may be different heads of loss which arise from the facts giving rise to the claim. In some older cases, the courts treated the existence of different heads of losses as giving rise to two separate causes of action. For example, in *Wilson v United Counties Bank Ltd*[1] the defendant bank was sued for breach of contract and negligence. The jury awarded £45,000 for the losses caused to Major Wilson's estate and £7,500 for the loss caused to his personal reputation. The decision in the case proceeded on the basis that the two heads of loss arose from separate causes of action. The right of action concerning the loss relating to the estate had vested in Major Wilson's trustee in bankruptcy, but the right of action concerning the loss to his personal reputation had not. Hence Major Wilson remained entitled both to pursue in his own name the claim concerning the loss to his personal reputation and to retain the damages awarded in respect of that claim. However, the premise that there were two causes of action, because there were two heads of loss, is no longer good law. In modern times, where the same facts give rise to more than one head of loss, there is nevertheless only one cause of action[2]. If the single cause of action includes a head of loss relating to property or some other matter which vests in the trustee then the single cause of action which has accrued vests in the trustee, even though other heads of loss are heads of loss concerning losses of a personal nature. The trustee, therefore, has the sole right to bring the action[3]. The trustee may retain any damages awarded in respect of the heads of loss relating to property or other matter vested in him, but any damages which are recovered in respect of the heads of loss which are of a personal nature, are held by the trustee on constructive trust for the bankrupt[4]. Accordingly a claim for damages caused by personal injury to the bankrupt which included, as one head of loss, a claim for loss of earnings, vested in the trustee. For claims for loss of earnings fall into the estate and are not claims of a personal nature.

1   [1920] AC 102.
2   *Ord v Upton* [2000] Ch 352, [2000] 1 All ER 193; *Stock v London Underground* (1999) Times, 13 August, CA.
3   *Mulkerrins v Pricewaterhouse Coopers* [2001] 05 LS Gaz R 36, CA.
4   *Ord v Upton* [2000] Ch 352, [2000] 1 All ER 193.

Practical impact of Ord v Upton

19.6 Many personal injury claims, especially where the injury is serious, will be capable of including a claim for loss of earnings. If they are capable of including such claim, then the cause of action will vest in the trustee. However, it appears that the bankrupt can avoid losing the ability to pursue even a hybrid claim by restricting the remedy sought to a remedy relating only to the part of the claim which is personal to the bankrupt. Thus in *Khan v Trident Safeguards Ltd*[1] the Court of Appeal held that a former employee was entitled to pursue his claim for race discrimination, even though it was a hybrid claim, because the relief which he sought was restricted to a declaration and compensation for injured feelings. Although reasons of policy may require that a bankrupt should be able to pursue such a claim, the result is difficult to square with the rule that a hybrid cause of action vests automatically and fully in the trustee.

1   [2004] EWCA Civ 624, [2004] ICR 1591, [2004] BPIR 881.

19.7 If a claim which is pursued by the trustee includes, as one head among several, a head of damage of a personal nature but is settled for a global sum, the amount of the sum which the trustee holds on trust for the bankrupt may be difficult to ascertain. In *Re Kavanagh, ex p Bankrupt v Jackson (Trustee)*[1], out of the proceeds of a claim by a bankrupt against her solicitor for breach of confidence and breach of contract, the bankrupt was entitled to retain part of the damages as representing the award in respect of the damage to her credit and reputation. The apportionment was made by splitting the award in half between her and the trustee. Although this may be appropriate as a last resort in some cases, it would seem likely that in most personal injury cases a more reasoned apportionment will be possible even where the settlement is made on the footing of a global sum. The heads of claim, apart from the claim for general damages, ought to be apparent from the schedule of special damages and the apportionment may be based on that.

[1]   [1949] 2 All ER 264.

19.8 The only heads of loss discussed in *Ord v Upton* were the general damages for pain and suffering, to which the bankrupt is clearly entitled, and the loss of earnings. Aldous LJ stated that, subject to retention for maintenance, damages for the loss of past and future earnings would naturally be money that ought to pass to the creditors because they do not relate to the pain and suffering of the bankrupt. The reference to maintenance is to the rule under the old law that a bankrupt was entitled to retain out of his post-bankruptcy earnings sufficient to maintain himself and his family[1]. How the amount which a bankrupt may keep for such needs is to be calculated is not clear.

[1]   Under the present law, there is no need for such a rule because income earned after the commencement of the bankruptcy does not fall automatically into the estate but must be claimed by way of an income payments order and the amount to be paid under such an order must not leave the bankrupt without him retaining what is necessary to meet his and his family basic domestic needs; see the IA 1986, s 310. See *Re Roberts* [1900] 1 QB 122; *Mercer v Vans Colina* [1900] 1 QB 130n; *Bailey v Thurston & Co* [1903] 1 KB 137; *Affleck v Hammond* [1912] 3 KB 162.

19.9 If the trustee does not wish to pursue a claim (whether it includes some personal element of loss or not), the bankrupt should ask the trustee to assign the cause of action back to him. If the trustee refuses to do so without good cause, the bankrupt may have grounds to complain to the court about the trustee's decision under the IA 1986, s 303(1)[1].

[1]   See also *Heath v Tang* [1993] 1 WLR 1421, 1423. The court has tended to permit the trustee (or liquidator of a company) to have a wide discretion in making decisions about the administration of the estate; see *Re a Debtor (No 400 of 1940), ex p Debtor v Dodwell (Trustee)* [1949] Ch 236, [1949] 1 All ER 510 and *Re Hans Place* [1992] BCC 737; *Re Edennote Ltd* [1996] BCC 718.

Claims where there are two causes of action

19.10 The decision in *Ord v Upton* concerns the situation where there is a single cause of action but plural heads of loss. Where the events give rise to more than one cause of action and one of those causes of action is a personal claim, it is open to the bankrupt to pursue that personal cause of action in isolation from the other causes of action. For example, in *Grady v Prison Service*[1] the circumstances of the claimant's dismissal from his employment gave rise to claims for wrongful dismissal, unfair dismissal and discrimination by reason of disability. He conceded that the wrongful dismissal and discrimination claims vested in his estate because they gave rise only to monetary remedies; but the Court of Appeal held that he was entitled to pursue his claim for unfair dismissal because it was a separate claim and the primary statutory remedy was reinstatement.

[1]   [2003] EWCA Civ 527, [2003] 3 All ER 745, [2003] BPIR 823.

Effect of bankruptcy set-off on causes of action

19.11 By the IA 1986, s 323 it is provided that where before the commencement of the bankruptcy there have been mutual credits, mutual debts or other mutual dealings between the bankrupt and any creditor of the bankrupt proving or claiming to prove for a bankruptcy debt, an account shall be taken of what is due from each party to the other in respect of the mutual dealings and the sums due from one party shall be set off against the sums due from the other. In *Stein v Blake*[1] the House of Lords held that this provision is self-executing in the sense that its operation is automatic, taking effect on the commencement of the bankruptcy, and not dependent upon either party invoking or consenting to it. In consequence where the bankrupt and the other party had, at the date of the bankruptcy's commencement, claims and cross-claims against each other, the causes of action which those claims and cross-claims individually comprised are replaced by a claim to a net balance, either provable in the bankruptcy or claimable by the trustee for the estate. For the purpose of determining the true position, the parties' claims and cross-claims may need to be pleaded for the purpose of litigation as if they continued to exist, or if the litigation is already under way, their cases would not require amendment, but such litigation is merely part of the retrospective calculation. In assessing the net balance, the creditor's claim for contingent or unascertained debts should be taken into account, estimated if necessary[2], but not the creditor's contingent liabilities to the bankrupt because to do so would advance the date on which the liability arose. It follows that the bankrupt's causes of action against the creditor do not survive the bankruptcy so as to be assignable, but the claim for the net balance on the account may be assigned.

[1]   [1996] AC 243, [1995] 2 All ER 961.
[2]   IA 1986, s 323(3).

Causes of action arising after bankruptcy

19.12 Where a cause of action arises after the commencement of the bankruptcy, then, unless it relates to property comprised in the bankrupt's estate, it will not automatically form part of the estate. For, after-acquired property does not fall into the estate, unless specifically claimed for the estate by the trustee[1]. By contrast, if the cause of action relates to property that has vested in the trustee as part of the estate, then, even though the cause of action may have arisen after the commencement of the bankruptcy, it is vested in the trustee as being derivative from property of which he holds the legal title. Therefore, in order to determine who has title to sue in respect of a cause of action accruing after the commencement of the bankruptcy, it is necessary to analyse the basis on which the cause of action arises. It will be apparent that the distinction here is not the same as between those causes of action which fall into the estate and those personal causes of action which are excepted discussed above. For example, the bankrupt may legitimately have entered into a contract with another person after the commencement of the bankruptcy. If that other person breaches the contract, the bankrupt will have a claim against him in respect of which the bankrupt will hold the title to sue even though it is not a personal claim in the exceptional sense discussed above.

[1]   IA 1986, s 307.

B PROCEDURAL ASPECTS

Bankruptcy after the commencement of proceedings brought by the bankrupt

19.13 Under the Rules of the Supreme Court 1965 it was expressly provided that an action did not abate by reason of the plaintiff's bankruptcy[1]. It is taken for granted that no abatement occurs under the Civil Procedure Rules 1998. If the trustee wishes to continue the proceedings where the cause of action has vested in him, the court may order his substitution as claimant, where it is desirable to make the substitution so that the court can resolve the matters in dispute in the proceedings[2]. If the trustee decides to continue the litigation, then he is at risk for the costs of the proceedings, including those costs which have arisen by virtue of steps taken before the bankruptcy[3]. The trustee must take the action as he finds it; he cannot adopt part and leave out the rest[4]. A trustee may adopt an action by taking steps to pursue it even though he is not made a party, and in such a case costs may be ordered against him[5].

[1]   RSC Ord 15 r 7(1).
[2]   CPR r 19.2(4).
[3]   *Watson v Holliday* (1882) 20 Ch D 780; *Borneman v Wilson* (1884) 28 Ch D 53.
[4]   *Borneman v Wilson* (1884) 28 Ch D 53.
[5]   *Vickery v Modern Security Systems Ltd* [1998] BPIR 164.

19.14 A trustee appointed after the commencement of proceedings may, however, decline to continue the action, for example because to do so would be detrimental to the body of creditors. If he does so, the action may be stayed subject to notice being given by the defendant to the trustee[1] or the defendant may raise the bankruptcy order as a defence[2]. A decision by the trustee not to continue the claim will form an election not to proceed with the action; if the action is then stayed but not dismissed, the trustee's election will bind any purported assignee of the claim[3].

[1]   *Wright v Swindon, Marleborough and Andover Rly Co* (1876) 4 Ch D 164.

²   *Champion v Formby* (1878) 7 Ch D 373; *Foster v Gamgee* (1876) 1 QBD 666; cf *Re Berry, Duffield v Williams* [1896] 1 Ch 939.
³   *Selig v Lion* [1891] 1 QB 513; *Clive Brooks & Col Ltd v Irvine Baynard* 1988 Times, 30 April, CA.

19.15 If the trustee continues the action, he will be in no better position on the pleadings than the bankrupt plaintiff. For this reason, if for no other, he may prefer not to become a party to the existing action, but rather to commence a fresh action in his own name founded on the same cause of action and claiming the same relief. To do this may prevent the trustee from accepting liability for costs orders in the original action. Under the rules of procedure in force before 26 April 1999, the trustee was not debarred from bringing fresh proceedings merely by reason of the fact that a second set of proceedings are being issued in respect of the same cause of action[1], but he may be barred from doing so, for example by the expiry of the relevant limitation period. Presumably a trustee could follow this course under the CPR, although it may be open to argument that it involves an abuse of process.

¹   *Bennett v Gamgee* (1877) 46 LJQB 204, CA.

Change of trustee

19.16 Where a new trustee is appointed during the course of proceedings commenced by the bankrupt claimant or a former trustee, he must apply to the court for an order that he be made a party to the action, in the same way as a trustee originally appointed[1]. Once he has obtained this order, he must serve notice of it on the other parties to the action. The former trustee will remain liable for so long as he is on the record until the new trustee is substituted in his place[2].

¹   Under the CPR r 19.2(4). See *Pooley's Trustee v Whetham* (1886) 33 Ch D 76.
²   *Pooley's Trustee v Whetham* (1886) 33 Ch D 76.

Joint contractors

19.17 Where an undischarged bankrupt is a contractor in respect of any contract jointly with any person, that person may sue or be sued in respect of the contract without the joinder of the bankrupt[1]. Where the bankrupt is a co-claimant, his trustee may apply to be made a party to the action in his place[2].

¹   IA 1986, s 345(4).
²   *Hoare & Co and Newton v Baker* (1887) 4 TLR 26.

Security for costs

19.18 Since 26 April 1999, the rules governing when a defendant may obtain security for his costs are contained in the CPR rr 25.12–25.14. The same rules apply to orders to provide security for costs against parties to appeals[1].

¹   CPR r 25.15.

Where the bankrupt is claimant

19.19 The fact alone that the claimant is a bankrupt, pursuing in his own name a cause of action against a defendant[1], does not entitle the court to order him to give security for the defendant's costs[2]. For, security may only be ordered where one of the conditions in the CPR r 25.13(2) applies and the court, having regard to all the circumstances of the case, is satisfied that it is just to make the order.

[1]   The principal cases in which the bankrupt may himself be claimant are: (1) in proceedings which concern a cause of action which accrued before bankruptcy but did not, because of its nature, form part of his estate; (2) in proceedings which concern a cause of action which accrued after the commencement of his bankruptcy and has not been claimed by the trustee as after-acquired property; or (3) in proceedings which concern a cause of action which vested in the trustee but which has been assigned by the trustee to the bankrupt.

[2]   See *Cook v Whellock* (1890) 24 QBD 658.

19.20 Where the trustee assigned a cause of action to the bankrupt in return for a share of the proceeds and the bankrupt brings proceedings in his own name, he was held not to be a nominal plaintiff within the meaning of RSC Ord 23 r 1(1)(b)[1]. There is no reason why the words 'nominal claimant' in CPR r 25.13(2)(f) should be interpreted differently. Conversely, where the claimant has assigned the benefit of proceedings to his creditors or a particular creditor but retains the legal right to sue, he will be a nominal claimant[2].

[1]   *Ramsay v Hartley* [1977] 2 All ER 673, [1977] 1 WLR 686.
[2]   *Lloyd v Hathern Station Brick Co* (1901) 85 LT 158; *Semler v Murphy* [1968] Ch 183, [1967] 2 All ER 185.

Where the trustee is claimant

19.21 A trustee in bankruptcy is not a nominal claimant even though he is necessarily, in virtue of his office, pursuing a claim in the interests of another person, namely the creditors[1]. But under the County Courts Act 1984, s 49 a trustee in bankruptcy who elects to continue a claim in the county court commenced by the bankrupt may be ordered to provide security for costs[2]. Given the extension to the jurisdiction of the county courts and the assimilation of procedure between the High Court and the county courts, it seems anomalous that this distinction between them should continue[3].

[1]   *Denston v Ashton* (1869) LR 4 QB 590; *Pooley's Trustee v Whetham* (1884) 28 Ch D 38; *Cowell v Taylor* (1885) 31 Ch D 34.
[2]   Where an enactment permits the court to require security for costs, it is not necessary to establish that one of the conditions in CPR r 25.13(2) is fulfilled: see CPR r 25.13(1)(b)(ii).
[3]   See *Hemming v Davies* [1898] 1 QB 660; *Talling v Lawrence* [1999] BPIR 414 (Barnet County Court).

Bankruptcy after judgment

19.22 An order that the name of the trustee in bankruptcy be substituted for that of the plaintiff may be made after judgment[1] unless the circumstances are such as to entitle the trustee to bring a fresh action.

[1]   *Re Clements, ex p Clements* [1901] 1 KB 260.

19.23   Where a claimant has obtained judgment but then becomes bankrupt, his trustee must obtain an order under RSC Ord 46 r 2[1] for leave to issue execution before he can issue execution in the High Court on behalf of the estate. It may be that, in the High Court, following the previous procedure the trustee need not first apply to be made a party to the action under CPR r 19.2(4)[2]. But, in a county court, it is probably necessary that he should be made a party because the rules governing enforcement in the county court are formulated by reference to the 'judgment creditor' who is defined as 'the person who has obtained or is entitled to enforce a judgment or order'[3]. The trustee must be substituted as a party if he wishes to present a bankruptcy petition against the judgment debtor[4]. The bankrupt judgment creditor is not entitled to issue execution once his trustee has been appointed[5].

[1]   Now contained in CPR Sch 1; see CPR r 50.1(1).
[2]   *Re Bagley* [1911] 1 KB 317, CA.
[3]   CCR Ord 24 r 1 contained in CPR Sch 2; see CPR r 50.1.
[4]   *Re Clements, ex p Clements* [1901] 1 KB 260.
[5]   *Re Carter, ex p Carter* (1876) 2 Ch D 806, CA.

Costs

19.24   A trustee in bankruptcy has no special protection against liability in costs. If for economic reasons he finds it prudent to discontinue proceedings, he will ordinarily incur liability for the opposing party's costs pursuant to CPR Pt 38[1].

[1]   *RBG Resources plc v Rastogi* [2005] EWHC 994 (Ch), [2005] 2 BCLC 592 where the liability was reduced because of the intransigence of the opposing party.

C ASSIGNMENT OF CAUSES OF ACTION

Introduction

19.25   It is common for a trustee in bankruptcy to assign causes of action vested in him as part of the bankrupt's estate. His ability to do so was recognised before the abolition of criminal and civil liability for maintenance and champerty[1]. Since the trustee's power to assign a cause of action was recognised as an exception to the general rule at law, that rule is set out first and then the trustee's power of assignment is discussed.

[1]   By the Criminal Law Act 1967, ss 13 and 14.

Rule at common law

19.26   Maintenance comprises the assisting or encouraging of a party to a suit by a third party who has no interest in the suit or any other interest which justifies his interference. The form of support ordinarily provided by the third party is money to fund the litigation. In more recent times, champerty has been classified as a species of maintenance[1] and defined as being a bargain made by a third party with a party to litigation to maintain the litigation in consideration of a share in the matter forming the subject of the dispute[2]. In origin, the object of prohibiting maintenance and champerty was to prevent the wrongful advantage which a person might achieve by embroiling another more vulnerable person in a multiplicity of suits, maintained or purchased for the purpose of oppressing him. But the application of the law has had wider effect than might be thought necessary to achieve the object of preventing abuse of process. Thus, Blackstone links the rule against champerty with the prohibition at common law of the assignment of choses in action, writing that the practice of purchasing a suit or a right of suing is 'so much abhorred by our law, that it is one main reason why a chose in action, or a thing of which one hath the right but not the possession, is not assignable at common law'[3]. Things in action may now be assigned at law by virtue of the Law of Property Act 1925, s 136 and, since the Criminal Law Act 1967 came into force on 1 January 1968, maintenance and champerty are no longer crimes or torts. But, because by virtue of the Criminal Law Act 1967, s 14(2) the abolition of criminal and civil liability under the law of England and Wales for maintenance and champerty does not affect any rule of law as to the cases in which a contract is to be treated as contrary to public policy or otherwise illegal, the common law rules as to what amounts to maintenance and champerty continue to have a living presence, in particular with respect to assignments of 'bare rights to sue'[4]. The effect, at common law, of the continuing rule that contracts involving maintenance or champerty may be illegal affects the enforceability of such agreements and, where a cause of action has been assigned under a contract rendered illegal because it involves maintenance or champerty, an action brought by the assignee to enforce the cause of action may be stayed. Moreover, despite the exemption recognised in the context of realising insolvent estates and discussed in the following paragraphs, the policy underpinning the rules about maintenance and champerty continues sometimes to affect the approach of courts even to arrangements made by office-holders in insolvency[5].

[1]   This may be an inversion of the historical sequence; see Winfield *The History of Conspiracy and Abuse of Legal Procedure* (Cambridge, 1921) ch VI.
[2]   See the definitions cited in *Guy v Churchill* (1888) 40 Ch D 481, 488.
[3]   Blackstone *Commentaries* vol 4, ch 10, para 10. In equity, such assignment was permissible, if the assignor was, at the time of the assignment, indebted to the assignee. Further, the assignability or negotiability of various instruments was recognised by the law merchant and this recognition was adopted by the common law.
[4]   *Giles v Thompson* [1994] 1 AC 142, [1993] 3 All ER 321.
[5]   See *Grovewood Holdings v James Capel & Co Ltd* [1995] Ch 80, [1994] 4 All ER 417; *Re Oasis Merchandising Services Ltd* [1995] 2 BCLC 493 (Robert Walker J); affd [1998] Ch 170, [1997] 1 All ER 1009, CA, discussed further below.

Trustee in bankruptcy's power to sell causes of action

19.27 Since the Bankruptcy Act 1869, a trustee in bankruptcy has had power to sell all the property of the bankrupt which vests in the trustee by the statutory assignment of the bankrupt's estate[1]. On the foundation that 'property' includes things in action by virtue of the relevant statutory definition, it has been held that the trustee in bankruptcy has power to realise the property which a cause of action represents by assigning it by way of sale[2]. This result is supported by the policies underlying the insolvency legislation because the trustee 'may have no funds, or be disinclined to run the risk of having to pay costs, or he may consider it undesirable to delay the winding-up of the bankruptcy until the end of the litigation'[3]. A liquidator of a company, on whom similar statutory powers are conferred, is thereby also enabled to assign causes of action belonging to the company before it is wound up[4]. The source of the exemption from the rules governing maintenance and champerty is, therefore, the insolvency legislation, but the exemption was and is not conferred expressly but inferred by judges from the policy of the legislation. The exemption may be taken to have the approval of Parliament because the legislation has been amended and consolidated on various occasions since the exemption was recognised.

[1] See the Bankruptcy Act 1869, s 25(6) conferring power to sell and s 4 defining property as including things in action.
[2] *Seear v Lawson* (1880) 15 Ch D 426; *Guy v Churchill* (1888) 40 Ch D 481; *Ramsay v Hartley* [1977] 2 All ER 673, [1977] 1 WLR 686; *Norglen Ltd v Reeds Rains Prudential Ltd* [1999] 2 AC 1, [1998] 1 All ER 218.
[3] *Seear v Lawson* (1880) 15 Ch D 426 at 433.
[4] *Re Park Gate Waggon Works Co* (1881) 17 Ch D 234.

What may be assigned

19.28 The trustee's power of sale may be exercised over 'any property for the time being comprised in the bankrupt's estate'[1]. Thus any cause of action for the time being comprised in the bankrupt's estate is capable of being assigned. But, the trustee could not assign any cause of action which did not vest in him because it was personal to the bankrupt[2]. Where the cause of action vests in the trustee subject, in respect of one or more of the heads of damage which arise under it, to such head or heads of loss being held by him on trust for the bankrupt[3], then any assignee would take subject to that trust.

[1] IA 1986, s 314, Sch 5, para 9.
[2] That is to say those claims within the exception recognised in *Beckham v Drake* (1849) 2 HL Cas 579 discussed above. For an example of a case where this point was taken in respect of a cause of action which did not fall within the exception, see *Empire Resolution Ltd v MPW Insurance Brokers Ltd* [1999] BPIR 486.
[3] See *Ord v Upton* [2000] Ch 352, [2000] 1 All ER 193 discussed above.

19.29 Secondly, a distinction must be drawn between causes of action which form part of the estate and claims arising by virtue of the rights and powers of the trustee in bankruptcy conferred on him by statute in virtue of his office. Claims falling into the latter category are not capable of assignment. Knox J drew this distinction in *Re Ayala Holdings (No 2) Ltd*[1] where a creditor of a company in liquidation sought to pursue a claim against the recipient of funds paid by the company after the presentation of the petition on which it was ordered to be wound up and which were therefore rendered void by the IA 1986, s 127. He held that such a claim could not be assigned since it arose after and only in virtue of the winding-up. Although the principle is unimpeachable, it is submitted that a claim under the IA 1986, s 127, in the case of the winding-up of a company or, in the case of bankruptcy, under IA 1986, s 284 is capable of assignment. For those provisions do not confer the right on the liquidator or trustee to make a claim in virtue of their office; what they provide is that a disposition of property by the company or the bankrupt is void. Hence title to the asset in question remains the company's or within the estate of the bankrupt and, it is submitted, should be capable of assignment. By contrast where an otherwise valid transfer of property has occurred but power is granted to the liquidator or trustee to seek an order setting that transfer aside and reversing its effect, the claim is one which can only be made by him in virtue of his office and is neither within the estate nor capable of assignment. In *Re Oasis Merchandising Ltd*[2] the purported assignment concerned a claim against the former directors of a company under the IA 1986, s 214 that they should contribute to the assets of the company on the basis that they had wrongfully permitted the company to continue trading after they should have known that insolvency was inevitable, the Court of Appeal distinguished between assets which were the property of the company at the commencement of the liquidation[3], including rights of action arising before that date, and 'assets which only arise after the liquidation of the company and are recoverable only by the liquidator pursuant to the statutory powers conferred on him'. Since an application under the IA 1986, s 214 might only be made by the liquidator, it was not assignable. It is submitted that the same reasoning will apply, in relation to the trustee in bankruptcy, so that applications which might be made by him, for example, to set aside transactions at an undervalue or a preference under the IA 1986, s 339 and s 340 respectively, are not capable of being assigned.

[1]   [1996] 1 BCLC 467.
[2]   [1998] Ch 170, [1997] 1 All ER 1009.
[3]   It is submitted that the reference to property being the company's at the commencement of the liquidation does not preclude the argument made above that claims for property under void dispositions are within the estate and capable of assignment because since the disposition is void the title to the property in question remains the bankrupt's (or the company's) at that time. Contrast where what is sought to be avoided by the trustee or liquidator is a voidable transaction as it was in *Re Yagerphone* [1935] Ch 392.

19.30 Thirdly, as mentioned above, where there have been mutual dealings between the bankrupt and a creditor and there are claims and cross-claims between them which are outstanding at the commencement of the bankruptcy, the setting off against each other of these claims and cross-claims takes effect simply by virtue of the bankruptcy. The causes of action on either side are replaced by a net balance due from one party to the other, taking into account the bankrupt's contingent liabilities, estimated if necessary, but not the creditor's contingent liabilities. If there is a net balance due (or alleged to be due) from the creditor, it may be assigned[1].

[1]   *Stein v Blake* [1996] AC 243, [1995] 2 All ER 961.

To whom a cause of action may be assigned

19.31 It is clear that the trustee may assign a cause of action to a third party. In *Seear v Lawson*[1] the assignment was made to a stranger and in *Guy v Churchill*[2] to a creditor in the bankruptcy. Under the Bankruptcy Act 1914 the trustee's power was expressed, in so far as material, as a power 'to sell all or any part of the property of the bankrupt ... with power to transfer the whole thereof to any person or company, or to sell the same in parcels'. In *Kitson v*

Hardwick, a case decided under the Bankruptcy Act 1869 which conferred a power in the same terms as contained in the Bankruptcy Act 1914, Willes J sitting in the Court of Common Pleas[3] held that the words 'any person' included the bankrupt himself, to whom the trustee had sold the entire estate. The Court of Appeal followed that decision in *Ramsay v Hartley*[4] in which the asset in question was a claim in tort for negligent misstatement against accountants that the trustee had assigned to the bankrupt. As contained in the IA 1986, Sch 5, para 9, the power no longer contains any reference to the person to whom the sale might be made. There is no reason to think that this changes the law, since if a restriction were to be imposed it would still have to be imposed by implication. Accordingly the cause of action may be assigned to the bankrupt.

[1]   (1880) 15 Ch D 426.
[2]   (1888) 40 Ch D 481.
[3]   (1872) LR 7 CP 43 sitting with Keating J.
[4]   [1977] 2 All ER 673, [1977] 1 WLR 686.

Consideration for which a cause of action may be assigned

19.32   The cause of action may be sold outright for a sum of money. The sale in *Seear v Lawson*[1] was such a case. The cause of action may also be sold on terms that the purchaser pay a share of the proceeds of the action to the trustee. This was the arrangement in *Guy v Churchill*[2] in which Chitty J rejected the argument that that feature rendered the assignment void for champerty because it involved sharing the proceeds of the action. Such an arrangement was accepted by the Court of Appeal in *Ramsay v Hartley*[3] to be a sale, within the meaning of the trustee's power of sale.

[1]   (1880) 15 Ch D 426.
[2]   (1888) 40 Ch D 481.
[3]   [1977] 2 All ER 673, [1977] 1 WLR 686. See *Weddell v JA Pearce & Major* [1988] Ch 26, [1987] 3 All ER 624.

Assignments of the recoveries of an action: champerty and the decision in Grovewood Holdings

19.33   In the cases mentioned in the preceding paragraph the asset assigned was the cause of action itself. In *Grovewood Holdings plc v James Capel & Co Ltd*[1] the liquidator of a company, who has power to sell the company's assets conferred on him in similar terms to those on which power of selling property comprised in the bankrupt's estate is conferred on the trustee in bankruptcy[2], entered into an agreement with a third party under which it was agreed that the third party, referred to in the agreement as 'the sponsor' would, at its expense, pursue the litigation in the company's name and that the proceeds of the action, after payment of costs, would be split in equal shares between the liquidator and the sponsor. Lightman J held that a transfer of a beneficial share in the recoveries of an action in return for a sale was a sale as that word was used in the context of the statutory power of sale. This is correct in that (1) the subject matter of the transaction is property and therefore capable of sale[3], and (2) there is consideration for the agreement to convey that property, ie the money, or the promise of it, to fund the action[4]. But he went on to hold that the transaction was not exempt from the general rule at law against maintenance and champerty and that therefore the action to which it related should be stayed. The basis on which he reached this conclusion may be summarised thus:

(1)   as a matter of general law, there is an unobjectionable method of assigning the fruits or recoveries of an action, namely to do so without giving the assignee any right to interfere in the action or to insist on its being continued;

(2)   there is also an objectionable method of assigning such property, namely to assign it together with such rights of interference[5];

(3)   since there is an unobjectionable method of assigning such property, a liquidator (or trustee) has no need to be granted a special exemption from the objections to the objectionable method for the purpose of enabling him to realise the value of such property.

[1]   [1995] Ch 80, [1994] 4 All ER 417.
[2]   Compare the IA 1986, Sch 4, para 6 (liquidator's power of sale) with Sch 5, para 9 (trustee's).
[3]   See *Glegg v Bromley* [1912] 3 KB 474, 484 where Vaughan Williams said with regard to the assignment of the fruits of an action, 'I think this was an assignment of property, and not of an expectancy. It is the assignment of property in the shape of the fruits of an action.'
[4]   In practical terms, a promise to pay the costs of an action is more helpful to the creditors of the bankrupt than the payment of a fixed sum set at the date of the assignment, since the costs might end up exceeding whatever fixed sum was then agreed.
[5]   See *Glegg v Bromley* [1912] 3 KB 474.

19.34 Doubt has been expressed about this aspect of the decision[1]. First, as a matter of practicality, it is unlikely that anyone would agree to fund an action without being given a measure of control over its conduct. Secondly, the exemption from the rules relating to maintenance and champerty is not an expressly granted exemption with any precise scope. What the courts have recognised is that the trustee in bankruptcy and the liquidator may exercise their power of selling the property of the bankrupt and the company respectively 'without any breach of the rules of public policy governing maintenance and champerty'[2]. If it is right, as it is suggested it is, that the transaction comprised in the assignment of part of the recoveries of an action in return for a promise to fund the costs of the action is a sale of the bankrupt's, or as it may be the company's, property, then no question should arise whether such sale is vitiated by the rules governing maintenance and champerty because the trustee or liquidator is empowered to make sales without offending those rules where they would otherwise apply.

[1]   See *Re Oasis Merchandising Services Ltd* [1995] 2 BCLC 493 (Robert Walker J); affd [1998] Ch 170, [1997] 1 All ER 1009, CA.
[2]   [1995] 2 BCLC 493, 504.

19.35 In *ANC Ltd v Clark Goldring & Page*[1], submissions were made as follows:

19.35 *Effect of bankruptcy on litigation and arbitration*

(1) The exemption from the rules of champerty arises from the liquidator's statutory power of sale under Schedule 4 to sell property as defined in the IA 1986, s 436.

(2) A legal assignment of a cause of action consists of the right to prosecute the action, to be named as the proper party to the action and to give good discharge to the judgement debtor: the Law of Property Act 1925, s 136.

(3) By contrast, an assignment of the fruits of an action is an equitable assignment being an agreement to assign such fruits if and when they are recovered in the future[2]. Such an agreement does not give the assignee any rights to prosecute or conduct the action and the assignee does not acquire any beneficial interest in the action itself[3].

(4) Since the assignment of the fruits of an action does not include any rights in the action itself nor any right to prosecute the action no question of champerty arises, nor does the scope of the liquidator's statutory exemption therefrom.

(5) Any agreement that an equitable assignee of the fruits should also have conduct of the action is entirely separate from and independent of the assignment of the fruits and nothing more than a funding agreement. It is subject to the usual rules on champertous agreements. It is entirely unconnected with the liquidator's exemption arising from the statutory power to sell property and is subject to the usual rules on champertous agreements.

[1] [2001] BPIR 568.
[2] *Tailby v Official Receiver* (1888) 13 App Cas 523.
[3] *Glegg v Bromley* [1912] 3 KB 474 at 484.

19.36 The Court of Appeal did not rule on the issue of champerty in that case but Robert Walker LJ commented that, whether or not the fifth step is correct (as to which he expressed no view) this analysis was a valuable aid to clarification of the position[1].

[1] See also *Farmer v Moseley Holdings Ltd* [2001] 2 BCLC 572.

Power to stay for abuse of process

19.37 In subsequent cases, applications for stays of proceedings funded by third parties on the ground that the funding was champertous have failed[1]. But the court retains power to stay litigation on the ground of abuse of process and the question whether the courts' process is affected or threatened by an agreement for the division of spoils is one to be considered in the light of the facts in each case. As regards an action brought by a trustee in bankruptcy, or other office-holder, one concern is whether he is acting in abuse of his office. Where the cause of action is vested in the trustee, the consequence of his assigning the recoveries of the action but not the cause of action itself would mean that the nominal claimant in the action would be the trustee. If he had granted the assignee of the recoveries control over the conduct of the action, an action apparently brought by the trustee in bankruptcy, on whom is conferred a certain status by virtue of his office, would in fact be conducted by the assignee. This could amount to an abuse of the trustee's office comparable to the abuse involved where a trustee brings possession proceedings over secured property solely for the benefit of the secured creditor[2]. So, where any action is to be brought by a trustee in bankruptcy, he should be careful to retain control over the conduct of the action.

[1]   *Faryab v Smith* (28 August 1998, unreported); *Stocznia Gdanska SA v Latreefers Inc (No 2)* [2001] 2 BCLC 116 at [60]–[61].
[2]   See *Re Zucco, ex p Cooper* (1875) 10 Ch App 510; *Re Ng (a bankrupt), Ng v Ng (trustee)* [1997] BCC 507 (Lightman J): 'a trustee in bankruptcy is not vested with the powers and privileges of his office so as to enable himself to accept engagement as a hired gun'; *Bukhari's Trustee v Bukhari* [1999] BPIR 157.

Indemnity against liability for costs

19.38   The trustee should ensure that he is adequately protected against any liability for costs. Although, if the cause of action is sold so as to enable the assignee to bring the action in his own name, it may be that the risk of an order being made against the trustee is reduced.

D THE BANKRUPT AS DEFENDANT

Stay of proceedings

19.39   At any time when proceedings on a bankruptcy petition are pending or an individual has been adjudged bankrupt, the court may stay any action, execution or other legal process against the property or person of the debtor or, as the case may be, of the bankrupt[1]. This provision is discussed at para **16.33** as one of the measures available to preserve the estate in as large a form as possible for the benefit of the creditors.

[1]   IA 1986, s 285(1).

Adoption by trustee of bankrupt's defence to pending proceedings

19.40   Where the trustee adopts the bankrupt's defence to pending proceedings, the trustee puts himself at risk of liability for the costs of that defence arising in the action both before and after his adoption of the defence[1].

[1]   *Watson v Holliday* (1882) 20 Ch D 780; *Borneman v Wilson* (1884) 28 Ch D 53 and see the discussion in para **19.13** above in relation to the adoption of claims made by the bankrupt in proceedings pending at the commencement of the bankruptcy.

Standing to pursue appeals

19.41   On bankruptcy the bankrupt loses his standing to pursue an appeal, even where the appeal is against the judgment on which the bankruptcy petition is founded[1]. Where the bankrupt is a defendant, this result occurs not because an asset of his has been divested from him but because he is protected by his bankruptcy from the claim which lies only against his estate and has therefore no recognised interest in defending it.

1   *Heath v Tang* [1993] 4 All ER 694, [1993] 1 WLR 1421; *James v Rutherford-Hodge* [2005] EWCA Civ 1580, [2006] BPIR 973.

Leave to commence proceedings

19.42 After a bankruptcy order is made, no person who is a creditor of the bankrupt in respect of a debt provable in the bankruptcy shall, before the discharge of the bankrupt, commence any action or other legal proceedings against the bankrupt except with the leave of the court and on such terms as it may impose[1]. In the most recent decision it was held that proceedings commenced without leave are a nullity and leave may not be granted retrospectively[2]. The prohibition is not expressed to relate only to proceedings to enforce provable debts.

1   IA 1986, s 285(3). The provision also denies the creditor any remedy against the property or person of the bankrupt in respect of the debt and is subject to the limited rights of enforcement and distress contained in IA 1986, ss 346 and 347.
2   *Taylor (a bankrupt), Re, Davenham Trust plc (t/a Booker Montagu Leasing) v CV Distribution (UK) Ltd* [2006] EWHC 3029 (Ch), [2007] Ch 150, [2007] 3 All ER 638; not following *Re Saunders (a bankrupt)* [1997] Ch 60, [1997] 3 All ER 992.

19.43 Leave will ordinarily be given where the claim is in respect of a liability from which the bankrupt will not be released by his discharge[1]. The prohibition does not affect proceedings commenced after discharge in respect of such claims. Leave should also be given where the action will enable the claimant to recover under the Third Parties (Rights against Insurers) Act 1930 from the bankrupt's insurers, who will be the effective defendants in such a case.

1   *Re Hutton* [1969] 2 Ch 201, [1969] 1 All ER 936.

19.44 Where leave is sought to commence proceedings against a company after it has been wound up, the court will as a matter of course impose a condition that any judgment obtained against the company shall not be enforced against its assets without the leave of the court. Such a condition is not necessary in bankruptcy because the IA 1986, s 285(3)(a) provides that (executions and distresses permitted under IA 1986, ss 346 and 347 apart) no creditor of the bankrupt in respect of a provable debt shall have any remedy against the property or person of the bankrupt in respect of that debt. 'Remedy' in that prohibition must be construed as not including proof in the bankruptcy. Hence if the proceedings for which leave is granted concern a claim for a debt provable in the bankruptcy and judgment is obtained, no remedy apart from proof will be available. But if the judgment concerns a claim which is neither provable in the bankruptcy nor a debt from which the bankrupt is discharged, the claimant, if he obtains judgment, will be entitled to enforce the judgment, in so far as he can against any assets which the bankrupt has retained as not forming part of the estate or against any assets subsequently acquired by the bankrupt. In *Re Davies (a bankrupt)*[1] where leave was granted for the purpose of pursuing the bankrupt's insurers under the Third Parties (Rights against Insurers) Act 1930, the decision of the district judge not to impose any condition that no enforcement proceedings should be taken against the person or property of the bankrupt in respect of any judgment or order for costs was upheld on appeal. The condition concerning enforcement of the judgment, which concerned a claim for a provable debt, was not necessary for the reason explained above. The condition regarding the costs was sought in order to protect the bankrupt against liability for the costs of the action since she would not be discharged by the bankruptcy from liability under an order for costs in the action because it would be a post-bankruptcy debt[2]. But the deputy judge held that it would be wrong, by imposing such a condition, to limit the discretion of the judge at trial to award costs as he thought fit. This must be right. If the claim was unsuccessfully contested by the insurers, then the appropriate order to make in respect of the costs of the trial might be that they should pay the costs; but the person and time to decide whether to make that order would be the judge conducting the trial at its conclusion who would then be in a position to assess who should bear them. Had the condition sought been granted when sought, the bankrupt would have a free hand to defend the proceedings without incurring any liability for costs.

[1]   [1997] BPIR 619.
[2]   See *Glenister v Rowe* [2000] Ch 76, [1999] 3 All ER 452 which confirms that liability for costs under a costs order made after the commencement of the bankruptcy is not a debt from which the bankrupt is discharged because, even though the action to which the order for costs relates may have been commenced before the bankruptcy, the risk that an order might be made does not render the debt a contingent liability within the IA 1986, s 382(1)(b).

Transfer of proceedings

19.45 The High Court has a special power to transfer proceedings where a bankruptcy order has been made by the High Court or an interim receiver has been appointed or bankruptcy proceedings have been transferred to that court from the county court. Pursuant to this provision a judge of any division of the High Court may, of his own motion, order the transfer to that division of certain proceedings pending against the bankrupt in another division of the High Court or in any court in England and Wales other than the High Court. Under the rules of procedure in force before 26 April 1999, a registrar in bankruptcy in the High Court was entitled to exercise the jurisdiction to order masters from county court of the High Court[1]. Relevant proceedings are those brought by or against the bankrupt for the purpose of enforcing a claim against the bankrupt's estate, or brought by a person other than the bankrupt for the purpose of enforcing any such claim, including in either case proceedings of any description by a mortgagee[2]. The transfer ought not to be made unless it is shown that it will be of advantage to the bankrupt's estate[3]. Where proceedings are transferred, the registrar may, subject to the special directions of the judge, dispose of any matter arising in the proceedings which would, but for the transfer, have been disposed of in chambers[4].

[1]   *Secretary of State for Trade and Industry v Guest* [1999] BPIR 587.
[2]   IR 1986, r 7.15(1)–(3).

19.45 *Effect of bankruptcy on litigation and arbitration*

3   *Re Ross, ex p Trustee* (1888) 5 Morr 281; *Re White & Co, ex p Official Receiver* (1884) 1 Morr 77; *Re Champagne, ex p Kemp* (1893) 10 Morr 285; see also *Re Kay and Lovell* [1941] Ch 420, [1941] 2 All ER 67.
4   IR 1986, r 7.15(4).

Payments into court

19.46 Payments may be made into court by a defendant either:

(1)   under CPR Pt 36 for the purpose of seeking to settle a claim or in support of a plea that payment has been tendered but not accepted;
(2)   pursuant to an order, as a condition of a defendant's being permitted to continue to defend an action; or
(3)   pursuant to an order for security for costs.

19.47 Where the payment into court is made before the presentation of the petition, the effect in each of these cases is to put the claimant into the position of a secured creditor.

19.48 In respect of the first case, although Vaughan Williams J in *Re Gordon, ex p Navalchand*[1] held that money paid into court under RSC Ord 22 was subject to a 'conventional charge' in favour of the plaintiff pending either the outcome of the proceedings or, if overtaken by bankruptcy, the admission of his proof, a subsequent decision of the Court of Appeal[2] put the point in doubt. But the Court of Appeal settled the law in *WA Skerratt Ltd v John Bromley Ltd*[3] in which Oliver LJ held that a defendant who made a payment into court under RSC Ord 22 parted outright with his money which became 'subject to whatever order the court may see fit to make and to treat it as the defendant's property available for distribution in his bankruptcy is to assume, for the purposes of exercising the court's discretion, the very situation which will only arise if the court exercises its discretion in a particular way'. There is no reason why the position should be different under CPR Pt 36.

1   [1897] 2 QB 516.
2   *Peal Furniture Ltd v Adrian Share (Interiors) Ltd* [1977] 2 All ER 211, [1977] 1 WLR 464.
3   [1985] QB 1038, [1985] 1 All ER 216; applied in *Cleaver v Delta American Reinsurance Co* [2001] UKPC 6, [2001] 2 AC 328.

19.49 As to the second and third cases, the purpose of requiring the payments into court in each case is to give the claimant security in the one case for his claim and in the other, for his costs and it is clear that such money in court does not form part of the estate[1]. If the claimant establishes his claim or entitlement to costs in the proceedings or by admission of his proof, the court should order that the money be paid out to the claimant; alternatively if he does not, the court should order its payment out to the trustee. But while it remains in court, the claimant is secured in respect of the contingent debt which his substantive claim represents or of the possible liability which might arise on a subsequent order for costs[2].

786

¹ See *Re Ford, ex p Trustee* [1900] 2 QB 211 (payment into court as condition of defending); *Re Gordon, ex p Navalchand* [1897] 2 QB 516 (security for costs).
² See *Glenister v Rowe* [2000] Ch 76, [1999] 3 All ER 452.

19.50 If a payment were made into court after the presentation of the petition on which a bankruptcy order was later made, the payment would be rendered void unless approved by the court by virtue of IA 1986, s 284. The fact that the payment had been ordered by the court with conduct of the action as a condition of defending the claim or as security for costs would not amount to the approval required which, it is submitted, means the approval of the court with conduct of the bankruptcy proceedings. It is unlikely that approval would be given since the effect would be to promote a creditor from being unsecured to one holding security and it is difficult to imagine circumstances in which that could be justified¹.

¹ For the position under the old law of bankruptcy where petitions would ordinarily be stayed pending the outcome of proceedings to determine whether a disputed debt was owed, see *Re Gentry* [1910] 1 KB 825.

Freezing injunctions

19.51 A freezing injunction does not give the claimant who has obtained it any security over the assets to which the injunction pertains¹. Where a defendant company paid money into an account to be held pending further order of the court in substitution for a freezing order which was in consequence discharged, the fund was not held as security for the claimant's claim but as the defendant's own funds held on the same footing as they would have been had the injunction remained in force². Once the trustee in bankruptcy is appointed, it will be open to him and usually necessary to apply for the discharge of the injunction in order that he may deal freely with the assets. But, given the prior need to restrain the bankrupt from dissipating his assets, the trustee will wish first to ensure that the assets are sufficiently within his control.

¹ *Cretanor Maritime Co Ltd v Irish Marine Management Ltd* [1978] 3 All ER 164, [1978] 1 WLR 966.
² *Flightline Ltd v Edwards* [2003] EWCA Civ 63, [2003] 1 WLR 1200; *Technocrats International Inc v Fredic Ltd* [2003] 3 All ER 1200, [2005] 1 BCLC 467.

Execution

19.52 The extent to which a judgment creditor is entitled under the IA 1986, s 346 to retain property on which he is in the course of executing his judgment at the commencement of the bankruptcy is discussed at para **16.50**.

Interim orders and voluntary arrangements

19.53 Both an interim order made in order to protect a debtor while he prepares and puts a proposal to his creditors for a voluntary arrangement and the voluntary arrangement itself, if the creditors accept the proposal, have an effect on actions proceeding against the debtor. These effects are discussed more fully in **Chapter 6**. In outline the following effects may be noted.

19.54 While an application for an interim order is pending, the court may stay any action, execution or other legal process against the debtor or his property[1]. This power is exercisable not only by the bankruptcy court in which the application for an interim order is pending, but also by the court in which the action against the debtor is proceeding[2]. The court may either stay the proceedings or allow them to continue on such terms as it thinks fit.

[1]   IA 1986, s 254(1).
[2]   IA 1986, s 254(2).

19.55 If an interim order is made, no bankruptcy petition may be presented or proceeded with against the debtor and no other proceedings, execution or other legal process may be commenced or continued against the debtor or his property except with the leave of the court[1].

[1]   IA 1986, s 252(2).

19.56 Where the debtor's proposal for a voluntary arrangement is approved at the creditors' meeting, that arrangement comes into effect as if made by the debtor on the date of the meeting[1] and every creditor who had notice of the meeting is bound by the arrangement whether he attended the meeting or not and irrespective of whether or how he cast his vote. No such creditor may then proceed with any action or execution against the debtor, save under the arrangement.

[1]   IA 1986, s 260(2).

19.57 Where the debtor's proposal is rejected by the creditors, the court may discharge any interim order in force[1]. After the discharge of the interim order proceedings may be instituted or continued against the debtor without leave or risk of stay. The court may, however, extend the force of the interim order where a challenge is made to the meeting's decision[2].

[1]   IA 1986, s 259(2).
[2]   Under the IA 1986, s 262.

E THE TRUSTEE'S POWERS IN RESPECT OF LITIGATION

19.58 The powers of a trustee in bankruptcy have been discussed in **Chapter 18**, section F. In relation to litigation and resolution of disputes the trustee in bankruptcy may, with the permission of the creditors' committee or of the court[1]:

(1)   bring, institute or defend any action or legal proceedings relating to the property comprised in the bankrupt's estate;

(2) refer to arbitration, or compromise on such terms as may be agreed, any debts, claims or liabilities subsisting or supposed to subsist between the bankrupt and any person who may have incurred any liability to the bankrupt;

(3) make such compromise or other arrangement as may be thought expedient with the creditors, or persons claiming to be creditors, in respect of any bankruptcy debts; and

(4) make such compromise or other arrangements as may be thought expedient with respect to any claim arising out of or incidental to the bankrupt's estate made or capable of being made on the trustee by any person or by the trustee of any person[2].

[1] The court will be unwilling to overrule the views of the creditors' committee or the creditors generally; *Re Ridgway, ex p Hurlbatt* (1889) 6 Morr 277; *Re Ridgway, ex p Clarke* (1891) 8 Morr 289; *Re Pilling, ex p Salaman* [1906] 2 KB 644; and see also *Re Geiger* [1915] 1 KB 439 at 450, 451, 456, CA; *Re Salmon, ex p Official Receiver* [1916] 2 KB 510 at 516.

[2] IA 1986, s 314(1)(a), Sch 5, paras 2, 6, 7 and 8.

The permission of the creditors' committee or the court

19.59 In order to secure his right to be paid out of the bankrupt's estate the costs and expenses of any legal proceedings, the trustee should obtain the permission of either the creditors' committee or the court, before instituting, adopting or defending any action or legal proceedings relating to the property comprised in the bankrupt's estate[1]. When giving the trustee such permission, the creditors' committee may limit the amount of money to be expended[2]. If this limit is exceeded, or if the trustee has proceeded with the action or defence without first obtaining the required permission, he may firstly lose his right to an indemnity out of the estate for the expenses incurred by him in excess of the permitted limit, and secondly lose his right to any indemnity at all[3].

[1] *Re White, ex p Nichols* (1902) 46 Sol Jo 569; *Re Duncan, ex p Official Receiver* [1892] 1 QB 879, CA; and see also *Re A Debtor (No 26A of 1975)* [1984] 3 All ER 995, [1985] 1 WLR 6 in which the trustee did not require permission because the costs of litigation were going to be met by the defendant or the legal aid fund.

[2] *Re Duncan, ex p Official Receiver* [1892] 1 QB 879.

[3] *Re White, ex p Nichols* (1902) 46 Sol Jo 569; *Re Duncan, ex p Official Receiver* [1892] 1 QB 879.

19.60 The requirement to obtain the sanction of the creditors' committee or the court is a matter between the trustee and the creditors. If the trustee brings an action without obtaining the sanction, the action is not a nullity. For in bringing the action the trustee is not strictly speaking acting ultra vires but rather acting improperly in such a way that he may be denied his costs from the estate; alternatively, perhaps, any resulting transaction, although not void, may be voidable[1].

[1] *Lee v Sangster* (1857) 2 CBNS 1; *Re Branson, ex p Trustee* [1914] 2 KB 701; *Leeming v Lady Murray* (1879) 13 Ch D 123; *Clark v Smith* [1940] 1 KB 126, [1939] 4 All ER 59, CA; *Re A Debtor (No 26A of 1975)* [1984] 3 All ER 995, [1985] 1 WLR 6; and see also *Weddell v JA Pearce & Major* [1987] 3 All ER 624, [1988] Ch 26.

19.61 Where the trustee has omitted to obtain the permission of the creditors' committee, he may obtain subsequent ratification either from the committee or from the court in order to recoup his expenses[1]. The trustee's action may only be ratified if ratification is sought without undue delay and the trustee shows that he acted in an emergency. In other cases, he will be ordered to bear personally the cost of his actions.

¹   IA 1986, s 314(4).

Trustee's title in litigation

19.62 The trustee should sue or be sued in his official name, i e 'the trustee of the estate of AB, a bankrupt'[1].

¹   IA 1986, s 305(4).

Γ ARBITRATION

Introduction

19.63 Arbitration in private law is a method of resolving disputes which depends upon a contract between the relevant parties to refer present or future disputes to arbitration[1]. Since bankruptcy does not ordinarily discharge contracts to which the bankrupt is party, the contract comprised in an arbitration agreement remains extant despite the bankruptcy.

¹   See *Heyman v Darwins Ltd* [1942] AC 356, [1942] 1 All ER 337 and *Harbour Assurance Co (UK) Ltd v Kansa General International Assurance Co Ltd* [1993] 3 All ER 897 for discussion of the separability of an arbitration contained in the same document as other contractual terms and see the Arbitration Act 1996, s 7.

Where the bankrupt is party to an arbitration agreement

19.64 Where a bankrupt had become party to a contract containing an arbitration agreement before the commencement of his bankruptcy, his trustee may choose whether to adopt the contract or not[1]. The trustee is more likely to face the question whether to adopt a contract or not before any dispute to which the arbitration agreement would relate has arisen. If he does adopt the contract, the arbitration agreement is enforceable by or against him in matters arising from or connected with the contract[2]. By adopting a contract, the trustee substitutes himself for the bankrupt and, as well as receiving whatever benefits may accrue under the contract for the estate, the trustee takes on the bankrupt's obligation to perform the contract and risks personal liability under it. It is therefore he who is then the appropriate party to any arbitral proceedings.

¹   IA 1986, s 349A.
²   IA 1986, s 349A(2).

Where the bankrupt is interested as claimant in an arbitration pending at the commencement of the bankruptcy

19.65 A claimant in an arbitration, just like a claimant in court proceedings, has commenced the process in order to pursue a claim comprising a cause of action. As discussed above and at para **14.55**, a cause of action is an item of property which forms part of the estate and vests in the trustee on his appointment. Hence title to pursue the claim is automatically transferred from the bankrupt to the trustee who may choose whether to continue the claim or not. Where the claim arises under a contract that contains an arbitration agreement, if the trustee decides to pursue the claim under the contract which the bankrupt had commenced, his decision would amount to a decision to adopt the contract and, since the arbitration agreement is enforceable against him[1], he must continue to pursue the claim by way of the arbitration. If the trustee decides not to pursue the claim, then this may give rise to a liability for the other party's costs of the arbitration to date. But that liability will only be a debt provable in the bankruptcy[2].

[1]   IA 1986, s 349A.
[2]   See *Re Smith, ex p Edwards* (1886) 3 Morr 179.

Where the bankrupt is the respondent in an arbitration pending at the commencement of the bankruptcy

19.66 If the bankrupt is the respondent in an arbitration pending at the commencement of the bankruptcy, there is unlikely to be any good purpose served by the trustee's adopting any contract containing the arbitration agreement pursuant to which the dispute was referred (although the position may be different if the bankrupt was also pursuing a counterclaim with good prospects of success). The choice faced by the trustee is described by Cave J in *Re Smith, ex p Edwards*[1]. In that case Edwards had commenced arbitral proceedings against the bankrupt before his bankruptcy, but the trustee had purported to revoke the arbitrator's authority. The arbitrator had ignored the attempted revocation and awarded a sum in respect of the claim and £600 in respect of the costs of the arbitration. The court held that the revocation was ineffective and that Edwards was entitled to prove both for the award (which the trustee did not dispute) and for the costs because they represented a debt arising 'by reason of an obligation incurred before the date of the receiving order'[2]. However, Cave J described the courses available to the trustee in the situation which had arisen as follows:

> 'he might have gone to a judge and expressed his willingness to pay what was right if the litigation was put a stop to. He might have desired to save the estate unnecessary expense, and have obtained an order of the court staying the reference. If he had done so, one of the terms would have been to allow Edwards to prove as for damages for the reference coming to an end. Another course was to take no notice; to leave Edwards to go on if he wished, and if he did go on, to leave him to prove.'

[1]   (1886) 3 Morr 179.
[2]   Bankruptcy Act 1883, s 37(3); see IA 1986, s 382(1)(b) which is in the same terms though the relevant date is that of the commencement of the bankruptcy.

19.67 It is generally assumed that the court's power to stay the arbitration in such circumstances is contained in the IA 1986, s 285(1) which enables the court to stay 'any action, execution or other legal process' at any time when proceedings on a bankruptcy petition are pending or an individual has been adjudged bankrupt. The assumption is that legal process includes arbitrations.

Bankruptcy does not revoke the arbitrator's authority

19.68 It has long been the law that the bankruptcy of a party to a pending arbitration does not revoke the arbitrator's authority and that the trustee in bankruptcy has no power to revoke the submission[1]. Under the Arbitration Act 1996, subject to the court's power to remove an arbitrator, an arbitrator's authority may only be revoked by the court where there has been a failure in the process of appointment or by the parties acting jointly or by an arbitral or other institution or person vested with powers of revocation[2].

[1]   *Hemsworth v Brian* (1845) 1 CB 131. See *Russell on Arbitration* (1891, 7th edn), p 162. Arguments to opposite effect in nineteenth century cases harked back to the position at common law before the Act of 3 & 4 W IV c 42, s 39. Before that Act, the position at common law was that the authority of the arbitrator might be revoked at any time before the award was made at the pleasure of any party to the submission. The Act made it necessary to obtain the leave of the court in respect of certain categories of submissions. Occasionally, but not usually, bankruptcy was taken as a ground for permitting revocation: *Gaffney v Killen* 12 Ir C L Rep App xxv. For other cases where revocation was not permitted by reason of a party's bankruptcy, see *Andrews v Palmer* (1821) 4 B & Ald 250; *Snook v Hellyer* (1818) 2 Chit 43 and *Re Smith, ex p Edwards* (1886) 3 Morr 179.
[2]   Arbitration Act 1996, s 23(3). The court's powers of revocation and removal are contained in s 18 and s 24 respectively.

References made after the commencement of the bankruptcy

19.69 Where no reference has been made before the commencement of the bankruptcy but either there is at that date a dispute to which the arbitration agreement relates or such a dispute subsequently arises, the position is as follows:

(1)   The trustee may, with the sanction of the creditors' committee or the court, refer to arbitration any debts, claims or liabilities subsisting or supposed to subsist between the bankrupt and any person who may have incurred any liability to the bankrupt[1]. Although the exercise of this power is not restricted to cases where there is an agreement to refer disputes made before bankruptcy by the bankrupt, it enables the trustee to commence arbitrations against a respondent who is or may be liable to the bankrupt.

(2)   If the trustee has adopted a contract entered into by the bankrupt containing an arbitration agreement, then the arbitration agreement is enforceable both by him and against him[2]. This raises the following two questions:

(a)   If the trustee who has adopted a contract containing an arbitration clause wishes to refer a dispute to arbitration, does he need to obtain the sanction of the creditors' committee or the court? It is suggested that the prudent trustee should do so in order to secure his right to the costs of the arbitration from the estate. But whether it is necessary for him to do so, is not wholly clear. The possibilities seem to be: (i) that he is exercising his power to bring 'legal proceedings' under the IA 1986, Sch 5, para 2 and therefore does require sanction[3]. So to construe 'legal proceedings' is consistent with the construction of 'legal process' mentioned above. Or (ii) that he is exercising the power under the IA 1986, Sch 5, para 6 to refer to arbitration a claim subsisting between the bankrupt and a person who may have incurred liability to the bankrupt. But this does not seem an apt description of the liability which the other party may have incurred under a contract adopted by the trustee. Or (iii) that the IA 1986, s 349A(2) confers on him power to refer disputes relating to adopted contracts without sanction from the creditors' committee or the court and is to be contrasted with the case where he has not adopted a contract but wishes to refer a dispute in which case he must obtain the consent of the creditors' committee before applying for an order from the court referring the dispute to arbitration[4].

(b)   If the other party to the adopted contract wishes to refer a dispute to arbitration, does he need the leave of the court before doing so? The possible answers are: (i) that such leave is necessary because of the restriction imposed by the IA 1986, s 285(3)(b). But that provision only applies to a person who is a creditor of the bankrupt in respect of a provable debt. If the contract has been adopted by the trustee and the claim which the other party seeks to arbitrate has arisen after the trustee's adoption of the contract, the other party may not be, or at least may not be acting in a capacity as, a creditor of the bankrupt in respect of a provable debt. Or (ii) that such leave is not necessary because the IA 1986, s 349A(2) enables the other party to make the reference without restriction.

It is submitted that the better view is that the trustee should obtain sanction before making a reference to arbitration. For although he may have adopted the contract and thereby have obtained power to enforce the arbitration agreement contained in it, his exercise of that power ought to remain subject to sanction because of the expense to the estate which the reference will entail. Conversely the other party ought to be able to enforce the arbitration agreement, without seeking the leave of the court, because it forms part of a contractual scheme which the trustee has adopted since the commencement of the bankruptcy. But the point is not free from doubt.

(3)   If the trustee has not adopted the contract and a matter to which the arbitration agreement applies requires to be determined in connection with or for the purposes of the bankruptcy proceedings either the trustee acting with the consent of the creditors' committee or any other party to the agreement may apply to the court which may, if it thinks fit in all the circumstances of the case, order that the matter be referred to arbitration in accordance with the arbitration agreement[5]. The court is the court which has jurisdiction in the bankruptcy proceedings. The

court would probably exercise its discretion in a similar way to how it decides whether to permit proceedings in court to be commenced under the IA 1986, s 285(3)(b).

1   IA 1986, s 314, Sch 5, para 6.
2   IA 1986, s 349A(2).
3   IA 1986, s 314(1)(a).
4   See the IA 1986, s 349A(3).
5   IA 1986, s 349A(3).

The award

19.70 Where the trustee has adopted a contract containing an arbitration agreement and an award is made against him under it, the award will be enforceable against him, with the leave of the court, in the same manner as a judgment[1]. Where the trustee has not adopted the contract, but the validity of a claim arising under a pre-bankruptcy contract made against the bankrupt has been determined by arbitration, the other party in whose favour the award has been made will be entitled to prove in the estate for the amount awarded. If the award is in favour of the trustee, then he may enforce it subject to obtaining the leave of the court.

1   Arbitration Act 1996, s 66(1).

G OTHER FORMS OF ALTERNATIVE DISPUTE RESOLUTION

19.71 A variety of methods by which disputants may seek to resolve their differences out of court have become current because of the policy, voiced in the CPR, to encourage settlement out of court. Such procedures, which in essence are supervised or formalised negotiations, depend on the consent of the parties both as to whether to commence the procedure and as to whether a settlement of the dispute should be agreed. It is submitted that no special considerations arise but that by application of the ordinary rules of bankruptcy law the possible situations are as follows:

(1)   If before the bankruptcy order is made, the bankrupt has settled a claim against him by agreement with the claimant but has made no payment pursuant to the settlement to the claimant, the claimant will be an unsecured creditor in respect of his claim and will have to prove for it. It is submitted that the trustee would not be bound by the bankrupt's settlement agreement in such a case but would be entitled to look at the substance of the claim and admit or reject the proof in whole or part according to the merit of the substantive claim[1].

(2)   If the bankrupt had made a payment to the claimant pursuant to the settlement before the presentation of the petition, then the trustee would be entitled to apply to set aside the payment as a transaction at an undervalue or as a preference and an order made to set the payment aside if the circumstances justified it[2], although if the claim was made in good faith and the payment was similarly made in settlement of it, it is unlikely that they would.

(3)   If the bankrupt made a payment to the claimant pursuant to the settlement between the presentation of the petition on which the bankruptcy order was made and the making of the bankruptcy order, the payment would be void unless approved by the court[3].

(4)   If the bankrupt had embarked on a procedure of negotiation but the dispute has not been settled before the bankruptcy order was made, the trustee would not be obliged to continue with the procedure. If he did not, the claimant would be entitled to prove his claim and the trustee would be entitled to admit or reject the proof in whole or in part as appropriate and any further dispute might be resolved according to the usual procedures for resolving disputed proofs of debt[4].

(5)   Since the trustee has power (with the sanction of the creditors' committee or the court) to make such compromise or other arrangement as may be thought expedient with persons claiming to be creditors in respect of bankruptcy debts and has ancillary power to do any other act which is expedient in connection with the exercise of that power[5], he has power to commence or continue a procedure of negotiation of this sort.

[1]   Compare the trustee's power to look behind judgments discussed at para **22.8**.
[2]   See the IA 1986, ss 339 and 340.
[3]   IA 1986, s 284.
[4]   IA 1986, s 322.
[5]   IA 1986, s 314 and Sch 5, paras 6 and 14.

Chapter 20

ADJUSTMENT OF PRIOR TRANSACTIONS

A INTRODUCTION

General

20.1 The Insolvency Act 1986 ('IA 1986') contains provisions which aim both to protect the assets comprising the bankrupt's estate at the date of the bankruptcy order and to recover assets or their value which have been transferred away from his estate by the debtor in the pre-bankruptcy period. The statutory protection afforded to the various assets making up the bankrupt's estate is discussed in **Chapter 16**. This chapter considers the statutory powers available to the court on the application of the trustee in bankruptcy to recover assets which have passed out of the debtor's control before he becomes bankrupt.

20.2 The Insolvency Act 1986[1] also amends the law, previously contained in the Law of Property Act 1925, s 172, under which transactions designed to defraud creditors may be set aside irrespective of whether the debtor has become insolvent. These provisions apply to both individual and corporate debtors and are considered in **Chapter 21**.

[1]   IA 1986, ss 423–425.

Fraud on a debtor's creditors

20.3 Equality is the essential principle underpinning all insolvency law. Any agreement or arrangement whereby one creditor obtains a secret collateral

796

advantage over other creditors, whether directly from the debtor or indirectly on behalf of the debtor, in connection with a composition or scheme of arrangement for the settlement of an individual's debts is a fraud on the other creditors. Such an agreement will be unenforceable between the parties to it, and is voidable at the instance of any creditor not similarly advantaged. The principle is scarcely surprising, being 'consistent with the ordinary principles of morality recognised by all mankind'[1] and save for one recent case the authorities have become reverend with age, pre-dating for the most part the Bankruptcy Act 1914 and the Deeds of Arrangement Act 1914 if not the Bankruptcy Act 1883. The growth of the market for 'distressed debt' does perhaps warrant a forceful reminder of the principle.

[1]   Per Stuart V-C in *Mare v Sandford* (1859) 1 Giff 288, 65 ER 923.

20.4 The recent case is that of *Somji v Cadbury Schweppes plc*[1] at first instance. The facts found by the deputy judge[2] revealed collateral payments made by a friend of a debtor who was proposing a voluntary arrangement in order to induce previously dissenting creditors to vote for the arrangement. Reviewing a number of the authorities the deputy judge concluded that the position 'as at the close of the nineteenth century' could be summarised in six principles:

(1)   any secret deal made in connection with a composition, or other similar arrangement for the settlement of debts, whereby a creditor was to receive more than the other creditors in return for supporting (or not opposing) the composition or arrangement, was illegal and void[3];

(2)   the existence of such a deal rendered the composition or arrangement voidable at the instance of an aggrieved creditor;

(3)   moreover, such a deal was wholly unenforceable as between the parties to it[4];

(4)   the principle was of entirely general application, and covered all forms of composition and arrangement, whether statutory or otherwise[5];

(5)   the principle was based on the fundamental rule that there must be equality between creditors in the distribution of the debtor's assets, and *additionally* on the equally fundamental rule that there should be complete good faith between the debtor and his creditors, and between the creditors inter se. It was therefore irrelevant that the inducement to the creditor came from a third party, and not out of the debtor's estate[6];

(6)   if the secret deal was not made by the debtor himself, all that was required was that it should have been made to his knowledge, and therefore with his concurrence, since concurrence must obviously be inferred where the debtor knows of the deal and does nothing either to stop it, or to inform his other creditors of it. The basis for this aspect of the principle was that, once the debtor knew of the secret deal, it became his duty to speak up and inform the other creditors of it[7].

[1]   [2001] 1 WLR 615, [2001] 1 BCLC 498.
[2]   Mr Anthony Boswood QC.
[3]   *McKewan v Sanderson* (1875) LR 20 Eq 65 at 72–73.
[4]   *Cockshott v Bennett* (1788) 2 Term Rep 763, 100 ER 411, where Lord Kenyon CJ, at 412–413, stressed that this was a principle of law as well as of equity; *McKewan v Sanderson* (1875) LR 20 Eq 65.

⁵ *Re Milner, ex p Milner* (1885) 15 QBD 605; *Mare v Sandford* (1859) 1 Giff 288, 65 ER 923.
⁶ *Knight v Hunt* (1829) 5 Bing 432, 130 ER 1127; *Dauglish v Tennent* (1866) LR 2 QB 49.
⁷ *Re EAB* [1902] 1 KB 457.

20.5 It is not necessary that the secret deal is for the payment of a greater sum than that available to other creditors. A secret agreement to provide one creditor with security for instalments which the debtor agrees to pay all his creditors is also illegal and void[1].

¹ *Leicester v Rose* (1803) 4 East 372, 102 ER 874; *ex p Sadler and Jackson* (1808) 15 Ves 52, 33 ER 675.

20.6 The Court of Appeal in *Somji v Cadbury Schweppes plc*[1] described the deputy judge's survey as impressive and accepted that in relation to compositions and arrangements with creditors before the advent of the individual voluntary arrangement the court did impose a strict requirement of good faith as between competing unsecured creditors, and prohibited any secret inducement to one creditor even if that inducement did not come from the debtor's own estate[2]. The court however overturned the deputy judge's finding that the result of the secret deal made the arrangement void, because this would open the door to challenges to individual voluntary arrangements long after the 28-day period allowed by IA 1986, s 262(3) had elapsed[3]. The basic principle however, that a secret deal by one creditor over the others is illegal and open to challenge by any party to it or any creditor affected by it, remains in place.

¹ [2001] 1 BCLC 498.
² Per Jonathan Parker LJ at [24]. He added: 'There is no strong presumption that a similar principle must be found in the new regime set out in Pt VIII of the Act, but (to put it at its lowest) it would be no great surprise to find it there in one form or another.' See also Judge LJ at [44]:

> 'The principles laid down in the cases decided in the 18th and 19th centuries, accurately summarised by the judge below, have not, as he rightly put it, 'become outmoded or unnecessary in modern times'. By contrast with the simple language of the section perhaps some of the eloquent flourish in these judgments may appear a little extravagant to us. Nevertheless s 276 and the rules encapsulate the principles of transparency and good faith and make proposed secret deals or confidential arrangements of the kind referred to by Robert Walker LJ as unacceptable today as they were in Victorian England.'

³ See para **6.232**.

B TRANSACTIONS AT AN UNDERVALUE AND PREFERENCES

General

20.7 Following the recommendations of the Cork Committee[1] the powers of the court to declare invalid transactions completed before the commencement of bankruptcy were substantially extended by the Insolvency Act 1986 over those previously in force. The provisions of the Bankruptcy Act 1914[2], which rendered voidable certain settlements and dispositions were altered and extended, and the court has been given an extensive discretion to make orders which have the aim of restoring the position to what it would have been if the bankrupt had not entered into the relevant transaction. The extent to which the powers of the court have been altered by the Insolvency Act 1986 means that this is new law to be construed independently of the previous law[3]. Orders which have the effect of avoiding or adjusting completed transactions will inevitably affect the rights of third parties, some of whom may be entirely innocent of any wrongdoing. The statutory protection originally afforded to innocent parties, either as purchasers of property interests which have been transferred as part of undervalue transactions or recipients of benefits, proved deficient in practice[4] and was improved by amendment by the Insolvency (No 2) Act 1994[5].

[1]   Report, Cmnd 8558, chapter 28.
[2]   Bankruptcy Act 1914, s 42 (avoidance of settlements) and s 44 (avoidance of preferences).
[3]   In *Re MC Bacon Ltd* [1990] BCLC 324 at p 335 Millett J stated that he:

> 'emphatically protested against the citation of cases decided under the old law. They cannot be of any assistance when the language of the statute has been so completely and deliberately changed. It may be that many of the cases which will come before the courts in future will be decided in the same way that they would have been decided under the old law. That may be so, but the grounds of decision will be different.'

> See also *Smith (a bankrupt) v Braintree District Council* [1990] 2 AC 215, at 238; *Re a Debtor (No 784 of 1991)* [1992] Ch 554, at 558–9, where Hoffmann J warned of the need to be wary of carrying over meanings given to similar words in earlier legislation but added that this did not mean that 'the language of the new Act comes entirely free of any of the intellectual freight which was carried by words and phrases in earlier bankruptcy and other legislation'. See also *Somji v Cadbury Schweppes plc* [2001] 1 BCLC 498, at 525 paras [23]–[24].

[4]   For a discussion of the problems inherent in the original drafting of IA 1986, s 342(2) see [1992] Gazette 22 and [1994] Gazette 23.
[5]   In respect of interest acquired or benefits received after 26 July 1994.

20.8 The provisions under which transactions at an undervalue and preferences may be challenged have extra-territorial effect[1].

[1]   See *Re Paramount Airways Ltd (in administration)* [1993] Ch 223, [1992] 3 All ER 1 and para **20.78** et seq.

Criminal proceedings

20.9 In cases involving criminal conduct the making of an order may be delayed by proceedings under the Proceeds of Crime Act 2002, and any subsequent orders have to take into account any realisation of property consequent upon confiscation proceedings[1].

[1]   See paras **20.98–20.100**.

Corporate insolvency decisions

20.10 The statutory provisions by which the court may adjust transactions at an undervalue and preferences in bankruptcy[1] closely mirror[2] the equivalent

20.10 *Adjustment of prior transactions*

provisions in corporate insolvency[3]. Decisions of the Companies Court on the corresponding corporate insolvency provisions will therefore frequently be directly relevant to bankruptcy cases.

1   Ie IA 1986, s 339 (transactions at an undervalue), s 340 (preferences), s 342 (orders under s 339 or s 340).
2   In the case of individual debtors who are traders the provisions which protect an undervalue transaction entered into by companies in good faith with reasonable grounds for belief that the transaction would benefit the company are not available. IA 1986, s 238(5) has no counterpart in IA 1986, s 339.
3   Ie IA 1986, s 238 (transactions at an undervalue), s 239 (preferences), s 241 (orders under s 238 or s 239).

Right of action in trustee

20.11 An application in respect of a transaction at an undervalue or a preference may only be made by a trustee in bankruptcy; a victim may not bring an application[1]. The trustee in bankruptcy may apply for an order under the appropriate section of the Insolvency Act 1986[2] and on a successful application the court makes such order as it thinks fit for the benefit of the creditors as a whole to restore the position to what it would have been[3] if the individual debtor had not entered into the transaction at an undervalue[4] or given the preference[5].

1   IA 1986, s 339(1) (transaction at an undervalue), s 340(1) (preference).
2   Ie s 339 (transaction at an undervalue), s 340 (preference).
3   So far as practicable. Inability to restore the position precisely is no reason for the court not to do what is possible and right in the circumstances, *Chohan v Saggar* [1994] 1 BCLC 706, CA.
4   IA 1986, s 339(2).
5   IA 1986, s 340(2).

20.12 These statutory provisions vest the trustee in bankruptcy with a right of action to bring proceedings in respect of transactions at an undervalue or preferences. This is a right which arises only after the debtor's bankruptcy and as such is not a right which can be assigned by the trustee in bankruptcy, neither does it constitute an asset of the estate which may be subject to a charge entered into by the debtor before bankruptcy[1].

1   Attempts to charge such rights are rather more likely to arise in corporate insolvency than in bankruptcy. See *Re Oasis Merchandising Services Ltd, Ward v Aitken* [1998] Ch 170, [1997] 1 BCLC 689, CA, following *Re Yagerphone Ltd* [1935] Ch 392 and *N W Robbie & Co Ltd v Witney Warehouse Co Ltd* [1963] 2 All ER 199, [1963] 1 WLR 1324, CA. In *Re Oasis Merchandising* the liquidator attempted to assign the fruits of a proposed action under IA 1986, s 214 (which permits claims against directors for wrongful trading) but the principle is of general application. Assets which are not the property of a company at the time of the commencement of its liquidation are recoverable only by the liquidator pursuant to the statutory powers which are conferred on him. The same must apply in personal insolvency.

20.13 An application in respect of a transaction defrauding creditors under IA 1986, s 423 may be brought by a victim where the debtor is bankrupt, but only with the leave of the court[1].

1   IA 1986 s 424(1), see para **21.26**.

The relevant time

20.14 The court may make an order[1] in respect of a transaction at an undervalue or a preference only if the transaction was entered into or the preference given at a 'relevant time'. Relevance is determined by reference to specified periods of time and the individual's solvency. A time is 'relevant' if:

(1)

    (a)   the individual is insolvent or becomes insolvent in consequence of the transaction or preference[2], and

    (b)   it is within the following periods ending with the day of the presentation of the bankruptcy petition on which the individual is adjudged bankrupt:

        (i)   in the case of a transaction at an undervalue, five years;

        (ii)   in the case of a preference which is not a transaction at an undervalue and is given to an associate[3] of the individual, two years;

        (iii)   in the case of a preference which is not a transaction at an undervalue and is not given to an associate, six months[4],

or

(2)   the individual enters into a transaction at an undervalue within two years of the day of the presentation of the bankruptcy petition on which the individual is adjudged bankrupt[5].

[1]   See para **20.87** et seq.
[2]   IA 1986, s 341(2).
[3]   Otherwise than by reason only of being an employee, IA 1986, s 341(1)(b); for 'associate' see **Appendix 2**.
[4]   IA 1986, s 341(1)(a), (b), (c).
[5]   IA 1986, s 341(2), irrespective of his solvency at the date of the transaction.

20.15 Accordingly a transaction at an undervalue made within two years of the date of the presentation of the bankruptcy petition may be the subject of an order whatever the individual's financial circumstances at the date he entered into the relevant transaction. In all other cases it is necessary to establish insolvency either at the time, or in consequence, of the transaction or preference.

Statutory presumption in the case of associates

20.16 The individual is presumed, subject to the contrary being shown, to be insolvent for the purposes of determining whether a transaction took place at a relevant time in relation to any transaction which is entered into by him with a person who is an associate for a reason other than by the fact that he is an employee[1].

[1]   IA 1986, s 341(2), and see para **20.22**.

Is insolvent or becomes insolvent

20.17 Insolvent for the purpose of determining whether a transaction was entered into or preference given at a relevant time means either that the individual is unable to pay his debts as they fall due, 'cash flow insolvency', or that the value of his assets is less than the amount of his liabilities, taking into account his contingent and prospective liabilities[1], 'balance sheet insolvency'. These provisions mirror the definition of inability of a company to pay its debts for the purposes of making a winding-up order[2], and the same test is used for determining the relevant time for the purposes of an order in respect of a transaction at an undervalue or preference in corporate insolvency[3].

1   IA 1986, s 341(3).
2   See IA 1986, s 123(1)(e), (2).
3   See IA 1986, s 240(2).

Unable to pay his debts as they fall due

20.18 It will usually be a fairly straightforward matter to determine whether or not the individual was able to pay his debts as they fell due at the date under consideration. The court will take a broad and realistic view. Unpaid invoices amount to evidence from which insolvency may be inferred[1]. Where however there is continuing business activity, one or even more unpaid invoices may have to be considered in context. While unpaid invoices may well demonstrate insolvency, such a conclusion is not inevitable[2].

1   *Re Taylor's Industrial Flooring Ltd v M & H Plant Hire (Manchester) Ltd* [1990] BCLC 216, CA; *Re DKG Contractors Ltd* [1990] BCC 903, 911.
2   See eg *Re Taylor Sinclair (Capital) Ltd* [2001] 2 BCLC 176, at [23] where the court stated that it would not be right to find an inability to pay debts because of one £5,500 debt where there were numerous later credits and debits, albeit for modest amounts.

Balance sheet insolvency

20.19 An individual is insolvent for these purposes if the value of his assets is less than the amount of his liabilities taking into account his contingent and prospective liabilities. Where the court is considering balance sheet insolvency difficult questions can arise, primarily because of the requirement that the court should 'take into account' any contingent and prospective liabilities. There is as yet no clear guidance on the manner in which the court should take such liabilities into account for the purposes of undervalue transactions and preferences[1]. Plainly the court cannot simply add the contingent and prospective liabilities to the present liabilities and strike a balance between the resultant total and the individual's assets[2]. Neither may the court ignore contingent and prospective liabilities because they are not present liabilities, for the statute expressly requires them to be taken into account. But on what basis are they to be taken into account? This is an area of particular concern in corporate insolvency because the same test applies in relation to the making of a winding-up order[3].

1 To the extent that it is ever permissible to consider authorities under the 'old' law, there is no assistance to be gained there in the present instance. The provisions of the Bankruptcy Act 1914, s 42 allowed the court to set aside voluntary settlements which amounted to fraudulent preferences, these provisions applying to corporate insolvency by virtue of the Companies Act 1985, s 615. Under the 1914 Act the court placed a reasonable estimate on contingent and future liabilities, see e g *Re Ridler* (1882) 22 Ch D 74 and *Re Densham* [1975] 1 WLR 1519. However, the wording of s 42 protected parties to the settlement who could prove that the settlor 'was able to pay all his debts without the aid of the property comprised in the settlement', and did not expressly incorporate a balance sheet approach. Further, in *Re Baker* [1936] Ch 61 the court held that where the settlement reserved to the settlor the power to raise a sufficient sum to meet his debts at the date of the settlement the settlor was not insolvent for the purposes of the Bankruptcy Act 1914, s 42.

2 This obvious point was stressed by Nourse J in *Re a Company (No 6794 of 1983)* [1986] BCLC 261 when considering a petition under the Companies Act 1985, s 223. The wording of s 223 was not precisely the same as that of IA 1986, s 123(2) but there is no material difference.

3 A winding-up order will be made against a company which is unable to pay its debts and a company is deemed to be unable to pay its debts, inter alia, if it is proved to the satisfaction of the court that the value of the company's assets is less than the amount of its liabilities, taking into account its contingent and prospective liabilities, IA 1986, s 123(2).

20.20 In *Re a Company (No 6794 of 1983)*[1] the court stated that it was necessary to 'consider whether, and if so when, [prospective liabilities] are likely to become present liabilities', but offered no guidance as to what regard should then be had to the result. In that case the petitioner for a winding-up order was the original tenant under a lease which had been assigned to the company. For many quarters the petitioner had had to pay the rent to the landlord and then recover it from the company, and the evidence was that the company had only managed to pay the rent by borrowing money from associated companies and others. The court, after holding that the company was just in a position to show that it could pay its existing debts, considered the effect of the contingent and prospective liabilities which the company faced. On the evidence the court found that the loans from the associated companies would not be withdrawn and that interest due would be waived, and decided that the company's financial position should be approached on the footing that the loans would not be called in until a date 18 months after the hearing of the winding-up petition. On this basis the petition was dismissed, in effect ignoring entirely liabilities which fell due at least 18 months after the date in question, an approach which is surely entirely unobjectionable. It offends common sense to suggest that an individual is insolvent because he cannot demonstrate how he will meet a liability which will not arise for another 18 months. Equally it would be quite unreasonable to suggest that an individual was solvent when he has net assets of £1,000 the day before a quarter day when rent of £25,000 would fall due, and cannot show how he will find the rent. But it is very difficult to see how a comprehensive principle may be developed, or indeed how cases away from the rather extreme examples given should be determined.

1 [1986] BCLC 261, at p 263.

20.21 The problem is the more acute in the light of the decision in *Byblos Bank v Al-Khudairy*[1] where the Court of Appeal stated that there is no scope on the statutory wording for the debtor's prospective assets to be taken into account as well as its prospective liabilities. Many companies will have prospective if not contingent liabilities, rent being the prime example. If the evidence demonstrates that in the past such liabilities have been met out of current income it seems harsh to ignore prospective assets when undertaking a balance sheet solvency exercise which includes prospective liabilities. The Act does undoubtedly refer to prospective and contingent liabilities while making no reference to prospective assets, but the words 'take into account' are extremely wide and should yet give the court the opportunity to take a fully practical approach to the question of balance sheet insolvency when it arises.

[1]   [1987] BCLC 232, see Nicholls LJ at p 246h.

Presumption of insolvency where transaction is with an associate

20.22 There is a statutory presumption which arises in transactions between the individual who has become bankrupt and a person who is an associate[1] of his, whether such transactions are challenged as undervalue transactions or preferences. The individual is presumed, subject to the contrary being shown, to be insolvent for the purposes of determining whether a transaction took place at a relevant time in relation to any transaction at an undervalue which is entered into by him with a person who is an associate otherwise than by reason only of being an employee[2]. The exemption of employee associates from the presumption reflects the difficulties that may arise in the payment of wages in the period leading up to bankruptcy. The shift of the burden of proof where an associate is involved in the transaction may be of considerable importance in many cases where the precise financial position of the individual is difficult to determine with accuracy.

[1]   'Associate' is defined in IA 1986, s 435, and this section is set out, annotated, in **Appendix 2**.
[2]   IA 1986, s 341(2).

Transaction at an undervalue

20.23 Where an individual is adjudged bankrupt and he has entered into a transaction at an undervalue with any person at a relevant time[1], the trustee in bankruptcy may apply to the court for an order to restore the position to what it would have been if the individual had not entered into that transaction[2]. An individual enters into a transaction with a person at an undervalue if:

(a)   he makes a gift to that person or otherwise enters into a transaction with that person on terms that provide for him to receive no consideration;

(b)   he enters into a transaction with that person in consideration of marriage; or

(c)   he enters into a transaction with that person for a consideration the value of which, in money or money's worth, is significantly less than the value, in money or money's worth, of the consideration provided by the individual[3].

[1]   See paras **20.14–20.16**.
[2]   IA 1986, s 339(1), (2).
[3]   IA 1986, s 339(3).

Gift or no consideration

20.24 The Insolvency Act 1986 here covers transactions where the individual receives no consideration, whatever the reason. The wording of the Act ('making a gift'; 'enters into a transaction') suggests that positive acts only are encompassed by these provisions. Mere acquiescence would be insufficient to ground an application for relief. Thus, for example, an office-holder may not be able to challenge as a transaction at an undervalue a default judgment in circumstances where there were plainly grounds for defending the action[1]. The assumption of liabilities under a mortgage will prevent the transfer of the property with its equity of redemption without further consideration from being a gift, but a comparison of the respective values of the consideration moving in each direction may lead to the conclusion that there is an element of bounty to the transferee, and thus that the transaction is one at an undervalue[2]. The receipt of monies by a third party from the debtor which are then lent back to the debtor or someone associated with him represent a transaction at an undervalue where no consideration is provided by the third party[3]. A decision by a debtor to incur interest retrospectively on a loan which had been made interest-free would be a transaction for no consideration[4]. Where the debtor is the trustee of property and he is directed by the beneficiary to transfer the bare legal estate in the property for no consideration to a third party[5], that is a transaction on terms that provide for the debtor to receive no consideration on a literal reading of the IA 1986, s 339 or s 423. The fact that the transferor is a trustee is no reason why that literal interpretation should not be applied[6].

[1] For a company to permit the entry of a default judgment in circumstances where it had reasonable grounds of defence might constitute a preference, as a preference may be given by a company 'suffering' something to be done, see paras **20.54–20.55**. However, the relevant time periods for a preference to be voidable (two years where given to an associate, six months otherwise) are considerably shorter than those that apply to a transaction at an undervalue (five years), see paras **20.14–20.16**.

[2] *Re Kumar, ex p Lewis v Kumar* [1993] 2 All ER 700, [1993] BCLC 548.

[3] *Re Barton Manufacturing Co Ltd* [1999] 1 BCLC 740.

[4] See *Re Shapland Inc* [2000] BCC 106; the loan was some 10 years old and the interest specified 1% per month compounded.

[5] Note that where a transfer of property to two or more persons is expressed in terms that they should take as beneficial joint tenants, that declaration is conclusive in the absence of fraud, mistake or some other reason for rectification, *Goodman v Gallant* [1986] Fam 106, [1986] 1 All ER 311, and see *Anglo Eastern Trust Ltd v Kermanshahchi* [2003] BPIR 1229, paras 76, 77.

[6] *Beckenham MC Ltd v Centralex Ltd* [2004] EWHC 1287 (Ch), [2004] 2 BCLC 764 at para 23 (a s 423 case): Hart J observed that unless D's creditor has for some reason a right to enforce against trust property he will be unaffected by the transaction, and continued, at para 24, 'D's creditor will have a right to enforce against the trust property in two possible situations. The first is where D has himself a right to be indemnified against his liability out of the trust property. The creditor may then be entitled by subrogation to stand in D's shoes as against the trust property. The second is where s 2(1)(b)(i) of the Charging Orders Act 1979 applies.'

20.25 Where the transferor transfers the bare legal title to the property to a transferee who already holds the entire beneficial interest, he has transferred nothing of value and there will be no transfer at an undervalue[1].

[1] The case is regularly advanced that a husband transferor already held the entire property on constructive trust for the wife transferee in accordance with the principles laid down by the House of Lords in *Lloyd's Bank plc v Rosset* [1991] 1 AC 107, [1990] 1 All ER 1111.

Such arguments often fail, see eg *Re Schuppan (a bankrupt)* [1996] 2 All ER 664, [1997] 1 BCLC 256 and *Kubiangha v Ekpenyong* [2002] EWHC 1567 (Ch), [2002] 2 BCLC 597.

In consideration of marriage

20.26 Any transaction in consideration of marriage is at an undervalue, whether the marriage is that of the individual debtor or not.

Significant difference in consideration

20.27 The more uncertain cases will fall under this head. Here the Act requires a comparison to be made between the value acquired by the individual from the transaction and the value provided by the individual. Both these values are measured in money or money's worth from the point of view of the individual debtor[1].

1   See paras **20.37–20.44**.

Gifts

20.28 An effective gift inter vivos is completed by a transfer of property without consideration by one person, the donor, to another, the donee, who accepts the gift. Gifts of a chose in possession, that is a tangible chattel, may be made by any donor of full age who is not under a legal disability. Minors may accept gifts, and, indeed, a gift to a child cannot be revoked[1]. There is a presumption in favour of the validity of a gift by a parent or grandparent or if the donor stands in loco parentis to the child[2]. The presumption of gift may be rebutted by showing that there was no intention to give[3]. A child may avoid gifts which are onerous or clearly to his prejudice to accept[4]. A husband and wife may give valid gifts to each other[5].

1   *Smith v Smith* (1836) 7 C&P 401.
2   *Wirth v Wirth* (1956) 98 CLR 228.
3   *Forrest v Forrest* (1865) 11 LT 763; *Goodfriend v Goodfriend* [1972] SCR 640.
4   *Re Blakely Ordnance Co, Lumsden's Case* (1868) 4 Ch App 31.
5   Being separate persons in law: Law of Property Act 1925, s 37.

20.29 An inter vivos gift of a chose in possession may be made by deed or delivery[1]. Delivery may be actual or constructive. An effective constructive delivery requires there to be a clear present intention to give and an intention to accept the property as a gift. The fact that the recipient regards the property as a loan and intends to give it back does not necessarily prevent the transaction being effective as a gift[2]. Delivery may be symbolic, for example giving means of access to property by delivering a key[3], or any article comprising or representing a part of a larger whole[4], or documents of title. Constructive delivery may take place where there is no change in the physical control of the possession but there is change in the purpose of that control. For example, if the donor utters words presenting the gift to the donee and declares himself bailee of the relevant chattel[5]. If the gift is made by deed, it is effective as soon as signed and delivered[6] even if the donee is unaware of the gift. If the donor retains possession, the deed of gift may require registration as a Bill of Sale[7]. A future interest in chattels cannot be the subject of a valid gift, though it is possible to contract to assign such property if and when the donor acquires it[8].

1   *Re Cole, ex p Trustees in Bankruptcy v Cole* [1964] Ch 175, [1963] 3 All ER 433, CA.
2   *Dewar v Dewar* [1975] 2 All ER 728, [1975] 1 WLR 1532.
3   *Re Craven's Estate, Lloyds Bank v Cockburn* [1937] Ch 423, 428; *Re Wasserberg* [1915] 1 Ch 195.
4   *Lock v Heath* (1892) 8 TLR 295, all furniture symbolised by a chair; *Re Harcourt* (1883) 31 WR 578.
5   *Re Stoneham* [1919] 1 Ch 149.
6   For the requirements of a deed see the Law of Property (Miscellaneous Provisions) Act 1989, s 1.
7   Bills of Sale Act 1878.
8   *Re Ellenborough* [1903] 1 Ch 697.

20.30 A gift may be made of a chose in action by absolute assignment to the donee. The instrument of gift must be executed in writing under the hand of the donor, and written notice must be given to the person liable to the donor in respect of the chose[1].

1   Law of Property Act 1925, s 136.

20.31 A gift may be made of an equitable interest in choses in possession or action by a donor who has legal title to the property making a clear declaration of trust for the donee so as to create a completely constituted trust[1]. An imperfect attempt to transfer the legal title to the donee will not normally be construed as a declaration of trust as 'Equity will not perfect an imperfect gift'[2], except where the donor has done all he alone can do to perfect the donee's legal title, but some act by someone else has yet to be done to complete the gift[3]. If the donor is only an equitable owner of the subject matter of the gift the donee may receive an equitable chose in action if the donor directly assigns his equitable interest to the donee, declares himself a trustee of his own equitable interest for the donee or instructs trustees to hold on behalf of the donee[4].

1   *Jones v Lock* (1865) 1 Ch App 25; for the requirements of a valid express trust see the Law of Property Act 1925, s 53.
2   *Richards v Delbridge* (1874) LR 18 Eq 11.
3   *Re Rose* [1952] Ch 499, [1952] 1 All ER 1217; *Re Paradise Motor Co Ltd* [1968] 2 All ER 625.
4   *Grey v IRC* [1960] AC 1, [1959] 3 All ER 603, HL.

20.32 In the case of wedding or anniversary presents where the donor's intention is not clear as to whether only one or both of the spouses should be the donee, it is presumed that presents from the husband's family were intended for the husband, and the wife's family given to the wife[1]. The nature of the gift may show the donor's intention[2].

1   *Samson v Samson* [1960] 1 All ER 653, [1960] 1 WLR 190, CA.
2   *Re Jamieson, ex p Pannell* (1889) 60 LT 159. There is a rebuttable presumption that a gift of an engagement ring is absolute, Law Reform (Miscellaneous Provisions) Act 1970, s 3(2).

20.33 Once made the gift will be irrevocable[1], unless it is given subject to some condition precedent which remains unfulfilled or condition subsequent which is not performed[2]. A gift may be avoided if it is induced by the donee's fraud, misrepresentation or undue influence[3]. Mistake can render a gift void at law or voidable in equity[4]. Gifts may also be avoided if under the Bills of Sale Act 1878 the donor retains possession and the title is not registered as a bill of sale.

1   *Bill v Cureton* (1835) 2 My & K 503.
2   *Cohen v Sellar* [1926] 1 KB 536.
3   *Zamet v Hymen* [1961] 1 WLR 1442.
4   *Ogilvie v Littleboy* (1897) 13 TLR 399, CA, (1899) 15 TLR 294, HL, where a widow sought to set aside two charitable deeds on the basis of mistake as to their effect and meaning. It was held that the trustees had satisfied the burden on them to establish the validity of the gift; a mistake had to be very serious before the court would set the gift aside.

Transaction

20.34 A 'transaction' is not exhaustively defined in the Insolvency Act. It includes a gift, agreement or arrangement[1]. An 'arrangement' is apt to include an agreement or understanding between parties, whether formal or informal, oral or in writing[2]. The provision of services or the loan of property for no or inadequate consideration may be the subject of a transaction at an undervalue, as well as a transfer of property. An appointment under a power contained in a policy of insurance is not a 'transaction' for the purpose of IA 1986, s 339[3]. Where a debtor paid receipts into a separate bank account and so created a trust in favour of a few specified creditors there was no transaction, and therefore no transaction at an undervalue[4]. A transaction, other than a gift, will be something that involves some element of dealing between the parties to the transaction[5]. Although it might be thought that a wide interpretation of 'transaction' is not suggested by the wording of IA 1986, s 339(3), as the statute refers to a 'transaction with a person', the courts have been willing to take a wide view and look at the debtor's dealing as a whole[6].

1   IA 1986, s 436.
2   Per Jonathan Parker LJ in *Feakins v Department for Environment, Food and Rural Affairs* [2005] EWCA Civ 1658, [2006] BPIR 895.
3   *Clarkson v Clarkson* [1994] BCC 921, 926.
4   *Re Lewis's of Leicester Ltd* [1995] 1 BCLC 428, 439.
5   *Re Taylor Sinclair (Capital) Ltd* [2001] 2 BCLC 176 at para 20; here it was held that the transmission by the company and receipt of cheques by the recipient stockbroker to the creditor of a third party involved no element of dealing and was therefore not a transaction on which IA 1986, s 238 might bite. It is possible that the court took too narrow a view of the overall dealings between the various parties concentrating as it did solely on relations between the company and the recipient.
6   See paras **20.35–20.36**.

Enters into a transaction

20.35 Where there is a dealing between the individual debtor and a third party it is permissible for the court to look at the whole dealing; the court's review need not be restricted to individual transactions nor need the court restrict the review to the debtor and the one or more parties who it is suggested have benefited at the debtor's expense where the overall dealings involve other persons. As a matter of construction, entirely consonant with the purposes of the IA 1986[1], 'enters into a transaction' may be interpreted as including 'participate in an arrangement', and an arrangement may comprise several individual transactions. As Hart J put it in *Secretary of State for the Environment, Food and Rural Affairs v Feakins*[2]:

> 'If the reason behind the linkage of two or more transactions is to achieve by that means the object which the section[3] is designed to frustrate, that may itself in my judgment be a justification for treating them as one composite arrangement for the purpose of the section.'

1   Whether IA 1986, s 339 or s 423.
2   [2004] EWHC 2735 (Ch), [2005] BPIR 292 at para 45, distinguishing *Re Brabon* [2000] BPIR 537.
3   This was a IA 1986, s 423 case but the principle will be equally applicable to IA 1986, s 339.

20.36 The transaction must have been entered into by the individual debtor. Plainly normal principles of agency will apply. Difficulties can however arise as in *Re Brabon, Treharne v Brabon*[1] where after contracting to sell a property the individual debtor was made bankrupt and the sale was completed by a chargee under a power of sale. The court held that the relevant transaction was not the contract but the actual disposal of the property. It followed that the transfer which the trustee sought to impugn had not been entered into by the individual debtor and so was not susceptible to an application to set it aside as a transaction at an undervalue.

1   [2001] 1 BCLC 11 at 33. The chargee was in fact the bankrupt's wife, but the court held that the charge was valid and rejected the trustee's submission that the sale by the mortgagee was 'mere conveyancing mechanics' and should be viewed as a sale by the bankrupt. This decision was distinguished in *Secretary of State for the Environment, Food and Rural Affairs v Feakins* [2004] EWHC 2735 (Ch).

Consideration

20.37 There is no statutory definition of the word 'consideration'. It refers to that which a party agrees to provide under the transaction[1], although that which is provided and received should be seen in its full context. What constitutes consideration should be interpreted widely, with the court having regard to the realities of the situation. The court should look at the real economic effect of the transaction and assess the true benefit and detriment of the transaction[2]. Where the owner of a farm having fallen into arrears with his mortgage created a tenancy at a full market rent to his wife, the Court of Appeal held that the 'ransom' position that this created, that is the likelihood that the mortgagee would have 'to negotiate with and no doubt pay a high price' to the wife before it could obtain vacant possession for the purposes of sale, amounted to consideration and resulted in the owner conferring on his wife a consideration significantly greater in value in money or money's worth than the value of the consideration provided by her[3]. Where a director caused a company to sell an asset to another company controlled by him and part of the purchase consideration was the satisfying of the director's loan account, the fact that the company was insolvent and was likely shortly to enter an insolvent liquidation in which the director could only expect a small dividend on his loan account should be taken into account when considering the consideration provided to the company[4].

1   *Pagemanor Ltd v Ryan* [2002] EWCA Civ 1518, [2002] All ER (D) 21 (Oct), per Arden LJ.
2   *Agricultural Mortgage Corpn v Woodward* [1995] 1 BCLC 1, CA see pp10–12; *Pena v Coyne (No 1)* [2004] 2 BCLC 703, para 114.
3   *Agricultural Mortgage Corpn v Woodward* [1995] 1 BCLC 1. In the circumstances of the case the court considered it unnecessary to attempt to calculate the value of the surrender value, see also *Barclays Bank plc v Eustice* [1995] 4 All ER 551, [1995] 2 BCLC 630, CA; *National Westminster Bank v Jones* [2001] EWCA Civ 1541, [2002] 1 BCLC 55, CA.
4   *Pena v Coyne* [2004] EWHC 2684 (Ch), [2004] 2 BCLC 703, para [113]; the deputy judge was considering the merits of the defence in the context of an application to set aside a default judgment.

20.38 A payment by the debtor which amounts to a preference, voidable at the instance of the trustee in bankruptcy, cannot amount to valuable consideration for the purposes of defeating a claim that the payment amounted to a transaction at an undervalue[1]. In *Barber v CI Ltd*[2] a third party had lent money to a director who had lent it on to a company. Shortly before its liquidation the company paid back the majority of the loan directly to the third party. At first instance the court held that there was no preference to the third party as it was not a creditor of the company, but that the repayment to the third party amounted to a transaction at an undervalue. On appeal, *Re Sonatacus Ltd*[3], the Court of Appeal considered the analysis below to be 'not at all satisfactory' but did not state how it was wrong. The Court of Appeal preferred the analysis that in making a payment directly to the third party the company had discharged its debt to the director, that discharge constituting a preference. An order could then be made against the third party as a person who had received benefits from the company other than in good faith[4].

1   *Barber v CI Ltd* [2006] BCC 927.
2   [2006] BCC 927.
3   [2007] EWCA Civ 31, [2007] All ER (D) 203 (Jan).
4   Ie under IA 1986, s 342(2), see para **20.92**.

Consideration received by the debtor

20.39 The Act requires a comparison to be made between the value acquired by the individual debtor from the transaction and the value provided by the individual debtor. Both these values are measured in money or money's worth from the debtor's standpoint. Accordingly consideration which cannot be valued in such terms falls outside the statutory provisions[1] and cannot be brought into account to save the transaction from being one at an undervalue. Any matter relevant to valuation will be brought into account in assessing the value of consideration in accordance with generally accepted valuation principles[2].

1   Ie of IA 1986, s 339(3)(c).
2   *Pagemanor v Ryan* [2002] BPIR 593 (approved on appeal [2002] EWCA Civ 1518, [2002] All ER (D) 21 (Oct)) a case under IA 1986, s 423, where, on the sale of a right-to-buy property within the period during which the discount might have to be repaid, completion

being deferred some three years, a substantial sum (50% of the discount) was taken into account to reduce the value of the property to the purchaser as representing the risk that the full value of the discount might become repayable to the local authority.

20.40 The consideration must pass to the individual debtor for otherwise the transaction will be one at an undervalue by reason of him entering into a transaction 'on terms that provide for him to receive no consideration'[1]. This has implications for guarantees given by the debtor of third party debts. On the face of it the debtor receives no consideration on becoming such a guarantor, even where it may be greatly in his interest to guarantee the obligations of, say, a company with which he is concerned or an essential supplier. In such cases the court may be satisfied on the facts that no order should be made[2]. Where the guarantee is part only of a series of interconnected transactions it might be thought that the court might look further than the immediate transaction between the debtor and the creditor and bring into account consideration passing to the debtor from other parties to the interconnected transactions. There is no stipulation in the statute that the only consideration which may be considered as having been received by the debtor is that given directly by the person to whom the debtor's consideration is provided. Where the debtor enters into linked transactions with different persons, the identification of the consideration passing to the debtor is a question of fact whether or not it also involves an issue of law; it may be appropriate to consider all the linked transactions together[3]. The transaction between the debtor and the 'person' in question[4] should be looked at as a whole. Accordingly where the debtor had participated in an arrangement whereby his property was sold by mortgagees to another party subject to an agricultural tenancy in favour of the debtor's company at a valuation which took account of the tenancy, with the debtor's company subsequently surrendering the tenancy to leave the purchaser with vacant possession, the debtor had entered into a transaction at an undervalue[5].

[1] IA 1986, s 339(3)(a), see para **20.23**.
[2] See para **20.87**.
[3] *Phillips v Brewin Dolphin Bell Lawrie Ltd* [2001] 1 WLR 143, [2001] UKHL 2, [2001] 1 All ER 673 (affirming the CA decision at [1999] 2 All ER 844, [1999] 1 WLR 2052 but on different grounds) where the sale of a stockbroking business was carried out under three separate agreements. When assessing the value of the consideration involving future payments Lord Scott, at para 26, stated that the court should take into account what had actually happened after the transaction was entered into. It is for the party who relies on the consideration to establish its value, para 27.
[4] '... an individual enters into a transaction with a person at an undervalue ...' IA 1986, s 339(3).
[5] *Feakins v Department for Environment, Food and Rural Affairs* [2005] EWCA Civ 1658, [2006] BPIR 895 – a case under IA 1986, s 423.

20.41 The wording of IA 1986, s 339(3)(c) (see para **20.23**) does not require the consideration passing to the individual debtor to have been provided by the other party to the transaction. In the case of a guarantee of a third party liability therefore consideration passing to the debtor by that or some other party, for example by way of security or cross guarantee, would fall to be valued and taken into account in a determination of possible undervalue.

Comparison of value: significantly less

20.42 Where the debtor has provided some consideration in respect of the transaction the Insolvency Act requires the value of that consideration to be compared with the value of the consideration acquired by the debtor from the transaction. An order to restore the pre-transaction position is to be made only if the value to the debtor is 'significantly less' than the value provided by the debtor. The comparison between the value of the consideration provided by and to the debtor is to be undertaken as at the date of entry into the transaction[1]. This exercise may present difficulty where the transaction involves future or contingent benefits or liabilities[2]. To take the case of a guarantee, the court will have to take into account on the one hand the likelihood of the debtor being called upon to make payment to the creditor by reference both to the events which might give rise to the liability, and the ability of the principal debtor to meet all or part of its liability, and on the other hand the value to the debtor of any security or co-guarantor or other remedies that it may have available. By the time the debtor is in bankruptcy it may well appear to the trustee in bankruptcy that the debtor's guarantee liability was incurred at a considerable undervalue. However, a comparative valuation conducted by reference to the date of the guarantee may present a rather different picture.

1   This is plain from the wording of IA 1986, s 339(1), and see *Phillips v Dolphin Bell Lawrie Ltd* [2001] UKHL 2, [2001] 1 All ER 673, [2001] 1 WLR 143 at [30], and *Doyle v Saville* [2002] BPIR 947 where the district judge had taken into account later values and the appeal was allowed.
2   The possibility that valuable planning permission may be obtained may be a relevant consideration in assessing the value of land being transferred, but this 'hope value' should be proved as a matter of fact, *Pinewood Joinery v Starelm Properties Ltd* [1994] 2 BCLC 412.

Date for valuation

20.43 At the risk of stating the obvious, the date on which the consideration is to be valued is the date on which the debtor entered into the transaction[1].

1   *Doyle v Saville* [2002] BPIR 947, para 44. It is not clear why the district judge had taken a later date.

Not essential to arrive at precise values

20.44 It has been suggested that the court must assess precise values for the value of the consideration provided by and received by the debtor in making a determination as to whether the latter is significantly less than the former[1]. There will be cases however where precision is not possible and yet it is plain that the debtor has given away more than he has received. For the court to refuse any relief because a precise determination of the value of the consideration passing to or from the debtor might seem unjust. In *Ramlort Ltd v Reid*[2] the Court of Appeal held that while it is preferable for the court to arrive at precise figures for the value of the consideration provided by and received by the debtor where it is able to do so, it is not essential that the court do so in every case. The court may, from a range of values, take those which are most favourable to the party seeking to uphold the transaction and then make findings of comparative value on that basis. In the absence of findings as to precise values the court may find that the range of remedies available to it are circumscribed, but if precise values cannot be assessed in cases where there is plainly a significant difference between the consideration provided by and received by the debtor, that is no reason either to refuse the application or deny a remedy.

¹   In reliance on the passage quoted in the next footnote from the judgment of Mummery LJ in *National Westminster Bank v Jones* [2001] EWCA Civ 1541, [2002] 1 BCLC 55 at [29].
²   [2005] 1 BCLC 331; Jonathan Parker LJ at para 106 stated that the comment of Mummery LJ in *National Westminster Bank v Jones* [2001] EWCA Civ 1541, [2002] 1 BCLC 55 at [29] to the effect that the court 'must ascertain from the evidence the actual value against which the consideration for the transaction must be measured' should not be taken out of context.

What constitutes significantly less

20.45 By using the term 'significantly' less when comparing the consideration provided by each side to the transaction the Insolvency Act gives the court a margin of discretion before it has to act and seek to restore the pre-transaction position. No clear guidance has yet emerged as to what constitutes significance for these purposes, and while courts will doubtless use indicative expressions of a general nature from time to time, the dividing line between 'less' and 'significantly less' in any individual case will depend substantially on the circumstances of that case. In *Re Kumar, ex p Lewis*¹ the court suggested that a transaction would be set aside where there was a 'substantial element of bounty'. This gives little assistance in determining what amounts to 'significantly less'; indeed it is suggested that any element of 'bounty', substantial or not, would amount to there being 'significantly less' consideration provided to the debtor and should warrant the court granting relief. An agreement for the sale of assets which provides for deferred payment without interest is capable of rendering the consideration received as being significantly less than the value of the goods sold².

¹   [1993] BCLC 548 at p 564.
²   *Barclays Bank plc v Eustice* [1995] 2 BCLC 630, 636, [1996] BPIR 1, 6, CA, where the deferred price was to be paid in 10 annual instalments.

20.46 In *National Westminster Bank plc v Jones*¹ the transaction under review was the grant of a tenancy of a farm of which the mortgagees wished to take possession. The tenancy was at an open market rent, as advised by an agricultural valuer, and in addition a base rent was reserved to represent a payment by the tenant for the benefit of obtaining the ransom value arising in consequence of the creation of the tenancy². The court undertook a detailed valuation exercise of the open market rental value of the farm, the surrender value of the tenancy, and the value of the tenancy, applying a discount rate of 6.5% to the deferred right of possession at the end of the tenancy, and an 8% discount rate to the right to receive rent to take into account the comparatively weak nature of the tenant's covenant³. The court also had to consider the value of the farming assets the price for which was payable in instalments over 20 years. Here the court applied a discount rate of 10% pa[4]. This exercise produced differentials of 15.5%, 18.6% and 47% in the tenant's favour, all of which were held to represent significantly less consideration for the purposes of the IA 1986[5]. A consideration received by the debtor of 80% of the value assessed by the court to have been provided by the debtor is plainly significantly less for the purposes of the IA 1986[6]. In *Pagemanor Ltd v Ryan*[7] differences amounting to 2.6% and 5.9% were considered not to amount to considerably less consideration. A sale at 7% below an expert valuation was not a sale at a substantial undervalue[8].

[1]   [2001] EWCA Civ 1541, [2001] 1 BCLC 98.
[2]   See *Agricultural Mortgage Corpn v Woodward* [1995] 1 BCLC 1 where the Court of Appeal held that the existence of this 'ransom' or 'surrender' value rendered the transaction one at an undervalue.
[3]   [2001] EWCA Civ 1541, [2001] 1 BCLC 98 at 127 para [95].
[4]   On the evidence. The court, Neuberger J, expressed scepticism as to whether 10% pa was a high enough rate to take where there was no security for the repayments, and stated, p 130 para 104, that 13% pa was a 'rather more likely rate than 10%'.
[5]   *National Westminster Bank plc v Jones* [2001] 1 BCLC 98 was a case under IA 1986, s 423.
[6]   *Gil v Baygreen Properties Ltd* [2004] EWHC 1732 (Ch), [2005] BPIR 95, a s 423 case. The fact that the company had made very little effort to sell the property on the market and had sold the property quickly at the time when the applicant was seeking to join the company as a defendant to proceedings were also indicative factors.
[7]   [2002] BPIR 593 (and on appeal [2002] EWCA Civ 1518, [2002] All ER (D) 21 (Oct)) where the 1998 transaction is considered in more detail than at first instance.
[8]   *Re London Local Residential (No 2)* [2005] BPIR 163 at para 17. In this case an order for the sale of property by a liquidator contained a provision that the co-owner might apply to restrain any proposed sale which was 'substantially below' market value.

The application of discounts

20.47 Where a transaction involves property which has been acquired by a tenant under the 'right to buy' provisions, there is no absolute rule that the discount obtained by the purchaser is to be treated as a contribution by the tenant, although it may be so treated in appropriate cases[1]. It is anticipated that in most such cases the discount will be credited to the account of the person who was entitled to it. In *Pozzuto v Iacovides*[2] the debtor was a shareholder in a company which owned the freehold reversion of a residential property. The company was dissolved and the reversion vested in the Crown as bona vacantia. The debtor wished to take advantage of the scheme operated by the Treasury Solicitor which enables former members of a dissolved company to purchase the reversion at a substantial discount. The purchase was wholly funded by the debtor's daughter, and the reversion was then transferred to the daughter for no consideration. On the bankruptcy of the debtor the trustee applied to set aside the transfer. The court rejected the argument that the debtor had transferred nothing of value because the daughter held the whole beneficial interest in the property under a resulting trust. It was wrong to ignore the fact that the substantial discount at which the property was acquired was available to the debtor but not the daughter. The court held that the beneficial interest acquired by the daughter under a resulting trust was limited to her contribution to the price without the discount, a mere 3.2% of the property's value and accordingly set the transfer aside as a transaction at an undervalue. Individual cases will throw up their own valuation issues and no summary of valuation principles may be attempted here. It may be noted however that the value of a life policy on assignment is likely to be more than its surrender value, and very much more where the person whose life is assured is not in good health[3].

[1] *Ashe v Mumford* [2001] BPIR 1, CA. Here the right to buy discount was not treated as a contribution to the purchase price of the property for the purposes of the creation of a resulting trust. However, this was in the context of the court's finding that this was a sham transaction.
[2] [2003] EWHC 431 (Ch), [2003] BPIR 999.
[3] *Ramlort Ltd v Reid* [2004] BPIR 985, CA at para 113.

Debtor granting security over his assets

20.48 The giving of security by the debtor over his assets is not of itself a transaction at an undervalue[1]. This is because the creation of the security does not deplete the debtor's estate or diminish its value. The debtor loses the right to deal with the secured assets as he wishes, but this loss is not capable of valuation in monetary terms. As Millet J put it in *Re MC Bacon Ltd*[2] in the case of a company:

> 'The mere creation of a security over a company's assets does not deplete them and does not come within [the definition of a transaction at an undervalue]. By charging its assets the company appropriates them to meet the liabilities due to the secured creditor and adversely affects the rights of other creditors in the event of insolvency. But it does not deplete its assets or diminish their value. It retains the right to redeem and the right to sell or remortgage the charged assets. All it loses is the ability to apply the proceeds otherwise than in satisfaction of the secured debt. That is not something capable of valuation in monetary terms and is not customarily disposed of for value. In the present case the company did not suffer that loss by reason of the grant of the debenture. Once the bank had demanded a debenture the company could not have sold or charged its assets without applying the proceeds in reduction of the overdraft ... By granting the debenture the company parted with nothing of value, and the value of the consideration which it received in return was incapable of being measured in money or money's worth.'

[1] *Re MC Bacon Ltd* [1990] BCLC 324, 340; approved by the Court of Appeal in *National Bank of Kuwait v Menzies* [1994] 2 BCLC 306, 319, a case on the equivalent provisions of IA 1986, s 423(1)(c); see also *Agricultural Mortgage Corpn v Woodward* [1994] 1 BCLC 1, CA.
[2] [1990] BCLC 324 at 340–341.

20.49 In *Re Brabon, Treharne v Brabon*[1] Jonathan Parker J stated that the converse also applies:

> 'Just as the grant of security rights over an asset does not diminish the value of that asset in the hands of the grantor of those rights, with the consequence that in granting such rights the grantor has not parted with anything of value, so (in my judgment) on a sale of the asset the value of the consideration provided by the seller is the value of the asset free from the security rights. I therefore reject the ... submission that on a sale of mortgaged property by the mortgagor the value of the consideration provided by the mortgagor for the purposes of [IA 1986 s 238(4)(b)] is the value of the land subject to the mortgage, i e the value

of the mortgagor's equity of redemption. The value of the consideration provided by the mortgagor in such circumstances is the value of the land free from the mortgage.'

1   [2001] 1 BCLC 11 at 36.

20.50 Accordingly where the debtor in return for granting security to a bank receives in return the bank's continued support by honouring cheques and forbearance in respect of the overdraft, this was held to be consideration incapable of monetary valuation[1]. These decisions indicate a strict approach to the question of valuation in money and money's worth. They may not accord with a businessman's commercial view of the value of assets, and may ignore the very real value to a creditor of security where a debtor is facing insolvency, but they do follow the strict terms of the statute. Undoubtedly there is an apparent, and very probably real, unfairness to the remaining unsecured creditors when one of their number become secured. However, IA 1986, s 339 requires a money or money's worth comparison between the consideration provided to and by the debtor and the courts have approached this by looking at the debtor's overall position before and after the transaction and considering whether any alteration has a monetary value[2]. There is no such value in the restrictions the debtor imposes on itself in respect of the charged assets[3]. The fact that the creditor will be in a better position relative to his fellow creditors is not, on the authorities, consideration provided by the debtor. The remaining unsecured creditors' complaint of unfairness is met by noting that the debtor's grant of security may be challenged as a preference. The relevant time for challenging a preference is shorter and any challenger must show an intention to prefer, but these differences between transactions at an undervalue and preferences are the result of parliamentary decision.

1   As in the case of *Re MC Bacon Ltd* [1990] BCLC 324.
2   'I do not see how [the company's] *position* is worse off on an overall basis merely because a debt is converted from an unsecured debt to a secured debt. The people who suffer are a category of creditors who would otherwise participate in the proceeds of sale of the charge security' per Peter Smith QC in *Re Mistral Finance Ltd* [2001] BCC 27, para 37.
3   Similarly, there was no transaction at an undervalue where the company paid receipts due to certain creditors into a separate bank account and created a trust in favour of those creditors, *Re Lewis's of Leicester Ltd* [1995] 1 BCLC 428, 439b: 'The company's assets were not diminished by what was in substance an arrangement for accelerated payment of future – and I emphasise only future – sums due to concession holders in respect of trading which took place in the future' per Robert Walker J. Although the learned judge emphasised the future nature of the sums paid into the separate account there would not have been a transaction susceptible to attack under IA 1986, s 238 [s 339] had there been no future element involved.

20.51 Once the security has been granted to the third party, previously unsecured, it cannot be ignored in subsequent transactions between the debtor and the third party. In *Doyle v Saville*[1] the debtor, together with his wife, transferred the legal estate in two properties to a third party who had already lent them significant sums of money and who then discharged the debtor's indebtedness to his bank. The court found the third party to have been an equitable chargee of one of the properties before the transfer, and on an application to set aside the transfer as being at an undervalue, assessed the value of the consideration provided by the debtor as the value of his beneficial interest in the property 'taking into account the equitable charge in favour of the third party. As the value of the debtor's beneficial interest was exceeded by the amount of the third party's charge it followed that the debtor's interest in the property he transferred was of no value'[2].

1   [2002] BPIR 947.
2   With respect to the second property the debtor's interest was valued at £30,000 and the value of the consideration provided by the third party in payments to the bank was £28,344.36. The court held that this was not 'significantly less' and made no order on application.

Negative equity cases

20.52 The impact of the approach of the courts in cases such as *Re MC Bacon Ltd* and *Re Brabon* is felt strongly in 'negative equity' cases. Where the equity of redemption in a mortgaged property is worth nil (or even less) the value of the property on a sale by the insolvent mortgagor is the value of the property free from mortgage; any transfer for a significantly lower sum than the full value of the property unencumbered will be at an undervalue. This result may seem strange. The court's answer to this 'apparent conundrum'[1] is that once it is established that no part of the proceeds of sale are receivable by the insolvent mortgagor the issue of undervalue becomes academic so far as the office-holder is concerned. Negative equity is therefore fatal to a claim that a sale has been at an undervalue, because there is no basis on which a court might grant relief even though the sale is at an undervalue[2]. It seems unlikely that this will be the last word on the effect of security on the value of assets for the purpose of assessing the value of consideration for the purposes of applications to impugn transactions as being at an undervalue. The court's wide discretion on granting relief should however ensure that a just result is reached in any particular case.

1   Per Jonathan Parker J in *Re Brabon, Treharne v Brabon* [2001] 1 BCLC 11 at 37c.
2   *Re Brabon, Treharne v Brabon* [2001] 1 BCLC 11 at 36–37.

20.53 The transfer by the lessor of leasing agreements together with assets needed to manage the business comprising the leasing agreements in consideration for payments, quarterly in arrears, to meet the sums due by the lessor to his financiers constitutes a transaction at an undervalue[1].

1   *Arbuthnot Leasing International Ltd v Havelet Leasing Ltd (No 2)* [1990] BCC 636.

Preference

20.54 An individual debtor gives a preference to a person which may be impeached under the provisions of the Insolvency Act where:

(a)   that person is one of the debtor's creditors or a surety or guarantor for any of the debtor's debts or other liabilities[1];

(b)   the debtor does anything or suffers anything to be done which, in either case, has the effect of putting that person into a position which, in the event of the debtor's bankruptcy, will be better than the position he would have been in if that thing had not been done[2]; and

(c) the debtor in giving the preference was influenced in deciding to give it by a desire to put that person into a better position in a subsequent bankruptcy than he would have been in had the preference not been given[3].

[1] IA 1986, s 340(3)(a).
[2] IA 1986, s 340(3)(b).
[3] IA 1986, s 340(4).

20.55 There is as yet no authority on what constitutes a debtor suffering anything to be done for the purposes of the statute. In other areas of the law, primarily landlord and tenant, the courts have stated that 'suffer' means the same as 'permit', and while 'suffer' is used in a passive not an active sense it will usually import some act or omission on the part of the person suffering[1]. The essential feature of suffering an action in the law generally is that the party concerned fails to take such steps as are reasonably available to him to prevent the action. It is no answer that the steps available to the party cannot be certain of success, but neither need a party take steps which have no realistic prospect of thwarting the relevant action[2]. Where a director lends money to a company which he himself has borrowed from the third party, the repayment by the company directly to the third party discharges the debt it owes to the director and the repayment may constitute a preference to the director[3].

[1] *Re Throckmorton, Ex p Eyston* (1877) 7 Ch D 145, 149, CA; *Re Moore's Estate* (1885) LR 17 IR 549, 551; *Wilson v Twamley* [1904] 2 KB 99, 103, CA.
[2] *Berton v Alliance Economic Investment Co* [1922] 1 KB 742, 759, CA per Atkin LJ: the court was considering covenants in a lease (i) not to permit the premises to be used for non-residential purposes, and (ii) not to suffer anything to be done which may be a nuisance to the lessors or adjoining occupiers:

> 'It is not suggested that there is any difference between the words "permit" and "suffer" in this context and I treat them as having the same meaning ... To my mind the word "permit" means one of two things, either to give leave for an act which without that leave could not legally be done, or to abstain from taking reasonable steps to prevent the act where it is within a man's power to prevent it. Acts which fall short of that, though they be acts of sympathy or assistance, do not amount to permission at any rate in the covenants with which we are dealing'.

[3] *Re Sonatacus Ltd* [2007] EWCA Civ 31, [2007] All ER (D) 203 (Jan) and see para **20.92**.

Improving the position of a creditor

20.56 Whether an act or sufferance by the individual debtor constitutes a preference is determined objectively. Where a creditor is involved as the other party to the transaction it must be ascertained whether the transaction improves the position of that creditor as against other creditors on a winding up either by enabling him to take a priority to which he is not entitled or by allowing him in effect to receive a greater dividend than other creditors of the same class[1]. There must be an actual improvement in the creditor's position. The fact that a chargee has transferred to him the proprietorship of the charged property does not necessarily improve his position[2]. Where a company's directors have given guarantees to the company's bank to secure loans to the company, a sale of company assets with payment direct to the bank has the effect of reducing the director's liability under his guarantee. However, as the bank had security over the company's assets on which it would have relied had the company then entered an insolvent liquidation the directors' position was no different to that it would have been had the company been wound up. Accordingly the payment of the proceeds of sale to the bank did not amount to a preference[3]. The fact that an improvement in the creditor's position may turn out to be more apparent than real is not fatal to an application. It is no answer to a preference claim that the fund from which particular creditors have been preferred is in fact subject to a security in the hands of another party; if, as between the unsecured creditors, the debtor prefers some over others an appropriate order should be made[4].

[1]   IA 1986, s 340(3)(b).
[2]   *Doyle v Saville* [2002] BPIR 947, para 57.
[3]   *Re Hawkes Hill Publishing Co Ltd, Ward v Perks* (2007) 151 Sol Jo LB 743, [2007] All ER (D) 422 (May).
[4]   *G&M Aldridge Pty Ltd v Walsh* [2002] BPIR 482 (a decision of the High Court of Australia). The preferential payments had been made out of a fund subject to a bank's floating charge after it had crystallised but before the bank appointed a receiver. At the hearing of the preference claim it was an open question whether on the facts the bank had waived its rights or was otherwise estopped from claiming the fund for itself.

20.57 Examples of potential preferences include returning goods which have not been paid for to a supplier where title has passed to the debtor[1]. The right to obtain property which he would be unable to claim otherwise will improve the creditor's position[2]. It may be noted that while preferences are defined as putting a creditor or surety in a better position in a debtor's bankruptcy, the 'better position' is not itself expressly restricted to one relating to the debt or guarantee in question. Any act or sufferance which improves the creditor's or surety's position in a bankruptcy may be a preference, such as the generation of a cross-claim or the giving of a guarantee to a creditor in respect of another person's debt to that creditor where that other person is unlikely to be able to pay that debt[3]. The fact that the debtor enters into an agreement which provides for the acceleration of rights and obligations in the event of the debtor's bankruptcy does not of itself amount to a preference[4].

[1]   See Cork Report para 1208.
[2]   See eg *Goel v Pick* [2006] EWHC 833 (Ch), [2007] 1 All ER 982 where the debtor attempted, in the event unsuccessfully, to assign the right to a valuable cherished number plate.
[3]   Eg where more than one company in a group faces insolvency, cross-guarantees by the debtor companies could improve a creditor's position in the insolvency of any one of the companies.
[4]   *Re Mistral Finance Ltd* [2001] BCC 27; although, of course, the terms on which rights and obligations are accelerated could amount to a preference in appropriate cases.

20.58 There must be a preference in fact before the court may make an order. A debtor does not grant a preference merely by entering into an agreement which may have that effect; it is the performance of that agreement which constitutes the preference[1].

[1]   *Re Ledingham-Smith* [1993] BCLC 635, 640.

20.59 The fact that the debtor has acted or allowed an act to be done in pursuance of a court order does not by itself prevent there being a preference[1]. It is possible therefore for the court to look behind an order when investigating an alleged preference. A debtor may for example allow judgment to be entered in default or summarily in circumstances where there was a good defence to all or part of the creditor's claim. This will allow the creditor to levy execution before the commencement of the bankruptcy. Such a judgment will be no answer to a claim that there has been a preference.

[1]   IA 1986, s 340(6).

Improving the position of a surety

20.60 Where a surety or guarantor is involved a comparison should be drawn between what the surety would be liable to pay had the act or sufferance alleged to be a preference not been done or permitted and what he has or would have to pay were the alleged preference allowed to stand. Acts constituting preferences include the payment or part payment of the debt of an unsecured creditor, thereby preferring the creditor over other creditors who are not being paid[1] and any person who has guaranteed the debt. Payment of a secured creditors' debt will not amount to a preference provided the sum paid does not exceed the value of the security. Giving a security or extra security for an existing debt will usually amount to a preference, and a preference may be granted by allowing a creditor to perfect a security when he is out of time to do so[2]. Where a company entered into a further agreement with a third party immediately before liquidation because the charge created by the initial agreement had become void for lack of registration, the security granted under the further agreement constituted a preference, even though the company had an existing obligation to execute the security[3].

[1]   As in *Re Cohen* [1924] 2 Ch 515, CA.
[2]   As in *Sir William Henry Peat v Gresham Trust Ltd* [1934] AC 252 where the company withdrew its opposition to the creditor's application to register a charge out of time. On the facts it was held that there was no fraudulent preference under the provisions of the Bankruptcy Act 1914, s 44.
[3]   *Re Mistral Finance Ltd* [2001] BCC 27, para 49.

Requisite intention and statutory desire

20.61 For the grant to be a preference the debtor must intend to do the act or permit the sufferance which comprises the preference. A voluntary act or forbearance must be shown. Furthermore, in undertaking that act or showing that forbearance the debtor must have been influenced by the statutory desire. A court may not make an order in respect of a preference unless it is established that the debtor was influenced by a desire to improve the position of the creditor or surety in the event of the debtor's bankruptcy[1]. ' "Desire" and "influenced by" are ordinary English words which are not susceptible of further useful definition'[2]. In contrast with 'intention', which requires an objective assessment, 'desire' imports a subjective element into the test for a preference. The desire on the part of the debtor has to be to put the creditor or surety into a better position in the event of bankruptcy and not simply to do the act which would constitute the preference. A careful distinction has to be drawn between the inevitable consequences of a debtor's actions and its desire to achieve those consequences. Some consequences from a course of action may be desired and others not, and a preferential effect for a creditor may be foreseen by the debtor without it being desired. 'If the [debtor] is influenced by 'proper commercial considerations' and not by a 'positive wish to improve the creditor's position in the event of [a bankruptcy]' then the debenture [or charge, payment or other benefit] will be valid'[3]. In *Re Lewis's of Leicester Ltd*[4] a company traded as a department store licensing some of its floor space to other traders, concessionaires, who operated as shops within a shop under a variety of different arrangements, some involving payments into the company's tills with later accounting to the concessionaire. The lease of the company's premises was coming to an end in February, and the company's financial position was uncertain. In the lead up to Christmas the company paid receipts relating to some concessionaires into a separate account which the court held was impressed with a trust. Although the position of the relevant concessionaires was thereby improved in the company's subsequent administration the court accepted that there was no intention, still less any desire, to grant a preference to the concessionaires[5]. In *Re Branston & Gothard Ltd*[6] a stockbroking company in financial difficulties opened a separate account to provide a fund which might be used to make good any deficiencies in client cash and investments held by the company. The court held that this account was impressed with a trust[7] in favour of investor clients to the extent necessary to make good any such deficiencies, and in the circumstances there was not the necessary desire on the part of the company for the payments into this account to amount to a voidable preference.

1   IA 1986, s 340(4).
2   *Re Ledingham-Smith* [1993] BCLC 635, per Morritt J at 641; see also *Weisgard v Pilkington* [1995] BCC 1108 at 1113.
3   *Re Fairway Magazines Ltd* [1993] BCLC 643, per Mummery J at 649g.
4   [1995] 1 BCLC 428.
5   The court accepted that the company 'took the action that it did on the advice of experienced insolvency practitioners for two principal reasons: first in the company's interests because the company was, no doubt rightly, concerned that a sudden defection of licence holders, possibly just before Christmas, would make the store look more like a morgue than a market during its final weeks of trading; and secondly, because the company thought that the concession holders who were believed to have this right [to separate accounting] were entitled to have this action taken ...' see p 438d.
6   [1999] 1 All ER (Comm) 289, [1999] BPIR 466.
7   As to the creation of a trust there is no requirement for any particular form to be used. What is required is a sufficient intention to create a trust and the existence of the 'three certainties' (the subject matter of the trust, the beneficiaries, and the beneficial interests), see eg *Re Kayford Ltd* [1975] 1 WLR 279, and *Re Chelsea Cloisters Ltd* (1980) 41 P&CR 98. Payment of monies into a separate account is a 'useful (although by no means conclusive) indication of an intention to create a trust', per Megarry J in *Re Kayford Ltd* [1975] 1 WLR 279. In *Multi Guarantee Co Ltd* [1987] BCLC 257, CA, premiums paid for warranties for domestic appliances were paid into a designated account by the company marketing the warranties while negotiations took place with the retailers as to the level of insurance cover the company had to support the warranty scheme. The court held that the company did not use sufficiently certain words to manifest a sufficient intention to create a trust.

20.62 Direct evidence of the requisite desire will only occasionally be available but its existence may be inferred from all the circumstances[1].

1   *Re MC Bacon Ltd* [1990] BCLC 324 at p 336, and see *Re Fairway Magazines Ltd* [1993] BCLC 643.

20.63 In any particular case, except where the presumption to prefer arises where the preference is given to an associate[1], it will be for the office-holder to show on a balance of probabilities that the debtor had the necessary desire. It will nevertheless be advisable for debtors and creditors entering into transactions in which it is foreseeable that the creditor's position will be improved in a subsequent bankruptcy to record what advantageous result was desired by the debtor when entering into the transaction.

1   See para **20.67**.

20.64 Once the requisite desire is established it need only be shown that it 'influenced' the act or sufferance challenged as a preference. Any influence, provided presumably that it cannot be dismissed as minimal, is sufficient, and the fact that there was some other predominating even decisive[1] influence on the mind of the debtor does not protect the transaction from being impugned as a preference[2]. The proper approach to the construction of IA 1986, s 340(4) was considered in *Re MC Bacon Ltd*[3]. In refusing to set aside a debenture granted by the corporate debtor to its bank taken when providing further assistance to the debtor which was in financial difficulties, Millet J underlined the subjective nature of the requirement that the debtor should be influenced by a desire to better the creditor's position[4], and stated that it would still be possible to provide assistance to a debtor in financial difficulties, provided that the parties were actuated only by proper commercial considerations:

> 'A man is not to be taken as desiring all the necessary consequences of his actions. Some consequences may be of advantage to him and be desired by him: others may not affect him and be matters of indifference to him; while still others may be positively disadvantageous to him and not be desired by him, but be regarded by him as the unavoidable price of obtaining the desired advantages ... Under [the Insolvency Act 1986] a transaction will not be set aside as a voidable preference unless the [debtor] positively wished to improve the creditor's position in the event of [his bankruptcy].'[5]

1   In *Re MC Bacon Ltd* [1990] BCLC 324. Millett J rejected the suggestion that it was necessary to prove that if the requisite desire had not been present the company would not have entered into the transaction as 'too high a test'.
2   'It is not necessary for the [office-holder] to show that the decision was the dominant factor or even the factor which 'tipped the scales' in persuading the debtor to enter into the transaction. On the other hand it must be shown to have been one of the factors which operated on the mind of the [debtor] in entering into the transaction.' *Doyle v Saville* [2002] BPIR 947, para 60.
3   [1990] BCLC 324.
4   Ie the requirement of IA 1986, s 340(3)(b).
5   Per Millett J *Re MC Bacon Ltd* [1990] BCLC 324 pp 335–6.

20.65 In cases where the person preferred is an associate of the debtor[1], the legal onus of proof that the debtor was influenced by the necessary desire is on the trustee in bankruptcy[2].

¹ See para **20.67**.
² *Re Ledingham-Smith* [1993] BCLC 635, 640.

Date on which intention formed

20.66 An agreement to make a payment or the entry into a transaction may pre-date the making of the payment or the execution of the transaction by a considerable time. The financial position of the debtor may well have deteriorated in the intervening period. The date on which the debtor's mental state in making the relevant payment or otherwise making a potential preference is to be considered may therefore be of considerable importance. It is not entirely clear from the statute which date should apply. The wording of IA 1986, s 340(4) ('the court shall not make an order ... unless the individual which gave the preference was influenced in deciding to give it') would suggest that the date on which the original decision was made is the relevant date. This was held to be the position in *Re MC Bacon Ltd*¹. However, as the definition of a preference in IA 1986, s 340(3) is where 'the individual does anything *or suffers anything to be done* which (in either case) has the [relevant] effect' it is arguable that an individual debtor gives a preference even when he is honouring existing obligations². In *Wills v Corfe Joinery Ltd*³ the board of a company resolved in a meeting held in January 1994 that the company be given notice that it was the intention of the directors to withdraw their loans in full in January 1995, but not before. The loans were repaid in February 1995. The court held that the relevant date for considering the mental state of the company in making the payments was February 1995 when the repayment cheques were duly signed. Even though there was an obligation on the company from January 1994 to make the repayments, it would have been necessary for the board to review whether to honour that obligation on the date of payment. If on that date the board knew that the company was insolvent or would become insolvent by honouring an existing obligation it should not have made the payment. By February 1995 the company could not afford to pay all its outstanding creditors, and in the absence of evidence to show that the payment was purely for commercial reasons there was nothing to rebut the statutory presumption⁴ in the case of a director, as a person connected with the company, that the company was influenced in repaying its directors by a desire to put them in a better position than that in which they would otherwise have been in should the company enter into insolvent liquidation. In *Re Brian Pierson (Contractors) Limited*⁵ the directors made short-term loans to the company on terms that they would be repaid in a few days. They would not have made the loans except on this basis. The question arose whether the court should consider the mental state of the company solely on the date of repayment, or whether it could have regard to the short-term nature of the transaction and consider the mental state of the company when agreeing to take the short-term loan. The court left open the possibility that a director might be able safely to tide the company over a particular problem, for example by making a personal payment of a company debt when the co-signatories for a company cheque were not available, without having the repayment of such a short-term loan voided as a preference. In the *Pierson* case however the purpose of the loan was to make funds available generally to the company in substitution for money which could not be borrowed from the bank because of its overdraft limit. The repayment was held to be a preference, the company having the necessary mental element on the date of repayment, and, arguably, throughout the short-term transaction.

¹ [1990] BCLC 324, per Millet J, see also *Re Fairway Magazines Ltd* [1993] BCLC 643 (Mummery J).
² As to the meaning of 'suffers' see para **20.55**.
³ [1998] 2 BCLC 75.
⁴ See para **20.67**.
⁵ [1999] BPIR 18. In this case one of the directors also paid insolvency practitioners for advice by personal cheque, the insolvency practitioner being unwilling to take a company cheque. He thereby became an unsecured creditor for this amount and his reimbursement by the company at a relevant time constituted a preference. The deputy judge (at p 41) considered the possibility that the director might be able to retain this payment on the grounds that it might properly be considered to be an expense of the liquidation with its attendant priority. The possibility was rejected on the facts however, in particular because the advice given was substantially concerned with assisting the directors personally as opposed to the company.

Presumption where preference given to an associate

20.67 An associate is given a wide definition¹. Where an individual debtor has given a preference to a person who is an associate, except where that person is an associate only by reason of being an employee, it is presumed, unless the contrary is shown, that the debtor was influenced in deciding to give the preference by the requisite desire for the purposes of IA 1986, s 340(4)². The person must be an associate of the debtor at the time that the preference is given³.

¹ See IA 1986, s 435; see **Appendix 2** below where s 435 is annotated.
² IA 1986, s 340(5); and see *Re Shapland Inc* [2000] BCC 106.
³ IA 1986, s 340(6). Note that a partner will remain an associate of the debtor after dissolution until the affairs of the partnership are fully wound up, *Goel v Pick* [2006] EWHC 833 (Ch), [2007] 1 All ER 982, [2006] BPIR 827 at [30].

Decisions of the Companies Court

20.68 There is an equivalent presumption in corporate insolvency where a preference is given by the company to a person who is connected with the company. The presumption of influence will therefore apply where a director who has guaranteed the company's overdraft advances money to the company secured by a debenture¹. The presumption also applied where the company created leases some four months before liquidation in favour of directors who had guaranteed the company's overdraft the consideration for which was the repayment of sums owed to them by the company². However, a declaration of trust in favour of a retirement benefit scheme of which the trustee and beneficiaries were the members of the company and their families was not a preference to a person connected with the company. The 'creditor' for the purposes of IA 1986, s 239(4) [s 340(3)] was the trustees, not the beneficiaries, and as trustees the members of the company came within the express exception for a trustee in his capacity as trustee of a pension scheme provided for in the Insolvency Act³. A belief at the date of the making of the payment asserted to be a preference that the company was not insolvent is in no way inconsistent with the application of the presumption of an intention to improve the position of the recipient in the event of insolvency supervening[4]. Where the company sold a property to directors at a proper value but with payment made partly in cash and partly by discharging loans made by the directors to the company, the directors failed to satisfy the burden of disproving that the company had been influenced by a desire to prefer them in ensuring that their loans to the company were repaid in full; the fact that the directors had been optimistic about the prospects for rescuing the company and had indeed continued to support the company to a considerable extent with some cash and more credit was insufficient to rebut the presumption of a preference[5]. Two further cases may be mentioned where the presumption also applied. In the first, the director of a ground-works company operated the company's business by interposing himself as, in effect, a subcontractor supplying labour, plant, and machinery for the company's contracts. The payments the director received from the company as supplier put him in a better position than other suppliers and while accepting that commercial considerations may also have influenced the company's method of operation and payments to the director, the court held the payments to have been a preference[6]. In the second, the company, which had received financial assistance from an associated company for many years, granted the associated company a debenture both to secure existing indebtedness and to cover future support some 14 months before it went into liquidation. The associated company argued that the debenture was the result of the exercise of legitimate commercial pressure. The court accepted that this may have been a factor in the debenture's grant, but as the associated company was aware of the company's difficult financial position and the inherent risk of insolvency the court held that it did not discharge the burden necessary to overcome the presumption[7].

1 *Re Fairway Magazines Ltd* [1993] BCLC 643, where the presumption was successfully rebutted.
2 *Weisgard v Pilkington* [1995] BCC 1108; the court found the directors' explanation that they were restructuring the company's affairs to be wholly unconvincing.
3 Ie IA 1986, s 435(5), (6), see **Appendix 2**; *Re Thirty Eight Building Ltd* [1999] 1 BCLC 416.
4 *Re Exchange Travel (Holdings) Ltd (in liquidation) (No 3)* [1996] 2 BCLC 524, at p 541c, expressly approved by the Court of Appeal on an application to stay execution and cross application for security for costs reported at [1997] 2 BCLC 579 at p 593g, and also on the appeal itself, reported as *Katz v McNally* at [1999] BCC 291 at 296.
5 *Re Conegrade Ltd* [2003] BPIR 358; the court found that there had been a preference even without regard to the burden of proof and 'the more so having regard to that'.
6 *Re DKG Contractors Ltd* [1990] BCC 903, 910.
7 *Re Transworld Trading Ltd* [1999] BPIR 628.

20.69 In seeking to rebut the presumption that the individual debtor was influenced by the requisite desire, the associate is likely to face a heavy evidential onus of proof. Much will undoubtedly depend upon the cogency of the explanation given by the individual debtor in evidence. But the court will naturally be slow to leave in place an arrangement which has the effect of preferring one creditor above the general body of creditors[1]. On the facts however where a tenant made payments in respect of rent to an associate seven days before the rent was due and 28 days before the right to re-enter could be exercised, the presumption was rebutted and it was found that there was not the requisite desire on the part of the tenant[2].

1   *Re Exchange Travel (Holdings) Ltd (in liquidation) (No 3)* [1996] 2 BCLC 524, on appeal [1997] 2 BCLC 579; *Re Agriplant Services Ltd (in liquidation)* [1997] 2 BCLC 598.
2   *Re Beacon Leisure Ltd* [1991] BCC 213; the court accepted the evidence of the remaining directors that they had no intention to prefer the director to whom the rent was paid.

20.70 In cases where the person preferred is not an associate of the individual debtor, the legal onus of proof that the individual debtor was influenced by the necessary desire is on the trustee in bankruptcy[1].

1   See e g *Re Ledingham-Smith* [1993] BCLC 635, 640.

C ORDERS ON APPLICATION

Applications for relief

20.71 In granting relief, whether in respect of a transaction at an undervalue or a preference, the court is required to restore the previous position, the status quo ante[1]. The court may make any order which has this aim, although without restricting the scope of the court's ingenuity, a number of possible orders are set out in the Act[2]. An application for an order under the Insolvency Act 1986 in respect of a transaction at an undervalue or a preference should be commenced by originating application[3]. It is usual to seek an order setting aside the transaction in question as being at an undervalue or a preference together with such further relief as the office-holder considers appropriate for restoring the pre-transaction position. Logically, the court should first make an order setting aside the relevant transaction before it makes further orders aimed at restoring the pre-transaction or preference position, such as an order for the sale of property[4], and in complex cases the question of the precise relief to be granted will frequently be considered at a separate hearing after the merits have been determined. In straightforward cases it should not be necessary to have two applications or two hearings for setting aside the order and the consequential relief.

1   IA 1986, s 339(2) (transaction at an undervalue), s 340(2) (preference).
2   IA 1986, s 342, and see para **20.87** et seq.
3   IR 1986, r 7.1; for a form of application see para **3.35**; as to the procedure see **Chapter 3**. Where an ordinary application is used the proceedings will be validated (under IR 1986, r 7.55) if the respondents have not been prejudiced, see e g *Re Buildlead Ltd Quicksave (South & West) Ltd v Katz (No 2)* [2004] EWHC 2443, [2006] 1 BCLC 9. It is difficult to envisage circumstances in which a respondent will be prejudiced by the use of the wrong form of application.
4   *Re Kumar (a bankrupt)* [1993] 1 WLR 224, 243.

20.72 The right of a trustee in bankruptcy to institute proceedings to set aside a transaction at an undervalue or a voidable preference does not form part of the bankrupt's estate[1]. It cannot therefore be assigned by the trustee in bankruptcy[2].

¹   *Re Yagerphone Ltd* [1935] Ch 392; *NW Robbie & Co v Witney Warehouse Co Ltd* [1963] 2 All ER 199, [1963] 1 WLR 1324, 1334; *Re Oasis Merchandising Services Ltd* [1998] Ch 170, [1997] 1 All ER 1009.
²   *Re Exchange Travel (Holdings) Ltd (in liquidation) (No 3)* [1997] 2 BCLC 579, 596.

Preliminary issue

20.73 It is possible for the court to order the determination of a preliminary issue. However, practitioners should take care to ensure that any preliminary issue put before the court does not limit the scope of the fact-finding exercise to be conducted by the judge at trial[1].

¹   *Re Thoars (deceased), Reid v Ramlort* [2002] EWHC 2416 (Ch), [2003] 1 BCLC 499, where Sir Andrew Morritt V-C declined to give an answer to the preliminary issue for this reason.

Burden of proof

20.74 The burden of proof is on the trustee in bankruptcy to make good his claim for relief on a balance of probabilities. The fact that the debtor has been shown to have been dishonest in the past does not by itself satisfy the burden of proof[1]. An applicant trustee must expect to do more than raise a strong suspicion that a transaction was at an undervalue. The court will be comparing consideration given with value transferred, and in the usual case the trustee should adduce valuation evidence specifically direct to the point[2].

¹   *Stone and Rolls Ltd v Micro Communications Inc* [2005] EWHC 1052 (Ch), [2005] All ER (D) 390 (May).
²   See eg *Mears v Latif* [2005] EWHC 1146 (Ch), [2006] BPIR 80 where the liquidator relied on an estate agent's letter suggesting a figure at which a long leasehold flat might be marketed. The deputy judge suggested, at [30], that such a letter 'with a specific disclaimer of such figure being a valuation would be a most unsatisfactory plank on which to find … the actual value. There was no direct evidence, for example from a property valuer, as to what the actual value of [the property] was at [the relevant date]. One may perhaps have suspicions that that figure represented a good deal for a buyer. But the evidence would not justify anything more than that'.

Disclosure

20.75 The court will normally order disclosure of documents passing between a party to a transaction under scrutiny and his legal advisers where the documents relate to the setting up of the transaction[1].

¹   *Barclays Bank plc v Eustice* [1995] 2 BCLC 630, 642c, 644h, CA. Documents obtained or created for the dominant purpose of being used in pending or contemplated proceedings will be protected by legal professional privilege, unless a prima facie case of fraud can be established, see eg *Royscott Spa Leasing Ltd v Lovett* [1995] BCC 502, 506 (a IA 1986, s 423 case) where the order for disclosure was discharged on appeal because no prima facie case of fraudulent purpose could be established.

20.76 *Adjustment of prior transactions*

Restored hearing

20.76 In cases of some complexity the court will often make findings on the merits of the claim and then, if an undervalue transaction or preference is found, adjourn to consider the precise relief to be granted at a further hearing. It will usually be too late to raise new arguments on the merits, however persuasive, on the restored hearing to consider the terms of the relief[1].

[1]   *Shreeve v Taylor* [2003] EWCA Civ 1197, [2003] BPIR 1421, CA.

Costs

20.77 Ordinary principles as to the award of costs will apply to applications under IA 1986, ss 339, 340 or 423. If a court is to deprive a successful party of his costs it should be on the basis of misconduct within the proceedings and not misbehaviour in connection with the transaction the subject matter of the proceedings[1]. Neither is it right to deprive the successful trustee of his costs because the respondent has acted honourably in creating the charge which is a preference or because the person benefiting from the charge has failed to provide evidence to resist the application[2].

[1]   *Hall v Rover Financial Services (GB) Ltd* [2002] EWCA Civ 1514, (2002) Times, 8 November (a hire purchase case).
[2]   *Cork v Gill* [2005] BPIR 272.

Respondent abroad

20.78 An application for relief under these provisions may be served on a respondent who is resident abroad. In *Re Paramount Airways Ltd (in administration)*[1] it was held that for the purposes of the equivalent provision in corporate insolvency, IA 1986, s 238(2) (which provides that an office-holder, ie a liquidator or administrator, may apply for an order 'where the company has ... entered into a transaction *with any person* at an undervalue'), the highlighted words should be construed without limitation. Accordingly there was an unrestricted extra-territorial jurisdiction, and service was permitted on a Jersey Bank[2]. The Court of Appeal stressed that there were two safeguards to the use of this unrestricted jurisdiction, the need for there to be a sufficient connection with England, and the need to obtain the court's leave[3] before serving abroad.

[1]   [1993] Ch 223, [1992] 3 All ER 1, CA.
[2]   Under IR 1986, r 12.12 which governs service outside the jurisdiction in insolvency proceedings.
[3]   Under IR 1986, r 12.12.

20.79 As to the first safeguard, a 'sufficient connection with England' the court stated that the grant of relief was discretionary[1]. Before an order was made the court would need to be satisfied that the defendant was sufficiently connected with England for it to be just and proper to make the order against him despite the foreign element:

'..in considering whether there is a sufficient connection with this country the court will look at all the circumstances, including the residence and place of business of the defendant, his connection with the insolvent, the nature and purpose of the transaction being impugned, the nature and locality of the property involved, the circumstances in which the defendant became involved in the transaction or received a benefit from it or acquired the property in question, whether the defendant acted in good faith, and whether under any relevant foreign law the defendant acquired an unimpeachable title free from any claims even if the insolvent had been adjudged bankrupt or wound up locally. The importance to be attached to these factors will vary from case to case. By taking into account and weighing these and any other relevant circumstances, the court will ensure that it does not seek to exercise oppressively or unreasonably the very wide jurisdiction conferred by [IA 1986, ss 339–340].'[2]

1   That the grant of relief is discretionary is plain under IA 1986, s 423(2) which provides that the court 'may' make an order. IA 1986, ss 238, 239 (and ss 339, 340 for personal insolvency) however provide that the court 'shall' make an order, but the requirement is that the court must make 'such order as it thinks fit'. This is 'apt to confer on the court an overall discretion', per Nicholls V-C [1992] 3 WLR 690, 702.
2   Per Nicholls V-C at [1993] Ch 223, 240.

20.80 The second safeguard is the need for leave for service abroad, and on an application for leave the court will take into account the strengths and weaknesses of the applicant's claim, including the applicant's claim that the respondent has a sufficient connection with England. There must be 'a real issue' which the applicant may reasonably ask the court to try. A sufficiently strong case must be made out to justify leave to serve abroad, although how strong that case needs to be will depend on the circumstances of the particular case[1].

1   Per Nicholls V-C at [1993] Ch 223, 241.

20.81 There is authority in corporate insolvency that the court will not restrain an office-holder of an insolvent English company from bringing proceedings in a foreign court to recover assets under equivalent provisions of the local law to IA 1986, ss 238, 239[1] save in exceptional circumstances[2]. A similar approach will be adopted in personal insolvency.

1   Ie transaction at an undervalue, IA 1986, s 238, and preference, IA 1986, s 239, corresponding with IA 1986, ss 339 and 340 in personal insolvency.
2   *Re Maxwell Communications Corpn plc* [1992] BCC 757, CA; the English court can properly grant an injunction preventing the claimant from pursuing his action in a foreign court if, exceptionally, it concludes that the pursuit of the action in the foreign court would be vexatious and oppressive and that the English court is the more appropriate forum for the trial of the action, see p 773H.

Limitation

20.82 There are two sections of the Limitation Act 1980 which may be relevant to claims for relief under IA 1986, ss 339–342. By the Limitation Act 1980, s 8 an action on a specialty may not be brought more than 12 years after the date on which the cause of action accrued, while the Limitation Act 1980, s 9 limits to six years from the accrual of the cause of action the period within which an action may be brought to recover any sum recoverable by virtue of any enactment. A statute is a form of specialty[1] and accordingly actions to assert a non-pecuniary right are subject to the 12-year limitation period. Statutory claims for money sums become statute-barred after six years[2]. It follows that where the application under the IA 1986 is to set aside a transaction, or to release or discharge a security given by the individual debtor, or for some other form of non-pecuniary relief there will be a 12-year limitation period, and for purely money claims there will be a six-year limitation period[3]. Where there is doubt as to the appropriate category in which to place any particular claim the court should look to see what is the substance or essential nature of the relief truly sought by the applicant and the limitation period determined accordingly[4]. The date of accrual of the cause of action will be the date on which the bankruptcy order is made[5].

[1] *Central Electricity Generating Board v Halifax Corpn* [1963] AC 785, [1962] 3 All ER 915; *Collin v Duke of Westminster* [1985] QB 581.
[2] Limitation Act 1980, s 8(2) provides that the 12-year period for a claim on a specialty does not affect any action for which a shorter period of limitation is prescribed.
[3] *Re Priory Garage (Walthamstow) Ltd* [2001] BPIR 144, 160 (IA 1986, ss 238–241 [ss 339–342]); the court agreed with the conclusions of the deputy judge as to limitation for claims under IA 1986, ss 238–241 [ss 339–342] in *Re Yates* [2005] BPIR 476 at para 183 (a case under IA 1986, ss 423–425). See generally the comments of the Court of Appeal in *Hill v Spread Trustee Co Ltd* [2006] EWCA Civ 542, [2007] 1 All ER 1106 on limitation in connection with a IA 1986, s 423 application, commented upon at paras 21.29–21.30.
[4] *Re Priory Garage (Walthamstow) Ltd* [2001] BPIR 144, 160–1.
[5] This being the date of the commencement of the bankruptcy, IA 1986, s 278.

20.83 It is important that trustees in bankruptcy do not delay in bringing applications to set aside undervalue transactions or preferences. Where trustees are guilty of inordinate and inexcusable delay in instituting and proceeding with their claims they may be struck out for want of prosecution, even where the limitation period has not yet expired and it would be open to the office-holder to commence fresh proceedings[1].

[1] *Re Farmizer (Products) Ltd* [1996] 2 BCLC 462; *Hamblin v Field* [2000] BPIR 621, CA.

Trustee in bankruptcy's costs

20.84 There is now express provision in the Insolvency Rules entitling a trustee in bankruptcy bringing proceedings under IA 1986, ss 339 or 340 to an indemnity out of the bankrupt's estate for costs properly incurred including the costs of the other side. This was the view of the Court of Appeal in *Re Exchange Travel (Holdings) Ltd (No 3)*[1]. In that case the Court of Appeal, noting that their views were obiter and reached without the benefit of any depth of argument, suggested that the reason this was the position was because any recoveries would be assets forming part of the estate for the purposes of the IA 1986 and the IR 1986. The costs incurred in such proceedings would accordingly be expenses of the bankruptcy[2] and as such payable first under the general rule as to priority of expenses payable out of the bankrupt's estate in the bankruptcy[3]. In contrast, in *Mond v Hammond Suddards*[4] the Court of Appeal[5], following the reasoning of Millett J in *Re*

MC Bacon Ltd (No 2)[6], held that a claim under IA 1986, ss 339 or 340 was not a claim to realise or get in any asset of the bankrupt[7] and so IR 1986, r 6.224(1)(a) which provided for the bankruptcy expenses to include 'expenses properly chargeable or incurred by the trustee in preserving, realising or getting in any of the assets of the bankrupt' could have no application to the costs of such an application[8]. Accordingly it was not permissible for the trustee to use the assets in the estate to fund his costs. Both these decisions were considered by the Court of Appeal in *Lewis v IRC*[9], where it was held that the decision in *Mond v Hammond Suddards* was binding. The court therefore ruled that the trustee had no entitlement as of right to recoup the costs of proceedings brought by him under IA 1986, ss 339 or 340, and it was doubted whether the court had a discretion to permit the trustee to be paid his costs out of the assets of the estate.

1   [1997] 2 BCLC 579.
2   Being 'fees, costs charges and other expenses incurred in the course of the bankruptcy', IR 1986, r 12.2.
3   IR 1986, r 6.224(1), see *Re Exchange Travel (Holdings) Ltd* [1997] 2 BCLC 579, CA. where the decision in *Re MC Bacon Ltd (No 2)* [1991] Ch 127, [1990] BCLC 607 was (wrongly) doubted; the Court of Appeal also stated that as the liquidator is a fiduciary he would in any case be entitled in accordance with the ordinary rule of equity to such indemnity as would protect him against the consequences of properly performing his fiduciary duty. This would apply equally to an administrator.
4   [2000] Ch 40, [1999] 3 WLR 697.
5   Without *Re Exchange Travel (Holdings) Ltd* [1997] 2 BCLC 579 being cited.
6   [1991] Ch 127, [1990] BCLC 607.
7   See *Re Yagerphone Ltd* [1935] Ch 392; any realisations do not become assets of the company but are received by the liquidator impressed with a trust in favour of those creditors amongst whom he has to distribute the assets of the company.
8   This was a corporate insolvency case and the further argument that the liquidator could recoup his costs by an order of the court under IA 1986, s 115 (voluntary liquidation) or s 156 (compulsory liquidation) was rejected on the basis that these provisions are concerned with priority and do not give the court power to authorise or direct the payment of costs not otherwise authorised by the Act or the Rules.
9   [2001] 3 All ER 499.

20.85 The decisions in *Mond* and *Lewis* were overruled by the Insolvency (Amendment) (No 2) Rules 2002[1]. It is now provided by IR 1986, r 6.224(1) that 'the expenses of the bankruptcy are payable out of the estate in the following order of priority – (a) expenses or costs which – (i) are properly chargeable or incurred by the official receiver or the trustee in preserving, realising or getting in any of the assets of the bankrupt or otherwise relating to the conduct of any legal proceedings which he has power to bring or defend whether the claim on which the proceedings are based forms part of the estate or otherwise'[2].

1   SI 2002/2712, as from 1 January 2003.
2   In corporate insolvency the understandable concern that this change in the rules may permit a liquidator who contests the validity of a floating charge or of assets falling within it to do so, where unsuccessful, using the chargee's own money has been mitigated by the House of Lords decision in *Buchler v Talbot* [2004] UKHL 9, [2004] AC 298, [2004] 1 All ER 1289; it is now settled that the company's assets do not include assets covered by a floating charge.

20.86 In many cases the assets of the bankrupt's estate are insufficient to fund contested litigation. It is common practice for the trustee to obtain an indemnity from one or more of the more substantial creditors before commencing proceedings on terms which entitle those creditors to be reimbursed any sums which they have to pay before the net recovery is distributed amongst the creditors generally. Such an arrangement is neither champertous nor an abuse of the process[1]. Furthermore, anyone who lends money to the trustee for the purposes of proceedings to recover money or other assets under the provisions relating to undervalue transactions or preferences will be entitled to be subrogated to the trustee's right of indemnity[2].

[1] *Re Exchange Travel (Holdings) Ltd (No 3)* [1997] 2 BCLC 579, where, by implication, this practice was approved by the Court of Appeal.
[2] *Re Exchange Travel (Holdings) Ltd (No 3)* [1997] 2 BCLC 579, 596.

Orders for restoring position

20.87 The court is to make such order as it thinks fit for restoring the position to what it would have been if the individual debtor had not entered into the transaction or given the preference[1]. The statute is framed in mandatory terms ('the court shall ... make such order as it thinks fit') but 'despite the use of the verb 'shall', the phrase 'such order as it thinks fit' is apt to confer on the court an overall discretion. The discretion is wide enough to enable the court, if justice so requires, to make no order against the other party to the transaction or the person to whom the preference was given'[2]. In appropriate cases therefore the court may make no order on an application even where it is found that assets have been transferred for no consideration[3]. It may not of course be possible to restore the pre-transaction position exactly. This is no reason for the court not to make an order[4]; the court should seek to restore the original position so far as practicable[5]. Without prejudice to this general power of the court the IA 1986 sets out a number of specific orders which might be made to achieve this purpose. The court may[6]:

(a) require any property transferred as part of the transaction, or in connection with the giving of the preference, to be vested in the trustee of the bankrupt's estate as part of that estate;

(b) require any property to be so vested if it represents in any person's hands the application either of the proceeds of sale of property so transferred or of money so transferred;

(c) release or discharge, in whole or in part, any security given by the individual;

(d) require any person to pay, in respect of benefits received by him from the individual, such sums to the trustee in bankruptcy as the court may direct;

(e) provide for any security or guarantor whose obligations to any person were released or discharged, in whole or in part, under the transaction, or by the giving of the preference, to be under such new or revived obligations to that person as the court thinks appropriate;

(f) provide for security to be provided for the discharge of any obligation imposed by or arising under the order, for such an obligation to be charged on any property and for the security or charge to have the same priority as a security or charge released or discharged, in whole or in part, under the transaction or by the giving of the preference; and

(g)   provide for the extent to which any person whose property is vested by
      the order in the trustee of the bankrupt's estate, or on whom obliga-
      tions are imposed by the order, is to be able to prove in the bankruptcy
      for debts or other liabilities which arose from, or were released or
      discharged, in whole or in part, under or by, the transaction or the
      giving of the preference.

1   IA 1986, ss 339(2), 340(2).
2   Per Nicholls V-C in *Re Paramount Airways Ltd* [1993] Ch 223, at 239, [1992] BCLC 710
    at 721.
3   *Singla v Brown* [2007] EWHC 405 (Ch), [2007] BPIR 424.
4   *Lord v Sinai Securities Ltd* [2004] EWHC 1764 (Ch), [2005] 1 BCLC 295.
5   See *Chohan v Saggar* [1994] 1 BCLC 706, a decision under IA 1986, s 423, but applicable
    to s 342.
6   See IA 1986, s 342(1).

20.88 In considering the appropriate remedy in any particular case the court
should not start from any a priori position, and there is certainly no
presumption in favour of monetary compensation as opposed to setting the
transaction aside and re-vesting any asset transferred[1]. There is, quite rightly,
concern that if the courts routinely order that the transferee makes good any
benefit he has obtained in the transaction by monetary compensation, this will
encourage undervalue transactions or preferences. There should be no encour-
agement to an 'if I get away with it all well and good and if not I still have the
asset and merely have to pay full value' attitude on the part of prospective
transferees of insolvent debtor's assets:

> 'The court would be slow to allow a transferee, who has entered into a
> transaction with an insolvent [debtor] when on notice that the transaction may
> be challenged by the [trustee] as being at an undervalue, to retain his purchase
> simply by means of paying a further sum at a later date. I suggest that the court
> would look carefully at allowing a transferee in these circumstances to buy his
> way out of the problem if the court were to consider that he went into the
> transaction with his eyes open and took a calculated risk.'[2]

1   *Re Thoars (deceased), Ramlort Ltd v Reid (No 2)* [2004] EWCA Civ 800, [2005] 1 BCLC
    331 para 126; *Walker v WA Personnel Ltd* [2002] BPIR 621.
2   Per His Honour Judge Havelock-Allan QC in *Walker v WA Personnel Ltd* [2002] BPIR
    621 quoted, with apparent approval, by Jonathan Parker LJ in *Re Thoars (deceased),
    Ramlort Ltd v Reid (No 2)* [2004] EWCA Civ 800, [2005] 1 BCLC 331.

20.89 Indeed, given the express words of the statute: 'the court shall ... make
such order as it thinks fit for restoring the position to what it would have been
if the individual debtor had not entered into that transaction'[1] there is if
anything a presumption against monetary compensation.

1   IA 1986, s 339(2) (transaction at an undervalue), s 340(2) (preference).

What position is to be restored?

20.90 Care must be taken in interpreting the requirement of the statute that
the order is to restore the position to what it would have been if the individual
debtor had not entered into the transaction. It is suggested that 'position' here
means no more than 'financial position'. It can surely not be required of the

court that it attempts to assess what would have happened to the debtor in the absence of the relevant transaction. In *Re MDA Investment Management Ltd*[1] the company, having become the sole owner of a business previously run by a partnership, sold the business to a third party for a proper consideration, but arranging for the partnership to be a party to the sale agreement and to receive a substantial proportion of the proceeds of sale. Park J after citing the words of the statute[2] stated: 'That requires me to assume that [the company] had not entered into the sale transaction at all and to ask: what would the position have been in that eventuality?'. On the facts of the case the learned judge concluded that had the company not entered into the transaction it would have had to close down its business and would have received nothing for it. Accordingly although the company did not receive full value for the sale of its business the learned judge refused the claim under IA 1986, s [339][3]. It is submitted that this is taking analysis too far. For the purposes of IA 1986, s 339(2) the court need not ask what would have happened to the debtor had the relevant transaction not been entered into. Indeed it is dangerous to do so. In any case considered by the court it will inevitably be the case that subsequent to the transaction the debtor has become bankrupt; no question of IA 1986, s 339 would otherwise arise. If, without the transaction, the debtor would have become insolvent anyway it may always be argued that the debtor suffered no loss in entering into the transaction. On the other hand if, without the transaction, the debtor would have remained solvent and traded, perhaps for many years, the court might find itself ordering compensation out of all proportion to the benefits lost and received on the particular transaction. On the facts of *Re MDA Investment Management Ltd* the company sold a business of which it was the sole owner and arranged for a third party to share the proceeds of sale. As at the date of the transaction the company owned a business of a particular value, as evidenced by the sale agreement, and were the court to have made an order by reference to IA 1986, s [342](1)(d)[4] it is suggested that the court would have sufficiently restored the position for the purposes of IA 1986, s [339(2)]. Certainly it would be unfortunate were it possible to meet an IA 1986, s 339 application with the defence that although the debtor did not receive full value he could not have done any better. The facts of *Re MDA Investment Management Ltd* were however unusual; in the more normal case of a purchaser paying too little for an asset it is likely that the issue will resolve itself into one of proper valuation.

1   [2003] EWHC 2277 (Ch), [2004] 1 BCLC 217.
2   'the court shall ... make such order as it thinks fit for restoring the position to what it would have been if the company had not entered into that transaction'.
3   In the circumstances this mattered little because the learned judge found the director responsible for the transaction liable for misfeasance.
4   See (d) at para **20.87**.

Events subsequent to the transaction

20.91 In deciding how to exercise its statutory discretion as to remedy the court must have regard to subsequent events and to the facts as they are at the date of the order[1].

1   *Re Thoars (deceased), Ramlort Ltd v Reid (No 2)* [2004] EWCA Civ 800, [2005] 1 BCLC 331 at [126].

Effect on third parties

20.92 An order by the court for restoring the position may affect both other parties to the relevant transaction or preference and any third party who may have acquired property or rights and interests as a result of the transaction or preference. Any order made by the court may affect the property of, or impose any obligation on, any person whether or not he is the person with whom the debtor in question entered into the transaction, or, as the case may be, the person to whom the preference was given[1]. The wording of the statute ('any person') makes it plain that the class of persons against whom orders may be made is unrestricted whether as to category or territory[2]. However, whereas in the case of a party to the transaction it is immaterial whether or not he is aware of the debtor's insolvency or the circumstances in which the transaction was entered into or preference made by the debtor, protection is afforded to bona fide third parties who have given value. The IA 1986[3] provides that any order made by the court:

(a)   must not prejudice any interest in property which was acquired from a person other than the individual debtor and was acquired in good faith and for value[4], or prejudice any interest deriving from such an interest, and

(b)   shall not require a person who received a benefit from the transaction or preference in good faith and for value to pay a sum to the trustee of the bankrupt's estate, except where that person was a party to the transaction or the payment is to be in respect of a preference given to that person at a time when he was a creditor of the individual debtor.

1   IA 1986, s 342(2).
2   *Re Paramount Airways Ltd* [1993] Ch 223, [1992] 3 All ER 1, CA, although in the case of extra-territorial persons the court emphasised the safeguards to the operation of this unrestricted jurisdiction, see paras **20.78–20.80**. In *Agriplant Services Ltd* [1997] 2 BCLC 598 it was suggested, at p 610f, that orders may be made only against a person or persons to whom a preference has been given. This does not appear to conform with the general intention of the Insolvency Act 1986, and while the circumstances in which the court will be considering making an order against someone other than the immediate beneficiary of the preference are likely to arise less often than in the cases of transactions at an undervalue, it would be unduly restrictive if not wrong to interpret the statute in this way. The court's overriding duty must be to make an order which restores the position to what it would have been had the company not given the preference, so far as this is practicable and having regard to the provisions of s 342(2), (2A), see text.
3   IA 1986, s 342(2)(a), (b).
4   The requirement originally in the IA 1986 that the acquisition should have been without notice of the relevant circumstances was removed by the Insolvency (No 2) Act 1994 as from 26 July 1994.

Insolvency (No 2) Act 1994

20.93 As originally enacted these provisions followed the well-known requirements of equity 'good faith, for value, and without notice of the relevant circumstances'. However, the requirement that the third party should have no notice of the relevant circumstances was capable of causing difficulty in the case of purchasers and mortgagees of interests in land, and the absolute nature of this requirement was mitigated by the Insolvency (No 2) Act 1994[1].

It is now open to a person who, for value, has acquired an interest in property from someone other than the individual debtor in question, or has received a benefit from the transaction and preference and who had notice of the 'relevant surrounding circumstances' and of the 'relevant proceedings' to demonstrate that he did in fact act in good faith. There is a statutory presumption that such a person acquired his interest or received a benefit otherwise than in good faith, but he may show the contrary and so avoid being the subject of an order[2]. The statutory presumption of absence of good faith also applies to any person or company who at the time he acquired property or received a benefit was an associate of, or was connected with, either the individual or the person with whom the individual entered into the transaction or to whom the individual gave the preference[3].

1   In relation to interests acquired and benefits received after 26 July 1994.
2   IA 1986, s 342(2A)(a). There is as yet no authority on the operation of these provisions.
3   IA 1986, s 342(2A)(b); for 'connected with' a company see **Appendix 2**. It is expressly provided by IA 1986, s 342(6) that the definition of 'connected with' a company contained in IA 1986, s 249 is to apply to the provisions of IA 1986, s 342(2A)(b).

20.94 The 'relevant surrounding circumstances' are, as relevant:

(a)   the fact that the individual in question entered into the transaction at an undervalue; or

(b)   the circumstances which amounted to the giving of the preference by the individual in question[1].

1   IA 1986, s 342(4).

20.95 A person has notice of the 'relevant proceedings' if he has notice:

(i)   of the fact that the petition on which the individual in question is adjudged bankrupt has been presented; or

(ii)   of the fact that the individual in question has been adjudged bankrupt[1].

1   IA 1986, s 342(5).

20.96 Any sums which the court may order to be paid to the trustee by way of an order in respect of a transaction at an undervalue or a preference are to be comprised in the bankrupt's estate[1].

1   IA 1986, s 342(3).

20.97 The case of *Re Sonatacus Ltd*[1] provides an interesting decision on the question of good faith in the present context. In *Re Sonatacus Ltd* the company, which had received a loan from a director who had himself borrowed the money from a third party, repaid a substantial portion of the loan directly to the third party shortly before it went into liquidation. The Court of Appeal held that in repaying the third party the company discharged part of its debt to the director and in so doing preferred him to other creditors. Faced with an application for an order in respect of the payment, the third party's evidence was that it did not appreciate that the repayment (which was by CHAPS payment directly to the third party's bank account) had come from the company rather than the director, its creditor. On the basis however that the third party was aware of the repayment and that the company was in financial difficulty, the Court of Appeal held that the third party company had not received the repayment in good faith because the third party must have been aware that it was likely that the director had been repaid by the company or at least shut his eyes to that possibility[2].

1   [2007] EWCA Civ 31, [2007] All ER (D) 203 (Jan).
2   A fact-sensitive decision, but it is surely right that a lender who lends to a director as principal knowing that the director will lend on to the company should not be in a better position than a lender to the company who takes a guarantee from the director.

Criminal conduct: 'tainted gifts'

20.98 The Proceeds of Crime Act 2002 ('POCA 2002') provides a statutory code[1] to cover the investigation and confiscation of the proceeds of crime, and may prohibit the making of an order under IA 1986, ss 339, 340 or 423. Under the provisions of POCA 2002 the Crown Court may make a confiscation order against a convicted defendant after determining whether the defendant has a criminal lifestyle[2] and has benefited from his general criminal conduct, or does not have a criminal lifestyle but has benefited from his particular criminal conduct[3]. Once a criminal investigation has been started with regard to an offence, or criminal proceedings have been instituted[4], the Crown Court may make a restraint order prohibiting any person from dealing with any realisable property which he holds[5] and where a restraint order is made a receiver may be appointed in respect of any realisable property subject to the restraint order[6]. Should a confiscation order be made but not satisfied it may be enforced by the appointment of an enforcement receiver[7] or by appointing the Director of the Assets Recovery Agency to act as enforcement authority.

1   As from 24 March 2003.
2   As defined in POCA 2002, s 75 and Sch 2.
3   POCA 2002, s 6.
4   POCA 2002, s 40.
5   POCA 2002, s 41; a restraint order is closely akin to a freezing order.
6   POCA 2002, s 48.
7   POCA 2002, s 50.

20.99 POCA 2002 introduces the concept of the 'tainted gift'[1]. Where a court has decided that the defendant has a criminal lifestyle, or no decision has been made as to whether the defendant has such a lifestyle or not, a gift is tainted if made at any time within six years of the date on which proceedings were started against the defendant[2], and if there are two or more offences and proceedings were started on different days, the earliest date on which proceedings were started[3]. Where a court has decided that the defendant does not have a criminal lifestyle a gift is tainted if made at any time after the date on which the relevant offence was committed, or the earliest such date where there are two or more offences[4]. A 'gift' is defined as a transfer of property for a consideration whose value is significantly less than the value of the property at the time of the transfer[5].

1   POCA 2002, s 77.
2   Even where that day pre-dates the passing of POCA 2002.

³   POCA 2002, s 77(2)(9).
⁴   POCA 2002, s 77(5).
⁵   POCA 2002, s 78, see also the provisions as to assessing value, ss 77–81.

20.100 Where an individual debtor becomes bankrupt having made a tainted gift, whether directly or indirectly, no order may be made under IA 1986, ss 339, 340 or 423 in respect of the making of the gift at any time when either any property of the recipient of the tainted gift is the subject of a restraint order, or there is an order in force appointing either an enforcement receiver or the Director of the Assets Recovery Agency to be the enforcement authority in respect of a confiscation order[1]. After any such order has been discharged the Bankruptcy Court or county court (or in the case of an order under IA 1986, s 423 the High Court) may then proceed to make an order under IA 1986, ss 339, 340 or 423, but any such order must take into account any realisation of property held by the recipient of the tainted gift under POCA 2002[2].

¹   POCA 2002, s 427(2), (3).
²   POCA 2002, s 427(4).

Other remedies

20.101 An application for an order in respect of a transaction at an undervalue or a preference may be accompanied by an application[1] for a freezing injunction or a search order to prevent dissipation of assets or the destruction of relevant documents pending the hearing of the application[2]. It may be possible for a creditor to obtain an injunction to restrain a prospective transaction at an undervalue. In *Customs & Excise Comrs v Anchor Foods Ltd*[3] the defendant proposed selling its business at a price which, although supported by an independent valuation, was asserted by the claimants as being at a serious undervalue. The court stated that while the provisions of IA 1986, ss 339 and 423 are of some assistance on the question of discretion in granting an injunction they did not go to the issue of jurisdiction[4]. In granting relief to restrain the sale of the debtor company's business to an associated company, the court stressed the importance of the cross undertaking in damages, which in this case was being given by an emanation of the Crown. The court may, in appropriate circumstances, appoint a receiver and manager pending the hearing of the application[5].

¹   Under CPR Pt 25, which applies in insolvency proceedings by virtue of IR 1986, r 7.51.
²   For an example of a worldwide freezing order (Mareva injunction) including an order for the disclosure of worldwide assets see *Aiglon Ltd and L'Aiglon SA v Gau Shan Co Ltd* [1993] 1 Lloyd's Rep 164; and see *Dora v Simper* [2000] 2 BCLC 561.
³   [1999] 3 All ER 268, [1999] 1 WLR 1139.
⁴   'The fact that relief would only be available after the transaction took place in certain limited circumstances according to statute does not mean that the court has no jurisdiction to grant relief before the transaction takes place unless those limited circumstances exist or are credibly said to exist', per Neuberger J at p 1148.
⁵   *Walker v WA Personnel Ltd* [2002] BPIR 621.

20.102 After a transaction has been carried out but before the hearing of an application to set it aside under IA 1986, ss 339, 340 or 423 injunctive relief may be sought to restrain particular use of the transferred asset, for example re-branding a business which has been transferred[1]. Such an application will proceed on *American Cyanamid* principles[2]. The nature of undervalue and preference claims are such that the court will usually be able to form a clear view as to the merits and thus of the trustee's prospects of success, and the requirement of the statute that the court should seek to restore the position to what it would have been if the individual debtor had not entered the transaction will readily lead to the conclusion that damages will not be an adequate remedy.

[1]   See eg *Walker v WA Personnel Ltd* [2002] BPIR 621; the court appointed a receiver and manager so the injunction was granted for a short period 'until the receiver's manager is in the driving seat', p 651.
[2]   *American Cyanamid Co v Ethicon Ltd* [1975] AC 396, [1975] 1 All ER 504, HL; the applicant needs to demonstrate (1) a real prospect of success, and (2) damages will not be an adequate remedy.

20.103   An application for an order in respect of a transaction at an undervalue may be made together with an application in respect of an extortionate credit transaction[1].

[1]   See para **20.138** and IA 1986, s 343(6).

Matrimonial cases

20.104   The fact that a disposal of property or payment of money has been made 'in order to comply with' a property adjustment order in matrimonial proceedings does not prevent it being set aside or adjusted as a transaction at an undervalue or preference[1]. In so providing the Matrimonial Causes Act 1973, s 39 appears to proceed upon the basis that it is the disposition by the party against whom an order is made which effects the transfer of the property in question. However, the Court of Appeal has held that it is the order of the family court which effects a transfer of beneficial interest, with the result that the subsequent disposition by the relevant spouse would be only of the bare legal estate[2]. The importance of the distinction will arise only rarely, in cases where the start date of the relevant time[3] falls after the date of the court order but before the date on which the spouse against whom the ancillary relief order was made executed the relevant transfer[4]. Accordingly a trustee in bankruptcy may apply to set aside an order for ancillary relief where the requirements for setting aside a transaction at an undervalue or a preference are met. An order which is the product of collusion between the spouses designed to affect adversely the interests of the creditors will be set aside[5]. An ancillary relief order, like any other order, whether made by the court after a contested hearing or by consent, may be set aside if a vitiating factor such as fraud, mistake or misrepresentation can be established, quite irrespective of whether it can be shown that the party responsible for the relevant vitiating conduct had the purpose of defeating or adversely affecting the creditors of one or other spouse. A trustee in bankruptcy, standing in the shoes of the bankrupt, will be in a position to challenge the validity of an order affecting the bankrupt where he is able to demonstrate the presence of a vitiating factor. It is not essential to show collusion or a vitiating factor, but it will be a rare case in which an ancillary relief order will be susceptible to challenge as a transaction at an undervalue, as opposed to a preference where different considerations apply, without there being collusion or a vitiating factor present.

1   Matrimonial Causes Act 1973, s 39, as amended by the Insolvency Act 1985, Sch 8. It is implicit in this provision of the 1973 Act that any transfer of property or payment of money pursuant to a property adjustment order amounts to a transaction for the purposes of IA 1986, s 339.
2   See eg *Maclurcan v Maclurcan* (1897) LT 474 and *Mountney v Treharne* [2003] Ch 135.
3   See para **20.14**.
4   In *Haines v Hill* [2007] EWCA Civ 1284 at [8] the wife conceded that the order of the matrimonial court is the relevant transaction for the purpose of IA 1986, s 339; it is open for argument that on a proper interpretation of the statute the relevant transaction is the transfer made by the spouse 'in order to comply with the property adjustment order', see the Matrimonial Causes Act 1973, s 39.
5   *Re Kumar (a bankrupt)* [1993] 1 WLR 225, *Haines v Hill* [2007] EWCA Civ 1284.

Hill v Haines: first instance

20.105 Under the pre-1986 law it was established that any financial benefit obtained by [the wife] under a post-nuptial settlement made by [the husband] within two years[1] of his bankruptcy in consideration of the wife refraining from taking divorce or ancillary relief proceedings against him was valid against the trustee in bankruptcy[2]. Following the introduction of the law on transactions at an undervalue, however, the suggestion was made that a post-nuptial settlement might not constitute consideration for the purposes of IA 1986, s 339(3)(a)[3], or if did, such consideration could not be measured in money or money's worth for the purposes of IA 1986, s 339(3)(c)[4]. In *Hill v Haines*[5], at first instance, the court held that neither an agreement compromising the spouse's claims for ancillary relief under the Matrimonial Causes Act 1973[6] nor a court order giving such relief were capable of amounting to consideration for the purposes of the law governing transactions at an undervalue[7]. Accordingly any payment or transfer of property by the bankrupt to his spouse either under an agreement compromising the spouse's claims for ancillary relief or under a property adjustment order, even an order obtained after a contested hearing, was likely to constitute a transaction at an undervalue. This decision, which caused some considerable controversy when it became highly publicised, proceeded on the basis that no spouse has a right (or cause of action) to ancillary relief against the other party to the marriage[8]. It followed that when two parties to a marriage reach an agreement for the compromise of an ancillary relief application, such an agreement could not give rise to a contract enforceable in law[9]. The only way for the parties to ensure that the terms of the agreement were complied with was to convert the agreement into an order of the court. However, the court does not then give effect to the bargain reached by the parties. Rather it carries out an independent assessment[10] for the purposes of its statutory function to make provision for ancillary relief by reference to the relevant statutory criteria[11]. Accordingly, the argument ran, there can be no consideration passing from the applicant spouse to the bankrupt spouse under the agreement to compromise the ancillary relief claim. The result was that any property passing from the bankrupt spouse to the applicant spouse passes under a transaction which does not provide for the bankrupt to receive any consideration[12]. Even where the family court made an ancillary relief order after a contested hearing, the court at first instance in *Hill v Haines* was of the view, based on dicta as to the status of the parties to ancillary relief hearings[13], that a court order for ancillary relief does not vest in a spouse rights which can amount to consideration.

1   The relevant period for the purposes of the Bankruptcy Act 1914, s 42(1):

> 'Any settlement of property, not being a settlement made in favour of a purchase or incumbrancer in good faith and for valuable consideration shall, if the settler becomes bankrupt within two years after the date of the settlement, be void against the trustee in bankruptcy.'

2   *Re Pope* [1908] 2 KB 169; *Re Abbott (a bankrupt)* [1983] 1 Ch 45.

3   See para **20.23.**

4   See para **20.23.**

5   [2007] EWHC 1012 (Ch), [2007] BPIR 727.

6   Matrimonial Causes Act 1973, ss 23–25, as amended.

7   See the discussion at paras **15.37–15.41** (property adjustment orders in family proceedings.

8   There is, or used to be, a common law right to maintenance, a husband owing his wife a duty to support his wife 'according to his estate and condition': *Manby and Richardson v Scot* (1685) 83 ER 1065, *Povey v Povey* [1972] Fam 40, 50. There were limitations to this right. It was lost if the parties lived apart or if the wife committed adultery (however badly her husband treated her, *Grovier v Hancock* (1796) 6 Term 603) and on a practical level the courts would not order the husband to make payments to his wife. (Enforcement was seen more as an ecclesiastical matter). The wife was however able to pledge her husband's credit for the supply of necessaries. In *Re C (a Minor)* [1994] 1 FLR 111, at 116 Ward J observed that there 'may be a so-called common law duty to maintain, but when one analyses what that duty is it seems effectively to come to nothing ... the common law has no remedy. The remedies to enforce a duty to maintain are the statutory remedies.' Given the existence of statutory remedies however it is perhaps surprising that the court cannot marry the common law duty with a statutory remedy and find that a spouse has a right to maintenance during marriage and, by extension, to ancillary relief after divorce.

9   *Xydhias v Xydhias* [1999] 2 All ER 386, CA.

10   See *Xydhias v Xydhias* [1999] 2 All ER 386, at 394 per Thorpe LJ:

> 'My cardinal conclusion is that ordinary contractual principles do not determine the issues in this appeal. This is because of the fundamental distinction that an agreement for the compromise of an ancillary relief application does not give rise to a contract enforceable in law. The parties seeking to uphold a concluded agreement of the compromise of such an application cannot sue for specific performance. The only way of rendering the bargain enforceable, whether to ensure that the applicant obtains the agreed transfers and payments, or whether to protect the respondent from future claims, is to convert the concluded agreement into an order of the court ... An even more singular feature of the transition from compromise to order in ancillary relief proceedings is that the court does not, either automatically or invariably, grant the application to give the bargain the force of an order. The court conducts an independent assessment to enable it to discharge its statutory function to make such orders as reflect the criteria list in s 25 of the 1973 Act, as amended.'

11   In the Matrimonial Causes Act 1973, s 25.

12   And is therefore at an undervalue, IA 1986, s 339(3)(a).

13   See in particular G v G *(Financial Provision: Equal Division)* [2002] EWHC 1339 (Fam), [2002] 2 FLR 1143 where the court held that a transfer of shares pursuant to an order made in ancillary relief proceedings would not attract capital gains tax because the wife gave no consideration for the shares; no business hold-over relief was available and no capital gains tax liability would arise:

> 'In an ancillary relief hearing neither party has any 'rights' as such at all. All powers are vested in the court which may or may not exercise them. The parties may make suggestions as to how those powers are to be exercised. That is all. So

when I order a transfer of shares in favour of the wife on a clean break basis she is not giving up her claim for maintenance as a quid pro quo. I am simply exercising my statutory powers in the way I consider to be fair. This would equally be the case where the court is making a consent order, for although the parties may have made their agreement, it is for the court independently to adjudge its fairness.'

20.106 On the question whether, if an agreement to compromise an ancillary relief claim or an order for ancillary relief could indeed amount to consideration, such consideration was measurable in money or money's worth, the court at first instance in *Hill v Haines*[1] held that such consideration would not be so capable of assessment[2]. The judge relied on dicta in *Re Abbott*[3] and *Re Pope*[4]. Consideration which cannot be assessed in money or money's worth cannot amount to value for the purpose of assessing whether the bankrupt has received consideration which is significantly less than the consideration he has provided under the transaction[5].

1   [2007] EWHC 1012 (Ch), [2007] BPIR 727.
2   [2007] EWHC 1012 (Ch), [2007] BPIR 727 at [15]–[16]. In *Re Kumar* [1993] 1 WLR 224, Ferris J considered that *Re Abbott,* a decision under the Bankruptcy Act 1914, s 42, was authority for the proposition that a compromise of a claim to a provision in matrimonial proceedings was capable of being consideration in money or money's worth for the purposes of IA 1986, s 339(3)(c), but his observations were obiter and distinguished in *Hill v Haines* [2007] EWHC 1012 (Ch).
3   [1983] Ch 45, where Peter Gibson J described the consideration provided by the wife under an agreement to compromise her claim for ancillary relief as '... a compromise of rights not measurable in money terms'.
4   [1908] 2 KB 169, CA, where Buckley LJ (dissenting) suggested that valuable consideration was given only when the consideration is 'money, or property or something capable of being measured in money. It does not, I think, extend to the surrender of ... the right to relief for matrimonial offences'. In *Re Kumar* [1993] 1 WLR 224, Ferris J considered that *Re Abbott,* a decision under the Bankruptcy Act 1914, s 42, was authority for the proposition that a compromise of a claim to a provision in matrimonial proceedings was capable of being consideration in money or money's worth for the purposes of IA 1986, s 339(3)(c), but his observations were obiter and distinguished in *Hill v Haines* [2007] EWHC 1012 (Ch).
5   For the purposes of IA 1986, s 339(3)(c).

20.107 The consequences of the first instance decision in *Hill v Haines*[1] were significant. It meant that a wife who divorced her bankrupt husband and obtained an ancillary relief order within two years of his bankruptcy order (five years if she could not show that her husband was solvent immediately after the order took effect[2]) was most inevitably going to find that she would lose the benefit of her property adjustment order at the instance of her former husband's trustee. Not even the residual discretion of the court not to make an order would come to her aid[3]. In *Hill v Haines* the judge[4] rejected the suggestion that the fact that an order was made against the context of matrimonial breakdown was a reason why the discretion in the Bankruptcy Court not to make an order should be exercised so as to protect the spouse, but held that in the normal course an order restoring the position to what it would have been without the relevant payments or transfers of property to the spouse should be made for the benefit of the creditors.

1   [2007] EWHC 1012 (Ch), which was followed without further consideration in *Segal v Pasram* [2007] BPIR 881.
2   See para **20.14**.

³   As to the discretion not to make an order see para **20.87**.
⁴   His Honour Judge Pelling QC.

Hill v Haines: Court of Appeal

20.108 'Normality', as understood by most practitioners, was restored by the Court of Appeal¹. As previously noted the essential issues for consideration were first whether the spouse transferring the property under the provisions of an ancillary relief order is doing so 'on terms that provide for him to receive no consideration', and second whether any such consideration is 'in money or money's worth' so as to enable a comparison of value given and received by the bankrupt². In giving the leading judgment the Chancellor stated that the starting point on the issue of the giving of consideration was the right of spouses to financial provision and property adjustment orders under the Matrimonial Causes Act 1973. Each party to the marriage has an entitlement to a fair share of the available property³. Although this entitlement is not of itself a proprietary right, 'it has value in that its exercise may, and commonly does, lead to court orders entitling one spouse to property or money from or at the expense of the other. That money and property is, prima facie, the measure of the value of the right'⁴. In cases where the spouses reach agreement to compromise the claim the applicant spouse's forbearance to bring [her] ancillary relief claim can and does constitute consideration on [her] part⁵. Neither the fact that a claim for ancillary relief does not constitute a cause of action⁶ nor the fact that a transfer ordered by the court does not give rise to a payment of consideration so as to reduce the value of holdover relief for capital gains tax dictates a conclusion that a property adjustment order must be regarded as made for no consideration⁷. An agreement to compromise an ancillary relief claim is not devoid of any legal effect on the basis that the jurisdiction of the court to make ancillary relief orders cannot be ousted by the agreement of the spouses. The existence of such an agreement is a relevant circumstance for the court when determining what order to make; indeed provided the court is satisfied that the agreement has been properly and fairly arrived at its terms should not be displaced unless there are good and substantial grounds for concluding that injustice will be done by holding the parties to their agreement⁸. Accordingly the Chancellor concluded that parties to an ancillary relief order (whether arrived at after a contested hearing or an agreement between the spouses) do give 'consideration' for the purposes of the IA 1986 provisions relating to transactions at an undervalue.

¹   *Haines v Hill* [2007] EWCA Civ 1284.
²   Ie for the purposes of IA 1986, s 339(3)(c), see para **20.23, 20.42**.
³   *White v White* [2001] 1 AC 596, *Miller v Miller, McFarlane v McFarlane* [2006] 2 AC 618; an entitlement measured by the 'yardstick of equality' as tempered by the threefold principles of 'need, compensation and sharing'.
⁴   *Haines v Hill* [2007] EWCA Civ 1284 at [29].
⁵   The court here followed the pre-1986 Act decisions of the Court of Appeal in *Re Pope* [1908] 2 KB 169 and the Divisional Court in *Re Abbott (a bankrupt)* [1983] 1 Ch 45 both holding that an agreement to forebear from taking matrimonial proceedings constituted valuable consideration for the purposes of the Bankruptcy Act 1883, s 47 and the Bankruptcy Act 1914, s 42 respectively.
⁶   For the purposes of the Law Reform (Miscellaneous Provisions) Act 1934, s 1(1).

20.109 On the issue whether consideration provided by way of an ancillary relief order was capable of being 'in money or money's worth' the Chancellor looked to the economic realities of such orders: '... the order of the court quantifies the value of the applicant spouse's statutory right by reference to the value of the money or property thereby ordered to be paid or transferred by the respondent spouse to the applicant. In the case of such an order, whether following contested proceedings or by way of compromise, in the absence of the usual vitiating factors of fraud, mistake or misrepresentation the one balances the other'[1]. The Chancellor noted that if the applicant spouse is not treated as providing consideration for the transfer either at all or in money's worth all transfers of property under an ancillary relief order will be void:

> 'I cannot accept that Parliament intended that what must be one of the commonest orders made by courts exercising their matrimonial jurisdiction, namely that the husband do transfer his beneficial interest in the matrimonial home to the wife, should be capable of automatic nullification at the suit of the trustee in bankruptcy of the husband against whom a bankruptcy order was subsequently made on his own petition.'[2]

Concurring, Rix LJ observed that although claims in contract for breach of contract or in tort for damages for personal injury may be very difficult to measure in financial terms, the court is required to put a monetary value on any claim where the loss is not entirely speculative. A claim, such as a claim for ancillary relief, that is founded entirely in statute and is in the exercise of the court's discretion is a claim like any other. It can be assessed in monetary value even if the award lies peculiarly in the discretion of the court[3].

1   *Haines v Hill* [2007] EWCA Civ 1284 at [35]. The Chancellor continued 'But if any such factor [ie fraud, mistake or misrepresentation] is established by a trustee in bankruptcy on an application under s 339 then it will be apparent that the prima facie balance was not the true one and the transaction may be liable to be set aside.'
2   *Haines v Hill* [2007] EWCA Civ 1284 at [36].
3   *Haines v Hill* [2007] EWCA Civ 1284 at [77]. See also at [79] where Rix LJ considers the question of consideration and concludes that there is nothing foreign to the concept of consideration in the idea that the compromise of an ancillary relief claim can provide good consideration – 'even if for section 339 purposes the question of adequacy can be reviewed, especially where there is room to find collusion, fraud or concealment'.

20.110 The result is that a wife who obtains a settlement or transfer of property from her husband[1] pursuant to a court order following a contested hearing, or an order based on a genuine assessment of her entitlement to a fair share of the property available to both spouses, need have little concern that her husband's trustee in bankruptcy will be able to interfere and set the settlement or transfer aside as a transaction at an undervalue. Where, however, the wife has colluded with her husband, or there is a vitiating factor such as fraud, mistake or misrepresentation, the fact that the wife has a court order in her favour will not prevent the trustee from challenging the settlement or transfer. Creditors may well be concerned that the wife's 'entitlement' to a share of the matrimonial property may be a right to share in property which has been built up at their expense, although the family court should assess the wife's entitlement in the context of the husband's existing and future liabilities. Financial hardship and matrimonial difficulties are regularly found together, and it is always open to a trustee in bankruptcy to challenge a settlement or transfer of property to the wife within two years of the bankruptcy as a preference where it appears that the reaching of the post-nuptial compromise agreement or obtaining of the ancillary relief order has been arrived at with the desire to put the wife in a better position on her husband's bankruptcy than she would have been in without the agreement or order[2]. It remains to be seen whether *Hill v Haines* will go to the House of Lords, but the combination of legal argument and policy considerations[3] are likely to ensure that the Court of Appeal's decision is upheld.

1   'Husband' in this paragraph does of course include 'former husband', and the same applies where the roles are reversed and it is the husband who received the benefit of a transfer of property from his (former) wife.
2   See paras **20.54–20.67**.
3   As to which see *Haines v Hill* [2007] EWCA Civ 1284 at [82] and the fact that if the bankrupt's creditors 'succeed' against the wife there is likely to be an increased burden on the state.

D RECOVERY OF EXCESSIVE PENSION CONTRIBUTIONS

Pension legislation: requirement of inalienability

20.111 In order to qualify for the available tax privileges an individual's pension, whether a retirement annuity, personal pension or stakeholder pension, must be inalienable. This requirement of inalienability gave rise to uncertainty whether an individual's pension became part of his estate on his bankruptcy. This uncertainty was resolved in *Re Landau, Pointer v Landau*[1], subsequently confirmed by the Court of Appeal in *Krasner v Dennison*[2], the court holding that a bankrupt's rights in his pension plan did form part of his estate. The requirement of inalienability did not prevent the bankrupt's interest in his pension plans passing to his trustee as this took place by operation of law. The subsidiary question whether the trustee could obtain an income payments order[3] in respect of pension payments being made to a bankrupt was answered in the negative. As the bankrupt's rights in the pension passed to his trustee payments due to the bankrupt under any annuity purchased under the terms of the pension were not income of the bankrupt within the relevant provisions of the IA 1986, and could not therefore be the subject of an income payments order.

1   [1998] Ch 223, [1997] 3 All ER 322.
2   [2001] Ch 76, [2000] 3 All ER 234; the Court of Appeal rejected the argument that the vesting of pension policies in the trustee without there being jurisdiction in the court to direct that the trustee pay some or all of the pension to the bankrupt constituted a breach of article 1 of the First Protocol to the European Convention on Human Rights.
3   Under IA 1986, s 310.

20.112 Concern that a bankrupt might lose his entire pension provision, with a consequent dependence on the state, resulted in statutory intervention. The legislative scheme[1] is for a bankrupt's rights under any pension arrangement to be excluded from his estate[2], but to enable the trustee both to recover excessive pension contributions made by the individual before his bankruptcy[3] and also apply for an income payments order which takes into account any payments received by the bankrupt under a pension scheme[4]. A court exercising the powers of the IA 1986 enabling the recovery of excessive pension contributions is not constrained by any provision of the Pension Schemes Act 1993, s 159 or the Pensions Act 1995, s 91 or any other pension legislation[5] which prevent assignment or the making of orders which restrain a person from receiving anything which he is prevented from assigning, or any corresponding provision of the arrangement itself[6]. The bankrupt's personal pension rights are also protected against any provision in the pension scheme which either forfeits rights, or involves any manner of deprivation or suspension of rights, on bankruptcy[7].

[1] Initially enacted in the Pensions Act 1995, see ss 95 and 122, Sch 3, para 15. These provisions were not brought into force, and the statutory scheme is now enacted in the Welfare Reform and Pensions Act 1999.

[2] Welfare Reform and Pensions Act 1999, s 11(1) excludes rights under an approved pension arrangement from the estate; s 12(1) enables the Secretary of State to make regulations to exclude rights under an unapproved pension arrangement from the estate, and such rights may be excluded under the Occupational and Personal Pension Schemes (Bankruptcy) (No 2) Regulations 2002, SI 2002/836, reg 4. Note that by s 11(3) rights arising under a personal pension scheme approved under Chapter IV of Part XIV of the Income and Corporation Taxes Act 1988 which does not comprise approved personal pension arrangements are not excluded from falling into the estate. Such rights and also rights arising under a retirement benefit scheme which is being considered for approval at the date of the bankruptcy order but which does not subsequently obtain approval vest in the trustee in bankruptcy, subject to protection for transactions entered into by the trustees or managers of the scheme in good faith without notice of the relevant decision of the Commissioners not to approve the scheme; see s 11(3)–(12).

[3] IA 1986, ss 342A–342C inserted by the Welfare Reform and Pensions Act 1999, s 14 and ss 342D–342F inserted by the Welfare Reform and Pensions Act 1999, Sch 12, para 71 in respect of pension-sharing cases.

[4] IA 1986, s 310 as amended by the Pensions Act 1995, s 122, Sch 3, para 15. Note that payments by way of guaranteed minimum pension and payments giving effect to the bankrupt's protected rights as a member of a pension scheme are not to be taken into account when assessing the bankrupt's income for the purpose of an income payments order, IA 1986, s 310(7), (8) as amended. See para **14.173**.

[5] Whether passed or made before or after the passing of the Welfare Reform and Pensions Act 1999.

[6] IA 1986, s 342C(2).

[7] Pension Schemes Act 1993, s 159A, inserted by the Welfare Reform and Pensions Act 1999, s 14(1).

Approved pension arrangements

20.113 Any rights of a bankrupt under an approved pension arrangement are excluded from his estate[1]. An 'approved pension arrangement' means:

(a)   an exempt approved scheme[2];
(b)   a relevant statutory scheme[3];
(c)   a retirement benefits scheme[4] set up by a government outside the United Kingdom for the benefit, or primarily for the benefit, of its employees;

(d)   a retirement benefits scheme which is being considered for approval under Chapter I of Part XIV of the Income and Corporation Taxes Act 1988 ('ICTA 1988');

(e)   a contract or scheme which is approved under Chapter III, Part XIV, ICTA 1988 (retirement annuities);

(f)   a personal pension scheme which is approved under Chapter IV, Part XIV, ICTA 1988;

(g)   an annuity purchased for the purpose of giving effect to rights under a scheme falling within any of paragraphs (a) to (c) and (f);

(h)   any pension arrangements of any description which may be prescribed by regulations made by the Secretary of State.

[1]   Welfare Reform and Pensions Act 1999, s 11(1).
[2]   As defined in ICTA 1988, s 592, namely (a) any approved scheme which is shown to the satisfaction of the HMRC Board to be established under irrevocable trusts, or (b) any other approved scheme as respects which the HMRC Board, having regard to any special circumstances, direct that this section shall apply.
[3]   As defined in ICTA 1988, s 612(1) namely a retirement benefits scheme established by or under any enactment (a) the particulars of which are set out in any enactment, or in any regulations made under any enactment, or (b) which has been approved as an appropriate scheme by a Minister or government department.
[4]   As defined in ICTA 1988, s 611(1) namely a scheme for the provision of benefits consisting of or including relevant benefits, but which does not include any national scheme providing such benefits.

20.114 For the purposes of paragraph (h) (para **20.113**) pension arrangements have been prescribed by the Occupational and Personal Pension Schemes (Bankruptcy) (No 2) Regulations 2002[1], reg 2 covering a variety of pension schemes including schemes funded by foreign emoluments.

[1]   SI 2002/836.

Unapproved pension arrangements

20.115 Although a bankrupt's rights under an unapproved pension arrangement are not automatically excluded from his estate it is open to the bankrupt to apply for an exclusion order which will protect his pension rights by excluding them from his estate[1]. To qualify as an unapproved pension arrangement the arrangement must meet the following conditions, namely:

(a)   be established under (i) an irrevocable trust, or (ii) a contract, agreement or arrangement made with the bankrupt;

(b)   have as its primary purpose the provision of relevant benefits; and

(c)   be the bankrupt's sole pension arrangement or his main means of pension provision (other than a contributory benefits pension under Part II of the Social Security Contributions and Benefits Act 1992)[2].

[1]   Welfare Reform and Pensions Act 1999, s 12(1).
[2]   The Occupational and Personal Pension Schemes (Bankruptcy) (No 2) Regulations 2002, SI 2002/836, reg 3 as amended by SI 2006/744, art 21(1), (4) as from 6 April 2004.

20.116 The pension arrangement will be an unapproved arrangement for the purposes of an order excluding it from a bankrupt's estate if it is a pension arrangement falling within:

20.116 *Adjustment of prior transactions*

(a)   the Finance Act 2004, s 157 (de-registration);
(b)   the Finance Act 2004, Sch 36, paras 52–57; or
(c)   the Finance Act 2003, s 393A[1].

[1]   The Occupational and Personal Pension Schemes (Bankruptcy) (No 2) Regulations 2002, SI 2002/836, reg 3 as amended by SI 2006/744, art 21(1), (4) as from 6 April 2004.

Excluding rights under unapproved pension arrangements

20.117 A bankrupt who wishes to exclude from his estate his rights under an unapproved pension arrangement has a choice. He may either:

(a)   make an application to the court for an exclusion order[1]; or
(b)   enter into a qualifying agreement with his trustee in bankruptcy[2].

[1]   In accordance with the provisions of the Occupational and Personal Pension Schemes (Bankruptcy) (No 2) Regulations 2002, SI 2002/836, reg 5.
[2]   In accordance with the provisions of the Occupational and Personal Pension Schemes (Bankruptcy) (No 2) Regulations 2002, SI 2002/836, reg 6.

20.118 An application for an exclusion order has to be made to the court within a period of 13 weeks beginning with the date on which the bankrupt's estate vests in the trustee in bankruptcy[1]. In most cases this will be the automatic vesting under the provisions of the Insolvency Act 1986[2]. However, in cases where the bankrupt's pension rights were in an approved scheme but have become unapproved arrangements because HMRC have withdrawn the registration of the relevant pension scheme[3] the bankrupt's pension rights will vest in his trustee in bankruptcy under the Welfare Reform and Pensions Act 1999[4]. The court may extend the time for the bankrupt to apply for an exclusion order either before or after the 13-week period has expired, where good cause is shown[5].

[1]   The Occupational and Personal Pension Schemes (Bankruptcy) (No 2) Regulations 2002, SI 2002/836, reg 5(1)(a)(i).
[2]   IA 1986, s 306.
[3]   Under the provisions of the Finance Act 2004, s 157.
[4]   Welfare Reform and Pensions Act 1999, s 11(5) or s 11(7); the bankrupt has 13 weeks from the vesting of his rights in the trustee to bring his application, The Occupational and Personal Pension Schemes (Bankruptcy) (No 2) Regulations 2002, SI 2002/836, reg 5(1)(a)(ii).
[5]   The Occupational and Personal Pension Schemes (Bankruptcy) (No 2) Regulations 2002, SI 2002/836, reg 5(2).

20.119 In exercising its discretion whether or not to make an exclusion order and, if so, whether to make it in respect of all or part of the excludable rights, the court is required to have reference to (a) the future likely needs of the bankrupt and his family, and (b) whether any benefits by way of pension or otherwise[1] are likely to be received by virtue of rights of the bankrupt which have already accrued under any other pension arrangements at the date on which the application for an exclusion order is made and the extent to which they appear likely to be adequate for meeting any such needs[2].

[1]   But excluding contributory benefits of an income-related benefit pension under the Social Security Contributions and Benefits Act 1992, Pt II.

2   The Occupational and Personal Pension Schemes (Bankruptcy) (No 2) Regulations 2002,
     SI 2002/836, reg 5(3).

Qualifying agreements

20.120 The bankrupt may make a 'qualifying agreement' with his trustee in
bankruptcy excluding his right in an unapproved pension arrangement from
his estate. There are no statutory requirements to be met in the making of such
an agreement. Presumably the trustee will have regard to the statutory scheme
which is to exclude pension rights from the estate, provided the bankrupt did
not make excessive pension contributions before his bankruptcy to the
detriment of his creditors, and to the matters of which the court should have
regard when making an exclusion order[1]. To the extent that his contributions
were reasonable given his income and circumstances the trustee should permit
the bankrupt to exclude his pension rights from his estate. Any qualifying
agreement made between the bankrupt and his trustee in bankruptcy must be
by deed and must incorporate all the terms which have been expressly agreed[2].

1   See para **20.117**.
2   The Occupational and Personal Pension Schemes (Bankruptcy) (No 2) Regulations 2002,
     SI 2002/836, reg 6(2).

20.121 A qualifying agreement is to be made within a period of nine weeks
beginning with the date on which the bankrupt's estate vests in his trustee in
bankruptcy[1] or, if later, the date on which the estate vests in the trustee[2] after
the de-registration of an approved scheme[3] by HMRC[4].

1   Under IA 1986, s 306.
2   The pension rights vest in the trustee under the provisions of the Welfare Reform and
     Pensions Act 1999, s 11(5) or s 11(7).
3   Under the provisions of the Finance Act 2004, s 157.
4   The Occupational and Personal Pension Schemes (Bankruptcy) (No 2) Regulations 2002,
     SI 2002/836, reg 6(1).

20.122 Should the bankrupt fail to make full disclosure of all material facts
in respect of any pension arrangement which is the subject of a qualifying
agreement for the purpose of enabling his rights to be excluded from his
estate, the trustee in bankruptcy may revoke the qualifying agreement on the
ground that the rights would not have otherwise been excluded[1]. The trustee
revokes the qualifying agreement by giving the bankrupt notice of revocation[2],
which notice must:

(a)   be dated;
(b)   be in writing;
(c)   specify the reasons for revocation of the qualifying agreement;
(d)   specify the date on which the agreement shall be revoked, such date not
       being one falling within a period of 30 days beginning with the date of
       the notice; and
(e)   inform the bankrupt that he has the right to apply for an exclusion
       order within a period of 30 days beginning with the date referred to in
       (d) above[3].

¹ The Occupational and Personal Pension Schemes (Bankruptcy) (No 2) Regulations 2002, SI 2002/836, reg 6(3).
² The Occupational and Personal Pension Schemes (Bankruptcy) (No 2) Regulations 2002, SI 2002/836, reg 6(3).
³ The Occupational and Personal Pension Schemes (Bankruptcy) (No 2) Regulations 2002, SI 2002/836, reg 6(4).

20.123 The trustee in bankruptcy is required to notify the person responsible for the pension arrangement¹ that a qualifying agreement has been made, or revoked, within 30 days of the date of the agreement or the date of a notice of revocation².

¹ Who may be the trustees, managers or provider of the arrangement, IA 1986, s 342C(6).
² The Occupational and Personal Pension Schemes (Bankruptcy) (No 2) Regulations 2002, SI 2002/836, reg 6(5).

20.124 Should the bankrupt wish to apply to the court for an exclusion order¹ he must do so within the 30-day period beginning with the date on which his qualifying agreement is revoked².

¹ See paras **20.117–20.119**.
² The Occupational and Personal Pension Schemes (Bankruptcy) (No 2) Regulations 2002, SI 2002/836, reg 5(1)(b).

Recovery of excessive pension contributions

20.125 The trustee of a bankrupt's estate may apply for an order where the bankrupt has made excessive contributions to his pension arrangements. The application may be made in respect of rights under an approved pension arrangement or excluded rights¹ under an unapproved pension arrangement². On an application by the trustee the court may make such order as it thinks fit for restoring the position to what it would have been had the excessive contributions not been made provided it is satisfied:

(a)   that the rights under the pension arrangements are to any extent, and whether directly or indirectly, the fruits of relevant contributions; and
(b)   that the making of any of the relevant contributions has unfairly prejudiced the individual's creditors³.

¹ Ie rights under an unapproved pension arrangement which are excluded from the bankrupt's estate under regulations pursuant to the Welfare Reform and Pensions Act 1999, s 12, IA 1986, s 342A(7). The Occupational and Personal Pension Schemes (Bankruptcy) (No 2) Regulations 2002, SI 2002/836, reg 10(1).
² IA 1986, s 342A(1).
³ IA 1986, s 342A(2); such contributions are styled 'the excessive contributions', s 342A(2).

20.126 For these purposes 'relevant contributions' means contributions to the individual's pension arrangements or any other pension arrangement which the individual has at any time made on his own behalf, or which have at any time been made on his behalf¹. In considering whether the making of any relevant contribution has unfairly prejudiced the individual's creditors the court is to consider 'in particular':

(a)   whether any of the contributions were made for the purpose of putting assets beyond the reach of the individual's creditors or any of them; and

(b)   whether the total amount of any contributions (i) made by or on behalf of the individual to pension arrangements, and (ii) represented, whether directly or indirectly, by rights under approved pension arrangements or excluded rights under unapproved pension arrangements, is an amount which is excessive in view of the individual's circumstances when those contributions were made[2].

1   IA 1986, s 342A(5).
2   IA 1986, s 342A(6).

20.127 In considering (a) above the court will presumably adopt the same approach to that used in respect of the similar provision with regard to transactions defrauding creditors[1].

1   Ie IA 1986, s 423(3)(a), see para **21.19**.

Excessive in individual's circumstances

20.128 There is no statutory guidance as to when the making of any relevant contribution, or the total amount of contributions, may be in an amount which is excessive in view of the individual's circumstances when that contribution or those contributions were made, neither have there been any relevant reported decisions. The test, 'has the contribution unfairly prejudiced the creditors', is essentially an objective one. Although the court is required to consider whether the individual had an intent to put assets beyond the reach of creditors[1], such an intent, where proved, will go to ensuring that an order is far more likely, it is not pre-requisite to an order being made. It will not be necessary for the trustee to demonstrate that the individual appreciated that he was prejudicing his creditors, merely that they were unfairly prejudiced. It also follows from a strict interpretation of the statute[2] that the date at which the court should consider whether or not the contribution has unfairly prejudiced the creditors is the date of the bankruptcy, and not the date on which the contribution was made. Any contributions which have been made to a pension arrangement, particularly in the years immediately preceding bankruptcy will, at least to some extent, have prejudiced the creditors. The critical question will be whether this prejudice is 'unfair'. It is in this context that the consideration of the individual's circumstances at the date of making the contribution will be relevant[3]. In each individual case where specific intent to defraud the creditors cannot be proved, the issue of unfairness will be determined primarily by the circumstances in which individual pension contributions were made (with reference here to such matters as the apparent state and future of the individual's business, whether trade or profession, and whether in making the contributions it can be demonstrated that the individual has left his business short of working capital, or himself with cash-flow difficulties), but with these circumstances seen against a background of the overall pension provision made by the individual in comparison with his total income over time. To state the obvious, an individual who has already made reasonable[4] pension provision may be held to have made an excessive contribution in a situation where another individual who is in all other respects similar to the first individual, but who has made no pension provision, will not.

1   IA 1986, s 342A(6).
2   Ie IA 1986, s 342A(2)(b).
3   IA 1986, s 342A(6), see para **20.126**.
4   'Reasonable' being judged by reference to the individual's overall standard of living.

20.129 Before making any order the court must be satisfied that the rights under any pension arrangement on which the order will bite are 'to any extent, and whether directly or indirectly' the fruits of 'relevant contributions'[1]. Where the court is satisfied that as a result of pension-sharing the value of the rights of the bankrupt have been subject to a debit[2] and is therefore less than it would otherwise have been, the court may treat the rights from the debited contributions as fruits of the individual's rights[3]. Should the court determine that not all the relevant contributions involved excessive contributions, the court is to treat as excessive the rights which have not been the subject of pension-sharing as excessive before it treats the debited contributions in that way[4].

1   IA 1986, s 342A(2)(a), see para **20.125**.
2   Under the Welfare Reform and Pensions Act 1999, s 29(1)(a).
3   IA 1986, s 342A(3), (4)(a).
4   IA 1986, s 342A(4)(b).

20.130 The trustee is entitled, by written request, to require any person who is responsible for an approved pension arrangement under which a bankrupt has rights, or an unapproved pension arrangement under which a bankrupt has excluded rights, or a pension arrangement under which a bankrupt has at any time had rights ('the responsible person'), to provide him with such information about the arrangement or rights as he may reasonably require[1]. Where the responsible person receives such a request he has nine weeks in which to comply, this period beginning with the day on which the request is received[2]. The court may extend this period where good cause is shown on an application made either before or after the period has expired[3].

1   IA 1986, s 342C(1); this information may be required 'for, or in connection with, the making of applications under IA 1986, s 342A'.
2   The Occupational and Personal Pension Schemes (Bankruptcy) (No 2) Regulations 2002, SI 2002/836, reg 10(1).
3   The Occupational and Personal Pension Schemes (Bankruptcy) (No 2) Regulations 2002, SI 2002/836, reg 10(2).

Restoration orders

20.131 The court is given a wide discretion to make such order as it thinks fit for restoring the position to what it would have been had the excessive contributions not been made[1], a 'restoration order'[2]. Without prejudice to this wide discretion, a restoration order may include provision:

(a)   requiring the person responsible for the arrangement to pay an amount to the individual's trustee in bankruptcy;
(b)   adjusting the liabilities of the arrangement in respect of the individual;

(c)   adjusting any liabilities of the arrangement in respect of any other person that derive, directly or indirectly, from rights of the individual under the arrangement;

(d)   for the recovery by the person responsible for the arrangement (whether by deduction from any amount which that person is ordered to pay or otherwise) of costs incurred by that person in complying in the bankrupt's case (i) with any requirement of the IA 1986, s 342C or (ii) in giving effect to the order[3].

[1]   IA 1986, s 342A(2).
[2]   Restoration orders are not so termed in the IA 1986, but an 'order made under IA 1986, s 342A' is called a restoration order in the Occupational and Personal Pension Schemes (Bankruptcy) (No 2) Regulations 2002, SI 2002/836 as amended by SI 2006/744, reg 1(4), as from 6 April 2006.
[3]   IA 1986, s 342B(1).

20.132 The 'person responsible for the arrangement' means the trustees, managers, or provider of the arrangement, or the person having the corresponding functions in relation to the arrangement[1]. In respect of (b) above (para **20.131**) 'adjusting the liabilities of the arrangement in respect of the individual' means, essentially, reducing the amount of any benefit payable immediately or in the future to the individual, but is not necessarily so limited[2]. As for 'adjusting any liabilities of the arrangement' in respect of another person under (c) above (para **20.131**) this does not enable a court to interfere with any pension-sharing order or agreement[3]. A restoration order requiring the person responsible for an arrangement to pay an amount to the individual's trustee (known as 'the restoration amount') must also provide for the liabilities of the arrangement to be correspondingly reduced[4]. Accordingly the difference between the amount of the liabilities immediately before and immediately after the reduction must be equal to the restoration amount[5]. A restoration order is binding on the person responsible for the arrangement. It overrides any provision of the arrangement to the extent that it may be in conflict with a provision of the order[6], and must be complied with by the responsible person within 17 weeks of the date of the service of the order on him[7].

[1]   IA 1986, s 342C(6).
[2]   IA 1986, s 342B(2).
[3]   IA 1986, s 342B(3).
[4]   IA 1986, s 342B(5).
[5]   IA 1986, s 342B(6).
[6]   IA 1986, s 342B(7).
[7]   The Occupational and Personal Pension Schemes (Bankruptcy) (No 2) Regulations 2002, SI 2002/836, reg 8.

20.133 The maximum amount which the person responsible for the arrangement may be required to pay by a restoration order is the lesser of:

(a)   the amount of the excessive contributions; and

(b)   the value of the individual's rights[1] under the relevant arrangement[2].

[1]   See para **20.132**, footnote 5 above. The value is calculated under the Occupational and Personal Pension Schemes (Bankruptcy) (No 2) Regulations 2002, SI 2002/836, reg 7(2).
[2]   IA 1986, s 342B(4).

20.134 The calculation of the value of the individual's rights under an approved pension arrangement is provided for by regulation[1].

1   The Occupational and Personal Pension Schemes (Bankruptcy) (No 2) Regulations 2002, SI 2002/836, which, by reg 7(2) import the valuation provisions of the Pensions on Divorce etc (Provision of Information) Regulations 2000, SI 2000/1048, reg 3. It is doubtless possible for someone with the appropriate mathematical skills who is not an actuary to carry out the calculation by reference to SI 2000/1048, reg 3. However, except where dealing with cash equivalents, see reg 3(9), the regulations require any calculation to be 'calculated and verified in such manner as may be approved in a particular case by (a) a Fellow of the Institute of Actuaries, (b) a Fellow of the Faculty of Actuaries, or (c) a person with actuarial qualifications approved by the Secretary of State, reg 3(7). In all but the exceptional case an individual lawyer or insolvency practitioner will have simply to pass the matter of valuation over to an appropriate actuary.

20.135 Any sum required to be paid by the order to the trustee in bankruptcy forms part of the bankrupt's estate[1].

1   IA 1986, s 342C(3).

Pension-sharing cases

20.136 A pension-sharing transaction comprises an order or agreement for pension sharing within the scope of the Welfare Reform and Pensions Act 1999[1] by parties to a divorce or order of nullity. It is open to a trustee to seek orders in respect of a pension-sharing transaction either as a transaction at an undervalue or a preference. A pension-sharing transaction is to be treated as a transaction for the purposes of IA 1986, s 339, entered into by the transferor with the transferee, by which the appropriate amount[2] is transferred by the transferor to the transferee, and is capable of being a transaction at an undervalue only so far as it is a transfer of so much of the appropriate amount as is recoverable[3]. The court may make an order requiring payments to be made or liabilities to be adjusted[4] where it appears that one or more contributions giving rights under a pension-sharing transaction have unfairly prejudiced the transferor's creditors[5]. A pension-sharing transaction is to be treated as a transfer of the appropriate amount to the transferee for the purposes of IA 1986, s 340, and is capable of being a preference only so far as it is a transfer of so much of the appropriate amount as is recoverable[6]. The trustee is entitled to require the person responsible for the pension-sharing arrangement to give information about the arrangement, the transferee's rights under the arrangement, and the transferor's rights under the arrangement by written request for the purpose of or in connection with the making of an application seeking orders in respect of the arrangement whether as a transaction at an undervalue or a preference[7].

1   Welfare Reform and Pensions Act 1999, Pt IV, see in particular s 28.
2   Ie for the purposes of the Welfare Reform and Pensions Act 1999, s 29 which creates credits and debits.
3   IA 1986, s 342D(1)(3), as amended by the Welfare Reform and Pensions Act 1999, s 84, Sch 12, para 71.
4   See IA 1986, s 342E, as amended by the Welfare Reform and Pensions Act 1999, s 84, Sch 12, para 71.
5   IA 1986, s 342D(4)–(7).
6   IA 1986, s 342D(2).

7   IA 1986, s 342F, as amended by the Welfare Reform and Pensions Act 1999, s 84, Sch 12, para 71.

E EXTORTIONATE CREDIT TRANSACTIONS

General

20.137 A trustee in bankruptcy may apply to reopen any credit transaction entered into by the bankrupt within the period of three years of the date of the commencement of the bankruptcy on the ground that it was or is extortionate[1]. The bankrupt must be, or have been, a party to the transaction for or involving the provision of credit to himself[2]. It is immaterial whether the credit transaction contributed to the bankrupt's financial difficulties which led to the bankruptcy[3]. Provided credit has been provided to the bankrupt under the agreement the fact that it was provided to him jointly with another person is no bar to an application by the trustee for an order on the basis that the credit provided was extortionate[4].

1   IA 1986, s 343(2).
2   IA 1986, s 343(1).
3   Contrast transactions at an undervalue and preferences, see the definition of 'relevant time' at paras **20.14–20.15**.
4   IA 1986, s 343(1). As long as the transaction involves the provision of credit to the bankrupt it is open to challenge; it is immaterial what other provision may also be made under the transaction.

20.138 The powers conferred on the court to reopen credit transactions by the Insolvency Act 1986 may be exercised concurrently with those relating to transactions at an undervalue[1].

1   IA 1986, s 343(6).

20.139 These powers are closely in line with the equivalent provisions of the Consumer Credit Act 1974 as originally enacted[1]. The definition of 'extortionate' is similar, and in both cases the onus is on the creditor to prove that the transaction, or 'bargain' under the Consumer Credit Act, is not extortionate[2]. As from 6 April 2007[3], however, the extortionate credit bargain provisions of the Consumer Credit Act 1974 have been replaced with a more general power in the court to make orders where it determines that the relationship between the creditor and the debtor is unfair to the debtor[4]. An order may be made in respect of an unfair relationship on the application of the debtor or a surety where the relationship of the debtor with the creditor is unfair because of one or more of the following:

(a)   any of the terms of the agreement or of any related agreement;
(b)   the way in which the creditor has exercised or enforced any of his rights under the agreement or any related agreement;
(c)   any other thing done (or not done) by, or on behalf of, the creditor (either before or after the making of the agreement or any related agreement)[5].

1   Ie ss 137–139, 171(7).
2   IA 1986, s 343(3); Consumer Credit Act 1974, s 171(7).

20.139 *Adjustment of prior transactions*

3   See the Consumer Credit Act 2006 (Commencement No 2 and Transitional Provisions and Savings) Order 2007, SI 2007/123, art 3, Sch 2.
4   Consumer Credit Act 1974, ss 140A, 140B, 140C, inserted by the Consumer Credit Act 2006, ss 19–21.
5   Consumer Credit Act 1974, s 140A(1).

20.140 There is no overlap in practice between the provisions of the Consumer Credit Act 1974 and the extortionate credit transaction provisions of the Insolvency Act 1986. The former do not apply after insolvency because the rights and obligations under any credit or related agreement will pass to the debtor's trustee in bankruptcy, and the trustee is not a person who may make an application under the Consumer Credit Act 1974. The latter cannot apply until after insolvency. Decisions on the issue of what constitutes an extortionate credit transaction under the Consumer Credit Act 1974 have in the past had a clear relevance to equivalent decisions under the Insolvency Act 1986. Decisions on the amended provisions of the Consumer Credit Act 1974 may continue to have some bearing on applications under the Insolvency Act 1986, because in determining whether any credit transaction is extortionate the court will have to look at the conditions prevailing in the market at the time the relevant transaction was entered into, and such considerations will inevitably be relevant to a consideration of what is and is not unfair to a debtor. However, the new Consumer Credit Act test of unfairness would appear to be rather less stringent than a test of what is extortionate. It may be that in future a trustee in bankruptcy will find himself less able to obtain an order protecting the estate against an adverse credit bargain than the individual debtor was before the commencement of his bankruptcy. If so this would be a strange result of the changes to the Consumer Credit Act 1974.

Credit transaction

20.141 There is no definition of 'credit transaction' in the IA 1986. For the purposes of the Consumer Credit Act 1974 'credit' is given a very broad definition as including 'a cash loan, and any other form of financial accommodation'[1]. Within the context of insolvency there is no reason to suppose that the court will not adopt an equally wide definition. A 'financial accommodation' will include not only the common forms of instalment credit transactions with which individuals may acquire goods such as hire-purchase, instalment sale, and conditional sale, but any agreement under which the time for payment of the purchase price is extended after delivery. It is not necessary for there to be a charge for the credit, although in such a case it is unlikely that the transaction will be extortionate. A true hiring of goods will not amount to the provision of credit. However, in the case of many leases of chattels the plain purpose of the lease is to provide the debtor hiring the chattel with finance, and over the term of the lease the debtor lessee will fully reimburse the lessor for the cost of the chattel and the financial facility provided to the lessee. It is open to the court under IA 1986, s 343 to hold that such an agreement involves the provision of credit to the bankrupt.

1   Consumer Credit Act 1974, s 9.

20.142 As IA 1986, s 343 applies to 'a transaction for, or involving, the provision of credit to the bankrupt' it will cover ancillary dealings to the agreement to provide credit. The provision of security is plainly envisaged by the Act to form part of the credit transaction as the court is expressly empowered[1] to vary the terms on which any security for the purposes of the transaction is held or to require that security to be surrendered. The IA 1986 does not import the concept of the 'linked transaction' which is to be found in the Consumer Credit Act 1974[2], but examples of such transactions as life or other insurance policies or maintenance contracts which provide financial advantages to the creditor are likely to be held to form part of the credit transaction.

1   See IA 1986, s 343(4)(b)(d).
2   Consumer Credit Act 1974, s 19.

Extortionate credit

20.143 A transaction is extortionate if, having regard to the risk accepted by the person providing the credit, either:

(a)   the terms of the transaction require grossly exorbitant payments to be made (whether unconditionally or in certain contingencies) in respect of the provision of credit, or
(b)   the transaction otherwise grossly contravenes ordinary principles of fair dealing[1].

1   IA 1986, s 343(3).

20.144 It may be noted that the question whether the transaction was responsible in whole or in part to the individual debtor's insolvency is not a relevant consideration. It is open to a trustee in bankruptcy to apply to re-open credit transactions which have been fully completed or have been terminated for any reason, provided always that the transaction was entered into within three years of the commencement of the bankruptcy[1]. This provision prevents agreements which are expressed to terminate on the insolvency of the individual debtor from escaping the provisions of the IA 1986[2].

1   IA 1986, s 343(2).
2   The Consumer Credit Act 1974 originally applied only to existing agreements, but as amended applies to completed agreements without limit in time, the Consumer Credit Act 1974, s 140A(4).

20.145 It is to be presumed, unless the contrary is proved, that a transaction with respect to which an application is made is or was extortionate[1].

1   IA 1986, s 343(3).

20.146 For the purposes of the Consumer Credit Act 1974 the Court of Appeal held, in *Paragon Finance v Staunton, Paragon Finance plc v Nash*[1], that where the interest rate varied during the course of the agreement the question whether the credit bargain was extortionate or not was to be determined by reference solely to the terms of the agreement at its inception; subsequent interest changes were irrelevant[2]. This decision was founded on the provisions of the Consumer Credit Act 1974 and the Consumer Credit (Total Charge for Credit) Regulations 1980[3], and is therefore not directly applicable to applications under the IA 1986. However, it is suggested that the wording of IA 1986, s 343(3) would lead to the same result in an insolvency application.

[1]   [2001] EWCA Civ 1466, [2002] 2 All ER 248, [2002] 1 WLR 685; as to the varying of interest rates (and the disclosure of the policy adopted by the lender as to variation) see also *Broadwick Financial Services Ltd v Spencer* [2002] EWCA Civ 35, [2002] 1 All ER (Comm) 446, and *Paragon Finance plc v Pender* [2005] EWCA Civ 760, [2005] 1 WLR 3412.

[2]   Although the court also held that the agreement was subject to an implied term that the discretion to vary interest rates was not to be exercised dishonestly, for an improper purpose, capriciously, arbitrarily, or in a way which no reasonable lender would act.

[3]   SI 1980/51.

What amounts to an extortionate interest rate

20.147   In the absence of decisions under the extortionate credit transaction provisions of the Insolvency Act 1986 it was natural to turn to decisions under the Consumer Credit Act 1974 for guidance given that the IA 1986 definition of 'extortionate' followed so closely[1] that originally in the Consumer Credit Act 1974. There would appear to be no good reason why the fact that it will be the bankrupt's creditors rather than the individual debtor himself who benefit from the order should constitute a distinction between the two statutory schemes. It remains to be seen whether the approach of the courts consequent on the amendments to the Consumer Credit Act 1974 will result in case law which will have little relevance to Insolvency Act 1986 applications. For the present however regard may safely be had to pre-amendment Consumer Credit Act 1974 decisions.

[1]   The two statutory schemes were not exactly parallel however. Under IA 1986, s 343 the court is required to have regard to 'the risk accepted by the provider of the credit' when determining whether the transaction is extortionate. Under the Consumer Credit Act 1974, s 138 the court is to have regard to a number of specified matters (which include the risk accepted by the creditor) and any other relevant considerations.

20.148   This is an area of the law primarily dealt with by district judges in the county court. Few of the decisions in respect of extortionate credit bargains under the Consumer Credit Act 1974 have been widely reported. No clear judicial guidelines have emerged[1]. The difference between an 'exorbitant' rate (which is permissible) and a 'grossly exorbitant' rate (which is not) has yet to be explored in any detail. In *A Ketley Ltd v Scott*[2] the court held that an interest rate of 48% pa was not extortionate under the Consumer Credit Act 1974. The debtor there had borrowed £20,800 at very short notice in order to buy a house in which he was a protected tenant. The debtor was unable to raise a mortgage and was at risk of losing his deposit. From the creditor's viewpoint he had accepted a substantial risk, having no time to investigate the debtor's financial position, and lending over 80% of the value of the property. The court found that the debtor knew what he was doing and in the circumstances a loan over three months at 12% interest was not extortionate. In *Wills v Wood*[3] a distinction was drawn between 'extortionate' and 'unwise', the court stating that the jurisdiction to reopen credit transactions seemed to contemplate at least a substantial imbalance in bargaining power of which one party had taken advantage. The Court of Appeal in *Coldunell Ltd v Gallon*[4], a case concerned with a son exercising undue influence over his father to secure a loan for the son's business, stated that a lender could not be expected to do more than properly and fairly point out to the guarantor the desirability of obtaining independent advice and to require the documents to be executed in the presence of a solicitor. A lender could not be expected to take steps to ensure that the guarantor did obtain legal advice or to guard against interception of documents[5]. The transaction was a proper commercial bargain, the interest charged being 20% pa, and the lenders acted in an ordinary commercial manner. It could not therefore be an extortionate bargain because undue influence was exerted and improper behaviour took place without the knowledge or connivance of the lenders[6]. In *Davies v Directloans Ltd*[7] a rate of 21.6% (APR)[8] was held not to be extortionate. The borrower had been warned that the cost of credit would be high and there was a significant risk to the lender in advancing the money.

[1]   Some guidance may be had from decisions under the Moneylenders Acts, see The Digest Vol 34(2) (3rd Reissue) pp 486–504 and *Meston on Moneylenders* (5th edn) pp 172–190.
[2]   [1981] ICR 241.
[3]   (1984) 128 Sol Jo 222, CA.
[4]   [1986] QB 1184, [1986] 1 All ER 429.
[5]   See generally the cases concerning the execution of bank charges and guarantees; *Barclays Bank v O'Brien* [1994] 1 AC 80, [1993] 4 All ER 417; *National Westminster Bank v Morgan* [1985] AC 686, [1985] 1 All ER 821; *Avon Finance Co v Bridger* [1985] 2 All ER 281; *Midland Bank v Shepherd* [1988] 3 All ER 17; *Bank of Credit and Commerce International SA v Aboody* [1990] 1 QB 923, [1992] 4 All ER 955.
[6]   The position would presumably be different where it could be shown that the person exercising undue influence was acting as the lender's agent, see eg *Kingsnorth Trust v Bell* [1986] 1 All ER 423, [1986] 1 WLR 119.
[7]   [1986] 2 All ER 783, [1986] 1 WLR 823.
[8]   See the Consumer Credit (Total Charge for Credit) Regulations 1980, SI 1980/51.

20.149 An interest rate of 100% pa on loans to develop properties made in 1999 was reduced to 25% under the provisions of the Consumer Credit Act 1974, s 138 in *Batooneh v Asombang*[1]. Expert evidence was adduced in *London North Securities v Meadows*[2] that in 1989 an APR of 34.9% was not unusual in the non-status market. However, while such a rate was therefore not by itself extortionate, it was combined with a provision entitling the lender to charge interest at the same rate on the arrears and on costs and charges and also to compound the interest. The court held that this contravened the principles of fair dealing and amounted to extortionate credit. The agreement was not set aside however in *Woodstead Finance Ltd v Petrou*[3] where an APR of 42½ % was found to be usual for a short-term loan to a borrower in a perilous financial situation and with a poor payment record[4].

[1]   [2003] EWHC 2111 (QB), [2003] All ER (D) 557 (Jul) (Buckley J).
[2]   (25 November 2004, unreported) HHJ Howarth, Lawtel Doc No AC 0107408.
[3]   (1986) 136 NLJ 188, CA.
[4]   It is not apparent from the report when the loan was made.

Applications

20.150 An application may be brought for an order in respect of an alleged extortionate credit transaction at the same time as an application asserting that a transaction was at an undervalue[1]. There being a statutory presumption that any credit transaction entered into by the individual debtor within three years of the commencement of his bankruptcy is extortionate the onus will be on the lender to prove that his agreement with the debtor was not extortionate, either by requiring grossly exorbitant payments to be made or by otherwise grossly contravening ordinary principles of fair dealing[2]. Unless there are existing proceedings within which an application under IA 1986, s 343 may be properly brought the application should strictly be commenced by originating application[3]. However, it is more usual for the applicant to use an ordinary application[4]. As there is a statutory presumption that a credit agreement is extortionate the applicant need do no more than serve a witness statement exhibiting the agreement the subject of the application and showing that it was entered into within the three-year period before the commencement of the bankruptcy[5], and specifying the order or orders which will be sought. It is plainly sensible however for the trustee in bankruptcy to set out the basis of his case that the agreement was indeed an extortionate transaction, either by reference to the payments which had to be made under it or by reference to the terms and circumstances which it is suggested amount to a gross contravention of ordinary principles of fair dealing. The respondent will need to serve evidence justifying the credit terms, at least to the extent of showing that even if they are exorbitant they are not 'grossly' exorbitant, usually by reference to the terms, and in particular interest rates, available on equivalent loans at the relevant time. In many applications it will be necessary to consider the need for expert evidence as to the rates of interest prevailing in the relevant market at the time of the making of the agreement.

1   IA 1986, s 343(1).
2   IA 1986, s 343(3).
3   IR 1986, r 7.2, Form 7.1.
4   IR 1986, r 7.2, Form 7.2.
5   IA 1986, s 343(2).

Orders

20.151 An order may be made on the application of the trustee in bankruptcy in respect of a credit transaction provided it was entered into by the individual debtor within three years of the commencement of the bankruptcy[1]. Such an order may include one or more of the following provisions as the court thinks fit, namely that[2]:

(a)   the whole or any part of any obligation created by the transaction be set aside;

(b)   the terms of the transaction, or the terms on which any security held for the purposes of the transaction, be varied;

(c)   any person who is or was a party to the transaction be required to pay to the trustee in bankruptcy any sums received from the individual debtor by virtue of the transaction;

(d)   any person holding any property held by him as security for the purposes of the transaction be required to surrender it to the trustee in bankruptcy;

(e)   accounts be taken between any persons.

¹   IA 1986, s 343(2).
²   IA 1986, s 343(4).

20.152 There is no statutory requirement that the order should apply only to the payment of any sum in excess of that fairly due and reasonable¹. But while the court's discretion is not so expressly limited, it would be contrary to general principle for the court to punish a creditor by leaving him with less than that which was reasonable and fairly due².

¹   Compare the Consumer Credit Act 1974, s 139(2) (repealed as from 4 April 2007, see para **20.139**) which contained an overriding qualification that the purpose of any order of the court should be the relief of the debtor or a surety from payment of any sum in excess of that fairly due and reasonable.
²   Such a penalty would be in the nature of exemplary damages for outrageous conduct as to the awarding of which see *Rookes v Barnard* [1964] AC 1129, [1964] 1 All ER 367.

20.153 There remains a discretion in the court whether or not to make an order at all, even where credit has been provided at an extortionate rate. It is possible that the court may refuse to make an order because of misconduct on the part of the individual debtor when obtaining the credit¹. However, as the effect of an order will be to increase the assets available for distribution to the bankrupt's creditors generally, and the court is able to make an order setting aside only that part of the credit which is extortionate, it should be rare for an order to be refused on this basis. As the IA 1986 provisions are limited in their application in time (three years before commencement of the bankruptcy) and do not require the extortionate nature of the credit to have contributed to the individual debtor's financial difficulties, it would appear that the causative effect, or lack of it, of the extortionate credit on the debtor's eventual insolvency is not a relevant factor to the making of an order.

¹   Misconduct such as misrepresentation as to the debtor's financial position; see eg *A Ketley Ltd v Scott* [1981] ICR 241.

F ASSIGNMENT OF BOOK DEBTS

Avoidance of general assignment of book debts

20.154 Where an individual debtor engaged in business makes a general assignment to another person of his existing or future book debts or any class of them, the assignment is void against the debtor's trustee in bankruptcy in respect of book debts which were not paid before the presentation of the bankruptcy petition, unless the assignment has been registered under the Bills of Sale Act 1878¹. An 'assignment' includes an assignment by way of security or charge on book debts². A 'general assignment' is not defined in the Act, but it does not include either (a) an assignment of book debts due at the date of the assignment from specified debtors or of debts becoming due under specified contracts, or (b) an assignment of book debts included either in a transfer of a business made in good faith and for value or in an assignment of assets for the benefit of creditors generally[3].

¹ IA 1986, s 344(1), (2).
² IA 1986, s 344(3)(a).
³ IA 1986, s 344(3)(b).

20.155 Many standard forms of factoring agreement require the debtor to make both a general assignment of all existing and future book debts, and also assign specific debts which are entered onto a list or schedule to the factoring agreement which is updated from time to time, often on a monthly basis. It is only against specific identified debts that money is advanced to the debtor, usually an agreed percentage of the debt thereby giving the factoring company its profit. The general assignment will be void unless registered under the Bills of Sale Act 1878, but the specific assignments will be effective against the bankrupt's trustee provided they are themselves valid and comply with the provisions of the Law of Property Act 1925, s 136. In *Hills v Alex Lawrie Factors Ltd*[1] the issue arose whether the fact that there was a (void) general assignment of all book debts which pre-dated the specific assignments of individual debts rendered the later specific assignments ineffective. The court held that the specific assignments were valid. They operated to assign the specific debts if and to the extent that the general assignment was ineffective. The specific assignments were valid legal assignments, being absolute assignments under the hand of the assignor of which express notice in writing had been given to the debtor[2], whereas the general assignment was merely equitable, no notice having been given to the debtor. The court also observed that the policy of the IA 1986 avoidance provisions was to protect the bankrupt's estate from the vagueness and uncertainty which is likely to surround an assignment of unspecified debts and the difficulty inherent in any investigation of whether a proper price or other consideration was received for the general assignment.

¹ [2001] BPIR 1038.
² Being the three requirements for a valid legal assignment under the Law of Property Act 1925, s 136.

Book debts

20.156 'Book debts' are debts which in the ordinary course of business would be entered in well-kept trade books[1]. The fact that the debts have not been entered in books by the trader is of no relevance. Book debts include future debts and future rent under hire agreements[2], and bills of exchange entered in the books as due to be paid[3]. Sums due under an export credit guarantee policy do not qualify as book debts[4], neither does a bank balance standing to the credit of the trader[5]. To constitute a 'class of book debts' the debts in question must presumably have a common nature or similar characteristics or other clear means of identification.

¹ *Shipley v Marshall* (1863) 14 CBNS 566.
² *Blakey v Pendlebury Trustees* [1931] 2 Ch 255.
³ *Siebe Gorman v Barclays Bank Plc* [1979] 2 Lloyd's Rep 142.

Registration as a bill of sale

20.157 For the purposes of registration under the Bills of Sale Act 1878 an assignment of book debts is to be treated as if it were a bill of sale given otherwise than by way of security for the payment of a sum of money[1], and the assignment must be registered as required by the 1878 Act[2]. A person who wishes to register a bill of sale must make an application to a Queen's Bench Master[3] accompanied by payment of the prescribed fee[4]. The application is to be made by claim form under CPR Pt 8 or by witness statement[5]. Where the application is made by witness statement, it is made under CPR Pt 23 and the witness statement constitutes the application notice[6]. The witness statement does not have to be served on any other person, and the application will normally be dealt with on paper without a hearing[7].

1   The relevance of this provision is that the amendments to the Bills of Sale Act 1878 effected by the Bills of Sale Act (1878) Amendment Act 1882 to such bills do not apply to an assignment of book debts under IA 1986, s 344.
2   IA 1986, s 344(4).
3   Local registration may be possible with the county court district judge, Bills of Sale Act (1878) Amendment Act 1882, s 11 and see the Bills of Sale (Local Registration) Rules 1960, SI 1960/2326.
4   CPR PD 8 para 15B.3.
5   CPR PD 8 para 15B.2.
6   CPR PD 8 para 15B.4(1), (2).
7   CPR PD 8 para 15B.4(3), (4).

20.158 Whether under CPR Pt 8 or Pt 23 the application must:

(1)   exhibit a true copy of the assignment and of every schedule to it;
(2)   set out the particulars of the assignment and the parties to it; and
(3)   verify the date and time of the execution of the assignment, and its execution in the presence of a witness[1].

1   CPR PD 8 para 15B.5.

20.159 The court may accept a defective witness statement, but this will not validate an assignment which is itself void, for example for failing to comply with the requirements of the Law of Property Act 1925, s 136[1]. The court may raise points on the assignment, but it is not the job of the court to inquire whether the assignment and witness statement comply with the statutory provisions[2]. The court, if satisfied that the requirements of the rules have been complied with, will file the assignment and any schedule to it, and enter particulars of the assignment and the parties to it in the register[3].

1   *Brown v London and County Advance and Discount Co* (1889) 5 TLR 199.
2   *Re Bills of Sale Act 1866, Needham to Johnson, Taylor to Bentley* (1867) 8 B & S 190. A decision well before the recent rule change on 1 October 2007 when an applicant had to comply with statutory requirements as to filing the original assignment, a copy, and an affidavit proving the execution and attestation of the assignment and the time it was made.
3   CPR PD 8 para 15B.6.

20.160 The registration of a bill of sale, and therefore of an assignment of book debts, must be renewed every five years otherwise it becomes void[1]. Renewal is effected by filing an affidavit or witness statement stating the date of the assignment, the last registration of it, a statement that the assignment is still subsisting, and the names, residences and occupations of the parties to the assignment[2]. A purported renewal in default of the statutory requirements is invalid[3].

1 Bills of Sale Act 1878, s 11.
2 Bills of Sale Act 1878, s 11.
3 *Re Morris, ex p Webster* (1882) 22 Ch D 136, CA (misstatement of address in the affidavit).

20.161 Where there is a failure to register or renew the registration of the assignment through accident or inadvertence an application may be made to a Queen's Bench Master to rectify the omission[1]. The Master may in his discretion order the time for registration to be extended, if appropriate on terms, as he thinks fit[2]. The court will not make an order that would defeat the rights of any third party which have accrued after the period in which the assignment should have been registered[3].

1 Under CPR PD 8 para 10A which replaced CPR Sch 1 RSC Ord 95 on 1 October 2007.
2 Bills of Sale Act 1878, s 14.
3 *Crew v Cummings* (1888) 21 QBD 420; *Re Parsons, ex p Furber* [1893] 2 QB 122; *Re Spiral Globe Ltd* [1902] 1 Ch 396.

Chapter 21

TRANSACTIONS DEFRAUDING CREDITORS

A   The law prior to the Insolvency Act 1986
B   The Insolvency Act 1986, ss 423–425

A THE LAW PRIOR TO THE INSOLVENCY ACT 1986

Introduction

21.1 In addition to the statutory provisions enabling a trustee in bankruptcy to apply to the court to set aside or adjust transactions to which the individual debtor was party without receiving full consideration or which prefer one or more creditors above the general body of creditors after the debtor has become bankrupt, there has since 1571[1] been a statutory power in the court to set aside any transaction made with intent to defraud creditors irrespective of whether the person responsible for the transaction has become insolvent. There is no need to show that the individual entering into the transaction is or became insolvent on making it in order to obtain a remedy.

[1]   13 Elizabeth c 5.

21.2 Prior to the commencement of the Insolvency Act 1986 ('IA 1986') this general power of the court was exercisable by virtue of s 172 of the Law of Property Act 1925 ('LPA 1925'). The Cork Committee in its Review of Insolvency Law and Practice[1] made a number of criticisms of this provision and proposed its replacement in a more clear and certain form. This proposal led to IA 1986, ss 423–425, which give the court a wide power to make orders where it is satisfied that a transaction has been entered into for the purpose of putting assets beyond the reach of creditors. The powers of the court under IA 1986, ss 423–425, which can be exercised alongside the insolvency provisions relating to transactions at an undervalue and preferences[2], came into force on the commencement date of the Insolvency Act 1986[3] on which date LPA 1925, s 172 was repealed. Transactions entered into before that date may only be set aside under the LPA 1925, s 172[4].

[1]   Cmnd 8558 paras 1210–1220.
[2]   IA 1986, ss 339–342.

3   29 December 1986.
4   IA 1986, Sch 11, para 20; these earlier provisions therefore remain relevant to all pre-IA
    1986 transactions, even though the debtor becomes insolvent under the provisions of the
    IA 1986.

The law before 1986

21.3 'Every conveyance of property made ... with intent to defraud creditors,
shall be voidable, at the instance of any person thereby prejudiced'[1]. Protection is afforded to innocent purchasers of property which has been conveyed
by a debtor with intent to defraud his creditors. Excluded from avoidance is
'any estate or interest in property conveyed for valuable consideration and in
good faith to any person not having, at the time of the conveyance, notice of
intent to defraud creditors'[2]. The existence of this provision does not affect the
operation of the law of bankruptcy[3].

1   LPA 1925, s 172(1).
2   LPA 1925, s 172(3).
3   LPA 1925, s 172(2).

Conveyance of property

21.4 Section 172 refers expressly only to 'conveyances'. It has therefore been
questioned whether the jurisdiction applied only to written conveyances of
real or personal property or whether it extended to any disposition of
property. The original statutory provision of 13 Eliz c 5 was 'for the avoiding
and abolishing of feigned, covinous and fraudulent feoffments, gifts, grants,
alienations, conveyances, bonds, suits, judgments, and executions, as well of
lands and tenements as of goods and chattels ...'. It is well arguable in the
context of the 1925 legislation that LPA 1925, s 172 was intended to be as
wide as the statute it replaced, and that in the light of the wording of the
earlier statute any transfer of property, whether by written conveyance or
otherwise, would be caught by the section. This view appears to have been
accepted by Harman J in *Re Eichholz, Eichholz's Trustee v Eichholz*[1] although
in that case he found that there had been a written conveyance. Harman J's
reasoning has been criticised on the ground that he was wrong to proceed on
the basis that the LPA 1925 was a consolidating statute[2], but as Charles J
pointed out in *Re Yates*[3] this incorrect reference to the LPA 1925 being a
consolidating statute is not a vital element of his reasoning. Noting that the
definition of 'conveyance' in the LPA 1925, s 205 begins with 'includes' and
that all the definitions in the LPA 1925 are subject to the proviso 'unless the
context otherwise requires', Charles J expressed the view that the context did
otherwise require and adopted the opinion of Harman J that LPA 1925, s 172
was not restricted to a conveyance in writing. It seems therefore that the
conveyance of any type of property conveyed by a grantor may be avoided.
The section has been applied to equitable reversionary interests in personal
property[4] and the proceeds recoverable in a pending action[5]. It would appear
unlikely, however, that the section could be applied to the payment of money,
but it does extend to gifts or transfers of money which are applied in the
purchase of property in the name of another or improvements to such a
property[6].

1   [1959] Ch 708, [1959] 1 All ER 166.
2   See *Lloyds Bank v Marcan* [1973] 3 All ER 754, [1973] 1 WLR 339, 344.
3   [2005] BPIR 476.
4   *Ideal Bedding Co Ltd v Holland* [1907] 2 Ch 157.
5   *Glegg v Bromley* [1912] 3 KB 474.
6   *Re Yates* [2005] BPIR 476.

Intent to defraud

21.5 It is necessary for the creditor seeking to set aside the conveyance under the LPA 1925, s 172 to prove intent to defraud. That intent may, however, be presumed from the circumstances of the transaction[1]. The intention to defraud may be inferred from the fact that the conveyance was made with an eye to the future, as when the conveyance is made by an individual who is about to engage in a hazardous endeavour[2]. While a fraudulent intent may readily be presumed when the individual making the conveyance cannot pay his debts without the property conveyed[3], that is not sufficient by itself to obtain an order. Even where the grantor is unable to pay his debts the conveyance will not be avoided where it appears that he had no intention to defraud[4]. In *Lloyds Bank Ltd v Marcan*[5] the Court of Appeal was divided as to whether an intent to deprive creditors of assets was sufficient without actual deceit or dishonesty[6]. There is no need to show an intent to defraud any particular creditor. A fraudulent intention to prefer one creditor over others is not sufficient under the LPA 1925, s 172 to avoid a conveyance which is not caught by the law of bankruptcy, except perhaps where the individual debtor concerned is himself in some way benefited by the conveyance[7].

1   *Godfrey v Poole* (1888) 13 App Cas 497, 503 PC.
2   *Mackay v Douglas* (1872) LR 14 Eq 106; and see *Re Butterworth, ex p Russell* (1882) 19 Ch D 588 at 598 (Jessel MR).
3   *Freeman v Pope* (1870) 5 Ch App 538.
4   *Re Wise, ex p Mercer* (1886) 17 QBD 290; *Maskelyne and Cooke v Smith* [1902] 2 KB 158; affirmed [1903] 1 KB 671.
5   [1973] 3 All ER 754.
6   Russell LJ followed Pennycuick VC at first instance in stating that it was not necessary to show actual deceit or dishonesty. Cairns LJ disagreed. In *Re Yates* [2005] BPIR 426 at para 206 Cairns LJ was described as a 'lone voice' in suggesting that dishonesty on the part of the transferor was a necessary ingredient to a claim under LPA 1925, s 172.
7   See *Re Lloyds Furniture Palace Ltd, Evans v Lloyds Furniture Palace* [1925] Ch 853.

Avoidance application

21.6 An application to avoid a conveyance under LPA 1925, s 172 can be made by any person prejudiced by it except where the individual debtor is bankrupt in which case it may only be made by the trustee in bankruptcy[1]. A creditor will be and remain prejudiced as long as his debt remains enforceable by action and is not statute-barred. He is not precluded from applying for relief because he has known about the conveyance for nearly ten years without taking proceedings[2] or because the grantor has died[3]. A creditor whose debt subsisted at the time of the conveyance has an undoubted right to apply, and provided any debt which existed at the date of the conveyance remains unpaid subsequent creditors may apply to avoid the conveyance[4]. Where only subsequent debts remain unpaid it may be necessary for the relevant creditors to show an intention to defraud them[5]. A subsequent creditor who can show that the grantor was able to pay existing debts by incurring the subsequent debt will be subrogated to the rights of existing creditors and may apply himself to avoid the conveyance[6].

1   *Re Crossley* [1954] 3 All ER 296, [1954] 1 WLR 1353.
2   *Re Maddever, Three Towns Banking Co v Maddever* (1884) 27 Ch D 523.
3   See *Re Gould, ex p Official Receiver* (1887) 19 QBD 92.
4   *Freeman v Pope* (1870) 5 Ch App 538.
5   *Cadogan v Cadogan* [1977] 1 All ER 200, [1977] 1 WLR 1041; *Re Butterworth, ex p Russell* (1882) 19 Ch D 588.
6   *Spirett v Willos* (1864) 3 De G J & S 293.

Effect on transferee

21.7 An innocent transferee who takes an estate or interest in the property in good faith for valuable consideration and without notice of the intent to defraud has statutory protection[1]. Similarly a bona fide purchaser from the transferee without notice of the fraudulent intent is protected against an order[2]. Where a transferee takes for value knowing of the fraud he is not protected[3]. The avoidance of the settlement does not, however, extend any further than is necessary to pay the creditors. Any property remaining after paying the creditors still vests in the transferee[4]. The proper form of order in such circumstances is to direct the transferee to join and concur in all acts and things necessary for making the property available for satisfying the claims of the creditors[5]. A transferee who is aware that the conveyance to him prejudices the grantor's creditors may be presumed to have notice of an intent to defraud on the part of the grantor[6].

1   LPA 1925, s 172(3), see para **21.3**. By LPA 1925, s 205(1)(xxi) valuable consideration includes marriage.
2   LPA 1925, s 172(3) and see *Harrods Ltd v Stanton* [1923] 1 KB 516.
3   *Kevan v Crawford* (1877) 6 Ch D 29; *Re Holland, Gregg v Holland* [1902] 2 Ch 360.
4   *Ideal Bedding Co Ltd v Holland* [1907] 2 Ch 157.
5   *Ideal Bedding Co Ltd v Holland* [1907] 2 Ch 157.
6   *Cornish v Clarke* (1872) LR 14 Eq 184.

B THE INSOLVENCY ACT 1986, SS 423–425

The Cork Committee's recommendations

21.8 These recommendations[1] were that the Law of Property Act 1925, s 172 should be re-enacted so amended as to make clear that:

(a)   the section applies to the mere payment of money, as well as to any disposition of property whether effected by an instrument in writing or not;
(b)   the necessary intent is an intent on the part of the debtor to defeat, hinder, delay or defraud creditors, or to put assets belonging to the debtor beyond their reach, and that such intent may be inferred whenever this is the natural and probable consequence of the debtor's

       actions, in the light of the financial circumstances of the debtor at the time, as known, or taken to have been known to him;

(c)   the section applies to any disposition made with the necessary intent, even if supported by valuable consideration, where that does not consist of full consideration in money or money's worth received by the debtor; but that

(d)   no disposition may be set aside if made in favour of a bona fide purchaser for money or money's worth without notice, at the time of the disposition of the debtor's fraudulent intent.

1   Cmnd 8558 para 1220.

21.9 The recommendations have been met in the provisions of the IA 1986, ss 423–425, with one exception. There is no express provision that the necessary intent may be inferred whenever this is the natural and probable consequence of the debtor's actions in the light of his financial circumstances. The courts were however prepared to infer intent from the circumstances prevailing at the time the transaction was entered into under the previous law[1], and a similar approach has been adopted with applications under the Insolvency Act 1986[2].

1   See para **21.5**.
2   See para **21.14** et seq and *Moon v Franklin* [1996] BPIR 196 where Mervyn-Davies J stated the court would assess the facts objectively and on this assessment might disregard the debtor's own evidence as to his purpose in entering into the transaction.

Requirements for relief

21.10 An applicant[1] for an order under IA 1986, ss 423–425 must establish that the 'debtor'[2], which term covers individual, corporate body or unincorporated association:

(a)   has entered into a transaction with another person at an undervalue[3]; and

(b)   has done so for the purpose either (i) of putting assets beyond the reach of a person who is making or may at some time make a claim against him, or (ii) of otherwise prejudicing the interests of such a person in relation to the claim which he is making or may make[4].

1   As to a person who may apply for an order, see paras **21.23–21.25**.
2   in IA 1986, ss 423–425 the person entering into the transaction is referred to as 'the debtor', IA 1986, s 423(5).
3   IA 1986, s 423(1).
4   IA 1986, s 423(3).

21.11 If these requirements are established the court may make such order as it thinks fit for restoring the position to what it would have been if the transaction had not been entered into and of protecting the interests of those who are victims of the transaction[1]. A 'victim' of a transaction is a person who is, or is capable of being, prejudiced by the transaction[2]. A victim may be someone not contemplated by the transferor at the date of the transaction, and may indeed be someone of whose existence the transferor was unaware at that date[3]. No order may be made under IA 1986, ss 423–425 in respect of a market contract to which a recognised investment exchange or recognised clearing house is a party or is entered into under its default rules, or a disposition of property in performance of such a market contract[4].

1   IA 1986, s 423(2). The making of an order is discretionary, but note Scott J in *Arbuthnot Leasing International Ltd v Havelet Leasing (No 2)* [1990] BCC 636, 645:

> 'There is an element of discretion involved here implicit in the use of the word "may". But in my judgment the courts must set their faces against transactions which are designed to prevent plaintiffs in proceedings, creditors with unimpeachable debts, from obtaining the remedies by way of execution that the law would normally allow them.'

quoted with approval by the Court of Appeal in *Chohan v Saggar* [1994] 1 BCLC 706.
2   IA 1986, s 423(5).
3   *Hill v Spread Trustee Co Ltd* [2006] EWCA Civ 542, [2007] 1 All ER 1106 at [101].
4   Companies Act 1989, s 165.

Transactions at an undervalue

21.12 The same definition is specified as applies for the purposes of setting aside or adjusting transactions entered into by individual debtors before bankruptcy[1]. A debtor enters into a transaction with another person at an undervalue if:

(a)   he makes a gift to that other person, or the terms of the transaction provide for him to receive no consideration;

(b)   he enters into a transaction with that other person in consideration of marriage[2]; or

(c)   he enters into a transaction with that other person for a consideration, the value of which, in money or money's worth, is significantly less than the value, in money or money's worth, of the consideration provided by the debtor[3].

1   IA 1986, s 339.
2   The transaction does not have to be between the parties to the marriage; any marriage settlement will be covered.
3   IA 1986, s 423(1).

21.13 The definition being the same the authorities as to what constitutes a transaction at an undervalue arising on applications made under IA 1986, s 339 will apply equally to applications under IA 1986, ss 423–425, see paras **20.23–20.53**[1]. For the purposes of (c) above the 'consideration' provided by both sides to the transaction has to be valued in money or money's worth and is therefore used to mean benefit in financial terms; consideration which cannot be valued in such terms cannot be brought into account when assessing whether or not the transaction was at an undervalue. However, where a single creditor is the intended victim of the transaction and he is indeed prejudiced by the transaction, the transaction may be held to be at an undervalue even though the overall asset position of the debtor is not reduced as a result of the particular transaction and there is no prejudice to the general body of creditors[2].

¹   Several of the cases there referred to are cases under IA 1986, ss 423–425.
²   *National Westminster Bank plc v Jones* [2001] 1 BCLC 98.

The debtor's purpose

21.14 Before making an order under IA 1986, ss 423–425 the court must be satisfied that the transaction being impugned was entered into by the debtor 'for the purpose:

(a)   of putting assets beyond the reach of a person who is making, or may at some time make, a claim against him; or

(b)   of otherwise prejudicing the interests of such a person in relation to the claim which he is making or may make'¹.

¹   IA 1986, s 423(3).

21.15 It follows from the statutory wording that there is no need for the trustee in bankruptcy to establish a dishonest intent on the part of the debtor when entering into the transaction in question¹. When assessing the debtor's purpose the court will consider all the objective circumstances, and in particular the size of any disposition made by the debtor in comparison with his then available resources²; such an assessment naturally takes precedence over the debtor's own evidence as to the purpose of the transaction³. It is immaterial that the creditor may have had other motives than that required by IA 1986, s 423(3). It is sufficient that the debtor, in acting as he did, had the purpose of putting assets beyond the reach of creditors⁴:

> 'As Lord Oliver in the well-known case of *Brady v Brady* [1989] AC 755 acknowledged, the word "purpose" is a word of wide content. But he went on to say that it must be construed bearing in mind the mischief against which the section in which that word appears is aimed. Here, the purpose or mischief against which the section is aimed, namely s 423, is the removal of assets by their owner, in anticipation of claims being made or contemplated, out of the reach of such claimants if those claims ultimately prove to be successful. It would defeat that purpose if it were possible successfully to contend that if the owner was able to point to another purpose, such as the benefit of his family, friends or the advantage of business associated, the section could not be applied.'⁵

¹   See also *Arbuthnot Leasing v Havelet Leasing (No 2)* [1990] BCC 637, at 644 and *Re Brabon, Treharne v Brabon and others* [2001] 1 BCLC 11, at 44.
²   See e g *Trowbridge v Trowbridge* [2002] EWHC 3114 (Ch), [2004] 2 FCR 79, where on an application by the former wife under IA 1986, s 423 the court looked carefully at the level of financial support provided by the husband to his second wife before concluding that the husband was aware that the monthly payments he was making to his second wife were materially larger than necessary for their joint living expenses and that in making them he was motivated by a desire to avoid providing financial support to his former wife.
³   *Moon v Franklin* [1996] BPIR 196; *Re Yates* [2005] BPIR 476.
⁴   *Chohan v Saggar* [1992] BCC 306.
⁵   Per Mr Evans-Lombe QC in *Chohan v Saggar* [1992] BCC 306 at 321. This passage was cited with approval by the Court of Appeal both in *Royscott Spa Leasing Ltd v Lovett* [1995] BCC 502 and in *Barclays Bank plc v Eustice* [1996] BPIR 1 at 9.

21.16 While the burden of proof remains on the applicant, establishing the necessary purpose should be less difficult to achieve than proving intent to defraud under the previous law, particularly with the breadth of purpose (b) quoted above. The inclusion of persons who 'may at some time make a claim' against the debtor envisages potential future creditors who, individually unknown to the debtor at the time of the transaction, become victims of a risky business enterprise against the consequences of failure of which the debtor seeks to protect himself at the outset[1]. In extending the purposes of the debtor which may be impeachable to include the prejudicing of the interests of present or future claimants, the ambit of the section is made very wide, and will cover cases where the debtor makes it more difficult, though not impossible, for a creditor to execute on an asset, or renders the asset less valuable when realised in the process of execution[2].

1   And see *Hill v Spread Trustee Co Ltd* [2006] EWCA Civ 542, [2007] 1 All ER 1106 at [101].
2   In *Hill v Spread Trustee Co Ltd* [2006] EWCA Civ 542, [2007] 1 All ER 1106 the Court of Appeal accepted that a distinction could be made between a hope and an intention, see [132]. A person cannot be said to have an intention merely because he contemplates something as a possibility which he would wish to come to pass. But it will be a rare case where the distinction between a hope and a purpose can properly be made, and a transferor with an illegitimate hope will (in practical terms) have to demonstrate a strong legitimate purpose if he is to avoid an order under IA 1986, ss 423–425.

21.17 In *Hill v Spread Trustee Co Ltd*[1] the Court of Appeal stressed that the correct approach to any particular case is to apply the statutory wording (see above) and not look for any causal connection between the relevant transfer and the particular victim. Accordingly if the transferor enters into the transaction with the intention of putting assets beyond the reach of creditors, but is mistaken in thinking that the transaction will prejudice a particular creditor, it is nevertheless within the scope of IA 1986, ss 423–425[2]. Or if the transferor enters into the transaction with the requisite purpose knowing that his entry into the transaction together with the happening of another event will prejudice creditors, again his transaction is within the scope of IA 1986, s 423[3]. The court does not have to consider the relative causal effect of the transaction and the other event.

1   [2006] EWCA Civ 542, [2007] 1 All ER 1106.
2   The example given at [2006] EWCA Civ 542, [2007] 1 All ER 1106 at [102] is the man A who thinks that if he gifts his property to his wife, his creditor B will be prejudiced. If unbeknown to A his wife has agreed to pay the monies she receives to B the purpose will not be achieved. But if B takes the benefit of this transaction solely for himself without sharing it among A's other creditors they are, or are likely to be, prejudiced by the transaction.
3   'It is enough if the transaction sought to be impugned was entered into with the requisite purpose. It is entry into the transaction, not the transaction itself, which has to have the necessary purpose', per Arden LJ at [102].

21.18 A father who transferred his house by deed of gift to his children shortly before his discharge from hospital into a nursing home was open to a finding that he acted as he did for the purpose of putting his house beyond the reach of the local authority who became liable for his nursing home charges[1].

1   *Derbyshire County Council v Akrill* [2005] EWCA Civ 308, [2005] All ER (D) 334 (Mar) – any other finding would have been 'perverse' but the father's appeal was allowed to enable him to pursue the public law argument that the local authority's decision to revisit an earlier decision in respect of a placing agreement should be reviewed.

Transferor with more than one purpose

21.19 Putting assets beyond the reach of creditors need not therefore be shown to be the sole purpose of the transaction before the court will intervene. But the question arises where the debtor has more than one purpose in entering into the relevant transaction whether the 'statutory purpose', that of putting assets beyond the reach or otherwise prejudicing the interests of creditors[1], needs to be the dominant purpose of the debtor, or a substantial purpose of his, or whether it is sufficient that it is the natural result of the debtor's intentions in entering into the transaction. It is evident that to meet the requirements of IA 1986, ss 423–425 the statutory purpose must be a real purpose behind the transaction. Anything less cannot properly be described as a purpose. 'It is not sufficient to quote something which is a by-product of the transaction under consideration or to show that it was simply a result of it ... or an element which made no contribution of importance to the debtor's purpose of carrying out the transaction under consideration'[2]. Once it is established that the debtor had, as a real substantial purpose, the statutory purpose of defeating or prejudicing creditors, does a proper interpretation of IA 1986, ss 423–425 require more, and necessitate the proving by the applicant for an order that the statutory purpose was the debtor's 'dominant' or 'predominant' purpose? In *Chohan v Saggar*[3], an early decision under the IA 1986, the court interpreted the statutory requirement as requiring the debtor to have the statutory purpose as his dominant purpose while not excluding the possibility that there might be other purposes behind the relevant transfer. In an even earlier decision, *Moon v Franklin*[4], it was suggested that 'predominant' was the right test. The correctness of these decisions was soon doubted[5] and they may now be discounted. In *IRC v Hashmi*[6] the court found that the debtor had two purposes in entering into the relevant transaction; he wanted to secure the future of his son financially and he wanted to put the relevant property beyond the reach of creditors should they emerge. Hart J., at first instance, observed that it will often be the case that the motive to ensure family financial protection and the motive to defeat creditors will co-exist. They may indeed be two sides of the same coin, with the transferor unable to say which was the more important in his own mind. Giving the leading judgment in the Court of Appeal Arden LJ, expressly having regard to the role of IA 1986, ss 423–425 in insolvency legislation said, at para 23:

> 'In my judgment there is no warrant for excluding the situation where purposes of equal potency are concerned ... One purpose can co-exist with another ... the section does not require the inquiry to be made whether the purpose was a dominant purpose. It is sufficient if the statutory purpose can properly be described as a purpose and not merely as a consequence, rather than something which was indeed positively intended.'

[1]   The wording of IA 1986, s 423(3), quoted at the start of this paragraph, referring as they do to putting assets beyond the reach of 'a person', have encouraged the submission that a particular person, whether creditor or otherwise, must be identified as a potential victim as at the time of the transaction. There can surely be no merit in such a submission which, if correct, would drive the proverbial coach and horses through the provisions of IA 1986, ss 423–425. It is a submission which could not have been made under LPA 1925, s 172, see para **21.3**, and in enacting the IA 1986 Parliament expressed no intention to restrict the jurisdiction; rather the reverse.
[2]   Per Arden LJ in *IRC v Hashmi* [2002] 2 BCLC 489, para 25.

3 [1992] BCC 306, at 323 followed in *Jyske Bank (Gibraltar) Ltd v Spjeldnaes* [1999] 2 BCLC 101.
4 [1996] BPIR 196.
5 See eg *Pinewood Joinery v Starelm Properties* [1994] 2 BCLC 412, 418; *Royscott Spa Leasing Ltd v Lovett* [1995] BCC 502 (where, for the purposes of an interlocutory appeal as to discovery, the Court of Appeal were prepared 'to assume, though without deciding the point, that the relevant purpose which has to be established in the application of s 423 is *substantial* purpose, rather than the stricter test of dominant purpose' see p 507H); *National Bank of Kuwait v Menzies* [1994] 2 BCLC 306, at p 317 and *Re Brabon, Treharne v Brabon* [2001] 1 BCLC 11.
6 [2002] 2 BCLC 489; and see *Kubianga v Ekpenyong* [2002] EWHC 1567 (Ch), [2002] 2 BCLC 597 at [12].

21.20 The other members of the Court (Laws, Simon Brown LJJ) also made it clear that there was no room for the argument that the statutory purpose had to be one which caused the transaction to be entered into before the court could intervene. Where the court is satisfied that, in truth, the statutory purpose substantially motivated the debtor it will intervene and make an appropriate order regardless of the fact that the debtor would have entered into the transaction for legitimate purposes in any event[1].

1 'Assume, say, that the debtor makes a gift partly out of a wish to avoid inheritance tax and partly to escape his creditors; and assume further that the debtor would have made it in any event purely for inheritance tax purposes. That, to my mind should not save the gift from being set aside ... No more should a gift, in my opinion, be saved merely because the debtor would in any event have made it to benefit the donee', per Simon Brown LJ at [2002] 2 BCLC 489, at para 38. See also *Hill v Spread Trustee Co Ltd* [2006] EWCA Civ 542, [2007] 1 All ER 1106 at [61][133].

The state of mind of the transferee

21.21 The presence or absence of bad faith or knowledge on the part of the other party to the transaction is not relevant when considering whether an order may be made[1], merely the debtor's personal purpose. If this purpose is established, it is irrelevant that the other party believed that the debtor was acting lawfully in entering into the transaction in question, for example in expressing his gratitude[2], or acting in accordance with professional advice as to appropriate family trust arrangements[3]. Neither are the debtor's good intentions relevant to an assessment whether the statutory purpose is behind the transaction. In *Arbuthnot Leasing International Ltd v Havelet Leasing Ltd (No 2)*[4] the managing director of the debtor company stated in his affidavit to the court that transfers of the debtor's assets comprising leasing agreements were made to protect the debtor's assets which were under threat by virtue of hostile litigation pursued by the victim. He was concerned that the assets would themselves become valueless by virtue of the victim's litigation and wanted to preserve them as a viable business in the hands of the transferee so as to fund the debtor's indebtedness to all its creditors including the victim[5]. Although the transaction may have been carried out without dishonest motive, on the advice of the debtor's lawyers, and in what was considered to be the best interests of the debtor's creditors, it was nevertheless evidently under-taken for the express purpose of putting assets beyond the reach of the victim who had obtained judgment on his debt, and who could not then levy execution on the transferred assets. The court accordingly reversed the transaction.

1 But note the protection given to bona fide purchasers for value under IA 1986, s 425(2), see paras **21.52–21.53**.
2 *Moon v Franklin* [1996] BPIR 196.
3 *Midland Bank plc v Wyatt* [1997] 1 BCLC 242.
4 [1990] BCC 636, Scott J.
5 The court made the point that the appropriate way to achieve this end would be by way of a voluntary arrangement, not imposed on a creditor as a fait accompli, see [1990] BCC 636, at p 645.

Alternative claim

21.22 In some cases it will be open to the applicant to challenge the relevant transaction as a sham, ie on the basis that all the parties to the transaction had the common intention that the acts and documents making up the transaction were not to create the rights and obligations which they give the appearance of creating[1]. If the relevant transaction is a sham there is nothing to set aside, and in the context of insolvency the trustee in bankruptcy may then acquire the relevant asset for the benefit of creditors. But the legal position may not always be straightforward. For a summary of the principles involved in the legal concept of a sham or pretence[2] and a discussion of the issues that can arise in bringing an alternative claim that the relevant transaction was a sham, see *Re Yates*[3].

1 See *Snook v London & West Riding Investments Ltd* [1967] 2 QB 786, [1967] 1 All ER 518; *Midland Bank plc v Wyatt* [1997] 1 BCLC 242.
2 Drawn from the judgment of Neuberger J in *National Westminster Bank v Jones* [2000] BPIR 1092.
3 [2005] BPIR 476, paras 168–178 and 217–222.

Applicant for an order

21.23 The following persons are entitled to make an application for an order under IA 1986, ss 423–425[1]:

Where the debtor is:

(1) an individual who is bankrupt: the official receiver or the trustee of the bankrupt's estate;
(2) a company in liquidation: the official receiver or the liquidator;
(3) a company in administration: the official receiver or the administrator;
(4) in any of the above three cases: any victim of the transaction, but only with the leave of the court[2];
(5) an individual or company which has entered into an approved voluntary arrangement and a victim of the transaction is bound by the arrangement: the supervisor of the arrangement;
(6) an individual or company which has entered into an approved voluntary arrangement: any victim of the transaction whether or not he is bound by the arrangement;

21.23 *Transactions defrauding creditors*

(7)   in any other case: by any victim of the transaction[3].

1   IA 1986, s 424(1).
2   If no objection is taken by the respondent the court may deal with the question of leave at the substantive hearing, see eg *National Bank of Kuwait v Menzies* [1994] 2 BCLC 306, 313. However, it is essential that leave be obtained before an order can be obtained and it would be unwise for a victim applicant in this situation to proceed without first obtaining leave in the hope that the court will deal with the requirement of leave at a substantive hearing of the application, even though leave may be given retrospectively, see *Re Saunders (a bankrupt)* [1997] Ch 60, [1997] 3 All ER 992. Leave will presumably not be given unless the trustee (or official receiver, liquidator, or administrator) has elected not to bring proceedings himself, compare *Re Crossley* [1954] 3 All ER 296, [1954] 1 WLR 1353.
3   Where the debtor is being wound up or is in administration (or as an individual is bankrupt) a victim may only make an application with the leave of the court, IA 1986, s 424(1)(a).

21.24 A 'victim' of a transaction is a person who is, or is capable of being, prejudiced by it[1]. These words are, intentionally, very wide. Victims who have brought IA 1986, s 423 proceedings include former clients bringing a professional negligence action against an accountant[2], a creditor of an insolvent company in compulsory liquidation[3], a creditor of a company not in liquidation[4], a corporate creditor of individuals not in bankruptcy[5], and a bank encountering difficulties in enforcing its security against a customer[6]. There is no need to show that the victim was a person who the transferor contemplated would be prejudiced by the transaction when he entered into it; a victim may indeed be a person of whose existence the transferor was unaware at that time[7].

1   IA 1986, s 423(5); quite plainly it is not restricted to those persons the transferor might have had in mind when he entered into the transaction, and see *Sands v Clitheroe* [2006] BPIR 1000.
2   *Moon v Franklin* [1996] BPIR 196.
3   *Re Ayala Holdings Ltd* [1993] BCLC 256.
4   *Pinewood Joinery v Starelm Properties Ltd* [1994] 2 BCLC 412.
5   *Pagemanor Ltd v Ryan* [2002] BPIR 593; *Anglo Eastern Trust Ltd v Kermanshahchi* [2003] BPIR 1229.
6   *Habib Bank Ltd v Ahmed* [2004] BPIR 35.
7   *Hill v Spread Trustee Co Ltd* [2005] EWCA Civ 542, [2007] 1 All ER 1106 at [101].

21.25 In *Hill v Spread Trustee Co Ltd*[1] the Court of Appeal acknowledged the possibility that an application might be made under IA 1986, s 423 even though it could not be shown at the date of the application that there was a person who could benefit by a finding that the transaction came within the provisions of IA 1986, ss 423–425.

1   [2005] EWCA Civ 542, [2007] 1 All ER 1106 at [136].

Leave required by victim

21.26 Leave to commence proceedings is required by any applicant victim where the debtor is bankrupt[1]. As any application is to be treated as being made on behalf of every victim of the transaction it is plainly sensible that the court should not give leave without considering the interests of all the debtor's creditors, and ascertaining whether or not the trustee in bankruptcy himself wishes to commence proceedings. The trustee will in most cases be the appropriate applicant. Leave should be sought by an applicant victim as a first step in any application[2], but there is no reason to suppose that the court cannot grant leave retrospectively when appropriate to do so[3]. If proceedings under IA 1986, s 423 are commenced before an individual becomes insolvent, his subsequent bankruptcy does not result in an automatic stay of the proceedings; they continue subject to an application for a stay[4].

[1] IA 1986, s 424(1)(a).
[2] *National Bank of Kuwait v Menzies* [1994] 2 BCLC 306, CA.
[3] See *Re Saunders* [1997] Ch 60, [1997] 3 All ER 992, a case on IA 1986, s 285, but stating the general principle that in the absence of clear words prior leave is not an absolute condition precedent to the issue of proceedings. In *National Bank of Kuwait v Menzies* [1993] BCLC 256 Chadwick J gave retrospective leave to the applicant victim to commence proceedings under IA 1986, s 423. Although the grant of leave was reversed in the Court of Appeal, [1994] 2 BCLC 306, this was on the basis that the claim was unsustainable. It would appear, see p 313d per Sir Christopher Slade, that the court was not critical of the judge agreeing to deal with the question of leave at the hearing of an interim application. In *Dora v Simper* [2000] 2 BCLC 561 at 572, Buckley J was plainly not impressed with counsel's attempt to distinguish *Re Saunders*, and while not expressing a considered view, suggested that the jurisdiction to grant leave retrospectively should exist. In the event he did not consider it appropriate to give leave on the merits.
[4] Under IA 1986, s 285, and see *Godfrey v Torpy* [2007] EWHC 919 (Ch), [2007] Bus LR 1203. The position is otherwise where proceedings have been commenced against a corporate debtor who becomes insolvent, for an automatic stay on the continuing of legal proceedings is imposed on the company entering either administration (by IA 1986, Sch B1, para 43 – proceedings may be continued with the consent of the administrator or with the permission of the court) or liquidation (IA 1986, s 130(2) imposes an automatic stay on the continuation of any proceedings on the making of a winding-up order, although this may be lifted by the court).

Court for applications

21.27 An application under IA 1986, ss 423–425 may be brought in any division of the High Court. If there are no existing proceedings in the Bankruptcy Court, the Insolvency Rules will not apply to the application; it will proceed under the CPR[1]. It is in the nature of the jurisdiction that IA 1986, s 423 applications are often made in conjunction with applications under IA 1986, ss 339–342, and such applications have regularly since the commencement of the Act been brought and continue to be brought under the Insolvency Rules[2]. There is here a difficulty in the drafting of the statute. Part 7, Chapter 1 of the Insolvency Rules[3], rule 7.1 provides that Chapter 1 applies 'to any application made to the court under the Act or Rules'[4]. Furthermore 'insolvency proceedings' are defined[5] as any proceedings under the Act or the Rules. But while applications under IA 1986, ss 423–425 are plainly applications under the Act, the authority under which the Insolvency Rules were made, namely IA 1986, ss 411–412, state expressly that the power to make rules is for the purpose of giving effect to Parts I to XI inclusive of the Insolvency Act 1986. As ss 423–425 comprise Part XVI of the Insolvency Act 1986, it may be questioned whether the Insolvency Rules can legitimately apply to applications under these sections[6]. If such applications have to be brought by claim form under the CPR, it would be an anomaly which may give rise to no little inconvenience if, as is often the case, an application is brought by a trustee in bankruptcy who wishes also to make an application under IA 1986, s 339. In *TSB Bank plc v Katz*[7], where the applicability of the Insolvency Rules to an application where there were no pending proceedings in the Bankruptcy Court was considered, the court was of the view that had there been such pending proceedings the application under IA 1986, s 423 could properly have proceeded under the IR 1986. Where an application is wrongly commenced by originating application under IR 1986 the court is likely to treat the originating application as a claim form, and allow the application to proceed under CPR[8].

[1] *TSB Bank plc v Katz* [1997] BPIR 147. For examples of IA 1986, s 423 applications made other than in the Companies Court or Bankruptcy Court see *Aiglon Ltd v Gau Shan Co Ltd* [1993] 1 Lloyd's Rep 164 (Commercial Court) and *Jyske Bank (Gibraltar) Ltd v Spjeldnaes* [1999] 2 BCLC 101 (Chancery Division).
[2] And are thus made to the High Court or any county court having a bankruptcy jurisdiction in relation to the debtor, see para **1.18** above.
[3] Which deals with applications.
[4] With the express exceptions of (a) an administration order, (b) a winding-up order, or (c) a bankruptcy order.
[5] IR 1986, r 13.7.
[6] *TSB Bank plc v Katz* [1997] BPIR 147.
[7] [1997] BPIR 147.
[8] See eg *Banca Carige SpA v Banco Nacional de Cuba* [2001] 1 WLR 2039 at para 16.

Limitation

21.28 The Cork Committee[1] expressed the view that there was no period of limitation applicable to claims under LPA 1925, s 172. The scheme of s 172 is to avoid the offending transaction as opposed to providing for the court to give relief to the victim(s) of the transaction. There is no provision of the Limitation Act 1980 ('LA 1980') which imposes a limitation period on such applications[2]. The position has changed however with the enactment of IA 1986, s 423–425. Under IA 1986, s 423(2), as expanded by s 425(1), on a successful application the court does not simply avoid the original transaction, leaving the resulting position to be determined by the general law, but makes specific orders actively to restore the position to what it would have been if the transaction had not been entered into and to protect the interests of victims. Although in *Law Society v Southall*[3] the Court of Appeal was content to proceed on the footing that there was no applicable limitation period to an application under IA 1986, s 423, it is difficult to see how such applications can escape the effect of LA 1980, ss 8 and 9[4]. An application under IA 1986, s 423 is 'an action upon a specialty' for the purposes of LA 1980, s 8 or, occasionally, 'an action to recover any sum recoverable by virtue of any enactment' for the purposes of LA 1980, s 9[5].

[1] Cmnd 8338 paras 1278–1282.
[2] Under LPA 1925, s 172 it was possible that delay in seeking to avoid the transaction might have been held to bar the claim, although only if the position of the relevant parties had altered in the meantime, see *Re Pullen, ex p Williams* (1870) LR 10 Eq 57, but the better view is that mere delay could not be a defence, avoidance under LPA 1925, s 172 being a legal right, and laches being an equitable remedy, *Re Maddever, Three Towns Banking Company v Maddever* (1884) 27 Ch D 523. In this case the Court of Appeal noted that the plaintiff's claim as a creditor against the defendant in respect of the deed in question was not itself barred by the statute of limitation. The court drew the distinction between a claim to set aside the relevant deed on equitable grounds, where the delay in question (almost 10 years) would have been a good defence, and the statutory claim to set aside the

deed as a fraud on the creditors, which was a legal claim. Both the court at first instance and the Court of Appeal were of the opinion that the legal claim under the statute would have been subject to the Statute of Limitations.

3   [2000] BPIR 336 at para 6.
4   As to which see para **20.82**.
5   Some consideration was given to the question of limitation in IA 1986, s 423 claims in *Re Yates* [2005] BPIR 476, at paras 180–187 but on the facts it was not necessary for any limitation point to be decided.

21.29 The applicability of a statutory period of limitation to claims under IA 1986, s 423 was considered by the Court of Appeal in *Hill v Spread Trustee Co Ltd*[1]. The court was unanimous that such claims are subject to the statute of limitations, either LA 1980, s 8 or s 9 (as above), but disagreed as to when the limitation period begins to run. The majority, agreeing with the judge at first instance, held that where the application is brought by the trustee in bankruptcy the period begins to run on the date of the bankruptcy order[2]. In her judgment dissenting on this point[3] Arden LJ well demonstrated the difficulties in arriving at an appropriate conclusion. There can be no cause of action without a victim but there may be many victims of the fraudulent transfer, and they may well become victims at different times. When the transferor becomes bankrupt and a trustee in bankruptcy is appointed he may bring proceedings, but this may be after the expiry of the period of limitation applicable to proceedings brought by an early victim of the transferor. But Arden LJ's conclusion[4] that the period of limitation commences as soon as there is one victim whoever is the actual applicant for relief could, occasionally, severely limit the usefulness of IA 1986, s 423. And while Arden LJ acknowledged that the limitation period may be postponed under LA 1980, the effect of having a limitation period commencing with the first victim could lead to capricious results. Different victims may have differing states of knowledge, or differing ability to discover that there is a right of action with reasonable diligence. Does the possibility of postponement depend solely on the first victim? How is the court to determine issues of postponement if the first victim in time is not a party?

1   [2006] EWCA Civ 542, [2007] 1 All ER 1106.
2   For the supervisor of an IVA or PVA the cause of action will accrue on the date on which the arrangement is approved.
3   [2006] EWCA Civ 542, [2007] 1 All ER 1106 at [106]–[129], the majority were Sir Martin Nourse with whom Waller LJ agreed.
4   [2006] EWCA Civ 542, [2007] 1 All ER 1106 at [126].

21.30 The decision of the majority, that where the applicant is the trustee in bankruptcy the limitation period begins to run on the date of the insolvency order, has the benefit not only of clarity but of meeting what are surely the purposes of both the IA 1986, s 423 remedy and of insolvency law generally. Where a transferor arranges his affairs so as to defeat potential creditors at some unspecified time in the future, he cannot realistically complain if he is held to account when creditors suffer however long that time may be in coming. But once an individual debtor has become bankrupt, it is in accordance with the general scheme of insolvency law that his insolvency brings his affairs to a conclusion and enables him to start again without liabilities, albeit in this case after a rather long limitation period. Of course this approach to the limitation period does mean that there will be separate limitation periods for different applicants under IA 1986, s 423[1]. An application by the individual victim will be subject to a limitation period which commences when the applicant becomes a victim. It might be suggested that it would be wrong for a victim whose claim is statute-barred to benefit from a recovery on a collective remedy by a subsequent victim or trustee in bankruptcy. However, a victim will effectively cease to be a victim if the legal right on which his victim status depends cannot be enforced because it itself is statute-barred. It would in theory be open to the court to make an order specifically in such a person's favour, for the court has such a wide discretion in making orders[2]. But a creditor with a statute-barred debt will not be able to prove in a debtor's bankruptcy.

[1] In *Hill v Spread Trustee Co Ltd* [2006] EWCA Civ 542, [2007] 1 All ER 1106 at [149] Sir Martin Nourse stated 'I see no inherent objection to the notion that there may be separate limitation periods for different applicants under s 423. While it has always been the policy of the Limitation Acts to put an end to stale claims, it has not been part of their policy to provide that time shall run against a claimant or applicant before he has been able to commence his action'.

[2] See IA 1986, s 423(2).

21.31 A further important issue arising in connection with limitation is the ability of an applicant to rely on the deliberate concealment provisions of the LA 1980. By LA 1980, s 32(1)(b) where any fact relevant to the applicant's right of action has been deliberately concealed from him by the defendant, the period of limitation does not begin to run until the applicant has discovered the concealment, or could with reasonable diligence have discovered it[1]. 'Deliberate concealment' is not restricted to but does include a deliberate commission of a breach of duty in circumstances in which it is unlikely to be discovered for some time[2]. In other words even where there are no acts which involve deliberately concealing what it is that the transferor has done there may be deliberate concealment for the purposes of the LA 1980. There must however be a deliberate breach of duty[3]. The position of a defrauding transferor for the purpose of a claim under IA 1986, s 423 was considered in *Giles v Rhind and Rhind*[4] and, in holding that such a transferor was in deliberate breach of duty so that the postponement provisions of LA 1980, s 32 applied, David Richards J said, at [41]:

> 'A transaction to which section 423 applies clearly involves the deliberate commission of an actionable wrong but does it involve a "breach of duty" within the meaning of section 32(2)? In my judgment, it does. It is true that "breach of duty" most obviously connotes a breach of a duty owed by the defendant to the claimant, such as a contractual, fiduciary or tortious duty. Section 423 is in a sense more amorphous. If a person enters into a transaction to which it applies, a range of possible claimants, including many who may not exist as such at the date of the transaction, may subsequently apply to set it aside or for other relief. It would however be unjustifiably restrictive to construe breach of duty as confined in the way indicated above. In my view, it is no more than the obverse of 'right of action' in s 32(1)(b) and means simply legal wrongdoing, that is acts or omissions giving rise to a right of action'.

[1] NB it will not be possible for an applicant to rely on LA 1980, s 32(1)(a), postponement in case of fraud, because fraud, even if present, is not an essential element of a claim under IA 1986, s 423, see *Beaman v ARTS Ltd* [1949] 1 KB 550, [1949] 1 All ER 465, CA.

² LA 1980, s 32(2).
³ *Cave v Robinson, Jarnis & Rolf* [2002] UKHL 18, [2003] 1 AC 384.
⁴ [2007] EWHC 687 (Ch), [2007] All ER (D) 474 (May).

21.32 In *Giles v Rhind* the transferor had transferred a beneficial interest in the matrimonial home to his wife (the classic IA 1986, s 423 transfer) by executing a deed of transfer which was not registered. The court held that the start of the limitation period was postponed to a date when the applicant could have discovered the essential facts[1].

¹ [2007] EWHC 687 (Ch) at [42]. The fact that it is now possible for anyone to search HM Land Registry could have a bearing in individual cases on the date on which the exercise of reasonable diligence could lead to the ascertainment of the relevant facts.

21.33 It is perhaps worth noting that the great majority of claims under IA 1986, ss 423–425 are brought within the context of insolvency, and if neither the trustee in bankruptcy, nor (with leave) a victim, has commenced proceedings within 12 years (or even six years) of the commencement of the bankruptcy something is seriously amiss.

Applications

21.34 If an application is made under the Insolvency Rules it should be commenced by originating application[1]. An application under the IR 1986 requires the 'nature of the relief or order applied for' to be stated in the application form[2]. This is a procedural not a substantive requirement, and the failure of the applicant to list each transaction to which the application related was not fatal to the application where the scheme of transactions which the applicant sought to impugn was evident from the evidence in support[3].

¹ IR 1986, r 7.2, and note prescribed Form 7.1, 7.2.
² IR 1986, r 7.3.
³ *Ashe v Mumford and others* (2000) Times, 7 March; on appeal [2001] BPIR 1, CA

21.35 Every application, whoever is the applicant, is to be treated as made on behalf of every victim of the transaction[1]. This provision, which will secure equality as between victims, may well require careful consideration being given in cases where the debtor is not in insolvency. It will usually be necessary to give directions to ensure that all potential victims of the transaction are notified of the making of the application, if necessary by advertisement, and are permitted to be heard. Such considerations are not addressed by the Insolvency Rules. A creditor of a deceased donor has no standing to apply for a declaration that a third party holds property the subject of a gift from the deceased on trust for the deceased's estate; it is necessary to join the deceased's estate as a party to the proceedings[2].

¹ IA 1986, s 424(2).
² *The Law Society v Southall* [2001] BPIR 303.

21.36 The onus of establishing the elements of the application remains on the applicant in all cases, whether or not the other party to a transaction under

21.36 *Transactions defrauding creditors*

review is a connected person or associate[1]. It is necessary therefore that the applicant strictly proves the 'hope' value of a property transferred for a nominal consideration when asserting that the transaction was at an undervalue[2].

[1]   See *Habib Bank Ltd v Ahmed* [2004] BPIR 35 upheld on appeal [2004] BPIR 864 CA. Contrast the position under IA 1986, ss 339–342, see paras **20.23–20.55**. Note that the burden of proof in showing cause why a charging order nisi should not be made absolute lies on the judgment debtor or third party, *Habib Bank Ltd v Ahmed* following *Roberts Petroleum Ltd v Bernard Kenny Ltd* [1982] 1 WLR 301, 307E–F, *Midland Bank plc v Wyatt* [1996] BPIR 288.
[2]   *Pinewood Joinery v Starelm Properties Ltd* [1994] 2 BCLC 412.

21.37 It may be appropriate to consider interim relief by way of freezing injunction or search order when bringing the application[1].

[1]   The power of the court to grant a freezing (mareva) injunction in support of a claim under IA 1986, s 423 was confirmed in *Aiglon Ltd v Gau Shan Co Ltd* [1993] 1 Lloyd's Rep 164; see also *Dora v Simper* [2000] 2 BCLC 561, CA.

Service out of the jurisdiction

21.38 Whether proceedings are brought under IR 1986 or CPR permission is required to serve out of the jurisdiction. Where the IR 1986 apply, see above, the court has a general discretion to order service out of the jurisdiction within such time, on such person, at such place and in such manner as it thinks fit[1]. Where proceedings are brought under CPR permission is required under CPR r 6.20. Reliance may not be placed on CPR r 6.19(2), which authorises service of a claim form on a defendant out of the jurisdiction 'where each claim included in the claim form against the defendant to be served is a claim, which, under any other enactment, the court has power to determine' because IA 1986, s 423 does not expressly contemplate proceedings against persons outside the jurisdiction[2].

[1]   IR 1986, r 12.12(3); an application for leave is to be supported by affidavit or witness statement stating the grounds of the application and identifying the place or country the person to be served is, or is probably, to be found, IR 1986, r 12.12(4).
[2]   *In re Banco Nacional de Cuba* [2001] 1 WLR 2039 paras 17–19, Lightman J relying on *Re Harrods (Buenos Aires) Ltd* [1992] Ch 72, 116, a decision under RSC Ord 11 r 1(2)(d) the predecessor of CPR r 6.19(2). The application for permission in this case was refused because the claimant failed to demonstrate that there was a serious issue to be tried on each of the four limbs of a successful claim, namely (i) the transaction was at an undervalue, (ii) the transaction was for the purpose of prejudicing the position of present or future claimants in relation to their claims, (iii) the claimant was a victim of the transaction, (iv) the court would exercise its discretion to grant the relief sought.

Disclosure

21.39 The court will normally order disclosure of documents passing between a party to a transaction under scrutiny and his legal advisers where the documents relate to the setting up of the transaction[1].

1   *Barclays Bank plc v Eustice* [1995] 2 BCLC 630, 642c, 644h CA. The court left open the possibility that the applicant for disclosure need only make out a prima facie case as opposed to a strong prima facie case. Documents obtained or created for the dominant purpose of being used in pending or contemplated proceedings will be protected by legal professional privilege, unless a prima facie case of fraud can be established, see e g *Royscott Spa Leasing Ltd v Lovett* [1995] BCC 502, 506 (a IA 1986, s 423 case) where the order for disclosure was discharged on appeal because no prima facie case of fraudulent purpose could be established.

Public law defence

21.40 A respondent has the right to raise as a defence to proceedings under IA 1986, s 423 an issue of public law which undermines the basis of the claim[1].

1   *Derbyshire County Council v Akrill* [2005] EWCA Civ 308, [2005] All ER (D) 334 (Mar) applying *Wandsworth London Borough Council v Winder* [1985] 1 AC 461, [1984] 3 All ER 976. In *Akrill* the respondent had gifted his house to his children shortly before entering a nursing home in order to avoid contributing to the cost of his care. He wished to challenge the propriety of the assessment made by the local authority for his contribution.

Financial Services

21.41 The Financial Services Authority may apply for an order under IA 1986, s 423 in relation to a debtor if:

(a)   at the time the relevant transaction was entered into the debtor was carrying on a regulated activity under the Financial Services and Markets Act 2000, s 22 (whether or not in contravention of the general prohibition); and

(b)   a victim of the transaction is or was party to an agreement entered into with the debtor where the making or performance of the agreement constituted or was part of a regulated activity carried on by the debtor[1].

1   Financial Services and Markets Act 2000, s 375(1).

21.42 Any application brought by the Financial Services Authority is to be treated as made on behalf of every victim of the transaction who comes within (b) above (para **21.41**)[1].

1   Financial Services and Markets Act 2000, s 375(2).

Compromise of claim

21.43 A claim under IA 1986, s 423 is brought for the benefit of all the creditors, and it will be unusual for the applicant to be in a position safely to compromise the claim with the debtor. In an appropriate case however the court has jurisdiction to approve proposals for settlement agreed by the parties, creditors and victims in place of order the setting aside of the relevant transaction[1].

1   *Pena v Coyne (No 2)* [2004] 2 BCLC 730.

21.44   *Transactions defrauding creditors*

Third party costs

21.44   Where a transfer is made in order to defeat creditors, a third party costs order[1] may be appropriate against a non-party whose actions may have deprived a claimant of a realistic opportunity to recover its costs. A third party costs application may be made where facts are in dispute, provided the court is able to determine the issues arising in the course of the application, and it is not essential that the transaction under challenge caused the claimant to incur the costs claimed against the third party[2].

[1]   Under the Supreme Court Act 1981, s 51.
[2]   *Re Total Spares and Supplies Ltd v Antares SRL* [2006] EWHC 1537 (Ch), [2006] All ER (D) 314 (Jun).

Orders under IA 1986, ss 423–425

21.45   In making an order the court must seek both:

(1)   to restore the position to what it would have been if the transaction had not been entered into; and
(2)   to protect the interests of victims of the transactions[1].

[1]   IA 1986, s 423(2).

21.46   In seeking to achieve these aims the court may make such order as it thinks fit[1]. Without prejudice to the generality of this discretion, IA 1986, s 425 specifies a number of orders which may be made, a list which follows closely the provisions relating to transactions at an undervalue and preferences[2]. Thus the court may:

(a)   require property which has been transferred to be vested in a particular person either absolutely or for the benefit of others;
(b)   require property acquired from the proceeds of transferred property to be so vested;
(c)   release or discharge any security[3] given by the relevant person, in whole or in part;
(d)   require a transferee or beneficiary of property transferred to pay money to a particular person;
(e)   revive the obligations of any surety or guarantor released through the transfer by the debtor; and
(f)   provide for security to be provided for the discharge of any obligation imposed or arising under the order. Such security may be charged on particular property, such charge to have the same priority as any security or charge released or discharged under the transaction.

[1]   IA 1986, s 423(2); 'the object being to remedy the avoidance of debts the "and" between paras (a) and (b) of s 423(2) must be read conjunctively and not disjunctively' per Nourse LJ in *Chohan v Saggar* [1994] 1 BCLC 706 at p 714c.
[2]   See IA 1986, s 342, and see para 20.87.
[3]   'Security' means any mortgage, charge, lien or other security, IA 1986, s 425(4).

21.47 An order should seek, so far as practicable, both to restore the position to what it would have been if the transaction had not been entered into, and to protect the interests of the victims:

> 'It is not a power to restore the position generally, but in such a way as to protect the victims' interests; in other words, by restoring assets to the debtor to make them available for execution by the victims. So the first question the judge must ask himself is what assets have been lost to the debtor. His order should, so far as practicable, restore that loss.'[1]

1   Per Nourse LJ, *Chohan v Saggar* [1994] 1 BCLC 706, 714d.

21.48 The whole or any part of the relevant transaction may be set aside, but the court must have a care to protect the position of third parties when determining what relief to grant[1]. Where the business and business assets of the debtor were transferred to an associated company which then conducted the business and incurred debts the court ordered the associated company to hold the business and assets on trust for the debtor without prejudice to the claims of creditors of the associated company whose debts arose after the date of transfer[2]. In *Feakins v Department for Environment, Food and Rural Affairs*[3] a debtor was party to an arrangement whereby his property was sold by mortgages to a third party subject to an agricultural tenancy in favour of the debtor's company at a valuation which took account of the tenancy. Subsequent to the sale the debtor's company surrendered the tenancy leaving the purchaser with vacant possession. The Court of Appeal held that this constituted a transaction at an undervalue for the purpose of IA 1986, s 423, but that as the surrendered tenancy was not a sham it ordered the reinstatement of the tenancy[4].

1   *Chohan v Saggar* [1994] 1 BCLC 706, 713–715, CA, and see *Midland Bank plc v Wyatt* [1997] 1 BCLC 242 where it was held that a family trust was a sham, but would have been set aside under IA 1986, s 423 had it been a valid declaration of trust as it was entered into to screen the family against the unknown risks of a new commercial adventure.
2   *Arbuthnot Leasing International Ltd v Havelet Leasing Ltd (No 2)* [1990] BCC 636.
3   [2005] EWCA Civ 1658, [2006] BPIR 895.
4   [2005] EWCA Civ 1658, [2006] BPIR 895 at [87].

21.49 Where the debtor is insolvent and the application is made by the trustee in bankruptcy or official receiver the proceeds of any execution will naturally be applied to swell the assets available to creditors in the insolvency. In other cases however, except where the court can be confident that the applicant(s)/claimant(s) before it are the only victims of the transaction in question, the order made on a successful application ought to make provision for the proceeds of any execution to be held on trust for all victims of the transaction. It will then be necessary to give directions to enable other victims to make their claims. A 'victim' claimant would be well advised to seek directions with respect to other victims at an early stage of the proceedings.

21.50 A transaction which is liable to be impeached under the provisions of IA 1986, ss 423–425 is not void ab initio but voidable and so takes effect until avoided by the order of the court[1].

[1]   *Chohan v Saggar* [1993] BCLC 661 at p 667e, relying on *Harrods Ltd v Stanton* [1923] 1 KB 516.

Criminal conduct: 'tainted gifts'

21.51 Where criminal conduct has been involved or is suspected, an application under IA 1986, s 423 may be delayed pending the resolution of confiscation proceedings in the Crown Court, and any eventual order under IA 1986, s 423 will have to take into account any realisation of property in such confiscation proceedings[1].

[1]   See the discussion of 'tainted gifts' in para **20.98–20.100**.

Effect on transferee and third parties

21.52 An order under IA 1986, s 423 may affect the property of or impose any obligation on the transferee or any third party even though he was not the person with whom the debtor entered into the transaction. Innocent third parties are given protection, however, and orders may not be made by the court which:

(a)   prejudice any interest in property which was acquired from a person other than the debtor and was acquired in good faith, for value and without notice of the relevant circumstances, or prejudice any interest deriving from such an interest; or

(b)   require a person who received a benefit from a transaction in good faith, for value and without notice of the relevant circumstances to pay any sum unless he was a party to the transaction[1].

[1]   IA 1986, s 425(2)(a)(b).

21.53 The 'relevant circumstances' are those circumstances which give rise to the making of an order under IA 1986, s 423 ie those circumstances which enable the court to find that the transaction impugned was at an undervalue and was entered into for the purpose of putting assets beyond the reach of claimants or prejudicing their interests in respect of present or future claims[1]. The terms in which s 425(2)(b) is drafted (noted above) would, strictly, enable the court to make an order against a party to the transaction even where he had given full value. The drafting of s 425(2)(a) and (b) largely follows the wording of IA 1986, s 342(2) as originally enacted. As noted in the previous chapter[2], the provisions of s 342(2) were amended by the Insolvency (No 2) Act 1994 primarily to protect purchasers and mortgagees of interests in land. There is no obvious reason why similar amendments should not have been made to IA 1986, s 425(2).

[1]   IA 1986, s 425(3).
[2]   See para **20.93**.

21.54 Where the transaction is entered into for the purpose of prejudicing the interests of a creditor in respect of a liability incurred on behalf of a trust, relief may be granted which has an adverse effect on the beneficiaries of the trust. They are, of course, unlikely to be innocent third parties[1].

[1]   See e g *Beckenham MC v Centralex Ltd* [2004] EWHC 1287 (Ch), [2004] 2 BCLC 764.

Chapter 22

PROOF OF DEBTS

A DEBTS PROVABLE IN BANKRUPTCY

General

22.1 The essence of bankruptcy is that it protects the debtor who becomes bankrupt against the claims of his creditors and ensures that, subject to certain exceptions[1], all unsecured creditors are treated equally. The protection of the bankrupt debtor is twofold. First, after the making of a bankruptcy order no creditor of the bankrupt may, in respect of a debt provable in the bankruptcy, exercise any remedy against the property or person of the bankrupt in respect of that debt, or commence any action or other legal proceedings against the bankrupt except with the leave of the court and on such terms as the court may impose[2]. Secondly, after the bankrupt receives his discharge he is released from any further liability in respect of all debts which could have been proved in his bankruptcy whether or not they were proved[3]. From the unsecured creditors' point of view, their equal treatment is achieved by the process whereby first, they may each establish the amount which, had the bankruptcy not occurred, the bankrupt would have had to pay them and secondly, the estate is divided amongst them in proportion to the respective values of their individual claims. The present chapter is concerned with the first part of that process: establishing the amount of each unsecured claim.

888

¹ These exceptions are (1) preferential debts which are given priority by statute; and (2) where the unsecured creditor has a right of set-off.
² IA 1986, s 285(3).
³ IA 1986, s 281(1).

Provable debts

22.2 Under the heading 'Provable debts' the Insolvency Rules 1986 ('IR 1986'), r 12.3 sets out which claims are provable in bankruptcy[1]. The general principle is that all claims by creditors are provable as debts against the bankrupt, whether they are present or future, certain or contingent, ascertained or sounding only in damages. But the rule goes on to identify claims which are not provable. These are:

(a) any fine[2] imposed for an offence, and any obligation (other than an obligation to pay a lump sum or to pay costs) arising under an order made in family proceedings[3] or any obligation arising under a maintenance assessment made under the Child Support Act 1991;

(b) any obligation arising under a confiscation order made under the Drug Trafficking Offences Act 1986, s 1 or the Criminal Justice (Scotland) Act 1987, s 1 or the Criminal Justice Act 1988, s 71 or under the Proceeds of Crime Act 2002, Pts 2, 3 or 4.

¹ And in winding up and administration.
² Defined by reference to the Magistrates' Courts Act 1980 in IA 1986, s 281(8).
³ Defined in IA 1986, s 281(8).

22.3 The generality of the principle as to the claims which are provable does not override, but is subject to, any enactment or rule of law under which a particular kind of debt is not provable, whether on grounds of public policy or otherwise[1].

¹ IR 1986, r 12.3(3).

Provable debts proof of which is postponed

22.4 IR 1986, r 12.3(2) contains provision postponing proof of a restitution order made under the Financial Services and Markets Act 2000, s 382(1)(a) pursuant to which the bankrupt has been ordered to disgorge to the Financial Services Authority profits which he has made through conducting business in contravention of requirements imposed by that Act. Although the rule provides for the postponement of the proof of a debt of this kind until all the other claims of the creditors in the bankruptcy have been paid in full with interest under IA 1986, s 328(4), the effect of the rule is to postpone the distribution of any dividend in respect of the debt until after all the other debts have been paid with interest.

Bankruptcy debts

22.5 But in order to see which debts may be proved in a bankruptcy, it is also necessary to bring into play the definition in IA 1986, s 382 of 'bankruptcy debt'. This is justified because in IA 1986, s 322(1) it is provided that the proof of any bankruptcy debt is to take place in accordance with the Insolvency Rules 1986. Secondly, the definition of 'provable debt' in IR 1986, r 12.3 does not include any reference to the time when any particular debt arose. The definition of 'bankruptcy debt' fills that deficiency by requiring that the bankrupt should be subject to the debt, or to an obligation which may render him subject to it, at the commencement of the bankruptcy[1].

[1] IA 1986, s 382(1)(a) and (b).

Definition of 'bankruptcy debt'

22.6 IA 1986, s 382 provides that any of the following are bankruptcy debts:

(1) any debt or liability to which the debtor is subject at the commencement of the bankruptcy[1];

(2) any debt or liability to which he may become subject after the commencement of the bankruptcy, including after discharge from bankruptcy, by reason of any obligation incurred before the commencement of the bankruptcy;

(3) any interest due in respect of the debt for any period prior to the commencement of the bankruptcy.

[1] Ie the date of the bankruptcy order, IA 1986, s 278.

22.7 It is immaterial whether the debt or liability is present or future, whether it is certain or contingent or whether its amount is fixed or liquidated, or is capable of being ascertained by fixed rules or as a matter of opinion[1]. A 'liability' is defined[2] as a liability to pay money or money's worth, including any liability under an enactment, any liability for breach of trust, any liability in contract, tort or bailment and any liability arising out of an obligation to make restitution. An unliquidated liability in tort may be a bankruptcy debt[3]. For these purposes the bankrupt is deemed to become subject to the tortious liability by reason of an obligation incurred at the time when the cause of action accrued[4].

[1] IA 1986, s 382(3).
[2] IA 1986, s 382(4).
[3] In contrast to the position under the Bankruptcy Act 1914.
[4] IA 1986, s 382(2).

B GENERAL PRINCIPLES APPLICABLE TO PROOF OF DEBTS

Investigation by the trustee

22.8 The role of the trustee is to get in, realise and distribute the bankrupt's estate[1] and in doing so he should investigate each proof of debt and determine whether it may properly be admitted in the bankruptcy. No debt which would not be enforceable against the bankrupt will be admissible for proof[2]. The trustee is in no way bound by the bankrupt's own statement of affairs and he may reject a claim which the bankrupt has admitted in his sworn statement[3].

The trustee may go behind a judgment, even a final judgment obtained by the creditor[4], and refuse to accept the proof if he discovers that it does not represent a bona fide claim, because of inadequate consideration[5], or because the debt on a true analysis should be postponed[6], or because the debt arises under a sham transaction designed to reduce the bankrupt's assets paid to creditors[7]. A trustee may also reopen a compromise which was not entered into in good faith between the creditor and the bankrupt. Provided however that there is no evidence of bad faith a trustee may not challenge a compromise on the ground that the creditor obtained too advantageous a settlement[8]. A bankrupt may not ask the court in effect to reopen a case and listen to further arguments; so where a judgment debt was founded upon an arbitration award made without the bankrupt advancing all his arguments, the bankrupt could not go behind the award in the bankruptcy proceedings in the absence of fraud or improper conduct on the part of the arbitrator[9]. The trustee must be in a similar position to that of the bankrupt. A trustee may not go behind an HMRC proof for assessed taxes[10]. Where the trustee finds that such a proof is in respect of an estimated assessment or reached without full knowledge of the bankrupt's affairs the appropriate course will be to apply or appeal to the HMRC for reassessment.

1   IA 1986, s 305(2).
2   *Re Benzon, Bower v Chetwynd* [1914] 2 Ch 68.
3   *Re Tollemache, ex parte Revell* (1884) 13 QBD 720, CA; *Re Browne, ex p Official Receiver v Thompson* [1960] 2 All ER 625.
4   *Re Menastar Ltd* [2002] EWHC 2610 (Ch), [2003] 1 BCLC 338; *Re Shruth Ltd* [2005] EWHC 1293 (Ch), [2006] 1 BCLC 294.
5   *Re Van Laun, ex p Chatterton* [1907] 2 KB 23. And see *Re Onslow, ex p Kibble* (1875) 10 Ch App 373; and the *Re Tollemache* cases; *Re Tollemache, ex p Revell* (1884) 13 QBD 720, CA; *Ex p Edwards* (1884) 14 QBD 415, CA; *Ex p Bonham* (1885) 14 QBD 604, CA; and *Ex p Anderson* (1885) 14 QBD 606, CA; *Re Lennox, ex p Lennox* (1885) 16 QBD 315, CA; *Re Flatau, ex p Scotch Whisky Distillers Ltd* (1888) 22 QBD 83, CA; *Re Beauchamp, ex p Beauchamp* [1904] 1 KB 572.
6   *Re Lupkovics, ex p Trustee v Freville* [1954] 2 All ER 125, [1954] 1 WLR 1234.
7   *Re Myers, ex p Myers* [1908] 1 KB 941.
8   *Re Cole* [1931] 2 Ch 174; *Re Maundy Gregory, ex p Norton* [1935] Ch 65; and see *Re A Debtor (No 12 of 1958)* [1968] 2 All ER 425. An unfavourable compromise might constitute a transaction at an undervalue if the creditor's consideration is 'significantly less' than that provided by the debtor, IA 1986, s 339(3).
9   *Re Newey, ex p Whiteman* (1912) 107 LT 832.
10 *Re Calvert, ex p Calvert* [1899] 2 QB 145, applied in *Re B Moschi, ex p R Moschi v IRC* (1953) 35 TC 92.

22.9 A trustee may be liable for misfeasance or breach of duty if the bankrupt's estate suffers loss in consequence of the manner in which he has carried out his functions[1]. Failure to take proper steps to investigate a proof may cause loss to the estate and render the trustee liable to compensate the estate for any loss[2].

1   IA 1986, s 304(1).
2   See e g *Re Home and Colonial Insurance Co* [1930] 1 Ch 102.

Control by court

22.10 The court has a general power to determine any question of law or fact arising in a bankruptcy[1]. Like the trustee, as described in the preceding

22.10 *Proof of debts*

paragraph, the court looks to the substance of the matter and may look behind a debt, even a judgment debt, and inquire into the consideration for the debt and generally into its validity for the purposes of proof[2]. The court may investigate any judgment or compromise and refuse to admit a claim based upon a debt which would not itself have been admissible for proof[3]. It has been held however that the court should not go behind an assessment for taxes made against the bankrupt[4]. The court is also concerned with questions of priorities and a debt which is postponed under the rules[5] continues to be postponed even after the creditor has obtained judgment upon it[6].

1 IA 1986, s 363(1).
2 *Re Onslow, ex p Kibble* (1875) 10 Ch App 373; and the *Re Tollemache* cases; *Re Tollemache, ex p Revell* (1884) 13 QBD 720, CA; *Ex p Edwards* (1884) 14 QBD 415, CA; *Ex p Bonham* (1885) 14 QBD 604, CA; and *Ex p Anderson* (1885) 14 QBD 606, CA; *Re Lennox, ex p Lennox* (1885) 16 QBD 315, CA; *Re Flatau, ex p Scotch Whisky Distillers Ltd* (1888) 22 QBD 83, CA; *Re Beauchamp, ex p Beauchamp* [1904] 1 KB 572, CA; *Re Van Laun, ex p Pattullo* [1907] 1 KB 155; affd at [1907] 2 KB 23, CA.
3 *Re Blythe, ex p Banner* (1881) 17 Ch D 480, CA; *Miles v New Zealand Alford Estate Co* (1886) 32 Ch D 266, CA; *Re Hawkins, ex p Troup* [1895] 1 QB 404, CA; *Re Mead* [1916] 2 IR 285, CA.
4 See *Re Calvert, ex p Calvert* [1899] 2 QB 145, applied in *Re B Moschi, ex p R Moschi v IRC* (1953) 35 TC 92.
5 See paras **23.20** and **23.21** below.
6 *Re Lupkovics, ex p Trustee v Freville* [1954] 2 All ER 125, [1954] 1 WLR 1234.

Unliquidated damages

22.11 A claim for unliquidated damages is a provable debt[1] whether the liability is one to which the bankrupt is subject at the commencement of the bankruptcy or one to which he may become subject after the commencement of the bankruptcy by reason of any obligation incurred before the commencement of the bankruptcy[2]. In determining whether any liability in tort is a bankruptcy debt, the bankrupt is deemed to become subject to that liability by reason of an obligation incurred at the time when the cause of action accrued[3].

1 See IA 1986, s 382(1), (4) and IR 1986, r 12.3(1).
2 IA 1986, s 382(1)(a), (b).
3 IA 1986, s 382(2).

Contingent debts

22.12 To be a contingent debt provable in the bankruptcy there must be a debt or liability to which the bankrupt may become subject after the commencement of the bankruptcy, including any period likely to be after the bankrupt's discharge, by reason of any obligation incurred before the date of the bankruptcy order[1]. For the purposes of voting and dividend a contingent debt has to be valued. The responsibility for valuation rests with the trustee[2] with a right of appeal to the court[3], and the sum estimated by the trustee or the court is then provable in the bankruptcy[4]. Generally, all contingent liabilities which may end in the payment of money, and which have not been declared incapable of being fairly estimated, are provable[5]. Examples are:

(a)   A supplier under a contract where the bankrupt has covenanted to purchase goods over a number of years may prove in respect of the goods which were to have been supplied in the future[6].

(b)   The beneficiary of a covenant to pay a sum of money out of the covenantor's estate within six months of his death may prove in respect of the covenant[7].

(c)   An annuitant may prove for the value of his annuity[8].

1   IA 1986, s 382(1)(b).
2   IA 1986, s 322(3).
3   Ie following an application under the IA 1986, s 303 by the trustee for directions or by any person dissatisfied with the trustee's decision in respect of the debt.
4   IA 1986, s 322(4).
5   *Hardy v Forthergill* (1888) 13 App Cas 351 at 360, 361, HL.
6   *Re Allen & Co, ex p Strong and Hanbury* (1893) 10 Morr 84; *Re Moore and Thomas, ex p Beer* (1868) 18 LT 418.
7   *Barnett v King* [1891] 1 Ch 4, CA.
8   *Re Gieve, ex p Shaw* (1899) 80 LT 737, 6 Mans 249, CA, where the goodwill of a business was sold in consideration of an annuity not expressly payable out of the profits of the business. The court held that account should be taken of the precarious nature of the business which would fund the annuity when assessing the amount of the proof.

The rule against double proof

22.13 A creditor may not prove in respect of every claim which he has against the bankrupt if by doing so he submits more than one proof in respect of the same debt or liability. There is a well-established principle against 'double proof' which applies even where there are separate contracts in respect of the same debt. The reason for the rule is, as stated by Mellish LJ in *Re Oriental Commercial Bank, Ex p European Bank*[1]:

'... that an insolvent estate ought not to pay two dividends in respect of the same debt appears to me to be a perfectly sound principle. If it were not so, a creditor could always manage, by getting his debtor to enter into several distinct contracts with different people for the same debt, to obtain higher dividends than the other creditors, and perhaps get his debt paid in full. I apprehend that is what the law does not allow; the true principle is, that there is only to be one dividend in respect of what is in substance the same debt, although there may be two separate contracts.'

1   (1871) 7 Ch App 99, at p 103.

22.14 So by way of example where a bankrupt charged his house direct to a mortgagee and conveyed the equity of redemption to his wife subject to a covenant that he would discharge the mortgage liability, it was held that for both the mortgagee and the wife to prove in respect of their separate rights to have the mortgage liability discharge would constitute double proof[1]. The most common, though not the only[2], situation in which the rule against double proof applies is that of suretyship. A surety will have a contingent claim against an insolvent principal debtor in the event that the surety pays the debt to the creditor, but the surety may not make that claim until the debt is paid in full. Accordingly the surety may not prove in the debtor's bankruptcy in any way which is in competition with the creditor[3]. However, where the surety has guaranteed part only of a debt, he may prove once he has paid that part in full[4]. The position of a surety who has guaranteed a specified part of a debt is to be contrasted with the surety who guarantees the whole debt subject to a limit. The surety in this situation may not prove in competition with the creditor even after paying his liability under the guarantee in full[5]. The difference in the surety's position has been explained by reference to there being separate contracts with the debtor in respect of the part of the debt which is guaranteed and the part which is not, and by invoking the doctrine of subrogation on behalf of the surety who has paid his obligations in full in respect of the specified part of the debt he has guaranteed[6]. However, in *Barclays Bank v TSOG Trust Fund Ltd*[7], Oliver LJ suggested that the test for the applicability of the rule against double proof was not to be found in an analysis of overlapping liabilities resulting from separate and independent contracts, but 'a much broader one which transcends a close jurisprudential analysis of the persons by and to whom the duties are owed. It is simply whether the two competing claims are, in *substance*, claims for payment of the same debt twice over.'

1   *Re Hoey, ex p Hoey* (1918) 88 LJKB 273; see also *Deering v Bank of Ireland* (1886) 12 App Cas 20, HL, and *Steamship Enterprises of Panama Inc, Liverpool (Owners) v Ousel, The Liverpool (No 2)* [1963] P 64. The principle was discussed in *Barclays Bank Ltd v TOSG Trust Fund Ltd* [1984] AC 626, [1984] 1 All ER 628, CA and HL.
2   See e g *Steamship Enterprises of Panama Inc, Liverpool (Owners) v Ousel, The Liverpool (No 2)* [1963] P 64.
3   See e g *Re Sass* [1896] 2 QB 12.
4   See *Re Sass* [1896] 2 QB 12 at p 15, and *Barclays Bank Ltd v TOSG Trust Fund Ltd* [1984] AC 626, [1984] 1 All ER 628.
5   See the cases cited above and *Ellis v Emmanuel* (1876) 1 Ex D 157.
6   See e g *Westpac Banking Corpn v Gollin & Co Ltd* [1988] VR 397, 405–406.
7   [1984] AC 626 at p 636D.

22.15 *In Re Polly Peck International plc*[1] Robert Walker J conveniently set out some elementary rules as to suretyship in the following terms (adapted to bankruptcy):

(1)   So long as any money remains due under the guaranteed loan, the principal creditor can proceed against either the debtor or (after any requisite notice) the surety.
(2)   If the debtor and the surety are both bankrupt, C can prove in both bankruptcies and hope to receive a dividend in both, subject to not recovering in all more than 100p in the £. This is sometimes called a 'double-dipping' and is permissible.
(3)   The surety's trustee in bankruptcy can prove in the debtor's bankruptcy (under an express or implied right of indemnity) only if the surety has paid the principal creditor in full (so that the principal creditor drops out of the matter and the surety stands in his place).
(4)   As a corollary of (3), the surety's trustee in bankruptcy cannot, because of the rule against double proof, prove in the debtor's bankruptcy in any way that is in competition with the principal creditor; though the surety has a contingent claim against the debtor (in the event of the principal creditor being paid off by the surety) the surety may not make that claim if it has not in fact paid off the principal creditor.

1   [1996] 2 All ER 433, [1996] 1 BCLC 428

22.16 As Robert Walker J explained, the underlying basis of the rule is that 'the surety's contingent claim is not regarded as an independent, free-standing debt, but only as a reflection of the "real" debt – that in respect of the money which the principal creditor had loaned to the principal debtor'.

22.17 Where tripartite contractual arrangements are made under which payments are made by a third party referable to the outstanding liability of a debtor to a creditor but not in discharge of such liability, on a true analysis the relationship between the parties is not analogous to that of a debtor-creditor-surety relationship and the rule against double proof is not applicable[1]. Where trust money entrusted to a firm for investment has been converted by it, proof may be allowed both against the firm's estate on its contract to invest or restore, and also against that of a partner who was trustee, on his contract to perform his trust[2].

[1]   *Re Parkfield Group plc, Bridisco Ltd v Jordan* [1997] BCC 778.
[2]   *Re Parkers, ex p Sheppard* (1887) 19 QBD 84; *Re Lake, ex p Howe Trustees* [1903] 1 KB 439.

Foreign creditors

22.18   There is no general bar on a foreign creditor proving in the bankruptcy of an English bankrupt in England, and on his discharge from bankruptcy an English creditor is released, so far as the English court is concerned, from his liability to foreign creditors[1]. The EC Insolvency Regulation overrides any rule preventing a creditor who has his habitual residence, domicile or registered office in a Member State to whom the regulation applies from proving[2]. The Cross-Border Insolvency Regulations 2006 provide similarly that foreign creditors are to have the same rights of participation as creditors in Great Britain[3].

[1]   *Royal Bank of Scotland v Cuthbert* (1813) 1 Rose 462; *Edwards v Ronald* (1830) 1 Knapp 259, 12 ER 317; *Armani v Castrique* (1844) 13 M & W 443, 153 ER 185; *New Zealand Loan and Mercantile Agency Co v Morrison* [1898] AC 349, PC; *Swiss Bank Corpn v Boehmische Industrial Bank* [1923] 1 KB 673.
[2]   EC Insolvency Regulation, art 39.
[3]   Cross-Border Insolvency Regulations 2006, SI 2006/1030, reg 3(1), Sch 1, art 13.

Hotchpot

22.19   At common law, where a creditor, in proceedings for the administration of the bankrupt's property abroad, had received any sum which would in England be divisible amongst the bankrupt's creditors generally, that receipt had to be brought into account before he was allowed to prove in a bankruptcy proceeding in England[1]. Bringing the receipt into account means that until all the other creditors of the same rank had received the same proportion of their debt as the creditor in question had received by the payment in the foreign proceedings, that creditor could not receive any dividend in the English bankruptcy. The hotchpot rule applies only however to foreign assets which would have been divisible amongst the bankrupt's creditors had they been available to the trustee in England. Therefore, for

22.19 *Proof of debts*

example, if under the foreign law the creditor is a secured creditor the value of his security need not be taken into account; the creditor may value the security and prove for the balance of his debt against the English estate[2].

1 *Re Douglas, ex p Wilson* (1872) 7 Ch App 490; *Re Hooper, Banco de Portugal v Waddell* (1880) 5 App Cas 161, HL; *Cleaver v Delta American Reinsurance Co* [2001] 2 AC 328.
2 *Re Somes, ex p De Lemos* (1896) 3 Mans 131, and note *Re Suidair International Airways Ltd* [1951] Ch 165, [1950] 2 All ER 920.

22.20 The EC Insolvency Regulation imposes a rule to the same effect, precluding a creditor who has received a dividend on his claim in an insolvency proceeding in one State from obtaining a dividend in proceedings in another State before creditors of the same ranking or category have obtained an equivalent dividend[1]. A similar rule is contained in the Cross-Border Insolvency Regulations 2006[2].

1 EC Insolvency Regulation, art 20(2).
2 Cross-Border Insolvency Regulations 2006, SI 2006/1030, reg 3(1), Sch 1, art 32.

Foreign revenue and social security claims

22.21 A general rule of English private international law precludes the enforcement of foreign revenue and penal laws[1]. However, as regards foreign tax and social security authorities this rule is no longer absolute. Where the EC Insolvency Regulation applies, it no longer applies as regards the tax authorities and social security authorities of Member States[2]. Further, under the Cross-Border Insolvency Regulations 2006 a proof cannot be challenged solely on the ground that it is a claim by a foreign tax or social security authority although it may be challenged on the basis that it is a penalty[3]. And, pursuant to art 6 of the Model Law, the court can refuse to take action if the action would be manifestly contrary to public policy in Great Britain; so, if a trustee in bankruptcy were rightly to reject a proof on a ground of public policy, the court ought to refuse to overturn his decision on appeal by the claiming authority[4].

1 *Government of India, Ministry of Finance (Revenue Division) v Taylor* [1955] AC 491, [1955] 1 All ER 292, HL; *Metal Industries (Salvage) Ltd v ST Harle* 1962 SLT 114; *Re Gibbons, ex p Walter* [1960] Ir Jur Rep 60; and see *Brokaw v Seatrain UK Ltd* [1971] 2 QB 476, [1971] 2 All ER 98, CA. See also *Re State of Norway's Application* [1987] QB 433, [1986] 3 WLR 452, CA; *Williams and Humbert Ltd v W & H Trade Marks (Jersey) Ltd* [1986] AC 368, [1985] 2 All ER 208, HL.
2 EC Insolvency Regulation, art 39.
3 Cross-Border Insolvency Regulations 2006, SI 2006/1030, reg 3(1), Sch 1, art 13(3).
4 Cross-Border Insolvency Regulations 2006, SI 2006/1030, reg 3(1), Sch 1, art 6.

Proof of residual claim where law has intervened

22.22 Where the bankrupt has given a preference to a creditor which has been set aside, the creditor may prove for his original debt with the other creditors[1]. Where a trustee successfully challenges as a penalty a sum specified in a contract as payable for breach by the debtor the creditor may prove for such sum as represents the actual damage sustained[2]. In cases where a bankruptcy order is made against a debtor who is insured against liabilities to third parties, the bankrupt's rights against the insurers in respect of the liability are transferred to and vest in the third party[3]. Should the insurer's liability to the bankrupt be less than the bankrupt's liability to the third party, the third party may prove for the balance due to him. A release given to a debtor in a deed of arrangement which is afterwards superseded by a bankruptcy will not prevent proof in the bankruptcy, unless it is clear that it was intended that it should do so[4].

[1]   *Re Stephenson, ex p Official Receiver* (1888) 20 QBD 540, and see *Re Tonnies, ex p Bishop* (1873) 8 Ch App 718.
[2]   *Re Newman, ex p Capper* (1876) 4 Ch D 724, CA. See also *Wallis v Smith* (1882) 21 Ch D 243, CA, and *Wilson v Love* [1896] 1 QB 626, CA.
[3]   See **Chapter 28** below.
[4]   *Re Stephenson, ex p Official Receiver* (1888) 20 QBD 540, DC, and see *Re Clement, ex p Goas* (1886) 3 Morr 153, CA; *Re Stock, ex p Amos* (1896) 3 Mans 324.

Secured debts

22.23 Proof is not available in so far as a debt is secured unless the security is given up. A debt is secured for bankruptcy purposes to the extent that the person to whom the debt is owed holds any security for the debt over the property of the person by whom the debt is owed[1]. Security includes a mortgage, charge, lien or any other security but does not include a lien on books, papers or other records except to the extent that they consist of documents which give a title to property and are held as such[2]. The security must be held over the debtor's property, and accordingly a creditor who holds security for his debt over the property of a third party is not a secured creditor for bankruptcy purposes. Neither does a guarantee of the bankrupt's debts by a third party constitute security[3]. A landlord's right of re-entry does not make him a secured creditor of his insolvent tenant[4]. If a secured creditor realises his security, he may prove for the balance of his debt, after deducting the amount realised[5]. If a secured creditor voluntarily surrenders his security for the general benefit of creditors, he may prove for his whole debt, as if it were unsecured[6]. If a secured creditor omits to disclose his security in his proof of debt, he must surrender his security for the general benefit of creditors, unless the court on his application relieves him from the effect of this provision on the ground that the omission was inadvertent or the result of honest mistake[7].

[1]   IA 1986, s 383(2).
[2]   IA 1986, s 383(2), (4).
[3]   *Re a Debtor (No 310 of 1988), ex p Debtor v Arab Bank Ltd* [1989] 2 All ER 42, [1989] 1 WLR 452.
[4]   *Christopher Moran Holdings plc v Bairstow* [2000] 2 AC 172, at 186C.
[5]   IR 1986, r 6.109(1).
[6]   IR 1986, r 6.109(2).
[7]   IR 1986, r 6.116(1).

Statute-barred debts

22.24 A debt barred by the Limitation Acts is not provable in bankruptcy[1]. However, a creditor's rights in respect of any lien held by him may be enforceable, even though the debt is barred[2]. Except for the petitioning creditor's debt time ceases to run for limitation purposes in respect of provable debts on the making of the bankruptcy order[3]. The petition is an 'action' for the purposes of the Limitation Act 1980 and accordingly time stops running on the petitioning creditor's debt at the date of presentation of the petition[4]. The court may refuse to admit proof of a debt if the creditor's delay before proving inhibits a proper inquiry as to whether it should be admitted for proof[5]. Where time has begun to run before the bankruptcy, it continues to run in respect of any rights to pursue any other remedies which are not caught by the bankruptcy proceedings[6]. It appears that neither the listing by the bankrupt of a debt in his statement of affairs[7], nor his answers at his examination[8], may amount to an acknowledgement sufficient to postpone the running of time for the purpose of proceedings apart from the bankruptcy. A payment of a dividend in bankruptcy will not amount to a part payment, so as to prevent the running of time in favour of the debtor[9].

[1] *Ex p Dewdney, ex p Seaman* (1809) 15 Ves 479; *Re Dewdney, ex p Roffey* (1815) 2 Rose 245.
[2] *Re Hepburn, ex p Smith* (1884) 14 QBD 394 at 400.
[3] *Re Westby, ex p Lancaster Banking Corpn* (1879) 10 Ch D 776 at 784; *Re Crosley, Munns v Burn* (1887) 35 Ch D 266, CA; *Re Cullwick, ex p London Senior Official Receiver* [1918] 1 KB 646 (right of trustee in prior bankruptcy to prove in subsequent bankruptcy) and see *Re General Rolling Stock Co Ltd* (1872) 7 Ch App 646; *Re Cases of Taffs Well Ltd* [1992] Ch 179.
[4] Cf *Re Karnos Property Co Ltd* [1989] BCLC 340; *Re Cases of Taffs Well Ltd* [1992] Ch 179.
[5] *Re Tollemache, ex p Revell* (1884) 13 QBD 720, CA, applied in *Re Browne (a bankrupt), ex p Official Receiver v Thompson* [1960] 2 All ER 625, [1960] 1 WLR 692; *Re Tollemache, ex p Edwards* (1884) 14 QBD 415, CA.
[6] *Re Benzon, Bower v Chetwynd* [1914] 2 Ch 68 at 75, 76, CA; *Cotterell v Price* [1960] 3 All ER 315, [1960] 1 WLR 1097, where a mortgagee lost his right to recover possession but may not have lost his right to prove on the covenant.
[7] *Everett v Robertson* (1858) 1 E & E 16; *Pott v Clegg* (1847) 16 M & W 321; *Courtenay v Williams* (1844) 3 Hare 539; affd (1846) 15 LJ Ch 204; approved in *M'Donnell v Broderick* [1896] 2 IR 136 at 167; *Re Levey, ex p Topping* (1865) 4 De GJ & Sm 551 (scheduling of debt to deed of arrangement not sufficient to entitle creditor to prove in subsequent bankruptcy). These decisions were decided on the ground that an acknowledgment in respect of a simple contract debt must import a promise to pay. Under the Limitation Act 1980, ss 29(5), 30, 31(6) such a promise need not be imported for an effective acknowledgment. However, the debtor's statement of affairs is a compulsory document which must contain a list of all his creditors and be submitted to the official receiver: see the IA 1986, s 272 (debtor's petition), s 288 (creditor's petition). The official receiver is not the agent of the creditor and irrespective of authority the provisions of the Limitation Act 1980, s 30 as to 'acknowledgment' do not appear to be satisfied merely by the inclusion of a debt in a statement of affairs.
[8] *Courtenay v Williams* (1844) 3 Hare 539; affd (1846) 15 LJ Ch 204.
[9] See *Davies v Edwards* (1851) 7 Exch 22 (dividend in insolvency paid to holder of promissory note; held not to have preserved right of action on note); *Re Levey, ex p Topping* (1865) 4 De GJ & Sm 551 (payment of dividend under deed of arrangement held not to have preserved right of proof in subsequent bankruptcy); *Taylor v Hollard* [1902] 1 KB 676 (action on English judgment; right of action held not to have been preserved by payment to claimant by foreign sequestrators of defendant's estate in respect of foreign judgment on same matter). Again however it should be noted that these cases were decided on the principle that a promise to pay the remainder must be imported if the part payment were to be effective which is no longer the law.

Unenforceable transactions

22.25 Debts founded on an illegal consideration are not provable[1]. Proof may be allowed in part where the consideration was in part legal[2]. Proof was allowed where a genuine debt existed, founded on an independent contract for a bank overdraft, antecedent to an illegal arrangement whereby forged bills were deposited as security[3]. A claim which is not supported by consideration may not be proved and the court may look behind a judgment obtained by consent or default and refuse its acceptance for proof if there was no consideration to support the claim[4]. Where on a proper construction of a contract a stipulation that certain sums be paid in the event of breach by way of ascertained damages is held to be a penalty[5], proof may be made only for the actual damage sustained[6].

[1] *Ex p Thompson* (1746) 1 Atk 125; *Re Scott, ex p Bell* (1813) 1 M & S 751; *Re Aldebert & Co, ex p Schmaling* (1817) Buck 93; *Re Grazebrook, ex p Chavasse* (1865) 4 De GJ & Sm 655.
[2] *Ex p Mather* (1797) 3 Ves 373; *Ex p Bulmer, Ex p Ellis* (1807) 13 Ves 313. However, as to the effect of the consideration being partly illegal see *Kearney v Whitehaven Colliery Co* [1893] 1 QB 700, CA.
[3] *Re Guerrier, ex p Leslie* (1882) 20 Ch D 131, CA.
[4] *Re Onslow, ex p Kibble* (1875) 10 Ch App 373 (default judgment); *Re Blyth* (1881) 17 Ch D 315; and *Lennox, Re, ex p Lennox* (1886) 16 QBD 315 (consent judgment).
[5] See *Dunlop Pneumatic Tyre Co Ltd v New Garage and Motor Co Ltd* [1915] AC 79 especially at 86–88; *Bridge v Campbell Discount Co Ltd* [1962] AC 600, [1962] 1 All ER 385.
[6] *Re Newman, ex p Capper* (1876) 4 Ch D 724, CA, *Wallis v Smith* (1882) 21 Ch D 243, CA; and *Wilson v Love* [1896] 1 QB 626, CA.

22.26 Proof may be allowed on a contract made abroad, even though because of some defect, such as want of registration of the contract, no remedy lies on it abroad[1]. A contract made with one of its members by an unregistered society requiring registration as a company under the Companies Act 1985[2] may give a right to prove where the member has recognised, acquiesced in and ratified the subsequent registration of the company[3].

[1] *Re Melbourn, ex p Melbourn* (1870) 6 Ch App 64. See also *Thurburn v Steward* (1871) LR 3 PC 478.
[2] Under the Companies Act 1985, s 716.
[3] *Re Thomas, ex p Poppleton* (1884) 14 QBD 379.

Agreements in fraud of other creditors

22.27 A right of proof may be affected or lost where it is based on an agreement the effect of which is a fraud on the other creditors[1]. Where a debtor accepts bills drawn on him by his agent who then sells the bills on for less than their face value to a purchaser who is aware of the debtor's financial difficulties that purchaser may only prove for the amount that he paid for them[2]. A voluntary bond, which had been entered into by the debtor in good faith is not by reason only of its voluntary nature a fraud on the creditors generally and will be provable equally with the bankrupt's other debts[3].

1   *Re Gomersall* (1875) 1 Ch D 137, CA; affd as *Jones v Gordon* (1877) 2 App Cas 616, HL. See also *Hall v Dyson* (1852) 17 QB 785; *Murray v Reeves* (1828) 8 B & C 421; *Kearley v Thomson* (1890) 24 QBD 742, CA; *Re McHenry, McDermott v Boyd, Levita's Claim* [1894] 3 Ch 365, CA; *Re Stewart, ex p Pottinger* (1878) 8 Ch D 621, CA; *Re Myers, ex p Myers* [1908] 1 KB 941.
2   *Re Gomersall* (1875) 1 Ch D 137, CA; affd sub nom *Jones v Gordon* (1877) 2 App Cas 616, HL.
3   *Re Stewart, ex p Pottinger* (1878) 8 Ch D 621, CA; *Re Coates, ex p Scott* (1892) 9 Morr 87.

Interest

22.28 Where a bankruptcy debt expressly bears interest, any interest due prior to the commencement of the bankruptcy may be proved as part of the debt[1]. Interest may also be included as part of the provable debt even though not previously agreed or reserved[2] where:

(1)   the debt is due under a written instrument and is payable on a certain date, in which event interest may be claimed for the period between that date and the date of the bankruptcy order[3]; or

(2)   in cases where the debt is not due under a written instrument, the creditor has made a written demand for payment of the debt and has given notice that interest will be charged from the date of demand to the date of payment. The demand must have been made before the presentation of the bankruptcy petition. The creditor may then prove for interest accruing between the date of the demand and the date of the bankruptcy order[4].

1   IA 1986, s 322(2).
2   IR 1986, r 6.113(1).
3   IR 1986, r 6.113(2).
4   IR 1986, r 6.113(3), (4).

22.29 In either case the rate of interest which may be claimed by the creditor may not exceed the rate applicable under the Judgments Act 1838, s 17 on the date of the bankruptcy order[1]. Where the rate of interest has been agreed contractually that rate may be proved for by the creditor, subject always to the trustee's right to apply to reduce the rate on the grounds that it represents an extortionate credit transaction[2].

1   IR 1986, r 6.113(5).
2   IA 1986, s 343.

22.30 After the commencement of the bankruptcy all debts carry interest which will only be payable as dividend in the event that all ordinary debts are paid in full[1]. The rate of interest will be either judgment rate[2] or the relevant contractual rate, if greater[3].

1   IA 1986, s 328(4).
2   Ie the rate applicable under the Judgments Act 1838, s 17 on the date of the bankruptcy order.
3   IA 1986, s 328(5).

Treatment of delayed proofs

22.31 There is no time limit for submitting proofs or for the trustee to investigate them once submitted. However, a proof submitted after years of delay after further funds have become available to the estate and the death of the bankrupt will arouse suspicion even when based on a judgment, and may be rejected if it is too late to carry out an investigation of the underlying transaction[1]. Equally a trustee should not delay in his investigation, and the court may not allow him to reopen a proof previously admitted if he wishes to reconsider the proof after the estate acquires further funds years after the proof was submitted[2].

---

[1] See *Re Tollemache, ex p Revell* (1884) 13 QBD 720, CA; *Re Tollemache, ex p Anderson* (1885) 14 QBD 606, CA; *Re Tollemache, ex p Bonham* (1885) 14 QBD 604.
[2] *Re Browne, ex p Official Receiver v Thompson* [1960] 2 All ER 625.

C PARTICULAR KINDS OF DEBTS

22.32 The following paragraphs discuss points which may arise on various kinds of debts, arranged alphabetically, for which proof may be made in the bankruptcy.

Annuities

22.33 An annuity is a contingent liability[1], the value of which may be estimated for proof[2]. Examples of annuities which have been held to be capable of valuation and therefore provable include:

(a) an annuity to a wife in lieu of repayment by her husband of money lent by her for his business[3];

(b) an annuity to a retiring partner, determinable on breach of covenant not to trade within a limited area[4];

(c) an annuity payable for so long as the bankrupt continued to work a salt pit which might cease at any time[5]; and

(d) an annuity payable until the annuitant should do some act whereby the annuity, if belonging to him absolutely, would have become vested in another[6].

---

[1] See for example *Greeves v Tofield* (1880) 14 Ch D 563, CA where an unregistered annuity charged on land was held to be valid against a trustee in bankruptcy.
[2] Estimates have been made of the value of an annuity defeasible on a woman's marrying again, *Re Blakemore, ex p Blakemore* (1877) 5 Ch D 372, CA or on a resumption of cohabitation by husband and wife, or on dissolution of marriage by any future act of either, or on the wife leading an unchaste life, *Re Batey, ex p Neal* (1880) 14 Ch D 579, CA; *Victor v Victor* [1912] 1 KB 247, CA; *McQuiban v McQuiban* [1913] P 208. As to the valuation of a tax-free annuity secured by the covenant of a deceased person see *Re Viscount Rothermere, Mellors, Basden & Co v Coutts & Co* [1945] Ch 72, [1944] 2 All ER 593.
[3] *Re Slade, Crewkerne United Breweries Ltd v Slade* [1921] 1 Ch 160.
[4] *Re Jackson, ex p Jackson* (1872) 27 LT 696.
[5] *Re Borron, ex p Parratt* (1836) 1 Deac 696.
[6] *Re Sinclair, Allen v Sinclair, Hodgkins v Sinclair* [1897] 1 Ch 921.

22.34 In estimating the value, all proper contingencies should be taken into account[1]. If the annuitant dies after the receipt of a dividend, the proof or dividend cannot be disturbed even where the dividend is greater than the amount which the bankrupt would have had to pay had he remained solvent[2]. Where the annuitant dies before the proof has been dealt with, the value of the annuity will be taken to be the amount of the payments falling due up to the date of the death[3].

1   *Re Grieves, ex p Pearce* (1879) 13 Ch D 262 at 265, CA. In *Re Grieves*, the annuity to be valued was a covenant by the bankrupt to pay his estranged wife an annuity during their joint lives to cease if they resumed cohabitation. *Re Gieve, ex p Shaw* (1899) 80 LT 359 (reversed on another point (1899) 80 LT 359) where the precarious nature of the business which was to fund the annuity had to be taken into account.
2   *Re Pannell, ex p Bates* (1879) 11 Ch D 914, CA. Cf *Re Miller, ex p Wardley* (1877) 6 Ch D 790, where the bankrupt died before any dividend was paid.
3   *Re Dodds, ex p Vaughan's Executors* (1890) 25 QBD 529. See also *Re Bridges, Hill v Bridges* (1881) 17 Ch D 342; *Re Northern Counties of England Fire Insurance Co, MacFarlane's Claim* (1880) 17 Ch D 337; *Re Beecham's Settlement, Johnson v Beecham* [1934] Ch 183.

Calls on shares

22.35 A company, and if insolvent its liquidator acting on its behalf[1], may prove against a bankrupt's estate for the estimated value of the bankrupt's liability to future calls on partly paid shares, as well as for calls already made[2]. Where shares are disclaimed, proof may be allowed for the whole balance unpaid on them, deducting the value of anything accruing to the company by reason of the disclaimer[3]. Where the bankrupt is under contract to take up shares, and this contract is disclaimed, the company may only prove in respect of damages for breach of contract[4]. If a contributory becomes bankrupt, either before or after he has been placed on the list of contributories, his trustee in bankruptcy represents him for all purposes of the winding up, and is a contributory accordingly[5]. The trustee may be called upon to admit to proof against the bankrupt's estate any money due from the bankrupt in respect of his liability to contribute to the company's assets[6].

1   *Re Mercantile Mutual Marine Insurance Association* (1883) 25 Ch D 415; *Re McMahon, Fuller v McMahon* [1900] 1 Ch 173. As for a liquidator acting on behalf of the company in proving in a bankruptcy, see the IA 1986, s 167(1)(b), Sch 4, para 8.
2   IA 1986, s 82(4).
3   *Re Hallett, ex p National Insurance Co* (1894) 1 Mans 380.
4   *Re Hooley, ex p United Ordnance and Engineering Co Ltd* [1899] 2 QB 579.
5   IA 1986, s 82(1), (2).
6   IA 1986, s 82(3).

22.36 Where a company under its articles of association has forfeited shares for non-payment of money due on allotment and for calls, and the articles provide that notwithstanding forfeiture the ex-shareholder is liable to pay all calls or other money owing upon the shares at the time of the forfeiture, then, if the shares are subsequently sold and re-allotted to other persons at a loss, the company, on the subsequent bankruptcy of the ex-shareholder, is entitled to prove only for the actual loss suffered, that is, the difference between the amount received on the re-allotment of the forfeited shares and the amount due at the date of the forfeiture[1].

1   *Re Bolton, ex p North British Artificial Silk Ltd* [1930] 2 Ch 48.

22.37 If a dividend is paid to the company which is less than 100 pence in the pound, its payment does not entitle the bankrupt's estate to rank as a fully paid shareholder in the company's liquidation[1].

1   *Re West Coast Gold Fields Ltd, Rowe's Trustee's Claim* [1906] 1 Ch 1, CA.

Costs of legal proceedings

Where the creditor is claimant

22.38 A claimant's costs in an action to recover a sum which does not give rise to a provable debt, are not themselves provable, unless judgment has been entered before the bankruptcy order with an order for costs to be paid[1]. It does not matter that the costs have not been agreed or assessed at the date of the bankruptcy order[2]. Where the action is in respect of a claim which is provable, provided the claimant has obtained judgment prior to the bankruptcy order, or is in a position to enter judgment as of right as a result of the defendant debtor having failed to acknowledge service or serve a defence, or having admitted liability by paying money into court, then the claimant's costs are provable[3]. In disputed proceedings against the debtor which are pending on the date of the bankruptcy order the claimant may have a choice. He may accept the stay which is automatically imposed on his action[4] and prove for his debt, in which event he will be unable to prove for his costs of the action to the date of the bankruptcy order[5]; alternatively he may seek the leave of the court to proceed with the action and hope to obtain an award of costs against the estate. The claimant may not however seek to prove for his costs incurred up to the date of the bankruptcy order as a contingent debt[6]. Except where interim awards of costs have been made payable in any event, liability to costs of an action does not accrue during the course of the action. It is only when an order of costs is made that such a liability arises. Accordingly an order of costs which might have been made against the bankrupt in the future had the action proceeded to finality cannot be a debt or liability of the bankrupt by reason of any obligation incurred before the commencement of the bankruptcy[7].

1   *Re Newman, ex p Brooke* (1876) 3 Ch D 494, CA; *Re Bluck, ex p Bluck* (1887) 57 LT 419; and *Re British Gold Fields of West Africa* [1899] 2 Ch 7, CA, where Lindley MR reviews the relevant principles.
2   *Re Fletcher, ex p Simpson* (1789) 3 Bro CC 46, 29 ER 400, and *Lewis v Piercy* (1788) 126 ER 18.
3   See the principles laid down in *Re Duffield, ex p Peacock* (1873) 8 Ch App 682, and the statement by Lindley MR of the rules as to proof for costs of proceedings taken against a bankrupt, in *Re British Gold Fields of West Africa* [1899] 2 Ch 7, CA.
4   By IA 1986, s 285(3).
5   *Re Pitchford* [1924] 2 Ch 260 a decision of the Divisional Court based on the definition of provable debt in the Bankruptcy Act 1914, s 30(3), but which appears to hold good under IA 1986, s 382(1). The claimant's costs in the pending action do not constitute a 'debt or liability to which the bankrupt is subject at the commencement of the bankruptcy', IA 1986, s 382(1)(a).

⁶   *Vint v Hudspith* (1885) 30 Ch D 24; *Re A Debtor (No 68 of 1911)* [1911] 2 KB 652.
⁷   IA 1986, s 382(1)(b).

Where the bankrupt is claimant

22.39 Where an action brought by a person subsequently adjudged bankrupt is unsuccessful, but neither judgment for the defendant on the claim nor an order for costs is given against him until after the bankruptcy order, the defendant's costs are not provable¹. If in such an action there has been a judgment on the claim or a judgment or an order for costs before the bankruptcy order, the costs will be provable even though they have not been assessed and judgment has not been formally entered².

¹   *Vint v Hudspith* (1885) 30 Ch D 24, CA; *Re Bluck, ex p Bluck* (1887) 57 LT 419; *Re British Gold Fields of West Africa* [1899] 2 Ch 7, CA.
²   *Re Duffield, ex p Peacock* (1873) 8 Ch App 682; *Re British Gold Fields of West Africa* [1899] 2 Ch 7, CA. As to the estimate of costs for voting purposes see *Re Dummelow, ex p Ruffle* (1873) 8 Ch App 997.

Arbitration

22.40 On a reference by consent to arbitration, the costs of the reference are provable, even though not awarded until after the bankruptcy order¹.

¹   *Re Smith, ex p Edwards* (1886) 3 Morr 179. See also *Re Pickering, ex p Harding* (1854) 5 De GM & G 367.

Counsel's fees

22.41 The old rule that counsel's fees are deemed to be an honorarium¹ and counsel has no right of proof for his fees, whether for litigious or non-litigious work, against the client's estate², is abolished by the Courts and Legal Services Act 1990³. There appears to be no entitlement for counsel to prove in the bankruptcy of a solicitor who becomes bankrupt having received fees due to counsel⁴. It has been suggested, however⁵, that the client should prove in the bankruptcy for return of the fees paid by him and then transmit the proceeds directly to counsel. If however counsel's fees are received by the trustee after bankruptcy, they should be paid to counsel⁶. If the trustee receives a lump sum from the client in settlement of the solicitor's whole bill of costs, it may be that a proportionate amount of it should be paid to counsel for his fees⁷.

¹   See *Rondel v Worsley* [1969] 1 AC 191, [1967] 3 All ER 993, HL.
²   *Mostyn v Mostyn* (1870) 5 Ch App 457; *Rondel v Worsley* [1969] 1 AC 191, [1967] 3 All ER 993, HL.
³   Courts and Legal Services Act 1990, s 61(1).
⁴   *Wells v Wells* [1914] P 157 at 166, CA; *Re Sandiford (No 2), Italo-Canadian Corpn Ltd v Sandiford* [1935] Ch 681; both those decisions were approved in *Rondel v Worsley* [1969] 1 AC 191, [1967] 3 All ER 993, HL, see, eg at 279 and at 1031, per Lord Upjohn, but these cases are all ripe for reconsideration.
⁵   See Clauson J in *Re Sandiford (No 2), Italo-Canadian Corpn Ltd v Sandiford* [1935] Ch 681 at p 692.
⁶   *Re Hall* (1856) 2 Jur NS 1076; see further *Wells v Wells* [1914] P 157, CA.
⁷   *Re Clift, ex p Colquhoun* (1890) 38 WR 688.

22.42 In the case of direct access work, counsel will presumably enter into an enforceable agreement with his client and will be able to prove in the client's bankruptcy as would any other creditor[1].

1   Subject to any rules promulgated by the General Council of the Bar.

Executors

22.43 One of several executors may prove on behalf of himself and the others[1]. If an executor refuses to submit a proof, a residuary legatee or other person interested may apply to the court and be given leave to prove subject to a direction that any dividend be paid to the executor[2]. Where a sole executor becomes bankrupt, he cannot prove in his representative capacity against himself without a court order, as this would infringe the principle that the assets of the estate should not come into the hands of the bankrupt[3]. In such a case, a legatee may apply for leave to prove, and the court will give directions as to the disposal of any dividends received[4]. A proof may be made by the legatee in respect of a legacy against an executor who has committed a devastavit[5].

1   *Re Manning, ex p Smith and Anderdon* (1836) 1 Deac 385; *Re Wright, ex p Phillips* (1837) 2 Deac 334. See *Re Davis, ex p Courtney* (1835) 2 Mont & A 227 (where one of two executors became bankrupt).
2   *Re Strahan, Paul and Bates, ex p Caldwell* (1865) 13 WR 952.
3   *Re Howard and Gibbs, ex p Shaw* (1822) 1 Gl & J 127; *Re Colman, ex p Colman* (1833) 2 Deac & Ch 584.
4   *Re Warne, ex p Moody* (1816) 2 Rose 413; *Re Boyes, ex p Beilby, Re Boyes, ex p Hall and Boyes* (1821) 1 Gl & J 167.
5   *Walcott v Hall* (1788) 2 Bro CC 305; *Re Warne, ex p Moody* (1816) 2 Rose 413.

Gaming debts

22.44 A gaming debt may not be proved in bankruptcy, even after judgment has been obtained in respect of it[1]. The assignee of such a debt is in no better position than the assignor[2]. The position that the gaming debt may not be proved in the bankruptcy is not altered by a subsequent agreement between the parties, the consideration for which is an undertaking to abstain from taking some action detrimental to the debtor. If the enforcement of any subsequent agreement would in fact result in the payment in any form of a sum of money alleged to have been won on a wager no provable debt arises[3]. The courts will look behind the immediate transaction to see whether in fact the debt or liability which is sought to be proved is tainted by gaming. Thus the following liabilities have been held to be unenforceable and therefore not capable of being proved or relied on in bankruptcy:

(a)   An account based on betting transactions[4].
(b)   A security given for losses on such transactions[5].
(c)   Money lent to the bankrupt to game or bet with[6], unless the money was lent for gaming purposes in countries where gaming is not illegal[7].
(d)   Money paid at the bankrupt's request to persons with whom the bankrupt has lost bets[8].

22.44 *Proof of debts*

(e)   A claim for half of a sum of money paid by the claimant to the bankrupt to meet losses on bets made by the bankrupt for him on joint account[9].

(f)   Money paid to a stakeholder at the bankrupt's request to abide the result of a wager, on the terms that the money is to be repaid by the bankrupt if he wins[10], but money deposited with a stakeholder to abide the result of a wager, being recoverable by the depositor before it has been paid over, is provable[11].

[1]   *Re Lopes, ex p Hardway and Topping* (1889) 6 Morr 245. It should be noted however that the judgment was obtained on a summons under RSC Ord 14 (now CPR Pt 24) after the debtor failed to comply with the terms on which he had obtained conditional leave to defend.

[2]   *Re Deerhurst, ex p Seaton* (1891) 8 Morr 97, CA.

[3]   See *Hill v William Hill (Park Lane) Ltd* [1949] AC 530, HL; which disapproved *Re Browne, ex p Martingell* [1904] 2 KB 133, where proof was allowed in respect of bills given as the price of the withdrawal of a complaint which had actually been sent to the debtor's club, is now of very doubtful authority. See also *Coral v Kleyman* [1951] 1 All ER 518.

[4]   *Alberg v Chandler* (1948) 64 TLR 394, approved in *Law v Dearnley* [1950] 1 KB 400, [1950] 1 All ER 124, CA.

[5]   *William Hill (Park Lane) Ltd v Hofman* [1950] 1 All ER 1013.

[6]   *Re Lister, ex p Pyke* (1878) 8 Ch D 754, CA.

[7]   *Saxby v Fulton* [1909] 2 KB 208, CA; *Societe Anonyme des Grands Etablissements de Touquet Paris-Plage v Baumgart* (1927) 96 LJKB 789.

[8]   *Tatam v Reeve* [1893] 1 QB 44, DC; *Woolf v Freeman* [1937] 1 All ER 178.

[9]   *Saffery v Mayer* [1901] 1 KB 11, CA.

[10] *Carney v Plimmer* [1897] 1 QB 634, CA.

[11] *O'Sullivan v Thomas* [1895] 1 QB 698; *Burge v Ashley and Smith Ltd* [1900] 1 QB 744, CA. See also *Shoolbred v Roberts* [1900] 2 QB 497, CA.

22.45 The fact that money lent to the bankrupt has been used to enable him to pay bets which he has lost does not prevent proof[1], provided that it is not a condition of the loan that the borrower must apply it to the payment of a debt or debts incurred by wagering[2]. Money received by an agent for his principal in respect of a wager is also provable[3]. Where a trustee admits a proof based on a gaming debt that proof is improperly admitted[4] and may be expunged[5].

[1]   *Re Lister, ex p Pyke* (1878) 8 Ch D 754, CA; *Re O'Shea, ex p Lancaster* [1911] 2 KB 981, CA.

[2]   *Macdonald v Green* [1951] 1 KB 594, [1950] 2 All ER 1240, CA.

[3]   *De Mattos v Benjamin* (1894) 63 LJQB 248.

[4]   For the purposes of the IR 1986, r 6.107.

[5]   *Re Browne (a bankrupt), ex p Official Receiver v Thompson* [1960] 2 All ER 625, [1960] 1 WLR 692, where however the trustee failed through lack of evidence to expunge a proof admitted many years previously by a former trustee on the basis that it was in respect of a gaming debt because of lack of evidence.

Gratuitous payments

22.46 No payment should in ordinary circumstances be made from the bankrupt's estate in respect of a purely gratuitous claim. The court did however sanction a payment of an ex gratia dividend based upon a fair sum for the services supplied to a claimant who had rendered useful services to a Russian bank and assisted in the protection of its assets[1] after having first rejected the claimant's proof[2]. There is no reason to suppose that the court would not follow this example in appropriate, albeit exceptional, circumstances.

¹   *Re Banque des Marchands de Moscou* [1953] 1 All ER 278, [1953] 1 WLR 172.
²   *Re Banque des Marchands de Moscou, Wilenkin v Liquidator* [1952] 1 All ER 1269.

Negotiable instruments

22.47 The holder of a bill of exchange or promissory note may proceed against all parties liable on the instrument until he has received 100 pence in the pound[1]. The holder may prove in the bankruptcy of any person liable, and need not take into account sums received from other parties after proof until he is paid in full[2]. Payments received or dividends declared before proof must be given credit for when proving[3].

¹   *Re Fothergill, ex p Turquand* (1876) 3 Ch D 445, CA.
²   *Ex p Rushforth* (1805) 10 Ves 409.
³   *Ex p Leers* (1802) 6 Ves 644; *Re Stein, ex p Royal Bank of Scotland* (1815) 2 Rose 197; *Re Watson, ex p Todd* (1815) 2 Rose 202n; *Cooper v Pepys* (1741) 1 Atk 107; *Ex p Rushforth* (1805) 10 Ves 409; *Re Houghton, ex p Tayler* (1857) 1 De G & J 302; *Re Blackburne* (1892) 9 Morr 249; *Re Houlder* [1929] 1 Ch 205.

22.48 Where the creditor is the holder of a bill of exchange which has been accepted by the debtor and indorsed by a third party, that third party is in an analogous position to a guarantor[1]. The creditor may pursue claims against both acceptor and the third party indorser, but may not prove in the bankruptcy of the acceptor without giving credit for any payments received before proof from the third party indorser[2]. Credit does not have to be given however in respect of payments received after the proof has been submitted[3].

¹   *Duncan Fox & Co v North & South Wales Bank* (1880) 6 App Cas 1.
²   *Re Blackburne* (1892) 9 Morr 249.
³   *Re London, Bombay & Mediterranean Bank* (1874) 9 Ch App 686; *Re Houlder* [1929] 1 Ch 205.

22.49 Unless the trustee allows, a proof in respect of money owed on a bill of exchange, promissory note, cheque or other negotiable instrument or security cannot be admitted unless there is produced the instrument or security itself or a copy of it, certified by the creditor or his authorised representative to be a true copy[1].

¹   IR 1986, r 6.108.

Rates and community charge

22.50 A liability to pay community charge under the Local Government Finance Act 1988 on the freeholder of empty property which arises after the bankruptcy order is not a provable debt[1].

¹   *Re Kentish Homes Ltd* [1993] BCLC 1375.

Rent and other payments of a periodical nature

22.51 In the case of rent and other periodical payments the creditor may prove for any amounts due and unpaid up to the date of the bankruptcy order[1]. Where at that date any payment was accruing due, the creditor may prove for so much as would have fallen due at that date, if accruing from day to day[2]. The landlord's right of distress is limited to six months' accrued rent before the commencement of the bankruptcy[3] after taking the benefit of which the landlord may prove for the balance, or if he prefers not to levy distress he may prove for all the arrears of rent.

1   IR 1986, r 4.92(1).
2   IR 1986, r 4.92(2).
3   IA 1986, s 437(1).

22.52 Where the trustee of an insolvent tenant continues to occupy the premises for the benefit of the estate, for example while looking for an assignee who might pay a premium, the landlord is entitled to receive his rent in full during such period as the trustee beneficially occupies the premises, and to have the covenants in the lease performed[1].

1   See generally *Re ABC Coupler and Engineering Co Ltd (No 3)* [1970] 1 All ER 650, [1970] 1 WLR 702. The court considers the liquidator's 'motivation' in holding the lease, and the obligation to pay rent in full extends only for that period after the commencement of the winding up during which the liquidator holds the lease for the benefit of the winding up.

22.53 In proving against the estate of an insolvent tenant in respect of a continuing lease, the landlord is not entitled to claim for the whole of the future rent and other obligations under the remaining term of the lease; he can only prove for the arrears of rent and for breaches of covenant committed before the date of his proof[1]. This principle was explained by Lord Millett[2] as resting on the fact that:

> 'rent is not a simple debt. It is the consideration for the right to remain in possession. The tenant's liability to pay future rent is not *debitum in praesenti solvendum in futuro*. Its existence depends upon future events. Rent in respect of a future rental payment may never become payable at all. Rent payable in future under a subsisting lease cannot be treated as a series of future debts making up a pure income stream.'

1   *Re London and Colonial Co Horsey's Claim* (1868) LR 5 Eq 561; *Re New Oriental Bank Corp (No 2)* [1895] 1 Ch 753; *Metropolis Estates Co Ltd v Wilde* [1940] 2 KB 536, [1940] 3 All ER 522, CA. The landlord would however be entitled to prove in respect of both past and future obligations of the tenant where he was willing to treat the lease as at an end, *Re Panther Lead Co* [1896] 1 Ch 978, and see *Re House Property and Investment Co* [1954] Ch 576, [1953] 2 All ER 1525.
2   In *Re Park Air Services plc, Christopher Moran Holdings Ltd v Bairstow* [2000] 2 AC 172, at 187E.

22.54 His Lordship then drew an analogy with the creditor who has contracted to supply goods or services which have yet to be supplied at the date of insolvency. Such a creditor cannot prove for the sum due under the contract unless it is adopted by the trustee. He has merely the right to prove for the compensation by way of damages he is entitled to on breach of the contract.

22.55 If the trustee disclaims the lease, then the landlord has a statutory right to prove for compensation in respect of the losses caused by the disclaimer[1].

1   See IA 1986, s 315(5).

22.56 In the case of a lease made before 1 January 1996[1], the landlord of a bankrupt who has assigned his lease before becoming bankrupt is entitled to prove in the bankruptcy in respect of the original covenants in the lease which has been assigned[2]. In these circumstances a proof may be lodged for the difference between the market value of the lease at the date of the bankruptcy with the benefit of the original tenant's covenants, and of the same lease without the benefit of those covenants[3].

1   Landlord and Tenant (Covenants) Act 1995, ss 1(1) and 31 and the Landlord and Tenant (Covenants) Act 1995 (Commencement) Order 1995, SI 1995/2963.
2   *Re House Property and Investment Co* [1954] Ch 576, [1953] 2 All ER 1525.
3   *Molit (No 55) Pty Ltd v Lam Soon* [1996] [BPIR] 614, see also *James Smith & Sons (Norwood) Ltd v Goodman* [1936] Ch 216. As the Landlord and Tenant (Covenants) Act 1995 increasingly takes effect on leases, and the landlord is unable to call on assignors, there will no longer be a market value differential for which to prove.

22.57 After a disclaimer of the lease the landlord is deemed to be a creditor of the company in respect of any losses he suffers as a result of the disclaimer[1]. This loss is calculated in accordance with general principles of damages for breach of contract[2]. An under-lessee whose rent was less than that reserved by the original lease and who becomes liable to pay the full rent may prove for the difference between the two[3]. In the case of a lease made before 1 January 1996[4], the assignor of a lease holding a covenant of indemnity from an insolvent assignee may prove in respect of rent payable until the premises can be re-let, for any loss in the letting value, and also for a sum in respect of his liability for dilapidations against which he has been indemnified[5].

1   IA 1986, s 315(5).
2   *Re Park Air Services plc, Christopher Moran Holdings Ltd v Bairstow* [2000] 2 AC 172.
3   *Re Levy, ex p Walton* (1881) 17 Ch D 746, CA; see also *Hardy v Fothergill* (1883) 13 App Cas 351, HL.
4   Landlord and Tenant (Covenants) Act 1995, ss 1(1) and 31 and the Landlord and Tenant (Covenants) Act 1995 (Commencement) Order 1995, SI 1995/2963.
5   *Re Carruthers, ex p Tobit* (1895) 2 Mans 172.

Trustees and beneficiaries

22.58 Where trustees are the proving creditor, they should if possible join in a proof[1].

1   *Re Manning, ex p Smith and Anderdon* (1836) 2 Mont & A 536; *Re Wright, ex p Phillips* (1837) 2 Deac 334.

22.59 Where one of two trustees who have committed a breach of trust becomes bankrupt, proof for the full amount of the trust money lost may be made against the bankrupt's estate, even though a sum by way of compromise has been received from the other trustee[1]. A proof may be allowed both against the separate estate of a defaulting trustee and the joint estate of his firm[2].

[1]   *Edwards v Hood-Barrs* [1905] 1 Ch 20.
[2]   *Re Macfadyen, ex p Vizianagaram Mining Co Ltd* [1908] 2 KB 817, CA.

D GUARANTEES AND SURETYSHIP

Bankruptcy of the principal debtor

The rights of the creditor

22.60 The bankruptcy of the principal debtor does not of itself affect the creditor's rights against the guarantor. The creditor may prove in the bankruptcy for the full balance due to him under the principal debt and may at the same time proceed against the guarantor for the sums due under the guarantee, obtain judgment against the guarantor for any sum outstanding at the date of the judgment, and then proceed to enforce his judgment until he is paid in full from all sources. Neither does the bankrupt debtor's discharge from bankruptcy have any effect on the guarantor's liability[1]. Although he will usually wish to call in the guarantee and proceed against the guarantor, a creditor cannot be obliged to exercise his rights against a guarantor by the trustee in bankruptcy or the other creditors either in law or in equity[2]. A creditor holding a guarantee is not a 'secured creditor' for the purposes of the IA 1986, s 383. He cannot therefore be made to value or surrender the guarantee or charge on the guarantor[3] even where the guarantor has a security on the estate of the principal debtor[4].

[1]   IA 1986, s 281(7).
[2]   *Re Dawes, ex p Kendal* (1811) 1 Rose 71.
[3]   As for valuing and surrendering securities see the IR 1986, rr 6.115–6.119 and para **22.150**ff below.
[4]   *Midland Banking Co v Chambers* (1869) 4 Ch App 398. And generally see *Re Melton, Milk v Towers* [1918] 1 Ch 37, CA and in particular the judgment of Scrutton LJ in its approach to problems of this nature.

Proof of creditor

22.61 The creditor is entitled to prove in the bankruptcy of the principal debtor irrespective of his ability to recover against the guarantor. On the question whether the creditor has to give credit for any sums received by him from the guarantor or other third party before he submits his proof of debt there is some divergence on the authorities. The better view is that in general the creditor when proving for his debt does not have to deduct sums received from the guarantor or from the realisation of any securities provided by the guarantor whether these sums are received before or after the bankruptcy occurred and, if after the commencement of the bankruptcy, whether before or after proof[1]. There have been cases however where the court has proceeded on the basis that the creditor should give credit for all payments received from the guarantor before proof and for the realisation of securities or securities as yet unrealised[2]. There is also authority that should the guarantor also be bankrupt the creditor must give credit for any dividend declared out of the guarantor's estate even where it has yet to be paid[3]. While it might seem unjust that the creditor should not have to give credit for sums received by him from the guarantor when proving in the debtor's bankruptcy, the rule may stem from the fact that were the creditor obliged to give credit for the guarantor's pre-proof payments neither the creditor nor the guarantor could then prove in respect of these amounts, the guarantor being unable to do so because he may not prove against the bankrupt debtor's estate until he has paid the guaranteed debt in full. Even in those cases where the court has proceeded on the basis that the creditor does have to give credit for sums received from the guarantor, mere receipt is not enough. The creditor must have actually applied the sums in formal reduction of the debt due from the debtor before credit need be given. In *Re Walker & Co, ex p Watson*[4] the creditor realised a security deposited by the guarantor on both his own and the principal debtor's account and after satisfying the guarantor's account placed the balance on a suspense account. It was held that this was not a receipt of the balance by the creditor who did not, therefore, need to give credit in his proof in the bankruptcy of the principal debtor. To be on the safe side a creditor receiving payments from the guarantor toward the discharge of the principal debt where the debtor is or is likely to become insolvent should not apply the payments in partial discharge of the debt but place them on suspense account. This approach is almost universally adopted by the English clearing banks. It is common procedure for the banks to place the proceeds of realised securities and guarantor's payments on a 'suspense' or 'securities realised' account and such sums are appropriated by the bank when it thinks fit, and only after the bank has received dividends on its proof against the principal debtor's estate.

1   *Ellis v Emmanuel* (1876) 1 Ex D 157; *Re Bunyard, ex p Newton, ex p Griffin* (1880) 16 Ch D 330, CA; *Re Blackburne, ex p Strouts* (1892) 9 Morr 249; *Re Sass, ex p National Provincial Bank of England Ltd* [1896] 2 QB 12.
2   *Re Oriental Commercial Bank, ex p Maxoudoff* (1868) LR 6 Eq 582; *Re Daunt, ex p Joint Stock Discount Co* (1871) 6 Ch App 455; *Re Bedell, ex p Gilbey* (1878) 8 Ch D 248; *Re Blakeley, ex p Aachener Disconto Gesellschaft* (1892) 9 Morr 173. This also appears to be the position under Scots law, see *McKinnon's Trustee v Bank of Scotland* (1915) SC 411.
3   *Ex p Leers* (1802) 6 Ves 644.
4   (1880) 42 LT 516; and see *Re Sass, ex p National Provincial Bank of England Ltd* [1896] 2 QB 12.

22.62 The creditor may not however receive more than 100p in the pound. As soon as he has received the full amount due under the principal debt he may not receive further dividends, but the guarantor will be entitled to the benefit of the proof for any further dividends[1].

1   *Re Milton, Milk v Towers* [1918] 1 Ch 37.

22.63 The creditor is not entitled to the benefit of a security provided by the debtor to the guarantor, and need not therefore have any regard to it in his proof[1].

22.63   Proof of debts

1   *Re Walker, Sheffield Banking Co v Clayton* [1892] 1 Ch 621; *Re Yewdall, ex p Barnfather* (1877) 46 LJ Bcy 87, 109, CA.

Proof by the guarantor

22.64   The common law rule is that the guarantor becomes subrogated to the rights of the creditor when he has paid the full amount due from the principal debtor[1]. Only then may he prove at all in the debtor's bankruptcy. In most cases however the guarantor will have an express or implied contractual right of indemnity against the principal debtor which arises quite separately from the common law right of subrogation[2]. The guarantor will then be entitled to be indemnified by the principal debtor in respect of such sums as he has paid to the creditor. If the principal debtor has become bankrupt, the guarantor may prove in the bankruptcy, but such proof is subject to the creditor's proof in respect of the principal debt. There must be no double proof[3]. The generally accepted view is that the creditor's proof prevails and that once the creditor has submitted a proof the guarantor may not even submit a proof until he has paid the creditor or the creditor has otherwise received 100p in the pound[4]. It has however been suggested that the guarantor may lodge a proof even while the creditor is proving and that the rule against double proof only comes into operation when the creditor is paid a dividend. As the 'rule against double proof' is in reality a rule against double dividend[5] the suggestion is that only when a dividend payment is to be made to creditors should the trustee consider whether to pay a dividend on a proof submitted by a guarantor[6]. There is therefore no good reason why a guarantor should not be permitted to lodge a proof alongside the creditor's proof in respect of what is in substance the same debt. There are practical implications dependent upon which is the correct approach. First, proofs are lodged in respect of the debt due at the commencement of the bankruptcy. Where suretyship, or situations analogous to suretyship, is concerned the position between the respective parties may change between the commencement of the bankruptcy and the date on which any dividend is paid[7]. There is no obvious reason why the trustee should not take account of such change of position, but a bankruptcy debt in respect of which a proof is submitted is defined by reference to the commencement of the bankruptcy[8] and the IR 1986 require the creditor's proof of debt to state the total amount of the creditor's claim as at the date of the bankruptcy order[9]. Secondly, if the guarantor is permitted to lodge a proof even though he has no immediate right to a dividend he may nevertheless be able to invoke any right of insolvency set-off he may have against the principal debtor. This is because of the wording of the IA 1986, s 323(1) which provides that the statutory set-off provisions apply where there have been mutual credits, debts or dealing before the commencement of the bankruptcy between the bankrupt and 'any creditor of the bankrupt proving or claiming to prove for a bankruptcy debt'. Plainly it would be quite wrong for the guarantor to be permitted to invoke a statutory set-off before he has a proof which may be properly admitted to dividend. If in the event the guarantor is never in a position to receive a dividend the rule against double proof (or double dividend) would indeed be infringed[10]. Thirdly, there are practical considerations involved in the guarantor's ability, or lack of it, to submit a proof alongside a proof by the creditor. A guarantor does not wish to find that when he proves after paying off the creditor he misses out on a dividend because the creditors' proof has been withdrawn or rejected by the trustee for some technical reason. Whether or not he seeks to submit a formal proof it is advisable for a guarantor to advise the trustee that he expects in due course to prove in his own right when he discharges the debt and pays off the creditor. However, the guarantor ought never to suffer from being prevented from submitting a proof before the creditor is paid in full, because once the creditor has been paid in full from all sources[11] the guarantor is entitled to the benefit of the creditor's proof for any remaining dividends[12]. If the creditor has been paid in full by the guarantor without giving credit for any dividends received, the guarantor will have a restitutionary claim against the creditor. Where the guarantor has guaranteed part only of the whole debt due to the creditor he may prove against the bankrupt's estate when he has paid that part in full unless precluded from doing so by the terms of the guarantee[13].

1   *Re Oriental Commercial Bank, ex p European Bank* (1871) 7 Ch App 99, 102; *Re Fenton Ltd, ex p Fenton Textile Association Ltd* [1931] 1 Ch 85, 115.
2   As where the guarantee has been given at the express or implied request of the principal debtor, see *Davies v Humphreys* (1840) 6 M&W 153; *Re Fox Walker & Co, ex p Bishop* (1880) 15 Ch D 400.
3   *Hardy v Fothergill* (1888) 13 App Cas 351; *Re Fitzgeorge, ex p Robson* [1905] 1 KB 462; *Re Lennard, Lennard's Trustee v Lennard* [1934] Ch 235.
4   *Re Fenton Ltd, ex p Fenton Textile Association Ltd* [1931] 1 Ch 85 where the Court of Appeal reviewed the authorities.
5   'The true principle is that there is only to be one dividend in respect of what is in substance the same debt', per Mellish LJ in *Re Oriental Commercial Bank, ex p European Bank* (1871) 7 Ch App 99, 103.
6   *Barclays Bank v TOSG Fund Ltd* [1984] 1 All ER 628, CA at 636 (Oliver LJ).
7   This is clearly recognised by Oliver LJ in *Barclays Bank v TOSG Fund Ltd* [1984] 1 All ER 628 at 637e: 'Now if ... the true rule is that there are not to be two dividends in respect of what is in substance the same debt, I can see no logical justification for seeking to fix the position at the commencement of the insolvency. One has, as it seems to me, to look at the position at the point at which the dividend is actually about to be paid and to ask the question then whether two payments are being sought for a liability which, if the company were solvent, could be discharged as regards both claimants by one payment.'
8   See the IA 1986, s 382(1).
9   See the IR 1986, r 6.98(1)(b).
10   It was for this reason that the Court of Appeal held in *Re Fenton, ex p Fenton Textile Association Ltd* [1931] 1 Ch 85 that the guarantor could not submit a contingent proof in respect of liabilities yet to fall due under a guarantee.
11   Eg set-off of obligations owed to the bankrupt debtor, realisation of securities given by the guarantor, payment by the guarantor directly or by dividend in the guarantor's own bankruptcy, or dividend in the principal debtor's bankruptcy.
12   *Re Fothergill, ex p Turquand* (1876) 3 Ch D 445; *Re Sass* [1896] 2 QB 12; *Re Pyke, Davis v Jeffreys* (1910) 55 Sol Jo 109; *Re Melton, Milk v Towers* [1918] 1 Ch 37.
13   *Re Sass* [1896] 2 QB 12 at 15. Many standard forms of guarantee will prohibit the guarantor from proving in competition with the creditor.

22.65 Once he is permitted to prove the guarantor may prove in respect of any claim which may arise under his guarantee whether present or future, certain or contingent[1]. He may not however submit a proof for the cost of maintaining a security where the principal debt has been extinguished[2]. The guarantor's position *qua* guarantor does not affect his ability to prove in respect of any other debt which may be owed to him by the debtor independently of the guarantee.

22.65 *Proof of debts*

1   IA 1986, ss 332, 382.
2   *Re Moss, ex p Hallett* [1905] 2 KB 307.

Guarantor holding security

22.66 Where the guarantor holds a security upon the principal debtor's estate, he is limited in his rights to benefit from the creditor's proof to the amount by which the guarantee liability exceeds the value of the security. Should the creditor take dividends from the estate and call on the guarantee to enable him to recover the debt in full, the guarantor will be entitled to realise any security he has on the principal debtor's estate. Should the realisation of this security result in the estate paying more than the amount of the debt the guarantor must account for the balance to the estate[1]. It is common form today for bank guarantees to provide that the bank may receive dividends from the principal debtor's estate and still hold the guarantor liable to the full extent of the guarantee. In this event proof by the bank (or other creditor holding a similar guarantee) does not affect any security held by the guarantor over the principal's estate[2].

1   *Baines v Wright* (1885) 16 QBD 330.
2   *Midland Banking Co v Chambers* (1869) 4 Ch App 398; *Re Lennard, Lennard's Trustee v Lennard* [1934] Ch 235.

Position of guarantor who has paid the principal debt in full

22.67 Where the guarantor has made only a partial payment to the creditor he may not prove in the principal's debtor's bankruptcy until the creditor has been paid in full[1]. A guarantor who has paid the whole indebtedness due to the creditor is subrogated to the rights of the creditor[2]. He is entitled to the benefit of any securities held by the creditor in respect of the guaranteed debt. He may succeed to the creditor's proof and receive any further dividends paid in the bankruptcy. If the creditor had a preferential status for his debt the guarantor will also be a preferential creditor[3]. The guarantor may set off his guarantee payments against debts due by him to the principal debtor[4] but the set-off extends only to the extent of payments made and not to prospective liabilities under the guarantee. This is because until the creditor has finally exercised his rights of proof in the estate a contingent set-off by the guarantor might effectively become a double proof[5]. Neither is a set-off allowed in respect of payments made after the commencement of the bankruptcy[6].

1   See para **22.64** above.
2   This is by agreement, express or implied, or in law.
3   *Re Lamplugh Iron Ore Co Ltd* [1927] 1 Ch 308.
4   Under the IA 1986, s 323(1).
5   *Re Fenton, ex p Fenton Textile Association Ltd* [1931] 1 Ch 85.
6   IA 1986, s 323(1) and see *Re a Debtor (No 66 of 1955), ex p Debtor v Trustee of Property of Waite* [1956] 3 All ER 225.

Position of guarantor who has paid less than the full principal debt

22.68 The distinction must first be drawn between the guarantor who has paid only part of his liability under the guarantee and the guarantor who has paid all that he is liable to pay, although this is less than the full principal debt. The guarantor who has paid only part of his liability under the guarantee may not prove in the principal debtor's insolvency, unless his obligations as guarantor arise under a negotiable instrument. It is immaterial whether his payment was made before or after the commencement of the bankruptcy[1], the guarantor may not prove in the bankruptcy, at least until the creditor has been paid in full[2]. The basis of the rule is clear. The guarantor has agreed to meet the liability due to the creditor under the principal debt to the full amount guaranteed, and it would therefore be wrong for him to prove or receive a dividend in competition with the creditor. The result may well be that the guarantor loses all rights of indemnity in respect of the sums paid; the creditor is not paid in full so the guarantor cannot prove and receive a dividend, and the principal debtor's liability to indemnify is discharged by the bankruptcy[3]. Neither will the guarantor necessarily be able to prove for his part payment after the creditor receives payment in full from all sources. If he has no right to an indemnity from the principal debtor arising by express or implied contract[4] the guarantor will have no right of proof. This is because he has no right of subrogation in law where he has paid part only of the principal debt[5]. Where, however, as will often be the case, the guarantor has a contractual right to an indemnity against the principal debtor, the guarantor will be able to prove[6] for any outstanding dividends once the creditor has been paid in full.

¹ *Re Sass* [1896] 2 QB 12.
² *Re Fenton (No 2)* [1932] 1 Ch 178.
³ *Re Fenton* [1931] 1 Ch 85.
⁴ See para **22.64** above.
⁵ *Re Oriental Commercial Bank, ex p European Bank* (1871) 7 Ch App 99, 102; *Re Fenton Ltd, ex p Fenton Textile Association Ltd* [1931] 1 Ch 85, 115.
⁶ The guarantor will usually be permitted to take over the creditor's proof – for there must be no double proof.

22.69 Different rules apply where the guarantee liability arises under a negotiable instrument. Both the drawer and an indorser of a bill of exchange are sureties for the acceptor, and will have a primary liability to the holder should the bill not be met on presentation[1]. Where the drawer or indorser of a bill pays part of the sum due to the holder before the holder submits a proof in the acceptor's bankruptcy the drawer or indorser may prove for the amount he has paid; the holder must then prove for the net amount due after giving credit for the sum received[2]. After the holder has submitted his proof however he need not give credit for any sums subsequently received, and the drawer or indorser may not prove for any amounts paid by them[3].

¹ Bills of Exchange Act 1882, s 55(1), (2). The drawer is also liable as surety to any indorser who is compelled to pay on the bill, provided the requisite proceedings on dishonour have been duly taken, Bills of Exchange Act 1882, s 55(1).
² *Re Blackburne* (1892) 9 Morr 249; *Re Houlder* [1929] 1 Ch 205.
³ *Re London, Bombay and Mediterranean Bank* (1874) 9 Ch App 686; *Re Fothergill, ex p Turquand* (1876) 3 Ch D 445.

22.70 Where the guarantor has paid all that he is liable to pay, although this is less than the principal debt, a further distinction needs to be drawn, on a true construction of the guarantee. This is between (1) the case where the guarantor guarantees part of an ascertained debt, and (2) the case where the guarantor has guaranteed the whole debt but subject to a limitation of liability which is less than the whole debt. In case (1) the payment of the amount guaranteed entitles the guarantor to stand, *pro tanto* in the creditor's shoes in the insolvency, since he has discharged the whole of his liability to the creditor[1]. The court treats the part of the debt guaranteed as a separate debt distinct from the part which has not been guaranteed. Accordingly when the guarantor pays the guaranteed part in full he has paid the entire 'principal debt' and so becomes subrogated to the creditor's right to prove for that 'debt'[2]. In case (2) so long as any part of the whole debt remains outstanding, the guarantor, although he has paid up to the limit of his financial liability, is treated as not having discharged his liability to the creditor 'presumably on the footing that there nevertheless remains an outstanding obligation on him to see that the whole debt is paid'[3]. The creditor may therefore prove for the full amount of the principal debt in the debtor's bankruptcy without having to give credit for the sums received from the guarantor, and the guarantor may not prove at all, at least until the creditor has received payment in full from all sources.

[1]   *Barclays Bank Ltd v TOSG Fund Ltd* [1984] 1 All ER 628 at 641h; and see *Ex p Rushforth* (1805) 10 Ves 409; *Bardwell v Lydall* (1831) 7 Bing 489; *Hobson v Bass* (1871) 6 Ch App 792; *Gray v Seckham* (1872) 7 Ch App 680 and *Re Sass, ex p National Provincial Bank of England* [1896] 2 QB 12.
[2]   See *Re Sass, ex p National Provincial Bank of England* [1896] 2 QB 12, 15.
[3]   Per Oliver LJ in *Barclays Bank Ltd v TOSG Fund Ltd* [1984] 1 All ER 628 at 641j. The learned judge continued: 'The distinction may seem over-subtle, but it is clearly established by authority: see the judgment of Blackburn J in *Ellis v Emmanuel* (1876) 1 Ex D 157, where the authorities are reviewed'. See also *Re Sass, ex p National Provincial Bank of England* [1896] 2 QB 12; *Midland Banking Co v Chambers* (1869) 4 Ch App 398; *Re Rees* (1881) 17 Ch D 98.

22.71 There is however a qualification to the rule applying to case (2) (para **22.70**)[1]. Where the guarantee is of the whole of a fluctuating balance, as in the case of a guarantee of the debtor's current account with a bank, and there is a limit on the guarantor's liability, such a guarantee is to be construed as a guarantee of part only of the debt. The guarantor who pays up to the limit of his liability will then be entitled to that extent to stand in the creditor's shoes and prove in the debtor's bankruptcy in priority to the creditor[2]. However, the guarantor's right in these circumstances to prove in priority to the creditor can, and usually will in bank guarantees, be excluded by the express terms of the guarantee. A provision that the guarantee is to be in addition and without prejudice to any other securities held from or on account of the debtor and that it is to be a continuing security notwithstanding any settlement of account is probably sufficient for this purpose[3]; there must at least be some express clause in the contract which can fairly be construed as a waiver by the guarantor of his rights in favour of the creditor[4]. A provision of this nature will not be readily inferred merely from the form which the transaction takes[5].

[1]   See *Barclays Bank Ltd v TOSG Trust Fund* [1984] 1 All ER 628 at 641–642 per Oliver LJ from whose judgment this text is taken.

2   *Ex p Rushforth* (1805) 10 Ves 409, 32 ER 903; *Gray v Seckham* (1872) 7 Ch App 680.
3   See *Re Sass* [1896] 2 QB 12; note however that in *Re Butlers Wharf Ltd* [1995] 2 BCLC 43 the deputy judge suggested that this reading of *Re Sass* was erroneous. He held that a provision in the guarantee that the granting of the guarantee was additional to other security held from the principal debtor did not prevent the guarantors from exercising rights of subrogation and sharing rateably in dividends paid by the debtor's estate.
4   See *Hobson v Bass* (1871) 6 Ch App 792 and cf *Midland Banking Co v Chambers* (1869) 4 Ch App 398.
5   *Gray v Seckham* (1872) 7 Ch App 680.

The guarantor's equity of exoneration

22.72 Where the principal debtor and the guarantor both charge their properties for the principal debt, the guarantor's equity of exoneration is to have the debt paid out of the principal debtor's property before the guarantor's property is appropriated for the debt. This principle is effective against the principal debtor's trustee in bankruptcy.

22.73 An example of the application of this principle may be found in the decision of the Bankruptcy Divisional Court in *Re Debtor (No 24 of 1971), ex p Marley v Trustee of Property of Debtor*[1]. There the father conveyed his freehold house into the joint names of himself and his son so that his son could obtain a bank loan. A charge was then executed on the house by both father and son in the bank's favour. The son's business failed and he became bankrupt. It was accepted that the father was in the position of a guarantor. The court held that an intention should be implied that the son's beneficial interest should bear the burden of the debt and that the father could be regarded as having an actual charge on the bankrupt son's interest in the house[2]. On the sale of the property the father was entitled to insist as against the son's trustee in bankruptcy, that the son's share was used to meet the outstanding bank loan in priority to the father's share.

1   [1976] 2 All ER 1010, [1976] 1 WLR 952, Foster and Fox LJ.
2   Following the principle discussed in *Gee v Liddell* [1913] 2 Ch 62 at 72. For a spouse's equity of exoneration see *Re Pittortou, ex p Trustee of Property of Bankrupt v Bankrupt* [1985] 1 All ER 285, [1985] 1 WLR 58.

Bankruptcy of the guarantor

Proof by creditor

22.74 The bankruptcy of the guarantor does not by itself revoke the guarantee[1], neither is the guarantee affected by the discharge of a bankrupt's guarantor[2]. The creditor may prove for any amount due and payable by the guarantor at the commencement of the bankruptcy, or, where the guarantor becomes bankrupt before the principal debt is due, for the guarantor's contingent liability under the guarantee[3]. The creditor must give credit for any payments or the value of any securities or dividends received from the principal debtor or the debtor's estate before the date on which the proof is submitted[4]. Credit need not be given however for payments received after submission of proof[5], but the creditor may not retain any dividend which results in him receiving more than 100p in the pound. It is the date of submission of proof that is relevant for these purposes, not the date on which the proof is admitted by the trustee in bankruptcy[6]. Where there are a number of co-guarantors jointly and severally liable for the principal debt the creditor may prove in the bankruptcy of one guarantor for the whole amount then due under the principal debt. He need not give credit for money or value received from the other co-guarantors whenever he receives it provided he does not recover more than the total debt due[7]. Neither need the creditor who has a security from another co-guarantor apply it to reduce the proof in the co-guarantor's bankruptcy. This includes money in a suspense account[8]. Where, however, the guarantor's liability arises under a negotiable instrument, the creditor must give credit for any payments received from co-guarantors. Accordingly a holder who has a claim against the estate of an insolvent drawer or indorser must deduct any sums received from other indorsers or the drawer, as the case may be, when lodging his proof[9]. The holder must also give credit for any sums received from the acceptor before lodging his proof[10].

1   *Boyd v Robins and Langlands* (1859) 5 CBNS 597.
2   IA 1986, s 281(7).
3   See *Re Fitzgeorge* [1905] 1 KB 462; assessing the value of the contingent proof may be extremely difficult.
4   *Re Blakeley, ex p Aachener Disconto Gesellschaft* (1892) 9 Morr 173; *Re Amalgamated Investment and Property Co Ltd* [1985] Ch 349, [1984] 3 All ER 272.
5   *Re Amalgamated Investment and Property Co Ltd* [1985] Ch 349, [1984] 3 All ER 272.
6   *Re Amalgamated Investment and Property Co Ltd* [1985] Ch 349, [1984] 3 All ER 272.
7   *Re Houlder* [1929] 1 Ch 205 and see *Re Blackburne* (1892) 9 Morr 249.
8   *Commercial Bank of Australia v John Wilson & Co's Estate, Official Assignee* [1893] AC 181.
9   *Re Blackburne* (1892) 9 Morr 249 and see *Re Houlder* [1929] 1 Ch 205.
10 *Re Stein, ex p Royal Bank of Scotland* (1815) 2 Rose 197, 19 Ves 310.

22.75 Where a creditor has waived his remedy against one guarantor he is not precluded from proof in the co-guarantor's bankruptcy, but an allowance must be made for the contribution which may have been had from the released co-guarantor[1].

1   *Ex p Gifford* (1802) 6 Ves 805.

22.76 Where the guarantee extends to only part of a debt and the debtor makes a payment towards the total debt the creditor is entitled to appropriate that payment either to the guaranteed part of the debt or to that part which has not been guaranteed at his election, and the guarantor's trustee in bankruptcy may not intervene and require the payment to be applied in reduction of the guaranteed part of the debt[1].

1   *Re Sherry* (1884) 25 Ch D 692, CA.

Proof by co-guarantor

22.77 One of several co-guarantors who pays the principal debt, or more than his proportionate share of the principal debt, is entitled to contributions in respect of the excess paid by him from the other guarantors. In taking proceedings for that excess the co-guarantor should make the principal debtor a party to the action unless the principal debtor is insolvent. The rule against double proof precludes a co-guarantor who has paid more than his due proportion of the guaranteed debt proving for his right of contribution until the creditor has received 100p in the pound[1]. A co-guarantor who has paid the creditor in full is subrogated to the rights of the creditor[2]. He can therefore prove for the full amount of the debt due to the creditor even if this is more than the amount to which he is entitled to contribute, so long as he does not receive more than 100p in the pound[3]. A co-guarantor also has a right to prove in respect of his contingent claim against another guarantor when no liability has yet arisen on behalf of that or any guarantor[4]. However, the rule against double proof prevents a co-guarantor proving in respect of any sum for which the creditor may prove, so this right is not one which in practice is likely to be exercisable.

1   *Hardy v Fothergill* (1888) 13 App Cas 351, HL.
2   Mercantile Law Amendment Act 1856, s 5.
3   *Re Parker, Morgan v Hill* [1894] 3 Ch 400, CA.
4   *Wolmerhausen v Gullick* [1893] 2 Ch 514.

Guarantor as mortgagor

22.78 When the creditor is secured by a legal charge executed by the guarantor he may enforce that security, subject to the provisions of the charge, in the event of the guarantor's bankruptcy. Where the guarantor has given an equitable mortgage or charge by way of security for the guarantee, any deed creating the charge may contain an irrevocable power of attorney clause enabling the creditor to make title when the guarantor mortgagor becomes bankrupt. Such a clause cannot be revoked by the guarantor's bankruptcy and the creditor mortgagee is able to make title without the co-operation of the guarantor's trustee in bankruptcy[1]. Other equitable charges without such a clause have to be enforced against the trustee.

1   Powers of Attorney Act 1971, s 4.

Bankruptcy of both principal debtor and guarantor

The rights of the creditor

22.79 The creditor is entitled to prove against both the principal debtor and the guarantor for the full amount due at the date of proof. He can take dividends from either or both estates until he is repaid in full[1].

1   *Ex p Rushforth* (1805) 10 Ves 409; *Re Fothergill, ex p Turquand* (1876) 3 Ch D 445; *Re Rees, ex p National Provincial Bank of England* (1881) 17 Ch D 98.

22.80 Where the debtor and guarantor are both liable on the same negotiable instrument, for example where the debtor is the acceptor and the guarantor an indorser of a bill of exchange, and the creditor proves against one estate before the second, the creditor must give credit for sums received or dividends declared in the first estate when proving in the second[1]. The creditor need not revise either proof however on receiving payments or dividends after the proof has been submitted[2].

[1] *Re Stein, ex p Royal Bank of Scotland* (1815) 2 Rose 197; *Re Houghton* (1857) 26 LJ Bcy 58.
[2] *Re London, Bombay & Mediterranean Bank* (1874) 9 Ch App 686; *Re Fothergill, ex p Turquand* (1876) 3 Ch D 445.

22.81 When both the drawer and the acceptor of a bill of exchange are insolvent and the drawer has given security to the acceptor to cover his acceptances, the holder of the acceptances is entitled to have the security applied in the discharge of the acceptances, the 'rule in Waring's Case'[1]. This is in order that there be equity between the two estates[2]. The basis of the rule is that the security provided by the drawer has been made for the specific purpose of securing payment to the holder so as to protect the position of the acceptor; it is accordingly impressed with a trust for this purpose and cannot become an asset in the acceptor's estate[3]. The holder must give credit for any sums received from realising the security in his proof of debt, and prove only for the balance due[4].

[1] *Re Brickwood, ex p Waring, Re Bracken, ex p Inglis* (1815) 19 Ves 345.
[2] *Re Burrough, ex p Sargeant* (1810) 1 Rose 153; *Thompson v Giles* (1824) 2 B & C 422; *Re Harrison, ex p Barkworth* (1858) 2 De G & J 194.
[3] *Re Suse, ex p Dever* (1885) 14 QBD 611; see also *Re Burrough, ex p Sargeant* (1810) 1 Rose 153; *Thompson v Giles* (1824) 2 B & C 422; *Re Harrison, ex p Barkworth* (1858) 2 De G & J 194.
[4] *Re Barned's Banking Co* (1875) 10 Ch App 198.

The rights of the guarantor's estate

22.82 No proof can be made on behalf of the guarantor's estate in the principal debtor's bankruptcy in respect of dividends declared out of the guarantor's estate once the creditor has proved in the principal debtor's estate[1]. However, when the creditor has been paid in full from all sources, the guarantor's estate is entitled to the benefit of the creditor's proof in the principal debtor's estate in respect of any further dividends paid[2].

[1] *Re Oriental Commercial Bank, ex p European Bank* (1871) 7 Ch App 99.
[2] *Re Whitehouse, Whitehouse v Edwards* (1887) 37 Ch D 683.

E BILLS OF EXCHANGE

22.83 The principal problems to which bills of exchange give rise in relation to bankruptcy concern the circumstances in which a party to a bill may prove in the bankruptcy of another party who is liable on the bill. The Bills of Exchange Act 1882 provides that 'the rules in bankruptcy relating to bills of exchange, promissory notes and cheques shall continue to apply' to such instruments notwithstanding anything contained in that Act[1]. By 'the rules in bankruptcy' is meant the general law of bankruptcy[2].

[1] Bills of Exchange Act 1882, s 97(1).

2   *Re Keever, ex p Trustee of the Property of the Bankrupt v Midland Bank Ltd* [1967] Ch 182.

Parties to a bill of exchange

22.84 The person who is entitled to be paid on a bill is the holder, ie the payee or indorsee who is in possession of it or the bearer of a bill or note payable to bearer[1]. Where the bill has been accepted the party primarily liable to the holder is the acceptor[2]. The liability of the drawer and of any indorser is a liability by way of suretyship, in that they engage by drawing or indorsing the bill as the case may be that it will be accepted on due presentment and that it will be paid according to its tenor[3]. If the bill is dishonoured by non-acceptance or by non-payment, the drawer is liable to compensate the holder and any indorser who is compelled to pay, and an indorser is liable to compensate the holder and any subsequent indorser. If the drawee does not accept the bill on presentment, there is no acceptor, but this does not change the nature of the liability of the drawer and any indorser since they remain liable for the failure of the drawee to accept albeit that the drawee incurs no liability on the instrument[4] himself and that, by reason of the non-acceptance, there is no acceptor.

1   Bills of Exchange Act 1882, s 2.
2   Bills of Exchange Act 1882, s 54.
3   Bills of Exchange Act 1882, s 55.
4   Bills of Exchange Act 1882, s 53. He may be liable under a collateral agreement to accept the bill.

22.85 In order to render the drawer or an indorser of the bill liable for dishonour, it is necessary to give notice of dishonour to them[1]. Where the drawer or indorser of the bill is bankrupt, the holder may give that notice either to the party himself or to his trustee in bankruptcy[2].

1   Bills of Exchange Act 1882, s 48(1).
2   Bills of Exchange Act 1882, s 49(10).

Proving in bankruptcy

22.86 The holder of a bill of exchange or promissory note may proceed against the various parties liable on it until he has received payment in full. Thus where any party liable is bankrupt he may prove in that party's bankruptcy. In doing so he may prove for the full sum due on the bill even though there remain other parties liable on it, but it must give credit for any payment he receives before he makes his proof[1]. Once the holder has received the dividend, he may proceed against the other parties liable on the bill for the balance of the debt due on it[2].

1   *Re Thompson and Mildred, ex p Prescott Grote & Co* (1834) 4 Deac & Ch 23; *Re Corson, ex p De Tastet* (1810) 1 Rose 10; *Re Stein, ex p Royal Bank of Scotland* (1815) 2 Rose 197.
2   *Re Fothergill, ex p Turquand* (1876) 3 Ch D 445, CA.

22.87 A debt is a bankruptcy debt and therefore is provable even though it is due in the future or on a contingency so long as the obligation which gives rise to it was incurred before the commencement of the bankruptcy[1]. Accordingly, so long as the bill was drawn, accepted or indorsed before the commencement of the bankruptcy of the drawer, acceptor or indorser, as the case may be, the holder may prove in the bankruptcy even if the bill is not yet due. For example the holder of a bill or note payable on demand or on notice may prove in the bankruptcy even though no demand was made or notice given before the commencement of the bankruptcy. Similarly where the bill or note is due on a fixed date, proof may still be made in respect of it. However, in such cases the trustee must make adjustment in calculating the dividend payable for the fact that the debt was not yet due at the commencement of the bankruptcy[2].

[1] IA 1986, s 382.
[2] IR 1986, rr 6.114, 11.13.

22.88 A holder who has purchased a bill in good faith for less than its face value may prove against the estate of any part for the full sum due on the bill[1]. Where the holder has bought a bill or promissory note after the commencement of the bankruptcy he may prove against the estate provided that at the commencement of the bankruptcy it was held by a person entitled to prove[2].

[1] *Jones v Gordon* (1877) 2 App Cas 616, HL.
[2] *Re Bowles, ex p Rogers* (1820) Buck 490; *Re Hardcastle, ex p Botten* (1833) Mont & B 412.

22.89 Where the holder of a bill has received it from the bankrupt as security for a debt due to him which is smaller than the sum payable under the bill, the holder may prove against the bankrupt drawer's estate for the whole amount of the bill though he may not receive dividends beyond the amount of the debt[1].

[1] *Re Bunyard, ex p Newton* (1880) 16 Ch D 330, CA.

22.90 A proof in respect of money owed on a bill of exchange, promissory note, cheque or other negotiable instrument cannot be admitted unless the instrument or a copy certified by the creditor or his authorised representative to be a true copy is produced, unless the trustee allows otherwise[1].

[1] IR 1986, r 6.108.

Secured bills of exchange

22.91 Secured bills are bills accepted by a person who has received goods from the drawer by way of security enabling the drawer to discount the bill and obtain cash. The drawer is entitled to redeem his goods by paying back the amount due and, where the goods are sold, he is entitled to receive back any surplus above the amount due to the acceptor. The acceptor becomes a creditor of the drawer on paying the bill and can realise his security[1].

[1] *Re Suse, ex p Dever* (1884) 13 QBD 766; *Re Broad, ex p Neck* (1884) 13 QBD 740, CA.

22.92 On the bankruptcy of the drawer his trustee is in no better position than the drawer and may only recover the goods by paying the amount due. The acceptor is a secured creditor and therefore may only prove against the drawer's estate for the unsecured balance of his debt after realisation of the security or, if he gives up his security and returns the goods, for the full amount[1].

1   IR 1986, r 6.109.

22.93 Where the acceptor becomes bankrupt his trustee is entitled to enforce the security if it is not redeemed by the drawer. Should the goods realise less than the amount due on the bill the trustee may recover the difference from the drawer; if the goods realise more, the surplus must be paid over.

22.94 Where both drawer and acceptor are bankrupt, the goods pledged are applied in making payment to the holder on the bill which was drawn against them. This follows the rule in *Ex p Waring*[1] that if both drawer and acceptor of a bill of exchange become bankrupt, the holder is entitled to have any securities given by the drawer to the acceptor for accepting the bill applied in paying the amount due on the bill.

1   *Ex p Waring* (1815) 19 Ves 345; see also *City Bank v Luckie* (1870) 5 Ch App 773; *Royal Bank of Scotland v Commercial Bank of Scotland* (1882) 7 App Cas 366, HL.

Accommodation bills

22.95 An accommodation bill is a bill signed by a party as drawer, acceptor or indorser who has received no value for rendering himself liable on the bill and has signed for the purpose of lending his name to some other person[1]. Although the accommodation party is liable to a holder on the bill, he is effectively the guarantor of the person to whom he has lent his name and if that person becomes bankrupt, the accommodation party may prove in his bankruptcy[2].

1   Bills of Exchange Act 1882, s 28.
2   *Re Fothergill, ex p Turquand* (1876) 3 Ch D 445.

22.96 Where there is mutual accommodation by cross-acceptances and one party becomes bankrupt, the other being solvent must take up his acceptance. Provided this is done the solvent party may prove in the bankruptcy of the bankrupt acceptor[1]. Where both parties become bankrupt, neither trustee can prove in the bankruptcy of the other until the holders of the bills have been fully paid, irrespective of any inequality in the accommodation transactions[2].

1   *Re Bowness and Padmore* (1789) Cooke's Bkpt Laws, 8th edn 183.
2   *Ex p Walker* (1798) 4 Ves 373.

Promissory notes

22.97 A promissory note is an unconditional promise in writing made by one person to another signed by the maker, engaging to pay, on demand or at a fixed or determinable future time, a sum certain in money, to, or to the order of, a specified person or bearer[1]. Where, without more, the maker of the note is adjudged bankrupt, the note will give rise to an unsecured debt in respect of which the only recourse will be to prove in the bankruptcy. But promissory notes are negotiable and may be indorsed. Subject to the provisions of the Bills of Exchange Act 1882, ss 83–89, the provisions of that Act relating to bills of exchange apply, with necessary modifications, to promissory notes[2]. For the purpose of applying those provisions, the maker of the note is deemed to correspond with the acceptor of a bill, and the first indorser of a note is deemed to correspond with the drawer of an accepted bill payable to drawer's order[3]. That means, amongst other things, that the maker of the note engages that he will pay it according to the tenor of the note[4] and that the first indorser engages that it will be paid according to its tenor and that if it be dishonoured, he will compensate the holder or any indorser who is compelled to pay it, provided that the requisite proceedings on dishonour be duly taken[5]. Hence where the note is indorsed, the first indorser guarantees the liability of the maker of the note; subsequent indorsers will take on similar liabilities. Accordingly, the rules concerning proof of debt relating to guaranteed debts will be applicable.

[1] Bills of Exchange Act 1882, s 83(1).
[2] Bills of Exchange Act 1882, s 89(1).
[3] Bills of Exchange Act 1882, s 89(2).
[4] Bills of Exchange Act 1882, s 54(1) as modified.
[5] Bills of Exchange Act 1882, s 55(1)(a).

Cheques

22.98 A cheque is a bill of exchange drawn on a banker payable on demand[1]. Although, therefore, cheques are a species of bill of exchange and in theory negotiable, in practice, because banks print cheques crossed and bearing the words 'account payee' or 'a/c payee' either with or without the word 'only', cheques are not transferable[2]. If a cheque is crossed and bears the words, it is only valid as between the parties to it, that is to say the drawer and the payee. In the event of the drawer's bankruptcy, the payee must prove for the debt to which the cheque gives rise.

[1] Bills of Exchange Act 1882, s 73.
[2] Bills of Exchange Act 1882, s 81A, inserted by the Cheques Act 1992, s 1.

F MUTUAL CREDITS AND SET-OFF

Statutory right of set-off

22.99 The ability to set off in bankruptcy gives a creditor an advantage akin to security. Instead of having to prove for his debt and recover, if anything, a dividend for it, he is entitled to set off his claim against the estate pound for pound against his indebtedness[1]. Set-off in bankruptcy occurs where, before the commencement of the bankruptcy[2], there have been mutual credits, mutual debts or other mutual dealings between the bankrupt and any creditor. It involves the taking of an account of what is due from each party to the other in respect of the mutual dealings and the sums due from one party shall be set off against the sums due from the other[3].

1 *Stein v Blake* [1996] AC 243, 251.
2 Ie the date on which the bankruptcy order was made, IA 1986, s 278(a).
3 IA 1986, s 323(1) and (2).

Automatic and self-executing operation of set-off

22.100 Set-off in insolvency occurs automatically without any step being taken to trigger the process apart from the commencement of the bankruptcy[1]. It ensues from this feature that the effect of the bankruptcy is to replace the causes of action formerly subsisting between the bankrupt and the creditor with a single claim for the net balance after the set-off by the creditor against the bankrupt where his claim exceeds his indebtedness or by the bankrupt's trustee against the creditor where the creditor's indebtedness is greater than his claim. In the former case, the creditor may prove for the balance of his claim and receive a dividend in respect of it; in the latter, the creditor must pay the amount outstanding into the estate and if he does not the trustee may sue for it in its entirety[2].

1 *Stein v Blake* [1996] AC 243, [1995] 2 All ER 961; *MS Fashions Ltd v Bank of Credit and Commerce International SA* [1993] Ch 425.
2 IA 1986, s 323(4).

Mandatory operation

22.101 The operation of set-off in insolvency is mandatory. In consequence, parties cannot contract out of it[1]. This is the case even where the monies owed by the creditor are stated in the agreement to be held on trust[2]. Neither can statutory set-off be waived by either party, so money which has been paid over without taking into account the operation of the set-off is recoverable[3]. Further, it has been held that the court has no power to disapply the provisions requiring insolvency set-off: hence the court was obliged to apply statutory set-off in an English winding-up, even where the winding-up in England was ancillary to insolvency proceedings in Luxembourg where the insolvency law does not allow set-off of mutual debts[4].

1 See in particular *National Westminster Bank Ltd v Halesowen Presswork and Assemblies Ltd* [1972] AC 785, [1972] 1 All ER 641, HL where there was a set-off as between separate bank accounts; *Re Vaughan, ex p Fletcher* (1877) 6 Ch D 350 at 356, CA; *British Guiana Bank v Official Receiver* (1911) 104 LT 754 at 755, PC; *Victoria Products Ltd v Tosh & Co Ltd* (1940) 165 LT 78; *Re EJ Morel (1934) Ltd* [1962] Ch 21, [1962] 1 All ER 796; *Rolls Razor Ltd v Cox* [1967] 1 QB 552, [1967] 1 All ER 397, CA; See also *British Eagle International Airlines Ltd v Compagnie Nationale Air France* [1975] 2 All ER 390, [1975] 1 WLR 758, HL. Parties may exclude the right of set-off where it would arise outside insolvency as a legal or equitable set-off: see eg *Coca Cola Financial Corpn v Finsat International Ltd* [1998] QB 43, [1996] 3 WLR 849, CA; *Hong Kong & Shanghai Banking Corpn v Kloeckner & Co AG* [1990] 2 QB 514.
2 *Re ILG Travel Ltd* [1995] 2 BCLC 128, [1996] BCC 21; the case concerned monies owed to travel agents by the company who wished to set off monies received by customers for holidays. The terms of the agreements between the insolvent company and the travel agents provided that the customers' payments should be held on trust. On the facts the agreement was held to give the agent a contractual right to deduct its claim against the customers'

payments. The court also considered the position on the basis that the agency agreements created a bare trust of the customers' payments in favour of the company, and held that this would not prevent the application of the statutory set-off. An agreement which is framed so as to create a trust will not exclude mutuality in circumstances where an express exclusion of statutory set-off would have been wholly ineffective.

3   *Re Cushla Ltd* [1979] 3 All ER 415.
4   *Re Bank of Credit and Commerce International SA (No 11)* [1997] 1 BCLC 80; *Re Bank of Credit and Commerce International SA (No 10)* [1997] Ch 213, noted with approval by the House of Lords in *Re Bank of Credit and Commerce International SA (No 8)* [1998] 1 BCLC 68, at p 73.

22.102 Nor can the extent of the right of set-off be extended. The fundamental principle of *pari passu* distribution of the bankrupt's assets must not be subverted and therefore there can be no set-off of claims by third parties, even with their consent[1], nor any contractual right of set-off which extends beyond the statutory right[2].

1   *British Eagle International Airlines Ltd v Compagnie Nationale Air France* [1975] 1 WLR 758, HL; *Re BCCI SA (No 8)* [1998] 1 BCLC 68, HL.
2   *Re Bank of Credit and Commerce International SA (No 8)* [1998] AC 214, [1998] 1 BCLC 68, HL.

Date at which the set-off takes effect

22.103 The notional date for the application of the set-off is the date on which the bankruptcy commenced[1]. This has implications as to the quantification of debts which are not at that time liquidated, which are discussed below. Secondly, set-off is not available with respect to debts arising after the commencement of the bankruptcy, not in consequence of any obligation in being at the commencement[2].

1   *Stein v Blake* [1996] AC 243, [1995] 2 All ER 961; *Re Dynamics Corpn of America* [1976] 2 All ER 669, [1976] 1 WLR 757.
2   *Kitchen's Trustee v Madders* [1950] Ch 134, [1949] 2 All ER 1079, CA explained in *Bradley-Hole v Cusen* [1953] 1 QB 300, sub nom *Hole v Cuzen* [1953] 1 All ER 87, CA.

Mutuality

22.104 In order that debts or the effect of dealings may be set off, they must be due respectively from the creditor and the debtor in the same right. By way of example, if the trustee in bankruptcy claims money paid to a creditor by way of preference, the creditor cannot set off the debt because the trustee claims in virtue of his statutory right to reclaim the money paid by way of preference[1]. Accordingly debts due to or from executors personally cannot be set off against debts due from or to them in their capacity as executors[2]. It has been held that if the creditor holds funds on trust for the bankrupt, which therefore form part of his estate, such money cannot be brought into account for the purpose of set-off[3].

1   See *Lister v Hooson* [1908] 1 KB 174, CA; *Re a Debtor (No 82 of 1926)* [1927] 1 Ch 410; *Re BP Fowler* [1938] Ch 113, [1937] 3 All ER 781.

²   *Bishop v Church* (1748) 3 Atk 691; *Re Willis Percival & Co, ex p Morier* (1879) 12 Ch D
      491, CA; *Middleton v Pollock, ex p Nugee* (1875) LR 20 Eq 29; and cf *Bailey v Finch*
      (1871) LR 7 QB 34.
³   *Elgood v Harris* [1896] 2 QB 491.

22.105 Mutuality will be absent where the creditor holds funds for a special
purpose or upon trust¹. Three cases illustrate this situation. In *Re Pollitt*² the
creditor, a solicitor, held money entrusted to him by the bankrupt for future
costs; he could not set this off against costs already incurred. In *Re Mid-Kent
Fruit Factory*³ the fund which could not be set off represented a surplus held
by a solicitor out of a sum specially provided by the bankrupt for the
satisfaction of claims made prior to bankruptcy. And in *Re City Equitable Fire
Insurance Co Ltd (No 2)*⁴ a fund held by way of guarantee against the
carrying out of specific obligations was held to be 'special' in this sense. In all
these cases the funds may be said to have been impressed with quasi-trust
purposes which destroyed the mutuality prerequisite to the right to set off⁵.

¹   *Re Asphaltic Wood Pavement Co, Lee & Chapman's case* (1885) 30 Ch D 216.
²   [1893] 1 QB 455.
³   [1896] 1 Ch 567.
⁴   [1930] 2 Ch 293.
⁵   *National Westminster Bank v Halesowen Presswork and Assemblies Ltd* [1972] AC 785,
      820. Note the comment of Lord Simon at 808: 'My only quarrel with this way of putting
      it [ie 'quasi-trust'] is that quasi anything gives uncertain guidance in the law. I would prefer
      to say that money is paid for a special (or specific) purpose so as to exclude mutuality of
      dealing if the money is paid in such circumstances that it would be a misappropriation to
      use it for any other purpose than that for which it is paid.'

22.106 The test of mutuality for the purpose of the application of the
statutory set-off is an objective one to be determined in the light of all the
circumstances; thus it is not possible to impress a special purpose on a fund if
in substance it is not held for such purpose¹.

¹   *Re ILG Travel Ltd* [1995] 2 BCLC 128, [1996] BCC 21.

Debt

22.107 Set-off is concerned only with claims for money. Each credit must be
of such a nature that it will eventually become a debt, and a mere deposit of
property without there being any agreement by which it might be turned into
money is not a credit for these purposes¹.

¹   *Rose v Hart* (1818) 8 Taunt 499; *Rose v Sims* (1830) 1 B & Ad 521.

22.108 But the debt need not be liquidated before the commencement of the
bankruptcy. In bankruptcy, 'debt' is to be construed in accordance with the
definition of 'bankruptcy debt' as defined in IA 1986, s 382¹. Section 382(3)
gives debt the same wide meaning for the purpose of set-off in bankruptcy.
Hence a sum should be regarded as being due to or from the bankrupt's estate
for the purpose of set-off whether it is payable at present or in the future;
whether the obligation by virtue of which it is payable is certain or contingent;
or whether its amount is fixed or liquidated, or is capable of being ascertained

by fixed rules or as a matter of opinion[2]. The mutual dealings may therefore extend to claims arising in tort[3] or pursuant to statute[4].

1 IA 1986, s 385(1).
2 With effect from 1 April 2005, IR 1986, r 4.90, governing set-off in a winding up or administration of a company in England and Wales, was amended so as to make clear that the same position applied under both those regimes. Cf the similar definition of debt for the purpose of winding up in IR 1986, r 13.12.
3 *Re T & N Ltd* [2005] EWHC 2870 (Ch), [2006] 3 All ER 697, [2007] 1 WLR 1728 at [63].
4 *Re West End Networks Ltd, Secretary of State for Trade and Industry v Frid* [2004] 2 AC 506, [2004] 2 All ER 1042.

22.109 Examples may be found of set-off of future debts[1]; and of claims for unliquidated damages[2]. Thus where a company which had contracted to deliver goods by instalments sued for the price and then went into liquidation the defendant was able to set off its counterclaim for non-delivery[3], and a claim for unliquidated damages for fraudulent misrepresentation by a bankrupt on the sale of a chattel was set off against a claim by the trustee for the unpaid price[4].

1 *Rolls-Razor Ltd v Cox* [1967] 1 QB 522, [1967] 1 All ER 397, CA.
2 *Re Prescot, ex p Prescot* (1753) 1 Atk 230; *Booth v Hutchinson* (1872) LR 15 Eq 30; *Peat v Jones & Co* (1881) 8 QBD 147, CA; *Jack v Kipping* (1882) 9 QBD 113, DC; *Re Daintrey, ex p Mant* [1900] 1 QB 546, CA; *Re Rushforth, ex p Holmes & Sons* (1906) 95 LT 807; *Tilley v Bowman Ltd* [1910] 1 KB 745; see also *Rolls Razor Ltd v Cox* [1967] 1 QB 552, [1967] 1 All ER 397, CA.
3 *Peat v Jones* (1881) 8 QBD 147, CA.
4 *Jack v Kipping* (1882) 9 QBD 113, CA.

Contingent debts

22.110 Debts which are contingent at the date of the bankruptcy order, being debts provable in bankruptcy[1], are capable of set-off where they have resulted from mutual dealings[2]. In *Hiley v Peoples Prudential Assurance Co Ltd*[3] Dixon J stated:

> 'In the first place the general rule does not require that at the moment when the [bankruptcy] commences there should be two enforceable debts, a debt provable in the [bankruptcy] and a debt enforceable by the [trustee] against the creditor claiming to prove. It is enough that at the commencement of the [bankruptcy] mutual dealings exist which involve rights and obligations *whether absolute or contingent*[4] of such a nature that afterwards in the events that happen they mature or develop into pecuniary demands capable of set off. If the end contemplated by the transaction is a claim sounding in money so that, in the phrase employed in the cases, it is commensurable with the cross-demand, no more is required than that at the commencement of the [bankruptcy] liabilities shall have been contracted by the [bankrupt] and the other party respectively from which cross money claims accrue during the course of the [bankruptcy][5].'

1 See the IA 1986, s 382 for the definition of bankruptcy debt.
2 *Re Charge Card Services Ltd* [1987] Ch 150, [1986] 3 All ER 289.
3 (1938) 60 CLR 468 at 496.
4 This emphasis was added by Millett J when citing this passage in *Re Charge Card Services Ltd* [1987] Ch 150, [1986] 3 All ER 289.

[5]   This passage was expressly approved in *Re Charge Card Services Ltd* [1987] Ch 150, [1986] 3 All ER 289.

Mutual credits, mutual debts and other mutual dealings

22.111 'Mutual debts' arise where the bankrupt and the other party each owe the other a liquidated sum payable immediately or in the future[1]. 'Mutual dealings' is a wide phrase which covers most transactions between the bankrupt and the other party which may give rise to rights or liabilities between them. Equitable rights will be set off with other mutual dealings[2], and an equitable debt may be set off against a legal debt[3]. It has been stated that the essential feature is that the parties each intend, expressly or by implication, to extend credit to the other in respect of individual transactions and liabilities with a view to an account being taken in due course and the balance payable as it is then due[4]. But intention is not the touchstone given that liability arising in tort or pursuant to statute may be included[5]. The claims on each side must be such as to result in pecuniary liabilities in respect of which the account may be taken[6]. There can therefore be no set-off where the claim on the one side is for the specific return of goods[7], or the right to appropriate property under a party's control[8], or in respect of money or goods deposited for a specific purpose which has not been carried out[9] or of a balance of such money remaining when it has been carried out[10]. However, there will be set-off where there is a debt on one side and a delivery of property with directions to turn it into money on the other[11].

[1]   Eg *Clark v Cort* (1840) Cr & Ph 154.
[2]   *Forster v Wilson* (1843) 12 M & W 191; *Bailey v Finch* (1871) LR 7 QB 34; *Bailey v Johnson* (1872) LR 7 Exch 263; *Bankes v Jarvis* [1903] 1 KB 549.
[3]   *Mathieson's Trustee v Burrup, Mathieson & Co* [1927] 1 Ch 562.
[4]   See generally *Rolls Razor v Cox* [1967] 1 QB 552, [1967] 1 All ER 397, CA and *National Westminster Bank Ltd v Halesowen Presswork Ltd* [1972] AC 785, [1972] 1 All ER 641, HL.
[5]   *Re West End Networks, Secretary of State for Trade and Industry v Frid* [2004] UKHL 24, [2004] 2 AC 506, [2004] 2 All ER 1042; *Re DH Curtis (Builders) Ltd* [1978] Ch 162 at 170, [1978] 2 All ER 183; *Re Cushla Ltd* [1979] 3 All ER 415.
[6]   *Rose v Hart* (1818) 8 Taunt 499; *Naoroji v Chartered Bank of India* (1868) LR 3 CP 444; *Palmer v Day & Sons* [1895] 2 QB 618.
[7]   *Re Robinson, ex p Flint* (1818) 1 Swan 30; *Rose v Hart* (1818) 8 Taunt 499; *Re Winter, ex p Bolland* (1878) 8 Ch D 225; *Eberle's Hotels and Restaurant Co Ltd v Jonas* (1887) 18 QBD 459, CA; *Lord's Trustee v Great Eastern Rly Co* [1908] 2 KB 54, CA; *Ellis & Co's Trustee v Dixon-Johnson* [1925] AC 489, HL; *Rolls Razor Ltd v Cox* [1967] 1 QB 552, [1967] 1 All ER 397, CA; see also *Handley Page Ltd v Customs and Excise Comrs and Rockwell Machine Tool Co Ltd* [1970] 2 Lloyd's Rep 459; affd [1971] 2 Lloyd's Rep 298, CA.
[8]   *Re Bank of Credit and Commerce International SA (No 8)* [1998] 1 BCLC 68, 79.
[9]   *Buchanan v Findlay* (1829) 9 B & C 738; *Re Pollitt, ex p Minor* [1893] 1 QB 455, CA; *National Westminster Bank Ltd v Halesowen Presswork and Assemblies Ltd* [1972] AC 785, [1972] 1 All ER 641, HL where, at 808, 812 and at 651, 663 respectively, the cases on 'special purpose' are discussed: money is paid for a special or specific purpose so as to exclude mutuality of dealing within the IA 1986, s 323 if the money is paid in such circumstances that it would be a misappropriation to use it for any other purpose than that for which it is paid.
[10]   *Re Mid-Kent Fruit Factory Ltd* [1896] 1 Ch 567; *Re City Equitable Fire Insurance Co (No 2)* [1930] 2 Ch 293, CA.

22.111 *Proof of debts*

11 *Naoroji v Chartered Bank of India* (1868) LR 3 CP 444; *Astley v Gurney* (1869) LR 4 CP 714; *Palmer v Day & Sons* [1895] 2 QB 618, CA; *Rolls Razor Ltd v Cox* [1967] 1 QB 552, [1967] 1 All ER 397, CA; *Eberle's Hotels and Restaurant Co Ltd v Jonas* (1887) 18 QBD 459, CA.

Creditor proving or claiming to prove

22.112 It is not necessary that the creditor should file a proof for the set-off to apply. The set-off is self-executing independently of any step, such as filing a proof, being taken and, secondly, it applies in the case where the creditor's claim is extinguished by his indebtedness, in which case the creditor having no claim against the estate may well not file any proof. The question is whether the creditor is entitled to prove[1].

1 *Re Bank of Credit and Commerce International SA (No 8)* [1998] AC 214, 228; *Mersey Steel and Iron Co Ltd v Naylor Benzon & Co* (1882) 9 QBD 648, CA.

Secured debt

22.113 The fact that the indebtedness of the creditor is secured by security granted to the bankrupt does not prevent the set-off from occurring. If the consequence of the set-off is that the debt owed by the insolvent is extinguished, the security is released. Thus in *ex p Barnett, in re Deveze*[1] the creditor had dealings with a trader who became bankrupt; at the time of the bankruptcy the bankrupt owed the creditor £3,010, and the creditor owed the bankrupt £88; but the bankrupt held goods of the creditor's upon which he had a lien for that amount of £88. His trustee in the bankruptcy insisted that the creditor should pay the debt of £88 before the goods were delivered up to them, and that they should prove for the whole sum of £3,010 against the bankrupt's estate. It was held that the creditor was entitled to set the sum of £88 off against the debt owed by the bankrupt, thereby freeing the lien and to prove for the balance of £2,922[2]. However, in the contrary situation where the creditor holds security in respect of one debt owed to him by the insolvent but proves in respect of another unsecured debt, it appears that the set-off only applies to the unsecured debt[3]. But, although it would equally be true that a creditor holding security for the indebtedness of the insolvent is not obliged to prove for his debt because it is secured, it is difficult to see why if that is his only indebtedness to the insolvent, there should not be a set-off where the creditor is indebted to the insolvent estate.

1 (1874) LR 9 Ch App 293.
2 A more complicated illustration is afforded by *Re ILG Travel Ltd* [1995] 2 BCLC 128.
3 *Re Norman Holding Co Ltd* [1990] 3 All ER 757, [1991] 1 WLR 10.

Claim arising from wrongdoing

22.114 A person indebted to the bankrupt has no right of set-off where his indebtedness arises from wrongdoing which gives the bankrupt or his estate a cause of action enabling him to pursue a proprietary claim or a claim to vindicate an interest in property. Thus, by analogy with cases involving companies, where the indebtedness arises from misappropriation of the bankrupt's assets[1] or conversion of chattels[2] belonging to the bankrupt, the indebtedness is not subject to set-off against a bankruptcy debt.

1   *Manson v Smith (liquidator of Thomas Christy Ltd)* [1997] 2 BCLC 161.
2   *Smith (Administrator of Cosslett (Contractors) Ltd) v Bridgend County Borough Council* [2002] 1 AC 336.

Excluded debts

22.115 The account must not, however, include any sums due to the creditor by the bankrupt if at the time that they became due the creditor had notice that a bankruptcy petition was pending against the bankrupt[1]. The creditor will have to prove separately for such debts.

1   IA 1986, s 323(3). See *Re SSSL Realisations (2002) Ltd* [2006] Ch 610.

Impact of rule against double proof

22.116 The right to set-off is subject to the rule against double proof[1]. Accordingly it is not available in favour of a surety when the principal creditor's right of proof in respect of the debt guaranteed is still subsisting[2].

1   See *Re Oriental Commercial Bank, ex p European Bank* (1871) 7 Ch App 99.
2   *Re Fenton, ex p Fenton Textile Association* [1931] 1 Ch 85 at 112, CA; *Re A Debtor (No 66 of 1955), ex p Debtor v Trustee of the Property of Waite (a bankrupt)* [1956] 2 All ER 94, [1956] 1 WLR 480; affd [1956] 3 All ER 225, [1956] 1 WLR 1226, CA.

Market contracts

22.117 A debt arising out of a market contract which is the subject of default proceedings under the Companies Act 1989, s 159 is not provable in the bankruptcy and may not be taken into account for the purpose of any set-off under IA 1986, s 323 until the completion of the default proceedings[1]. Once the default proceedings are complete, a net sum will, if due, be certified as due; that sum is provable and may be taken into account for the purpose of set-off in the same way as a debt due before the commencement of the bankruptcy[2].

1   Companies Act 1989, s 159(4).
2   Companies Act 1989, s 163(2).

Effect of set-off

22.118 Set-off in bankruptcy operates automatically. The creditor's claim is reduced by his indebtedness and replaced by the remaining balance. In consequence, if the creditor seeks to assign his claim, he cannot assign the whole claim for, after the commencement of the bankruptcy, it no longer subsists and all that may be assigned is the remaining balance after the set-off[1]. Equally, if the creditor's claim is exceeded by his indebtedness, the result is that the trustee is left with a reduced claim against him on behalf of the estate for the remaining part of the indebtedness.

¹   *Stein v Blake* [1996] AC 243.

Quantification

22.119 Where debts are liquidated and due for payment before the commencement of the bankruptcy, no difficulty arises in quantifying them. But where the debt is a future or contingent debt, two techniques are available to determine its amount. First, events occurring after the bankruptcy which result in the amount being ascertained may be relied on. Thus, if an insurance policy matures and becomes payable after the commencement of the bankruptcy, the amount of the payment then revealed may be taken into account. Secondly, if it is impracticable to wait for the event or contingency to occur, the trustee may estimate the value of the bankruptcy debt pursuant to IA 1986, s 322(3). But, it is not competent to estimate the amount of the creditor's indebtedness because there is no statutory or other authority enabling the trustee or the court to require him to pay in advance of the occasion on which his liability will accrue¹.

¹   *Stein v Blake* [1996] AC 243, 253.

Rule in Cherry v Boultbee

22.120 If a legatee becomes bankrupt after the testator's death and owes money to his estate, the trustee in bankruptcy, if he claims the legacy for the estate¹, can be in no better position than the legatee and may only claim the balance of the legacy, if any, after giving credit for the debt owed to the testator's estate². This is not a true case of set-off, as there are no mutual debts³, nor is it a case of the former right of retainer in a personal representative⁴. The principle is that a person who owes money which would swell the mass of the deceased's estate is bound to make his contribution to the estate before taking a part share out of it, such as a share of the residuary estate⁵. The principle does not, therefore, prevent a legatee taking a specific legacy before contributing to the general residuary estate⁶. It extends to the right of a deceased's estate to indemnity in respect of payments made as surety for the legatee⁷.

¹   As after-acquired property under IA 1986, s 307, see para **14.161** above.
²   *Bousfield v Lawford* (1863) 1 De GJ & Sm 459; *Re Batchelor, Sloper v Oliver* (1873) LR 16 Eq 481; *Re Watson, Turner v Watson* [1896] 1 Ch 925.
³   *Courtenay v Williams* (1846) 15 LJ Ch 204.
⁴   *Re Akerman, Akerman v Akerman* [1891] 3 Ch 212 at 219. The personal representative's former right of retainer was abolished by the Administration of Estates Act 1971, s 10, though there remains protection for personal representatives who pay debts of the estate in good faith and without reason to believe that the estate was insolvent, Administration of Estates Act 1971, s 10(2).
⁵   *Cherry v Boultbee* (1839) 4 My & Cr 442 at 448; *Courtenay v Williams* (1846) 15 LJ Ch 204; *Re Akerman, Akerman v Akerman* [1891] 3 Ch 212.
⁶   *Re Akerman, Akerman v Akerman* [1891] 3 Ch 212; and see *Re Richardson, ex p Thompson v Hutton* [1902] 86 LT 25 where a legacy was held not to be specific.

7   *Re Watson, Turner v Watson* [1896] 1 Ch 925; *Re Melton, Milk v Towers* [1918] 1 Ch 37, CA.

22.121 If, however, the legatee becomes bankrupt before the testator's death, there is no right to withhold the bankrupt's share as beneficiary, there being no enforceable debt due from the legatee[1], except to the extent of any dividend declared or composition payable in the bankruptcy[2]. Where the testator has expressly directed that debts from the legatee should be deducted from his share in the estate, the personal representative should make the deduction, giving credit for any dividend received by the testator in his lifetime[3].

1   *Cherry v Boultbee* (1839) 4 My & Cr 442; *Re Hodgson, Hodgson v Fox* (1878) 9 Ch D 673; *Re Rees, Rees v Rees* (1889) 60 LT 260. See also *Re Pink, Pink v Pink* [1912] 1 Ch 498; *varied* [1912] 2 Ch 528, CA.
2   *Cherry v Boultbee* (1839) 4 My & Cr 442 at 448; *Re Orpen, Beswick v Orpen* (1880) 16 Ch D 202; cf *Re Peruvian Railway Construction Co Ltd* [1915] 2 Ch 442, CA.
3   *Re Ainsworth, Millington v Ainsworth* [1922] 1 Ch 22.

22.122 The principle may also be applicable in the distribution of a fund in insolvent administration[1].

1   In *Re SSSL Realisations (2002) Ltd* [2006] EWCA Civ 7, [2006] Ch 610.

G PROCEDURE FOR PROVING DEBTS

Meaning of 'prove'

22.123 Proving is the process by which a person who is or claims to be a creditor of the bankrupt in respect of any bankruptcy debt makes his claim for payment out of the assets of the estate. A person claiming to be a creditor of the bankrupt and wishing to recover his debt in whole or in part has to submit his claim in writing to the official receiver, where acting as receiver and manager, or to the trustee[1]. The creditor is referred to as 'proving' for his debt; and the document by which he seeks to establish his claim is his 'proof'[2]. In exceptional circumstances the court may order that it is not necessary to prove a claim or a class of claims[3]. The creditor's proof must be in the form known as 'proof of debt', whether the form prescribed or a substantially similar form, which must be made out by or under the directions of the creditor, and signed by him or a person authorised for that purpose[4]. Where a debt is due to a Minister of the Crown or a government department, the proof need not be in the prescribed form, provided that the creditor makes a written claim giving all the particulars of the debt as are required in the prescribed form used by other creditors, and as are relevant in the circumstances[5]. The trustee may require the proof to be in the form of an affidavit[6].

1   IR 1986, r 6.96(1); the official referee may become the trustee.
2   IR 1986, r 6.96(1), (2).
3   IR 1986, rr 6.93(2), 6.96(1); proofs were dispensed with for claims for interest on money accepted as deposit in *Re Theo Garvin Ltd* [1969] 1 Ch 624, [1967] 3 All ER 497.
4   IR 1986, r 6.96(3). For the prescribed form of general proof of debt see Form 6.37, and **Appendix 3** below. Where an existing trustee proves in a later bankruptcy under the IA 1986, s 335(5), a different form is prescribed; see IR 1986, Sch 4, Form 6.38.

22.123 *Proof of debts*

IR 1986, r 6.96(4).
IR 1986, r 6.96(6).

22.124 No time limit is specified for submitting a proof. It would be open to a trustee if he considered it appropriate to seek a direction from the court under its general powers of control over all matters arising in any bankruptcy[1] that proofs should be lodged by a particular date. In the absence of any such direction a creditor will be able to lodge a proof at any time, but will not be able to disturb any dividends which have already been paid[2]. A creditor who delays proving his debts without good reason cannot expect the court to order a stay of the payment of a dividend while he submits his proof[3]. A creditor who delayed proving her debt until after a dividend had been declared in reliance on the trustee's promise to inform her of the progress of the bankruptcy was given a month by the court to prove her debt, and in the meanwhile payment of the dividend was suspended[4]. The court has even allowed a creditor to prove after the completion of the administration and the payment of a final dividend. The bankrupt received a substantial legacy before obtaining his discharge. The creditor's name had appeared on the bankrupt's statement of affairs but he had failed to submit a proof until he became aware of the legacy[5].

1 IA 1986, s 363(1).
2 See eg *Re Fenton, ex p Day* (1831) Mont 212; *Re Holland, ex p Dilworth* (1842) 3 Mont D & De G 63.
3 *Re Smith, ex p Brees* (1833) 3 Deac & Ch 283; *Re Boutland, ex p Todd* (1837) 2 Deac 416.
4 *Re Hirst, ex p Colton* (1833) 3 Deac & Ch 194; see also *Re Graham and Tate* (1833) 2 Deac & Ch 554.
5 *Re Westby, ex p Lancaster Banking Corpn* (1879) 10 Ch D 776.

EC Insolvency Regulation liquidator

22.125 A liquidator appointed in insolvency proceedings opened in another Member State may prove in the bankruptcy[1]. The Insolvency Rules 1986 provide that a Member State liquidator is to be deemed to be a creditor for the purpose of proving[2].

1 EC Insolvency Regulation, art 32(2).
2 IR 1986, r 6.238 and r 13.13(11).

Forms of proof

22.126 Where the bankruptcy order was made on or after 1 April 2004, the official receiver or the trustee is required to send out forms of proof to every creditor of the bankrupt who asks for one[1].

1 IR 1986, r 6.97; for the transitional provision, see the Insolvency (Amendment) Rules 2004, SI 2004/584. Where the bankruptcy order was made before that date, the previous version of r 6.97 remains applicable and the official receiver or the trustee is required to send out forms of proof to every creditor of the bankrupt who is known to the sender, or is identified in the bankrupt's statement of affairs. If the trustee is aware of a bankruptcy debt in respect of which the creditor has not submitted a claim it is his duty, provided he can communicate with him, to invite the creditor to prove in the bankruptcy;

Re Compania de Electricidad de la Provincia de Buenos Aires Ltd [1980] Ch 146, [1978] 3 All ER 668. The forms of proof sent out pursuant to this duty by the official receiver or trustee must accompany, whichever is first:

(1) the notice to creditors of the official receiver's decision not to call meetings of creditors;
(2) the first notice calling a meeting of creditors; or
(3) where a trustee is appointed by the court, the notice of his appointment sent by him to creditors,

unless the trustee advertises his appointment, with the leave of the court, in which case he must send proofs to the creditors within four months after the date of the bankruptcy order. These provisions are subject to any order of the court dispensing with the requirement to send out forms of proof, or altering the time at which the forms are to be sent.

Contents of proof

22.127

The contents of the proof are closely prescribed by the rules[1]. The following matters must be stated in a creditor's proof of debt:

(1) the creditor's name and address and, if a company, its company registration number;
(2) the total amount of his claim (including any VAT) as at the date of the bankruptcy order[2];
(3) whether or not that amount includes outstanding uncapitalised interest[3];
(4) particulars of how and when the debt was incurred by the debtor;
(5) particulars of any security held, the date when it was given and the value which the creditor puts upon it;
(6) details of any reservation of title in respect of goods to which the debt refers; and
(7) the name, address and authority of the person signing the proof, if other than the creditor himself.

1   IR 1986, r 6.98.
2   Ie the date of commencement of the bankruptcy, IA 1986, s 278.
3   A proof of debt in respect of a moneylending transaction made before 27 December 1980, ie the date on which the Moneylenders Acts 1927, s 9 was repealed by the Consumer Credit Act 1974, s 192(3)(b), (4), Sch 5 where the creditor was at the time of the transaction a licensed moneylender, must have indorsed on or annexed to it a statement setting out in detail the particulars mentioned in the Moneylenders Act 1927. IR 1986, r 6.102; the particulars are those contained in the Moneylenders Act 1927, s 9(2).

22.128 There must be specified in the proof any documents by reference to which the debt can be substantiated[1]. It is not essential that such documents be attached to the proof or submitted with it, but the trustee, or the convenor or chairman of any meeting of creditors may call for any document or other evidence to be produced to him, where he thinks it necessary for the purpose of substantiating the whole or any part of the claim made in the proof[2].

1   IR 1986, r 6.98(2).
2   IR 1986, r 6.98(3).

Verification of proof by affidavit

22.129 If he thinks it necessary, the trustee may require a claim of debt, ie a bankruptcy debt of whatever nature, to be verified by means of an affidavit[1]. The affidavit may be sworn before an official receiver or deputy official receiver, or before a duly authorised officer of the Department of Trade and Industry or of the court[2].

1   IR 1986, r 6.99; for this purpose the form known as 'affidavit of debt' is prescribed, IR 1986, Sch 4, Form 6.39. Note that an affidavit may be required notwithstanding that a proof of debt has already been lodged, IR 1986, r 6.99(2).
2   IR 1986, r 6.99(3).

Transmission of proofs to trustee

22.130 On the appointment of a trustee the official receiver is required to send the trustee all the proofs which have so far been lodged, duly itemised on a list of proofs[1]. From then on, all proofs of debt must be sent to the trustee and retained by him[2]. Where the relevant insolvency practitioner ceases to be trustee, he must immediately deliver up to his successor the proofs of debt, amongst other documents[3]. When the administration of the bankrupt's estate is for practical purposes complete, the trustee must file in court all the proofs he has in the proceedings[4].

1   IR 1986, r 6.103(1). The trustee must sign the list by way of receipt for the proofs, and return it to the official receiver, IR 1986, r 6.103(2).
2   IR 1986, r 6.103(3).
3   See IR 1986, r 6.146(1).
4   IR 1986, r 6.146(2).

Cost of proving

22.131 Subject to any order of the court[1], every creditor bears the cost of proving his own debt, including such costs as may be incurred in providing documents or evidence substantiating the claim made in the proof[2]. Any costs incurred by the trustee in estimating the value of a debt not bearing a certain value[3] fall on the estate, as an expense of the bankruptcy[4].

1   The court has a discretion as to where the costs of proving or estimating debts should lie, IR 1986, r 6.100(3).
2   IR 1986, r 6.100(1).
3   Under the IA 1986, s 322(3).
4   IR 1986, r 6.100(2).

Trustee's decision on proofs

22.132 The trustee has to determine whether to admit or reject each proof submitted for the purpose of dividend and voting. This is not a mere administrative function. The trustee should examine every proof and consider the validity of the grounds of the debt being proved[1]. This is the case even where the proof is based on a judgment, a covenant or an account stated[2]. The trustee should also consider any set-off which may arise to ascertain the proper sum in which the proof may be admitted[3]. In valuing the proof the trustee is not bound by any representations made by the debtor which would have given rise to estoppels in favour of the creditor had the debtor not become bankrupt[4]. A trustee may not reject a proof for tax on the grounds that there were no taxable profits or that reliefs are available to reduce or extinguish the liability[5]. The trustee may be liable for misfeasance in not investigating a claim thoroughly[6].

1   *Re Lupkovics, ex p Trustee v Freville* [1954] 2 All ER 125; *Re Home and Colonial Insurance Co* [1930] 1 Ch 102.
2   *Re Van Laun, ex p Chatterton* [1907] 2 KB 23, CA; *Re Lupkovics, ex p Trustee v Freville* [1954] 2 All ER 125, [1954] 1 WLR 1234.
3   *Re National Wholemeal Bread and Biscuit Co* [1892] 2 Ch 457.
4   *Re Exchange Securities and Commodities Ltd* [1988] Ch 46.
5   *Re Calvert, ex p Calvert* [1899] 2 QB 145; *Re Ayr Picture Houses Ltd* (1928) 13 TC 675; the trustee should appeal to the appropriate revenue authority.
6   *Re Home and Colonial Insurance Co* [1930] 1 Ch 102.

22.133 A proof may be admitted for dividend either for the whole amount claimed by the creditor, or for part of that amount[1]. If the trustee rejects a proof in whole or in part, he must prepare a written statement of his reasons for doing so, and send it forthwith to the creditor[2].

1   IR 1986, r 6.104(1).
2   IR 1986, r 6.104(2).

Appeal against trustee's decision

22.134 If a creditor is dissatisfied with the trustee's decision with respect to his proof, including any decision on the question of preference[1], he may apply to the court for the decision to be reversed or varied provided he does so within 21 days of his receiving the statement of reasons for rejecting the proof[2]. An application may also be made by the bankrupt or any other creditor if dissatisfied with the trustee's decision admitting or rejecting the whole or any part of a proof; again the application must be made within 21 days of the applicant becoming aware of the trustee's decision[3]. The court may make an order that the applicant give security for the trustee's costs, as for example where the applicant is ordinarily resident out of the jurisdiction[4]. On the making of such an application, the court fixes a date for the application to be heard, and the applicant must send notice of the hearing to the creditor who lodged the proof in question, if it is not himself, and to the trustee[5]. The trustee must, on receipt of the notice, file in court the relevant proof, together, if appropriate, with a copy of the statement of reasons rejecting the proof[6]. The court will decide the issue on the merits of the evidence before it; the court's function is not that of deciding merely whether the rejection was right or wrong on the evidence available to the trustee[7]. Accordingly, the trustee is not restricted before the court to the reasons he has given for rejecting the proof, and provided that the decision has been taken fairly[8] the court may uphold the trustee's decision on the basis of a ground not included in the statement of reasons[9]. In appropriate cases, where necessary for the fair disposal of the issue, the court may make orders for disclosure and cross examination of witnesses[10]. As cross examination is available the court will not normally order an examination under the IA 1986, s 366 for the purpose of enabling the trustee to test a disputed proof[11].

1   See para **23.11**ff below.
2   IR 1986, r 6.105(1).
3   IR 1986, r 6.105(2).
4   *Re Pretoria Pietersburg Rly Co (No 2)* [1904] 2 Ch 359.
5   IR 1986, r 6.105(3).
6   IR 1986, r 6.105(4).
7   *Re Kentwood Construction Ltd* [1960] 2 All ER 655n, [1960] 1 WLR 646; *Re Trepca Mines Ltd* [1960] 3 All ER 304n, [1960] 1 WLR 1273, CA.
8   Note the Human Rights Act 1998 implications to the trustee's decision.
9   *Re Thomas Christy Ltd* [1994] 2 BCLC 527, 530.
10 *Re Bank of Credit and Commerce International SA (No 6), Mahfouz v Morris* [1994] 1 BCLC 450, Nicholls V-C noting at p 454 that IR 1986, rr 7.7 and 7.10 expressly contemplated that cross examination may be ordered with regard to affidavits filed in support of applications, see also *Re Bank of Credit and Commerce International SA (No 5)* [1994] 1 BCLC 429.
11 *Re Bank of Credit and Commerce International SA (No 7)* [1994] 1 BCLC 455.

22.135   After the application has been heard and determined, the proof must, unless it has been wholly disallowed, be returned by the court to the trustee[1]. The official receiver, whether while acting as trustee or before a trustee is appointed, may not personally be liable for costs incurred by any person in respect of any such application; and the trustee, if other than the official receiver, is not so liable unless the court makes an order to that effect[2].

1   IR 1986, r 6.105(5).
2   IR 1986, r 6.105(6).

Inspection of proofs

22.136   The trustee must, so long as proofs lodged with him are in his hands, allow them to be inspected, at all reasonable times on any business day, by any of the following persons:

(1)   any creditor who has submitted his proof of debt (unless his proof has been wholly rejected for purposes of dividend or otherwise);
(2)   the bankrupt; and
(3)   any person acting on behalf of either of the above[1].

1   IR 1986, r 6.101.

22.137   'Business day' means any day other than a Saturday, a Sunday, Christmas Day, Good Friday or a day which is a bank holiday in any part of Great Britain[1].

1   IR 1986, rr 13.1, 13.13(1).

Withdrawal or variation of proof

22.138   A creditor's proof may at any time, by agreement between himself and the trustee, be withdrawn or varied as to the amount claimed[1]. Such an agreement is presumably open to challenge by any other creditor or the bankrupt[2]. If the trustee refuses to agree a variation the creditor may apply to the court, or if he prefers submit a further proof in respect of any additional sum claimed, and make an application in respect of any refusal by the trustee to admit this further proof[3].

1 IR 1986, r 6.106; this represents a change in the law, the amendment or withdrawal of proofs having previously been under the control of the court, see e g *Re Safety Explosives Ltd* [1904] 1 Ch 226, CA.
2 Ie under the IR 1986, r 6.105(2), although this rule makes no specific reference to variations of existing proofs, and there is no obligation on the trustee to give reasons for a refusal to agree to a variation of an existing proof.
3 IR 1986, r 6.105(1).

Expunging of proof by the court

22.139 The court may expunge a proof or reduce the amount claimed (1) on the trustee's application, where he thinks that the proof has been improperly admitted[1], or ought to be reduced; or (2) on the application of a creditor, if the trustee declines to interfere in the matter[2]. Where any such application is made to the court, the court must fix a date for the application to be heard, notice of which must be sent by the applicant (a) in the case of an application by the trustee, to the creditor who made the proof; and (b) in the case of an application by a creditor, to the trustee and to the creditor who made the proof, if not himself[3]. No time limit for an application is prescribed by the Insolvency Rules 1986 and mere lapse of time does not bar the court's right to expunge or reduce a proof[4]. If a proof is expunged or reduced, a creditor may retain any dividend previously received, but he is not entitled to receive any further dividend without giving credit for the overpayment in respect of his original proof[5]. The proof of a limited company which is dissolved after the company has proved will not be expunged, but the dividends after dissolution devolve on the Crown as *bona vacantia*[6] subject to the rights of any unsatisfied debenture holders at the time of the dissolution[7].

1 This may have been by the official receiver, an earlier trustee or the trustee himself.
2 IR 1986, r 6.107(1).
3 IR 1986, r 6.107(2).
4 *Re Tait, ex p Harper* (1882) 21 Ch D 537, CA.
5 *Re Tait, ex p Harper* (1882) 21 Ch D 537, CA. *Re Searle, Hoare & Co* [1924] 2 Ch 325; and see *Re Pilling, ex p Ogle, ex p Smith* (1873) 8 Ch App 711; *Re Browne (a bankrupt), ex p Official Receiver v Thompson* [1960] 2 All ER 625, [1960] 1 WLR 692.
6 *Re Higginson and Dean, ex p A-G* [1899] 1 QB 325; and see *Re Wells, Swinburne-Hanham v Howard* [1933] Ch 29, CA.
7 *Gough's Garages Ltd v Pugsley* [1930] 1 KB 615.

H QUANTIFICATION OF CLAIM

Estimate of quantum

22.140 Where a debt is uncertain by reason of its being subject to any contingency or contingencies or for any other reason, the trustee must estimate its value as at the date of the commencement of the bankruptcy[1]. In valuing the debt however the trustee should have regard to relevant events which have happened since the date of the bankruptcy order[2]. The amount provable in the bankruptcy in respect of any debt is the amount admitted or estimated by the trustee[3]. Should the creditor submitting the proof, or the bankrupt or any other creditor, be dissatisfied by the amount of the trustee's estimate he may apply to the court, and the court will estimate the value of the debt in substitution of the estimate given by the trustee[4].

1   IA 1986, s 322(3); where, for example, there are claims for future breaches of covenant the trustee should make 'a just estimate so far as possible of their value', per Buckley J in *Re Lucania Temperance Billiard Halls (London) Ltd* [1966] Ch 98, 106.
2   'The hindsight principle'; *MS Fashions Ltd v BCCI* [1993] Ch 425, 432.
3   IA 1986, s 322(4).
4   IA 1986, s 303.

22.141   In considering the proper quantum to allow on any proof the trustee should take all reasonable steps to arrive at the appropriate figure as between the debtor and the creditor[1]. Any trade or other discount which would have been available to the debtor but for his bankruptcy must be deducted from the claim, except any discount for immediate, early or cash settlement[2].

1   *Re Van Laun* [1907] 2 KB 23; *Re Home and Colonial Insurance Co* [1930] 1 Ch 102, the trustee may be liable in misfeasance proceedings for failing to take proper steps to investigate a creditor's claim.
2   IR 1986, r 6.110.

Debt payable at future time

22.142   A creditor may prove for a debt of which payment was not yet due at the date of the bankruptcy order, such a debt being a bankruptcy debt from which the bankrupt will eventually be discharged.

Debts in foreign currency

22.143   Debts which are payable in a foreign currency must be converted into sterling for the purposes of proof[1]. The debt is to be converted at the middle market rate at the Bank of England published for the day on which the bankruptcy order is made, or in the absence of any such published rate at such rate as the court determines[2]. Where the creditor is proving in respect of a claim for damages in tort in a foreign currency[3] the bankrupt is deemed to become subject to the relevant liability by reason of an obligation incurred at the time the cause of action accrued[4]. It appears probable that in such cases the date on which the cause of action accrued would be the appropriate date for conversion, presumably at the official exchange rate.

1   IR 1986, r 6.111 and see *Re Lines Bros* [1983] Ch 1, [1982] 2 All ER 183, CA.
2   IR 1986, r 6.111.
3   See *The Despina R* [1979] AC 685, [1979] 1 All ER 421, HL.
4   See IA 1986, s 382(2).

Periodical payments

22.144 In the case of rent and other payments of a periodical nature, the creditor may prove for any amounts due and unpaid up to the date of the bankruptcy order[1]. Where at that date any payment was accruing due, the creditor may prove for so much as would have fallen due at that date, if accruing from day to day[2].

[1] IR 1986, r 6.112(1).
[2] IR 1986, r 6.112(2).

Proof for interest

22.145 Where a bankruptcy debt bears interest, that interest is provable as part of the debt except in so far as it is payable in respect of any period after the commencement of the bankruptcy[1]. The IR 1986 provide that the creditor's claim may include interest on the debt at the prescribed rate[2] for periods before the bankruptcy order, although not previously reserved or agreed, in the following circumstances[3]:

(1) If the debt is due by virtue of a written instrument, and payable at a certain time, interest may be claimed for the period from that time to the date of the bankruptcy order[4].

(2) If the debt is due other than by a written instrument and payable at a certain time, interest may be claimed only if, before the presentation of the bankruptcy petition, a demand for payment was made in writing by or on behalf of the creditor, and notice given that interest would be payable from the date of the demand to the date of payment[5]. In this case, interest may only be claimed for the period from the date of the demand to that of the bankruptcy order[6].

[1] IA 1986, s 322(2). As to the payment of interest on debts proved in the bankruptcy see para **23.19** below.
[2] The rate of interest to be claimed is the rate specified in the Judgments Act 1838, s 17 on the date of the bankruptcy order: IR 1986, r 6.113(5).
[3] IR 1986, r 6.113(1).
[4] IR 1986, r 6.113(2).
[5] IR 1986, r 6.113(3).
[6] IR 1986, r 6.113(4).

22.146 Where the contract contains provisions for the capitalisation of interest falling due before bankruptcy these are to be applied in the quantification of a creditor's claim, but such provisions cannot be applied to interest payments falling due after the commencement of the bankruptcy[1].

[1] *Re Amalgamated Investment and Property Co Ltd* [1985] Ch 349, [1984] 3 All ER 272.

22.147 For all the purposes of the IA 1986 and the IR 1986, the rate of interest charged may not exceed the prescribed rate[1] namely the rate specified in the Judgments Act 1838, s 17[2].

[1] IR 1986, r 6.113(3).
[2] At the date of the bankruptcy order; IR 1986, r 6.113(5).

I PROOF BY SECURED CREDITORS

Proof by secured creditor

22.148 A secured creditor has various options open to him. He does not have to participate in the bankruptcy process. He may prefer to rely entirely on his security and not prove in the bankruptcy. He may realise or value his security and prove for any balance, or he may surrender his security for the benefit of the general body of creditors and prove for his entire debt. Where a secured creditor realises his security, he must deduct the amount realised before proving his debt which will be for the balance[1]. If the secured creditor has a number of claims against the bankrupt, he may appropriate the proceeds of realisation of his security as he thinks fit between the claims including between those claims which are provable and not provable[2], or between preferential and non-preferential claims in the bankruptcy[3]. The net proceeds of the realisation may not be applied to interest accrued after the date of the bankruptcy order[4], but profits made from an unrealised security may be applied to meet such interest[5]. If a secured creditor has realised his security for a particular debt and has a balance over in his hands at the commencement of the bankruptcy, he may set off this balance against another, unsecured, debt due to him by the bankrupt[6]. A creditor who holds several securities in respect of different debts must apply the proceeds of each security to its particular debt, and the surplus funds of one security may not be applied to make good the deficiency of another[7]. A creditor who values his security[8] proves for the balance as an ordinary unsecured creditor.

[1]   IR 1986, r 6.109(1).
[2]   *Re Foster, ex p Dickin* (1875) LR 20 Eq 767; *Re William Hall (Contractors) Ltd* [1967] 2 All ER 1150.
[3]   *Ex p Hunter* (1801) 6 Ves 94; *Re Fox and Jacobs, ex p Discount Banking Co of England and Wales* [1894] 1 QB 438.
[4]   *Re Bulmer, ex p Johnson* (1853) 3 De G M & G 218; *Re William Hall (Contractors) Ltd* [1967] 2 All ER 1150, [1967] 1 WLR 948.
[5]   *Re London, Windsor and Greenwich Hotels, Quartermaine's Case* [1892] 1 Ch 639; *Re Savin* (1872) 7 Ch App 760.
[6]   *Re H E Thorne and Son* [1914] 2 Ch 438.
[7]   *Re Newton, ex p Bignold* (1836) 2 Deac 66.
[8]   See para **22.150** below.

22.149 Where a secured creditor voluntarily surrenders[1] his security for the general benefit of creditors, he may prove for the whole debt, as if it were unsecured[2]. The surrender of the security does not discharge a surety[3]. The surrender by a first mortgagee of his security puts the trustee in his place, and does not accelerate the rights of subsequent mortgagees[4].

[1]   Voluntary surrender may appear unlikely if the security has any real value, but note that the creditor may by required to surrender his security if he submits a proof without referring to it: IR 1986, r 6.116(1).
[2]   IR 1986, r 6.109(2).
[3]   *Rainbow v Juggins* (1880) 5 QBD 422, CA.
[4]   *Cracknall v Janson* (1877) 6 Ch D 735. Cf *Moor v Anglo-Italian Bank* (1879) 10 Ch D 681 at 690. See also *Bell v Sunderland Building Society* (1883) 24 Ch D 618; *Re Pidcock, Penny v Pidcock* (1907) 51 Sol Jo 514.

Valuing the security

22.150 A creditor holding security must give particulars of the security in his proof and state the value that he puts on it[1]. The value placed on the security may be altered by the creditor at any time with the agreement of the trustee or the leave of the court[2]. The leave of the court to a revaluation is necessary however in two cases: first where the secured creditor was the petitioner for the bankruptcy order and he has put a value on his security in the petition, and second where the secured creditor has voted[3] in respect of the unsecured balance of his debt[4].

[1] IR 1986, r 6.98(1)(g).
[2] IR 1986, r 6.115(1).
[3] A secured creditor may vote only in respect of any unsecured balance of the debt due to him after deducting the value of the security: IR 1986, r 6.93(4).
[4] IR 1986, r 6.115(2).

22.151 Should the trustee be dissatisfied with the value which a secured creditor has put on his security, whether in his proof or by way of revaluation, the trustee may require any property comprised in the security to be offered for sale[1]. The terms of sale are to be agreed between the bankrupt and the creditor, or as the court may direct; and, if the sale is by auction, the trustee on behalf of the estate, and the creditor on his own behalf, may appear and bid[2]. The trustee may not test the value of the security by requiring sale however, if the security has been revalued and the revaluation has been approved by the court[3].

[1] IR 1986, r 6.118(1).
[2] IR 1986, r 6.118(2).
[3] IR 1986, r 6.118(3).

22.152 If a creditor who has valued his security subsequently realises it, whether or not at the instance of the trustee, the net amount realised must be substituted for the value previously put by the creditor on the security, and that amount must be treated in all respects as an amended valuation made by the creditor[1].

[1] IR 1986, r 6.119.

22.153 The revaluing of a security will not have the effect of disturbing dividends already paid or votes already taken. However, the trustee will be able to recover money paid to a partly secured creditor whose security is revalued upwards as money had and received to the trustee's use.

Rights in rem protected under the EC Insolvency Regulation, art 5

22.154 In the following paragraphs the consequences of a secured creditor's proving in the bankruptcy without disclosing his security and the trustee's ability to redeem security or insist on the property subject to the security being sold are discussed. These measures are capable of adversely affecting the security-holder's rights: non-disclosure in a proof will result in the security being lost and the other measures may result in the security-holder receiving less for his security than he might obtain if left freely to deal with his security as he might wish. If the English bankruptcy is a main proceeding within the meaning of the EC Insolvency Regulation, then the application of these measures, which form part of the English law of bankruptcy, to assets situated in another Member State, over which a creditor has rights in rem would conflict with the protection afforded to such rights by art 5 of the regulation. Although this results in any event under the regulation because it is directly effective, the position is made clear by IR 1986, r 6.116(3).

Surrender for non-disclosure

22.155 If a secured creditor omits to disclose his security in his proof of debt, he must surrender his security for the general benefit of creditors. Such surrender is subject to the power of the court, on the creditor's application, to relieve him from the required surrender on the ground that the omission was inadvertent or the result of honest mistake[1]. Inadvertence covers a case where the omission is accidental[2], the onus of proof being on the creditor[3]. It does not matter that the creditor has voted in respect of his whole debt provided that he has not had a deciding influence on a vote on an important issue[4]. Inadvertence is a question of fact[5]. It was held not to be inadvertence where a company having first proved in the bankruptcy in respect of partly paid shares on which it had a paramount lien, later amended its articles to extend the lien to fully paid shares held by the holder of partly paid shares, and then sought to lodge a fresh proof relying on the more extensive lien[6]. If the court grants relief, it may require or allow the creditor's proof of debt to be amended, on such terms as may be just[7].

[1] IR 1986, r 6.116(1): see *Re Burr, ex p Clarke* (1892) 67 LT 232; *Re Henry Lister & Co Ltd* [1892] 2 Ch 417.
[2] *Re Small, Westminster Bank v Trustee* [1934] Ch 541.
[3] *Re Safety Explosives Ltd* [1904] 1 Ch 226, CA; *Re Maxson, ex p Trustee, Re Maxson, ex p Lawrence and Lawrence Ltd* [1919] 2 KB 330.
[4] *Re Henry Lister and Co Ltd* [1892] 2 Ch 417.
[5] *Re Pawson* [1917] 2 KB 527.
[6] *Re Rowe, ex p West Coast Gold Fields Ltd* [1904] 2 KB 489.
[7] IR 1986, r 6.116(2).

Redemption of security by trustee

22.156 The trustee may at any time give notice to a creditor whose debt is secured that he proposes, at the expiration of 28 days from the date of the notice, to redeem the security at the value put upon it in the creditor's proof[1]. The creditor then has 21 days, or such longer period as the trustee may allow, in which to exercise his right to revalue his security if he so wishes, with the leave of the court where this is required[2]. If the creditor revalues his security, the trustee may only redeem at the new value[3]. If the trustee redeems the security, the cost of transferring it is borne by the estate[4]. A secured creditor may at any time, by a notice in writing, call on the trustee to elect whether he will or will not exercise his power to redeem the security at the value then placed on it; and the trustee then has six months in which to exercise the power or determine not to exercise it[5].

1   IR 1986, r 6.117(1).
2   IR 1986, r 6.117(2).
3   IR 1986, r 6.117(2).
4   IR 1986, r 6.117(3).
5   IR 1986, r 6.117(4).

Third party interests in property

22.157   Where a security is granted over a property which belongs to the bankrupt and a third party jointly, then, in so far as the bankrupt's interest is a beneficial one, the creditor is secured to that extent, and he may not prove in the bankruptcy without acknowledging the security[1]. There is no difference between property owned by the bankrupt as tenant in common and property owned by the bankrupt as joint tenant with the third party. If the property when given up would augment the bankrupt's estate, credit must be given for its value as security[2]. Where a creditor has realised a security granted by a third party on property which was in fact the property of the bankrupt, but represented by him to be his wife's, he must deduct the amount realised before proving[3]. A creditor who obtains judgment for the purchase price of specific shares is a secured creditor in respect of the judgment debt, because he is entitled to keep the shares until the purchaser, having become the equitable owner, pays the price[4]. Where consignors sent goods to the debtor for sale, drawing bills on him which they indorsed to bankers to whom they sent the bills of lading, and the bills were accepted 'payable on the delivery up of the bills of lading', this form of acceptance made the goods the property of the debtor; in proving against the debtor's estate, therefore, the bank had to treat them as such and prove as secured creditors[5].

1   *Re Rushton (a bankrupt), ex p National Westminster Bank Ltd v Official Receiver* [1972] Ch 197, [1971] 2 All ER 937.
2   *Re Turner, ex p West Riding Union Banking Co* (1881) 19 Ch D 105, CA; *Re Rushton (a bankrupt), ex p National Westminster Bank Ltd v Official Receiver* [1972] Ch 197, [1971] 2 All ER 937.
3   *Re Cooksey, ex p Portal & Co* (1900) 83 LT 435 and cf *Re Clarke, ex p Connell* (1838) 3 Deac 201; *Re Collie, ex p Manchester and County Bank* (1876) 3 Ch D 481, CA; and *Re Cooksey, ex p Portal & Co* (1900) 83 LT 435, 556.
4   *Re A Debtor (No 6 of 1941)* [1943] Ch 213, [1943] 1 All ER 553, CA.
5   *Re Howe, ex p Brett* (1871) 6 Ch App 838.

22.158   No credit need be given by a creditor in his proof for a voluntary payment made by a stranger in respect of a loss caused by the bankrupt[1].

1   *Re Rowe, ex p Derenburg & Co* [1904] 2 KB 483, CA.

Chapter 23

DISTRIBUTION OF BANKRUPT'S ESTATE

A   Priority of debts
B   Manner of distribution
C   Dividends
D   Second bankruptcy

A PRIORITY OF DEBTS

Order of priority

23.1 After satisfying the claims of secured creditors the trustee must distribute the remaining assets in accordance with the prescribed order of payment[1], which is as follows:

(1)   the costs and expenses of the bankruptcy;
(2)   debts with pre-preferential priority;
(3)   the debts of preferential creditors;
(4)   the debts of ordinary creditors;
(5)   interest arising on the debts of both preferential and ordinary creditors since the commencement of the bankruptcy;
(6)   any debts due to the bankrupt's spouse, any other postponed debts and any interest payable in respect of such debts;
(7)   any balance to be returned to the bankrupt[2].

[1]   See the IA 1986, ss 328, 329; IR 1986, rr 6.46A, 6.224, 10.4, 12.2.
[2]   IA 1986, s 330(5).

23.2 With respect to interest a distinction is to be made between interest arising on a debt prior to the commencement of the bankruptcy which is itself part of the bankruptcy debt provable in the bankruptcy[1], and interest on a bankruptcy debt from the commencement of the bankruptcy which is payable at the prescribed rate, but is postponed to the payment of ordinary debts whether it is interest payable on preferential or ordinary debts[2].

[1]   IA 1986, s 322(2).
[2]   IA 1986, s 328(4).

23.3 To be entitled to share in the distribution, a creditor must have proved his debt and, if he is a secured creditor, he must have complied with the various provisions governing secured debts[1].

[1] See para **22.148** above.

23.4 All debts proved in the bankruptcy in the same category of priority rank equally among themselves, without reference to the date on which they were respectively incurred[1]. That all debts in the same category should rank equally for a share in the assets available for distribution is a fundamental principle in bankruptcy law. An agreement which has the effect of securing a higher dividend to some creditors than the dividend received by others in the same class will be void[2]. Thus an agreement between a trustee and certain creditors that the trustee would allow part of his remuneration to be applied in paying them a larger dividend than the other creditors would receive in consideration and that the creditors concerned would consent to his acting as trustee, is not enforceable[3]. A garnishee order which has the effect of giving the claimant creditor a preference over other creditors should not be made absolute[4].

[1] IA 1986, s 328(2), (3).
[2] *Farmers' Mart Ltd v Milne* [1915] AC 106, HL.
[3] *Farmers' Mart Ltd v Milne* [1915] AC 106, HL.
[4] *Pritchard v Westminster Bank Ltd* [1969] 1 All ER 999, [1969] 1 WLR 547, CA.

23.5 It may be noted that except for those categories of debt which are preferential the Crown has no priority in bankruptcy over other unsecured creditors[1].

[1] *Food Controller v Cork* [1923] AC 647, HL.

Bankruptcy expenses

23.6 The expenses of the bankruptcy are paid first out of the available assets[1]. These expenses include all fees, costs, charges and other expenses incurred in the course of the bankruptcy proceedings[2]. They also include:

(a)   any expenses, including damages[3], incurred by the official receiver in connection with any proceedings taken against him in the bankruptcy in whatever capacity he may have been acting[4];
(b)   any expenses properly incurred in the administration of a voluntary arrangement where the bankruptcy order is made on a petition by the supervisor of, or any person other than the individual, who was bound by the arrangement[5].

[1] IA 1986, s 328(2).
[2] IR 1986, r 12.2.
[3] See IR 1986, r 10.4.
[4] IR 1986, r 10.4(1), the official receiver has a charge over the estate to secure any sums due to him, r 10.4(2).
[5] IA 1986, s 276(2).

23.7 The Insolvency Rules 1986[1] specify the precise order of priority of the various costs and expenses which may arise in the course of bankruptcy in 18 separate categories, namely:

(1) expenses or costs which:
  (i) are properly chargeable or incurred by the official receiver or the trustee in preserving, realising or getting in any of the assets of the bankrupt or otherwise relating to the conduct of any legal proceedings which he has power to bring (whether the claim on which the proceedings are based forms part of the estate or otherwise)[2] or defend, including those incurred in acquiring title to after-acquired property;
  (ii) relate to the employment of a shorthand writer, if appointed by an order of the court made at the instance of the official receiver in connection with an examination;
  (iii) are incurred in holding an examination under IR 1986, r 6.174 (where the examinee was unfit for examination) where the application was made by the official receiver;
(2) any other expenses incurred or disbursements made by the official receiver or under his authority, including those incurred or made in carrying on the business of a debtor or bankrupt;
(3) (i) the fee payable under any order made for the performance by the official receiver of his general duties as official receiver; (ii) any repayable deposit lodged by the petitioner under any such order as security for such fee, except where the deposit is applied to the payment of the remuneration of an insolvency practitioner appointed[3] by the court on a debtor's petition;
(4) any other fees payable under any order made, including those payable to the official receiver, and any remuneration payable to him under general regulations;
(5) the cost of any security provided by an interim receiver, trustee or special manager;
(6) the remuneration of the interim receiver, if any;
(7) any deposit lodged on an application for the appointment of an interim receiver;
(8) the costs of the petitioner, and of any person appearing on the petition whose costs are allowed by the court;
(9) the remuneration of the special manager, if any;
(10) any amount payable to a person employed or authorised[4] to assist in the preparation of a statement of affairs or of accounts;
(11) any allowance made, by order of the court, towards costs on an application for release from the obligation to submit a statement of affairs, or for an extension of time for submitting such a statement;
(12) the costs of employing a shorthand writer in any case other than one appointed by an order of the court at the instance of the official receiver in connection with an examination;
(13) any necessary disbursements by the trustee in the course of his administration, including expenses incurred by members of the creditors' committee or their representatives and allowed[5] by the trustee, but not including any payment of capital gains tax in circumstances referred to in head (15) below;

(14) the remuneration or emoluments of any person, including the bankrupt, who has been employed by the trustee to perform any services for the estate;

(15) the remuneration of the trustee, up to any amount not exceeding that which is payable to the official receiver under general regulations;

(16) the amount of any capital gains tax on chargeable gains accruing on the realisation of any asset of the bankrupt, without regard to whether the realisation is effected by the trustee, a secured creditor or a receiver or manager appointed to deal with a security;

(17) the balance, after payment of any sums due under head (14) above, of any remuneration due to the trustee;

(18) any other expenses properly chargeable by the trustee in carrying out his functions in the bankruptcy.

1 IR 1986, r 6.224(1).
2 The amendment to the rule avoids the previous difficulty that expenses of an unsuccessful attempt by a trustee to get in assets by seeking to set aside a prior transaction as a transaction at an undervalue or preference were not be recoverable out of the estate, see *Re MC Bacon Ltd* [1991] Ch 127.
3 Ie under IA 1986, s 273.
4 Ie under IR 1986, rr 6.58–6.72.
5 Ie under IR 1986, r 6.164.

23.8 Whether expenditure by a trustee should count as an expense of the bankruptcy is not a matter which the court has any discretion to determine; it depends on whether the expenditure in question falls within one of the categories enumerated above[1].

1 *Re Toshoku Finance UK plc* [2002] UKHL 6, [2002] 3 All ER 961, [2002] 1 WLR 671.

Pre-preferential debts

23.9 This is a class of debts given priority next after the payment of the bankruptcy costs and expenses by specific statutory authority, which is expressly preserved by the IA 1986[1]. Five categories of pre-preferential debts are noted:

(1) A claim for expenses of the trustee of a deed of arrangement which has been avoided by the bankruptcy of the debtor[2].

(2) A claim by a trustee savings bank against an officer of the bank who becomes bankrupt holding money or other things belonging to the bank by virtue of his office[3].

(3) A claim by a friendly society against an officer of the society who becomes bankrupt while in possession of money or property belonging to the society by virtue of his office[4].

(4) Reasonable funeral, testamentary and administration expenses where the estate of a deceased insolvent is being administered in bankruptcy[5].

(5) Repayment of fees paid to a bankrupt employer by an apprentice or to a bankrupt principal by an articled clerk where the trustee does not transfer the indenture or articles to another person[6].

1 IA 1986, s 328(6).
2 Deeds of Arrangement Act 1914, s 21.

23.9 *Distribution of bankrupt's estate*

3   Trustee Savings Bank Act 1969, s 72.
4   Friendly Societies Act 1974, s 59.
5   Administration of Insolvent Estates of Deceased Persons Order 1986, SI 1986/1999, art 4(2).
6   IA 1986, s 348(4).

23.10 In the case of an officer or trustee[1] of a friendly society becoming bankrupt it is essential for pre-preferential status that the society's claim is in respect of money or property of the society held by virtue of his office[2]. It is immaterial that the money or property cannot be traced[3], or that the officer has behaved wrongfully[4], or that there has been carelessness on the society's part[5], or that at the date of the bankruptcy he has ceased to be an officer of the society[6]. This preferential right in the trustees of the society applies only in the case of properly constituted officers[7], and does not apply in the case of a society's bankers[8]. Neither does it apply if the transaction amounted in substance to a loan to the bankrupt[9].

1   Friendly Societies Act 1974, s 111(1).
2   *Re Aberdein, Hagon v Aberdein* [1896] WN 154; *Re Thick, ex p Buckland* (1818) Buck 214; *Re Jardine, ex p Fleet* (1850) 4 De G & Sm 52; *Re West of England and South Wales District Bank, ex p Swansea Friendly Society* (1879) 11 Ch D 768.
3   *Re Miller, ex p Official Receiver* [1893] 1 QB 327, CA.
4   *Re Welch, ex p Trustees of the Oddfellows Society* (1894) 63 LJQB 524.
5   *Moors v Marriott* (1878) 7 Ch D 543. Cf *Re Welch, ex p Trustees of the Oddfellows Society* (1894) 63 LJQB 524.
6   *Re Eilbeek, ex p Trustees of the Good Intent Lodge No 987 of the Grand United Order of Oddfellows* [1910] 1 KB 136.
7   *Re Thick, ex p Buckland* (1818) Buck 214; *Re Aberdein, Hagon v Aberdein* [1896] WN 154.
8   *Re Rufford and Wragge, ex p Orford* (1852) 1 De GM & G 483; *Re West of England and South Wales District Bank, ex p Swansea Friendly Society* (1879) 11 Ch D 768.
9   *Ex p Amicable Society of Lancaster* (1801) 6 Ves 98; *Ex p Stamford Friendly Society* (1808) 15 Ves 280; *Re Shattock, ex p Long Ashton Junior Friendly Society* (1861) 5 LT 370.

Preferential debts

23.11 The categories of preferential debts under the IA 1986 were curtailed from the position under the previous law and have been further culled by the Enterprise Act 2002[1], pursuant to which the preferential treatment of Crown debts has been abolished. Preferential debts, which rank equally among themselves, must be paid in full before any dividend is payable to ordinary creditors[2]. If there are insufficient assets in the estate to meet the preferential debts in full they abate in equal proportions[3]. Where a surety discharges a preferential debt he is entitled to the priority which the creditor had with the debt in question[4]. A preferential creditor has no priority to or rights over a secured creditor[5]. The various categories of preferential debts are specified in the IA 1986, Sch 6 and are in summary:

(a)   contributions to occupational pension schemes and state scheme pensions;
(b)   remuneration due to employees;
(c)   EC levies on coal and steel production.

1   Enterprise Act 2002, s 251.

2   IA 1986, s 328(3).
3   *Richards v Kidderminster Corpn* [1896] 2 Ch 212; *Banister v Islington London Borough Council* (1972) 71 LGR 239.
4   Mercantile Law Amendment Act 1856, and see *Re Lamplugh Iron Ore Co Ltd* [1927] 1 Ch 308; *Re Lord Churchill, Manisty v Churchill* (1888) 39 Ch D 174.
5   *Richards v Kidderminster Overseers, Richards v Kidderminster Corpn* [1896] 2 Ch 212.

23.12 Also by way of preferential debt, miners employed wholly or in part in or about a mine in the stannaries of Devon and Cornwall have a first charge upon all mining effects pertaining to the mine and upon all money held by the mining company[1] in respect of their wages not exceeding an amount equal to three months' wages, and this charge has priority over all claims by creditors of the company which owns or works the mine[2].

1   For these purposes 'company' includes any person, or partnership body, Stannaries Act 1887, s 2.
2   Stannaries Act 1887, s 4.

Remuneration of employees

23.13 IA 1986, Sch 6 provides that the following sums due to employees constitute preferential debts:

(1)   Unpaid remuneration due to a employee whether or not employed at the date his employer became bankrupt in respect of any part of the four months next before the relevant date[1] which does not exceed the prescribed amount[2]. Remuneration is defined widely[3].
(2)   An amount owed by way of accrued holiday remuneration, in respect of any period of employment before the relevant date, to a person whose employment by the bankrupt has been terminated, whether before, on or after that date[4].
(3)   Any sum owed in respect of money advanced for the purpose of paying employees' remuneration or holiday pay[5].
(4)   Any sum which has been ordered to be paid by the bankrupt in respect of a default made by him under the Reserve Forces (Safeguard of Employment) Act 1985[6].

1   IA 1986, s 387(6): This will be the date of the bankruptcy order unless an interim receiver was appointed earlier, if so, it is the date of the interim receiver's appointment.
2   IA 1986, Sch 6, para 9, the prescribed amount is currently £800; Insolvency Proceedings (Monetary Limits) Order 1986, SI 1986/1996.
3   See IA 1986, Sch 6, para 13.
4   IA 1986, Sch 6, para 10.
5   IA 1986, Sch 6, para 11.
6   IA 1986, Sch 6, para 12.

23.14 The purpose of allowing sums arising under category (3) listed in para **23.13** above to be preferential is to safeguard banks or other lenders who advance money to the proprietor of a business to pay wages and other sums due to employees at a time when the business is in financial difficulties. Whether a wages cheque drawn by a bankrupt on an overdrawn account is regarded as paid out of money advanced for the purpose depends upon the way in which the account is kept and an overdrawn ordinary current account out of which wages cheques were regularly drawn did not constitute money advanced for the purpose of paying employees' remuneration[1]. Where the bank froze the existing current account and opened two further accounts, including a wages account no debit on which was allowed to become more than four months old, the balance due on the wages account after setting off sums in credit on the second account were held to be preferential[2]. Where a lending bank arranged for another bank to cash a company's cheques for any purposes but principally for wages the overdraft was held to have been advanced for wages[3].

1 *Re Primrose (Builders) Ltd* [1950] Ch 561, [1950] 2 All ER 334.
2 *Re E J Morel (1934) Ltd* [1962] Ch 21, [1961] 1 All ER 796.
3 *Re Rampgill Mill Ltd* [1967] Ch 1138, [1967] 1 All ER 56.

23.15 When an employer becomes bankrupt there will inevitably be an appreciable delay before a trustee is able to meet claims from employees for unpaid remuneration. To protect employees against hardship the Employment Rights Act 1996 ('ERA 1996'), s 182 requires the Secretary of State, on the written application of the employee, to pay to the employee out of the redundancy fund an amount in respect of all or any of the following[1]:

(a)   any arrears of pay in respect of a period or periods not exceeding eight weeks;

(b)   any amount which the employer is liable to pay the employee for the relevant statutory period of notice[2];

(c)   any holiday pay in respect of a period or periods of holiday, not exceeding six weeks in all, to which the employee became entitled during the 12 months immediately preceding the employer's insolvency;

(d)   any basic award of compensation for unfair dismissal[3];

(e)   any reasonable sum by way of reimbursement of the whole or part of any fee or premium paid by any apprentice or articled clerk.

1 See ERA 1996, s 184.
2 Or so much of an award under a designated dismissal procedures agreement as does not exceed any basic award of compensation for unfair dismissal to which the employee would be entitled but for the agreement, ERA 1996, s 184(1)(d).
3 ERA 1996, s 184(1)(d).

23.16 The amount payable under these provisions is limited by reference to the weekly maximum amount prescribed for the purposes of the ERA 1996[1]. Having made a payment under these provisions the Secretary of State is subrogated to the preferential rights of the employee concerned[2].

1 See the current Employment Protection (Variation of Limits) Order.
2 ERA 1996, s 189.

Ordinary debts

23.17 All debts which are neither preferential debts nor debts owed in respect of credit provided by the bankrupt's spouse nor debts which are otherwise postponed in law[1] are ordinary debts. They rank equally between themselves and each ordinary creditor is entitled to the same dividend on his debt provided that he has proved his debt before the distribution of any dividend[2]. Only after the ordinary debts are paid in full is interest payable on both preferential and ordinary debts, with all interest ranking equally.

[1]   See para **23.21**ff.
[2]   IA 1986, s 328(3); as to the position where a creditor proves his debt after a dividend has been declared, see para **23.39** below.

Debt payable at a future time

23.18   Where a creditor has proved in respect of a debt payable at a future time he is entitled to be paid his debt, calculated by a special formula, in full before any other creditor is entitled to interest[1]. For the purpose of establishing what dividend is due to such a creditor, the amount of his proof is to be reduced by applying the following formula:

$$X \div 1.05^n$$

where X is the value of the proof and n is the period beginning with the relevant date and ending with the date on which the payment of the creditor's debt would otherwise be due expressed in years and months in a decimalised form[2]. In bankruptcy, the relevant date is the date of the bankruptcy order[3]. Where a distribution has previously been made to the creditor, X will be the amount outstanding in respect of the proof. This formula was introduced in response to the criticism made by the House of Lords in *Re Park Air Services Ltd, Christopher Moran Holdings v Bairstow*[4].

[1]   IR 1986, r 11.13(3).
[2]   Using a scientific calculator, the calculation may be carried out by entering 1.05, pressing the button marked 'x^y', entering the value of n, and pressing the button marked '='. The same exercise may be carried on on a Windows calculator on a PC by going to calculator, going to 'view', selecting 'scientific' and then following the foregoing instruction.
[3]   IR 1986, r 11.13.
[4]   [2000] 2 AC 172, 187–188; [1999] 1 BCLC 155, 165.

Interest on debts

23.19   Any surplus remaining after the payment in full of both preferential and ordinary debts is to be applied in paying interest on those debts in respect of the periods during which they have been outstanding since the commencement of the bankruptcy[1]. For this purpose interest on preferential debts ranks equally with interest on ordinary debts[2]. The rate of interest payable is whichever is the greater of the rate specified in the Judgments Act 1838, s 17 at the commencement of the bankruptcy, and any rate applicable to that debt by reason of contract or otherwise[3].

[1]   IA 1986, s 328(4).
[2]   IA 1986, s 328(4).
[3]   IA 1986, s 328(5).

Debts due to bankrupt's spouse or civil partner

23.20   Debts owed in respect of credit provided by a person who, whether or not the bankrupt's spouse or civil partner at the time the credit was provided, was the bankrupt's spouse or civil partner at the commencement of the bankruptcy are postponed and rank in priority after preferential and ordinary debts and interest payable on such debts[1]. If there are sufficient funds in the estate the debts due to the bankrupt's spouse are payable with interest in respect of the period during which they have been outstanding since the commencement of the bankruptcy[2].

1   IA 1986, s 329(1), (2).
2   IA 1986, s 329(2).

Other postponed debts; commercial venture loans

23.21   Where a loan is made to a person engaged or about to engage in any business, on the basis that the lender is to receive either a rate of interest varying with the profits[1], or a share of the profits arising from carrying on the business, the debt represented by that loan is a postponed debt for bankruptcy purposes. It is immaterial whether the contract for the loan was made orally or in writing[2], or whether a continuing business is contemplated or merely an individual commercial venture or transaction[3]. Such a contract will not of itself make the lender a partner, provided it be in writing and signed by or on behalf of all the parties to it[4]. Where such a loan is made and the borrower is made bankrupt, or enters into an arrangement to pay his creditors less than 100 pence in the pound, or dies insolvent, the lender will not be entitled to recover anything in respect of his loan[5], until the claims of the borrower's other creditors have been satisfied in full[6].

1   For the meaning of 'profits' see *Re Spanish Prospecting Co Ltd* [1911] 1 Ch 92 at 98, CA.
2   *Re Fort, ex p Schofield* [1897] 2 QB 495, CA.
3   *Re Abenheim, ex p Abenheim* (1913) 109 LT 219.
4   Partnership Act 1890, s 2(3)(d).
5   *Re Grason, ex p Taylor* (1879) 12 Ch D 366, CA; *Re Tew, ex p Mills* (1873) 8 Ch App 569.
6   Partnership Act 1890, s 2(3)(d), note that this provision is not affected by the IA 1986, see s 328(6).

23.22   The creditor who is party to such a contract will have his debt postponed, even if the contract is for payment of a fixed sum out of the profits[1], or the sum due is described as a salary[2]. The relevant date is the date on which the loan was made[3], and if the case falls within the Partnership Act 1890, s 2 under the terms of the original contract no subsequent variation short of a repayment of the loan and the making of a fresh one will take the case out of s 2[4].

1   *Re Young, ex p Jones* [1896] 2 QB 484.
2   *Re Stone* (1886) 33 Ch D 541.
3   *Re Stone* (1886) 33 Ch D 541; *Re Tew, ex p Mills* (1873) 8 Ch App 569.
4   *Re Tew, ex p Mills* (1873) 8 Ch App 569; *Re Grason, ex p Taylor* (1879) 12 Ch D 366, CA; *Re Hildesheim, ex p Trustee* [1893] 2 QB 357; *Re Mason, ex p Bing* [1899] 1 QB 810.

23.23 Although the debt representing the loan is postponed to other creditors the lender's rights in any security given for the loan will not be affected by the borrower's bankruptcy[1].

1   *Re Lonergan, ex p Sheil* (1877) 4 Ch D 789, CA; *Badeley v Consolidated Bank* (1888) 38 Ch D 238, CA.

23.24 A person who sells the goodwill of his business in consideration for a portion of the profits of the business, by way of annuity or otherwise, is in a similar position. He will not be a partner in the business or liable as such[1] but he cannot prove for his unpaid profits until the claims of all the other creditors for valuable consideration in money or money's worth have been satisfied[2]. Where a person sells a business in consideration of an annuity which is not stated to be payable out of the profits, the seller's right of proof against the buyer's estate will not be postponed[3].

1   Partnership Act 1890, s 2(3)(e).
2   Partnership Act 1890, s 3.
3   *Re Gieve, ex p Shaw* (1809) 80 LT 737, CA.

23.25 A person who advances money to another, not by way of loan but as a contribution to the capital of a business carried on for their joint benefit, is precluded from proving in the bankruptcy of the recipient of the money in competition with the creditors of the business[1].

1   *Re Meade, ex p Humber v Palmer* [1951] Ch 774, [1951] 2 All ER 168, DC.

Surplus

23.26 In the unlikely event that there are any surplus funds available after payment of all fees and expenses, all preferential and ordinary debts which have been proved[1] and interest, postponed debts and interest, that surplus is payable to the bankrupt[2].

1   See *Re Ward, ex p Hammond & Son v Official Receiver and Debtor* [1942] Ch 294, [1942] 1 All ER 513.
2   IA 1986, s 330(5).

B MANNER OF DISTRIBUTION

Payment by dividend

23.27 Whenever the trustee has sufficient funds in hand to do so he is required to declare and distribute dividends among the creditors who have proved their debts, subject to the retention of sufficient money to meet the expenses of the bankruptcy[1]. For this purpose a Member State liquidator appointed in relation to the bankrupt is deemed to be a creditor[2] and if he has proved will be entitled to the appropriate dividend. Dividends are paid by 'payment instruments'[3] which are prepared by the Department of Trade and Industry at the trustee's request[4]. The Department provides a form on which the trustee may make his application for payment instruments[5]. The trustee must keep proper records to explain the receipts and payments made by him in the administration of the estate[6], and these records must include the total amount of every dividend which the trustee wishes to pay[7]. On vacating office the trustee is required to endorse 'cancelled' on any payable orders still in his possession before returning them to the Department[8].

1   IA 1986, s 324(1).
2   IR 1986, r 11.1(3).
3   Ie a cheque or payable order, Insolvency Regulations 1994, SI 1994/2507, reg 3(1).
4   Insolvency Regulations 1994, SI 1994/2507, reg 23(1).
5   Insolvency Regulations 1994, SI 1994/2507, reg 23(2).
6   Insolvency Regulations 1994, SI 1994/2507, reg 24(1).
7   Insolvency Regulations 1994, SI 1994/2507, reg 23(3).
8   Insolvency Regulations 1994, SI 1994/2507, reg 23(4).

Distribution of property in specie

23.28   In appropriate cases, which will be rare, the trustee has power, with the permission of the creditors' committee, to divide the bankrupt's property in its existing form amongst the creditors according to its estimated value[1]. The property must be such that from its peculiar nature or other special circumstances it cannot readily or advantageously be sold. The creditor's committee may not give the trustee a general sanction to divide property *in specie*; each particular proposed exercise of the power must be separately authorised[2]. A person dealing with the trustee in good faith and for value need not be concerned to inquire whether any requisite permission has been given[3].

1   IA 1986, s 326(1).
2   IA 1986, s 326(2).
3   IA 1986, s 326(2).

23.29   The trustee may obtain subsequent ratification of any division of the bankrupt's goods undertaken without authorisation either from the creditor's committee, provided it is satisfied that the trustee acted in a case of urgency and has sought its ratification without undue delay, or from the court[1]. If he does not obtain ratification the trustee will not be entitled to have his expenses paid out of the bankrupt's estate.

1   IA 1986, s 326(3).

Unclaimed funds and dividends

23.30   Any moneys representing unclaimed or undistributed assets of the bankrupt or dividends in the hands of the trustee in bankruptcy at the date of his vacation of office, or which comes into the hands of any former trustee in bankruptcy at any time after his vacation of office, must be paid by him into the Insolvency Services Account[1]. From this account money is paid from time to time into the Consolidated Fund[2]. A creditor who wishes to make a claim for an unpaid dividend after the trustee has paid it into the Insolvency Services Account must apply to the Secretary of State for payment, providing such evidence of his claim as the Secretary of State may require[3]. If dissatisfied with the Secretary of State's decision the creditor may appeal to the court[4].

1   Insolvency Regulations 1994, SI 1994/2507, reg 31.
2   IA 1986, s 407.
3   Insolvency Regulations 1994, SI 1994/2507, reg 32(1).
4   Insolvency Regulations 1994, SI 1994/2507, reg 32(2).

C DIVIDENDS

Notice of intended dividend

23.31 Before declaring a dividend, the trustee must give notice of his intention to do so to all creditors whose addresses are known to him and who have not proved their debts and where a Member State liquidator has been appointed in relation to the bankrupt, to him[1]. Before declaring a first dividend, the trustee must give notice of the intended dividend by public advertisement unless he has previously by public advertisement invited creditors to prove their debts[2]. Any such notice and any notice of a first dividend must give at least 21 days' notice of a specified date ('the last date for proving') up to which proofs may be lodged. This date must be the same for all creditors[3]. The trustee must in his notice state his intention to declare a dividend, whether interim or final, within the period of four months from the last date for proving[4].

1   IA 1986, s 324(2); IR 1986, r 11.2(1).
2   IR 1986, r 11.2(1A).
3   IR 1986, r 11.2(2).
4   IR 1986, r 11.2(3).

Final admission and rejection of proofs

23.32 Within seven days from the last date for proving the trustee must deal with every creditor's proof, in so far as not already dealt with, by admitting or rejecting it in whole or in part, or by making such other provision as he thinks fit[1]. The trustee is not obliged to deal with proofs lodged after the last date for proving; but he may do so in his own discretion[2]. In the declaration of a dividend no payment shall be made more than once by virtue of the same debt. Where a creditor has proved and a Member State liquidator has proved in relation to the same debt, then payment shall only be made to the creditor (subject to any assignment which he may have made pursuant to IR 1986, r 11.11)[3]. The risk of double payment arises because a Member State liquidator has the right to prove on behalf of creditors who have lodged claims in the proceedings in which he was appointed; those creditors also have the right to prove in the English bankruptcy. A trustee will have to scrutinise carefully the proofs lodged by creditors directly with the proof lodged by the Member State liquidator.

1   IR 1986, r 11.3(1).
2   IR 1986, r 11.3(2).
3   IR 1986, r 11.3(3) and (4).

Declaration of dividend

23.33 If the trustee has not had cause to postpone or cancel the dividend in the four-month period stated in his notice of intended dividend, he must within that period proceed to declare the dividend of which he gave notice[1]. The trustee may have to postpone or cancel a proposed dividend if in the period of four months stated in the notice of dividend:

(1) he has rejected a proof in whole or in part and application is made to the court for his decision to be reversed or varied; or

(2) application is made to the court for the trustee's decision on a proof to be reversed or varied, or for a proof to be expunged, or for a reduction of the amount claimed[2].

[1] IR 1986, r 11.5(1).
[2] IR 1986, r 11.4.

23.34 Except with the leave of the court, the trustee may not declare the dividend so long as there is pending any application to the court to reverse or vary a decision of his on a proof, or to expunge a proof or to reduce the amount claimed. If the court gives leave for a dividend to be declared it may direct the trustee to make provision in respect of the proof in question[1]. In the calculation and distribution of a dividend the trustee must make provision for: (a) any bankruptcy debts which appear to him to be due to persons who, by reason of the distance of their place of residence, may not have had sufficient time to tender and establish their proofs; (b) any bankruptcy debts which are the subject of claims which have not yet been determined; and (c) disputed proofs and claims[2].

[1] IR 1986, r 11.5(2).
[2] IA 1986, s 324(4).

Notice of declaration

23.35 The creditors who have proved their debts and any Member State liquidator who has been appointed are entitled to notice of dividend from the trustee[1] and this notice must inform them of:

(1) the amounts realised from the sale of assets, indicating, so far as practicable, amounts raised by the sale of particular assets;

(2) any payments made by the trustee in the administration of the bankrupt's estate;

(3) any provision made for unsettled claims, or funds retained for particular purposes;

(4) the total amount to be distributed, and the rate of dividend;

(5) whether, and if so when, any further dividend is expected to be declared[2].

[1] IA 1986, s 324(3).
[2] IR 1986, r 11.6(2).

23.36 The dividend may be distributed simultaneously with the notice of dividend[1]. Payment of dividend may be made by post, or arrangements may be made with any creditor for it to be paid to him in another way, or held for his collection[2]. In cases where the dividend is paid on a bill of exchange or other negotiable instrument, the amount of the dividend must be indorsed on the instrument, or on a certified copy of it, if required to be produced by the holder for that purpose[3].

1   IR 1986, r 11.6(3).
2   IR 1986, r 11.6(4).
3   IR 1986, r 11.6(5).

23.37 If the trustee gives notice to creditors that he is unable to declare any dividend or any further dividend, he must explain in his notice whether this is because no funds have been realised or that the funds realised have already been distributed or used or allocated for defraying the expenses of administration[1].

1   IR 1986, r 11.7.

23.38 Where a creditor has proved for a debt of which payment is not due at the date of the declaration of dividend, he is entitled to dividend equally with other creditors, but subject to a reduction of 5% pa calculated on a monthly basis in respect of his admitted proof[1]. The IR 1986 expressly provide that other creditors are not entitled to interest out of surplus funds until any such creditor has been paid the full amount of his debt[2]. What constitutes the full amount is not defined. The point will usually be of purely academic interest, but it would seem that this provision is unnecessary if the 1986 Rules did not intend that the future creditor should have the whole of the face value of his debt paid before other creditors are paid interest on past debts, but unfair in favouring future creditors over past creditors if it should be interpreted in this way[3].

1   IR 1986, r 11.13(1).
2   IR 1986, r 11.13(3).
3   It is to be interpreted in this way. This provision was criticised by the House of Lords in *Re Christopher Moran Holdings Ltd v Bairstow* [2000] 2 AC 172 at 187.

Proof made or altered after payment of dividend

23.39 Neither a creditor who has not proved his debt before the declaration of any dividend nor a creditor who increases the amount claimed in his proof after a payment of dividend is entitled to disturb dividends which have already been distributed[1]. He will however be entitled to be paid such dividend as he has not yet received out of any available money and in any event before any further dividend is paid[2]. In cases where a creditor's proof is withdrawn, expunged, or reduced after a dividend has been paid the creditor is liable forthwith to repay to the trustee any sum to which he is not entitled[3].

1   IA 1986, s 325(1).
2   IA 1986, s 325(1)(a), (b); see also IR 1986, r 11.8(1), (2).
3   IR 1986, r 11.8(3).

23.40 Similarly where a secured creditor revalues his security after payment of a dividend has been declared, he may not disturb payments made where he is entitled to further payment, and must repay to the trustee any sum to which in the light of the revaluation he is no longer entitled[1]. If a creditor contravenes any provision relating to the revaluation of securities, the court may, on the application of the trustee, order that the creditor be wholly or partly disqualified from participation in any dividend[2].

[1] IR 1986, r 11.9(1)–(3).
[2] IR 1986, r 11.10.

Assignment of right to dividend

23.41 If a person entitled to a dividend gives notice[1] to the trustee that he wishes the dividend to be paid to another person, or that he has assigned his entitlement to another person, the trustee must pay the dividend to the person or assignee concerned[2]. A notice so given must specify the name and address of the person to whom payment is to be made[3].

[1] Notice may be sent by post or served personally, IR 1986, r 13.3.
[2] IR 1986, r 11.11(1).
[3] IR 1986, r 11.11(2).

Preferential creditors

23.42 The trustee declares and pays dividends to preferential creditors in the same way as with ordinary creditors, but he is entitled to adapt the procedure as he considers appropriate considering that preferential creditors are of a limited class[1]. The notice of an intended dividend for preferential creditors need only be given to those creditors whose debts the trustee believes to be preferential, and public advertisement of the intended dividend need only be given if the trustee thinks fit[2].

[1] IR 1986, r 11.12(1).
[2] IR 1986, r 11.12(2).

Liability of trustee for dividend

23.43 No action lies against the trustee for a dividend whether declared or not[1]. In the event that the trustee refuses to pay a dividend, the creditor concerned may apply to the court for an order that it be paid, and the court may, if it thinks fit, also order the trustee to pay, out of his own money, interest at judgment rate[2] on the dividend from the time it was withheld, and the costs of the proceedings[3].

[1] IA 1986, s 325(2).
[2] Ie the rate specified for the Judgments Act 1838, s 17.
[3] IA 1986, s 325(2).

Final distribution and meeting of creditors

23.44 The trustee's task is to realise all the bankrupt's estate, but he may bring his administration to an end when he has realised as much of the estate as he is able 'without needlessly protracting the trusteeship'[1]. On completing his administration the trustee must give notice[2] either of his intention to declare a final dividend or that no dividend, or further dividend, will be declared[3]. This notice must contain the prescribed particulars[4] and require claims against the bankrupt's estate to be established by a date ('the final date') specified in the notice[5]. After the final date, which may be postponed by the court on the application of any interested person[6], the trustee must: (1) defray any outstanding expenses of the bankruptcy out of the bankrupt's estate; and (2) declare and distribute any final dividend without regard to any claims not already proved in the bankruptcy[7].

1   IA 1986, s 330(1).
2   In the manner prescribed by IR 1986, r 11.2.
3   IA 1986, s 330(1).
4   Under IR 1986, r 11.6(2).
5   IA 1986, s 330(2).
6   IA 1986, s 330(3).
7   IA 1986, s 330(4).

23.45 When a trustee other than the official receiver considers that his administration is for practical purposes complete he must summon a final general meeting of the bankrupt's creditors to receive his report of his administration of the bankrupt's estate and determine whether the trustee should have his release[1]. The notice summoning the final general meeting may be given at the same time as the notice of final distribution[2].

1   IA 1986, s 331(1), (2).
2   IA 1986, s 331(3).

D SECOND BANKRUPTCY

A second bankruptcy

23.46 An undischarged bankrupt may be made bankrupt, and the creditors of this second or subsequent bankruptcy will be those creditors whose debts arose after the date of the preceding bankruptcy order and before the making of the subsequent bankruptcy order. The creditors of the first or previous bankruptcy have no rights as creditors in the later bankruptcy[1] but the trustee of the earlier bankruptcy may prove in the later bankruptcy for any unsatisfied balance of debts and expenses of the earlier bankruptcy ranking in priority after all the debts and interest in the later bankruptcy. The IA 1986 refers to the trustee of the earlier bankruptcy as 'the existing trustee'[2].

1   IA 1986, s 335(5).
2   IA 1986, s 334(1).

23.47 *Distribution of bankrupt's estate*

Stay of distribution in case of second bankruptcy

23.47 Where a bankruptcy order is made against an undischarged bankrupt and the existing trustee[1] has been given the prescribed notice[2] of the presentation of the petition for the later bankruptcy, any distribution or other disposition by him after receiving the notice, of:

(1)　any property which is vested in the existing trustee as after-acquired property;

(2)　any money paid to the trustee in pursuance of an income payments order; and

(3)　any property or money which is, or in the hands of the existing trustee represents, the proceeds of sale or application of property or money falling within either of the above heads,

is void except to the extent that it was made with the consent of the court or is or was subsequently ratified by the court[3].

1　Ie the trustee of the earlier bankruptcy.
2　For the prescribed form see IR 1986, r 12.7, Sch 4, Form 6.78.
3　IA 1986, s 334(1), (2).

Adjustment between earlier and later bankrupt estates

23.48 On the making of a bankruptcy order against an undischarged bankrupt the following property ceases to form part of the existing estate and is treated as being comprised in the estate of the later bankruptcy, namely:

(1)　any property which is vested in the existing trustee as after-acquired property;

(2)　any money paid to the existing trustee in pursuance of an income payments order; and

(3)　any property or money which is, or in the hands of the existing trustee represents, the proceeds of sale or application of property or money falling within heads (1) or (2) above[1].

1　IA 1986, ss 334(1), 335(1).

23.49 Until there is a trustee of the later estate, the property is to be dealt with by the existing trustee[1]. Any sums which in pursuance of an income payments order are payable after the commencement of the later bankruptcy to the existing trustee form part of the bankrupt's estate for the purposes of the later bankruptcy, and the court may give directions for the modification of the income payments order as may be appropriate[2].

1　IA 1986, s 335(1).
2　IA 1986, s 335(2).

23.50 All other property which is, or is capable of being comprised in the bankrupt's estate for the purposes of the earlier bankruptcy remains property in the earlier bankruptcy[1].

1　IA 1986, s 335(4).

23.51 The creditors of the bankrupt in the earlier bankruptcy may not prove in the later bankruptcy in respect of the same debts, but the existing trustee may prove in the later bankruptcy for:

(a) the unsatisfied balance of the debts provable against the bankrupt's estate in the earlier bankruptcy;
(b) any interest payable on that balance; and
(c) any unpaid expenses of the earlier bankruptcy[1].

¹   IA 1986, s 335(5).

23.52 Any amount so provable ranks in priority after all the other debts provable in the later bankruptcy and after interest on those debts and, accordingly, may not be paid unless those debts and that interest have first been paid in full[1].

¹   IA 1986, s 335(6).

Expenses of trustees of earlier estate

23.53 Any property comprised in a bankrupt's second estate which had formed part of his first estate prior to the commencement of the second bankruptcy is subject to a first charge in favour of the existing trustee for any bankruptcy expenses incurred by him in relation to the property[1]. Any expenses so incurred by the existing trustee must be defrayed out of, and are a charge on any property or money which the existing trustee has received as after-acquired property or in pursuance of an income payments order or which represents the proceeds of sale or application of such property or money, whether in the hands of the existing trustee or of the trustee of the later bankruptcy[2].

¹   IA 1986, s 335(3).
²   IR 1986, r 6.228.

Chapter 24

BANKRUPTCY OFFENCES

A   Offences committed by bankrupt
B   Defence of innocent intention
C   Specified offences
D   Offence by debtor in relation to proposal for IVA
E   Offences committed by other persons
F   Practice and procedure

A OFFENCES COMMITTED BY BANKRUPT

Prosecution by Secretary of State or DPP

24.1 The Insolvency Act 1986 ('IA 1986')[1] specifies a number of offences which may be committed by the bankrupt either (a) by his acts or omissions occurring after an order has been made on a bankruptcy petition presented against him, or (b) by his acts occurring before the commencement of the bankruptcy which may become offences by virtue of the bankruptcy order being made. As is explained below some bankruptcy offences are absolute offences, but with a defence of innocent intention, and others require the prosecution to prove the necessary *mens rea*. All require the accused to have been bankrupt at the relevant time. As to whether it may be a defence that the accused did not believe that he was bankrupt at the relevant time, there is no authority under the IA 1986. It is likely that the courts will hold that the bankruptcy element of these offences is strict, and reject as a defence any belief asserted by the bankrupt that he was not an undischarged bankrupt[2]. Proceedings for any of those offences may only be instituted by the Secretary of State or by, or with the consent of, the Director of Public Prosecutions[3].

---

[1]   IA 1986, Part XI, Chapter VI, ss 350–360.
[2]   See *R v Brockley* (1993) 99 Cr App Rep 385, CA, a case under CDDA 1986, s 11, following the propositions as to when the courts should hold that offences are absolute set out in *Gammon (Hong Kong) Ltd v A-G of Hong Kong* [1985] AC 1 at 14. See also *R v Doring* [2002] EWCA Crim 1695, [2003] 1 Cr App Rep 143.
[3]   IA 1986, s 350(5).

964

Acts committed outside the jurisdiction

24.2 It is no defence to a bankruptcy offence that anything relied on, in whole or in part, as constituting the relevant offence was done outside England and Wales[1].

[1]   IA 1986, s 350(4).

Annulment no bar to prosecution

24.3 A bankrupt may be prosecuted for a bankruptcy offence even if his bankruptcy order is annulled; but the prosecution must be instituted before the annulment[1].

[1]   IA 1986, s 350(2).

Liability to prosecution after discharge

24.4 A bankrupt is not liable to be prosecuted for anything done after his discharge[1]. A prosecution for a bankruptcy offence may, however, be instituted after the bankrupt's discharge for an offence committed before his discharge[2].

[1]   IA 1986, s 350(3).
[2]   IA 1986, s 350(3).

Bankruptcy restrictions order

24.5 Introduced by the Enterprise Act 2002[1] at the same time as the period before automatic discharge was reduced to one year, a bankruptcy restrictions order may be imposed on any bankrupt whose conduct in becoming bankrupt or after the making of a bankruptcy order is considered to be blameworthy in some relevant respect[2]. A court may grant a bankruptcy restrictions order if it thinks it appropriate having regard to the bankrupt's conduct generally[3], but in considering whether or not to make an order the court is required to take into account any behaviour of the bankrupt which comes within 13 kinds of behaviour specified by the statute[4]. The specified behaviours include the failure to keep proper records and the carrying on of any gambling or rash and hazardous speculation which previously constituted but are now no longer separate bankruptcy offences[5]. The fact that a bankruptcy restrictions order is in force in relation to a former bankrupt does not preclude his prosecution for an offence committed before his discharge[6].

[1]   EA 2002, s 257 and Sch 21.
[2]   Bankruptcy restrictions orders are covered in **Chapter 11**.
[3]   IA 1986, s 281A, Sch 4A, para 2(1).
[4]   IA 1986, s 281A, Sch 4A, para 2(2).
[5]   IA 1986, ss 361 (no proper accounting records) and 362 (gambling, rash and hazardous speculation) were repealed with effect from 1 April 2004 by EA 2002, s 263.
[6]   IA 1986, s 350(3A).

B DEFENCE OF INNOCENT INTENTION

The statutory defence

24.6 Many of the offences created by IA 1986 are drawn both widely and without the inclusion of any specific element of *mens rea*. The *actus reus* of individual offences may be committed without culpability on the part of the individual bankrupt. To avoid possible injustice in such cases IA 1986 provides a general defence, the 'defence of innocent intention'. The defence is contained in IA 1986, s 352 which provides:

> 'Where in the case of an offence under any provision of this Chapter[1] it is stated that this section applies, a person is not guilty of the offence if he proves that, at the time of the conduct constituting the offence, he had no intent to defraud or to conceal the state of his affairs'.

[1]   Ie IA 1986, Part XI, Chapter VI, ss 350–360.

24.7 The application of this defence to individual offences is set out in the text below. It will be seen that the offences excepted from this defence[1] are all offences which incorporate a specific *mens rea* element requiring the prosecution to prove dishonesty before the offence is made out.

[1]   Namely the offences of failure to account for or explain loss of property (see para **24.32**), failure to inform of false proof (see para **24.47**), advancing fictitious losses (see para **24.48**), fraudulently obtaining creditors' consent (see para **24.49**), obtaining credit without disclosing status as undischarged bankrupt (see para **24.57**), and use of business name other than name in which adjudicated bankrupt (see para **24.64**).

24.8 The wording of the defence suggests that the burden of proof in relation to any dishonesty involved in the *mens rea* of the offence is transferred to the accused. Prior to the coming into force of the Human Rights Act 1998 the defence of innocent intention was interpreted in the 'conventional' manner. The prosecution had first to prove, beyond reasonable doubt, the elements of the offence with which the accused is charged. If the accused wished to rely on the defence of innocent intention he had then to discharge a legal or persuasive burden of proof by showing on a balance of probabilities that he had no intent to defraud or to conceal the state of his affairs. A legal or persuasive burden of proof may be contrasted with an evidential burden of proof. 'Evidential burden of proof' is 'a convenient way of describing a requirement that a party adduce some evidence in support of his case on any particular issue before that issue is left to the jury'[1].

[1]   Per Lord Devlin in *Jayasena v R* [1970] AC 618 PC at 624C–E: the phrase is 'otherwise meaningless'.

The impact of the Human Rights Act 1998

24.9 Interpreted conventionally, in the absence of the Human Rights Act 1998, the combined effect of the offence and the statutory defence is to reverse the burden of proof on an essential element of the offence. It will be for the accused to prove lack of fraud or dishonesty[1]. Article 6(2) of the

European Convention on Human Rights provides that everyone charged with a criminal offence shall be presumed innocent until proved guilty according to law. The burden of proof in criminal cases has therefore to be on the prosecution. Placing a persuasive burden on an accused to prove a particular defence will, to a greater or lesser extent depending upon the crime in question, amount to a breach of the presumption of innocence. The European Court of Human Rights has however permitted the principle enshrined in art 6(2) to be qualified in cases where the law requires an accused to prove a specific defence to a charge which has otherwise been proved by the prosecution[2] or where the law makes presumptions of law or fact against an accused in circumstances which are not incompatible with the European Convention[3]. To be compatible with the European Convention presumptions of fact or law against the accused or requirements placed on an accused to prove a specific defence must be kept within reasonable limits and must not be arbitrary:

> 'It is open to states to define the constituent elements of a criminal offence, excluding the requirement of *mens rea*. But the substance and effect of any presumption adverse to an accused must be examined, and must be reasonable. Relevant to any judgment on reasonableness or proportionality will be the opportunity given to the accused to rebut the presumption, maintenance of the rights of the defence, flexibility in application of the presumption, retention by the court of a power to assess the evidence, the importance of what is at stake and the difficulty which a prosecutor may face in the absence of a presumption'.[4]

1   See *R v Daniel* [2002] EWCA Crim 959, [2003] 1 Cr App Rep 99 at [15].
2   See, for example, *Lingens v Austria* (1981) 4 EHRR 373.
3   See, for example, *Salabiaku v France* (1988) 13 EHRR 379.
4   Per Lord Bingham in *Sheldrake v DPP, A-G's Reference (No 4 of 2002)* [2004] UKHL 43, [2003] 1 AC 264 at [21].

24.10 It follows that no uniform approach may be adopted in all cases where the legislation enacting a crime seeks to impose a persuasive burden on an accused to prove a specific defence. Each enactment imposing such a burden has to be considered on its merits. Where the courts consider that it is reasonable and proportionate to impose a persuasive burden of proof on the accused that requirement stands. Where the courts take the opposite view the relevant statutory provision may be declared incompatible with the Convention right enshrined in art 6(2)[1], or, more probably, will be construed as creating merely an evidential burden on the accused so as to give effect to the provision in a way which is compatible with the accused's Convention right[2].

1   Under the Human Rights Act 1998, s 4.
2   Such an approach to construction is required by the Human Rights Act 1998, s 3; though see the comments of the Court of Appeal in *R v Daniel* [2002] EWCA Crim 959, [2003] 1 Cr App Rep 99 where the court suggested the words of the statutory defence '[an accused] is not guilty if he proves' or 'it is a defence for the [accused] to prove' must, 'as a matter of plain English', mean more than the evidential raising of an issue for the prosecution to refute beyond reasonable doubt. While noting that the courts are required, by HRA 1998, s 3(1), to strive for compatibility through the medium of interpretation the Court stated 'where there is plain incompatibility between the ordinary and natural meaning of statutory words *whatever the context* and art 6(2), the court should take care not to strive for compatibility by so changing the meaning of those words as to give them a sense that they cannot, in the sense intended by section 3(1), *possibly* bear'. The court

suggested that the distinction between what are *procedural* guarantees in art 6(2) and the *substantive* elements of the offence has not been clearly made, quoting with apparent approval the suggestion that art 6(2) has no bearing on substantive law requirements. Accordingly reversing the burden of proof on elements of the offence and even offences of strict or absolute liability would not be contrary to the accused's art 6(2) Convention right.

24.11 The principles upon which courts should interpret statutory provisions which impose burdens of proof on the accused have been considered by the House of Lords in *R v Johnstone*[1] and *Sheldrake v DPP, A-G's Reference (No 4 of 2002)*[2] and the decision of a five-man Court of Appeal in *A-G's Reference (No 1 of 2004), R v Edwards*[3]. In this last appeal, heard after *Johnstone* but before *A-G's Reference (No 4 of 2002)* the Court of Appeal gave general guidance to be followed in individual cases[4], but this guidance was expressly not endorsed by the House of Lords in *A-G's Reference (No 4 of 2002)*[5]. In particular, concern was expressed with the particular guidance that 'the assumption should be that Parliament would not have made an exception without good reason'[6]. This approach, it was felt, may lead the court to give too much weight to the enactment under review and too little to the presumption of innocence and the obligation imposed by the Human Rights Act 1998, s 3 to read and give effect to domestic legislation in a way which is compatible with Convention rights. Their Lordships were 'inclined to agree' with the Court of Appeal's conclusion in each of the cases before them[7] but were clearly not prepared to go further than provide a general canvas by reference to which courts should determine individual cases as and when they arise.

1   [2003] UKHL 28, [2003] 3 All ER 884 a case concerning the defence available to an accused under the Trade Marks Act 1994, s 92(5): 'it is a defence for a person ... to show that he believed on reasonable grounds that the use of the sign in the manner in which it was used, or was to be used, was not an infringement of the registered trade mark'.
2   [2004] UKHL 43, [2005] 1 AC 264 concerning the defences available under the Terrorism Act 2000, s 11(2) and the Road Traffic Act 1988, s 5.
3   [2004] EWCA Crim 1025, [2005] 4 All ER 457 concerning two bankruptcy offences (failing to inform the official receiver of the disposal of property – IA 1986, s 353(1) and transferring property within five years of the commencement of the bankruptcy – IA 1986, s 357(1)); the Protection from Eviction Act 1977, s 1(2); the Homicide Act 1957, s 4(2); the Criminal Justice and Public Order Act 1994, s 51(7).
4   [2004] EWCA Crim 1025, [2005] 4 All ER 457 at [52].
5   [2004] UKHL 43, [2005] 1 AC 264 at [32], [55], [56].
6   [2004] UKHL 43, [2005] 1 AC 264 at [52]D.
7   And most importantly for insolvency lawyers '... and would in particular agree that *R v Carass* [2001] EWCA Crim 2845, [2002] 1 WLR 1714 was wrongly decided' per Lord Bingham at para 32.

The defence of innocent intention in practice

24.12 The approach indicated by the House of Lords to the proper interpretation of reverse burdens of proof together with approval, albeit cautiously given, to the individual conclusions of the Court of Appeal in *A-G's Reference (No 1 of 2004)* (and in particular the express agreement of the House of Lords that *R v Carass*[1] was wrongly decided) should provide a strong indication as to the status of the defence of innocent intention with respect to the various offences to which it applies. The Court of Appeal in *A-G's Reference (No 1 of*

2004) recognised that insolvency offences, both in corporate and individual insolvency, have long been regarded as subject to special rules:

> 'The reasons for this are not difficult to see. The law gives those involved in the affairs of a company the benefit of its corporate personality and in the case of most companies the additional very great benefit of limited liability. In the case of individual insolvency, the law relieves the bankrupt of personal liability for his debts, which are met out of his estate. These benefits drastically affect the rights and remedies of the creditors. The proper working of our insolvency law depends on the inclusion in the assets of an insolvent company and in the estate of a bankrupt of all the assets that should be comprised in them. In can be tempting for those involved in the management of a company or bankrupt to conceal or to dispose of such assets to the disadvantage of creditors. Furthermore, such concealment or disposal may be done by a person alone and in private: a failure to record or to disclose any assets, or a disposal of stock at an undervalue or the making of a disposal for nil consideration, may be known only to those involved in the transaction. There may well be no independent witnesses to the act in question. Whether there had been fraud will often be known only to the individual or individuals who are alleged to have committed the fraud.'[2]

1   [2001] EWCA Crim 2845, [2002] 1 WLR 1714; In *R v Carass* the Court of Appeal had suggested that in *all* cases where an intent to defraud was an ingredient the defendant faced only an evidential burden (a requirement 'to adduce evidence sufficient to raise an issue that he had no intent to defraud') leaving the prosecution having to prove the contrary beyond reasonable doubt.
2   [2004] EWCA Crim 1025, [2005] 4 All ER 457 at [81].

24.13 These considerations will normally be sufficient to justify imposing a persuasive burden on a defendant to prove that when he deliberately acted in a way which may be inferred to involve a fraud on his creditors he did not in fact have fraudulent intent. In cases where there is no deliberate act from which a fraudulent inference may be drawn it will be less easy to justify imposing a persuasive burden on the defendant to prove that he had no fraudulent intention[1].

1   [2004] EWCA Crim 1025, [2005] 4 All ER 457 at [82].

24.14 In *A-G Reference (No 1 of 2004)* and *R v Edwards*[1] the Court of Appeal considered two cases involving the defence of innocent intention as it applied to two offences:

(1)   failing to inform the official receiver of the disposal of property which would but for the disposal have been comprised in the bankrupt's estate[2];
(2)   making a transfer of property within five years of the commencement of the bankruptcy[3].

1   [2004] EWCA Crim 1025, [2005] 4 All ER 457.
2   Contrary to IA 1986, s 353(1)(b), see para **24.21**.
3   Contrary to IA 1986, s 357(1), see para **24.50**.

24.15 The court noted that with respect to the first of these offences the prosecution had to prove:

(i) that the bankrupt failed to inform the official receiver of a disposal of property that but for the disposal would be comprised in his estate; and

(ii) that the disposal was not in the ordinary course of business or made in payment of his ordinary living expenses.

24.16 Once those matters have been proved it would follow that the disposal in question would be an unusual disposal, and therefore a perfectly acceptable inference that the disposal was intended to defeat creditors:

> 'We see nothing unreasonable for a bankrupt against whom the above facts have been proved beyond reasonable doubt to have to establish on a balance of probabilities that when he failed to inform the official receiver of the disposal he did not intend to defraud or to conceal the state of his affairs. The intention of the defendant when he failed to inform the official receiver of the unusual transaction will be peculiarly within his knowledge and he will know what his motive was'.[1]

[1] [2004] EWCA Crim 1025, [2005] 4 All ER 457 at [95].

24.17 Accordingly the Court of Appeal held that the defence of innocent intention was compatible with art 6(2) when read together with IA 1986, s 353(1)(b) in imposing a persuasive burden of proof.

24.18 With respect to the second of the above offences the Court of Appeal noted that the ambit of the relevant provision, IA 1986, s 357(1), is very wide indeed. It applies to disposals of property made long before the commencement of the bankruptcy, and possibly at the time when there was no indication of insolvency. There is no minimum value of the gift or transfer for which the bankrupt may be called to account, neither does the prosecution have to establish anything unusual or irregular in the making of the gift or the disposal. There is no requirement on the prosecution to prove that the bankrupt was aware of the possibility of his insolvency when he made the gift or disposal. There is no time limit on prosecutions, and they are unlikely to be brought until a considerable time after the individual has been made bankrupt. The Court of Appeal concluded that to make the bankrupt prove that he had no intent to defraud was not justified and infringed art 6(2). Accordingly the court held that the defence of innocent intention should, when applied to IA 1986, s 357(1), be interpreted as imposing merely an evidential burden on the defendant[1].

[1] [2004] EWCA Crim 1025, [2005] 4 All ER 457 at [90], [99].

C SPECIFIED OFFENCES

Failure to disclose property

24.19 The bankrupt commits an offence if he does not disclose all the property comprised in his estate to the best of his knowledge and belief to the official receiver or trustee[1]. Although after-acquired property no longer comprises property of the bankrupt's estate, it may become part of the estate if the trustee serves a notice claiming it under the IA 1986, s 307. The trustee may also claim property which the bankrupt is using for his business or household needs under the IA 1986, s 310. The Act[2] provides that any property which the trustee may claim under either of these sections is included as property comprised in the bankrupt's estate for the purposes of this offence. The disclosure must be to the official receiver or trustee, so disclosure to creditors will not suffice though it may well be strong evidence in support of a defence of innocent intention. The primary place for disclosure is the statement of affairs which the bankrupt must submit to the official receiver within 21 days of the commencement of the bankruptcy[3]. The statement of affairs and any other statement made by the bankrupt when required to do so may be used in evidence against the bankrupt in any proceedings against him[4].

[1] IA 1986, s 353(1)(a).
[2] IA 1986, s 351(a).
[3] IA 1986, s 288.
[4] IA 1986, s 433.

24.20 The defence of innocent intention applies to this offence[1].

[1] IA 1986, s 353(3), and see paras **24.6–24.8**.

Failure to disclose disposal of property

24.21 The bankrupt commits an offence if he does not inform the official receiver or trustee of any disposal of property which, but for that disposal, would be comprised in his estate[1]. Full details of the disposal must be given showing how, when, to whom and for what consideration the property was disposed. The offence does not cover the disclosure of any disposal in the ordinary course of the bankrupt's business, or any payment of the ordinary expenses of the bankrupt or his family[2]. The IA 1986 does not specify how far back the disclosure should go. It will be noted that the court has jurisdiction to set aside any transaction which was entered into for the purpose of putting assets beyond the reach of creditors and this jurisdiction is not limited in time[3]. Plainly, disclosure of any such transaction may be required of the bankrupt irrespective of its age.

[1] IA 1986, s 353(1)(b) and see **Chapter 14** for what property is comprised in the estate.
[2] IA 1986, s 353(2).
[3] IA 1986, s 423, although individual claims will be subject to a limitation period, see **21.28** et seq.

24.22 The 'ordinary course of a bankrupt's business' and the 'ordinary expenses of the bankrupt and his family' will usually be easy to recognise in practice, although providing a comprehensive definition is not straightforward. The previous offence of this nature[1] referred to 'the ordinary way of [the bankrupt's] trade' and over a century of enactment no difficulties worthy of a reported appellate decision appear to have been encountered. Earlier, under the Debtors' Act 1869, s 11(15), it had been an offence for 'a trader to pawn, pledge or dispose of any property obtained on credit otherwise than in the ordinary way of trade, unless the jury was satisfied that he had no intent to defraud'. In this connection it was held that a trader who executed a bill of sale over goods acquired on credit in favour of his sister to meet a debt owing to her was not disposing of the goods in the ordinary way of trade; furthermore that assigning the whole of the property to one creditor while reserving nothing for the others showed an intent to defraud[2]. It was open to the jury to find that a toolmaker who ordered six tons of steel worth 18s. a cwt. and sold it on for 14s. per cwt. was not disposing of goods in the ordinary way of trade[3]. Disposing of goods obtained on credit before they were paid for does not constitute the offence where this was the trader's normal way of conducting business[4], neither was an offence committed by a trader who, while completely insolvent, bought goods on credit, exported them, and obtained advances on the bills of lading[5].

[1] Under the Bankruptcy Act 1914, s 154(1).
[2] *R v Thomas* (1870) 22 LT 138, 11 Cox CC 535.
[3] *R v Bolus* (1870) 23 LT 339, 11 Cox CC 610.
[4] *R v Juston* (1897) 61 JP 505.
[5] *Re Hodgson, ex p Brett* (1875) 1 Ch D 151, CA.

24.23 The defence of innocent intention applies to this offence[1].

[1] IA 1986, s 353(3) and see paras **24.6–24.8**.

Failure to deliver up property

24.24 The bankrupt commits an offence if he fails to deliver up any property to the official receiver or trustee which he is required by law to deliver up and which is in his possession or under his control[1]. The official receiver or trustee may direct the bankrupt to give possession of only part of his property in which case only that part is relevant for the purposes of this offence.

[1] IA 1986, s 354(1)(a).

24.25 The defence of innocent intention applies to this offence[1].

[1] IA 1986, s 354(1) and see paras **24.6–24.8**.

Concealment of debts or property

24.26 The bankrupt commits an offence if he conceals any debt due to or from him or conceals any property which he is required to deliver up to the official receiver or trustee, the value of which is not less than the prescribed amount[1].

[1] IA 1986, s 354(1)(b); the prescribed amount is £1,000; see the Insolvency Proceedings (Monetary Limits) (Amendment) Order 2004, SI 2004/547, art 2, Schedule.

24.27 The defence of innocent intention applies to this offence[1].

[1] IA 1986, s 354(1) and see paras **24.6–24.8**.

Concealment prior to bankruptcy

24.28 The bankrupt commits an offence if he conceals debts or property valued at not less than the prescribed amount during the 12 months preceding the presentation of the petition or between the presentation of the petition and the commencement of the bankruptcy[1].

1   IA 1986, s 354(1)(c); the prescribed amount is £1,000; see the Insolvency Proceedings (Monetary Limits) (Amendment) Order 2004, SI 2004/547, art 2, Schedule.

24.29 The defence of innocent intention applies to this offence[1].

1   IA 1986, s 353(3) and see paras **24.6–24.8**.

Removal of property

24.30 The bankrupt commits an offence if he removes any property the value of which is not less than the prescribed amount and which he is required to deliver up to the official receiver or trustee at any time after the presentation of the petition against him[1].

1   IA 1986, s 354(2); the prescribed amount is £1,000; see the Insolvency Proceedings (Monetary Limits) (Amendment) Order 2004, SI 2004/547, art 3, Schedule, Pt II.

24.31 The defence of innocent intention applies to this offence[1].

1   IA 1986, s 354(2) and see paras **24.6–24.8**.

Failure to account for or explain loss of property

24.32 The bankrupt commits an offence if, on being required to do so by the official receiver, or by the court, he fails without reasonable excuse to account for the loss of any substantial part of his property incurred during the 12 months prior to the presentation of the petition or between the presentation of the petition and the commencement of the bankruptcy, or to give a reasonable explanation of the manner in which such a loss was incurred[1]. The equivalent offence under the Bankruptcy Act 1914 was construed by the Court of Appeal as one of strict liability; this was justified because the purpose of the offence is to 'put in peril the man who goes bankrupt without having so conducted his affairs as to be able satisfactorily to explain why some substantial loss has been incurred[2]'. This is in the interests of the business community as a whole and the defence of innocent intention does not apply to this offence.

1   IA 1986, s 354(3).
2   *R v Salter* [1968] 2 QB 793, [1968] 2 All ER 951, CA.

24.33 In *R v Kearns*[1] the Court of Appeal dismissed a complaint that the provisions of IA 1986, s 354(3), compelling as they do a bankrupt to give information to the official receiver, was a breach of ECHR, art 6. The court drew the distinction between the compulsory production of documents or other material which have an existence independent of the will of the accused and statements that he has had to make under compulsion. In the former case there is no infringement of the right to silence and the right not to incriminate oneself; in the latter case there could be, depending on the circumstances. Further, the court observed that a law will not be likely to infringe the right to silence or against self-incrimination if it demands the production of information for an administrative purpose or in the course of an extra-judicial inquiry. Nevertheless, if the information so produced is or could be used in subsequent judicial proceedings, whether criminal or civil, then the use of the information in such proceedings could breach those rights and so make that trial unfair[2]. For the purposes of IA 1986, s 354(3) it will usually be the case that the official receiver required information for the purpose of investigation of the bankrupt's estate, not for an enquiry into any possible criminal conduct of the bankrupt[3]. Accordingly there would be no breach of an art 6 right.

[1]   [2002] EWCA Crim 748, [2002] 1 WLR 2815.
[2]   [2002] EWCA Crim 748, [2002] 1 WLR 2815 at [53].
[3]   See *Saunders v UK* (1997) 23 EHRR 313, 2 BHRC 358, where the ECtHR drew the distinction between the use of answers compulsorily obtained during an insolvency investigation in a subsequent criminal trial and extrajudicial inquiries which are essentially investigative. In the court's view to subject preparatory investigation to the guarantees of a judicial procedure would in practice unduly hamper the effective regulation in the public interest of complex financial and commercial activities. See also *R v Kearns* [2002] EWCA Crim 748, [2002] 1 WLR 2815 at [34] onwards where the Court of Appeal considered relevant European and UK authorities.

Concealment of records

24.34 The bankrupt commits an offence if he does not deliver up to the official receiver or trustee all the books, papers and other records of which he has possession or control and which relate to his estate and affairs or such books, papers, etc which the official receiver or trustee direct him to deliver up[1].

[1]   IA 1986, s 355(1).

24.35 The defence of innocent intention applies to this offence[1].

[1]   IA 1986, s 355(1) and paras **24.6–24.8**.

Destruction, mutilation, falsification, etc of records

24.36 The bankrupt commits an offence if he[1]:

(1)   prevents the production of any books, papers or records relating to his estate and affairs at any time after the presentation of the petition;
(2)   conceals, destroys, mutilates or falsifies any such books, papers or other records or causes or permits such concealment, destruction, mutilation or falsification at any time after the date 12 months prior to the presentation of the petition; or
(3)   makes any false entries in any book, document or record relating to his estate or affairs or causes or permits the making of any such false entry at any time after the date 12 months prior to the presentation of the petition[2].

1   IA 1986, s 355(2).
2   IA 1986, s 355(3).

24.37 Where the false entries are made in a trading record the period of 12 months prior to the presentation of the petition is extended to two years[1]. A 'trading record' is defined as a 'book, document or record which shows or explains the transactions or financial position of a person's business including (a) a periodic record of cash paid and received, (b) a statement of periodic stock-taking, and (c) except in the case of goods sold by way of retail trade, a record of goods sold and purchased which identifies the buyer and seller or enables them to be identified'[2].

1   IA 1986, s 355(4).
2   IA 1986, s 355(5).

24.38 The defence of innocent intention applies to this offence[1].

1   IA 1986, s 355(2) and see paras **24.6–24.8**.

Causes or permits

24.39 The proper interpretation of 'causes or permits' has come before the courts on a number of occasions, both in connection with road traffic legislation[1] and other regulatory statutes. In a case concerning the Road Traffic Act 1935, *McLeod v Buchanan*[2], Lord Russell stated[3]:

> 'To "cause" the user involves some express or positive mandate from the person "causing" to the other person, or some authority from the former to the latter, arising in the circumstances of the case. To "permit" is a looser and vaguer term. It may denote an express permission, general or particular, as distinguished from a mandate. The other person is not told to use the vehicle in the particular way, but he is told that he may do so if he desires. However, the word also includes cases in which permission is merely inferred.'

1   It has for many years been an offence to 'use or cause or permit any other person to use' a motor vehicle without a valid policy of insurance.
2   [1940] 2 All ER 179, HL.
3   [1940] 2 All ER 179 at p 187.

24.40 In *Attorney-General of Hong Kong v Tse Hung-Lit*[1], the Privy Council had to consider the nature of the relationship which was required before a defendant could be said to have caused another person to have acted in contravention of a statutory prohibition. Lord Bridge cited with approval the conclusion of the High Court of Australia in *O'Sullivan v Truth and Sportsman Ltd*[2] after reviewing the English authorities:

> 'This appears to mean that when it is made an offence by or under statute for one man to "cause" the doing of a prohibited act by another the provision is not to be understood as referring to any description of antecedent event or condition produced by the first man which contributed to the determination of the will of the second man to do the prohibited act. Nor is it enough that in producing the antecedent event or condition the first man was actuated by the desire that the second should be led to do the prohibited act. The provision

should be understood as opening up a less indefinite inquiry into the sequence of anterior events to which the forbidden result may be ascribed. It should be interpreted as confined to cases where the prohibited act is done on the actual authority, express or implied, of the party said to have caused it or in consequence of his exerting some capacity which he possesses in fact or law to control or influence the acts of the other. He must moreover contemplate or desire that the prohibited act will ensue.'

1   [1986] AC 876, [1986] 3 All ER 173.
2   (1957) 96 CLR 220, at 228.

24.41 It is open to interpretation in individual cases whether 'permits' requires mens rea solely to the extent that the defendant has a power to control whether the actus reus is committed or not, or whether there has to be mens rea as to the commission of all the various acts which comprise the offence. The former can be seen as a form of absolute liability. In *Gammon (Hong Kong) Ltd v A-G of Hong Kong*[1] Lord Scarman considered when the law should require the proof of mens rea as to all the elements of the actus reus, and formulated five propositions of general application[2]. In the case of an offence relating to the books and records of the bankrupt however as the defence of innocent intention applies the proper approach would appear to be to treat an offence of 'permitting' as one of absolute liability subject to the application of the defence.

1   [1985] AC 1, [1984] 2 All ER 503.
2   [1985] AC 1 at p 14: (1) there is a presumption of law that mens rea is required before a person can be held guilty of a criminal offence; (2) the presumption is particularly strong where the offence is 'truly criminal' in character; (3) the presumption applies to statutory offences, and can be displaced only if this is clearly or by necessary implication the effect of the statute; (4) the only situation in which the presumption can be displaced is where the statute is concerned with an issue of social concern, and public safety is such an issue; (5) even where a statute is concerned with such an issue, the presumption of mens rea stands unless it can also be shown that the creation of strict liability will be effective to promote the objects of the statute by encouraging greater vigilance to prevent the commission of the prohibited act.

Disposal or alteration of records

24.42 The bankrupt commits an offence if he disposes of, alters or makes any omission in any book, document or record relating to his estate or affairs or causes or permits such disposal, alteration or making any omission at any time after the date 12 months prior to the presentation of the petition[1].

1   IA 1986, s 355(3).

24.43 Where the false entries are made in a trading record the period of 12 months prior to the presentation of the petition is extended to two years[1]. A 'trading record' is defined as a 'book, document or record which shows or explains the transactions or financial position of a person's business including (a) a periodic record of cash paid and received, (b) a statement of periodic stock-taking, and (c) except in the case of goods sold by way of retail trade, a record of goods sold and purchased which identifies the buyer and seller or enables them to be identified'[2].

24.44 The defence of innocent intention applies to this offence[1].

1 IA 1986, s 355(3) and see paras **24.6–24.8**.

False statements

24.45 The bankrupt commits an offence if he makes any material omission in his statement of affairs or any other statement relating to his affairs required of him under the IA 1986[1].

1 IA 1986, s 356(1).

24.46 The defence of innocent intention applies to this offence[1].

1 IA 1986, s 356(1) and see paras **24.6–24.8**.

Failure to inform of false proof

24.47 The bankrupt commits an offence if knowing or believing that a false debt has been proved by any person under the bankruptcy, he fails to inform the trustee as soon as practicable[1].

1 IA 1986, s 356(2)(a).

Advancing fictitious losses

24.48 The bankrupt commits an offence if he attempts to account for any part of his property by fictitious losses or expenses. This offence may be committed by the bankrupt at any meeting of his creditors at any time after the date 12 months prior to the presentation of the petition or by a fictitious account in any circumstances after the presentation of the petition[1].

1 IA 1986, s 356(2)(b) and (c).

Fraudulently obtaining creditors' consent

24.49 The bankrupt commits an offence if he makes any false representation or perpetuates any other fraud designed to obtain the consent of his creditors or any of them to an agreement relating to his affairs or his bankruptcy[1].

1 IA 1986, s 356(2)(d).

Fraudulent disposal of property

24.50 The bankrupt commits an offence if he makes or causes to be made at any time after the date five years prior to the commencement of the bankruptcy any gift or transfer of or any charge on his property[1]. Although the offence is termed 'fraudulent' disposal of property there is no express requirement of fraud. The statutory defence of innocent intention applies[2], and will be the critical consideration for this offence. Making a transfer of or charge on property includes causing or conniving at the levying of execution against that property[3].

1   IA 1986, s 357(1).
2   IA 1986, s 357(1), and see paras **24.6–24.8**.
3   IA 1986, s 357(2).

Concealment or removal of property to defeat a judgment

24.51 The bankrupt commits an offence if he conceals or removes any part of his property after or within two months before the date on which a judgment or order for the payment of money has been obtained against him where that judgment or order is not satisfied before the commencement of the bankruptcy[1].

1   IA 1986, s 357(3).

24.52 The defence of innocent intention applies to this offence[1].

1   IA 1986, s 357(3) and see paras **24.6–24.8**.

Absconding with property

24.53 The bankrupt commits an offence if he leaves or makes preparations to leave England and Wales with any property the value of which is not less than the prescribed amount and possession of which he is required to deliver to the official receiver or trustee at any time after the date six months prior to the presentation of the petition[1].

1   IA 1986, s 358; the prescribed amount is £1,000. See the Insolvency Proceedings (Monetary Limits) (Amendment) Order 2004, SI 2004/547, art 3, Schedule, Pt II.

24.54 The defence of innocent intention applies to this offence[1].

1   IA 1986, s 358 and see paras **24.6–24.8**.

Dealing with property on credit

24.55 The bankrupt is guilty of an offence if he disposes of any property which he had obtained on credit at a time when he has not paid for it, at any time after the date 12 months prior to the presentation of the petition[1]. The offence is not committed where the acquisition and disposal of the property was in the ordinary course of business of the bankrupt. In determining whether the acquisition or disposal is in the ordinary course of business, regard may be had in particular to the price paid for the property[2]. The 'disposal' of property includes pawning or pledging the property[3].

¹   IA 1986, s 359(1).
²   IA 1986, s 359(3) and (4).
³   IA 1986, s 359(5).

24.56   The defence of innocent intention applies to this offence[1].

¹   IA 1986, s 359 and see paras **24.6–24.8**.

Obtaining credit without disclosure of status

24.57   The bankrupt commits an offence if either alone, or jointly with another person, he obtains credit at or above the prescribed amount without 'giving the person from whom he obtains it the relevant information about his status' ie that he is an undischarged bankrupt (or that his estate has been sequestrated in Scotland) and that he has not been discharged)[1]. Obtaining credit includes both:

(a)   obtaining goods on hire purchase or conditional sale terms; and
(b)   being paid in advance for the supply of goods or services[2].

¹   IA 1986, s 360(1)(a), (4); the prescribed amount is £500, see the Insolvency Proceedings (Monetary Limits) (Amendment) Order 2004, SI 2004/547, art 3, Sch, Pt II.
²   IA 1986, s 360(2).

24.58   All forms of credit are covered by the offence; the above particular forms of 'credit' are specified for clarity and to overrule contrary authority[1].

¹   See eg *R v Garlick* (1958) 42 Cr App Rep 141, CCA where the court held that entry into a hire-purchase agreement did not amount to obtaining credit, and *Fisher v Raven* [1964] AC 210, [1963] 2 All ER 389, HL where the bankrupt took deposits from customers to make paintings from photographs and this was held not to amount to obtaining credit.

24.59   Whether or not the bankrupt obtains credit for the purposes of the offence depends upon the nature of the agreement not on the intention of the bankrupt. The obtaining of credit means obtaining some benefit from another without immediately giving the consideration in return for which that benefit is provided[1]. Accordingly there was no obtaining of credit where the bankrupt defaulted on his obligations under a hire-purchase agreement and became liable to pay arrears[2] (although now an offence would be committed by the initial entry into the agreement, see above), because on the happening of the default the finance company did not provide credit, but had an instant cause of action for the overdue instalment; 'the antithesis of giving credit'[3]. By the same logic the bankrupt did not obtain credit by falsely representing that the capital provided by a third party would be applied to a joint business venture; the third party obtained an immediate cause of action to avoid the agreement and recover his money[4]. 'Obtaining' must involve 'some conduct, either by words or otherwise, which amounts to an obtaining'[5]. Whether there is an obtaining in circumstances where the bankrupt's bank account became overdrawn after the dishonouring of cheques paid into the account and the payment of cheques drawn by the bankrupt is a question of fact for the jury[6].

¹   *R v Miller* [1977] 3 All ER 986, at 991.
²   *R v Miller* [1977] 3 All ER 986.

24.59 *Bankruptcy offences*

3   *R v Miller* [1977] 3 All ER 986, at 991; the Court of Appeal made the point that the position might have been different had the bankrupt written to the finance company asking for and obtaining an extension of time to make the overdue payment.
4   *R v Ramzan* [1998] 2 Cr App Rep 328, CA.
5   *R v Hayat* (1976) 63 Cr App Rep 181.
6   *R v Hayat* (1976) 63 Cr App Rep 181.

24.60 The bankrupt commits the offence if he obtains credit in excess of the prescribed amount by a series of instalments[1]. Neither is it necessary that all the goods supplied on credit are ordered or supplied at the same time[2]. It is not a defence, though it may go to mitigation, if the bankrupt repays the credit and thereby reduces the debt below the prescribed amount.

1   *R v Hartley* [1972] 2 QB 1, [1972] 2 WLR 101, following *R v Juby* (1886) 16 Cox CC 160; cf also *R v Peters* 16 Cox CC 36.
2   *R v Juby* (1886) 16 Cox CC 160.

24.61 In *R v Godwin*[1] the Court of Appeal held that it was a question for the jury to determine on the evidence whether the bankrupt held himself out as the person for whom credit was sought or whether the credit was sought for a genuine and separate business and not as a charade to disguise the fact that the bankrupt was in truth the person seeking credit. The context in which the issue arose in that case was that a company had been incorporated after the commencement of bankruptcy which was owned by the bankrupt's wife but which the bankrupt managed ostensibly on her behalf. Such an arrangement, although once common[2], would no longer be lawful by virtue of the Company Directors Disqualification Act 1986, s 11.

1   (1980) 71 Cr App Rep 97; no offence is committed where the bankrupt obtains credit for a third party not associated with him.
2   For another example see *R v Goodall* (1958) 43 Cr App Rep 24.

Victim's knowledge not relevant to liability

24.62 The offence is committed when the defendant's status as a bankrupt is not made clear to the credit provider irrespective of that person's actual knowledge. This offence is the successor to the offence under the Bankruptcy Act 1914, s 155, which was held to be an offence of strict liability committed where the bankrupt fails to disclose his status as undischarged bankrupt even though the provider of the credit is aware of the true position[1]. It could not therefore be a defence for the bankrupt to prove that he genuinely believed that the credit provider knew of his status[2]. The aim of the statute is to ensure that the credit provider's attention is drawn to the bankrupt's status when giving credit:

> '... to require a bankrupt to tell a person what that person already knows – that the informant is an undischarged bankrupt – is not to impose an empty ritual, it is to ensure, at the risk of needless repetition on occasions, that the credit provider is told or reminded of a most material fact.'

1   *R v Duke of Leinster* [1924] 1 KB 311.
2   *R v Duke of Leinster* [1924] 1 KB 311; see eg *R v Scott* [1998] BPIR 471, a decision of the Supreme Court of South Australia, Court of Criminal Appeal, on a similar offence to the Bankruptcy Act 1914, s 155 under Australian bankruptcy law.

24.63 That the credit provider's actual knowledge is irrelevant is even clearer under the IA 1986 offence. Under the Bankruptcy Act 1914 the offence was committed if credit were obtained without 'informing' the credit provider of the bankrupt's status. This permitted argument, albeit unsuccessful, that a person could not 'inform' another of something he already knew. Now under the IA 1986 the offence is committed if credit is obtained without 'giving' the relevant information. The provisions of IA 1986, s 360 do not specify the precise time at which the information has to be given. It is probably still good law that provided that the bankrupt has disclosed his status to the credit provider within a reasonable time of his obtaining credit he need not disclose it again at the time he receives the credit[1]. Given the purpose of the statute however a 'reasonable time' will be a short period, such that it can fairly be said that the information was given at about the time of the credit transaction or otherwise in circumstances where the credit provider can be confidently said to have had the bankrupt's status in front of him when extending the credit.

[1]   *R v Zeitlin* (1932) 23 Cr App Rep 163, CCA. The defendant had, in June, given a cheque post-dated to September and the judge's summing up may have suggested to the jury that the relevant date for informing the credit provider was September. Hewart LCJ stated. at p 165:

> 'Certainly the appellant gave evidence that just before the time when he obtained this credit he had a conversation ... which, if it took place, showed clearly that he was an undischarged bankrupt. In those circumstances, if the jury accepted the version of the matter given by the appellant, it was quite clear that the offence had not been committed ... The statute does not require that the information should be given at the very moment of obtaining.'

Use of business name

24.64 A bankrupt commits an offence if he engages either directly or indirectly in any business under a name other than that in which he was adjudged bankrupt without disclosing to all persons with whom he enters into any business transactions the name in which he was so adjudged[1].

[1]   IA 1986, s 360(1)(b).

Acting as a director or being concerned in activities of a company

24.65 It is an offence for a person who is an undischarged bankrupt to act as director of, or directly or indirectly to take part in or be concerned in the promotion, formation or management of, a company, except with the leave of the court[1]. This is an offence of absolute liability. Accordingly it is not a defence to show that the accused believed that he was not bankrupt at the material time[2], nor is it a defence that the accused did not appreciate that his conscious or deliberate actions would or might amount to 'management' for the purposes of this offence[3].

[1]   Company Directors Disqualification Act 1986, s 11.
[2]   *R v Brockley* (1993) 99 Cr App Rep 385, CA.
[3]   *R v Doring* [2002] EWCA Crim 1695, [2003] 1 Cr App Rep 143 at [23].

Maximum penalties

24.66 For convictions under offences listed in paras **24.19–24.31, 24.34– 24.49** and **24.55–24.56** above the penalty on summary conviction is up to six months' imprisonment or a fine not exceeding the statutory maximum or both, and on conviction on indictment imprisonment for up to seven years or a fine or both. For conviction under offences listed in paras **24.32–24.33, 24.50–24.54** and **24.57–24.65** above the penalty on summary conviction is up to six months' imprisonment or a fine not exceeding the statutory maximum or both and on conviction on indictment, imprisonment for a term not exceeding two years or a fine or both[1].

[1] IA 1986, s 430, Sch 10, and for para **24.65**, Company Directors Disqualification Act 1986, s 13.

D OFFENCE BY DEBTOR IN RELATION TO PROPOSAL FOR IVA

Fraud in obtaining voluntary arrangements

24.67 On the introduction of the voluntary arrangements regime it was an offence for a debtor to make any false representation or commit any other fraud for the purposes of obtaining the approval of his creditors to a proposed voluntary arrangement[1]. The amendments introduced by IA 2000 replaced this offence in more specific terms, and in addition introduced a duty on the nominee or supervisor of an arrangement to report any possible offence to the Department of Trade. An individual debtor commits an offence if, for the purpose of obtaining the approval of the creditors to a proposal for a voluntary arrangement, he either (a) makes any false representation, or (b) fraudulently does, or omits to do, anything[2]. This wide wording should catch any fraudulent behaviour engaged in with the aim of securing a voluntary arrangement. An offence may be committed even if the proposal is not approved[3]. The penalty is imprisonment or a fine, or both[4]. A notable omission from these provisions is criminal liability in respect of false representations or fraudulent acts in connection with obtaining the approval of creditors to a variation to a voluntary arrangement.

[1] IR 1986, r 5.30, (repealed).
[2] IA 1986, s 262A(1).
[3] IA 1986, s 262A(2).
[4] On indictment, seven years, unlimited fine; on summary conviction six months or the statutory maximum, or both, IA 1986, Sch 10.

24.68 In PVA there is an offence in similar terms[1]. It may be committed by any person who is an officer of the partnership or an officer (including shadow director[2]) of a corporate member of a partnership who either (a) makes a false representation, or (b) fraudulently does, or omits to do, anything for the purposes of obtaining the approval of the members or creditors of an insolvent partnership or of the members or creditors of any of the insolvent partnership's members or creditors to a proposal for voluntary arrangement whether or not the proposal is approved.

¹   IA 1986, s 6A(1) as modified by the Insolvency Partnerships (Amendment) (No 2) Order 2002, SI 2002/2708, art 4. There is an immaterial difference. In IA 1986, s 6A(1) the offence is to make 'any' false representation. As modified the offence is to make 'a' false representation.
²   That is a person in accordance with whose directions or instructions the directors of a company are accustomed to act, but excluding professional advisers, IA 1986, s 251.

Duty of nominee or supervisor to report fraud

24.69   A duty is imposed on the nominee or supervisor to report possible fraud in relation to a voluntary arrangement. This duty arises only where a voluntary arrangement has been approved by the creditors and has taken effect[1]. The nominee or supervisor must report an individual debtor where it appears to him that the debtor 'has been guilty of any offence' in connection with a voluntary arrangement 'for which he is criminally liable'[2]. The report is to be made to the Secretary of State and is to be made 'forthwith' that is immediately upon it appearing to the nominee or supervisor that there is guilt on the part of the individual debtor[3].

¹   IA 1986, s 262B(1).
²   IA 1986, s 262B(2).
³   IA 1986, s 262B(2).

24.70   The duty to report is subject therefore to two questionable restrictions. First, although an offence may be committed in connection with the obtaining of a voluntary arrangement whether or not the relevant proposal was in fact approved, the duty to report criminal behaviour arises only where the proposal is approved and the voluntary arrangement takes effect. Secondly, the duty is to report 'guilt of an offence for which he *is* criminally liable'. The distinction may therefore be made between clear cases of guilt and cases where the nominee or supervisor merely considers that there might be guilt on the part of an officer or individual debtor. It would make a nonsense of the duty to report criminal activity if insolvency practitioners, perhaps reluctant to become involved in a criminal investigation, were to stick rigidly to reporting only the clearest possible cases. It would have been possible for the duty to have been drafted in rather wider terms, and this may yet become necessary if the Secretary of State is determined to take a rather firmer line on criminality in connection with voluntary arrangements than has been the case in the past.

Duty to provide assistance by nominee or supervisor

24.71   The nominee or supervisor is also obliged to assist in any prosecution which may follow his report of criminal behaviour. Any information of relevance must be provided to the Secretary of State if required of the relevant practitioner, and he must also give such access to and facilities for inspecting and taking copies of any relevant documents which may be in his possession or under his control[1]. Should either the Director of Public Prosecutions or the Secretary of State institute criminal proceedings following a report by the nominee or the supervisor of an IVA, the practitioner concerned must give all assistance in connection with the prosecution which he is reasonably able to give[2]. The relevant practitioner may also be directed to assist in the prosecution by the court on the application of the prosecuting authority concerned[3].

1   IA 1986, s 262B(2)(b).
2   IA 1986, s 262B(3).
3   IA 1986, s 262B(4).

E OFFENCES COMMITTED BY OTHER PERSONS

General

24.72 There are no specific bankruptcy offences relating to false claims in the bankruptcy or fraudulent behaviour generally in respect of another's bankruptcy. Such offences are likely to be covered by the general criminal law. The offences most likely to be charged in such circumstances are, the Theft Act 1968, ss 15–17, obtaining property or pecuniary advantage by deception, the Theft Act 1978, ss 1 and 2 obtaining services or evading liabilities by deception, the law regarding aiding and abetting criminal offences[1], and the Fraud Act 2006. The Fraud Act 2006 creates a general offence of fraud[2], with three possible ways of committing it. These are fraud by false representation[3], fraud by failing to disclose information[4], and fraud by abuse of position[5].

1   See eg *R v Dawson* [2001] EWCA Crim 1554, [2001] All ER (D) 342 (Jun); an intent to default on liabilities subject to an IVA correctly charged under the Theft Act 1978, s 2(1)(b).
2   Fraud Act 2006, s 1.
3   Fraud Act 2006, s 2.
4   Fraud Act 2006, s 3.
5   Fraud Act 2006, s 4.

Receiving property from a bankrupt

24.73 While criminal conduct by persons other than the bankrupt falls to be dealt with by the general law the IA 1986 does provide for a specific offence when another person obtains property from the bankrupt which the bankrupt had obtained on credit. The offence is committed where the person concerned acquires or receives property from the bankrupt knowing or believing that the bankrupt:

(a)   owed money in respect of that property; and
(b)   did not intend or was unlikely to be able to pay the money he owed on the property.

24.74 The offence may be committed at any time during the period commencing 12 months before the presentation of the petition and ending on the commencement of the bankruptcy[1]. The offence is not committed where the bankrupt dealt with the property in the ordinary course of his business[2]. In determining whether his dealing was in the ordinary course of business, particular regard may be had to the price paid for the property[3].

1   IA 1986, s 359(2); the penalty is seven years' imprisonment or a fine or both on indictment, and on summary conviction six months' imprisonment or the statutory maximum fine, or both, IA 1986, Sch 10.
2   IA 1986, s 359(3).
3   IA 1986, s 359(4).

Wrongful payment by trustee under deed of arrangement

24.75 If a trustee under a deed of arrangement[1] pays to any creditor out of the debtor's property a sum larger than that paid to other creditors entitled to the benefit of the deed, unless the deed authorises him to do so, or unless such payments are either made to a creditor entitled to enforce his claim by distress or are such as would be lawful in a bankruptcy, the trustee is guilty of an offence which is triable either way[2].

1   Ie a deed under the Deeds of Arrangement Act 1914.
2   Deeds of Arrangement Act 1914, s 17 and Magistrates' Courts Act 1980, s 17(1) and Sch 1.

Fraudulent disposal or concealment of property before bankruptcy

24.76 A person is guilty of an offence if he has, with intent to defraud his creditors or any of them, made or caused to be made any gift, delivery, or transfer of or any charge on his property or if he has, with intent to defraud his creditors, concealed or removed any part of his property since or within two months before the date of any unsatisfied judgment or order for payment of money obtained against him[1]. The person concerned need not be or become bankrupt in order to be guilty of either of these offences[2].

1   Debtors Act 1869, s 13.
2   *R v Rowlands* (1882) 8 QBD 530.

F PRACTICE AND PROCEDURE

Criminal proceedings

24.77 A criminal prosecution begins with a bill of indictment. This becomes an indictment, without which no Crown Court trial is valid, when the bill of indictment is signed by the proper officer of the court[1]. Insolvency Act offences are all 'either way' offences, that is they may be tried summarily or on indictment and accordingly they commence in the magistrates' court and are either committed or transferred to the Crown Court[2].

1   Administration of Justice (Miscellaneous Provisions) Act 1933, s 2(1); the judge being satisfied that the requirements of s 2(2) have been complied with.
2   Committal proceedings were abolished for offences triable only on indictment by the Crime and Disorder Act 1998, s 51.

24.78 At the magistrates' court the charge must be written down and read to the accused[1]. The court must then explain to the accused in ordinary language that he may indicate whether he would plead guilty or not guilty if the case were to proceed to trial, and that if he indicates a guilty plead then the court will proceed as if the proceedings were summary from the start, that he has pleaded guilty, and that he may be committed[2] to the Crown Court for sentence[3]. If the accused indicates a not guilty plea, or fails to indicate any plea, the court must then consider what mode of trial should be adopted[4]. The magistrates have a discretion to allow the accused to change his election; he is not lightly to be deprived of his right to a trial by jury[5]. The accused must be in court at the initial hearing to indicate a plea[6] save where he has a legal representative and the court considers it should proceed in the accused's absence by reason of his disorderly conduct[7].

[1]   Magistrates' Court Act 1980, s 17A(3).
[2]   Under the Powers of Criminal Courts (Sentencing) Act 2000, s 3.
[3]   Magistrates' Court Act 1980, s 17A(4)(6).
[4]   Magistrates' Court Act 1980, ss 18, 19(1).
[5]   *R v Craske, ex p Metropolitan Police Commr* [1957] 2 QB 591, [1957] 2 All ER 772, DC; as to considerations on change of election see *R v Bourne JJ, ex p Cope* (1988) 153 JP 161, DC.
[6]   Magistrates' Court Act 1980, s 17A(2).
[7]   Magistrates' Court Act 1980, s 17B(1).

24.79   In determining the mode of trial the magistrates' court is to have regard to (a) the nature of the case, (b) whether the circumstances make the offence one of serious character, (c) whether the powers of punishment available to magistrates are adequate, (d) any circumstances which make it appear to the court to make it more suitable for the offence to be tried one way rather than the other[1]. The magistrates should have regard to the mode of trial guidelines[2]. For offences of theft and fraud the guidelines provide:

> 'Cases should be tried summarily unless the court considers that one or more of the following features is present in the case *and* that its sentence powers are insufficient.
> (a)   Breach of trust by a person in a position of substantial authority, or in whom a high degree of trust is placed.
> (b)   Theft or fraud which has been committed or disguised in a sophisticated manner.
> (c)   Theft or fraud committed by an organised gang.
> (d)   The victim is particularly vulnerable to theft or fraud, eg the elderly or infirm.
> (e)   The unrecovered property is of high value[3].
>
> Magistrates should take account of their powers to commit for sentence (and to commit during the course of the hearing if information emerges which leads the magistrates to conclude that their powers of sentence are inadequate).'

[1]   Magistrates' Court Act 1980, s 19(3).
[2]   Now forming paragraph 51 of the *Practice Direction (Criminal Proceedings: Consolidation)* [2002] 1 WLR 2870.
[3]   'High value' means a figure equal to at least twice the amount of the limit imposed by statute on a magistrates' court when making a compensation order, *Practice Direction (Criminal Proceedings: Consolidation)*, para 51.4. At present this limit is £5,000.

24.80   Where the accused faces more than one charge, any charge which warrants a trial on indictment will take the other charges with it to the Crown Court. Contested issues as to the disclosure of sensitive material may be a factor in committing a matter for trial[1]. The Crown should not invite the magistrates to deal with serious offences summarily for the sake of convenience[2]. It is inappropriate for the magistrates to accept jurisdiction in a case charging the fraudulent evasion of some £200,000 of value added tax[3].

[1]   *R v Burnley JJ, ex p Smith and Wilkins* [1995] 2 Cr App Rep 285, DC.
[2]   *R v Norfolk JJ, ex p DPP* [1950] 2 KB 558, 567, DC; *R v Coe* [1969] 1 All ER 65, [1968] 1 WLR 1950.
[3]   *R v Northamptonshire Magistrates' Court, ex p Comrs of Customs & Excise* [1994] Crim LR 598, DC.

24.81 If a summary trial is considered to be more suitable the accused must be told that he may consent to such a trial or, if he wishes, be tried by a jury[1]. If he consents, a summary trial will follow. However even where the magistrates embark on a summary trial, they may, at any time before the conclusion of the prosecution's evidence discontinue the trial and, adjourning the hearing, proceed as examining magistrates[2]. Equally, if the magistrates begin to inquire into the information as examining justices with a view to committal to the Crown Court, they may after considering the material before them ask the accused whether he consents to be tried summarily and if so proceed with a summary trial[3].

[1]   Magistrates' Court Act 1980, s 20(1), (2)(a); the accused must be warned that if convicted in a summary trial he may be committed to the Crown Court for sentence, s 20(2)(b).
[2]   Magistrates' Court Act 1980, s 25(2).
[3]   Magistrates' Court Act 1980, s 25(3); this power may not be exercised in prosecutions brought by the Attorney-General or DPP without the consent of the Attorney-General.

Trial on indictment

24.82 Cases may be sent to the Crown Court for trial on indictment by their committal by magistrates or by notice of transfer by a designated authority. Examining magistrates may commit a case for trial after considering all admissible evidence put before them by the Crown if of the opinion that there is sufficient evidence to put the accused on trial by jury[1]. For these purposes written statements, exhibits, depositions and other documents are admissible[2].

[1]   Magistrates' Court Act 1980, s 6.
[2]   See the Magistrates' Court Act 1980, ss 5A–5F.

Transfer to Crown Court

24.83 Serious fraud cases may be transferred to the Crown Court by the service of a notice of transfer by a designated authority[1]. The relevant authority must be of the opinion that the evidence is sufficient to justify a committal for trial and that it reveals a case of fraud of such seriousness or complexity that it is appropriate that the management of the case should without delay be taken over by the Crown Court[2]. There is no appeal against a notice of transfer[3]. The procedure to be followed is governed by statute, regulations and rules[4]. Serious or complex fraud cases may be heard only in certain court centres[5].

24.83 *Bankruptcy offences*

1   Criminal Justice Act 1987, s 4(1); the relevant authorities are the DPP, Director of the Serious Fraud Office, Commissioners of Inland Revenue, Commissioners of Customs & Excise and the Secretary of State, s 4(2).
2   Criminal Justice Act 1987, s 4(1)(b).
3   Criminal Justice Act 1987, s 4(3).
4   Criminal Justice Act 1987, s 5, the Criminal Justice Act 1987 (Notice of Transfer) Regulations 1988, SI 1988/1691, the Magistrates' Courts (Notice of Transfer) Rules 1988, SI 1988/1701.
5   See *Practice Direction (Criminal Proceedings: Consolidation)* [2002] 1 WLR 2870.

24.84 After a notice of transfer has been given an accused may apply to the relevant Crown Court for one or more charges to be dismissed on the ground that the evidence is insufficient for a jury properly to convict him[1]. Notice of such an application may be given orally or in writing, but if given orally written notice of intention must be given to the Crown Court[2]. A dismissal hearing is usually conducted on the written statements, exhibits and other documents, but the judge may give leave for the hearing of oral evidence[3]. If an order for dismissal is made no further proceedings may be brought on a dismissed charge except by means of the preferment of a voluntary bill of indictment[4]. Dismissal applications are governed by rules which provide for the form of written application, prosecution reply, application for oral hearings and the service of documents[5].

1   Criminal Justice Act 1987, s 6(1).
2   Criminal Justice Act 1987, s 6(2).
3   Criminal Justice Act 1987, s 6(3).
4   Criminal Justice Act 1987, s 6(5); only a High Court judge may grant a voluntary bill.
5   The Criminal Justice Act 1987 (Dismissal of Transferred Charges) Rules 1988, SI 1988/1695.

Preparatory hearings

24.85 The judge may order a preparatory hearing if it is considered beneficial for one or more of the following purposes:

(a)   identifying issues which are likely to be material to the verdict of the jury;
(b)   assisting their comprehension of any such issues;
(c)   expediting the proceedings before the jury; or
(d)   assisting the judge's management of the trial[1].

1   Criminal Justice Act 1987, s 7(1).

24.86 The trial begins with a preparatory hearing, and accordingly arraignment must take place at the start of such a hearing[1]. Preparatory hearings may be used to determine questions of law relating to the case, issues of admissibility of evidence, and to give directions to both prosecution and defence as to the provision of case statements and the preparation and presentation of evidence[2]. The careful preparation of case statements is important. If any party departs from his case statement during the trial the judge, and with his leave any other party, may comment on the fact to the jury and the jury may draw such inference as is proper[3]. Save in exceptional circumstances the judge presiding at a preparatory hearing must be the judge who conducts the trial[4]. The judge may not prohibit the Crown from re-interviewing witnesses after receipt of a defence case statement, but may exclude their evidence, if appropriate, on the ground of unfairness[5]. With the leave of the judge or the Court of Appeal an appeal lies to the Court of Appeal from any order or ruling of a judge at a preparatory hearing on an issue of admissibility of evidence or any question of law[6].

[1]   Criminal Justice Act 1987, s 8.
[2]   Criminal Justice Act 1987, s 9.
[3]   Criminal Justice Act 1987, s 10.
[4]   See *R v Crown Court at Southwark, ex p Customs & Excise Comrs* [1993] 1 WLR 764, 97 Cr App R 266, DC; 'exceptional circumstances' is not necessarily the test where the indictment has been severed, *R v Lord Chancellor, ex p Maxwell* [1996] 4 All ER 751, [1997] 1 WLR 104, DC.
[5]   *R v Nadir and Turner* [1993] 4 All ER 513, [1993] 1 WLR 1322, CA.
[6]   Criminal Justice Act 1987, s 9(11).

Disclosure of documents

24.87 The duty of the Crown to disclose documents is twofold. First there is the duty to give primary disclosure[1]. Primary disclosure comprises any material which in the prosecutor's opinion might undermine the case against the accused[2]. After compliance, or purported compliance, by the Crown of the duty to give primary disclosure the accused must give a defence statement both to the prosecutor and to the court[3]. A defence statement must set out the nature of the accused's defence in general terms, indicate the matters on which he takes issue with the prosecution, and set out the reason why he takes issue with each such matter[4]. It should not simply comprise a general legal description of the defence[5]. Having received the defence statement the Crown should review its disclosure by reference to the issues raised in the statement and give secondary disclosure, that is disclose any material which might be reasonably expected to assist the accused's defence as it appears from the defence statement[6]. At any time after serving a defence statement and the prosecutor has purported to give secondary disclosure or failed to give such disclosure the accused may apply for specific disclosure of any material of which the accused has at any time had reasonable cause to believe is material which might be reasonably expected to assist his defence[7]. There is a continuing duty on the Crown to disclose any material which might undermine its case against the accused[8]. Disclosure in criminal cases is governed by rules[9] and the prosecution and defence should comply with the Protocol on Disclosure in criminal cases[10].

[1]   Criminal Procedure and Investigations Act 1996, s 3.
[2]   Criminal Procedure and Investigations Act 1996, s 3(1); material which has already been disclosed to the accused, for example in the witness statements or exhibits, need not be disclosed again, s 3(1); If there is no material to disclose a written statement to that effect must be given to the accused. 'Material' is defined and the manner of disclosure is specified, see s 3(2)–(8).
[3]   Criminal Procedure and Investigations Act 1996, s 5.
[4]   Criminal Procedure and Investigations Act 1996, s 5(6).
[5]   *R v Tibbs* [2000] 2 Cr App R 309, CA.
[6]   Criminal Procedure and Investigations Act 1996, s 7; If there is no material to disclose a written statement to that effect must be given to the accused.

7   Criminal Procedure and Investigations Act 1996, s 8; material within this section is defined, s 8(3).
8   Criminal Procedure and Investigations Act 1996, s 9.
9   The Crown Court (Criminal Procedure and Investigations Act 1996) (Disclosure) Rules 1997, SI 1997/698.
10 20 February 2006.

Case management

24.88 Whether or not the court orders a preparatory hearing judges of the Crown Court are now encouraged to exercise a degree of case management and control previously alien to the criminal trial process. It is expected that the issues which will be contested at trial should be identified and directions given, including where appropriate the timetabling of evidence, to ensure that the trial process does not drift; fairness now goes hand in hand with due expedition[1]. As the Court of Appeal put it in *R v Jan Jisl and others*[2]:

> 'Active, hands on, case management, both pre-trial and throughout the trial itself, is now regarded as an essential part of the judge's duty. The profession must understand that this has become and will remain part of the normal trial process, and that cases must be prepared and conducted accordingly ... To enable the trial judge to manage the case in a way which is fair to every participant, pre-trial, the potential problems as well as the possible areas for time saving, should be canvassed. In short, a sensible informed discussion about the future management of the case and the most convenient way to present the evidence, whether disputed or not, and where appropriate, with admissions by one or other or both sides, should enable the judge to make a fully informed analysis of the future timetable, and the proper conduct of the trial. The objective is not haste and rush, but greater efficiency and better use of limited resources by closer identification of and focus on critical rather than peripheral issues.'

1   *R v Chaaban* [2003] EWCA Crim 1012, [2003] Crim LR 658; *R v K and others* [2006] EWCA Crim 724, [2006] 2 All ER 552n.
2   [2004] EWCA Crim 696, (2004) Times, 19 April.

The hearing

24.89 Trials of insolvency offences will usually follow the pattern set for other criminal cases. There is however an increasingly flexible attitude to trial management in serious fraud cases, including such areas as hours of sitting[1], the hearing of evidence by reference to issues, and the use of electronic aids[2].

1   Where defendants have not been remanded in custody 'Maxwell hours' (9.15 – 1.30pm with applications in the absence of the jury put over to an afternoon hearing) may be ordered with the consent of the presiding judge.
2   Judges trying serious fraud cases are now required to be computer literate, and courts are now extensively wired for electronic presentation of evidence under the Courts and Tribunals Modernisation programme.

Use of compelled evidence at a criminal trial

24.90 As enacted in the IA 1986, s 433 provided that in any proceedings (whether under the IA 1986 or not) (a) a statement of affairs prepared for the purposes of any provision of the IA 1986 which is derived from the Insolvency Act 1985, and (b) any other statement made in pursuance of a requirement imposed by or under rules made under the IA 1986, may be used in evidence against any person making or concurring in making the statement. Thus, in both criminal and civil proceedings, the statements in question might be adduced as evidence in chief. The bankrupt making the statement is compelled by law to make the statements and therefore the statements stand in the same category as statements made to inspectors appointed under the Companies Act 1985. In *Saunders v United Kingdom*[1] the European Court of Human Rights held that the use of transcripts of evidence given to such inspectors, when adduced at length as evidence in chief against an accused, infringed his right to a fair trial under art 6(1) of the Convention, specifically in that it infringed the accused's right not to incriminate himself. In consequence, the IA 1986, s 433 has been amended so as to provide that, subject to certain exceptions[2], in criminal proceedings no evidence relating to the statement may be adduced and no question relating to it may be asked by or on behalf of the prosecution, unless evidence relating to it is adduced, or a question relating to it is asked in the proceedings by or on behalf of the accused[3].

[1] (1996) 23 EHRR 313.
[2] See para **24.91**.
[3] IA 1986, s 433(2) as inserted by the Youth Justice and Criminal Evidence Act 1999, s 59 and Sch 3, para 7. The change renders the decision in *R v Kansal* [1993] QB 244, [1992] 3 All ER 844, CA in which the inter-relation of the IA 1986, s 433 (as originally enacted) and the Theft Act 1968, s 31 no longer good law. Indeed the conviction in that case was quashed by the Court of Appeal; see *R v Kansal* [2001] 28 LS Gaz R 43 where, on an appeal initiated by a reference made by the Criminal Cases Review Commission, the Court of Appeal gave retrospective effect to the Human Rights Act 1998 (specifically to art 6(1) of Sch 1, as interpreted in the light of *Saunders v United Kingdom* (1996) 23 EHRR 313). In permitting the Human Rights Act 1998 to have retrospective effect, the Court of Appeal relied on the reasoning of the majority in *R v DPP, ex p Kebilene* [2000] 2 AC 326, [1999] 4 All ER 801, HL. Following the decision of the House of Lords in *R v Lambert* [2001] UKHL 37, [2001] 3 All ER 577, it would seem that the Human Rights Act 1998 is not to be given such retrospective effect (save where s 22(4) of that Act applies).

Excepted cases

24.91 In certain specified criminal proceedings, the restriction imposed by the IA 1986, s 433(2) on the use of statements compulsorily given does not apply[1]. These are criminal proceedings in which the accused is charged with an offence:

(a) under IA 1986, ss 22(6), 47(6), 66(6), 67(6), 95(8), 98(6), 99(3)(a), 131(7), 192(2), 208(1)(a) or (d) or (2), 210, 235(5), 353(1), 354(1)(b) or (3) or 356(1) or (2)(a) or (b) or para 4(3)(a) of Sch 7;

(b) which is (i) created by rules made under the IA 1986, and (ii) designated for the purposes of the IA 1986, s 433(3) by such rules or by regulations[2] made by the Secretary of State;

(c) which is (i) created by regulations made under any such rules, and (ii) designated for the purposes of the IA 1986, s 433(3) by such regulations;

(d) an offence under the Perjury Act 1911, ss 1, 2 or 5;

[1] The exceptions are listed in the IA 1986, s 433(3).

2   Such regulations must be made by statutory instrument and after being made must be laid before each House of Parliament.

Pre-bankruptcy documents

24.92 Pre-existing documents obtained from the bankrupt pursuant to his compulsory duty to deliver such documents to the official receiver may be used as evidence in chief by the prosecution in criminal proceedings[1].

1   *A-G's Reference (No 7 of 2000)* [2001] EWCA Crim 888, [2001] 1 WLR 1879.

Use of statements in civil proceedings

24.93 The statements made by the bankrupt which are referred to in the IA 1986, s 433(1) may be used for any purpose in civil proceedings[1]. Proceedings under the Company Directors Disqualification Act 1986 are civil proceedings for this purpose[2].

1   Cf *R v Hertfordshire County Council, ex p Green Environmental Industries Ltd* [2000] 2 AC 412, [2000] 1 All ER 773 where a challenge to local authority's request for information, which the applicant was compelled by law to provide, was based on the local authority's refusal to undertake not to use the information for the purpose of any subsequent prosecution. The House of Lords upheld the dismissal of the challenge on the ground that the information was required for the legitimate purpose of protecting public health and the environment and that the subsequent use of the information in criminal proceedings was a matter within the scope of the trial judge's discretion.
2   *Re Westminster Property Management Ltd, Official Receiver v Stern* [2001] 1 All ER 633, [2000] 1 WLR 2230.

Sentencing

24.94 While older cases show that short prison sentences (three to nine months) frequently followed conviction for insolvency offences, the shortage of prison accommodation and the resultant requirement of the Court of Appeal that custodial sentences should be imposed only where really necessary[1] should result in fewer such sentences. Often defendants are of previous good character and the conviction itself will represent a not inconsiderable punishment. Furthermore, the ability to disqualify the defendant from acting as a director[2] provides an additional form of punishment not previously available. The imposition of a disqualification order may well serve to reduce any sentence of imprisonment which might otherwise have been imposed. The Home Office Crown Court statistics indicate that about 55 to 60 sentences are passed each year for bankruptcy offences, with about half that number again for company director frauds. About one-fifth of defendants are given custodial sentences, the average length being nine months. There are few reported cases of sentences in bankruptcy matters. The following examples will give an indication of the approach of the courts.

1   *R v Kefford* [2002] EWCA Crim 519, [2002] Cr App Rep (S) 495.
2   Under the Company Directors Disqualification Act 1986.

Immediate imprisonment

24.95 In *R v Bevis*[1] the defendant made a late guilty plea to failing to disclose company property and details of its disposal to the liquidator[2]. He was 53, of good character, and did not himself benefit financially. The Court of Appeal reduced the sentence of imprisonment from 18 months to nine months and the period of disqualification from four years to two years stating that the element of dishonesty in the offence justified a custodial sentence even where there was no intent of personal enrichment. The defendant in *R v Mungroo*[3] failed to disclose a £31,000 gratuity received on leaving the army three months before his bankruptcy[4], using it to pay off gambling and family debts and meeting the cost of an extension to the family home. A man of good character with an exemplary army record, the defendant pleaded guilty to fraudulent disposal of property[5]. The Court of Appeal upheld an immediate custodial sentence of two months stating that it was 'clearly to be understood that in all normal circumstances such conduct crossed the custody threshold'. The defendant in *R v Teece*[6] pleaded guilty to concealing property while bankrupt and taking part in the management of a company run by his wife. On liquidation the wife's company owed £186,000 and on being made bankrupt for a second time the defendant failed to disclose his liability on a guarantee in the sum of £22,000. An immediate custodial sentence of nine months was upheld by the Court of Appeal. A sentence of four years' imprisonment was upheld in the Court of Appeal in *R v Vanderwell*[7]. There had been a late guilty plea by a 53 year old man with one similar previous conviction to offences of management of a company while bankrupt, obtaining by deception, failing to keep proper accounts, and concealment of debts. The defendant had commenced trading through a company immediately on release from prison for his previous offence and was described by the sentencing judge as 'a thoroughly dishonest fraudster'.

[1]   [2001] EWCA Crim 9, [2001] Cr App Rep (S) 257.
[2]   Contrary to IA 1986, s 208(1)(a); cf IA 1986, s 354(1).
[3]   [1998] BPIR 784.
[4]   The petitioning and main creditor being a finance company with a judgment debt of £18,300.
[5]   Contrary to IA 1986, s 357(1), see para **24.50**.
[6]   (1994) 13 Cr App Rep (S) 302.
[7]   [1998] 1 Cr App Rep (S) 439.

Suspended imprisonment

24.96 When considering previous cases it should be borne in mind that between the implementation of the Criminal Justice Act 1991, s 5(1)[1] and the coming into force of the Criminal Justice Act 2003, s 189[2] the court was able to suspend a custodial sentence only where it could be 'justified by the exceptional circumstances of the case'. 'Exceptional circumstances' was strictly defined and few suspended sentences were passed. Under the 2003 Act it is likely that the suspended sentence, to which a full range of community sentence requirements may be added[3], will be more frequently employed. The court may now suspend a sentence of between 14 days' and 12 months' imprisonment for between six months and two years[4]. Under the previous

24.96 *Bankruptcy offences*

provisions, in *R v Wood*[5] it was discovered on the liquidation of the defendant's company that some £97,000 stock and £7,500 cash belonging to his company could not be accounted for. The Court of Appeal upheld the sentence of three months' imprisonment suspended for 12 months on a guilty plea on a defendant who failed to keep proper accounting records[6].

1 Which amended the Powers of Criminal Courts Act 1973, s 22(2).
2 On 4 April 2005.
3 Criminal Justice Act 2003, s 189(1)(a), s 190. The court may also order periodic reviews of a suspended sentence order, s 191, and on a review may amend any community requirement imposed under the order, s 192.
4 Criminal Justice Act 2003, s 189(1), as amended by the Criminal Justice Act 2003 (Sentencing) (Transitory Provisions) Order 2005, SI 2005/643. Where an unpaid work requirement is imposed the sentence must be suspended for at least 12 months, s 200(2).
5 (1992) 13 Cr App Rep (S) 317.
6 Contrary to CA 1985, s 223.

Community penalty

24.97 In *R v Dawes*[1] the defendant, of previous good character, obtained credit for goods and services worth about £3,000 without disclosing he was bankrupt. Sentenced to three months' imprisonment, the Court of Appeal substituted a community penalty with an unpaid work requirement of 80 hours.

1 [1997] 1 Cr App Rep (S) 149.

Managing a company while bankrupt

24.98 For the appropriate sentence for this offence[1] guideline comments may be found in *R v Theivendran*[2]. 'If the contravention has been flagrant, that is to say deliberate or reckless, a custodial sentence would in principle be appropriate. If, on the other hand, there are no aggravating features, such as previous offences of the same kind or personal profit gained in fraud of creditors, that may be taken into account as justifying suspension of the sentence in whole or part.' The defendant had there traded honestly for many years but completely ignoring the fact that he had been made bankrupt. He was found to have given false evidence to the effect that he had been told by an official receiver that he might trade. The Court of Appeal reduced the sentence of nine months' imprisonment to one of six months suspended for two years, and the period of disqualification from ten years to five years. A suspended sentence, six months suspended for two years, was also given to the defendant in *R v Brockley*[3], who had carried on his hotel business for several years while bankrupt. The defendant maintained that he had believed that he had been discharged because he had been told that he would have had an automatic discharge by the relevant date by an unqualified member of his solicitors' staff, a suggestion he had not thought to check with the official receiver. In *R v Thompson*[4] the defendant acted as a director while bankrupt for the second time, the companies with which he was associated defaulting on some £73,000 worth of debts. The Court of Appeal reduced the sentence of

15 months on a guilty plea to eight months' imprisonment, with a disqualification order of seven years. The defendant in *R v Ashby*[5] was convicted of managing four companies which constituted Tottenham Hotspur FC while bankrupt. He had turned the companies round from near insolvency to some prosperity, there was no personal enrichment, and the defendant was of previous good character. The judge described the offences as wholly flagrant, blatant because repeated over several years and considered that there was a need to give a clear warning to others and sentenced the defendant to four months' imprisonment. This was upheld by the Court of Appeal, but it was noted that the then current legislation prevented the suspending of the sentence[6]. The period of disqualification was reduced from seven to five years.

1   Company Directors Disqualification Act 1986, s 11.
2   (1992) 13 Cr App Rep (S) 601.
3   (1993) 99 Cr App Rep (S) 385.
4   (1993) 14 Cr App Rep (S) 89.
5   [1998] 2 Cr App Rep (S) 37.
6   This is now possible under the provisions of the Criminal Justice Act 2003, s 189, see above.

Chapter 25

PARTNERSHIP

A INTRODUCTION

Statutory framework: Insolvent Partnerships Order 1986

25.1 Under the law prior to the coming into force of the Insolvency Act 1986 ('IA 1986'), insolvent partnerships were dealt with under the law of bankruptcy[1]. Under the IA 1986, partnerships as entities separate from the members who make up the partnership were brought into the general framework for corporate insolvency. This was achieved through subordinate legislation. IA 1986, s 420 empowers the Lord Chancellor, with the concurrence of the Secretary of State, to make an order providing that specified provisions of the Insolvency Act should apply to insolvent partnerships with such modifications as may be considered appropriate[2].

[1]   See the Bankruptcy Act 1914, s 116, the Bankruptcy Rules 1952, rr 279/296; note that a firm comprising eight or more partners could be wound up as an unregistered company: Companies Act 1985, s 665(1).
[2]   The order has to be made by statutory instrument subject to annulment in pursuance of a resolution of either House of Parliament: IA 1986, s 420(3). There is a complete discretion given to the Lord Chancellor and Secretary of State to make different provisions for different cases and provide for incidental, supplemental, and transitional provisions as may appear necessary or expedient: IA 1986, s 420(2).

25.2 The first Order made was the Insolvent Partnerships Order 1986[1] ('IPO 1986'). It introduced the concept that an insolvent partnership could be wound up as an unregistered company under the IA 1986, s 221, with the

996

partners liable as contributories where the partnership assets were insufficient to meet its liabilities. Under IPO 1986, insolvency proceedings might be commenced against an insolvent partnership or its members in four different ways:

(1)   the partnership itself, independently of its members, could be wound up as an unregistered company[2];
(2)   the partnership could be wound up as an unregistered company together with the bankruptcy or liquidation of two or more of its individual or corporate members[3];
(3)   a partnership comprising only individual members, none of whom was a limited partner, could present a joint petition for the insolvency of all the members without the partnership being wound up as an unregistered company[4];
(4)   one or more members of a partnership could be made bankrupt or put into liquidation without involving other members and without winding up the partnership as an unregistered company[5].

[1]   SI 1986/2142; this Order did not apply in relation to any case in which a petition for bankruptcy or winding up was presented before 29 December 1986 or where bankruptcy proceedings were pending on that date against any member, including cases where a bankruptcy notice had been served against the partnership or any member of it: IPO 1986, art 15(1), (2).
[2]   IPO 1986, art 7.
[3]   IPO 1986, art 8.
[4]   IPO 1986, art 13(1).
[5]   IPO 1986, art 15(3).

25.3 IPO 1986 was subject to three particular criticisms. First, on a purely practical note, the statutory provisions as modified for insolvent partnerships were difficult to follow. Individual words or phrases from sections in the IA 1986 were amended without setting out the amended section as a whole. Secondly, the IPO 1986 provided no mechanism for the partnership as opposed to its members to enter into voluntary arrangements. Although the practice developed of arranging IVAs for all members of the partnership[1] with identical provision for the partnership debts and a common supervisor, this was often difficult to arrange for large partnerships. Thirdly, the recommendations of the Cork Committee as to the treatment of creditors in the joint estate was not implemented. IPO 1986[2] kept to the long-standing rule that whenever there was a joint estate the creditors of the joint estate could not receive a dividend out of the separate estates of the members of the partnership until all the creditors of the separate estates had been paid in full.

[1]   A company voluntary arrangement could be proposed by the corporate members of the partnership.
[2]   IPO 1986, art 10.

25.4 IPO 1986 was replaced, with effect from 1 December 1994, with the Insolvent Partnerships Order 1994 ('IPO 1994')[1].

[1]   Insolvent Partnerships Order 1994, SI 1994/2421.

Insolvent Partnerships Order 1994 ('IPO 1994')

25.5 IPO 1994[1] introduced a number of changes from the regime in place under IPO 1986, meeting much of the criticism to which the earlier Order had been subject. On a purely practical level, IPO 1994 is much easier to follow than its predecessor, because the full text of the various sections and schedules to the 1986 Act which are modified by IPO 1994 are set out in the schedules to the Order. The main changes introduced by IPO 1994 were:

(1) *'Member'*. The definition of 'member' in the Order is extended and means: 'a member of the partnership and any person who is liable as a partner within the meaning of s 14 of the Partnership Act 1890'[2].
The Partnership Act 1890, s 14 provides that a person who has held himself out, or has allowed himself to be held out, as a member of the partnership is liable as a partner to anyone who in reliance of the holding out has given credit to the firm[3]. Such a person is a member for the purposes of IPO 1994, although not a partner under the terms of the partnership whether formal documents have been prepared or not[4]. Where separate practices use the same name under a group management agreement, there is a holding out of the various practices and their members as partners of each other[5]. 'Member' includes both partners as individual members and companies as corporate members[6].

(2) *Voluntary arrangements*. It is now possible for an insolvent partnership to enter into a voluntary arrangement, the provisions relating to company voluntary arrangements being extended to partnerships[7].

(3) *Administration*. A partnership may now be the subject of an administration order[8].

(4) *Joint and separate estates*. The rules governing the priority of payments as between joint and separate creditors have been varied[9].

[1]   SI 1994/2421.
[2]   IPO 1994, art 2(1).
[3]   Partnership Act 1890, s 14(2) provides that, where the partnership business is continued in the same name after the death of a partner, that fact does not of itself make the deceased partners' personal representatives liable for partnership debts contracted after the partner's death.
[4]   Eg 'salaried partners', 'associate partners'.
[5]   *Bass Brewers Ltd v Appleby* [1997] 2 BCLC 700.
[6]   IPO 1994, art 2.
[7]   IPO 1994, art 4(1). A 'PVA' can now take place under the protection of a moratorium. The individual members of the partnership are able to enter IVAs; IPO 1994, art 5(1).
[8]   IPO 1994, art 6.
[9]   See para **25.127**.

25.6 Other changes introduced by the IPO 1994 include:

(i)   it is now possible to wind up an insolvent partnership with a concurrent petition against one member, whereas under IPO 1986 there had to be concurrent petitions against at least two members[1]; and

(ii)   a secured creditor with the power to appoint an agricultural receiver[2] is in the same position as a debenture-holder having the power to appoint an administrative receiver, and his consent is needed before an administration order may be made in respect of the partnership[3].

1   IPO 1994, art 8; cf IPO 1986, art 8.
2   Ie a receiver appointed under a power in an agricultural charge pursuant to the Agricultural Credits Act 1928.
3   IPO 1994, Sch 2, paras 2, 3, 6, 7, 8, 11, 15.

25.7 The various changes to the insolvency regime affecting companies implemented by the Enterprise Act 2002, including in particular the complete revision of the administration procedure, are brought into partnership insolvency by the Insolvent Partnerships (Amendment) Order 2005[1] as from 1 July 2005.

1   SI 2005/1516.

25.8 IPO 1994 specifies new forms which must be used both in the High Court or a county court, with such variations as the circumstances may require[1].

1   IPO 1994, art 17. The forms are contained in Sch 9.

25.9 While the above changes are important, IPO 1994 does not represent any radical change to the approach of the IPO 1986 to partnership insolvency. This is to apply the Insolvency Act 1986 and the Company Directors Disqualification Act 1986 by way of modification of the primary legislation in various schedules[1]. While the task of digesting the modifications is made easier by setting out the modified sections in full, there remain difficulties with this approach. Most importantly, a partnership is treated as if it were a company, with the persons having the management and control of the partnership being considered to be officers of the partnership. IPO 1994 assumes that the appropriate equivalents will be found for company terms and procedures. Partnerships are self-evidently not companies, however, and without the statutory framework which governs companies, there is not the same uniformity of practice which enables all partnerships to be comfortably equated with companies. It is also to be noted that a particular section of the IA 1986 may be modified differently in different parts of IPO 1994. Care has to be taken to ensure that the provisions relating to the particular insolvency procedure under IPO 1994 under consideration have been correctly identified.

1   This approach is dictated by the provisions of the governing legislation, IA 1986, s 420.

What constitutes a partnership?

25.10 Partnership is not defined for the purposes of IPO 1994. 'Partnership property', however, is defined[1] as having the same meaning as in the Partnership Act 1890[2]. This definition of 'partnership property' provides that partnership property 'must be held and applied by the partners exclusively for the purposes of the partnership and in accordance with the partnership agreement'[3]. The reference to the partnership in this context is a reference to the definition of partnership in the Partnership Act 1890, s 1[4]. For the purposes of IPO 1994, partnership may be taken to mean formal partnership within the definition in the Partnership Act 1890. Where a person is held out as a partner of another, this is sometimes referred to as 'partnership by estoppel'. Such a partnership, if properly described as a partnership at all, does not come within the IPO 1994[5].

1   IPO 1994, art 2(1).
2   See the Partnership Act 1890, s 20.
3   Partnership Act 1890, s 20(1).
4   Which is subject to the rules for determining the existence of partnership set out in the Partnership Act 1890, s 2.
5   *Re C & M Ashberg* (1990) Times, 17 July – Jurisdiction cannot be conferred on the court by estoppel any more than by the partners' consent, Gavin Lightman QC.

The procedures available for partnership insolvency

25.11 After 1 December 1994, where an insolvent partnership does not enter into a voluntary arrangement or administration, a creditor has the option to seek either:

(1)   the winding up of the partnership as an unregistered company without instituting insolvency proceedings against any of the firm's members[1] (pursuant to an 'Article 7 Petition');
(2)   the winding up of a partnership as an unregistered company together with the bankruptcy or liquidation of one or more of the firm's members[2] (pursuant to an 'Article 8 Petition');
(3)   the bankruptcy or liquidation of any one or more members of the partnership without formal proceedings against the partnership itself[3].

1   IPO 1994, art 7.
2   IPO 1994, art 8 (under the IPO 1986 there had to be petitions against at least two members).
3   IPO 1994, art 19(5).

25.12 In the last of these cases, the proceedings will follow bankruptcy or liquidation procedures as appropriate and it will be for the trustee(s) in bankruptcy or liquidator(s) to decide what, if any, proceedings are brought against the remaining partners. In *Schooler v Customs and Excise Comrs*[1] the Court of Appeal rejected the argument that because the liability of partners for the debts of the partnership is joint and not joint and several[2], the court had no jurisdiction to bankrupt one individual member of the firm in the absence of a petition against the partnership or a previous judgment against the partnership for which the member would have a personal liability[3]. A creditor who has obtained judgment against a partnership is able to issue execution by presenting a petition against any member of the partnership:

(a)   without the need for leave from the court where the member has acknowledged service of the claim form as a partner, or, having been served as a partner has failed to acknowledge service, or has admitted in his statement of case that he is a partner or has been adjudged to be a partner[4]; and
(b)   with the leave of the court on an application under CPR Pt 23 on the grounds that the partner was liable to satisfy the judgment as being a member of the partnership[5].

1   [1995] 2 BCLC 610.

1000

²   See the Partnership Act 1890, s 9.

³   The court relied on the provisions of IPO 1986, art 15(3), which stated that:

> 'Nothing in this Order is to be taken as preventing any creditor or creditors owed one or more debts by an insolvent partnership from presenting a petition under the Act against one or more members of the partnership without including the others and without presenting a petition for the winding up of the partnership as an unregistered company, *and in such a case the debt or debts shall be treated as a debt or debts of the member in question.*'

> IPO 1994, art 19(5) is in similar terms, except that (for no obvious reason) the words in italics are omitted. Nourse LJ in *Schooler* noted the difference in wording but expressed the view that it would still be open to a creditor to take proceedings only against one partner under IPO 1994, even though the others are jointly indebted with him; p 615.

⁴   CPR Sch 1 RSC Ord 81 r 5(2).

⁵   CPR Sch 1 RSC Ord 81 r 5(4).

Consolidation of bankruptcy proceedings

25.13 The court has power to consolidate bankruptcy proceedings where petitions have been issued against two or more partners[1], and this consolidation may be ordered even where the proceedings have been commenced under the Bankruptcy Act 1914, the Insolvency Act 1986, IPO 1986, or IPO 1994[2]. The application for consolidation may be made by the official receiver, any responsible insolvency practitioner, the trustee of the partnership, or any other interested person[3]. The court may, and in the case of a consolidation of procedures under different Acts or Orders must[4], make provision for the manner in which the consolidated proceedings are to be conducted. The court will usually prefer to apply the provisions of IPO 1994.

¹   IA 1986, s 303(2B) inserted by IPO 1994, art 14(2).

²   IPO 1994, art 19(6).

³   IA 1986, s 303(2C) inserted by IPO 1994, art 14(2).

⁴   IPO 1994, art 19(6).

25.14 Where a member wishes to take insolvency proceedings IPO 1994 enables him:

   (i)   to wind up the partnership without presenting a petition against another member[1];

  (ii)   to wind up the partnership with concurrent petitions against *all* the other members[2];

 (iii)   together with all the other members of the firm, to present a joint petition for bankruptcy of all members without the winding up of the partnership itself[3].

¹   IPO 1994, art 9 and Sch 5.

²   IPO 1994, art 10 and Schs 4 and 6.

³   IPO 1994, art 11 and Sch 7.

25.15 IPO 1994[1] does not prevent the presentation of a petition against an insolvent partnership under the Financial Services and Markets Act 2000, s 367, or any other enactment[2]. As from 1 December 1994, IA 1986, s 168(5C)[3] provides that where the court makes an order under the Financial Services Act 1986, s 72(1)(a), the Banking Act 1987, s 92(1)(a) or the

25.15 *Partnership*

Financial Services and Markets Act 2000, s 367(3)(a), it may order that the provisions of IPO 1994 are to apply to the winding up; however, this jurisdiction is not extended to winding up under the Insurance Companies Act 1982, or other provisions of the Financial Services Act 1986 or Banking Act 1987. By virtue of the provisions of IA 1986, Sch A1, para 12, a petition to wind up a partnership cannot be presented during the period for which a moratorium is in force under the procedure for partnership voluntary arrangements[4].

[1]   As amended by the Financial Services and Markets Act 2000 (Consequential Amendments and Repeals) Order 2001, SI 2001/3649, art 467 and the Insolvent Partnerships (Amendment) (No 2) Order 2002, SI 2002/2708, art 5.
[2]   IPO 1994, art 19(4) as amended. Examples of other enactments under which particular types of partnership may be made insolvent include the Insurance Companies Act 1982, ss 53, 54, and the Banking Act 1987, s 92.
[3]   As inserted by IPO 1994, art 14(1).
[4]   IPO 1994, art 19(4) as amended.

Voluntary liquidation

25.16 Voluntary liquidation is not available to an insolvent partnership, being expressly prohibited by IA 1986, s 221(4)[1].

[1]   As modified by IPO 1994, Sch 3, para 3 (art 7 petitions); Sch 4, para 3 (art 8 petitions); Sch 5, para 2 (art 9 petitions); Sch 6, para 4 (art 10 petitions).

Territorial jurisdiction

25.17 By virtue of the IPO 1994[1], and subject to the provisions of the EC Insolvency Regulation[2], the High Court has jurisdiction to wind up any insolvent partnership as an unregistered company and any corporate member of an insolvent partnership as a registered or unregistered company, as appropriate, which the courts in England and Wales have jurisdiction to wind up. The High Court also has jurisdiction extending only to England and Wales in respect of bankruptcy and other insolvency proceedings in relation to individual members of insolvent partnerships[3]. Two conditions must be met before the courts of England and Wales have jurisdiction to wind up an insolvent partnership as an unregistered company:

(1)   the partnership must have or at any time have had:
    (a)   a principal place of business in England or Wales (this need not be the firm's only principal place of business); or
    (b)   a place of business in England or Wales at which business is or has been carried on[4] in the course of which the debt (or part of the debt) arose which forms the basis of the winding-up petition[5]; and
(2)   the partnership must have been carrying on business at any time during the period of three years ending on the day on which the winding-up petition is presented[6].

[1]   IPO 1994, art 1(2)(a).
[2]   See para **25.21**.
[3]   IPO 1994, art 1(2)(b).

⁴ For the meaning of 'carrying on business within England and Wales' see *Re A Company (No 7816 of 1994)* [1995] 2 BCLC 539; *Scher v Policyholders Protection Board* [1994] 2 AC 57; *Grant v Anderson* [1892] 1 QB 108, CA; *Re Dagnall* [1896] 2 QB 407; *Theophile v Sol-General* [1950] AC 186, [1950] 1 All ER 405; *Re Bird, ex p Debtor v IRC* [1962] 2 All ER 406, [1962] 1 WLR 686; *Re A Debtor (No 784 of 1991)* [1992] Ch 554, [1992] 3 All ER 376.
⁵ IA 1986, s 221(1) as modified by IPO 1994, Sch 3, para 3 and Sch 4, para 3; s 117(1), as modified by Sch 3, para 6.
⁶ IA 1986, s 221(2), modified as above.

25.18 In the case of a partnership with a principal place of business in Scotland or Northern Ireland, the partnership must have had a principal place of business in England and Wales within the periods of one year and three years respectively ending with the day on which the winding-up petition is presented[1].

¹ IA 1986, s 221(3), modified as above.

25.19 The county court has a concurrent jurisdiction with the High Court if within its insolvency district the partnership has either:

(a) a principal place of business (which need not be the firm's only principal place of business); or
(b) a place of business at which business is or has been carried on, in the course of which the debt (or part of the debt) arose which forms the basis of the winding-up petition[1].

¹ IA 1986, s 117(2), modified as above.

25.20 Where the county court has jurisdiction, it has for that purpose all the powers of the High Court[1]. High Court petitions must be presented in London as the District Registries do not have a partnership insolvency jurisdiction[2].

¹ IA 1986, s 117(6), modified as above.
² IA 1986, s 117(6), modified as above.

EC Insolvency Regulation: effect on partnership insolvency

25.21 On 31 May 2002, Council Regulation (EC) 1346/2000 on Insolvency Proceedings came into effect throughout the EU, except in Denmark. It is not a harmonisation instrument. It controls the exercise of the jurisdiction to commence insolvency proceedings in respect of EU debtors, and provides uniform rules for the choice of law. Insolvent partnerships are not expressly mentioned in the EC Insolvency Regulation, but they plainly come within the scope of the regulation[1], and the subordinate legislation which carried the EC Insolvency Regulation into effect proceeds on the basis that insolvent partnerships do come within its provisions[2]. The scheme of the regulation is to ensure primacy for insolvency proceedings opened in the debtor's state, that is the Member State in which the debtor[3] has his 'centre of main interests'. Once main proceedings have been opened against the debtor, the liquidator[4] in those proceedings may involve himself in any insolvency proceedings opened in other Member States. The liquidator may seek a stay of the realisation of assets[5], propose a rescue plan or composition in those proceedings[6], or apply for a voluntary arrangement or administration to be converted into formal insolvency[7]. The EC Insolvency Regulation also contains provisions relating to the lodgement of claims against the insolvent partnership and its members[8].

[1]   EC Insolvency Regulation, art 1.1 provides: 'This Regulation shall apply to collective insolvency proceedings which entail the partial or total divestment of a debtor and the appointment of a liquidator'. By art 2 'liquidator' is defined as 'any person or body whose function is to administer or liquidate assets of which the debtor has been divested or to supervise the administration of his affairs'.

[2]   See the Insolvent Partnerships (Amendment) Order 2002, SI 2002/1308.

[3]   'Debtor' includes an insolvent partnership, see (by necessary implication) IPO 1994, arts 7(1), 8(1), as modified by the Insolvent Partnerships (Amendment) Order 2002, SI 2002/1308.

[4]   EC Insolvency Regulation, art 2(b) provides an extended definition of 'liquidator'.

[5]   EC Insolvency Regulation, art 33.

[6]   EC Insolvency Regulation, art 34, provided the secondary law allows it. A liquidator in foreign main proceedings could propose a voluntary arrangement in England and Wales. There is no express provision for this in the IR 1986, but presumably he would proceed as would an office-holder in the debtor's English insolvency.

[7]   EC Insolvency Regulation, art 37.

[8]   EC Insolvency Regulation, art 39.

25.22 The jurisdictional provisions of the EC Insolvency Regulation take precedence when considering the jurisdiction of the courts in the United Kingdom over insolvent partnerships[1]. Jurisdiction to open proceedings in respect of insolvent partnerships is vested in the courts of the Member State in which the partnership has its centre of main interests[2]. Such proceedings are 'main proceedings'. Proceedings may be commenced in a Member State other than that in which the insolvent partnership has its centre of main interests only if the insolvent partnership has an establishment within the territory of that state. Such proceedings may be either 'secondary proceedings' or 'territorial proceedings'. Proceedings commenced after the main proceedings are opened are termed 'secondary proceedings' and 'territorial proceedings' are proceedings commenced before the main proceedings.

[1]   Under the EC Insolvency Regulation the UK is regarded as one jurisdiction. This precedence is achieved by inserting an additional subsection in IA 1986, ss 117, 221 and 265 in IPO 1994, Schs 3, 4, 5, and 6, which provides that the section is subject to art 3 of the EC Insolvency Regulation.

[2]   EC Insolvency Regulation, art 3(1).

25.23 The effects of territorial proceedings must be restricted to the assets of the partnership situated in that state[11]. Territorial proceedings may be issued only if (a) main proceedings cannot be opened because of conditions laid down by the law of the relevant Member State, or (b) the opening of territorial proceedings is requested by a creditor who has his domicile, habitual residence or registered office in the Member State within the territory of which the relevant establishment of the insolvent partnership is situated, or whose claim arises from the operation of that establishment[1].

[1]   EC Insolvency Regulation, art 3(4).

25.24 Secondary proceedings must be restricted to winding-up proceedings[1], which for these purposes comprise winding up by or subject to the supervision of the court, creditors' voluntary winding up with confirmation by the court, or bankruptcy[2]. There can therefore be no partnership voluntary arrangement or administration in England and Wales after main proceedings have been commenced in another Member State if the insolvent partnership's centre of main interests is in that Member State.

1 EC Insolvency Regulation, art 3(3).
2 EC Insolvency Regulation, art 2(c) and Annex B.

Subordinate legislation

25.25 IPO 1994 goes further than the IPO 1986 did in applying subordinate legislation to partnership insolvency. The following Rules, Orders and Regulations are applied[1]:

(a) The Insolvency Practitioners Tribunal (Conduct of Investigations) Rules 1986[2].

(b) The Insolvency Practitioners (Recognised Professional Bodies) Order 1986[3].

(c) The Insolvency Rules 1986[4].

(d) The Insolvency Regulations 1986[5] (now Insolvency Regulations 1994[6]).

(e) The Insolvency Proceedings (Monetary Limits) Order 1986[7].

(f) The Administration of Insolvent Estates of Deceased Persons Order 1986[8].

(g) The Insolvency (Amendment of Subordinate Legislation) Order 1986[9].

(h) The Insolvency Fees Order 1986[10].

(i) The Companies (Disqualification Orders) Regulations 1986[11].

(j) The Co-operation of Insolvency Cause (Designation of Relevant Countries and Territories) Order 1986[12].

(k) The Insolvent Companies (Reports on Conduct of Directors) No 2 Rules 1986[13].

(l) The Insolvent Companies (Disqualification of Unfit Directors) Proceedings Rules 1987[14].

(m) The Insolvency Practitioners Regulations 1990[15].

1 By IPO 1994, art 18(1).
2 SI 1986/952.
3 SI 1986/1764.
4 SI 1986/1925.
5 SI 1986/1994.
6 SI 1994/2507.
7 SI 1986/1996.
8 SI 1986/1999.
9 SI 1986/2001.
10 SI 1986/2030.
11 SI 1986/2067.
12 SI 1986/2123.
13 SI 1986/2134.
14 SI 1987/2023.
15 SI 1990/439.

25.26 This is a wide range of subordinate legislation drafted in some cases to deal with detailed procedures involving companies. This legislation is to be applied 'as from time to time in force and with such modifications as the context requires for the purpose of giving effect to the provisions of the [Insolvency Act 1986] and of the Company Directors Disqualification Act 1986 which are applied by this Order'[1]. It is left to the courts to resolve the differences that are likely to arise in individual cases. In the case of any conflict between any provision of the subordinate legislation and any provision of IPO 1994, the latter provision is to prevail[2].

[1] IPO 1994, art 18(1).
[2] IPO 1994, art 18(2).

Transitional provisions

25.27 Where a winding-up or bankruptcy order was made against a partnership or insolvent membership of a partnership before 1 December 1994, the procedure remains subject to the provisions of IPO 1986[1]. Proceedings which were pending on 1 December 1994 are governed by the provisions of IPO 1994 unless the court directs that the proceedings should continue under IPO 1986[2]. In any procedure continuing under the provisions of IPO 1986, however, the court may apply any provisions of IPO 1994, with any necessary modifications[3]. The new administration regime which applied to companies as from 15 September 2003 was not extended to partnerships until 1 July 2005[4], and to limited liability partnerships on 1 October 2005[5].

[1] IPO 1994, art 19(1).
[2] IPO 1994, art 19(2).
[3] IA 1986, s 168(5A). Any interested person may apply for an order applying the IPO 1994, s 168(5B).
[4] Insolvent Partnerships (Amendment) Order 2005, SI 2005/1516, art 2.
[5] The Limited Liability Partnerships (Amendment) Regulations 2005, SI 2005/1989.

B PARTNERSHIP VOLUNTARY ARRANGEMENTS

General

25.28 Introduced by IPO 1994, the partnership voluntary arrangement ('PVA') treats the partnership as if it were a limited company, and applies the provisions of the Insolvency Act 1986, Part I relating to company voluntary arrangements ('CVA') to the insolvent partnership. There is, however, no bar to an individual partner proposing an individual voluntary arrangement ('IVA') either by himself, or as one of a group of partners acting together proposing a series of interlocking IVAs. Interlocking IVAs have similar provisions in the case of joint debts and in making available the joint estate to the joint creditors together with individual provisions tailored to the needs of separate debts and the separate estates. The fact that any individual debtor is liable on his debts jointly with others is no bar to his obtaining an interim order and proceeding to an IVA[1]. The partner of an insolvent partnership and any insolvency practitioner advising him must take into account the fact that a PVA will protect the individual partner's estate from the claims of joint (ie partnership) creditors, but will not protect the individual's estate from the claims of any separate creditor. The entry into an IVA by one partner does not protect the other partners from enforcement procedures by a partnership creditor against their separate estates[2].

1   *Re Cupit* [1996] BPIR 560, CA.
2   *Schooler v Customs & Excise Comrs* [1995] 2 BCLC 610, 616.

25.29 It is open to the members of an eligible insolvent partnership to obtain a moratorium. To be eligible the insolvent partnership must meet two or more of the following qualifying conditions in the period of the year ending with the date of filing of the moratorium documents or in the tax year of the insolvent partnership which ended last before that date[1]. There are three qualifying conditions, namely: (1) turnover not exceeding £5.6 million; (2) assets not exceeding £2.8 million; and (3) no more than 50 employees[2]. The exclusions from eligibility applicable to an insolvent company apply equally to an insolvent partnership.

1   IPO 1994, art 4(1) and Sch 1, Part II, para 3.
2   IA 1986, Sch A1, para 3(1), (2).

Procedure for PVA

25.30 By the IPO 1994, art 4, the provisions of IA 1986, Part I, as modified in IPO 1994, Sch 1, apply to insolvent partnerships. The provisions of IA 1986, Part I include the ability of an eligible partnership to obtain a moratorium, in which event the voluntary arrangement proceeds under the provisions of IA 1986, Sch A1. Only essential modifications have been made to the IA 1986 for the purpose of PVA and the procedure closely follows that for CVA. In essence a PVA is proposed for, approved or rejected at meetings of the partnership's creditors and members, and is subject to challenge in the same way as is provided for a CVA. Thus the members of the insolvent partnership[1] may propose a PVA as may an administrator of the partnership, the liquidator of a partnership being wound up as an unregistered partnership, or a trustee of the partnership appointed[2] following a joint petition to the court by the members for the bankruptcy of each of them in his capacity as a member of the partnership. Where the nominee is not the liquidator, administrator or trustee he must submit a report to the court stating whether, and if so when and where, meetings should be held for members and the partnership's creditors[3]. This report is also to state whether there are in existence any insolvency proceedings in respect of the insolvent partnership or any of its members[4]. Meetings are then summoned of the members of the partnership and the partnership's creditors, and if the PVA is approved it takes effect as if made by the members of the partnership at the creditors' meeting, binding every person who in accordance with the rules was entitled to vote at the meeting irrespective of whether he was present or represented[5]. The approval of a PVA may be challenged within 28 days by any person entitled to vote at either meeting, the nominee, or where appropriate the liquidator, administrator, or trustee of the partnership[6]. An approved PVA is then implemented by the supervisor of the PVA. Any act, omission, or decision of the supervisor may be challenged by any of the partnership's creditors or any other dissatisfied person[7].

1 Rather than the directors of a company.
2 Under IPO 1994, art 11.
3 IA 1986, s 2(1), (2) as modified by IPO 1994, art 4, Sch 1.
4 IA 1986, s 2(3) as modified by IPO 1994, art 4, Sch 1.
5 IA 1986, s 5(2) as modified by IPO 1994, art 4, Sch 1.
6 IA 1986, s 6(2) as modified by IPO 1994, art 4, Sch 1.
7 IA 1986, s 7(3) as modified by IPO 1994, art 4, Sch 1.

Applicable rules and statutory provisions

25.31 The relevant provisions of the Insolvency Rules 1986, ie Part I[1], apply to PVAs 'with such modifications as the context requires'[2]. At the meeting of the partnership's members, voting will be in accordance with the voting rights in the partnership[3], a simple majority being sufficient to approve the PVA[4]. Where there is a partnership deed with provision for voting rights, those provisions will apply. Otherwise partners will be entitled to vote in accordance with their rights to share in capital and profits, this right being equal as between the partners where there is no agreement expressed or implied to the contrary[5]. There may be partners, eg 'salaried partners', who have no right to vote within the partnership. Members who have no voting rights in the partnership may neither vote at the meeting nor challenge the meeting's decision[6]. The requisite majority required to approve the proposal or any modification to it at the creditors' meeting is 75 per cent[7], provided also that the resolution is not opposed by 50 per cent of those voting when omitting the votes of persons to whom notice of the meeting was not sent, whose debt is wholly or partly secured, and anyone whom the chairman of the meeting believes to be connected with the partnership[8]. In determining either of these majorities the chairman must leave out: (a) the claim of any creditor who does not give written notice of his claim either before or at the meeting to the convenor or chairman; (b) the secured part of any creditor's claim; and (c) the claim of any creditor which is secured by a current bill of exchange or promissory note, unless the creditor is prepared to treat the liability of every person liable on the bill antecedently to the partnership and who is not insolvent as security, and to estimate the value of such security and deduct it from the value of his claim for voting purposes[9].

1 IR 1986, rr 1.1–1.54 inclusive.
2 IPO 1994, art 18(1).
3 IR 1986, r 1.18(1) (no moratorium), r 1.51 (moratorium).
4 IR 1986, r 1.20(1) (no moratorium), r 1.53 (moratorium).
5 Partnership Act 1890, s 24(1).
6 This follows the revocation of IR 1986, r 1.18(2) (by the Insolvency (Amendment) (No 2) Rules 2002, SI 2002/2712, para 3(1)), which had allowed a member to vote solely to protect his right to challenge the decision of the meeting.
7 IR 1986, r 1.19(1) (no moratorium), r 1.52 (moratorium).
8 IR 1986, r 1.19(4) (no moratorium), r 1.52(5) (moratorium).
9 IR 1986, r 1.19(3) (no moratorium), r 1.52(4) (moratorium).

25.32 IPO 1994 also provides[1] that the following provisions of the Insolvency Act 1986 should apply to PVAs:

(a)   s 233, which enables the supervisor to obtain supplies of gas, electricity, water, and telecommunication services from a public authority or operator;

(b)   ss 247, 248, 249 and 251 which provide definitions;
(c)   ss 386 and 387 which define preferential debts and the relevant date for determining the existence and amount of a preferential debt;
(d)   ss 388–398 which make provision for insolvency practitioners to be qualified;
(e)   ss 411, 413, 414, and 419 which provide for subordinate legislation covering the Insolvency Rules, the Insolvency Rules Committee, Fees Orders and Regulations governing insolvency practitioners;
(f)   ss 423–425 (provision against debt avoidance), ss 426–434 (co-operation between insolvency courts, criminal offences, etc), s 435 (the definition of associate), s 436 (general definitions) and ss 437–444 (final provisions).

¹   IPO 1994, art 4(2), (3).

25.33 As to the definition of 'associate', it may be noted that the definition is in the present tense: 'A person is an associate of any person with whom he *is* in partnership, and of the husband or wife or a relative of any individual with whom he *is* in partnership'¹ (emphasis added). Former partners are not associates. Thus where a vote is to be taken on an IVA or PVA, a person who has ceased to be a partner by the date of the vote, even if by one day, is not an associate. Where insolvency has arrived or is looming there could well be little to inhibit partners dissolving or terminating their relationship and so being able to vote on the same terms as wholly independent creditors on their partners' proposals for IVA. However, in *Goel v Pick*² the court held that a former partner remained an associate until the affairs of the partnership had been fully wound up, referring to the provisions of the Partnership Act 1890, s 38:

> 'After the dissolution of a partnership the authority of each party to bind the firm, and the other rights and obligations of the partners, continue notwithstanding the dissolution as far as may be necessary to wind up the affairs of the partnership, and to complete transactions begun but unfinished at the time of the dissolution, but not otherwise.'

¹   IA 1986, s 435(3).
²   [2006] EWHC 833 (Ch), [2007] 1 All ER 982 (Sir Francis Ferris), a case concerned with the transfer of a vehicle registration mark.

25.34 Even after the winding up of the partnership the court may, in appropriate circumstances, conclude that the termination of the partnership was a sham.

Implementation of PVA

25.35 The supervisor administers the PVA subject to the power of the court to confirm, reverse or modify any act, omission or decision of the supervisor on the application of any creditor or other person dissatisfied, or to give directions at the instance of any dissatisfied person or on the application of the supervisor¹. The court has power to appoint an insolvency practitioner as supervisor either in substitution for an existing supervisor or to fill a vacancy².

¹   IA 1986, s 7(3), (4) as applied by IPO 1994, art 4(1), Sch 1.
²   IA 1986, s 7(5) as applied by IPO 1994, art 4(1), Sch 1.

Failure of PVA

25.36 In the event of failure of a PVA, the creditors, subject to the precise terms of the PVA, will be able to petition for the winding up of the partnership as an unregistered company and for the insolvency of any member under IPO 1994, Part IV.

25.37 Where a winding-up petition is presented solely against the partnership, the available grounds for the petition are:

  (i)   that the partnership is unable to pay its debts;
  (ii)   that it is just and equitable for the partnership to be wound up;
  (iii)   that the partnership has ceased to carry on business or is carrying on business only for the purpose of winding up its affairs; or
  (iv)   at the time at which a moratorium comes to an end, no voluntary arrangement has been approved in respect of the insolvent partnership¹.

¹   IA 1986, s 221(7) as modified by IPO 1994, art 7, Sch 3, para 3.

25.38 Where concurrent petitions are presented against the partnership and one or more of its members, the ground for the winding-up petition will have to be that the partnership or corporate member is unable to pay its debts¹, or a moratorium comes to an end without a PVA being approved, for there is no provision in IPO 1994 which makes a default in connection with a PVA a ground for seeking a winding-up order. In the case of an individual, the IPO 1994 proceeds on the basis that the bankruptcy petition must be grounded in respect of one or more joint debts owed by the insolvent partnership². In cases where the PVA is so drafted that the partnerships' joint debts are compromised in return for a dividend to be paid out of assets provided both by the partnership and particular members of the partnership, and the partnership has duly made available its assets, it would appear to be necessary to establish that the failure of the PVA is such that the creditor is entitled to rely on his original joint debt. It is the case that IPO 1994, art 8(5) applied the provisions of IA 1986, Part IX, including ss 264(1)(c) and 276 (which permits a bankruptcy petition to be presented on the ground of a default in connection with an IVA), but the former provision is not modified so as to extend to a PVA.

¹   IA 1986, s 221(8), as modified by IPO 1994, art 8, Sch 4, para 3 (partnership); IA 1986, s 122, as modified by IPO 1994, art 8, Sch 4, para 3 (corporate member).
²   IA 1986, s 267(1), as modified by IPO 1994, art 8, Sch 4, para 6 (individual).

C PARTNERSHIP ADMINISTRATION ORDERS

General

25.39 Any partnership which the courts of England and Wales have jurisdiction to wind up may be the subject of an administration¹. The procedure closely follows the procedure which applies to companies, and, although there was a delay in its implementation, the new administration procedure for companies introduced in the Enterprise Act 2002 now applies to partnerships by virtue of the Insolvent Partnerships (Amendment) Order 2005 ('IP(A)O 2005')[2]. An administrator may therefore be appointed out of court. Partnership administrations which commenced before 1 July 2005 continue to be governed by IA 1986, ss 8–27 as amended by IPO 1994, Sch 2[3]. The administration regime applicable to companies is applied to partnerships with only minor amendments. The relevant provisions of the Insolvency Rules[4] apply to partnership administration orders 'with such modifications as the context requires'[5].

[1]   IPO 1994, Arts 1(2), 6.
[2]   SI 2005/1516, see the Insolvent Partnerships (Amendment) Order 2005, art 3 which came into effect on 1 July 2005. Minor amendments were made to the 2005 Order with effect from 6 April 2006 to correct mistakes, in particular to ensure that the prescribed part for unsecured creditors provisions (IA 1986, s 176A) does not apply to the insolvent partnership itself and the priority of agricultural charges is determined by the time of registration; the Insolvent Partnerships (Amendment) Order 2006, SI 2006/622.
[3]   Before amendment by the 2005 Order. IPO 1994 made only minor amendments to the IA 1986, ss 8–15 and Sch 1, and ss 17–27 were not amended at all.
[4]   Ie IR 1986, Part 2.
[5]   IPO 1994, art 18(1).

The IPO 1994 scheme for applying the IA 1986 administration provisions to insolvent partnerships

25.40 IPO 1994, art 6(1), as substituted by IP(A)O 2005, art 3 provides that IA 1986, Part II and Sch B1: 'shall apply to an insolvent partnership, certain of those provisions being modified in such manner that, after modification, they are as set out in Schedule 2 to this Order'. The application of Sch B1 is subject to two general changes. For every reference to 'administrative receiver' and 'floating charge' is to be substituted, respectively, 'agricultural receiver' and 'agricultural floating charge'[1]. In reading the provisions of IA 1986 in the context of an insolvent partnership, IPO 1994, art 3 provides that references to companies are to be construed as references to insolvent partnerships, all references to the registrar of companies are to be omitted, and other expressions appropriate to companies are to be construed, in relation to the insolvent partnership, to corresponding persons, officers, documents or organs, as the case may be, appropriate to a partnership.

[1]   IPO 1994, art 6(3), as amended. An 'agricultural floating charge' is to be construed as a reference to a floating charge created under the Agricultural Credits Act 1928, s 5: IPO 1994, art 6(6).

25.41 IPO 1994 also provides[1] that the following provisions of the Insolvency Act 1986 should apply to partnership administration orders:

(a)   Part VI: Miscellaneous provisions:
    –   ss 230–232 qualifications and appointment of an administrator;
    –   s 233 supplies of gas, water, electricity and telecommunications;
    –   s 234 powers to get in the partnership property;
    –   s 235 duty to co-operate with official receiver or liquidator;

- ss 236, 237 power to inquire into the dealings of the partnership and enforcement by the court;
- ss 238–245 powers to adjust prior transactions;

(b)   Part VII: Interpretation:
- s 247 (definition of insolvency); s 248 (secured creditor); s 249 (connected person); and s 251 (expressions used generally);

(c)   Part XII: Preferential debts:
- s 386 (categories of preferential debts); s 387 (the 'relevant date');

(d)   Part XIII: Insolvency practitioners:
- ss 388–398 which make provision for insolvency practitioners to be qualified;

(e)   Part XV: Subordinate legislation:
- ss 411, 413, 414 and 419, which provide subordinate legislation covering Insolvency Rules, the Insolvency Rules Committee, Fees Orders and Regulations governing insolvency practitioners;

(f)   Parts XVI–XIX:
- ss 423–425 provisions against debt avoidance;
- ss 426–434 co-operation between Insolvency Courts, disqualifications and exemptions, offences and punishment, admissibility of statement of affairs in evidence and application to the Crown;
- s 435 definition of 'associate';
- s 436 general definitions;
- ss 437–444 transitional provisions, savings, repeals, amendments, commencement and citation.

1   IPO 1994, art 6(4), (5), as amended by IP(A)O 2005, art 3.

Obtaining a partnership administration order

25.42   The procedure for obtaining a partnership administration order closely follows that which applies to companies. An administrator of a partnership may be appointed by the court[1], or by the holder of a qualifying agricultural floating charge[2], or by the members of an insolvent partnership[3]. An agricultural floating charge qualifies if created by an instrument which expressly states that IA 1986, Sch B1, para 14 (as modified by IPO 1994) applies to the agricultural floating charge and which purports to empower the holder of the charge to appoint both an administrator and an agricultural receiver in respect of the partnership[4].

1   IA 1986, Sch B1, para 11, applied by IPO 1994, art 6 as substituted by IP(A)O 2005, art 3 and modified by IP(A)O 2005, Sch 2.
2   IA 1986, Sch B1, para 14, applied by IPO 1994, art 6 as substituted by IP(A)O 2005, art 3 and modified by IP(A)O 2005, Sch 2.
3   IA 1986, Sch B1, para 22, applied by IPO 1994, art 6 as substituted by IP(A)O 2005, art 3 and modified by IP(A)O 2005, Sch 2.
4   IA 1986, Sch B1, para 14(2), applied by IPO 1994, art 6 as substituted by IP(A)O 2005, art 3 and modified by IP(A)O 2005, Sch 2. A person is the holder of a qualifying agricultural floating charge in respect of partnership property if he holds one or more charges of the partnership secured by: (a) a qualifying agricultural floating charge relating to the whole or substantially the whole of the partnership property; or (b) a number of qualifying agricultural floating charges which together relate to the whole or substantially the whole of the partnership property; or (c) charges and other forms of security which

together relate to the whole or substantially the whole of the partnership property and at least one of which is a qualifying agricultural floating charge; IA 1986, Sch B1, para 14(3), applied by IPO 1994, art 6 as substituted by IP(A)O 2005, art 3 and modified by IP(A)O 2005, Sch 2.

Appointment by the court

25.43 The court may make an administration order in relation to a partnership only if satisfied: (a) that the partnership is unable to pay its debts; and (b) that the administration order is reasonably likely to achieve the purpose of administration[1]. This provision mirrors the requirement for making an administration order in respect of an insolvent company. Requirement (a), inability to pay its debts[2], raises the question as to the status of member's own assets. Unlike a company, a partnership will have partners who will have personal obligations to meet the partners' debts where the partnership itself is insolvent. The question arises, therefore, whether members' personal assets should be taken into account before the court can be satisfied that the partnership 'is unable to pay its debts'. In *Re H S Smith & Sons*[3] it was held that only the partnership's assets should be taken into account when the court was considering whether or not the partnership was unable to pay its debts. A partnership administration order was therefore made for the purpose of securing the survival of the undertaking of the partnership as a going concern even though one of the partners had ample personal assets to pay off the partnership debts. The order was made to hold off the creditors from presenting winding-up petitions while the partner concerned realised personal assets to recapitalise the partnership.

[1]   IA 1986, Sch B1, para 11, applied by IPO 1994, art 6 as substituted by IP(A)O 2005, art 3 and modified by IP(A)O 2005, Sch 2.
[2]   Which also applied to partnership administration before the introduction of the new administration regime.
[3]   (1999) Times, 7 January, Park J.

25.44 As for requirement (b) (para **25.43**), reasonable likelihood that an administration order will achieve the purpose of administration, the 'purpose of administration' is defined as the administrator performing his functions with one of three possible objectives, namely: (1) rescuing the partnership as a going concern; (2) achieving a better result for the partnership's creditors as a whole than would be likely if the company were wound up without first being in administration; or (3) realising property in order to make a distribution to one or more secured or preferential creditors[1].

[1]   IA 1986, Sch B1, para 3.

25.45 Objective (2) (para **25.44**) above, 'achieving a better result for the partnership's creditors than would be likely if the partnership were wound up', may be compared with the ground for making an administration order under the original administration regime that the order was likely to achieve a more advantageous realisation of assets than in a winding up[1]. Where this original ground was made out, the court refused to adjourn the petition in order to allow the partnership to attempt to sell its own assets without the intervention of an administrator[2]. As a pending petition has the effect of providing the partnership with an interim moratorium, it would require exceptional facts before the court acceded to a request for an adjournment of the hearing of the petition. The effect of an adjournment is to give the partnership the benefits of an administration order without the appointment of an administrator.

[1]   IA 1986, s 8(3)(d).
[2]   *Re Kyrris* [1998] BPIR 103; see also *Re Greek Taverna* [1999] BCC 153.

Procedure

25.46 An 'administration application' may be made only by the members of the insolvent partnership, or by one or more of the partnership's creditors[1], or by a combination of members and creditors[2]. A members' administration application must be made by or on behalf of all the members of the partnership[3], and an individual member who wishes to make an administration application against the wishes of other members may only do so in conjunction with a partnership creditor. Once made, an administration application may not be withdrawn without the permission of the court[4]. Notification of the application must be given as soon as is reasonably practicable to any person who has appointed, or who is or may be entitled to appoint, an agricultural receiver of the partnership, or any person who as holder of a qualifying agricultural floating charge is, or may be entitled to appoint, an administrator of the partnership[5]. On the hearing of the application the court may make the order sought, or an interim order, or any order which the court thinks appropriate[6]. In cases where the court concludes that an application is improperly presented and is an abuse of the process, the application may be dismissed forthwith, before the date fixed for its hearing[7].

[1]   'Creditor' includes contingent or prospective creditors; IA 1986, Sch B1, para 12(5), applied by IPO 1994, art 6 as substituted by IP(A)O 2005, art 3 and modified by IP(A)O 2005, Sch 2.
[2]   IA 1986, Sch B1, para 12(1), applied by IPO 1994, art 6 as substituted by IP(A)O 2005, art 3 and modified by IP(A)O 2005, Sch 2.
[3]   An application on behalf of all members will be made in accordance with the partnership deed or other rules governing the administration of the affairs of the individual partnership.
[4]   IA 1986, Sch B1, para 12(3), applied by IPO 1994, art 6 as substituted by IP(A)O 2005, art 3 and modified by IP(A)O 2005, Sch 2.
[5]   IA 1986, Sch B1, para 12(2), applied by IPO 1994, art 6 as substituted by IP(A)O 2005, art 3 and modified by IP(A)O 2005, Sch 2.
[6]   IA 1986, Sch B1, para 13, applied by IPO 1994, art 6 as substituted by IP(A)O 2005, art 3 and modified by IP(A)O 2005, Sch 2. Lest there be any doubt on the matter, para 13 also provides that the court may dismiss the application or adjourn the hearing with or without conditions.
[7]   *Re West Park Golf & Country Club* [1997] 1 BCLC 20, where a creditor applied for leave to enforce his security while a petition for an administration order was pending.

Appointment by charge-holder

25.47 The holder of a qualifying agricultural floating charge may appoint an administrator under the terms of his charge, provided always that his charge is enforceable[1]. He must, however, first give at least two business days' written notice to the holder of any prior agricultural floating charge, or have the written consent of any prior charge-holder to the making of the appointment[2]. Having made an appointment, the charge-holder must file a notice of appointment with the court[3]. This notice must: (a) include a statutory declaration that the appointer holds a qualifying floating charge and that this charge is enforceable, and that the appointment has been made in accordance with IA 1986, Sch B1, as applied by IPO 1994; (b) identify the administrator; and (c) be accompanied by a statement by the administrator that he consents to the appointment, that in his opinion the purpose of the administration is likely to be achieved, and giving such other information as may be prescribed[4]. The administrator's appointment takes effect on the filing of the notice of appointment with the court, it being the duty of the charge-holder to notify the administrator that the notice has been filed[5].

[1]   IA 1986, Sch B1, paras 14 and 16, applied by IPO 1994, art 6 as substituted by IP(A)O 2005, art 3 and modified by IP(A)O 2005, Sch 2. A partnership cannot create a floating charge; *Re West Park Golf & Country Club* [1997] 1 BCLC 20.
[2]   IA 1986, Sch B1, para 15(1), applied by IPO 1994, art 6 as substituted by IP(A)O 2005, art 3 and modified by IP(A)O 2005, Sch 2; a 'prior charge' is one which was either created first or which is to be treated as having priority by agreement between the relevant charge-holders, para 15(2).
[3]   IA 1986, Sch B1, para 22, applied by IPO 1994, art 6 as substituted by IP(A)O 2005, art 3 and modified by IP(A)O 2005, Sch 2.
[4]   IA 1986, Sch B1, para 18, applied by IPO 1994, art 6 as substituted by IP(A)O 2005, art 3 and modified by IP(A)O 2005, Sch 2.
[5]   IA 1986, Sch B1, paras 19 and 20, applied by IPO 1994, art 6 as substituted by IP(A)O 2005, art 3 and modified by IP(A)O 2005, Sch 2.

Appointment by members

25.48 The entitlement to make an appointment is vested in 'the members' of an insolvent partnership, that is the membership as a whole[1]. However, the provisions of Schedule B1, as amended, governing the making of the application refer to 'a person' proposing to make an appointment. Presumably what is intended is a person ('the applicant') acting on behalf of all the members. The applicant must give at least five business days' notice in writing to any person who is or may be entitled to appoint an agricultural receiver of the partnership and any person entitled to appoint an administrator of the partnership[2]. The notice must identify the proposed administrator and be in the prescribed form[3]. As soon as reasonably practicable after giving notice of intention to appoint an administrator, the applicant must file at a court a copy of the notice, together with any document accompanying it, and a statutory declaration made by the applicant or someone on his behalf stating that the partnership is unable to pay its debts, that the partnership is not in liquidation, and that the application is not prevented by the terms of Schedule B1[4]. There are two statutory preventions. First, an administrator may not be appointed within 12 months of the end of any previous appointment whether by the members or by the court on the application of the members[5]. Secondly, an administrator may not be appointed while there is a pending petition to wind up the partnership or pending application to appoint an administrator, or while an agricultural receiver is in office[6]. On the making of an appointment the appointer must file at court a notice of appointment which notice must include a statutory declaration that the appointer is entitled to make the appointment, that the appointment is made in accordance with Schedule B1, and that the information in the statutory declaration is accurate[7]. The notice of appointment must identify the administrator and be accompanied by the administrator's statement that he consents to his appointment and that in his opinion the purpose of the administration is reasonably likely to be achieved[8].

[1]   IA 1986, Sch B1, para 22, applied by IPO 1994, art 6 as substituted by IP(A)O 2005, art 3 and modified by IP(A)O 2005, Sch 2.
[2]   IA 1986, Sch B1, para 26(1), applied by IPO 1994, art 6 as substituted by IP(A)O 2005, art 3 and modified by IP(A)O 2005, Sch 2; notice must also be given to any other person as may be prescribed, para 26(2).
[3]   IA 1986, Sch B1, para 22(3), applied by IPO 1994, art 6 as substituted by IP(A)O 2005, art 3 and modified by IP(A)O 2005, Sch 2. The prescribed form is Form 1A in IPO 1994, Sch 9.
[4]   IA 1986, Sch B1, para 27, applied by IPO 1994, art 6 as substituted by IP(A)O 2005, art 3 and modified by IP(A)O 2005, Sch 2.
[5]   IA 1986, Sch B1, para 23, applied by IPO 1994, art 6 as substituted by IP(A)O 2005, art 3 and modified by IP(A)O 2005, Sch 2.
[6]   IA 1986, Sch B1, para 25, applied by IPO 1994, art 6 as substituted by IP(A)O 2005, art 3 and modified by IP(A)O 2005, Sch 2.
[7]   IA 1986, Sch B1, para 29(1), (2), applied by IPO 1994, art 6 as substituted by IP(A)O 2005, art 3 and modified by IP(A)O 2005, Sch 2.
[8]   IA 1986, Sch B1, para 29(3), applied by IPO 1994, art 6 as substituted by IP(A)O 2005, art 3 and modified by IP(A)O 2005, Sch 2; the administrator's statement must also give such other information as may be prescribed. The notice of appointment must be in Form 1B to IPO 1994, Sch 9.

25.49 In corporate insolvency, while an administration application is pending, or between the date of filing a notice of intention to appoint an administrator by the holder of a floating charge or the members and the date on which such an appointment takes effect, an interim moratorium comes into effect. During this period no other insolvency proceedings or other legal process may be taken or enforced against the company without the permission of the court[1]. There are no express modifications to the IPO 1994, Sch B1 to extend the interim moratorium process to insolvent partnerships; the IPO 1994 achieves this result as a consequence of the general provision requiring any reference to companies in the IA 1986 to be construed as a reference to an insolvent partnership[2].

[1]   IA 1986, Sch B1, para 44.
[2]   See IPO 1994, art 3.

The effect of an administration order

25.50 The administration order has the effect of imposing a moratorium both on insolvency proceedings against the partnership and on all other legal process against the insolvent partnership's property. Accordingly, no order may be made for the winding up of the partnership[1], nor may an order be made for the dissolution of the partnership[2] and no order may be made on an 'Article 11 petition'[3]. The prohibition on legal process against partnership property is not absolute; such process may be taken with the consent of the administrator or with the permission of the court[4]. All forms of legal process are caught by the moratorium, whether legal proceedings, execution or distress and including the repossession of goods the subject of hire-purchase, the exercise of a right of forfeiture by any person to whom rent is payable[5]. An agricultural receiver may not be appointed to a partnership in administration[6], and any agricultural receiver who has been appointed must vacate office[7].

1 This does not preclude a petition by the Secretary of State to wind up the partnership in the public interest under IA 1986, s 124A, nor a petition by the Financial Services Authority under the Financial Services and Markets Act 2000, s 367.
2 Under the Partnership Act 1890, s 35.
3 IA 1986, Sch B1, para 42, applied by IPO 1994, art 6 as substituted by IP(A)O 2005, art 3 and modified by IP(A)O 2005, Sch 2.
4 IA 1986, Sch B1, para 43, applied by IPO 1994, art 6 as substituted by IP(A)O 2005, art 3 and modified by IP(A)O 2005, Sch 2. Where the court gives permission for any transaction to take place it may impose any condition or requirement in connection with that transaction that it thinks fit; para 43(7).
5 IA 1986, Sch B1, para 43(3), (4), (5), applied by IPO 1994, art 6 as substituted by IP(A)O 2005, art 3 and modified by IP(A)O 2005, Sch 2.
6 IA 1986, Sch B1, para 43(6), applied by IPO 1994, art 6 as substituted by IP(A)O 2005, art 3 and modified by IP(A)O 2005, Sch 2.
7 IA 1986, Sch B1, para 41(1), applied by IPO 1994, art 6 as substituted by IP(A)O 2005, art 3 and modified by IP(A)O 2005, Sch 2.

Process of administration; functions of administrator

25.51 The administration of an insolvent partnership proceeds as does that of an insolvent company. The modifications made to the administration regime by IPO 1994 merely accommodate the differences between a partnership and a company. The administrator of an insolvent partnership may do anything necessary or expedient for the management of the affairs, business or property of the partnership[1]. In the absence of some special relationship, an administrator owes no general common law duty of care to unsecured creditors in relation to his conduct of the administration[2]. In *Re Kyrris (No 2)*[3] the partnership ran 12 Burger King restaurants under a franchise agreement with Burger King Ltd, which was also the partnership's landlord. Burger King commenced forfeiture proceedings for non-payment of rent and the partnership sought relief from forfeiture. The partnership countered with proceedings for damages, including claims for abuse of dominant position under Article 86 of the EC Treaty, and in respect of overpayment of rent. Soon after the partnership's writ was issued, the Partnership Administration Order was made. The administrators considered that the partnership assets could be realised for a considerable sum, provided Burger King were prepared to co-operate in any sale. This Burger King was prepared to do only on the basis that all the various claims between it and the partnership were resolved. The partnership contended that the partnership claim for damages was not an asset of the partnership which the administrators could take over for the purpose of its compromise. In giving directions to the administrators[4], the court held that: (1) the administrators were entitled to seek relief from forfeiture of the partnership's leasehold premises; (2) the claims for damages were in respect of matters arising from the relationship between the partnership and Burger King, and could thereby be taken over by the administrators; and (3) the administrators were entitled to compromise the damages claims as part of an overall agreement with Burger King.

¹ IA 1986, Sch B1, para 59(1), not modified in the case of a partnership but it is to be assumed that the IPO 1994 intends that this paragraph applies to an insolvent partnership.
² *Kyrris v Oldham; Royle v Oldham* [2003] EWCA Civ 1506, [2004] 1 BCLC 305.
³ [1998] BPIR 111; the court had previously refused to adjourn the hearing of the petition which the partners had sought in order to attempt to sell the firm's assets; *Re Kyrris* [1998] BPIR 103.
⁴ See IA 1986, s 14(3), now IA 1986, Sch B1, para 63.

Ending the administration

25.52 The administration of an insolvent partnership automatically ceases at the end of the period of one year beginning with the date on which the administration takes effect¹. An administrator's term of office may be extended for a specified term not exceeding six months with the consent of each secured creditor and a majority of the unsecured creditors², and for any specified period by the court, even where his term has already been extended, provided that the order is made before the expiry of the administrator's term of office³. Where the objective of the administration is 'sufficiently' achieved, an administrator appointed by the court must apply to the court for his appointment to cease, and an administrator appointed by the members of the partnership or the holder of an agricultural charge may file a notice with the court⁴ in the prescribed form which brings his appointment to an end⁵. The court may end an administrator's appointment at any time on the administrator's application⁶. Such an application must be made if the administrator considers that the purpose of the administration cannot be achieved or that the partnership should not have entered administration, or he is required to do so by a creditors' meeting⁷. A creditor may apply to the court to end the administration on the ground that the applicant for his appointment or his appointer had an improper motive in making his application or appointment⁸.

¹ IA 1986, Sch B1, para 76(1), applied by IPO 1994, art 6 as substituted by IP(A)O 2005, art 3 and modified by IP(A)O 2005, Sch 2.
² IA 1986, Sch B1, paras 76(2)(b), 78, applied by IPO 1994, art 6 as substituted by IP(A)O 2005, art 3 and modified by IP(A)O 2005, Sch 2; in determining the majority of unsecured creditors the debts of any creditor who does not respond to the invitation to give or withhold consent are to be disregarded; para 78(1)(b).
³ IA 1986, Sch B1, paras 76(2), 77, applied by IPO 1994, art 6 as substituted by IP(A)O 2005, art 3 and modified by IP(A)O 2005, Sch 2.
⁴ And, apparently, with the registrar of companies because para 80 has not been modified to delete this requirement.
⁵ IA 1986, Sch B1, para 79(3), 80(2) applied by IPO 1994, art 6 as substituted by IP(A)O 2005, art 3 and modified by IP(A)O 2005, Sch 2.
⁶ IA 1986, Sch B1, para 79(1), applied by IPO 1994, art 6 as substituted by IP(A)O 2005, art 3 and modified by IP(A)O 2005, Sch 2.
⁷ IA 1986, Sch B1, para 79(2), applied by IPO 1994, art 6 as substituted by IP(A)O 2005, art 3 and modified by IP(A)O 2005, Sch 2.
⁸ IA 1986, Sch B1, para 81, applied by IPO 1994, art 6 as substituted by IP(A)O 2005, art 3 and modified by IP(A)O 2005, Sch 2.

D CREDITORS' PETITIONS

Petition against partnership alone: 'Article 7 petition'

25.53 A petition may be presented to wind up the insolvent partnership without seeking the insolvency of individual members at the same time¹. In many instances it might appear strange that a creditor takes the trouble to institute insolvency proceedings against the firm without also proceeding against its members. There will be cases, however, where such an approach may be tactically advisable. The individual partners may be engaged in other businesses which are or are likely to become profitable. Winding up the firm will not prevent the partners from working in their other enterprises, but preclude further losses to the firm against which the petition is issued. If the individual partners do not make good the insolvent partnership's losses, further petitions may be presented against one or more individual partners. Another use of the Article 7 petition (against the partnership alone) will be by the trustee of a bankrupt who has been in partnership with others who are not insolvent. The trustee will wish to get in those assets of the partnership that represent the bankrupt's share in order to make payments to the bankrupt's own creditors.

1   IPO 1994, art 7, Sch 3.

25.54 The winding up of the partnership proceeds under the IA 1986, Part V[1] as modified by IPO 1994[2]. The jurisdiction to wind up the partnership is referred to above.

1   IA 1986, ss 220–229.
2   IPO 1994, art 7, Sch 3, Parts I and II.

Article 7 petition and grounds

25.55 An Article 7 petition may be presented by:

(1)   A creditor, the partnership, one or more members of the partnership, or by all or any of those parties together or separately[1].
(2)   (a) The liquidator or administrator of a corporate member or former corporate member; (b) the administrator of the partnership; (c) the trustee of an individual member's estate or former individual member's estate; or (d) the supervisor of the partnership's PVA or of a CVA or an IVA of a member of the partnership[2].

1   IA 1986, s 221(5) as modified by IPO 1994, Sch 3, para 3. This provides that all the provisions of the IA 1986 and the Companies Act 1985 about winding up apply to the winding up of an insolvent company as an unregistered company with the exceptions and additions referred to in IA 1986, ss 221(6), (7), (8) and 221A, and subject to modifications specified in IPO 1994, Sch 3, Part II. IA 1986, s 124 ('application for winding up') is neither excluded nor modified.
2   IA 1986, s 221A(1) as modified by IPO 1994, Sch 3, para 3.

25.56 In the case of a petition presented by one of the practitioners specified in category (2) above, the IA 1986 refers to the petitioner as the 'petitioning insolvency practitioner'[1]. No form is prescribed by IPO 1994 for a petition in category (1) above; the petitioner should therefore use IR 1986, Form 4.2[2] suitably amended and verified by affidavit in Form 2 in IPO 1994, Sch 9[3]. A petitioning insolvency practitioner in category (2) above must petition in Form 3 in IPO 1994, Sch 9[4], again verified by affidavit in Form 2[5].

1   IA 1986, s 221A(2) as modified by IPO 1994, Sch 3, para 3.

2   See IR 1986, r 4.7 and IR 1986, Sch 4, Part 4, Form 2.
3   The use of an affidavit in this form is prescribed; see IA 1986, s 221(8) as modified by IPO 1994, Sch 3, para 3.
4   IA 1986, s 221A(1) as modified by IPO 1994, Sch 3, para 3.
5   See note 3 above.

25.57 The grounds on which an insolvent partnership may be wound up as an unregistered company are the following[1]:

(a)   the partnership is dissolved, or has ceased to carry on business, or is carrying on business only for the purpose of winding up its affairs;
(b)   the partnership is unable to pay its debts;
(c)   the court is of the opinion that it is just and equitable that the partnership should be wound up.
(d)   at the time at which a moratorium for the insolvent partnership under IA 1986, s 1A comes to an end, no voluntary arrangement has been approved in relation to the insolvent partnership[2].

1   IA 1986, s 221(7) as modified by IPO 1994, Sch 3, para 3.
2   A winding-up petition on this ground may only be presented by one or more creditors; IA 1986, s 221(7A).

25.58 The court has jurisdiction to make a winding-up order against an insolvent partnership (as an unregistered company) of its own motion without there being a petitioning creditor. Such an order may only be made under grounds (a), (b) or (c) above (para **25.57**) and only in exceptional cases[1]. The Article 7 petition follows essentially the same procedure as does a petition to wind up a company. Where there is a petitioning insolvency practitioner he may be appointed as a provisional liquidator[2] and/or liquidator[3] of the partnership, and if the partnership property is insufficient to pay his costs he may recover them from the assets of the corporate or individual member in respect of whom he has been appointed, in the same order of priority as expenses properly chargeable for getting in any assets of the member[4].

1   *Lancefield v Lancefield* [2002] BPIR 1108; in this case the partnership carried on the business of a residential letting agency and held deposits made by tenants. Neuberger J considered it difficult, if not impossible, to envisage any grounds on which a winding-up order might be opposed by anyone entitled to object and felt that this was a business which should be in the hands of an independent third party as soon as possible.
2   IA 1986, s 221A(4) as modified by IPO 1994, Sch 3, para 3.
3   IA 1986, s 221A(5) as modified by IPO 1994, Sch 3, para 3.
4   IA 1986, s 221A(6) as modified by IPO 1994, Sch 3, para 3.

Inability to pay debts: Article 7 petition

25.59 IPO 1994 repeats the statutory definition of inability to pay debts by an unregistered company contained in IA 1986, ss 222–224 inclusive, ss 222 and 223 being reproduced in their modified form in IPO 1994, Sch 3. The modifications essentially concern service.

25.60 Inability to pay debts is proved:

(1) by the failure of the partnership to comply with a written demand which has been served by a creditor requiring payment of a debt in a sum exceeding £750[1];

(2) by the failure of the partnership to pay a debt after proceedings in respect of that debt had been instituted, notice of those proceedings having been served on the partnership and the partnership not having within three weeks thereafter paid, secured, or compounded the debt or procured a stay of the proceedings[2];

(3) where execution or other process issued on a judgment against the partnership is returned unsatisfied[3]; or

(4) if it is proved to the satisfaction of the court that the partnership is unable to pay its debts as they fall due[4].

[1] IA 1986, s 222(1) as modified by IPO 1994, Sch 3, Part I.
[2] IA 1986, s 223(1) as modified by IPO 1994, Sch 3, Part I.
[3] IA 1986, s 224(1)(a).
[4] IA 1986, s 224(1)(d).

25.61 In the case of a petition under category (2) above where the ground of the petition is that the partnership is unable to pay its debts, and the petitioning insolvency practitioner is able to show that the insolvency of the member concerned is the result of that member's inability to pay a joint debt, the insolvency order against the member is proof of the partnership's inability to pay its debts, unless it is proved otherwise to the satisfaction of the court[1].

[1] IA 1986, s 221A(3) as modified by IPO 1994, Sch 3, para 3.

25.62 Service of the demand for (1) above or of the notice for (2) above may be effected in one of the following ways:

(a) by leaving it at a principal place of business of the partnership in England and Wales;

(b) by leaving it at a place of business of the partnership in England and Wales which business is carried on in the course of which the debt or demand (or part of the debt or demand) arose; or

(c) by delivering it to an officer of the partnership; or

(d) by otherwise serving it in such manner as the court may approve or direct[1].

[1] IA 1986, ss 222(2), 223(2) as modified by IPO 1994, Sch 3, para 4.

Petitions against partnerships where concurrent petitions presented against member(s) ('Article 8 petition')

25.63 An Article 8 petition is presented against the partnership of an unregistered company concurrently with a petition against any one or more of the members or former members of the partnership, either corporate or individual. The jurisdiction to present a petition against a partnership is referred to above. The petition(s) against one or more members must all be presented to the same court and, unless the court permits otherwise, on the same day[1]. There are only two grounds on which an insolvent partnership may be wound up on an Article 8 petition: (1) that the partnership is unable to pay its debts; and (2) no PVA has been approved at the time at which a moratorium for the insolvent partnership under IA 1986, s 1A comes to an end[2]. Similarly, these are the only two grounds on which a corporate member or former corporate member of an insolvent partnership may be wound up[3]. Inability to pay one or more debts is the only ground on which bankruptcy petitions may be presented, but in the case of the individual member of a partnership IA 1986, s 267 is modified to provide that the creditor's petition must be in respect of one or more joint debts owed by the partnership, and the petitioner must be a person to whom at least one of the debts is owed[4].

[1] IA 1986, s 124(3) as modified by IPO 1994, Sch 4, Part II, para 8.
[2] IA 1986, s 221(8) as modified by IPO 1994, Sch 4, Part I, para 3.
[3] IA 1986, s 122 as modified by IPO 1994, Sch 4, Part II, para 6(a). For a winding-up order to be made on this ground there must be a creditor, by assignment or otherwise, to whom the insolvent partnership is indebted and the corporate member or former corporate member must be liable in relation to that debt at the time when the moratorium comes to an end.
[4] IA 1986, s 267(2)(c) as modified by IPO 1994, Sch 4, Part II, para 6(b).

25.64 Article 8 petitions may be presented by any creditor or creditors to whom the partnership and the member or former member in question is indebted in respect of a liquidated sum payable immediately[1]. It is not open to a creditor to rely on prospective inability to pay, as it would be in the case of a bankruptcy petition[2].

[1] IA 1986, s 124(2) as modified by IPO 1994, Sch 4, Part II, para 8.
[2] IA 1986, s 267(2)(b).

Inability to pay debts: Article 8 petition

25.65 The primary ground on which the partnership can be wound up with a concurrent winding up or bankruptcy of members or former members of the partnership under an Article 8 petition is inability to pay debts[1]. A partnership is deemed to be unable to pay its debts if:

(1) it owes a debt exceeding £750 to a creditor and a written demand in proper form has been served upon the partnership and a similar demand upon either a corporate member or an individual member; and

(2) the partnership and its members fail within three weeks after service of the demand to pay the sum due or to provide security for it or to compound it[2].

[1] IA 1986, ss 122(1), 221(8) as modified by IPO 1994, Sch 4.
[2] IA 1986, s 222(1) as modified by IPO 1994, Sch 4, Part II.

25.66 A corporate member is deemed unable to pay its debts if:

(1) the partnership owes a debt exceeding £750 to a creditor and a written demand in proper form has been served upon the partnership and corporate member; and

(2)   the corporate member and the partnership fail, within three weeks after service of the demand, to pay the sum due or to provide security for or to compound it[1].

¹   IA 1986, s 123(1) as modified by IPO 1994, Sch 4, Part II.

25.67 An individual member is deemed unable to pay his debts if:

(1)   the partnership owes a debt exceeding £750 and a written demand in proper form has been served on both the partnership and the individual member;

(2)   the partnership and its individual member fail within three weeks after service of the demand, to pay the sum due or to provide security for or to compound it or, in the case of an individual member, if he fails to set aside the demand[1].

¹   IA 1986, s 268(1) as modified by IPO 1994, Sch 4, Part II.

25.68 For these purposes, a member, whether corporate or individual, includes a former member. IPO 1994, does not attempt to harmonise the statutory provisions relating to the written demands which must be served. There is therefore no procedure whereby the partnership or corporate member may apply to set aside any demand served upon it. An individual member may, however, apply within 18 days[1] to set aside the demand ('the statutory demand') on the ground that (a) he has a counterclaim set-off or cross-demand which equals or exceeds the amount of the debt or debts specified in the statutory demand; (b) the debt is disputed on substantial grounds; (c) the creditor holds security of at least equal value to his debt; or (d) the court is satisfied on other grounds that the debt should be set aside[2].

¹   The individual debtor may apply out of time by originating application for leave supported by an affidavit explaining why he is out of time and giving his grounds to set the statutory demand aside, provided he does so before a petition has been presented against him; *Practice Direction: Insolvency Proceedings*; see **Appendix 1**.
²   IR 1986, r 6.5.

Service of the demand

25.69 As modified by IPO 1994, the Insolvency Act 1986 provides that the demand for payment by the partnership must be served on the partnership, whereas the demand for payment by the member or former member must be served both on the member or former member and on the partnership. It is possible that this is too strict an interpretation of the statutory provisions and that service of one demand on the partnership will suffice[1]. Service of the demand or demands upon the partnership is effected[2]:

(a)   by leaving it at a (not the) principal place of business of the partnership in England and Wales;

(b)   by leaving it at a place of business of the partnership in England and Wales at which business is carried on in the course of which the debt or part of the debt arose;

(c)   by delivering it to an officer of the partnership; or

(d)   by otherwise serving it in such manner as the court may direct.

¹   See IA 1986, s 222 as modified by IPO 1994, Sch 4, para 4 (partnership); IA 1986, s 123 as modified by IPO 1994, Sch 4, para 7(a) (company corporate member); IA 1986, s 268 as modified by IPO 1994, Sch 4, para 7(b) (individual member).
²   See IA 1986, ss 222(2), 123(2), 268(2), modified as above.

25.70   An 'officer' of an insolvent partnership means either a member or a person who has management or control of the partnership business¹. A 'member' means a member or any person who is liable as a partner by holding out².

¹   IPO 1994, art 2(1).
²   IPO 1994, art 2(1); and see Partnership Act 1890, s 14:

> 'Everyone who by words spoken or written or by conduct represents himself or who knowingly suffers himself to be represented, as a partner in a particular firm, is liable as a partner to anyone who has on the faith of any such representation given credit to the firm, whether the representation has or has not been made or communicated to the person so giving credit by or with the knowledge of the apparent partner making the representation or suffering it to be made.'

25.71   Service of the demand on a corporate member or former member is effected by leaving the demand at its registered office¹. Service of the demand on an individual member is governed by the Insolvency Rules². So far as practicable there should be personal service, but in limited cases newspaper advertisement may be permitted by the court³.

¹   IA 1986, s 123(2), modified as above.
²   IR 1986, rr 6.3(1), (2), 6.11(1)(3).
³   IR 1986, r 6.3(3).

Article 8 petitions

25.72   The forms of Article 8 petitions are specified by IPO 1994¹, with the petition against the partnership to be in Form 5, that against a corporate member or former member in Form 6, and that against an individual member in Form 7 in IPO 1994, Sch 9². They must be presented to the same court and, except as the court otherwise permits or directs, on the same day³, and be advertised in the prescribed form⁴. With the leave of the court the petitioner may add other members or former members of the partnership as parties to the proceedings in relation to the insolvent partnership after presentation of the petition⁵. Each petition presented must contain particulars of the other petitions being presented in relation to the partnership, identifying the partnership and members concerned⁶.

¹   IA 1986, ss 124(1), 264, as modified by IPO 1994, Sch 4, Part II, para 8.
²   See Atkins Court Forms, vol 30(1).
³   IA 1986, s 124(3) as modified by IPO 1994, Sch 4, Part II, para 8.
⁴   IA 1986, s 124(3)(b); IPO 1994, Sch 9, Form 8; NB only petitions against the partnership and a corporate member need be advertised.
⁵   IA 1986, s 124(4) as modified by IPO 1994, Sch 4, Part II, para 8.
⁶   IA 1986, s 125(5) as modified by IPO 1994, Sch 4, Part II, para 8.

25.73 Article 8 petitions may be presented by:

(1)   any creditor or creditors to whom the partnership and the member or former member in question is indebted in respect of a liquidated sum payable immediately;

(2)   a liquidator, within the meaning of EC Insolvency Regulation, art 2(b), appointed in proceedings by virtue of EC Insolvency Regulation, art 3(1); or

(3)   a temporary administrator, within the meaning of EC Insolvency Regulation, art 38.

25.74 For the purposes of the EC Insolvency Regulation[1], a liquidator means any person or body whose function is to administer or liquidate assets of which the debtor has been divested, or to supervise the administration of his affairs. In England and Wales this covers a liquidator, a supervisor of a PVA, an administrator, the official receiver, or a trustee in bankruptcy. Article 3(1) proceedings are 'main proceedings', that is, proceedings in respect of a debtor whose centre of main interests is in England and Wales. A temporary administrator is a person appointed to preserve the debtor's assets between the time of the presentation and the time of the determination of the petition.

[1]   EC Insolvency Regulation, art 2(b).

Hearing of Article 8 petitions

The partnership hearing

25.75 The hearing of an Article 8 petition against the partnership takes place before the hearing of the one or more petitions against corporate or insolvent members[1]. At the hearing the petitioner is required to inform the court of the progress of the other petitions presented under art 8 by handing in to the court a prescribed form[2] duly completed. The petitioner can withdraw the petition at the hearing provided he withdraws all the Article 8 petitions against members and gives notice to the court at least three days beforehand of his intention to do so[3]. Notice is not required, however, where the petitioner is able to satisfy the court on the application to withdraw a petition that because of difficulties in serving that petition on an insolvent member or for any other reason the continuance of that particular petition would be likely to prejudice or delay the proceedings on the petition against the partnership or on any petition which has been presented against another member of the insolvent partnership[4]. Where notice of intended withdrawal has been given, the court may, on such terms as it thinks just, substitute as petitioner in respect of both the petition issued against the partnership and against each insolvent member any creditor of the partnership who has a right to present a petition[5]. The hearing itself is in open court before the registrar or district judge, but if the petition is opposed it must be adjourned to the Judge. At the hearing the court may make a winding-up order against the partnership or dismiss the petition, or adjourn it with or without conditions, or make any other order it thinks fit[6].

1   IA 1986, s 124(6) as modified by IPO 1994, Sch 4, Part II; the practice in London has been
    each fortnight to list the petition against the partnership on a Wednesday morning and the
    petitions against the members on the Wednesday afternoon.
2   IPO 1994, Sch 9, Form 9.
3   IA 1986, s 124(9)(a), (b) as modified by IPO 1994, Sch 4, para 8.
4   IA 1986, s 124(10) as modified by IPO 1994, Sch 4, para 8.
5   IA 1986, s 124(11) as modified by IPO 1994, Sch 4, para 8.
6   IA 1986, s 125(1), (2) as modified by IPO 1994, Sch 4, para 9.

The hearing against a member

25.76   The hearing is before the registrar or district judge and is in open court
for a petition against a corporate member, but in chambers for a petition
against an individual member. If opposed, it must be adjourned to the judge.
Petitions against a corporate member or individual member are heard after the
petition against the partnership. At the hearing the petitioner must draw the
court's attention to the result of the hearing of the winding-up petition against
the partnership[1]. In cases of petitions to wind up an individual member, a
certificate of continuing debt must also be lodged with the court[2]. At the
hearing of the petition against the partnership and its member(s) the court
may dismiss the petition or adjourn the hearing conditionally or unconditionally or make any other order it thinks fit[3]. If the court has not made a
winding-up order or dismissed the winding-up petition against the partnership
it may adjourn the hearing of the petitions against any insolvent member[4].
Where a winding-up order has been made against the partnership the court
may make a winding-up order against a corporate member or a bankruptcy
order against an individual member[5]. However, if no insolvency order is made
against any member within 28 days of the making of a winding-up order
against the partnership, then the proceedings against the partnership must be
conducted as if the petition had been presented to wind up the partnership by
itself, and no further proceedings continue against individual members[6].
Where the winding-up petition against the partnership is dismissed, the
petition to wind up a corporate member or make an individual member
bankrupt may also be dismissed, but dismissal of the petition against the
member is not automatic; the proceedings may continue against a corporate
member as a normal winding up or against an individual member as in
bankruptcy[7].

1   IA 1986, s 125A(1) as modified by IPO 1994, Sch 4, para 9; and note *Practice Direction:
    Insolvency Proceedings*; see **Appendix 1**.
2   IR 1986, r 6.25(1).
3   IA 1986, s 125(1) as modified by IPO 1994, Sch 4, para 9.
4   IA 1986, s 125A(2) as modified by IPO 1994, Sch 4, para 9.
5   IA 1986, s 125A(3) as modified by IPO 1994, Sch 4, para 9.
6   IA 1986, s 125A(4) as modified by IPO 1994, Sch 4, para 9.
7   IA 1986, s 125A(5) as modified by IPO 1994, Sch 4, para 9.

25.77   In the case of a petition against a member who is a limited partner, the
court may dismiss the petition if (a) the member lodges in court the benefit of
creditors of the partnership's sufficient money or security to the court's

satisfaction to meet his liability for the debts and obligations of the partnership; or (b) the member satisfies the court that he is no longer under any liability in respect of the debts and obligations of the partnership[1].

1   IA 1986, s 125A(7)(a), (b) as modified by IPO 1994, Sch 4, para 9.

25.78 The court is given the power[1] to dismiss a petition against an insolvent member if it considers it just to do so because of a change in circumstances since the making of the winding-up order against the partnership. This provision provides a solution to the problem which arose under IPO 1986 in *Re Marr*[2], where at first instance it was held that bankruptcy orders had to be made against the individual partners where the partnership had been wound up, despite the fact that the debt had been paid in full before the hearing of the petitions against the individual members.

1   IA 1986, s 125A(6).
2   [1990] Ch 773, [1990] 2 All ER 880, CA; the Court of Appeal allowed the appeal on the basis that despite the express provisions of IA 1986, s 271(2A), (2B), as modified, the court may never make a bankruptcy order unless it is satisfied that the petition debt has not been paid, secured or compounded for.

E MEMBERS' PETITIONS

Petition against partnership alone: ('Article 9 petition')

25.79 Provided that the partnership consists of at least eight members[1], a member of the partnership may present a petition to wind up the partnership as an unregistered company without a concurrent petition against any member[2]. The grounds on which an Article 9 petition may be served are:

(1)   the partnership is dissolved, or has ceased to carry on business, or is carrying on business only for the purpose of winding up its affairs[3];
(2)   the partnership is unable to pay its debts[4];
(3)   that it is just and equitable that the partnership be wound up[5];
(4)   only with the leave of the court, that the partnership is indebted to the petitioning member in respect of a joint debt exceeding £750[6] due from the partnership but paid by the member[7].

1   IA 1986, s 221A(1) as modified by IPO 1994, Sch 5, para 2.
2   IPO 1994, art 9 modifying the IA 1986 as provided in Sch 5 and Sch 3, Part I.
3   IA 1986, s 221(7)(a) as modified by IPO 1994, Sch 5, para 2.
4   IA 1986, s 221(7)(b) as modified by IPO 1994, Sch 5, para 2.
5   IA 1986, s 221(7)(c) as modified by IPO 1994, Sch 5, para 2.
6   Or the minimum debt required to support a petition if raised by the Secretary of State under IA 1986, s 416.
7   IA 1986, s 221A(2) as modified by IPO 1994, Sch 5, para 2.

25.80 Before a member may apply for leave to present a petition under ground (4) above (para **25.79**), he must not only serve a written demand in the prescribed form[1] on the partnership[2] which has remained unpaid, or has not been secured or compounded for to the members' satisfaction, but also demonstrate that he has obtained a judgment decree or order of the court against the partnership for reimbursement of the amount of the joint debt and taken all reasonable steps to enforce that judgment decree or order, other than take insolvency proceedings[3]. IPO 1994, art 9(b) incorporates the modifications to the IA 1986 made by Sch 3, Part I for Article 7 petitions. Thus, for example, the partnership is unable to pay its debts for the purposes of ground (2) above (para **25.79**) where a creditor has duly served a written demand in the prescribed form and the debt has remained unpaid for three weeks. Further, for the purposes of presenting an Article 9 petition a member of the partnership includes a 'petitioning insolvency practitioner', ie the liquidator, administrator or supervisor of a CVA of a corporate member, and the trustee in bankruptcy or supervisor of an IVA of an individual member[4].

[1]   Ie IPO 1994, Sch 9, Form 9; IA 1986, s 221A(2)(a) as modified by IPO 1994, Sch 5, para 2.
[2]   For service on the partnership, see IA 1986, s 222(2) as modified by IPO 1994, Sch 3, para 4.
[3]   IA 1986, s 221A(2) as modified by IPO 1994, Sch 5, para 2.
[4]   IA 1986, s 221A(1) as modified by IPO 1994, Sch 3, para 3.

25.81 The jurisdiction to wind up a partnership is referred to above.

Petition against partnership where concurrent petitions are presented against all members: ('Article 10 petition')

25.82 A petition may be presented by a member to wind up the partnership as an unregistered company under IPO 1994, art 10 only on the grounds that the partnership is unable to pay its debts and provided also that petitions are at the same time presented by that member for insolvency orders against every member of the partnership, including himself or itself, and each member is willing to enter into insolvency[1]. The petitions must be in the prescribed form[2], must, in the case of a petition against a member, contain a statement to the effect that the member is willing to have an insolvency order made against him[3], and must also contain particulars of all the other petitions being served concurrently with it[4]. The jurisdiction to present a petition against a partnership is referred to above. All the petitions must be presented to the same court and unless the court otherwise permits or directs, on the same day[5]. The petitions against the partnership and any corporate member must be advertised in the prescribed form[6], and the procedure relating to a petition against the company duly followed[7].

[1]   IA 1986, s 124(2) as modified by IPO 1994, Sch 6, para 2.
[2]   Ie IPO 1994, Sch 9, Form 11 (partnership); Form 12 (corporate member) and Form 13 (individual member).
[3]   IA 1986, s 124(2) as modified by IPO 1994, Sch 6, para 2.
[4]   IA 1986, s 124(5) as modified by IPO 1994, Sch 6, para 2.
[5]   IA 1986, s 124(4)(a) as modified by IPO 1994, Sch 6, para 2.
[6]   IA 1986, s 124(4)(b), Sch 9, Form 8.
[7]   And see IR 1986, r 4.11–4.15.

Hearing of Article 10 petition

25.83 The hearing of the petition against the partnership is to be fixed before the hearing of the other petitions[1], although if practicable all the petitions may be heard on the same day. On the day fixed for the hearing of the petition against the partnership the petitioner must hand in a completed Form 9[2], which explains the current position of all the various petitions against the members. The hearing will be before the registrar or district judge in open court and, if opposed, will be adjourned to the judge. Any member (who will of course have had a petition presented against him) is entitled to appear and be heard on the petition to wind up the partnership[3]. The court has power to dismiss the petition, adjourn the hearing with or without conditions, or make any other order it thinks fit, but it may not refuse a winding-up order against the partnership or a corporate member on the ground only that: (i) the partnership property or corporate members' assets had been mortgaged to an amount equal to or in excess of that property or assets; or (ii) the partnership has no property or the corporate member no assets[4]. In the case where an insolvency order has already been made against a member of the partnership, ie on a petition other than an Article 10 petition, the court on making any order in respect of the partnership may make directions as to the future conduct of the insolvency proceedings against the member[5]. Once a winding-up order has been made against the partnership the court may proceed to make orders against the members[6]. The court must, however, make insolvency orders against all the members within 28 days of the order against the partnership, and if it fails to do so the proceedings against the partnership continue as if the winding-up petition had been presented under art 7, and the proceedings against the member(s) who have not had orders made against them continue as if an 'ordinary' liquidation or bankruptcy[7]. In this event, however, the court will have power to make directions in all sets of proceedings so that it will be possible to preserve the concurrent nature of the various proceedings[8].

1 IA 1986, s 124(6) as modified by IPO 1994, Sch 6.
2 IA 1986, s 124(7); Sch 9, Form 9.
3 IA 1986, s 124(8) as modified by IPO 1994, Sch 6.
4 IA 1986, s 125(1) as modified by IPO 1994, Sch 6, para 3.
5 IA 1986, s 125(2) as modified by IPO 1994, Sch 6, para 3.
6 IA 1986, s 125A(3) as modified by IPO 1994, Sch 6, para 3.
7 IA 1986, s 125A(4) as modified by IPO 1994, Sch 6, para 3.
8 IA 1986, ss 168, 303 as amended by IPO 1994, art 14.

25.84 At the hearing, the petitioner may withdraw the petition if he withdraws all the other petitions presented concurrently with the petition and has given three days' notice of his intention to withdraw[1]. The requirement that all other petitions must be withdrawn may be waived by the court in the case of a petition against a member if the petitioner can demonstrate that because of difficulties in effecting service or any other reason the continuance of that petition would be likely to prejudice or delay any petition which has been presented against the partnership or any member[2].

1 IA 1986, s 125(9) as modified by IPO 1994, Sch 6, para 3.
2 IA 1986, s 125(10) as modified by IPO 1994, Sch 6, para 3.

25.85 While in most cases it is likely that the petition against the partnership and its members will stand or fall together, this need not necessarily be the case. The court may dismiss a petition against an insolvent member even though an order has been made to wind up the partnership, if it is just to do so because of a change in circumstances since the making of the winding-up order against the partnership[1]. Where the member is a limited partner, the court may dismiss the petition if the member either: (a) lodges in court for the benefit of the partnership creditors sufficient money or security to the court's satisfaction to meet his liability for the debts and obligations of the partnership; or (b) satisfies the court that he is no longer under any liability in respect of the debt or obligations of the partnership[2].

1 IA 1986, s 125A(6) as modified by IPO 1994, Sch 6, para 3.
2 IA 1986, s 125A(7) as modified by IPO 1994, Sch 6, para 3.
3 IA 1986, s 125A(5) as modified by IPO 1994, Sch 6, para 3.
4 IA 1986, ss 168, 303 as modified by IPO 1994, art 14.

25.86 It is envisaged that the court might make an insolvency order against a member even after dismissing the winding-up petition against the partnership[1]. In this event the insolvency will proceed as an ordinary liquidation or bankruptcy subject to the power of the court to make orders or give directions in the insolvency in conjunction with orders or directions in other insolvency proceedings against members or former members[2].

1 IA 1986, s 125A(5) as modified by IPO 1994, Sch 6, para 3.
2 IA 1986, ss 168, 303 as modified by IPO 1994, art 14.

Joint bankruptcy petition by individual members: ('Article 11 petition')

25.87 Provided they have no corporate or limited partners, and have carried on business in England and Wales within three years of its presentation[1], all the individual members of the partnership may present a joint bankruptcy petition without winding up the partnership as a limited company[2]. No such petition may be presented by the members of an insolvent partnership if the partnership: (a) has permission under the Financial Services and Markets Act 2000[3] to accept deposits[4]; or (b) continues to have a liability in respect of a deposit which was held by it in accordance with the Banking Act 1979 or the Banking Act 1987[5]. The petition must be in prescribed form[6], and must contain a request that the trustee will wind up the partnership business and administer the partnership property without the partnership being wound up as an unregistered company[7], a request which does not appear (in full) on the prescribed form. The petition may be presented to the High Court or to a county court if the partnership has, or at any time has had, a, but not necessarily its only, principal place of business within the insolvency district of that court[8]. The Article 11 petition may be *signed* either: (i) by all the members, stating that they are all individual members; or (ii) by only one member, in which event the petition must be accompanied by an affidavit in the prescribed form[9], showing that all the members are individuals, none are limited partners, and all concur in the presentation of the petition[10]. The Article 11 petition should be presented by all the members, unless the court is satisfied on the application of any member that its presentation by all members would be impracticable, in which event the court may direct that it may be presented by one or more specified members[11]. The court's leave is required to withdraw an Article 11 petition[12], and there is a general power in the court to dismiss or stay the petition on any terms thought fit, on the grounds that there has been a contravention of the rules or for any other reason[13].

1   IA 1986, s 265(2) as modified by IPO 1994, Sch 7, para 3.
2   IA 1986, s 264(1) as modified by IPO 1994, Sch 7, para 2.
3   Financial Services and Markets Act 2000, Part 4.
4   Other than such a permission only for the purpose of carrying on another regulated activity in accordance with that permission; IA 1986, s 264(2)(a), as modified by IPO 1994, Sch 7, para 2.
5   IA 1986, s 264(2).
6   IPO 1994, Sch 9, Form 14.
7   IA 1986, s 265(1) as modified by IPO 1994, Sch 7, para 3.
8   IA 1986, s 265(1) as modified by IPO 1994, Sch 9, para 3.
9   IPO 1994, Sch 9, Form 15.
10   IA 1986, s 264(4) as modified by IPO 1994, Sch 7, para 2.
11   IA 1986, s 266(1) as modified by IPO 1994, Sch 7, para 4.
12   IA 1986, s 266(2) as modified by IPO 1994, Sch 7, para 4.
13   IA 1986, s 266(3) as modified by IPO 1994, Sch 7, para 4.

25.88 The sole ground on which an Article 11 petition may be presented is that the partnership is unable to pay its debts[1], and the petition must be accompanied by statements of affairs of each member and the partnership in the prescribed forms[2].

1   IA 1986, s 272(1) as modified by IPO 1994, Sch 9, para 5.
2   IA 1986, s 272(2) as modified by IPO 1994, Sch 7, para 5, ie Sch 9, Form 17 for an individual partner's statement of affairs and Sch 9, Form 18 for the partnership's statement of affairs, the latter being deposed to by one or more members of the partnership.

25.89 The Article 11 petition will be heard ex parte. The form of the bankruptcy orders is prescribed[1], providing for the bankruptcy of the members and the winding up of the partnership business and administration of its property[2].

1   IPO 1994, Sch 9, Form 16.
2   IA 1986, s 264(5) as modified by IPO 1994, Sch 7, para 2.

Summary administration

25.90 The summary administration procedure was repealed for individual bankruptcies by the Enterprise Act 2002 as from 1 April 2004[1]. It survived for bankruptcies of members of partnerships until 1 July 2005 when it was abolished by the Insolvent Partnerships (Amendment) Order 2005[2].

1   See the Enterprise Act 2002, ss 269, 278(2); Sch 23, paras 1, 2; Sch 26.
2   SI 2005/1516, art 5.

F POSITION OF MEMBERS ON INSOLVENCY OF PARTNERSHIP

Member as contributory

25.91 When a partnership is wound up pursuant to an Article 8 petition any present or former member who has not been the subject of an insolvency order and is liable to pay or contribute to the payment of any debt will be a contributory[1]. A person who has been held out as a member[2] will also be a contributory. A member's liability as a contributory to meet calls made by the liquidator of the partnership is a speciality debt accruing at the date such liability commences[3]. If a contributory dies or becomes bankrupt either before[4] or after he has been placed on the list of contributories, his personal representatives or trustee in bankruptcy (but not the liquidator in the case of a corporate member) will be liable as contributories[5]. The extent to which a member is liable to creditors as a contributory will be unlimited, and within the terms of the partnership agreement will be subject to any adjustments that may be necessary as between members[6]. Where the contributory is a former member he will be liable to creditors for those debts which were incurred while he remained a member, subject to any indemnity he may have from the continuing members[7]. The liquidator is responsible for drawing up a list of contributories, making calls upon them and adjusting the rights of the contributories inter se[8]. A member of the partnership who has been made insolvent under a concurrent petition is not to be treated as a contributory, 'unless the contrary intention appears'[9]. There is no need for the insolvent member to be made a contributory because the separate estate of such a member will be available to meet any shortfall there may be in the partnership estate[10].

[1] IA 1986, s 226, as applied by IPO 1994, art 8(1).
[2] Within the context of the Partnership Act 1890, s 14.
[3] IA 1986, s 80, applied in the case of an unregistered company by IA 1986, s 221(1), as applied by IPO 1994, art 8(1). It follows that the limitation period is 12 years; Limitation Act 1980, s 8.
[4] 'If a contributory dies ... before ... he has been placed on the list of contributories'; IA 1986, s 81(1) extends back to before the winding-up order.
[5] IA 1986, ss 80–81, applied in the case of an unregistered company by IA 1986, s 226(4).
[6] IA 1986, s 226(1), (2).
[7] IA 1986, s 226(2), which presumably overrides the provisions of IA 1986, s 74 (applied by virtue of IA 1986, s 221(1)), which exclude from liability as a contributory any past member who ceased to be a member at least one year before the commencement of a winding up.
[8] IR 1986, rr 4.195–4.200.
[9] IA 1986, s 221(7) as modified by IPO 1994, Sch 4, para 3.
[10] IA 1986, ss 175A–175C, as modified by IPO 1994, Sch 4, para 23.

Member as officer

25.92 Where an insolvent partnership is being wound up as an unregistered company, any member or former member of the partnership or any other person who has, or has had, control or management of the partnership business is deemed to be an officer or director of the company for the purposes of the Insolvency Act 1986[1] and the Company Directors Disqualification Act 1986 ('CDDA 1986')[2]. A partner who is himself the subject of an insolvency order may therefore face criminal liability in respect of the offences which may be committed by officers and directors of a company under the Insolvency Act 1986[3], and may be made liable for misfeasance, fraudulent trading, or wrongful trading[4]. The sanction for these latter provisions is to restore property and make personal contribution to the company's assets, a sanction which would seem to have little relevance to a partner with unlimited liability[5]. Of more relevance perhaps is the possibility that a partner may be disqualified to act as a director of a company without the leave of the court[6]. A disqualification order may be made against a former member[7]. The ground for making a disqualification order is that the member's conduct as a member, taken alone or together with his conduct as a member of any other partnership, makes him unfit to be concerned in the management of a company[8]. An application for a disqualification order may be made only by the Secretary of State or, at his direction, the official receiver[9]. The sanction for becoming a director while disqualified is to become personally liable for the debts of the company. The criminal penalties for acting on contravention of a disqualification order imposed by CDDA 1996[10] are not applied in the case of partnership, but the former member who does so act will be guilty of contempt of court. There will also be personal responsibility for the debts of the company on the part of any person who acts or is willing to act on instructions given by a disqualified director without the leave of the court[11].

[1]   IPO 1994, Arts 2(1), 3.
[2]   IPO 1994, art 16.
[3]   And in particular see IA 1986, ss 206–211.
[4]   IA 1986, ss 212–214; applied by IPO 1994, Arts 8(5), 10(3).
[5]   It might, however, be open to a court to make an order which requires a 'guilty' member to contribute more than his share of the members' liability so that he does not, as against other members, obtain the benefit of his misfeasance. In any given circumstances there is likely to be given an alternative, and more direct, approach to such a problem.
[6]   IPO 1994, art 16 applies the provisions of CDDA 1996, ss 6–10, 15, 19(c) and 20 and Sch 1 to partnerships as if any member of the partnership was a director of a company, and the partnership were a company as defined by CDDA 1996, s 22(2)(b), which definition includes unregistered companies. These sections are set out, as modified, in IPO 1994, Sch 8. Note that s 1 is not included. This defines the scope of a disqualification order. It appears that the court can disqualify a member of an insolvent partnership from being a company director or an office-holder in insolvency.
[7]   CDDA 1986, s 6(1) as applied by IPO 1994, art 16.
[8]   CDDA 1986, s 6(1) as applied by IPO 1994, art 16.
[9]   CDDA 1986, s 7 as applied by IPO 1994, art 16.
[10]   CDDA 1986, s 13.
[11]   CDDA 1986, s 15(1)(b) as applied by IPO 1994, art 16.

G ADMINISTRATION OF ASSETS AND ESTATES

General

25.93 The conduct of the winding up of the partnership, the bankruptcy or winding up of any insolvent members, and the administration of the partnership assets and the members' assets or estates will in general terms follow the same course as the bankruptcies and liquidations of individuals and companies who are not partners. The Insolvent Partnerships Order 1994 modifies the statutory provisions relating to the appointment of liquidators and trustees and the appointment of liquidation and creditors' committees. It further provides rules governing the priority of expenses and debts where insolvency orders are made in relation to an insolvent partnership. These modifications and rules, together with the proof of debts against the joint and separate estates of the partnership and its members are considered in the following paragraphs, with particular reference to the concurrent winding up of the partnership and of the insolvency of one or more of its members, which will be the most common form of partnership insolvency.

Statement of affairs and public examination

25.94 Following the making of a winding-up order or the appointment of a provisional liquidator in respect of an insolvent partnership or corporate member of that partnership, or a bankruptcy order against an individual member of that partnership, the official receiver may require one or more specified persons to make out and submit a statement, in the prescribed form[1], as to the affairs of the partnership or member[2]. The persons specified by the Act[3] are persons who: (a) are or have been officers of the partnership; (b) are or have been officers of the corporate member; (c) have taken part in the formation of the partnership or corporate member within one year of the relevant date[4]; (d) are or have in the past year been in the employment of the partnership or corporate member and are in the official receiver's opinion capable of giving the information required; (e) are or have within the past year been officers of or in the employment of the company which is or was within the year an officer of the partnership or corporate member[5]. The statement of affairs must be submitted within 21 days of the requirement to do so[6], unless the official receiver extends the time for submission[7].

[1] Ie for the partnership or a corporate partner, the form prescribed for a company's statement of affairs, see IR 1986, rr 4.32, 4.35, Form 4.17; for an individual member form prescribed in bankruptcy, see IR 1986, r 6.59, Form 6.33.
[2] IA 1986, s 131(1), (2) as modified by IPO 1994, Sch 4, para 10.
[3] IA 1986, s 131(4).
[4] The relevant date is the date of the winding-up order unless a provisional liquidator has been appointed, in which case it is the date of that appointment; IA 1986, s 131(7) as modified by IPO 1994, Sch 4, para 10.
[5] IA 1986, s 131(4) as modified by IPO 1994, Sch 4, para 10.
[6] IA 1986, s 131(5) as modified by IPO 1994, Sch 4, para 10.
[7] IA 1986, s 131(6) as modified by IPO 1994, Sch 4, para 10.

25.95 The company winding-up provisions for the public examination of officers and former officers are extended to officers of the partnership[1], and the court may direct that the public examination of any person under these powers may be combined with a public examination in relation to the affairs of a corporate or individual member[2]. Subject to the court's direction the official receiver must make an application to the court for a public examination when requested to do so by one half in value of the creditors of the partnership[3]. At a public examination questions may be put by the official receiver, the partnership liquidator, any special manager of the partnership's business and any creditor of the partnership who has tendered a proof in the winding up[4].

[1] IA 1986, s 133(1) as modified by IPO 1994, Sch 4, para 11.
[2] IA 1986, s 133(5) as modified by IPO 1994, Sch 4, para 11.
[3] IA 1986, s 133(2) as modified by IPO 1994, Sch 4, para 11.
[4] IA 1986, s 133(4) as modified by IPO 1994, Sch 4, para 11.

Functions of official receiver

25.96 Following insolvency orders against the partnership and one or more of its members, the official receiver becomes the responsible insolvency practitioner both of the partnership and any insolvent member[1]. He continues in office until an insolvency practitioner is appointed[2], and resumes office during any vacancy[3]. He may summon a combined meeting of creditors of the partnership and any insolvent member for the purpose of choosing an insolvency practitioner to replace him[4].

[1]   IA 1986, s 136(1) as modified by IPO 1994, Sch 4, para 12.
[2]   IA 1986, s 136(2) as modified by IPO 1994, Sch 4, para 12.
[3]   IA 1986, s 136(3) as modified by IPO 1994, Sch 4, para 12.
[4]   IA 1986, s 136(4) as modified by IPO 1994, Sch 4, para 12.

25.97 As soon as practicable within 12 weeks of the date of the partnership winding-up order, the official receiver must decide whether or not to call a creditors' meeting[1]. If he decides not to call a meeting the official receiver must so inform the creditors and explain to them that they have the power under the Insolvency Rules[2] to require him to summon a meeting at the instance of one quarter in value of the partnership's creditors or the creditor of any insolvent member[3]. Where the official receiver decides to summon a meeting it must be held within four months of the date of the partnership winding-up order[4].

[1]   IA 1986, s 136A(1) as modified by IPO 1994, Sch 4, para 12.
[2]   IR 1986, r 4.57.
[3]   IA 1986, s 136A(1)(b), (2) as modified by IPO 1994, Sch 4, para 12.
[4]   IA 1986, s 136A(3) as modified by IPO 1994, Sch 4, para 12.

Appointment of responsible insolvency practitioner

25.98 The appointment may, and will normally, be made by the creditors in the creditors' meetings. If the creditors do not make an appointment, the official receiver may apply to the Secretary of State to appoint a person to act as the responsible insolvency practitioner of both the partnership and the insolvent members[1]. The Secretary of State is under no obligation to make an appointment[2]. Should he make an appointment and an insolvency order is subsequently made against any further insolvent partners by virtue of IPO 1994, art 8, then the insolvency practitioner concerned automatically becomes the insolvency practitioner of the insolvent member[3]. The insolvency practitioner, once appointed, must either summon a combined meeting of creditors[4] for the purpose of considering whether or not to establish a creditors' committee or notify the creditors that he has decided not to do so. He must explain that the creditors have the power to require him to summon such a meeting at the request of one tenth in value of either the partnership's creditors or the creditors of any member against whom an insolvency order has been made[5]. Should a further member be made insolvent, an insolvency practitioner appointed by the Secretary of State must state in his advertisement of the appointment whether or not a creditors' committee has been established and whether he proposes to appoint additional members of the committee[6] or, if no creditors' committee has been appointed, the power of the creditors to require a meeting must be explained[7].

1   IA 1986, s 137 as modified by IPO 1994, Sch 4, para 13.
2   IA 1986, s 137A(1) as modified by IPO 1994, Sch 4, para 13.
3   IA 1986, s 137A(3) as modified by IPO 1994, Sch 4, para 13.
4   Under IA 1986, s 141 as modified by IPO 1994, Sch 4, para 16.
5   IA 1986, s 137A(5) as modified by IPO 1994, Sch 4, para 13.
6   Under IA 1986, s 141A(3) as modified by IPO 1994, Sch 4, para 16.
7   IA 1986, s 137A(6) as modified by IPO 1994, Sch 4, para 13.

25.99 Where insolvency orders are made pursuant to an Article 8 petition on the discharge of a partnership administration order in the course of a PVA, the court may appoint an insolvency practitioner who has been acting as administrator[1], or supervisor[2], to be the responsible insolvency practitioner of the partnership and insolvent members.

1   IA 1986, s 140(1), (2) as modified by IPO 1994, Sch 4, para 15.
2   IA 1986, s 140(1)(3) as modified by IPO 1994, Sch 4, para 15.

Creditors' meeting and creditors' committee

25.100 The rules governing creditors' meetings in company liquidations are applied both to separate meetings of the creditors of the partnership and any insolvent corporate member, and combined meetings of all creditors[1]. Such combined meetings are to be conducted as if all the creditors of the partnership and its insolvent member(s) were a single set of creditors[2]. Separate meetings of an insolvent individual member are governed by the bankruptcy rules on such meetings[3].

1   IA 1986, s 139(1), (2) as modified by IPO 1994, Sch 4, para 14.
2   IA 1986, s 139(4) as modified by IPO 1994, Sch 4, para 14.
3   IA 1986, s 139(3) as modified by IPO 1994, Sch 4, para 14.

25.101 The creditors may establish a creditors' committee at a combined meeting of creditors whether summoned for the purpose of choosing a responsible insolvency practitioner of the partnership and insolvent members[1], or at the instance of the responsible insolvency practitioner[2], or at the request of one tenth in value of the partnership's creditors or the creditors of any insolvent member[3].

1   IA 1986, s 141(1), (2) as modified by IPO 1994, Sch 4, para 16.
2   IA 1986, s 141(3) as modified by IPO 1994, Sch 4, para 16.
3   IA 1986, s 141(3) as modified by IPO 1994, Sch 4, para 16.

25.102 The creditors' committee acts as the liquidation committee for the partnership and any corporate member and as the creditors' committee for any bankrupt individual member, exercising these committees' respective functions[1]. Additional creditors may be appointed to the creditors' committee by the responsible insolvency practitioner when appointed in respect of a further insolvent member[2], provided always that the creditor consents to his appointment, or by the court on the application of any creditor of the insolvent partnership or any insolvent member³. The creditors' committee may not carry out its functions at any time when the official receiver is acting as the responsible insolvency practitioner⁴, in which event the creditors' functions are vested in the Secretary of State⁵, who also exercises the relevant functions where there is no committee appointed⁶.

1   IA 1986, s 141A(2) as modified by IPO 1994, Sch 4, para 16.
2   IA 1986, s 141A(3) as modified by IPO 1994, Sch 4, para 16.
3   IA 1986, s 141A(4) as modified by IPO 1994, Sch 4, para 16; the appointment may take place even though the maximum number of members under the rules of the committee is thereby exceeded, IA 1986, s 141A(5).
4   Eg during a vacancy.
5   IA 1986, s 141A(6) as modified by IPO 1994, Sch 4, para 16.
6   IA 1986, s 141A(7) as modified by IPO 1994, Sch 4, para 16.

The responsible insolvency practitioner

25.103 The responsible insolvency practitioner is defined by IPO 1994¹ as: '(a) in winding up, the liquidator of an insolvent partnership or corporate member; and (b) in bankruptcy, the trustee of the estate of an individual member, and in either case includes the official receiver when so acting'. His functions, as with a company liquidator or individual's trustee in bankruptcy, are to secure the realisation of the assets and the distribution to the respective creditors and, should there be a surplus in the estate, the distribution of such surplus to the persons entitled to it². The responsible insolvency practitioner is entitled to use his own discretion in the carrying out of his functions and in the management of the property and assets, subject to the provisions of the IA 1986 and IR 1986. Where he is an insolvency practitioner³ it is his duty to furnish the official receiver with such information, and produce for the official receiver's inspection such books, papers and other records as the official receiver may reasonably require, and to give him such other assistance as may reasonably be required for the purposes of carrying out the official receiver's functions in relation to the winding up of the partnership and any corporate member or the bankruptcy of any individual member⁴.

1   IPO 1994, art 2(1).
2   IA 1986, s 143(1), as modified by IPO 1994, Sch 4, para 17.
3   Ie not the official receiver.
4   IA 1986, s 134(3) modified as above.

25.104 The responsible insolvency practitioner may at any time summon either separate or combined general meetings of the creditors or contributories of the partnership or insolvent members to ascertain their wishes on any aspect of his administration¹. Meetings of creditors must be summoned by the responsible insolvency practitioner either as separate creditors of the partnership or insolvent member or the combined creditors whenever requested to do so by one tenth in value of the relevant creditors². The responsible insolvency practitioner may apply to the court for directions in respect of any particular matter arising during the partnership or members' insolvency³, and any person aggrieved by an act or decision of the responsible insolvency practitioner may apply to the court to review the act or decision complained of, on which application the court may make any order it thinks fit⁴.

1   IA 1986, s 168(1), (2) as modified by IPO 1994, Sch 4, para 20.
2   IA 1986, s 168(3) modified as above.
3   IA 1986, s 168(4) modified as above.
4   IA 1986, s 168(5) modified as above.

25.105 When the responsible insolvency practitioner[1] considers that the winding up of the partnership or of any corporate member or the administration of any individual member's estate is, for practical purposes, complete, he is required to summon a final general meeting of the creditors of the partnership or the insolvent member(s), or alternatively a combined final general meeting of the creditors of the partnership and of the insolvent members to:

(a)   receive the practitioner's report for the winding up of the insolvent partnership or of any corporate member or for the administration of the estate of an individual member; and

(b)   determine whether the practitioner should have his release[2].

1   Other than the official receiver, as to the release of whom see IA 1986, s 174, as modified by IPO 1994, Sch 4, para 22.
2   IA 1986, s 146(2) as modified by IPO 1994, Sch 4, para 18.

25.106 The responsible insolvency practitioner may, if he thinks fit, at the same time as giving the notice summoning the final general meeting, give notice of any final distribution of the partnership property, or the property of the insolvent members, to the creditors. The final general meeting may not be concluded until such date as the responsible insolvency practitioner is able to report to the meeting for the winding up of the partnership or corporate member or administrator of the individual member's estate is complete for practical purposes[1]. Accordingly, if the final meeting of creditors is summoned before the responsible insolvency practitioner is able to make such a report it will have to be adjourned as may be necessary. It is the duty of the responsible insolvency practitioner to retain sufficient funds from the partnership property and the property of any insolvent member to cover the expenses of summoning and holding the final meeting of creditors[2].

1   IA 1986, s 146(3) modified as above.
2   IA 1986, s 146(4) modified as above.

25.107 The responsible insolvency practitioner may be removed from or vacate office only by order of the court[1] or in one of the following circumstances:

(i)   if appointed by the Secretary of State he may be removed only by direction of the Secretary of State[2];

(ii)   if he is not the official receiver he must vacate office if he ceases to be a person who is qualified to act as an insolvency practitioner in relation to the insolvent partnership or any insolvent member of it against whom an insolvency order has been made[3];

(iii) he may resign his office with the leave of the court or where appointed by the Secretary of State with the leave of the court or the Secretary of State, giving notice of his resignation to the court[4];

(iv) where a final meeting has been held, the practitioner whose report was considered at the meeting must vacate office as liquidator or as trustee, as the case may be, as soon as he has given notice to the court[5] that the meeting has been held and the decisions, if any, of the meeting[6];

(v) he must vacate office as trustee of the estate of an individual member if the Insolvency Order against that member has been annulled[7].

[1] IA 1986, s 172(1), (2) as modified by IPO 1994, Sch 4, para 21.
[2] IA 1986, s 172(3) modified as above.
[3] IA 1986, s 172(4) modified as above.
[4] IA 1986, s 172(5) modified as above.
[5] And, in the case of a corporate member, to the Registrar of Companies.
[6] IA 1986, s 172(6) modified as above.
[7] IA 1986, s 172(7) modified as above.

25.108 The responsible insolvency practitioner obtains his release under the provisions of the IA 1986, s 174[1].

[1] As modified by IPO 1994, Sch 4, para 22, which modified both IA 1986, s 174 and s 299 to provide for the circumstances in which the responsible insolvency practitioner should obtain his release.

Power of court to stay proceedings

25.109 The court has a general power to stay insolvency proceedings against a partnership, either generally or for a limited time, and if thought fit on terms, on the ground that the proceedings ought to be stayed[1]. An application for a stay may be made by the responsible insolvency practitioner, official receiver, any creditor or any contributory[2]. On being satisfied that an application for a stay of the proceedings against the partnership has been or will be made, the court may adjourn a petition against an insolvent member[3]. On staying proceedings against the partnership, the court may dismiss a petition against a member, annul or rescind an insolvency order made against a member, or may make any order it thinks fit[4]. Before making an order for a stay, the court may require the official receiver to furnish it with a report on any facts or matters which are in his opinion relevant to the application[5].

[1] IA 1986, s 147(1) as modified by IPO 1994, Sch 4, para 19.
[2] IA 1986, s 147(1) modified as above.
[3] IA 1986, s 147(2) modified as above.
[4] IA 1986, s 147(3) modified as above.
[5] IA 1986, s 147(4) modified as above.

Administration following an order on Article 7 petition[1]

25.110 The winding up of the insolvent partnership follows the administration of the winding up of an unregistered company with few modifications. The official receiver may require any person who: (i) is a present or former officer of the partnership; (ii) took part in the formation of the partnership within one year of the partnership's insolvency; (iii) is or was within one year of its insolvency employed by the partnership or a company which was an officer of the partnership, to prepare a statement of affairs of the insolvent partnership[2]. Any officer, person involved in the formation, liquidator or administrator of the partnership may be publicly examined[3]. The liquidator or provisional liquidator of the partnership has the same rights to get in partnership property as he would as a liquidator or provisional liquidator of a company, and any officer, former officer, or personal representative of a deceased officer is similarly obliged to hand over possession of partnership property to the liquidator or provisional liquidator[4]. Also expressly modified for the purposes of the partnership insolvency are the incorporate insolvency provisions governing:

(1)　the powers of the court to require delivery up of partnership assets;

(2)　the immunity of the liquidator or provisional liquidator from liability for loss or damage in seizing or disposing of property which he believes to be partnership property in the absence of negligence;

(3)　the imposing of a lien on property, or the proceeds of sale, for such expenses as were incurred in connection with seizing and disposing of the property[5].

[1]　Ie a petition presented by a creditor against the partnership alone.
[2]　IA 1986, s 131 as modified by IPO 1994, Sch 3, para 7.
[3]　IA 1986, s 133 as modified by IPO 1994, Sch 3, para 8.
[4]　IA 1986, s 234(1), (2) as modified by IPO 1994, Sch 3, para 9.
[5]　IA 1986, s 234(3)–(5) as modified by IPO 1994, Sch 3, para 9.

Administration following order on an Article 9 petition[1]

25.111 The winding up of the insolvent partnership proceeds as a winding up of an unregistered company under the IA 1986, Part V without express statutory modification but with such modifications as the court considers are appropriate to the insolvency of a partnership[2].

[1]　Ie a petition presented by a member against the partnership alone.
[2]　IPO 1994, art 9.

25.112 Unregistered companies are wound up under the same rules as those governing the winding up of companies registered under the Companies Act 1985 with a few modifications which are of little relevance to an insolvent partnership. An unregistered company cannot be wound up voluntarily[1].

[1]　IA 1986, s 221(4).

Administration following order on an Article 10 petition[1]

25.113 The winding up of the insolvent partnership proceeds as a winding up of an unregistered company under the IA 1986, Part V, and the insolvency of the corporate and individual members proceed as liquidations or bankruptcies as appropriate with the same modifications to the IA 1986 as are made to such insolvencies following insolvencies consequent on an order on a creditor's Article 8 petition[2].

[1]　Ie a petition presented by a member against both the partnership and all its members.
[2]　IPO 1994, art 10 incorporating Sch 4, Part II of the Order.

Administration following order on an Article 11 petition[1]

25.114 The bankruptcies of the individual members of the partnership proceed in accordance with the provisions of the IA 1986 relating to bankruptcy, subject to the various modifications made in IPO 1994, Sch 7. In summary, these modifications are the following:

(a) *Definition of individual member's estate*[2]. The definition is modified to make clear that the exempted items, ie tools of trade, clothes and household equipment, do not include any property belonging to the partnership.

(b) *Restrictions on dispositions of property*[3]. Where a person who is subsequently adjudged bankrupt or has been adjudged bankrupt makes a disposition of property, including a cash payment, between the date of the presentation of the petition and the vesting of his estate in his trustee that disposition is void. The IA 1986 is modified so as to make clear that a disposition of property is void whether or not the property concerned would form part of the individual member's estate, save the dispositions of property held on trust for a beneficiary other than the partnership.

(c) *Public examination of member*[4]. The right of the official receiver to hold a public examination, and his duty to do so when requested by one half in value of the creditors, are modified to enable public examinations of the individual members to be combined and held together. How practical this will be in the usual case is, however, open to question.

(d) *Power to appoint trustee*[5]. The creditors' power to appoint an insolvency practitioner to act as trustee of the insolvent members and of the partnership[6] is vested in a combined general meeting of the creditors of the partnership and the individual members. This provision may enable former partners, salaried partners with indemnity claims against equity partners, and partners who have acted as guarantors of other members to vote in the appointment of their own trustee. Their claims will of course have a very low priority and in the usual case will have a negligible or nominal value for voting purposes.

(e) *Conflicts of interest*. The trustee may find that there is a conflict of interest between his functions as trustee of the members' estates and of the partnership. IA 1986 is modified[7] to enable the trustee in such a position to apply to the court for directions and for the court to appoint one or more insolvency practitioners to act for the estates in conflict or as joint trustee.

(f) *Appointment of the trustee*. The official receiver by virtue of his office becomes the trustee of the estates of the members and of the partnership and continues in office until an insolvency practitioner is appointed[8]. The official receiver has 12 weeks to decide whether or not to summon a combined meeting of all the creditors of the partnership and the members, and if he does not do so he must notify the creditors of their power to require a meeting at the request of one quarter of the creditors of the partnership or of any individual member[9]. Should a combined meeting of the creditors fail to appoint a trustee, or at any time when the official receiver is acting as trustee, the official receiver may refer the need for an appointment of the Secretary of State, who may make an appointment or decline to do so[10].

(g) *Rules applicable to meetings of creditors.* Creditors' meetings proceed subject to the rules governing meetings of creditors in bankruptcy[11], with any combined meeting of creditors conducted as if the various creditors of the partnership and the members were a single set of creditors[12].

(h) *Removal and release of trustee.* The trustee of the estates of the members and the partnership may be removed only by order of the court and not by a meeting of creditors summoned specially for the purpose as is permitted in 'ordinary' bankruptcies[13]. Where the trustee is appointed by the Secretary of State he may be removed by the Secretary of State[14]. IPO 1994 also makes minor modifications to the provisions relating to the trustee vacating office[15], the position on a vacancy in the office of a trustee[16], and the obtaining of his release by the official receiver and the trustee[17].

[1] Ie the presentation of a joint bankruptcy petition by all the individual members of a partnership without winding up the partnership itself.
[2] IA 1986, s 283 as modified by IPO 1994, Sch 7, para 7.
[3] IA 1986, s 284 as modified by IPO 1994, Sch 7, para 8.
[4] IA 1986, s 290 as modified by IPO 1994, Sch 7, para 9.
[5] IA 1986, s 292 as modified by IPO 1994, Sch 7, para 10.
[6] In certain circumstances the Secretary of State has the power to appoint the trustee; see IA 1986, s 292(1)(b), modified as above.
[7] IA 1986, s 292A as modified by IPO 1994, Sch 7, para 10.
[8] IA 1986, s 293(1)–(3) as modified by IPO 1994, Sch 7, para 11.
[9] IA 1986, s 293(4), (5) as modified by IPO 1994, Sch 7, para 11.
[10] IA 1986, ss 295, 296 as modified by IPO 1994, Sch 7, paras 12, 13.
[11] See IR 1986, rr 6.79–6.95.
[12] IA 1986, s 297 as modified by IPO 1994, Sch 7, para 14.
[13] IA 1986, s 298(1) as modified by IPO 1994, Sch 7, para 15.
[14] IA 1986, s 298(2) as modified by IPO 1994, Sch 7, para 15.
[15] IA 1986, s 298(3)–(7) as modified by IPO 1994, Sch 7, para 15.
[16] IA 1986, s 300 as modified by IPO 1994, Sch 7, para 17.
[17] IA 1986, s 299 as modified by IPO 1994, Sch 7, para 16.

25.115 Where all the members of a partnership present individual bankruptcy petitions it is open to the court to direct that the partnership's affairs should be administered as if the partners had presented a joint bankruptcy petition under art 11[1]. This can be a useful provision. For when bankruptcy orders are made against all the partners the partnership is dissolved and none of the former partners, or their trustees, has any power to dispose of the partnership's assets. It is necessary for the court to direct that the partnership's affairs be administered as if an Article 11 petition had been presented to enable the trustee to collect in and realise the property of the former partnership[2].

[1] IA 1986, s 303(2A)–(2C); IPO 1994, art 14(2).
[2] *Official Receiver v Hollens* [2007] EWHC 754 (Ch), [2007] 3 All ER 767. Here the district judge had refused to give the direction sought by the official receiver because it would mean that the property comprising tools of the trade which would be exempt in an individual bankruptcy would nevertheless be realisable on behalf of the creditors as partnership property. As Blackburne J said at [25]:

'If a person chooses to trade through a partnership or a limited company and the relevant tool of the trade is an asset of that partnership or limited company, the item in question is liable to be realised for the benefit of creditors in the event of the insolvent winding up of the partnership or company. The fact that the item would have been exempt if the person in question had traded on his own account and had become insolvent is nothing to the point.'

H PRIORITY OF EXPENSES AND DEBTS

General

25.116 IPO 1994 modifies IA 1986 to provide a uniformed set of rules for the priority of expenses and debts in the insolvency of the partnership and of any corporate or individual member[1]. The order of priority is as follows:

(1)   costs and expenses of the insolvency;
(2)   preferential debts;
(3)   ordinary debts[2];
(4)   interest on preferential and ordinary debts;
(5)   postponed debts;
(6)   interest on postponed debts;
(7)   the members of the partnership as contributories, in accordance with their respective rights and interest in the surplus.

[1]   See IPO 1994, Sch 4, paras 23, 24; IPO 1994, Sch 7, para 21. The overall order of priority is provided for as follows: IA 1986, s 175A(2), as modified by IPO 1994, Sch 4, para 23 (Article 8 petitions, joint estate); IA 1986, s 175B(1), as modified by IPO 1994, Sch 4, para 23 (Article 8 petitions, separate estates); IA 1986, s 328A(2), as modified by IPO 1994, Sch 7, para 21 (Article 11 petitions); IA 1986, s 328B(1), as modified by IPO 1994, Sch 7, para 21 (Article 11 petitions, separate estates).
[2]   Ie 'debts which are neither preferential nor postponed debts'; IA 1986, s 175A(2)(b), as modified by IPO 1994, Sch 4, para 23.

25.117 It is necessary when determining priorities to ascertain with respect to any particular debt whether it is a joint debt of the partnership, a separate debt of a member, or a joint or several debt. This is because the scheme of the IA 1986 as amended by IPO 1994 is for joint debts to be proved against the joint estate and any shortfall becomes a provable debt in the separate estate of each member of the insolvent partnership ranking equally with that partner's separate debts. This provision, coupled with the obligation on the responsible insolvency practitioner to adjust the member's rights among themselves as members of the partnership should ensure that all creditors, both of the partnership and its members, receive equivalent treatment in the distribution of the assets available both from the partnership and its members.

25.118 For partnership insolvencies prior to 1 December 1994 the rule as to separation of estates applied, namely that the partnership's assets ('the joint estate') went first to the partnership creditors, and the member's personal estate ('the separate estate') went first to his personal creditors, before the surplus in either estate, if any, being made available to the other creditors. The relevant provisions are set out in IPO 1986, Arts 9 and 10. They are not discussed in this text.

25.119 As with all insolvencies the debts within each category rank equally amongst themselves, and if the available estate is insufficient to meet them in full they abate in equal proportions between themselves[1]. Interest on any category of debt is payable on the debt in question in respect of the period during which the debt has been outstanding since the winding-up order was made against the partnership or any corporate member, or the bankruptcy order was made against any individual member[2]. It is payable at judgment rate, ie the rate specified for the Judgments Act 1838, s 17 applying on the day on which the winding-up or bankruptcy order was made or, if higher, any rate of interest which applies to the debt apart from the insolvency whether contractual or statutory[3].

[1]   IA 1986, ss 175A(4) and 175B(2), as modified by IPO 1994, Sch 4, para 23 (Article 8 petitions); IA 1986, ss 328A(4) and 328B(2) as modified by IPO 1994, Sch 7, para 21 (Article 11 petitions).
[2]   IA 1986, s 189(1), (2), as modified by IPO 1994, Sch 4, para 24 (Article 8 petitions); IA 1986, s 328D(1), (2), as modified by IPO 1994, Sch 7, para 21 (Article 11 petitions).
[3]   IA 1986, ss 189(3) and 328D(3), modified as above.

25.120 An individual member may not prove in his own partnership's insolvency in competition with the partnership creditors whether for a joint or several debt[1]. Any sums due to individual members whether by way of profit share, return of monies advanced or repayment of capital rank after all the creditors, and may only be paid after all creditors have been paid in full. A member who discharges the debt of any particular creditor is not subrogated to the rights of such creditor[2], he merely improves his rights against his fellow members as contributories in the repayment of any surplus after all debts and interest have been paid. In the case, however, where a member has rescinded the partnership agreement for fraud or misrepresentation by any of his fellow members, he is entitled to be subrogated to the rights of any creditors of the partnership to whom he has made payment in respect of partnership liabilities[3].

[1]   IA 1986, s 175C(2), as modified by IPO 1994, Sch 4, para 23. There are two exceptions to this rule, namely where the debt has arisen (a) as a result of fraud, and (b) in the ordinary course of a business carried on separately from the partnership's business.
[2]   *R v Connor* (1906) Exch CR 183.
[3]   Partnership Act 1890, s 41.

Secured creditors

25.121 A secured creditor of the partnership or of a member has four options open to him:

(1)   he may rely on his security and enforce it as the law may allow without reference to the insolvency;

(2)   he may voluntarily surrender his security for the general benefit of creditors and prove for the whole of his debt as if unsecured[1];

(3)   he may value his security and prove for any unsecured balance[2] as to the power of the responsible insolvency practitioner to estimate the value of the unsecured debt, or the ability of the secured creditor to revise the value which he has put upon his security in his proof of debt[3]; or

(4)   he may realise his security and prove for the balance of the debt[4].

1   IR 1986, r 4.88(2) (partnership), r 6.109(2) (member).
2   IR 1986, r 4.75(1) (partnership), r 6.98(1) (member).
3   See IR 1986, rr 4.86, 4.95 (partnership), r 6.115 (member).
4   IR 1986, r 4.88(1), r 6.109(1).

25.122 A creditor who omits to disclose his security in his proof of debt must surrender it for the general benefit of creditors, subject to the power of the court to allow him to keep his security on the grounds that the omission was inadvertent or the result of honest mistake[1]. The responsible insolvency practitioner may redeem the security[2] or require any property comprised in the security to be offered for sale so as to test the value put on it by the secured creditor[3].

1   IR 1986, r 4.96, r 6.116.
2   IR 1986, r 4.97, r 6.117.
3   IR 1986, r 4.98, r 6.118.

25.123 A secured creditor whose security is over an asset of the partnership may enforce any separate debt owed to him by one or more members of the partnership without reference to his security. He need neither release his security nor give credit for its value against any separate debt owed by a member[1]. In a situation where a partnership asset is held in the name of one member only, a security over that asset is in reality a security over a partnership asset and will be treated as such[2]. Where the secured creditor's security is over one or more assets of members of the partnership, he may prove for joint debt against the joint estate without reference to the security[3], but will presumably be required to bring it into account if the joint estate is insufficient to pay the joint debts and the aggregate value of the unsatisfied joint debts becomes a claim against the separate estate of the member whose assets is held as a security[4].

1   *Re Fraser, Trenholm & Co* (1868) 4 Ch App 49; *Rolfe v Flower Salting & Co* (1865) LR 1 PC 27.
2   *Re Collie, ex p Manchester and County Bank* (1876) 3 Ch D 481.
3   *Re Dutton, Massey & Co* [1924] 2 Ch 199, CA; *Re Hart* (1884) 25 Ch D 716; *Re Turner* (1881) 19 Ch D 105, CA.
4   See IA 1986, ss 175A(5), 328A(5).

25.124 In a case where a creditor is owed both a joint debt by the partnership and a separate debt by a member and has been given one security to cover both debts, he may enforce the security and appropriate the proceeds to whichever debt he chooses, retaining any balance in a suspense account while proving for the whole of the other debt[1].

1   *Re Walker & Co* (1880) 42 LT 516; *Re Foster* (1875) LR 20 Eq 767.

Set-off: mutual debts and credits

25.125 Set-off of mutual debts and credits in insolvency is discussed above[1]. For set-off to arise in insolvency the liabilities must be mutual. Accordingly, there is no set-off between a member's separate debts and debts due to the firm[2]. The statutory requirement of mutuality applies to whatever personal arrangements that may have been made between particular parties by way of set-off, as the operation of the principle of set-off will affect all the other creditors of the same class[3]. Where a member is liable to a creditor both jointly and severally, insolvency set-off will operate automatically on the insolvency of either of them[4]. There is no provision in the IA 1986 or IR 1986 which would suggest that a debt should not be the subject of the insolvency set-off provision on the basis that it is a postponed debt, even though the application of the set-off will have the effect of giving the creditor priority over other non-postponed debts[5].

[1] See para **22.99**ff.
[2] *Re Pennington & Owen Ltd* [1925] Ch 825; *Piercy v Fynney* (1871) LR 12 Eq 69.
[3] See generally *National Westminster Bank v Halesowen Press Work* [1972] AC 785, [1972] 1 All ER 641.
[4] *M S Fashions v Bank of Credit and Commerce International (No 2)* [1993] Ch 425, [1993] 3 All ER 769.
[5] See *Re Lonergan* (1877) 4 Ch D 789, 791 (James LJ obiter suggesting a set-off), but cf *Atlantic Acceptance Corpn v Burns* (1970) 14 DLR (3D) 175 to the contrary.

Priority of costs and expenses

25.126 As between the various costs and expenses which may be incurred in the insolvency of the partnership of any member, the standard rules of priority apply[1]. The priority for payment for costs and expenses as between the joint estate of the partnership and the separate estates of the insolvent members is provided for by IPO 1994[2] in the following manner:

(1) the joint estate of the partnership shall be applicable in the first instance in payment of the joint expenses and the separate estate of each insolvent member shall be applicable in the first instance in payment of the separate expenses relating to that member;

(2) where the joint estate is insufficient for the payment in full of the joint expenses, the unpaid balance shall be apportioned equally between the separate estates and the insolvent members against whom insolvency orders have been made and shall form part of the expenses to be paid out of those estates;

(3) where any separate estate of an insolvent member is insufficient for the payment in full of the separate expenses to be paid out of that estate, the unpaid balance shall form part of the expenses to be paid out of the joint estate;

(4) where, after the transfer of any unpaid balance in accordance with (2) or (3) above, any estate is insufficient for the payment in full of the expenses to be paid out of that estate, the balance then remaining unpaid shall be apportioned equally between the other estates;

(5) where, after an apportionment under (4) above, one or more estates are insufficient for the payment in full of the expenses to be paid out of those estates, the total of the unpaid balances of the expenses to be paid out of the estate shall continue to be apportioned equally between the other estates until provision is made for the payment in full of the

expenses or there is no estate available for the payment of the balance finally remaining unpaid, in which case it abates in equal proportions between all the estates;

(6)   without prejudice to (2) to (5) above, a responsible insolvency practitioner, may, with the sanction of the creditors' committee, if any[3], or with the leave of the court obtained on application:

    (a)   pay out of the joint estates part of the expenses to be paid out of that estate any expenses incurred for any separate estate of an insolvent member; or

    (b)   pay out of any separate estate of an insolvent member any part of the expenses incurred for the joint estate which affects that separate estate.

[1]   See IR 1986, r 4.218 (partnership and corporate member), r 6.224 (individual member).
[2]   See IA 1986, s 175, amending IA 1986, ss 175, 328(1)–(3), (6) by Sch 4, para 23 for Article 8 petitions and IA 1986, s 328 as modified by Sch 7, para 21 for Article 11 petitions (in identical terms).
[3]   Ie a creditors' committee established under IA 1986, s 141 (partnership/corporate member), IA 1986, s 301 (individual member).

Priority of debts as between joint and separate estates

25.127 The responsible insolvency practitioner (or in Article 11 petition cases, the trustee) should first administer the joint estate and pay the preferential and joint creditors and then, if there is sufficient estate available, the ordinary joint creditors and then the interest on all joint debts[1] from the joint estate. Where the joint estate is insufficient to meet the joint preferential creditors and the joint ordinary creditors, the aggregate amount of the unpaid debts constitutes a claim against the separate estate of each insolvent member and, as a debt provable by the responsible insolvency practitioner (or trustee) in each such estate, ranks equally with the ordinary debt provable in the insolvent members' estates[2]. Unpaid joint preferential debts thus lose their preferential status when proved in the insolvent members' estates. Similar provisions apply to the payment of interest on joint debts, postponed debts and interest on postponed debts. In each case, maintaining its strict order of priority, where the joint estate is insufficient to pay interest or joint preferential or ordinary debts, postponed debts or interest on postponed debts, the aggregate balance is provable in the separate estates of the insolvent members ranking equally for the interest on the separate preferential and ordinary debts, separate postponed debts or interest on such postponed debts respectively in the various separate estates of the insolvent members[3].

[1]   Interest on both preferential and ordinary debts has the same priority and is payable after payment of the ordinary debts but before the postponed debts.
[2]   IA 1986, s 175A(5), as modified by IPO 1994, Sch 4, para 23 (Article 8 petitions); IA 1986, s 328A(5), as modified by IPO 1994, Sch 7, para 21 (Article 11 petitions).
[3]   IA 1986, s 175A(6) (interest), s 175A(7) (postponed debts), s 175A(8) (interest on postponed debts), as modified by IPO 1994, Sch 4, para 23. Article 8 petitions: IA 1986, s 328A(6) (interest), s 328A(7) (postponed debts), s 328A(8) (interest on postponed debts), as modified by IPO 1994, Sch 7, para 21 (Article 11 petitions).

25.128 Any payment by way of distribution from the separate estate of any member in respect of the joint debt or interest on such debt becomes part of the joint estate[1].

¹ IA 1986, s 175A(9), as modified by IPO 1994, Sch 4, para 23, s 328A(9), as modified by IPO 1994, Sch 7, para 21.

General provisions applying to the distribution of the estates

25.129 The following provisions apply to the distribution of the joint and separate estates by the responsible insolvency practitioner, or trustee in the case of administration, following an Article 11 petition:

(1)   distinct accounts shall be kept of the joint estate of the partnership and/or the separate estate of each member of that partnership against whom an insolvency order is made[1];

(2)   no member of the partnership may prove for a joint or separate debt in competition with joint creditors, unless the debt has arisen (a) as a result of fraud, or (b) in the ordinary course of business carried out separately from the partnership business[2];

(3)   the provisions governing the order of priority of debts are without prejudice to any provision of the IA 1986 or of any other enactment concerning the ranking between themselves of postponed debts and interest on postponed debts, but in the absence of any such provisions postponed debts and interest rank equally between themselves[3];

(4)   'sub-partnerships' of any two or more members of an insolvent partnership constitute a separate partnership, the creditors of such a separate partnership shall be deemed to be a separate set of creditors and subject to the same statutory provisions as for separate creditors of any member of the insolvent partnership[4];

(5)   where any surplus remains after the administration of the estate of a separate partnership, the surplus shall be distributed to the members or, where applicable, to the separate estates of the members of that partnership according to their respective rights and interests in it[5];

(6)   no fees are payable whether to the responsible insolvency practitioner, the official receiver or the Secretary of State, in connection with (a) the transfer of a surplus from the joint estate to a separate estate, (b) a distribution from the separate estate to the joint estate, or (c) a distribution from the estate of a separate partnership to the separate estate to the members of that partnership[6].

¹ See IA 1986, s 175(1) as modified by IPO 1994, Sch 4, para 23; IA 1986, s 328C as modified by IPO 1994, Sch 7, para 21.
² See IA 1986, s 175(2) as modified by IPO 1994, Sch 4, para 23; IA 1986, s 328C as modified by IPO 1994, Sch 7, para 21.
³ See IA 1986, s 175(5) as modified by IPO 1994, Sch 4, para 23; IA 1986, s 328C as modified by IPO 1994, Sch 7, para 21.
⁴ See IA 1986, s 175(6) as modified by IPO 1994, Sch 4, para 23; IA 1986, s 328C as modified by IPO 1994, Sch 7, para 21.
⁵ See IA 1986, s 175(7) as modified by IPO 1994, Sch 4, para 23; IA 1986, s 328C as modified by IPO 1994, Sch 7, para 21.
⁶ See IA 1986, s 175(8) as modified by IPO 1994, Sch 4, para 23; IA 1986, s 328C as modified by IPO 1994, Sch 7, para 21.

Postponed debts

25.130 The following categories of postponed creditors arise by virtue of the provisions of the Partnership Act 1890[1]:

(1)   a creditor who has advanced money by way of a loan in consideration of (a) a share of the profits, (b) a payment varying with the profits, or (c) a rate of interest which varies with the profits of the partnership business;
(2)   an employee or agent of the partnership who is remunerated by a share of the partnership's profits;
(3)   a seller of goodwill and consideration of the share in the profits of the partnership business.

¹   Partnership Act 1890, ss 2(2), 3.

25.131 The fact that the debt is postponed does not affect any security the creditor or seller may have taken, which may be enforced ahead of the rights of unsecured creditors¹. It may also be the case that a postponed debt may be set off against a partnership debt under the insolvency set-off provisions². The courts have tended to restrict the operation of the postponement provisions of the Partnership Act 1890. A provision that an allowance, not specified, ought to be made in the event that the profits were insufficient to enable repayment of a loan at fixed interest was void for uncertainty and outside the 1890 Act provisions³. Further, advances not clearly within the provisions of the original loan will not be postponed⁴ and where a loan is made in consideration both of interest payment at a fixed rate and also a share in the profits, only the profit share payments will be postponed⁵. Where a widow sold her late husband's business on terms that included the payment of a fixed annuity by the purchaser, the debt was held not to be postponed because the annuity was fixed and did not vary with the profits⁶. However, a debt comprising a fixed sum stated to be payable out of the profits will be postponed⁷. A debt is not postponed where the creditor has agreed to waive payments in consideration of the payment to another person of a share in the profits⁸, and where a loan was made on terms which included payment of a share of the profits, but no profits were made so that the lender released the partnership from the loan on the terms that the partners agreed to repay the loan at fixed interest with a guarantee from the partnership, it was held that the transaction for releasing liability on the original loan was not subject to postponement⁹.

¹   *Re Vince, ex p Baxter* [1892] 2 QB 478.
²   *Re Lonergan* (1877) 4 Ch D 789 (James LJ obiter suggested that there would be a set-off) but cf *Atlantic Acceptance Corpn v Burns* (1970) 14 DLR (3d) 175 to the contrary.
³   *Re Vince, ex p Baxter* [1982] 2 QB 478.
⁴   *Re Mason* [1899] 1 QB 810; *Re Tew, ex p Mills* (1873) 8 Ch App 569.
⁵   *Re Mason* [1899] 1 QB 810; *Re Tew, ex p Mills* (1873) 8 Ch App 569.
⁶   *Re Gieve, ex p Shaw* (1899) 80 LT 737.
⁷   *Re Young* [1896] 2 QB 484.
⁸   *Re Pinto Leite & Nephews* [1929] 1 Ch 221.
⁹   *Re Abenheim* (1913) 109 LT 219.

25.132 In the separate estate of an individual member, a debt owed to a person who at the commencement of the bankruptcy¹ was the spouse of the bankrupt member is a postponed debt².

¹   Ie the date of the bankruptcy order; IA 1986, s 278.
²   IA 1986, s 329.

Members as contributories: partner's lien

25.133 Any surplus of the joint estate after payment of the various creditors is distributed to the members in accordance with their respective rights and interest. Where a member has a lien over partnership property this will bind the responsible insolvency practitioner or trustee of the estate[1], and the lien will take priority over the rights of separate creditors of other members[2] or a mortgagee of a members' share in the partnership[3]. In no case does a partner's lien prejudice the rights of joint creditors[4]. A partner's lien may arise:

(i)   where a member rescinds the partnership agreement on the grounds of fraud or misrepresentation, he has a lien for the capital introduced into the business or money paid by him for the purchase of a partnership share[5];

(ii)   at any time during the term of the partnership in respect of partnership property improperly disposed of, or to secure the share of a member who has not made his required capital contribution[6];

(iii) on dissolution of the partnership to protect the right of each member to have the partnership's assets properly applied to the discharge of debts and liabilities and distribution among the members[7].

[1] *Ex p Reeve* (1804) 9 Ves 588; *Re Bland, ex p Reid* (1814) 2 Rose 84; *Holderness v Shackels* (1828) 8 B&C 612; *Re Butterworth* (1835) 4 Deac & Ch 160.
[2] *Ex p King* (1810) 17 Ves 115.
[3] *Cavander v Bulteel* (1873) 9 Ch App 79.
[4] See the Partnership Act 1890, ss 39, 41.
[5] Partnership Act 1890, s 41.
[6] *Re White, ex p Morley* (1873) 8 Ch App 1026; *Steward v Blakeway* (1869) 4 Ch App 603.
[7] Partnership Act 1890, s 39.

25.134 The partner's lien is equitable and ceases to apply to property properly disposed of or mortgaged to secure a partnership debt[1] and does not prejudice the rights of a purchaser or mortgagee in good faith of any specific partnership asset[2]. A lien over partnership land comes within the definition of a mortgage[3] for the purposes of the Land Charges Act 1972[4] and should be protected by registration as a land charge or by a caution against dealings[5].

[1] *Re Bourne* [1906] 2 Ch 427.
[2] *Re Langmead's Trust* (1855) 20 Beav 20; affd (1855) 7 De G & M G 353.
[3] Law of Property Act 1925, s 205(1).
[4] Land Charges Act 1972, ss 2, 4.
[5] See generally *United Bank of Kuwait v Sahib* [1997] Ch 107, [1995] 2 All ER 973.

Members as contributories: adjustment of liabilities

25.135 The responsible insolvency practitioner is required to 'adjust the rights among themselves of the members of the partnership as contributories, and shall distribute any surplus to the members, or, where applicable, to the separate estate of the members according to their respective rights and interests in it'[1]. The members' 'rights among themselves' will be governed by any agreements between them and, in the absence of any agreement, the Partnership Act 1890, s 44, which provides that after payment of the firm's debts and liabilities any remaining assets should be applied first in repayment of any advances made by members, secondly in repayment of capital, and finally any ultimate residue divided amongst the members in the proportions in which the profits are divisible.

1   IA 1986, s 175A(3), as modified by IPO 1994, Sch 4 (Article 8 and 10 petitions); IA 1986, s 328A(3), as modified by IPO 1994, Sch 7 (Article 11 petitions).

25.136 No member may prove for a joint or separate debt in competition with a joint creditor, subject to two exceptions, for this would have the effect of reducing the debt owed by the member himself[1]. The first exception is where the debt has arisen 'as a result of fraud'[2]. IPO 1994 does not restrict the circumstances in which the fraud has to arise to come within the exception, and these circumstances will include cases where the member has been fraudulently induced to contribute capital to the partnership[3], or has been fraudulently deprived of his own property by the partnership[4]. The second exception is where the member's debt has arisen 'in the ordinary course of a business carried on separately from the partnership business'[5]. The business must be quite distinct from the partnership business and 'the question, what is dealing in a distinct trade, is always to be looked at with great care'[6]. If in reality one business is a branch of the partnership business and is carrying on part of the partnership's business, albeit a distinct aspect of that business, it is not being carried on separately from the partnership's business[7]. A banking business is not a distinct trade where its purpose is to finance the commercial trading of the partnership[8].

1   IA 1986, s 175C(2) and s 328(2), modified as above; this continues the common law rule, see eg *Nanson v Gordon* (1876) 1 App Cas 195; *Re Blythe* (1881) 16 Ch D 620; and see *In re Beale, ex p Corbridge* (1876) 4 Ch D 246, where the trader's co-habitee who had provided money for the business was not allowed to prove in competition with the creditors.
2   IA 1986, s 175C(2)(a) and s 328C(2)(a) as modified by IPO 1994, Schs 4 and 7.
3   See eg *Bury v Allen* (1845) 1 Coll 589.
4   See eg *Re Goodchilds & Co, ex p Sillitoe* (1824) 1 Gl & J 374.
5   IA 1986, s 175C(2)(b) and s 328C(2)(b), as modified by IPO 1994, Schs 4 and 7.
6   Per Ld Eldon in *Ex p Sillitoe* (1824) 1 Gl & J 374 at 383.
7   *Ex p Hargreaves* (1788) 1 Cox Eq Cas 440.
8   *In re Braginton, ex p Maude* (1867) 2 Ch App 550.

I LIMITED LIABILITY PARTNERSHIPS

The limited liability partnership

25.137 From 6 April 2001 it has been possible for partnerships to enjoy limited liability under the terms of the Limited Liability Partnerships Act 2000 ('LLPA 2000'). This form of legal entity is called the limited liability partnership ('LLP'). Any two or more persons who have agreed to be associated for the purpose of carrying on a lawful business with a view to profit may establish an LLP[1]. An LLP is formed by being incorporated under the LLPA 2000[2], and will in most respects be governed by company law, rather than the law relating to partnership[3]. Incorporation is by delivering to the registrar of companies an incorporation document in an approved form which states the name of the LLP, the address of the registered office of the

LLP[4], the name and address of each person who is to be a member of the LLP on incorporation, and specifies which of those persons are to be designated members[5]. There must be at least two designated members, and all the members may be designated members[6]. The mutual rights and duties of the members of an LLP and of the LLP and its members will be governed by an agreement made between them, and in the absence of agreement on any matter, by regulation[7]. An LLP has unlimited capacity[8], and every member of an LLP is the agent of that partnership[9]. However, an LLP will not be bound by any act of a member in dealing with the third party if (a) the member did not have authority for the act in question, and (b) the third party is aware of the lack of authority or does not know or believe him to be a member of the partnership[10].

1 LLPA 2000, s 2(1)(a).
2 LLPA 2000, s 1(2).
3 See LLPA 2000, ss 1(5) and 15 which enable regulations to be made to apply or incorporate any law relating to companies or partnerships to LLPs.
4 Which must be in England and Wales, or Wales or Scotland; LLPA 2000, s 2(2).
5 LLPA 2000, s 2(2); the designated members are responsible for due compliance by the LLP with its statutory duties such as the signing and filing of annual accounts, the removal of auditors, and the preparation of a statement of affairs in the event of insolvency.
6 LLPA 2000, s 8(2), (3); the incorporation document may state that every person who is from time to time a member of the LLP should be a designated member.
7 LLPA 2000, s 5; regulations incorporating provisions of company law may be made under s 15, see the Limited Liability Partnerships Regulations 2001, SI 2001/1090, Part II (accounts and audit) and Part III (the remainder of the provisions of the Companies Act 1985).
8 LLPA 2000, s 1(3).
9 LLPA 2000, s 6(1).
10 LLPA 2000, s 6(2).

Insolvency of limited liability partnership

25.138 The provisions of the IA 1986 as to company voluntary arrangements, administration and winding up are applied to the LLPs by regulation with modifications as appropriate[1]. The modifications are set out in the Limited Liability Partnerships Regulations 2001, SI 2001/1090, Sch 3[2]; the salient features being set out below.

1 LLPA 2000, s 14; see the Limited Liability Partnerships Regulations 2001, SI 2001/1090, Part IV.
2 As amended by the Limited Liability Partnerships (Amendment) Regulations 2005, SI 2005/1989, art 3, Sch 2.

Voluntary arrangements

25.139 An LLP may propose for a voluntary arrangement, with the designated members making the proposal in place of the directors. The designated members will be acting on behalf of the LLP who, it is assumed, will have agreed to the proposal for a voluntary arrangement in accordance with its own decision-making procedures. Accordingly, no meetings of the LLP need be held, only meetings of the LLP's creditors. In the event that the meeting of creditors approves the proposal with modifications, these have to be agreed by the LLP as a whole. Any member of the LLP is entitled to challenge the decision of the creditors' meeting. An LLP may seek a voluntary arrangement under the moratorium provisions of IA 1986[1].

[1] As from 1 October 2005; see the Limited Liability Partnerships (Amendment) Regulations 2005, SI 2005/1989, art 3, Sch 2, para 2.

Administration

25.140 The new administration regime introduced by the Enterprise Act 2002 has been extended to LLPs[1]. The administrator has power to prevent any member of the LLP from taking part in the management of the LLP's business and to appoint any person to be a manager of that business.

[1] As from 1 October 2005; see the Limited Liability Partnerships (Amendment) Regulations 2005, SI 2005/1989, art 3, Sch 2. The prohibition on the appointment of an administrative receiver (IA 1986, s 72) applies to an LLP as it does to a company; and the same exceptions also apply, eg *Feetum v Levy* [2005] EWCA Civ 1601, [2006] Ch 585.

Winding up

25.141 An LLP may be wound up voluntarily or compulsorily, with every present and past member liable to contribute to the assets of the LLP to such extent as he may have agreed. In the case of past members, the liability to contribute is dependent upon his agreement to do so surviving his ceasing to be a member. The liquidator of an LLP must be a qualified insolvency practitioner.

Voluntary winding up

25.142 A voluntary winding up commences upon a determination by the LLP that it be wound up voluntarily, a copy of which determination must be forwarded to the registrar of companies within 15 days of it being made. Any transfer of the interest of any member in the property of the LLP after the determination to enter voluntary liquidation is void. There may be a members' voluntary winding up where a statutory declaration of solvency is made by the designated members. The LLP as a whole and not just the designated members appoint the liquidator. The statement of affairs to be laid before the creditors' meeting in a creditors' voluntary liquidation is to be prepared by the designated members, and one of the designated members must attend and preside over the creditors' meeting. The liquidator retains the power to accept shares or other benefits as consideration for the sale of the assets of the LLP. Any member may dissent from the sale and require its abandonment or the purchase of his interest at a price to be determined by agreement or arbitration.

Winding up by the court

25.143 Any LLP, whatever the size of its assets, may be wound up in the county court as well as in the High Court. An LLP may be wound up by the court if it so determines, it does not commence business within a year from its incorporation or suspends its business for one year, the number of members reduces below two, it is unable to pay its debts, or the court is of the opinion that it is just and equitable that it be wound up[1]. Inability to pay debts is determined as in the case of corporate insolvency, and the liquidation proceeds in the same manner as would a company liquidation with the members of the LLP taking the place of the general meeting of the company. Members of an LLP who have been guilty of misfeasance or misappropriation, fraudulent trading or wrongful trading may be required to make such contribution to the assets of the LLP as the court may order. The Limited Liability Partnerships Regulations 2001, SI 2001/1090, insert an additional provision enabling the court to order a member of an LLP to make contribution to the assets available for creditors.

[1]   As in the case of companies where a petition brought on the just and equitable ground relies on the assertion that the substratum of the enterprise has been lost, the petition will be dismissed unless it can be shown that it is 'utterly impossible to carry on the business'; *Marsden v Tower Taxi Technology LLP* [2005] EWCA Civ 1503, [2005] All ER (D) 162 (Oct).

25.144 A new provision in the IA 1986, s 214A ('adjustment of withdrawals') applies to any member of the LLP who withdrew property of the LLP for his own benefit during the period of two years prior to the commencement of the winding up, whether in the form of share of profits, salary, repayment, or payment, of interest on a loan to the LLP or any other withdrawal of property[1]. If the liquidator proves to the court's satisfaction that at the time of withdrawal the member knew or had reasonable grounds for believing that the LLP was unable to pay its debts as they fell due, or was insolvent on a balance-sheet basis, or would become insolvent as a result of the member's withdrawal either taken by itself or together with all other contemporaneous withdrawals by other members or together with withdrawals in contemplation when that withdrawal was made[2], the court may order that member to make a contribution to the LLP's assets[3]. The amount of contribution so ordered may not exceed the aggregate amount of the member's withdrawals during the two years immediately prior to the commencement of the winding up[4]. Such an order is not to be made where the court is satisfied that there remained, after the relevant withdrawal, a reasonable prospect that the LLP would avoid going into insolvent liquidation[5]. This provision may be enforced against shadow members of an LLP[6], and an order may be made to adjust a withdrawal under this provision without prejudice to an order against the member concerned in respect of fraudulent trading[7]. The liquidator has the same power to seek orders in respect of antecedent trading (transactions at an undervalue, preferences, exorbitant credit transactions, disclaimer of onerous contracts, etc) as he would in a company winding up. The definition of 'associate'[8] is extended to include, as under IA 1986, s 435(3A), the provision that a member of an LLP is an associate of that LLP and of every other member of that LLP and of the husband or wife or relative of every other member of that LLP.

1   IA 1986, s 214A(1), (2).
2   IA 1986, s 214A(2).
3   IA 1986, s 214A(3).
4   IA 1986, s 214A(4), as amended.
5   IA 1986, s 214A(5).
6   IA 1986, s 214A(7).
7   IA 1986, s 214A(8).
8   IA 1986, s 435; see **Appendix 2**.

Chapter 26

ADMINISTRATION OF INSOLVENT ESTATES OF DECEASED PERSONS

A   General
B   Administration otherwise than in bankruptcy
C   Death of debtor before presentation of bankruptcy petition
D   Death of debtor after presentation of bankruptcy petition
E   Effect of death on individual voluntary arrangements

A GENERAL

26.1 The estate of a deceased person is insolvent if, when realised it will be insufficient to meet in full all debts and other liabilities to which it is subject[1]. Where an estate is found to be or is likely to be insolvent after an individual's death it has to be administered for the benefit of the deceased's creditors and not for those entitled under a will or on intestacy until all the debts are paid. There are three regimes under which the administration of an insolvent estate may proceed:

(1)   the executors may administer the estate in accordance with the law of bankruptcy as to the rights of creditors and priorities;
(2)   the estate may be administered pursuant to an administration action; or
(3)   the estate may be administered in bankruptcy pursuant to an insolvency administration order.

[1]   IA 1986, s 421(4).

26.2 Insolvent estates, whether a debtor dies insolvent or a bankrupt dies during the course of his bankruptcy, are regulated by the Administration of Insolvent Estates of Deceased Persons Order 1986 ('DPO 1986').

26.3 The general effect of an insolvency administration order is that the deceased estate is administered in the same way as is the estate of a living bankrupt. The administration will be subject to the control of the bankruptcy court which will have the same powers and the same procedures as in bankruptcy[1]. The appropriate court for the insolvent administration will be the court within the jurisdiction of which the debtor resided or carried on business for the greater part of the six months immediately before his death[2].

1   DPO 1986, art 3, Sch1, Pt II, para 30.
2   IA 1986, s 385(1) modified by the DPO 1986, art 3, Sch 1, Pt II, para 33.

B   ADMINISTRATION OTHERWISE THAN IN BANKRUPTCY

26.4 An insolvent estate does not have to be administered under an insolvency administration order. An executor or administrator may if he wishes administer the estate outside formal bankruptcy[1] but if he does so he must comply with the bankruptcy rules as to administration of the estate, the rights of secured and unsecured creditors, proof of debts, the priority of debts and payments, etc[2]. The executor or administrator will prove the will or take out letters of administration in the normal way and may then proceed to administer the estate. Where the deceased has died intestate, or there are executors under a will who have renounced, a creditor may apply for letters of administration. An executor or administrator who is administering the estate outside formal bankruptcy does not have to be a qualified insolvency practitioner[3].

(1)   The personal representative will gather in the assets. Where there were mutual dealings between the deceased and a person indebted to him, the mutual indebtedness will be subject to set-off. The personal representative is not entitled to bring proceedings to set aside any preference or transaction at an undervalue; if there are grounds for taking such course, that would be a reason for presenting an insolvency administration petition in order that a trustee in bankruptcy may be appointed and pursue such claims.

(2)   The order of distribution will follow the same order as in bankruptcy save that the reasonable funeral, testamentary and administration expenses have priority over the preferential debts and are therefore paid first. Once those expenses are paid the distribution will follow the order set out in IA 1986, s 328.

1   DPO 1986, art 4(1) ie without the making of an insolvency administration order.
2   DPO 1986, art 4(1); if the deceased was a joint tenant of property immediately before his death it may be necessary for a petition for an insolvency administration order to be presented so that it will be possible for the trustee of the estate to apply for an order under IA 1986, s 421A, see para **26.17** below, against the survivor to reimburse the estate the value of the deceased's beneficial interest lost by reason of the operation of the doctrine of survivorship.
3   DPO 1986, art 4(3).

26.5 Unless letters of administration were granted solely by reason of his being a creditor, a personal representative who, in good faith and at a time when he has no reason to believe that the deceased's estate is insolvent, pays the debt of any person (including himself) who is a creditor of the estate shall not, if it subsequently appears that the estate is insolvent, be liable to account to a creditor of the same degree as the paid creditor for the sum so paid. But he may be liable to a creditor of a superior degree[1]. This protection also applies where letters of administration were granted to the personal representative as a creditor if in good faith and not believing at the time of payment that the estate is insolvent, he pays the debt of another person who is a creditor of the estate. However, subject to the court's power under the Trustee Act 1925, s 61[2] to relieve a personal representative who has acted honestly and reasonably and ought fairly to be relieved, a personal representative will otherwise be liable if he does not distribute the estate according to the priorities laid down in IA 1986, s 328.

[1]   Administration of Estates Act 1971, s 10(2).
[2]   This provision is applicable to personal representatives by virtue of the definition of 'trustee' in the Trustee Act 1925, s 68(1) and see s 69(1).

C DEATH OF DEBTOR BEFORE PRESENTATION OF BANKRUPTCY PETITION

The insolvency administration petition

26.6 A petition for an insolvency administration order may be presented to the court by one or more of the deceased debtor's creditors, or by the supervisor or any person who is bound by an approved voluntary arrangement[1]. The petition must be in the prescribed form[2]. An insolvency administration petition must be served on (1) if a liquidator, within the meaning of the EC Insolvency Regulation, has been appointed in main proceedings under art 3(1) of the regulation, that liquidator; (2) unless the court directs otherwise, the debtor's personal representative; and (3) such other persons as the court may direct[3]. As the court has power to dispense with service of the petition on the personal representative it would appear that an order may be made on the petition where there is no personal representative in place. Once served, an insolvency administration petition may not be withdrawn without the leave of the court[4]. The court does have a general power, if it appears appropriate to do so on the grounds that there has been a contravention of the rules or for any other reason, to dismiss or stay an insolvency administration petition and make any appropriate order for costs[5].

[1]   See IA 1986, s 264, modified by the DPO 1986, art 3, Sch 1, Pt II, para 1. The petition is deemed to have been presented on the date of the deceased debtor's death, see para **26.15** below.
[2]   Ie DPO 1986, Sch 3, Form 1 or 2.
[3]   IA 1986, s 266(1), modified by the DPO 1986, art 3, Sch 1, Pt II, para 2.
[4]   IA 1986, s 266(2), modified by the DPO 1986, art 3, Sch 1, Pt II, para 2.
[5]   IA 1986, s 266(3), modified by the DPO 1986, art 3, Sch 1, Pt II, para 2.

26.7 A petition for an insolvency administration order may not be presented to the court after proceedings have been commenced in any court for the administration of the deceased debtor's estate[1]. Where such proceedings have been commenced, the court seised of those proceedings may, if satisfied that the estate is insolvent, transfer the proceedings to the court exercising bankruptcy jurisdiction[2]. On the transfer of the proceedings the bankruptcy court may make an insolvency administration order[3] as if a creditor's petition for such an order had been duly presented[4].

¹   IA 1986, s 271(2), modified by the DPO 1986, art 3, Sch 1, Pt II, para 5.
²   IA 1986, s 271(3), modified by the DPO 1986, art 3, Sch 1, Pt II, para 5.
³   The order made, must be in Form 5, set out in the DPO 1986, Sch 3.
⁴   IA 1986, s 271, modified by the DPO 1986, art 3, Sch 1, Pt II, para 5.

Grounds for petition

26.8 A creditor's petition must relate to one or more debts owed by the debtor, and the petitioning creditor, or each of the petitioning creditors must be a person to whom the debt or one of the debts is owed[1]. Subject to the rules relating to secured creditors[2], a creditor's petition may be presented to the court in respect of a debt or debts only if, at the time the petition is presented, and on the assumption that the debtor was alive[3], either (1) the amount of the debt, or the aggregate amount of the debts, owed by the debtor would have been equal to or exceeded the bankruptcy level[4]; or (2) the debt, or each of the debts, owed by the debtor would have been for a liquidated sum payable to the petitioning creditor, or one or more of the petitioning creditors, either immediately, or at some future time, and would have been unsecured.

¹   IA 1986, s 267(1), modified by the DPO 1986, art 3, Sch 1, Pt II, para 3.
²   IA 1986, s 269.
³   IA 1986, s 267, modified by the DPO 1986, art 3, Sch 1, Pt II, para 3.
⁴   £750, see para **8.51** above.

26.9 In cases where the debtor dies before the presentation of the petition, there is no need to serve a statutory demand, nor may reliance be placed on an incomplete execution to obtain an insolvency administration order[1].

¹   DPO 1986, Sch 1, Pt II does not include IA 1986, s 286 among the provisions applying to an insolvency administration petition.

Grounds upon which the court may make an insolvency administration order

26.10 The court may make an insolvency administration order if it is satisfied[1] that:

(a)   the debt, or one of the debts, in respect of which the petition was presented is a debt which:
   (i)   having been payable at the date of the petition or having since become payable, has neither been paid, nor secured, nor compounded for; or
   (ii)   has no reasonable prospect of being able to be paid when it falls due; and
(b)   there is a reasonable probability that the estate will be insolvent.

¹   IA 1986, s 271(1), modified by the DPO 1986, art 3, Sch 1, Pt II, para 5.

26.11 A 'reasonable probability' that the estate will be insolvent should speak for itself; there is no statutory guidance as to what is required. The making of an insolvency administration order does not invalidate any payment or act done in good faith by the personal representative before the date of the insolvency administration order[1]. Good faith involves a lack of awareness both of the presentation of the petition and of the insolvency of the deceased's estate.

[1]   IA 1986, s 271(5), modified by the DPO 1986, art 3, Sch 1, Pt II, para 5.

Personal representative's petition for insolvency administration order

26.12 A personal representative may present a petition[1] for an insolvency administration order only on the grounds that the estate of a deceased debtor is insolvent. Prospective insolvency is not a ground for an order. A personal representative who is uncertain as to the future solvency of the estate, because it has contingent liabilities, should take care not to make distributions until the position is clarified. If an insolvency administration order is eventually made it is deemed to have been made on the date of the debtor's death[2]. The insolvency administration petition must be accompanied by a statement of the deceased insolvent's affairs[3]. The court must make an insolvency administration order if satisfied that the deceased's estate is insolvent[4].

[1]   The petition must be in Form 6 set out in the DPO 1986, Sch 3.
[2]   See para **26.15** below.
[3]   See Form 7 set out in the DPO 1986, Sch 3.
[4]   IA 1986, s 273, substituted by the DPO 1986, art 3, Sch 1, Pt II, para 7. See also Form 4 of the DPO 1986, Sch 3 for the form of the order.

Duration

26.13 The administration in bankruptcy of the insolvent estate of a deceased debtor against which an insolvency administration order has been made, commences with the day on which the order is made[1], and continues unless annulled[2] until the completion of the administration of the estate.

[1]   IA 1986, s 278, modified by the DPO 1986, art 3, Sch 1, Pt II, para 10. The insolvency administration order is deemed to have been made on the date of the deceased debtor's death, see para **26.15** below.
[2]   There is no express provision as to when the order ceases. It would seem that because the DPO 1986 does not apply the IA 1986, s 278(b) but does apply s 282(1) and (4), the order continues unless annulled.

26.14 The court may annul an insolvency order at any time on the basis that (1) the order ought not to have been made in the first place[1]; or (2) the estate's debts have been paid or secured to the satisfaction of the court[2]. When the court annuls an insolvency administration order any sale or other disposition of property, payments or other acts of the official receiver or trustee remain valid. The annulment order will revest the estate's assets in the personal representative on such terms as may be appropriate[3].

[1]   IA 1986, s 282(1)(a), applied by the DPO 1986, art 3, Sch 1, Pt II, para 11.
[2]   IA 1986, s 282(1)(b), applied by the DPO 1986, art 3, Sch 1, Pt II, para 11.
[3]   IA 1986, s 282(4), applied by the DPO 1986, art 3, Sch 1, Pt II, para 11.

The deceased debtor's estate and its protection

26.15 The provisions of the IA 1986 which define the bankrupt's estate[1] and place restrictions on the disposition of property[2] and on proceedings and remedies against the property of the bankrupt[3], apply to the administration of an insolvent estate. The provisions are modified by the DPO 1986[4] so that they take effect as if the petition had been presented and the insolvency administration order had been made on the date of the death of the deceased debtor. The result of this modification is that all dispositions of property and payments made by the personal representative after the debtor's death are void unless ratified by the court[5]. This could involve a substantial period within which the personal representative may have made a number of dispositions of property unaware of the eventual petition and insolvency administration order. In *Re Vos, Dick v Kendall Freeman*[6] the deceased was a Lloyds name whose estate was administered for some eight years before an insolvency administration order was made on an insolvency administration petition presented by Lloyds. Payments made by the personal representative to solicitors appointed by him to act on behalf of the estate were held to be void. The personal representative could either have made an application for an order authorising him to use funds from the estate for the purpose of litigating with Lloyds by way of a Beddoe application[7] (which would involve persuading the court that the litigation was worthwhile) or by seeking authorisation from the court for any proposed disposition or, if the disposition had been made, validation. In the instant case, validation was refused in respect of dispositions made after the date on which the estate ought to have been put into insolvent administration.

[1] IA 1986, s 283.
[2] IA 1986, s 284.
[3] IA 1986, s 285.
[4] By the DPO 1986, art 3, Sch 1, Pt II, para 12.
[5] IA 1986, s 284(1), (2), applied by the DPO 1986, Sch 1, Pt II, para 12.
[6] [2006] BPIR 348.
[7] *Re Beddoe, Downes v Cottram* [1893] 1 Ch 547.

26.16 The recipient of a disposition rendered void because it was made after the presentation of the petition in the bankruptcy of a living person is protected against any remedy where he received the relevant property or payment before the making of the bankruptcy order in good faith for value and without notice that the petition had been presented[1]. In the case of an insolvent administration order this provision is modified to relate to dispositions made before the death of the debtor, and accordingly provides no protection at all for the third party who receives property or payments from a personal representative in good faith and for value before the date on which the petition for an insolvency administration order is presented.

[1] IA 1986, s 284(4).

26.17 The DPO 1986 made no specific provision for the relatively common incidence of the right of survivorship in the spouse of the deceased debtor who was the joint tenant of the matrimonial home or other property. It was confirmed by the Court of Appeal in *Re Palmer deceased* that by operation of the right of survivorship the beneficial share of a deceased joint tenant passed at the moment of death to the survivor and would not form part of the estate[1]. Once this was appreciated the general view was that it was inappropriate that the deceased's creditors should be deprived of the benefit of the deceased's share in any property he held as joint tenant at the date of his death. Altering the position was not however possible under the order making power available to the Lord Chancellor under the IA 1986, s 421[2]; this permits only modification of the IA 1986, and not the law generally. The law has now been changed by the Insolvency Act 2000[3] which inserts a new section, s 421A, into the IA 1986[4]. This enables the trustee to apply to the court for an order requiring the survivor[5] of a joint tenancy held with the deceased to pay to the trustee, for the benefit of the estate[6], an amount not exceeding the value lost to the estate by virtue of the operation of the law of survivorship[7]. Where there is more than one survivor an order may be made against all or any of them, but no individual survivor may be required to pay more than so much of the value lost to the estate as is properly attributable to him[8]. An application may be made in respect of any property to which the deceased was beneficially entitled immediately before his death where the petition for an insolvency administration order was presented within five years of the date of death[9]. An order is discretionary, the court being required to have regard to all the circumstances of the case, including the interests of the deceased's creditors and of the survivor[10]. However, unless the circumstances are exceptional, the court must assume that the interests of the deceased's creditors outweigh all other considerations[11]. The court may impose terms and conditions on any order made against the survivor or survivors as it thinks fit[12].

---

[1] *Re Palmer deceased (a debtor)* [1993] 4 All ER 812, [1994] Ch 316, CA. The court rejected the various arguments advanced on behalf of the trustee, in particular that the insolvency administration order (following decisions under the Bankruptcy Act 1914) should be deemed to be made at the earliest moment of the day on which it was actually made, and so should be deemed to precede the debtor's death (a fiction derived from the 'Hilary Rules' made by the judges in 1834). The court pointed out the absurdity of a fiction which deemed that an insolvency administration order was made before the debtor died: '... the time has come to say the fiction should have no place when the true facts are known, at least in cases where the court's jurisdiction is concerned', per Evans LJ at [1994] Ch 316 at 349C.

[2] The statutory authority for the DPO 1986.

[3] Insolvency Act 2000, s 11.

[4] The modifications of the IA 1986 which may be made by order under the IA 1986, s 421 may include any modifications which may be necessary or expedient in consequence of the IA 1986, s 421A: s 421A(6).

[5] Ie the person who, immediately before the deceased's death, was beneficially entitled as joint tenant with the deceased or, if the person who was so entitled dies after the making of the insolvency administration order, his personal representatives, IA 1986, s 421A(7).

[6] IA 1986, s 421A(5).

[7] IA 1986, s 421A(2).

[8] IA 1986, s 421A(8).

[9] IA 1986, s 421A(1).

[10] IA 1986, s 421A(3); the survivor will usually be the widow.

[11] IA 1986, s 421A(3); the same formulation is used by the IA 1986, s 335A in relation to an application under the Trusts of Land and Appointment of Trustees Act 1996, s 14 for the sale of land comprising the home or former home of the bankrupt or his (or her) spouse or former spouse. Decisions of the court in respect of the IA 1986, s 335A may have relevance to an application under the IA 1986, s 421A(2).

[12] IA 1986, s 421A(4).

26.18 The definition of the deceased debtor's estate is modified by restricting the personal and household equipment and provisions which are exempted from comprising part of the estate[1] to those belonging to the family of the deceased debtor, and by including in the estate the capacity to exercise and take proceedings for exercising all such powers over and in respect of property as might have been exercised by the deceased's personal representative for the benefit of the estate on the date of the insolvency administration order[2].

[1] IA 1986, s 283(2), modified by the DPO 1986, art 3, Sch 1, Pt II, para 12.
[2] IA 1986, s 283(4A), enacted by the DPO 1986, art 3, Sch 1, Pt II, para 12.

Investigation of the affairs of the deceased debtor

26.19 Between the making of the insolvency administration order and the date on which the deceased debtor's estate vests in a trustee, the official receiver becomes the receiver and manager of the estate[1]. The court has the power to appoint an interim receiver in the administration of an insolvent estate, if it is considered necessary to protect the deceased debtor's property[2].

[1] IA 1986, s 287, applied by the DPO 1986, art 3, Sch 1, Pt II, para 14.
[2] IA 1986, s 286(1), applied by the DPO 1986, art 3, Sch 1, Pt II, para 13.

26.20 Once an insolvency administration order has been made, the personal representative, or if there is no personal representative such person as the court may direct on the application of the official receiver, must submit to the official receiver a statement of the deceased debtor's affairs containing particulars of the assets and liabilities of the estate as at the date of the insolvency administration order together with other particulars of the affairs of the deceased debtor in the prescribed form[1] or as the official receiver may require[2]. The statement must be submitted before the end of the period of 56 days beginning with the date of a request by the official receiver for the statement or such longer period as he or the court may allow[3]. The official receiver may if he thinks fit release a personal representative or such person who has been directed by the court from the duty to submit a statement of affairs or extend the period within which it must be submitted, and where the official receiver has refused to exercise either such power the court, if it thinks fit, may exercise it[4].

[1] Ie Form 7 set out in the DPO 1986, Sch 3. The DTI produce a guidance booklet (Form B44.24) to assist generally anyone who has to complete a statement of affairs form.
[2] IA 1986, s 288(1), modified by the DPO 1986, art 3, Sch 1, Pt II, para 15.
[3] IA 1986, s 288(2), modified by the DPO 1986, art 3, Sch 1, Pt II, para 15.
[4] IA 1986, s 288(2), applied by the DPO 1986, art 3, Sch 1, Pt II, para 15, and construed through the DPO 1986, Sch 1, Pt I.

26.21 The official receiver is not under any duty to investigate the conduct or affairs of the deceased debtor but may if he thinks fit report to the court on the activities of the deceased debtor[1].

[1] IA 1986, s 289, substituted by the DPO 1986, art 3, Sch 1, Pt II, para 16.

26.22 The personal representative, or such other person as the court may order, is under a duty to deliver to the official receiver possession of the insolvent estate, all books, papers and records which relate to the insolvent estate and which are in his possession or control[1], and to assist the official receiver in the protection of property which cannot be delivered to him[2].

[1] IA 1986, s 291(1), applied by the DPO 1986, art 3, Sch 1, Pt II, para 17.
[2] IA 1986, s 291(2), applied by the DPO 1986, art 3, Sch 1, Pt II, para 17.

The appointment and control of a trustee of the deceased debtor's estate

26.23 A trustee may be appointed to, or removed or released from a deceased person's insolvent estate in a similar manner to that applying in a living bankrupt's bankruptcy[1]. The creditors may form a creditors' committee for the control of the trustee[2], and any meeting of creditors summoned for any purposes relating to the trustee and his administration of the estate is governed by the rules regarding the trustee in bankruptcy and the creditors' committee[3]. The trustee of a deceased debtor's estate is under the general control of the court[4] and may be held liable by the court where he has misapplied or retained or become accountable for any money or other property comprised in the insolvent estate or when the deceased debtor's estate has suffered any loss in consequence of any misfeasance or breach of fiduciary or other duty by a trustee of the estate in the carrying out of his functions[5].

[1] IA 1986, ss 292–297, applied by the DPO 1986, art 3, Sch 1, Pt II, para 18. The trustee must be a qualified insolvency practitioner in relation to the deceased, DPO 1986, art 3, Sch 1, Pt II, para 36.
[2] IA 1986, ss 301, 302, applied by the DPO 1986, art 3, Sch 1, Pt II, para 18.
[3] DPO 1986, art 3, Sch 1, Pt II, para 18.
[4] IA 1986, s 303, applied by the DPO 1986, art 3, Sch 1, Pt II, para 19.
[5] IA 1986, s 304, applied by the DPO 1986, art 3, Sch 1, Pt II, para 19.

Distribution of deceased debtor's estate

26.24 The administration of the deceased debtor's estate by the trustee[1], the right to reclaim items of excess value[2], the proof of debts by creditors[3], (subject to the priority given to the reasonable funeral, testamentary and administration expenses)[4] the distribution of the assets of the deceased debtor's estate realised by the trustee[5], and the priority of debts[6] is in accordance with the same law and procedure as that which applies in the bankruptcy of an individual. The statutory provisions relating to the claim by the trustee of after-acquired property for the deceased debtor's estate apply from the date of death of the deceased debtor[7]. Similarly the date of calculation of preferential debts[8], and the date from which interest payable on bankruptcy debts is to be paid in its due order of priority[9] is the date of death of the deceased debtor.

[1] IA 1986, s 305, modified by the DPO 1986, art 3, Sch 1, Pt II, para 20.
[2] IA 1986, s 308, modified by the DPO 1986, art 3, Sch 1, Pt II, para 23.
[3] IA 1986, s 322, applied by the DPO 1986, art 3, Sch 1, Pt II, para 23.
[4] DPO 1986, art 4(2).

5   IA 1986, ss 324 and 326, applied by the DPO 1986, art 3, Sch 1, Pt II, para 23.
6   IA 1986, s 328, applied by the DPO 1986, art 3, Sch 1, Pt II, para 24.
7   IA 1986, s 307, modified by the DPO 1986, art 3, Sch 1, Pt II, para 22.
8   IA 1986, s 328, modified by the DPO 1986, art 3, Sch 1, Pt II, para 24.
9   IA 1986, s 328, modified by the DPO 1986, art 3, Sch 1, Pt II, para 24.

26.25 In the exercise of his functions in the administration of a deceased debtor's estate, the trustee must have regard to any claim by the personal representative to payment of reasonable funeral, testamentary and administration expenses incurred by him in respect of the deceased debtor's estate or, if there is no such personal representative, to any claim by any other person for payment of any such expenses incurred by him in respect of the estate, provided that the trustee has sufficient funds in hand for the purpose, and such claims shall have priority over any preferential debts[1].

1   IA 1986, s 305(5), modified by the DPO 1986, art 3, Sch 1, Pt II, para 20.

26.26 Any surplus remaining after payment in full with interest of all the creditors of the deceased debtor's estate, and the payment of the expenses of the insolvent estate's administration is to be paid to the personal representative unless the court orders otherwise[1].

1   IA 1986, s 330(5), modified by the DPO 1986, art 3, Sch 1, Pt II, para 25.

Effect of insolvency administration order on prior rights and transactions

26.27 The effect of an insolvency administration order on the right of occupation of the deceased debtor's spouse[1], transactions at an undervalue[2], preferences[3], extortionate credit transactions[4], a general assignment of book debts[5], contracts to which the deceased debtor was a party[6], distress[7], apprenticeships[8] and liens on books, papers and other documents[9] is the same as that of a bankruptcy order. For the purposes of transactions at undervalue and preferences, the relevant time is assessed by reference to the appropriate period ending with the date of death of the deceased debtor[10].

1   IA 1986, s 336, applied by the DPO 1986, art 3, Sch 1, Pt II, para 26.
2   IA 1986, s 339, applied by the DPO 1986, art 3, Sch 1, Pt II, para 26.
3   IA 1986, s 340, applied by the DPO 1986, art 3, Sch 1, Pt II, para 26.
4   IA 1986, s 343, applied by the DPO 1986, art 3, Sch 1, Pt II, para 28.
5   IA 1986, s 344, applied by the DPO 1986, art 3, Sch 1, Pt II, para 28.
6   IA 1986, s 345, applied by the DPO 1986, art 3, Sch 1, Pt II, para 28.
7   IA 1986, s 347, applied by the DPO 1986, art 3, Sch 1, Pt II, para 28.
8   IA 1986, s 348, applied by the DPO 1986, art 3, Sch 1, Pt II, para 28.
9   IA 1986, s 349, applied by the DPO 1986, art 3, Sch 1, Pt II, para 28.
10   IA 1986, s 341, modified by the DPO 1986, art 3, Sch 1, Pt II, para 27.

Insolvency administration offences

26.28 The deceased debtor will be beyond the jurisdiction of the court, but a third party is guilty of an offence[1] if, in the 12 months before the date of the death of the deceased debtor he acquired or received property[2] from the deceased debtor knowing or believing that the deceased debtor owed money in respect of the property and that the deceased debtor did not intend, or was unlikely to be able to pay the money which he so owed[3]. A person is not guilty of this offence if the acquisition or receipt of the property was in the ordinary course of business carried on by the deceased debtor at the time of the disposal, acquisition or receipt[4]. In determining whether any property is acquired or received in the ordinary course of a business carried on by the deceased debtor, regard may be had, in particular, to the price paid for the property[5].

1   IA 1986, s 430, applied by the DPO 1986, art 3, Sch 1, Pt II, para 36.
2   Note that it is not a defence in any proceedings for one of the acts that anything relied on was done outside England and Wales, see the IA 1986, s 350(4), applied by the DPO 1986, art 3, Sch 1, Pt II, para 28.
3   IA 1986, s 359(2), modified by the DPO 1986, art 3, Sch 1, Pt II, para 29.
4   IA 1986, s 359(3), modified by the DPO 1986, art 3, Sch 1, Pt II, para 29.
5   IA 1986, s 359(4), modified by the DPO 1986, art 3, Sch 1, Pt II, para 29.

26.29 The fact that an insolvency administration order has been annulled does not preclude a conviction for an offence[1], but criminal proceedings may not be instituted after annulment[2]. Proceedings for an offence must not be instituted except by the Secretary of State, or either by or with the consent of the Director of Public Prosecutions[3].

1   IA 1986, s 350(1), applied by the DPO 1986, art 3, Sch 1, Pt II, para 28.
2   IA 1986, s 350(2), applied by the DPO 1986, art 3, Sch 1, Pt II, para 28.
3   IA 1986, s 350(5), applied by the DPO 1986, art 3, Sch 1, Pt II, para 28.

D DEATH OF DEBTOR AFTER PRESENTATION OF BANKRUPTCY PETITION

Continuation of proceedings

26.30 Unless the court orders otherwise, if a debtor by or against whom a bankruptcy petition has been presented dies, the proceedings continue as if he were alive[1]. Should a debtor die between presentation of a petition and service the court may order service to be effected on his personal representative or such other person as it thinks fit[2]. The court may dispense with service on a personal representative, as for example where there is none appointed[3]. The personal representative of the deceased debtor's estate, or such other person as the court on the application of the official receiver may direct, must then prepare a statement of the deceased debtor's affairs as at the date of the order containing the prescribed particulars[4]. The IR 1986[5] apply to this statement as they apply to the statement of affairs required of a living bankrupt[6]. The time limit for the submission of the statement of affairs to the official receiver is 56 days from the date of the request for the statement by the official receiver, but either he or the court may allow further time[7].

1   DPO 1986, art 5(1) subject to the modifications to the IA 1986 contained in the DPO 1986, Sch 2.
2   DPO 1986, art 5(3).
3   DPO 1986, art 5(3).
4   See DPO 1986, Sch 3, Form 7.
5   Ie IR 1986, rr 6.58–6.66.

6   IA 1986, ss 288(1) and 330(4)(b) modified by the DPO 1986, art 5(1), Sch 2.
7   IA 1986, s 288(2) modified by the DPO 1986, art 5(1), Sch 2.

Priority of reasonable funeral, testamentary and administration expenses

26.31 The reasonable funeral, testamentary and administration expenses relating to the deceased debtor have priority over preferential debts[1].

1   Ie the DPO 1986, art 5(1), Sch 2.

Final distribution

26.32 Although the reasonable funeral and testamentary expenses have priority over any preferential debts it is essential that the personal representative of the deceased debtor gives notice of such expenses to the trustee. After the final date for claims against the estate to be established the trustee must defray any outstanding expenses of the insolvency administration out of the deceased debtor's estate. If he intends to declare a final dividend, the trustee must declare and distribute that dividend without regard to the claim either of any creditor in respect of a debt not already proved in the insolvency administration or of the personal representative in respect of any funeral and testamentary expenses of which notice has not already been given to the trustee[1].

1   IA 1986, s 330(4)(b) modified by the DPO 1986, art 5, Sch 2, para 2.

E EFFECT OF DEATH ON INDIVIDUAL VOLUNTARY ARRANGEMENTS

Death before IVA is approved

26.33 The DPO 1986 brings a proposed IVA[1] to an end if the arrangements have not been approved by the creditors before the death of the debtor making the proposal for an IVA. Thus where an interim order has been made[2], but the debtor dies before he has submitted his proposal, the nominee must give notice to the court of the death of the debtor[3] and on receiving such notice the court must discharge the interim order[4]. Where an interim order has been made[5], and the nominee has submitted a report to the court on receipt of which the court is satisfied that a creditors' meeting should be summoned to consider the debtor's proposal, but the debtor dies before a creditors' meeting has been held, then the meeting is cancelled and, if the debtor was at the date of his death an undischarged bankrupt, the personal representative must give notice of the death to the trustee of his estate and to the official receiver[6].

1   For IVAs generally see **Chapter 6** above.
2   IA 1986, s 252.
3   IA 1986, s 256(1A) added by the DPO 1986, art 3, Sch 1, Pt III, para 1.
4   IA 1986, s 256(1B) added by the DPO 1986, art 3, Sch 1, Pt III, para 1.
5   IA 1986, s 252.
6   IA 1986, s 257 modified by the DPO 1986, art 3, Sch 1, Pt III, para 2.

Death after approval of voluntary arrangement

26.34 Where the creditors' meeting summoned to consider the IVA approves the proposals[1] and the chairman of the meeting has reported the result to the court, the voluntary arrangement takes effect and, subject to any provision in the arrangement to the effect that the death of the debtor brings the IVA to an end, is then implemented by the supervisor notwithstanding the subsequent death of the debtor[2]. It would appear however that if the debtor dies after the approval by the creditors' meeting, but before the report to the court, then because the IA 1986, ss 260–262 are disapplied on the death of the debtor[3], the voluntary arrangement cannot be enforced as a valid and binding arrangement[4], the court is not required to act on the basis of the approval[5], and the approval cannot be challenged by any of the interested parties[6]. It is somewhat strange that the DPO 1986 should apparently permit an IVA to continue after approval by creditors but only if the chairman has reported the meeting's decision to the court. The report to the court would seem to be merely an administrative function so that, if appropriate, the court may discharge the interim order. It is not for the court to review or interfere with the creditors' decision. In the ordinary course the IVA takes effect as if made by the debtor at the meeting[7] not when the result of the meeting is reported to the court. There is no obvious advantage in preventing an IVA approved by the creditors before the death of the debtor taking effect, and it is to be hoped that the court will construe para 4 of Pt III of the DPO 1986 in a purposive way to enable such a result to be achieved.

[1]   IA 1986, s 258.
[2]   IA 1986, s 263 modified by the DPO 1986, art 3, Sch 1, Pt III, para 5.
[3]   DPO 1986, art 3, Sch 1, Pt III, para 4.
[4]   Ie IA 1986, s 260.
[5]   Ie IA 1986, s 261.
[6]   Ie IA 1986, s 262.
[7]   See IA 1986, s 260(2).

26.35 Where the debtor dies after the arrangement has been approved, the personal representative succeeds to the deceased debtor's rights to challenge any act or decision of the supervisor in the course of his implementation of the IVA[1].

[1]   IA 1986, s 263 modified by the DPO 1986, art 3, Sch 1, Pt III, para 5(a).

Chapter 27

SOLICITORS ACTING IN BANKRUPTCY MATTERS

A   The solicitor and his client
B   Privilege
C   Lien
D   Undertakings

A THE SOLICITOR AND HIS CLIENT

27.1 Solicitors acting in bankruptcy or other personal insolvency matters will often find themselves in very different roles and there are particular pitfalls in each role.

The individual voluntary arrangement

27.2 The most common problem arising for the solicitor in the individual voluntary arrangement (IVA) stems from the very identity of his own client. If an insolvency practitioner, as nominee or supervisor, needs the assistance of a solicitor then the solicitor's duty is simply and clearly to his client. However, a very common situation arises in which a debtor consults a solicitor who either advises him in relation to, or assists him in the formulation of, a proposal for an IVA. He will occasionally secure an interim order. He will sometimes assist in seeing through the proposal at a creditors' meeting. Thereafter, with knowledge of the circumstances surrounding the debtor's affairs, the solicitor will often be instructed by the supervisor. Here lies a clear potential for a conflict of interest. If all goes smoothly, with no conflicting information coming to the attention of the supervisor, and with the debtor co-operating in all respects, and fulfilling his arrangement in accordance with the proposal, no professional difficulties arise.

Petitioning for bankruptcy

27.3 However, not all IVAs go smoothly and many fail, leaving the supervisor with a duty to petition for the debtor's bankruptcy. The solicitor thus moves from a potential to a real conflict. At first view, there is no difficulty. The solicitor will recognise that he should not act for the supervisor against his former client. However, the reality is that in many cases insolvency practitioners introduce, or invoke the assistance of, solicitors in formulating the more complex proposals and in seeing through applications for interim orders. This may be necessary where there is, for example, a current bankruptcy petition pending before the court. When the insolvency practitioner introduces the debtor he is introducing a client to the solicitor. This is so even if, as often happens, the costs involved are dealt with as part of the proposal itself.

27.4 If there is a subsequent difference between the debtor and his supervisor the supervisor often feels a proprietorial interest in the services of the solicitor he has introduced, and worked with, on the IVA. Solicitors acting for the debtor before an IVA, and anticipating acting for the supervisor in the course of that IVA, should be careful at the outset to warn their debtor client of the possibility of a subsequent conflict arising and must, of course, be careful not to act at all if that conflict actually arises.

Acting for the petitioning creditor

27.5 The most commonly overlooked problem faced by solicitors acting for creditors is that concerned with the acceptance of payments on account. The passing of the old concept of the doctrine of relation back whereby, under the Bankruptcy Act 1914 a bankruptcy was deemed to commence at a date, often several months, before the making of the receiving order, caused many solicitors to proceed on the basis that payments on account can be received and safely accounted for to the client. However, dispositions by a debtor between the presentation of a petition and the vesting of his property in the trustee require ratification. IA 1986, s 284 contains provisions for the subsequent ratification of dispositions but payments on account to only one creditor are unlikely to obtain that ratification and should be repaid to the trustee in bankruptcy[1]. If a solicitor has accounted to his client for such payments on account, at a time when a petition was still pending against the debtor, he must warn his client, clearly, of the prospect of a repayment having to be made to the bankrupt's estate if the petition is going to proceed to a bankruptcy order. The extent of payments on account can clearly affect a creditor's decision about whether or not to proceed to a bankruptcy order at all.

[1] See para **16.28** above.

Public examination

27.6 A solicitor acting for a creditor who wishes to ask questions at a public examination should bear in mind that creditors are only permitted to question the bankrupt 'with the approval of the court (made known at the hearing or in advance of it)'[1]. These days public examinations, especially those at which a creditor or creditors wish to appear or be represented, are sufficiently rare for it to be impossible to set out any helpful guidelines for when or when not such questioning may be approved. Under the 1914 Act, when there was invariably a public examination, but when this qualification did not apply, there was no difficulty over creditors being represented. In case there is doubt, and so that costs are not wasted in preparing for an attendance which may not be approved by the court, an application should be made to the court in advance of the public examination, so that a particular creditor may secure leave to be represented in good time.

1   IR 1986, r 6.175(2).

Acting for the debtor

27.7 A solicitor is entitled to receive money from his debtor client for the purposes of funding the costs of opposing the bankruptcy proceedings themselves[1]. However, this does not extend to the conduct of an appeal[2]. Where a solicitor is holding funds for his client for a particular purpose those funds cannot be set off by the solicitor against his claim for costs incurred in the bankruptcy or other matters[3]. However, if monies are held by a solicitor in his client account for or on account of costs then those monies can be applied to the proper costs of dealing with the bankruptcy proceedings[4].

1   *Re Sinclair, ex p Payne* (1885) 15 QBD 616.
2   *Re A Debtor (No 490 of 1935)* [1937] Ch 92.
3   *Re Pollitt, ex p Minor* [1893] 1 QB 455, CA and see *Re British Folding Bed Company, ex p Trustee v NA Woodiwiss & Co* [1948] Ch 635, [1948] 2 All ER 216.
4   See *Prekookeaska Plovidba v LNT Lines SrL* [1988] 3 All ER 897, [1989] 1 WLR 753.

27.8 If possible, solicitors should protect themselves by requesting third party funds to cover their costs, satisfying themselves, insofar as they can, that any such payments come from third party funds.

27.9 In cases where a public examination is held the debtor may employ a solicitor or counsel 'who may put to him such questions as the court may allow for the purposes of enabling him to explain or qualify any answers given by him and may make representations on his behalf'[1].

1   IR 1986, r 6.175(3).

Acting for the trustee

27.10 A trustee in bankruptcy has authority to employ a solicitor or other agent to assist him in the carrying out of his duties. This power is ancillary to the carrying out of his other duties as trustee[1]. He has no need to secure the prior authority of the committee of creditors, if there is one. However, if he employs a solicitor he must inform the committee that he has done so[2].

1   See IA 1986, s 314 and Sch 5, Pt III.
2   IA 1986, s 314(6).

27.11 It is not uncommon for a trustee in bankruptcy to instruct the solicitors who act for, or acted for, the petitioning creditors. Where there are difficulties in locating or recovering assets this can be of great advantage to the creditors generally and was approved in principle in *Re Schuppan*[1]. But the court retains a supervisory jurisdiction over the solicitor and, although it should exercise the jurisdiction with caution given the interference entailed with a party's choice of representative, may order a solicitor not to act where justified by his holding information confidential to the opposing party or being subject to some other conflict of interest or duty[2].

[1]   [1996] BPIR 486. See also *Re Baron Investments (Holdings) Ltd (in liqn)* [2000] 1 BCLC 272.
[2]   *Re Recover Ltd, Hornan v Latif Group SL* [2003] EWHC 536 (Ch), [2003] 2 BCLC 186.

27.12 The trustee has authority to agree his solicitor's fees but he may, as may the committee of creditors, call for the solicitor to have his costs assessed by the court[1].

[1]   IR 1986, r 7.34.

27.13 If a solicitor is required to submit his bill for detailed assessment, he must deliver his bill to the appropriate officer within three months of being requested to do so, or he forfeits his claim entirely[1].

[1]   IR 1986, r 7.35(4).

B PRIVILEGE

The bankrupt's papers

27.14 The Insolvency Act 1986 ('IA 1986') provides for the delivery to the official receiver, on a bankruptcy order being made[1] and to the trustee on the acquisition of control by the trustee[2], of all books, papers and other records which relate to the bankrupt's estate or affairs 'including any which would be privileged from disclosure in any proceedings'. IA 1986, s 291 also refers to documents 'under the control' of the bankrupt.

[1]   IA 1986, s 291(1)(b).
[2]   IA 1986, s 306.

27.15 If the bankrupt's solicitor's costs have been paid, so that no question of lien arises, then the solicitor's files, other than (as some would argue, attendance notes and solicitor's own records) are under the theoretical control of the trustee. Ownership will have passed to the official receiver or the trustee who may simply call for their delivery up.

27.16 This simple proposition can however lead to some awkward problems for solicitors in connection with privilege attaching to certain types of documents and information, particularly as between husbands and wives or between business partners. A trustee in bankruptcy must be treated as standing in the shoes of the bankrupt for the purposes of privilege in relation to matters in which the solicitor acted for the bankrupt. Thus, as between spouses or partners against whom a trustee might have a claim, that spouse or partner cannot assert legal privilege against the trustee[1]. Accordingly the trustee is in the same position as the bankrupt would have been, so that the rule which recognises that joint clients cannot maintain privilege against each other is preserved. The privilege of the bankrupt is thus devolved to the trustee, who is entitled to obtain privileged information from the bankrupt. This can be very relevant in cases relating to the transfer of the matrimonial home, as was the case in *Re Konigsberg*[2].

[1] See *Re Konigsberg, ex p Trustee v Konigsberg* [1989] 3 All ER 289, [1989] 1 WLR 1257.
[2] [1989] 3 All ER 289, [1989] 1 WLR 1257.

27.17 It does not follow from the fact that legal privilege passes to a trustee in bankruptcy that he has power to waive privilege in relation to matters which do not concern the estate or affairs of the bankrupt. He can however waive privilege in relation to the bankrupt's financial affairs generally so as to render the bankrupt's solicitor obliged to provide privileged information concerning the bankrupt to the Serious Fraud Office[1].

[1] *Re Cook (Dennis Michael)* [1999] BPIR 881.

27.18 There can be no legal privilege for a communication with or from a solicitor in preparation for or in furtherance of a fraud or other crime. Detailed analyses of legal professional privilege and the circumstances in which the court will override it in cases of fraud are contained in the judgment of Vinelott J in *Derby & Co Ltd v Weldon (No 7)*[1], and of Schiemann LJ in *Barclays Bank v Eustice*[2].

[1] [1990] 3 All ER 161, [1990] 1 WLR 1156; see also *Finers (a firm) v Miro* [1991] 1 All ER 182, [1991] 1 WLR 35, CA.
[2] [1995] 4 All ER 511, [1996] BPIR 1, CA.

Examination of solicitor

27.19 If a trustee in bankruptcy decides to invoke his investigatory powers under IA 1986, s 366, by an examination of a solicitor, it is the usual practice (to the extent that most courts require it in the case of witnesses from the professions) to send to that solicitor a questionnaire which sets out the questions being examined. This gives the solicitor the opportunity of considering in advance any questions of privilege which may arise. However, where there is genuine urgency, not of the trustees in bankruptcy own making, and where highly sensitive information might justify it, the court may order an s 366 examination of a solicitor without notice, but such an order is very rarely justified[1].

[1] *Re Cook (Dennis Michael)* [1999] BPIR 881.

27.20 If he has acted for the bankrupt then in respect of most information the privilege which was formerly that of the bankrupt will have passed to the trustee and, therefore, cannot be claimed against him.

27.21 It should be borne in mind that the records which pass to the trustee by virtue of the operation of IA 1986, s 311 are the records which relate to the bankrupt's estate. Those records which might relate to his personal status, or perhaps to advice concerning the commission of a criminal offence by the bankrupt, or to claims in damages for libel or to property not falling into the bankrupt's estate, such as property which he holds as a trustee, are not covered by the provisions of IA 1986, s 311 and are not therefore available to the trustee.

27.22 When a solicitor is caught in 'cross fire' between his former client, now bankrupt, and a trustee or some outside agency, such as the Serious Fraud Office, the solicitor may 'at the extremity of' the class of persons who may be so described be a 'person dissatisfied' by the acts of a trustee in bankruptcy and apply to the court under IA 1986, s 303 for directions in respect of trustees' conduct.

27.23 Although no solicitor can be made to assist a trustee save under the formal statutory provisions, the fact is that official receivers and trustees in bankruptcy very often ask solicitors to a bankrupt for informal assistance on certain questions. It may be that no questions of privilege arise or that the bankrupt simply waives any possible question which might arise. The provision of information requested by the trustee might be very time-consuming, requiring research into files going back for months or years. Trustees often indicate that they are not willing to pay fees for the provision of information while in cases where there is no trustee (often because there are no funds) the official receiver understandably indicates that he can incur no fee because he has no funds to pay such a fee.

27.24 In formal examinations under IA 1986, s 366, where an order for examination is made, a solicitor is entitled to a fee as a professional witness. In a remark made in *Re Aveling Barford Ltd*[1] Hoffmann J likened the position of solicitors who were requested to provide an administrative receiver with information under the provisions of IA 1986, s 236 with the recipient of a *subpoena duces tecum* or *ad testificandum*, by which a citizen is required to perform a public duty in aid of the administration of justice, than with, say, a Norwich Pharmacal order or Mareva injunction affecting a third party at the instance of a private litigant. Though leaving the question open, he suggested that there was no reason why there should be a presumption under IA 1986, s 236 that a respondent is entitled to be indemnified against his costs of complying with the order.

[1]   [1988] 3 All ER 1019, [1989] 1 WLR 360 (obiter).

27.25 When solicitors sought to set aside orders for their oral examination and the production of documents in circumstances where the court found that they had made unjustified claims to legal professional privilege they were ordered to pay the costs of the trustee in bankruptcy on an indemnity basis[1].

[1]   *Re Murjani* [1996] 1 All ER 65, [1996] BPIR 325.

Solicitors' costs

27.26 In cases which fall short of a formal statutory examination, the question of the cost of the provision of information can cause problems.

27.27 One practical solution employed in appropriate cases is for the solicitor to deliver up his file or files to the trustee or official receiver, securing an undertaking to return it on being asked to do so. The research can then be carried out by the trustee or official receiver who can copy what information he needs and return the file in due course.

27.28 This may be of use in cases where there are limited funds but the trustee is willing to invest his own time in investigations. Where there are funds there may be genuine disagreement on whether or not a fee should be payable for the provision of information. Before the current legislation came into force, the Law Society took the advice of leading counsel and published a summary of that advice in its 1974 Guide to Professional Conduct. Whilst that Guide is no longer in force, there is no reason to suppose that the advice therein reflected is not good today. That summary advice, with the new statutory provisions inserted where appropriate, is set out (with the kind permission of the Law Society) below:

'(a)   Except under s 366 of the Insolvency Act 1986, the solicitor is under no obligation to supply information or documents (other than documents of title to property which has vested in the trustee) to the trustee. Accordingly, if the trustee asks for information or documents (other than as aforesaid) it would be proper for the solicitor, before complying, to ask the trustee to pay his reasonable costs of complying with the trustee's request, and it would be proper for the solicitor to refuse to comply with the trustee's request if the trustee has refused to pay the solicitor's reasonable costs of complying.

(b)   It is, in practice, not uncommon for a trustee to agree to pay a modest fee, where the matters on which the information is requested are of some considerable age and the work of looking out files and searching through them is involved, and for the solicitor to be reimbursed the costs of any copying work he is asked to carry out. Should the solicitor refuse to co-operate with the Official Receiver or trustee, except at a fee greater than that which the trustee is able or willing to pay, he may well be faced with an application to the court for his examination under s 366.

(c)   If an examination under s 366 is ordered, the solicitor who attends is entitled not merely to conduct money tendered with the summons, but also to be paid his witness allowance under r 9.6(4). A solicitor is entitled to expenses as a professional witness.

(d)   In cases of examination under s 366 there is no general right to be reimbursed the costs of appearing by counsel or another solicitor. It would seem in any event that a solicitor would only need representation in the exceptional circumstances that he was being examined by the trustee in a potentially adverse capacity. Awards of costs in favour of witnesses are rare, although they have been known to be made.'

27.29 It should be borne in mind that it is now available to the court to make orders for the costs of an examination against the witness[1].

¹ IR 1986, r 9.6.

27.30 The above should be read bearing in mind that the current provisions of IA 1986, s 311 concerning the delivery up of documents, which may in the ordinary course be privileged documents, was not a provision which applied in the 1914 legislation.

C LIEN

Operation of lien

27.31 A solicitor's lien entitles him to retain documents as against his client and includes the right to refuse to produce the documents under a *subpoena duces tecum* at the instance of a client who has become involved in litigation. However, it was never possible to decline to answer a particular question, put under a statutory examination, now under IA 1986, s 366, because the provision of an answer would have the effect of defeating that lien.

27.32 IA 1986, s 349 makes the position clear in relation to any lien save one which applies to documents which give title to property and which are held as such. IA 1986, s 349 provides that a lien over the papers or records of the bankrupt, and this must include his solicitor's file, is unenforceable to deprive the official receiver or the trustee of the bankrupt's estate of such documentation. This statutory assistance to office holders came into effect not long before the court assisted an administrative receiver to overcome a solicitor's lien by applying the dicta in *Re Toleman and England, ex p Bramble*[1] to find that a solicitor's lien only entitled him to retain documents as against his client and that he could not assert it against third parties, such as administrative receivers[2].

¹ (1880) 13 Ch D 885.
² *Re Aveling Barford Ltd* [1988] 3 All ER 1019, [1989] 1 WLR 360.

27.33 The exception to IA 1986, s 349 relating to documents which prove title to property, 'and are held as such', extends to documents of title, for example share certificates or deeds and documents giving legal title, such as mortgages or debentures which might be lodged with solicitors as security for their fees. It appears that such a lodgment by way of security would enable a solicitor to assert his lien. Such a claim was upheld in a company in liquidation case (where the statutory provisions are the same) in *Brereton v Nicholls*[1].

¹ [1993] BCLC 593.

D UNDERTAKINGS

Liability on undertaking

27.34 An innumerable quantity of business, conveyancing and other financial transactions proceed, these days, upon the basis of solicitors' undertakings. Similarly when a debtor's financial position is bleak, a solicitor's undertaking, perhaps to preserve a fund, or dispose of a fund in a particular way, may be the only thing which will stop a creditor from pressing on to the bankruptcy of his debtor.

27.35 In many cases, the bankruptcy of a client supervening an undertaking given by a solicitor will not affect the undertaking or the solicitor's legal or professional obligation to comply with it. If the solicitor holds deeds, or a fund of money, on trust for a bank or other interested party, the bankruptcy of his client will not place the solicitor in jeopardy. However, where a solicitor gives an undertaking for payment out of an indicated fund not relating to a property in which the recipient of the undertaking has an interest (as would a bank or building society) then the bankruptcy of the solicitor's client can place the solicitor in grave difficulty. He may be liable professionally or legally on his undertaking while the fund on which he intended to rely will have passed to the official receiver or a trustee in bankruptcy by reason of the bankruptcy of the client.

27.36 The solicitor in this position may be able to argue that his undertaking has created an equitable charge over the fund in question. Unlike a company in liquidation where unregistered charges of particular assets are void against the liquidator if not registered, there are no provisions in the bankruptcy legislation requiring the registration of legal or equitable charges over the assets of a person who subsequently becomes bankrupt. Where solicitors in contested ancillary relief proceedings held funds in a designated deposit account against a payment ordered by the court to be made by the husband against whom a bankruptcy order was made to his wife, the court ordered that the sum once received by the solicitors no longer formed part of the husband's estate in bankruptcy because it was earmarked as the source of the ordered lump sum payment[1].

[1]   *Re Mordant, Mordant v Halls* [1996] BPIR 302.

27.37 The cautious solicitor, however, habitually limits any undertaking to his, or his firm, having legal control of the fund in question. The obvious problem with this, however, is that it may be unacceptable to the astute creditor as a satisfactory undertaking and may therefore not achieve for the client the necessary respite he needs.

Chapter 28

RIGHTS AGAINST BANKRUPT'S INSURERS

A   Statutory basis
B   Third Parties (Rights against Insurers) Act 1930

A STATUTORY BASIS

Assignment under statute

28.1 At common law an injured third party had no rights against the insurers of an insured person or company even where the risk insured against was damage or loss to a class of persons of which the third party was one. The third party, not being a party to the contract of insurance, could not enforce it for his own benefit. Neither could he attach or garnishee money payable by the insurers to the insured under the policy of insurance[1]. The rights of an insured against the insurer under a contract of liability insurance are rights to be indemnified against any payment the insured is legally liable to pay to the injured third party. If the insurer fails to honour his obligation under the policy the insured has a claim for damages for breach of contract. No debt however is due to the insured from the insurer, for even where the insurer accepts an obligation to indemnify he may discharge that obligation by making payment direct to the third party. Accordingly there is no debt which can be garnisheed in the hands of the insurers. Even where a claim by the insured in respect of the third party's injuries was met by insurers, the third party had no recourse to that fund either in law or equity. Therefore, when the insured became insolvent, the insurance money went into the insolvent insured's general fund of assets to which the third party ranked only as an ordinary creditor[2].

[1]   See eg *Israelson v Dawson* [1933] 1 KB 301, CA; *Chandris v Argo Insurance Co* [1963] 2 Lloyd's Rep 65; *Edmunds v ADAS* [1986] 2 All ER 249, [1986] 1 Lloyd's Rep 326.
[2]   *Re Law Guarantee Trust and Accident Society Ltd* [1914] 2 Ch 617, CA.

28.2 Under the Workman's Compensation Act 1897 a statutory right of subrogation had been given to a workman against his employer's insurers in the event of the employer's bankruptcy or liquidation. This right was limited to the workman's statutory compensation rights under the 1897 Act. To meet

1078

judicial criticism[1] of the hardship caused to injured third parties Parliament enacted statutory rights of assignment whereby the insured's rights under a contract of insurance passed to the person who he had injured. The relevant statutes were the Third Parties (Rights against Insurers) Act 1930 ('TP(RAI)A 1930'), which has general application, and the Road Traffic Act 1930[2], which modified those rights in respect of road traffic cases.

[1]   See in particular *Re Harrington Motor Co Ltd* [1928] Ch 105, CA and *Hoods' Trustees v Southern Union General Insurance Co* [1928] Ch 793, CA.
[2]   Amended by the Road Traffic Act 1934. The relevant provisions are now the Road Traffic Act 1988, ss 143–155.

28.3 Following the enactment of the Contracts (Rights of Third Parties) Act 1999 it might be possible for a third-party victim to enforce the relevant terms of an insurance contract as a member of a class of beneficiaries for whom the term purports to confer a benefit[1]. Under the express provisions of the 1999 Act it would not matter that the third party was not a victim and therefore not within the class of beneficiaries at the date on which the contract was made[2]. Were insurers to accept the prospect of direct actions by third-party victims, the TP(RAI)A 1930 could become otiose. However, it is probable that in the case of most if not all liability policies the court will hold that on a proper construction of the contract the insurer and insured did not intend the relevant terms of the contract to be enforceable by the third-party victim, and it may well be that insurers will rewrite their policies to ensure that the provisions of the Contracts (Rights of Third Parties) Act 1999 do not apply[3].

[1]   Contracts (Rights of Third Parties) Act 1999, s 1(1), (3).
[2]   Contracts (Rights of Third Parties) Act 1999, s 1(3).
[3]   As they are permitted to do, Contracts (Rights of Third Parties) Act 1999, s 1(2).

B THIRD PARTIES (RIGHTS AGAINST INSURERS) ACT 1930

Insolvency requirement

28.4 The TP(RAI)A 1930 takes effect where, under any contract of insurance, a person who is insured against particular liabilities to third parties incurs such liabilities and, in the case of an individual, the insured becomes bankrupt or makes a composition or arrangement with his creditors[1]. In the case of an insured company, the TP(RAI)A 1930 applies in the event of any of a winding-up or administration order, the passing of a resolution for a voluntary winding up[2], the appointment of a receiver or manager of the company's business or undertaking, the enforcement of a floating charge or the company entering into a voluntary arrangement[3].

[1]   TP(RAI)A 1930, s 1(1)(a).
[2]   Except where the voluntary winding up is solely for the purposes of reconstruction or amalgamation, TP(RAI)A 1930, s 1(6).
[3]   TP(RAI)A 1930, s 1(1)(b).

28.5 On the happening of any of these events, the TP(RAI)A 1930 operates to transfer to and vest in the third party the insured's rights under the contract of insurance against his insurers in respect of his liability to the third party. It is immaterial whether the liability to the third party was incurred before or after the relevant event of insolvency. The TP(RAI)A 1930 operates in either case[1].

1   TP(RAI)A 1930, s 1(1).

Deceased debtor

28.6 The death of the debtor liable to the third party does not prevent the operation of the statute. Where the insured debtor has died and his estate falls to be administered under the provisions of the Administration of Insolvent Estates of Deceased Persons Order 1986[1] the TP(RAI)A 1930[2] provides that where the deceased debtor has rights against insurers under a contract of insurance in respect of any debt provable in bankruptcy, those rights shall be transferred to and vested in the third party to whom the debt is owing.

1   SI 1986/1999.
2   TP(RAI)A 1930, s 1(2).

Application of the TP(RAI)A 1930: contract of insurance

28.7 For the TP(RAI)A 1930 to apply there must be a contract of insurance[1]. A 'contract of insurance' cannot be comprehensively defined, but the provisions of the statute presuppose liability insurance, which in general terms is a contract whereby the insurer undertakes in return for the payment of premium to indemnify the insured against any loss he may sustain on the happening of a specified event. In *Tarbuck v Avon Insurance plc*[2] the court held that the TP(RAI)A 1930 did not apply to legal expenses insurance covering the insured's own costs:

> 'I have to choose between construing the words "where a person is insured against liabilities to third parties which he may incur" as limited to insurance against liabilities which may be imposed on that person by operation of law, whether for breach of contract or in tort, or as including the underwriting of liabilities voluntarily undertaken by that person, ie the payment of contract debts. I do not believe that the words were intended to include the latter. So with regret on the facts of the present case[3], I would hold that the claimant has no right of claim against the insurers under the 1930 Act.'[4]

1   TP(RAI)A 1930, s 1(1).
2   [2001] 2 All ER 503.
3   The bankrupt had been in litigation with her landlord funded by legal expenses insurance. The solicitors' final bill was delivered after the date of the bankruptcy order. The insurers were prepared to pay the solicitors directly but the bankrupt would not consent. The learned judge expressed the view (508d) that it seemed only fair that the insurance money should go to the now bankrupt claimant's costs (ie to the solicitors) rather than to her general creditors, or, if the trustee did not make a claim in time under the period specified in the policy (which was the case) that the money should be retained by the insurers.
4   Per Toulson J at 509b.

28.8 The 1930 Act expressly provides[1] that the 'liabilities to third parties' of the insured under a contract of insurance to which it relates do not include any liability of the insured in the capacity of insurer under some other contract of insurance. Accordingly the 1930 Act does not apply to contracts of reinsurance. Mutual insurance, for example such as in a P & I Club, does come within the scope of the 1930 Act[2].

1   TP(RAI)A 1930, s 1(5).
2   See eg *Re Allobrogia Steamship Corpn* [1978] 3 All ER 423; *Firma C-Trade SA v Newcastle Protection and Indemnity Association* [1991] 2 AC 1, [1990] 2 Lloyd's Rep 191.

28.9 The TP(RAI)A 1930 will apply where the insured is a foreign national against whom a bankruptcy order is made in England and Wales. Bankruptcy jurisdiction under the Insolvency Act 1986 ('IA 1986') is exercisable without reference to nationality[1]. It is uncertain whether the court will allow a foreign trustee to rely on the provisions of the TP(RAI)A 1930 in the course of his administration of a foreign bankruptcy. There would appear to be no reason why the court should not interpret 'becoming a bankrupt' in the TP(RAI)A 1930, s 1(1) as including a foreign bankruptcy, and no other reason why the foreign trustee should not be able to rely on the provisions of the TP(RAI)A 1930. Should it be necessary to obtain a bankruptcy order in this country, and for this purpose show that the foreign debtor concerned has assets within the jurisdiction, the rights which will be transferred under the TP(RAI)A 1930 will be sufficient for the purpose. Assets include things in action and therefore include a claim under a contract of insurance against an insurer[2]. Within the corporate field a winding-up order may be made against a foreign corporation where the only asset is the right of action of the corporation against its insurers provided the petitioning third party is able to show that the action against the insurers has a reasonable possibility of success[3].

1   IA 1986, s 265, and EC Insolvency Regulation, art 3.
2   *Re Compania Merabello San Nicholas SA* [1973] Ch 75, [1972] 3 All ER 448.
3   *Re Allobrogia Steamship Corpn* [1978] 3 All ER 423.

28.10 The TP(RAI)A 1930 comes into effect only upon the insolvency[1] of the insured. Accordingly the third party is not entitled to an injunction to prevent a settlement of the insured's claim for an amount that is insufficient to meet the probable liability of the insured to the third party, even though the result of the settlement may be that the insured becomes insolvent when the third party establishes his claim[2].

1   For 'insolvency' for the purposes of the TP(RAI)A 1930 Act see para **28.4** above.
2   *Normid Housing Association Ltd v Ralphs* [1989] 1 Lloyds Rep 265, 21 Con LR 98, CA. Giving the judgment of the Court of Appeal Slade LJ (at p 272) suggested that different considerations might well have arisen had the insured architects been under a contractual or professional duty to the third-party building owners to effect the policies of insurance.

Operation of the TP(RAI)A 1930

28.11 The TP(RAI)A 1930 operates by transferring to the third party the rights of the insured under the contract of insurance. The TP(RAI)A 1930 does not transfer the insured's claim against the insurers, it effects a statutory assignment of the insured's rights under the policy in respect of the particular claim to the extent necessary to achieve the object of the Act[1]. Only those contractual rights of the insured in respect of the insured's liability to the third party are transferred[2]. Where the liability of the insurer to the insured exceeds the liability of the insured to the third party, nothing in the TP(RAI)A 1930 affects the rights of the insured against the insurer in respect of the excess, and if the liability of the insurer to the insured is less than the liability of the insured to the third party, the TP(RAI)A 1930 has no effect upon the rights of the third party against the insured in respect of the balance[3]. The result is that the insured is still able to make a claim under the policy in respect of insured losses other than his liability to the third party, and the third party is not restricted in his claim against the insured to the amount which may be recovered against the insurer[4]. The insurer is not entitled to set off against the third party's claim any outstanding premiums owed by the insured, unless a right to set off premiums is a condition of the policy[5].

1   See *Post Office v Norwich Union Fire Insurance Society Ltd* [1967] 2 QB 363, 376, 377, CA; *Murray v Legal and General* [1970] 2 QB 495, 503.
2   TP(RAI)A 1930, s 1(1).
3   TP(RAI)A 1930, s 1(4)(a), (b).
4   The third party will have to prove for any uninsured balance in the bankruptcy.
5   *Murray v Legal and General* [1970] 2 QB 495, [1969] 3 All ER 794.

28.12   Before an effective transfer of the insured's rights can take place, it is necessary either for the claim to be admitted by insurers or for the liability of the insured to the third party to be established by judgment or arbitration award. The third party may not bring proceedings against the insurance company before liability has been established[1]. In *Post Office v Norwich Union Fire Insurance Society Ltd*[2] the Court of Appeal held that the action was premature where the Post Office, which had a disputed claim against contractors for damaging its cables, took proceedings against the contractors' public liability insurers when the contractors went into liquidation before the claim against them had been heard. Lord Denning MR said[3]:

'Under [TP(RAI)A 1930, s 1] the injured person steps into the shoes of the wrongdoer. There are transferred to him the wrongdoer's "rights against the insurers under the contract". What are those rights? When do they arise? So far as the "liability" of the insured is concerned, there is no doubt that his liability to the injured person arises at the time of the accident, when negligence and damage coincide. But the "rights" of the insured person against the insurer do not arise at that time. The policy says that "the company will indemnify the insured against all sums which the insured shall be legally liable to pay as compensation in respect of loss of or damage to property". It seems to me that the insured only acquires a right to sue for the money when his liability to the injured person has been established so as to give rise to a right of indemnity. His liability to the injured person must be ascertained and determined to exist either by judgment of the court or by an award in arbitration or by agreement ... Under the section it is clear to me that the injured person cannot sue the insurance company except in such circumstances as the insured himself could have sued the insurance company. The insured could only have sued for an indemnity when his liability to the third person was established and the amount of the loss ascertained. In some circumstances the insured might sue earlier for a declaration, for example, if the insurance company were repudiating the policy for some reason. But where the policy is admittedly good, the insured cannot sue for an indemnity until his own liability to the third person is ascertained.'

1   *West Wake Price & Co v Ching* [1957] 1 WLR 45, per Devlin J at p 49, 'The insured cannot recover anything under the main indemnity clause or make any claim against the underwriters until they have been found liable and so sustained a loss'.
2   [1967] 2 QB 363, [1969] 3 All ER 794, CA.
3   At pages 373–374; the passage cited was expressly approved by the House of Lords in *Bradley v Eagle Star Insurance Co Ltd* [1989] AC 957, 966.

28.13   In the absence of agreement as to the insured's liability to the third party it will therefore be necessary for the third party to take proceedings against the insured. Where the insured is a debtor who becomes bankrupt in the course of proceedings brought by the third party it will be necessary for the third party to obtain the leave of the court to continue the proceedings; leave will be required to commence proceedings against a bankrupt[1]. Leave will automatically be given to allow the third party to establish his claim for the purposes of exercising his rights under the TP(RAI)A 1930[2].

1   IA 1986, s 285(1), (3); note that the court may impose terms on which an action may continue, IA 1986, s 285(2), or be commenced, IA 1986, s 285(3).
2   Per the Court of Appeal in *Post Office v Norwich Union Fire Insurance Society Ltd* [1967] 2 QB 363, 367, 375, 377–378.

28.14   The need for the third party first to establish his claim against the insured before he may exercise any rights under the TP(RAI)A 1930 is cumbersome, and entails risk. It is possible for the third party to expend time and money establishing his claim against the insured, only to find that the insured's rights against the insurer under the policy are worthless because, for example, of breach of condition or non-disclosure on the part of the insured. In *Re OT Computers Ltd (in administration)*[1] the Court of Appeal held that the insured is obliged under TP(RAI)A 1930, s 2 to give information about the insurance policy before the third party establishes liability against the insured. The third party should avail itself of this right before embarking on litigation against the bankrupt insured in order, as far as possible, to see that doing so is going to be worthwhile.

1   [2004] EWCA Civ 653, [2004] Ch 317, [2004] 2 BCLC 682, CA, overruling a series of decisions to the opposite effect.

28.15   Consistent with the law as stated above, a third party was held to have no *locus standi* to prevent a compromise between the insurer and the supervisor of the insured's voluntary arrangement while the insured's liability to the third party remained in dispute in pending proceedings[1]. It also follows that where the insured enters into a voluntary arrangement with his creditors involving a composition of his debts, the third party will only be able to bring proceedings against the insurer under the TP(RAI)A 1930 in respect of the debt as compounded. For this reason the third party was entitled to challenge the approval of the voluntary arrangement on the ground that his interests were unfairly prejudiced[2].

1   *Jackson v Greenfield* [1998] BPIR 699; the third party may have been able to prevent the settlement of the claim had it been able to adduce evidence of bad faith.
2   *Sea Voyager Maritime Inc v Bielecki* [1999] 1 All ER 628, [1999] 1 BCLC 133.

28.16 Where the bankrupt has potential liabilities to many third parties, such that the limit of indemnity under his policy with the insurer will be less than the total of the claims, and the various third parties all have claims before the court, the court may set up a scheme to ensure that no advantage is obtained by third parties who are able to establish liability before others by reason of their position in the court lists. However, such schemes are suitable only in relatively uncomplicated cases, and where, as in the Lloyd's litigation, there were many actions with many and varied complex issues, it was held that there was no obligation on the court to set up such a scheme; the claims would have to be met in the order in which liability and quantum were established[1].

1   *Cox v Bankside Members Agency Ltd* [1995] 2 Lloyd's Rep 437, CA.

Position of third party is no better than insured's

28.17 As stated above, the TP(RAI)A 1930 operates by transferring to the third party the rights of the insured under the contract of insurance. The third party cannot therefore place himself in a better position vis-à-vis the insurer than that of the insured before his insolvency. The point was graphically made by Harman LJ in the *Post Office v Norwich Union Fire Insurance Society Ltd*[1] case where, it should be noted from the quotation from Lord Denning's judgment above, the policy provided that the insurer's liability to indemnify the contractors only arose in respect of sums which the contractors were 'legally liable to pay as compensation in respect of loss of or damage to property'. Harman LJ stated[2]:

> '... the contract contains not only rights, but limitations of those rights. You cannot, I think, assign to somebody part of the rights under the contract without assigning to him the condition subject to which those rights exist. Consequently, I think the Post Office is saddled with the inability of Potters to sue direct themselves before the liability is ascertained, because that would amount to a breach of condition 3 of the policy which would in itself be a defence to the insurance company.
>
> Therefore, I would decide this case on the narrow ground that the right assigned to the Post Office by the statute must be coupled with the rest of the particular rights and obligations which make up the contract of insurance. You cannot pick out one bit – pick out the plums and leave the duff behind. Therefore I think that, as Potters could not sue, so their statutory assignees, the Post Office, cannot sue until the amount has been ascertained and quantified.'

1   [1967] 2 QB 363.
2   At p 376D.

28.18 Therefore, before the third party may recover against insurers, it is necessary that he establish both the insured's liability to the third party and also the insurer's liability to pay the insured under the terms of the policy. If, as in the *Post Office v Norwich Union* case the insurer has the right to require the insured's liability to the third party to be ascertained, the third party cannot enforce the policy until that liability has been determined. Where the policy of insurance contains an arbitration clause, the third party may be required by the insurer to go to arbitration[1]. It is no reason for the court to refuse the insurer's application to stay proceedings by reason of the arbitration clause that the third party is unable to afford to arbitrate[2]. On an application for a stay by the insurers the court should look at the matter as between the insured and the insurer without taking account of any consideration personal to the third party[3]. In exceptional cases, such as the Lloyd's litigation, where the questions under consideration were of wide interest to other parties, the court may refuse to order a stay of proceedings to enable a reference to arbitration[4].

1 *Freshwater v Western Australia Assurance Co Ltd* [1933] 1 KB 515, CA; *Denneby v Bellamy* [1938] 2 All ER 262, CA; *Schiffahrtsgesellschaft Detlev von Appen GmbH v Voest Alpine Intertrading GmbH* [1997] 1 Lloyd's Rep 179.
2 *Smith v Pearl Assurance Co Ltd* [1939] 1 All ER 95, CA.
3 *Smith v Pearl Assurance Co Ltd* [1939] 1 All ER 95 at p 97 per Slesser LJ.
4 *Rew v Cox* [1996] CLC 472.

28.19 The rights transferred by the TP(RAI)A 1930 to the third party are subject to any defences which would be available to the insurer against a claim by the insured[1]. The third party may for example find that the insured has in some way repudiated the policy or given the insurer ground to avoid it, by material non-disclosure, fraud, misrepresentation or breach of warranty[2]. Should the insurer accept the insured's repudiation or avoid the policy, the third party will lose his rights[3]. The insured may have been in reckless breach of a reasonable precautions clause in the policy[4]. The third party is bound by any condition precedent to liability including any procedural requirements of the contract of insurance and will be bound by any provision of the insurance policy which limits the insurer's liability[5]. In the absence of fraud, the third party will not be able to recover against an insurer who has compromised with or has been released by the insured[6], provided the compromise or release has been made before the insolvency of the insured. Any such agreement made after the insured's insolvency and the incurring of liability to the third party is void by reason of the provision of the TP(RAI)A 1930, s 3.

1 TP(RAI)A 1930, s 1(4).
2 See, for example, *Total Graphics Ltd v AGF Insurance Ltd* [1997] 1 Lloyd's Rep 599; *Abbey National plc v Solicitors Indemnity Fund Ltd* [1997] PNLR 306; *Arab Bank plc v Zurich Insurance Co* [1999] 1 Lloyd's Rep 262 where under the terms of a composite policy it was provided that the dishonesty of one insured would not be held against other insureds who were not complicit in the fraud.
3 *McCormick v National Motor and Accident Insurance Union Ltd* (1934) 40 Com Cas 76; *Cleland v London General Insurance Co* (1935) 51 LL Rep 156.
4 See, for example, *M/S Aswan Engineering Establishment Co v Iron Trades Mutual Insurance Co Ltd* [1989] 1 Lloyd's Rep 289; *Aluminium Wire and Cable Co v Allstate Insurance Co* [1985] 2 Lloyd's Rep 280.
5 *Avandero v National Transit Insurance Co Ltd* [1984] 2 Lloyd's Rep 613.
6 *Farrell v Federated Employers' Insurance Association Ltd* [1970] 3 All ER 632, [1970] 1 WLR 1400, CA; *Hassett v Legal and General Assurance Society Ltd* (1939) 63 Lloyd's Rep 278.

28.20 A third party will also be bound, and will be defeated, by a 'pay to be paid' or 'pay first' clause. Such clauses, commonly found in contracts of mutual insurance, provide that the insured must first discharge his liability to the third party before the insurer becomes liable to indemnify the insured under the policy. In *The Fanti*[1] the House of Lords rejected the arguments that such clauses were contrary to the contracting out provisions of the TP(RAI)A 1930[2] or should be struck down because performance had become impossible. The suggestion that the TP(RAI)A 1930 operated to transfer to the third party a right of indemnity contingent upon payment by the third party was also rejected. Accordingly, unless the clause is drawn in a most unusual form, the Act will be of no effect to a third party whose claim is against an insured with a policy subject to a pay first or pay to be paid clause[3].

[1] *Firma C-Trade SA v Newcastle Protection and Indemnity Association, The Fanti* [1991] 2 AC 1.
[2] Ie TP(RAI)A 1930, s 1(3).
[3] A case for reform is argued by Sir Jonathan Mance at 'Insolvency at Sea' [1995] LMCLQ 34, at 43–49.

28.21 The third party will not be liable on a counterclaim which the insurer may have against the insured for unpaid premiums, unless the right to set off premiums which have fallen due is a condition of the policy[1].

[1] *Murray v Legal and General Assurance Society Ltd* [1970] 2 QB 495, [1969] 3 All ER 794. It is not clear from the judgment why the insurer was not able to exercise his general right of equitable set-off which would appear to be as much a defence as any other available to him, see *Hanak v Green* [1958] 2 QB 9, [1958] 2 All ER 141, CA.

No contracting out

28.22 The TP(RAI)A 1930, by s 1(3), makes of no effect any provisions in a contract of insurance which purport directly or indirectly to avoid the consequences of the 1930 Act or alter the rights of the parties of the contract in the event that the 1930 Act becomes operable. Insurers may not therefore preclude their liability to third parties on the insolvency of the insured by express provision in the contract of insurance. Where it is a condition precedent to liability on the part of the insurer under the policy that the insured must first satisfy the liability he has to the third party, the 'pay to be paid' or 'pay first' clause, the House of Lords has held that TP(RAI)A 1930, s 1(3) does not operate to permit the third party to recover directly against the insurers[1]. In such cases the insured has only contingent rights against the insurers in respect of their liabilities to the third party until the insured has discharged such liabilities. Accordingly on the insured's insolvency no accrued rights to indemnity can be transferred under the TP(RAI)A 1930 to the third party, and as the third party cannot have a greater right against the insurers than did the insured immediately, before the insured's insolvency, no claim can pass under the 1930 Act.

[1] See *Firma C-Trade SA v Newcastle Protection and Indemnity Association* [1991] 2 AC 1, [1990] 2 Lloyd's Rep 191, HL.

Procedural or administrative requirements of policy

28.23 The third party will be bound by any procedural or administrative requirement of the insured's policy. This can be a serious matter for the third party, particularly in the case of notice clauses. It is common for policies of insurance to require the insured to notify the insurer of any circumstances which might give rise to a claim within a relatively short time period and to require the insured to forward immediately a copy of any writ or other proceedings served on him in respect of which he will seek indemnity.

28.24 If these requirements are conditions precedent to liability, the insured, and in turn the third party, may lose the cover provided under the policy in the event of non-compliance by the insured irrespective of whether the insurer has been prejudiced by the breach[1]. The third party is of course unlikely to be in any position to ensure that the policy requirements are adhered to, and even if he is aware of the insured's insurers and the terms of the policy, he may be unable to satisfy the requirements of the policy by giving notice of his own claim against the insured to the insurers. In *The Vainqueur José*[2] the court held that the notice of claim required by the insured's P & I Club had to be given by the insured or his duly authorised agent. Notice by another interested party, in that case a firm of New York attorneys who had previously acted for the insured but had not been expressly instructed for this particular matter, was insufficient for the purposes of the insurance. The terms of the policy may not however preclude the third party giving effective notice of his own claim to insurers[3]. Even after notice is given however the third party remains at risk of the insured's rights of indemnity being lost for failure by the insured to comply with the various procedural or administrative requirements under the policy, in particular clauses requiring the co-operation of the insured and the provision of all such evidence as the insurers may properly require for the purpose of ascertaining the extent of the claim and matters relevant to its defence[4]. Where the insurer has the right in his discretion to make a deduction from any claim because the insured has not taken proper steps to protect his interests this right may be enforced against the third party. The court will not interfere with the insurer's exercise of his discretion provided he acted honestly, fairly and legally[5].

[1]   *Farrell v Federated Employers' Insurance Association Ltd* [1970] 3 All ER 632, [1970] 1 WLR 1400, CA (breach of condition that writ be notified immediately); *Hassett v Legal and General Assurance Society Ltd* (1939) 63 Ll L Rep 278; *Alfred McAlpine plc v BAI (in run off) Ltd* [1998] 2 Lloyd's Rep 694 (clause requiring notice of claim not a condition precedent); *Pioneer Concrete (UK) Ltd v NEM General Insurance Association Ltd* [1985] 2 All ER 395, [1985] 1 Lloyd's Rep 274 (clause requiring notice of claim a condition precedent); *Saunders v Royal Insurance Inc* 1999 SLT 358 (notification 'on receipt'); *Horne v Prudential Assurance Co Ltd* 1997 SLT (Sh Ct) 75 (notification 'as soon as reasonably possible').

[2]   *CVG Siderugicia del Orinoco SA v London Steamship Owners' Mutual Insurance Association* [1979] 1 Lloyd's Rep 557.

[3]   *Barrett Bros (Taxis) Ltd v Davies* [1966] 2 Lloyd's Rep 1, CA.

[4]   See eg *Pioneer Concrete (UK) Ltd v NEM General Insurance Association Ltd* [1985] 1 Lloyd's Rep 274 where the third party gave notice of the claim to insurers but not his subsequent service of proceedings.

[5]   *CVG Siderugicia del Orinoco SA v London Steamship Owners' Mutual Insurance Association ('The Vainqueur José')* [1979] 1 Lloyd's Rep 557.

28.25   *Rights against bankrupt's insurers*

28.25 In the case of employer's liability insurance the effects of this rule on the third party employee seeking to recover damages for injuries sustained at work against an insolvent employer are mitigated by the Employer's Liability (Compulsory Insurance) General Regulations 1971[1]. Regulation 2(1) prohibits any condition in an employer's liability policy which provides, in whatever terms, that no liability shall arise under the policy 'in the event of some specified thing being done or omitted to be done after the happening of the event giving rise to a claim under the policy'. This wording should be wide enough to nullify any procedural requirement likely to defeat a third-party employee's claim.

[1]   SI 1971/1117.

Duty of insured to give information

28.26 The TP(RAI)A 1930 requires an insured who becomes insolvent to give information to any third party claiming that the insured is under a liability to him. In the case of an individual insured the duty arises on his becoming bankrupt, entering into an individual voluntary arrangement or making some other composition or arrangement with his creditors[1]. The personal representative of an insolvent estate is under a similar obligation upon the making of an insolvency administration order[2].

[1]   TP(RAI)A 1930, s 2(1).
[2]   TP(RAI)A 1930, s 2(1).

28.27 The duty imposed by the TP(RAI)A 1930 requires the provision of such information as may reasonably be required by the third person for the purpose of ascertaining whether any rights against an insurer have been transferred to and vested in the third person by the 1930 Act, and arises on the making of a request by the third party[1]. The third person is also entitled to information reasonably required to enable him to enforce his statutory rights against the relevant insurer. Any provision in the contract of insurance which seeks to prohibit the giving of such information or to alter the rights of the parties to the contract on giving such information is void[2].

[1]   TP(RAI)A 1930, s 2(1).
[2]   TP(RAI)A 1930, s 2(1).

28.28 Should the information obtained by the third person disclose reasonable ground for supposing that third party rights have been transferred to him under the TP(RAI)A 1930, the duty extends to the insurers concerned and they too can be required to give such information as the third person reasonably requires[1]. The duty extends to disclosure of documents including 'all contracts of insurance, receipts for premiums, and other relevant documents in the possession or power of the person on whom the duty is so imposed'[2]. Documents may be inspected and copies taken[3].

[1]   TP(RAI)A 1930, s 2(2).
[2]   TP(RAI)A 1930, s 2(3).
[3]   TP(RAI)A 1930, s 2(3).

28.29 Before establishing that the insured is liable to him[1], the third party may obtain from the insolvent insured or the insolvency office-holder such information as the third party reasonably requires for the purpose of seeing what rights have vested in him and enforcing them[2]. Information which may assist includes the policy itself and any information which bears on whether the insurer could avoid the policy or deny liability.

[1] *Re OT Computers Ltd (in administration)* [2004] EWCA Civ 653, [2004] Ch 317, [2004] 2 BCLC 682, CA (overruling a series of decisions in which it had been held that the third party had to establish liability against the insured before he could seek information under TP(RAI)A 1930, s 2).
[2] TP(RAI)A 1930, s 2.

Settlement between insurer and insured

28.30 Where the insured has become bankrupt, no agreement made between the insurer and the insured after liability has been incurred to a third party and after the commencement of the bankruptcy, nor any waiver, assignment or other disposition made by, or payment made to, the insured after the commencement of the bankruptcy, shall be effective to defeat or affect the rights transferred to the third party under the TP(RAI)A 1930. These rights remain vested in the third party as if no such agreement, waiver, assignment, disposition or payment had been made[1]. These provisions do not apply to agreements made before the commencement of the bankruptcy, even where the insured has entered into voluntary arrangements, a scheme of arrangement or composition with his creditors. Under the Insolvency Act 1986 an agreement benefiting the insurers made before the presentation of the petition may be liable to be avoided by the trustee as a preference or undervalue transaction.

[1] TP(RAI)A 1930, s 3.

Extent and prosecution of claims

28.31 The rights vested by the TP(RAI)A 1930 in the third party against the insurer do not affect the third party's rights against the insured where the insurer's liability is less than the total of the third party's claim on the insured. The third party will be entitled to prove in the bankruptcy of the insured for the balance and interest as an ordinary creditor. Conversely, should there be a liability on the part of the insurers to the insolvent insured greater than the insured's liability to the third party, the trustee in bankruptcy may recover any balance on behalf of the insured for the benefit of the estate[1].

[1] TP(RAI)A 1930, s 1(4).

28.32 Subject to the fulfilment of any conditions precedent in the insurance policy and due compliance by the insured with any conditions or warranties, once the insured's rights have vested in the third party he may sue the insurers to recover his loss. The insurers may have declined to become involved in initial proceedings in which event they will be unable to contest the quantum of any judgment obtained by the third party against the insured or any bona fide settlement between them. On the other hand, the insurers may have become involved in the defence of the third party's proceedings, at least initially, until some fact emerged which allowed them to avoid liability under the policy. In circumstances where the insurers exercise their right to conduct the insured's defence, it is improbable, in the light of the decision in *Soole v Royal Insurance Co*[1] that, as between the insured and the insurer, the insurer will have compromised his rights to avoid the policy and be stopped from denying liability to indemnify the insured. As between the insurer and the third party however, it is possible that in the conduct of the defence, the insurer or his solicitor may have represented that the insured would be indemnified and thereby encouraged the third party to continue an action against a defendant whom he knew or suspected would be unable to meet a judgment personally. Should the insurer disclaim liability to the insured during the course of the proceedings, he would be advised to inform the third party.

1   [1971] 2 Lloyd's Rep 332, 339–340, 342; the fact that the insurer defends the action is not an acceptance of liability under the policy. In *Soole* the insurer unsuccessfully defended proceedings against the insured taken by neighbours seeking to enforce a restrictive covenant. The insurer then successfully disputed liability on the ground that a claim had been first intimated to the insured before the inception of the policy.

Insolvency of the insurer

28.33 Decisions of the courts under the subrogation provisions of the Workman's Compensation Acts suggest that a third party's rights against the insurers are not affected by the insurers going into liquidation or becoming bankrupt, whether this is before or after the liquidation, administration or other operative event affecting the insured[1]. The liability of the insurers is determined at the date of their insolvency and the third party can then prove in the liquidation or bankruptcy[2].

1   *Re Renishaw Iron Co Ltd* [1917] 1 Ch 199 and *Re Pethick, Dix & Co* [1915] 1 Ch 26.
2   *Re Law Car and General Insurance Corpn Ltd* (1913) 110 LT 27.

Limitation

28.34 The period of limitation for an action by a third party to enforce rights which have been transferred to him under the TP(RAI)A 1930 will be six years[1], unless, unusually, the rights transferred to the third party are rights under a specialty in which case the limitation period will be 12 years[2]. Potentially more difficult is the question when the limitation period begins to run. The rights transferred by the TP(RAI)A 1930 are the insured's 'rights against the insurer under the contract in respect of the liability'[3]. The more natural interpretation is that the rights transferred to the third party are the rights which previously existed in the insured in respect of the liability to the third party, and not equivalent but distinct rights under the contract. An insured's cause of action against the insurer under a liability insurance policy, being a contract of indemnity, accrues when the loss is incurred. This is when the insured's liability to the third party is determined by agreement, judgment or arbitration award[4]. If on this date the insured has not yet become insolvent it would follow that when the rights are transferred to the third party on a subsequent insolvency of the insured these will be rights which are subject to a limitation period which has already begun to run. It is necessary that the third-party issues proceedings within six years of the accrual of the insured's right of action against the insurer, for otherwise his claim will be statute barred[5]. The third party's cause of action against the insurer will not accrue until the insured becomes insolvent, and in extreme cases, this may be more than six years after the accrual of the insured's cause of action against the insurer. It is possible therefore that the third party will inherit rights that are already statute-barred. But the contrary argument, that the limitation period only begins to run on the date of the accrual of the third party's cause of action against the insurer, while more attractive in the result, does not sit readily with the words of the statute[6]. The fact that the insured has commenced proceedings against the insurer does not preserve the third party's position in relation to limitation[7]. However, there would appear to be no objection in principle to the third party applying to be substituted in any existing proceedings commenced by the insured[8].

[1]   Limitation Act 1980, s 5.
[2]   Limitation Act 1980, s 8.
[3]   TP(RAI)A 1930, s 1(1).
[4]   *Bradley v Eagle Star Insurance Co Ltd* [1989] 1 All ER 961, [1989] AC 957, HL.
[5]   *Lefevre v White* [1990] 1 Lloyd's Rep 569, 578.
[6]   In *London Steamship Owners Mutual Insurance Association Ltd v Bombay Trading Co Ltd, The Felice* [1990] 2 Lloyd's Rep 21n Phillips J may have taken the contrary view. The insured had commenced an arbitration just within the six-year limitation period, and went into liquidation just after this period expired. An application by the third party for a declaration that it had the right to continue the arbitration in its own name was refused, the court stating that the insured should commence a new arbitration. As the court indicated that the result might have been different had it considered that the new arbitration would be statute-barred, without however explaining how and when this would occur, the learned judge must either have taken the view that the limitation period commenced when the insured went into liquidation or that the limitation position was in some way preserved by the first arbitration proceedings.
[7]   *Lefevre v White* [1990] 1 Lloyd's Rep 569, 578.
[8]   Under CPR Pt 19 see *Montedipe SpA v JTP-RO Jugotanker, The Jordan Nicolov* [1990] 2 Lloyd's Rep 11 a case outside the TP(RAI)A 1930 where the court (Hobhouse J) held that an assignee could intervene in a pending arbitration commenced by his assignor. See also *Baytur SA v Finagrain Holding SA* [1992] QB 610, [1992] 1 Lloyd's Rep 134, CA.

28.35 The commencement of the insolvency proceedings does not stop time from running for the purpose of making a claim under the TP(RAI)A 1930[1].

[1]   *Financial Services Compensation Scheme Ltd v Larnell (Insurance Ltd)* [2006] QB 808, [2005] EWCA Civ 1408.

Part IV

ADMINISTRATION ORDERS AND OTHER DEBT MANAGEMENT ARRANGEMENTS

Chapter 29

ADMINISTRATION ORDERS

A   General
B   Procedure on application

A GENERAL

Power to make administration order

29.1 The county court has jurisdiction[1] to make an order providing for the administration of a debtor's estate where the debtor is unable to satisfy a judgment against him and his whole indebtedness does not exceed £5,000, inclusive of the debt for which the judgment was obtained[2]. The order is known as an administration order[3]. Any county court may make an administration order, not just the court in which judgment was obtained, but there must be a judgment entered against the debtor before an order may be made[4]. The effect of an administration order is to put the debtor in what has been described as a 'mini-bankruptcy'. The aim of the order is to enable a debtor who owes several debts, including a judgment debt, to discharge his debts by making regular payments into court for distribution among his creditors. While he does so the debtor obtains protection from those debts which are scheduled to the order; the relevant creditors are prevented from enforcing their debts without the leave of the court. It is a jurisdiction which has not been much used, partly perhaps because only the debtor may apply for an order, and partly because £5,000 is today a rather low level of indebtedness.

[1]   County Courts Act 1984, s 112.
[2]   County Courts Act 1984, s 112(1).
[3]   County Courts Act 1984, s 112(2).
[4]   Either in the High Court or the county court.

29.2 There has for some time been widespread agreement that there ought to be a simplified procedure for small bankruptcies. The extension of the administration order jurisdiction has been seen as the way to achieve that aim. Indeed the Courts and Legal Services Act 1990 ('CLSA 1990')[1] contains detailed provision for significant amendments to be made to administration orders. Were these amendments to be brought into force the administration order jurisdiction would be considerably increased enabling any debtor to be the subject of an administration order whatever his level of indebtedness, protected by an enforcement restriction order which would prevent any creditor specified in the order pursuing any remedy against the debtor without the leave of the court. The CLSA 1990 provisions would enable the debtor to apply for an order before judgment has been entered against him, or for an administration order to be made on the application of a judgment creditor or on the court's own motion. The scope of the order would be widened with the court having power to add a composition provision to an administration order, but the order would cease to have effect if the debtor made an individual voluntary arrangement ('IVA'). An administration order would differ from an IVA in that it could be made without the need for the consent of 75% in value of the debtor's creditors and it would have the advantage of avoiding the expense of the services of an insolvency practitioner as supervisor[2]. Quite how the expanded administration order envisaged in the CLSA 1990 would have fitted into the overall scheme for personal insolvency provided by the Insolvency Act 1986 ('IA 1986') is far from clear, but this would now seem to be an academic concern. The CLSA 1990 reforms have not been brought into force, and it is now clear that they never will be.

[1] CLSA 1990, s 13, not yet in force, and unlikely ever to be brought into force.
[2] Costs not exceeding ten pence in the pound may be recovered by the court, County Courts Act 1984, s 117(1).

Administration order

29.3 Before an administration order is made, the court[1] must send to every person whose name the debtor has notified the court as being one of his creditors, a notice that that person's name has been included on the debtor's list of creditors[2].

[1] The powers of the court may be exercised by the district judge, or in specified circumstances the court manager, CPR Sch 2 CCR Ord 39 r 1.
[2] County Courts Act 1984, s 112(3).

29.4 There is a prescribed form for the administration order[1], but the court has a wide discretion in framing its terms. An administration order may provide for the payment of the debts of the debtor by instalments, either in full or to such extent as appears practicable to the court under the circumstances of the case. Provision may be made that the debtor make payments from his future earnings or income, such payments usually being made into court[2]. The order must ensure that there is a pro rata division of the debtor's available property among all his creditors[3].

[1] CPR, County Court Form No 94.
[2] County Courts Act 1984, s 112(6).
[3] *Re Frank* [1894] 1 QB 9.

29.5 Where a county court makes an administration order in respect of a debtor's estate, it may also make an attachment of earnings order to secure the payments required by the administration order[1]. This is indeed the usual method employed to ensure that the administration order is enforced. The county court has the duty of enforcing the order and accordingly an attachment of earnings order may be made on the court's own motion; it is not necessary for a creditor to make an application for such an order[2]. On the revocation of an administration order, any attachment of earnings order made to secure the payments required by the administration order must be discharged[3].

1   Attachment of Earnings Act 1971, s 5(1).
2   Attachment of Earnings Act 1971, s 5(2).
3   CPR Sch 2 CCR Ord 39 r 16.

29.6 An administration order is not invalid should it be found that the total level of indebtedness exceeds the £5,000 limit, but in this event the court may set aside the administration order if it thinks fit[1].

1   County Courts Act 1981, s 112(5).

Administration order on application for attachment of earnings order

29.7 Where, on an application to a county court by a creditor for an attachment of earnings order against a debtor to secure the payment of a judgment debt, it appears to the court that the debtor also has other debts, the court:

(1)   must consider whether the case may be one in which all the debtor's liabilities should be dealt with together and that for that purpose an administration order should be made; and

(2)   if of the opinion that it may be such a case, has power to order the debtor to furnish to the court a list of all his creditors and the amounts owed to them with a view to making an administration order, whether or not the court makes an attachment of earnings order.

29.8 If the list of creditors suggests that the debtor's whole indebtedness amounts to not more than the £5,000 limit[1], the court may make an administration order in respect of the debtor's estate[2].

1   Were the Courts and Legal Services Act 1990, s 13 to be brought into force this limit would go, but it now appears that the amendments enacted by s 13 will never be implemented.
2   Attachment of Earnings Act 1971, s 4(2).

Effect of administration order

29.9 When an administration order is made, no creditor has any remedy against the person or property of the debtor in respect of any debt of which the debtor notified the court before the administration order was made, or which has been scheduled to the order, except with the leave of the court and on such terms as that court may impose[1]. Any county court in which proceedings are pending against the debtor in respect of any debt so notified or scheduled (other than bankruptcy proceedings) must stay the proceedings on receiving notice of the administration order, although the court may allow costs already incurred by the creditor and provide that such costs may be added to the debt[2].

1 County Courts Act 1984, s 114(1).
2 County Courts Act 1984, s 114(2).

29.10 Proceedings in bankruptcy against the debtor may proceed despite the making of an administration order[1], but so long as an administration order is in force, a creditor whose name is included in the schedule to the order may not, without the leave of the appropriate court, be entitled to present, or join in, a bankruptcy petition against the debtor. There is an important exception to this bar on the presenting of a bankruptcy petition. A creditor who receives notice from the county court that his debt has been included in the schedule to an administration order has 28 days to present, or join in, a petition for the debtor's bankruptcy. The petition debt must however exceed £1,500[2]. The creditor thus has a short period within which to commence bankruptcy proceedings against the debtor, and after 28 days have elapsed the debtor may be reasonably confident that the administration of his affairs under the administration order will proceed without challenge by a creditor. The fact that this restricted period is allowed for presenting a petition suggests that a court should not give leave to review a petition when the 28-day period has expired unless the creditor is able to show good cause, for example that the debtor is paying other debts owed by him which are not scheduled to the order preferentially to those other creditors, or that there is reason to believe that the powers of the court in bankruptcy, for example to set aside an undervalue transaction or a preference, might be usefully employed against the debtor[3].

1 County Courts Act 1984, s 114(3).
2 County Courts Act 1984, s 112(4)(b); the Secretary of State may by regulation increase or reduce this sum but no such increase may affect any case in which the bankruptcy petition is already presented, County Courts Act 1984, s 112(7), (8). The requirement for a debt or debts totalling £1,500 is in contrast to the minimum debt of £750 ordinarily required for a bankruptcy petition, see para **8.51** above.
3 County Courts Act 1984, s 112(4), amended by the IA 1986, s 220(1), (2).

29.11 An application under the County Courts Act 1984, s 112(4) for leave to present or join in a bankruptcy petition must be made on notice to the debtor[1] but the court may, if it thinks fit, order that notice be given to any other creditor whose debt is scheduled to the administration order[2].

1 CPR Sch 2 CCR Ord 13 r 1.
2 CPR Sch 2 CCR Ord 39 r 12.

29.12 Money paid into court under an administration order must be appropriated first in satisfaction of the costs of administration, which may not exceed ten pence in the pound on the total amount of the debts, and then in liquidation of debts in accordance with the order[1].

1 County Courts Act 1984, s 117(1).

Execution by district judge

29.13 Where it appears to the district judge of the court, which has made an administration order at any time while the order is in force, that the debtor has property the value of which exceeds £50[1], he must, at the request of any creditor[2], and without fee, issue execution against the debtor's goods[2]. This power enables the court to ensure that any assets which the debtor has not previously disclosed or which come into his possession during the course of the administration order may be seized for the benefit of creditors. There is however no statutory obligation on the debtor subject to an administration order to notify the court of the fact that he has acquired property, in contrast to the position in bankruptcy where the bankrupt is required to give notice to his trustee of any property which he acquires or which devolves on him within 21 days of his becoming aware of the relevant facts[3]. The court may overcome this drawback by imposing a provision in the administration order that the debtor notifies the court of any acquisition of property, and (or alternatively) by directing that the order should be reviewed at regular intervals so as to enable the court to investigate any change in the debtor's affairs[4].

1   £50 is 'the minimum amount' which may be altered by order by the Lord Chancellor.
2   County Courts Act 1984, s 115(1).
3   IA 1986, s 333(2); IR 1986, r 6.200.
4   Such a direction may be given under CPR Sch 2 CCR Ord 39 r 8.

Right of landlord to distrain

29.14 A landlord or other person to whom any rent is due from a debtor in respect of whom an administration order is made, may at any time, either before or after the date of the order, distrain upon the goods or effects of the debtor for the rent due to him from the debtor. There is however this limitation, that if the distress for rent is levied after the date of the order, it is available only for six months' rent accrued due prior to the date of the order and is not available for rent payable in respect of any period subsequent to the date when the distress was levied, but the landlord or other person to whom the rent may be due from the debtor may prove under the order for the surplus due for which the distress may not have been available[1].

1   County Courts Act 1984, s 116.

B PROCEDURE ON APPLICATION

Request by debtor for administration order

29.15 A debtor wishing to obtain an administration order must file a request in the court for the district in which he resides or carries on business[1]. The court may proceed as if the debtor had filed such a request where in the course of an oral examination he provides the court on oath with a list of his creditors and the amounts which he owes to them respectively and sufficient particulars of his resources and needs[2]. On the filing of a request or list the court[3] should appoint a day for consideration of the question whether an

29.15 *Administration orders*

administration order should be made and give not less than 14 days' notice thereof to the debtor and to each creditor mentioned in the list provided by the debtor[4].

1   CPR Sch 2 CCR Ord 39 r 2(1); for the prescribed form of request see the County Court Form No 92.
2   CPR Sch 2 CCR Ord 39 r 2(2).
3   The county court will usually appoint the court manager to have the conduct of the order, and he must take all proper steps to enforce the order or to bring to the attention of the court any matter which may make it desirable to review the order: CPR Sch 2 CCR Ord 39 r 13(1).
4   CPR Sch 2 CCR Ord 39 r 5; for the prescribed form of notice of hearing see the County Court Form No 373.

29.16 Any creditor to whom notice has been given and who objects to any debt included in the list provided by the debtor must, not less than seven days before the day of hearing, give notice of his objection, stating the grounds thereof, to the court, the debtor and the creditor to whose debt he objects[1]. Except with the leave of the court, no creditor may object to a debt unless he has so given notice of his objection[2].

1   CPR Sch 2 CCR Ord 39 r 6(1).
2   CPR Sch 2 CCR Ord 39 r 6(2).

Procedure to administration order

29.17 The Insolvency Rules 1986 ('IR 1986') provide that an administration order may be made without a hearing in cases where the debtor files a request for an order and it appears that the debtor's means are sufficient to discharge his debts in full within a reasonable period[1]. This order is made by the 'proper officer' (usually the court manager) rather than the district judge. The proper officer may determine the amount and frequency of the payments to be made. He is then to notify the debtor of the proposed rate of payment, and give each creditor notice of the request for an administration order, the list of creditors and the proposed rate of payment. Both the debtor and the creditors have 14 days in which to make objection, either as to the proposed rate of payment or as to the inclusion of any particular debt in the proposed order[2]. If no objection is received within 14 days of service of this notification the proper officer may then make an administration order on the terms proposed[3]. If objection is received a hearing is fixed before the judge, with not less than 14 days' notice to the debtor and each creditor[4]. Where the proper officer considers that the debtor's means are insufficient to pay all the debts in full, or for some other reason the proper officer considers that he is unable to fix a rate of payment, he must refer the request for an administration order to the district judge[5]. The district judge may then fix a proposed rate of payment of the debtor's debts either in full or to such extent and within such period as appears 'practicable in the circumstances of the case'[6]. The debtor and the creditors then have 14 days to object and require a hearing[7].

1   CPR Sch 2 CCR Ord 39 r 5; there is no guidance in the rules as to what constitutes a 'reasonable period'.
2   CPR Sch 2 CCR Ord 39 r 5(2).
3   CPR Sch 2 CCR Ord 39 r 5(3).

4 CPR Sch 2 CCR Ord 39 r 5(4).
5 CPR Sch 2 CCR Ord 39 r 5(6).
6 CPR Sch 2 CCR Ord 39 r 5(6).
7 CPR Sch 2 CCR Ord 39 r 5(7).

29.18 On the day of the hearing:

(1) any creditor, whether or not he is mentioned in the list furnished by the debtor, may attend and prove his debt or object to any debt included in that list[1];

(2) every debt included in that list must be taken to be proved unless it is objected to by a creditor or disallowed by the court or required by the court to be supported by evidence[2];

(3) any creditor whose debt is required by the court to be supported by evidence must prove his debt[3];

(4) the court may adjourn the proof of any debt and, if it does, may either adjourn consideration of the question whether an administration order should be made or proceed to determine the question, in which case, if an administration order is made, the debt, when proved, must be added to the debts scheduled to the order[4];

(5) any creditor whose debt is admitted or proved, and, with the leave of the court, any creditor the proof of whose debt has been adjourned, is entitled to be heard and to adduce evidence on the question of whether an administration order should be made and, if so, in what terms[5].

1 CPR Sch 2 CCR Ord 39 r 7(a).
2 CPR Sch 2 CCR Ord 39 r 7(b).
3 CPR Sch 2 CCR Ord 39 r 7(c).
4 CPR Sch 2 CCR Ord 39 r 7(d).
5 CPR Sch 2 CCR Ord 39 r 7(e).

29.19 Where an administration order is made, the court must send a copy to:

(a) the debtor;

(b) every creditor whose name was included in the list furnished by the debtor;

(c) any other creditor who has proved his debt; and

(d) every other court in which, to the knowledge of the district judge, judgment has been obtained against the debtor or proceedings are pending in respect of any debt scheduled to the order[1].

1 CPR Sch 2 CCR Ord 39 r 9.

Notice of order and proof of debts

29.20 Where an administration order has been made:

(1) notice of the order must be posted in the office of the county court for the district in which the debtor resides, and must be sent to every person whose name the debtor has notified as being a creditor of his or who has proved[1];

(2)   any creditor of the debtor, on proof of his debt before the registrar, is
        entitled to be scheduled as a creditor of the debtor for the amount of his
        proof[2];

(3)   any creditor may object in the prescribed manner[3] to any debt sched-
        uled, or to the manner in which payment is directed to be made by
        instalments[4];

(4)   any person who, after the date of the order, becomes a creditor of the
        debtor must, on proof of his debt before the registrar, be scheduled as a
        creditor of the debtor for the amount of his proof, but is not entitled to
        any dividend under the order until the creditors who are scheduled as
        having been creditors before the date of the order have been paid to the
        extent provided by the order[5].

[1]   County Courts Act 1984, s 113(a).
[2]   Under CPR Sch 2 CCR Ord 39 r 6(1).
[3]   County Courts Act 1984, s 113(b).
[4]   County Courts Act 1984, s 113(c).
[5]   County Courts Act 1984, s 113(d).

Subsequent objection by creditor

29.21   After an administration order has been made, a creditor who has not
received notice of the appointment for consideration whether an administration order should be made and who wishes to object to a debt scheduled to the
order, or to the manner in which payment is directed to be made by
instalments, must give notice to the court of the nature and grounds of his
objection[1]. The court acts by its proper officer[2]. On receipt of such notice the
court must consider the objection and may allow it, dismiss it, or adjourn it
for hearing on notice being given to such persons and on such terms as to
security for costs or otherwise as the court thinks fit[3]. The court may also
dismiss an objection if it is not satisfied that the creditor gave notice of it
within a reasonable time of his becoming aware of the administration order[4].

[1]   CPR Sch 2 CCR Ord 39 r 10(1).
[2]   CPR Sch 2 CCR Ord 39 r 10(1); the proper officer is usually the court manager.
[3]   CPR Sch 2 CCR Ord 39 r 10(2).
[4]   CPR Sch 2 CCR Ord 39 r 10(3).

Subsequent proof by creditor

29.22   Both a creditor whose debt is not scheduled to an administration order,
and a person who became a creditor after the date of the order, may prove his
debt by sending particulars of his claim to the proper officer of the court. The
court then gives notice[1] of the creditor's proof to the debtor and to every
creditor whose debt is scheduled to the order[2].

[1]   In the prescribed form, see the CPR, County Court Form No 375.
[2]   CPR Sch 2 CCR Ord 39 r 11(1).

29.23   If neither the debtor nor any creditor gives notice to the proper officer
that he objects to the claim within seven days after receipt of such notice, and

the court does not require it to be supported by evidence, the claim is to be taken as proved[1]. If the debtor or a creditor gives notice of objection within the said period of seven days or the court requires the claim to be supported by evidence, the proper officer must fix a day for consideration of the claim and give notice thereof to the debtor, the creditor by whom the claim was made and the creditor, if any, making the objection. On the hearing the court may either disallow the claim or allow it in whole or in part[2]. If a claim is proved or allowed, the debt must be added to the schedule to the order and a copy of the order must then be sent to the creditor by whom the claim was made[3].

1   CPR Sch 2 CCR Ord 39 r 11(2).
2   CPR Sch 2 CCR Ord 39 r 11(3).
3   CPR Sch 2 CCR Ord 39 r 11(4).

Conduct of order

29.24 The court manager, or such other officer of the court as the court making an administration order from time to time appoints, has the conduct of the order. He must take all proper steps to enforce the order or to bring to the attention of the court any matter which may make it desirable to review the order[1]. Any creditor whose debt is scheduled to the order may, with the leave of the court, take proceedings to enforce the order[2]; and the debtor or, with the leave of the court, any creditor, may apply to the court to review the order[3].

1   CPR Sch 2 CCR Ord 39 r 13(1).
2   CPR Sch 2 CCR Ord 39 r 13(2).
3   CPR Sch 2 CCR Ord 39 r 13(3).

29.25 The officer having the conduct of the administration order must from time to time declare dividends and distribute them among the creditors. When a dividend is declared, notice must be sent by the officer to each of the creditors[1]. A debtor who changes his residence must forthwith inform the court of his new address; and, where the debtor becomes resident in the district of another court, the court in which the administration order is being conducted may transfer the proceedings to that other court[2].

1   CPR Sch 2 CCR Ord 39 r 17.
2   CPR Sch 2 CCR Ord 39 r 19.

Review of order

29.26 On making an administration order or at any subsequent time, the court may direct that the order shall be subject to review on a particular date or at specified intervals[1]. The debtor or, with the leave of the court, any creditor whose debt is scheduled to the administration order may apply to the court to review the order[2]. Where the court has directed that an administration order shall be subject to review, or where the debtor or a creditor applies to the court to review the order, the court must give seven days' notice of the hearing to the debtor and to every creditor who appeared when the order was made[3]. On the review of an administration order, the court may:

(1) if satisfied that the debtor is unable from any cause to pay any instalment due under the order, suspend the operation of the order for such time and on such terms as it thinks fit;

(2) if satisfied that there has been a material change in any relevant circumstances since the order was made, vary any provision of the order;

(3) if satisfied that the debtor has failed without reasonable cause to comply with any provision of the order or that it is otherwise just and expedient to do so, revoke the order, either forthwith or on failure to comply with any condition specified by the court; or

(4) make an attachment of earnings order to secure the payments required by the administration order or vary or discharge any such attachment or earnings order already made[4].

[1] CPR Sch 2 CCR Ord 39 r 8(1).
[2] CPR Sch 2 CCR Ord 39 r 13(3).
[3] CPR Sch 2 CCR Ord 39 rr 8(2), 13(4).
[4] CPR Sch 2 CCR Ord 39 r 14(1).

29.27 The court manager is required to send a copy of any order varying or revoking an administration order to the debtor, to every creditor whose debt is scheduled to the administration order and, if the administration order is revoked, to any other court to which a copy of the administration order was sent[1].

[1] CPR Sch 2 CCR Ord 39 r 14(2).

Revocation of administration order

29.28 Where a person fails to make any payment which he is required to make under an administration order, the court which is administering that person's estate under the order may revoke the administration order and make an order directing that the debtor shall be restricted in obtaining credit and precluded from acting as a director of a limited liability company for a period not exceeding two years[1]. Where the debtor is precluded from acting as a director pursuant to such an order, he may not, without the leave of the court, act as a director or liquidator of, or directly or indirectly take part or be concerned in the promotion, formation or management of, a company[2]. Contravention of this prohibition is an offence[3].

[1] IA 1986, s 429(1), (2).
[2] Company Directors Disqualification Act 1986, s 12.
[3] Company Directors Disqualification Act 1986, s 13.

29.29 A person who is the subject of such an order may not (1) either alone or jointly with another person, obtain credit[1] to the extent of the prescribed amount[2] or more; or (2) enter into any transaction in the course of, or for the purposes of, any business in which he is directly or indirectly engaged, without disclosing to the person to whom he is dealing the fact that these provisions apply to him[3]. Breach of the order is a criminal offence[4].

1   'Obtaining credit' includes (1) a case where goods are bailed or hired to the debtor under a hire purchase agreement or agreed to be sold to him under a conditional sale agreement; and (2) a case where the debtor is paid in advance, whether in money or otherwise, for the supply of goods or services, IA 1986, s 429(4).
2   Ie the amount prescribed for IA 1986, s 360(1)(a), currently £250.
3   IA 1986, s 429(3).
4   IA 1986, s 429(5).

29.30 On the revocation of an administration order an attachment of earnings order made to secure the payments required by the administration order must be discharged[1].

1   CPR Sch 2 CCR Ord 39 r 16.

Discharge of administration order

29.31 The debtor may obtain a discharge of the administration order by paying sufficient money into court to pay: (1) each creditor scheduled to the order to the extent provided by the order; (2) the costs of the claimant in the action in respect of which the order was made; and (3) the costs of the administration[1]. On the discharge of the order the debtor is discharged from his debts to the scheduled creditors.

1   County Courts Act 1984, s 117(2).

Chapter 30
NEW DEBT MANAGEMENT ARRANGEMENTS

A INTRODUCTION

30.1 There has for some time been widespread concern that there ought to be a simplified procedure for small bankruptcies. The Courts and Legal Services Act 1990 contained detailed provision for significant amendments to be made to administration orders towards this aim, but that provision was never brought into force[1]. In 2004 the Department for Constitutional Affairs issued a consultation document entitled 'A Choice of Paths – better options to manage over-indebtedness and multiple debt'[2]. And in 2005 the Insolvency Service issued a consultation paper 'Relief for the Indebted – An Alternative to Bankruptcy'[3]. These activities have borne fruit in the Tribunal, Courts and Enforcement Act 2007 ('TCEA 2007') which provides for four new procedures for the management of individual over-indebtedness or insolvency.

[1]   Courts and Legal Services Act 1990, s 13 (not in force).
[2]   July 2004.
[3]   March 2005.

Commencement

30.2 None of the provisions discussed in this chapter are yet in force. Commencement orders will be made pursuant to TCEA 2007, s 148.

Regulations

30.3 There is power to make regulations in respect of all the new procedures. It is likely that in the same way that the Insolvency Act 1986 can only be half understood without reference to the Insolvency Rules 1986, so the various provisions discussed below can only be half understood without reference to the rules and regulations to be made with regard to them. At the time of writing these regulations have not yet been made.

The new procedures

30.4 The four new procedures are:

(1)   debt relief orders[1];
(2)   county court administration orders in an amended form in place of the administration orders described in **Chapter 29**[2];
(3)   enforcement restriction orders[3];
(4)   debt repayment plans provided pursuant to debt management schemes[4].

[1]   IA 1986, Part 7A, ss 251A–251X and Schs 4ZA and 4ZB, inserted by TCEA 2007, s 108 and Schs 17–19 (not yet in force).
[2]   County Courts Act 1984, Part 6, ss 112A–112AI, inserted by TCEA 2007, s 106 (not yet in force) in substitution for the existing Part 6.
[3]   County Courts Act 1984, Part 6A, ss 117A–117X, inserted by TCEA 2007, s 107 (not yet in force).
[4]   TCEA 2007, ss 109–133 (not yet in force).

Comparisons between the regimes

30.5 The new regimes have in common the aim of providing relief from indebtedness to consumers or non-business debtors as they are termed. But they have considerable differences, not all readily apparent amongst the detailed statutory provisions, and cater for different types of debtor accordingly.

Debt relief orders

30.6 Debt relief orders are appropriate for a debtor with no substantial assets and no income over what is needed to meet his reasonable domestic needs. The order will result in the debtor's discharge from his relevant debts and give him protection against their enforcement. It cannot impose any obligation on him to make payments; nor does it entail any distribution of assets to creditors because the basis for making the order includes the condition that the debtor's property is limited in value.

Administration orders

30.7 Administration orders protect the debtor from enforcement proceedings for up to a maximum of five years. But it is a requirement of an administration order that the debtor should make repayments and to obtain his discharge from his debts, the debtor must make the repayments required in the administration order. Accordingly, he must have surplus income over that which he needs for his reasonable needs as a condition of the order's being made. Such orders are appropriate for debtors who will, if given sufficient time and protection from enforcement, be able to pay their debts out of their income.

Enforcement restriction orders

30.8 An enforcement restrictions order is only available where the debtor is suffering from a sudden and unforeseen deterioration in his financial circumstances and there is a realistic prospect of an improvement within six months. Thus, it is a regime which will assist a debtor whose problems in paying his debts are, in the short term, acute, but are likely to be overcome in the medium term. While the order will restrict the ability of creditors to pursue the debtor while it is current, it does not provide for any discharge from his debts which he must still pay, including any interest on them, in full.

Debt repayment plans

30.9 Of all the new regimes, debt repayment plans are the most inscrutable. They represent a form of privatised debt relief administered by private operators supervised by a regulatory authority, the Lord Chancellor until other authorities are appointed, and subject only to limited express rights of recourse to the court. Like the other regimes they are aimed at the consumer debtor but, until the rules governing them are promulgated and the schemes under which they are to be offered are drawn up, it remains to be seen precisely what their remit will be.

B DEBT RELIEF ORDERS

Debt relief order

30.10 Debt relief orders provide protection from indebtedness similar to bankruptcy in that they prohibit further legal process against the debtor without the court's permission in respect of his debts and at the end of one year discharge the debtor from those debts. They differ from bankruptcy in that, since they are only available to debtors with no substantial assets and no income over that which is necessary to meet the debtor's reasonable needs, there is no provision relating to the collection, realisation and distribution of the debtor's estate. The assumption is that there will be nothing to distribute. They also differ from bankruptcy in that they are primarily conducted as an administrative exercise carried out by the official receiver. The role of the court is only supervisory and this supervision will only occur where the official receiver or some interested party invokes it. A further difference to note is that an application for a debt relief order may only be initiated by a debtor, not by a creditor; and the debtor may only make his application through an approved intermediary. Approved intermediaries are to be individuals approved to act as intermediaries by a supervising authority; their role will be twofold: to assist the debtor, but also to provide a further check on the truth of what the debtor tells the official receiver in his application.

Insolvency Act 1986, Part 7A

30.11 The provisions relating to debt relief orders are contained in a new part, Part 7A, inserted into IA 1986 by TCEA 2007, s 108. The new Part 7A comprises ss 251A–251X and is supplemented by two new schedules, Sch 4ZA and Sch 4ZB. As mentioned above, these provisions are not yet in force, but they are described below as if they were.

Application for a debt relief order

Applicant

30.12 An individual who is unable to pay his debts may apply for a debt relief order to be made in respect of his qualifying debts[1].

[1]   IA 1986, s 251A(1).

Qualifying debts

30.13 A 'qualifying debt' means a debt which is for a liquidated sum payable either immediately or at some certain future time and is not an excluded debt[1]. Regulations not yet made will prescribe the meaning of 'excluded debt'[2]. A debt is not a qualifying debt to the extent that it is secured[3].

[1]   IA 1986, s 251A(2).
[2]   IA 1986, s 251A(3).
[3]   IA 1986, s 251A(4).

Application

30.14 An application for a debt relief order must be made to the official receiver through an approved intermediary[1].

[1]   IA 1986, s 251B(1).

Required information

30.15 The application must include:

(a)   a list of the debts to which the debtor is subject at the date of the application, specifying the amount of each debt (including any interest, penalty or other sum that has become payable in relation to that debt on or before that date) and the creditor to whom it is owed;
(b)   details of any security held in respect of any of those debts; and

(c)   such other information about the debtor's affairs (including his credi-
         tors, debts and liabilities and his income and assets) as may be
         prescribed[1].

[1]   IA 1986, s 251B(2).

Procedure

30.16 Details of the procedure to be followed will be contained in regulations
which may make further provision as to:

(a)   the form of an application for a debt relief order;
(b)   the manner in which an application is to be made; and
(c)   information and documents to be supplied in support of an applica-
         tion[1].

[1]   IA 1986, s 251B(3).

When the application is treated as having been made

30.17 An application is not to be regarded as having been made until it has
been submitted to the official receiver and any fee required in connection with
it has been duly paid[1]. Until both these steps have been taken and the
application is in consequence recognised as having been made, the official
receiver will not come under any duty to consider and determine the
application. In the interpretation section[2], 'the application date' is defined, in
relation to a debt relief order or an application for a debt relief order, as
meaning the date on which the application for the order is made to the official
receiver. This must therefore mean the date on which either the application is
submitted and the appropriate fee duly paid or if those steps are taken on
different dates, the later of the two dates.

[1]   IA 1986, s 251B(4).
[2]   IA 1986, s 251X(1).

Criminal law

30.18 Offences may be committed if the debtor knowingly gives false
information given in or in support of the application. These are mentioned
further below.

Approved intermediaries

Definition

30.19 As mentioned, a debtor may only apply for a debt relief order through
an approved intermediary. That means an individual for the time being

approved by a competent authority to act as an intermediary between a person wishing to make an application for a debt relief order and the official receiver[1].

1   IA 1986, s 251U(1).

The function of the approved intermediary

30.20 The role of the approved intermediary is important. First, he will be a source of help and advice to individuals in financial distress. But secondly, when the official receiver comes to determine the application he is obliged to presume that the application is justified if the information supplied in the application appears to justify it[1]. The approved intermediary should therefore take care, as far as he can, to ensure that the information given is correct and addresses all the points which need to be covered.

1   IA 1986, s 251D.

Competent authority

30.21 The Secretary of State will designate persons or bodies for the purposes of granting approvals to individuals to act as approved intermediaries. Designation as a competent authority may be limited so as to permit the authority only to approve persons of a particular description[1].

1   IA 1986, s 251U(2) and (3).

Regulations relating to designation of competent authorities

30.22 The Secretary of State may by regulations make provision as to the procedure for designating persons or bodies as competent authorities and for the withdrawal of designations. The regulations may include provision requiring the payment of fees[1].

1   IA 1986, s 251U(4)(a).

Regulations relating to approval of intermediaries

30.23 The Secretary of State may also make regulations containing provision as to descriptions of individuals who are ineligible to be approved under IA 1986, s 251U; the procedure for granting approvals to intermediaries and for the withdrawal of approvals. The regulations may include provision requiring the payment of fees[1].

1   IA 1986, s 251U(4)(b) and (c).

Regulations relating to the activities of intermediaries

30.24 The regulations to be made by the Secretary of State may make provision about the activities to be carried out by an approved intermediary in connection with an application for a debt relief order, which may in particular include assisting the debtor in making the application; checking that the application has been properly completed; and sending the application to the official receiver. The rules may also make provision about other activities to be carried out by approved intermediaries[1].

[1]   IA 1986, s 251U(5) and (6).

Prohibition on intermediaries' charging fees

30.25 An approved intermediary may not charge a debtor any fee in connection with an application for a debt relief order[1].

[1]   IA 1986, s 251U(7).

Immunity from suit

30.26 An approved intermediary is not liable to any person in damages for anything done or omitted to be done when acting (or purporting to act) as an approved intermediary in connection with a particular application by a debtor for a debt relief order, unless the act or omission was in bad faith[1].

[1]   IA 1986, s 251U(8) and (9).

Conditions for making a debt relief order

Conditions which must be met

30.27 Schedule 4ZA, Part 1 contains a series of conditions which must be satisfied in respect of a debtor in order to obtain a debt relief order. As discussed below, the official receiver is charged with deciding whether the conditions are met. If he is not satisfied that they are all met, he must refuse the application[1]. The conditions which must be met are set out in the following paragraphs.

[1]   IA 1986, s 251C(5)(c).

Connection with England and Wales

30.28 The debtor must:

(1)   be domiciled in England and Wales on the application date;
(2)   at any time during the period of three years ending with that date have been ordinarily resident, or have had a place of residence, in England and Wales; or
(3)   at any time during that three-year period, have carried on business in England and Wales[1].

[1]   IA 1986, Sch 4ZA, para 1.

30.29 Obviously if the debtor trades as a sole trader, he is carrying on business. But he is also treated as carrying on business where business is carried on by a firm or partnership of which the debtor is a member; or by an agent or manager for him or for such a firm or partnership.

30.30 This requirement corresponds with some[1] of the jurisdictional conditions imposed by IA 1986, s 265(1) which must be satisfied before a bankruptcy petition may be presented.

[1] Personal presence in the jurisdiction is omitted.

Debtor's previous insolvency history: his current status

30.31 On the determination date, the debtor must not be an undischarged bankrupt; subject to an interim order or voluntary arrangement under Part 8; or subject to a bankruptcy restrictions order or a debt relief restrictions order[1].

[1] IA 1986, Sch 4ZA, para 2.

Debtor's previous insolvency history: prior petitions presented by the debtor

30.32 Where a debtor has presented a petition for his own bankruptcy before the determination date, a debt relief order may not be made unless proceedings on the petition have been finally disposed of before that date; or, on hearing the petition, the court has referred the debtor under IA 1986, s 274A(2) for the purposes of making an application for a debt relief order. On a literal reading of the provision, it would seem that any prior debtor's petition will prevent the making of a debt relief order; but the better reading, taking the immediately preceding paragraph with its reference to being an undischarged bankrupt into account, seems to be that if the debtor had previously presented his own petition, been made bankrupt on it and in due course been discharged, he would be eligible for a debt relief order. The proceedings on the petition referred to in the first exception must mean the proceedings on the petition which come to an end with a bankruptcy order or the dismissal or withdrawal of the petition[1].

[1] IA 1986, Sch 4ZA, para 3.

Debtor's previous insolvency history: creditor's petitions

30.33 Equally where a creditor's petition for the debtor's bankruptcy under Part 9 is pending at the determination date, no debt relief order may be made unless proceedings on the petition have been finally disposed of before that date; or the person who presented the petition has consented to the making of an application for a debt relief order[1].

[1] IA 1986, Sch 4ZA, para 4.

30.34 *New debt management arrangements*

Debtor's previous insolvency history: prior debt relief orders

30.34 A debtor is not eligible for a debt relief order if an earlier debt relief order has been made in relation to him in the period of six years ending with the determination date[1].

1   IA 1986, Sch 4ZA, para 5.

Limit on debtor's overall indebtedness

30.35 The total amount of the debtor's debts on the determination date, other than unliquidated debts and excluded debts, must not exceed the prescribed amount. Regulations prescribing the relevant amount have not yet been made. For this purpose an unliquidated debt is a debt that is not for a liquidated sum payable to a creditor either immediately or at some future certain time[1].

1   IA 1986, Sch 4ZA, para 6.

Limit on debtor's monthly surplus income

30.36 The debtor's monthly surplus income (if any) on the determination date must not exceed the prescribed amount. Regulations prescribing the relevant amount have not yet been made. For this purpose 'monthly surplus income' is the amount by which a person's monthly income exceeds the amount necessary for the reasonable domestic needs of himself and his family. The rules to be made may make provision as to how the debtor's monthly surplus income is to be determined; and provide that particular descriptions of income are to be excluded for the purposes of this determination[1].

1   IA 1986, Sch 4ZA, para 7.

Limit on value of debtor's property

30.37 The total value of the debtor's property on the determination date must not exceed the prescribed amount. Regulations prescribing the relevant amount have not yet been made. The rules to be made may make provision as to how the value of a person's property is to be determined; and provide that particular descriptions of property are to be excluded for the purposes of this determination[1].

1   IA 1986, Sch 4ZA, para 8.

Other conditions

30.38 IA 1986, Sch 4ZA, Part 2 contains other conditions to the effect that the debtor has not at a material time entered into a transaction at an undervalue or given a preference. If the official receiver is not satisfied that these conditions are fulfilled, meaning if the official receiver is not satisfied

1114

that the debtor has not entered into a transaction at an undervalue or given a preference at a material time, then the official receiver may refuse the application for a debt relief order[1].

¹ IA 1986, s 251C(6).

Transactions at an undervalue

30.39 The condition relating to transactions at an undervalue is that the debtor has not entered into a transaction with any person at an undervalue during the period between the start of the period of two years ending with the application date; and the determination date. This is a much shorter period than the five years before presentation of the petition applicable in bankruptcy[1]. For this purpose a debtor enters into a transaction with a person at an undervalue if:

(a) he makes a gift to that person or he otherwise enters into a transaction with that person on terms that provide for him to receive no consideration;

(b) he enters into a transaction with that person in consideration of marriage or the formation of a civil partnership; or

(c) he enters into a transaction with that person for a consideration the value of which, in money or money's worth, is significantly less than the value, in money or money's worth, of the consideration provided by the individual[2].

¹ See IA 1986, s 341(1)(a).
² IA 1986, Sch 4ZA, para 9.

Preferences

30.40 The condition relating to preferences is that the debtor has not given a preference to any person during the period between the start of the period of two years ending with the application date; and the determination date. For this purpose a debtor gives a preference to a person if that person is one of the debtor's creditors to whom a qualifying debt is owed or is a surety or guarantor for any such debt, and the debtor does anything or suffers anything to be done which (in either case) has the effect of putting that person into a position which, in the event that a debt relief order is made in relation to the debtor, will be better than the position he would have been in if that thing had not been done[1].

¹ IA 1986, Sch 4ZA, para 10.

Determination of the application

Duty of the official receiver to determine an application

30.41 Once the application has been duly made, the official receiver must determine it. The decision which he is positively required to make is the decision whether to refuse the application[1]. The grounds on which a refusal may be based are specified in the statute. In some cases, if the specified grounds obtain, the official receiver has a discretion whether to refuse the application; in others, he is obliged to refuse the application. If the official receiver does not refuse the application, then he must make a debt relief order in relation to the specified debts he is satisfied were qualifying debts of the debtor at the application date.

[1]   IA 1986, s 251C(3)(a).

Stay of determination

30.42 The official receiver may stay consideration of the application until he has received answers to any queries raised with the debtor in relation to anything connected with the application[1].

[1]   IA 1986, s 251C(2).

Mandatory grounds for refusing an application

30.43 The official receiver must refuse the application if he is not satisfied that:

(a)   the debtor is an individual who is unable to pay his debts;
(b)   at least one of the specified debts was a qualifying debt of the debtor at the application date;
(c)   each of the conditions set out in Sch 4ZA, Part 1 is met[1].

[1]   IA 1986, s 251C(5).

30.44 For the purpose of satisfying himself as to these requirements, it is provided that the official receiver must make certain presumptions. The effect of the presumptions is to give considerable weight to the information supplied in the application; they also serve to reduce the scope of the inquiries which the official receiver needs to make in a routine case.

The presumptions

30.45 First, the official receiver must presume that the debtor is an individual who is unable to pay his debts at the determination date if that appears to him to be the case at the application date from the information supplied in, or in support of, the application and he has no reason to believe that the information supplied is incomplete or inaccurate; and he has no reason to believe that, by virtue of a change in the debtor's financial circumstances since the application date, the debtor may be able to pay his debts[1].

[1]   IA 1986, s 251D(2).

30.46 Secondly, he must presume that a specified debt (of the amount specified in the application and owed to the creditor so specified) is a qualifying debt at the application date if that appears to him to be the case from the information supplied in, or in support of, the application; and he has no reason to believe that the information supplied is incomplete or inaccurate[1].

1   IA 1986, s 251D(3).

30.47 Thirdly, he must presume that the condition specified in Sch 4ZA, para 1, concerning the debtor's connection with England and Wales, is met if that appears to him to be the case from the information supplied in, or in support of, the application; any prescribed verification checks relating to the condition have been made; and he has no reason to believe that the information supplied is incomplete or inaccurate[1].

1   IA 1986, s 251D(4).

30.48 Finally, he must presume that any other condition specified in Sch 4ZA, Part 1 or 2 is met if that appears to him to have been the case as at the application date from the information supplied in, or in support of, the application and he has no reason to believe that the information supplied is incomplete or inaccurate; any prescribed verification checks relating to the condition have been made; and he has no reason to believe that, by virtue of a change in circumstances since the application date, the condition may no longer be met[1].

1   IA 1986, s 251D(5).

Discretionary grounds for refusing an application

30.49 The official receiver may refuse the application if he considers that:

(a)   the application does not meet all the requirements imposed by or under IA 1986, s 251B;
(b)   any queries raised with the debtor have not been answered to the satisfaction of the official receiver within such time as he may specify when they are raised;
(c)   the debtor has made any false representation or omission in making the application or on supplying any information or documents in support of it[1].

1   IA 1986, s 251C(4).

30.50 The official receiver may refuse the application if he is not satisfied that each condition specified in Sch 4ZA, Part 2 is met[1].

1   IA 1986, s 251C(6).

30.51 *New debt management arrangements*

Reasons for refusal

30.51 If the official receiver refuses an application he must give reasons for his refusal to the debtor in the prescribed manner[1].

¹ IA 1986, s 251C(7).

The order

Form and content

30.52 The order must be made in the prescribed form. It must include a list of the debts which the official receiver is satisfied were qualifying debts of the debtor at the application date, specifying the amount of the debt at that time and the creditor to whom it was then owed[1]. References to a creditor who is specified in a debt relief order as the person to whom a qualifying debt is owed by the debtor include a reference to any person to whom the right to claim the whole or any part of the debt has passed, by assignment or operation of law, after the date of the application for the order[2].

¹ IA 1986, s 251E(2) and (3).
² IA 1986, s 251X(2).

Official receiver's duty to give a copy to the debtor

30.53 The official receiver must give a copy of the order to the debtor[1].

¹ IA 1986, s 251E(4)(a).

Official receiver's duty to register the order

30.54 The official receiver must make an entry for the order in the register containing the prescribed information about the order or the debtor[1]. Registration is an important step because the date on which an entry relating to the making of a debt relief order is first made in the register is referred to in IA 1986 Part 7A as 'the effective date'[2]. The effective date is the date from which the moratorium imposed by the order takes effect[3].

¹ IA 1986, s 251E(4)(b).
² IA 1986, s 251E(7).
³ IA 1986, s 251G(1).

Other steps to be taken by the official receiver

30.55 The rules, yet to be made, may make provision as to other steps to be taken by the official receiver on the making of the order. Those steps may include, in particular, notifying each creditor to whom a qualifying debt

1118

specified in the order is owed of the making of the order and its effect, the grounds on which a creditor may object under IA 1986, s 251K, and any other prescribed information[1].

1   IA 1986, s 251E(5) and (6).

Other steps to be taken by the debtor

30.56 The rules, yet to be made, may also make provision as to other steps to be taken by the debtor on the making of the order[1].

1   IA 1986, s 251E(5) and (6).

The effect of the order

Effect on other debt management arrangements

30.57 A debt relief order overrides any other debt management arrangements which are in force in respect of the debtor immediately before the order is made. In this context, 'other debt management arrangements' means (a) an administration order under the County Courts Act 1984, Part 6; (b) an enforcement restriction order under the County Courts Act 1984, Part 6A; and (c) a debt repayment plan arranged in accordance with a debt management scheme that is approved under the Tribunals, Courts and Enforcement Act 2007, Part 5, Ch 4. Any of these debt management arrangements cease to be in force when the debt relief order is made[1].

1   IA 1986, s 251F.

Moratorium from qualifying debts

30.58 On the effective date for the debt relief order a moratorium commences in relation to each qualifying debt specified in the order. Each of these debts is referred to as 'a specified qualifying debt'[1].

1   IA 1986, s 251G(1).

Prohibition on commencing proceedings without permission

30.59 During the moratorium, any creditor to whom a specified qualifying debt is owed has no remedy in respect of the debt, and may not commence a creditor's petition in respect of the debt, or otherwise commence any action or other legal proceedings against the debtor for the debt, except with the permission of the court and on such terms as the court may impose. References here to the debt include a reference to any interest, penalty or other sum that becomes payable in relation to that debt after the application date[1].

1   IA 1986, s 251G(2).

30.60 *New debt management arrangements*

Pending proceedings

30.60 If, on the effective date, a creditor to whom a specified qualifying debt is owed has any petition, action or other proceeding pending in any court against the debtor for the debt, the court may stay the proceedings on the petition, action or other proceedings (as the case may be), or allow them to continue on such terms as the court thinks fit[1]. If a creditor's petition against the debtor is pending at the determination date[2], then that application could only be made if the creditor consented to the making of the application for the debt relief order[3]. But it is possible that a creditor's petition might be presented between the determination date and the effective date. If the creditor's petition had been presented before the determination date and was still pending on that date, then an application for a debt relief order could only be made with the consent of the petitioning creditor[4].

1   IA 1986, s 251G(3).
2   IA 1986, s 251X(1).
3   IA 1986, Sch 4ZA, para 4(c).
4   IA 1986, s 251C(5)(c) and Sch 4ZA, para 4(c).

Saving for secured creditors

30.61 The moratorium does not affect the right of a secured creditor of the debtor to enforce his security[1].

1   IA 1986, s 251G(5).

Period of the moratorium

30.62 The moratorium relating to the qualifying debts specified in a debt relief order continues for the period of one year beginning with the effective date for the order, unless the moratorium terminates early; or the moratorium period is extended by the official receiver or by the court[1]. Early termination means the order's terminating before the end of what would otherwise be the moratorium period, whether on the revocation of the order or by virtue of any other enactment[2]. The moratorium period may be extended more than once, but any extension (whether by the official receiver or by the court) must be made before the moratorium would otherwise end[3].

1   IA 1986, s 251H(1).
2   IA 1986, s 251H(6).
3   IA 1986, s 251H(5).

Official receiver's power to extend the moratorium

30.63 The official receiver may only extend the moratorium period for the purpose of (a) carrying out or completing an investigation under IA 1986, s 251K; (b) taking any action he considers necessary (whether as a result of an investigation or otherwise) in relation to the order; or (c) in a case where he has decided to revoke the order, providing the debtor with the opportunity to make arrangements for making payments towards his debts[1]. The official receiver may not extend the moratorium period for the purpose of pursuing an investigation under IA 1986, s 251K without the permission of the court[2]. He may not extend the moratorium period beyond the end of the period of three months beginning after the end of the initial period of one year beginning with the effective date[3].

1   IA 1986, s 251H(2).
2   IA 1986, s 251H(3).
3   IA 1986, s 251H(4).

Discharge from qualifying debts

30.64 At the end of the moratorium applicable to a debt relief order the debtor is discharged from all the qualifying debts specified in the order (including all interest, penalties and other sums which may have become payable in relation to those debts since the application date)[1]. But the debtor is not discharged from any of those debts if the moratorium terminates early[2]. And, even if the moratorium runs its course, he is not discharged from any qualifying debt which he incurred in respect of any fraud or fraudulent breach of trust to which he was a party[3]. Further, if the debt relief order is revoked by the court after the end of the moratorium period, the qualifying debts specified in the order shall (so far as practicable) be treated as though the statutory discharge had never applied to them[4].

1   IA 1986, s 251I(1).
2   IA 1986, s 251I(2).
3   IA 1986, s 251I(3).
4   IA 1986, s 251I(5).

Preservation of third parties' liabilities

30.65 The discharge of the debtor at the end of the moratorium period does not release any other person from any liability (whether as partner or co-trustee of the debtor or otherwise) from which the debtor is released by the discharge; or any liability as surety for the debtor or as a person in the nature of such a surety[1]. Thus, even where the liability is a joint liability, a third party who is jointly liable with the debtor will not be released from his liability by reason of the debtor's discharge.

1   IA 1986, s 251I(4).

Debtor's duties

30.66 Once the debtor has made an application for a debt relief order he becomes subject to certain duties with which he must comply[1].

1   IA 1986, s 251J(1).

30.67 *New debt management arrangements*

General duty to co-operate with the official receiver

30.67 He must give to the official receiver such information as to his affairs, attend on the official receiver at such times, and do all such other things, as the official receiver may reasonably require for the purpose of carrying out his functions in relation to the application or, as the case may be, the debt relief order made as a result of the application[1]. This duty continues to apply after (as well as before) the determination of the application, for as long as the official receiver is able to exercise functions in relation to the application or the ensuing debt relief order[2].

1   IA 1986, s 251J(2).
2   IA 1986, s 251J(4).

Duty to give notice of errors, omissions and material changes

30.68 He must notify the official receiver as soon as reasonably practicable if he becomes aware of any error in, or omission from, the information supplied to the official receiver in, or in support of, the application; or any change in his circumstances between the application date and the determination date that would affect (or would have affected) the determination of the application[1]. This duty continues after the determination of the application, like the duty mentioned in the preceding paragraph[2].

1   IA 1986, s 251J(3).
2   IA 1986, s 251J(4).

Duty to give notice of increase in income, after-acquired property, etc

30.69 If a debt relief order is made, the debtor must notify the official receiver as soon as reasonably practicable if there is an increase in his income during the moratorium period applicable to the order; he acquires any property or any property is devolved upon him during that period; or he becomes aware of any error in or omission from any information supplied by him to the official receiver after the determination date[1].

1   IA 1986, s 251J(5).

Non-compliance

30.70 Non-compliance with any of the duties forms a ground on which the official receiver can revoke the debt relief order[1].

1   IA 1986, s 251L(2)(b).

Criminal law

30.71 Intentional failure to comply with the duties to provide information is an offence[1].

1   IA 1986, s 251O(2)(a) and (4)(a).

Objections to the official receiver

Creditor's entitlement to object

30.72 Any person specified in a debt relief order as a creditor to whom a specified qualifying debt is owed may object to (a) the making of the order; (b) the inclusion of the debt in the list of the debtor's qualifying debts; or (c) the details of the debt specified in the order[1].

[1]   IA 1986, s 251K(1).

Regulation of objections

30.73 The creditor's entitlement to object is not at large. An objection must be:

(a)   made during the moratorium period relating to the order and within the prescribed period for objections, which must not be less than 28 days after the creditor in question has been notified of the making of the order;

(b)   made to the official receiver in the prescribed manner;

(c)   based on a prescribed ground;

(d)   supported by any information and documents as may be prescribed[1].

[1]   IA 1986, s 251K(2).

Duty to consider objections

30.74 The official receiver must consider every objection made to him[1].

[1]   IA 1986, s 251K(3).

Official receiver's power to investigate

Power to investigate

30.75 The official receiver may, either as part of his consideration of an objection, or on his own initiative, carry out an investigation of any matter that appears to the official receiver to be relevant to the making of certain specified decisions in relation to a debt relief order or the debtor. The decisions to which an investigation may be directed are (a) whether the order should be revoked or amended under IA 1986, s 251L; (b) whether an application should be made to the court under IA 1986, s 251M; or (c) whether any other steps should be taken in relation to the debtor[1].

[1]   IA 1986, s 251K(4) and (5).

When exercisable

30.76 The power to carry out an investigation under IA 1986, s 251K is exercisable after (as well as during) the moratorium relating to the order[1].

¹ IA 1986, s 251K(6).

Obtaining information

30.77 The official receiver may require any person to give him such information and assistance as he may reasonably require in connection with an investigation under IA 1986, s 251K[1].

¹ IA 1986, s 251K(7).

Conduct of the investigation

30.78 Subject to anything prescribed in the rules as to the procedure to be followed in carrying out an investigation pursuant to this power, an investigation may be carried out by the official receiver in such manner as he thinks fit[1].

¹ IA 1986, s 251K(8).

Official receiver's power to revoke the order

The power to revoke

30.79 The official receiver may revoke a debt relief order during the applicable moratorium period only on one or more of a number of specified grounds[1].

¹ IA 1986, s 251L(1).

Grounds for revocation

30.80 First, the official receiver may revoke the order on the ground that:

(a) any information supplied to him by the debtor in, or in support of, the application, or after the determination date, was incomplete, incorrect or otherwise misleading;

(b) the debtor has failed to comply with one of the duties imposed on him by IA 1986, s 251J;

(c) a bankruptcy order has been made in relation to the debtor; or

(d) the debtor has made a proposal for an IVA under IA 1986, Part 8 (or has notified the official receiver of his intention to do so)[1].

¹ IA 1986, s 251L(2).

30.81 Secondly, he may revoke the order on the ground that he should not have been satisfied:

(a)   that the debts specified in the order were qualifying debts of the debtor as at the application date;
(b)   that the conditions specified in Sch 4ZA, Part 1 were met;
(c)   that the conditions specified in Sch 4ZA, Part 2 were met or that any failure to meet such a condition did not prevent his making the order.

This ground is most likely to come into play where a creditor has objected to the order and adduced evidence negating the information supplied in, or in support of, the application[1].

¹   IA 1986, s 251L(3).

30.82 Thirdly, he may revoke the order on the ground that either or both of the conditions in Sch 4ZA, paras 7 and 8 (monthly surplus income and property) are not met at any time after the order was made. For this purpose those paragraphs are to be read as if references to the determination date were references to the time in question. This ground enables the official receiver to revoke the order on the basis that the debtor's financial circumstances have improved in relevant respects since the order was made. This would seem to put a disincentive on the debtor's trying to change his position for the better during the period of the moratorium. Nor does there seem to be a means whereby the debtor could offer to pay the surplus income or after-acquired property to the benefit of his creditors because the scheme does not include any power or machinery for distributions to be made to creditors[1].

¹   IA 1986, s 251L(4).

When the revocation is to take effect

30.83 Where the official receiver decides to revoke the order, he may revoke it either (a) with immediate effect, or (b) with effect from such date (not more than three months after the date of the decision) as he may specify. In considering when the revocation should take effect the official receiver must consider (in the light of the grounds on which the decision to revoke was made and all the other circumstances of the case) whether the debtor ought to be given the opportunity to make arrangements for making payments towards his debts. It might be appropriate to give this opportunity where the decision to revoke is based on a ground that the debtor is earning surplus income or has received property since the order was made the extent of which prompts its revocation[1].

¹   IA 1986, s 251L(5) and (6).

30.84 If the order has been revoked with effect from a specified date the official receiver may, if he thinks it appropriate to do so at any time before that date, revoke the order with immediate effect[1].

¹   IA 1986, s 251L(7).

Official receiver's power to amend the order

30.85 The official receiver may amend a debt relief order for the purpose of correcting an error in or omission from anything specified in the order. But the official receiver may not amend the order so as to add any debts that were not specified in the application for the debt relief order to the list of qualifying debts[1].

[1] IA 1986, s 251L(8) and (9).

Applications to the court

Persons dissatisfied with the official receiver's decisions

30.86 Any person may make an application to the court if he is dissatisfied by any act, omission or decision of the official receiver in connection with a debt relief order or an application for such an order[1].

[1] IA 1986, s 251M(1).

Applications by the official receiver

30.87 The official receiver may make an application to the court for directions or an order in relation to any matter arising in connection with a debt relief order or an application for such an order.

30.88 Matters which may be the subject of an application for directions include, among other things, matters relating to the debtor's compliance with any duty arising under IA 1986, s 251J[1].

[1] IA 1986, s 251M(2) and (3).

When applications may be made

30.89 An application under IA 1986, s 251M may, subject to anything in the rules, be made at any time[1].

[1] IA 1986, s 251M(4).

Extension of moratorium period while application pending

30.90 The court may extend the moratorium period applicable to a debt relief order for the purposes of determining an application under IA 1986, s 251M[1].

[1] IA 1986, s 251M(5).

Orders which may be made

30.91 On an application either by a dissatisfied person or by the official receiver, the court may dismiss the application or do one or more of the following:

(a)   quash the whole or part of any act or decision of the official receiver;
(b)   give the official receiver directions (including a direction that he reconsider any matter in relation to which his act or decision has been quashed under paragraph (a));
(c)   make an order for the enforcement of any obligation on the debtor arising by virtue of a duty under IA 1986, s 251J;
(d)   extend the moratorium period applicable to the debt relief order;
(e)   make an order revoking or amending the debt relief order;
(f)   make an order under IA 1986, s 251N; or
(g)   make such other order as the court thinks fit[1].

[1]   IA 1986, s 251M(6).

30.92 An order for the revocation of a debt relief order may be made during the moratorium period applicable to the debt relief order or at any time after that period has ended; may also be made on the court's own motion if the court has made a bankruptcy order in relation to the debtor during that period; and may provide for the revocation of the order to take effect on such terms and at such a time as the court may specify[1].

[1]   IA 1986, s 251M(7).

30.93 An order for the amendment of a debt relief order may not add any debts that were not specified in the application for the debt relief order to the list of qualifying debts[1].

[1]   IA 1986, s 251M(8).

Inquiries by court order

30.94 The court has similar powers to make orders for the purpose of investigating the financial affairs of a person subject to a debt relief order to those available in bankruptcy by way of private examination. The orders may be made, and it appears only made, on application by the official receiver[1].

[1]   IA 1986, s 251N(1).

Orders to appear for examination

30.95 The court may order any of the following persons to appear before it: the debtor; the debtor's spouse or former spouse or the debtor's civil partner or former civil partner; and any person appearing to the court to be able to give information or assistance concerning the debtor or his dealings, affairs and property. Persons in the third category may be required to provide a written account of his dealings with the debtor; or to produce any documents in his possession or under his control relating to the debtor or to the debtor's dealings, affairs or property[1].

1   IA 1986, s 251N(2) and (3).

Arrest warrants

30.96 Where a person fails without reasonable excuse to appear before the court when he is summoned to do so the court may cause a warrant to be issued to a constable or prescribed officer of the court for the arrest of that person, and for the seizure of any records or other documents in that person's possession. The court may authorise a person arrested under such a warrant to be kept in custody, and anything seized under such a warrant to be held, in accordance with the rules, until that person is brought before the court under the warrant or until such other time as the court may order[1].

1   IA 1986, s 251N(4) and (5).

Offences

30.97 With the debt relief regime are introduced a series of new criminal offences intended as a bulwark against abuse. Proceedings for any of these offences may only be instituted by the Secretary of State or by or with the consent of the Director of Public Prosecutions[1]. It is not a defence that anything relied on, in whole or in part, as constituting the offence was done outside England and Wales[2].

1   IA 1986, s 251T(1).
2   IA 1986, s 251T(2).

Offences in connection with applications

30.98 Offences may be committed by a person who makes an application for a debt relief order if he knowingly or recklessly makes any false representation or omission in making the application or providing any information or documents to the official receiver in support of the application; or if he intentionally fails to comply with a duty to notify the official receiver of an error or omission in the information given in or in support of the application or of a material change in his circumstances[1]. The offences may still be committed even if no debt relief order is made as a result of the application[2]. Although these offences would seem to be aimed primarily at the applicant rather than an approved intermediary because it is the applicant who makes the application, an approved intermediary would no doubt be guilty of aiding and abetting the offence if he knowingly assisted the applicant in, for example, making a false representation. The approved intermediary's immunity from suit only applies to civil claims for damages[3]. The relevant offence may still be committed even though no debt relief order is made.

1   IA 1986, s 251O(1) and (2).

2   IA 1986, s 251O(3).
3   IA 1986, s 251U(8).

Offences concerning non-disclosure of information

30.99 Once the debt relief order is made, the debtor to whom it relates is guilty of an offence if he intentionally fails to comply with a duty under IA 1986, s 251J(5) to inform the official receiver of increases in his income or the acquisition of property or of any error or omission in any information given to the official receiver after the determination date; or he knowingly or recklessly makes any false representation or omission in providing information to the official receiver in connection with such a duty or otherwise in connection with the performance by the official receiver of functions in relation to the order[1].

1   IA 1986, s 251O(4).

Offences relating to the debtor's books and records

30.100 Offences may also be committed if the debtor fails to provide his records to the official receiver when requested to provide them or if he prevents their production or conceals or destroys them. Failure to keep proper records in the period preceding the application for the debt relief order may also involve an offence. A defendant has a defence if he proves that, in respect of the conduct constituting the offence, he had no intent to defraud or to conceal the state of his affairs[1].

1   IA 1986, s 251P.

Offences relating to transfers of property

30.101 A person in respect of whom a debt relief order is made is guilty of an offence if he made or caused to be made any gift or transfer of his property during the period between the start of the period of two years ending with the application date and the end of the moratorium period.

30.102 A transfer of any property includes causing or conniving at the levying of any execution against that property. It is a defence if the debtor proves that, in respect of the conduct constituting the offence, he had no intent to defraud or to conceal the state of his affairs[1].

1   IA 1986, s 251Q.

Offences relating to property obtained on credit

30.103 The debtor in respect of whom a debt relief order has been made may commit an offence if he disposes of any property which he has obtained on credit and for which, at the time of the disposal, he has not paid. The person receiving the property may also be guilty of an offence if he receives the property knowing or believing that the debtor owed money in respect of the property, and that the debtor did not intend, or was unlikely to be able, to pay the money he so owed. These offences may be committed if the disposal or receipt occurred during the period between the start of the period of two years ending with the application date and the determination date. No offence is committed if the disposal, acquisition or receipt of the property was in the ordinary course of a business carried on by the debtor. In determining whether any property is disposed of, acquired or received in the ordinary course of a business carried on by the debtor, regard may be had, in particular, to the price paid for the property.

30.104 The debtor has a defence if he proves that, in respect of the conduct constituting the offence, he had no intent to defraud or to conceal the state of his affairs. Disposing of property includes pawning or pledging it; and references to acquiring or receiving property are to be similarly construed[1].

[1] IA 1986, s 251R.

Offences relating to obtaining credit or engaging in business

30.105 A person in respect of whom a debt relief order is made is guilty of an offence if, during the relevant period he obtains credit (either alone or jointly with any other person) without giving the person from whom he obtains the credit the relevant information about his status; or he engages directly or indirectly in any business under a name other than that in which the order was made without disclosing to all persons with whom he enters into any business transaction the name in which the order was made. The relevant information about a person's status is the information that a moratorium is in force in relation to the debt relief order, a debt relief restrictions order is in force in respect of him, or both a moratorium and a debt relief restrictions order is in force, as the case may be. The relevant period is the moratorium period relating to the debt relief order, or the period for which a debt relief restrictions order is in force in relation to the person in respect of whom the debt relief order is made, as the case may be. Obtaining credit includes taking possession of goods under a hire-purchase agreement or a conditional sale agreement and payment in advance (in money or otherwise) for the supply of goods or services. No offence is committed if the amount of the credit is less than the prescribed amount (if any)[1].

[1] IA 1986, s 251S.

Debt relief restrictions orders and undertakings

30.106 Although in general it is now accepted that falling into financial distress is not of itself a justification for social reproach, it remains possible that the causes of an individual's indebtedness are to be found in his own irresponsible behaviour. As in bankruptcy, so with respect to persons subject to debt relief orders, a regime of debt relief restrictions orders is to be implemented for the purpose of imposing on individuals, where justified, a regime of disqualification from holding public or financial offices.

Persons against whom debt relief restrictions orders may be made

30.107 A debt relief restrictions order may be made by the court in relation to a person in respect of whom a debt relief order has been made[1]. Where a debt relief order has been made and then revoked, an application for a debt relief order which was instituted before the revocation is unaffected by the revocation unless the court orders otherwise[2].

1   IA 1986, s 251V, Sch 4ZB, para 1(1).
2   IA 1986, s 251V, Sch 4ZB, para 10(b).

Persons who may apply

30.108 A debt relief restrictions order may be made only on the application of the Secretary of State, or the official receiver acting on a direction of the Secretary of State[1].

1   IA 1986, s 251V, Sch 4ZB, para 1(2).

When applications may be made

30.109 An application for a debt relief restrictions order in respect of a debtor may be made at any time during the moratorium period relating to the debt relief order in question, or after the end of that period, but only with the permission of the court[1]. In the context of directors disqualification orders, a restrictive approach is taken to granting permission for applications made out of time; a similar approach may be taken here.

1   IA 1986, s 251V, Sch 4ZB, para 3(1).

Grounds for making order

30.110 The basis on which the court is to act is similar to that applicable in respect of bankruptcy restrictions orders and company director disqualification orders. The court is bound to make an order if it thinks it appropriate to do so having regard to the conduct of the debtor (whether before or after the making of the debt relief order)[1].

1   IA 1986, s 251V, Sch 4ZB, para 2(1).

Particular behaviour to be considered

30.111 Although the court is entitled to take into account any conduct which it regards as relevant, there are certain specific kinds of behaviour which the court must take into account. These are:

(a) failing to keep records which account for a loss of property by the debtor, or by a business carried on by him, where the loss occurred in the period beginning two years before the application date for the debt relief order and ending with the date of the application for the debt relief restrictions order;

(b) failing to produce records of that kind on demand by the official receiver;

(c) entering into a transaction at an undervalue in the period beginning two years before the application date for the debt relief order and ending with the date of the determination of that application[1];

(d) giving a preference in the period beginning two years before the application date for the debt relief order and ending with the date of the determination of that application[2];

(e) making an excessive pension contribution[3];

(f) a failure to supply goods or services that were wholly or partly paid for;

(g) trading at a time, before the date of the determination of the application for the debt relief order, when the debtor knew or ought to have known that he was himself to be unable to pay his debts;

(h) incurring, before the date of the determination of the application for the debt relief order, a debt which the debtor had no reasonable expectation of being able to pay;

(i) failing to account satisfactorily to the court or the official receiver for a loss of property or for an insufficiency of property to meet his debts;

(j) carrying on any gambling, rash and hazardous speculation or unreasonable extravagance which may have materially contributed to or increased the extent of his inability to pay his debts before the application date for the debt relief order or which took place between that date and the date of the determination of the application for the debt relief order;

(k) neglect of business affairs of a kind which may have materially contributed to or increased the extent of his inability to pay his debts;

(l) fraud or fraudulent breach of trust;

(m) failing to co-operate with the official receiver[4].

[1] 'undervalue' shall be construed in accordance with Sch 4ZA, para 9(2); IA 1986, s 251V, Sch 4ZB, para 2(4).

[2] 'preference' shall be construed in accordance with Sch 4ZA, para 10(2); IA 1986, s 251V, Sch 4ZB, para 2(4).

[3] 'excessive pension contribution' shall be construed in accordance with IA 1986, s 342A; IA 1986, s 251V, Sch 4ZB, para 2(4).

[4] IA 1986, s 251V, Sch 4ZB, para 2(2).

Previous bankruptcy

30.112 The court must also, in particular, consider whether the debtor was an undischarged bankrupt at some time during the period of six years ending with the date of the application for the debt relief order[1].

[1] IA 1986, s 251V, Sch 4ZB, para 2(3).

Duration of order

30.113 A debt relief restrictions order comes into force when it is made, and ceases to have effect at the end of a date specified in the order. The date specified in a debt relief restrictions order must not be before the end of the period of two years beginning with the date on which the order is made, or after the end of the period of 15 years beginning with that date[1]. Where an interim debt relief restrictions order has been made, the reference to the date on which the order was made should be treated as a reference to the date on which the interim debt relief restrictions order was made[2].

¹   IA 1986, s 251V, Sch 4ZB, para 4.
²   IA 1986, s 251V, Sch 4ZB, para 2(3).

Effect of a debt relief restrictions order

30.114 There is no single statement of the effect of a debt relief restrictions order. The various disqualifications which ensue have to be gathered from a multiplicity of statutes. In general, it appears that the effect will be the same as a bankruptcy restrictions order and statutes referring to bankruptcy restrictions orders will be amended so as also to refer to debt relief restrictions order. For example, IA 1986, s 426A is to be amended to disqualify those who are the subject of debt relief restrictions orders from participating in Parliament[1]. These, or at least many of them, are mentioned in **Chapter 11**.

¹   TCEA 2007, s 108(3), Sch 20, para 12.

Interim debt relief restrictions order

30.115 At any time between the institution of an application for a debt relief restrictions order, and the determination of the application, the court may make an interim debt relief restrictions order if the court thinks that there are prima facie grounds to suggest that the application for the debt relief restrictions order will be successful, and it is in the public interest to make an interim debt relief restrictions order[1]. An interim debt relief restrictions order may only be made on the application of the Secretary of State, or the official receiver acting on a direction of the Secretary of State[2].

¹   IA 1986, s 251V, Sch 4ZB, para 5(1) and (2).
²   IA 1986, s 251V, Sch 4ZB, para 5(3).

Effect and duration of an interim debt relief restrictions order

30.116 An interim debt relief restrictions order has the same effect as a debt relief restrictions order, and comes into force when it is made. It ceases to have effect either on the determination of the application for the debt relief restrictions order, on the acceptance of a debt relief restrictions undertaking made by the debtor, or if the court discharges the interim debt relief restrictions order on the application of the person who applied for it or of the debtor[1].

[1] IA 1986, s 251V, Sch 4ZB, para 5(6).

Debt relief restrictions undertaking

30.117 Provision is made to enable debtors to give undertakings with the same effect as a debt relief restrictions order and thereby save the expense and trouble of proceedings. The undertaking may be offered to the Secretary of State[1]. In determining whether to accept a debt relief restrictions undertaking the Secretary of State is obliged to have regard to the matters mentioned above to which the court must have regard[2].

[1] IA 1986, s 251V, Sch 4ZB, para 7(1).
[2] IA 1986, s 251V, Sch 4ZB, para 7(2); ie the kinds of behaviour specified in Sch 4ZB, para 2(2) and any relevant previous bankruptcy as specified in Sch 4ZB, para 2(3).

Duration of a debt relief restrictions undertaking

30.118 A debt relief restrictions undertaking comes into force on being accepted by the Secretary of State, and ceases to have effect at the end of a date specified in the undertaking. The date specified as the end date must not be before the end of the period of two years beginning with the date on which the undertaking is accepted, or after the end of the period of 15 years beginning with that date[1].

[1] IA 1986, s 251V, Sch 4ZB, para 9(1) and (2).

Annulment of or release from an undertaking

30.119 On an application by the debtor the court may annul a debt relief restrictions undertaking or provide for a debt relief restrictions undertaking to cease to have effect before the date specified in it as the date when it ceases to have effect[1].

[1] IA 1986, s 251V, Sch 4ZB, para 9(3).

Effect of a debt relief restrictions undertakings

30.120 The effect of an undertaking is the same as that of a debt relief restrictions order. This is achieved by providing that a reference in an enactment to a person in respect of whom a debt relief restrictions order has effect (or who is 'the subject of' a debt relief restrictions order) includes a reference to a person in respect of whom a debt relief restrictions undertaking has effect[1].

[1] IA 1986, s 251V, Sch 4ZB, para 8.

Effect of revocation of debt relief order

30.121 Unless the court directs otherwise, the revocation at any time of a debt relief order does not:

(a) affect the validity of any debt relief restrictions order, interim debt relief restrictions order or debt relief restrictions undertaking which is in force in respect of the debtor;

(b) prevent the determination of any application for a debt relief restrictions order, or an interim debt relief restrictions order, in relation to the debtor that was instituted before that time;

(c) prevent the acceptance of a debt relief restrictions undertaking that was offered before that time; or

(d) prevent the institution of an application for a debt relief restrictions order or interim debt relief restrictions order in respect of the debtor, or the offer or acceptance of a debt relief restrictions undertaking by the debtor, after that time[1].

1   IA 1986, s 251V, Sch 4ZB, para 10.

Registration

30.122 The Secretary of State must maintain a register of matters relating to debt relief orders, debt relief restrictions orders and debt relief restrictions undertakings[1]. Power to amalgamate this register with other registers may be conferred under rules yet to be made[2].

1   IA 1986, s 251W.
2   TCEA 2007, s 108(3), Sch 20, para 14(5).

C NEW COUNTY COURT ADMINISTRATION ORDERS

County Courts Act 1984, Part 6

30.123 The new regime relating to administration orders is contained in a new Part 6 of the County Courts Act 1984 which is substituted for the current Part 6 by TCEA 2007, s 106(1). The current Part 6 of the County Courts Act 1984 comprises ss 112–117. The new Part 6 comprises ss 112A–112AI. As mentioned above, these provisions are not yet in force but are described below as if they were.

Regulations

30.124 The statutory provisions will be supplemented by regulations to be made pursuant to CCA 1984, s 112AI.

Transitional provision

30.125 The new regime does not apply in any case where an administration order was made or an application made for such an order before the day on which TCEA 2007, s 106 comes into force[1].

¹ TCEA 2007, s 106(3).

Administration orders

30.126 There are three essential elements to an administration order[1]. First, there must be scheduled to it, the declared debts of the debtor[2]. Debts arising after the order may be added to the schedule so long as the debtor applies for their addition and they do not bring the total amount of the relevant debts above the prescribed maximum[3]. Undeclared debts existing at the time of the order may also be added subject again to the condition that their addition does not take the total debt above the prescribed maximum[4]. Secondly, the order must impose a requirement on the debtor that he makes repayments during the currency of the order[5]. Thirdly, the order must impose certain requirements on creditors that they may not, during the currency of the order, pursue the debtor by legal process without the permission of the court, charge him with interest in respect of any scheduled debt, or, in the case of suppliers of gas or electricity for domestic use, stop that supply[6].

¹ CCA 1984, s 112A.
² CCA 1984, s 112C.
³ CCA 1984, s 112D.
⁴ CCA 1984, s 112Y(3).
⁵ CCA 1984, s 112E.
⁶ CCA 1984, ss 112F–112I.

Application for an administration order

Who may apply

30.127 A county court may make an administration order only on the application of the debtor. The debtor may make an application for an administration order whether or not a judgment has been obtained against him in respect of any of his debts[1].

¹ CCA 1984, s 112J.

Proper court

30.128 Rules of court will specify to which county court the application should be made[1]. The county court which makes the administration order is referred to as the proper county court[2].

¹ CCA 1984, s 112AA(4).
² CCA 1984, s 112AA(3).

Conditions for an administration order

30.129 A number of conditions must be met before a county court may make an administration order[1].

1   CCA 1984, s 112B(1).

The debtor

30.130 An administration order may only be made in respect of an individual who is a debtor under two or more qualifying debts[1]. He must not be a debtor under any business debts[2]. All debts are qualifying debts, except for any debt secured against an asset and any debt of a description specified in regulations[3]. A business debt is any debt (whether or not a qualifying debt) which is incurred by a person in the course of a business[4]. This must mean in the course of the debtor's business. In this context, only debts that have already arisen are included in references to debts; and accordingly such references do not include any debt that will arise only on the happening of some future contingency[5]. Where the debtor has entered into an agreement, such as a hire-purchase agreement, where instalments will become due at regular intervals, the full amount payable under the agreement should be treated as the debt because a debt that is repayable by a number of payments becomes due when the time for making the first of the payments is reached[6].

1   CCA 1984, s 112B(2).
2   CCA 1984, s 112B(3).
3   CCA 1984, s 112AB(1).
4   CCA 1984, s 112AB(2).
5   CCA 1984, s 112AB(3).
6   CCA 1984, s 112AF(2).

Inability to pay

30.131 The debtor must be unable to pay one or more of his qualifying debts[1]. In a case where an individual is the debtor under a debt that is repayable by a single payment, the debtor is to be regarded as unable to pay the debt only if the debt has become due, the debtor has failed to make the single payment, and the debtor is unable to make that payment[2]. A debt that is repayable by a single payment becomes due when the time for making that payment is reached[3]. In a case where an individual is the debtor under a debt that is repayable by a number of payments, the debtor is to be regarded as unable to pay the debt only if the debt has become due, the debtor has failed to make one or more of the payments, and the debtor is unable to make all of the missed payments[4]. A debt that is repayable by a number of payments becomes due when the time for making the first of the payments is reached[5]. These definitions do not explain what the test for inability to pay is: the usual cash-flow concept of not having liquid funds to pay when the debt falls due will no doubt apply.

1   CCA 1984, s 112B(5).
2   CCA 1984, s 112AC(1).
3   CCA 1984, s 112AF(1).

⁴   CCA 1984, s 112AC(2).
⁵   CCA 1984, s 112AF(2).

Total qualifying debts

30.132 The total amount of the debtor's qualifying debts must be less than, or the same as, the prescribed maximum[1]. Detailed provision for calculating the debtor's qualifying debts will be made in regulations[2]. All of the debtor's qualifying debts which have arisen before the calculation must be taken into account (whether or not the debts are already due at the time of the calculation).

¹   CCA 1984, s 112B(2).
²   CCA 1984, s 112AD.

Surplus income

30.133 The debtor's surplus income must be more than the prescribed minimum[1]. It is essential that the debtor should have some surplus income in order for him to be able to meet the repayment requirement which is an essential element of an administration order. The debtor's surplus income is to be calculated in accordance with regulations[2].

¹   CCA 1984, s 112B(7).
²   CCA 1984, s 112AE.

Exclusions

30.134 The debtor must not be excluded under what are referred to as the AO exclusion; the voluntary arrangement exclusion; and the bankruptcy exclusion[1]. These exclusions apply respectively:

(1)   if an administration order currently has effect in respect of him, or, subject to certain qualifications, had effect in the previous 12 months; the impact of the qualifications just referred to is that a prior administration order which was in effect during the previous 12 months will not exclude a new administration order being made if the previous administration order ceased to have effect on the making of an enforcement restriction order or a debt relief order or if the prior order was revoked because the debtor no longer had any qualifying debts;

(2)   if an interim order under IA 1986, s 252 has effect in respect of him, or he is bound by an IVA; and

(3)   if a petition for a bankruptcy order to be made against him has been presented but not decided, or he is an undischarged bankrupt[2].

¹   CCA 1984, s 112B(4).
²   CCA 1984, s 112AH.

Representations by creditors and others

30.135 Before making an administration order, the county court must have regard to any representations made by any person about why the order should not be made, or by a creditor under a debt about why the debt should not be taken into account in calculating the total amount of the debtor's qualifying debts[1].

1   CCA 1984, s 112B(8).

Scheduling debts to the administration order

Generally

30.136 A debt is scheduled to an administration order if the relevant information is included in a schedule to the order and a scheduled debt is a debt that is scheduled to an administration order[1]. The relevant information is the amount of the debt, and the name of the creditor under the debt[2].

1   CCA 1984, s 112AG(1) and (4).
2   CCA 1984, s 112AG(3).

Scheduling declared debts

30.137 The first category of debts to consider are those labelled 'declared debts'[1]. These have to be qualifying debts, meaning any debts which are not secured against an asset or falling into a description specified in regulations[2]. If an administration order is made, and, when the order is made, the debt is taken into account in calculating the total amount of the debtor's qualifying debts for the purposes of CCA 1984, s 112B(6), then:

(1)   If the declared debt is already due at the time the administration order is made, it must be scheduled to the order when the order is made; and
(2)   If the declared debt becomes due after the administration order is made, it must be scheduled to the order if the debtor, or the creditor under the debt, applies to the court for the debt to be scheduled[3].

1   CCA 1984, s 112C(1).
2   CCA 1984, s 112AB(1).
3   CCA 1984, s 112C(2) and (3).

30.138 The court must not schedule a debt to an administration order unless the court has had regard to any representations made by any person about why the debt should not be scheduled[1].

1   CCA 1984, s 112C(4) and 112AG(5).

Scheduling new debts

30.139 A 'new debt' is a debt which arises after an administration order is made, and becomes due during the currency of the order[1]. The court may schedule the new debt to the administration order if the debtor, or the creditor under the new debt, applies to the court for the debt to be scheduled and the total amount of the debtor's qualifying debts (including the new debt) is less than, or the same as, the prescribed maximum[2].

1   CCA 1984, s 112D(1).
2   CCA 1984, s 112D(2).

Scheduling undeclared debts

30.140 It may happen that an administration order is made, but it becomes apparent that the total amount of the debtor's qualifying debts was not properly calculated for the purposes of CCA 1984, s 112B(6), because of an undeclared debt. In this context, a debt is undeclared if it ought to have been, but was not, taken into account in the calculation for the purposes of 1984, s 112B(6). So long as the undeclared debt does not bring the total debt over the prescribed maximum the court must schedule the undeclared debt to the order, either straightaway, if the undeclared debt is due (whether it became due before or after the making of the order), or, when the debt becomes due, if it is not yet due[1]. Here 'total debt' means the total amount of the debtor's qualifying debts (including the undeclared debt)[2]. The court must not schedule an undeclared debt to an administration order unless the court has had regard to any representations made by any person about why the debt should not be scheduled[3]. But the court need not take into account any representations which are made by the debtor in relation to the scheduling of an undeclared debt[4]. If the total debt is more than the prescribed maximum, the court must revoke the administration order (whether or not the undeclared debt is due)[5].

1   CCA 1984, s 112Y(6).
2   CCA 1984, s 112Y(1)–(4).
3   CCA 1984, ss 112Y(7) and 112AG(5).
4   CCA 1984, s 112AG(6).
5   CCA 1984, s 112Y(5).

De-scheduling debts

30.141 The court has power to vary an administration order on the application of the debtor or a qualifying creditor or of its own motion. This includes power to vary the order by de-scheduling a debt. A debt is de-scheduled if the relevant information is removed from a schedule in which it was included[1]. But the debt may be de-scheduled only if it appears to the proper county court that it is just and equitable to do so[2] and the court must not de-schedule a debt unless it has had regard to any representations made by any person about why the debt should not be de-scheduled[3].

1   CCA 1984, s 112AG(2).
2   CCA 1984, s 112T.
3   CCA 1984, s 112AG(7).

30.142 A scheduled debt must be de-scheduled where the debt has been repaid to the extent required by the administration order[1]. In such a case the court does not have to have regard to any representations[2].

¹   CCA 1984, s 112Q(1).
²   CCA 1984, s 112AG(8).

The repayment requirement

30.143 An administration order must, during the currency of the order, impose a repayment requirement on the debtor, meaning a requirement for the debtor to repay the scheduled debts. The repayment requirement may provide for the debtor to repay a particular scheduled debt in full or to some other extent. It may provide for the debtor to repay different scheduled debts to different extents¹. The repayment requirement must provide that the repayments which the debtor is required to make are to be made by instalments. The court must decide when the instalments are to be made. It must determine the amount of the instalments in accordance with repayment regulations. These regulations will make provision for instalments to be determined by reference to the debtor's surplus income. The repayment requirement may provide that the repayments are to be made by other means (including by one or more lump sums) in addition to the instalments. The repayment requirement may include provision in addition to any that is required or permitted by CCA 1984, s 112E².

¹   CCA 1984, s 112E(1)–(4).
²   CCA 1984, s 112E(6)–(11).

Postponement of repayment of new debts

30.144 Where a new debt is scheduled to the order in accordance with CCA 1984, s 112D, the repayment requirement may provide that no due repayment in respect of the new debt is to be made until the debtor has made all due repayments in respect of declared debts¹.

¹   CCA 1984, s 112E(5).

Requirements affecting creditors

Generally

30.145 An administration order must contain a series of requirements affecting the rights of creditors. They apply during the currency of the order. That means during the period which begins when the order first has effect, and ends when the order ceases to have effect¹. These requirements must be imposed by the order and derive their force from the order, not from the statute. Presumably if a court purported to make an administration order but it inadvertently failed to contain these or some of these requirements, it could be amended in order to do so pursuant to CPR r 40.12 on the basis that the omission was accidental. The requirements are described below on the assumption that they have been properly included in the administration order.

¹   CCA 1984, s 112AA(2).

Presentation of bankruptcy petition

30.146 During the currency of the order, no qualifying creditor[1] of the debtor is to present a bankruptcy petition against the debtor in respect of a qualifying debt, unless the creditor has the permission of the proper county court. Permission may be given subject to conditions[2].

1   Meaning a creditor under a qualifying debt; see CCA 1984, s 112AA(1).
2   CCA 1984, s 112F.

Remedies other than bankruptcy

30.147 No qualifying creditor of the debtor may, during the currency of the order, pursue any remedy for the recovery of a qualifying debt unless either regulations provide otherwise, or the creditor has the permission of the proper county court. Regulations may specify classes of debt which are exempted (or exempted for specified purposes) from this restriction. Permission may be given subject to conditions[1].

1   CCA 1984, s 112G.

Charging of interest, etc

30.148 No creditor under a scheduled debt may, during the currency of the order, charge any sum by way of interest, fee or other charge in respect of that debt[1].

1   CCA 1984, s 112H.

Stopping supplies of gas or electricity

30.149 During the currency of the order, no domestic utility creditor is to stop the supply of gas or electricity[1], or the supply of any associated services, except in certain specified cases. A domestic utility creditor is any person who provides the debtor with a supply of mains gas or mains electricity for the debtor's own domestic purposes, and is a creditor under a qualifying debt that relates to the provision of that supply. The excepted cases where supply may be stopped are: first, where the reason for stopping a supply relates to the non-payment by the debtor of charges incurred in connection with that supply after the making of the administration order; secondly, where the reason for stopping a supply is unconnected with the non-payment by the debtor of any charges incurred in connection with that supply, or any other supply of mains gas or mains electricity, or of associated services, that is provided by the domestic utility creditor; and thirdly, where the proper county court gives permission to stop a supply. Conditions may be imposed on any permission which is given[2].

1   In this context, a supply of mains gas is a supply of the kind mentioned in the Gas Act 1986, s 5(1)(b); and a supply of mains electricity is a supply of the kind mentioned in the Electricity Act 1989, s 4(1)(c); see CCA 1984, s 112I(8) and (9).
2   CCA 1984, s 112I.

Stay of existing county court proceedings

30.150 If an administration order is made; proceedings in a county court (other than bankruptcy proceedings) are pending against the debtor in respect of a qualifying debt; by virtue of a requirement included in the order by virtue of CCA 1984, s 112G, the creditor under the qualifying debt is not entitled to continue the proceedings in respect of the debt; and the county court receives notice of the administration order, then the county court must stay the proceedings. It may also allow costs already incurred by the creditor, and, if it does so, it may on application or of its motion add them to the debt, or if the debt is a scheduled debt, to the amount scheduled to the order in respect of the debt. But the court may not add the costs in the case of a scheduled debt if the court is under a duty[1] to revoke the order because the total amount of the debtor's qualifying debts (including the costs) is more than the prescribed maximum[2].

[1]   Under CCA 1984, s 112U(6)(b).
[2]   CCA 1984, s 112O.

Duration of an administration order

30.151 An administration order may last for up to a maximum period of five years beginning with the day on which the order is made. The court which makes the order may, when it makes the order, specify a day on which the order will cease to have effect. But it may not specify a date falling after the last day of the maximum five-year period and if it does not specify any day, the order will last for that five-year period and cease to have effect at the end of it[1].

[1]   CCA 1984, s 112K(1)–(4).

Variation of the period

30.152 The court has power to substitute a different termination date, on the application of the debtor or a qualifying creditor or on its own motion. But the substituted date must fall on or before the end of the maximum five-year period[1].

[1]   CCA 1984, ss 112K(6)(a), 112R and 112S.

Early termination

Revocation of the administration order

30.153 In certain circumstances, discussed below, an administration order must or may be revoked. Where the court revokes the order, the order will cease to have effect in accordance with the terms of the revocation[1].

[1]   CCA 1984, ss 112K(6)(b) and 112W

30.154 *New debt management arrangements*

Subsequent enforcement restriction order or debt relief order

30.154 If an enforcement restriction order is made at a time when an administration order is in force, the administration order will cease to have effect[1]. Similarly the making of a debt relief order will bring an administration order to an end[2].

1   CCA 1984, s 112M(1), (2) and (6)(a).
2   IA 1986, s 251F.

Effects of an administration order

Effect on other debt management arrangements

30.155 'Other debt management arrangements' means any of the following: an enforcement restriction order under CCA 1984, Part 6A; a debt relief order under IA 1986, Part 7A; and a debt repayment plan arranged in accordance with a debt management scheme that is approved under TCEA 2007, Part 5. The making of an administration order will cause any other debt management arrangements then in force to cease to be in force. For this purpose, a debt relief order is 'in force' if the moratorium applicable to the order under IA 1986, s 251H has not yet ended[1].

1   CCA 1984, s 112L(1), (2), (6) and (8).

Court's duty to give notice

30.156 The county court which makes the administration order must give notice of the order to the relevant authority either, if it is aware of the other debt management arrangements when it makes the administration order, as soon as practicable after making the order, or if it becomes aware of the other arrangement later, as soon as practicable after becoming aware of them. In this context 'the relevant authority' means in relation to an enforcement restriction order: the proper county court (within the meaning of CCA 1984, Part 6A); in relation to a debt relief order: the official receiver; and, in relation to a debt repayment plan: the operator of the debt management scheme in accordance with which the plan is arranged[1].

1   CCA 1984, s 112L(3)–(5) and (7).

Duty to provide information to the court

Generally

30.157 During the whole period that an administration order has effect in respect of a debtor, he must, at the prescribed times, provide the proper county court with particulars of his earnings, income, assets, and outgoings. He must provide particulars of those matters as the matters are at the time the particulars are provided, and as the debtor expects the matters to be at such times in the future as are prescribed[1].

1 CCA 1984, s 112M(1)–(3).

Disposals of property

30.158 If the debtor intends to dispose of any of his property he must, within the prescribed period, provide the proper county court with particulars of the following matters: the property he intends to dispose of; the consideration (if any) he expects will be given for the disposal; such other matters as may be prescribed; such other matters as the court may specify. But this requirement does not apply to goods in certain specified classes. These classes are:

(a) goods that are exempt goods for the purposes of TCEA 2007, Sch 12; this means goods which are to be exempt from the new procedure of enforcement provided for in that schedule and which are to be specified in regulations by description or circumstances or both[1];

(b) goods that are protected under any other enactment from being taken control of under that schedule, or

(c) prescribed property.

1 TCEA 2007, s 62(1), Sch 12, para 3(1).

30.159 The debtor must comply with this duty whether he is the sole owner, or one of several owners, of the property in question[1].

1 CCA 1984, s 112M(4)–(6).

Offence if information not provided

30.160 A person commits an offence if he fails to comply with his duties to provide the information described in the preceding paragraphs. The offence may be dealt with and punished in the county court as if it were a contempt of court[1].

1 CCA 1984, s 112N.

Appropriation of money paid

30.161 Any money paid into court under an administration order is to be appropriated, first, in satisfaction of any relevant court fees, and then in liquidation of debts. The relevant court fees are any fees under an order made under the Courts Act 2003, s 92 which are payable by the debtor in respect of the administration order[1].

1 CCA 1984, s 112P.

Discharge from debts

30.162 If the debtor repays a scheduled debt to the extent provided for by the administration order, the proper county court must order that the debtor is discharged from the debt, and de-schedule the debt. Thus discharge from a scheduled debt depends on making the repayments required by the administration order and upon the court making a further order to the effect that the debtor is discharged from the debt or debts in question. If the debtor repays all of the scheduled debts to the extent provided for by the administration order, the proper county court must revoke the order. The debtor is only obliged to pay as much as is required by the administration order; that may not involve their being repaid to their full extent, but even so, if he has paid what the administration order requires, he is entitled to be discharged from the debts in question and once he has repaid all of the scheduled debts to the extent required by the administration order he is entitled to have it revoked as well[1].

[1]   CCA 1984, s 112Q.

Variation of an administration order

30.163 The proper county court may vary an administration order on the application of the debtor; on the application of a qualifying creditor; or of the court's own motion[1]. The particular powers to vary the duration of the order[2] and to vary the order by scheduling new or undeclared debts[3] or by de-scheduling debts[4] have been mentioned above.

[1]   CCA 1984, s 112R.
[2]   CCA 1984, s 112S.
[3]   CCA 1984, ss 112D and 112Y.
[4]   CCA 1984, s 112T.

Revocation of an administration order

Generally

30.164 Revoking an administration order means bringing the order to an end. Where an order is revoked, the effect is not that the order is treated as not having been made nor any other automatic effect; the effect of the revocation depends on the terms on which the revocation is made[1]. Secondly, revocation does not carry any pejorative connotation: where the debtor has made all the repayments which the administration order requires, he is entitled to be discharged from the scheduled debts and to have the administration order revoked[2].

[1]   CCA 1984, s 112W.
[2]   CCA 1984, s 112Q(2).

Circumstances in which the court has a duty to revoke the order

30.165 The proper county court must revoke an administration order in any of the following cases[1]:

(1)   where it becomes apparent that, at the time the order was made, the condition in CCA 1984, s 112B(2), that the debtor had two or more qualifying debts, was not met;
(2)   where the debtor is no longer a debtor under any qualifying debts;
(3)   where it becomes apparent that, at the time the order was made, the condition in CCA 1984, s 112B(3) was not met because the debtor in fact had one or more business debts, and he is still a debtor under the business debt, or any of the business debts, in question;
(4)   where the debtor subsequently becomes a debtor under a business debt, and he is still a debtor under that debt;
(5)   where it becomes apparent that, at the time the order was made, the condition in CCA 1984, s 112B(4) was not met (ie the debtor was in fact excluded under the AO, voluntary arrangement or bankruptcy exclusion);
(6)   where, after the order is made either the debtor becomes excluded under the voluntary arrangement exclusion, or a bankruptcy order is made against the debtor, and is still in force;
(7)   where it becomes apparent that, at the time the order was made, the condition in CCA 1984, s 112B(5) was not met (ie the debtor was in fact able to pay his qualifying debts);
(8)   where the debtor is now able to pay all of his qualifying debts;
(9)   where it becomes apparent that, at the time the order was made, the condition in CCA 1984, s 112B(6) was not met (ie the debtor's qualifying debts were in fact more than the prescribed maximum);
(10)   where the total amount of the debtor's qualifying debts is now more than the prescribed maximum[2];
(11)   where it becomes apparent that, at the time the order was made, the condition in CCA 1984, s 112B(7) was not met (ie the debtor's surplus income was in fact less than, or the same as, the prescribed minimum);
(12)   where the debtor's surplus income is now less than, or the same as, the prescribed minimum.

[1]   CCA 1984, s 112U.
[2]   See also CCA 1984, s 112Y(5).

30.166 The court must also revoke the order where the debtor has made all the repayments required under the administration order[1].

[1]   CCA 1984, s 112Q(2).

Prompting the court to act

30.167 The court is under a duty to revoke the order where any of the specified cases are made out. Although it will be open to the court to act of its own initiative, it will be more likely that the facts will be brought to the court's attention by an interested party. This is a matter on which the rules, once promulgated, may provide an answer.

Circumstances in which the court has power to revoke order

30.168 The proper county court has a general power to revoke an administration order in any case where there is no duty under this Part to revoke it. Good reason would be required to exercise the power, which is exercisable on the application of the debtor; on the application of a qualifying creditor; or of the court's own motion. But in particular it may be exercised in any of the following cases:

(1)   where the debtor has failed to make two payments (whether consecutive or not) required by the order;
(2)   where the debtor has failed to provide the proper county court with the particulars required pursuant to any duty imposed on him by CCA 1984, s 112M(2)–(4)[1].

[1]   CCA 1984, s 112V.

Effect of revocation

30.169 Where the proper county court revokes an administration order, the order ceases to have effect in accordance with the terms of the revocation[1].

[1]   CCA 1984, s 112W.

Notification to creditors

30.170 The court must, when certain events relating to an administration order occur, give notice of them to every creditor under any scheduled debt. These events occur in each of the following cases:

(1)   when the administration order is made;
(2)   when a debt is scheduled to the administration order at any time after the making of the order;
(3)   when the administration order is varied;
(4)   when the administration order is revoked;
(5)   when the proper county court is given notice under any of the provisions listed in CCA 1984, s 112K(7) of the effect on the administration order of a subsequent enforcement restriction order or debt relief order[1].

[1]   CCA 1984, s 112X.

D ENFORCEMENT RESTRICTION ORDERS

County Courts Act 1984, Part 6A

30.171 The Tribunals, Courts and Enforcement Act 2007 introduces a third new regime, enforcement restrictions orders, by inserting a new Part 6A into the County Courts Act 1984[1]. The provisions contained in that new Part 6A, comprising ss 117A–117X are not yet in force but are described below as if they were.

[1] TCEA 2007, s 107(1) (not yet in force).

Regulations

30.172 The statutory provisions will be supplemented by regulations to be made pursuant to CCA 1984, s 117X.

Enforcement restrictions orders

30.173 An enforcement restrictions order must, as its label implies, impose restrictions on the ability of the debtor's creditors to pursue proceedings against him. The order may also, but need not, impose a requirement on the debtor to make repayments[1].

[1] CCA 1984, s 117A.

Application for an enforcement restrictions order

Who may apply

30.174 A county court may make an enforcement restrictions order only on the application of the debtor. The debtor may make an application for an enforcement restrictions order whether or not a judgment has been obtained against him in respect of any of his debts[1].

[1] CCA 1984, s 117G.

Proper court

30.175 Rules of court will specify to which county court the application should be made[1]. The county court which makes the enforcement restrictions order is referred to as the proper county court[2].

[1] CCA 1984, s 117T(4).
[2] CCA 1984, s 117T(3).

Conditions for an enforcement restrictions order

30.176 A number of conditions must be met before a county court may make an enforcement restrictions order[1].

[1] CCA 1984, s 117B(1).

The debtor

30.177 An enforcement restrictions order may only be made in respect of an individual who is a debtor under two or more qualifying debts[1]. He must not be a debtor under any business debts[2]. All debts are qualifying debts, except for any debt secured against an asset and any debt of a description specified in regulations[3]. A business debt is any debt (whether or not a qualifying debt) which is incurred by a person in the course of a business[4]. This must mean in the course of the debtor's business. In this context, only debts that have already arisen are included in references to debts; and accordingly such references do not include any debt that will arise only on the happening of some future contingency[5]. So long as the debts do not include any business debts, there is no limit set in the statutory provisions as to the total amount of the debts.

[1]   CCA 1984, s 117B(2).
[2]   CCA 1984, s 117B(3).
[3]   CCA 1984, s 117U(1).
[4]   CCA 1984, s 117U(2).
[5]   CCA 1984, s 117U(3).

Inability to pay

30.178 The debtor must be unable to pay one or more of his qualifying debts[1]. In a case where an individual is the debtor under a debt that is repayable by a single payment, the debtor is to be regarded as unable to pay the debt only if the debt has become due, the debtor has failed to make the single payment, and the debtor is unable to make that payment[2]. In a case where an individual is the debtor under a debt that is repayable by a number of payments, the debtor is to be regarded as unable to pay the debt only if the debt has become due, the debtor has failed to make one or more of the payments, and the debtor is unable to make all of the missed payments[3]. These definitions do not explain what the test for inability to pay is: the usual cash-flow concept of not having liquid funds to pay when the debt falls due will no doubt apply.

[1]   CCA 1984, s 117B(5).
[2]   CCA 1984, s 117V(1).
[3]   CCA 1984, s 117V(2).

Sudden and unforeseen financial problem

30.179 In order to obtain an enforcement restrictions order, the debtor must be suffering from a sudden and unforeseen deterioration in his financial circumstances[1]. This condition and the next differentiate enforcement restrictions orders from other debt management arrangements. An obvious example of an event which may cause a sudden deterioration of this sort is the loss of the debtor's job. But there are many other events which may occasion the same problem: illness suffered by the debtor or the illness or death of another person who contributes significantly to the household budget. Divorce may also have a deteriorating effect on a person's finances, but there may be more difficulty in showing that the deterioration is sudden or unforeseen.

¹ CCA 1984, s 117B(5).

Realistic prospect of improvement within six months

30.180 There must also be a realistic prospect that the debtor's financial circumstances will improve within the period of six months beginning when the order is made[1]. Establishing such a prospect will involve adducing evidence showing why and how the improvement is likely to occur. There is no limit on what assets the debtor may have. So, it may be, and this is likely to be typical, that the debtor can show that his problem is simply one of liquidity and that within six months he will be able to realise assets which will enable him to pay his debts.

¹ CCA 1984, s 117B(6).

Fairness

30.181 It must be fair and equitable to make the order[1]. Thus the court has a general discretion whether to make the order and will look at the matter from the point of view of creditors as well as the debtor. A creditor may be specially hard-pressed himself and it may overall be unfair to keep him from his remedy against the debtor.

¹ CCA 1984, s 117B(7).

Exclusions

30.182 The debtor must not be excluded under what are referred to as the ERO exclusion; the voluntary arrangement exclusion; and the bankruptcy exclusion[1]. These exclusions apply respectively:

(1)   if an enforcement restrictions order currently has effect in respect of him, or, subject to certain qualifications, had effect in the previous 12 months; the impact of the qualifications just referred to is that a prior enforcement restrictions order which was in effect during the previous 12 months will not exclude a new enforcement restrictions order being made if the previous enforcement restrictions order ceased to have effect on the making of an administration order or a debt relief order or if the prior order was revoked because the debtor no longer had any qualifying debts;

(2)   if an interim order under IA 1986, s 252 has effect in respect of him, or he is bound by an IVA; and

(3)   if a petition for a bankruptcy order to be made against him has been presented but not decided, or he is an undischarged bankrupt[2].

¹ CCA 1984, s 117B(4).
² CCA 1984, s 117W.

Representations by others

30.183 Before making an enforcement restrictions order, the county court must, subject to provision made in the CPR, have regard to any representations made by any person about why the order should not be made[1].

1   CCA 1984, s 117B(9) and (10).

Requirements affecting creditors

Generally

30.184 An enforcement restrictions order must contain a series of requirements affecting the rights of creditors. They apply during the currency of the order. That means during the period which begins when the order first has effect, and ends when the order ceases to have effect[1]. These requirements must be imposed by the order and derive their force from the order, not from the statute. As mentioned in connection with administration orders an inadvertent failure to include these or some of these requirements could be amended in order to do so pursuant to CPR r 40.12 on the basis that the omission was accidental. The requirements are described below on the assumption that they have been properly included in the enforcement restrictions order.

1   CCA 1984, s 117T(2).

Presentation of bankruptcy petition

30.185 During the currency of the order, no qualifying creditor[1] of the debtor is to present a bankruptcy petition against the debtor in respect of a qualifying debt, unless the creditor has the permission of the proper county court. Permission may be given subject to conditions[2].

1   Meaning a creditor under a qualifying debt; see CCA 1984, s 117T(1).
2   CCA 1984, s 117C.

Remedies other than bankruptcy

30.186 No qualifying creditor of the debtor may, during the currency of the order, pursue any remedy for the recovery of a qualifying debt unless either regulations provide otherwise, or the creditor has the permission of the proper county court. Regulations may specify classes of debt which are exempted (or exempted for specified purposes) from this restriction. Permission may be given subject to conditions[1].

1   CCA 1984, s 117D.

Stopping supplies of gas or electricity

30.187 During the currency of the order, no domestic utility creditor is to stop the supply of gas or electricity[1], or the supply of any associated services, except in certain specified cases. A domestic utility creditor is any person who provides the debtor with a supply of mains gas or mains electricity for the debtor's own domestic purposes, and is a creditor under a qualifying debt that relates to the provision of that supply. The excepted cases where supply may be stopped are: first, where the reason for stopping a supply relates to the non-payment by the debtor of charges incurred in connection with that supply after the making of the enforcement restriction order; secondly, where the reason for stopping a supply is unconnected with the non-payment by the debtor of any charges incurred in connection with that supply, or any other supply of mains gas or mains electricity, or of associated services, that is provided by the domestic utility creditor; and thirdly, where the proper county court gives permission to stop a supply. Conditions may be imposed on any permission which is given[2].

[1] In this context, a supply of mains gas is a supply of the kind mentioned in the Gas Act 1986, s 5(1)(b); and a supply of mains electricity is a supply of the kind mentioned in the Electricity Act 1989, s 4(1)(c); see CCA 1984, s 117E(8) and (9).
[2] CCA 1984, s 117E.

Stay of existing county court proceedings

30.188 If an enforcement restrictions order is made; proceedings in a county court (other than bankruptcy proceedings) are pending against the debtor in respect of a qualifying debt; by virtue of a requirement included in the order by virtue of CCA 1984, s 117G, the creditor under the qualifying debt is not entitled to continue the proceedings in respect of the debt; and the county court receives notice of the enforcement restrictions order, then the county court must stay the proceedings. It may also allow costs already incurred by the creditor, and, if it does so, it may on application or of its own motion add them to the debt[1].

[1] CCA 1984, s 117L.

Charges

30.189 During and after the currency of an enforcement restriction order a qualifying creditor may not make any charge in respect of a protected qualifying debt, unless the charge is interest, or, if not, relates to a time before or after the currency of the order. A 'protected qualifying debt' means any qualifying debt under which the debtor was a debtor at some time during the currency of the enforcement restriction order. Any charge made in breach of this provision is not recoverable[1]. This restriction on creditors derives its force from the statute not the order.

[1] CCA 1984, s 117M.

The repayment requirement

Power to include a repayment requirement

30.190   An enforcement restrictions order may impose a repayment requirement on the debtor, meaning a requirement for the debtor to make payments,
in respect of one or more of his qualifying debts, to the person or persons to
whom he owes the debt or debts. A county court may include a repayment
requirement in an order only if the debtor has surplus income at the time of
the inclusion of the requirement, and the inclusion of the requirement would
be fair and equitable. The debtor's surplus income is to be calculated in
accordance with regulations. These must make provision about what is
surplus income; and about the period by reference to which the debtor's
surplus income is to be calculated. They may, in particular, provide for the
debtor's assets to be taken account of for the purpose of calculating his surplus
income[1].

[1]   CCA 1984, s 117F(1), (5) and (6)–(9).

Time when the requirement may be imposed

30.191   The county court may include the requirement in the order at the time
it makes the order. But it may also, at any time after an enforcement
restriction order has been made, vary the order so as to include a repayment
requirement[1].

[1]   CCA 1984, s 117F(2) and (3).

Other variations

30.192   The order may also be varied by the proper county court, at any time
when an enforcement restriction order includes a repayment requirement, so
as to remove the repayment requirement, or to include a different repayment
requirement[1].

[1]   CCA 1984, s 117F(4).

Occasions for variation in respect of a repayment requirement

30.193   The proper county court may vary an enforcement restriction order in
one of the ways mentioned above of its own motion; on the application of the
debtor; or on the application of a qualifying creditor[1].

[1]   CCA 1984, s 117F(10).

Duration of an enforcement restriction order

30.194   An enforcement restriction order may last for up to a maximum
period of 12 months beginning with the day on which the order is made. The

court which makes the order may, when it makes the order, specify a day on which the order will cease to have effect. But it may not specify a date falling after the last day of the maximum five-year period and if it does not specify any day, the order will last for that five-year period and cease to have effect at the end of it[1].

¹   CCA 1984, s 117H(1)–(4).

Variation of the period

30.195 The court has power to substitute a different termination date on the application of the debtor or a qualifying creditor or on its own motion. But the substituted date must fall on or before the end of the maximum five-year period[1].

¹   CCA 1984, s 117N.

Early termination

Revocation of the enforcement restriction order

30.196 In certain circumstances, discussed below, an enforcement restriction order must or may be revoked. Where the court revokes the order, the order will cease to have effect in accordance with the terms of the revocation[1].

¹   CCA 1984, s 117Q.

Subsequent administration order or debt relief order

30.197 If an administration order is made at a time when an enforcement restriction order is in force, the enforcement restriction order will cease to have effect[1]. Similarly the making of a debt relief order will bring an enforcement restriction order to an end[2].

¹   CCA 1984, s 112L(1), (2) and (6)(a).
²   IA 1986, s 251F.

Effects of an enforcement restrictions order

Effect on other debt management arrangements

30.198 'Other debt management arrangements' means any of the following: an administration order under CCA 1984, Part 6; a debt relief order under IA 1986, Part 7A; and a debt repayment plan arranged in accordance with a debt management scheme that is approved under TCEA 2007, Part 5. The making of an enforcement restrictions order will cause any other debt management arrangements then in force to cease to be in force. For this purpose, a debt relief order is 'in force' if the moratorium applicable to the order under IA 1986, s 251H has not yet ended[1].

[1]   CCA 1984, s 117I(1), (2), (6) and (8).

Court's duty to give notice

30.199 The county court which makes the enforcement restrictions order must give notice of the order to the relevant authority either, if it is aware of the other debt management arrangements when it makes the enforcement restrictions order, as soon as practicable after making the order, or if it becomes aware of the other arrangement later, as soon as practicable after becoming aware of them. In this context 'the relevant authority' means in relation to an administration order: the proper county court (within the meaning of CCA 1984, Part 6); in relation to a debt relief order: the official receiver; and, in relation to a debt repayment plan: the operator of the debt management scheme in accordance with which the plan is arranged[1].

[1]   CCA 1984, s 117I(3)–(5) and (7).

Duty to provide information to the court

Generally

30.200 During the whole period that an enforcement restrictions order has effect in respect of a debtor, he must, at the prescribed times, provide the proper county court with particulars of his earnings, income, assets, and outgoings. He must provide particulars of those matters as the matters are at the time the particulars are provided, and as the debtor expects the matters to be at such times in the future as are prescribed[1].

[1]   CCA 1984, s 117J(1)–(3).

Disposals of property

30.201 If the debtor intends to dispose of any of his property he must, within the prescribed period, provide the proper county court with particulars of the following matters: the property he intends to dispose of; the consideration (if any) he expects will be given for the disposal; such other matters as may be prescribed; such other matters as the court may specify. But this requirement does not apply to goods in certain specified classes. These classes are:

(a)   goods that are exempt goods for the purposes of TCEA 2007, Sch 12; this means goods which are to be exempt from the new procedure of enforcement provided for in that schedule and which are to be specified in regulations by description or circumstances or both[1];

(b)   goods that are protected under any other enactment from being taken control of under that schedule, or

(c)   prescribed property.

1   TCEA 2007, s 62(1), Sch 12, para 3(1).

30.202 The debtor must comply with this duty whether he is the sole owner, or one of several owners, of the property in question[1].

1   CCA 1984, s 117J(4)–(6).

Offence if information not provided

30.203 A person commits an offence if he fails to comply with his duties to provide the information described in the preceding paragraphs. The offence may be dealt with and punished in the county court as if it were a contempt of court[1].

1   CCA 1984, s 117K.

Revocation of an enforcement restrictions order

Generally

30.204 Revoking an enforcement restrictions order means bringing the order to an end. Where an order is revoked, the effect is not that the order is treated as not having been made nor any other automatic effect; the effect of the revocation depends on the terms on which the revocation is made[1].

1   CCA 1984, s 117Q.

Circumstances in which the court has a duty to revoke the order

30.205 The proper county court must revoke an enforcement restrictions order in any of the following cases[1]:

(1)   where it becomes apparent that, at the time the order was made, the condition in CCA 1984, s 117B(2) was not met (ie the debtor in fact did not have two or more qualifying debts);
(2)   where the debtor is no longer a debtor under any qualifying debts;
(3)   where it becomes apparent that, at the time the order was made, the condition in CCA 1984, s 117B(3) was not met (ie the debtor in fact had one or more business debts), and he is still a debtor under the business debt, or any of the business debts, in question;
(4)   where the debtor subsequently becomes a debtor under a business debt, and he is still a debtor under that debt;
(5)   where it becomes apparent that, at the time the order was made, the condition in CCA 1984, s 117B(4) was not met (ie the debtor was in fact excluded under ERO, voluntary arrangement or bankruptcy exclusion);

(6)   where, after the order is made either the debtor becomes excluded under the voluntary arrangement exclusion, or a bankruptcy order is made against the debtor, and is still in force;

(7)   where it becomes apparent that, at the time the order was made, the condition in CCA 1984, s 117B(5) was not met (ie the debtor is in fact able to pay his qualifying debts);

(8)   where the debtor is now able to pay all of his qualifying debts;

(9)   where it becomes apparent that, at the time the order was made, the condition in CCA 1984, s 117B(6) was not met (ie the debtor was in fact not suffering from sudden and unforeseen deterioration in his financial circumstances);

(10)   where the debtor is no longer suffering from the deterioration in financial circumstances which was taken into account for the purposes of CCA 1984, s 117B(6) (even if he is suffering from some other sudden and unforeseen deterioration in his financial circumstances);

(11)   where it becomes apparent that, at the time the order was made, the condition in CCA 1984, s 117B(7) was not met (ie there was in fact no realistic prospect of an improvement in the debtor's financial circumstances);

(12)   where there is no longer a realistic prospect that the debtor's financial circumstances will improve during the period within which the order would continue to have effect (if it were not revoked);

(13)   where it becomes apparent that, at the time the order was made, the condition in CCA 1984, s 117B(8) was not met (ie it was not in fact fair and equitable to make the order);

(14)   where it is not fair and equitable for the order to continue to have effect[2].

[1]   CCA 1984, s 112U.
[2]   CCA 1984, s 117O.

Prompting the court to act

30.206 The court is under a duty to revoke the order where any of the specified cases are made out. Although it will be open to the court to act of its own initiative, it will be more likely that the facts will be brought to the court's attention by an interested party. This is a matter on which the rules, once promulgated, may provide an answer.

Circumstances in which the court has power to revoke order

30.207 The proper county court has a general power to revoke an enforcement restrictions order in any case where there is no duty under this Part to revoke it. Good reason would be required to exercise the power, which is exercisable on the application of the debtor; on the application of a qualifying creditor; or of the court's own motion. But in particular it may be exercised in any of the following cases:

(1)   where the order includes or has included a repayment requirement and the debtor has failed to comply with that requirement;

(2)   where the debtor has failed to provide the proper county court with the particulars required pursuant to any duty imposed on him by CCA 1984, s 117J(2)–(4)[1].

[1]   CCA 1984, s 117P.

Effect of revocation

30.208 Where the proper county court revokes an enforcement restrictions order, the order ceases to have effect in accordance with the terms of the revocation[1].

[1]   CCA 1984, s 117Q.

Notification to creditors

30.209 The court must, when certain events relating to an enforcement restrictions order occur, give notice of them to every creditor under any scheduled debt. These events occur in each of the following cases:

(1)   when the enforcement restrictions order is made;
(2)   when the enforcement restrictions order is varied;
(3)   when the enforcement restrictions order is revoked;
(4)   when the proper county court is given notice under any of the provisions listed in CCA 1984, s 117H(7) of the effect on the enforcement restrictions order of a subsequent administration order or debt relief order[1].

[1]   CCA 1984, s 117R.

E DEBT MANAGEMENT SCHEMES AND DEBT REPAYMENT PLANS

Tribunals, Courts and Enforcement Act 2007, Part 5, Ch 4

30.210 Finally, the Tribunals, Courts and Enforcement Act 2007 introduces a fourth new regime, debt management schemes and debt repayment plans made under such schemes[1]. Again, these provisions are not yet in force but are described below as if they were.

[1]   TCEA 2007, ss 109–133 (not yet in force).

Regulations

30.211 The statutory provisions will be supplemented by regulations to be made pursuant to the various provisions specifically empowering regulations to be made and generally pursuant to TCEA 2007, s 130.

Outline of the regime

30.212 The purpose of this regime is to enable private or commercial operators to establish schemes called debt management schemes pursuant to which they may provide debt repayment plans to non-business debtors. The operators of these schemes will be supervised by a regulatory authority, at first the Lord Chancellor. They may charge for their reasonable costs incurred in connection with the approved schemes and are entitled to recover those costs from debtors or affected creditors, if willing to pay. The debt repayment plans provided under the schemes will relate to all of the debtor's relevant debts, will give him protection against enforcement of those debts, must require him to make payments in respect of them and will, if he makes the required payments, result in his discharge from those debts. Provision is made for creditors affected by a debt repayment plan to appeal to the county court. But in essence and effect, the arrangements represent a privatised form of debt relief not under the control of the court but provided by an operator subject to supervision by a regulatory authority.

Debt management schemes

30.213 A debt management scheme is a scheme under which the scheme operator provides debt repayment plans to non-business debtors. It must meet certain conditions. First, it must be operated by a body of persons (whether a body corporate or not). Secondly, it must be open to some or all non-business debtors. What being open to a non-business debtor means is that the scheme must allow such a debtor to make a request to the scheme operator for a debt repayment plan to be arranged for him. Thirdly, the scheme must provide that, if such a request is made a decision must be made about whether a debt repayment plan is to be arranged for the non-business debtor, and such a plan must be arranged (if it is decided to do so)[1].

[1]   TCEA 2007, s 109.

Non-business debtor

30.214 A 'non-business debtor' means any individual who is a debtor under one or more qualifying debts, but is not a debtor under any business debts[1]. All debts are qualifying debts, except any debt secured against an asset; and in relation to a debt repayment plan which has been requested or arranged, any debt which could not, by virtue of the terms of the debt management scheme, be specified in the plan. A business debt is any debt (whether or not a qualifying debt) which is incurred by a person in the course of a business[2].

[1]   TCEA 2007, s 131(1).
[2]   TCEA 2007, s 132(1) and (2).

Debt repayment plans

30.215 Similarly a debt repayment plan must meet certain conditions. These are addressed further below but in outline the plan must specify all of the debtor's qualifying debts and must require the debtor to make payments in respect of each of the specified debts[1].

[1] TCEA 2007, s 110.

Supervision of scheme operators and approval of schemes

The supervising authority

30.216 The supervising authority is the Lord Chancellor, or any person that the Lord Chancellor has authorised to approve debt management schemes under TCEA 2007, s 111. Where an authorisation is started or ended, the validity of an approval that is then in force at the relevant time is unaffected and the new supervising authority may exercise all of its functions in relation to an approval that is then in force as though it had given the approval itself[1].

[1] TCEA 2007, s 129.

Approval by supervising authority

30.217 The supervising authority may approve one or more debt management schemes. Regulations may make provision about conditions that must be met before the supervising authority may approve a debt management scheme; and considerations that the supervising authority must, or must not, take into account in deciding whether to approve a debt management scheme. They may, in particular, make provision about conditions or considerations that relate to any matter listed in TCEA 2007, Sch 21[1]. These include:

(1) in relation to the scheme operator, the constitution of the scheme operator; the governance of the scheme operator; the size of the scheme operator's undertaking; the financial standing of the scheme operator; and whether or not a scheme operator is a profit-making organisation;

(2) as regards the terms of a debt management scheme, the non-business debtors to whom the scheme is open; and the kinds of debts which may be specified in a plan arranged in accordance with the scheme;

(3) as regards the operation of a debt management scheme, how decisions are made about whether debt repayment plans are to be arranged; how debt repayment plans are arranged; how decisions are made about the terms of debt repayment plans, including decisions about (i) what payments will be required in relation to the specified debts; (ii) the amounts, times and recipients of payments; (iii) the duration of the plan; the format of debt repayment plans; when debt repayment plans begin to have effect; how changes are to be made to debt repayment plans (including the specification of debts after a plan has been arranged); how decisions are made about whether debt repayment plans are to be terminated; how debt repayment plans are terminated;

(4)   as regards changes affecting a scheme operator, whether and how
         changes may be made to the terms or operation of a debt management
         scheme; and whether and how the operation of a debt management
         scheme may be transferred to another body.

¹   TCEA 2007, s 111(1)–(3).

30.218 The supervising authority may approve a debt management scheme
whether a body seeking approval is operating the scheme at the time of the
approval, or proposing to operate the scheme from a time in the future¹.

¹   TCEA 2007, s 111(4).

Applications for approval

30.219 Regulations may specify a procedure for making an application for
approval of a debt management scheme and may, in particular, specify a
procedure that requires any or all of the following: an application to be made
in a particular form; information to be supplied in support of an application;
and, inevitably, a fee to be paid in respect of an application¹.

¹   TCEA 2007, s 112.

Terms of approval

30.220 The approval of a debt management scheme has effect subject to any
relevant terms. These are the terms (if any) specified in regulations that relate
to the approval, and the terms (if any) that the supervising authority includes
in the approval. They may deal with all or any of the following: the start of
the approval; the expiry of the approval; and the termination of the approval,
including termination because of the breach of some other term. They may
impose requirements on the scheme operator and they may relate to any
matter listed in Sch 21, which are set out above. Regulations may make
provision about terms that the supervising authority must, or must not,
include in an approval¹.

¹   TCEA 2007, s 113.

Termination of approval

30.221 The approval of a debt management scheme may be terminated only
if the termination is in accordance with any terms to which the approval is
subject by virtue of TCEA 2007, s 113; any provision made in regulations
under TCEA 2007, s 125; any other provision made in other regulations
under TCEA 2007, ss 109–133¹.

¹   TCEA 2007, s 126.

Procedure for termination

30.222 Regulations may specify a procedure for terminating the approval of a debt management scheme and may, in particular, specify a procedure that requires any or all of the following: notice of, or the reasons for, an intended termination to be given (whether to the supervising authority, the scheme operator, the Lord Chancellor or any other person); conditions to be met before a termination takes effect; and a particular period of time to elapse before a termination takes effect[1].

[1]   TCEA 2007, s 125.

Alternatives to termination

30.223 Regulations may make provision to allow the supervising authority to deal with a case in which the supervising authority would be entitled to terminate the approval of a debt management scheme other than by terminating the approval. Regulations under this section may, in particular, make provision to allow the supervising authority to transfer the operation of the scheme to itself or to any other body[1].

[1]   TCEA 2007, s 127.

Effects of end of approval

30.224 Regulations may make provision about the effects if the approval of a debt management scheme comes to an end and may, in particular, make provision about the treatment of debt repayment plans arranged for non-business debtors before the scheme came to an end. This includes provision to treat a plan as though the approval had not come to an end, or as though the plan had been made in accordance with a different approved scheme. Regulations may make provision about cases where, at the time the scheme comes to an end, the scheme operator is in breach of an obligation relating to the scheme, including its operation, the approval of the scheme and the termination of the scheme. This includes provision to ensure that the operator is not released from any of those obligations by virtue of the termination[1].

[1]   TCEA 2007, s 128.

Request to a scheme operator

Consequences of making a request: period of protection

30.225 Making a request to a scheme operator that it consider whether to arrange a debt repayment plan brings interim protection to the non-business debtor who makes the request. This is because making that request opens what is referred to as the period of protection. The period of protection, in relation to a non-business debtor, is the period which begins if, and when, the debtor makes a request to the operator of an approved scheme for a debt repayment plan to be arranged in accordance with the scheme. It ends either if a debt repayment plan is not arranged in consequence of the request: when the decision is made not to arrange the plan; or if a debt repayment plan is arranged in consequence of the request: when that plan ceases to have effect. But if other debt management arrangements[1] are in force in relation to the debtor immediately before he makes the request, the period does not begin unless, and until, a debt repayment plan is arranged in consequence of the request, and comes into effect in accordance with TCEA 2007, s 121(2)[2].

[1]   Other debt management arrangements mean an administration order, an enforcement restrictions order and a debt relief order; see TCEA 2007, s 121(7).
[2]   TCEA 2007, s 133.

Protection afforded during the period of protection

30.226 The following protections are granted to non-business debtors during the period of protection.

(1) PROTECTION AGAINST REMEDIES OTHER THAN BANKRUPTCY

30.227 First, no qualifying creditor of the debtor may pursue any remedy for the recovery of a qualifying debt, unless regulations provide otherwise, or the creditor has the permission of a county court, which, if given, may be subject to such conditions as the court thinks fit. This protection does not have any effect in relation to bankruptcy proceedings.

(2) CHARGING OF INTEREST, ETC

30.228 Secondly, no qualifying creditor may charge any sum by way of interest, fee or other charge in respect of a qualifying debt, unless regulations provide otherwise, or he obtains the permission of a county court which may again, if given, be subject to such conditions as the court thinks fit.

(3) STOPPING SUPPLIES OF GAS OR ELECTRICITY

30.229 No domestic utility creditor may stop the supply of gas or electricity[1], or the supply of any associated services, except in certain specified cases. A domestic utility creditor is any person who provides the debtor with a supply of mains gas or mains electricity for the debtor's own domestic purposes, and is a creditor under a qualifying debt that relates to the provision of that supply. The excepted cases where supply may be stopped are: first, where the reason for stopping a supply relates to the non-payment by the debtor of charges incurred in connection with that supply after the making of the enforcement restriction order; secondly, where the reason for stopping a supply is unconnected with the non-payment by the debtor of any charges incurred in connection with that supply, or any other supply of mains gas or mains electricity, or of associated services, that is provided by the domestic utility creditor; and thirdly, where regulations allow the supply to be stopped; and fourthly, where the proper county court gives permission to stop a supply. Conditions may be imposed on any permission which is given[2].

1   In this context, a supply of mains gas is a supply of the kind mentioned in the Gas Act 1986, s 5(1)(b); and a supply of mains electricity is a supply of the kind mentioned in the Electricity Act 1989, s 4(1)(c); TCEA 2007, s 118(9) and (10).
2   TCEA 2007, s 118.

Content and effect of debt repayment plans

Content of a debt repayment plan

30.230 As mentioned above, a debt repayment plan must specify all of the debtor's qualifying debts[1]. These are all the debtor's debts except those which are secured against an asset or by virtue of the terms of the debt management scheme under which the plan is arranged, cannot be specified in the plan[2]. The plan must also require the debtor to make payments in respect of the debts[3]. But the plan may require payments of different amounts to be made in respect of a specified debt at different times; and it does not matter if the payments that the plan requires to be made in respect of a specified debt would, if all made, repay the debt only in part[4]. So a plan may involve the compounding of debts.

Other terms

1   TCEA 2007, s 110(2).
2   TCEA 2007, s 132(1).
3   TCEA 2007, s 110(3).
4   TCEA 2007, s 110(4).

30.231 The plan should specify when it will cease to have effect. It may, and no doubt will, include other terms such as the conditions in which the plan may be modified or terminated without running its full intended course. Save where a matter may be the subject of an appeal to the court under TCEA 2007, s 122, it is not clear how disputes about a plan are to be resolved; it may be that this is something which will be made clear in subordinate legislation or it may be that the terms of the plan itself will indicate a method of dispute resolution.

Discharge from specified debts

30.232 If a debt repayment plan is arranged for a non-business debtor in accordance with an approved scheme, and the plan comes into effect, it will result in the discharge of the debtor from the debts that are specified in the plan. However, the discharge from a particular specified debt only takes effect at the time when all the payments required by the plan in respect of that debt have been made[1]. It appears, therefore, that discharge is not a general

30.232   *New debt management arrangements*

consequence of the plan, but depends on the required payments being made in respect of the debts to which they relate.

1   TCEA 2007, s 114.

Protection against the presentation of a bankruptcy petition

30.233   During the currency of a debt repayment plan arranged in accordance with an approved scheme, no qualifying creditor of the debtor may present a bankruptcy petition against the debtor in respect of a qualifying debt, unless regulations provide otherwise, or the creditor has obtained the permission of a county court. A debt repayment plan is current during the period which begins when the plan first has effect, and ends when the plan ceases to have effect. Where a county court may give permission to a creditor to present a bankruptcy petition it may give permission subject to such conditions as it thinks fit[1].

1   TCEA 2007, s 115.

Continuation of the period of protection

30.234   If a debt repayment plan is arranged in consequence of a non-business debtor's request to a scheme operator, the period of protection begun on the making of that request will continue until the plan ceases to have effect (unless there are other debt management arrangements in force, in which case the plan and the protection will not begin until those arrangements have been brought to an end)[1]. During the continuing period or protection, the debtor will have protection from remedies other than bankruptcy[2], the charging of interest[3], and the stopping of supplies of gas and electricity[4].

1   TCEA 2007, s 133(3)(b) and (4).
2   TCEA 2007, s 116.
3   TCEA 2007, s 117.
4   TCEA 2007, s 118.

Stay of existing county court proceedings

30.235   If a debt repayment plan is arranged for a non-business debtor in accordance with an approved scheme; proceedings in a county court (other than bankruptcy proceedings) are pending against the debtor in respect of a qualifying debt; by virtue of TCEA 2007, s 116, the creditor under the qualifying debt is not entitled to continue the proceedings in respect of the debt; and the county court receives notice of the debt repayment plan, then the county court must stay the proceedings. It may also allow costs already incurred by the creditor. If the court allows such costs, and the qualifying debt is a specified debt, then the operator of the approved scheme may add the costs to the amount specified in the plan in respect of the debt, if requested to do so by either the non-business debtor, or the creditor under the qualifying debt. But the operator may not add the costs to that amount if, under the terms of the approved scheme, the operator is under a duty to terminate the plan[1].

1   TCEA 2007, s 119.

Effect on other debt management arrangements in force

30.236 If a debt repayment plan is arranged for a debtor in accordance with an approved scheme, and immediately before the plan is arranged, other debt management arrangements are in force in respect of the debtor, then the plan will not come into effect unless the other debt management arrangements cease to be in force. 'Other debt management arrangements' means any of an administration order under the County Courts Act 1984, Part 6; an enforcement restriction order under the County Courts Act 1984, Part 6A; or a debt relief order under IA 1986, Part 7A. Any provision (whether in the plan or elsewhere) about when the plan is to come into effect is subject to this restriction[1]. A debt relief order is 'in force' if the moratorium applicable to the order under IA 1986, s 251H has not yet ended[2].

1   TCEA 2007, s 121(1)–(3).
2   TCEA 2007, s 121(9).

Notification of the plan to the relevant authority

30.237 If the operator of the approved scheme is or becomes aware of the other debt management arrangements, the operator must give the relevant authority notice that the plan has been arranged. 'The relevant authority' means in relation to an administration order: the proper county court (within the meaning of the County Courts Act 1984, Part 6); in relation to an enforcement restriction order: the proper county court (within the meaning of the County Courts Act 1984, Part 6A); and in relation to a debt relief order: the official receiver. Where the operator is aware of other debt management arrangements at the time the plan is arranged, it must give the notice as soon as practicable after the plan is arranged; where the operator becomes aware of those arrangements after the plan is arranged, it must give the notice as soon as practicable after becoming aware of them[1].

1   TCEA 2007, s 121(4)–(8).

Registration

30.238 Regulations may make provision about the registration of either or both of the following: any request made to the operator of an approved scheme for a debt repayment plan to be arranged in accordance with the scheme; and any debt repayment plan arranged for a non-business debtor in accordance with an approved scheme. Here, 'registration' means registration in the register maintained under the Courts Act 2003, s 98 (the register of judgments and orders, etc)[1].

1   TCEA 2007, s 120.

Appeals by affected creditors

Right of appeal

30.239 A right of appeal is conferred on affected creditors if a debt repayment plan is arranged for a debtor in accordance with an approved scheme. In this context, 'affected creditor' means the creditor under any debt which is specified in the plan. Such a creditor may appeal to a county court against any of the following matters:

(a)   the fact that the plan has been arranged;
(b)   the fact that a debt owed to the affected creditor has been specified in the plan;
(c)   the terms of the plan, including any provision included in the plan in accordance with TCEA 2007, s 110(3), ie the requirements for repayments by the debtor[1].

[1]   TCEA 2007, s 122(1), (2) and (4).

30.240 But an affected creditor may not appeal against the fact that a debt owed to any other creditor has been specified in the plan[1]. This would appear to prevent a creditor from appealing against the inclusion of a debt alleged to be due to another person but which the affected creditor contends is not truly due. It is not clear what the creditor's remedy in such a case is intended to be. Perhaps the provision could be construed as only biting in cases where there is truly a debt owed to another creditor; or perhaps it is intended that the creditor should have some entitlement to make representations to the scheme operator, subject perhaps to judicial review of the operator's decision, if it is flawed.

[1]   TCEA 2007, s 122(3).

Dealing with appeals

30.241 If an appeal is made to a county court by an affected creditor, the county court may determine the appeal in any way that it thinks fit and may make such orders as may be necessary to give effect to the determination of the appeal. In particular, it may order the scheme operator to do any of the following: to reconsider the decision to arrange the plan; to reconsider any decision about the terms of the plan; to modify the debt repayment plan; or to revoke the debt repayment plan. The county court may make such interim provision as it thinks fit in relation to the period before the appeal is determined[1]. Rules will identify which county court the appeal should be made to[2].

[1]   TCEA 2007, s 123.
[2]   TCEA 2007, s 131(2).

Charges by operator of approved scheme

30.242 The operator of an approved scheme may recover its costs by charging debtors or affected creditors (or both). In this context, 'debtors' means both debtors who make requests for debt repayment plans to be arranged in accordance with the approved scheme, and debtors for whom debt repayment plans are arranged in accordance with the approved scheme[1].

[1]   TCEA 2007, s 124(1) and (2).

Relevant costs

30.243 The costs in view here are the costs which the operator incurs, taking one year with another, in connection with the approved scheme, so far as those costs are reasonable[1]. This means that the operator is entitled to determine the charges it makes in a particular case, not by reference to the costs incurred specifically in relation to that case, but by reference to the overall costs of running the approved scheme on an annual basis. This may, in some cases, result in one debtor subsidising other debtors' plans because the charge levied is higher than the cost of administering his particular plan; but the cost involved in identifying the costs incurred with respect to each request handled or plan implemented may well exceed any difference which a more refined approach to costs would identify.

[1]   TCEA 2007, s 124(1) and (2).

Part V
APPENDICES

Appendix 1

PRACTICE DIRECTION: INSOLVENCY PROCEEDINGS[1]

PART ONE

1. General

1.1 In this Practice Direction:

(1)   'The Act' means the Insolvency Act 1986 and includes the Act as applied to limited liability partnerships by the Limited Liability Partnerships Regulations 2001;

(2)   'The Insolvency Rules' means the rules for the time being in force and made under s 411 and s 412 of the Act in relation to insolvency proceedings;

(3)   'CPR' means the Civil Procedure Rules and 'CPR' followed by a Part or rule by number means the Part or rule with that number in those Rules;

(4)   'RSC' followed by an Order by number means the Order with that number set out in Schedule 1 to the CPR;

(5)   'Insolvency proceedings' means any proceedings under the Act, the Insolvency Rules, the Administration of Insolvent Estates of Deceased Persons Order 1986 (SI 1986/1999), the Insolvent Partnerships Order 1986 (SI 1986/2124), the Insolvent Partnerships Order 1994 (SI 1994/2421) or the Limited Liability Partnerships Regulations 2001.

(6)   References to a 'company' shall include a limited liability partnership and references to a 'contributory' shall include a member of a limited liability partnership.

1.2 This Practice Direction shall come into effect on 26th April 1999 and shall replace all previous Practice Notes and Practice Directions relating to insolvency proceedings.

1.3 Except where the Insolvency Rules otherwise provide, service of documents in insolvency proceedings in the High Court will be the responsibility of the parties and will not be undertaken by the court.

1.4 Where CPR Part 2.4 provides for the court to perform any act, that act may be performed by a Registrar in Bankruptcy for the purpose of insolvency proceedings in the High Court.

1.5 A writ of execution to enforce any order made in insolvency proceedings in the High Court may be issued on the authority of a Registrar.

[1]   Up to date as at 1 October 2007.

1.6

(1)   This paragraph applies where an insolvency practitioner ('the outgoing office holder') holds office as a liquidator, administrator, trustee or supervisor in more than one case and dies, retires from practice as an insolvency practitioner or is otherwise unable or unwilling to continue in office.

(2)   A single application may be made to a Judge of the Chancery Division of the High Court by way of ordinary application in Form 7.2 for the appointment of a substitute office holder or office holders in all cases in which the outgoing office holder holds office, and for the transfer of each such case to the High Court for the purpose only of making such an order.

(3)   The application may be made by any of the following:
    (i)   the outgoing office holder (if he is able and willing to do so);
    (ii)   any person who holds office jointly with the outgoing office holder;
    (iii)   any person who is proposed to be appointed as a substitute for the outgoing office holder; or
    (iv)   any creditor in the cases where the substitution is proposed to be made.

(4)   The outgoing office holder (if he is not the applicant) and every person who holds office jointly with the office holder must be made a respondent to the application, but it is not necessary to join any other person as a respondent or to serve the application upon any other person unless the Judge or Registrar in the High Court so directs.

(5)   The application should contain schedules setting out the nature of the office held, the identity of the Court currently having jurisdiction over each case and its name and number.

(6)   The application must be supported by evidence setting out the circumstances which have given rise to the need to make a substitution and exhibiting the written consent to act of each person who is proposed to be appointed in place of the outgoing office holder.

(7)   The Judge will in the first instance consider the application on paper and make such order as he thinks fit. In particular he may do any of the following:
    (i)   make an order directing the transfer to the High Court of those cases not already within its jurisdiction for the purpose only of the substantive application;
    (ii)   if he considers that the papers are in order and that the matter is straightforward, make an order on the substantive application;
    (iii)   give any directions which he considers to be necessary including (if appropriate) directions for the joinder of any additional respondents or requiring the service of the application on any person or requiring additional evidence to be provided;
    (iv)   if he does not himself make an order on the substantive application when the matter is first before him, give directions for the further consideration of the substantive application by himself or another Judge of the Chancery Division or adjourn the substantive application to the Registrar for him to make such order upon it as is appropriate.

(8)   An order of the kind referred to in sub-paragraph (6)(i) shall follow the draft order in Form PDIP 3 set out in the Schedule hereto and an order granting the substantive application shall follow the draft order in Form PDIP 4 set out in the schedule hereto (subject in each case to such modifications as may be necessary or appropriate).

(9)   It is the duty of the applicant to ensure that a sealed copy of every order transferring any case to the High Court and of every order which is made on a substantive application is lodged with the court having jurisdiction over each case affected by such order for filing on the court file relating to that case.

(10)   It will not be necessary for the file relating to any case which is transferred to the High Court in accordance with this paragraph to be sent to the High Court unless a Judge or Registrar so directs.

PART TWO
COMPANIES

[paras 2–8 deal only with company matters]

PART THREE
PERSONAL INSOLVENCY – BANKRUPTCY

9. Distribution of business

9.1 The following applications shall be made direct to the Judge and unless otherwise ordered shall be heard in public:

(1)   Applications for the committal of any person to prison for contempt;
(2)   Application for injunctions or for the modification or discharge of injunctions;
(3)   Applications for interlocutory relief or directions after the matter has been referred to the Judge.

9.2 All other applications shall be made to the Registrar or the District Judge in the first instance. He shall give any necessary directions and may, if the application is within his jurisdiction to determine, in his discretion either hear and determine it himself or refer it to the Judge.

9.3 The following matters shall be heard in public:

(1)   The public examination of debtors;
(2)   Opposed applications for discharge or for the suspension or lifting of the suspension of discharge;
(3)   Opposed applications for permission to be a director;
(4)   In any case where the petition was presented or the receiving order or order for adjudication was made before the appointed day, those matters and applications specified in Rule 8 of the Bankruptcy Rules 1952;
(5)   All matters and applications heard by the Judge, except matters and applications referred by the Registrar or the District Judge to be heard by the Judge in private or directed by the Judge to be so heard.

9.4 All petitions presented will be listed under the name of the debtor.

9.5 In accordance with Directions given by the Lord Chancellor the Registrar has authorised certain applications in the High Court to be dealt with by the Court Manager of the Bankruptcy Court pursuant to Insolvency Rule 13.2(2). The applications are:

(1)   by petitioning creditors: to extend time for hearing petitions (s 376 of the Act).
(2)   by the Official Receiver:
   (a)   To transfer proceedings from the High Court to a County Court (Insolvency Rule 7.13);
   (b)   to amend the full title of the proceedings (Insolvency Rules 6.35 and 6.47).

[NB In District Registries all such applications must be made to the District Judge.]

10. Service abroad of statutory demand

10.1 A statutory demand is not a document issued by the Court. Leave to serve out of the jurisdiction is not, therefore, required.

10.2 Insolvency Rule 6.3(2) ('Requirements as to service') applies to service of the statutory demand whether outside or within the jurisdiction.

10.3 A creditor wishing to serve a statutory demand outside the jurisdiction in a foreign country with which a civil procedure convention has been made (including the Hague Convention) may and, if the assistance of a British Consul is desired, must adopt the procedure prescribed by CPR Part 6.25. In the case of any doubt whether the country is a 'convention country', enquiries should be made of the Queen's Bench Masters' Secretary Department, Room E216, Royal Courts of Justice.

10.4 In all other cases, service of the demand must be effected by private arrangement in accordance with Insolvency Rule 6.3(2) and local foreign law.

10.5 When a statutory demand is to be served out of the jurisdiction, the time limits of 21 days and 18 days respectively referred to in the demand must be amended. For this purpose reference should be made to the table set out in the practice direction supplementing Section III of CPR Part 6.

10.6 A creditor should amend the statutory demand as follows:

(1)   For any reference to 18 days there must be substituted the appropriate number of days set out in the table plus 4 days, and
(2)   for any reference to 21 days there must be substituted the appropriate number of days in the table plus 7 days.

Attention is drawn to the fact that in all forms of the statutory demand the figure 18 and the figure 21 occur in more than one place.

11. Substituted service

Statutory demands:

11.1 The creditor is under an obligation to do all that is reasonable to bring the statutory demand to the debtor's attention and, if practicable, to cause personal service to be effected. Where it is not possible to effect prompt personal service, service may be effected by other means such as first class post or by insertion through a letter box.

11.2 Advertisement can only be used as a means of substituted service where:

(1)   The demand is based on a judgment or order of any Court;
(2)   The debtor has absconded or is keeping out of the way with a view to avoiding service and,
(3)   There is no real prospect of the sum due being recovered by execution or other process.

As there is no statutory form of advertisement, the Court will accept an advertisement in the following form:

STATUTORY DEMAND

(Debt for liquidated sum payable immediately following a judgment or order of the Court)

To (Block letters)

of

TAKE NOTICE that a statutory demand has been issued by:

Name of Creditor:

Address:

The creditor demands payment of £ the amount now due on a judgment or order of the (High Court of Justice Division)(......... County Court) dated the day of 199 .

The statutory demand is an important document and it is deemed to have been served on you on the date of the first appearance of this advertisement. You must deal with this demand within 21 days of the service upon you or you could be made bankrupt and your property and goods taken away from you. If you are in any doubt as to your position, you should seek advice immediately from a solicitor or your nearest Citizens' Advice Bureau. The statutory demand can be obtained or is available for inspection and collection from:

Name:

Address:

(Solicitor for) the Creditor

Tel. No. Reference:

You have only 21 days from the date of the first appearance of this advertisement before the creditor may present a Bankruptcy Petition. You have only 18 days from that date within which to apply to the Court to set aside the demand.

11.3 In all cases where substituted service is effected, the creditor must have taken all those steps which would justify the Court making an order for substituted service of a petition. The steps to be taken to obtain an order for substituted service of a petition are set out below. Failure to comply with these requirements may result in the Court declining to file the petition: Insolvency Rule 6.11(9).

Petitions

11.4 In most cases, evidence of the following steps will suffice to justify an order for substituted service:

(1)   One personal call at the residence and place of business of the debtor where both are known or at either of such places as is known. Where it is known that the debtor has more than one residential or business address, personal calls should be made at all the addresses.

(2)   Should the creditor fail to effect service, a first class prepaid letter should be written to the debtor referring to the call(s), the purpose of the same and the failure to meet with the debtor, adding that a further call will be made for the same purpose on the day of 19 at hours at (place). At least two business days' notice should be given of the appointment and copies of the letter sent to all known addresses of the debtor. The appointment letter should also state that

     (a)   in the event of the time and place not being convenient, the debtor is to name some other time and place reasonably convenient for the purpose;

     (b)   (Statutory Demands) if the debtor fails to keep the appointment the creditor proposes to serve the debtor by [advertisement] [post] [insertion through a letter box] or as the case may be, and that, in the event of a bankruptcy petition being presented, the Court will be asked to treat such service as service of the demand on the debtor;

     (c)   (Petitions) if the debtor fails to keep the appointment, application will be made to the Court for an order for substituted service either by advertisement, or in such other manner as the Court may think fit.

(3)   In attending any appointment made by letter, inquiry should be made as to whether the debtor has received all letters left for him. If the debtor is away, inquiry should also be made as to whether or not letters are being forwarded to an address within the jurisdiction (England and Wales) or elsewhere.

(4)   If the debtor is represented by a Solicitor, an attempt should be made to arrange an appointment for personal service through such Solicitor. The Insolvency Rules enable a Solicitor to accept service of a statutory demand on behalf of his client but there is no similar provision in respect of service of a bankruptcy petition.

(5)   The written evidence filed pursuant to Insolvency Rule 6.11 should deal with all the above matters including all relevant facts as to the debtor's whereabouts and whether the appointment letter(s) have been returned.

11.5 Where the Court makes an order for service by first class ordinary post, the order will normally provide that service be deemed to be effected on the seventh day after posting. The same method of calculating service may be applied to calculating the date of service of a statutory demand.

12. Setting aside a statutory demand

12.1 The application (Form 6.4) and written evidence in support (Form 6.5) exhibiting a copy of the statutory demand must be filed in Court within 18 days of service of the statutory demand on the debtor. Where service is effected by advertisement in a newspaper the period of 18 days is calculated from the date of the first appearance of the advertisement. Three copies of each document must be lodged with the application to enable the Court to serve notice of the hearing date on the applicant, the creditor and the person named in Part B of the statutory demand.

12.2 Where, to avoid expense, copies of the documents are not lodged with the application in the High Court, any order of the Registrar fixing a venue is conditional upon copies of the documents being lodged on the next business day after the Registrar's order otherwise the application will be deemed to have been dismissed.

12.3 Where the statutory demand is based on a judgment or order, the Court will not at this stage go behind the judgment or order and inquire into the validity of the debt nor, as a general rule, will it adjourn the application to await the result of an application to set aside the judgment or order.

12.4 Where the debtor (a) claims to have a counterclaim, set off or cross demand (whether or not he could have raised it in the action in which the judgment or order was obtained) which equals or exceeds the amount of the debt or debts specified in the statutory demand or (b) disputes the debt (not being a debt subject to a judgment or order) the Court will normally set aside the statutory demand if, in its opinion, on the evidence there is a genuine triable issue.

12.5 A debtor who wishes to apply to set aside a statutory demand after the expiration of 18 days from the date of service of the statutory demand must apply for an extension of time within which to apply. If the applicant wishes to apply for an injunction to restrain presentation of a petition the application must be made to the Judge. Paragraphs 1 and 2 of Form 6.5 (Affidavit in Support of Application to set Aside Statutory Demand) should be used in support of the application for an extension of time with the following additional paragraphs:

('3)   That to the best of my knowledge and belief the creditor(s) named in the demand has/have not presented a petition against me.

(4)   That the reasons for my failure to apply to set aside the demand within 18 days after service are as follows: ...'

If application is made to restrain presentation of a bankruptcy petition the following additional paragraph should be added:

('5)   Unless restrained by injunction the creditor(s) may present a bankruptcy petition against me'.

13. Proof of service of a statutory demand

13.1 Insolvency Rule 6.11(3) provides that, if the Statutory Demand has been served personally, the written evidence must be provided by the person who effected that service. Insolvency Rule 6.11(4) provides that, if service of the demand (however effected) has been acknowledged in writing, the evidence of service must be provided by the creditor or by a person acting on his behalf. Insolvency Rule 6.11(5) provides that, if neither paragraphs (3) or (4) apply, the written evidence must be provided by a person having direct knowledge of the means adopted for serving the demand.

13.2 Form 6.11 (Evidence of personal service of the statutory demand): this form should only be used where the demand has been served personally and acknowledged in writing (see Insolvency Rule 6.11(4)). If the demand has not been acknowledged in writing, the written evidence should be provided by the Process Server and Paragraphs 2 and 3 (part of Form 6.11) should be omitted (See Insolvency Rule 6.11(3)).

13.3 Form 6.12 (Evidence of Substituted Service of the Statutory Demand): this form can be used whether or not service of the demand has been acknowledged in writing. Paragraphs 4 and 5 (part) provide for the alternatives. Practitioners are reminded, however, that the appropriate person to provide the written evidence may not be the same in both cases. If the demand has been acknowledged in writing, the appropriate person is the creditor or a person acting on his behalf. If the demand has not been acknowledged, that person must be someone having direct knowledge of the means adopted for serving the demand.

Practitioners may find it more convenient to allow process servers to carry out the necessary investigation whilst reserving to themselves the service of the demand. In these circumstances Paragraph 1 should be deleted and the following paragraph substituted:

> ('1) Attempts have been made to serve the demand, full details of which are set out in the accompanying affidavit of ...'.

13.4 'Written evidence' means an affidavit or a witness statement.

14. Extension of hearing date of petition

14.1 Late applications for extension of hearing dates under Insolvency Rule 6.28, and failure to attend on the listed hearing of a petition, will be dealt with as follows:

(1) If an application is submitted less than two clear working days before the hearing date (for example, later than Monday for Thursday, or Wednesday for Monday) the costs of the application will not be allowed under Insolvency Rule 6.28(3).

(2) If the petition has not been served and no extension has been granted by the time fixed for the hearing of the petition, and if no one attends for the hearing, the petition will be re-listed for hearing about 21 days later. The Court will notify the petitioning creditor's solicitors (or the petitioning creditor in person), and any known supporting or opposing creditors or their solicitors, of the new date and times. Written evidence should then be filed on behalf of the petitioning creditor explaining fully the reasons for the failure to apply for an extension or to appear at the hearing, and (if appropriate) giving reasons why the petition should not be dismissed.

(3) On the re-listed hearing the Court may dismiss the petition if not satisfied it should be adjourned or a further extension granted.

14.2 All applications for extension should include a statement of the date fixed for the hearing of the petition.

14.3 The petitioning creditor should attend (by solicitors or in person) on or before the hearing date to ascertain whether the application has reached the file and been dealt with. It should not be assumed that an extension will be granted.

15. Bankruptcy petition

To help in the completion of the form of a creditor's bankruptcy petition, attention is drawn to the following points:

15.1 The petition does not require dating, signing or witnessing.

15.2 In the title it is only necessary to recite the debtor's name eg Re John William Smith or Re J W Smith (Male). Any alias or trading name will appear in the body of the petition. This also applies to all other statutory forms other than those which require the 'full title'.

15.3 Where the petition is based on a statutory demand, only the debt claimed in the demand may be included in the petition.

15.4 In completing Paragraph 2 of the petition, attention is drawn to Insolvency Rule 6.8(1)(a) to (c), particularly where the 'aggregate sum' is made up of a number of debts.

15.5 Date of service of the statutory demand (paragraph 4 of the petition):

(1)   In the case of personal service, the date of service as set out in the affidavit of service should be recited and whether service is effected *before/after* 1700 hours on Monday to Friday or at any time on a Saturday or a Sunday: see CPR Part 6.7(2) and (3).
(2)   In the case of substituted service (otherwise than by advertisement), the date alleged in the affidavit of service should be recited: see '11. Substituted service' above.
(3)   In the strictly limited case of service by advertisement under Insolvency Rule 6.3, the date to be alleged is the date of the advertisement's appearance or, as the case may be, its first appearance: see Insolvency Rules 6.3(3) and 6.11(8).

15.6 There is no need to include in the petition details of the person authorised to present it.

15.7 Certificates at the end of the petition:

(1)   The period of search for prior petitions has been reduced to eighteen months.
(2)   Where a statutory demand is based wholly or in part on a County Court judgment, the following certificate is to be added:

'I/We certify that on the of 19 I/We attended on the County Court and was/were informed by an officer of the Court that no money had been paid into Court in the action or matter v Claim No pursuant to the statutory demand.'

This certificate will not be required when the demand also requires payment of a separate debt, not based on a County Court judgement, the amount of which exceeds the bankruptcy level (at present £750).

15.8 Deposit on petition: the deposit will be taken by the Court and forwarded to the Official Receiver. In the High Court, the petition fee and deposit should be handed to the Supreme Court Accounts Office, Fee Stamping Room, who will record the receipt and will impress two entries on the original petition, one in respect of the Court fee and the other in respect of the deposit. In the County Court, the petition fee and deposit should be handed to the duly authorised officer of the Court's staff who will record its receipt.

In all cases cheque(s) for the whole amount should be made payable to 'HM Paymaster General'.

15.9 On the hearing of a petition for a bankruptcy order, in order to satisfy the Court that the debt on which the petition is founded has not been paid or secured or compounded the Court will normally accept as sufficient a certificate signed by the person representing the petitioning creditor in the following form:

'I certify that I have/my firm has made enquiries of the petitioning creditor(s) within the last business day prior to the hearing/adjourned hearing and to the best of my knowledge and belief the debt on which the petition is founded is still due and owing and has not been paid or secured or compounded save as to ...'

Signed .... Dated .....

For convenience in the High Court this certificate will be incorporated in the attendance slip, which will be filed after the hearing. A fresh certificate will be required on each adjourned hearing.

15.10 On the occasion of the adjourned hearing of a petition for a bankruptcy order, in order to satisfy the Court that the petitioner has complied with Insolvency Rule 6.29, the petitioner will be required to file written evidence of the manner in which notice of the making of the order of adjournment and of the venue for the adjourned hearing has been sent to:

(i)   the debtor, and
(ii) any creditor who has given notice under Insolvency Rule 6.23 but was not present at the hearing when the order for adjournment was made.

16. Orders without attendance

16.1 In suitable cases the Court will normally be prepared to make orders under Part VIII of the Act (Individual Voluntary Arrangements), without the attendance of either party, provided there is no bankruptcy order in existence and (so far as is known) no pending petition. The orders are:

(1)   A fourteen day interim order with the application adjourned 14 days for consideration of the nominee's report, where the papers are in order, and the nominee's signed consent to act includes a waiver of notice of the application or a consent by the nominee to the making of an interim order without attendance.

(2)   A standard order on consideration of the nominee's report, extending the interim order to a date 7 weeks after the date of the proposed meeting, directing the meeting to be summoned and adjourning to a date about 3 weeks after the meeting. Such an Order may be made without attendance if the nominee's report has been delivered to the Court and complies with Section 256(1) of the Act and Insolvency Rule 5.10(2) and (3) and proposes a date for the meeting not less than 14 days from that on which the nominee's report is filed in Court under Insolvency Rule 5.10 nor more than 28 days from that on which that report is considered by the Court under Insolvency Rule 5.12.

(3)   A 'concertina' Order, combining orders as under (1) and (2) above. Such an order may be made without attendance if the initial application for an interim order is accompanied by a report of the nominee and the conditions set out in (1) and (2) above are satisfied.

(4)   A final order on consideration of the Chairman's report. Such an order may be made without attendance if the Chairman's report has been filed and complies with Insolvency Rule 5.22(1). The order will record the effect of the Chairman's report and may discharge the interim order.

16.2 Provided that the conditions as under 16.1(2) and (4) above are satisfied and that the appropriate report has been lodged with the Court in due time the parties need not attend or be represented on the adjourned hearing for consideration of the Nominee's report or of the Chairman's report (as the case may be) unless they are notified by the Court that attendance is required. Sealed copies of the order made (in all four cases as above) will be posted by the Court to the applicant or his Solicitor and to the Nominee.

16.3 In suitable cases the Court may also make consent orders without attendance by the parties. The written consent of the parties will be required. Examples of such orders are as follows:

(1)   On applications to set aside a statutory demand, orders:
  (a)   dismissing the application, with or without an order for costs as may be agreed (permission will be given to present a petition on or after the seventh day after the date of the order, unless a different date is agreed);
  (b)   setting aside the demand, with or without an order for costs as may be agreed; or
  (c)   giving permission to withdraw the application with or without an order for costs as may be agreed.
(2)   On petitions: where there is a list of supporting or opposing creditors in Form 6.21, or a statement signed by or on behalf of the petitioning creditor that no notices have been received from supporting or opposing creditors, orders:
  (a)   dismissing the petition, with or without an order for costs as may be agreed, or
  (b)   if the petition has not been served, giving permission to withdraw the petition (with no order for costs).
(3)   On other applications, orders:
  (a)   for sale of property, possession of property, disposal of proceeds of sale
  (b)   giving interim directions
  (c)   dismissing the application, with or without an order for costs as may be agreed
  (d)   giving permission to withdraw the application, with or without an order for costs as may be agreed.

If, (as may often be the case with orders under subparagraphs (3)(a) or (b) above) an adjournment is required, whether generally with liberty to restore or to a fixed date, the order by consent may include an order for the adjournment. If adjournment to a date is requested, a time estimate should be given and the Court will fix the first available date and time on or after the date requested.

16.4 The above lists should not be regarded as exhaustive, nor should it be assumed that an order will be made without attendance as requested.

16.5 The procedure outlined above is designed to save time and costs but is not intended to discourage attendance.

16.6 Applications for consent orders without attendance should be lodged at least two clear working days (and preferably longer) before any fixed hearing date.

16.7 Whenever a document is lodged or a letter sent, the correct case number, code (if any) and year (for example 123/SD/99 or 234/99) should be quoted. A note should also be given of the date and time of the next hearing (if any).

16.8 Attention is drawn to Paragraph 4.4(4) of the Practice Direction relating to CPR Part 44.

16A. Bankruptcy restrictions orders

Making the application

16A.1 An application for a bankruptcy restrictions order is made as an ordinary application in the bankruptcy.

16A.2 The application must be made within one year beginning with the date of the bankruptcy order unless the court gives permission for the application to be made after that period. The one year period does not run while the bankrupt's discharge has been suspended under section 279(3) of the Insolvency Act 1986.

16A.3 An application for a bankruptcy restrictions order may be made by the Secretary of State or the Official Receiver ('the Applicant'). The application must be supported by a report which must include:

(a)   a statement of the conduct by reference to which it is alleged that it is appropriate for a bankruptcy restrictions order to be made; and

(b)   the evidence relied on in support of the application (r. 6.241 Insolvency Rules 1986).

16A.4 The report is treated as if it were an affidavit (r. 7.9(2) Insolvency Rules 1986) and is prima facie evidence of any matter contained in it (r. 7.9(3)).

16A.5 The application may be supported by evidence from other witnesses which may be given by affidavit or (by reason of r. 7.57(5) Insolvency Rules 1986) by witness statement verified by a statement of truth.

16A.6 The court will fix a first hearing which must be not less than 8 weeks from the date when the hearing is fixed (r. 6.241(4) Insolvency Rules 1986).

16A.7 Notice of the application and the venue fixed by the court must be served by the Applicant on the bankrupt not more than 14 days after the application is made. Service of notice must be accompanied by a copy of the application together with the evidence in support and a form of acknowledgment of service.

16A.8 The bankrupt must file in court an acknowledgment of service not more than 14 days after service of the application on him, indicating whether or not he contests the application. If he fails to do so he may attend the hearing of the application but may not take part in the hearing unless the court gives permission.

Opposing the application

16A.9 If the bankrupt wishes to oppose the application, he must within 28 days of service on him of the application and the evidence in support (or such longer period as the court may allow) file in court and (within three days thereof) serve on the Applicant any evidence which he wishes the court to take into consideration. Such evidence should normally be in the form of an affidavit or a witness statement verified by a statement of truth.

16A.10 The Applicant must file any evidence in reply within 14 days of receiving the evidence of the bankrupt (or such longer period as the court may allow) and must serve it on the bankrupt as soon as reasonably practicable.

Hearings

16A.11 Any hearing of an application for a bankruptcy restrictions order must be in public (r. 6.241(5) Insolvency Rules 1986). The hearing will generally be before the registrar or district judge in the first instance who may:

(1) adjourn the application and give directions;
(2) make a bankruptcy restrictions order; or
(3) adjourn the application to the judge.

Making a bankruptcy restrictions order

16A.12 When the court is considering whether to make a bankruptcy restrictions order, it must not take into account any conduct of the bankrupt prior to 1 April 2004 (art. 7 Enterprise Act (Commencement No 4 and Transitional Provisions and Savings) Order 2003).

16A.13 The court may make a bankruptcy restrictions order in the absence of the bankrupt and whether or not he has filed evidence (r. 6.244 Insolvency Rules 1986).

16A.14 When a bankruptcy restrictions order is made the court must send two sealed copies of the order to the Applicant (r. 6.244(2) Insolvency Rules 1986), and as soon as reasonably practicable after receipt, the Applicant must send one sealed copy to the bankrupt (r. 6.244(3)).

16A.15 A bankruptcy restrictions order comes into force when it is made and must specify the date on which it will cease to have effect, which must be between two and 15 years from the date on which it is made.

Interim bankruptcy restriction orders

16A.16 An application for an interim bankruptcy restrictions order may be made any time between the institution of an application for a bankruptcy restrictions order and the determination of that application (Sch 4A para. 5 Insolvency Act 1986). The application is made as an ordinary application in the bankruptcy.

16A.17 The application must be supported by a report as evidence in support of the application (r. 6.246(1) Insolvency Rules 1986) which must include evidence of the bankrupt's conduct which is alleged to constitute the grounds for making an interim bankruptcy restrictions order and evidence of matters relating to the public interest in making the order.

16A.18 Notice of the application must be given to the bankrupt at least two business days before the date fixed for the hearing unless the court directs otherwise (r. 6.245).

16A.19 Any hearing of the application must be in public (r. 6.245).

16A.20 The court may make an interim bankruptcy restrictions order in the absence of the bankrupt and whether or not he has filed evidence (r. 6.247).

16A.21 The bankrupt may apply to the court to set aside an interim bankruptcy restrictions order. The application is made by ordinary application in the bankruptcy and must be supported by an affidavit or witness statement verified by a statement of truth stating the grounds on which the application is made (r. 6.248(2)).

16A.22 The bankrupt must send the Secretary of State, not less than 7 days before the hearing, notice of his application, notice of the venue, a copy of his application and a copy of the supporting affidavit. The Secretary of State may attend the hearing and call the attention of the court to any matters which seem to him to be relevant, and may himself give evidence or call witnesses.

16A.23 Where the court sets aside an interim bankruptcy restrictions order, two sealed copies of the order must be sent by the court, as soon as reasonably practicable, to the Secretary of State.

16A.24 As soon as reasonably practicable after receipt of sealed copies of the order, the Secretary of State must send a sealed copy to the bankrupt.

Bankruptcy restrictions undertakings

16A.25 Where a bankrupt has given a bankruptcy restrictions undertaking, the Secretary of State must file a copy in court and send a copy to the bankrupt as soon as reasonably practicable (r. 6.250).

16A.26 The bankrupt may apply to annul a bankruptcy restrictions undertaking. The application is made as an ordinary application in the bankruptcy and must be supported by an affidavit or witness statement verified by a statement of truth stating the grounds on which it is made.

16A.27 The bankrupt must give notice of his application and the venue together with a copy of his affidavit in support to the Secretary of State at least 28 days before the date fixed for the hearing.

16A.28 The Secretary of State may attend the hearing and call the attention of the court to any matters which seem to him to be relevant and may himself give evidence or call witnesses.

16A.29 The court must send a sealed copy of any order annulling or varying the bankruptcy restrictions undertaking to the Secretary of State and the bankrupt.

PART FOUR
APPEALS

17. Appeals in insolvency proceedings

17.1 This Part shall come into effect on 2nd May 2000 and shall replace and revoke Paragraph 17 of, and be read in conjunction with the Practice Direction: Insolvency Proceedings which came into effect on 26th April 1999 as amended.

17.2

(1)   An appeal from a decision of a County Court (whether made by a District Judge or a Circuit Judge) or of a Registrar of the High Court in insolvency proceedings ('a first appeal') lies to a Judge of the High Court pursuant to s 375(2) of the Act and Insolvency Rules 7.47(2) and 7.48(2) (as amended by s 55 of the Access to Justice Act 1999).
(2)   The procedure and practice for a first appeal are governed by Insolvency Rule 7.49 which imports the procedure and practice of the Court of Appeal. The procedure and practice of the Court of Appeal is governed by CPR Part 52

and its Practice Direction, which are subject to the provisions of the Act, the Insolvency Rules and this Practice Direction: see CPR Part 52 rule 1(4).

(3)   A first appeal (as defined above) does not include an appeal from a decision of a Judge of the High Court.

17.3

(1)   Section 55 of the Access to Justice Act 1999 has amended s 375(2) of the Act and Insolvency Rules 7.47(2) and 7.48(2) so that an appeal from a decision of a Judge of the High Court made on a first appeal lies, with the permission of the Court of Appeal, to the Court of Appeal.
(2)   An appeal from a Judge of the High Court in insolvency proceedings which is not a decision on a first appeal lies, with the permission of the Judge or of the Court of Appeal, to the Court of Appeal (see CPR Part 52 rule 3);
(3)   The procedure and practice for appeals from a decision of a Judge of the High Court in insolvency proceedings (whether made on a first appeal or not) are also governed by Insolvency Rule 7.49 which imports the procedure and practice of the Court of Appeal as stated at Paragraph 17.2(2) above.

17.4 CPR Part 52 and its Practice Direction and Forms apply to appeals from a decision of a Judge of the High Court in insolvency proceedings.

17.5 An appeal from a decision of a Judge of the High Court in insolvency proceedings requires permission as set out in Paragraph 17.3(1) and (2) above.

17.6 A first appeal is subject to the permission requirement in CPR Part 52, rule 3.

17.7 Except as provided in this Part, CPR Part 52 and its Practice Direction and Forms do not apply to first appeals, but Paragraphs 17.8 to 17.23 inclusive of this Part apply only to first appeals.

17.8 Interpretation:

(a)   the expressions 'appeal court', 'lower court', 'appellant', 'respondent' and 'appeal notice' have the meanings given in CPR Part 52.1(3);
(b)   'Registrar of Appeals' means:
in relation to an appeal filed at the Royal Courts of Justice in London, a registrar in bankruptcy; and
in relation to an appeal filed in a district registry, a district judge of that district registry.
(c)   'appeal date' means the date fixed by the appeal court for the hearing of the appeal or the date fixed by the appeal court upon which the period within which the appeal will be heard commences.

17.9 An appellant's notice and a respondent's notice shall be in Form PDIP 1 and PDIP 2 set out in the Schedule hereto.

17.10

(1)   An appeal from a decision of a registrar in bankruptcy must be filed at the Royal Courts of Justice in London.
(2)   An appeal from a decision of a district judge sitting in a district registry may be filed:
(a)   at the Royal Courts of Justice in London; or
(b)   in that district registry.
(3)   An appeal from a decision made in a county court may be filed:

(a)   at the Royal Courts of Justice in London; or

(b)   in the Chancery district registry for the area within which the county court exercises jurisdiction.

(There are Chancery district registries of the High Court at Birmingham, Bristol, Caernarfon, Cardiff, Leeds, Liverpool, Manchester, Mold, Newcastle upon Tyne and Preston. The county court districts that each district registry covers are set out in Schedule 1 to the Civil Courts Order 1983.)

17.11

(1)   Where a party seeks an extension of time in which to file an appeal notice it must be requested in the appeal notice and the appeal notice should state the reason for the delay and the steps taken prior to the application being made; the court will fix a date for the hearing of the application and notify the parties of the date and place of hearing;

(2)   The appellant must file the appellant's notice at the appeal court within:

    (a)   such period as may be directed by the lower court; or

    (b)   where the court makes no such direction, 21 days after the date of the decision of the lower court which the appellant wishes to appeal.

(3)   Unless the appeal court orders otherwise, an appeal notice must be served by the appellant on each respondent:

    (a)   as soon as practicable; and

    (b)   in any event not later than 7 days, after it is filed.

17.12

(1)   A respondent may file and serve a respondent's notice.

(2)   A respondent who wishes to ask the appeal court to uphold the order of the lower court for reasons different from or additional to those given by the lower court must file a respondent's notice.

(3)   A respondent's notice must be filed within:

    (a)   such period as may be directed by the lower court; or

    (b)   where the court makes no such direction, 14 days after the date on which the respondent is served with the appellant's notice.

(4)   Unless the appeal court orders otherwise a respondent's notice must be served by the respondent on the appellant and any other respondent:

    (a)   as soon as practicable; and

    (b)   in any event not later than 7 days, after it is filed.

17.13

(1)   An application to vary the time limit for filing an appeal notice must be made to the appeal court.

(2)   The parties may not agree to extend any date or time limit set by:

    (a)   this Practice Direction; or

    (b)   an order of the appeal court or the lower court.

17.14 Unless the appeal court or the lower court orders otherwise an appeal shall not operate as a stay of any order or decision of the lower court.

17.15 An appeal notice may not be amended without the permission of the appeal court.

17.16 A Judge of the appeal court may strike out the whole or part of an appeal notice where there is compelling reason for doing so.

17.17

(1)   In relation to an appeal the appeal court has all the powers of the lower court.
(2)   The appeal court has power to:
    (a)   affirm, set aside or vary any order or judgment made or given by the lower court;
    (b)   refer any claim or issue for determination by the lower court;
    (c)   order a new trial or hearing;
    (d)   make a costs order.
(3)   The appeal court may exercise its powers in relation to the whole or part of an order of the lower court.

17.18

(1)   Every appeal shall be limited to a review of the decision of the lower court.
(2)   Unless it orders otherwise, the appeal court will not receive:
    (a)   oral evidence; or
    (b)   evidence which was not before the lower court.
(3)   The appeal court will allow an appeal where the decision of the lower court was:
    (a)   wrong; or
    (b)   unjust because of a serious procedural or other irregularity in the proceedings in the lower court.
(4)   The appeal court may draw any inference of fact which it considers justified on the evidence.
(5)   At the hearing of the appeal a party may not rely on a matter not contained in his appeal notice unless the appeal court gives permission.

17.19 The following applications shall be made to a Judge of the appeal court:

(1)   for injunctions pending a substantive hearing of the appeal;
(2)   for expedition or vacation of the hearing date of an appeal;
(3)   for an order striking out the whole or part of an appeal notice pursuant to Paragraph 17.16 above;
(4)   for a final order on paper pursuant to Paragraph 17.22(8) below.

17.20

(1)   All other interim applications shall be made to the Registrar of Appeals in the first instance who may in his discretion either hear and determine it himself or refer it to the Judge.
(2)   An appeal from a decision of a Registrar of Appeals lies to a Judge of the appeal court and does not require the permission of either the Registrar of Appeals or the Judge.

17.21 The procedure for interim applications is by way of ordinary application (see Insolvency Rule 12.7 and Sch 4, Form 7.2).

17.22 The following practice applies to all first appeals to a Judge of the High Court whether filed at the Royal Courts of Justice in London, or filed at one of the other venues referred to in Paragraph 17.10 above:

(1)   on filing an appellant's notice in accordance with Paragraph 17.11(2) above, the appellant must file:
    (a)   two copies of the appeal notice for the use of the court, one of which must be stamped with the appropriate fee, and a number of additional

        copies equal to the number of persons who are to be served with it pursuant to Paragraph 17.22(4) below;

(aa)   an approved transcript of the judgment of the lower court or, where there is no official record of the judgment, a document referred to in paragraph 5.12 of the Practice Direction supplementing CPR Part 52.

(b)   a copy of the order under appeal; and

(c)   an estimate of time for the hearing.

(2)   the above documents may be lodged personally or by post and shall be lodged at the address of the appropriate venue listed below:

(a)   if the appeal is to be heard at the Royal Courts of Justice in London the documents must be lodged at Room 110, Thomas More Building, The Royal Courts of Justice, Strand, London WC2A 2LL;

(b)   if the appeal is to be heard in Birmingham, the documents must be lodged at the District Registry of the Chancery Division of the High Court, 33 Bull Street, Birmingham B4 6DS;

(c)   if the appeal is to be heard in Bristol the documents must be lodged at the District Registry of the Chancery Division of the High Court, Third Floor, Greyfriars, Lewins Mead, Bristol, BS1 2NR;

(ca)   if the appeal is to be heard in Caernarfon the documents must be lodged at the District Registry of the Chancery Division of the High Court, Llanberis Road, Caernarfon, LL55 2DF;

(d)   if the appeal is to be heard in Cardiff the documents must be lodged at the District Registry in the Chancery Division of the High Court, First Floor, 2 Park Street, Cardiff, CF10 1ET;

(e)   if the appeal is to be heard in Leeds the documents must be lodged at the District Registry of the Chancery Division of the High Court, The Court House, 1 Oxford Row, Leeds LS1 3BG;

(f)   if the appeal is to be heard in Liverpool the documents must be lodged at the District Registry of the Chancery Division of the High Court, Liverpool Combined Court Centre, Derby Square, Liverpool L2 1XA;

(g)   if the appeal is to be heard in Manchester the documents must be lodged at the District Registry of the Chancery Division of the High Court, Courts of Justice, Crown Square, Manchester, M60 9DJ;

(ga)   if the appeal is to be heard in Mold the documents must be lodged at the District Registry of the Chancery Division of the High Court, Law Courts, Civic Centre, Mold, CH7 1AE;

(h)   if the appeal is to be heard at Newcastle Upon Tyne the documents must be lodged at the District Registry of the Chancery Division of the High Court, The Law Courts, Quayside, Newcastle Upon Tyne NE1 3LA;

(i)   if the appeal is to be heard in Preston the documents must be lodged at the District Registry of the Chancery Division of the High Court, The Combined Court Centre, Ringway, Preston PR1 2LL.

(3)   if the documents are correct and in order the court at which the documents are filed will fix the appeal date and will also fix the place of hearing. That court will send letters to all the parties to the appeal informing them of the appeal date and of the place of hearing and indicating the time estimate given by the appellant. The parties will be invited to notify the court of any alternative or revised time estimates. In the absence of any such notification the estimate of the appellant will be taken as agreed. The court will also send to the appellant a document setting out the court's requirement concerning the form and content of the bundle of documents for the use of the Judge. Not later than 7 days before the appeal date the bundle of documents must be filed by the appellant at the address of the relevant venue as set out in sub-paragraph 17.22(2) above and a copy of it must be served by the appellant on each respondent.

(4)   the appeal notice must be served on all parties to the proceedings in the lower court who are directly affected by the appeal. This may include the Official Receiver, liquidator or trustee in bankruptcy.

(5)   the appeal notice must be served by the appellant or by the legal representative of the appellant and may be effected by:

(a)   any of the methods referred to in CPR Part 6 rule 2; or

(b)   with permission of the court, an alternative method pursuant to CPR Part 6 rule 8.

(6)   service of an appeal notice shall be proved by a Certificate of Service in accordance with CPR Part 6 rule 10 (CPR Form N215) which must be filed at the relevant venue referred to at Paragraph 17.22(2) above immediately after service.

(7)   Subject to sub-paragraphs (7A) and (7B), the appellant's notice must be accompanied by a skeleton argument and a written chronology of events relevant to the appeal. Alternatively, the skeleton argument and chronology may be included in the appellant's notice. Where the skeleton argument and chronology are so included they do not form part of the notice for the purposes of rule 52.8.

(7A)   Where it is impracticable for the appellant's skeleton argument and chronology to accompany the appellant's notice they must be filed and served on all respondents within 14 days of filing the notice.

(7B)   An appellant who is not represented need not file a skeleton argument nor a written chronology but is encouraged to do so since these documents may be helpful to the court.

(8)   where an appeal has been settled or where an appellant does not wish to continue with the appeal, the appeal may be disposed of on paper without a hearing. It may be dismissed by consent but the appeal court will not make an order allowing an appeal unless it is satisfied that the decision of the lower court was wrong. Any consent order signed by each party or letters of consent from each party must be lodged not later than 24 hours before the date fixed for the hearing of the appeal at the address of the appropriate venue as set out in sub-paragraph 17.22(2) above and will be dealt with by the Judge of the appeal court. Attention is drawn to paragraph 4.4(4) of the Practice Direction to CPR Part 44 regarding costs where an order is made by consent without attendance.

17.23 Only the following paragraphs of the Practice Direction to CPR Part 52, with any necessary modifications, shall apply to first appeals: 5.10 to 5.20 inclusive.

17.24

(1)   Where, under the procedure relating to appeals in insolvency proceedings prior to the coming into effect of this Part of this Practice Direction, an appeal has been set down in the High Court or permission to appeal to the Court of Appeal has been granted before 2nd May 2000, the procedure and practice set out in this Part of this Practice Direction shall apply to such an appeal after that date.

(2)   Where, under the procedure relating to appeals in insolvency proceedings prior to the coming into effect of this Part of this Practice Direction, any person has failed before 2nd May 2000 either:

(a)   in the case of a first appeal, to set down in the High Court an appeal which relates to an order made (County Court) or sealed (High Court) after 27th March 2000 and before 2nd May 2000, or

(b)   in the case of an appeal from a decision of a Judge of the High Court, to obtain any requisite permission to appeal to the Court of Appeal which relates to an order sealed in the same period, the time for filing an appeal notice is extended to 16th May 2000 and application for any such permission should be made in the appeal notice.

17.25 This paragraph applies where a judge of the High Court has made a Bankruptcy order or a winding-up order or dismissed an appeal against such an order and an application is made for a stay of proceedings pending appeal.

(1)   the judge will not normally grant a stay of all proceedings but will confine himself to a stay of advertisement of the proceedings.

(2)   where the judge has granted permission to appeal any stay of advertisement will normally be until the hearing of the appeal but on terms that the stay will determine without further order if an appellant's notice is not filed within the period prescribed by the rules.

(3)   where the judge has refused permission to appeal any stay of advertisement will normally be for a period not exceeding 28 days. Application for any further stay of advertisement should be made to the Court of Appeal.

THE INSOLVENCY ACT 1986, SECTIONS 380 TO 385 AND 435 TO 436A

380 Introductory

The next five sections have effect for the interpretation of the provisions of this Act which are comprised in this Group of Parts; and where a definition is provided for a particular expression, it applies except so far as the context otherwise requires.

381 'Bankrupt' and associated terminology

(1) 'Bankrupt' means an individual who has been adjudged bankrupt and, in relation to a bankruptcy order, it means the individual adjudged bankrupt by that order.

(2) 'Bankruptcy order' means an order adjudging an individual bankrupt.

(3) 'Bankruptcy petition' means a petition to the court for a bankruptcy order.

382 'Bankruptcy debt', etc

(1) 'Bankruptcy debt', in relation to a bankrupt, means (subject to the next subsection) any of the following—

    (a) any debt or liability to which he is subject at the commencement of the bankruptcy,

    (b) any debt or liability to which he may become subject after the commencement of the bankruptcy (including after his discharge from bankruptcy) by reason of any obligation incurred before the commencement of the bankruptcy,

    (c) *any amount specified in pursuance of section 39(3)(c) of the Powers of Criminal Courts Act 1973 in any criminal bankruptcy order made against him before the commencement of the bankruptcy, and*

    (d) any interest provable as mentioned in section 322(2) in Chapter IV of Part IX.

(2) In determining for the purposes of any provision in this Group of Parts whether any liability in tort is a bankruptcy debt, the bankrupt is deemed to become subject to that liability by reason of an obligation incurred at the time when the cause of action accrued.

(3) For the purposes of references in this Group of Parts to a debt or liability, it is immaterial whether the debt or liability is present or future, whether it is certain or contingent or whether its amount is fixed or liquidated, or is capable of being ascertained by fixed rules or as a matter of opinion; and references in this Group of Parts to owing a debt are to be read accordingly.

(4) In this Group of Parts, except in so far as the context otherwise requires, 'liability' means (subject to subsection (3) above) a liability to pay money or money's worth, including any liability under an enactment, any liability for breach of trust, any liability in contract, tort or bailment and any liability arising out of an obligation to make restitution.

Amendment

Sub-s (1): para (c) prospectively repealed by the Criminal Justice Act 1988, s 170(2), Sch 16, as from a day to be appointed.

383   'Creditor', 'security', etc

(1)   'Creditor'—

    (a)   in relation to a bankrupt, means a person to whom any of the bankruptcy debts is owed (*being, in the case of an amount falling within paragraph (c) of the definition in section 382(1) of 'bankruptcy debt', the person in respect of whom that amount is specified in the criminal bankruptcy order in question*), and

    (b)   in relation to an individual to whom a bankruptcy petition relates, means a person who would be a creditor in the bankruptcy if a bankruptcy order were made on that petition.

(2)   Subject to the next two subsections and any provision of the rules requiring a creditor to give up his security for the purposes of proving a debt, a debt is secured for the purposes of this Group of Parts to the extent that the person to whom the debt is owed holds any security for the debt (whether a mortgage, charge, lien or other security) over any property of the person by whom the debt is owed.

(3)   Where a statement such as is mentioned in section 269(1)(a) in Chapter I of Part IX has been made by a secured creditor for the purposes of any bankruptcy petition and a bankruptcy order is subsequently made on that petition, the creditor is deemed for the purposes of the Parts in this Group to have given up the security specified in the statement.

(4)   In subsection (2) the reference to a security does not include a lien on books, papers or other records, except to the extent that they consist of documents which give a title to property and are held as such.

Amendment

Sub-s (1): in para (a) words in italics prospectively repealed by the Criminal Justice Act 1988, s 170(2), Sch 16, as from a day to be appointed.

384   'Prescribed' and 'the rules'

(1)   Subject to the next subsection [and sections 342C(7) and 342F(9) in Chapter V of Part IX], 'prescribed' means prescribed by the rules; and 'the rules' means rules made under section 412 in Part XV.

(2)   References in this Group of Parts to the amount prescribed for the purposes of any of the following provisions—

    [section 251S(4);]
    section 273;
    [section 313A;]
    section 346(3);
    section 354(1) and (2);
    section 358;
    section 360(1);
    section 361(2); *and*
    section 364(2)(d),
    [paragraphs 6 to 8 of Schedule 4ZA,]

and references in those provisions to the prescribed amount are to be read in accordance with section 418 in Part XV and orders made under that section.

Amendments

Sub-s (1): words 'and sections 342C(7) and 342F(9) in Chapter V of Part IX' in square brackets inserted by the Welfare Reform and Pensions Act 1999, s 84(1), Sch 12, Pt II, paras 70, 72.

Sub-s (2): words 'section 251S(4);' in square brackets inserted by the Tribunals, Courts and Enforcement Act 2007, s 108(3), Sch 20, Pt 1, paras 1, 4(a). Date in force: to be appointed: see the Tribunals, Courts and Enforcement Act 2007, s 148(2).

Sub-s (2): words 'section 313A;' in square brackets inserted by the Enterprise Act 2002, s 261(5).

Sub-s (2): word 'and' in italics repealed by the Tribunals, Courts and Enforcement Act 2007, s 108(3), Sch 20, Pt 1, paras 1, 4(b). Date in force: to be appointed: see the Tribunals, Courts and Enforcement Act 2007, s 148(2).

Sub-s (2): words 'paragraphs 6 to 8 of Schedule 4ZA' in square brackets inserted by the Tribunals, Courts and Enforcement Act 2007, s 108(3), Sch 20, Pt 1, paras 1, 4(c). Date in force: to be appointed: see the Tribunals, Courts and Enforcement Act 2007, s 148(2).

385 Miscellaneous definitions

(1) The following definitions have effect—

'the court', in relation to any matter, means the court to which, in accordance with section 373 in Part X and the rules, proceedings with respect to that matter are allocated or transferred;

'creditor's petition' means a bankruptcy petition under section 264(1)(a);

'criminal bankruptcy order' means an order under section 39(1) of the Powers of Criminal Courts Act 1973;

'debt' is to be construed in accordance with section 382(3);

'the debtor'—

[(za) in relation to a debt relief order or an application for such an order, has the same meaning as in Part 7A,]

(a) in relation to a proposal for the purposes of Part VIII, means the individual making or intending to make that proposal, and

(b) in relation to a bankruptcy petition, means the individual to whom the petition relates;

'debtor's petition' means a bankruptcy petition presented by the debtor himself under section 264(1)(b);

['debt relief order' means an order made by the official receiver under Part 7A;]

'dwelling house' includes any building or part of a building which is occupied as a dwelling and any yard, garden, garage or outhouse belonging to the dwelling house and occupied with it;

'estate', in relation to a bankrupt is to be construed in accordance with section 283 in Chapter II of Part IX;

'family', in relation to a bankrupt, means the persons (if any) who are living with him and are dependent on him;

['insolvency administration order' means an order for the administration in bankruptcy of the insolvent estate of a deceased debtor (being an individual at the date of his death);

'insolvency administration petition' means a petition for an insolvency administration order;

'the Rules' means the Insolvency Rules 1986.]

'secured' and related expressions are to be construed in accordance with section 383; and

'the trustee', in relation to a bankruptcy and the bankrupt, means the trustee of the bankrupt's estate.

(2) References in this Group of Parts to a person's affairs include his business, if any.

Amendments

Sub-s (1): definition 'criminal bankruptcy order' prospectively repealed by the Criminal Justice Act 1988, s 170(2), Sch 16, as from a day to be appointed.

Sub-s (1): definition 'the debtor' para (za) inserted by the Tribunals, Courts and Enforcement Act 2007, s 108(3), Sch 20, Pt 1, paras 1, 5(1), (2). Date in force: to be appointed: see the Tribunals, Courts and Enforcement Act 2007, s 148(2).

Sub-s (1): definition 'debt relief order' inserted by the Tribunals, Courts and Enforcement Act 2007, s 108(3), Sch 20, Pt 1, paras 1, 5(1), (3). Date in force: to be appointed: see the Tribunals, Courts and Enforcement Act 2007, s 148(2).

Sub-s (1): definitions 'insolvency administration order', 'insolvency administration petition' and 'the Rules' inserted by SI 1986/1999, art 6.

...

435   Meaning of 'associate'

(1)   For the purposes of this Act any question whether a person is an associate of another person is to be determined in accordance with the following provisions of this section (any provision that a person is an associate of another person being taken to mean that they are associates of each other).

[(2)   A person is an associate of an individual if that person is—

    (a)   the individual's husband or wife or civil partner,

    (b)   a relative of—
        (i)   the individual, or
        (ii)   the individual's husband or wife or civil partner, or

    (c)   the husband or wife or civil partner of a relative of—
        (i)   the individual, or
        (ii)   the individual's husband or wife or civil partner.]

(3)   A person is an associate of any person with whom he is in partnership, and of the husband or wife [or civil partner] or a relative of any individual with whom he is in partnership; and a Scottish firm is an associate of any person who is a member of the firm.

(4)   A person is an associate of any person whom he employs or by whom he is employed.

(5)   A person in his capacity as trustee of a trust other than—

    (a)   a trust arising under any of the second Group of Parts or the Bankruptcy (Scotland) Act 1985, or

    (b)   a pension scheme or an employees' share scheme (within the meaning of the Companies Act),

is an associate of another person if the beneficiaries of the trust include, or the terms of the trust confer a power that may be exercised for the benefit of, that other person or an associate of that other person.

(6)   A company is an associate of another company—

    (a)   if the same person has control of both, or a person has control of one and persons who are his associates, or he and persons who are his associates, have control of the other, or

    (b)   if a group of two or more persons has control of each company, and the groups either consist of the same persons or could be regarded as consisting of the same persons by treating (in one or more cases) a member of either group as replaced by a person of whom he is an associate.

(7)   A company is an associate of another person if that person has control of it or if that person and persons who are his associates together have control of it.

(8)   For the purposes of this section a person is a relative of an individual if he is that individual's brother, sister, uncle, aunt, nephew, niece, lineal ancestor or lineal descendant, treating—

(a)   any relationship of the half blood as a relationship of the whole blood and the stepchild or adopted child of any person as his child, and
(b)   an illegitimate child as the legitimate child of his mother and reputed father;

and references in this section to a husband or wife include a former husband or wife and a reputed husband or wife [and references to a civil partner include a former civil partner] [and a reputed civil partner].

(9)   For the purposes of this section any director or other officer of a company is to be treated as employed by that company.

(10)   For the purposes of this section a person is to be taken as having control of a company if—

(a)   the directors of the company or of another company which has control of it (or any of them) are accustomed to act in accordance with his directions or instructions, or
(b)   he is entitled to exercise, or control the exercise of, one third or more of the voting power at any general meeting of the company or of another company which has control of it;

and where two or more persons together satisfy either of the above conditions, they are to be taken as having control of the company.

(11)   In this section 'company' includes any body corporate (whether incorporated in Great Britain or elsewhere); and references to directors and other officers of a company and to voting power at any general meeting of a company have effect with any necessary modifications.

Amendments

Sub-s (2): substituted by the Civil Partnership Act 2004, s 261(1), Sch 27, para 122(1), (2).
Sub-s (3): words 'or civil partner' in square brackets inserted by the Civil Partnership Act 2004, s 261(1), Sch 27, para 122(1), (3).
Sub-s (8): words 'and references to a civil partner include a former civil partner' in square brackets inserted by the Civil Partnership Act 2004, s 261(1), Sch 27, para 122(1), (4).
Sub-s (8): words 'and a reputed civil partner' in square brackets inserted by SI 2005/3129, art 4(4), Sch 4, para 8.

436   Expressions used generally

In this Act, except in so far as the context otherwise requires (and subject to Parts VII and XI)—

'the appointed day' means the day on which this Act comes into force under section 443;
'associate' has the meaning given by section 435;
'business' includes a trade or profession;
'the Companies Act' means the Companies Act 1985;
['the Companies Acts' means the Companies Acts (as defined in section 2 of the Companies Act 2006) as they have effect in Great Britain;]
'conditional sale agreement' and 'hire-purchase agreement' have the same meanings as in the Consumer Credit Act 1974;
['the EC Regulation' means Council Regulation (EC) No 1346/2000;]
['EEA State' means a state that is a Contracting Party to the Agreement on the European Economic Area signed at Oporto on 2nd May 1992 as adjusted by the Protocol signed at Brussels on 17th March 1993;]
'modifications' includes additions, alterations and omissions and cognate expressions shall be construed accordingly;

'property' includes money, goods, things in action, land and every description of
property wherever situated and also obligations and every description of
interest, whether present or future or vested or contingent, arising out of, or
incidental to, property;

'records' includes computer records and other non-documentary records;

'subordinate legislation' has the same meaning as in the Interpretation Act 1978;
and

'transaction' includes a gift, agreement or arrangement, and references to entering
into a transaction shall be construed accordingly.

Amendments

Definition 'the Companies Acts' inserted by SI 2007/2194, art 10(1), (2), Sch 4, Pt 3, para 45.
Definition 'the EC Regulation' inserted by SI 2002/1037, regs 2, 4.
Definition 'EEA State' inserted by SI 2005/879, reg 2(1), (3).

[436A   Proceedings under EC Regulation: modified definition of property]

[In the application of this Act to proceedings by virtue of Article 3 of the EC
Regulation, a reference to property is a reference to property which may be dealt with
in the proceedings.]

Amendment

Section 436A inserted by SI 2002/1240, regs 3, 18.

Appendix 3

SELECTED STATUTORY FORMS

The forms follow on the next page.

Appendix 3 *Selected statutory forms*

FORM 6.1 STATUTORY DEMAND UNDER IA 1986, S 268(1)(A) – DEBT FOR LIQUIDATED SUM PAYABLE IMMEDIATELY

Rule 6.1

Statutory Demand under section 268(1)(a) of the Insolvency Act 1986. Debt for Liquidated Sum Payable Immediately

Form 6.1

Notes for Creditor

- If the creditor is entitled to the debt by way of assignment, details of the original creditor and any intermediary assignees should be given in part C on page 3.
- If the amount of debt includes interest not previously notified to the debtor as included in the debtor's liability, details should be given, including the grounds upon which interest is charged. The amount of interest must be shown separately.
- Any other charge accruing due from time to time may be claimed. The amount or rate of the charge must be identified and the grounds on which it is claimed must be stated.
- In either case the amount claimed must be limited to that which has accrued due at the date of the demand.
- If the creditor holds any security the amount of the debt should be the sum the creditor is prepared to regard as unsecured for the purposes of this demand. Brief details of the total debt should be included and the nature of the security and the value put upon it by the creditor, as at the date of the demand, must be specified.
- If signatory of the demand is a solicitor or other agent of the creditor the name of his/her firm should be given.

*Delete if signed by the creditor himself

Warning

- This is an **important** document. You should refer to the notes entitled "How to comply with a statutory demand or have it set aside".
- If you wish to have this demand set aside you must make application to do so **within 18 days** from its service on you.
- If you do not apply to set aside **within 18 days** or otherwise deal with this demand as set out in the notes **within 21 days** after its service on you, you could be made bankrupt and your property and goods taken away from you.
- Please read the demand and notes carefully. If you are in any doubt about your position you should seek advice **immediately** from a solicitor, a Citizen Advice Bureau, or a licensed insolvency practitioner.

Demand

To _____

Address _____

_____

This demand is served on you by the creditor:

Name _____

Address _____

_____

The creditor claims that you owe the sum of £ _____ , full particulars of which are set out on page 2, and that it is payable immediately and, to the extent of the sum demanded, is unsecured.

The creditor demands that you pay the above debt or secure or compound for it to the creditor's satisfaction.

[The creditor making this demand is a Minister of the Crown or a Goverment Department, and it is intended to present a bankruptcy petition in the High Court.]

Signature of individual _____

Name _____
(BLOCK LETTERS)

Date _____

*Position with or relationship to creditor _____

_____
*I am authorised to make this demand on the creditor's behalf.

Address _____

_____

Tel. No. _____ Ref. _____

N.B. The person making this demand must complete the whole of pages 1, 2 and parts A, B and C (as applicable) on page 3.

Particulars of Debt

(These particulars must include (a) when the debt was incurred, (b) the consideration for the debt (or if there is no consideration the way in which it arose) and (c) the amount due as at the date of this demand.)

Note for Creditor

Please make sure that you have read the notes in page 1 before completing this page.

Note:

If space is insufficient continue on page 4 and clearly indicate on this page that you are doing so.

Part A
Appropriate Court for Setting Aside Demand

Rule 6.4(2) of the Insolvency Rules 1986 states that the appropriate court is the court to which you would have to present your own bankruptcy petition in accordance with Rule 6.40(1) and 6.40(2). In accordance with those rules on present information the appropriate court is [the High Court of Justice] [County Court]

Any application by you to set aside this demand should be made to that court.

Part B

The individual or individuals to whom any communication regarding this demand may be addressed is / are:

Name _____
        (BLOCK LETTERS)
Address _____

_____

Telephone Number _____

Reference _____

Part C
For completion if the creditor is entitled to the debt by way of assignment

	Name	Date(s) of Assignment
Original creditor		
Assignees		

How to comply with a statutory demand or have it set aside (ACT WITHIN 18 DAYS)

If you wish to avoid a bankruptcy petition being presented against you, you must pay the debt shown on page 1, particulars of which are set out on page 2 of this notice, within the period of **21 days** after its service upon you. Alternatively, you can attempt to come to a settlement with the creditor. To do this you should:

- inform the individual (or one of the individuals) named in part B above immediately that you are willing and able to offer security for the debt to the creditor's satisfaction; or
- inform the individual (or one of the individuals) named in part B immediately that you are willing and able to compound for the debt to the creditor's satisfaction.

If you dispute the demand in whole or in part you should:

- contact the individual (or one of the individuals) named in part B immediately.

THERE ARE MORE IMPORTANT NOTES ON THE NEXT PAGE

If you consider that you have grounds to have this demand set aside or if you do not quickly receive a satisfactory written reply from the individual named in part B whom you have contacted you should **apply within 18 days** from the date of services of this demand on you to the appropriate court shown in part A above to have the demand set aside.

Any application to set aside the demand (Form 6.4 in Schedule 4 to the Insolvency Rules 1986) should be made within 18 days from the date of service upon you and be supported by an affidavit (Form 6.5 in Schedule 4 to those Rules) stating the grounds on which the demand should be set aside. The forms may be obtained from the appropriate court when you attend to make the application.

Remember! – From the date of service on you of this document

     (a) you have only 18 days to apply to the court to have the demand set aside, and

     (b) you have only 21 days before the creditor may present a bankruptcy petition

---

Appendix 3 *Selected statutory forms*

FORM 6.7 CREDITOR'S BANKRUPT PETITION ON FAILURE TO COMPLY WITH A STATUTORY DEMAND FOR A LIQUIDATED SUM PAYABLE IMMEDIATELY

Rule 6.6   Form 6.7

Creditor's Bankruptcy Petition on Failure to Comply with a Statutory Demand for a Liquidated Sum Payable Immediately
(Title)

(a) Insert full name(s) and address(es) of petitioner(s)

I/We (a) _____

_____

_____

(b) Insert full name, place of residence and occupation (if any) of debtor

petition the court that a bankruptcy order may be made against (b)_____

_____

(c) Insert in full any other name(s) by which the debtor is or has been known

[also known as (c)_____]

(d) Insert trading name (adding "with another or others", if this is so), business address and nature of business

[and carrying on business as (d) _____

_____]

(e) Insert any other address or addresses at which the debtor has resided at or after the time the petition debt was incurred

[and lately residing at (e)_____

_____]

(f) Give the same details as specified in note (d) above for any other businesses which have been carried on at or after the time the petition debt was incurred

[and lately carrying on business as (f) _____

_____]

and say as follows:-

(g) Delete as applicable

1. (g) [The debtor's centre of main interests has been][The debtor has had an establishment] at _____

OR

The debtor carries on business as an insurance undertaking; a credit institution; an investment undertaking providing services involving the holding of funds or securities for third parties; or a collective investment undertaking as referred to in Article 1.2 of the EC Regulation

OR

The debtor's centre of main interests is not within a member State

2. The debtor has for the greater part of six months immediately preceding the presentation of this petition (g) [resided at] [carried on business at]

_____

(h) Or as the case may be following the terms of Rule 6.9

within the district of this court (h)

Under the EC Regulation:
(i) The centre of main interests should correspond to the place where the debtor conducts the administration of his interests on a regular basis.
(ii) Establishment is defined as "any place of operations where the debtor carries out a non-transitory economic activity with human means and goods".

<table>
<tr><td>(j) Please give the amount of the debt(s), what they relate to and when they were incurred. Please show separately the amount or rate of any interest or other charge not previously notified to the debtor and the reasons why you are claiming it</td></tr>
</table>

3. The debtor is justly and truly indebted to me [us] in the aggregate sum of

£(j) _____

4. The above-mentioned debt is for a liquidated sum payable immediately and the debtor appears to be unable to pay it

(k) Insert date of service of a statutory demand

5. On (k) _____ a statutory demand was served upon the debtor by

(l) State manner of service of demand

(l) _____
in respect of the above-mentioned debt. To the best of my knowledge and belief the demand has neither been complied with nor set aside in accordance with the Rules and no application to set it aside is outstanding

(m) If 3 weeks have not elapsed since service of statutory demand give reasons for earlier presentation of petition

(m)

6. I/We do not, nor does any person on my/our behalf, hold any security on the debtor's estate, or any part thereof, for the payment of the above-mentioned sum

OR

I/We hold security for the payment of (g) [part of] the above-mentioned sum. I/We will give up such security for the benefit of all the creditors in the event of a bankruptcy order being made.

OR

I/We hold security for the payment of part of the above-mentioned sum and I/we estimate the value of such security to be £   . This petition is not made in respect of the secured part of my/our debt.

Endorsement
This petition having been presented to the court on _____ it is ordered that the petition shall be heard as follows:-

Date _____

Time _____ hours

Place _____

(n) Insert name of debtor

and you, the above-named (n) _____ , are to take notice that if you intend to oppose the petition you must not later than 7 days before the date fixed for the hearing:

    (i)   file in court a notice (in Form 6.19) specifying the grounds on which you object to the making of a bankruptcy order; and

    (ii)   send a copy of the notice to the petitioner or his solicitor.

The solicitor to the petitioning creditor is:- (o)

(o) Only to be completed where the petitioning creditor is represented by a solicitor

Name _____
Address _____
_____

Telephone Number _____

Reference _____

FORM 6.11 AFFIDAVIT OF PERSONAL SERVICE OF STATUTORY DEMAND

Rule 6.11   **Form 6.11**

Affidavit of Personal Service of Statutory Demand

Date of Statutory Demand

(a) Insert name, address and description of person making the oath and whether the creditor or a person acting on his behalf

I (a)

make oath and say as follows:—

(b) Delete "I" and insert name and address of person who effected service, if applicable

1. (b) [I][_____]
did on (c) _____ (d) [before] [after]   hours, at (e)_____

(c) Insert date

personally serve the above-named debtor with the demand dated

(d) Insert time which must be either before or after 16.00 hours Monday to Friday or before or after 12.00 hours Saturday

(f) [2. That on (c) _____ the debtor acknowledged service of
the demand by (g) _____]

(e) Insert address

(f) Delete words in [   ] if no acknowledgement of service has been received

3. A copy of the demand marked "A" (f) [and the acknowledgement of service marked "B"]
is/are exhibited hereto.

(g) Give particulars of the way in which the debtor acknowledged service of the demand

Sworn at

FORM 6.13 AFFIDAVIT OF TRUTH OF STATEMENTS IN
BANKRUPTCY PETITION

Rule 6.12   **Form 6.13**

Affidavit of Truth of Statements
in Bankruptcy Petition

(a) Insert name, address and description of person making oath

I (a)_____

_____

_____

make oath and say as follows:

[1. I am the petitioner. The statements in the petition now produced and shown to me marked "A" are true to the best Of my knowledge, information and belief.

(b) If petition is based upon a statutory demand, and more than 4 months have elapsed between service of the demand and presentation of the petition, give reason(s) for delay and explanation of circumstances which have contributed to the late presentation of the petition.

2. (b)

]

OR

(c) State the capacity eg. director, secretary, solicitor etc.

[1. I am (c)_____
of the petitioner; or

(d) Delete as applicable

2. I am duly authorised by the petitioner to make this affidavit on (d) [its] [his] behalf.

3. I have been concerned in the matters giving rise to the presentation of the petition and I have the requisite knowledge of the matters referred to in the petition because (e)

(e) State means of knowledge of matters sworn to in the affidavit

4. The statements in the petition now produced and shown to me marked "A" are true to the best of my knowledge, information and belief.

5. (b)   ]

Sworn at

FORM 6.17 AFFIDAVIT OF PERSONAL SERVICE OF BANKRUPTCY PETITION

Rule 6.15   **Form 6.17**

Affidavit of Personal Service of Bankruptcy Petition

(TITLE)

(a) Insert date In the matter of a bankruptcy petition filed on (a)

(b) Insert full name, address and description of person making oath I (b)

(c) Insert name and address and for the purpose of service instructed by (c)

(d) Delete as applicable (d) [Solicitor(s) for] the

make oath and say as follows:—

1. That I did on (a)   serve the above-named debtor with a copy of the above-mentioned petition, duly sealed with the seal of the court
(e) Insert name of debtor as in title by delivering the same personally to the said (e)
(f) State exact place of service at (f)

2. A sealed copy of the said petition is now produced and shown to me marked
(g) Sealed copy must be marked as an exhibit "A" (g)

Sworn at

NOTE: This affidavit and exhibit should be filed in court immediately after service (Rule 6.15.(2))

FORM 6.22 DISMISSAL OF BANKRUPTCY PETITION

**Rule 6.25, 6.27,
6.32**   **Form 6.22**

Dismissal of Bankruptcy Petition
(TITLE)

Mr Registrar   in chambers

(a) Insert date   In the matter of a bankruptcy petition filed on (a)

(b) Insert full name,   Upon the application of (b)
address and
description of
applicant

And upon hearing

And upon reading the evidence

(c) Delete as applicable   It is ordered that (c) [this petition be dismissed] [the petitioner has leave to withdraw
this petition].
(d) Insert any further   [And that (d)   ]
terms of the order eg.
as to costs

And it is ordered that the registration of the petition as a pending action at the Land

(e) Insert date of   charges Department of Land Registry, on (e)
registration
under Reference No.   be vacated upon the application of the debtor
under the Land Charges Rules.

Dated
_____

Notice to Debtor

It is your responsibility and is in your interest to ensure that the registration of the
petition as an entry, both in the Land Charges Register and your registered titles, is
cancelled.

Appendix 3 *Selected statutory forms*

FORM 6.25 BANKRUPTCY ORDER ON CREDITOR'S PETITION

Rule 6.33   Form 6.25

Bankruptcy Order on Creditor's Petition
(TITLE)

(a) Insert name and address of petitioning creditor

Upon the petition of (a) ....

....

a creditor, which was presented on ....

And upon hearing

And upon reading the evidence

(b) Insert full description of debtor as set out in the petition

It is ordered that (b) ....

....

be adjudged bankrupt.

(c) Delete as applicable
(d) Insert whether main, secondary or territorial proceedings

(c) And the Court being satisfied that the EC Regulation does apply declares that these proceedings are

(d) .... proceedings as defined in Article 3 of the EC Regulation.

OR

(c) The court is satisfied that the EC Regulation does not apply in relation to these proceedings.

Dated ....

Time .... hours

Important Notice to Bankrupt

(c) [The][One of the] official receiver(s) attached to the court is by virtue of this order receiver and manager of the bankrupt's estate. You are required to attend upon the Official Receiver of the court at

(e) Insert address of Official Receiver's office

(e) _____

_____

immediately after you have received this order.

The Official Receiver's offices are open Monday to Friday (except on Holidays) from 09.00 to 17.00 hours.

(f) Order to be endorsed where petitioning creditor is represented by a solicitor

Endorsement on Order (f)

The solicitor to the petitioning creditor is:-

Name_____

Address_____

Telephone No._____

Reference _____

FORM 6.33 STATEMENT OF AFFAIRS (CREDITOR'S PETITION)

Form 6.33

Rule 6.59

Statement of Affairs (Creditor's Petition)
Insolvency Act 1986

NOTE:
These details will be the same as those shown at the top of your petition

In the _____

In Bankruptcy   No_____ of _____

Re _____

The 'Guidance Notes' Booklet tells you how to complete this form easily and correctly

Show your current financial position by completing all the pages of this form which will then be your Statement of Affairs.

Affidavit

This Affidavit must be sworn before a Solicitor or Commissioner of Oaths or an officer of the court duly authorised to administer oaths when you have completed the rest of this form

a) Insert full name and occupation

I (a)_____

_____

(b) Insert full address

of (b) _____

_____

Make oath and say that the attached pages exhibited hereto and marked _____are to the best of my knowledge and belief a full, true and complete statement of my affairs as at _____the date of the bankruptcy order made against me.

Sworn at _____

Date_____   Signature(s)_____

Before me_____

A Solicitor or Commissioner of Oaths or Duly authorised officer

Before swearing the affidavit the Solicitor or Commissioner is particularly requested to make sure that the full name, address and description of the Deponent are stated, and to initial any crossings-out or other alterations in the printed form. A deficiency in the affidavit in any of the above respects will mean that it is refused by the court, and will need to be re-sworn.

Appendix 3 _Selected statutory forms_

A

List of Secured Creditors

Is anyone claiming something of yours to clear or reduce their claim?

Tick Box
Yes ☐ No ☐

If **'YES'** give details below: ⟵

Name of creditor	Address (with postcode)	Amount owed to creditor £	What of yours is claimed and what is it worth?
1.			
2.			
3.			
4.			

Signature ⟵

Date

B

List of Unsecured Creditors

1. No.	2. Name of creditor or claimant	3. Address (with postcode)	4. Amount the creditor says you owe him/her £	5. Amount you think you owe £

Signature _____   Date _____

C

Assets

Now show anything else of yours which may be of value:

	£
a) Cash at bank or building society	
b) Household furniture and belongings	
c) Life policies	
d) Money owed to you	
e) Stock in trade	
f) Motor vehicles	
g) Other property (see Guidance Notes):—	
TOTAL	

Signature_____   Date_____

FORM 6.37 PROOF OF DEBT – GENERAL FORM

Rule 6.96   Form 6.37

Proof of Debt – General Form

(TITLE)		
Date of Bankruptcy Order		No.
1	Name of Creditor (If a company please also give company registration number.)	
2	Address of creditor for correspondence	
3	Total amount of claim, including any Value Added Tax and outstanding uncapitalised interest as at the date of the bankruptcy order.	£
4	Details of any documents by reference to which the debt can be substantiated. (Note: There is no need to attach them now but the trustee may call for any document or evidence to substantiate the claim at his discretion as may the official receiver whilst acting as receiver and manager, or the chairman or convenor of any meeting.)	
5	If the amount in 3 above includes outstanding uncapitalised interest, please state amount	£
6	Particulars of how and when debt incurred (If you need more space append a continuation sheet to this form.)	
7	Particulars of any security held, the value of the security, and the date it was given	
8	Particulars of any reservation of title claimed, in respect of goods supplied to which the claim relates.	
9	Signature of creditor or person authorised to act on his behalf	
	Name in BLOCK LETTERS	
	Position with or in relation to creditor	
	Address of person signing (if different from 2 above)	

Admitted to vote for	Admitted for dividend for
£	£
Date	Date
Official Receiver/Trustee	Trustee

Appendix 3 *Selected statutory forms*

10	Particulars of any security held, the value of the security, and the date it was given	
11	Particulars of any reservation of title claimed, including details of goods supplied, their value and when supplied	

12	Signature of creditor or person authorised to act on his behalf
	Name in BLOCK LETTERS
	Position with or relation to creditor

Admitted to vote for

£

Date

Official Receiver/Trustee

Admitted preferentially for

£

Date

Trustee

Admitted non-preferentially for

£

Date

Trustee

FORM 6.39 AFFIDAVIT OF DEBT

Form 6.39

Rule 6.96, 6.99   **Affidavit of Debt**

(TITLE)

(a) Insert full name, address and description of person making oath

I (a)

make oath and say:

(b) Delete as applicable

(1) That (b) [I am a creditor of the above-named bankrupt] [I am (c)

(c) State capacity eg director, secretary, solicitor etc

of (d)

(d) Insert full name and address of creditor

a creditor of the above-named bankrupt.

(e) State means of knowledge of matters sworn to in affidavit

I have been concerned in this matter (e)

and am authorised by the creditor to make this affidavit on its/his behalf]

(f) Insert name of bankrupt

(2) That the said (f)

(g) Insert date

on (g)   the date of the bankruptcy order, was and still is justly and truly indebted (b) [to me] [to the said creditor] in the sum of £   as shown in the proof of debt exhibited hereto marked "A".

Sworn at

Originating Application

Form 7.1

Rule 7.2

Originating Application

(TITLE)

Between

Applicant _____

and

Respondent _____

(a) Insert name and address of respondent

Let (a)

attend

before the Judge/Registrar on:—

Date _____

Time _____ hours

Place _____

(b) Insert name of applicant

On the hearing of an application by (b)
the applicant for an order in the following terms:—

(c) State the terms of the order to which the applicant claims to be entitled

(c)

The grounds on which the applicant claims to be entitled to the order are:—

(d) Set out grounds or refer to an affidavit in support

(d)

The names and addresses of the persons upon whom it is intended to serve this application are:—

(e) State the names and addresses of the persons intended to be served

(e)

OR

It is not intended to serve any person with this application.

(f) State the applicant's address for service

The applicant's address for service is: (f)

Dated _____

Signed: _____
(SOLICITOR FOR THE) APPLICANT

If you do not attend, the court may make such order as it thinks fit.

FORM 7.2 ORDINARY APPLICATION

Form of ordinary application

Form 7.2

Rule 7.2   **Ordinary Application**
(TITLE)

Between

Applicant _____
and
Respondent _____

Take notice that I intend to apply to the Judge/Registrar on:

Date _____

Time _____ hours

Place _____

(a) State nature and   for (a)
grounds of application

Signed: _____
            (SOLICITOR FOR THE) APPLICANT

My/Our address for service is:-

(b) Give the name(s)   To: (b)
and address(es) of the
person(s) (including
the respondent) on
whom it is intended to
serve the application   **OR**
It is not intended to serve any person with this application

If you do not attend, the court will make such order as it thinks fit

FORM 8.1 PROXY – COMPANY OR INDIVIDUAL
VOLUNTARY ARRANGEMENTS

Proxy (Company or Individual Voluntary Arrangements)
(TITLE)

Notes to help completion
of the form

Please give full name and
address for communication

Name of creditor/member _____

Address _____

_____

Name of proxy-holder _____

Please insert name of
person (who must be 18 or
over) or the "chairman of the
meeting" (see note
below) If you wish to
provide for alternative
proxy-holders in the
circumstances that your first
choice is unable to attend
please state the name(s) of
the alternatives as well

1 _____

_____

2 _____

_____

3 _____

_____

Please delete words in
brackets if the proxy-holder
is only to vote as directed ie
he has no discretion

I appoint the above person to be my/the creditor's/member's proxy-holder at the meeting of creditors/members to be held on _____ , or at any adjournment of that meeting. The proxy-holder is to propose or vote as instructed below [and in respect of any resolution for which no specific instruction is given, may vote or abstain at his/her discretion].

Voting instructions for resolutions

*Please delete as
appropriate

1. For the acceptance/rejection* of the proposed voluntary arrangement [with the following modifications:—]

Any other resolutions which
the proxy-holder is to
propose or vote in favour of
or against should be set out
in numbered paragraphs in
the space provided below
Paragraph 1. If more room
is required please use the
other side of this form.

_____

_____

_____

_____

_____

_____

_____

This form must be signed

Signature _____   Date _____

Name in CAPITAL LETTERS_____

Only to be completed if the
creditor/member has not
signed in person

Position with creditor/member or relationship to creditor/member or other authority for signature _____

_____

Remember: there may be resolutions on the other side of this form

FORM 8.4 PROXY – WINDING UP BY THE COURT OR BANKRUPTCY

Form 8.4

Rule 8.1 Insolvency Act 1986
Proxy (Winding up by the Court or Bankruptcy)
(TITLE)

Notes to help completion of the form

Please give full name and adress for communication

Name of creditor/contributory _____

Address _____

_____

Please insert name of person (who must be 18 or over) or the "Official Receiver". If you wish to provide for alternative proxy-holders in the circumstances that your first choice is unable to attend please state the name(s) of the alternatives as well.

Name of proxy-holder _____

1 _____

_____

_____

2 _____

_____

3 _____

_____

Please delete words in brackets if the proxy-holder is only to vote as directed ie he has no discretion

I appoint the above person to be my/the creditor's/contributory's proxy-holder at the meeting of creditors/contributories to be held on_____, or at any adjournment of that meeting. The proxy-holder is to propose or vote as instructed below [and in respect of any resolution for which no specific instruction is given, may vote or abstain at his/her discretion].

Voting instructions for resolutions

Please complete paragraph 1 if you wish to nominate or vote for a specific person as a trustee/liquidator

1 For the appointment of_____of
_____as liquidator of the company/trustee of the bankrupt 's estate.

Please delete words in brackets if the proxy-holder is only to vote as directed ie he has no discretion

(in the event of a person named in paragraph 1 withdrawing or being eliminated from any vote for the appointment of a liquidator/trustee the proxy-holder may vote or abstain in any further ballot at his/her discretion)

Any other resolutions which the proxy-holder is to propose or vote in favour of or against should be set out in numbered paragraphs in the space provided below paragraph 1. If more room is required please use the other side of this form.

_____

_____

_____

_____

_____

This form must be signed.

Signature _____ Date _____

Name in CAPITAL LETTERS _____

Only to be completed if the creditor/contributory has not signed in person

Position with creditor/contributory or relationship to creditor/contributory or other authority for signature _____

Remember: there may be resolutions on the other side of this form.

1221

PDIP1 APPELLANT'S NOTICE – INSOLVENCY PROCEEDINGS

Appellant's notice

In the High Court of Justice

For use in connection ONLY with an Appeal from a decision of the County Court or a Registrar of the High Court in insolvency proceedings

Notes for guidance are available which will help you complete this form. Please read them carefully before you complete each section.

Seal

For Court use only	
Appeal Court Reference No.	
Date filed	

Section 1 — Details of the case

Name of court	Case number

Case name

Names of claimant/ applicant/ petitioner		Names of defendant(s)/ respondent(s)/ debtor(s)	

In the case, were you the (tick only one box)

☐ claimant   ☐ applicant   ☐ petitioner

☐ defendant   ☐ respondent   ☐ debtor   ☐ other (please specify) _____

Section 2 — Your (appellant's) name and address

Your (Appellant's) name

Your Solicitor's name *(if you are legally represented)*

Your (your solicitor's) address

	Reference or contact name
	Contact telephone number
	DX number

Section 3	Respondent's name and address

First respondent's name

Solicitor's name
(if legally represented)

First respondent's (solicitor's) address

Reference or contact name

Contact telephone number

DX number

Second respondent's name

Solicitor's name
(if legally represented)

Second respondent's (solicitor's) address

Reference or contact name

Contact telephone number

DX number

Details of other respondents are attached ☐ Yes ☐ No

Section 4	Permission to appeal and time estimate for appeal hearing

Do you need permission to appeal? ☐ Yes ☐ No

Has permission to appeal been granted?

☐ **Yes**   ☐ **No**

Date of order granting permission

Name of Judge granting permission

I

the Appellant('s solicitor) seek permission to appeal.

2

	Days	Hours	Minutes
How long do you estimate it will take to put your appeal to the appeal court at the hearing?			

Who will represent you at the appeal hearing? ☐ Yourself ☐ Solicitor ☐ Counsel

Section 5	Details of the order(s) or part(s) of order(s) you want to appeal

Name of District Judge/Circuit Judge/Registrar   Date of order(s)

If only part of an order is appealed, write out that part (or those parts)

Section 6	Grounds for appeal

I (the appellant) appeal(s) the order(s) at **section 5** because:

Does your appeal include any issues arising from the Human Rights Act 1998? ☐ Yes ☐ No

Signed _____   Date _____
    Appellant('s Solicitor)

3

Section 7	What decision are you asking the appeal court to make?

I am (the appellant is) asking that:-

(tick appropriate box)

☐ the order(s) at **section 5** be set aside

☐ the order(s) at **section 5** be varied and the following order(s) substituted:-

☐ a new trial be ordered

☐ the appeal court makes the following additional orders:-

Appendix 3 *Selected statutory forms*

Section 8	Application for extension of time for filing Appellant's Notice

I apply (the appellant applies) for an application for extension of time for filing this Appellant's notice.

I wish (the appellant wishes) to reply on the following evidence in support of this application:-

---

Statement of Truth

I believe that the facts stated in Section 8 of this Appellant's Notice - Insolvency Proceedings are true.

Full name _____

Name of appellant's solicitor's firm _____

Signed _____   Position or office held _____

       Appellant ('s solicitor)   (if signing on behalf of firm or company)

5

1226

PDIP2 RESPONDENT'S NOTICE – INSOLVENCY PROCEEDINGS

Respondent's notice

In the High Court of Justice

For use in connection ONLY with an Appeal from a decision of the County Court or a Registrar of the High Court in insolvency proceedings

Notes for guidance are available which will help you complete this form. Please read them carefully before you complete each section.

Seal

For Court use only	
Appeal Court Reference No.	
Date filed	

Section 1	Details of the case

Name of court _____   Case number _____

Case name _____

In the case, were you the (tick only one box)

☐ claimant   ☐ applicant   ☐ petitioner

☐ defendant   ☐ respondent   ☐ debtor   ☐ other (please specify) _____

Section 2	Your (respondent's) name and address

Your (respondent's) name _____

Your Solicitor's name
(if you are legally represented) _____

Your (your solicitor's) address

	Reference or contact name	
	Contact telephone number	
	DX number	

Details of other respondents are attached   ☐ Yes   ☐ No

Section 3	Permission to appeal and time estimate for appeal hearing

Do you need permission to appeal?   ☐ Yes   ☐ No

Has permission to appeal been granted?

☐ **Yes**   ☐ **No**

Date of order granting permission

Name of Judge granting permission

I

the Respondent('s solicitor) seek permission to appeal.

	Days	Hours	Minutes
How long do you estimate it will take to put your appeal to the appeal court at the hearing?			

Who will represent you at the appeal hearing?   ☐ Yourself   ☐ Solicitor   ☐ Counsel

Section 4	Details of the order(s) or part(s) of order(s) you want to appeal

Name of District Judge/Circuit Judge/Registrar   Date of order(s)

If only part of an order is appealed, write out that part (or those parts)

Section 5	Grounds for appeal or for upholding the order

I (the respondent)

☐ appeal(s) the order   ☐ wish(es) the appeal court to uphold the order on different or additional grounds

because:-

Does your appeal include any issues arising from the Human Rights Act 1998? ☐ Yes ☐ No

Signed _____   Date _____

        Respondent('s Solicitor)

3

Appendix 3 *Selected statutory forms*

Section 6	What decision are you asking the appeal court to make?

I am (the respondent is) asking that:-

(tick appropriate box)

☐ the order(s) at **section 4** be set aside

☐ the order(s) at **section 4** be varied and the following order(s) substituted:-

```



```

☐ a new trial be ordered

☐ the appeal court makes the following additional orders:-

```



```

☐ the appeal court upholds the order but for the following different or additional reasons

```



```

4

1230

Section 7	Application for extension of time for filing Respondent's Notice

I apply (the respondent applies) for an application for extension of time for filing this Respondent's notice.

I wish (the respondent wishes) to reply on the following evidence in support of this application:-

Statement of Truth

I believe that the facts stated in Section 7 of this Respondent's Notice - Insolvency Proceedings are true.

Full name _____

Name of respondent's solicitor's firm _____

Signed _____   Position or office held _____

       Respondent ('s solicitor)   (if signing on behalf of firm or company)

Appendix 4

SELECTED PRECEDENTS

PRECEDENT 1: ORIGINATING APPLICATION[1] PURSUANT TO IA 1986, S 253 SEEKING INTERIM ORDER BY A DEBTOR WHO IS NOT AN UNDISCHARGED BANKRUPT

In the [...] County Court[2]

No ... of ...

In the matter of the Insolvency Act 1986[3]

Re AB[4]

Between

	AB	
		Applicant
	and	
	(1) CD	
	(2) EF	
		Respondents

Let CD[5] of [address] and EF[6] of [address] attend before the District Judge on:

Date:

Time:

Place:

On the hearing of an application by AB, the applicant for:

1. an interim order pursuant to section 252 of the Insolvency Act 1986 in respect of the applicant; and
2. a direction pursuant to section 256 of the Insolvency Act 1986 that the period for which the interim order has effect shall be extended until [date] for the purpose of enabling the applicant's proposal to be considered by his creditors[7].

The grounds on which the applicant claims to be entitled to the order are set out in the witness statement[8] of the applicant dated [*date*].

The names and addresses of the persons upon whom it is intended to serve this application are:

(1)   CD of [*address*]
(2)   EF of [*address*]

The applicant's address for service is [*address*].

Dated:

Signed:

(Solicitor for the) applicant.

If you do not attend, the court may make such order as it thinks fit.

[1]   Based on the general form of an originating application, Form 7.1; see IR 1986, r 12.7(1) and Sch 4, Form 7.1.
[2]   The court where the application should be made is the court to which the debtor could present his own bankruptcy petition; see IR 1986, r 5.8(1) referring to r 6.40 (which sets out where a debtor should present his own petition).
[3]   An application for an interim order by a debtor who is not an undischarged bankrupt should not be headed 'In Bankruptcy' because the application is made under the IA 1986, Pt VIII; see the IR 1986, r 7.26(2).
[4]   The debtor.
[5]   The nominee; see IR 1986, r 5.7(4)(c).
[6]   Any creditor who has, to the debtor's knowledge, presented a petition against him must be given notice of the application; see IR 1986, r 5.7(4)(b).
[7]   Where the nominee has already prepared his report and recommended that the debtor's proposal be put to his creditors before the application for the interim order is made, it is appropriate to seek the direction extending the period for which the interim order has effect until after the date on which the creditors' meeting is to be held. If the interim order is sought before the nominee's report has been prepared, a second hearing will be necessary at which the court will consider the report and direct that the period be extended if appropriate.
[8]   The application must be supported by a witness statement; see IR 1986, r 5.7(1) and r 7.57(5).

PRECEDENT 2: WITNESS STATEMENT[1] IN SUPPORT OF APPLICATION AT PRECEDENT 1

In the [...] County Court

No ... of ...

In the matter of the Insolvency Act 1986[2]

Re AB[3]

Between

AB

Applicant

and
(1) CD
(2) EF

Respondents

I, AB, of [*address*], state as follows[4]:

1.   I am the applicant in this matter. I make this witness statement in support of my application for an interim order pursuant to section 252 of the Insolvency Act 1986.
2.   Attached to this statement marked 'AB1' is a copy of my proposal for an individual voluntary arrangement and a copy of the notice to my intended nominee, CD, duly endorsed with her agreement to act in relation to my proposed voluntary arrangement.
3.   My reasons for seeking an individual voluntary arrangement are set out in my proposal[5]. In summary I believe that my creditors will receive a better return if my affairs are administered under the proposed arrangement than they would if I were made bankrupt.
4.   A bankruptcy petition was presented against me on [*date*] by EF of [*address*] in respect of an undisputed debt of £20,000 due as rent for business premises at Unit 4, Industrial Park. No execution or other legal process has, to my knowledge, been commenced against me.
5.   I am able to petition for my own bankruptcy.
6.   No previous application for an interim order has been made by or in respect of me in the period of 12 months ending with the date of this application.
7.   Ms D is willing to act in relation to the proposal and, as she has informed me, is qualified to act as an insolvency practitioner in relation to the proposal *or* is authorised to act as nominee in relation to the proposal[6].
8.   I have not submitted to the official receiver the document referred to at section 263B(1)(a) of the Insolvency Act 1986 or the statement referred to at section 263B(1)(b) of that Act[7].

Statement of truth [*etc*].

[1]   A witness statement may be made instead of an affidavit; IR 1986, r 7.57(5).
[2]   An application for an interim order by a debtor who is not an undischarged bankrupt should not be headed 'In Bankruptcy' because the application is made under the IA 1986, Pt VIII; see the IR 1986, r 7.26(2).
[3]   The debtor.
[4]   For the required contents of the witness statement see the IR 1986, r 5.7(1).
[5]   For the required contents of the proposal, see IR 1986, r 5.3 and the following checklist.

⁶ Delete as appropriate; for the qualification to act as an insolvency practitioner, see IA 1986, s 390; and for authorisation of individuals who are not so qualified to act as a nominee or supervisor in relation to an IVA, see IA 1986, s 389A.

⁷ The purpose of this statement is to confirm that the debtor has not sought to implement a fast track IVA. By IA 1986, s 263B(1) a debtor is enabled to submit to the official receiver (a) a document setting out the terms of the IVA which he is proposing, and (b) a statement of his affairs containing prescribed particulars.

CHECKLIST: MATTERS TO BE INCLUDED IN A PROPOSAL FOR AN INDIVIDUAL VOLUNTARY ARRANGEMENT

A proposal for an individual voluntary arrangement must include the following matters[1]. Other matters may be added, for example, provision to enable meetings to be held to amend the arrangement and provision defining events of default and the consequences of default.

1. A short explanation of why, in his opinion, an IVA is desirable.
2. Reasons why his creditors may be expected to concur with the IVA.
3. A statement by the debtor of, so far as within his immediate knowledge:
   (1)   what his assets are, with an estimate of their respective values;
   (2)   the extent, if any, to which the assets are charged in favour of creditors;
   (3)   the extent, if any, to which particular assets are excluded from the IVA.
4. Particulars of any property, other than his own assets, which is proposed to be included in the IVA, the source of that property and the terms on which it is to be made available for inclusion.
5. Particulars of any property, other than assets of the debtor himself, which is proposed to be included in the arrangement, the source of such property and the terms on which it is to be made available for inclusion.
6. A statement as to (a) the nature and amount of his liabilities (so far as within his immediate knowledge), (b) the manner in which they are proposed to be met, modified, postponed or otherwise dealt with by means of the arrangement and (in particular):
   (1)   how it is proposed to deal with preferential creditors (defined in section 258(7)) and creditors who are, or claim to be, secured,
   (2)   how associates of the debtor (being creditors of his) are proposed to be treated under the arrangement, and
   (3)   in any case where the debtor is an undischarged bankrupt, whether, to the debtor's knowledge, claims have been made under section 339 (transactions at an undervalue), section 340 (preferences) or section 343 (extortionate credit transactions), *or* where the debtor is not an undischarged bankrupt, whether there are circumstances which would give rise to the possibility of such claims in the event that he should be adjudged bankrupt, and *in either case*, where any such circumstances are present, whether, and if so how, it is proposed under the voluntary arrangement to make provision for wholly or partly indemnifying the insolvent estate in respect of such claims.
7. A statement whether any, and if so what, guarantees have been given of the debtor's debts by other persons, specifying which (if any) of the guarantors are associates of his.
8. A statement as to the proposed duration of the voluntary arrangement.
9. A statement as to the proposed dates of distributions to creditors, with estimates of their amounts.
10. A statement of how it is proposed to deal with the claims of any person who is bound by the arrangement by virtue of section 260(2)(b)(ii), ie those persons

who do not get notice of the creditors' meeting to consider the proposal but who would be entitled to vote if they had such notice.

11. A statement of the amount proposed to be paid to the nominee (as such) by way of remuneration and expenses.

12. A statement of the manner in which it is proposed that the supervisor of the arrangement should be remunerated, and his expenses defrayed.

13. A statement whether, for the purposes of the arrangement, any guarantees are to be offered by any persons other than the debtor, and whether (if so) any security is to be given or sought.

14. A statement as to the manner in which funds held for the purposes of the arrangement are to be banked, invested or otherwise dealt with pending distribution to creditors.

15. A statement as to the manner in which funds held for the purpose of payment to creditors, and not so paid on the termination of the arrangement, are to be dealt with.

16. If the debtor has any business, a statement as to the manner in which it is proposed to be conducted during the course of the arrangement.

17. Details of any further credit facilities which it is intended to arrange for the debtor, and how the debts so arising are to be paid.

18. A statement of the functions which are to be undertaken by the supervisor of the arrangement.

19. The name, address and qualification of the person proposed as supervisor of the voluntary arrangement, and confirmation that he is, so far as the debtor is aware, qualified to act as an insolvency practitioner in relation to him *or* is an authorised person in relation to him.

20. A statement whether the EC Regulation[2] will apply and, if so, whether the proceedings will be main proceedings or territorial proceedings.

[1] IR 1986, r 5.3(1) and (2).
[2] Council Regulation of 29 May 2000, 1346/2000/EC.

PRECEDENT 3: INTERIM ORDER INCLUDING EXTENSION[1]

In the [...] County Court

No ... of ...

In the matter of the Insolvency Act 1986

Re AB

Between

AB

Applicant

and
(1) CD
(2) EF

Respondents

Upon the application of AB

And upon hearing [counsel/the solicitor for] the debtor, AB, and the nominee, CD, and [counsel/the solicitor for] the second respondent, EF

And upon reading the evidence

It is ordered that during the period of [...] days beginning with the day after the date of this order and during any extended period for which this interim order has effect:

(i)   no bankruptcy petition relating to the above-named debtor, AB, may be presented or proceeded with;

(ii) proceedings upon the petition presented against the debtor on [*date*] by the second respondent are stayed;

(iii) no landlord or other person to whom rent is payable may exercise any right of forfeiture by peaceable re-entry in relation to premises let to the debtor in respect of a failure by the debtor to comply with any term or condition of his tenancy of such premises, except with leave of the court; and

(iv) no other proceedings, and no execution or other legal process, may be commenced or continued and no distress may be levied against the debtor or his property except with the leave of the court[2]

And the court having this day considered the report of the nominee submitted pursuant to section 256 of the Insolvency Act 1986 and filed on [*date*]

It is ordered that the period for which the interim order hereby made has effect be extended[3] to [*date*] to enable a meeting of the debtor's creditors to be summoned to consider the debtor's proposal, such meeting as proposed by the nominee to be held on

Date:

Time:

Place:

And it is ordered that this application is adjourned to:

Date:

Time:

Place:

For consideration of the report of the chairman of the creditors' meeting

Dated [*date*]

1 Adapted from the IR 1986, Sch 4, Forms 5.2 and 5.3. This form of order is appropriate where the nominee has prepared his report before the debtor seeks an interim order. Alternative approaches are for the debtor to apply for an interim order before the nominee has prepared her report in which case there will have to be a separate hearing for the court to receive and consider that report or for the debtor to propose an IVA without obtaining an interim order (see IA 1986, s 256A).

2 For the effect of an interim order, see IA 1986, s 252(2).

3 For the court's power, on receipt of the nominee's report, to extend the period for which the interim order has effect in order that the creditors may consider the proposal; see IA 1986, s 256(5).

PRECEDENT 4: ORDINARY APPLICATION BY THE DEBTOR PURSUANT TO IR 1986, R 5.17 CHALLENGING THE RIGHT OF A CREDITOR TO VOTE[1]

In the [...] County Court

No ... of ...

In the matter of the Insolvency Act 1986

Re AB

Between

AB

Applicant

and
GH

Respondent

Take notice that AB intends to apply to the District Judge on:

Date:

Time:

Place:

for:

1.   a declaration that the respondent's vote in respect of a claimed debt of £100,000 at the meeting of creditors held on [*date*] to consider the applicant's proposal for an individual voluntary arrangement was invalid;
2.   alternatively, a declaration that the debt owed by the applicant to the respondent be valued at £50,000 or such other sum as the court may determine;
3.   a declaration that the resolution passed at the meeting of creditors held on [*date*] to reject the applicant's proposal be revoked;
4.   a direction that a further meeting of the applicant's creditors be held to reconsider the applicant's proposal;
5.   such further or other orders as the court may think just.

The grounds on which the applicant claims to be entitled to the relief sought are set out in the witness statement of the applicant dated [*date*][2].

To: (1) GH of [*address*] and (2) [*name of the chairman*][3] of [*address*]

Dated:

Signed:

(Solicitor for the) applicant.

My address for service is [*address*].

To: [*name and address of respondent*].

If you do not attend, the court may make such order as it thinks fit.

1   Where a creditor's right to vote is disputed and the chairman is in doubt whether to admit the claim on which it is based, he should admit the claim but mark it as objected to. The debtor, or another creditor, may then apply by way of appeal under the IR 1986, r 5.17 to the court for a determination whether the objection should be sustained or not; *Re a Debtor (No 222 of 1990), ex p the Bank of Ireland* [1992] BCLC 137.

2   The application must be supported by a witness statement in which the maker of the statement (1) explains why the debt is disputed either in its entirety or as to the value put on it; (2) shows that the outcome of the relevant vote would have differed had the chairman treated the debt differently; and (3) sets out any other relevant circumstances. Appropriate supporting evidence should be exhibited to the statement.

3   Notice of the application must be given to the chairman but he need not be joined as a party unless a specific allegation is made as to his conduct, but should be served in order that he may participate if he wishes.

PRECEDENT 5: ORDINARY APPLICATION UNDER IA 1986, S 262 BY A
CREDITOR TO CHALLENGE THE DECISION OF THE MEETING TO
APPROVE THE DEBTOR'S PROPOSAL

In the [...] County Court

No ... of ...

In the matter of the Insolvency Act 1986

Re AB

Between

JK

and
AB[1]

Applicant

Respondent

Take notice that JK intends to apply to the District Judge on:

Date:

Time:

Place:

for:

1.   an order revoking the approval given by the meeting of creditors held on [*date*] to the respondent's proposal for an individual voluntary arrangement as modified at the meeting on the ground that there was a material irregularity at the meeting because the modification made at the meeting to the respondent's proposal affects the applicant's right to enforce his security over the respondent's freehold interest in [*address of charged premises*] and, contrary to section 258(4) of the Insolvency Act 1986, was approved without the applicant's concurrence;
2.   a direction that CD[2] summon a further meeting of the respondent's creditors to consider any revised proposal which the respondent may make;
3.   such further or other orders as the court may think just.

The grounds on which the applicant claims to be entitled to the order are set out in the witness statement of the applicant dated [*date*][3].

To: (1) AB of [*address*] and (2) [*name of the chairman*][4] of [*address*]

The applicant's address for service is [*address*].

Dated:

Signed:

(Solicitor for the) applicant.

If you do not attend, the court may make such order as it thinks fit.

1   The debtor should be made respondent, but unless there is special reason to join the chairman, the chairman should not be joined as a party, but should be served in order that he may participate if he wishes.

2   Ie the nominee who acted as chairman.

3   The application must be supported by a witness statement (see IR 1986, r 7.57(5)) in which the maker of the statement (1) explains what the material irregularity was, and (2) sets out any other relevant circumstances. Appropriate supporting evidence should be exhibited to the statement. In the example on which the precedent is based the failure to obtain the secured creditor's consent is both irregular and necessarily material to him. In other cases, it may be necessary to show separately that the irregularity was material in the sense that the outcome of the relevant vote would have differed had the irregularity not occurred.

4   Notice of the application must be given to the chairman but he need not be joined as a party unless a specific allegation is made as to his conduct.

PRECEDENT 6: ORDINARY APPLICATION[1] UNDER IA 1986, S 282(1)(B) BY THE BANKRUPT TO ANNUL THE BANKRUPTCY ORDER ON THE BASIS THAT THE BANKRUPTCY DEBTS AND EXPENSES HAVE ALL BEEN PAID OR SECURED

In the [...] County Court

No ... of ...

In Bankruptcy[2]

Re AB

Between

AB

Applicant

and
(1) The official receiver
(2) The trustee of the estate of AB, a bankrupt[3]

Respondent

Take notice that AB intends to apply to the District Judge on:

Date:

Time:

Place:

for:

1. an order that the bankruptcy order dated [*date*] against AB [*give the full name and description of bankrupt as set out in petition*] be annulled;
2. an order that the petition filed on [*date*] be dismissed;
3. an order permitting vacation of the registration of the petition as a pending action and of the bankruptcy order in the register of writs and orders affecting land[4].

The ground on which the applicant claims to be entitled to the orders sought is that the bankruptcy debts and the expenses of the bankruptcy have all been paid or secured to the satisfaction of the court[5] as is further set out in the witness statement[6] of [*name*] dated [*date*].

Signed:

(Solicitor for the) applicant

My address for service is:

To:

The official receiver of [*address*]

The trustee of the estate of AB, a bankrupt, of [*address*]

If you do not attend, the court may make such order as it thinks fit.

1 An ordinary rather than originating application is appropriate because the application is made in the bankruptcy proceedings; see IR 1986, r 7.2(1).
2 The title should include the words 'In Bankruptcy' by virtue of IR 1986, r 7.26(2).
3 The applicant must give notice of the application to the official receiver and, if another person has been appointed as trustee in bankruptcy, the trustee in bankruptcy; see IR 1986, r 6.206(4). For the official name of the trustee, see IA 1986, s 305(4).
4 See IR 1986, r 6.213(1).
5 The basis for annulment under IA 1986, s 282(2)(b) is that the bankruptcy debts and expenses have been paid. Giving security is only available where the debt is disputed or a creditor who has proved cannot be traced; see IR 1986, r 6.211(3). Statutory interest will ordinarily be required upon the bankruptcy debts.
6 The application must be supported by a witness statement in which the debts are set out and evidence of their payment is given.

Appendix 4   *Selected precedents*

PRECEDENT 7: ORDINARY APPLICATION[1] UNDER IA 1986, S 282(1)(A) BY THE BANKRUPT TO ANNUL THE BANKRUPTCY ORDER ON THE BASIS THAT THE BANKRUPTCY ORDER OUGHT NOT TO HAVE BEEN MADE, INCLUDING AN APPLICATION PURSUANT TO IR 1986, R 6.208 FOR STAY OF ADVERTISEMENT AND PROCEEDINGS PENDING APPLICATION TO ANNUL A BANKRUPTCY ORDER

In the [...] County Court

No ... of ...

In Bankruptcy[2]

Re AB

Between

AB

and
(1) The official receiver
(2) The trustee of the estate of AB, a bankrupt[3]

Applicant

Respondent

Take notice that I intend to apply to the District Judge on:

Date:

Time: hours

Place:

For:

1.   an interim order that the advertisement of and proceedings under the bankruptcy order made herein on [*date*] be stayed until [*date*] or further order[4];
2.   an order that the bankruptcy order dated [*date*] against AB [*give the full name and description of bankrupt as set out in petition*] be annulled;
3.   an order that the petition filed on [*date*] be dismissed;
4.   an order permitting vacation of the registration of the petition as a pending action and of the bankruptcy order in the register of writs and orders affecting land.

The ground on which this order is sought is that the bankruptcy order ought not to have been made.

Signed:

(Solicitor for the) applicant

My address for service is:

To[5]:

1246

The official receiver of [*address*]

If you do not attend, the court may make such order as it thinks fit.

1   An ordinary rather than originating application is appropriate because the application is made in the bankruptcy proceedings; see IR 1986, r 7.2(1).
2   The title should include the words 'In Bankruptcy' by virtue of IR 1986, r 7.26(2).
3   The applicant must give notice of the application to the official receiver and, if another person has been appointed as trustee in bankruptcy, the trustee in bankruptcy; see IR 1986, r 6.206(4). For the official name of the trustee, see IA 1986, s 305(4).
4   In order that this interim order should be effective, the bankrupt must apply for it as soon as possible and before the hearing of the substantive application to annul; but he should give notice of the interim application to the official receiver (and the trustee if different); see IR 1986, r 6.208(1) and (3).
5   Where the application is made to stay all or any of the proceedings in the bankruptcy it may not be made ex parte; IR 1986, r 6.208(2).

PRECEDENT 8: ORIGINATING APPLICATION TO SET ASIDE A
TRANSACTION AT AN UNDERVALUE

In the High Court of Justice

In Bankruptcy

Re AB

Between

The trustee of the estate of AB, a bankrupt[1]

Applicant

and

(1) CD
(2) EF
(3) AB

Respondents

Let CD of [*address*], EF of [*address*] and AB of [*address*] attend before the Registrar on:

Date:

Time:

Place:

On the hearing of an application by TB the trustee in bankruptcy of the above-named bankrupt for an order in the following terms:

1.   a declaration that the transfer by the bankrupt of the freehold property [*address*] ('the Property') registered in the [...] District Land Registry under title number [...] to the first respondent on [*date*] constitutes a transaction at an undervalue within the meaning of section 339 of the Insolvency Act 1986;
2.   an order that the property be vested in the applicant as part of the estate of the bankrupt;
3.   alternatively to (2) above, such order as the court thinks fit for restoring the position to what it would have been had the bankrupt not made the said transfer;
4.   an order that the first respondent do give vacant possession of the property to the applicant and directions for sale;
5.   a declaration that the sale by the bankrupt of the various items of stock and other chattels listed in the schedule hereto to the second respondent on [*date*] constitutes a transaction at an undervalue within the meaning of section 339 of the Insolvency Act 1986;
6.   an order that the said sale be set aside, alternatively such relief as the court thinks fit for restoring the position to what it would have been if the bankrupt had not entered into such sale;
7.   all such consequential directions as the court may consider necessary;
8.   an order that the first and second respondents do pay the costs of this application.

The grounds on which the applicant claims to be entitled to this order are set out in the witness statement of TB dated [*date*] a true copy of which is served herewith[2].

The names and addresses of the persons upon whom it is intended to serve this application are:

(1)   CD of [*address*]
(2)   EF of [*address*]
(3)   AB of [*address*]

The applicant's address for service is:

Dated:

Signed:

(Solicitor for the) applicant

If you do not attend, the court may make such order as it thinks fit.

[1]   The applicant must give notice of the application to the official receiver and, if another person has been appointed as trustee in bankruptcy, the trustee in bankruptcy; see IR 1986, r 6.206(4). For the official name of the trustee, see IA 1986, s 305(4).

[2]   The application must be supported by a witness statement setting out the evidence upon which it is contended that the transactions in question were at an undervalue. Where the disposition was gratuitous, it will not be necessary to adduce valuation evidence in order to show that it was at an undervalue, but where the contention is that the value given as consideration was lower than the true value, then valuation evidence will be required.

Appendix 4 *Selected precedents*

PRECEDENT 9: ORDER ON APPLICATION TO SET ASIDE A TRANSACTION
AT AN UNDERVALUE

In the High Court of Justice in Bankruptcy

The Honourable Mr Justice [*name*]

[*date*]

Between

The trustee of the estate of AB, a bankrupt

Applicant

and
(1) CD
(2) EF
(3) AB

Respondents

ON HEARING counsel for the applicant, counsel for the first respondent, counsel for
the second respondent and the third respondent appearing in person:

THIS COURT DECLARES that the transfer by the third respondent of the freehold
property [*address*] ('the Property') registered in the [...] District Land Registry under
title number [...] to the first respondent on [*date*] is void as against the applicant as a
transaction at an undervalue within the meaning of section 339 of the Insolvency
Act 1986;

AND THIS COURT FURTHER DECLARES that the sale by the third respondent of
the items listed in the schedule hereto to the second respondent on [*date*] constitutes a
transaction at an undervalue within the meaning of section 339 of the Insolvency
Act 1986.

AND IT IS ORDERED THAT

1. the Property be vested in the applicant, as trustee of the estate of the third
    respondent;
2. the first respondent do give vacant possession of the Property on or before
    [*date*];
3. the second respondent do pay the sum of £50,000 to the applicant as further
    payment due for the items listed in the schedule hereto within 14 days of this
    order.

AND IT IS ORDERED that the costs of the applicant be the subject of detailed
assessment by a costs officer of this court and that the amount so assessed be paid by
the second respondent to the applicant.

Dated this [ ] day of [ ]

Index

References are to paragraph numbers.

Index

Index

Index

Index

Index

Index

Index

Index

Index

Index

Index

Index

Index

1301

Index

Index

Index

Index